سلسلة المعاجم المصوَّرة

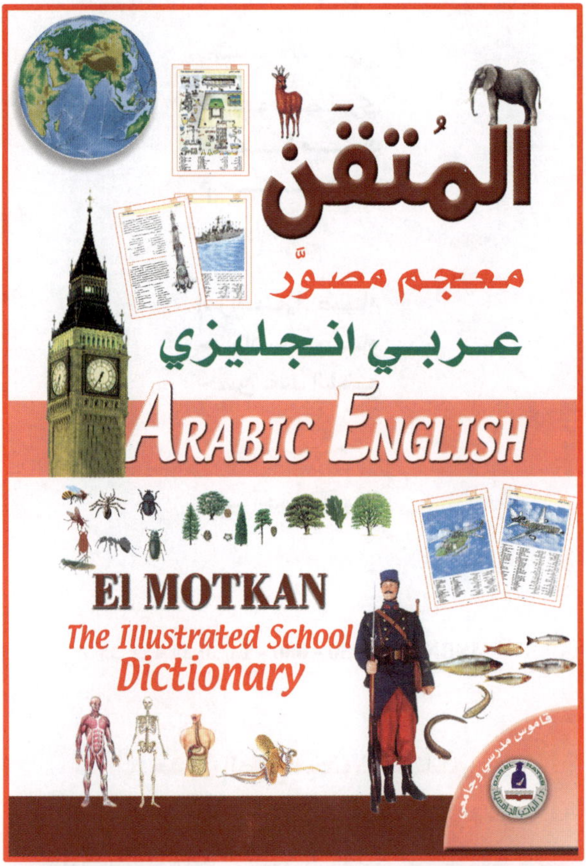

المتقن: عربي إنجليزي

DAR EL RATEB
دار الراتب الجامعية

الإعداد

جيرار موسى
طلعت قبيعة
هزار أحمد
فائدة مرجان

التنقيح والتصحيح

ج. أبو نصري
ليا مراد
م. مراد

الرسوم

إبراهيم أ. صيام
جاد سرياو
حسن عبد الشفيع

المشرف العام

راتب أحمد قبيعة

الترقيم الدولي: ISBN 9953 - 30 - 080 - 1

دار الراتب الجامعية
DAR El-RATEB

صندوق بريد: 229 5 14 / 2020 5 110 ـ بيروت ـ لبنان
هاتف/ فاكس: 853993 01 / 853895 01 ـ جوال: 877180 03 / 887181 03
E-mail: el-rateb@cyberia.net.lb

تمهيد

اتبعنا في إعداد مفردات هذا المعجم طريقة إيراد الكلمة في حالة المفرد بدون ذكر مصدرها، ويجيء الفعل قبل الاسم والصفة وبالأخص عند تشابه الحروف. اعتبرنا الألف الممدودة ألفًا عادية في عملية التنسيق. واعتبرنا الهمزة ألفاً بأي صورة وردت في المتن بين أحرف الكلمة. أما بالنسبة للفعل فقد أوردناه في صيغة الماضي وأوردنا الصفات في صيغة المذكر إلا ما كان إيراده ضرورياً بصيغة المؤنث.

التزمنا في هذا المعجم الشامل مراجع اللغة، وقام بإعداد مواده مجموعة من الأدباء والمختصين في اللّغة ليجيء وافيًا شاملاً لا تشوبه أخطاء لغوية، وقام بالتصحيح أفراد دائرة النشر والترجمة في دارنا وهم أفراد من خرّيجي الجامعات، اكتسبوا خبرة واسعة خلال عملهم في الدار فكان إنتاجهم ممتازاً بحق.

اعتمدنا في متن المعجم الرموز التالية للدلالة على: (ج) صيغة الجمع، (أ) الاسم، (ص) صفة، (نب) نبات، (حو) حيوان، (حش) حشرة، (قا) قانون، (ل) لغة، (طي) طير.

وهكذا يجد القارئ مثلاً فعل «دَرَسَ»، تحت حرف «د»، وكلمة «مَدْرَسَة» تحت حرف الميم، وكلمة «تَدْريس» تحت حرف «ت».

فصَّلنا معاني الكلمة باللغة الإنكليزية باستعمال الشولة المنقوطة (؛) للدلالة إلى المعاني المختلفة التي قد تتضمّنها الكلمة العربية.

تحتوي مفردات اللغة العربية كافة الكلمات والمصطلحات والعبارات المعاصرة التي دخلت في صلب اللغة العربية إما بفعل الشيوع أو التداول، وبالأخصّ في علوم الفيزياء والكيمياء والطب والكهرباء والاقتصاد والموسيقى.

أهملنا في هذا القاموس الكلمات التي باتت مهجورة بسبب كونها قد ابتعدت عن حاجات العصر، وبالمقابل أضفنا المعاني المستحدثة للعديد من الكلمات.

وقد أضفنا إلى متن هذا العمل المعجميّ رسوماً ملوّنة، وضعنا لها تعليقات باللغتين العربية والإنكليزية تُفيد الطالب في تركيب جملةٍ مفيدة حَسَنةِ الصِّياغة.

ولقد ذيلناه بأطلسٍ وافٍ للمرافق العامة من كافة أمور الحياة، المنزل، المدرسة، المطعم، المسرح، السفر جواً، الإبحار، السوق، والأمور العلمية والتكنولوجية من طاق ومواقع الإنشاء، والسيارات والأجهزة الكهربائية والالكترونية والطائرات والبواخر والسفن، وعالم النبات والحيوانات.

كما وضعنا فيه كافة التفاصيل عن جسم الإنسان وختمناه ببعض الأدباء والشعراء العالميين.

وبالرغم من العناية الفائقة التي أحطنا هذا المعجم إعداداً وطباعةً، فإنّنا نقرّ بأن العمل المعجمي يحتاج دائماً إلى تصحيح وتحسين، وخاصةً في عالمٍ سريع التطور.

دائرة النشر والترجمة

حرف الألف

أ — a; the first letter of the Arabic Alphabet; a particle introducing direct and indirect questions; a particle indicating or implying doubt.

اِئْتَزَرَ — wear a loincloth.

اِئْتِلاف — harmony; agreement; unity; symphony.

اِئْتَلَفَ (مع) — to harmonize with; to agree with; to suit; to match; to be consistent with; to merge; to form a coalition.

اِئْتِمان — reliance; faith; credit.

اِئْتَمَرَ — to confer; to consult; to plot; to scheme; to obey; to submit to.

اِئْتَمَنَ — to entrust someone with; to confide to; to place one's confidence; to rely on.

آب — August

يُعرف شهر آب بشهر أغسطس عند الفرنجة

The month of «AB» is called «August» by foreigners

آبَ — to come back; to return.

أَبَّ — to long for; to yearn; to get ready to.

أ ب ت ث ج ح خ د ذ ر ز س ش ص ض ط ظ ع غ ف ق ك ل م ن هـ و ي

أب — father; priest; ancestor; originator; author; a male parent.

أبو البَشَر — Adam.

أبو الهول — sphinx.

أَبى — to refuse, decline, reject, deny; to spurn.

تأبى نفسي أكل الأطعمة الحارة
I refuse to eat hot meals

إباء — refusal; rejection; denial; disdain; pride.

أَباحَ — to reveal, divulge, disclose; to permit, allow, authorize.

إباحِيّ — licentious; uninhibited; unrestrained; lewd; dissolute; profligate; pornographic.

إباحِيَّة — licentiousness; profligacy; pornography; dissoluteness.

أَبادَ — to exterminate, eradicate, destroy, annihilate, extirpate.

إِبادَة — extermination, eradication, destruction; annihilation; extirpation.

أَبانَ — to elucidate; to render clear; to expose, demonstrate, explain; to distinguish, expound.

إبَّان — during; at the time of.

ابْتاعَ — to buy; to purchase.

نبتاع السلع التي نحتاج إليها من المخازن
We purchase consumer items from the stores

ابْتَدَأ — to begin; to start; to arise; to speak first.

ابْتِداءً من — starting from; beginning from; effective from.

ابْتِدائيّ — primary; preliminary; primitive; preparatory; original; initial.

ابْتِداع — invention; innovation; creation; novelty; heresy.

ابْتِذال — abuse; triteness; banality, misuse; platitude; degradation, debasement.

ابْتَذَلَ — to make trite; to violate accepted standards of good manners; to be indecent; to use abusive language; to demean oneself; to sacrifice one's dignity; to hackney.

أ ب ت ث ج ح خ د ذ ر ز س ش ص ض ط ظ ع غ ف ق ك ل م ن هـ و ي

أَبْتَر	amputated; cut-off; severed; broken; curtailed; amputee; tailless; childless; mutilated; imperfect; incomplete.
ابْتَزَّ	to snatch from; to outstrip; to take away; to steal, rob, fleece, extort from, usurp from; to pilfer; to blackmail.
ابْتِزاز	extortion; usurpation; blackmailing; theft; robbery; pilferage; racket.
ابْتِسام	smile; smiling.
ابْتِسامَة	smile.
ابْتَسَمَ	to smile.

ابتسم الأب في وجه ابنه

The father smiled in the face of his son

ابْتِعاد	going away; leaving; keeping away; separation; detachment; avoidance; remoteness; departure.
ابْتَعَدَ	to move away; to depart; to stay away from; to distance oneself from; to quit, leave; to avoid, keep off; to withdraw.

ابتعد وهو يركض مسرعاً

He departed running quickly

ابْتَغى	to desire, seek, aspire to, covet.
ابْتِغاء	seeking, desiring, aspiring to, coveting; for the purpose of; in the aim of; wishing.
ابْتِكار	innovation, creativity, ingenuity; novelty, invention; creative ability.
ابْتَكَرَ	to innovate; to create; to invent; to contrive; to design; to make; to coin (a phrase).
ابْتَلَّ	to become wet; to be moistened.
ابْتَلى	to put to the test; to afflict; to torment; to test; to try; to be afflicted; to suffer; to undergo; to experience.
ابْتِلاع	swallowing; gulping down; holding back.
ابْتَلَعَ	to swallow; to gulp down; to catch one's breath.
ابْتِهاج	jubilation, joy, delight; cheerfulness, happiness.

ابْتَهجَ — to rejoice at; to be happy; to be delighted; to be merry about; to cheer up.

ابْتَهَلَ — to supplicate, pray, invoke, implore, beseech.

أَبْجَدِيّ — alphabetical; abecedarian.

أَبْجَدِيًا — alphabetically.

أَبْجَدِيَّة — alphabet.

إِبْحَار — navigation; sailing.

أَبْحَرَ — to sail; to navigate; to make a voyage by sea.

تبحر المراكب في عرض البحر

Ships sail in the high seas

أَبْحَرَت السفينة — to depart; to leave; to set sail.

أَبَدُ الآبدين — for ever and ever.

أَبَد — eternity; perpetuity.

أَبَدُ الدَهْر — forever, permanently.

أبداً — never, absolutely not, always, ever.

أَبْدَى — to show, display, manifest, disclose, express; to bring out.

إِبْداء — demonstration; presentation; disclosure; declaration; expression; bringing into view.

إِبْداع — creation, innovation; ingenuity; excellence; invention; originality; perfection.

إِبْدَال — replacement, permutation, substitution; exchange; transference.

أَبْدَعَ — to excel; to be or to become outstanding in; to bring to perfection.

أَبْدَلَ — to exchange; to commute for; to substitue for; to alter; to change; to commute.

أَبَدِيّ — everlasting; eternal.

أَبَدِيَّة — eternity; perpetuity.

إِبْراء ذِمّة — discharge, release.

إِبْرَاز — manifestation; bringing into view; showing; accentuation; emphasis; protrusion; bringing out.

إِبْرَاق — telegraphy.

إِبرَام — ratification; sanctioning; legalization; conclusion.

إِبْرَة — needle; indicator; pointer; injection.

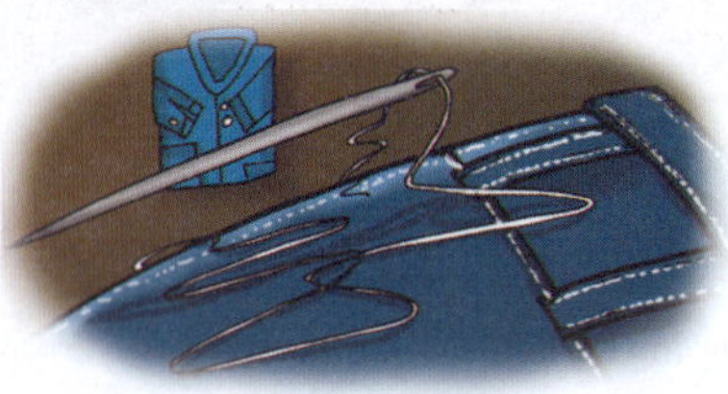

تخيط والدتي الملابس بالإبرة

My mother sews clothes with a needle

إِبْرَة مَغْنَطِيسِيَّة magnetic needle.

أَبْرَدَ to mail; to send by mail.

أَبْرَزَ to show, present, display; to accentuate; to underline; to point out; to project; to stick out; to publish; to expose; to produce; to stress.

أَبْرَشِية diocese; parish.

أَبْرَص leper.

أَبْرَقَ to telegraph.

أَبْرَقَ وَجْهُهُ to radiate; to brighten.

أَبْرَمَ to ratify; to endorse; to validate; to conclude; to annoy; to irritate; to weary.

إِبْرِيز pure gold.

إِبْريق pitcher; jug.

كان المصريون القدامى يضعون إبريقاً من الماء بجوار جثة الميت

Ancient Egyptians used to put a pitcher of water in the coffin

إِبْريقُ الشاي teapot.

إِبْزِيم buckle, fastener.

أَبْشَرَ to bring good tidings; to announce.

إِبْصار vision, eyesight.

أَبْصَرَ to see,notice, perceive; to catch sight of.

إِبْط armpit.

أَبْطَأَ to be slow; to linger; to tarry; to slow down; to delay, retard.

أَبْطَأ (ص) slower.

إِبْطاء deceleration; slackening; slowing down; lag.

إِبْطال invalidation, annulment, cancellation; rescission, revocation; frustration; abrogation.

أَبْطَلَ to cancel; to rescind; to abrogate; to invalidate; to frustrate,foil, annul, void.

إِبْعاد removal; elimination; expulsion; banishment; exclusion; alienation; repulsion.

أَبْعَدَ to put aside; to keep away; to dismiss; to exclude; to alienate; to repel.

أَبْعَد (ص) farther away; beyond; more distant.

الأَبْعَد farthest; outermost; most distant.

أَبْغَضَ to hate; to abhor; to dislike; to detest.

أَبْقَى to retain, preserve, hold; to leave over; to make stay; to keep up; to spare; to maintain.

إِبْقاء retention, preservation, holding; maintenance; asking someone to stay; to save someone's life.

أبْكى to make someone weep.

أبْكَمَ to silence; to reduce to silence.

أبْكَم (ص) mute, dumb.

أبَلَّ من المرض to recover, convalesce, regain health, recuperate; to get well.

أبْلى الثوب to wear out.

أبْلى بلاءً حَسَناً to fare well in battle; to fight courageously.

إبْلاغ notification, information; declaration; notice; denunciation; reporting.

إبْلال (من مرض) recovery, convalescence, recuperation.

أبْلَغَ to inform, notify, report, convey, declare, announce; to serve (a summons); to denounce; to tell about.

أبْلَه idiot, stupid, feebleminded, fool, simpleton; empty-headed; dumb; silly.

إبْليس Satan; Devil.

أبَّنَ الميت to eulogize; to praise (a dead person).

إبْن son; boy; offspring.

إبْنُ الأخ أو الأُخت nephew.

إبْنُ آدم human being.

إبْنٌ بالتَّبَنّي adoptive child.

إبْنٌ بالمَعْمودِيَّة godson.

إبْنُ البَلَد native.

إبْنُ الزوج أو الزوجة stepson, stepchild.

إبْنُ ساعتِهِ spontaneous; extemporaneous; transient.

إبْنُ السبيل passer-by; vagrant; wanderer.

إبْنُ العم أو الخال أو العمة أو الخالة cousin.

إبْنُ زِنًى bastard.

إبْنُ حرام illegitimate child.

إبْنَة daughter, girl.

إبْنَةُ الزوج أو الزوجة stepdaughter.

إبنةٌ بالمعمودية goddaughter; godchild.

أبْنوس أو أَبَنوس ebony.

إبهامُ اليد thumb.

نشير بالإبهام إلى سيارة الأجرة كي تتوقف
We point to a taxi to stop using our thumb

إبهامُ الرِّجْل big toe.

أبَهة splendor; pomposity.

أبْهَجَ to cheer up, make happy, fill with joy.

أبْهَر aorta.

أبْهَظَ to overburden; to weigh down; to load; to oppress; to surcharge, to overload.

أبْهَمَ to make obscure, make dubious, make vague.

أُبُوَّة fatherhood.

أَبَوِيّ paternal; fatherly.

أَبِيّ haughty; proud.

ابْيَضَّ to whiten; to become white.

أَبْيَض (ص) white; empty; unmarked; clear; pure.

ابْيِضاض whitening; becoming white.

آتٍ coming; next; forthcoming; arriving.

الآتي following.

أتى to come, arrive; to bring forward; to produce; to achieve; to give; to do; to perform (a deed); to commit (a crime); to mention (something); to finish, complete; to destroy, eliminate; to do away with; to elaborate on; to tackle in the right way; to offer; to furnish, provide, supply with; to suit, befit; to agree with; to grant (something to someone); to derive; to result from; to progress, to ask (someone to come); to happen; to consume; to refer to.

أتاحَ to allow; to make possible for; to make available; to grant, to provide with; to predetermine; to afford; to give the opportunity (to someone).

اتَّأَدَ to be slow; to be deliberate; to act slowly or deliberately; to take one's time.

إتاوة royalty; tax; bride.

اتِّباع comming or proceeding after; following; observing; compliance with; adherence to; pursuing; chasing; going after; tracking; adopting.

إتْباع following up; annexation; joining; attaching.

أَتْبَعَ to annex to; to join to; to send after; to attach to.

اتَّبَعَ to come after; to follow; to adopt; to observe; to abide by; to stick to; to imitate; to follow someone's example; to follow suit; to pursue; to track; to run after; to proceed after; to comply with.

اتِّجار trade; business; commercial deal.

اتِّجاه direction; heading; tendency; attitude; inclination, orientation; approach; sense.

اتِّجاهِيّ directional.

اتَّجَرَ to trade; to do business; to deal in.

اتَّجَهَ to turn toward; to head for; to proceed to; to follow (an action or plan); to be aimed at; to consider.

اتِّحاد union; merger; consolidation; association; alliance, federation; unity; unanimous (resolution); trust; syndicate, trade union, confederation; amalgamation; harmony; oneness; concord, unison.

أَتْحَفَ to offer to, bestow upon, present with.

اتَّخَذَ to assume, adopt; to make use of; to take (steps); to acquire (a form or shape); to decide; to take the initiative; to begin, set out to, undertake; to take one's seat; to have in mind; to occupy.

أَتْخَمَ to satiate; to overstuff; to overfeed; to cause indigestion to; to glut.

أَتْرَحَ to grieve, aggrieve, sadden.

أَتْرَعَ to fill to the brim; to overfill; to fill up.

أَتْرَفَ to spoil; to make reckless or careless; to surround with luxury.

اتِّزَان poise; balance; judiciousness; sobriety; equilibrium; equanimity; rationality.

اتَّزَرَ to wear a loincloth; to put on a garment; to commit a sin.

اتَّزَنَ to be composed, judicious, of sound judgment; to be weighed; to be in equipose, in equilibrium; to be rythmically balanced; to be evenly poised.

اتِّساع expansion; extention; stretch; extensiveness; vastness, amplitude, wideness; extent, scope, range; sufficiency; vagueness of expression; compass.

اتِّساق harmony, symmetry, uniformity.

اتَّسَخَ to be or to become dirty, filthy or unclean.

اتَّسَعَ to broaden; to be enlarged or extensive; to be or to become wide, ample, spacious, widespread, farreaching, comprehensive.

اتَّسَقَ to be or to become consistent, harmonious, symmetrical, uniform, even.

اتَّشَحَ to wear a sash; to throw on loosely a cloak; to put on a garb; to assume a name.

اتِّصال connection, link; contact; liaison; intersection; continuance; communication with someone; juncture; getting in touch with.

اتِّصالٌ جماهيرِيّ mass communication.

اتِّصالٌ جِنْسِيّ sexual intercourse, coition, copulation.

اتَّصَفَ to be characterized by; to carry a mark, quality, attribute, property; to be distinguished by.

اتَّصَلَ to join, unite, connect, link, communicate; to be or to become connected, attached, joined; to relate to; to be concerned with; to belong, pertain to.

اتَّضَحَ to be or to become plain, distinct, clear, manifest; to be concerned with; to belong, pertain to.

أَتْعاب remuneration, retainer, fee.

اتِّعاظ taking an example from; taking a warning from.

أَتْعَبَ to overburden, overwork, overstrain someone; to make tired; to wear away; to tire out; to disturb; to annoy; to irk; to inconvenience.

أتْعَسَ — to make unhappy; to destroy; to make miserable.

اتّفاق — agreement; contract, treaty; convention; accord, covenant, deal, settlement; concert, concord, harmony; concurrence; correspondance; chance; accident, fortuity.

اتّفاقاً — by chance, by accident; by agreement.

اتّفاقُ الآراء — consensus; unanimity.

اتّفاقُ تحكيم — arbitration agreement.

اتّفاقُ عَدَمِ اعْتِداء — nonagression pact.

اتّفاقيّ — accidental; conventional, fortuitous; random; casual; occasional; consensual; contingent.

اتّفاقِيّة — treaty; agreement, pact, convention; concordat; deal, covenant, accord, entente.

اتّفَقَ — to agree; to suit; to concur with; to be consistent with; to correspond; to be analogous to; to be in harmony with; to coincide; to consent; to subscribe; to confirm, approve, sanction, authorize, ratify; to reconcile; to reach an agreement; to fall in line with; to come to terms about something; to chance, happen, occur; to turn out successfully; to be destined to someone; to come to pass.

اتّقى — to beware of, be cautious of; to seek protection in; to shield, protect, shelter oneself; to avoid, avert, obviate, fend off, prevent; to fear God.

اتّقاء — precaution; protection; avoidance, obviation; fending off; safeguarding; caution, wariness.

اتّقاد — kindling, ignition, setting on fire, burning; vehemence; zeal, ardor; flame.

إتْقان — proficiency; dexterity; workmanship; excellence; precision; skill, mastery, command; exactness.

اتّقَدَ — to burn; to flare up; to glow; to rage.

أتْقَنَ — to master; to have command of; to become skilled in, well-versed in, proficient in.

اتّكأ — to recline on, rest on, lean on.

اتّكال — reliance, trust.

اتّكالِيّة — reliance, dependence.

اتّكَلَ — to rely on; depend on, lean on; to trust (in God).

إتْلاف — damaging; wearing out; wrecking.

أتْلَفَ — to damage, wear out, destroy, devastate, wreck, spoil, ravage.

أتَمَّ — to finish, terminate, finalize, end; to execute, carry out, implement; to achieve, fulfill, complete, bring to an end, bring to perfection.

إتْمام — finishing, completion, termination, carrying out; fulfilment; windup; ending; rounding off.

اتّهام — accusation, indictment, charge.

اتَّهَم to accuse of; to charge with; to indict for; to impeach.

أتُون kiln; furnace.

إتيمُولُجيّ (ص) etymological.

إتيمُولُجي (اسم) etymologist.

إتيمُولُوجيا etymology.

أَثَابَ to recompense; to reward.

أَثَاث furniture.

اشتريت أثاث المنزل بالتقسيط المريح

I bought my house furniture by instalments

أَثَارَ to arouse, kindle, inflame, excite, irritate, provoke, incite, instigate; to actuate, motivate, drive, impel; to evoke, elicit, bring forth, cause, produce, generate, induce; to raise, put forth, (a question); to enrage, madden, irritate (a person); to thrill, move, touch (feelings).

إثارَة excitation, stirring up; kindling; agitation, incitement,provocation, arousing; awakening; irritation; stimulation; triggering; putting forth; enraging, vexation.

آثارِيّ (اسم) archeologist.

آثارِيّ (ص) archeological.

إِثْبات proof, evidence; verification; confirmation; putting down; insertion; assertion; attestation; registration; authentication, affirmation.

إِثْباتٌ شَخْصِيّ testimonial; proof of evidence.

إِثْباتُ الهُوِيَّة identification; evidence of identity.

أَثْبَتَ to confirm, corroborate, substantiate; to prove, establish, demonstrate; to fix one's eyes on; to determine; to assert as valid; to furnish evidence for; to bear witness; to attest, acknowledge, concede; to record, register, list something (in a book, roster, list); to identify, ascertain, verify; to consider carefully; to proceed with caution; to seek confirmation of; to prove guilty; to convict.

أَثَّثَ to furnish, provide with furniture; to prepare, fix up, arrange.

أَثْخَنَ to enfeeble; to give a sound thrashing; to massacre the enemy; to weaken by inflicting wounds; to exaggerate, overdo; to wound, injure.

آثَرَ to prefer, like, favor, choose; to think proper, deem wise; to hope for the best for oneself.

أ ب ت ث ج ح خ د ذ ر ز س ش ص ض ط ظ ع غ ف ق ك ل م ن هـ و ي

أَثَّرَ to affect, influence, act upon; to make an impression on; to induce; to prefer; to pursue, follow up (a question, a problem); to engross (the attention).

أَثَر track, trace, vestige; sign, mark; touch; impression, effect; influence; work of art, ancient monument, remnants, vestiges; touch, trace, consequence, result; prophetic tradition.

أَثَرُ الجُرْح scar (of a wound); cicatrix.

أَثَرُ القَدَم footprint.

أَثَرٌ رَجْعِيّ retroactive effect.

إِثْرَ immediately after; right after.

أَثْرَى to be or become rich, wealthy; to enrich.

أَثَرِيّ (ص) archeological; ancient; antique; vestigial.

أَثَرِيّ (اسم) archeologist.

إِثْقال adding weight to; overburdening; disturbance; molestation; annoyance; encumbering; oppression.

أَثْقَلَ to make heavy; to add weight to ;to overburden; to weigh down on; to oppress, encumber, disturb, trouble, molest, harass, annoy, irritate.

أَثْلَجَ to snow; to please; to cool with ice; to turn into ice; to delight, gratify someone; to become icy.

أَثِمَ to sin, err, offend; to commit (a crime, a misdeed); to be wicked, evil, criminal.

آثِم sinful; criminal; wicked; evil, sinner.

إِثْم sin; offence; misdeed; crime.

أَثْمَرَ to bear fruit; to yield, produce, pay off; to bring in; to benefit; to result, gain, produce profit.

أَثْنَى to praise; to appreciate; to dissuade, prevent, divert (someone from); to extol; to laud; to speak appreciatively of; to compliment.

أَثْنَاء during; at the time of; while; when; as; meantime.

إِثْنَا عَشَر (إِثْنَتَا عَشْرَة) twelve.

إِثْنَان (إِثْنَتَان) two; pair; couple.

إِثْنولُوجِيّ ethnologist.

إِثْنِيّ ethnical.

إِثْنِيَّة ethnicity.

الإِثْنَيْن Monday.

أَثِير (اسم) ether; air.

أَثِير (ص) favorite; preferred; chosen; honored; venerable.

الأَثِير the preferred, the favored.

أَثِيل deep-rooted; firmly established; of noble origin.

أَثِيم sinner; offender; wicked; evil; guilty; criminal.

أَجَابَ to reply, respond, comply with, accede, answer; to hear; to fulfill, grant (a wish);to consent, agree to; to echo, ring out (voices); to react, listen, pay attention to; to show interest in.

إجَابَة answering, replying; response; compliance; granting (of a request); consent; satisfaction.

أَجَادَ to make better; to improve; to ameliorate; to recite (the Koran); to do well; to master; to be conversant with (an art or field of knowledge); to achieve exellent results.

إجَادَة excellence; skill, mastery; command; proficiency.

أَجَارَ to shelter; to harbor; to grant refuge to; to help, assist, support, rescue, save, defend; to stand by someone; to grant a sanctuary to someone.

أَجَازَ to allow, approve, sanction, warrant, authorize; to cross, exceed, surpass; to disregard; to give up; to relinquish; to endorse (a decision); to tolerate, suffer, bear; to refrain from; to cut across.

إجَازَة allowance; approval; permission, authorization, licensing; endorsement; leave, permit, licence; vacation.

إجَازَةُ سَوْق driving licence.

إجَازَةٌ مَرَضِيَّة sick leave.

إجَازَةُ مُرُور laissez-passer.

أَجَالَ to circulate; to pass around; to ponder; to let one's eyes wander about; to look around; to roam, rove, move around, patrol, cruise, tour, travel about; to rotate; to contemplate, consider carefully.

إجْبَار compulsion, coercion.

إجْبَارِيّ compulsory, obligatory, mandatory, imperative.

أَجْبَرَ to force, compel, oblige, constrain (someone to do something).

اجْتَاحَ to annihilate, destroy, ruin; to flood, inundate (the land);to carry away, sweep away; to subdue; to overwhelm, overcome, eradicate; to pervade, infest, swarm over; to trespass.

اجْتَازَ to cross, traverse, pass through; undergo, suffer, endure; to surmount, get over, cope with; to overstep, leave behind, surpass.

اجْتَثَّ to uproot; to tear out; to deracinate; to extirpate.

اجْتِثَاث tearing out; uprooting, deracination, extirpation.

اجْتِذَاب attraction; drawing; enticement, lure, seduction.

اجْتَذَبَ to attract, draw, entice, lure, seduce.

اجْتَرَّ to ruminate.

اجْتَرَأَ to dare, venture, risk; to take the risk (of doing something), to be or become bold, audacious, daring, reckless.

اجْتَرَحَ to achieve, accomplish, carry out, bring about, perform; to commit, do, perpetrate.

اجْتَرَفَ to carry along; to sweep away; to wash away; to tear away; to carry off.

اجْتَزَّ to cut off; to shear off (the wool of sheep).

اجْتَزَأَ to divide; to cut up; to partition; to separate; to substract; to shorten; to deduct; to be content.

اجْتَلَى to observe; to look at; to contemplate; to reflect; to bring to light; to manifest itself; to clear up; to reveal; to regard; to clarify.

اجْتِلاب bringing; getting; importation.

اجْتَلَبَ to bring; to get; to fetch; to import.

اجْتِماع meeting; get-together, gathering, assembly; reunion; rally, convention; conjunction; constellation (astronomy); confluence (of rivers); human society; crossroads.

اجْتِماعِيّ social; community; group; socialist; sociological.

اجْتِماعِيّ اقْتِصادِيّ socioeconomic.

اجْتِماعِيّ سِياسِيّ sociopolitical.

اجْتَمَعَ to meet; to gather, assemble, congregate, rally, flock together; to accumulate; to unite.

اجْتَنَى to collect; to derive (a profit); to realize (an advantage); to incur (harm); to harvest; to earn; to obtain, acquire, win, gain, secure.

اجْتِناب avoidance; shunning, warding off; evasion; sidestepping; dodging; steering clear of.

اجْتَنَبَ to avert, ward off, keep out of the way; to steer clear, get out of the way; to avoid, parry; to prevent, evade, elude, dodge.

اجْتِهاد effort, exertion, endeavor; pains; trouble; industry, diligence; independent judgment (in a legal or theological question); individual judgment; jurisprudence; discretion; hardwork.

اجْتَهَدَ to endeavor, strive, fight; to tire, wear out; to exert oneself, work too hard.

اجْتِياح invasion; encroachment (upon); pervasion; plaguing; sweeping away; overflowing, flooding, overwhelming; devastation, destruction, eradication.

اجْتِياز crossing, traversing, passing through; covering (of a distance); undergoing; passing (an exam); surmounting (difficulties); endurance, sufferring.

أَجَّجَ to kindle, light, inflame (fire); to stir up (sentiments).

إجْحاف injustice; prejudice, bias; harm, injury.

أَجْحَفَ to harm, hurt, injure, prejudice; to ruin, destroy; to wrong; to eradicate, exterminate, wipe out.

أَجْدَى more useful; more beneficial; more profitable; more instrumental; more favorable.

أَجْدَبَ to be or become barren, sterile, arid (for land); to suffer from poverty (for people).

أَجْدَب (ص) barren; sterile; infertile; arid.

أَجْدَر (ص) more deserving; more suitable.

أَجْدَع mutilated; maimed.

أَجْذَلَ to gladden, delight, rejoice; to make happy.

آجَرَ to reward, recompence, remunerate; to lease, rent; to take a lease on; to employ, hire, engage the services of.

أَجَّرَ to rent out; to lease; to charter (a ship).

أَجَّرَ من الباطِن to sublet, sublease, subcharter.

آجُرّ tiles; bricks.

أَجْر wages, emolument, fee, remuneration , charge, reward, salary; stipend.

أَجْرَى to perform, carry out, execute, effect; to cause to flow; to set running (water); to impose a punishment; to grant to, donate to , bestow upon; to conduct an investigation; to hold talks.

أَجْرَى الكَلِمَةَ to inflect a word (grammar).

أَجْرَى له الحِساب to credit with.

أَجْرَى عليه الحِساب to debit with.

أَجْرَى مجرى كذا to treat in the same manner as.

أَجْرَى اتصالاً هاتفياً to call; to telephone.

أَجْرَى القُرْعَة to draw lots.

أَجْرَى مقابَلةً مع to interview; to meet with; to have a meeting with.

إِجْراء performance (of an action); execution; enforcement; measure, step, proceeding.

إِجْرائيّ procedural; executive.

إِجْرام criminality; crime; delinquency.

إِجْرامِيّ criminal; delinquent.

أَجْرَب scabby; scabious.

أُجْرَة rent; salary; wages; remuneration; fee.

أُجْرَةُ السَّفَر أو الشَّحْن charge; fare; freight.

أَجْرَد bald; hairless; barren; waste; shabby; worn.

أَجْرَمَ to commit a crime.

أَجْزَى to replace; to serve instead; to suffice.

أَجْزَلَ to give generously.

أَجَشّ hoarse; harsh; throaty.

أَجْفَلَ to scare away; to rouse; to make jump with fright.

أَجَلَّ to glorify, exalt, dignify, honor; to respect, revere, venerate; to regard far beyond something.

أَجَّلَ to postpone; to delay; to adjourn.

أَجَل term, period, date, dateline, duration, due date.

أَجَل moment of death, death.

أَجَل yes, indeed, certainly.

آجِل — future, delayed, deferred, put off, later.

آجِلاً أو عاجِلاً — sooner or later.

أَجْل — cause, reason.

أَجْلَى — to evacuate, expel, evict, force out, dislodge; to dispel, disperse, dissipate, remove.

إجْلاء — eviction, expulsion, driving away; dispersal, dissipation, removal, getting rid of.

إجلال — esteem, respect, veneration, exaltation, reverence.

أَجْلَسَ — to seat; to ask to sit; to make someone sit.

إجماع — unanimity, consensus.

إجْمَال — summing up, condensation, summation; generalization.

إجْمالاً — on the whole, in general, generally speaking, in the main, as a whole, overall.

إجْماليّ — general, total, aggregate, thorough; gross, entire, overall.

إجْماليُّ المبيعات — turnover.

أَجْمَع — all, whole, entire, altogether.

أَجْمَلَ — to sum up; to summarize; to condense; to add up; to generalize; to treat as a whole.

أَجْمَلَ في العمل — to do right; to do expertly.

أَجْنَبِيّ (ص) — foreign, extraneous, alien.

أَجْنَبِيّ (اسم) — foreigner, alien, stranger.

إجْهاد — stress, pressure, exhaustion, strain.

إجْهَاض — abortion, miscarriage; induced abortion.

أَجْهَدَ — to strain, stress, exert, overwork; to exhaut.

أَجْهَدَ نَفْسَه — to put one's mind to; to put oneself out for; to work hard; to go to great lengths; to go out of one's way for.

أَجْهَرَ — to announce, disclose, proclaim, declare openly, express frankly; to avow in public.

أَجْهَزَ — to finish off; to deliver the coup de grace to; to finish, ruin someone; to put to death.

أَجْهَشَ — to be about to weep; to break into tears; to sob, cry, weep.

أَجْهَضَ — to miscarry; to abort; to cause to have an abortion.

أَجْوَف — hollow, empty, deceitful.

أجيج — burning, blazing, flaming.

أجير — worker, servant, laborer, hireling.

آح — albumen.

أحادِيُّ التَّكافُؤ — monovalent.

أَحادِيُّ الجانِب — unilateral, one-sided.

أحادِيُّ الخَلِيَّة — unicellular.

أحادِيُّ الطور — monophase.

أَحادِيُّ القُطْب — unipolar.

أَحادِيُّ اللُّغة — monolingual.

أَحادِيُّ اللَّون — monochromatic.

أ ب ت ث ج ح خ د ذ ر ز س ش ص ض ط ظ ع غ ف ق ك ل م ن هـ و ي

أَحَاطَ to surround, encompass, encircle, enclose; to close in from all sides; to comprise; to ring; to know thoroughly, comprehend, grasp completely, understand fully; to be thoroughly acquainted with; to have comprehensive knowledge; to take note of; to bring to someone's notice.

إِحَاطَة encirclement, encompassment, comprehension, grasp, understanding, cognizance of; acquaintance, familiarity with; information, communication.

أَحَاقَ to surround, encompass, encircle, enclose, embrace.

أَحَالَ to refer to; to transfer; to assign; to forward.

أَحالَ إلى التَّقاعُد to pension off.

إِحَالَة referring, reference, relegation, submission, forwarding, referral, assignment, transmittal, transfer, cession.

أَحَبَّ to love, like, endear; to wish, want, like to do something; to show love; to reveal one's affection; to court, woo; to deem desirable; to prefer; to be fond of; to take a fancy to; to wish to, love to, want to do something.

إِحْبَاط frustration, foiling, blocking.

أَحْبَطَ to frustrate, thwart, foil, block, forestall.

أُحْبُولَة snare, trap, net, trick, ruse, ploy.

اِحْتَاجَ to need, require, demand, want.

اِحْتَارَ to become confused; to be at a loss; to know nothing; to waver, hesitate; to be unable to choose between; to be bewildered, baffled, dismayed, startled, appalled, stunned; to be at one's wit end; to be uncertain, helpless, perplexed.

اِحْتَاطَ to take precautions; to take care; to be on one's guard against; to make provision for; to surround; to encircle; to protect, guard, preserve.

اِحْتَالَ to trick; to deceive, fool, delude, beguile; to cheat, defraud, outwit; to contrive; to manage to work out; to resort to trickery.

اِحْتِبَاس retention, restraint, inhibition, impediment, obstruction, stoppage.

اِحْتِبَاسُ البول ischuria.

اِحْتَبَسَ to be withheld, detained, put away; to be restrained, held back, confined; to be impeded, stopped, interrupted.

اِحْتَجَّ to protest; to advance as an argument, a plea, an excuse, a pretext; to invoke, claim, maintain; to dispute, argue; to allege in support or vindication; to remonstrate, object, raise objections.

اِحْتِجاب hiding, disappearance, withdrawal, occultation.

اِحْتِجاج protest, excuse, pretext; plea, pretence, remonstrance; objection, exception to, claim, pleading; expostulation, demurral.

اِحْتِجاز arrest, detention, seizure, confiscation, sequestration; reservation of seats; separation.

اِحْتَجَب to be hidden, concealed, withdrawn, veiled, sheltered; to cease publication (newspaper, magazine).

اِحْتَجَزَ to confiscate, impound, seize, sequester; to safeguard, reserve, retain; to detain, arrest.

اِحْتَدَّ to get angry, furious, exasperated, excited, upset; to intensify, heighten, build up; to become more serious, more intense, more severe, more infuriated.

اِحْتِدام burning, ardor, vehemence, violence.

اِحْتَدَمَ to glow, flare, flame, burn; to flare up, erupt, break out (the battle); to become furious; to burn with anger, rage.

اِحْتَذَى to imitate, emulate, follow the example of, copy; to put on shoes.

اِحْتِذاء imitation, emulation, following the example of; putting on shoes.

اِحْتِراز caution, prudence, alertness, protection.

اِحْتِرازِيّ precautionary; preventive; protective.

اِحْتِراس circumspection, prudence, vigilence, precaution.

اِحْتِراف professionalism, professional pursuit of (a trade, etc).

اِحْتِراق burning, combustion, fire, conflagration.

اِحْتِرام respect, deference, regard, esteem; dignity, gravity, solemnity; observance of; compliance with; adherence to; carrying out, standing by, making good (one's words).

اِحْتِرامُ الذَّات self-respect, self-esteem.

اِحْتَرَزَ to be on one's guard against; to be wary of; to be careful; to watch out; to be on the alert, on the look-out; to take precautions.

اِحْتَرَسَ to be on one's guard against; to be wary of; to be careful; to take precautions.

اِحْتَرَفَ to practise something as a profession; to do something professionally; to strive for success.

اِحْتَرَقَ to burn, catch fire, kindle, ignite; to be on fire, aflame, ablaze; to be burned by fire.

اِحْتَرَمَ to honor, revere, venerate, esteem, respect, admire, prize; to hold in esteem; to think highly of.

اِحْتَرَمَ to observe, honor, live up to, comply with, abide by, conform to; to fulfill, meet (one's obligations).

اِحْتَسَى to drink; to sip.

احْتِساب satisfaction, contentment.

احْتِسَاب calculation, computation, counting.

احْتَسَبَ to calculate, compute, reckon, count.

احْتَسَبَ to consider, deem, count, regard as, think, suppose, take for.

احْتِشَاد gathering, assembling, crowding together, trooping, swarming; crowd; concentration (of troops).

احْتَشَدَ to gather; to concentrate; to mobilize (an army); to assemble, gather, show together; to be rallied, crowded, assembled, concentrated; to be heaped up.

احْتَشَمَ to be modest, decent, decorous, chaste, reserved.

احْتِضَار demise, agony of death.

احْتِضَان embrace, accolade, hugging.

احْتَضَنَ to take in the bosom; to bring up a child

احتضنت الأمّ رضيعها بحنان
The mother hugs her baby lovingly

احْتَفَى to receive hospitably; to entertain cordially; to honor, welcome; to celebrate (an occasion); to greet.

احْتِفاء welcome, greeting, honoring, celebration.

احْتِفَاظ retention, maintenance, conservation, protection, vindication; keeping, holding, safeguarding.

احْتِفَال celebration, ceremony, festival, reception.

احْتِفَالِيّ ceremonial, ceremonious, ritual, solemn, festive.

احْتَفَظَ to keep, retain, hold, maintain; to preserve, conserve, hold in custody; to safeguard, shelter.

احْتَفَلَ to celebrate, commemorate; to honor, welcome, receive someone kindly.

احْتِقَار contempt, disdain, scorn, humiliation; to regard with contempt; to look down one's nose at someone.

احْتِقان congestion.

احْتَقَرَ to despise, scorn, disdain; to have a low opinion of; to humiliate; to look with contempt (someone).

احْتَقَنَ to be congested; to flush, glow, redden (the face); to take an enema.

احْتَكَّ to rub oneself against; to come in close contact with; to be in contact with; to mingle with.

احْتِكَار monopoly, monopolization.

احْتِكَارِيّ monopolistic.

احْتِكَاك friction, rubbing, chafing; getting in contact; mingling, mixing with.

احْتَكَرَ to monopolize; to hoard and withhold (merchandise); to corner (the market); to have exclusive possession of something.

احْتَكَمَ to appeal to; to go to court; to seek a judgment from.

احْتَلَّ to occupy the place of someone; to occupy (a territory); to assume, take over, hold (place, rank, office); to seize unlawfully; to misappropriate, usurp (something).

احْتِلال occupation; takeover; seizure; usurpation; taking possession of ; appropriation.

احْتَمَى to seek protection from; to seek shelter in; to protect oneself from.

احْتِمَال possibility, probability, likelihood, potentiality; bearing, standing, suffering, toleration.

احْتِمَالِيّ likely, probable, conceivable, prospective.

احْتَمَلَ to bear, assume, take upon oneself; to sustain, endure; tolerate, undergo; to put up with.

احْتَوَى to contain, include, comprise, comprehend, encompass, enclose, embody, hold, cover, imply; to possess, own.

احْتِواء inclusion, containment.

احْتِياج need, want, requirement, necessity.

احْتِياط caution, prudence, precaution, reservation; provision, care, prevention, precautionary measures.

احْتِياطِيّ precautionary, preventive; replacement, spare; stand-by; reserve funds, reserves.

احْتِياطِيُّ الاستهلاك depreciation reserve.

احْتِياطِيُّ الذهب gold reserve.

احْتِياطِيُّ رأس المال capital reserve.

احْتِياطِيٌّ قانونيٌّ legal reserve.

احْتِيال trickery, cunning, subtlety; malice, treachery, perfidy, deception, fraud.

احْتِيالِيّ fraudulent, deceptive, malicious.

إِحْجام refrainment, abstention, forbearance, recoiling; reluctance, unwillingness, restraint, aloofness.

أَحْجَمَ to refrain from; to abstain from; to retreat; to desist; to shrink, recoil.

أُحْجِيَة riddle, mystery, puzzle.

أَحَدَّ النظرَ إلى to scrutinize; to look sharply at.

أَحَدَّ السِّكِّين to sharpen; to make sharp.

أَحَد one; unique, singular, individual; matchless.

أَحَد alone, single, lone.

أَحَدٌ ما somebody, someone, anybody, anyone.

الأَحَد (يوم) Sunday.

أَحَدُ الشعانين Palm Sunday.

أَحَدُ العَنْصَرَة Pentecost.

أَحَدَ عشَرَ (إِحْدى عَشْرَة) eleven.

إِحْدَاث production, creation, invention, origination, effectuation, causation.

إِحْدَاثِيّ coordinate (mathematics).

أَحْدَب (ص) humpbacked; hunchbacked.

في حيِّنا صبيٌّ أحدب الظهر

In our quarter lives a hunchbacked boy

أَحْدَب (اسم) hunchback, humpback.

أَحْدَب convex, arched, vaulted, protruding, bent, crooked.

أَحْدَثَ to produce, create, invent, originate, generate; to give rise to, bring about; to provoke, induce, trigger, work out, result in.

أَحْدَقَ to surround, encircle, enclose, embrace.

أَحْدَقَ النظرَ to look sharply at; to scrutinize.

أَحَرّ hotter, warmer.

أَحْرَى more appropriate, more suitable, more adequate.

بالأَحْرَى more precisely, strictly speaking, more explicitly, with greater reason, the more so, rather.

إِحْرَاج embarrassment, disconcertion, putting in an awkward position.

إِحْرَاق burning, incineration, setting on fire, ignition, kindling,; cremation (of dead bodies); arson (burning buildings on purpose).

إِحْرام state of ritual consecretion of a Mecca pilgrim; garment of a Mecca pilgrim.

أَحْرَجَ to embarrass; disconcert; to put in an embarrassing situation; to forbid, prohibit.

أَحْرَزَ to acquire, obtain, win, gain, attain, achieve.

أَحْرَزَ قَصَبَ السَّبْق to score a great success; to win a victory; to prevail over, overpower, beat, defeat.

أَحْرَقَ to burn; to destroy by fire; to set on fire; to set ablaze; to ignite, light, kindle.

أَحْزَنَ to sadden, grieve, depress, deject; to make someone sad.

أَحَسَّ to feel, sense, perceive, notice, experience; to be affected by; to be deeply touched by.

إِحْسَاس feeling, sensation, perception, sensitivity, emotion, sentiment, compassion.

إحْسَان charity, beneficence, philanthropy,almsgiving, kind act; performance of good deeds.

أَحْسَنَ to do well; to act well or right; to do expertly, proficiently one's job; to master; to be proficient (in a language, an art, a handicraft); to be charitable; to do favors; to do good (to someone); to give alms.

أَحْسَنْتَ! well done!.

أَحْسَن (ص) better, surperior, nicer, more beautiful.

الأَحْسَن the best; the finest; the nicest; the most beautiful; the most superior.

أَحْسَنُ حَالاً مِنْ better off than.

أَحْشَاء bowels, intestines, entrails; interior, inside.

أَحْصَى to calculate, compute, reckon, enumerate.

إِحْصَاء counting; enumeration, statistics.

إِحْصَاءُ السُّكَّان census.

إِحصائيّ statistical; stastistician.

إِحضار bringing; procurement; supply; summon.

إِحْضارٌ إلى المَحْكَمة arraingnment, summoning, subpoening.

أَحْضَر to bring, get, fetch, introduce, bring forward; to procure, supply, provide; to call for; to send for; to summon; to carry with.

أُحْفُور fossil.

أَحَقُّ worthier, more deserving.

إِحْقَاق enforcement, execution, carrying out.

إِحْكَام accuracy, precision, exactness, perfection.

أَحْكَمَ to consolidate, fortify, tighten, fasten; to master, excel in, make perfect; to compact; to make firm, solid, tight.

أَحَلَّ to absolve from; to discharge, release, disengage from; to relieve, exempt, exonerate, free from; to enjoin on; to make incumbent on; to impose as a duty upon.

أَحَلَّ to make stay (at a place); to place, set, position, locate.

أَحَلَّ to replace by; to substitute for; to subrogate.

إِحْلاَل substitution for someone; replacement, substitution; subrogation of a debtor by another.

احْلَوْلَى to sweeten; to become sweet, pretty, charming, pleasant.

إِحْليل urethra.

إِحْليليّ urethral.

أَحَمَّ to heat, make hot; to bathe someone or something.

أَحْمَى to heat, make hot.

احْمَرَّ to redden; to become red; to make red.

احْمَرَّ to blush, flush, glow (from shyness, timidity).

أَحْمَر red; purple, scarlet

أ ب ت ث ج ح خ د ذ ر ز س ش ص ض ط ظ ع غ ف ق ك ل م ن هـ و ي

أَحْمَرُ الشِّفاه lipstick.

احْمِرَار redness, blushing, glowing.

أَحْمَق stupid, foolish, fatuous, dumb, idiot, silly.

أَحْنَقَ to infuriate, anger, irritate, vex, madden.

أَحْوَجَ to impoverish; to reduce to poverty; to compel to; to oblige to ; to make necessary for to.

أَحْوَج in greater need of.

أَحْوَر having eyes with a marked contrast of white and black.

احْوَلَّ to become cross-eyed.

أَحْوَل cross-eyed, squint-eyed, cockeyed.

أَحْيَا to give life to; to revive, reanimate; to celebrate a festival; to commemorate a deceased person; to spend the night in prayer; to throw a party; to resurrect.

إِحْيَاء animation, vitalization, resuscitation, reanimation; restoration, renewal; commemoration.

أَحْيَائِيّ (ص) biological.

أَحْيَائِيّ (اسم) biologist.

أَحْيَاناً sometimes, occasionally, at times.

أَخ brother, fellow man, neighbor, friend; member of a religious brotherhood.

أَخٌ شقيق brother-german.

أَخٌ لأب أو لأم half-brother.

الأخ هو الشقيق وأنا أكبر من أخي بسنة واحدة

I am older than my brother by one year

أخو الزَّوْج أو الزَّوْجَة brother-in-law.

إِخْوَة brethren, brothers.

آخَى to fraternize with.

إِخاء brotherhood, fraternity.

أَخَّاذ captivating, fascinating, attractive, breathtaking.

أَخافَ to intimidate, frighten, scare, alarm, fill with fear (someone).

إِخافَة act of frightening, scaring someone or something.

إِخْبار notification, information, transmission; declaration; denunciation; reporting (an event).

إِخْبارِيَّة news, information,

أَخْبَرَ to inform, notify, advise, tell; to report, relate; to denounce, inform against.

أُخت sister.

أُخْتٌ لأب أو لأُمّ half sister.

sister-in-law.	أُخْت الزَّوْج أو الزَّوْجَة	
to choose, select, elect, prefer, favor.	اخْتارَ	
to be conceited, vain; to show conceit, arrogance.	اخْتالَ	
to hide oneself, to vanish; to conceal oneself	اخْتبأَ	

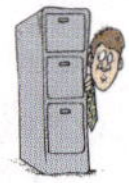

hiding, concealment. — اخْتِباء

experiment, examination, test, trial, investigation, research; practical knowldge. — اخْتِبار

experimental, empirical. — اخْتِبارِيّ

to test, examine, try out; to make an experiment; to investigate; to put to test; to experiment; to know thoroughly; to know by experience, by trial. — اخْتَبَرَ

to become crazy; to be or become mentally disturbed, insane; to become muddled, deranged, confused in his mind. — اخْتَبَلَ

conclusion, termination, finishing, completion, winding-up. — اخْتِتام

to conclude, terminate, finish, complete, wind-up. — اخْتَتَمَ

invention, creation, innovation. — اخْتِراع

patent. — اخْتِراع (براءةُ اخْتِراع)

penetration, piercing, disruption, crossing; percolation, infiltration, breakthrough. — اخْتِراق

to invent; to devise — اخْتَرَعَ

to penetrate, pierce, disrupt, cross; to pass through; to permeate, infiltrate; to break a blockade. — اخْتَرَقَ

اخترع ماركوني أجهزة عدّة أهمها التلغراف
Marconi invented several instruments of which the telegraph was the most important

stenography; cancellation, reduction; abbreviation, abridgment; shorthand. — اخْتِزال

storage, storing, accumulation, warehousing; hoarding. — اخْتِزان

to write in shorthand; to abbreviate; to reduce. — اخْتَزَلَ

to store, accumlate, hoard; to keep secret; to put in safe keeping; to keep in a store,warehouse. — اخْتَزَنَ

to specialize; to be competent in; to have special relevance to; to be devoted, dedicated in particular to; to have as a special function or task; to have jurisdiction in. — اخْتَصَّ

to set aside for oneself; to destine for oneself. — اخْتَصَّ

to bestow special honors upon someone in preference to others; to endow, confer, bestow. — اخْتَصَّ

to apportion, allot, assign, give accord to. — اخْتَصَّ

اخْتِصار abbreviation, summing up, abstraction, briefing; brevity, conciseness.

باخْتِصار in short, in brief, in summary.

اخْتِصاص specialization; jurisdiction; competence, authority; special field; function; sphere of interest.

اخْتِصاصيّ specialist, expert, technician.

اخْتَصَر to abbreviate, abridge, shorten, summarize, epitomize.

اخْتِطاف forcible seizure, rape, abduction, kidnapping.

اخْتَطَف to abduct, kidnap; to seize by force; to snatch, wrest, wrench from; to run away with; to dazzle the eyes.

اخْتَفَى to disappear, fade out, hide; to keep oneself out of view; to disguise oneself; to vanish ;to be absent.

اخْتِفاء disappearance, vanishing, fading out, hiding.

اخْتَلَّ to be mentally disordered, unbalanced, disturbed, deranged; to be or become defective, imperfect, faulty; to be or become unbalanced.

اخْتَلَج to quiver, tremble, quake, shake, twitch; to be filled with grief (heart).

اخْتَلَج to worry, disturb, preoccupy, affect deeply, penetrate, touch (because of something).

اخْتَلَس to embezzle, misappropriate, steal, pilfer.

اخْتَلَس السَّمع to eavesdrop on.

اخْتَلَس النَّظَر to peep at; to peek at; to steal a look at,

اخْتَلَط to be or become mixed, mingled, blended, combined; to be or become associated with; to be or become confused, muddled, unsettled, disordered, deranged; to be or become mentally deranged, lunatic, demented.

اخْتَلَف to differ, vary from; to be unlike, dissimilar, inconsistent, contrary, opposed.

اخْتَلَف to be diverse, varied.

اخْتَلَف to disagree, disaccord; to be at variance; to argue about; to dispute about.

اخْتَلَف to frequent a place; to visist frequently a place.

اخْتَلَق to fabricate, invent, create, fake, concoct, contrive, devise, trump up.

اخْتَمَر to undergo fermentation; to rise (dough); to be brewed (beer); to ripen; to become fully developed (idea); to wear a veil (for a woman).

اخْتِناق suffocation, asphyxia.

اخْتَنَق to be or become strangulated, suffocated, smothered, asphyxiated, throttled; to be choked to death; to be crammed, jammed, crowded (for a place).

اخْتِيار choice, selection, picking out; option; preference; free will; election.

اخْتِياريّ optional, facultative, voluntary; elective; volitional;

اخْتِيال arrogance, haughtiness; pride; vainglory; snobbism, conceit.

أخْجَل to embarrass; to put to shame.

أُخْدود furrow, ridge, groove, trench.

أُخْدودُ الوجه wrinkle.

أخَذَ to take, receive, obtain, seize, grab; to take hold of; to infer, deduce; to grip; to thrill; to acquire; to adhere to; to follow; to imitate someone; to accept; to admonish; to enjoin; to impose something on someone; to deprive someone of; to blame someone for; to hold against someone; to learn from; to study under someone; to begin, start, set out, get ready; to adopt; to take possession of; to sit down; to be on one's guard; to be complaisant toward someone; to punish; to consult; to deal with; to obstuct someone's way; to take something upon oneself; to put someone under an obligation; to be caught unawares; to help; to take care of someone; to treat harshly; to take into consideration.

أخَذَ شَكْلاً to take on a form or shape.

أخَذَ أُهبَتَه to get ready.

أخَذَ عِلماً to acknowledge; to take note of.

أخَذَ نَفَساً to inhale; to breathe.

آخَذَ to blame; to reproach; to punish.

أخْذُ الرأي dispute; debate; discussion.

أخَّرَ to delay, postpone; to hinder, obstruct, retard; to set back a watch; to dismiss.

آخَر another; last; ultimate; distinct; unlike others.

آخِرُ الأمر in the end; finally.

آخِر another; the other; end; termination; bottom.

إخْراج taking out, removal; emission; hauling off; evacuation; extraction; expulsion; direction; production; staging a motion picture or a theater presentation; output from a computer; exclusion; release, issuance.

الآخِرَة the hereafter, the afterlife.

أخْرَجَ to go out, emerge from, exude, depart, leave; stick out, step out; to discharge; to expel; to eliminate; to exclude; to issue, publish.

أخْرَجَ فضلات الجسم to excrete.

أخْرَجَ فيلماً أو مسرحية to direct; to stage.

أخْرَسَ to silence, muzzle, reduce to silence.

أخْرَس mute; dumb.

أخْرَق awkward; stupid; illegal; unlawful; clumsy; inept; unhandy; foolish.

أ ب ت ث ج ح خ د ذ ر ز س ش ص ض ط ظ ع غ ف ق ك ل م ن هـ و ي

أَخْزَى — to dishonor; to humiliate; to degrade; to debase; to put to shame; to disgrace.

إِخْصائيّ — specialist; technician.

إِخْصاب — fertilization; impregnation; insemination.

أَخْصَبَ — to fertilize, fecundate, impregnate.

إِخْضاع — subjugation; subordination; overcoming; subdual; subjection.

أَخْضَر — green; verdant.

اخْضِرار — greenness; verdancy.

أَخْضَعَ — to subjugate, subdue, conquer, overcome, overpower, to subject to; to impose upon.

أَخْطَأَ — to err; to make a mistake; to blunder; to sin; to be at fault; to miss a shot; to be incorrect or wrong.

إِخْطار — notice; notification; warning.

أُخْطُبُوط — octopus.

أَخْطَرَ — to notify, inform, warn; caution.

يعيش **الأخطبوط** في عمق البحر
ويقتات بالأسماك الصغيرة

The octopus is a sea animal
and feeds on small fish

أَخَفّ (ص) — lighter; milder; weaker; lesser.

أَخْفَى — to hide, conceal, keep secret; to disguise; to keep out of view; to cover up, veil, blind, mask.

إِخْفاء — hiding, concealment; secretion; sheltering; covering, veiling; disguising; lowering of the voice.

إِخْفاق — failure; fizzle; flop; flasco.

أَخْفَقَ — to be unsuccessful; to fail, miss, miscarry; to be abortive.

أَخَلَّ — to be deficient; to breach, violate, transgress, infringe.

أَخَلَّ بالأَمْن — to disturb the peace.

أَخَلَّ بالتَّوازُن — to upset; to disequilibrate.

أَخْلَى — to desert, leave, vacate, evacuate; to release; to empty, deplete; to cede.

أَخْلَى طَرَفَ الشَّخْص — to exonerate; to exculpate; to free.

إِخْلاء — vacating; emptying; clearing; evacuation; release.

إِخْلاد — perpetuation, immortalization; commemoration.

إِخْلاد — abiding; remaining; staying; lingering.

إِخْلاص — honesty, sincerity, devotion, loyalty; frankness, candor; faithfulness, fidelity.

أَخْلاق (ج) — character, temper; morals ethics; manners.

أَخْلاقِيَّة — morality; ethics; morals, moralism.

إخلال — breach, infraction, violation; offense, transgression; disturbance; impairment.

أَخْلَدَ — to remain; to stay; to rest; to make eternal; to perpetuate; to immortalize.

أَخْلَصَ — to be devoted to, sincere to, loyal to.

أَخْلَفَ — to renege; to break one's promise; to fail to keep one's word or commitment; to disappoint.

إخْماج — infectiousness, infection.

إخْمادٌ للنار أو للعاصفة — extinction; quenching; smothering.

إخْمادٌ للثورة — suppression, repression; putting down.

أَخْمَدَ الحريق — to extinguish, quench, smother.

أَخْمَدَ الثورة — to suppress, repress, put down, quell.

أَخْمَدَ نَفَسَ الشَّخْص — to stifle, smother, kill.

أَخْمَصُ القدم — sole of the foot; vola.

أَخْنَى على الشخص الدَّهْرُ — to afflict; to aggrieve; to crush; to ruin.

أُخُوَّة — brotherhood; fraternity.

أَخَوِيّ — brotherly; fraternal.

أَخَوِيَّة — brotherhood; fraternity.

أخير — last; latest; ultimate; extreme.

أخيرًا — finally; at last; in the end; eventually; recently; lately; of late; not long ago.

أخيرًا وليس آخِرًا — last but not least.

أَدَّى — to perform, carry out, fulfill, accomplish; to lead to, cause, bring about, generate, engender, create; to induce.

أَدَّى التحية — to salute.

أَدَّى خدمةً — to render a service.

أَدَّى دينًا — to settle; to pay.

أَدَّى شهادةً — to testify; to witness.

أَدَّى يمينًا — to swear; to take an oath.

أداء — performance; exercising; discharge; settlement of a debt; taking an oath; execution, carrying out.

آداب (ج) — literature; etiquette; decency; morals.

أداة — tool; device; apparatus; appliance; instrument.

أداة — means; medium.

أداة — particle.

أداةُ التعريف — definite article.

أدارَ — to run, administer, manage, direct; to operate, set in operation; to rotate, whirl; to aim; to circulate.

إدارة — administration, direction, management; setting in operation; department, office.

إدارةُ الأعمال — business administration.

إدارِيّ (ص) — administrative, managerial, executive; departmental.

إدارِيّ (اسم) — manager, director, administrator.

أَدامَ — to perpetuate, eternize, maintain, conserve; to hold, retain, preserve.

إدامة maintaining; preservation, conservation; maintenance; retention, keeping up.

أدانَ to condemn, incriminate, inculpate; to find guilty; to denounce, sensure.

أدانَ مالاً to lend; to loan.

إدانة condemnation, incrimination, denunciation.

أَدَّبَ to educate; to refine.

أدَّبَ to punish, chastise, discipline.

أَدَب good manners; courtesy; decency; politeness.

أَدَب literature.

إدْبار escape, flight; running away from; turning the back on.

أَدْبَرَ to turn the back on; to escape; to run away.

أَدَبِيّ literary; moral; ethical.

ادِّخار saving; storing, hoarding; accumulation.

إدْخَال admission, admittance; introduction, insertion, inclusion, incorporation; entering; input of data in a computer.

ادَّخَرَ to save; to keep; to store away; to amass, accumulate, reserve for future use.

أَدْخَلَ to let enter; to introduce, insert; to drive in; to include, embody.

أَدْرَى to inform of; to tell about; to notify of; to make someone aware of.

إدْرَاج inclusion, insertion, recording, incorporation; entry; registration.

إدْرَاك recognition, realization, discernment, awareness; comprehension, understanding; puberty; perception.

إدْرَاك overtaking, catching up with.

أَدْرَجَ to incorporate; to include; to insert; to enter; to embody; to register in a list; to fold up.

أَدْرَكَ to realize, understand, become aware of, perceive, comprehend, come to know.

أَدْرَكَ to mature; to ripen; to attain puberty.

أَدْرَكَ to reach and seize one another; to face, meet.

أَدْرَكَ to get, obtain, acquire, accomplish.

أَدْرَكَ to take steps to prevent; to put in order; to correct.

أَدْرَكَ to provide compensation; to repair; to redress.

ادَّعَى to claim, assume, presume, pretend.

ادَّعَى على to charge, accuse, prosecute, sue, bring suit against.

ادِّعاء على accusation, charge, prosecution in court, litigation; lawsuit.

إدْغام (لغة) diphtong; contraction; assimilation.

أَدْغَمَ to incorporate, embody, insert, introduce; to merge, amalgamate, join, integrate.

أَدْلى	to slander, calumniate; to express, utter, declare, state, announce; to deliver a speech; to adduce, present, advance, offer, plead; to testify, witness.
أَدْلى بِصَوْته	to vote, cast a vote.
ادْلَهَمَّ	to be pitch-dark, gloomy.
آدَم	Adam.
إدمان	addiction; mania.
إدمانٌ على الكحول	alcoholism.
إدمانُ المُخَدِّرات	drug addiction.
أَدَمَة	dermis; epidermis.
أَدْمَجَ	to incorporate, embody, include; to introduce, annex, interpolate; to merge, join, amalgamate, unite.
أَدْمَنَ	to be addicted to.
آدَمِيّ	human, human being.
أَدْنى	to approximate, measure up; to approach, draw near; to bring close; to lower.
أَدْنَى	nearer; closer; lower; inferior; minimum.
أَدْنَاه	below, hereunder, hereinbelow.
أَدْنَفَ	to be seriously ill.
أَدْهَشَ	to astonish, amaze, surprise, bewilder, startle, perplex, baffle, puzzle, constern; to dismay.
أَديب (اسم)	man of letters; writer; author.
أَديب (ص)	polite; cultured; well-bred, civil, courteous.

يؤلف الأديب كتباً يضمّ أبحاثه فيها

The author writes books in which he includes his researches

إذ	then; when; since; because; in view of the fact that; for.
إذْ ذاك	at that time; then.
إذا	if; when; whenever; whether; unless; if not; in case of ; in the event of; provided that.
إذاً	therefore; then; in that case; hence; consequently; accordingly; thus.
آذَى	to hurt, harm, damnify; to cause injury; to annoy, vex, offend, harass, molest; to offend, insult.
أَذًى	injury; detriment; evil; nuissance; harm; offense; insult; grievance; trouble.
أَذابَ	to dissolve, melt, liquefy, fuse.
إذابَة	dissolution; melting; liquefaction.
آذار	March.
أَذاعَ	to announce, proclaim, publish; to reveal, disclose, divulge, to spread, propagate, disseminate, diffuse; to broadcast, transmit by radio;

تكثر الزوابع والأمطار في شهر آذار

March is the month of hurricanes and rains

to telecast, transmit by television; to show, manifest, display.

إذاعة spreading; dissemination, propagation; announcement, proclamation; revelation, disclosure; broadcasting; transmission; publication; divulgence; telecasting; radio station.

أذاق to make someone taste something; to make someone suffer.

يستمع أبي إلى أخبار الإذاعة صباح كل يوم قبل أن يذهب إلى العمل

My father hears news of the local radio station every morning before he leaves for work

أذان call to prayer (in Islam).

أَذْبَلَ to make wither; to cause to dry up or fade.

إذْعان submission, yielding, giving in, obedience; acquiescence; compliance; pliability.

أَذْعَنَ to submit to, yield to, surrender to, give in to; to obey, comply with, acquiesce to; to accede to someone's wishes or orders.

أذْكى to kindle,light; to stir up, flare up; to cause to blaze.

أَذَلَّ to degrade, humiliate, debase, humble someone; to subject, subdue, conquer; to deride, flout, disgrace.

إذْلال degradation, humiliation, debasement; derision; subdual; subjection.

أَذِنَ to allow, permit, authorize; to call to prayer; to announce, inform, notify; to urge, admonish, exhort.

آذَنَ to be on the verge of doing something; to show signs of the imminent end; to herald, announce, indicate.

أَذَّنَ to call to prayers (in Islam).

أُذُن ear; handle.

إذَن therefore; hence; thus; consequently; accordingly.

إذْن permission; leave; licence; authorization.

أَذْنَبَ to commit a crime or an offense; to be guilty.

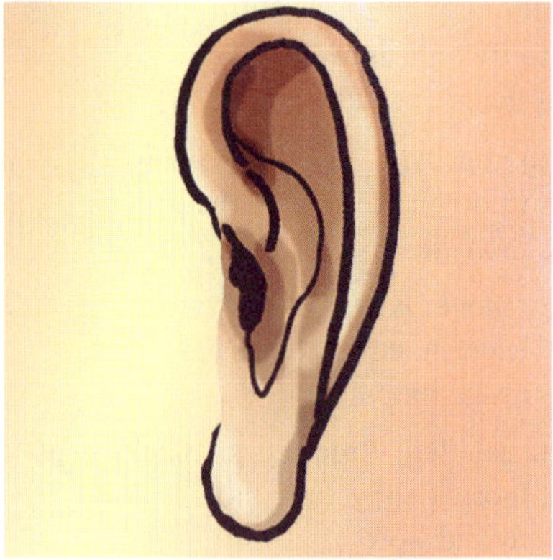

لكل إنسان أذنان يسمع بواسطتهما

Human beings have two ears for hearing

أذهَلَ to astonish, alarm, startle, surprise, amaze; to frighten, scare; to confuse, bewilder, stun, confound.

أذِيَّة harm; injury; evil; harassment; damage; insult; prejudice; nuisance; grievance; pain.

أُذَيْنُ القلب atrium; auricle.

أَرَى to show, exhibit, present, bring out.

أراجيف (ج) false rumors; lies.

أَراحَ to relieve; to give rest; to put at ease; to soothe; to calm down; to relax; to please.

إراحَة relief; soothing; relaxation; resting; easement.

أَرادَ to intend, have in mind, wish, desire; to seek, aim at, covet, strive for.

إرادَة will, wish, desire; intent, volition.

إرادِيّ voluntary, volitional, intentional, willful.

أَراقَ to shed, spill, pour; to make a liquid flow.

أَراقَ ماءَ وجهه to sacrifice one's honor; to lose face.

إراقَة shedding; spilling; pouring out.

إراقَةُ الدِّماء bloodshed.

أَرَب aim; goal; wish; need; purpose.

إِرْب limb; organ; need; sense; mind.

أَرْبَى to exceed; to be more than; to increase, grow, augment.

إِرْبَاك confusion, embarassment, muddle, upsetting; bewildering; complicating; entanglement.

الأَرْبِعاء Wednesday.

أَرْبَعَة (عدد) four.

أَرْبَعَة عَشَر (عدد) fourteen.

أَرْبَعُون (عدد) forty.

الأَرْبَعون the fortieth.

أَرْبَكَ to confuse, disconcert, disturb, befuddle, embarrass, perplex, puzzle, baffle, bewilder; to complicate, upset; to involve.

أُرْبِيَّة groin.

ارْتَأَى to believe, think, consider, judge; to suggest, propose; to contemplate, ponder on; to see, behold.

ارْتابَ to show suspicion; to doubt; to suspect; to be suspicious, doubtful, skeptical; to be distrustful.

ارْتاحَ to be satisfied with; to feel at ease; to have a rest; to relax; to be pleased, happy, glad.

ارْتَادَ to frequent a place; to visit often a place.

ارْتَاعَ to be frightened, scared, terrified, alarmed, dismayed, shocked, horrified.

ارْتِباط correlation; connection, linkup, conjunction; tie; relation; attachment.

ارْتِباط engagement, commitment, obligation.

ارْتِباك confusion, embarrasment, puzzlement; muddle; mess; upset; entanglement; tangle; disconcertation; perplexity; bewilderment; snarl.

ارْتَبَطَ to connect or to be connected to; to be joined, linked, attached, coupled with; to be moored, fastened to.

ارْتَبَكَ to be confused, disconcerted, disturbed, upset, agitated. embarrassed; to feel perplexed, puzzled. at a loss; to become involved in.

ارْتَجَّ to shake, tremble; to be shaken, convulsed.

ارْتِجاج shock, convulsion, tremor, shaking.

ارْتِجاف tremor, quaking, trembling, quavering.

ارْتِجال improvisation; extemporisation.

ارْتِجاليّ impromptu; offhanded; improvised, extemporary.

ارْتَجَعَ to restitute, return, refund; to react; to retrieve, revoke; to recall.

ارْتَجَفَ to tremble, quiver, shiver, shake.

ارْتَجَلَ to improvise; to extemporize; to do on the spur of the moment.

ارْتَحَلَ to move away; to depart; to leave; to emigrate; to pass away, die.

ارْتَخَى to sag, flag, droop; to be slack, loose, flabby, limp, lax, flaccid, soft.

ارْتِخَاء sagging; relaxation; limpness; lassitude, laxity, slackness; abatement, mitigation.

ارْتَدَّ to return back; to waver; to fall back; to retrogress; to revert; to forsake one's faith; to withdraw; to renounce.

ارْتَدَى to wear, put on clothes; to dress.

ارْتِداد withdrawal; retreat; regress, return; reversion; renegation; rebound, bounce.

ارْتَدَعَ to be deterred from; to be inhibited from.

ارْتَسَمَ to manifest, show, reveal itself; to come out, appear, emerge; to be visible, evident, clear.

ارْتَشَى to accept a bribe; to be bribed.

ارْتِشَاء bribery.

ارْتَشَحَ to filter, percolate, leak.

ارْتَضَى to be satisfied, content, pleased; to accept; to consent, agree, approve willingly.

ارْتِطَام clash, impact, collision.

ارْتَطَمَ to collide with; to bump against; to run into.

ارْتعَاش tremor, quivering, shivering, shaking.

ارْتعَبَ to be frightened, terrified, scared, horrified.

ارْتَعَدَ to tremble, shake, quiver, shudder.

ارْتَعَشَ to tremble, shiver, quiver, flutter

ارْتِفَاع rising, ascension, ascent; height; altitude, elevation; loudness of voice.

ارْتَفَعَ to rise; to ascend; to become high, elevated; to soar; to climb; to uprise.

ارْتَقَى to go up; to progress; to rise in rank; to ascend; to climb; to make progress.

ارْتِقَاء progress; development; rising; promotion; climbing; mounting; accession.

ارْتَقَبَ to expect; to anticipate; to await; to look forward; to look out for; to lie in wait.

ارْتِكَاب perpetration, committing; pursuit; practice.

ارْتِكَاز support; resting on; dependence on; leaning on; reliance on.

ارْتِكَاس reaction; reflex; relapse; decline; regression; retrocession.

ارْتَكَبَ to commit; to perpetrate.

ارْتَكَزَ to lean on, rest on, found on; to be based on, founded on; to rely on, count on, settle on.

ارْتَكَسَ to relapse, regress, recede, deteriorate.

ارْتَمَى to be thrown, hurled, tossed; to fling oneself; to fall down; to prostrate oneself.

ارْتَهَنَ to receive in pledge; to be subject to; to be dependent on; to bind oneself; to be bound by.

ارْتَوَى to be given to drink; to be watered, irrigated; to quench one's thirst.

أَرْتُوازِيّ artesian (well).

ارْتِيَاب doubt, suspicion, distrust; misgiving; skepticism.

ارْتِيَاح satisfaction, relief, ease, grafication.

ارْتِيَاد frequentation.

إِرْث inheritance, legacy; bequest; patrimony.

أَرِج fragrant; perfumed; sweet-smelling.

أَرْجَأَ to postpone, delay, adjourn; to suspend execution.

إِرْجَاء postponement; deferment; delaying; adjournment; suspension.

إِرْجَاع restoration; restitutiuon; taking back; laying back; reinstatement.

أَرْجَح more likely; predominant; preferable; more acceptable.

أَرْجَحِيَّة likelihood; strong probability; prospects; preponderance; superiority.

أَرْجَعَ — to restore, send back, return, replace; to lay back, reinstall, reinstate.

أَرْجَعَ إلى — to attribute to, ascribe to, refer to.

أُرْجُوان — purple.

أُرْجُوحَة — swing; seasaw.

تُنصب الأرجوحة عادةً في حديقة المنزل

A seasaw is usually installed in the house garden

أَرَّخَ — to date; to write the history of.

إرْخاء — slackening; lowering; unloosing; relaxation.

أَرْخَبيل — archipelago.

أَرْخَص — cheaper; less expensive.

أَرْدَى — to bring about the fall of; to destroy; to kill; to throw to the ground; to knock down.

أَرْدَفَ — to follow with; to cause to follow; to come after; to add; to say further; to complement.

أَرْدُوَاز — slate.

أَرْذَل (ص) — lower; viler.

أَرْذَلُ العُمْر — old age.

أَرُزّ — rice (grain).

يعتبر الأرزّ الطعام الرئيسيّ في دول آسيا

Rice is a staple food in most Asian countries

أَرْز — cedar (tree).

الأرزة رمز لبنان السرمدي

The cedar tree is the eternal symbol of Lebanon

أَرْسَى — to anchor, moor, berth a ship.

أَرْسَى — to found, stabilize, anchor, secure firmly.

إرْسَاء — anchoring, mooring, berthing a ship.

إرْسَال — dispatching, forwarding, expedition; discharge; transmission; emission.

إرْسالِيَّة — consignment, shipment.

إرْسَالِيَّة — mission (religious mission).

أَرِسْتُقراطِيّ (ص) — aristocratic.

أَرِسْتُقراطيّ (اسم) — aristocrat.

أَرِسْتُقْراطِيَّة aristocracy.

أَرْسَلَ to send, dispatch, forward, transmit by radio; to pour forth; to shed tears; to issue; to diffuse.

أَرْسَلَ الشَّعْر to let hair hang down.

أَرْسَلَ في طلب الشخص أو الشيء to send for; to call for; to summon.

إرْشاد guidance; piloting; counselling.

إرْشادات (ج) instructions; directives.

أَرْشَدَ to guide, direct, pilot, advise; to counsel, teach, instruct; conduct.

أَرْشيف archives.

أَرْصادٌ جَوِّيَّة meteorology.

أَرْصَدَ to set aside. earmark funds; to balance the account.

أَرَّضَ to ground; to earth an electrical circuit.

أَرْض earth; land; ground; soil; terrain; country; territory; plot of land.

يسمى الكوكب الذي نعيش فيه بالأرض
Our planet is called the Earth

الأَرْض the Earth (planet).

إرْضاء satisfaction; gratification; fulfillment of a claim or a desire; a conciliation.

إرْضاع breast- feeding.

أَرْضَعَ to breast-feed.

أَرْضيّ terrestial, earthly.

أَرْضِيَّة ground; floor.

أَرْعَبَ to frighten, terrorize, intimidate, scare.

أَرْعَن frivolous; careless; reckless; rash; imprudent; inconsiderate; thoughtless.

ارْعَوى to desist from; to abstain from; to repent.

أَرْغى to foam; to produce a foam.

إرْغام coercion; compulsion; forcing.

أَرْغَمَ to compel, coerce, force, oblige to.

أَرْفَقَ to accompany with; to attach to; to enclose with; to append; to add.

أَرْفَقَ to be kind, friendly, nice; to treat gently; to show a friendly attitude toward someone.

أَرْفَقَ to profit; to benefit, make use, utilize.

أَرِقَ to be sleepless; to suffer insomnia.

أَرَّقَ to keep someone awake; to make someone sleepless.

أَرَق insomnia; sleeplessness.

أ ب ت ث ج ح خ د ذ ر ز س ش ص ض ط ظ ع غ ف ق ك ل م ن هـ و ي

أَرْقَدَ to put to sleep.

أَرْكَعَ to make someone kneel down.

أَرْكَنَ to rely on; to depend on; to trust.

أَرْمَل widower.

أَرْمَلَة widow.

أَرْنَب rabbit (animal).

أَرْنَبٌ بَرِّيّ hare.

أَرْنَبٌ هندِيّ guinea pig.

أَرْنَبَة female rabbit; tip of the nose.

إرْهَاب terrorrism; intimidation.

إرْهَابِيّ terrorist.

إرْهَاق fatigue; tiredness; stress, strain; burdening; oppression.

أَرْهَبَ to terrorize, horrify, scare, frighten.

أَرْهَفَ to thin out; to sharpen.

أَرْهَفَ السَّمْعَ to pay attention to; to give one's ear to.

أَرْهَقَ to exhaust; to weary; to tire out; to stress; to burden, encumber, oppress; to overexert; overwork.

إرْواء watering; irrigation; giving to drink; quenching one's thirst; moistening.

أَرُومَة root; lineage; strain; stock.

أَرُومَةُ الشجرة stump; stub.

أَرِيب skilled, dexterous, clever; intelligent; smart; cunning; resourceful.

أَرِيج fragrance, perfume, scent.

أَرْيَحِيّ generous; openhanded.

أَرْيَحِيَّة generosity; openhandedness.

أَرِيكَة couch; sofa; settee.

الأريكة مقعد بذراعين وظهر مريحة جداً

The sofa is a chair with two comfortable arms and back

أَزَّ to buzz, hum, hiss, whir, zoom.

إزاحَة removal; displacement; putting away.

إزار loincloth; veil.

أَزالَ to eliminate, get rid of, relieve, take away; to remove, disperse.

إزالَة removal; elimination; getting rid of; taking off; dispersion; clearing.

أَزْجَى to urge on; to push; to present greetings.

ازدادَ to increase; to become more intense; to grow.

ازْدانَ to be adorned, embellished, decorated.

ازْدِحام congestion; throng.

ازْدَحَمَ to overcrowd; to congest; to throng.

تزدحم الشوارع بالناس في منتصف النهار
A traffic congestion takes place usually at noon in the city

ازْدَرَى to despise, belittle, disdain, scorn.

ازْدِراء scorn, disdain, contempt.

ازْدَرَدَ to swallow, gobble, gulp.

ازْدَرَعَ to transplant, graft, culture.

ازْدَهَى to glow, gleam; to pride oneself; to show vanity, pride, beauty; to shine, glitter.

ازْدِهار boom; prosperity.

ازْدَهَرَ to flourish, thrive, prosper, boom; to blossom; to be in bloom.

ازْدِواج dualism; duplicity, duplication.

ازْدَوَجَ to pair; to come together forming a pair; to become double, dual.

ازْدِياد increase, increment, growth; swell; rise.

آزَرَ to support, assist, aid, help.

أَزْر strength; might; power; back.

ازْرَقَّ to become blue.

أَزْرَق blue.

إزْعاج annoyance; harrassment, inconvenience; vexation, nuisance.

أَزْعَجَ to disturb, annoy, harrass, vex, irk.

أَزْعَر (ص) despicable; malicious; thin-haired.

أَزْكَى to augment; to chasten; to praise; to grow.

أَزَل eternity.

أَزَلِيّ eternal; everlasting; timeless.

أَزَلِيَّة eternity.

أَزْمَة crisis; emergency; critical development.

أَزْمَعَ to decide to; to resolve; to be determined; to make up one's mind to.

إزْميل chisel.

أَزْهَى to bloom; to grow; to glow.

إزْهَار blooming; blossoming; radiancy; florescence.

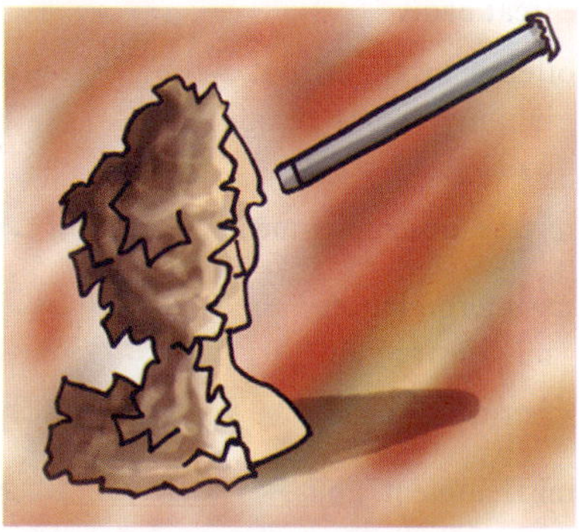

يستعمل الإزميل لنقر الخشب أو نحت الحجارة لصنع التماثيل
Chisels are used to carve wood or stone for making statues

أ ب ت ث ج ح خ د ذ ر ز س ش ص ض ط ظ ع غ ف ق ك ل م ن هـ و ي

أَزْهَرَ to bloom, blossom; to bear flowers.

أَزْهَر shining; luminous; radiant; brilliant.

أَزْهَقَ to kill; to suppress; to crush, destroy.

أزيز buzzing, zoom, whizzing.

أُسّ basis; foundation; base; exponent; index.

آسَى to nurse; to console, comfort; to assist, support; to express one's sympathy toward someone.

أَسًى grief; sorrow; distress; unhappiness.

أساءَ to oppress, do wrong to; to offend, insult, hurt, injure, spoil, disturb, trouble; to mismanage, misgovern; to misuse, misemploy; to misbehave; to misinterpret, misconstrue; to mistrust, doubt; to mistreat, abuse; to treat badly.

إساءَة offense, insult, affront; wrong; iniquity; injury, harm, damage.

إساءَةُ الاستعمال misuse, misemployment.

إساءَةُ التفسير misinterpretation, misconstruction.

إساءَةُ الظنّ mistrust, distrust.

إساءَةُ المعاملة mistreatment, abuse.

أَساس basis; base; foundation; root; bottom; origin; cause, radix (math).

أَساسِيّ fundamental; radical; basic; essential; principal; main; major; crucial; substantial.

أسالَ to cause to flow; to spill. shed; to liquefy. dissolve, melt; to flush, pour out.

إسالَة dissolution; melting; liquefaction.

أَسْبَغَ على to bestow; to grant lavishly to; to ascribe to; to give, impart to, lend to, attribute.

أَسْبَقِيَّة priority; seniority; precedence.

أَسْبَلَ to lower a curtain; to shed tears; to let fall.

أُسْبُوع week.

يتكوّن الأسبوع من سبعة أيام

A week has seven days

أُسبوعِيّ weekly.

أُسْبوعِيًّا every week; weekly; per week.

إسْت anus.

اسْتاءَ to resent; to be offended, hurt, displeased, vexed, upset, annoyed.

اسْتاتِيّ static.

اسْتِئْثار monopolization; appropriation; preoccupation; exclusive power.

اسْتَأْثَرَ to appropiate; to claim a monopoly; to possess alone; to take exclusive possession; to preoccupy, engross the atttention.

اسْتِئْجار rent; lease; tenure; tenancy; chartering a ship or a plane.

اسْتَأْجَرَ to rent, hire, lease, hold under a lease; to engage, take on someone; to charter a ship or a plane.

أُسْتاذ professor; teacher; master; mister.

أُسْتاذٌ مُساعِد assistant professor.

أُستاذ (دفتر الأستاذ) ledger.

اسْتِئْذان asking permission; taking leave.

اسْتَأْذَنَ to ask permission; to take leave.

اسْتَأْسَدَ to take courage; to become daring, tough, strong; to demonstrate one's power; to display the courage of a lion; to dominate, control, bully.

اسْتِئْصال extirpation; extermination; elimination; removal by surgery; pulling out, uprooting.

اسْتَأْصَلَ to extirpate, eliminate, uproot, deracinate; to pull out, extract, remove, ablate.

اسْتِمارَة form, application form.

اسْتِئْناف resumption; reopening; appeal of a court decision; renewal.

اسْتَأْنَسَ to be sociable, friendly, affable, polite; to become tame, domesticated (for an animal); to like someone's company; to feel at ease with; to become friendly with; to get used to; to be familiar with; to be accustomed to; to be acquainted with; to draw upon; to resort to ; to rely upon.

اسْتَأْنَسَ برأيِ شَخْص آخر to consult; to seek the advice of; to listen to; to pay attention to.

اسْتَأْنَفَ to resume, renew, recommence; to carry on with; to reestablish; to appeal a court decision.

اسْتَأْهَلَ to be worthy of; to be deserving; to be entitled, meriting; to be qualified, worthy of.

اسْتَباحَ to violate, defile; to deem permissible; to consider ownerless; to confiscate; to proscribe killing someone lawful; to appropriate.

اسْتِباحَة violation; appropriation; seizure; capture, confiscation; proscription; expropriation.

اسْتَبانَ الأمر to become clear, evident, plain, obvious; to be explained; to be clearly distinguished; to discover, find out, examine; to verify, get to know, recognize, discern.

اسْتَبَدَّ to be despotic, autocratic; to govern, rule, manage tyrannically; to oppress, overcome, overpower, take hold of.

اسْتَبَدَّ to possess alone, appropriate, monopolize.

اسْتَبَدَّ برأيه to be obstinate, stubborn.

اسْتِبْداد despotism, tyranny; autocracy; arbitrariness.

اسْتِبْدادِيّ despotic, tyrannical, arbitrary.

اسْتِبْدال substitution; replacement; exchange; barter; commutation; trade-off.

اسْتَبْدَل to exchange, substitute, replace,; to receive or give in exchange for; to barter, swap; to commute; to change.

اسْتِبْسال death defiance; heroism; risking one's life.

اسْتَبْسَل to defy death; to risk one's life.

اسْتَبْشَر to see a good omen in; to welcome; to be cheerful, happy about; to regard as auspicious.

اسْتَبْصَر to reflect on, ponder; to have the faculty to see; to be endowed with reason.

اسْتَبْطَأ to find slow; to be kept waiting.

اسْتِبْعاد taking away; disqualification; exclusion; setting aside; putting away.

اسْتَبْعَد to take away, put away, set aside; to exclude, rule out, eliminate, disqualify.

اسْتَبَق to foresee, anticipate, forestall.

اسْتَبْقى to detain; hold back, retain, keep; to ask someone to stay; to spare, save.

اسْتِبْقاء retention, detention; asking someone to stay; keeping; sparing; holding back.

اسْتِبْيان questionnaire.

اسْتَتَبَّ to settle; to be steady, orderly, calm, quiet; to be stable, constant, peaceful.

اسْتَتْبَع to entail; to imply; to ask to follow.

اسْتَتَر to hide; to seek cover; to hide oneself.

اسْتَثْقَل to find heavy, troublesome, onerous, unbearable; to consider oppressive, irritating, annoying.

اسْتِثْمار exploitation; utilization; capitalizing on; usufruct; investment of funds for profit.

اسْتَثْمَر to invest, exploit, utilize, capitalize on; to make use of; to turn to one's advantage.

اسْتَثْنى to exclude, except, rule out.

اسْتِثْناء exception; exclusion.

اسْتِثْنائِي exceptional; unusual; rare; special; extraordinary; uncommon.

اسْتَجاب to respond to; to show a favorable reaction to; to grant, comply with, accede to; to accept, agree, carry out, satisfy; to fulfill a request; to concur in; to echo from; to defer to the wish of; to show interest in; to meet, answer, reply.

اسْتِجَابَة response; compliance, accedence, consent; answering; carrying out; agreement.

اسْتَجَارَ to seek protection or refuge with; to ask for the help, aid, assistance of another.

اسْتَجَدَّ to come newly in to existence; to happen, occur, appear unexpectedly; to renew.

اسْتَجْدَى to beg for alms; to entreat, supplicate, solicit earnestly, implore.

جلس الشحّاذ على الرّصيف يستجدي المارة

The beggar sits on pavements to ask for alms

اسْتِجْدَاء begging for alms; imploring, beseeching.

اسْتَجْلَى to seek to clarify; to try to find out; to investigate, uncover, discover, detect matters.

اسْتِجْلاء investigation; clarification of matters; searching for, inquiring about.

اسْتِجْلاب calling for, sending for; summoning; acquisition; importation; attraction; drawing; fetching.

اسْتَجْلَبَ to call for, send for; to arraign, summon; to acquire, obtain, procure; to import; to attract; to draw; to bring over; to fetch.

اسْتِجْمَام recreation, rest, relaxation.

اسْتَجْمَعَ to gather, re-collect, summon, call forth; to pile up, amass, accumulate; to assemble, meet, convene; to contain, include, comprise, summarize.

اسْتِجْوَاب interrogation, questioning; hearing (in court); interview; interpellation (in parliament); inquiry, investigation.

اسْتَجْوَبَ to interrogate, question; to interpellate; to hear in court; to cross-examine a witness.

اسْتَحَى to be shy; timid, bashful, diffident.

اسْتَحَالَ to be impossible; to be absurd, inconceivable; to be transformed, changed, transmuted.

اسْتِحَالَة impossibility; absurdity; transition; change, transformation; turn, shift.

اسْتَحَثَّ to urge, incite, exhort, prompt, stimulate.

اسستِحْدَاث innovation, introduction, invention.

اسْتَحْدَثَ to innovate, originate, invent, introduce.

اسْتِحْسَان approval, approbation; consent; acclaim; discretion; to find pleasant, agreeable, commendable, advisable, good.

اسْتَحْسَنَ to approve, consent, acclaim, favor; to have a good opinion of; to admire, appreciate, think highly of; to consider right, suitable; to be pleased with.

اسْتِحْصَال obtainment; achievement; acquisition; collection; recovery of a debt; receipt.

اسْتَحْصَلَ to get, receive, achieve, come into possession; to collect, recover debts; to acquire, obtain.

اسْتِحْضَار sending for; calling for; summons; making; confection; formulation; conjuration of spirits; pleading; memorandum.

اسْتَحْضَرَ to send for, call for, call in, summon; to recall, recollect, remember; to conjure, evoke, invoke spirits; to prepare, combine, formulate.

اسْتَحَقَّ to deserve, merit; to have the right to; to be entitled to; to require, demand; to mature or become due (for bills); to be worth mentioning, noteworthy; to be due, worth, deserving.

اسْتِحْقَاق merit; worthiness; entitlement; maturity; becoming due for payment.

اسْتِحْكَام intensification; increase; strengthening; consolidation; fortification; reinforcement; rampart; stronghold.

اسْتَحْكَمَ to intensify, increase, grow, build-up; to strengthen, consolidate, fortify, reinforce; to be forceful, severe, deep-rooted, ingrained; to be compact, firm, solid, accurate, precise.

اسْتَحْلَبَ to milk; to emulsify.

اسْتَحْلَفَ to plead with; to appeal to; to beseech, entreat, conjure; to make someone swear; to administer an oath on.

اسْتَحَمَّ to bathe; to take a bath; to wash oneself.

اسْتِحْمَام bathing; taking a bath; washing oneself.

اسْتِحْوَاذ obsession; preoccupation; possession.

اسْتَحْوَذَ to possess; to occupy wholly; to take up; to overcome; to seize, take hold of; to preoccupy one's entire attention; to overpower.

اسْتَحيا to be ashamed of; to be bashful

اسْتِحْيَاء shame, diffidence, bashfulness, timidity, shyness.

اسْتِخْبَار investigation, examination, inquiry.

اسْتَخْبَرَ to investigate, inquire about; to seek or gather information about; to examine.

اسْتِخْدَام utilization; putting into operation; use, employment; hiring of an employee; service; position; job, occupation.

اسْتَخْدَمَ to employ, hire, engage the services of; to provide work for; to operate; to make use; to exploit; to apply; to avail oneself of.

اسْتِخْراج extraction, getting out, pulling out; conclusion, deduction; discovering; reproduction.

اسْتَخْرَجَ to extract, take out, pull out, to derive, infer, conclude, deduce, figure out; to discover, find out; to reproduce.

اسْتَخَفَّ to belittle, depreciate; undervalue; to despise, scorn, disdain; to find light in weight; to disparage.

اسْتِخْفاء keeping oneself out of view; disguise; disappearance, concealment.

اسْتِخْفاف disdain, scorn, contempt; levity; frivolity; disparagement; belittlement, underestimation.

اسْتِخْلاص extraction, drawing out, taking out; inference, deduction, conclusion; finding out.

اسْتَخْلَصَ to extract; to deduce, infer, conclude; to gather, figure out, discover; to select, pick out.

اسْتَدارَ to be round or circular; to turn around; to look back; to turn in a circle; to spin, whirl, revolve.

اسْتَدانَ to borrow; to incur debts.

اسْتِدانَة borrowing, loan.

اسْتِدْراج persuasion, inducement, enticement, temptation; invitation of offers.

اسْتِدْراك redress; reparation; correction; ratification; taking steps to prevent; putting in order; setting right; making amends; straightening out.

اسْتَدْرَجَ to persuade, induce, attract, allure, entice; to seduce, tempt, invite; to invite offers.

اسْتَدْرَكَ to repair, redress, correct, rectify; to evade; to become conscious; to take steps to prevent; to put in order; to make amends; to avert, ward off, avoid; to supplement.

اسْتَدْعَى to send for; to summon; to recall, call back; to call out; to call for, require, demand; to evoke, elicit; to make a formal request.

اسْتِدْعاء sending for, calling for; summoning; recalling; application, petition, request; need, want.

اسْتَدَلَّ to conclude, deduce, reason out, figure out; to draw a conclusion; to inquire about.

اسْتِدْلال conclusion, deduction, inference, reasoning.

اسْتراتيجِيّ strategic.

اسْتراتيجية strategy.

اسْتَراحَ to rest; to take a rest; to be satisfied with; to feel at ease about, glad about, pleased with.

اسْتِراحَة rest, recreation; rest-house; break.

اسْتِراقُ السَّمْع eavesdropping; peeping; snooping.

اسْتِرْجاع recovery; retrieval, recuperation; taking back; withdrawal; repeal.

اسْتَرْجَعَ to recover, retrieve, recuperate; to recall, call back, cancel. revoke.

اسْتِرْحَام supplication; plea for mercy; appeal, petition, request, application.

اسْتَرْحَمَ to plea for mercy; to implore, entreat, plead, solicit, appeal to.

اسْتَرْخَصَ to find inexpensive.

اسْتَرَدَّ to regain, get back, recuperate, recall; to withdraw; to extradite a criminal.

اسْتِرْدَاد recovery, retrieval, recuperation; recalling; extradition of a criminal.

اسْتِرْسَال letting oneself go; unrestraint; elaboration; expatiation.

اسْتَرْسَلَ to hang loose (for hair); to let oneself go unhibited; to act without affectation; to indulge in.

اسْتَرْسَلَ في الكلام to talk at great length; to expatiate on.

اسْتَرْشَدَ to seek guidance; to consult; to ask for advice from someone; to follow someone's action or opinion for guidance; to be guided by.

اسْتِرْضَاء conciliatory attitude; propitiation, conciliation.

اسْتَرْعَى to draw attention; to attract one's attention or interest.

اسْتَرَقَّ السَّمْعَ to eavesdrop; to listen secretly.

اسْتَرَقَّ النَّظَرَ to glance furtively; to peep at; to snoop at.

اسْتَسَاغَ to enjoy; to find agreeable; to approve of.

اسْتِسْلَام surrender, capitulation; submission; giving in; resignation.

اسْتَطَاعَ to be able to; to be capable of; to manage to.

اسْتِطَاعَة ability, capability, faculty, possibility.

اسْتِطْراد digress; to proceed to say.

اسْتِطْلَاع exploration, reconnoitering, reconnaissance; investigation, research; consultation; poll; survey.

اسْتَطْلَعَ to explore; reconnoiter; to inquire, investigate; to uncover; to consult; to poll; to survey public opinion.

اسْتِظْهَار memorization, learning by heart.

اسْتَظْهَرَ to memorize; to learn by heart; to commit to memory; to ask for help, assistance; to overcome, defeat.

اسْتَعَادَ to take back; to resume activity; to regain; to take up again; to revive memories; to recall; to demand back, recuperate, retrieve.

اسْتِعَادَة recovery, restitution, recuperation; recollection; regaining.

اسْتَعَارَ to borrow.

اسْتِعَارَة borrowing; metaphor (language).

اسْتَعَانَ to appeal for the aid, help or assistance of another; to have recourse to; to make use of.

اسْتِعْبَاد	enslavement; subjugation.
اسْتِعْجَال	hurry, haste; precipitation; acceleration.
اسْتَعْجَل	to hurry, rush, drive, urge; to demand a quick reply from someone; to speed up.
اسْتَعَدَّ	to get ready; to prepare oneself; to stand prepared; to be prepared.
اسْتِعْدَاد	readiness, preparedness; inclination; disposition, aptitude; susceptibility to a disease; convenience; willingness.

اسْتِعْرَاض	review, parade, show; survey; examination.
اسْتَعْرَض	to review; to survey, examine, explore; to discuss; to parade; to browse.
اسْتَعْصَى	to be incurable; to defy, oppose; to be difficult, intricate, hard to deal with.
اسْتِعْطَاف	imploring; conciliation; propitiation.
اسْتَعْطَف	to implore, entreat, supplicate, appeal to; to conciliate, propitiate, appease.
اسْتَعْفَى	to resign; to ask pardon; to apologize to.
اسْتِعْفَاء	resignation; apology.

اسْتِعْلَام	inquiry; asking information; seeking information.
اسْتِعْمَار	colonialism; imperialism.
اسْتِعْمَارٌ جديد	neocolonialism.
اسْتِعْمَارِيّ	colonial, imperial.
اسْتِعْمَال	use, application, employment, utilization, exploitation; handling; operating on.
اسْتَعْمَل	to use, employ, utilize, exploit; to handle, manage, operate.
اسْتِغَاثَة	call for help.
اسْتِغْرَاب	astonishment wonder, surprise, amazement.
اسْتَغْرَب	to be astonished, surprised, amazed.
اسْتَفْتَى	to ask for a legal opinion; to consult; to take counsel with; to poll, canvass people's opinions; to hold a; referendum or a plebiscite.

اسْتِفْتَاءٌ شَعْبِيّ	referendum; plebiscite; poll.
اسْتِفْتَاءٌ قانونيّ	request for a formal legal opinion.
اسْتَفْحَل	to worsen. become worse; to become severe; to intensify; to increase; to spread dangerously.
اسْتِفْرَاغ	vomiting; puking.
اسْتَفْرَغ	to vomit; to puke.

اسْتَفَزَّ	to provoke; to excite, arouse, instigate.
اسْتِفْزَازِيّ	provocative, instigative, rousing.
اسْتِفْسَار	inquiry; question.

اسْتَفْسَر	to ask for an explanation of; to inquire about; to seek an explanation for.
اسْتِفْهَام	asking; inquiry; interrogation.
اسْتَفْهَم	to enquire of someone about something; to seek or to ask for an explanation.

اسْتَقالَ to resign; to tender one's resignation.

اسْتِقالَة resignation; demission.

اسْتَقامَ to sit up; to stand erect; to be right, correct, proper, straight; to be honest, upright.

اسْتِقامَة honesty, integrity, rightness, sincerity; uprightness.

اسْتِقْبال reception; welcome; facing; taking in.

اسْتَقْبَلَ to receive, welcome, meet; to take in; to confront; to face.

اسْتَقَرَّ to settle; to reside at; to stay at; to be firmly established; to be fixed, steady, stable; to be stabilized, constant, orderly; to dwell on (mind); to resolve, determine; to sit down; to get seated; to take a seat; to be in a secure position.

اسْتِقْرار stability; sedentation; staying; sojourn; establishment; constancy; repose; stillness.

اسْتَقْرَضَ to ask for a loan; to obtain a loan.

اسْتِقْصاء examination; investigation; exploration; study; inquiry; fact-finding.

اسْتَقْطَبَ to polarize; to draw; to attract; to muster.

اسْتَقَلَّ to be independent; to possess alone; to board a bus, ship, plane; to mount; to find little; to consider insignificant, meager; to belittle; to underestimate, undervalue; to despise, scorn.

اسْتِقْلال independence.

اسْتَكانَ to surrender to; to succumb to; to submit to.

اسْتَكْثَرَ to consider as too much; to deem excessive; to ask for a lot.

اسْتِكْشاف scouting, exploration, discovery, reconnaissance.

اسْتَكْشَفَ to try to find, discover, explore; to search into; to detect, unearth.

اسْتَكْمَلَ to complete, conclude, complement; supplement.

اسْتَلَّ to unsheathe (a knife, sword).

اسْتِلام receipt; taking over; assumption.

اسْتَلْزَمَ to require; to necessitate, entail, involve; to be in need of; to demand.

اسْتَلَفَ to borrow; to contract a loan.

اسْتَلْقى to lie down; to lie back.

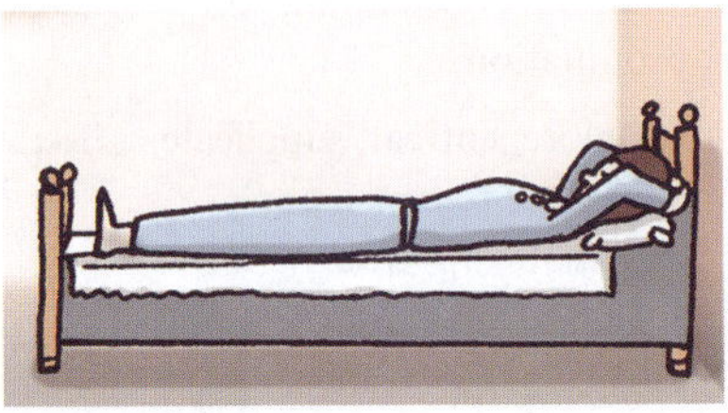

استلقى الرجل على سريره طلباً للراحة

The man lies down on his bed seeking rest

اسْتَلَمَ to receive; to get, obtain, have; to take over; to assume; to take possession of.

أ ب ت ث ج ح خ د ذ ر ز س ش ص ض ط ظ ع غ ف ق ك ل م ن هـ و ي

اسْتِمارَة form; application form.

اسْتِماع listening; audition; hearing.

اسْتَمالَ to attract; to win over; to conciliate.

اسْتَمَدَّ to obtain from; to derive from.

اسْتَمَرَّ to continue to do; to keep doing; to persist in.

اسْتِمْرار continuation; persistence; permanence; to keep doing without interruption.

اسْتَمَعَ to listen to; to eavesdrop; to hearken to.

استمع كل مساء إلى ما تبثُّه الإذاعة من موسيقى

I listen every evening to the music broadcast by the broadcasting station

---

اسْتِمْلاك appropriation; seizure.

اسْتَمْلَكَ to take possession of; to seize; to appropriate.

اسْتِمْناء masturbation.

اسْتِناد leaning on; dependence on.

اسْتِنادًا إلى based on; on the basis of; on the strength of; pursuant to; by virtue of.

اسْتِنْباط discovery, invention; devisal, design; contrivance; extraction; deduction, inference.

اسْتَنْبَطَ to invent; to devise, contrive, design; to extract, deduce, conclude, infer.

اسْتِنْتاج conclusion, deduction, inference.

اسْتَنْتَجَ to conclude, infer; to deduce; to draw a conclusion.

اسْتَنْجَدَ to appeal for; to ask the help of; to resort to.

اسْتَنَدَ to lean on; to be based on; to rely on; to trust.

اسْتَنْطَقَ to interrogate; to examine; to hear.

اسْتِنْفار mobilization; putting on the alert (troops); general call to arms; general alarm.

اسْتَنْفَدَ to deplete, exhaust, consume.

اسْتَنْفَرَ to mobilize; to put on the alert (troops); to call upon to fight; to keep away from; to have an aversion to; to clash; to be frightened away; to go to war.

اسْتِنْكار condemnation, censure, disapproval.

اسْتَنْكَرَ to condemn, denounce, disapprove, censure.

اسْتَنْكَفَ to disdain, spurn, refuse, abstain from; to be haughty, proud.

اسْتَهَانَ to underestimate; to belittle; to despise; to consider easy, of little value.

اسْتِهَانَة understimation, underrating; scorn, disdain.

اسْتِهْتَار recklessness, wantonness, unrestraint; disdain, scorn; licentiousness.

اسْتَهْتَرَ to be reckless, wanton, licentious; to despise, scorn; to slight.

اسْتِهْجَان disapproval, condemnation; censure.

اسْتَهْجَنَ to disapprove of; to reprehend, condemn, censure; to find offensive, objectionable.

اسْتَهْدَفَ to strive for; to aspire to; to aim at.

اسْتَهْدَفَ لِـ to be exposed to, liable to; to come under; to incur; to contract; to be subjected to.

اسْتَهَلَّ to initiate, begin, introduce; to fall heavily (rain); to set in; to raise one's voice; to undertake; to tackle, embark upon; to shed tears (eyes); to draw, unsheathe (a sword).

اسْتِهْلَاك consumption; attrition; wear and tear; amortization of an asset; depreciation; exhaustion; redemption of mortgage bonds.

اسْتِهْلَال starting, introduction, preface, preamble.

اسْتَهْلَكَ to consume, exhaust, wear away; to amortize; to write off debts; to redeem mortgage bonds.

اسْتَوَى to be straight, even, level; to be steady, regular, equal; to sit firmly on.

اسْتِوَائِيّ (ص) equatorial; tropical.

اسْتَوْجَبَ to require; to call for; to deem necessary; to deserve; to be worthy of.

اسْتَوْحَى to be inspired by; to seek inspiration from; to borrow, derive, draw from (ideas).

اسْتَوْرَدَ to import (goods, ideas).

اسْتَوْضَحَ to ask, seek for an explanation; to inquire about; to investigate.

اسْتَوْطَنَ to settle permanently in a country not his own; to establish a colony or residence in.

اسْتَوْعَبَ to contain; to hold; to have room or capacity for; to comprise, embody, enclose; to understand, comprehend; to absorb, assimilate.

اسْتَوْفَى to receive, get one's due in full; to collect; to satisfy, fulfill (conditions, terms of contract).

اسْتَوْقَفَ to catch the eye; to arrest attention; to be striking or eye-catching; to ask to stop; to bring to a stop; to detain, slow down.

اسْتَوْلَى	to capture, occupy, seize, confiscate; to appropriate; to take possession of; to overpower, dominate, overcome, take over.
اسْتِيَاء	discontent, displeasure, anger, dissatisfaction.
اسْتِيرَاد	import; importation of goods.
اسْتِيطَان	settlement; setting permanently in a country.
اسْتِيعَاب	capacity; understanding; assimilation.
اسْتَيْقَظ	to wake up; to get up; to awaken.
اسْتِيلَاء	seizure, takeover; appropriation; confiscation; requisitioning; usurpation; taking possession of.

أَسَد	lion (animal).

يُعرف الأسد بأنه ملك الغاب

The lion is known as the king of the jungle

أَسْدَى	to confer on; to render; to offer; to give an advice, a favor, a service.
أَسْدَلَ	to lower; to let hang; to drop.
أَسَرَ	to capture, arrest; to take a captive; to chain.
أَسَرَ	to captivate, fascinate, charm.
أَسَرَّ	to make happy; to keep secret; to confide a secret to someone.

أَسْر	captivity; arrest.
إِسْرَاء	nocturnal journey; Prophet Mohammad's midnight journey to the seven heavens.
إِسْرَاع	acceleration, hurrying.
إِسْرَاف	squandering, extravagance, prodigality; immoderation, intemperance.
أُسْرَة	family, household; dynasty (ruling family).
أَسْرَعَ	to hasten, rush, speed; to make haste; to be fast, rapid, quick.
أَسْرَفَ	to squander, waste, spend lavishly; to be extravagant, immoderate.
أَسَّسَ	to found; to establish; to set up; to lay the foundation for; to build, create, form; to base on; to rest on.

إِسْطَبْل	stable, barn.
أُسْطُوَانَة	cylinder; drum; roller; column; disc; musical disc or record.
أُسْطُوَانِيّ	cylindrical.

أُسْطُورَة	legend; myth.
أُسْطُورِيّ	legendary.
أُسْطُول	fleet (ships); squadron (planes).
إِسْعَاف	relief; aid; rescue.

تسير سيارة الإسعاف مسرعة لتنقذ المصابين

First aid cars drive speedily to the scene of the accident

إسْعَافٌ أوَّليّ first aid.

أَسْعَدَ to make happy.

أَسْعَفَ to relieve, aid, rescue, save.

أَسِفَ to feel sorry; to regret.

أَسَف regret; sorrow; grief.

آسِف sorry, sad, regretful; pardon me.

أَسْفَرَ عن to result in; to give rise to; to disclose, uncover, reveal, bring forth; to unveil; to illuminate.

أَسْفَل (اسم) bottom; foot; base; lower part.

أَسْفَل (ص) lower; inferior.

أَسْفَلْت asphalt.

إسْفين wedge; cotter.

إسْقَاط dropping; toppling (a government); omission, cancellation; deduction; abortion, miscarriage; projection.

إسقاطُ الحقّ waiver, renunciation.

أَسْقَطَ to let fall; to drop; to overthrow, topple (a government); to deduct; to omit, cancel; to fail in an exam; to waive, renounce one's right; to abort, miscarry; to project.

أَسْقَمَ to sicken; to make sick.

إسْكَات silencing.

إسْكَاف shoemaker.

إسْكَان quartering; housing.

أَسْكَتَ to silence; to muzzle; to hush.

أَسْكَنَ to house; to lodge someone.

الإسلام Islam.

إسلاميّ Islamic.

أَسْلَفَ to lend money; to harrow the land.

أَسْلَمَ to embrace Islam; to become a Moslem.

أَسْلَمَ to surrender; to yield; to give up; to resign oneself to; to present to; to hand over.

أَسْلَمَ الرُّوحَ to die; to pass away.

أُسْلُوب method, manner, mode, pattern, way, style; expression ; phrasing; technique; procedure.

إسْم name, designation; noun (language); reputation.

إسْمُ إشارة demonstrative pronoun.

إسْمٌ تِجاريّ goodwill, trade name, business name.

إسْمُ تَحَبُّبي pet name.

إسْمُ جَمْع collective noun.

إسْمُ جِنْس generic noun.

إسْمُ العَائِلة surname.

إسْمُ عَلَم proper noun.

إسْمٌ مُسْتَعار pseudonym; alias; pen name.

إسْمٌ مَوْصول relative pronoun.

أَسْمَى (ص) higher; loftier; more exalted; supreme; superior.

أَسْمَال (ج) rags; torn clothes.

أَسْمَر dark brown.

أَسْمَعَ to make hear; to insult, offend.

إِسْمَنْت cement; concrete.

إِسْمَنْتٌ مُسَلَّح reinforced concrete.

إِسْمِيّ nominal.

أَسَنَ to stagnate; to become stagnant.

آسِن stagnant; stinking; brackish.

إِسْنَاد attribution; imputation; investiture; predication (language); commissioning.

إِسْنَادِيّ predicative; predicate (language).

أَسْنَدَ to lean on; to support on; to attribute to; to ascribe to; impute to; to entrust to; to commission to; to rest on; to found on; to predicate (language).

إِسْهال diarrhea.

إِسْهَام participation; taking part; sharing.

أَسْهَبَ to elaborate on; to dwell upon; to discuss at length; to write or talk in detail; to expatiate.

أَسْهَمَ to share; to participate; to take part.

أُسْوَار bracelet; armlet.

أُسْوَة example; pattern; following the example of; similar to.

إِسْوَدَّ to become black; to get blacker; to blacken.

أَسْوَد black; negro.

آسيا Asia (continent).

آسيا الصُّغْرَى Asia Minor.

أَسِير captive; prisoner of war.

آسيَوِيّ Asian; Asiatic.

أَشَاحَ وَجْهَهُ to turn one's face away; to shun.

أَشَادَ to praise; to laud; to extol; to pay tribute to; to build, construct.

إِشادَة praise, eulogy, laudation; building, construction.

أَشَارَ to beckon to ;to motion, signal, gesticulate; to indicate, show, point out; imply, designate; to allude to, insinuate; to mention, refer to, state; to advise, counsel.

إِشارَة mark, sign, symbol, signal, gesture, hint; allusion; mentioning, stating; citation.

تُنصب الإشارات الضوئية عند مفترق الطرق في المدن
Trafic signals are installed on crossroads in cities

إِشارَةُ المُرور traffic signal, traffic light.

أَشَاعَ to spread a rumor; to publicize; to propagate; to disclose, divulge, reveal.

إشاعة rumor; disclosure; propagation.

إشْبَاع gratification; saturation; soaking, impregnation.

أَشْبَعَ to satiate, saturate; to soak, impregnate.

أَشْبَعَ to charge with; to load with.

أَشْبَعَ المَوْضُوع to treat exhaustively the subject.

أَشْبَعَ ضَرْباً to beat up; to strike repeatedly.

اشْتَاق to long for; to desire; to yearn.

اشْتِبَاك entanglement; involvement, scuffle; hand-to-hand fight; clash.

اشْتِباه resemblance, similarity; doubt; suspicion, dubiousness.

اشْتَبَكَ to clash; to be involved; to brawl, fight; to be engaged in a fight, in a battle; to be entangled, interlocked, intertwined.

اشْتَبَهَ to suspect; to doubt; to distrust; to resemble.

اشْتَدَّ to intensify, increase, become stronger, become more intense; to assault, bear down upon the enemy.

اشْتِدَاد intensification, aggravation, increase, deterioration.

اشْتَرَى to buy; to purchase.

اشْتِرَاط stipulating.

اشْتِرَاع legislation.

اشْتِراك partnership; participation; sharing; joining; collaboration in; interference in; subscription to; contribution in; complicity in a crime.

اشْتِرَاكات (ج) complications of a disease.

اشْتِرَاكِيّ Socialist.

اشْتِراكِيَّة Socialism.

اشْتَرَطَ to stipulate, specify or impose as a condition.

اشْتَرَعَ to legislate; to enact laws.

اشْتَرَكَ to participate in; to share in; to take part in; to collaborate with; to contribute to; to subscribe to; to engage in a fight, battle.

اشْتِعَال ignition; inflammation; burning, combustion.

اشْتَعَلَ to burn; to catch fire; to be on fire; to be ablaze; to be in flames; to flame with rage.

اشْتِغَال work, occupation with; state of being busy or occupied; activity, concern; anxiety.

اشْتَغَلَ to work, labor, operate, function; to act upon.

اشْتِقاق derivation; etymology (language).

اشْتَكَى to complain; to accuse; to suffer from; to raise a complaint of or against someone.

اشْتَمَلَ to contain; to include, comprise, comprehend; to enclose, enfold; to imply, implicate something; to wrap oneself in a cloak or shamla.

اشْتَهَى to wish; to lust; to desire; to yearn for; to feel appetite for; to have an ardent wish.

اشْتِهاء greed, craving, desire, longing, yearning; eagerness; passion, lust, carnal desire; appetite; ardent wish.

اشْتَهَرَ to be famous, well-known; to be widespread, common, renowned; to be characterised with; to be known by; to be notorious, famed by.

أَشْجَنَ to sadden; to grieve.

أَشَدّ (ص) stronger; harder; tougher; worse.

أَشَّرَ to mark; to put a mark on; to sign; to endorse by one's signature; to grant a visa on a passport.

إشْرَاف supervision; superintendence; control over; patronage; overlooking; closeness.

إشْرَاق radiance, brightness; shining.

إشْرَاكٌ بالله polytheism

أَشْرَفَ to supervise, watch over, control, direct, manage; to overlook, dominate; to be close to; to be on the brink of; to approach.

أَشْرَقَ to rise; to shine; to radiate.

إشْعَار notification, information, notice, note.

إشْعَاع radiation; irradiation.

إشْعَال lighting, illumination; burning, setting on fire, ignition, kindling.

أَشِعَّة rays.

أَشِعَّةٌ سينيَّة x-rays.

أَشِعَّةٌ تحت الحَمْرَاء infrared rays.

أَشِعَّةٌ فوق البَنَفْسَجِيَّة ultraviolet rays.

أَشْعَرَ to notify; to advise, inform, forwarn.

أَشْعَلَ to light, kindle, ignite; to burn; to set on fire.

أَشْفَى على to be about to, near to, on the verge of.

إشْفَاق compassion, pity, sympathy, tenderness; care; solicitude, concern, anxiety.

أَشْفَقَ to feel pity for; to have mercy upon; to sympathize with; to be anxious about; to be scared of; to beware of.

إشْكَال ambiguity, dubiosity; complication; problem; paradox.

أَشَمّ (ص) proud; haughty; honorable; lofty; high.

اشْمَأَزَّ to be disgusted by; to feel disgust at; to loathe.

إشْهَاد attestation.

إشْهَار declaration; proclamation; promulgation.

إشْهارُ الإفْلاس notice of bankruptcy.

أَصَابَ to hit a target; to score a goal; to be in the right; to be correct.

أَصَابَ to afflict; to gain, obtain, win, earn; to attain, achieve; to bestow upon.

أَصَابَ to afflict; to befall; to hit.

إصابَة hit, goal, score (in sports); injury, wound; attack of sickness; accident.

أَصَاخَ إلى to listen to.

أَصَالَة originality, firmness; steadfastness; nobility of descent; purity of origin; judiciousness; act in one's own name.

أَصْبَحَ to become; to reach a state; to come to a point where; to grow; to turn; to be; to come in the morning; to enter upon morning; to wake up; to get up; to rise; to emerge; to be evident, plain, clear.

إصْبَعُ اليد finger.

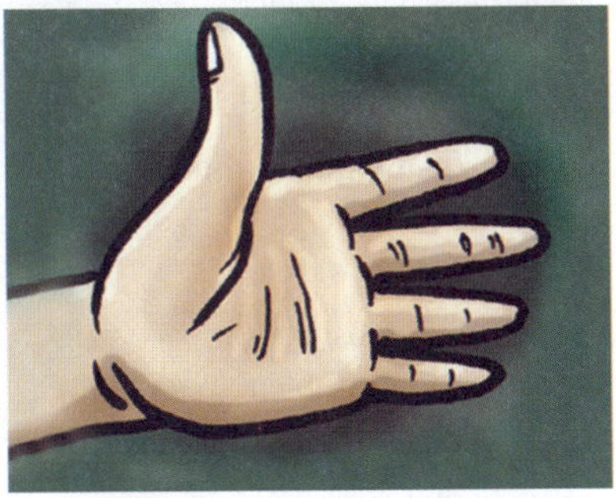

تحتوي يد الإنسان على خمسة أصابع

A human hand has five fingers

إصْبَعُ القَدَم toe.

إصْدَار issue; sending out; publication; release; production of a book.

إصْدارُ حُكْم giving of a sentence; rendering of a verdict.

أَصْدَرَ to release, issue, publish, produce a book; to issue, emit bonds, stamps etc; to pronounce, deliver; to give a sentence in court; to command; to issue an order, a statement.

أَصَرَّ to insist; to persist in; to resolve to; to decide, intend to.

إصْرَار insistence; persistance; resolution; decision; intention.

اصْطَادَ to hunt; to fish; to ensnare; to trap.

اصْطَافَ to spend summer at.

اصْطِحَاب accompaniment (music).

اصْطَحَبَ to befriend; to keep company with; to accompany.

يصطاد الصيّاد الطيور بالبندقية

The hunter hunts birds with a rifle

اصْطِدَام collision, crash; encounter; fight.

اصْطَدَمَ to collide, clash with; to strike against; to encounter; to fight; to hit against.

اصْطَفَّ to line up; to stand in formation.

اصْطَفَى to choose; select; cull.

اصْطَكَّ to chatter (teeth); to shake (knees).

اصْطِلاح usage; custom; term, expression.

اصْطِلاحِيّ conventional, formal, idiomatic.

اصْطَلَحَ to make peace with; to be reconciled with; to agree on; to accept.

اصْطِنَاعِيّ artificial; synthetic.

اصْطَنَعَ to synthetize, to affect, assume, simulate, feign an attitude; to create, fabricate, work out.

اصْطِيَاف summer vacationing.

أَصْغَى to listen attentively to; to hearken.

اصْفَرَّ to turn, become yellow; to be pale.

أَصْفَر (ص) yellow; pale.

أَصْل origin; source; root; basis; descent; ancestry; cause; original; radical (chemistry); asset.

أَصْلاً initially; not at all; not in the least.

إِصْلاح restoration; restitution, redressing, reparation; improvement, amelioration; reconditioning, renovation; establishment of peace and order; reform; conciliation; reclamation of land; reconciliation, peace-making between.

إِصْلاحِيَّة reformatory; penitentiary.

أَصْلَحَ to restore, restitute, repair, improve, ameliorate, renovate, rehabilitate, redress; to reform, conciliate; to reclaim land; to reconcile, make peace between.

يُصلح العامل الصنبور باستعمال مفتاح
The plumber repairs the faucet using a spanner

أَصْلَح (ص) more suitable, appropriate, adequate, qualified, efficient; more virtuous, pious.

أَصْلَع (اسم) baldhead.

أَصْلِيّ original; genuine; authentic; primary; principal; basic; radical; main; true.

أَصَمّ deaf.

أَصَمّ أَبْكَم deaf-mute.

أُصُول assets (accounts); ancestors; principles; basics; essentials; origins; roots.

أُصُولِيّ proper; confirming to principles; jurisprudent.

أَصِيص flowerpot; flower vase.

أَصِيل (ص) of pure origin; of noble descent; purebred (horses); thoroughbred (animals); authentic; pure; real; true; original; incumbent; judicious.

أَصِيل (اسم) late afternoon.

أَضاءَ to light up; to illuminate; to shine, beam.

إِضاءَة lighting; illumination.

أَضاعَ to lose; miss; mislay; to let slip; to omit; to fail to make use of; to waste, squander; to ruin, destroy; to kill time.

أَضافَ to append, supplement, add; to say further; to host a guest.

إِضافَة addition; appending; increase; addendum; annex; supplement

إِضافَة إلى in addition to; together with.

إِضافِيّ additional; supplementary; accessory; secondary; more; plus; auxiliary; spare.

إِضْبَارة file.

أَضْجَرَ to bore, annoy, irk, irritate.

أَضْحَى to become; to turn into.

الأَضْحَى Greater Bairam (Islam).

أُضْحوكَة laughingstock; joke.

أَضَرَّ to damage, hurt, injure.

أَضَرَّ to force, compel, coerce, oblige someone to.

إضراب strike; walkout.

تمنع دول عديدة حصول الإضراب فيها حمايةً لاقتصادها

Strikes are forbidden in several countries in order to protect their national economy

إِضْرار wrongdoing; harming; injuring.

إِضْرام kindling fire; lighting fire; ignition; setting fire to; causing fire to break.

أَضْرَبَ to go on strike; to walk out; to remain in.

أَضْرَمَ to kindle, light; to set to fire; to burn.

اضْطَجَعَ to lie down; to rest on one's side; to lie back.

اضْطَرَّ to compel, coerce, impel, oblige.

اضْطِراب disturbance, disorder, confusion, muddle; perturbation; disruption; trouble, commotion; unrest, riot; derangement, turmoil.

اضْطِرار compulsion, coercion; necessity, exigency.

اضْطِرَارِيّ compulsory, coercive. imperative, obligatory; urgent, emergency; forced (landing of plane).

اضْطَرَبَ to be disturbed, disorganized, muddled; to be mixed up, agitated, upset; to tremble, shake, quiver.

اضْطَرَمَ to burn; to catch fire; to be ablaze.

اضْطِلاع assumption of; taking upon onseslf.

اضْطَلَعَ to assume; to take upon oneself.

اضْطِهاد repression, oppression, persecution.

اضْطَهَدَ to persecute, oppress, tyrannize.

أَضْعَفَ to weaken, enfeeble, debilitate.

أَضْفَى to bestow upon; to reflect on; to ascribe to ;to grant, award.

اضْمَحَلَّ to fade away; to wane, decline, decay; to disappear; to vanish.

أَضْمَرَ to hide, conceal; to emaciate; to waste away; to make lean, thin, slender; to harbor a feeling.

أَضْنَى to emaciate; to wear out; to exhaust; to weaken, enervate, undermine, consume.

أَطَاحَ to overthrow, topple, bring down (a ruler).

إِطار frame; sphere; field; environment; rim.

توضع الصور داخل إطار وتعلّق على الجدار

Pictures are kept within frames and hanged on walls

إطار tire of a wheel.

أَطالَ to extend, elongate; to expatiate (speech); to prolong.

إطالَة elongation; extension; lengthening; expatiation (speech).

إطْباق closing, shutting; attack, assault, raid; occlusion of teeth.

أَطْبَقَ to close; to cover up; to darken; to fall upon; to attack, assail, clamp down on.

أَطْرَى to praise; to extol, laud; to lavish, praise on; to make moist, tender, soft; to moisten, wet.

إطْراء praise, extolment, laudation, commendation.

اطِّراد evenness; regularity; continuity, sequence.

أَطْرَبَ to delight, enrapture.

أَطْرَش deaf.

أَطْرَقَ to be silent; to stop talking; to bow one's head.

أُطْرُوحة thesis; dissertation.

إطْعام feeding; nourishing.

أَطْعَمَ to feed; to give food to.

أَطْفَأَ to put out, extinguish, smother, stifle a fire; to turn off, switch off light; to quench thirst.

إطْفاء extinction; extinguishing, fire-fighting.

إطْفائِيّ fireman.

يخاطر الإطفائيّ أحياناً بحياته لإخماد الحريق

The fireman risks his life sometimes to quench the fire

إطْفائيّة fire department; fire brigade.

أَطَلَّ to look down; to tower above; to command a view of; to overtop the surrounding area; to open upon or toward; to give on; to look out; to peek out; to appear, show, emerge, rise; to come, approach.

اطّلاع knowledge; awareness; conversance; seeing.

إطْلاق release, turning loose, freeing; undoing; launching, discharge, sending out, ejection.

إطْلاقُ الرَّصاصِ shooting, opening fire.

إطْلاقًا absolutely; without exception; never; on no account; by no means.

أطْلَسِيّ (الأَطْلَسِيّ) Atlantic.

أَطْلَعَ to inform of; to advise, notify of, report to; to disclose, show to; to sprout (plant); to explain.

اطَّلَعَ to study; to look at, inspect, view; to acquaint oneself with; to obtain information; to be informed of; to examine, look into, inspect; to be aware of; to find out, discover; to explore, inquire about, detect.

أَطْلَقَ to release, liberate, free, turn loose.

أَطْلَقَ to launch; to send out; to eject; to shoot; to fire shots; to let a laugh or a cry; to name or to give a name to; to give full rein; to let one's beard grow; to give a free hand to someone; to give generously to.

أَطْلَقَ to unleash (a war); to loosen one's bowels; to run away, bolt, dash off like the wind; to incite a crowd to demonstrations; to be radiant with joy.

اطْمَأَنَّ to be quiet, calm, reassured; to be appeased, soothed, assuaged; to reassure oneself of; to feel secure, safe; to rely on; to trust in.

إطْناب exaggeration, verbosity, redundancy.

أَطْنَبَ to expatiate; to overdo, exaggerate; to brag.

أَظْلَمَ to darken; to be dark, gloomy.

إظْهَار showing, demonstration; manifestation; exhibition; disclosure, display; developing photos.

أَظْهَرَ to show, demonstrate; to reveal, expose; to enlighten about; to let know about; to expound, explain, clarify, exhibit, uncover.

أَعَادَ to bring back; to revert someone or something to; to renew, resume an activity; to cause to return; to give back, put back, lay back something in its place; to repeat, reiterate, re-establish, restore.

إعادَة returning, sending back; reinstatement; repetition; repair, revision; resumption.

إعادةُ النَّظَر في review, revision, reconsideration, re-examination, reappraisal.

أَعَارَ to lend; to loan; to second an employee.

إعاشَة rations.

أَعَاقَ to hinder, detain, withhold, hold back someone from; to impede, hamper, defer, delay, put off, retard someone or something.

إعَاقَة hindering, detaining, impeding; stopping; delaying, retardation; deferment.

إعَالَة providing for a family; sustenance, support.

إعَانَة help, aid, assistance, succor, relief, support, subvention, subsidy; contribution; allowance; aid in money.

اعْتَادَ to get used to; to be accustomed to; to habituate oneself on; to make a habit of; to be used to doing something; to contract a habit.

اعْتَاق emancipation from slavery; release, discharge from a commitment.

اعْتِبَار respect, regard, esteem, consideration; point of view; taking into account; deeming; honor; holding in esteem; learning a lesson from.

اعْتِباراً من starting from; as of; from; effective from; beginning from.

باعْتِبار أَنَّ in view of the fact that; considering that; provided that; in terms of.

اعْتِباطِيّ arbitrary, random, haphazard.

اعْتَبَرَ to consider, weigh, take into account; to make allowances for; to deem, regard, look at; to esteem, honor, revere. value, respect; to hold in esteem; to have regard for.

اعْتَدَّ to consider; to calculate; to have confidence in oneself; to be self-reliant, self-conceited.

اعْتَدَى to commit an aggression; to act unjustly toward; to assault, attack; injure someone; to cross, transcend, overstep someone's right; to act hostilely; to contravene laws, principles; to transgress, violate, break laws; to act brutally, unlawfully against; to make an attempt on someone's life; to commit excesses against; to rape a woman.

اعْتِدَاء attack, assault, raid, inroad on; attempt to kill; outrage, rape, aggression upon a woman; transgressing limit or rights; contravening laws; acting brutally or unlawfully against another; wrongdoing.

اعْتِداد self-reliance; self-conceit; self-confidence.

اعْتِدال moderation; temperance; tenseness; evenness; symmetry of stature; equinox.

اعْتَدَلَ to be moderate, temperate, mild (for weather); to be straight, erect (in stature); to straighten up, sit up, sit straight; to act in moderation.

اعْتِذار apology, excuse.

اعْتَذَرَ to apologize; to excuse oneself; to plead in defense of; to make an apology.

اعْتَرَى to befall, afflict, seize, happen.

اعْتِراض opposition, objection, rebuttal; rejoinder; expostulation; remonstrance; protest, veto; resistance; counter argument, riposte; interception, rebuttal, demurral of a project law.

اعْتِراف recognition, acknowledgment, avowal, admission, confession, disclosure of one's intents.

اعْتَرَضَ to object, protest, expostulate, veto; to demur at; to take exception to; to rebut, challenge; to intercept; to obstruct, hinder, impede, hamper.

اعْتَرَفَ to confess, acknowledge, avow, admit, concede.

اعْتِزاز pride, boasting; glory.

اعْتِزال retirement; seclusion, retreat; privacy.

اعْتَزَمَ to be resolved; to be determined; to make up one's mind; to have an intent to do something; to plan to; to decide, resolve.

اعْتِصام sit-in; strike; adherence to; taking shelter in; seeking protection in.

اعْتَصَمَ to adhere to; to hang on to; to take refuge in; to seek protection in; to sit-in; to be patient; to maintain silence.

اعْتِقاد belief, faith, dogma; view; opinion.

اعْتِقال arrest, detention, internment.

اعْتَقَدَ to believe in; to consider, deem, regard as; to suppose; to think; to view.

اعْتَقَلَ to arrest; to put under arrest; to detain, intern , apprehend.

اعْتَكَفَ to isolate, seclude oneself in; to retire into; to live in seclusion, in retirement from; to apply oneself assiduously to something.

اعْتِلال illness, sickness, disease; disorder.

اعْتِماد reliance, dependence on; confidence; trust in; sanction, authorization; accreditation of diplomats; credit, loan; approbation in a balance sheet.

اعْتِمادٌ على النَّفس self-reliance, self-confidence.

اعْتَمَدَ to rely on; to depend on; to trust in; to be based on; to lean, recline, rest on; to adopt, observe, comply with; to sanction, authorize, approve; to accredit a diplomat; to take up; to be baptized.

اعْتَنَى to take interest in; to take care of; to take pains in doing something; to be concerned about; to care, provide, look after, see, tend, attend, devote one's attention to.

اعْتِناق adoption, embracement of a religion or doctrine.

اعْتِيادِيّ ordinary; common; usual; customary; habitual; normal; regular; plain; simple.

إعْجاب admiration; fancy; liking.

أُعْجِب بِـ to admire, think highly of; to like; to be pleased with; to have a liking for.

أُعْجُوبَة miracle; wonder; marvel.

أَعَدَّ to prepare; to arrange; to set up; to draft; to draw up; to design; to intend for a specified use or future use; to set in readiness; to make.

إعْدَاد preparation; readying; fixing; arrangement; setting up; making; drawing up; designing; adaptation.

إعْدَادِيّ preparatory (school);preliminary.

إعْدَام execution by hanging, electrocution or fire.

أعْرَاب Arabs of the desert.

إعْرَاب syntax, analysis, inflection, declension of words or sentences; expression; declaration; statement; proclamation; pronouncement.

إعْرَاض shunning, avoidance; evasion; reluctance.

أعْرَبَ to express, utter, voice, declare, state; to analyse; to parse (language).

أعْرَج (ص) crippled, lame.

أعْرَضَ to avoid, shun; keep away from; to renounce.

أعْزَب (ص) unmarried; celibate.

أعْزَب (اسم) bachelor.

أعْزَل (ص) unarmed; defenseless.

إعْصَار hurricance; tornado; cyclone.

دمّر الإعصار المنزل الريفيّ

The hurricane destroyed the country house

أعْطَى to give, present, hand over; to grant, award, accord; to bestow upon; to surrender, submit to someone; to administer a drug.

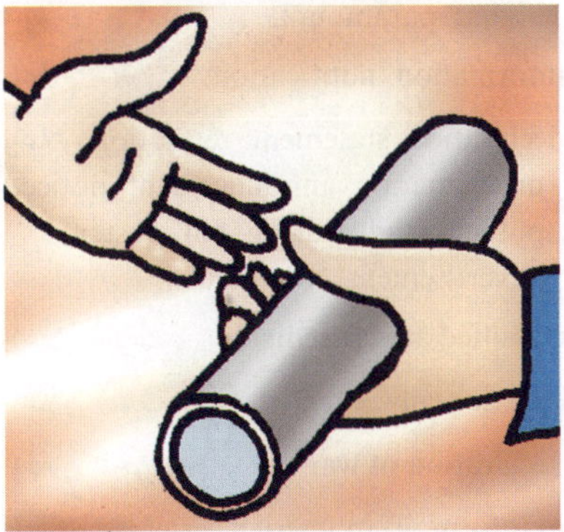

أعطيت الغرض إلى صاحبه فأخذه منّي

I handed over the thing to its owner and he took it from me

إعْطَاء giving, granting, awarding, handing over; bestowing upon; surrendering; administering a drug; according, donating, presenting.

أعْطَبَ to damage, spoil, wreck, impair.

أعْفَى to exempt from; to exonerate from; to release from; to relieve from; to discharge, dismiss from an office; to exempt, dispense of punishment.

إعْفَاء exemption (from a fee); excuse, dispense (of punishment); dismissal, discharge (from an office); remission; pardon, absolution, acquittal.

أَعْقَبَ to result from; to arise from; to follow, succeed, come after; to beget an offspring.

أَعْلَى (ص) maximum; highest; uppermost; superior; loftier; higher; paramount.

إعْلام information, notification.

إعْلان declaration, statement; revelation; proclamation; announcement, notice, publicity, advertising; bill, poster, advertisement, commercial.

إعْلانٌ مُبَوَّب classified advertisement.

إعْلانٌ ضَوْئِيّ electric sign.

إعْلانُ الحَرْب declaration of war.

أَعْلَمَ to inform of; to instruct, brief; to notify, advise of or about.

أَعْلَنَ to make known; to reveal, disclose, state, declare; to make public; to publish, announce, proclaim; to advertise; to declare war; to give evidence of.

أَعْمَى blind.

إعْمار development; construction; populating.

أَعْنَف (ص) harsher, more violent, more severe.

اعْوَجَّ to be crooked, bent, curved, twisted, distorted.

اعْوِجَاج bending, distortion; deviaton; crookedness; curvature, twist.

أَعْوَر one-eyed.

أَعْيا to exhaust, weary, tire out; to incapacitate; to perplex, puzzle; to be tired, feeble.

إعْياء fatigue, exhaution, weariness; inability; helplessness, tiredness.

أَغاثَ to succor; to aid, help, relieve.

إغاثَة succor; relief; help; aid.

إغارَة raid, attack, assault; invasion.

أَغاظَ to infuriate; to embitter, enrage, irritate; to vex, exasperate, incense.

اغْتابَ to slander, calumniate.

اغْتاظَ من to be furious at, angry with, irritated by.

اغْتالَ to kill, murder, assassinate.

اغْتِباط happiness, jubilation, joy, rejoicing, exultation.

اغْتَبَطَ to be glad, happy, delighted; to rejoice, jubilate, exult.

اغْتَرَّ to be deluded by; to be enticed by; to be conceited, vain.

اغْتِراب emigration; expatriation; alienation; westernism.

اغْتَرَبَ to emigrate; to go to live or work in a foreign country; to go westward; to be westernized.

اغْتِسال washing; taking a bath.

اغْتَسَلَ to wash up; to bathe.

اغْتِصاب rape (of a woman); usurpation, extortion.

اغْتَصَبَ to extort from; to usurp from; to seize unlawfully from; to rape (a woman).

اغْتَمَّ to be grieved, sad, gloomy, unhappy; to grieve, sadden, worry.

اغْتَنَمَ to seize the opportunity; to avail oneself of the occasion to.

أ ب ت ث ج ح خ د ذ ر ز س ش ص ض ط ظ ع غ ف ق ك ل م ن هـ و ي

اغْتِيال — assassination, murder, killing.

أَغْوَى — to incite; induce, prod; to seduce, tempt.

إغْراء — seduction, temptation, enticement; incitement, inducement, urging.

إغْراق — drowning, flooding, sinking, dumping of markets with goods; extravagance; hyperbole (language) exorbitance, immoderation.

أَغْرَقَ — to drown; to flood, inundate; to dump markets with goods; to overdo, exaggerate, to carry to excess; to laugh noisily.

أُغْرِمَ بِـ — to fall in love with; to be passionately attached to.

أَغْضَبَ — to annoy, exasperate, anger, enrage, infuriate; to vex, irritate, provoke, gall.

إغْفَال — omission, skipping, neglect; disregard, ignoring.

أَغْفَلَ — to omit, skip, neglect, disregard, ignore.

إغْلاق — closing, shutoff, lockup; foreclosure of a mortgage; barring; locking, bolting.

أَغْلَبُ الأحيان — mostly; in most cases; in general; most of the time; by and large.

أَغْلَبُ الظَّنّ — most likely; most probably.

أَغْلَبِيَّة — majority; greater portion.

أَغْلَبِيَّة سَاحِقَة — overwhelming majority.

أَغْلَبِيَّة مُطْلَقَة — absolute majority.

أَغْلَقَ — to close, bolt, shut off, lock.

أغلق الباب بعد خروجك من فضلك

Please close the door after you leave

إغْماء — swoon; faint; unconsciousness.

أَغْمَدَ — to sheathe, to put into the scabbard (sword); to plunge, thrust (a knife, sword) into someone's breast; to encompass, shelter, protect; to cover with God's grace.

أَغْمَضَ — to close, shut one's eyes in the face of; to sleep; to be asleep; to make someone blind to; to feign blindness; to overlook, wink, connive at; to bear, stand, tolerate something.

أُغْمِيَ عليه — to pass out; to lose consciousness; to faint.

أَغْنَى — to enrich; to suffice; to be of benefit; to serve instead of; to dispense of; to be helpful.

أُغْنِيَة أو أُغْنِيَّة song; melody; tune.

أَغْوَى to seduce, tempt, entice, mislead.

إغْوَاء seduction, temptation, enticement, misguidance.

أُفّ! ugh!

أَفَادَ to be useful, profitable, of help, of service; to benefit, profit; to utilize; to make use of.

أَفَادَ to mean; to inform; to report, tell about; to declare; to state; to testify under oath; to obtain, get, acquire, earn profit.

إفادَة usefulness, use, advantage, benefit.

إفادَة utilization; making use of; profiting from.

إفادَة reporting, informing, telling; statement, deposition; testimony, affidavit.

أَفَاضَ to dwell on; to speak extensively; to report in detail; to fill to overflowing; to pour out; to shed tears; to spread news; to expatiate.

أَفَاقَ to get up; to awaken; to be vigilant, on the alert; to recover, recuperate from sickness.

أَفَّاق tramp; vagabond.

أَفَّاك liar; scandalmonger; impostor.

آفَة epidemic; disease; evil; blight; pestilence.

أَفْتَى to deliver a formal legal opinion.

افْتَأَتَ to tell lies about someone; to accuse falsely of; to act on one's own judgment; to oppress, tyrannize, domineer.

افْتِتاح opening, inauguration, commencement, dedication; introduction.

افْتِتَاحِيَّة editorial; leader; overture (music).

افْتِتَان enchantment, fascination, infatuation.

افْتَتَحَ to dedicate; to address first; to open the talk with someone about; to open up; unfold; to inaugurate, introduce, begin; to occupy, conquer a country or region.

افْتَخَرَ to boast, brag of; to pride oneself upon; to be proud of; to vie in glory.

افْتَرَى to tell lies against; to accuse falsely of; to slander, defame, speak evil of.

افْتِراء falsehood; false accusation; calumny, slander.

افْتِراض assumption, supposition, premise, hypothesis, presupposition.

افْتِرَاضِيّ assumed; presumed; hypothetical.

افْتَرَسَ to prey upon; to devour; to rape, violate (a girl).

افْتَرَضَ to assume, presume, presuppose; to take for granted; to postulate.

افْتَرَقَ to separate, disengage oneself from; to be separated, split, disunited, dispersed; to be divided; to part company.

افتِضاح infamy, ignominy, disgracefulness; disclosure; bringing to light.

افتَضَحَ to be disclosed, revealed, divulged; to be disgraced, compromised, dishonored.

افتَعَلَ to fabricate, invent, contrive, plan; to do on purpose; to do deliberately; to forge, falsify.

افتِقار need, want, lack, insufficiency; becoming poor.

افتَقَرَ to be poor, needy, destitute; to need, want, require; to be lacking, deficient in, short of.

أفحَمَ to confute in argument; to dumbfound.

إفراج release; discharge; bail; freeing.

إفرادِيّ individual; separate; single.

إفراز secretion; exudation; discharge; expectoration; partition in kind.

إفراط immoderation; excess; exaggeration.

إفراغ vacating, discharge; evacuation; emptying, unloading.

أفرَجَ to release, discharge, let go, free a prisoner; to bail out, release on bail a detained person; to leave, quit, evacuate a place.

أفرَحَ to make happy; to gladden; to delight.

أفرَدَ to set aside, separate, segregate, isolate someone; to single out; to devote to; to perfom single-handedly; to allocate, allot, appropriate for a specific purpose.

أفرَزَ to secrete, excrete, exude, discharge; to separate, set, classify, screen; to select, pick out, muster.

أفرَطَ to go to excess; to be immoderate; to exceed proper limits.

أفرَغَ to empty, evacuate, discharge, unload a cargo; to pour out; to unload from a ship, truck, etc; to mold; to exert, oneself to the utmost; to make every effort; to occupy oneself exclusively with; to phrase, shape, form, express, articulate.

إفريز cornice; frieze; ledge.

إفساد spoiling, sabotaging, thwarting, undermining; corruption of characters; demoralization; vitiation; depravation; frustration

أفسَحَ to make room for; to make way for; to give an opportunity for; to enable, allow, permit; to extend, expand, dilate the scope of action.

أفسَدَ to spoil, corrupt, deprave someone's characters; to ruin, degrade, debase, tarnish, defile; to rot, decompose, putrefy; to thwart, foil, frustrate, undermine; to sow or stir up dissension among; to act wickedly; to distort; to devaluate, depreciate, degrade something for someone.

أَفْشَى to reveal, disclose, uncover, spread, propagate.

إفْشاء disclosure, propagation, dissemination; divulgence, revealing, disclosing.

إفْشال frustration; foiling.

أَفْشَلَ to frustrate, foil, abort, thwart.

إفْصاح uttering, utterance; declaration, statement.

أَفْصَحَ to express, voice, announce, declare, reveal; to express oneself in flawless Arabic style; to speak frankly about; to be clear, plain, evident, obvious.

أَفْضَى to conduce to; to lead to ;to bring about; to engender; to create, make, produce; to reach at; to inform, tell about, disclose to, reveal to someone of one's feelings or secrets.

أَفْضَلِيَّة precedence, priority.

إفْطار fast-breaking; breakfast.

أَفْعَى viper; snake; serpent.

تزحف الأفعى على بطنها لأن لا أرجل لها
The snake moves on its belly because it has no feet

أُفُق horizon; skyline.

تغيب الشمس في الأفق وتبرز أيضاً منه
The sun hides in the horizon and appears from it too

إفْقار impoverishment.

أَفْقَدَ to deprive of; to cause someone to lose something.

أَفْقَرَ to impoverish; to reduce to poverty.

أُفُقِيّ horizontal.

أَفَلَ to set, go down (sun); to fade, dim.

إفْلات escape; disengagement; getaway.

إفْلاس bankruptcy; insolvency.

أَفْلَتَ to escape, skip away, break away; to free oneself from; to set free, liberate; to let escape.

أَفْلَحَ to thrive, prosper; to be lucky, successful in.

أَفْنَى to annihilate, bring to nought; to destroy, ruin; to exhaust, consume, wear out, spend, deplete, waste, wear away.

إفْناء annihilation, extermination, wiping out; destruction; complete exhaustion, consumption, depletion.

أَفْهَمَ to make understand; to instruct, teach.

أَفْيون opium.

أَقَالَ to depose, discharge,remove from office; to free, release, exempt from an obligation; to demand the cancellation of a sale; to seek the abrogation of a contract; to steady someone who has stumbled.

إقالَة deposition, dismissal, discharge from an office; cancellation, abrogation, revocation of a sale or a contract; freeing, releasing, exemption from an obligation.

أَقَام to resurrect, raise from the dead; to lift up, raise, erect, elevate; to start, originate, found something; to fix, determine something; to appoint, nominate, install someone as; to put someone in charge of; to agitate, rouse, excite something; to hold a meeting; to celebrate, organize a festival; to give a reception; to occupy oneself constantly with; to abide, stay, reside in; to persist in; to stick to; to provide for someone's needs; to support someone to build, raise, establish, institute a building or business; to institute legal proceedings against; to sue, prosecute, litigate; to prove, demonstrate, substantiate a fact; to protest; to render account to someone; to administer justice; to attach importance to something; to stage a contest; to substitute someone for someone else; to upset someone; to throw someone in a state of violent emotion; to rise; to get up; to straighten up.

إقامَة (مكوث) stay; residence; residing; dwelling.

إقامَة (إنشاء) erection, building, construction, establishment, founding, installation.

إقامَةُ الدَّعْوَى institution of legal proceedings against; suing, prosecution; administration of justice.

إقامَةُ الصلاة performance of ritual prayers.

إقامَةُ القُدَّاس celebration of a mass (Christian Faith).

إقامَةُ الموتى resurrection of the dead.

إقْبال approach, drawing near; embarking upon; great demand; good fortune; attendance; concern for; coming, arrival; attention, response.

أَقْبَلَ to approach, draw near, come; to advance to; to attend, show up, come to; to embark upon, undertake, proceed to; to be lucky, prosperous.

اقْتِبَاس adaptation of a literary text; quotation, citation of another's literary work; learning; loaning, borrowing.

اقْتَبَسَ to quote, cite, borrow from, adapt from a literary work; to learn, acquire knowledge.

اقْتَتَلَ to fight one another; to battle; to make war.

اقْتِحَام breaking into; storming into; breakthrough.

اقْتَحَمَ to break into, storm into, break through; to embark boldly upon; to defy danger.

اقْتَدَى to emulate; to take after; to follow the example of; to imitate; to be guided by.

اقْتِدَاء emulation; following the example of; imitation.

اقْتَدَرَ to be able, apt, capable of; to have the aptitude, strength, power.

اقْتِرَاب approach; approximation; getting near or close to; advance; moving toward.

اقْتِرَاح suggestion, proposal, offer.

اقْتِرَاض borrowing, loan.

اقْتِرَاع voting, ballot, polling.

اقْتِرَاعٌ عامّ universal suffrage.

اقْتِرَان coupling, union, linkup; marriage; conjunction; mapping; function (math); conjugation (biology).

اقْتَرَبَ to approach, approximate, come near or close.

اقْتَرَحَ to propose, suggest, recommend.

اقْتَرَضَ to borrow; to obtain a loan.

اقْتَرَعَ to vote; to cast a vote; to poll; to draw lots; to choose by lot.

اقْتَرَفَ to commit, perpetrate.

اقْتَرَنَ to be coupled with; to be connected with; to unite with; to pair, couple, join.

اقْتَرَنَ to be married; to marry, wed; to take as a wife.

اقْتَسَمَ to divide, distribute among two or more persons; to share, partake with others.

اقْتَصَّ to take revenge on; to retaliate upon; to punish; to tell a story; to track; to follow the trail of.

اقْتِصَاد economy; saving; thriftiness; providence.

اقْتِصَادٌ كُلِّيّ macro economics.

اقْتِصَادٌ حُرّ free enterprise.

اقْتِصَادِيّ (ص) economic; economical.

اقْتِصَادِيّ (اسم) economist.

اقْتِصَادِيَّات economies; economics.

اقْتَصَدَ to economize; to save; to be frugal, thrifty, provident; to practise economy.

اقْتَصَرَ to be restriced to, confined to; to curtail, abridge.

اقْتَضَى to require, demand, call for.

اقْتِطَاع deduction, substraction; discount, rebate; appropriation.

اقْتَطَعَ to take a part of; to borrow, tear out; to appropriate, acquire, take possession of; to deduct, substract, take off.

اقتطع الحطاب جزءاً من جذع شجرة
The lumbertack cut a piece from the tree trunk

اقْتَطَفَ to select, choose, extract, quote; to pick, gather, harvest, pluck off.

اقْتَفَى to trace, trail, track; to follow, pursue, chase; to imitate, emulate, follow someone's example.

اقْتِلاع extraction, pulling out, uprooting; extermination; eradication; deracination.

اقْتَلَعَ to pluck out, pull out, weed out, extract, uproot; to exterminate, deracinate, eradicate.

اقْتَنَى to acquire, possess, have, own.

اقْتِناء acquisition, purchase, possession.

اقْتِناع conviction, satisfaction, contentment.

اقْتَنَعَ to be satisfied, content with; to be convinced; to be persuaded; to put a mask, veil on one's face.

إقْدام intrepidity, courage, initiative, audacity, daring, pluck, fearlessness.

أَقْدَمَ to venture, risk, dare; to set out; to embark boldy upon; to have the audacity to do something; to brave, attack.

أَقْدَم (ص) senior, older.

أَقْدَمِيَّة seniority.

أَقَرَّ to confess, to resolve; to decide, determine; to acknowledge, set up; affirm, agree, consent; to concede; to establish; to gladden someone's eyes; to uphold, sustain, maintain.

إقْرار confession, avowal, admission, recognition; ratification, endorsement, approval, consent; establishment, confirmation, declaration, attestation.

إقْراض lending.

أَقْرِباء (ج) relatives, kinsfolk, kindred, family.

أَقْرَبُون (ج) relatives, kinsfolk, kindred, family.

أَقْرَضَ to lend; to grant a loan.

أَقْرَع bald, baldheaded.

أَقْسَمَ to swear by, to take an oath.

أَقْسَمَ يميناً كاذِبَة to commit perjury.

أَقْصَى to put aside; to keep away; to remove, take away; to force out, exclude, dismiss, expel.

أَقْصَى (ص) farther away, ulterior. remotest, furthest, uttermost, extreme, ultimate, maximum.

إقْصاء removal, sending far away, dismissal, elimination, exclusion, forcing out, driving away.

أَقْصُوصَة short story or novel.

أحبّ قراءة الأقاصيص المشوّقة

I love reading exciting stories

إقْطاع feudalism.

إقْطاعِيّ (ص) feudal.

إقْطاعِيّ (اسم) feudal lord.

إقْطاعِيَّة feudalism, feudal estate.

أَقْعَدَ to seat; to make sit; to cripple, disable; to prevent someone from doing something.

إقْفال closure, shutdown; lockup, bolting.

أَقْفَرَ to be desolate, deserted, uninhabited; to be destitute of, devoid of, empty.

أَقْفَلَ to close, shut, lock, latch, bolt; to turn off; to hang up (telephone receiver); to cut a line of connection, of transport.

أَقَلَّ to carry, transport, raise, lift; to do little of.

إقْلاع sailing, departure, takoff; abstention; relinquishment; giving up a habit.

شاهدت إقلاع الطائرة من أرض المطار

I watched the airplane taking off from the airport's runway

إقْلاق troubling, disturbing, upsetting someone's peace of mind, comfort, sleep, etc.

أَقْلَعَ to desist from; to abstain from; to abandon, give up, relinquish (a habit, something, etc); to set sail (ship); to depart, take off (airplane).

أَقْلَقَ to worry, disquiet; upset, disturb someone's peace of mind, comfort, sleep, etc.

أَقَلِّيَّة minority.

إقْليم region, territory, area, district, province.

إقليمِيّ regional, territorial, provincial.

أَقْنَعَ to persuade, convince, induce, prevail upon; to give satisfaction; to satisfy, content.

أَقْوى (ص) stronger, mightier, more powerful.

أَكادِيمِيَّة academy.

أَكّال corrosive, erosive.

إكْبار reverence, admiration, esteem.

أَكْبَر (ص) greater, bigger, larger, superior.

أَكْبَرُ سِنًّا older, elder.

اكْتَأَبَ to be sad, grieved, depressed; to feel dejected, melancholic, sad.

اكْتِئاب depression, melancholy, grief, sorrow, sadness.

اكْتِتاب subscription, contribution; underwriting (shares).

اكْتَتَبَ to subscribe, contribute; underwrite (shares); to copy, transcribe; to write, compose, edit, draft a book, essay, article, thesis etc.

اكْتِراث concern, interest, care, attention.

اكْتَرَثَ to take an interest in; to care for; to heed, mind.

اكْتِسَاب acquisition, gaining, winning, earning.

اكْتَسَبَ to acquire, gain, earn, profit.

اكْتَسَحَ to sweep away; to invade, overrun; to flood, inundate; to overwhelm, crush.

اكْتِشاف disclosure, discovery, detection, spotting, uncovering, finding out.

اكْتَظَّ to be crowded, overcrowded (place, street); to be overpopulated, densely populated (a country, town, region).

اكْتِظاظ congestion; overcrowdedness.

أَكْتَع having crippled fingers.

اكْتِفاء satisfaction, contentment.

اكْتِفاءٌ ذاتِيّ self-sufficiency.

اكْتِمال completion, maturity, ripeness; termination.

اكْتَمَلَ to be complete, integral, perfect; to be accomplished, terminated, concluded; to be finished, done, fulfilled, matured.

أَكْثَرَ to increase, multiply, grow; to do much of; to give much of; to augment, compound.

أَكْثَر (ص) more; more numerous; longer; most.

أَكْثَرُ من exceeding; more than; over.

أَكْثَرِيَّة majority.

أَكْثَرِيَّة ساحِقَة overwhelming majority.

أَكْثَرِيَّةٌ مُطْلَقَة absolute majority.

أَكَّدَ to confirm, affirm, assert, corroborate, prove, assure; to emphasize, stress, underline; to give assurance; to make sure, definite, imperative.

أُكْذُوبَة lie.

إكْرامِيَّة fees, retainer, honorarium, bonus, tip, gratuity, premium.

إكْراه coercion, compulsion, duress, use of force.

أَكْرَمَ to honor, revere, venerate, exalt; to bestow honor upon; to meet with deference, respect, politeness; to treat reverentially, hospitably, politely.

أَكْرَهَ to compel, force, coerce, oblige to.

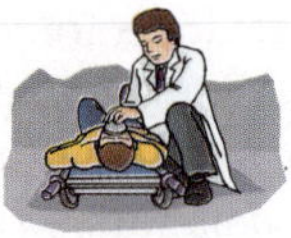

أُكْسِجين oxygen (gas).

أَكْسَدَ to oxidize.

أَكْسَدَة oxidation, oxidization.

أُكْسِيد oxide.

إكْسِير elixir.

أَكَلَ to eat; to consume, eat up; to devour; to erode, corrode, wear away.

أَكَلَ الدهْرُ عليه وشَرِبَ to be old, decrepit, timeworn, ancient.

أَكْل food, eating.

آكِل corrosive, erosive; eater.

إكْليل crown; wreath; garland (flowers); laurel; corona.

إكْمال completion, finishing, termination, conclusion.

أَكَمَة hillock, mound, hummock.

يسقط الثلج على أكمة الجبل

Snow falls over the mountain top

أَكْمَلَ to complete, finish, terminate, conclude.

أَكول glutton, voracious, greedy.

أَكيد (ص) certain, positive, sure, definite, firm.

أَكيدًا surely, certainly; for sure.

آلَ to revert to; to return to; to be traced back to; to lead, conduce to; to cause, result in; to end up with; to arrive, reach at; to come to; to devolve upon; vest in, accrue to; to govern, rule, lead the people.

آل family, relatives, people, kinsfolk.

آلَى to swear; to undertake, take upon oneself; to pledge, vow, promise; to engage, commit oneself.

إلَى to, toward, till; up to; until.

إلى آخِرِه and so on; etc; and so forth.

إلى مَتَى؟ till when?.

ألاَّ not to; so as not to; in order not to.

إلاَّ except, but, with the exception of; unless.

إلاَّ إذَا unless, if not, except when.

إلاَّ أَنَّ yet, however, but; nevertheless, still.

أَلَّبَ to incite against; to provoke, arouse against; to rally, band people against; to sow dissension among people; to plot, conspire against.

أَلْبَسَ to clothe; to dress; to drape, face, coat; to encrust, plate, line.

آلة machine, instrument, appliance, device; organ; agent, servant.

آلةُ تَسْجِيل الصَّوْتِ recorder, tape recorder.

آلةُ تَسْجِيل النَّقْدِ cash register.

آلةُ تَصْوير camera.

آلةُ تَفْقيس incubator.

آلةٌ حاسِبَة calculating machine.

آلةُ خِياطَة sewing machine.

آلةٌ كاتِبَة typewriter.

آلةٌ ناسِخَة photocopier, duplicating machine.

الْتَأَمَ to convene, meet, assemble; to heal up; to be joined, welded, connected; to be repaired, mended.

الْتِباس confusion, ambiguity, dubiosity, tangle, doubt.

الْتَجَأَ to take refuge; to ask for protection; to flee to; to resort to.

الْتِجاء recourse, resorting to; to seek refuge or protection in or with.

الْتِحاق affiliation, joining, entering.

الْتِحام cohesion, fusion, merger; welding; engagement in battle; close connection or link-up.

الْتَحَق to join, enter; to become a member of; to associate oneself with; to be affiliated with.

الْتَحَمَ to adhere, fuse, join, unite, merge; to clash, engage in battle; to heal, cicatrize; to weld; to get connected, joined, fused with.

الْتَذَّ to enjoy; relish; to take or derive pleasure from; to find delicious, pleasant, savoury; to be gratified, delighted, pleased by.

الْتِزام commitment, liability, duty, obligation; contract, concession, franchise; compliance with; respecting, honoring one's engagement; farming (land).

الْتَزَمَ to observe, comply with, maintain, honor; respect one's engagement; to bind, commit, obligate oneself; to undertake, assume; to be bound by; to abide by; to farm land; to keep silence.

الْتِصاق adhesion, cohesion.

الْتَصَقَ to adhere to, cohere to, cling to, stick to.

الْتَفَّ to wrap oneself in; to gather around; to surround, encircle, embrace, wrap; to wind, coil, twist; to intertwine, interweave, convolute.

الْتِفاف winding, coiling, convolution; surrounding, encirclement; gathering, assembly, rallying.

الْتَفَتَ to turn around; to look around; to heed, pay attention to, consider, take care of.

الْتَقَى to meet, band toghether; to come across; to hit upon; to encounter, meet unexpectedly.

الْتِقاء meeting; concurrence in opinion.

الْتِقاط gathering, collection, picking up; reception; taking photographs; snapping; filming.

الْتَقَطَ to gather, pick up, collect, receive; to photograph, take a picture, shoot, film.

الْتِماس request, solicitation, appeal, plea, petition.

الْتَمَسَ to request, ask for, solicit; to beseech, entreat, appeal to; to plead with; to search for, look for.

الْتِهاب inflammation, bursting into flames; infection.

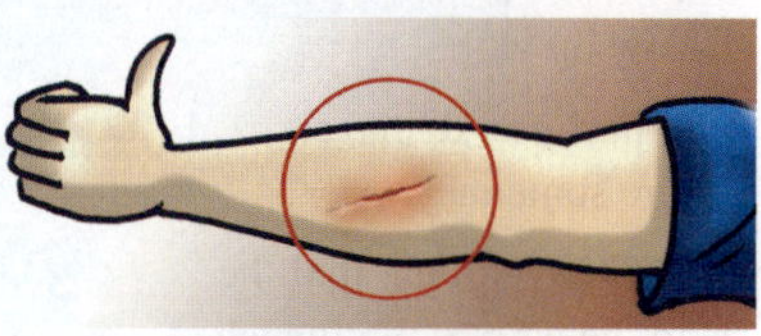

أصاب الالتهاب ذراعي فداويتها

Inflammation reached my arm and I treated it

اِلْتِهَام ingurgitation; devouring; gobbling.

اِلْتَهَبَ to inflame, flame, burn; to burst into flames; to be aflame; to catch fire; to be inflamed (medecine).

اِلْتَهَمَ to devour, gobble, ingurgitate.

اِلْتَوَى to be twisted, tortuous, bent, crooked; to be curved, warped, contorted, out of shape.

اِلْتِواء curvedness, bend, twist, curve; absurdity, perverseness; flexing, coil; warping; crook.

أَلَحَّ to pester, harass, urge, press someone to do something; to insist, solicit; to request earnestly.

إِلْحاح insistence, pressing, urging, emphasis, earnest request, urgent solicitation.

إِلْحاد atheism, apostasy, heresy.

إِلْحاق annexation, following up, addition, admission to an organization, enrollment in; joining; appending.

أَلْحَدَ to be an atheist, unbeliever; to apostatize; to be a heretic.

أَلْحَقَ to attach, append, annex to; to follow up with.

أَلْحَقَ ضَرَراً to do harm to, damage, injure someone.

اَلَّذي who, whom, which, that; he who, he whom, that which.

إِلْزام compulsion, coercion, forcing; binding, obligation, enjoining.

إِلْزَامِيّ compulsory, obligatory, mandatory.

أَلْزَمَ to bind, impose upon, enjoin on; to force, compel, coerce, oblige someone to; to force someone to stay in bed (sick person).

أَلْصَقَ to attach, affix, fix, stick, paste, glue; to post, affix a poster, a placard; to fit closely.

أَلْصَقَ تُهْمَةً to impute to, charge with, accuse of.

أَلْغَى to cancel, invalidate, nullify, revoke, rescind; to overrule.

أَلِفَ to get used to; to be accustomed to; to be familiar with, acquainted with; to like; to be tame, domesticated (animal).

آلَفَ to mix with; to be intimate with; to harmonize with; to get used to.

أَلَّفَ to compose, write, compile (a book); to set up, establish, (a business, company); to unite, join, link up, merge; to tame, domesticate an animal; to reconcile, make peace among, conciliate between.

أَلْف thousand.

أَلِفْباء alphabet.

أَلِفْبائِيّاً alphabetically.

أُلْفَة familiarity, intimacy, friendship, love, affection; union, harmony, concord, congeniality; affinity.

أَلْقى to throw, cast, drop, discard; to recite, play, sing (a song); to give a lecture; to burden with; to pay attention to; to make a statement about; to lay one's fate in someone's hands; to throw oneself into; to surrender to someone; to give oneself up to someone.

ألقى الخطيب خطاباً حماسياً أمام الجمهور
The speaker delivered a speech that aroused the audience

أَلْقى حُمولَةَ المَرْكِبِ to jettison.

أَلْقى البَيْضَ to lay eggs.

أَلْقى تَحِيَّةً to salute, greet.

أَلْقى قُرْعَةً to cast lots.

أَلْقى القَنابِلَ to drop bombs, bombard, bomb.

أَلْقى عليهِ القَوْلَ to dictate, to.

أَلْقى اللَّوْمَ على to blame; to put the blame on.

إلقاء throwing, casting, dropping, discarding; dictation, recitation, recital, lecturing.

الله God, the Lord, Allah.

الله أكْبَر God is the greatest.

اللّهُمّ! o God! o Lord!.

اللّهُمّ إذا if only; at least if.

اللّهُمَّ إلاَّ unless; except that.

آلَمَ to hurt, pain, ache someone; to cause pain or suffering to someone.

أَلَمَّ to be acquainted, familiar with; to get to know something; to commit, perpetrate a crime.

أَلَمَّ to befall, afflict, hit, affect; to visit; to call at someone's house.

أَلَم pain, suffering, agony, torment, ache.

أَلْماس diamond.

الألماس أصلب المعادن على الإطلاق
Diamonds are the hardest metals on earth

إلْمام knowledge, familiarity, cognizance.

أَلْمَعِيّ brilliant, intelligent, clever, sagacious.

أَلَّهَ to deify; to make a god of.

إلَه God, deity.

إلْهَاء distraction.

إلْهَام inspiration, revelation.

أَلْهَبَ to inflame, ignite, set on fire; to excite, stir, stir up, rouse (emotions).

أَلْهَمَ to inspire someone.

إلَهِيّ divine, from God.

ألومينيوم aluminium, aluminum.

في مطبخ منزلنا أوانٍ مصنوعة من الألومنيوم

Aluminium is used to produce a wide variety of utensils

آلِيّ mechanical, automatic, self-propelled, motorized.

أَلْيَة buttocks, rump, fat tail (of a sheep).

آلِيَّة mechanism; machinery; automation; vehicle.

أَلِيف tame, domestic (animal); friendly, genial, sociable, intimate, close, familiar (man).

أَمَّ to go to; to travel to; to lead in prayer (Islam); to become a mother (woman); to nationalize.

أَمْ or.

أُمّ mother; source; origin; basis; foundation; original version of a book; essence, gist; matrix.

أحبّ أمّي حبّاً عظيماً

I love deeply my mother

أَمَّا as to; as for; however; yet; on the other hand.

إمَّا either or; if.

أَمارَة sign, indication, token, mark.

إمارَة emirate.

أَماطَ to remove, pull away, move away from.

أَماطَ اللِّثَامَ عَن to unveil, unmask, disclose, reveal, expose.

إمَالَة inclination, tilting, sloping, bending.

أَمام in front of; opposite to; facing; before; forward.

إمام Imam (Islam); leader; model, example; guide; index; criterion.

أَمامِيّ front, forward, foremost; ahead, anterior; at a forward position; in the front.

أمان safety, peace, security; protection, safeguard; immunity, guarantee; pact, agreement.

أَمانَة faithfulness, fidelity, loyalty; honesty, integrity; trust, faith; deposit, charge; trusteeship, custody; care; protection.

أَمانَةُ السِّرّ secretariat.

إمْبَراطور emperor.

إمْبَراطورَة empress.

إمْبَراطوريّ imperial.

إمْبَراطوريَّة empire.

أَمَة slave girl, bondmaid.

أُمَّة nation, people.

امْتازَ بـِ to be distinguished, characterized by; to be peculiar to; to have a distinctive feature.

امْتازَ عن to excel, surpass, outclass.

امْتِثال submission; obedience; compliance; consent; abidance by; observance of.

امْتَثَلَ to obey, follow, submit to; to comply with; to take as a model; to imitate, copy.

امْتِحان examination, test, trial.

امْتَحَنَ to examine, test; to put to test; to subject to a trial; to afflict, distress.

امْتَدَّ to extend; to stretch out; to spread out; to be spread out; extended, stretched out, distended, protracted, prolonged, elongated.

امْتِداد extention, stretching, widening, distention, dilatation, elongation, prolongation; length, size; extent; spread; range, scope.

امْتَدَحَ to praise, commend, laud, extol, eulogize.

امْتِزاج mixture, mixing, blending.

امتزج to be mixed, blended, mingled with; to mix, blend, combine, mingle.

امْتَصَّ to absorb, imbibe, suck up, sip.

امْتِصاص absorption, soaking up, sucking, suction.

امْتِعاض displeasure, indignation, anger, resentment.

امْتَعَضَ to be displeased, indignant, angered, resentful.

امْتَقَعَ to be pale, pallid, wan.

امْتَلأَ to be full, filled with.

امْتِلاء fullness; fatness, obesity (body).

امْتِلاك taking possession; occupancy, seizure, possession.

امْتِناع refraining, abstention from; refusal, denial; impossibility, desistance; stoppage, ceasing.

امْتَنَعَ to abstain, refrain; keep from; to desist, stop, cease; to refuse, decline; to be impossible.

امْتَهَنَ to humble, degrade, treat in a humiliating manner; to revile, despise; to wear out by use; to practise as a profession; to employ someone for menial work.

امْتِياز	distinction, excellence; privilege; prerogative; concession, franchise; patent; lien, preference on a debtor's assets.
أُمْثولة	example, lesson.

أَمَدَّ	to supply, provide, equip with; to help, aid, assist; to grant a respite or delay; to postpone, put off a due date for payment of a debt, bill payable.

أَمَد	scope, period, duration.
إمْدَاد	supply, provision, equipping; help, aid, assistance.
أَمَرَ	to order, command, instruct; to commision, charge; to plot, conspire against; to decree, prescribe, dictate.
أَمَرَّ	to let pass; to cause to go through, get through; to be bitter (taste); to embitter.
أَمْر	order, command, instruction; decree, ordinance; condition, state,situation; thing; imperative (grammar).
أَمْرُ تَسْليم	delivery order.
أَمْرُ تَفْتيش	search warrant.
أَمرُ إحْضار (للمُتَّهَم أو للشَّاهِد)	subpoena; summons.
آمِر	commander, head, ruler, leader; warden (of a prison); commanding officer (army); master.
امْرُؤ	man, person, individual.
امْرَأة	woman; wife.

ترتدي هذه الإمرأة لباس أهل الريف

This woman wears the distinctive rural dress

إمْرَة	leadership, command, control, authority.
أَمْرَد	hairless, beardless, bald.
أَمْس	yesterday; immediate past; recently, newly.
أَمْسُ الأوَّل	the day before yesterday.
أَمْسَى	to come to be; to become; to enter into evening.
إمْسَاك	seizure, detention; stop, cessation, abstinence, avarice; constipation; time of the day which marks the beginning of the Ramadhan fast (Islam).
إمْساكِيَّة	calendar of fasting during Ramadhan (Islam).
أَمْسَكَ	to hold, grasp, seize, catch, clasp; to refrain, abstain, desist from; to withhold, detain, prevent; to possess alone; to constipate (bowels).
أُمْسِيَّة	evening; evening gathering, party, show.

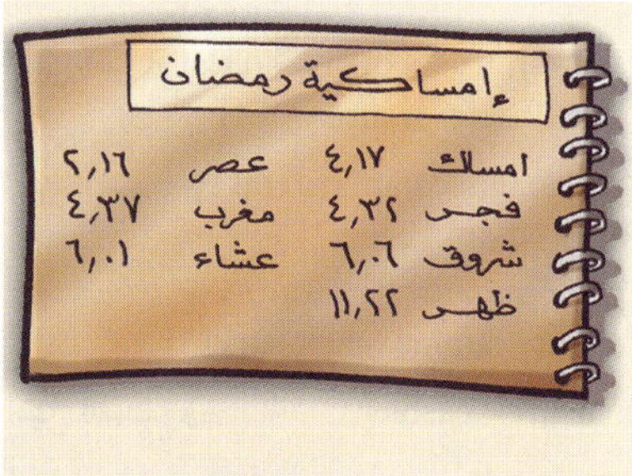

تحدّد إمساكية شهر رمضان مواعيد الصوم والإفطار
Ramadhan's diary specifies the times of prayers and fasting during the month

أَمْضَى — to spend, pass; to carry out, perform, accomplish; to sign a document.

إمْضاء — signature; conclusion, accomplishment.

وقّع المدير إمضاءه على رسالة تجارية
The manager put his signature on a commercial letter

أَمْطَرَ — to rain; to shower with rain (sky); to shower with a hail (of stones), with a flood of (abuses, threats etc).

أَمْعَنَ — to go to extremes; to carry too far; to apply oneself steady, assiduously to; to scrutinize, ponder over.

إمْكان — ability; faculty; possibility; potentiality.

أمطرت السماء فاختبأت داخل كوخ
Rain dropped and I had to take refuge in a hut

إمْكَانِيَّة — possibility; potentiality; probability.

أَمْكَنَ — to be possible, feasible; to be capable of; can; may; to enable someone to do something.

أَمَلَ — to hope; to expect, anticipate, look forward to.

أَمَل — hope, anticipation; expectation.

إمْلاء — dictation.

إمْلاق — abject poverty, destitution.

أَمْلَس (ص) — smooth, even, plain.

أَمْلَط (ص) — hairless.

أَمَّمَ — to nationalize.

أَمِنَ — to feel safe, secure, peaceful.

آمَنَ — to believe in; to have faith in.

أَمَّنَ — to insure; to safeguard; to guarantee; to entrust, to have faith in; to secure, warrant, ensure; to provide with; to procure, achieve, accomplish.

أَمْن — security, safety, peace, protection.

الأَمْنُ الداخِليّ — internal security.

الأَمْنُ العامّ — public security.

الأمْنُ القَوْمِيّ national security.

آمِن safe, secure, peaceful.

أُمْنِيَّة wish, aspiration, desire.

أمْهَلَ to grant a respite, time delay to someone.

أُمومَة motherhood.

أُمِّيّ illiterate, unlettered; maternal, motherly.

أُمِّيَّة illiteracy.

أمير prince, emir, leader, lord.

يجلس الأمير على كرسيّ الإمارة

The emir sits on the emirate's chair

أميرُ البَحر admiral.

أَميرُ المُؤْمِنين commander of the faithful; caliph.

أَميرة princess.

أَميرِيّ state-owned, public domain; fiscal; princely.

أمين (ص) faithful, trustworthy, honest, loyal; safe, secure.

أمين (اسم) trustee, guardian, caretaker, custodian, keeper, superintendent, curator, surety; amine (chemistry).

أَمينُ الصُّنْدوق treasurer, cashier.

أَمينٌ عامّ secretary- general.

أَمينُ مُسْتَوْدَع storekeeper.

آنَ to become ripe; to draw near; to approach; to come.

آنَ الأوانُ the time has come.

آنَ لَكَ أنْ it is time for you to.

أَنَّ to moan, wail, whine.

آن time, period, moment.

الآن now, at present, at this moment; presently, today, nowaday.

أنْ that; to.

إنْ if.

أَنَّ that.

إنَّ verily, indeed.

إنَّما verily, indeed; but; however, yet; rather.

أنا I.

أنّى؟ where from? why? where? how? wherever; when? whence; at what time?

أنْأى to remove; to move away; to distance from.

إناء vessel, container, receptacle, table utensil, dish, plate, pot, vase.

آنيةٌ خزفيّة pottery, chinaware, porcelain.

آنيةٌ زُجاجيّة glassware.

آنيةُ المَطْبخ kitchenware.

أناب to deputize, delegate, commission (a representative, an agent); to act for; to return from time to time to; to frequent, haunt, visit often or periodically.

أناة patience, tolerance.

أنار to light, illuminate; to shed light upon.

إنارة lighting, illumination; enlightenment.

أُناس people, human beings, mankind.

أناطَ to entrust with; to commission someone to do something; to authorize, empower someone to.

أناطَ to suspend, hang, attach.

أنانيّة selfishness, egoism, egocentricity.

أنّبَ to reprimand, rebuke, scold, reprove.

أنبأ to inform of; to tell about; to advise of; to notify to or of; to state, declare, tell.

أنبتَ to make grow; to grow, raise, plant, cultivate.

انبِثاق emanation, arising; outflow; effusion, outburst.

انبثقَ to emanate, spring, emerge, arise, stem from; to burst forth, gush out, flow out, effuse, spout.

انبرى to vie, compete, contend; to defy, oppose; to undertake, set out to do; to enter, embark upon.

انبَرى to abrade, scrape off, wear away; to be sharpened, worn away, trimmed, abraded, scraped off.

انبِساط extension, stretching, spreading; delight, happiness, pleasure; extroversion.

انبسَطَ to spread out, stretch, extend; to be spread out, extended, stretched; to be happy, gay, delighted.

انبطَحَ to lie face down, to lie down.

انبِعاث revival, renaissance, regeneration; emission, issue, emergence; resurrection from the dead.

انبعَثَ to be emitted, triggered; to arise, spring, proceed, develop from; to grow out of; to be revived, resuscitated, revitalized; to be resurrected from the dead.

انبهر to be dazzled, dazed; to be breathless.

أُنبوب pipe, tube, duct.

أُنبوبيّ tubular.

أنتَ ، أنتِ you, thou.

انتاب to befall, strike, come over or upon; to beset.

إنتاج production; manufacture; growing; cultivation; output; generation.

تُمدُّ أنابيب مياه الشرب في الأقنية
Potable water is supplied to consumers through pipes

الإنْتَاجُ القَوْمِيُّ الإجْمَالِيّ gross national product.

إنْتَان infection.

انْتِبَاه attention, attentiveness; vigilance, alertness; foresight, circumspection, carefulness.

انْتَبَهَ to be cautious, careful; to look out, watch out; to be on the alert, on the lookout; to pay attention to; to take notice of; to observe; to be aware of; to wake up (from sleep).

أَنْتَجَ to bring forth; to yield, produce, generate; to make, manufacture, fabricate; to create, originate, cause; to bring about; to give rise to; to bear, give birth to (animal).

انْتِحَار suicide.

انْتَحَبَ to sob, weep, cry, wail, lament, moan.

انْتَحَرَ to commit suicide.

انْتَحَلَ to impersonate; to pretend to be; to assume the identity of; to plagiarize; to ascribe to oneself what others have done; to embrace, adopt a faith, doctrine, principle.

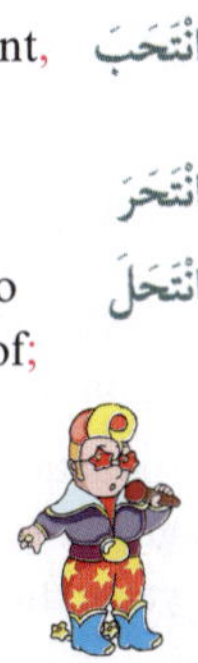

انْتِخَاب election, choice, selection; voting, ballot.

انْتِخَابِيّ electoral.

انْتَخَبَ to select, choose; to elect, vote, cast a ballot.

انْتِدَاب to deputize, delegate, accredit; to appoint, assign someone to an office; to commission, charge, entrust someone with; to empower, authorize; to give a country the mandate over another territory; region, area, district, etc.

انْتِزَاع extraction, pulling out, removal, withdrawal; expropriation; snatching, wresting from.

انْتَزَعَ to pull out, extract, uproot, remove; to snatch, wrest away; to extort, take by force.

انْتِسَاب affiliation, membership, belonging.

انْتَسَبَ to belong to; to be related to; to trace one's ancestry; to belong to a clan, party; to attach oneself to; to associate, affiliate, join oneself to; to become a member of.

انْتِشَار diffusion, propagation, spreading; outbreak of a disease; deployment of troops.

انْتَشَرَ to be spread out, unfolded; to be propagated, diffused, scattered, dispersed, to pervade, prevail; to deploy troops.

انْتَشَلَ to lift, raise up, rescue; to take away.

انْتِصَاب erection; getting up; rising, rise.

انْتِصَار victory, triumph.

انْتَصَبَ to stand erect, get up, rise.

انْتَصَرَ to triumph; to obtain victory; to be victorious; to conquer, vanquish, overpower, defeat; to take revenge on; to come to someone's aid; to side with.

انْتِظَار waiting; expectation; anticipation.

انْتِظَام regularity; uniformity; orderliness; constancy.

انْتَظَرَ to wait for; to await; to expect; to be patient with; to bide one's time.

انتظرت مدّة ساعة إلى أن وصل القطار

I waited for one hour the arrival of the train

انْتَظَمَ to be organized, put in order; to be adjusted; to be regular, uniform; to include, contain, involve; to join, become a member of.

انْتِعَاش recovery, revival, stimulation; invigoration; boost, boom; refreshment.

انْتَعَشَ to be refreshed, revived, invigorated, stimulated; to freshen up; to revive, recover.

انْتِفَاخ swelling; inflation; flatulence; tumefaction.

انْتِفَاضَة tremble, tremor, shudder, jerk; uprising, revolt.

انْتِفَاع utilization, use; profiting by or from; usufruct.

انْتَفَخَ to be inflated, blown up, filled with air; to swell, inflate; to become swollen.

انْتَفَضَ to shake, tremble, quiver.

انْتَفَعَ to utilise, to put to use; to profit from or by.

انْتِقَاء selection, choosing.

انْتِقَاد criticism; objection; disapproval; censure.

انْتِقَال change of location; locomotion; move; transfer; conveyance; transport; transition; demise, death; devolution, accrual.

انْتِقَام revenge, vengeance, retaliation, reprisal.

انْتَقَدَ to criticize, censure.

انْتَقَضَ to be revoked, abrogated, cancelled; to be destroyed, demolished, wrecked; to be broken, undone; to decay, fall down, collapse, wear off; to contradict each other; to rebel, revolt, attack.

انْتَقَلَ to move, shift, change one's residence; to change position; to travel about; to be spread, transplanted into; to go away, depart, leave; to pass away, die; to be transmitted, communicated (disease).

انْتَقَمَ to take revenge; to avenge oneself on; to make reprisals, take vengeance for.

أَنْتَ، أَنْتُمَا، أَنْتُم you.

انْتَمى to belong to; to be affiliated with; to be affiliated with; to be a member of (a race, tribe, cult, family).

أَنْتُنَّ you (for the female).

انْتَهى to come to an end; to be terminated, completed, ended, finished, concluded; to expire; to end up in; to result in; to come to; to lead to; to desist from; to stop, give up, leave off.

انْتِهاء conclusion, termination, end; expiry; completion.

انْتِهازِيّ (اسم) opportunist, timeserver.

انْتِهاك depletion, exhaustion; violation, profanation, desecration, rape, sacrilege; infraction, trespassing.

انْتَهَزَ to seize the opportunity; to take advantage of the opportunity

انْتَهَكَ to desecrate, defile, violate; to infringe, contravene (regulations, laws); to tresspass, encroach upon someone's rights, property.

أُنْثى female.

انْثَنى to be folded, doubled, bent, flexed, curved; to bend, incline, bow; to turn away from; to give up, relinquish, forsake; to abstain from, refrain from; to be flexible, pliable.

انْثِناء bending, curve, turn; giving up, relinquishment, desistance from, forsaking, abandonment; flexibility.

أُنْثَوِيّ feminine, female; effeminate.

أَنْجى to save, deliver from (evil, trap), rescue.

إنْجاب procreation; giving birth to

انْجابَ to be dispersed, dispelled, scattered; to split, dent, tear; to get torn, split.

إنْجاز execution, completion, realization, accomplishment; achievement, feat, exploit.

أَنْجَبَ to beget; to give birth to.

أَنْجَدَ to succor, help, support; to give aid, help to; to rescue, save.

انْجِراف drift; washout; erosion.

أَنْجَزَ to carry out, execute, complete, terminate, finish; to finish off; to kill someone.

انْجَلى to become clear, distinct, manifest, evident; to appear, come to light; to emerge, surface, manifest itself clearly; to become untroubled, cloudless (sky); to be dispelled, dispersed, dislodged; to wind up with; to result, end up in; to be polished, smoothed, glazed, scoured; to pull out, go away, depart.

الإنْجيل the New Testament (Christian).

أَنْحى to turn away one's eyes from; to assail; to blame, reproach.

انْحِباس occlusion, obstruction, confinement, interruption.

انْحَبَسَ to be confined, suppressed, obstructed, blocked; to be imprisoned, blocked, interned, jailed; to be separated, detached, isolated; to stop, cease.

انْحِدَار slope, descent; decline; decadence; gliding down, falling, slanting; declivity.

انْحَدَرَ to descend, come down, slope down, sink, dip; to decay, decline, deteriorate.

انْحِرَاف deviation, digression, inclination, slant; ailment, indisposition; corruption, perversion; depravity, turpitude, aberration, delinquency; declination, refraction (astronomy).

انْحَرَفَ to deviate from, deflect from; to change direction; to veer, warp; to go astray; to be corrupted, depraved, perverted; to incline, slant, slope, tilt; to turn toward; to dissuade someone from; to be indisposed, ill, out of humor, unwell.

انْحِسَار abatement, waning, decline; ebb (of water); retreat, withdrawal.

انْحَسَرَ to die down; to diminish, decline, shrink; to recede, withdraw; to disappear; to be dispelled, lifted, raised, pulled away; to subside, ebb (sea water).

انْحِصَار detention, condensation; encirclement; limitation, confinement, restrictedness; monopoly, monopolization, exclusivity; centralization.

انْحَصَرَ to be confined, encircled, constrained; to be shut in; to be concentrated, centralized, condensed; to be exclusive.

انْحَطَّ to degenerate, decline, degrade; to demean, low, debase oneself morally; to sink, descend, fall, drop.

انْحِطاط degeneration, degradation, decline; fall, descent; depression, feebleness of one's vitality.

انْحَلَّ to be untied, unfastened, undone, loosened; to be freed, disengaged, released; to be solved, resolved, settled; to dissolve, melt; to disintegrate, decompose, crumble, degenerate.

انْحِلاَل dissolution, disintegration, decomposition, putrefaction, decay; weakness; looseness.

انْحَنى to bend, bow, flex, tilt, incline; to be bent, curved, flexed; inclined, twisted, tilted; to stoop; to bow one's head.

انْحِيَاز partiality, prejudice, bias; seclusion, retirement, isolation; segregation, separation.

انحنى الفقير طلباً للصّدقة
He inclined himself asking for alms

انْخِراط entering; affiliation; joining.

انْخَرَطَ to join, enter; to become an affiliate with, a member of; to be turned, lathed.

انْخَفَضَ to sink, dip, decline, fall; to decrease, diminish, subside, dwindle; to be lowered, reduced, decreased.

انْدِثار extinction, oblivion, obliteration.

انْدَثَرَ to be extinct, obsolete; to fall into oblivion; to be obliterated, wiped out, exterminated.

انْدِحار defeat, debacle.

انْدَسَّ to slip into or among; to creep into or among; to infiltrate, penetrate; to be buried, concealed in, inserted into, put into.

انْدِفاع rushing, plunging into; outburst, outbreak; engagement in; zeal, enthusiasm; impetuosity, impulsiveness; temerity, rashness; impulse, verve, mettle.

انْدَفَعَ to rush, hurry, burst out, move rapidly, run; to flow, stream, pour forth, gush out; to start, set out; to plunge, rush into, penetrate, engage in; to give oneself over to; to be guided by.

انْدِلاع outbreak, eruption.

انْدَلَعَ to break out, erupt.

انْدِماج merger, consolidation, incorporation, inclusion, fusion, union.

انْدَمَجَ to merge, unite, join, fuse; to incorporate, combine, blend; to be consolidated, united, joined, fused, incorporated, blended.

انْدَهَشَ to be baffled, startled, astonished, amazed.

إنْذار warning, final notice.

آنَذاك at that time; then.

أَنْذَرَ to warn, alert, caution; to portend evil; to presage; to be a sign of something bad; to augur ill; to be a bad omen.

إنْزال bringing down, lowering; landing, debarkation; launching a ship; revelation; unloading of cargo; putting up in lodging; accomodation; reduction, lowering of prices; substraction, deduction; demotion in rank or position; devaluation of currency; revelation, inspiration.

انْزِعاج inconvenience, trouble, discomfort; disturbance, confusion.

انْزَعَجَ to be disturbed, annoyed, troubled, upset.

أَنْزَلَ to bring down; to lower, drop; to reveal to; to unload, discharge a cargo; to land, disembark from a ship; to reduce, decrease, lower prices, costs; to deduct, substract, discount; to demote, degrade (in rank, position, status); to impose upon, inflict harm on someone.

انْزَلَقَ to slide, glide, slip, skid; to skate on ice.

انْزَوَى to seclude, isolate oneself; to retire with; to hold a closed meeting with; to withdraw in a corner.

أَنِسَ to like someone's company; to be used, accustomed, habituated to; to notice, find a quality in; to sense, feel, recognize something in; to like to listen to someone; to be friendly to someone; to entertain, amuse; to be sociable; to become intimate, tame, friendly, nice, kind to; to take into consideration; to draw upon something; to listen to; to heed an opinion.

إِنْس mankind, human race, people, human beings.

أَنْسَى to make forget.

انْسَابَ to flow, stream, run; to pour into; to seep away; to speed along; to glide, slip between; to work fast, hurry.

انْسَاقَ to drift; to be swept away; to be driven.

إِنْسَان human being, man, person.

على الإنسان أن يحترم رفيقه الإنسان
Man should respect his fellow man

إِنْسَانٌ آلِيّ robot.

إِنْسانِيّ (ص) human, humanistic, humane, humanitarian.

إِنْسَانِيَّة humanity; politeness; civility; the human race; human attributes; human; humanitarianism; philanthropy.

آنِسَة young lady, miss.

انْسِجَام harmony; order; fluency; affinity; agreement; accord; compatibility.

انْسَجَمَ to harmonize with; to agree with; to be in conformity with; to be compatible with.

انْسِحَاب retreat, withdrawal; pullout; fallback; walkout.

انْسَحَبَ to retreat, withdraw; to pull out, fall back; to walk out; to leave; to be pulled, drawn, towed; to apply; to make applicable (law or regulation).

انْسَدَّ to be blocked up; to be plugged up, closed up; to be sealed, closed, stoppered.

انْسِداد blockage, obstruction, stoppage, occlusion; embolism (blood vessel); thrombosis (coronary artery).

انْسَلَخَ to be cast off, shed, peeled (skin); to strip off (clothing); to abandon, cast off (a quality, a habit); to get detached from; to withdraw, retire from; to secede from.

أَنْشَأَ to estalish, institute, found, form, generate; to give rise to, bring about; to build, construct, erect; to write, compose; to manufacture, make; to begin, start, proceed, initiate; to raise (child).

إنْشاء establishment, organization, institution; formation, setting up; making, manufacture; erection, construction, building; founding; compilation, composition, writing; art of composition; essay, treatise.

إنْشاءات (ج) installations, facilities.

إنْشاد recitation, recital, chanting.

انْشِراح ease, joy, delight, relaxation, gaiety.

انْشَرَحَ صَدْرُهُ to be pleased, delighted, happy, glad; to feel at ease, relaxed.

انْشِغال preoccupation, engrossment, being busy.

انْشَغَلَ to be occupied, busy; to busy oneself.

انْشِقاق splitting; fission; secession; separation; breakaway; schism, split, fissure.

أُنْشودَة song, chant, anthem.

أُنْشوطَة knot, loop, noose.

انْصاعَ to succumb to; to surrender to; to obey; to comply with; to abide by; to accede to someone's wishes or orders.

انْصِراف departure, leaving; turning away from; giving up; abstention from; devoting oneself to; engaging oneself in the pursuit of.

انْصَرَفَ to turn away; to go away; to depart, leave; to give up, abandon, relinquish; to flow off; to change over; to proceed to do something; to devote oneself to; to be spent (money).

انْصَرَمَ to pass, go by, expire, run out; to be cut off.

أَنْصَفَ to do justice to; to treat fairly; to be just; to cut in half.

انْصِهار fusion, melting.

انْصَهَرَ to fuse, melt.

انْصِياع submission, surrender, obedience, compliance.

انْضِباط discipline.

انْضِغاط compression.

انْضَمَّ to join, enter, become a member; to unite, join; to be affiliated, combined, united, merged.

انْضِمام affiliation, union, joining, merger, integration.

انْطِباع impression.

انْطِلاق outburst, outbreak; explosion; release; unrestraint, liberty; starting; departing.

انْطَلَق to dash along; to hurry; to rush; to explode, go off; to burst forth; to take off, decamp; to move off, pull out; to go on, proceed on one's way; to go away, leave, go by, elapse, pass; to set out to do something; to start with; to utter words against; to be fluent, eloquent; to cheer up; to be delighted.

انْطَوى to harbor, hold, contain; to be folded, turned over; to go by, pass, elapse (time); to be hidden, concealed under; to comprise, embrace, involve, include; to withdraw within oneself.

إنْعاش revival; resuscitation; invigoration, refreshment; reanimation.

انْعِزال isolation, seclusion, segregation.

انْعَزَل to be isolated, secluded; to seclude, isolate oneself; to be separated.

انْعَطَف to bend, curve, bow, turn; to make a turn.

انْعِقاد convention, assembly; coagulation; thickening.

انْعَقَد to convene, gather, assemble; to be convened, made, concluded; to coagulate, thicken.

انعطفت السيارة إلى اليمين بسرعة شديدة

The car turned abruptly to the left in great speed

انْعِكاس reversal; reflection of light; impact, bearing, reflex, repercussion.

انْعَكَس to be reversed, inverted; to be reflected (light); to affect, produce an effect; to have an impact upon.

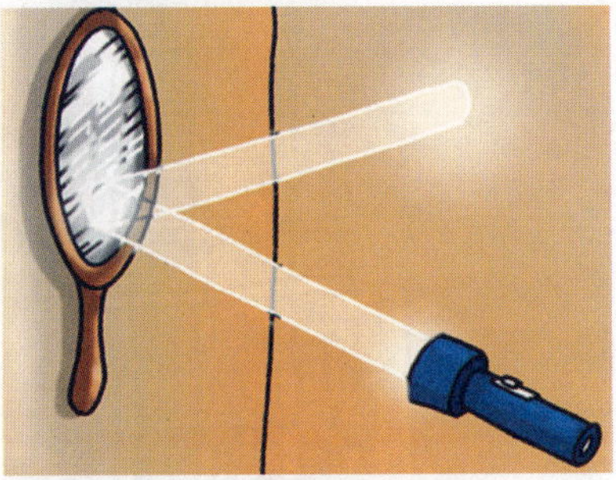

ينعكس الضوء المسلط على المرآة

Light is reflected by a mirror

أنْعَمَ to bestow upon; to confer upon; to look closely at; to regard attentively; to become engrossed in; to grant, award, favor with.

انْغَمَس to be dipped, immersed; to dive, plunge, sink; to throw oneself into; to be engrossed in; to be preoccupied with; to indulge in pleasures.

أنِف to disdain, scorn, reject haughtily.

أَنْف nose.

آنِف preceding; previous.

آنِفُ الذِّكْر above-mentioned; above; aforesaid.

آنِفًا previously; formerly; before.

إنْفاق spending; expenditure; disbursement.

انْفِجار explosion, blast; outbreak, eruption.

دمّر الانفجار الطوابق العليا من المبنى
The explosion demolished the upper storeys of the building

انْفَجَرَ to gush out, gush forth, burst out, burst forth; to explode, go off, detonate (bomb, bullet); to rupture (a blood vessel); to break out, erupt (war); to burst into tears; to explode with anger.

انْفِراج openness; relaxation; relief, detente; diversion.

انْفِراد seclusion, loneliness; privacy; being alone; meeting separately with.

انْفَرَجَ to open up, unfold, gape; to be wide open; to diverge; to be dispelled (worry); to relax, to decrease in intensity.

انْفَرَدَ to isolate oneself; to be alone with oneself; to meet separately with; to be distinguished by, characterized by; to be unique, singular, unequaled, incomparable.

انْفِصال separation, interruption, secession, disengagement.

انْفِصامُ الشَّخْصِيَّة schizophrenia.

انْفَصَلَ to separate oneself from; to secede from; to withdraw from; to break away, split, divide; to be separated, disengaged, detached, divided.

انْفَطَمَ to be weaned.

انْفِعال emotion, excitement; strain.

انْفَعَلَ to be affected, influenced; to react, respond; to get emotional, excited, nervous; to be done.

أَنْفَقَ to spend, pay out, disburse; to consume, exhaust.

انْفَكَّ to be undone, loosened, disengaged; to be disassembled, taken apart; to be separated, detached, disconnected; to become unscrewed (bolt).

ما انفكَّ not to cease doing; to keep doing, persist in.

انْقادَ to be led by; to yield to, submit to, comply with; to let oneself be carried away by.

إنْقاذ rescue, salvation.

أنْقاض (ج) debris, rubble, ruins.

انْقِباض contraction, shrinkage; depression, low spirits, gloominess; constipation; systole (heart); to be received, collected (money).

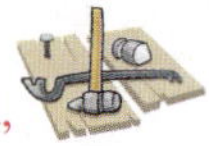

انْقَبَضَ to contract; to be contracted, shrunk.

انْقَبَضَ صَدْرُهُ to be depressed, downcast, dispirited.

أنْقَذَ to save from, rescue from, deliver from.

انْقِراض extinction, ceasing to exit, dying out.

انْقَرَضَ to become extinct, cease to exist, die out.

انْقِسام division, partition, splitting; schism; fission.

انْقَسَمَ to be divided, split, separated, partitioned; to be distributed, allotted, broken up.

انْقَضَّ to swoop down, pounce down; to strike, descend; to pounce, rush, hurl; to attack, assail.

انْقَضَى to expire, elapse, run out; to lay claim; to claim, exact, require; to be completed, finished, done.

انْقِضاء passing, elapsing, expiry, expiration; extinction (of an obligation).

انْقِضاض swooping down, pouncing down; attack, assault, onslaught; sudden attack.

انْقِطاع separation, break, rupture, rift; disruption, cessation; extinction, conclusion; withdrawal; abstention; devotion to; gasp (breath).

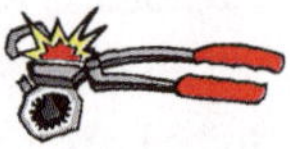

انْقَطَعَ to be cut off, separated, chopped off, sundered, severed, torn apart; to be disconnected, interrupted, shut off; to be blocked; to come to be an end; to be discontinued, stopped, ceased; to stay away; to devote oneself to; to occupy oneself exclusively to; to desist from; to gasp (breath).

انْقِلاب revolution, upheaval, overthrow; solstice; change, transformation, alteration.

انْقَلَبَ to topple over; to reverse; to be reversed, inverted, toppled over, overturned; to capsize; to be converted; to become transmuted.

انْقِياد obedience, submission; compliance.

إنْكار denial, repudiation, refusal.

إنْكارُ الذَّات self-denial; unselfishness.

إنْكارُ الجَميل ingratitude.

انْكَبَّ to bend down, bow down, prostrate oneself; to apply oneself eagerly to; to be overturned, knocked over, poured away.

انْكِبَاب devotion to; dedication to; pursuit of.

أَنْكَرَ to disavow, disclaim, repudiate, disprove, deny, renounce, renege; to censure, reproach, rebuke.

انْكَسَرَ to be broken, shattered, smashed, fractured; to be defeated, vanquished; to be refracted (light); to ease, abate, subside; to get bankrupt.

انْكَشَفَ to get uncovered, laid bare, revealed; to be removed, lifted, dispelled, driven away (worries).

انْكَمَشَ to recoil within oneself; to be self-absorbed; to contract, shrink; to cower.

إنَّما verily, indeed; but, yet; rather.

إنْماء development, promotion, improvement; enchancement, advancement.

أُنْمُلَة finger tip.

أَنْهَى to conclude, finish, terminate; to wind up, settle, abandon, cease, stop; to report, communicate, impart (news, orders).

إنْهاء ending, conclusion, termination, winding up; stopping, finalization, suspension.

انْهَارَ to collapse; to tumble down, crash down; to give way, crumple; to be destroyed, demolished; to elapse, go by (time).

انهار المبنى بعدما أصابه الزلزال

The house tumbled down as a result of the earthquake

إنْهَاك exhaustion, wearing out, wearing away, tiring out; overstraining, overtiring; attrition.

انْهَالَ to be poured in a heap; to rain down (bombs); to assail someone with (abusive language, blows).

انْهَدَّ to be demolished, destroyed, ruined; to fall down; to collapse; to be pulled down.

انْهَدَمَ to be demolished, wrecked, destroyed; to break down, collapse, crash.

انْهِزَام defeat, rout.

انْهَزَمَ to be defeated, routed, overcome, conquered; to lose (a battle, a tournament); to be put to flight.

انْهَضَمَ to be digested (food).

أَنْهَكَ to weary, tire out, wear away; to emaciate, waste away; to overstrain, overtax, overtire.

انْهَمَر to be poured out, poured down; to rain heavily; to be shed; to flow in torrents.

انهمر دمع الطفل لأنه أصبح وحيداً

The child's tears were shed heavily because of being alone

انْهَمَكَ to be engrossed in, wholly engaged in, preoccupied with; to dedicate oneself to, devote oneself (to a cause, a task, a thought).

انْهِيَار collapse, downfall, crash, breakdown; prostration (mental or physical).

انْهِيَارٌ عَصَبِيّ nervous breakdown.

أُنُوثَة feminity, womanhood.

آنِيّ present, actual, instantaneous, prompt; immediate, instant.

أَنِيس sociable, affable, gentle, tame (animal); intimate friend.

أَنِيق smart, stylish, elegant, spruce, well-dressed.

أَنِين moan, whimpering, whining.

أَهَابَ to call upon; to request; to appeal to, call out, shout to.

أَهَانَ to insult, abuse, disdain, belittle; to humiliate, abase, demean; to scorn, slight, to despise.

إِهَانَة insult, offense, affront, abuse, humiliation.

اهْتَدَى to be rightly guided; to be led; to find the way; to come upon something (idea); to be made aware of; to be on the right way.

اهْتَزَّ to tremble, quiver, shake; to be shaken, jolted, jiggled; to rock, sway, swing, wave, vibrate.

اهْتَمَّ to concern oneself with; to take an interest in; to be interested; to look after; to pay attention to ;to take notice of; to take care of; to assist, help, provide, watch over; to attend to, mind; to consider seriously; to attach importance to.

اهْتِمَام interest, concern, attention anxiety, endeavor, care, solicitude.

اهْتِيَاج agitation, excitement, uproar, turmoil, fury, tumult, commotion, excitement.

أَهْدَى to give as a present; to donate, bestow upon, confer upon; to dedicate (a book, etc); to award.

إِهْدَاء presentation, donation, offering; dedication of (a book, etc).

أَهْرَقَ to shed, spill (blood); to pour out (liquid).

أَهَّلَ to rehabilitate, prepare, qualify; to make fit; to greet, welcome.

أَهْل relatives, kinsfolk, people, family; household inhabitants, natives; followers, adherents; possessors, masters.

أَهْلُ الرَّجُل wife.

أَهْلاً وَسَهْلاً welcome.

آهِل inhabited, populated.

إِهْلاك destruction, perdition, ruin, annihilation.

أَهْلَكَ to annihilate, ruin, destroy, imperil.

أَهْلِيّ national, domestic, native.

أَهْلِيَّة competence, aptitude, capability, eligibility; efficiency, merit, worthiness, qualification.

إِهْلِيلَجِيّ elliptical, elliptic.

إِهْمَال negligence, disregard, ignoring, omission, oversight, heedlessness.

أَهْمَلَ to neglect, disregard, ignore, overlook, forget; to cease to use; to be careless, negligent, remiss, lazy.

أَهَمِّيَّة importance, significance, magnitude, worth, consequence, interest.

أَهْوَج reckless, careless, imprudent, frivolous, rash.

أَوْ or; unless; if not; until; except when.

أَوَى to lodge at; to stay at; to take shelter in; to retire, go to bed; to go to; to offer lodgings to; to accomodate.

آوَى to accomodate, provide lodgings for; to shelter.

أَوَان time, season.

أَوْب return, coming back; side, direction.

أَوْباش (ج) mob, scum.

أَوْتَدَ to drive or put or ram a peg, stake or wedge.

أُتوماتيكِيّ automatic, automotive, self-driven.

أَوْثَقَ to bind, fetter, enchain, fasten, tie up.

أَوْج peak; apogee; apex, crest; summit, zenith, aphelion (astronomy), pinnacle; top; crown.

أَوْجَبَ to impose, enjoin (something on someone); to obligate; to adjudge, adjucate, necessitate, entail, decree.

أَوْجَدَ to produce, create, generate, bring about; to acquire, attain; to force, oblige, compel someone (to do something); to bring into being, originate; to get, procure, obtain, make available(something).

أَوْجَزَ to abridge, summarize; to abstract, synopsize; to make brief, concise (speech).

أَوْجَسَ to be apprehensive of; to dread, fear; to feel worried; to have forebodings, presentiments of; to hide, conceal, perceive, feel, sense.

أَوْجَعَ to hurt; to cause pain to; to torment, anguish.

أَوْحى to inspire to; to suggest to; to give an idea or an impression of.

أَوْدى to destroy, kill; to cause to die.

أَوْدَعَ to deposit (money in a bank); to lodge; to entrust; to place, lay down; to incorporate, include; to throw (in prison); to consign, commit; to store in a warehouse (goods).

أَوْرَدَ to bring to; to mention, cite, quote; to import (goods).

أَوْرَقَ to foliate; to put forth leaves.

أَوْسَط middle, central, intermediate; mean.

أَوْسَعَ to widen; to make wider; to broaden, enlarge, extend, dilate; to make room for; to become wealthy; to heap (abuse) upon someone; to beat up, hit forcefully, to strike severely.

أَوْشَكَ to be on the point of doing something; to be about to do something; to be close to.

أَوْصى to bequeath, transfer by will; to make a point of something; to mean well; to enjoin on someone something; to order, advise, recommend.

أَوْصَدَ to close, shut.

أَوْصَلَ to bring to, lead to, conduct to, drive to; to transport, carry, deliver, hand over; to escort; to connect, link (electricity, sound, light).

أَوْضَحَ to clarify; to make clear, plain; to explain, expound, elucidate, illustrate, propound; to make visible, manifest; to indicate, denote, express, bring to light, state, set forth.

أَوْعَزَ to insinuate, suggest; to advise, recommend to; to instruct, enjoin, order someone to do something.

أَوْغَرَ to arouse someone's anger against; to arouse bitter feelings; to burn with rage.

أَوْغَلَ to penetrate deeply into; to intrude on someone; to come uninvited; to push, press, hurry; to walk briskly; to exaggerate.

أَوْفى to meet, fulfill, discharge (an engagement); to pay (a debt); to cover (expenses); to suffice, compensate, complete; to treat exhaustively (a subject); to supply, provide; to draw to a close; to go through with something; to present in detail; to exceed, be above, go beyond, surpass.

أَوْفَدَ to delegate, deputize, send, despatch someone.

أَوْقَدَ to kindle, light, start (a fire); to burn, set on fire, set fire to.

أَوْقَعَ to let fall; to cause to fall; to throw down, topple; to inflict on, cause to; to cause damages; to impose a punishment; to sow dissenssion between; to throw into; to hurl, plunge someone into; to ensnare, enmesh, catch in a trap.

لا توقد النار في مكان تكثر فيه الأشجار والنباتات

It is dangerous to light a fire in a place where trees and plants abound

أَوْقَفَ to make stand; to raise; to stop, halt, discontinue, suspend, end, terminate; to arrest, hold up; to hinder, obstruct; to estop (a law); to cancel; to desist from, abstain from; to acquaint someone with; to let someone know about; to disclose to; to brake (a car); to park (a car); to stay (the execution of a sentence).

أُوكسِيجين oxygen.

أَوْكَلَ to entrust something to someone; to assign (a task to someone); to delegate one's authority to another; to trust in God.

أَوَّلَ to interpret, construe, explain.

أَوَّل (ص) first, foremost; main; cardinal; earlier, former; beginning, outset.

أَوَّلاً in the first place; first of all; at first; originally; initially.

الأَوَّلُون forefathers; ancestors, forebears.

أَوَّلَ البارِحَة the day before yesterday.

أَوْلَى to entrust someone with; to commission someone with; to place one's confidence in; to render (a service to someone).

أُولاء these, those.

أَوْلَجَ to introduce, insert, interpose, thrust; to penetrate into; intercalate.

أَوْلَوِيَّة priority, precedence; seniority.

أَوَّلِيّ first, primary; earliest; fundamental, preliminary; introductory; elementary; rudimentary; primitive; raw, crude, unrefined (products).

أَوْمَأَ to motion, signal, beckon; to point out, indicate, point to; to make a gesture.

أَوْمَضَ to flash; to glance furtively; to wink, blink, sparkle, glint, gleam.

أَوْهَى to enfeeble; to make weak.

أَوْهَمَ to give the impression that; to deceive, delude, mislead, suggest.

أَوْهَنَ to enfeeble; to discourage; to weaken; to demoralize, dispirit, frustrate.

أَيْ that is; namely; to wit; in other words.

أَيّ which? what? any, every; no matter what; whoever, whatever; whatsoever, whosoever.

آي الذِّكرِ الحَكِيم verses of the holy Koran.

إيَاب comming back, return.

أيَّار May.

يتمتّع الناس في شهر أيار بطقس معتدل
People enjoy a moderate weather in May

آية sign; prodigy; miracle; warning; example; masterpiece; verse (of a holy book).

إيثار preference; unselfishness; altruism.

إيجاب affirmation; in conformity with; obligation, commitment; assertion; consent, compliance; to answer in the affirmative; offer of contract.

إيجابِيّ positive, affimative; constructive, active.

إيجَاد creation, production, procurement, supply; evaluation, calculation; giving rise to, causing.

إيجَار rent, lease.

إيجارٌ مِنَ البَاطِن sublease, subletting.

إيجَاز abridgement, brevity, shortness, conciseness, epitome, brief sketch, summary.

إيْحاء inspiration, suggestion.

أيَّدَ to back, support, confirm; to endorse, corroborate, approve, consent to; to accede to, subscribe to; to uphold, be in favor of.

إيدَاع depositing (money in bank); entrustment; lodging, bailment (of goods, bonds).

إيْذان declaration, announcement; indication, sign that the conversation is ended.

إيْراد allegation; citation, quotation; import, supply; revenue, income, proceeds; yield, gain, profit, takings.

إيْصَال connecting, joining; conveyance, transport; transmission; receipt, voucher.

إيصالِيَّة conductivity, conductance.

أَيْضًا also, too, as well, likewise; equally; again, besides, moreover; in addition.

إيضاح clarification, elucidation, explanation, explication.

إيعاز advice, counsel; recommendation; hint, suggestion; command, injunction, order.

إيفاء redemption (of a promise); discharge (of an obligation); payment (of a debt).

إيفاد delegation, deputization; sending; dispatching.

إيقاد kindling, lighting (of a fire); setting fire to.

إيقاظ awakening (from sleep); rousing, arousal, excitation; wakening; alerting, warning, cautioning; putting on the alert.

إيقاع dropping; causing to fall; bringing down; toppling; striking terror to someone's heart; inflicting a punishment.

إيقاعٌ موسيقِيّ rythm, harmony, cadence.

إيقاف stopping; raising, setting up; seizure, arrest, halting, stunting; hampering, obstruction; discontinuation; delay; notice, notification; putting an end to, termination; cancellation, calling off, cessation; desistance, abstention; detention, arrest; apprehension.

إيقافُ التَّنفِيذ stay of execution.

إيقافُ الحُكْم arrest of judgment.

إيقافُ الدَّفْع moratorium, respite.

إيْقَافُ العَمَل suspension of work.

أَيْقَظَ to awaken; to arouse from sleep; to provoke; to alert, warn, alarm, caution; to put on the alert.

أَيْقَنَ to ascertain, find out, become convinced of.

آيِلٌ إلى leading to; resulting in; accruing to; devolving upon; vested in.

إيلاج intromission, insertion, penetration, thrusting.

أَيْلول September.

إيماء gesture, sign, pantomime.

إيمان belief, faith.

أَيْمَن (ص) right-handed, dextral, right.

أَيْنَ where? at which place?.

أَيْنَعَ to ripen; to become ripe.

أَيْنَما wherever, anywhere, where.

إيْهام delusion, pretense, make-believe, deceit.

إيواء lodging, accomodating, sheltering.

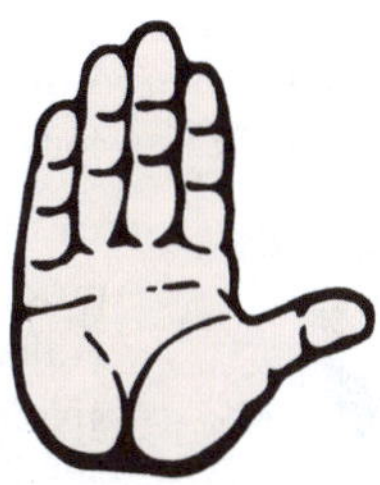

ب in, at, on, with, through, by means of.

بِلا without, excluding; deprived of, free from.

بِمَ، بِما with what? wherewith?.

بِما أَنَّ since, because, whereas.

باءَ to come back, return, bring back.

باءَ بالفشل to fail, to be unsuccessful.

بائِت stale.

بائِخ insipid, tasteless, colorless, banal, silly.

بائِد extinct, dead, bygone.

بائِر unsown, unplanted (land); unmarketable (goods); inactive, stagnant (market).

بائِس miserable, wretched, afflicted, sad, deplorable.

بائِع seller, vendor, dealer,

بائعُ تَجْزِئَة retailer.

بائعُ جُمْلَة wholesaler.

بائعٌ مُتَجَوِّل peddler, travelling salesman.

بائعٌ بِالمَزاد auctioneer.

بائِنَة dowry.

باب door, gate, entrance; section, chapter; category, grade, sort, kind; matter, affair, topic, issue.

لكل منزل ومبنى باب للدخول إليه
Each house or building has an entrance

بؤبؤ pupil (of the eye).

بابا daddy.

باتَ to stay overnight; to come to be; to continue to do; to stick to; to keep on doing.

باتّ absolute, unqualified, conclusive, final.

باحَ to reveal, divulge, disclose (a secret); to release, abandon; to declare; to allow, permit; to justify; to take as booty; to seize, confiscate.

باحَة open space, square, courtyard.

باحَثَ to discuss with; to negotiate with; to talk with.

باحِث scholar, researcher, investigator.

باخِرَة steamboat, steamship.

تنقل الباخرة المسافرين من بلد إلى آخر

Ships transport persons from one country to the other

بادَ to perish, cease to exist.

بادٍ apparent, visible, obvious, plain, distinct.

بادَأَ to make the first step; to begin, start; to speak first, to open the conversation; to greet first.

بادِئ initiator, starter, author; beginning.

بادِئَ الأمر at first, in the beginning.

بادِئَ ذي بَدءٍ first, first of all; to start with, above all.

بادِئَة prefix.

بادَرَ to take the initiative; to begin; to embark upon; to set about, undertake, act, resort to; to anticipate; to take by surprise; to speak first; to greet first.

بادِرَة sign, harbinger, precursor, indication, gesture.

بادَلَ to exchange, substitute, replace; to trade, barter; to reciprocate, repay, return in kind.

بادِيَة desert.

يعيش أهل البادية تحت خيام من وبر الجمال

Tribesmen live under tents woven with camel hair

باذِخ prodigal, extravagant, arrogant, high, exalted, lofty, elevated.

باذِنْجان eggplant (plant).

بارَ to die, perish; to be futile, unprofitable; to remain uncultivated (land); to be unmarketable (goods); to stagnate; to become dull (market).

بار bar, pub, tavern.

بارّ pious, faithful; obedient; upright.

بِئْر well.

يُستخرج الماء من البئر بواسطة دلو مربوط بحبل
Water is drawn from the well by way of a pail attached to a rope

بِئْرٌ ارتوازِيَّة artesian well.

بارى to compete with; to emulate; to try to outstrip someone; to contend; to defy, oppose.

بُؤْرَة focus, focal point, pit.

بارَحَ to leave, depart.

البارِحَة yesterday.

بارِد cold, cool; silly, dull; frigid; weak.

بارَزَ to duel, fence with; to compute in a contest with.

بارِز prominent, salient, noticeable, distinct; projecting, raised; embossed, in relief.

بارِع skilled, skillful, proficient, outstanding (work of art); efficient; clever, expert; ingenious; capable; masterful.

بارِقَة glimpse, gleam; thundercloud; twinkle.

بارَكَ to bless, to invoke a blessing on; to give one's blessing to; to sanction, approve, endorse.

بارود gunpowder.

باسَ to kiss.

بَؤُسَ to be or become strong, brave, valiant.

بَئِسَ to be or become miserable, poor, wretched.

بَأْس courage, valor, intrepidity; strength, might.

بَأْس fear, panic.

بأس harm, injury, hurt, detriment.

بُؤْس misery, wretchedness, suffering.

باسَطَ to speak out frankly; to be sincere, explicit; to explain, expound, set forth.

باسِق high, towering, lofty.

باسِل brave, bold, intrepid; fearless.

باشَرَ to carry out (a job); to practise, attend, pursue; to begin, start, embark upon; to launch, initiate.

باشَرَ to have sexual intercouse with.

باضَ to lay eggs (animal or bird); to remain in, settle down.

باطِل null, void, ineffective, obsolete; futile; vain; worthless, groundless; untrue; wrong; of no avail.

باطِل (اسم) falsehood, lie; injustice; triviality.

باطِن interior, within; essence, gist, bottom of.

باطِنُ القَدَم sole.

باطِنُ اليَد palm.

باعَ to sell; to auction; to peddle.

باعِث incentive, impulse, spur, cause, reason, motive.

باعَدَ to cause a separation between; to prevent someone from attaining something; to stare wide-eyed; to take away; to banish, exile; to set aside, single out.

باغٍ (الباغِي) oppressive; tyrant, despot; aspiring, desiring, coveting, wanting.

باغَتَ to surprise someone; to come unexpectedly.

باقٍ (الباقِي) remaining, lasting, everlasting; surviving; leftover, remainder, surplus; outstanding (balance).

باقَة bundle, bouquet (of flowers).

قدّمت إلى أمي باقة من الزهور في عيد الأمّ

I presented to my mother a beautiful bouquet of red roses on Mother's Day

باكٍ (الباكِي) weeping, crying; weeper, mourner.

باكِر early, premature.

باكِرًا early in the morning; soon.

باكورَة first produce, result, fruits; start, rise, beginning.

بال mind, thought, condition; attention, concern; patience, forbearance.

بالٍ (البالِي) old, ragged; dilapidated; decomposed, rotten; obsolete; antiquated, outdated.

بالَة bundle, bale.

بالَغَ to exaggerate, overdo, overstate.

بالِغ of age, adult; mature, ripe; serious, grave; acute, excessive.

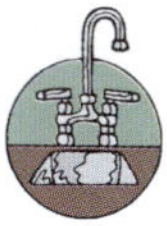

بالوعَة sink, gutter, sump.

باميا okra.

بانَ to appear, come out, emerge; to reveal itself; to be visible, manifest, obvious, distinct.

باهَى to vie with; to boast of; to flaunt, show off; to pride oneself on.

باهِت pale, pallid, faded (color); aghast, perplexed.

باهِر dazzling, overwhelming, splendid, superb, exquisite, marvellous.

باهِظ exorbitant, excessive (price); enormous, cumbersome; oppressive; expensive, costly.

بايَعَ to pay homage to; to acknowledge as sovereign or leader; to pledge allegiance; to conclude a bargain.

بايَنَ to be different; to be plain, evident; to differ, be unlike something; to contradict; to be at variance; to forsake; to desert, abandon, separate oneself from others.

بَبَّغاء parrot.

البَبغاء تقلد صوت الإنسان دون أن يكون كلامها مفهوماً
Parrots imitate human voices in a muddled manner

بَتَّ to decide, determine, settle, resolve a matter, question, topic; to have the final word; to cut, sever.

بَتاتًا definitely, absolutely not; never, not in the least; by no means, in no way.

بَتّار sharp, cutting.

البَتَّة absolutely not; never; not in the least; by no means; in no way, under no circumstances.

بَتَرَ to cut off, sever; to amputate (a limb); to maim, dismember.

بَتْر amputation (of a limb), cutting off, severance, mutilation.

بَتْرول petroleum.

بَتَلَة petal.

بَتول virgin, maiden.

بُتولَة virginity, maindenhood.

بَثَّ to disseminate, propagate, spread, diffuse; to broadcast (by radio); to transmit; to televise; to lay (mines in the sea); to reveal, divulge (a secret).

بَثّ broadcasting (radio); televising (television); transmission, diffusion, dissemination; grief, sorrow, anguish.

بَثْرَة pimple, pustule, blister, boil, blackhead.

بَجَّ to cut open, split open.

بَجَسَ to cause to flow or gush out (water); to pour forth copiously.

بَجَع، بَجعَة pelican (bird).

البَجعة طائر مائي جميل ورشيق
Pelicans are graceful and beautiful aquatic birds

بَجَّلَ to revere, venerate, esteem; to honor, glorify.

بُحَّ صَوْتُهُ to be hoarse; to have a husky voice.

بَحَّاثَة researcher, eminent scholar.

بَحَّار seaman, sailor, mariner.

يقود البحّار السفينة بواسطة الدفة
The seaman guides his ship by way of a rudder

بُحْبُوحَة affluence, prosperity; middle, center.

بُحَّة hoarseness.

بَحَثَ to search for, look for, hunt for; to investigate, study, explore; to discuss (a subject); to confer with; to drill for, prospect for; to inquire into, scrutinize.

بَحْث discussion, search, quest, study, examination; research; exploration; treatise, survey, report.

بَحْر sea; meter (in poetry); a noble man; a man of vast knowledge.

يقع لبنان على شاطئ البحر الأبيض المتوسط
Lebanon lies on the eastern shore of the Mediterranean Sea

البحرُ الأَبْيَضُ المُتَوسِّط the Mediterranean Sea.

البَحْرُ الأَحْمَر the Red Sea.

البحرُ المَيِّت the Dead Sea.

بحرُ البَلْطِيق the Baltic Sea.

البحرُ الأَسْوَد the Caspian Sea.

بَحْرَة pond.

بَحْرِيّ (ص) maritime, naval, marine.

بَحْرِيّ (اسم) sailor, seaman, mariner.

بَحْرِيَّة navy.

بَحْص pebbles, gravel, macadam.

بُحيرَة lake.

بُخَار vapor, steam.

بُخارِيّ steam-driven.

بَخْت luck, fortune.

بَخَّرَ to vaporize, evaporate, fumigate; to perfume with incence; to disinfect; to expose to aromatic smoke.

بَخَسَ to decrease, diminish, lessen the value of something; to neglect, belittle, undervalue.

يتصاعد البخار من الماء عند غليه
Vapor rises from boiling water

بَخْشيش gratuity, tip.

بَخُلَ ، بَخِلَ to be niggardly, stingy with someone; to withhold from; to give grudgingly.

بُخْل stinginess, avarice, cupidity, greed.

بَخُور incense, frankincense.

بخيل (ص) stingy, niggardly, miserly, avaricious, greedy.

بخيل (اسم) miser, niggard, skinflint.

بُدّ escape, alternative, way out.

بَدَأَ to begin, start, initiate, set about, launch; to create, generate, bring about; to arise, spring up.

بَدَا to appear; to come to light; to emerge, reveal itself; to be apparent, evident.

بَدْء start, beginning, onset, starting point; introduction, launching.

بَدَائِيّ ، بِدَائِيّ primitive, elementary, initial; primary.

بَدَانَة obesity, corpulence, overweight.

بَدَاهَة spontaneity, impulse, intuition.

بَدَاوَة nomadism, desert life.

بِدَايَة beginning, first step, first instance.

بَدَّدَ to disperse; scatter; squander, waste; to eliminate, dispose of arbitrarily.

بَدَرَ to come unexpectedly; to take by surprise; to overtake, overwhelm; to hasten, rush to, hurry to; to embark, set out without delay.

بَدْر full moon.

بِدْعَة fad, rage, innovation; heresy.

بَدَّلَ to change, substitute, replace, exchange; to convert; to give in exchange for; to compensate for; to trade, barter; to modify, alter, transform.

بَدَل substitute, alternate, replacement; price, rate; allowance; charge; equivalent.

بَدَل ؛ بدلاً من instead of; in place of; in lieu of; in replacement of; in return for.

بَدْلَة costume, suit, uniform.

بَدَن body, trunk, hull (of a ship).

بَدَنِيّ bodily, corporal, physical.

بَدَه to surprise, improvise, come suddenly; to appear unexpectedly before someone; to do on the spur of the moment.

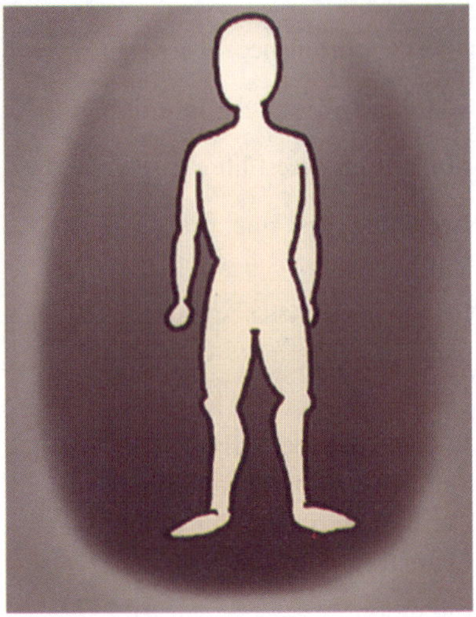

يتكوّن بدن الإنسان من لحم وعظام وعضلات ودم

The human body is formed of flesh, bones, muscles and blood

بَدْو bedouins, nomads.

بَدَوِيّ (اسم) bedouin, nomad.

بَدَوِيّ (ص) rural, nomadic

بديع (ص) wonderful, marvelous, amazing, unique.

بديع (اسم) creator, maker; rhetoric.

بَديل substitute, alternate, replacement; standby; understudy; double; reserve.

بَديهَة intuition, impulse, improvisation; inspiration; intuitive insight, perceptive faculty; presence of mind.

بَديهيّ self-evident, intuitive, a priori, obvious; undeniable, indisputable.

بَذَاءة obscenity, ribaldry, foulness (of language); disgust, loathing, contempt, aversion; bawdiness, indecency.

بَذَخ to be haughty, proud, lavish, prodigal.

بَذْخ prodigality, luxury, haughtiness, pride.

بَذَرَ to sow, seed; to disseminate, spread; to waste, squander, dissipate.

بَذَّر to squander, waste, dissipate; to sow, seed, spread.

بَذْر seed, pip, grain, pit, stone (of fruit).

بَذَلَ to give generously; to sacrifice; to offer, grant; to take pains; to do one's best; to fritter away one's fortune; to display vulgar manners; to abuse, degrade, demean; to sacrifice one's dignity; to give everything in order to; to make efforts; to grant assistance.

بَذْل granting, spending, generosity, sacrifice, effort.

بَذْلَة suit, costume, uniform.

بَذيء obscene, bawdy, ribald; foul; dirty, disgusting; shameless, lewd, abusive.

بَرَّ to be reverent, kind, devoted, charitable, beneficent; to obey, honor, respect; to be honest, truthful; to keep a promise, oath; to warrant, justify, vindicate; to acquit, absolve, exonerate, exculpate; to carry out (one's promise).

بَرّ land, mainland, earth, ground.

بُرّ wheat.

أعلق بذلتي بعد أن أخلعها عن جسمي
I hang my suit on a hanger after I undress

بِرّ charity, benevolence, piety, godliness, kindness, devoutness, probity, devotion, reverence.

بَرَأَ to create.

بَرِئَ to recover (from illness); to cause to recover, cure, heal; to be innocent of; to free (from responsibility); to rid oneself of.

بَرَى to sharpen, point, chafe, shave off, trim, shape; to wear out, emaciate, enervate; to vie, compete with; to contend; to meet in a contest.

بَرَّأَ to acquit from, exonerate from, free from, release from, discharge from; to cure, heal; to declare someone innocent from.

بَرَاءة innocence; naivete, artlessness; license, diploma, patent; credentials.

بَرَاءةُ ذِمَّة acquittance, discharge, quittance.

بَرَّاد icebox; cold storage plant.

بِرَاز excrement, feces, stool; competition, test, contest, duel, match (in sports).

بَرَاعَة skill, dexterity, adeptness, ability, workmanship, capacity.

بَرَّاق shining, sparkling, glittering.

بَرَّايَة pencil sharpener.

بَرْبَر Berbers.

بَرْبَرِيّ Berber; barbaric, barbarian, savage, uncivilized.

بَرْبَرِيَّة barbarism, savagery; wildness; inhumanity, cruelty.

بُرْتُقال orange.

بُرْتُقالِيّ orange, orange-colored.

بُرْثُن claw, talon.

بُرْج tower, castle; sign of the zodiac, constellation.

بُرْجُ الحَمَام pigeon-house.

بُرْجٌ عاجِيّ ivory tower.

بُرْجُ المُراقبة watch tower.

بُرْجُ المياه water tower.

بَرْجَل	compass, dividers.
بُرْجُمَة	knuckle.
بَرِحَ	to leave, go away, depart.
بَرِحَ (ما)	still, yet, to continue to do.
بَرَّحَ	to torment, afflict, trouble; to exhaust.
بَرَدَ	to be cold; to cool, cool off; to feel cold; to file; to mail, post.
بَرَّدَ	to cool, chill, refrigerate; to soothe, refresh, alleviate.
بَرَد	hail.
بَرْد	cold, coldness, cooling, coolness; alleviation, soothing.
بُرْد، بُرْدَة	garment, gown.
بَرْدَعَة	saddle.
بَرْدِيّ	papyrus.
بَرْدِيَّة	chill, fever, malaria.
بَرَّرَ	to justify, warrant, rationalize, vindicate; to acquit, absolve, exonerate.
بَرَزَ	to appear; to come out into view, emerge; to jut out, protrude, stand out, reveal itself; to occur, happen; to excel, surpass someone in; to distinguish oneself by; to compete in a duel.
بَرْزَخ	isthmus; screen; divider; interval, time; bar, obstruction; gap.
بُرْش	mat.
بِرْشام	rivet.

بِرْشامَة	capsule (containing medecine), wafer.
بَرَص	leprosy.
بُرْطاش	doorstep, threshold, doorsill.
بَرْطَلَ	to bribe; to corrupt, buy off.
بَرَعَ	to excel; to distinguish oneself; to be skillfull, proficient; to outdo, outshine.
بُرْعُم	bud, burgeon, sprout, shoot, blossom.

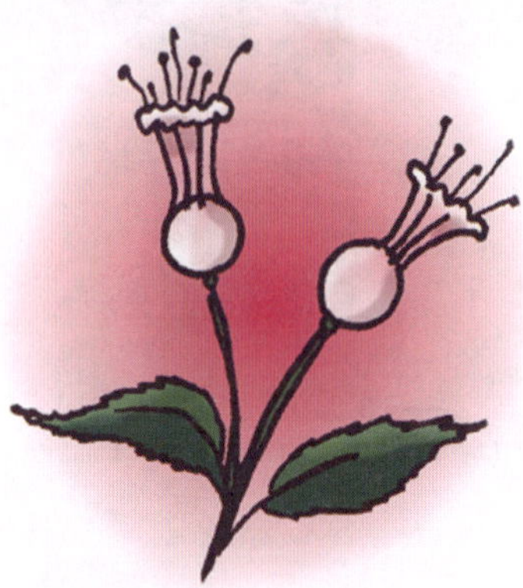

تتفتّح براعم الأزهار خلال شهر آذار

Flowers bloom usually in March

بَرْغَش	mosquitoes, gnats.
بُرْغُل	crushed wheat.
بُرْغُوث	flea (insect).
بُرْغِيّ	screw.
بَرَقَ	to flash; to sparkle, shine; to twinkle, glimmer.
بَرْق	lightning, flash of lightning; telegraph, cable.
بُرْقُع	veil, drape.

بُرْقوق	plum.
بَرْقيّ (ص)	telegraphic.
بَرْقِيَّة	telegram, cable, wire, telegraph.
بِرْكار	compass, dividers.

يرسم الخطاط الدوائر بواسطة البركار

The surveyor draws circles with a compass

بُرْكَان	volcano.

يقذف البركان الحمم عندما يثور

Volcanoes eject lava when they erupt

بَرَكَة	blessing, prosperity, felicity, benediction.
بِرْكَة	pond, pool.
بِرْكَةُ سِباحَة	swimming pool.

بَرَمَ	to twist, twine; to shape something round; to roll up the sleeves.
بَرِمَ	to be weary, tired, fed up, bored with; to find something annoying, wearisome.
بَرْمَجَ	to program.
بَرْمَجة	programming.
بَرْميل	barrel, keg, cask, tun.

تُحفظ السوائل في البرميل لحين استعمالها

Liquids are stored in barrels for future use

بَرْنامِج	program, plan; agenda; platform (political); software (computer); curriculum (study); list, index.
بَرْنَقَ	to varnish.
بَرْنِيَّة	clay pot or vessel.
بُرْنَيْطَة	hat.
بُرْهَان	proof, evidence.
بُرْهَة	a while, a time; short time; instant, moment.

بَرْهَنَ	to prove, demonstrate.
بِرْواز	frame.
بروتين	protein.
بُروجي	trumpeteer, bugler.
بُرودَة	coldness; frigidity; unfriendliness, apathy.
بَرْوَزَ	to frame.
بُروز	emergence, protrusion, prominence; happening; appearance, rise.
برونز	bronze.
بَرِّيّ	terrestial; wild; untamed.
بَرِيء	innocent, guiltless; naive, free from, clear of; exempt from.
بَرِيَّة	creation; mankind.
بَرِّيَّة	wilderness, desert, wasteland.
بَريد	mail, post.
بَريدٌ جَوِّيّ	air mail.
بَريدٌ عادِيّ	surface mail.
بَريدٌ مُسَجَّل	registered mail.
بَريق	shine, gloss, glitter, luster.
بَريمَة	drill, auger; corkscrew.
بَزَّ	to take away, steal, wrest, snatch; to rob.
بَزَّ	to defeat, beat; to excel, outstrip; to triumph.
بَزّاز	draper, cloth merchant.
بَزّاقَة	snail; cobra (reptile).
بَزْباز، بَزْبوز	nozzle, spout.

بِزَّة	clothing, clothes, attire, uniform.
بَزَرَ	to sow; to seed.
بِزْر	seed; spice.
بِزْرُ الكِتّان	linseed.
بِزْرَة	seed, pip, stone, kernel.
بَزَغَ	to rise (sun); to break forth; to appear, emerge.
بَزَلَ	to puncture, pierce, perforate; to tap a hole; to filter (liquid); to broach (a cask).
بُزوغ	appearance, emergence; rise (of the sun).
بَسّ، بِسّ	cat.
بِساط	carpet, rug, mat.
بَساطَة	simplicity, modesty, humbleness.
بَسالَة	courage, bravery, intrepidity.
بُسْتان	garden, orchard, grove.
بُسْتانِيّ	gardener.

يهتمّ البستاني بمزروعات حديقته من الأشجار والنبات

The gardener takes care of his orchard

بَسْتَر — to pasteurize.

بَسْتَرَة — pasteurization.

بَسْتَنَة — gardening, horticulture.

بَسَطَ — to spread out, level, flatten; to enlarge, extend; to unroll; to grant, offer, present; to submit, set forth, explain; to flog; to please.

بَسَطَ المائِدَة — to lay the table.

بَسَطَ ذِراعَيْه — to spread one's arms.

بَسَطَ يَدَ المُساعَدَة — to extend a helping hand.

بَسُطَ — to be simple, plain; to be trivial, artless, naive, ingenuous; to be generous, openhanded.

بَسَّطَ — to simplify, make simple; to explain; to make easy.

بَسْط — spreading, rolling, unfolding; levelling off, flattening; presentation; explanation; delight, amusement; numerator (of a fraction).

بَسْطَة — extension, magnitude, expanse, extent, scope; skill; abundance; statement, report, presentation.

بَسَقَ — to be towering, lofty, high; to excel, surpass.

بَسْكَويت — biscuit.

بَسُلَ — to be valiant, intrepid, brave; to be reckless.

بَسَمَ — to smile.

بَسْمَة — smile.

بَسْمَلَ — to utter the invocation (in the Name of God, the Beneficent, the Merciful).

بَسيط — simple, plain, naive; trivial, petty; natural, unadorned; unpretentious, modest; innocent, trifling.

بَشَّ — to display a cheeful face; to smile; to be friendly.

بِشارة — good news, glad tidings, good omen; gospel.

بَشاشَة — smile, happy mien, cheerful face.

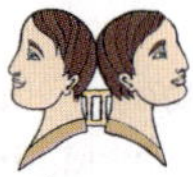

بَشاعَة — ugliness.

بَشَرَ — to grate, shave off, shred, scrape off.

بَشَّرَ — to announce good news; to propagate, preach (a religion, doctrine); to portend, herald, signal the approach of; to presage, forshadow.

بَشَر — human being, man, human; people, mankind.

بِشْر — happiness, glad tidings.

بُشْرى — good news, glad tidings.

بَشَرَة — epidermis, outer skin, complexion.

بَشَريّ — human, human being; epidermal, cutaneous.

بَشَرِيَّة — humankind, mankind, human race.

بَشِعَ — to be ugly, unsightly, loathsome.

بَشِع — ugly, offensive, repulsive, unpleasant; distasteful, repugnant, disgusting, hideous.

بَشْكير — towel.

بَشَّمَ — to rivet; to drive a rivet.

أ ب ت ث ج ح خ د ذ ر ز س ش ص ض ط ظ ع غ ف ق ك ل م ن هـ و ي

بَشُوش smiling, cheerful.

بَشِير harbinger, precursor, herald, presage; portend, omen, augury; bringer of good news.

بَصَّ to glow, sparkle, glitter, shine.

بَصَّار fortune-teller, soothsayer.

بُصَاق spit, spittle.

بَصَّة embers.

بَصُرَ to see, look, realize; to understand, comprehend, discern; to catch sight of; to make out, notice.

بَصَّرَ to tell the fortune; to enlighten; to make understand; to reflect, ponder.

بَصَر vision, eyesight; glance, look; insight, sight, discernment, perception.

بَصَرِيّ optical, visual, ocular.

بَصَرِيَّات optics (science).

بَصَقَ to spit.

بَصْقَة spit, spittle.

بَصَل onion.

بَصَلَة bulb.

بَصَمَ to print, imprint, stamp.

بَصْمَة imprint, stamp, impression.

بَصْمَةُ الإِصْبَع fingerprint.

بَصِير endowed with eyesight; acutely aware; discerning, perceptive; acute, keen; clear-sighted; knowledgeable, discriminating.

بَصِيرة keen insight, discernment, perspicacy; mental perception, foresight, prevision.

للبصل منافع عديدة
ويُستعمل في معظم الأطباق
Onions have several benefits and are used in the preparation of most meals

بَصِيص glow, sparkle, glitter, shine.

بُصَيلَة bulb.

بِضَاعة goods, merchandise, wares, commodities.

بَضَعَ to cut, amputate, dissect, incise.

بِضْع some, a few, several.

بَطّ duck.

بَطُؤَ to be slow; to go slowly; to lag, linger, tarry, hesitate; to slow down, decelerate.

بُطْء slowness, lag, sluggishness.

بَطَارِخ roe of fish, spawn of fish.

بَطَّارِيَّة battery, pile (electrical); flashlight.

بَطَّارِيَّة battery (military).

بَطَاطِس، بَطَاطَا potatoes.

بِطَاقَة card, ticket, label, tag.

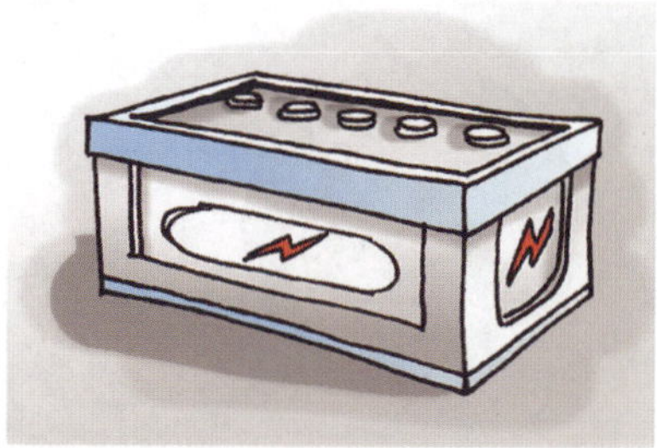

البطارية تولد الطاقة الكهربائية لتشغيل المحركات
The battery generates electrical power to operate engines

بِطاقَةٌ شَخْصِيَّة calling card.

بِطاقَةُ تَعْريف، بِطاقَةُ هَوِيَّة identity card.

بِطاقَةُ دُخول ticket, admission card.

بِطاقَةُ دَعْوَة invitation card.

بِطاقَةُ مُعايَدَة greeting card.

بَطَّال inactive, idle, unemployed, out of work, jobless.

بَطَالَة ، بِطَالَة inactivity, unemployment, free time.

بِطانَة lining (of a garment); retinue, entourage.

بَطَّانِيَّة blanket, quilt, cover.

بَطَّة duck (bird); leather flask.

بَطَّةُ الساق calf (of the leg).

بَطِرَ to be wild, wanton, reckless; to be ungrateful, thankless; to be dissatisfied, arrogant, proud, vain.

بَطَر ingratitude, ungratfulness; wantonness; discontent; arrogance, vanity, pride.

بَطْرَخ roe, spawn.

تسبح البطة في مياه البحيرة
وتقتات بالأسماك الصغيرة
Ducks swim in lakes and live on small fish they catch in the waters

بَطْرِيَرْك patriarch.

بَطْرِيَرْكِيَّة patriarchate.

بَطْرِيق penguin (bird).

يقتات البطريق بالسمك
ويعيش فقط في المناطق القطبية
Penguins live in the polar regions and catch fish swimming under the ice cover

بَطَشَ to knock out, strike sharply; to assult, devastate, crush, ruin, attack with violence; to hit, fall upon.

بَطْش strength, force, violence; tyranny; bravery.

بَطَل to be null, invalid, void, ineffective, vain, futile; to be abolished, cancelled; to fall into disuse; to become obsolete; to cease, stop; to thwart, foil, frustrate; to remain without work; to be jobless, idle.

بَطُل to be brave, heroic; to be a hero.

بَطَل (اسم) hero, champion, pioneer, protagonist; lead star (of a play, a film).

بُطْلان nullity, uselessness, futility, vanity; falsity, untruth.

بَطَلَة heroine; female lead, star (of a play, a film).

بَطَّنَ to line (a garment); to cover the inside.

بَطْن abdomen, belly; interior, inside; sept, subdivision of a tribe.

بَطْنُ القَدَم sole of the foot.

بَطْنُ الكَفّ palm of the hand.

بَطْنًا بِظَهْر upside down.

بَطْنِيّ abdominal.

بُطُولَة bravery, valor, heroism; leading role (in a play, a film).

بُطُولَةُ العالَم world championship.

بُطُولِيّ heroic.

بطيء slow, sluggish; lazy, slack; tardy, late.

بِطِّيخٌ أَحْمَر watermelon.

بِطِّيخٌ أَصْفَر melon, muskmelon.

بَظْر clitoris.

يطيب أكل البطيخ خلال فصل الصيف
Eating watermelon is delicious during the summer season

بَعَثَ to send, send out, dispatch, forward to; to emit; to delegate; to evoke, arouse, call forth; to stir up, provoke, bring on; to revive, resuscitate, resurrect (from death); to incite, induce, instigate, cause; to revitalize; to prompt, spur, urge on, trigger.

بَعْث sending out, emission, dispatching, delegation; resurrection; arousal, excitation, provocation; revival, reanimation, renaissance.

بَعْثَة mission, delegation; expedition; revival, rebirth; renaissance; rise.

بَعْثَرَ to disarrange, scatter, squander, waste, dissipate.

بَعَجَ to slit open; to groove, dent, notch.

بَعُدَ to be distant, far away, far off; to keep away; to be remote, improbable, unlikely.

بَعَّدَ to remove, banish, exile; to take away, eliminate; to send away, dismiss; to keep away; to single out, set aside.

بَعْدَ after, in addition to, beside; aside from.

بَعْدَ ذلك — afterwards, later on; besides; moreover.

بَعْدَ أن — after.

بَعْدَ الظُّهرِ — in the afternoon.

بَعْدُ — yet, still, so far; up to now.

بُعْد — remoteness, farness, distance, dimension, interval.

بُعْدُ الصِّيت — renown, fame, celebrity.

بُعْدُ النَّظر — farsightedness, foresight.

بَعْدَئِذ — then, thereafter; thereupon; after that; afterwards.

بَعر ، بَعَر — droppings, dung (of animals).

بَعْزَق — to scatter, waste, squander, dissipate, disperse.

بَعْض — some of, a little; rather.

بَعْضُهم بَعْضاً — one another, each other; mutually, reciprocally.

بَعْل — husband, spouse; lord, master; God, deity; land thriving on natural water supply (from rain).

بَعوض، بَعُوضة — gnats, mosquitos, bugs.

بَعيد — far, distant, faraway, remote, outlying; far-reaching, extensive, far-fetched; unlikely, unusual; strange, odd, queer, incompatible, inconsistent with.

بَعيدُ الأَثَر — of far-reaching consequence.

بَعيدُ التّاريخ — remote in time, ancient.

بَعيدُ الغَوْر — deep, unfathomable.

بَعيدُ المَدى — long-range, long-distance, extensive.

بَعيدُ النَّظَر — farsighted, farseeing.

يتكاثر البعوض بسرعة في المستنقعات
Mosquitoes thrive in stagnant waters

بَعيدُ المَنال — hardly attainable, hard to get at.

بُعَيْد — shortly after, soon after.

بَعير — camel.

البعير اسم آخر للجمل ذي السنام الواحد
Camels are of two kinds, single or double humped

بَغَى — to seek, covet, desire, want; to oppress, commit outrage upon; to treat unjustly; to wrong someone.

بَغى		to fornicate; to whore.
بِغاء		prostitution, whoredom.
بَغّال		mule driver, muleteer.
بَغَتَ		to come unexpectedly, descend unawares upon.
بَغْتَةً		unexpectedly; suddenly, unawares, all of a sudden; by surprise; without warning.
بَغَضَ		to loathe, detest, hate.
بَغُضَ، بَغِضَ		to be hateful, odious, abominable.
بَغَّضَ		to make someone hateful.
بُغْض		hatred, hate, disgust, antipathy.
بَغْل		mule (animal).

البغل حيوان أليف يستخدم في نقل الأثقال عبر الجبال

Mules are very useful animals for transporting loads across mountainous regions

بَغِيّ	prostitute, whore, harlot.
بَغْي	injustice, oppression, tyranny, outrage, aggression, offense, despotism, wrong.
بُغْيَة	wish, desire; for, for the purpose of, with the aim of; with a view to; in order that, so as, to.
بَغيض	hateful, odious, loathsome, abominable, repulsive, detested, abhorred, hated.
بَقَّ	to spout; to give off in abundance, eject, discharge.
بَقاء	remaining, staying, abiding; sojourn; continuance, continuation, duration; survival, existence; immortality, eternity; permanence.
بَقاءُ الأَصْلَح	survival of the fittest.
بَقّال	grocer, greengrocer.
بِقالَة	grocery, greengrocery; the grocery business.
بَقْبَقَ	to gurgle, bubble, sputter; to chatter, prattle.
بَقْبَقَة	chatter, prattle, gossip; bubble, sputter.
بَقّة	bug, bedbug, chinch (insect).
بُقْجَة	bundle, pack, package.

لا يطير البق لعدم امتلاكه جناحين كمعظم الحشرات الأخرى

Bugs have no wings like other insects and accordingly they cannot fly

بَقْدُونَس parsley.

بَقَرَ to slit open, cut open, rip open.

بَقَر ، بَقَرَة cow, cows; cattle, bovines.

نحصل على حليب صحّي من ضرع البقرة
Fresh milk is obtained from cows

بَقَرِيّ bovine, cow, cattle.

بَقْشِيش tip, gratuity.

بُقْعَة spot, stain; splotch, smudge.

بَقْل ، بَقْلَة legumes, plants, vegetables, herbaceous plants.

بَقِيَ to remain, stay; to be left over, left behind; to last, continue, go on; to continue to do; to keep doing something; to become.

بَقِيَ على قَيْدِ الحياة to survive; to stay alive.

بَقِيَّة remainder, rest, remnant, residue, remains.

بَكَى to cry, weep over; to bemoan, lament, bewail; to mourn; to shed tears.

بُكَاء crying, weeping.

بَكَارَة virginity, maidenhead.

بَكَّارة pulley, tackle, pulley block.

بَكَالُورِيا baccalaureate.

بَكَالُورِيُوس bachelor's degree.

بَكَّتَ to censure, blame; to reproach, reprimand, rebuke.

بَكْتِيرِيا bacteria.

بَكَرَ ، بَكَّرَ to set out early in the morning; to get up early; to come early; to be early; to do something ahead; to do something ahead of its time.

بِكْر firstborn. eldest; novel, first, new.

بِكْر virgin, maiden.

بَكَرَة ، بَكْرَة pulley, tackle; reel, coil, roller, spool.

يتمّ لفّ الحبل الطويل على بكرة
A long rope is reeled on a coil

بُكْرَة early morning; early in the morning; tomorrow; the following day.

بَكَّلَ to buckle, buckle up, button up; to fold, cross (the arms); to clasp, fasten.

بُكْلَة buckle, clasp, clip, fastener.

أ ب ت ث ج ح خ د ذ ر ز س ش ص ض ط ظ ع غ ف ق ك ل م ن هـ و ي

بَكَمَ، بَكِمَ to be silent; to become mute.

بَكَم muteness, dumbness.

بَكير coming early; early, premature; precocious.

بَلَّ to moisten, wet, make wet; to recover (from an illness).

بَلْ but, however; yet, even; rather.

بَلَى yes, yes indeed, certainly; for sure, truly.

بِلًى wear, loss, decay, erosion, corrosion, putrefaction, deterioration, shabbiness, decomposition.

بَلاء affliction, distress, misfortune, calamity, scourge, plague; evil, curse, ordeal.

بَلاء creditable performance; bravery, gallantry; heroric action, prowess; courage.

بَلادَة stupidity, silliness, dullness; laziness, indolence.

بَلاط pavement, tiled floor, floor tiles; slabs; paving.

بَلاط royal palace, royal court.

بَلاطَة floor tile, flagstone, slabstone, paving stone.

بَلاغ communique, bulletin; declaration, statement; notice, announcement; proclamation; message, edict; notification.

بَلاغَة eloquence, art of composition; art of good style.

بَلاهَة stupidity; simplemindedness, imbecility; silliness.

بَلْبَلَ to disquiet; to make uneasy; to stir up, rouse; to disturb, trouble, confuse; to perplex, puzzle, bewilder; to muddle, derange, complicate; to put into confusion.

بَلْبَلَة confusion, chaos; tangle, tumult; disturbance; anxiety; uneasiness; muddle, jumble, hubhub.

بَلَح unripe dates.

بَلُدَ to be dull, stupid; to become lazy, sluggish.

بَلَد country, town, city, place, community, village.

بَلَدُ المنشأ country of origin.

بَلْدَة town, village, borough.

بَلَدِيّ indigenous, local, domestic; municipal, provincial.

بَلَدِيَّة municipality.

بَلْسَم balm, balsam.

بَلْشُون heron, egret (bird).

يهاجر البلشون خلال فصل الشتاء إلى المناطق الحارة
Herons are migratory birds and leave cold toward warm regions during winter

بَلَّطَ to pave with tiles; to tile.

بَلْطَة ax, axe.

بَلَعَ to swallow, gulp down; to put up with; to stomach, brook something; to gobble.

بَلَعَ ريقه to catch one's breath; to have a break; to restrain, hold back one's rage.

بَلْع swallowing, gulping, absorption.

بُلْعُوم pharynx.

بَلَغَ to reach, arrive at, attain, get to; to inform; to attain manhood; to become an adult; to notify; to ripen; to become ripe, mature (fruit); to amount to; to add up to; to come of age; to come to one's knowledge, hear of, learn about, find out about; to lead to, convey to, drive to; to become serious, grave; to act, have its effect; to go far in; to convey, impart.

بَلَغَ السَّيْلُ الزُّبَى the matter reached a climax, things came to a head.

بَلَغَ أَشُدَّه to attain full maturity, come of age.

بَلَغَ مُنْتَهاه to reach its climax.

بَلُغَ to be eloquent.

بَلَّغَ to inform, notify, advise, convey (a message); to transmit, impart; to communicate, report; to tell, let know, give an account of; to denounce.

بَلَّغَ السلام to give one's regards to someone else .

بَلْغَم phlegm, expectoration, sputum.

بَلْكون balcony, veranda,

بَلَّلَ to wet, moisten; to make wet.

بَلَل wetness, moisture, humidity, dampness.

بَلَل recuperation, recovery, convalescence (from sickness).

بَلِهَ to be or become stupid, imbecile, foolish, simpleminded, idiotic.

بَلْوَى trial, tribulation, affliction, distress, calamity.

بَلْوَرَ to crystalize.

بَلُّور crystal; glass.

بَلُّوط oak (tree).

بُلُوغ arrival, achievement; puberty, maturity; ripeness.

بَلِيَ to be or become old, worn, tattered; to deteriorate, disintegrate, rot, degenerate, spoil, corrode, erode.

بَلِيَّة calamity, distress, affliction, trial, tribulation.

بَلِيد stupid, idiotic; dull-witted; imbecile; slow-witted; sluggish, lazy; languid, lethargic.

بَلِيغ eloquent, fluent, well-spoken; lasting, deep, profound; serious, grave, violent, drastic; sharp, acute, intense; substantial, far-reaching.

بُنّ coffee, coffee beans.

بَنَى to build, erect, construct, set up; to establish.

بَنَى to give the word an indeclinable ending (grammar).

بَنَّاء (اسم) mason, builder.

بِنَاء building, construction, erection, setting up, structure; set-up, make-up; edifice; forming, formation.

بِنَاءً على according to; in acccordance with; on the basis of; by virtue of; on the strength of; acccordingly; thus.

بِنَاءً عليه accordingly, thus, hence; consequently.

بَنَادُورة tomatoes (plant).

بِنَاية building, structure, edifice, premises.

بِنْت girl, daughter; queen (playing cards).

بِنْتُ الأخ أو الأخت niece.

بِنْتُ الزَّوْج أو الزَّوْجة stepdaughter.

بِنْتُ العمّ أو الخال أو العمّة أو الخالة cousin.

بِنْتُ الهوى prostitute, whore, harlot.

بَنَّجَ to anesthetize.

بَنْج anesthetic.

بَنْجَر beet, red beet, sugar beet.

بَنْد clause, article, paragraph, item; provision, term.

بَنْد banner, flag.

بَنْدَر seaport, harbor, port.

بُنْدُق hazelnuts, filberts.

بُنْدُقِيَّة rifle, gun, shotgun.

بَنَدُورَة tomatoes (plant).

بِنْزِين gasoline, gas, petrol, benzine.

بِنْصِر ring finger.

البنصر هو الإصبع الرابع في يد الإنسان

The fourth finger of the hand is called the ring finger

بَنْطَلُون trousers, pants.

بَنَفْسَج violet; pansy (flower).

بَنَفْسَجِيّ violet.

بَنْك bank; bench, seat.

بَنْكُ الدم blood bank.

بَنْكٌ مركزيّ central bank.

بُنُوَّة sonship.

بَنَوِيّ filial.

بُنِّيّ (ص) brown.

بُنْيَان	building, construction, erection; structure, edifice; physique, stature.
بِنْيَة	structure, setup, make-up; build, frame; physique, physical constitution.
بِنْيَةٌ تَحْتِيَّة	infrastructure.
بِنْيَةٌ فَوْقِيَّة	superstructure.
بِنْيَوِيّ	structural, constructional.
بَهَاء	beauty, splendor, magnificence; glory; radiance.
بَهَار	pepper, spice.
بَهَتَ	to astonish; to amaze, startle; to slander, defame, vilify; to speak evil of.
بَهِتَ	to fade, dim, wan, tarnish (color).
بُهِتَ	to be astonished, amazed, perplexed, surprised, stunned, shocked.
بُهْتَان	slander, false accusation; lie; untruth; calomny, defamation; falsehood, falsity.
بَهِجَ	to be glad, happy, delighted; to be beautiful, look wonderful.
بَهْجَة	joy, delight; beauty, grace.
بَهَرَ	to dazzle (the eyes); to shine, glitter, overwhelm; to flaunt, show off, parade.
بُهِرَ	to pant, gasp; to be dazzled, overwhelmed.
بَهْرَجَ	to adorn, dress up showily, decorate, embellish; to falsify, fake, counterfeit.

بَهْرَجَة	sham splendor; hollow pomp; showy adornment.
بَهْلَوان	acrobat, equilibrist, tightrope walker.
بَهْلَوَانِيَّات	acrobatics.
بُهْلُول	jester,clown, buffoon.
بَهْو	hall, parlor; reception hall.
بَهِيّ	beautiful, splendid, brillant; dazzling, pretty; charming; radiant.
بَهِيج	happy, glad, delighted; cheerful.
بَهِيمَة	beast, animal; quadruped.
بَهِيمِيَّة	bestiality, brutality, animalism.
بَوَّأَ	to take a place; to settle down; to install; to dwell in, live in, inhabit; to invest with an office; to inaugurate; to appoint to an office.
بَوَّاب	doorkeeper, gatekeeper, doorman; pylorus (med).
بَوَّابَة	gate, portal.
بَوَار	perdition, ruin; slump; stagnation; fallow land, wasteland, uncultivated land.
بَوَّبَ	to categorize, classify, tabulate, sort out, group; to divide into sections, chapters, parts.
بُوتَقَة	crucible, melting pot.
بَوْح	divulgence, disclosure, revelation, confession.
بُورجوازِيَّة	bourgeoisie.
بُورْصَة	stock exchange, stock market, exchange.
بُورِي	trumpet, bugle.

بَوْس — kissing.

بَوْسَة — kiss.

بُوْص — reed.

بُوْصَة — inch.

بُوْصُلَة — compass.

بُوْظَة — icecream.

أحبّ أكل البوظة في يوم حارّ

I like to eat icecream on a hot day

بَوَّق — to bugle, blow the trumpet, sound the horn.

بُوْق — horn; trumpet, bugle; mouthpiece, spokesman; tube.

بَوَّل — to urinate; to make water.

بَوْل — urine.

بُوْلِيس — police, police force; policeman.

بُوْلِيسُ الآداب — vice squad.

بُوْلِيسٌ حَرْبِيّ — military police.

بُوْلِيسٌ سِرِّيّ — detective, secret agent.

بُوْلِيسُ المُرُور — traffic police.

بُوْلِيصَة — policy.

بُوْلِيصَةُ تَأْمِين — insurance policy.

بُوْلِيصَةُ شحن — bill of lading.

بُوْم، بُوْمَة — owl (bird).

البوم طائر نتشاءم من سماع نعيبه

Owls are considered as birds of bad augury

بَوْن — interval, distance; difference.

بُوْيا — paint.

بُويَجِيّ — shoeblack, bootblack.

بِيْئَة — environment, surroundings, milieu, habitat.

بَيَّارَةُ بُرْتُقال — orange grove; orange plantation.

بَيَاض — whiteness; white; blank space.

بَياضُ البَيْض	albumen, white of egg.
بَياضُ العَيْن	white of the eye.
بَياضُ الجُدْران	whitewash.
بَياضات (ج)	linen goods, bed clothes.
بَيان	statement, declaration, announcement, explanation, illustration, information, report.
بَيان	index, catalog, list.
بَيان	style; eloquence.
بَيان (عِلْمُ البَيان)	rhetoric.
بِيان، بِيانو	piano.
بَيَّت	to scheme, plot, intrigue; to hatch, brood about; to hide, conceal, harbor; to lodge; to put up for the night.
بَيْت	house, room, apartment, flat; case, box, casing; covering, sheath; family, household.
بَيْتُ الإِبْرَة	compass.
البَيْتُ الحَرام	the Kaaba.
بَيْتُ الخَلاء	toilet, water closet, bathroom.
البَيْتُ العَتيق	the Kaaba.
بَيْتُ الدَّعارة	brothel, bordello.
بَيْتُ شَعْر	tent.
بَيْتُ شِعْر	verse, line of poetry.
بَيْتُ العَنْكَبوت	cobweb, spiderweb.
بَيْتُ المال	treasury, exchequer.
بَيْتُ المَقْدِس	Jerusalem.
بُيوتات تُجارِيَّة	firms, business establishments.

بَيْتِيّ	domestic, private; homemade; domesticated (animal).
بَيْداء	desert, wilderness, steppe.
بَيْدَ أَنَّ	but, yet, nevertheless; on the other hand, although; whereas; however.
بَيْدَر	threshing floor.
بَيْدَق	pawn (in chess).
بَيْرَق	flag, banner, standard.
بيرُوقراطِيَّة	bureaucracy.
بَيَّضَ	to whitewash; to exculpate, vindicate, justify someone; to make white; paint white, whiten; to bleach (textiles); to make a fair copy of; to make someone appear blameless.
بَيْض (ج)	eggs.
بَيْضَة	egg; testicle; helmet; main part; essence.
بَيْضَوِيّ	oval, ovoid, egg-shaped, elliptical.
بَيْطار	farrier; veterinarian.
بَيْطَرَة	farriery; veterinary medecine.
بَيْع	sale.
بَيْعٌ بالمُفرَّق	retail.
بَيْعُ التَّصْفِيَة	clearance sale, sale.
بَيْعٌ بالتقسيط	sale by intallments.
بَيْعٌ بالجملة	wholesale.
بَيْعٌ بالدَّين	sale on credit.
بَيْعٌ عَلَنِيّ	public sale.
بَيْعٌ بالمزاد	auction sale, public auction.
بَيْعٌ نَقْدِيّ	cash sale.

أ ب ت ث ج ح خ د ذ ر ز س ش ص ض ط ظ ع غ ف ق ك ل م ن هـ و ي

بَيْعَة agreement; business deal; commercial transaction; homage, pledge of allegiance.

بَيَّنَ to show, demonstrate; to make clear, plain, visible, evident; to announce, state; to explain, expound, elucidate, throw light on, indicate, set forth.

بَيِّن clear, plain, evident, obvious; eloquent, explicit, manifest, patent, apparent.

بَيْن separation, disunion; enmity, hostility; dissension, discord; difference.

بَيْنَ between, among, amidst.

بَيْنَ بَيْنَ just fair, mediocre, medium; neither good or bad.

بَيْنَما while as, at the time of, whereas.

بَيْنَ وقتٍ وآخر from time to time; now and then; sometimes.

بَيْنَ يدَيْه with him, in his hands; before him, in his presence.

بَيِّنَة evidence, proof, document serving as evidence.

بُيَيْضَة ovum, ovule.

حرف التاء

تَ by.

تاء «ت» name of the letter.

تائِب repentant, penitent, contrite.

تائِه absent-minded; lost, straying, roving, wandering; haughty, arrogant, conceited.

تَابَ to repent; to be penitent; to turn from sin; to be converted from; to turn to God in repentance; to forgive, pardon; to renounce, forsake.

تَأَبَّطَ to carry under one's arms.

تَابَعَ to follow (the news, a topic); to watch, pursue, trail, track (someone or something); to follow in succession; to be consecutive; to examine, investigate, study; to continue, attend (studies); to prosecute, sue, take legal action against.

تابع (ص) following, succeeding, subsequent; attached, joined, auxiliary, supplementary; adjunct, annex, supplement; secondary, subsidiary, accessory, attendant.

تابع (اسم) subordinate, subaltern, vassal, subject;. servant, follower, adherent, partisan, national, citizen (of a country); appositive (grammar); satellite, moon; function (math).

تابِعِيَّة citizenship, nationality.

تابِل spice, condiment, seasoning, dressing.

تابُوت coffin, casket; box, chest.

تَأْبيد eternization, immortalization.

تَأْبين eulogy, funeral oration.

تَأَثُّر state of being affected, impressed, influenced; emotion, feeling, stimulation; sensitivity, excitability.

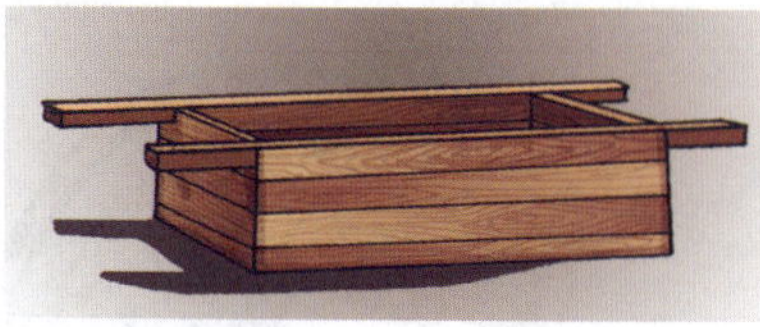

حمل المشيّعون التابوت إلى المقبرة
The coffin was carried on the shoulders to the cemetery

تَأْثِيث furnishing.

تَأْثِير influence, impact, impression; action, affect; efficacy, induction, effectiveness.

تَاج crown; corona.

يضع الملك التاج على رأسه في الاحتفالات الرسمية
The king puts the crown on his head during official receptions

تَأَجَّج to burn, blaze, flame.

تَاجَرَ to trade, do business, deal; to sell and buy.

تَاجِر merchant, trader, businessman, dealer.

تَاجِرُ الجُمْلَة wholesaler.

تَاجِرُ المُفَرَّق retailer.

تَأَجَّل to be postponed, deferred, delayed, adjounted.

تَأْجِير letting, letting out, leasing, rental, hire, lease.

تَأْجِيرُ سَفِينَة chartering.

تَأْجِيرٌ مِنَ البَاطِن subletting, sublease.

تَأْجِيل postponement, deferment, adjountment, respite.

تَآخٍ (التآخي) fraternization; brotherliness, fraternity.

تَآخَى to fraternize; to be on fraternal terms with.

تَأَخَّرَ to be late, delayed, lag behind; to tarry, linger, hesitate, default; to be in arrears with; to be behind in; to fall behind; to delay, retard.

تَأَخُّر delay, lag, retardation, lingering, tardiness, falling or staying behind; default, being in arrears, failure to pay; backwardness, underdevelopment.

تَاخَمَ to border on, abut upon; to be adjacent to.

تَأْخِير delay, postponement, deferment; retardation, obstruction, hindrance; setting back (the clock).

تَأَدَّبَ to be well-bred, well-educated, well-disciplined; to show oneself polite, courteous, civil; to educate oneself; to refine one's literary tastes by; to imitate, copy, take after, follow someone's example.

تَأْدِيب disciplining, discipline, education; chastisement, punishment.

تَأْدِيبِيّ disciplinary, retaliatory.

أ ب ت ث ج ح خ د ذ ر ز س ش ص ض ط ظ ع غ ف ق ك ل م ن هـ و ي

تَارَةً once, sometimes; once in a while.

تَأَرْجَحَ to swing back and forth; to rock, seasaw, teeter; to fluctuate, vibrate, wobble.

تَأَرْجُح swinging back and forth, fluctuation, vibration.

تَأْرِيخ chronology, chronicling, dating.

تاريخ history; date, time; chronicle, annals.

تاريخُ الاسْتِحْقاق due date, maturing date.

تاريخُ الحياة biopgraphy, curriculum vitae.

تاريخيّ historical, historic.

تَآزَرَ to help, assist one another; to cooperate, support, join forces.

تَآزُر cooperation, mutual support, combined effort, backing, help, aid, assistance.

تَأَزَّمَ to become critical; to be aggravated; to come to a head.

تَأَزُّم، تَأْزِيم aggravation; complication; worsening; critical development, deadlock.

تَأَسَّسَ to be founded, established, set up, constituted, built; to be based on, founded on.

تاسِع (التّسع) ninth.

تاسِعًا ninthly.

تَأَسَّفَ to regret; to feel sorry for; to be sad about.

تَأْسِيس foundation, setting up, establishment, founding; building, constitution, formation.

تَأْسِيسًا على based on, on the basis of; pursuant to.

تَأْسِيسيّ founding, foundational, fundamental; constitutional.

تَأْشِيرة visa; endorsement, stamping, signing.

تَأَصَّلَ to be firmly established, firmly rooted; to be deeprooted, ingrained; to take root; to derive one's origin from.

تَأَفَّفَ to grumble, complain, fuss, grouch; to show displeasure about; to express anger, displeasure.

تافِه، تَفِه insignificant, trivial, triffling, worthless; common, mediorce; vapid, insipid; trite, banal; stupid, silly, ridiculous, absurd.

تاقَ to long, yearn, wish for; to desire, crave, covet something; to strive, aspire for or to.

تَأَقْلَمَ to be acclimatized; to habituate oneself; to acclimatize oneself.

تَأَقْلُم acclimatization, adaptation; adjustment.

تَأَكَّدَ to be convinced, reassured; to be sure; to be certain, sure, true, correct; to ascertain, find out, make sure; to check, verify.

تَأَكُّد verification, assurance; ascertainment; checking.

تَآكَلَ to be corroded, eroded, worn, fretted; to be eaten away; to become old, worn, timeworn.

تَأْكِيد assurance, emphasis; confirmation, assertion.

بالتأكيد certainly, of course, surely; undoubtedly.

تالٍ (التّالي) following, subsequent, next.

تَأَلَّبَ to conspire against; to band together against.

تَأَلُّب conspiracy, plotting, rallying against.

تالِد old, time-honored; inherited.

تَأَلَّفَ to be formed, set-up, constituted of; to be composed, made of; to comprise, embrace, involve; to combine, unite, merge, join forces; to gather, band together; to be linked, in tune with.

تالِف damaged, ruined, spoiled; bad; decayed; worn.

تَأَلَّقَ to shine, radiate, glitter, sparkle, glisten.

تَأَلُّق radiance, brilliance; splendor, glory.

تَأَلَّمَ to feel pain; to suffer; to complain.

تأليب incitation against; incitement against; instigation against; sowing dissension among; conspiracy, plotting against.

تأليف formation; composition, compilation, writing (of a book); work, book, publication; union, junction, combination of separate things; synthesis, reconciliation, harmonization; domestication (of wild animals); written by.

تألّم الرّجل من وجع شديد في رأسه
The patient complained of a strong headache

تامّ perfect, complete, entire; concluded, finalized, accomplished; of full value; genuine; total, integral; consummated, performed, done; outright, utter.

تَآمَرَ to plot, conspire, connive against; to deliberate, confer, consult.

تَآمُر plotting, conspiring, colluding, intriguing against; conferring, consultation, talk; conspiracy, plot, intrigue.

تَأَمَّلَ to look attentively at; to regard, contemplate, meditate, think over; to think deeply about; to ponder on.

تَأَمُّل meditation, contemplation; pondering; speculation.

تأميم nationalization.

تأمين insurance, assurance; security, guarantee; pledge, mortgage; deposit; surety.

تأمين securing, ensuring, guaranteeing; procuring, furnishing with, providing with.

تأمين reassurance, assurance.

تأمينٌ اجْتماعِيّ social security.

تأمينٌ بَحْرِيّ maritime insurance.

تأمينٌ على الحَياة life insurance.

تَأَنّى to act slowly; to proceed unhurriedly; to bide one's time; to be patient, careful, deliberate.

تَأَنَّثَ to be effeminate; to display effeminate manners; to be put in the feminine form (word).

تَأَنَّقَ to be chic, elegant, meticulous, fastidious; to be smart, neat, spruce, comely (in dressing); to be stylish, fashionable, dainty (in speaking, writing).

تأْنِيب reprimand, reprehension, rebuke, reproach; blame, censure, castigation.

تاهَ to lose one's way; to go astray; to swagger, flaunt, boast; to be haughty, arrogant; to be perplexed, baffled; to perish.

تَأَهَّبَ to be ready, prepared; to get ready; to prepare oneself; to be equipped for; to be on the alert.

تَأَهُّب preparedness, readiness preparation.

تَأَهَّلَ to get married; to be qualified, prepared, suited; to be worthy of; to deserve; to be competent.

تَأْهِيل rehabilitation, qualifying, adaptation.

تَأْهيل welcoming, greeting.

تَأَوَّهَ to moan, sigh, wail, groan.

تَأْوِيل interpretation, explanation, construction.

تَأَيَّدَ to be supported by; to be corroborated, confirmed, affirmed, sustained by; to be endorsed, approved, seconded, sanctioned by.

تَأْيِيد support, backing; approval; sanction, assent, consent, corroboration, endorsement; confirmation.

تَبَاحَثَ to discuss with or together; to have a talk with someone about; to exchange views with someone; to argue, negotiate, confer, debate with.

تَبَاحُث negotiation, parley, conference, talk, discussion.

تَبَادَرَ to appear at first glance; to suggest itself strongly; to hurry, hasten, rush to.

تَبَادَلَ to exchange, reciprocate (words, greetings, views); to receive in exchange, barter (goods, chattels); to replace, substitute something or someone by; to alternate, rotate (roles, functions, positions).

تَبادُل exchange, interchange (of views, greetings); barter, swap, exchange (goods, chattels); reciprocation; alternation, rotation.

تَبادُلِيّ reciprocal, mutual, alternance.

تَبارَى to compute, vie, contest, contend with.

تَبارَكَ to be blessed; to ask the blessing of; to see a good omen in.

تَباشير (ج) presages, omens, portents; dawn, first appearace; glad tidings, good news.

تَباطَأَ to slow down, decelerate, delay; to go slowly; to loiter, lag, stall.

تَباطُؤ slowdown, slowness, retardation; reduction of speed, deceleration; tarrying, delay, lag, stalling.

تِباعاً successively, one by one, respectively.

تَباعَدَ to be separated; to lie apart, at some distance from one another; to part company; to become estranged; to move away, withdraw, depart, keep away, avoid.

تَباعُد separation, remoteness; dissimilarity, divergence; discord, dissention; alienation, mutual estrangement, keeping away, staying away; leaving, shunning, avoidance; keeping clear of, away from.

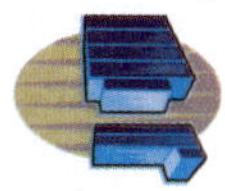

تَباكَى to pretend to be weeping, crying, lamenting.

تَباهٍ pride, vainglory, pomposity, boastfulness.

تَباهَى to be proud of; to pride oneself on; to flaunt, parade, show off; to boast of, brag of; to vie in boasting with one another.

تَبايَنَ to differ, vary; to be disparate, dissimilar; to be conflicting, contrary, opposed.

تَبايُن difference, unlikeness, disparity; inconsistency, disagreement; conflict, opposition, incongruity.

تَبْجيل veneration, reverence; esteem, exaltation; honor.

تَبَخْتَرَ to swagger, prance, mince, strut.

تَبَخَّرَ to be evaporated; to evaporate, volatilize; to be fumigated, perfumed with incense.

تَبَدَّدَ to be dispersed, scattered, driven away; to be wasted, squandered, lost; to disappear, scatter, dissolve.

تَبَدَّلَ to change, vary, transform; to be changed, varied, transfomed; to undergo change, transmutation, shifting; to turn into; to assume the form, shape or state of; to be substituted, replaced, converted

تَبَدُّل change, alteration, shift, turn, transformation; transmutation, conversion, transition.

أ ب ت ث ج ح خ د ذ ر ز س ش ص ض ط ظ ع غ ف ق ك ل م ن هـ و ي

تَبْديد dispersal, squandering, elimination; extravagance, prodigality, wasting.

تَبْديل change, alteration, mutation, modification, transformation, variation, conversion; alternation; replacement, substitution, commutation.

تَبْذير wasting, squandering, dissipation, prodigality.

تِبْر gold ore, raw gold, gold.

تَبَرَّأَ to clear oneself from (a charge); to free oneself from responsibility; to rid oneself of; to declare oneself innocent; to be acquitted, freed from a charge, exculpated, exonerated.

تَبْرِئَة acquittal, clearance, discharge; release.

تَبَرَّجَ to adorn, groom, preen, primp, spruce up (oneself, particularly a woman).

تَبَرُّج toilette, grooming, adorning, putting on makeup.

تَبَرَّزَ to excrete, defecate, evacuate the bowels.

تَبَرْطَلَ to take bribes; to be bribed.

تَبَرَّعَ to contribute, donate; to volunteer; to grant.

تَبَرُّع contribution, grant, donation, gift, present; volunteering.

تَبَرَّكَ to be blessed by; to get the blessing of; to see a good omen in.

تَبَرَّمَ to be fed up with; to be bored, sick, tired of; to become weary of; to find annoying, wearisome; to complain, growl, grumble from or of.

تَبَرُّم weariness, boredom, disgust; discontent, annoyance; discomfort; dissatisfaction; impatience, complaining.

تَبْرِيد cooling, refrigeration, freezing.

تَبْرِيدُ هَواء airconditioning.

تَبْرِير justification, rationalization.

تَبَسَّطَ to be simplified; to be made simple; to be extended, unfolded, stretched; to set forth, present, explain.

تَبَسَّطَ في الكلام to talk freely, frankly, in plain terms; to elaborate, expand on, speak at great length.

تَبْسيط simplification; facilitation.

تَبْشير announcement of glad tidings; preaching.

تَبَصَّرَ to be rational, reasonable, intelligent; to reflect, ponder on something; to be able to see, speculate; to scrutinize, meditate, consider carefully.

تَبْصير fortune-telling, sooth-saying; enlightenment, information, instruction, explanation.

تَبْطين lining, padding.

تَبِعَ to follow, succeed, come after; to trail, track; to go after someone; to walk behind someone; to pursue, adhere, stick to; to observe, enter upon, take (a road); to comply with; to belong, pertain; to be attached, under the authority of; to heed, obey, bear in mind.

تَبِعَ الدروس to follow classes or courses regularly.

تَبِعَ مِن to follow from, result from, ensue from; to be the result of; to be caused by.

تَبَعًا لِـ، تِبْعًا لِـ pursuant to, according to; depending on, owing to; as a result of; in view of; on account of.

تَبَعْثَرَ to be turned upside down; to be scattered, dispersed, strewn about; to be wasted, squandered.

تَبَعِيَّة subordination, dependency; citizenship, nationality.

تَبْغ، تِبْغ tobacco.

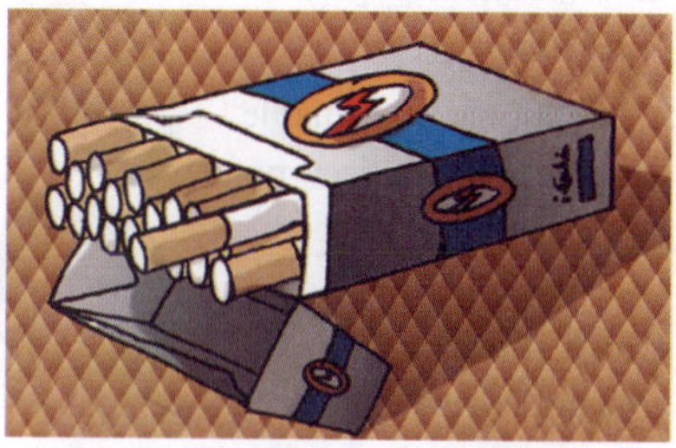

تُصنع السجائر من التبغ وهي تضرّ بالصحّة

Cigarettes are made from tobacco and are very harmful to the health

تَبْكِيت reproach, blame, uneasiness; remorse.

تَبَلْبُل anxiety, concern; confusion, chaos.

تَبَلَّغَ to be informed, notified, told; to content oneself with; to be satisfied with.

تَبَلَّلَ to become wet, moistened; drenched, showered (with water).

تَبَلْوُر crystallization

تَبْلِيط paving, tiling, flooring.

تَبْلِيغ transmission, conveyance, delivery; infomation about; report, notification of, communication, announcement, notice, proclamation.

تَبَنٍّ (التَّبَنِّي) adoption (of a child); embracement (of an idea).

تِبْن straw, hay.

تَبَنَّى to adopt (a child, an idea).

تَبَوَّأَ to hold, occupy, fill, take (a place, a position).

تَبَوَّأَ العَرْشَ to ascend the throne.

تَبَوَّلَ to urinate, make water.

تَبْوِيب classification, sectioning; grouping, systemic arrangement; division into chapters; grading; tabulation.

تَبَيَّنَ to become clear, evident, plain, distinct; to be perceived, noticed, observed, understood; to verify, examine, ascertain, recognize, see, identify.

تَبييض whitening.

تَبييضُ القماش bleaching.

تَبْييضُ النُّحاس tinplating.

تَبْييضُ الجُدران whitewashing.

تَبْيين demonstrating, showing, exhibitioning, presenting; clarification, explanation, elucidation.

تَتابَعَ to follow one another; to happen, take place consecutively; to occur repeatedly.

تَتابُع sequence, succession.

بالتَّتابُع consecutively, successively, one after the other, in turn, respectively; unceasingly; serially.

تَتالٍ (التَّتالي) succession, consecution.

بالتَّتالي successively, consecutively; one by one, one after the other; by turns, respectively; constantly.

تَتَبَّعَ to pursue; to trail, track; to watch, observe, take notice of, scrutinize; to look for; to prosecute, sue, take legal action against; to trace the origin of.

تَتَبُّع following, pursuit, chase, trailing; observation, scrutiny; prosecution; legal action.

تَتَلْمَذَ to be a pupil or apprentice of someone; to receive one's schooling or training from; to work as an apprentice under someone.

تَتِمَّة completion; accomplishment; epilogue; supplement, complement, continuation; end, conclusion .

تَتْويج coronation, crowning, enthronement; topping, capping.

تَثاءَبَ to yawn.

يتثاءب الطفل قبل أن ينام للتعبير عن نعاسه
The baby usually yawns before sleeping

تَثاقَلَ to lag, tarry, slacken; to be heavy, troublesome, burdensome; to disturb, molest, bother, annoy; to oppress, overburden; to bear down on, lie heavily on.

تَثَبَّتَ to make sure, establish, determine; to verify, ascertain; to consider carefully; to try to make sure, to find right, proven or true.

تَثَبُّت verification, making sure of, ascertainment.

تَثْبيت fixation; establishment; stabilization; consolidation; substantiation; demonstration, proving.

تَثبيط frustration, discouragement, demoralization.

تَثَقَّف to be trained, educated, enlightened; to learn, study, obtain education or knowledge.

تَثْقيف education, teaching, instruction, culture.

تَثْمين estimation, evaluation, appreciation, valuation.

تَثَنَّى to double; to become double; to be doubled, repeated; to bend, lean, incline, bow; to turn away from; to walk with a swinging gait; to swing, roll.

تَثْنِيَة duplication, germination, repetition; pleating, plaiting (of a dress); seconding (a decision).

تَجادَل to contend, squabble, dispute, debate with; to have an argument with; to carry on a dispute; to bicker, wrangle, discuss with.

تِجارَة commerce, trade, business; merchandise, goods, chattels.

تِجارَةُ الرَّقيقِ الأبيض white slavery.

تِجارِيّ commercial, mercantile, trade, trading.

تَجاسَر to dare, venture; to be bold, daring, insolent; to have the audacity to do something.

تَجاعيد (ج) wrinkles, furrows.

تَجانُس homogeneity, homogeneousness, resemblance, analogy, uniformity; conformity; similarity.

تُجاه، تِجاه in front of; facing, opposite.

تَجاهَل to disregard (a fact); to pretend ignorance of; to ignore, disregard, neglect, overlook; to abstain from recognizing (a fact); to feign ignorance of.

تَجاوَب to respond to; to accede to the request of; to concur; to reply to one another; to be favorable, propitious to someone; to listen, pay attention to; to harmonize with; to be in accord with.

تَجاوُب allergy (med).

تَجاوَر to be neighbors; to live near each other; to be adjacent, neighboring, close, near.

تَجاوَز to go past something; to go beyond something; to overstep, cross, leave behind; to exceed, surpass, disregard, pay no attention; to relinquish, give up, forgo; to traverse; to go too far, overstep all bounds; to encroach, make inroads, trespass, transgress upon; to pardon, excuse; to omit, leave out, waive; to abstain, refrain, desist from.

تجاورت العائلتان فأصبح أفرادها أصدقاء
The two families became neighbors and established friendship among their members

تَجاوُز passing, leaving behind, overtaking, getting beyond, surpassing; going too far, overstepping all bounds, exceeding the limits; trespassing, encroachment, making inroads upon; surmounting, overcoming, defeating, coping with; disregarding, pardon, remission, excuse; omission, neglect; giving up, relinquishment; abstention from, refraining from, overstepping the limits of authority, misuse of power.

تَجَبَّرَ to be haughty, arrogant, tyrannical; to tyrannize.

تَجَدَّدَ to become new; to be renewed; to revive; to be rejuvenated, regenerated, refreshed, rebuilt.

تَجَدُّد renewal, renovation, revival, regeneration.

تَجْديد renewal, renovation, revival, regeneration, reconstruction, modernization, reform; innovation; rejuvenation of youth.

تَجْديف blasphemy, profanity; imprecation.

تَجْديف rowing, oaring.

تَجْديل braiding, plaiting.

تَجْذير root extraction (math).

تَجَرَّأَ to dare, venture, risk; to take the risk of doing something; to have the courage for; to be venturesome, bold, audacious.

تَجْرِبَة experiment, test, trial; rehearsal, audition; experience, endeavor, attempt; tribulation, ordeal; proof (printting); probation, tryout.

تَجَرَّدَ to free oneself from; to give up something; to be free from; to devote oneself exclusively to; to give up, renounce, divest oneself of; to strip, undress, disrobe (clothes); to be impartial, unbiased, objective.

تَجَرُّد objectivity; impartiality; stripping, undressing; devotion to, dedication to do something.

تَجْرِيبيّ experimental, empirical.

تَجْريح deformation, slander, libel; contestation; refutation.

تَجْريد divestiture, deprivation, dispossessioning; freeing from; voiding, emptying; denudation, stripping, undressing.

تَجْريد abstraction (of an idea).

تَجْريدٌ مِن السِّلاح disarmament; demilitarization.

تَجْريدٌ مِن المِلْكِيَّة expropriation, confiscation, dispossession.

تَجْريم incrimination, inculpation; unloading (a ship).

تَجَزَّأَ to be divided, partitioned, split, sectioned.

تَجْزِئَة partitioning; splitting, division, dividing; dissociation; fragmentation.

تَجَسَّدَ to materialize, take shape, form; to be embodied, incorporated.

تَجَسَّسَ to spy on; to snoop on; to gather information for; to be engaged in espionage; to reconnoiter, scout, explore.

تَجَسُّس espionage, spying.

تَجْسيد embodiment, incorporation, materialization

تَجْسيم enlargement; exaggeration; incorporation; protrusion, embossment, relief.

تَجَشَّأ to belch, burp.

تَجَشَّم to suffer, endure; assume, undertake; to take pains to do something.

تَجَعَّد to curl, frizz (the hair); to crease, pleat, plait (cloth); to wrinkle (skin); to be wavy, curly, frizzed (hair); to be creased, pleated (cloth); to be wrinkled (skin).

تَجْفيف drying, desiccation, dehydratation; drainage.

تَجَلَّى to be clear, distinct, evident, explicit; to manifest, reveal, appear, emerge; to be revealed, expressed, manifested; to come to light.

تَجَلَّد to be frozen, be covered with ice; to take heart; to show toughness;to resign oneself; to bear, suffer with patience.

تَجَلَّل to be glorified, dignified, honored, venerated; to cover oneself in.

تَجْليد freezing; bookbinding.

تَجَمَّد to freeze, frost, congeal; to coagulate, harden, stiffen; to become frozen; to turn into ice; to become icebound; to freeze to death; to set (cement); to clot (blood); to curdle.

تَجَمَّع to gather, assemble, congregate, rally, band together; to pile up, accumulate; to come together, meet; to join, unite, combine.

تَجَمُّع gathering, congregation, meeting, coming together; concentration (of troops); crowd, throng, agglomeration.

تَجَمَّل to adorn oneself; to be adorned, embellished.

تَجَمَّل بالصَّبْر to be patient, forbearing; to endure, suffer with patience.

تَجَمْهَر to gather, assemble, congregate; to crowd together; to flock together; to team, rally, swarm, throng.

تَجْميد freezing, frosting, congelation, solidification, hardening; coagulation, clotting (of blood).

تَجْميع accumulation, amassment, collecting, assemblage, fitting together; uniting, grouping; crowding; concentration (of troops).

تَجْميل adornment; application of cosmetics (on face); prettying up, making beautiful.

تَجَنَّى to accuse falsely; to incriminate, blame, charge someone unjustly.

تَجَنَّب to avoid, shun, avert, ward off; to keep oneself out of the way of; to steer clear of; to prevent; to flee from, escape, evade, dodge.

تَجْنيد draft, enlistment, mobilization, conscription; compulsory service in the armed forces.

تَجْنيس naturalization.

تَجْهيز equipping supplying, providing; readying; equipment, furnishment.

تَجْهيزات (ج) equipments, supplies, provisions, gear, appliances, implements, fixtures, installations.

تَجَوَّل to roam, wander about, move around; to cruise, tour, travel about.

تَجْويع starving; starvation.

تَجْويف hollow, hole, cavity, bore, pocket, socket; excavation, hollowing up.

تَجْيير endorsement (cheque, bond).

تَحادَثَ to engage in a conversation with; to converse, chat, speak; to talk to someone about something.

تَحارَبَ to fight one another; to make war with; to be engaged in a war with.

تَحاشَى to avoid; to keep away, stand aloof from; to shun, beware, be on one's guard; to abstain from.

تَحالَفَ to join in alliance; to form an alliance with; to enter in a confederation, an alliance.

تَحالُف alliance, confederation.

تَحامَلَ to take sides against; to wrong, oppress; to treat unjustly, badly; to discriminate against.

تَحامَلَ على نَفْسِهِ to force oneself to do something; to gather one's strength, energy, power to do something; to overexert, strain oneself.

تَحاوَرَ to hold talks with someone; to argue, dialogue with another; to discuss, carry on a discussion with.

تَحايَلَ to dodge, evade something; to deceive by pretenses; to proceed cunningly; to employ artful means; to resort to tricks; to deceive, beguile, dupe, cheat.

تَحَبَّبَ إلى to endear oneself to; to flatter, court, woo, seek the affection of.

تَحَبَّبَ to granulate; to become granulated.

تَحَبُّب granulation.

تَحْبيذ advocacy, sanctioning, endorsement, support, acclaim, praise; recommendation, commendation.

تَحتَ ، تَحتُ under, below, beneath, down, dowstairs; on, in at, subject.

تَحتَ التَّجْرِبَة on probation.

تَحتَ التَّحْضير in preparation.

تَحتَ السِّلاح under arms.

تَحتَ تَصَرُّفِه at his disposal.

تَحتَ الطَّبْع in press.

تَحتَ التَّمْرين in training.

تَحْتَ اليَدّ at hand, available.

تَحْتَ الدَّرْس under consideration.

تَحْتَ رَحْمَةِ كَذا at the mercy of.

تَحْتَ الطَّلَب on demand.

تَحْتانِي lower, low, under; sub-; at the bottom of, underlying, inferior.

تَحَتَّم to be obligatory, necessary, mandatory, imperative; to be incumbent upon; to be someone's duty.

تَحَدَّى to challenge, compete, provoke, defy; to oppose, resist, withstand, stand up against; to incite, arouse.

تَحَدَّث to speak, talk to; to converse with someone about something; to address someone; to call up (by telephone); to have a conversation with.

تَحَدَّد to be defined, determined, fixed, designated, indicated, set, appointed; to be demarcated (boundaries); to be limited, restricted, confined.

تَحَدَّر to descend from, be born from, derive one's origins from; to come down , glide down; to be in decline; to decline; to flow down (tears); to slant down, slope down.

تَحْدِيث modernization, updating; speaking, talking.

تَحْدِيد definition, designation, taking down, appointment (of frontiers); limitation, restriction, confinement; sharpening, pointing.

تَحْدِيدُ الأَسْعار price fixing.

تَحْدِيدُ النَّسْل birth control.

تَحْدِيق staring, gazing, stare.

تَحْذِير warning, admonition, cautioning.

تَحَرٍّ (التَّحَرِّي) investigation, inspection; surveying, inquiry; detection; detective, investigator.

تَحَرَّى to examine, investigate, inquire; to make inquiries about; to take care of; to attend to; to look after; to try to find out, ascertain, detect, determine.

تَحَرَّر to be free, freed, liberated; to be released, relieved; to release oneself; to be emancipated, liberated, set free, released from bondage (slave).

تَحَرُّر freedom, emancipation; release, liberation.

تَحَرَّش to molest; to solicit; to pick a quarrel, start a brawl; to provoke, instigate, prod, incite; to meddle in, interfere in, intrude upon.

تَحَرَّق to be overcome with longing; to yearn ardently for; to hunger for; to long desperately for; to be aflame, consumed by fire, burned, pained.

تَحَرَّك to move, stir, get started; to be in motion, get moving, start out, depart, leave (train); to sail (ship); to react, respond, take a step, take action.

أ ب ت ث ج ح خ د ذ ر ز س ش ص ض ط ظ ع غ ف ق ك ل م ن هـ و ي

تَحَرُّك motion, movement, step, activity, reaction, response.

تَحْرِيج afforestation; tightening; prohibition; insistence.

تَحْرِير liberation, release, emancipation; writing, editing, redaction; letter, brief, record; discharge, disengagement; acquittal, absolution.

تَحْرِيض instigation, provocation, inducement, stirring up, prodding, urging; induction (electricity).

تَحْرِيف distortion, alteration; perversion, corruption (of a word); canting, tilting; deviation; swerving.

تَحْرِيك shaking, moving; stimulation, actuation, stirring; starting, initiation; awakening, fomenting; vowelization (grammar); revival; prosecution (lawsuit).

تَحْرِيم forbiddance, interdiction, prohibition, ban.

تَحَزُّب factionalism, advocacy, partisanship; favoritism, siding with; backing, patronage; formation of a party; coming together, rallying.

تَحَزَّز to be indented, grooved, fluted, notched, serrated.

تَحْزِيم packaging, packing; fastening, girding.

تَحَسَّر to regret; to be grieved, pained by; to sigh; to be distressed, sad, sorrowful.

تَحَسَّس to grope, probe for; to touch, run the hand over; to feel around; to seek information, make inquiries; to sense, perceive, experience; to search for, look for.

تَحَسُّس feeling, sensation, perception; seeking information.

تَحَسَّن to improve; to become better; to be more attractive, beautiful, nicer.

تَحَسُّن improvement, amelioration.

تَحْسِين improvement, amelioration, embellishment.

تَحَشَّم to be reticent, modest, shy, bashful, diffident.

تَحَصَّن to be fortified, strengthened; to become protected, immunized against.

تَحْصِيص allotment, allocation, distribution.

تَحْصِيل collection, raising, levying (of taxes, fees); attainment; gain; acquisition; learning, studying; income, revenue, receipts; resumé, summary; gist (of a speech, an opinion).

تَحْصِيلُ حاصِل in summary, beyond doubt; definite; indisputable.

تَحْصِين fortification, reinforcement; immunization.

تَحَضُّر civilization, urbanization.

تَحْضِير preparation, producing, readying.

تَحْضِيرِيّ preparatory, preliminary.

تَحَطَّم to break, go to pieces; to be broken, smashed, shattered; to crash; to be wrecked (ship); to be destroyed, crumbled.

تَحْطيم breaking, crashing, shattering, crushing.

تُحْفَة masterpiece, chef d'oeuvre, rarity; work of art; gift, present.

يحتوي المتحف على تحف أثرية ثمينة ونادرة

The museum contains many precious and rare pieces of antiquities

---

تَحَفَّزَ to get ready, prepare oneself for action; to be on the alert; to listen, pay attention.

تَحَفَّظَ to be mindful, heedful; to stay, suspend (a judicial investigation); to uphold, sustain, keep; to have reservations; to put away; to reserve for oneself; to memorize.

تَحَفُّظ reservation, caution, precautionary measure; conditional stipulation.

تَحَفُّظِيّ precautionary, protective (measures, actions).

تَحْفيز catalysis (chem).

تَحَقَّقَ to materialize; to become realized; to be achieved, fulfilled, effected, affirmed, established.

تَحَقَّقَ من to make sure, ascertain, check, verify; to recognize, find out, substantiate, assert.

تَحْقير contempt, disdain, scorn, humiliation; insult; depreciation.

تَحْقيق realization, accomplishment, execution; bringing about, putting into effect; securing, ensuring; satisfaction, fulfillment; verification, confirmation.

تَحْقيق inquiry, investigation, interrogation, inquest.

تَحْقيقٌ صُحُفِيّ reportage, press report.

تَحَكُّم arbitrariness, despotism; control, command; domination, rule, power, dominion.

تَحَكُّمٌ مِن بُعْد remote control.

تَحْكيم arbitration; award; arbitral decision.

تَحَلَّى to be sweet; to be adorned; to be sweetened; to be embellished; to be provided with; to be endowed with, distinguished by.

تَحَلَّلَ to disengage oneself from; to extricate oneself from; to become slack, limp, weak; to disintegrate, melt away; to be decomposed; to be legitimate, permissible.

تَحْلِيَة sweetening; decoration, embellishment.

تَحْليق flying, hovering (airplane); flying; flight (birds); ascending, rising.

تَحَلَّق to circle in the air; to gather in a circle; to form a circle around.

تَحْلِيل analysis, breaking down, disintegration.

تَحْلِيل legalization, sanctioning, allowing.

تَحْلِيلٌ كَهْرَبائِيّ electrolysis.

تَحْلِيلٌ كِيمْيائِيّ chemical analysis.

تَحْلِيلٌ نَفْسِيّ psychoanalysis.

تَحَمَّس to be enthusiastic, zealous, eager; to get excited; to be overzealous; to advocate fervently.

تَحَمَّل to bear, sustain, support, tolerate.

تَحَمَّل to assume, undertake, shoulder, carry.

تَحَمُّل endurance, supporting, fortitude, bearing.

تَحَمُّل assumption (of a mission, job); undertaking of; shouldering, carrying.

تَحَمُّل durability, burdening, encumbering.

تَحْمِيلَة suppository (med).

تَحْنِيط mummification; embalment; stuffing.

تَحَوُّط provision, care, attention; precaution; prudence.

تَحَوَّل to be changed, transformed, converted, made into; to turn away from; to change; to turn, grow into; to develop, evolve from; to withdraw, deviate from; to depart, digress, stray (from the way); to renounce, relinquish, disclaim; to switch from.

تَحْوِير alteration; distortion; conversion; changing.

تَحْوِيل alteration, change; switching; transformation, conversion; transposition, inversion; displacement; transfer, assignment.

تَحْوِيلُ النُّقُود remittance, transfer.

تَحْوِيلٌ عَنْ diversion, deviation, detraction from.

تَحِيَّة greeting, salute.

تَحِيَّات (ج) compliments, regards, respects.

تَحَيَّر to be confused, puzzled, perplexed, bewildered; to be at a loss; to hesitate; to be unable to choose (between); to be dismayed, embarrassed, startled.

تَحَيُّز partiality, favoritism; taking sides with; bias, prejudice; one-sidedness.

تَحَيَّن to wait for an opportunity; to bid one's time.

تَخَابَث to behave wickedly; to show malice; to be wicked, evil, wily, sly.

تَخَابَر to communicate with; to contact each other; to call one another (over the phone); to correspond, write to each other; to exchange letters, informations.

تَخَاذُل weakness, feebleness, languor; dissent, disagreement.

تَخَاصَم to quarrel, argue, dispute with; to bring legal action against; to have a fight with.

أ ب ت ث ج ح خ د ذ ر ز س ش ص ض ط ظ ع غ ف ق ك ل م ن هـ و ي

تَخَاطَبَ to talk to one another; to hold a conversation, discussion, communication.

تَخَالَصَ to be quits, even; to agree, come to an agreement; to come to terms; to be sincere, honest with one another.

تَخَالُط blending, mixing, mingling; association with.

تَخَالُف dissimilarity; variety; disagreement; divergence; contradiction; clash, variance; inconsistency.

تَخَبَّطَ to be lost, wander about; to grope about; to struggle, resist, fumble about, toss about; to fall victim to; to be immersed in; to run in disorder; to become disordered; to become disturbed, muddled; to get all mixed up.

تَخْت bedstead; sofa, couch; cabinet, chest, wardrobe.

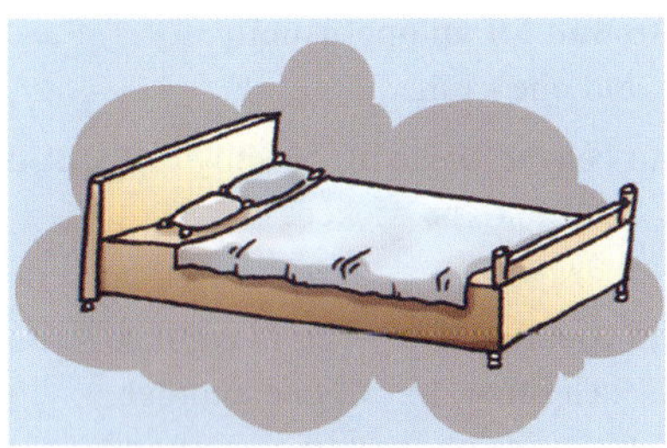

أنام في الليل على تختي الوثير
I sleep on a very cosy couch at night

تَخَثُّر coagulation, clotting (of blood); curdling, thickening (of milk).

تَخَدَّرَ to be anesthetized, doped, dazed, benumbed; to come to rest, calm down; to stay at a place.

تَخْدِير grooving, furrowing.

تَخْدِير anesthetization, doping; anesthesia.

تَخَرَّجَ to graduate from (a college); to be educated in.

تَخْرِيب destruction, devastation, wrecking; sabotage.

تَخْرِيج graduation; explanation; facing, lining (fabrics).

تَخْرِيم piercing; lace, lacework; punching, perforation.

تَخْزِين storage, storing, warehousing.

تَخَشَّعَ to show reverence; to display humility; to be humble, moved, touched; to implore, beg, supplicate.

تَخْشِيبة hut, wooden shed.

تَخَصَّصَ to specialize (in a scientific field); to devote all one's attention to; to apply oneself to; to be peculiar to; to be distinguished by; to be duly qualified, comptent.

تَخْصِيص singling out, setting aside, earmarking; allotment, allocation; dedication, consecretion.

تَخَضَّب to be dyed, colored, pigmented.

تَخَضَّب بالدَّم to be bloodstained, ensanguined.

أ ب ت ث ج ح خ د ذ ر ز س ش ص ض ط ظ ع غ ف ق ك ل م ن هـ و ي

تَخَطّى to overstep, transgress, cross; to ford (a river); to go beyond, exceed, transcend; to overtake, outdistance; to encroach upon; to skip, disregard, omit; to pass through.

تَخْطيط ruling, drawing of, marking with; lineation, marking; planning, marking out, laying out; plan, design, layout; sketch, outline; diagram.

تَخَفّى to disguise oneself; to be hidden; to disappear from sight; to keep oneself out of view; to be hidden, concealed.

تَخْفيض reduction, decrease, lowering; abatement, lessening; devaluation (of currency).

تَخْفيف decrease, lessening, lightening; mitigation, easing, alleviation; attenuation; tempering, toning down.

تَخْفيف dilution, thinning (of paint); reduction (of tension); deceleration (of speed); commutation (of punishment).

تَخَلّى to abandon, give up, surrender, renounce, quit; to abdicate (a throne); to desert, forsake (in time of need); to desist, refrain from; to cede, leave; to lay down; to step aside.

تَخَلْخَلَ to be shaken, rocked; to come off, become disjointed; to become loose, detached; to become shabby, tattered; to be rarefied (chem).

تَخَلَّصَ to get rid of, dispense with, dispose of; to discard, throw away, remove, eliminate; to be freed, delivered, saved, rescued; to extract, extricate oneself from.

تَخَلَّفَ to lag, fall behind; to tarry, linger; to fail to appear, show up; to be absent; to fail to come or arrive.

تَخَلُّف lag, falling behind, tarring, lingering; non attendance, absence, failure to attend (a meeting); default (in paying one's debt in time); failure to appear (in court).

تَخَلُّف underdevelopment, backwardness.

تَخَلُّفٌ عَقْليّ mental retardation, idiocy.

تَخَلَّلَ to pervade, percolate, infiltrate; to intervene; to lie in between; to pick one's teeth; to acetify.

تَخْلِية leaving, abandonment, giving up; desistance, abstention; vacating, evacuation; emptying, voiding, draining; relinquishment; exoneration, exculpation (of a culprit).

تَخْليد perpetuation, immortalization; commemoration.

تَخْليداً لِذِكْرى in commemoration of; in remembrance of.

تَخْليص salvation, rescue, saving; freeing, release, riddance; clearing; purification; clearance (of goods).

تَخَمَ to fix the limits of; to confine, bound; to border on; to be adjacent to.

تَخِمَ to suffer from indigestion; to feel sick from overeating; to surfeit, satiate (the stomach).

تَخْم، تُخْم boundary, frontier, border.

تُخْمَة indigestion, surfeit, satiety, dyspepsia.

تَخَمُّر fermentation.

تَخْمير fermentation; leavening (of dough); brewage (of beer).

تَخْمين guessing, surmise; assessment, appraisal, evaluation, estimation.

تَخَوَّفَ to fear; to be afraid, frightened, scared, anxious, alarmed, apprehensive for.

تَخْويف intimidation; bullying, cowing, frightening, scaring; terrifying.

تَخْويل authorization, accreditation; entrustment, delegation of authority; granting, bestowal.

تَخَيَّرَ to choose, select, pick; make one's choice, prefer.

تَخَيَّلَ to imagine, fancy, deem, believe that; to suspect good qualities in someone; to pretend; to feel self-important; to behave pompously; to conceive eccentric ideas.

تَخَيُّل imagination, fancying, conception; pretension; feeling self-important; behaving pompously; suspecting good qualities in someone; fantasy, delusion, whim, hallucination.

تَدَاخَلَ to overlap, interlock, interface, mesh; to be superimposed, merged, blended; to join, participate in, take part in; to meddle, interfere, intrude.

تَدَاخُل interference, interlock, interlacement, meshing, gearing; superimposition; pervasion; merger, blending.

تَدَارَسَ to study, consider carefully, look into; to discuss, deliberate, exchange views on something with another.

تَدَارَكَ to set right, put right, correct, amend; to repair, redress; to prevent, forestall, avert, ward off; to follow up with; to cause to be followed up; to follow in succession; to take steps to prevent; to provide indemnity (for a loss).

تَدَاعَى to falter; to be dilapidated; to sink, cave in, fall down; to collapse; to rally, flock together; to sue one another in court; to carry on a lawsuit.

تَدَافَعَ to push one another, to scramble; to shove one another; to gush forth, burst forth, rush out.

تَدَاوَى to be cured; to treat oneself; to receive medical treatment.

تَدَاوَلَ to confer, talk, discuss with someone about something; to hold a discussion with; to circulate, put into circulation; to alternate, rotate; to pass from hand to hand; to spread from mouth to mouth; to change hands.

تَدَبَّرَ	to ponder, reflect on; to consider carefully; to manage, contrive; to obtain, secure, take care of; to do with, get by with what one possesses; to plan, organize, devise; to manage well.

تَدْبِيج	embellishment, decoration; composition, writing.
تَدْبِير	planning, organization, management, mapping out; regulation; economization; measure, step, move; procurement, acquisition; accomplishment.
تَدْبِيرٌ مَنْزِلِيّ	housekeeping, home economics.
تَدْبِيرٌ وَقَائِيّ	precautionary measure, precaution; safety measure.
تَدَثَّرَ	to cover, envelop oneself with.
تَدَحْرَجَ	to roll along, to roll down.
تَدَخَّلَ	to interfere, intervene, meddle in; to intrude upon.
تَدَخُّل	intrusion, obtrusion, intervention, interference.
تَدْخِين	smoking; fumigation, fuming.
تَدَرَّبَ	to practise, exercise oneself; to be trained, coached, tutored; to be apprenticed; to get used to.
تَدَرُّب	training, practice; apprenticeship; habitation.
تَدَرَّجَ	to advance step by step; to make gradual progress; to become graded, gradated, graduated; to be apprenticed, trained.
تَدَرُّن	tuberculosis.
تَدْرِيب	training, coaching, tutoring; practice, habituation, schooling, drill, apprenticeship; rehearsal (play).
تَدْرِيج	graduation, grading, gradation; calibration; popularization, promotion, spreading.
تَدْرِيجِيًّا	gradually, step by step, bit by bit, progressively.
تَدْرِيس	teaching, instruction, tuition, educating.
تَدْشِين	inauguration, opening.
تَدْعِيم	support, strengthening, reinforcement, consolidation, buttressing, shoring up.
تَدْفِئَة	heating, warming.
تَدْفِئَةٌ مَرْكَزِيَّة	central heating

تَدَفُّق	flow, outflow, outpour, effluence; outbreak, inpour, outburst; exuberance, effusion; spurting.
تَدْقِيق	checking out, check up, verification; accuracy, precision, exactness; investigation, inquiry.
تَدْقِيقُ الحِسَابات	auditing of accounts.
تَدَلَّى	to hang down, dangle; to be suspended, lowered; to be low; to sink, descend.
تَدْلِيع	pampering, spoiling, coddling (a child); fondling, petting, caressing.
تَدْلِيك	massage, rubdown; embrocation.
تَدْلِيل	pampering, spoiling, coddling (a child); fondling, petting, caressing.

تَدْليل proving, verification; furnishing of evidence.

تَدْمير destruction, annihilation, demolition, wrecking.

تَدَنَّى to sink; to drop, fall, decline; to be mean, base, vile, despicable; to come closer, get close; to be near, close; to approach.

تَدْنيس soiling, dirtying, staining; profanation, desecration, sacrilege, defilement; pollution, contamination, disgracing.

تَدَهْوَرَ to fall, crash; to hurl down, topple, overthrow; to slump, sink to be lowest level.

تَدَهْوُر downfall, tumble, crash, drop, deterioration, decline.

تَدْوير turning, rotating, revolving; operation, start up; putting in operation; rounding, making round; winding (a clock); rounding off (a number).

تَدْويل internationalization.

تَدْويم spinning, whirling, rotation, turning; putting in operation; perseverence, perpetration.

تَدْوين registration, recording, writing down, putting in writing, entering, inscription; entry, in a register, record, book.

تَذَبْذَبَ to oscillate, vibrate, wobble; to hesitate, falter, fluctuate.

تَذَرَّعَ to use as a pretext; to use as a means; to plead, invoke, claim, allege.

تَذْكار token, souvenir, reminder; memorial; remembrance.

تَذَكَّرَ to remember, bear in mind, think of; recall.

تَذْكِرَة reminder; ticket, card.

تذكِرة دخول ticket, admission card.

تَذكِرَة ذهاب وإياب return ticket, round-trip ticket.

تذكِرَة مرور permit, laissez-passer.

تذكِرَة هُوِيَّة identity card; identification card.

تَذْكير reminding of; reminder.

تَذَلَّلَ to lower, debase, degrade, humiliate, humble oneself; to be humble, obsequious; to act in a servile manner.

تَذْليل overcoming, ironing out, smoothing out; derogation, degradation, surmounting (an obstacle).

تَذَمَّرَ to complain, grumble.

تَذَمُّر grumbling, complaint, grievance.

تَذَوَّقَ to taste, savor, relish.

تَذْييل appending, annexation; annotation; footnote, comment, commentary.

تُرى I wonder; do you think? what's your opinion?.

تَراءَى to appear to; to deem, think, believe; to be thought proper; to look at something; to contemplate; to be of the opinion that; to have, form an opinion; to see one another; to assume, suppose, envisage; to envision, visualize.

تُراب dirt; earth, soil; ground.

تَرابُط correlation, interrelation, linkup, coherence; association (of ideas); dependence, connection.

تُراث heritage, legacy, patrimony.

تَراجَعَ to retreat; to fall back; to refrain, withdraw, revoke, repeal (a decision); to retrace one's steps; to fall off, back off; to retrograde; to retract.

تَراجُع retreat, fallback, retraction; retrogression, backing down; going back on one's words.

تَراخى to slacken, droop, relax, sag.

تَرادُف synonymity; succession, sequence.

تَراسُل correspondence, exchange of letters.

تَراصَفَ to align, line up; to be aligned, lined up.

تَراضٍ (التَّراضي) mutual consent, mutual agreement.

تَرافَعَ to plead, argue a case in court; to defend in court.

تَرافَقَ to be associated with; to accompany one another.

تَراكُب overlapping, superimposition, overlaying.

تَراكَمَ to pile up, heap up, accumulate, gather, amass.

تَرامى to throw oneself at someone's feet; to throw oneself on the ground, on the bed; to fall to the ground; to extend, reach; to be wide, extensive; to come to one's knowledge; to learn about, hear off.

تَراوَحَ to fluctuate, alternate, vary between; to intervene, lie between two events; to sway, swing.

تَرِب dusty, full of earth; poor, needy.

تِرْب contemporary; comrade, friend, colleague.

تَرَبّى to be brought up (child); to be nursed, educated, taught, reared, bred, raised.

تُرْبَة soil, ground; cemetery, burial ground; grave, tomb.

تَرَبَّصَ to lurk, lie in wait for; to lay in ambush.

تَرْبَويّ educational.

تَرْبِيَة education, pedagogy, teaching; upbringing, raising, breeding (child, animal); pisciculture (fish); aviculture (birds).

تَرْبِيَةٌ بَدَنِيَّة physical education.

تَرْبِيَةٌ مَدَنِيَّة civics.

تَرْبِيَةٌ مِهَنِيَّة vocational education.

تَرَتَّبَ to result from; to be arranged, organized along the lines of; to be caused, grow out of, occasioned by; to be incumbent upon; to be someone's duty; to become necessary, obligatory, mandatory.

تَرَتَّبَ بِذِمَّتِهِ to be indebted; to owe.

تَرْتيب arrangement, order, array; setup, layout; organization, measure, step; classification; disposal; preparation, making ready; makeup, structure.

تَرتيبٌ ألفبائيّ alphabetical order.

تَرْتيبات (ج) arrangements, plans, measures.

تَرْتيبيّ ordinal (number).

تَرْتيل slow recitation of the Koran; intonation, hymning.

تَرْتيلَة hymn, psalm; chant, song.

تَرَجَّلَ to dismount, get down; to assume masculine manners (woman); to behave like a man (woman).

تَرْجَمَ to translate, interpret, explain.

تُرْجُمان translator, interpreter.

تَرْجَمَة translation, interpretation, explanation; biography; preface, foreword (of a book).

تَرَح grief, sadness, sorrow.

تَرِح sad, grieved, distressed.

تَرَحَّمَ to ask God to have mercy upon.

تَرْحيب welcome, greeting; hospitality.

تَرْحيل eviction, dislodgment, exile, deportation; posting (account books); moving, transportation.

تَرْخيص authorization, permission, license; leave, permit, granting of permission; concession; price cut, price reduction.

تَرَدَّدَ to hesitate; to be reluctant to do something; to waver, become doubtful; to be frequently discussed; to desist, refrain, give up, quit, leave.

تَرَدَّدَ to reverberate, rebound; to be reflected (sound, voice); to frequent, visit often (a place).

تَرَدُّد hesitation, wavering, irresolution; frequency (electricity); frequentation (of a place).

تَرْديد repetition, reiteration.

تِرْس sprocket wheel, pinion.

تَرَسَّخَ to take root; to be fixed firmly; to be secured in one's place; to be deeply rooted; to be solid, firm, stable; to be conversant, well versed in.

تَرَسَّمَ to follow someone's example; to imitate, copy, emulate; to be appointed (to a public office); to scrutinize, look attentively; to remember, recollect.

تَرْسيب precipitation, sedimentation.

تَرَشَّحَ to be nominated as a candidate; to be a nominee.

تَرَشَّحَ to catch a cold; to filter.

تَرْشيح filtration, percolation.

تَرْشيد rationalization; guidance, direction, directive; pointing out, calling someone's attention to; giving an advice to; to show the right way to.

تَرْضِيَة gratification; satisfaction; compensation.

تَرْطيب moistening, wetting, damping.

تُرْعَة canal, waterway, aqueduct.

تَرَعْرَعَ to grow up, develop, flourish, thrive.

تَرِفَ to lead a luxurious life; to live in opulence, luxury.

تَرَف luxury, opulence, affluence, high living.

تَرِف opulent, sumptuous, luxurious, ornate; living in ease and luxury.

تَرَفَّعَ to deem oneself above something; to be too proud; to bear one's head high; to be arrogant, snobbish, haughty; to look down upon; to disdain.

تَرَفَّعَ to be promoted, advanced (to the rank of).

تَرَفَّقَ to be kind, friendly, nice to; to treat gently; to display a friendly attitude toward someone; to proceed slowly or gently; to show leniency toward someone.

تَرْفيع promotion, advancement (in rank, position); uplifting.

تَرْفِيه amusement, entertainment, recreation.

تَرَقَّبَ to expect, watch, keep an eye on; to look forward to; to lie in wait, anticipate, wait, await.

تَرَقْرَقَ to overflow with tears; to flow; to ripple, wave; to glitter, glisten, glimmer.

تَرْقِيَة promotion, advancement (in rank, position); upgrading, elevation, raising; extension, development.

تَرْقيع patching (of dress); grafting (of skin).

تَرْقيم numbering; paging; punctuation.

تَرَكَ to leave, relinquish, renounce, abandon, abstain from, refrain from; to omit, leave out, neglect, skip; to allow, permit someone do as he pleases.

تَرْك leaving, abandonment, relinquishment; omission, overlooking, disregard.

تَرِكَة، تِرْكَة estate, inheritance, bequest.

تَرَكَّزَ to be concentrated on; to focus, center on; to settle down; to be settled, fastened, positioned.

تَرْكِيب assembling, assembly, fitting together, setting up; composition, fabrication; fixing, placing, fitting; structure, makeup, setup; constitution, formation.

تَرْكيز fastening, fixing, stabilization; centering, focusing; concentration, condensation; emphasis, highlighting.

تَرَمَّلَ to lose one's wife (man); to lose one's husband (woman); to become a widower (man), to become a widow (woman).

تَرْميم repair, overhauling; reconditioning; restoration.

تَرَنَّحَ to stagger, totter, sway, falter, reel, shake, rock.

تُرَّهَة triviality; farce, lie, hoax, trifle.

تَرَهَّلَ to be flabby, soft, bloated, fat.

تَرْهيب intimidation, threatening, scaring, alarming, terrorizing.

تَرَوَّى to ponder, reflect on, think over; to consider carefully; to act slowly or carefully.

تَرْوِيض taming, domesticating (an animal); breaking in, training (an animal); training, coaching someone; pacifying, placating someone.

تَرْوِيع frightening, scaring, alarming.

تَرَيَّثَ to hesitate, delay, tarry; to linger, bide one's time, wait; to be patient.

تَزَاحَمَ to compete, contend; to crowd, throng together; to jostle, shove, hustle, press.

تَزَامَنَ to coincide, concur, synchronize; to be simultaneous; to occur at the same time.

تَزَامُن synchronization, simultaneity, coincidence.

تَزَاوَرَ to exchange visits; to visit one another.

تَزَايَدَ to become more, greater; to augment, increase; to outbid one another; to be compounded.

تَزَايُد increase, growth, rise, intensification; raising, buildup, increment.

تَزْجِيج glazing, vitrification.

تَزَحْزَحَ to budge, move; to be dislodged, displaced.

تَزَحْلَقَ to slide, glide, slip, skid; to ski; to skate.

تَزَعْزَعَ to shake, totter; to be shaken, convulsed, unsettled; to become shaky, unsteady.

تَزَعَّمَ to lead; to be at the head of; to become the leader, chief, boss (of a group, a country, a team).

تَزْكِيَة recommendation; purification.

بالتَّزْكِيَة uncontested, unopposed.

تَزَلَّجَ to ski, skate, glide, slip (on snow).

تَزَلُّج skiing, skating, sliding, gliding.

تَزَلَّفَ to flatter, fawn upon, curry favor, ingratiate oneself.

تَزْلِيق lubrication, oiling, greasing.

تَزَمَّتَ to be prim, sedate, staid, grave, stern, narrowminded, puritanical, strict.

تَزَوَّجَ to marry, unite in matrimony; to get married, to wed; to take as spouse; to become husband and wife.

تَزَوَّدَ to be supplied with provisions; to equip oneself with; to provide oneself with.

تَزْوِيد providing, supplying, furnishing; supply, provision, equipment with.

تَزْوِير forgery, falsification.

تَزَيَّنَ to be adorned, embellished, decorated; to adorn oneself; to preen, primp, smarten up oneself; to put on makeup, use cosmetics; to shave, get a shave.

تَزْيِيت oiling, lubrication.

تَزْيِيف forgery, falsification, counterfeiting.

أ ب ت ث ج ح خ د ذ ر ز س ش ص ض ط ظ ع غ ف ق ك ل م ن هـ و ي

تَزْيين adornment, embellishment, decoration.

تَسارَعَ to hurry, hasten, rush, dash; to speed up, accelerate, expedite; to flow in succession.

تَسارُع acceleration, quickening, hurrying.

تَساقَطَ to fall down; to collapse, break down; to fall out (hairs).

تَساقُط falling down; dropping; collapse.

تَساقُطُ الشَّعْر loss of hair.

تَساقُطُ المَطَر rainfall, downpour.

تَسامَى to compete; to try to excel one another; to vie in glory with one another; to rise above; to be elevated, lofty, tall; to tower up.

تَسامُح indulgence, toleration, leniency, mercy, kindness.

تَساهَلَ to be lenient with; to be obliging toward; to be negligent, careless in something.

تَساوٍ (التَّساوِي) equality, parity, equivalence.

تَساوَى to be equal, even, balanced.

تَساوُق coherence, harmony, symmetry, congruity.

تَسَبَّبَ to cause, produce, bring about, effect; to be the cause, consequence, result of; to justify, motivate; to trade; to do business; to sell.

تَسْبِيح glorification, eulogy, extolment (of God).

تَسَتَّرَ to be veiled; to cover oneself; to hide, conceal oneself; to be hidden, concealed.

تَسَجَّلَ to be registered, recorded, listed, inscribed; to enroll as member; to be entered (in the commercial register, book of accounts); to be recorded on a tape.

تَسْجِيل registration, recording, entering (book of accounts); inscription; enrollment (in a club, school); writing down.

تَسْخِير utilization, subjugation, exploitation.

تَسْخِين heating, warming up.

تَسْدِيد payment (of a debt); paying up; aiming, pointing.

تَسَرَّبَ to leak, seep, ooze, flow out; to infiltrate into; to penetrate, sneak into, flow along, seep through.

تَسَرُّب leakage, seepage; infiltration, running out; sneaking.

تَسَرَّعَ to do in a hurry; to rush to; to be hasty, rash in; to be quick, fast, prompt; to hasten.

تَسَرُّع rashness, hurry, haste, hastiness.

تَسْرِيح discharge, dismissal, release; demobilization (of troops); permission, authorization.

تَسْرِيحَة hairdo, hairstyle (hair).

تَسْرِيع acceleration, speeding up, hurrying.

تَسْطِير ruling, lining; crossing, striping; jotting down; drawing up, recording, writing down.

تُسْع one-ninth (1/9).

تِسْعَة nine.

تِسْعَةُ عَشَرَ nineteen.

تِسْعُون ninety.

تَسْعِير pricing, quotation; flaring up; kindling.

تَسْعِيرَة price, quotation; price fixing, pricing.

تَسَقَّطَ to pick up information about; to gather information.

تَسْقِيف roofing.

تَسَكَّعَ to loiter, loaf, hang around; to proceed aimlessly, dawdle; to grope about in the dark.

تَسَكُّع loitering, loafing, hanging around, puttering.

تَسْكِين calming, quieting, soothing (pain); alleviation, allaying; mitigation; housing; making vowelless a consonant (grammar).

تَسَلَّى to amuse oneself; to console oneself; to have a good time.

تَسَلُّح armament, rearmament.

تَسَلْسُل sequence, progression, order, hierarchy.

تَسَلْسُل train of thought.

بالتَّسَلْسُل in proper sequence; successively, serially, one after the other; consecutively, in order.

تَسَلَّطَ to overpower, overwhelm; to prevail, gain the upper hand; to be absolute master of; to command, supervise, rule; to predominate, hold sway over, gain power over.

تَسَلُّط domination, predominance, supremacy, control, hegemony; power, command, sway, supervision.

تَسَلَّقَ to climb, scale, mount, go up; to creep (plant).

تَسَلَّلَ to sneak, slip, steal into; to infiltrate, penetrate, enter something; to slip away; to withdraw smoothly from.

تَسَلُّل infiltration, penetration, sneaking; offside (in football playing).

تَسَلَّمَ to receive, get, obtain; to take over, assume.

تَسَلُّم receipt, taking over, assumption.

تَسْلِيَة amusement, entertainment, pastime.

تَسْلِيف credit, lending; advance, loan.

تَسْلِيم handing over, handing in; submitting; delivery; salutation, greeting; approval, consent, admission, acknowledgment; submission, obedience; surrender, capitulation; extradition (of criminals).

تَسَمَّرَ to stand as if pinned to the ground; to be nailed; to be brown or tan (by sunrays).

تَسَمَّعَ to listen to, hearken to; to eavesdrop; to lend one's ear to; to pay attention to (a lecturer).

تَسَمُّم poisoning, toxication; toxicosis (med).

تَسْمِيَة naming, nomination, designation; name, title, nomenclature.

تَسْمِيد fertilization, using manure (in planting); fertilizing.

تَسْمِيع reciting (a lesson); letting someone hear what one says.

تَسَنَّى to be made easy, possible, feasible; to be facilitated to.

تَسَنَّمَ to mount, scale; ascend (to the throne).

تَسَهَّلَ to be easy, facilitated; to be made easy, possible.

تَسْهِيل facilitation, making easy.

تَسْهِيلات (ج) facilities.

تَسَوُّس dental caries, tooth decay; caries (bones).

تَسَوُّل begging, mendicancy, begging for alms.

تَسْوِيَة leveling; grading (ground); dressing, arranging, fixing up; settlement, equalization, equating; reconciliation, compromise, accomodation; adjustment.

تَسْوِيف procrastination, stalling, postponement, delay, deferment.

تَسْوِيق marketing, sale of mechandise.

تَسْيِيج surrounding with a hedge, fence; enclosing.

تَسْيِير driving forward; setting in motion; sending out; management; operating; forwarding; promotion, spreading.

تَشَاءَمَ to be pessimistic; to regard something as an evil portent; to foretell calamity; to be superstitious.

تَشَاؤُم pessimism.

تَشَابُك interlocking, tangle, confusion; interlacing, entanglement, intermeshing; overlapping, complexity, intertwining (branches).

تَشَابُه resemblance, similarity, analogy, parity, likeness; vagueness, haziness, obscurity.

تَشَاجَرَ to quarrel, fight, argue, dispute; to come to blows with, scuffle, brawl.

تَشَاحَنَ to wrangle, quarrel, fight, dispute; to hate one another; to have a feud with another.

تَشَاغَلَ to pretend to be busy; to occupy oneself with; to be preoccupied, absorbed, engrossed in.

تَشَاوَرَ to take counsel, deliberate, consult with; to ask for advice; to exchange views with.

تَشَاوُر consultation, deliberation, joint discussion.

تَشَبَّثَ to cling to, hang on to; to adhere to; to be obstinate, tenacious, stubborn.

تَشَبُّث tenacity, adherence, stubborness, obstinacy.

تَشَبَّعَ to be sated, saturated, filled with; to be loaded, charged with.

تَشَبَّه to imitate, resemble, bear a resemblance; to look alike someone; to be similar; to copy, ape, match.

تَشْبيه likening, comparison; allegory, simile (language); parable, assimilation.

تَشَتُّت dispersal, dispersion, scattering, breaking up (a crowd); distraction, absentmindedness.

تَشْتيت dispersion, dispersal; breaking up (a crowd).

تَشَجَّعَ to take heart, pluck up courage; to be encouraged.

تَشْجير afforestation, tree-planting.

تَشْجيع encouragement, heartening, promotion, advancement.

تَشْحيم greasing, lubrication, oiling (of a machine).

تَشْخيص diagnosis (of a sickness); personification; identification; performance of an actor; acting (in a play).

تَشَدُّد sternness, intensification, toughness.

تَشْديد emphasis; concentration; constraint, limitation, oppression; strengthening, intensification; doubling of a consonant (grammar); doubling sign over a consonant (grammar).

تَشْذيب trimming, pruning, polishing; clipping; modifying.

تَشَرَّدَ to roam, tramp about; to wander about; to be made homeless; to rave, straggle.

تَشَرَّفَ to have the honor to; to be honored with.

تَشْريح anatomy, dissection (body); autopsy, postmortem (dead); slicing, ripping open, dismembering.

تَشْريد displacement, making someone homeless; eviction, expulsion; vagrancy.

تَشْريع legislation, lawmaking; law, act, code, statute.

تَشْريف honoring, bestowing honors upon.

تِشْرينُ الأوَّل October.

تِشْرينُ الثاني November.

تَشْظِيَة fragmentation, splintering, chipping.

تَشَعَّبَ to form branches; to branch out; to ramify; to be ramified, divided into branches; to be subdivided; to separate, split, break out; to become disorganized, disrupted; to result from.

تَشَعُّب ramification, branching; disruption, disunion; divisioning, splitting.

تَشَعَّثَ to be disheveled, tousled, unkempt (hair); to disintegrate, fall apart.

تَشْغيل operation; employment, providing of employment, providing work, hiring; starting, putting in operation; investment (of money); manufacture, making.

تَشَفَّعَ to intercede for, plead for, mediate for, intervene on behalf of someone with someone else.

تَشَقَّقَ to be split, cracked, cleft.

تَشَكَّلَ to be formed, fashioned, worked; to take a form, shape; to be made, built, set up; to be variegated, graded; to appear in visible form of; to assume the form of; to develop, arise, come into being; to consist of, be composed of; to be embodied in, involved in.

تَشْكِيل forming, shaping, molding, creation; fashioning; diversification, variegation; formation; vowelization (grammar).

تَشَمَّعَ to be waxed; to be cirrhotic (med).

تَشَنَّجَ to contract, shrink; twitch; to suffer from a spasm, a cramp, convulsions.

تَشَنُّج spasm, convulsion, cramp; shriveling, shrinking (of the skin); twitch, jerk; fit, constriction.

تَشْنِيع calumny, slander, defamation, revilement, libel; distortion, disfigurement.

تَشْهِير calumny, slander, defamation, revilement; invective, libel, vetuperation.

تَشَوَّشَ to be confused, confounded, disturbed, disorganized; to run in disorder, confusion.

تَشَوُّش confusion, chaos, disorder.

تَشَوَّقَ to long, yearn, crave, covet, desire ardently.

تَشَوَّهَ to be disfigured, defaced, mutilated; to be distorted, misstated, corrupted, twisted, falsified.

تَشْوِيش confusion, disturbance, confounding, derangement; interference, jamming (broadcast, radio waves).

تَشْوِيق arousing of desire; fascination, thrilling, stimulation; excitement, suspense.

تَشْوِيه deformation, defacement, distortion, mutilation; perversion, faslsification (of the truth); defamation, slander, libel, defilement, tarnishing (of repute).

تَشَيَّعَ to side with; to support, patronize, advocate; to follow, adhere to, join, make common cause with; to become a Shiite; to pretend to be a Shiite.

تَشَيُّع partisanship, bias for, adherence to; taking sides with; partiality; factionalism.

تَشْيِيد building, construction, erection.

تَشْيِيع making known; seeing off; accompanying, escorting, bidding farewell.

تَشْيِيع to pay the last honors (to the deceased); funeral.

تَصَابَى to behave like a child; to act in a childish manner; to regain youth; to become young again; to woe, court, tempt, charm (a woman).

تَصادَفَ to happen by chance; to meet someone unexpectedly; to come across; to come to pass.

تَصارَعَ to wrestle with one another; to struggle, clash, fight with someone.

تَصاعَدَ to rise, ascend, lift; to be emitted, discharged, diffused (vapor).

تَصافَحَ to shake hands with.

تَصالُب intersection, crossing.

تَصالَحَ to make peace, become reconciled with.

تَصَبَّبَ to flow, gush forth, effuse.

تَصَبَّبَ عَرَقاً to sweat, perspire.

تَصَبُّر patience, forbearance; endurance, perseverance.

تَصَحَّفَ to misread, misspell; mispronounce (a word).

تَصْحيح correction, adjustment; mending, repairing; proofreading (printing).

تَصَدَّى to confront, face, resist, oppose; to occupy oneself with; to embark upon; to intercept, stand up to.

تَصَدَّرَ to head, lead, preside; to have a front seat (at a social gathering, meeting).

تَصَدَّعَ to get split; to go to pieces; to come apart; to be split, cracked, cleft, broken.

تَصَدَّقَ to give alms to; to be charitable; to donate.

تَصْدير export, exportation; preface, foreword, introduction; sending off, forwarding.

تَصْديق belief, faith in; consent, agreement to; approval, attestation, confirmation; ratification, authentication, legalization (of a document).

تَصَرَّفَ to behave, conduct oneself; to dispose freely in; to act without restriction; to be inflected, declined, conjugated (grammar).

تَصَرُّف disposal, usufruct, administration; demeanor, behavior, conduct; outflow, discharge.

تَصَرُّف adaptation (book).

تَصْريح statement, announcement, declaration; official permission; license, permit.

تَصْريف drainage, discharge (water); letting off; sale, disposal of; inflection, declension, conjugation (grammar); management, handling, administration.

تَصْعيد escalation; evaporation; sublimation.

تَصْغير reduction, diminution, decrease; diminutive.

تَصَفَّحَ to browse through, page through, run over (a newspaper, book); to skim through; to leaf, thumb (a book); to examine, scrutinize, study.

تَصْفِيَة clarification, purification, filtration, filtering; settlement, adjustment; liquidation, clearance sale; settlement of accounts.

تَصْفيفُ الشَّعْر combing, styling (hair).

تَصْفيق applause, hand clapping, acclaim.

تَصَلُّب inflexibility, hardness, callousness; stiffness, rigidity; stubbornness; obstinacy; intolerance.

تَصْليد hardening, induration, concretion.

تَصْميم determination, resolution, decision; resolute action; planning, projecting, design, designing.

تَصَنَّعَ to affect, feign, assume, fake, speak or write in an artificial manner.

تَصَنُّع affectation, mannerism, hypocrisy.

تَصَنَّفَ to be categorized, classed, arranged, tabulated; to be compiled, written (a book).

تَصْنيع industrialization.

تَصْنيف classification, categorization, sorting; compilation, composition, writing; literary work.

تَصَوَّرَ to imagine, fancy, conceive, think; to seem to; to present itself to; to visualize, envision, suppose.

تَصَوَّرَ to be shaped, formed, fashioned.

تَصَوُّر imagination, fancy, fantasy; idea, conception.

تَصَوُّف mysticism, Sufism; the Sufi way of life.

تَصْويب correction, rectification; aiming, pointing.

تَصْويت voting, polling, casting of ballots; raising one's voice about; shouting.

تَصْويتٌ بالإجماع unanimous vote.

تَصْويتٌ بِرَفْعِ الأيْدِي voting by show of hands.

تَصْويتٌ على الثِّقَة vote of confidence.

تَصْوير picturing, illustration; painting, portrayal; description, depiction; forming, formation, shaping, molding; photography; sketching.

تَصْويرٌ بالأشِعَّة radiography.

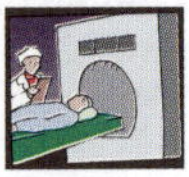

تَصْويرُ الدِّماغ encephalogy.

تَصْويرُ الشَّرايين arteriography.

تَصْويرُ الوَريد phlebography.

تَصْويرٌ زيتيّ painting, oil painting.

تَصْويرٌ فوتوغرافيّ photography, shooting, filming.

تَصْويرُ المُسْتَنَدات photocopying, reproduction.

تَضاءَلَ to dwindle, diminish, decrease, abate; to become small, meager, sparse.

تَضاؤُل dwindling, waning, meagerness, sparsity, decrease, shrinking, shrinkage; minute; scanty.

تَضارَبَ to fight, quarrel, come to blows with one another; to be divided; to differ, conflict, clash with one another.

تَضارُب conflict, opposition, contradiction, inconsistency, clash; hand to hand fighting, brawl, quarrel.

تَضاريس (ج) topographic relief, elevations; wrinkles (of face).

تَضَافَرَ to help one another; to be tightly interwoven; to be tied up, closely connected; to combine, unite, join forces with, collaborate, assist.

تَضَافُر cooperation, joining forces, mutual assistance.

تَضَامَنَ to be jointly liable; to have joint responsibility for; to be in accord, solidary, united.

تَضَامُن solidarity; joint liability.

بالتَّضامُن والتَّكافُل jointly and severally.

تَضَايَقَ to be or feel annoyed, vexed, upset.

تَضَايُق grievance, embarrassment, harassment; annoyance, vexation, irritation, nuisance.

تَضْحِيَة sacrifice, sacrificing, immolation.

تَضَخَّمَ to swell, become inflated; to expand, distend; to be enlarged, magnified, huge, big, large.

تَضَخُّم distention, inflation (economy); expansion; magnification, enlargement.

تَضْخِيم inflation, distention, enlargement; swelling; exaggeration; amplification (electricity).

تَضَرَّرَ to be damaged, harmed; to suffer damage or harm; to be injured, hurt, impaired, prejudiced.

تَضَرَّعَ to supplicate, implore, beg, beseech, entreat; to humiliate oneself, abuse oneself.

تَضَرُّع supplication, imploring, begging, entreaty.

تَضَعْضَعَ to become weak; to wane; to dissolve; to fall apart, decline, perish, decay.

تَضَلَّعَ to be versed in, skilled in, proficient in; to be throughly familiar or acquainted or conversant with; to assume, take over, (a job, an expense).

تَضْلِيل misguidance, misdirection; deception, delusion.

تَضَمَّخَ to perfume oneself; to be perfumed.

تَضَمَّنَ to comprise, include, embody, to imply, involve, contain; to comprehend, embrace.

تَضْمِيد dressing, bandaging (of a wound).

تَضْمِين implication, insertion, inclusion.

تَضْمِين modulation (electricity).

تَضْمِينات damages, reparation, redress, amends.

تَضَيُّق stricture, narrowing, stenosis (med).

تَضْيِيق narrrowing, constriction; hampering, restriction; limitation, oppression; tightening (rope, blockade).

تَطَابَقَ to be conforming, consistent, compatible with; to correspond to, agree with, conform to; to contrast with, adapt, adjust, suit, fit, match; to be arranged in strata.

تَطَابُق correspondence, conformity, consistency, compatibility, congruance, matching; stratification.

تَطاوَلَ to dare; to become insolent; to pretend, presume; to be long; to be presumptuous; to display an arrogant behavior toward someone; to attack, trespass.

تَطايَرَ to be scattered, dispersed, spread, diffused; to fly in all directions; to disappear, vanish; to volatize.

تَطَبُّع adaptability, acquired character.

تَطْبِيب art of healing, medical practice, medical profession.

تَطْبِيع normalization (of relations).

تَطْبِيق adaptation, accomodation, adjustment, application; implementation, enforcement, execution, putting into practice, putting into effect.

تَطَرُّف extremism, immoderation, extravagance, radicalism.

تَطَرَّقَ to discuss, treat of a topic; to approach, touch on a theme; to bring up, raise a subject.

تَطْرِيز embroidery, needlework.

تَطْعِيم grafting (plant); transplantation (tissue).

تَطْعِيم inoculation, vaccination, injection.

تَطَفَّلَ to intrude upon, to arrive uninvited; to be obtrusive; to live at another person's expense.

تَطَفُّل intrusion, forcing oneself upon others; meddling, interfering; sponging, parasitism.

تَطَلَّبَ to demand, exact, require; to make necessary.

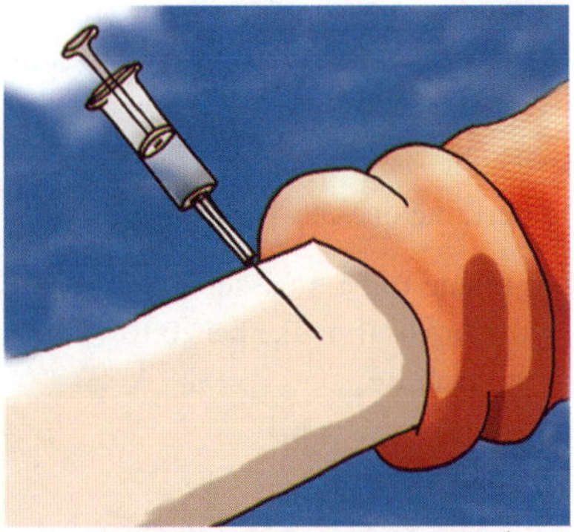

يتمّ تطعيم الأطفال الصغار لوقايتهم من الأوبئة
Small children are inoculated to protect them from diseases

تَطَلَّعَ to have an eye on; to wait, look out for; to gaze, stare, look attentively at; to seek, to discover, explore; to seek information about.

تَطَهَّرَ to clean oneself, clean up, wash up; to perform an ablution; to be sterilized, disinfected.

تَطَلُّع striving, aspiration, endeavor; curiosity; anticipation, hope, longing for, expecting.

تَطْهِير disinfection, sterilization; purge, purging, purification; chastening; clearing up.

تَطْهِير circumcision.

تَطَوَّرَ to develop, evolve, change; to be developed, advanced.

تَطَوُّر evolution, development, advancement.

تَطَوَّعَ to volunteer; to enlist (in the army).

تَطْوِير development, promotion, advancement.

تَطْويق encirclement, surrounding, circling; enclosure, encompassment.

تَطَيَّب to perfume oneself.

تَظاهَرَ to pretend to be; to assume, fake, act as if, make belief; to demonstrate.

تَظاهُرة demonstration, rally; assistance, support.

تَظَلَّمَ to complain about.

تَظْليل shading; hatching.

تَظْهير endorsement (of a cheque); development (of a photo).

تَعادَلَ to be balanced, equal; to be on a par; to be equal, equivalent to; to match, outweigh, equate.

تَعادُل equality, parity; balance; tie, draw (in a game).

تَعارَفَ top be acquainted with; to get to know each other.

تَعاسَة unhappiness, distress, misery, wretchedness.

تَعاضُد cooperation, mutual support, assistance.

تَعاطَى to practise, pursue, engage in, deal in; to be occupied with; to swallow, take (a medicine, narcotic).

تَعاطَفَ to sympathize with; to sway, swing (walking).

تَعاطُف sympathy.

تَعاظَمَ to intensify; to be intensified, proud, arrogant; to be increased; to be weighty, grave, serious.

تَعاظُم intensification, increase; pride, arrogance.

تَعافَى to recover, convalesce, recuperate (from illness); to regain health; to get well.

تَعاقَبَ to follow one another; to come successively; to alternate, rotate.

تَعَقُّب succession, sequence; alternation, rotation.

بالتَّعاقُب in succession, consecutively, one after the other; in rotation, successively, in turn.

تَعاقُد concluding a contract, an agreement.

تَعاقُدِيّ contractual.

تَعالَى to stress, further, rise; to be high, exalted (God); to look down on; to stay away from; to tower up, climb, scale; to master something.

تَعالَجَ to be treated; to be under medical treatment; to receive medical treatment.

تَعامَى to shut one's eyes; to pretend not to see; to be blind to.

تَعامَلَ to treat, do business with; to deal in, carry on business in; to sell, handle, transact business; to trade with one another.

تَعامُل intercourse, trade, business, transaction; treatment, treating, dealing with; usage, custom, practice.

تَعاهَدَ to enter into a covenant, a contract, an obligation; to engage, undertake, bind oneself, obligate oneself; to promise.

تَعاوُن collaboration, mutual assistance.

بِالتَّعاوُنِ مَع in collaboration with.

تَعاوَنَ to work together in executing work; to cooperate, collaborate; to unite, join forces.

تَعاوُنِيَّة cooperative.

تَعايَشَ to live together with; to coexist.

تَعِبَ to become tired, weary of; to irk, weary; to work hard; to toil, labor, sweat.

تَعَب fatigue, weariness; difficulty, hard work; inconvenience, hardship; exhaustion, burden.

تَعِب tired, fatigued, worn out.

تَعْبِئَة mobilization (of troops); filling, packing; boxing, encasement; bottling, canning; loading.

تَعَبَّدَ to devote oneself to worship (of God); to worship; to be paved (road).

تَعَبُّد piety, devotion, worship.

تَعْبيد paving (roads);. enslavement, subjugation; subjection.

تَعْبير expression, declaration, utterence of a feeling, phrase, term; phrasing, wording, formulation; term, idiom; wording, manner of expression.

تَعْتيم darkening, obscuring, clouding; blackout, hushing up.

تَعَثَّرَ to stumble, trip; to stutter, stammer (in his speech); to fail (in his endeavors); to meet with difficulties; to be hindered, obstructed.

تَعَجَّبَ to wonder at; to marvel at; to be astonished, amazed, surprised.

تَعَجْرَفَ to be presumptuous, arrogant, haughty.

تَعْجيل acceleration, speedup, expediting; hurrying, rushing.

تَعَدَّى to pass over, bypass, overstep, exceed, transcend; to go beyond, exceed the proper bounds; to act unjustly toward; to assail, assault; to make transitive (grammar); to transgress, violate, break (the law); to act outrageously against; to commit excesses against.

تَعْداد counting, listing, count; calculation, computation.

تَعْدادُ الأَنْفُس census.

تَعَدُّد multiplicity, variety, diversity, plurality.

تَعَدُّدُ الأَزْواج polygamy.

تَعَدُّدُ اللُّغات multilingualism, polyglotism.

تَعَدَّلَ to be adjusted, changed, set in order; to be equal, equivalent to; to undergo modification.

تَعْديل modification, straightening out, settling, setting right; alteration, change, amendment; regulation, improvement; reshuffle (of the cabinet); modulation (electricity).

تَعْدين mining.

تَعَذَّبَ to suffer; to be punished; to feel pain.

تَعَذَّرَ to be impossible, unfeasible, hopeless.

تَعْذيب tormenting, torture, punishment, chastisement.

تَعَرَّى to undress, disrobe, strip.

تَعَرَّضَ to be exposed, subjected to; to run the risk of; to face, encounter; to be confronted with, faced with; to resist, oppose, confront; to interfere with; to molest; to deal, treat, consider, study, discuss.

تَعَرَّفَ to recognize, perceive, know, identify; to discover, experience; to acknowledge; to distinguish, differentiate; to be acquainted with; to familiarize oneself with; to be definite (grammar).

تَعْرِفَة tariff.

تَعَرُّق perspiration, sweating; graining, veining; venation.

تَعَرْقَلَ to be blocked, hindered, obstructed, encumbered; to be complicated, hampered, impeded, delayed.

تَعْريب translation into Arabic; Arabization.

تَعْرِيَة disrobement, stripping off, uncovering; erosion, corrosion; deprivation, divestiture.

تَعْريض broadening, widening; exposure; insinuation.

تَعْريضٌ للخَطَر endangering, jeopardizing.

تَعْريف definition, introduction, announcement, notification, direction, determination, identification.

تَعَزَّزَ to be strong, powerful, mighty, strengthened, fortified, consolidated; to pride oneself; to be honored, exalted; to be supported, enhanced, fostered, furthered.

تَعْزِيَة condolence, consolation, solace.

تَعْزيز consolidation, support, backing, strengthening; boosting, furtherance, enhancement, reinforcement; promotion, fostering, bracing, strengthening.

تَعَسَّرَ to be hard, difficult, trying, adverse.

تَعَسُّر difficulty.

تَعَسُّف arbitrariness, despotism, tyranny.

تَعْشيق gearing, meshing; engagement; dovetailing, coupling, fitting tightly together.

تَعَصُّب fanaticism, bigotry, narrow-mindedness.

تَعَطَّشَ to thirst for, yearn for, hanker after; to desire ardently, eagerly; to crave, aspire to, long for, covet.

تَعَطُّش longing, yearning, hankering, ardent desire, eagerness, thirst, aspiration.

تَعَطَّفَ to feel, have compassion; to sympathize with; to deign to do something; to harbor affection toward.

تَعَطَّلَ to be idle, without work, unemployed; to be hindered, impeded, obstructed, suspended, interrupted; to be shut down, no longer operating (machine).

تَعْطِيل breakdown, disruption, putting out of action; defusing, deactivation; hindering, hampering; suspension (of a newspaper); impairment, destruction, ruining; stoppage, shutting off (a motor, machine); inactivity, unemployment, destitution.

تَعَظَّمَ to be exalted, dignified, honored, glorified; to flaunt, boast; to be arrogant, proud, haughty; to be great, grandiose, huge, prodigious.

تَعْظِيم glorification, exaltation; aggrandisement; veneration, esteem, honor.

تَعَفَّفَ to be abstinent, virtuous, chaste; to be decent, pure, modest.

تَعَفَّنَ to be rotten, putrid, decayed, decomposed, musty, mildewy.

تَعَفُّن rottenness, putridity, decay, spoiledness.

تَعَقَّبَ to pursue, follow, trail; to take turns, alternate; to ensue, come after; to succeed one another.

تَعَقَّلَ to be reasonable, sensible, rational, intelligent, judicious, wise.

تَعَقُّل judiciousness, rationality, discretion, carefulness.

تَعْقِيب commentary, review, remark.

تَعْقِيد complication, entanglement, intricacy.

تَعْقِيم sterilization, disinfection, pasteurization.

تَعْكِير muddying, muddling, disturbance, rendering turbid, troubled.

تَعَلَّقَ to be suspended, hanged to; to be attached, affixed; to be fond of; to depend on; to be dependent on; to be related to; to relate to; to be connected with; to concern, regard, belong to, have to do with.

تَعَلُّق dangling, suspension, hanging down; clinging to; sticking to; attachment, love, affection; relevance, concern, pertinence, relationship.

تَعَلُّل offering of an excuse, justification; explanation, argumentation.

تَعَلَّمَ to learn, come to know about; to be educated.

تَعَلُّم learning, studying, study, education.

تَعْلِيب canning, packing, casing, encasement.

تَعْليق hanging down, suspension, dangling; attachment, tying, fixing; keeping pending, undecided; holding in abeyance; cancellation; abeyance; adjournment (of a session, meeting); making conditional on.

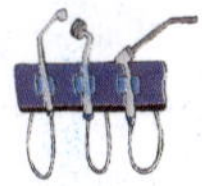

تَعْليق commentary, remark, review; annotation, caption, critique.

تَعْليل justification, explanation, motivation; entertainment, diversion, distraction.

تَعْليم teaching, instruction, training, schooling, education, apprenticeship; information.

تَعْليمٌ مُخْتَلَط coeducation.

تَعْليمٌ عالٍ higher education, academic studies.

تَعْليمٌ ابتدائيّ elementary education.

تَعْليمٌ ثانويّ secondary education; college education.

تَعَمَّدَ to intend, purpose; to do intentionally, on purpose; to approach with a definite aim in mind; to be baptized, christened.

تَعَمُّد intention, intent, resolution; determination, purpose; premeditation, willfulness; baptism, christening.

تَعَمَّقَ to penetrate deeply into; to delve into; to study thoroughly.

تَعَمَّمَ to be spread, diffused, popularized, circulated; to put on a turban.

تَعْمِيَة disguise; obscurity, blinding; puzzle, riddle.

تَعْميد baptizing, christening; settlement, confirmation.

تَعْمير construction, building; longevity.

تَعْميم popularization, spreading; circular; vulgarization, universalization.

تَعَنَّتَ to be obstinate, stubborn; to vex, annoy, trouble, molest; to confuse, puzzle, embarrass.

تَعَنُّت obstinacy, stubborness, inflexibility.

تَعْنيف rebuke, reprimand; reprehension, censure.

تَعَهَّدَ to cultivate, develop, improve; to sponsor, foster, patronize; to undertake, take upon onself; to promise, undertake; to make a contract with someone (concerned).

تَعَهُّد commitment, obligation, pledge, contract; care, charge; maintenance.

تَعَوَّدَ to get used to; to be accustomed to; to acquire a habit.

تَعَوُّق delay, retardation, deferment.

تَعْويض compensation, satisfaction, indemnity, reparation; replacement, reimbursement, restitution, substitution; consideration; equivalent, substitute, recompense.

تَعْويم floating, setting afloat.

تَعِيس miserable, wretched, unhappy, unfortunate.

تَعَيَّنَ to be nominated, appointed, assigned (to an office); to be allotted; to be destined, set aside, earmarked; to be incumbent upon.

تَعْيين appointment, assignment, scheduling; nomination, stipulation; allotment, apportion; allocation; specification, itemization; designation, determination.

تَغاضَى to overlook, ignore, disregard; to let pass; to pass over, wink at, pay no attention; to have no objection to; to forgive, pardon, excuse; to condone, connive.

تَغافَلَ to feign inattention, inadvertance, negligence; to pretend to be inattentive, negligent, careless; to ignore, pay no attention to; to be indifferent to.

تَغايُر difference, disparity, contrast, contradiction, variance, variation, inconsistency.

تَغَذَّى to be nourished, fed; to be provided with, supplied with; to feed, live on.

تَغْذِيَة feeding, nourishment, alimentation, nutrition; supply, provisioning; input, charging.

تَغَرَّبَ to emigrate; to live in a foreign country; to assimilate oneself to the western way of life; to travel westward; to become westernized.

تَغَرْغَرَ to gargle; to be bathed in tears (eyes).

تَغْرِيد singing; warbling; song.

تَغْرِير deception, delusion, blinding; alluring; exposure to danger; risking one's life; self-deception; seduction, dazzling; endangering.

تَغْرِيم fining; falling in love.

تَغَزَّلَ to speak words of love to a woman; to court, woo, flirt with a woman; to celebrate in love poems; to extol, laud, eulogize.

تَغْشِيَة hazing, enveloping, veiling, covering; overlaying.

تَغَضَّنَ to be wrinkled, creased, folded, corrugated, crumpled.

تَغْضِين wrinkling, creasing, crumpling, folding, corrugation.

تَغَطَّى to be covered, wrapped; to wrap oneself; to cover oneself; to be concealed, veiled.

تَغَطْرَسَ to be haughty, supercilious, to strut, prance, swagger (while walking).

تَغْطِيَة covering, casing, concealment; coverage (of news); wrapping, capping.

تَغْطِيس immersion, dipping, submersion.

تَغَلَّبَ to surmount, overcome, overwhelm; to defeat, vanquish, triumph over; to overpower, predominate.

تَغَلْغَلَ to permeate, pervade, infiltrate, spread into; to be deeply embedded in.

تَغْلِيف wrapping, covering, encasing, packaging, enveloping; binding (of books).

تَغَمَّدَ to cover, shelter, protect, conceal.

تَغَمَّدهُ اللّهُ بِرَحْمَتِهِ May God cover him with His grace.

تَغَوَّطَ to excrete, defecate.

تَغَيَّبَ to be absent, away; to stay away; to slander, calumniate; to be hidden, concealed; to absent oneself.

تَغَيَّرَ to be changed, modified, varied, altered; to be dissimilar, different; to differ, change, alter, vary.

تَغْيِير change, replacement, exchange, shifting.

تَفَّ to spit.

تَفَاءَلَ to be optimistic; to see a good omen in.

تَفَاؤُل optimism.

تُفَّاح، تُفَّاحَة apples, apple.

تُفَّاحَة آدم Adam's apple.

تَفَاخُر pride, vainglory, pomposity; boasting, bragging.

تَفَادَى to beware of, keep away from; to avoid, prevent, ward off; to avert, get away from, flee.

تَفَاضُل rivalry for superiority; differential.

تَفَاعُل reaction, interaction; chemical process.

تَفَاقَمَ to become grave, serious, critical, dangerous; to become aggravated, reach alarming proportions.

تَفَاقُم aggravation, worsening, intensification.

جاء في الأمثال: كلّ تفاحة كلّ يوم تبعد عنك الطبيب

The maxim says: one apple a day keeps the doctor away

تَفَانَى to dedicate, devote, sacrifice oneself completely for; to give oneself wholeheartedly to; to become totally absorbed by.

تَفَاهَة insipidity, paltriness, triviality, insignificance; stupidity, silliness, vapidity.

تَفَاهَمَ to understand one another; to reach an understanding with another; to agree, come to terms with one another.

تَفَاهُم mutual understanding, agreement, concurrence, accord; arrangement, entente.

تَفَاوُت difference, dissimilarity, disparity, contrast; variance, divergence, inequality.

تَفَاوَضَ to negotiate, confer, parley on with.

تَفاوُض negotiation, parley, talk.

تَفَتَّتَ to be crumbled, divided into small fragments; to crumble, disintegrate.

تَفَتَّحَ to be unfolded, opened; to bloom, blossom (flower).

تَفَتَّقَ to be unsewn, torn, slit; to produce, devise, innovate, bring about.

تَفْتيت crumbling, disintegration, breaking up into small fragments, fragmentation.

تَفْتيش inspection, search; looking for, seeking.

تَفَجَّعَ to be painfully affected, grieved, tormented; to lament, wail.

تَفْجير exploding, detonating, blasting.

تَفَحَّصَ to scrutinize, inspect, inquire into, inquire about; to examine, test, investigate, search for.

تَفْخيم exaltation, magnification, honoring.

تَفْخيم (الكلام) euphemism, grandiloquence, emphatic pronunciation of a consonant.

تَفَرَّدَ to do something alone; to possess something alone; to be unique, singular, unrivaled; to be isolated.

تَفَرُّد singularity; exclusive possession of; isolation.

تَفَرَّسَ to stare at; to look fixedly at.

تَفَرَّعَ to branch out, become ramified, spread in all directions.

تَفَرُّع ramification, branching.

تَفَرَّغَ to devote, occupy, engage oneself exclusively with; to become unoccupied.

تَفَرَّغَ to transfer the ownership of something to someone; to cede, deliver, assign (a deed).

تَفَرُّغ devoting oneself to; to occupy oneself with; transfer of ownership; disposal of, assignment (of a deed).

تَفَرَّقَ to separate; to be dispersed; to be disunited, split, divided, scattered, broken up.

تَفْرِقة separation, severance, sunderance; partition, dispersion, dispersal, scattering.

تَفْرِقةٌ عُنْصُرِيّة racial discrimination.

تَفْريط negligence, neglect, wasting, squandering; abuse, exaggeration, dissolution, renunciation.

تَفْريغ emptying, unloading, evacuation; discharge; drainage; disembarkation (from a ship); unpacking.

تَفْريق separation, dispersal, distribution; discrimination, differentiation; severance, partitioning.

تَفَسُّخ disintegration, decomposition, falling apart; decay, putrefaction, rot.

تَفْسير explanation, exposition; commentary; explication, elucidation, clarification; expounding, interpretation.

تَفَشّى to spread, diffuse, circulate; to be disseminated, spread, diffused; to be disclosed, revealed; to be epidemic, prevalent, massive.

تَفْصيل detail, detailing, elaboration; detailed statement, description, exposition; cutting out (garments).

بالتَّفْصيل in detail, elaborately, minutely.

تَفَضَّلَ to have the kindness of doing; to be kind; to deign, condescend; to be graciously disposed to do something; to oblige, favor, confer a benefit upon.

تَفَضَّل please! if you please! help yourself! come in, please.

تَفْضيل preference, favoring, esteem.

تَفَقَّدَ to visit, inspect, review (troops); to seek, search for.

تَفَكَّكَ to disintegrate, break up, to be disassembled, dismounted, shattered, split, disintegrated, loosened; to be unfastened, undone, disunited, disjoined.

تَفَكُّك disassembly, dissociation, rupture, split; disintegration, decomposition.

تَفْكير thinking, meditation; reflection, contemplation; thought; pondering.

تَفْكيك disassembly, dissociation, dismantlement.

تَفَلَ to spit.

تُفْل spit; sediment, residue.

تَفْليسة bankruptcy.

تَفَنَّنَ to be varied, diverse; to diversify; to be an expert in; to be versatile in.

تَفَنُّن diversity, versatility; varied activity, skillful manner.

تَفْنيد refutation, disproof.

تَفِهَ to be trivial, insignificant; to be tasteless, insipid, vapid, banal; to be silly, stupid.

تَفَهَّمَ to understand; to be sympathetic, considerate, understanding.

تَفَهُّم understanding; sympathy, consideration; comprehension, grasping; concurrence.

تَفَوَّقَ to excel, outmatch, surpass; to be superior; to transcend, exceed; to do excellent work; to show outstanding skill; to pass an examination with distinction.

تَفَوُّق superiority, preponderance, supremacy, talent.

بِتَفَوُّق with distinction, cum laude.

تَفَوَّهَ to utter, say, pronounce.

تَفْويض commissioning, empowerment, authority, authorization; mandate, proxy; power of attorney; deputation.

تَفَيَّأَ to seek shade under; to sit in the shadow of.

تَقابَلَ to get together with; to meet, interview with; to be opposite each other; to face each other; to have a meeting with.

تَقاتَل to fight one another; to combat, make war with.

تَقادُم prescription.

تَقارَبَ to approach one another; to get near to each other; to come near to; to approximate; to be almost equivalent with; to approximate each other; to advance, get close to.

تَقارُب mutual approach, mutual approximation, rapprochement.

تَقارُن coupling, union, linkage, connection.

تَقاسَمَ to share with; to distribute among themselves; to divide, partake with others.

تَقاضَى to summon before a judge; to arraign, prosecute, sue, take legal action against; to litigate; to claim; to get, receive (money, remuneration).

تَقاطَرَ to drip, dribble, trickle, soak, percolate into; to come in successive groups; to crowd, throng, flock (to a place).

تَقاطُع intersection, crossing; crossroads, junction.

تَقاعُد reticence; pension.

تَقاعَسَ to tarry, linger, neglect, fail to; to hesitate, waver; to be reluctant, uninterested in.

تَقَبَّلَ to accept, receive, take; to hear, fulfill, answer soneone's prayer (by God).

تَقَبُّل acceptance, reception, receipt, receiving; hearing, answering, fulfillment of someone's prayer.

تَقْبيل kissing.

تَقْتير stinginess, niggardliness, parsimony toward.

تَقْتيل killing, slaughtering, massacring; massacre, slaughter, carnage.

تَقَدَّمَ to precede, to go before, to be at the head of a group of people; to advance, progress, move nearer to.

تَقَدَّمَ في السِّنّ to get older; to be advanced in years.

تَقَدَّمَ إلى الامْتِحان to sit for an examination.

تَقَدُّم progress, advance, development; improvement; antecedence, priority.

تَقْدِمَة present, donation, grant.

تَقَدُّمِيّ progressive, liberal.

تَقْدير appraisal, evaluation, estimation, esteem; appreciation, taking in consideration; assumption, hypothesis; expectation; discretion; worth, standing.

تَقْديراً لِـ in appreciation of.

تَقْديرِيّ discretionary, estimative, assumed, hypothetical.

تَقْديم presentation, submission, offering up; dedication, offer; tender, bid; sending forward; advancing, moving forward; introducing; preface, introduction.

تَقَرَّبَ to approach, approximate; to come close to; to seek to gain someone's favor; to endear oneself to.

تَقَرَّر to be decided, determined, established, fixed.

تَقْرِيب approximation.

تَقْرِيبًا approximately, almost, about.

تَقْرِير report, account; establishment, confirmation, settlement, determination; decision.

تَقْرِيع scolding, chiding, rebuke, censure.

تَقْسِيط payment by installments.

تَقْسِيم division, splitting, partition; apportionment, portioning, sharing out.

تَقَشَّر to be peeled, skinned, scaled off, shaved off.

تَقَشُّر peeling off, scaling off, flaking off.

تَقَشُّف abstinence, austerity, asceticism.

تَقْشِير paring, skinning, scaling, peeling, shaving off.

تَقَصَّى to inspect, scrutinize, make inquiries about.

تَقْصِير curtailment, shortening; default, negligence, omission; failure (examination); bleaching.

تَقَطُّر dripping, dribbling, trickling, seepage.

تَقَطَّع to be severed, cut off, chopped to pieces; to be broken apart, divided, partitioned, sundered.

تَقَطُّع interruption, rupture, sunderance; irregularity, discontinuance; segmentation.

تَقْطِيب frowning, lowering, contracting the eyebrows; scowling, glowering; sewing together two pieces of cloth; stitching.

تَقْطِير distillation, filtering, refining, distilling.

تَقْطِيع cutting into pieces, carving, sectioning, segmentation; tearing, dismemberment; stature, figure, shape.

تَقَلَّب to toss about, move restlessly; to tumble, welter, writhe in one's bed; to turn inside out; to be changed; to hold numerous offices; to lead a life of ease; to be upturned, reversed; to fluctuate (price).

تَقَلُّب turning over, tossing, rolling about, tumbling; transformation, change; fluctation; instability; moodiness (character).

تَقَلَّد to assume; to take over (power, control); to be counterfeited, forged; to put on a necklace; to gird oneself with a cord.

تَقَلَّص to contract, shrink; to decrease, diminish; to dwindle, decline, recede.

تَقَلُّص contraction, shrinkage, decrease, decline.

تَقَلْقَل to be shaken, agitated, stirred, disturbed; to be shaky, unstable; to totter, falter, wobble.

تَقَلْقُل unrest, excitement, agitation, commotion; shakiness, unsteadiness, instability, tottering.

تَقْلِيب transformation, unsteadiness, change; turning.

تَقْليبُ الرَّأي	studying, medidating on, thinking over.
تَقْليد، تَقاليد	tradition, convention, custom.
تَقْليد	imitation, copying, mimicry.
تَقْليد	counterfeiting, forgery.
تَقْليدُ مَنْصَب	investiture, installation, appointment.
تَقْليديّ	traditional, conventional, customary.
تَقْلِيص	contraction, shrinking, shrinkage; decrease, reduction, diminution. 
تَقْليم	clipping (nails); trimming, pruning (trees); stripping, stripes.
تِقْنِيّ (ص)	technical, technological.
تِقْنِيّ (اسم)	technician.
تَقْنين	codifying; passing laws; rationing.
تَقَهْقَرَ	to fall back, retreat, withdraw; to recede, retrogress, decline, deteriorate.
تَقَهْقُر	backward movement, retrogression, retreat, withdrawal; degeneration; recession.
تَقْوَى	devoutness, piety, fearing God.
تَقَوَّسَ	to bend; to become bent, curved.
تَقَوَّضَ	to collapse; to be demolished; to fall in, cave in, break up; to be wrecked, destroyed, torn down, ruined, undermined.
تَقْوِيَة	fortification, reinforcement, bolstering, consolidation, hardening; encouragement.
تَقْوِيض	wrecking, pulling down, demolition, destruction, undermining, subversion, sapping (of force). 
تَقْوِيم	setting up, erection;appraisal, valuation; rectification, adjustment; modification, adaptation.
تَقْوِيم	calendar, almanac, chronology.
تَقِيّ	God-fearing, godly, pious, devout.
تَقَيَّأَ	to vomit, puke, throw up.
تَقَيُّح	purulence, suppuration.
تَقَيَّدَ	to bind oneself to; to be limited, restricted; to have one's name registered; to comply, observe, abide by; to undertake; to be committed, obligated; to be bound, tied, shackled; to be listed, registered, recorded.
تَقَيُّد	observance of, compliance with, adherence to; obligation, commitment; limitation, confinement. 
تَقْييد	tying, shackling, binding; limitation, restriction.
تَقْييد	recording, registering, entering, enrollment.
تَقْييدُ النَّسْل	birth control.
تَكاتَبَ	to exchange letters with; to write to each other.
تَكاتَفَ	to support one another; to unite, join forces, stand together; to be united in solidarity.

تَكاثَرَ to increase, proliferate, multiply, grow; to reproduce, propagate, breed.

تَكاسَلَ to be lazy, idle, negligent.

تَكافُؤ equivalence, evenness; valence; equality.

تَكافَلَ to vouch, stand as sponsor to; to be liable for; to guarantee each other; to join forces.

تَكافُل joint liability; solidarity.

بالتَّكافُلِ والتَّضامُن jointly and severally.

تَكامُل integration, perfection, integral.

تَكَبَّدَ to suffer, bear, endure, undergo, sustain; to defray costs; to take up the center; to be in the zenith; to culminate.

تَكَبَّرَ to be proud, haughty, arrogant, insolent.

تَكَبُّر pride, haughtiness, arrogance, insolence, conceit.

تَكَبَّلَ to be shackled, fettered; to be enchained, bound, tied.

تَكْبير enlargement, magnification; exaggeration; exclaiming God is Great; amplification (electricity).

تَكْبيل fettering, handcuffing, enchaining, binding, tying.

تَكَتَّلَ to be heaped up, piled up, clustered; to be pressed in a compact mass; to unite in a bloc; to band together, agglomerate.

تَكَتُّل agglomeration; bloc, front (political).

تَكَتَّمَ to hide, conceal; to keep silent, secretive, discreet.

تَكَتُّم secrecy, secretiveness, reserve, discretion.

تَكْتيكِيّ tactical.

تَكَثَّفَ to become thicker, denser, more concentrated; to become intense, concentrated; to thicken, condense, intensify.

تَكَثُّف condensation, intensification, thickening.

تَكَدَّرَ to be turbid, muddy, cloudy, brackish, grimy; to be dreary, unhappy, angry, annoyed, displeased, offended.

تَكَدَّسَ to pile up, accumulate; to be accumulated, piled up.

تَكْديس accumulation, piling up, amassment.

تَكْذيب denial, refutation, calling someone a liar.

تَكْرار repetition, reiteration, frequency.

تَكْرارًا repeatedly, frequently, time and again.

تَكَرَّرَ to be repeated, reiterated; to be refined.

تَكَرُّر frequency, repetition.

تَكَرَّسَ to be consecrated, dedicated to; to be sanctified, established as proof, set up, confirmed, corroborated.

تَكَرَّمَ to deign, condescend, oblige, favor; to donate, present graciously to.

تكرير repetition; clarification; refining, purification.

تكريس consecration, dedication; devoting, sanctification; establishing, founding; fixing, consolidation, confirmation; corroboration; inauguration.

تكريم honoring, tribute; honor, respect, welcoming, bestowal of honors upon; hospitality.

تكسّر to break, smash, crash,break up; to be shattered, smashed, broken into pieces.

تكسير breaking, shattering, fragmentation.

تكشّف to manifest, exhibit, expose, reveal, disclose; to be uncovered, bared, laid open, disclosed, revealed.

تكفّل to take upon oneself, assume, commit oneself; to be responsible for, liable for; to guarantee, sponsor; to be legal guardian; to warrant, ensure; to undertake, pledge oneself.

تكفير expiation, atonement, penance.

تكلّف to affect, feign, pretend; to burden oneself; to take the trouble to; to cost someone dearly; to take over; to force a laugh; to be affected, formal, ceremonious; to do something with difficulty.

تكلُّف affectation, mannerism, constraint, hypocrisy, unnatural manner.

تكلّم to speak, talk to; to converse with; to say.

تكلُّم speaking, talking; talk, conversation, speech.

تكليف charging, entrustment; instruction, order; task, assignment; overburdening; ceremony; formality; imposition of taxes; taxation; servitude.

تكمِلة supplement, complement, sequel, end, conclusion.

تكميليّ complementary, supplementary, additional.

تكنّى to be known by the surname of; to be surnamed.

تكهرُب electrification.

تكهّن to predict, forecast, foresee; to divine, augur.

تكهُّن prediction, prophecy, surmise, forecasting.

تكوّم to be piled up, stacked, accumulated.

تكوّن to be formed, created, produced; to come into existence; to be composed, made up; to consist of.

تكوُّن birth, rise, development, formation.

تكويم heaping up, piling up; accumulation.

تكوين forming, shaping, creating, making; bringing into being; origination, setting up, instituting; structure, setup, frame, form, shape, configuration.

تكيّف to adapt oneself to; to accomodate oneself to, conform to; to assume, aquire a form or shape; to be shaped.

تَكَيُّف adaptation, conformity, accomodation.

تَكْيِيف forming, shaping; adaptation, conditioning, modification, qualification; airconditioning.

تَلّ hill, mound.

تلا، تَلَى to follow, come after, succeed; to result from, arise from.

تَلاءَمَ to suit, fit, match with; to be suitable for, adequate to, suited to.

تَلاحَقَ to follow in close succession; to pursue each other; to come successively, consecutively; to occur repeatedly; to continue.

تَلاحَمَ to join in battle; to engage in a mutual massacre;. to cling closely together; to be intermeshed, closely united.

تَلازَمَ to accompany; to adhere, be attached, stick to; to be necessary, indispensable; to be inseparable, linked, coupled with.

تَلاشَى to vanish, disappear, fade away; to decline, die away; to be scattered, dispersed, destroyed.

تَلاصُق cohesion, adhesion, contact, contiguity.

تَلاطَفَ to be kind toward; to be amiable, friendly; to treat someone with kindness; to be civil and polite toward someone.

تَلاطَمَ to clash; to exchange blows; to fight, quarrel.

تَلاعَبَ to act fraudulently; to cheat, rig, manipulate; to tamper with; falsify, change (figures); to play on words; to move, play a trick.

تَلاعُب manipulation, rigging, falsification (figures); cheating, tampering with; play on words, pun, wordplay.

تَلافٍ (التَّلافِي) avoidance, obviation, prevention, staving off; redressing, making up for.

تَلافَى to put right, to repair; to eliminate, remedy, redress; to avoid, avert, stave off.

تَلاقٍ (التَّلاقِي) meeting, encounter, reunion, getting together.

تَلاقَى to get together; to meet with; to hold a meeting with; to bump into, encounter.

تَلاكَمَ to fight with the fists; to box.

تَلأْلأَ to glitter, sparkle, radiate, shine, glimmer.

تَلأْلُؤ shining, sparkling, glittering, radiance.

تَلامَسَ to touch each other; to be adjacent to; to contact with; to be in mutual contact.

تَلامُس touching, contact, adjacency, contiguity.

تِلاوَة recital, recitation, reading.

تَلَبَّدَ to stick together; to become matted, entangled, compressed, clouded, overcast (with clouds); to become gloomy; to get stuck.

تَلَبَّسَ to get mixed up with, involved in; to be obscure, dubious, ambiguous; to dress, overlay; to be attired, covered with, wrapped in.

تَلْبِيَة compliance, observance, obeying; in compliance with; consent, assent, carrying out.

تَلْبِيس dressing, garbing, draping; overlaying, inlaying; incrustation; coating, covering.

تَلّة hill, mound.

تَلْحين musical composition.

تَلَخَّصَ to be summarized, briefed, abridged, epitomized in.

تَلْخيص summing up, briefing, summary, epitome, abstract, synopsis, outline, condensation, abridgment.

تَلَذُّذ enjoyment, relish, pleasure, delight.

تَلَزَّزَ to be crammed together; to be united, jointed; to adhere, stick to; to be compacted, tied firmly to.

تَلْزيم granting a contract, a concession; obligation, commitment; contract, monopoly, farming out.

تَلَصَّصَ to spy; to snoop on, peek at.

تَلَطَّخَ to be soiled, stained, smeared, smudged.

تَلَطَّفَ to be kind and friendly toward; to be nice, amiable toward; to treat someone with kindness; to be polite to; to be obliging, indulgent toward; to have the kindness to give; to be alleviated, eased, soothed; to deign, be gracious enough to; to proceed gently, carefully, slowly, gracefully.

تَلْطيف softening, alleviation, soothing, toning down.

تَلَعْثَمَ to stutter, stammer, hesitate in one's speech.

تَلِفَ to be destroyed, ruined, damaged, spoiled.

تَلَف damage, ruin, wreckage, decay, wear and tear.

تَلَفَّتَ to turn one's face; to look around; to pay attention, heed, bear in mind.

تَلَفَّظَ to pronounce, utter, express in words, say.

تَلَفُّظ pronounciation, enunciation, articulation.

تَلَقَّى to receive, get, obtain; to encounter, meet.

تَلَقَّى العِلْمَ to take lessons in; to study at; to be taught; to acquire knowledge; to pursue studies at.

تِلْقاء opposite to; before.

تِلْقائي spontaneous, impulsive.

تِلقائيًا spontaneously; of one's own accord, willingly, voluntarily, automatically.

تَلَقَّبَ to be surnamed, nicknamed, called.

تَلَقَّحَ to be fertilized, fecundated; to be vaccinated, pollinated.

تَلَقَّفَ to snap at, snatch, grab, catch; to seize quickly.

تَلْقيح pollination, fertilization, fecundation; impregnation; inoculation, vaccination.

تَلْقيم spoon-feeding; feeding bit by bit; to load, charge (a weapon).

تَلْقين instruction, direction; dictation, suggestion, insinuation; prompting (an actor on stage).

تِلْكَ that, that one.

تَلَكَّأَ to lag, linger, loiter; to be tardy; to fail to meet one's obligations; to be in default.

تَلْمَذَة studentship, apprenticeship; school days.

تَلَمَّسَ to fumble, grope about; to look, search for; to ask for, solicit.

تَلْميح insinuation, allusion, hint, suggestion.

تِلْميذ student, pupil, schoolboy; apprentice (profession); disciple; trainee.

تَلْميع polishing, polish; lustering, glossing, brightening up.

تَلَهَّى to amuse oneself; to pass the time with; to seek distraction from; to be distracted, diverted from.

تَلَهَّفَ to yearn, pant after; to regret, deplore, lament, grieve, sigh for; to be eager for.

تَلَهُّف sigh, lament; concern; yearning, longing, desire; anxiety, apprehension.

تَلَوٍّ (التَّلَوِّي) writhing, twisting; tortuosity, wriggling.

تِلْوَ after, upon, immediately after.

تَلَوَّى to writhe, twist, wriggle; to squirm.

تَلَوَّثَ to be polluted, contaminated; to be unclean, soiled, stained, tarnished.

تَلَوُّث pollution, contamination, impurity.

تَلَوَّنَ to be colored, tinted, painted.

تَلَوَّنَ to be unsteady, capricious, inconstant, whimsical.

تَلْويح beckoning, brandishing, waving; allusion, insinuation; hint, sign, signal.

تَلْوين coloring, painting.

تَلْيين softening, tempering; mitigation, moderation.

تَمَّ to be complete, completed; to be concluded, finalized, terminated; to end; to be accomplished, executed, performed, realized, fulfilled.

تَماثُل similarity, homology, likeness, ressemblance.

تَماثُل recovery, recuperation (from illness).

تَمادَى to go too far; to go to extremes; to continue, persist, persevere in; to keep on doing.

تَمارَضَ to feign sickness; to pretend to be sick.

تَماسَكَ to hold together, stick together, cling together; to cohere, adhere.

تَماسُك coherence, cohesion, solidity, tenacity.

تَمالَكَ to control, restrain oneself; to refrain, keep from.

تَمالُك self-control, self-restraint.

تَمام completion, entirety; full, whole, complete; perfection, termination.

تَماماً	completely, entirely, wholly; perfectly; quite.
تَمايَلَ	to stagger, waver, swing, totter.
تَمَتَّعَ	to enjoy, savor, relish; to have for one's use or benefit.
تَمَتُّع	enjoyment, savoring, relish.
تَمْتَمَ	to mumble, murmur, mutter.
تَمْتِين	strengthening, consolidation.
تِمْثال	statue; bust.

نحت الفنّان تمثالاً نصفيّاً في الحجر

The artist carved a statue from a rock

تَمَثَّلَ	to imitate, take after; to take on the shape of someone; to imagine, fancy; to appear, show, manifest itself; to be represented, visible, assimilated (food).

تَمْثِيل	representation; description; exemplification; likening; torture, mutilation; assimilation (food); acting, playing, performance (on stage, in films).
تَمْثِيلِيَّة	play, drama, performance.
تَمْجِيد	glorification, praise, laudation.
تَمَخَّضَ	to bring forth, give rise to; to be churned (milk).
تَمَدَّدَ	to stretch out; to spread out; to be spread out, extended, stretched, lengthened, distended; to lie down.
تَمَدُّد	extension, expansion, stretching out; prostration.
تَمَدُّن	civilization, urbanization.
تَمْدِيد	lengthening, prolongation, extension; laying; protraction.
تَمْدِيدات (ج)	installations, fixtures, fittings.

تَمْر	dates.
تَمَرَّدَ	to rebel, revolt, mutiny against; to disobey orders; to be arrogant, insolent.
تَمَرُّد	recalcitrance, disobedience; uprising, revolt, mutiny, insurgence, insurrection.
تَمَرَّسَ	to be accustomed, get used to; to be oneself with, against.
تَمَرَّغَ	to roll in; to wallow (in dust); to waver, hesitate.
تَمَرَّنَ	to practise, exercise, rehearse; to become trained, coached, tutored; to be skilled, experienced; to get used to; to be accustomed to.

تَمَرُّن exercise, practise, training; habituation.

تَمْرِيض nursing; caring of the sick.

تَمرِين exercise, training, practise; rehearsal (of a play); drill (military).

تَمَزَّق to be torn, lacerated, shredded to pieces, ruptured.

تَمَزُّق laceration, rupture, tear.

تَمْزِيق tearing, shredding, ripping apart, rending.

تِمْساح crocodile, alligator.

يعيش التمساح في أنهر المناطق الاستوائية

Crocodiles abound
in the rivers of equatorial regions

تَمَسَّك to cling to, adhere to, stick to, hold to; to persist in; to clutch, cleave, hang on to; to grab fast.

تَمَسُّك clinging to, sticking to; adhering to; tenacity, attachment, persistence in.

تَمَشَّى to go, walk on foot; to proceed, march, keep pace with; to keep abreast; to walk slowly; to stroll, saunter; to stride along; to be appropriate, correspond to; to follow, observe (a principle, idea).

تَمْشِيط combing, dressing (hair); carding (cotton); combing, searching meticulously a place.

تَمَعَّن to look closely at; to examine carefully; to pore over attentively.

تَمَعُّن scrutiny, close examination.

تَمَغَّط to be stretched, extended, expanded.

تَمَغُّط elasticity.

تَمَغْنُط magnetization.

تَمَكَّن to be capable; to have the power to; to master, gain mastery of; to be firm, fixed, strong.

تَمَكُّن ability, capability, power, authority, mastery.

تَمْكِين consolidation, fixing, fastening, enabling.

تَمَلَّص to slip away, escape, dodge, free oneself; to rid oneself of; to evade, shirk.

تَمَلَّق to flatter, cajole, adulate.

تَمَلُّق adulation, flattery, cajolery, bootlicking.

تَمَلَّك to take over, acquire, lay hands on, possess; to appropriate, take possession, seize; to gain control over oneself; to restrain one's emotions; to rule, dominate, control.

تَمَلُّك possession, acquisition, domination, control.

تَمَلْمَل to fidget, mumble, grumble; to be disgruntled, angry, restless, fidgety, nervous, uncertain.

تَمْليك conveyance of property; alienation, cession of ownership; transfer of property.

تَمَنٍّ (التَّمَنّي) wishing, desiring.

تَمَنِّيات (ج) compliments, wishes.

تَمَنَّى to wish, desire, hope; to look forward to.

تَمَنَّعَ to decline to accept; to refuse, deny, withhold from; to abstain, refrain from doing something; to be strongly fortified, unconquerable; to resist, oppose, object; to avoid, keep from doing, forbear.

تَمَنُّع refraining, refusal; denial, abstention; resistance, desisting; impossibility.

تَمَهَّلَ to act slowly; to slacken one's pace, tarry, dawdle, take one's time.

تَمَهُّل slowness, deliberateness.

تَمْهيد leveling, grading (ground); paving; arrangement, preparing, facilitating.

تَمْهيد preface, foreword, preamble.

تَمْهيديّ preliminary, preparatory, provisional.

تَمَوُّج undulation, fluctuation, rippling, swaying, rising in waves.

تَمْويل financing.

تَمْوين food supply, provisioning, replenishment.

تَمْويه camouflaging; disguising; misrepresentation, falsification; coating, plating; dilution, weakening.

تَمَيَّزَ to be preferred, privileged, distinguished; to burst with rage; to be brought before a court of cassation (case); to be discriminated.

تَميمَة amulet, talisman, charm.

تَمْييز differentiation, discrimination; recognition, distinction; partiality, bias, favoritism; preference, setting aside, segregation; specification (language); cassation (law); discretion, common sense.

تَمْييع liquefaction; turning into liquid.

تَناثَرَ to be scattered about, strewn about; to be dispersed; to fall off, fall out.

تَناحَرَ to flight, combat, battle with each other.

تَناذُر syndrome.

تَنازَعَ to dispute, contend; to litigate; pull pack and forth; to snatch; to engross, absorb, engage, preoccupy; to contest, challenge.

تَنازُع struggle, strife, fight, contest, dispute.

تَنازَلَ to step down, give up, relinquish, surrender, waive, cede; to abdicate (a throne); to condescend, deign; to be gracious enough to do something; to attack, submit to someone; to abase, humble, demean oneself.

تَنازُل assault, giving up, surrender, yielding, resignation; abdication (of a throne); cession, assignment; deigning; concession.

أ ب ت ث ج ح خ د ذ ر ز س ش ص ض ط ظ ع غ ف ق ك ل م ن هـ و ي

تَنَاسَى to pretend to have forgotten; to try to forget.

تَنَاسَبَ to correspond, suit, fit; to be compatible, consistent with; to be in agreement with; to be related to one another by marriage; to be convenient with; to be appropriate, adequate, commensurate.

تَنَاسُب proportion, conformity, congruity; relationship.

تَنَاسُبِيّ proportional.

تَنَاسُخ transmigration (of souls); succession, sequence; metempsychosis.

تَنَاسُق coordination, consistency, harmony, congruity; order, symmetry.

تَنَاسُل reproduction, propagation, procreation.

تَنَاسُلِيّ genital, reproductive, sexual.

تَنَاظَرَ to debate, argue, discuss; to face each other; to be corresponding, similar, analogous; to be symmetrical (math).

تَنَاظُر difference of opinion, squabble, wrangle; symmetry (match); analogy, similarity, homology.

تَنَاغُم harmony, agreement, concord, congruity.

تَنَافَى to disagree; to be contradictory, inconsistent; to be incompatible with.

تَنَافُر mutual aversion, mutual antipathy, mutual alienation; dispute, quarrel, conflict; discord, disagreement, disharmony; repulsion (physics).

تَنَافَسَ to compete, vie, contend.

تَنَافُس competition, rivalry; fight, struggle.

تَنَافُسِيّ competitive, emulative.

تَنَاقَشَ to debate, argue, dispute.

تَنَاقَصَ to decrease, diminish, dwindle, lessen, reduce.

تَنَاقُص decrease, dwindling, lessening, decrement.

تَنَاقَضَ to contradict each other, to clash; to be contradictory, conflicting, disagreeing, contrasting.

تَنَاقُض contradiction, opposition, contrariety; inconsistency, discrepancy, contrast.

تَنَاقَلَ to carry away, transfer, relocate; to transmit, pass on; to communicate, spread, convey, relate (a story); to pass from mouth to mouth; to be on every body's lips; to pass from hand to hand.

تَنَاهَى to come to someone's knowledge; to get wind of.

تَنَاوُب alternation, succession.

بِالتَّنَاوُب by turns, successively, one by one.

تَنَاوَلَ to take, pick up, obtain, get, receive, get hold of; to eat (food); to treat, discuss (a subject); to include, encompass.

تَنَبَّأَ to predict, foretell, forecast, foresee.

تَنَبُّؤ prediction, foretelling, forecasting, prophecy.

تُنْبَاك tobacco.

تَنَبَّهَ to realize, notice; to be aware of, conscious of; to heed, mind; to pay attention to; to wake up; to beware; to be alerted; to be mindful, headful; to be on one's guard, be wary, cautious, careful.

تَنْبيه arousal; warning, monition, alarm, alert; awakening, rousing; note, remark.

تَنْجيد upholstery, upholstering.

تَنْجيم astrology, fortune-telling.

تَنَحَّى to retire, withdraw, step aside, make way; to abandon, give up, relinquish.

تَنْحِيَة dismissal, setting aside, putting aside.

تَنْدِيَة moistening, wetting.

تَنْديد condemnation, censure, denunciation, revilement.

تَنَزَّهَ to take a walk; to go on a picnic; to disdain; to be too proud for; to be honest.

تَنَزُّه going for a walk, picnicking; disdain; honesty, integrity; probity.

تَنَزُّهٌ عن الخَطأ infallibility.

تَنْزيل lowering, bringing down, unloading; reduction, decrease, deduction; demotion (in rank or status).

تَنْزيل revelation, inspiration.

التَنْزيل the Holy Koran.

تَنَسَّكَ to lead an ascetic life, to become an ascetic; to be pious; to devote oneself to the worship of God.

تَنَسُّك asceticism, reclusion; piety, devotion.

تَنَسَّمَ to breathe, respire; to blow gently (wind); to nose about, hunt for, pick up (news, information); to be fragrant; to exhale fragrance.

تَنْسيق arraying, setting up, disposition, arrangement; grouping, coordination, concert.

تَنْشِئَة upbringing, raising, rearing.

تَنَشَّقَ to sniff, inhale; to smell.

تَنْشيط encouragement, stimulation, activation; promotion (of sales); energizing.

تَنْشيف drying, desiccation; wiping.

تَنَصَّتَ to eavesdrop, listen secretly.

تَنَصَّلَ to renounce, disavow, vindicate oneself; to justify oneself; to refuse to take the responsibility; to disclaim.

تَنْصيب appointment, nomination, induction (in an official position); installation, installment; investiture.

تَنْضيد typesetting, composition (printing).

تَنَظَّمَ to be organized, arranged, arrayed; to become steady, uniform, regular; to be affiliated, enrolled; to be put together; to be grouped.

تَنْظير theorization, theorizing; observing, viewing.

تَنْظيف cleaning, cleansing, scrubbing.

تَنْظيم organization, arrangement, readjustment; control; laying out; preparation; planning.

تَنْظيم organization, formation.

تَنْظيمُ الأُسْرَة family planning.

تَنَعَّمَ to live in comfort and luxury; to lead a life of ease, a carefree life; to be delighted; to enjoy, savor, taste; to be smooth, soft, tender.

تَنَعُّم luxury, ease, comfort, enjoyment.

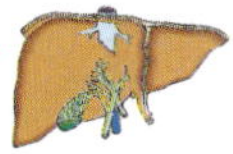

تَنَغَّصَ to be disturbed, ruffled, spoiled; to be embittered.

تَنَفَّسَ to breathe, respire, inhale.

تَنَفُّس respiration, breathing.

تنفيذ carrying out, implementation, accomplishment, realization, execution; sending, forwarding.

تَنفيذيّ executive.

تَنْفيس ventilation, airing, release, discharge, letting off (air, steam).

تَنَقَّلَ to move from its place; to change one's residence, to change position; to walk about, wander, migrate.

تَنَقُّل change of residence, locality; change of position, station, garrison; traveling, wandering, migration; moving, motion.

تَنْقيب drilling for metals; excavation in search of mineral deposits; research, investigation, search, hunt.

تَنْقِيَة purification, clarification, cleaning, refining.

تَنْقيح revision, rectification, redaction, editing, retouching, examination.

تَنْقيط pointing, dotting; punctuation (grammar); spotting, dotting, specking.

تحفر بئر في الأرض للتنقيب عن الماء أو النفط
A well is drilled in the ground in search of water or oil

تَنَك tin, tinplate.

تَنَكَّبَ to deviate, swerve (from a road); to avoid, shun; to refrain from; to take upon oneself; to assume; to lean on, recline on.

تَنَكَّرَ to be disguised, masked; to disapprove, reject; to disavow, deny; to renounce; to alienate oneself from; to treat with hostility; to feign ignorance; to detest, loathe.

تَنْكيل exemplary punishment, torture.

تَنْمِيَة development, promotion; cultivation; enhancement.

تَنْميق ornamentation, embellishment; composition in an elegant style (text); grandiloquence, pomposity (speech, writing).

تَنَهَّدَ to sigh.

تَنَهُّد sigh, sighing.

تَنُّور oven, furnace.

تَنَوُّع diversity, variety.

تَنْوِير enlightenment; illumination; blooming, blossoming, flowering.

تَنْوِيع modification, change; diversity, variety.

تَنْوِيم putting to sleep.

تَنْوِيمٌ مَغْنَطِيسِيّ hypnotism, hypnosis.

تَنْوِيه tribute, praise, mention; hint, allusion.

تِنِّين dragon, sea monster.

تَهَاتُر abuse, revilement, vituperation; confrontation of similar evidence (law).

تَهَادَى to exchange presents with; to sway, swing rythmically (while walking); to move forward.

تَهَادَنَ to make peace with; to be reconciled with; to conclude a truce; to quiet down.

تَهَافَتَ to follow in succession; to pounce, rush, plunge, fall; to throng; to cave in, collapse; to contradict.

تَهَافُت collapse, breakdown; rush; breakup; crowding, flocking; contradiction.

تَهَالَكَ to strive, endeavor, exert oneself; to do one's utmost; to pounce upon; to covet, crave; to feel enthusiasm; to devote oneself eagerly to; to break down, collapse; to drop, fall, throw oneself.

تَهَاوَى to collapse, break down, plunge into; to pounce, fall upon, drop; to be thrust down.

تَهَاوَنَ to attach no importance to; to belittle, deride, minimize; to be negligent, careless; to consider easy; to esteem lightly.

تَهَاوُن neglect, disdain, indifference, carelessness, laxity, remissness, slackness.

تَهَايُؤ adaptation, accomodation.

تَهَتَّكَ to be dissolute, uninhibited, immoral; to be shameless, impudent; to be exposed, disgraced; to be torn, lacerated.

تَهَتُّك immorality, dissoluteness; impudence, shamelessness, insolence.

تَهَجَّأَ to spell.

تَهَجَّمَ to assail, pounce, raid, assault; to invade, trespass.

تَهَجُّم attack, charge, assault, raid, agression, offense.

تَهْجِير eviction, displacing; emigration; expulsion.

تَهْدِئَة pacification, appeasement, soothing, alleviation, quieting; tranquilization, reassurance.

تَهَدَّلَ to hang down; to hang loose; to dangle; to flow.

تَهَدَّمَ to be torn down, razed, demolished, destroyed; to fall down, break down, collapse.

تَهْدِيد threat, menace, intimidation.

تَهْدِيم pulling down, wrecking, destruction, demolition.

تَهْدِيمِيّ destructive, subversive.

تَهَذَّبَ to be well-bred, well-raised, educated; to be courteous, refined; to be corrected, trimmed, polished, rectified.

تَهْذِيب instruction, education; upbringing; refinement, trimming, polishing; revision, correction; courtesy, politeness, discipline, good manners.

تَهَرَّبَ to elude, evade, dodge, desert, shirk.

تَهَرُّب elusion, escape, shirking, avoidance, evasion.

تَهْرِيب smuggling, illicit trade.

تَهْرِيج jesting, joking, making fun.

تَهَزْهَزَ to be moved, agitated, shaken; to quake, quiver.

تَهَشَّمَ to be smashed, shattered, broken into pieces, destroyed.

تَهْشِيم smashing, shattering, destruction, crushing.

تَهَكَّمَ to mock, scoff, make fun of; to ridicule, deride, jeer someone; to jeer at, snear at.

تَهَكُّم irony, ridicule, scorn, gibe, sarcasm, mocking.

تَهَلَّلَ to shout with joy; to exult, rejoice; to shine, gleam, glow, beam with joy (face); to be delighted, jubilant, exultant, cheerful.

تَهْلِيل acclaim, applause, hail, cheer; jubilation, exultation; to utter the formula «la Ilaha Illallah».

تُهْمَة accusation, charge.

تَهْنِئَة congratulation, felicitation.

تَهَوَّرَ to be destroyed, crashed; to rush headlong into danger; to be careless, rash, heedless, imprudent.

تَهَوُّر rashness, recklessness, carelessness; extravagance, irresponsibility, hastiness; breakdown, collapse.

تَهْوِيَة ventilation, airing.

تَهْوِيدَة lullaby.

تَهْوِيش excitation, agitation, rousing, incitation.

تَهْوِيل frightening, alarming, intimidation; phantom, nightmare, bogey.

تَهَاوِيل (ج) embellishments, ornamental florishes.

تَهَيَّأَ to be ready, prepared; to prepare, ready oneself; to be in fighting condition (in war); to be well-dressed; to be possible, feasible for.

تَهَيُّؤ preparedness, adaptation.

تَهْيِئَة preparation, readying, setting up; adaptation; adjustment, accomodation.

تَهَيَّبَ to fear, be afraid of, stand in awe by; to honor, respect; to inspire with awe, frighten.

تَهَيَّجَ to be excited, agitated, awakened, stirred; to be in a state of commotion; to be scared up.

أ ب **ت** ث ج ح خ د ذ ر ز س ش ص ض ط ظ ع غ ف ق ك ل م ن هـ و ي

تَهَيُّج excitement, agitation, commotion, disturbance; turmoil, irritation, uproar (of elements).

تَوًّا at once, right away, immediatly.

تَوَاءَمَ to be in harmony with; to suit, fit.

تَوَاتَرَ to be strained, stretched; to follow in succession; to recur; to repeat itself.

تَوَاتُر recurrence, frequency, succession, repetition.

تَوَاجَهَ to face each other; to meet face to face.

تَوَاحَدَ to be united, joined, brought together; to be one; to form a unity; to be amalgamated, combined.

تَوَارَى to hide, conceal oneself; to disappear; to disguise, mask oneself with; to disappear from the sight of.

تَوَارَدَ to arrive one after the other; to succeed one another; to coincide, happen; to be identical (ideas).

تَوَازَى to be parallel to each other; to be equivalent, correspond to, equal; to run side by side.

تَوَازَنَ to be balanced, in equilibrium, counterpoised; to be equal in weight, even up with; to be stabilized.

تَوَازُن equilibrium, balance, counterpoise; stability.

تَوَاصَلَ to continue; to form an uninterrupted sequence; to be joined, connected; to communicate with.

تَوَاصُل continuity, continuance; connection, contact, intercourse, communication.

تَوَاضَعَ to humble, humiliate, disparage oneself; to be low, lowly, humble; to behave modestly; to agree, to reach an agreement on.

تَوَاضُع humility, modesty, lowliness, humbleness.

تَوَاطُؤ connivance, collusion, agreement in secret.

تَوَاعَدَ to promise one another; to arrange for a meeting; to make an appointment with; to threaten, menace someone.

تَوَافَدَ to arrive successively; to arrive together; to flock.

تَوَافَرَ to be abundant, plentiful, ample; to be fulfilled (a condition); to be richly endowed with; to grow, multiply; to be available, obtainable.

تَوَافُر plenty, abundance, profusion; availability.

تَوَافَقَ to be right, proper, suitable, appropriate with; to be consistent with someone's interests, wishes; to be in line with, correspond to; to be in agreement, in accordance, in conformity with; to tally, coincide, to chance, happen, occur.

تَوَافُق agreement, congruence, congruity, consistency, harmony, conformity, entente.

تَوَّاق longing, yearning, eager for, craving something; desiring ardently, aspiring to.

تَوَالٍ (التَّوالِي) succession, sequence; alternation, rotation.

على التَّوالِي continuously, successively, consecutively, one by one, after the other.

تَوَالَى to follow in succession; to continue without interruption; to progress, continue; to rotate, alternate.

تَوَالَدَ to reproduce, propagate, procreate, generate.

تَوَالُد procreation, begetting, generation, propagation, reproduction, proliferation.

تَوْأَم twin, twins.

تَوَانٍ (التَّوانِي) lagging, slackness, limpness, negligence, tarrying, lingering, lassitude.

تَوَانَى to slacken, slack, tarry, linger; to be slow, slack, lax, negligent, limp; to hesitate, waver, wait.

تَوْبَة repentance, contrition, penitence.

تَوْبيخ scolding, reproach, reproof, reprimand, rebuke, censure.

تُوت mulberry (tree).

تُوتُ الأَرْض strawberry (plant).

تُوتُ العُلَّيق raspberry (plant).

تَوَتَّر to be strained, stretched, tight, taut, tense.

تَوَتُّر strain, stress, tension.

تَوَتُّرُ الأَعْصاب nervous tension.

تَوْتير straining, tightening, tensioning.

تَوْثيق consolidation, strengthening; documentation, authentication; registration, notarization.

تَوَّجَ to crown, enthrone; to top, cap.

تَوَجَّبَ to be necessary, obligatory, incumbent on; to be deemed worthy of, necessary, binding.

تَوَجَّسَ to be apprehensive, worried; to have forbodings, apprehensions, presentiments; to be afraid; to have a sensation of fear; to regard as an evil omen; to taste.

تَوَجُّس apprehensiveness, worry, presentiment, fright, sensation of fear, of anxiety.

تَوَجَّعَ to feel pain, suffer; to be tormented; to feel sorrow, pity, compassion for someone.

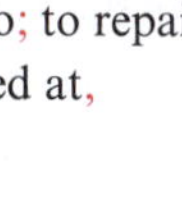

تَوَجُّع pain, lament, suffering.

تَوَجَّهَ to go to, head for, proceed to; to pursue, aim at, address oneself to; to turn one's face to; to repair to; to be directed, aimed at, turned toward.

تَوَجُّه direction, inclination, tendency, orientation.

تَوْجيه aiming, directing, orientation, guidance; steering, guiding, instruction; transfer, conveyance; forwarding; controlling.

تَوْجيهات (ج) directives, instructions.

تَوَحَّدَ to unite, to be united, connected, joined; to become one; to be merged, amalgamated with; to be consolidated, combined; to form a unity.

تَوَحَّدَ to be alone, seclude oneself, live in seclusion; to perform singlehandedly.

تَوَحُّد solitude, loneliness, singleness; isolation, seclusion.

تَوَحَّشَ to be deserted, desolute (region); to be filled with anxiety; to feel lonely, lonesome; to become wild, savage, brutal; to become estranged, afraid, repelled.

تَوْحيد unification, union, fusion, merger, amalgamation; standardization, integration.

التَّوْحيد monotheism, belief in the unity of God.

تَوَخَّى to have in mind; to seek to; to strive for.

تَوَدَّدَ to show love, affectation; to try to gain favor with; to curry favor; to flatter one's way into; to be on friendly terms with.

تَوْديع bidding farewell to; leavetaking.

تَوْراة، التَّوْراة Old Testament.

تَوَرَّدَ to become red; to glow, redden (cheek); to blossom.

تَوَرَّطَ to be or get involved in; to get oneself into trouble; to be entangled, embroiled in.

تَوَرُّط involvement, embroilment in.

تَوَرُّم swelling, tumefaction; edema.

تَوْريد provision, supplying; importation, import.

تَوْريط involvement, embroilment, entanglement.

تَوْريق foliation; wallpapering.

تَوْزيع distribution; apportionment; delivery; division.

تَوَسَّطَ to mediate; to intercede for; to be or sit in the middle of; to lie bettwen; to take a middle course; to act as a mediator or go-between.

تَوَسُّط mediation, intervention, intermediacy; moderation.

تَوَسَّعَ to expand, extend, widen, broaden; to be wide, roomy, spacious; to sit comfortably, make oneself at home in; to write at great length; to become rich; to discuss or write in detail; to elaborate; to give or grant generously; to spend lavishly.

تَوَسُّع expansion, enlargement, extension; increase, widening, stretching; expansionism.

تَوَسَّلَ to curry favor; to seek or solicit someone's favor; to implore, entreat, beseech, plead with; to use as a means; to make use of a means.

تَوَسُّل entreaty, beseeching, solicitation; petition; use of a means; request, plea, application.

أ ب ت ث ج ح خ د ذ ر ز س ش ص ض ط ظ ع غ ف ق ك ل م ن هـ و ي

تَوْسيع widening, expansion, extension, broadening, enlargement, elaboration.

تَوَصَّلَ to arrive; to reach; to come; to obtain access to; to attain to; to come to someone's knowledge.

تَوْصِيَة recommendation; exhortation; counsel, advice; proposal; mandate; commission.

تَوْصيل uniting, connecting; supply, feed; conductivity (elec.); transmission, delivery; conduction (elec.).

تَوَضَّأَ to perform the ritual ablution before prayer.

تَوَضَّحَ to become visible, to be made clear; to be clarified, to be shown, indicated, obvious; to come out, manifest itself; to be elucidated, explained.

تَوْضيب packing, boxing, packaging, arrangement.

تَوْضيح elucidation, illustration, explanation, clarification.

تَوْطِئَة preliminary step; introduction, preface; leveling, flattening; preparation.

تَوَطَّدَ to be firmly established, settled, stabilized, consolidated.

تَوْطين settlement, settling.

تَوَظَّفَ to be employed, hired; to get a job; to hold an office.

تَوْظيف employment, hiring, appointment.

تَوَعَّدَ to threat, menace, to intend firmly to.

تَوَعَّكَ to be indisposed, ill, sick.

تَوَعُّك indisposition, illness.

تَوْعِيَة enlightenment, edification; cautioning, alerting.

تَوَغَّلَ to penetrate deeply into; to come uninvited to.

تَوَغُّل penetration; preoccupation; thorough study.

تَوَفَّى to die, pass away, expire; to obtain one's dues.

تَوَفَّرَ to be available, abundant, plentiful; to be spared, saved (money); to be fulfilled (conditions).

تَوَفُّر abundance, augmentation; fulfillment, availability.

تَوْفير saving, economizing, providence; providing, furnishing, supply; ensuring, securing (peace, calm); increase, augmentation.

تَوْفيق conformation, adaptation, accomodation; success, happy outcome, gool luck; prosperity; reconciliation, arbitration, peacemaking.

تَوْق longing, yearning, craving, desire; striving for.

تَوَقَّعَ to expect, anticipate, forecast.

تَوَقُّع expectation, anticipation, forecast, presumption.

تَوَقَّفَ to stop, halt; to come to a standstill; to pause, halt, hesitate, waver; to abstain from, refrain from doing something; to depend on, be dependent on; to fail, stop working, break down (machine); to cease publication; to suspend payment.

تَوَقُّف halt, cessation, standstill; pause; hesitation, wavering; dependence on; suspension (of payment); breakdown, failure (machine).

تَوْقيت timing, reckoning of time; time.

تَوْقيع signature; dropping; performance, execution; discharge, undertaking; recording, registration.

تَوْقيعٌ بِالأَحْرُفِ الأُوْلَى initiating.

تَوْقيف detention, arrest; setting up, erection; stopping, halting; impeding, obstruction; interruption; deferment, delay; suspension from duty, work, job.

تَوَكَّلَ to be appointed as agent, proxy, representative; to act as agent, proxy, representative; to rely, depend on; to place one's confidence in; to be entrusted, charged, commissioned with; to guarantee, warrant, vouch for.

تَوَكُّل trust, confidence, reliance; representation, proxy, agency.

تَوْكيد confirmation, affirmation, assurance, assertion, emphasis, stress.

تَوْكيل empowerment, authorization; power of attorney; appointment as representative, deputy, agent; delegation of authority, power.

تَوَلٍّ (التَوَلِّي) assumption of; undertaking of; occupation of; be in charge of; seizing control of, coming into power.

تَوَلَّى to assume, undertake, take upon oneself; to take care of, to attend to; to be in charge of, to hold, occupy, take over, (a position); to come into power, assume power; to refrain from, desist from, leave off; to escape, flee, run away.

تَوَلَّدَ to be born, generated, produced from; to be brought forth, caused, occasioned by; to arise, proceed, result from, emanate from, spring from.

تَوَلُّد generation, production, procreation, genesis, origination, emanation.

تَوْلِيَة investiture, appointment, nomination to a position; installation; inauguration.

تَوْليد midwifery; obstetrics.

تَوْليد generation, production, bringing into being; giving birth to, begetting; causing, engendering.

تَوَهَّجَ to glow, flash, blaze; to be incadescent; to gleam, glitter, flicker (eyes).

تَوَهَّمَ to fancy, suppose, assume, believe, presume, surmise, misinterpret, misconstrue; to have a wrong idea of; to be under the delusion of.

تَوَهُّم imagining, fancying; delusion, illusion, suspicion, imagination, presumption, assumption.

تَيَّار current, stream; trend, tendency, inclination.

تَيَّارٌ مُسْتَمِرٌّ، مُتَواصِل direct current (elec.).

تَيَسَّرَ to become easy, available, simplified; to thrive, prosper, succeed.

تَيْسير facilitation, simplification, making available, accessible, obtainable.

تَيَقَّظ to be awake; to be on one's guard; to be watchful, alert.

تَيَقُّظ wakefulness, watchfulness, vigilance; caution.

تَيَّمَ to infatuate, captivate, fascinate, mesmerize; to be enthralled, enslaved by love.

تين fig (tree).

تَيَّهَ to mislead, misdirect; to puzzle, bewilder, confuse; to distract, divert, confound.

تيه pride, arrogance; maze, labyrinth; desert; deviation, error; straying, going astray.

تَيْهور avalanche.

حرف الثاء

ثائِر (اسم) rebel, revolutionary,
insurgent, mutineer.

ثائِر (ص) revolutionary; aroused,
agitated; wild, frantic;
enraged, furious, angry.

ثائِرة outburst, uproar; commotion,
disturbance.

ثَابَ to come back, return; to
recover, regain health;
to regain consciousness;
to recover one's senses.

ثَابِت firm, fixed, stationary; constant,
stable; proven, confirmed;
steadfast, fearless; permanent,
lasting; maintaining, keeping,
adhering to; persevering, diligent,
assiduous; remaining at, staying
at, residing at.

ثابَرَ to persevere, persist in.

ثَأَرَ to avenge the blood of; to take
vengeance; to get one's revenge;
to retaliate, make reprisals.

ثَارَ to be roused, excited; to rage,
storm; to fly into a rage; to become
furious; to stimulate, irritate; to
revolt against; to flare up with rage.

ثَأْر revenge, vengeance; reprisal,
retaliation.

ثاقِب penetrating, sharp; shrewd, clear-
headed, astute; perceptive,
discerning, clear-sighted.

ثالِث third, tertiary; third party.

ثالِثًا thirdly, in the third place.

ثالوث triad; triple, triplet; trinity.

ثُؤْلُول wart.

ثامِن eighth.

ثامِنًا eighthly, in the eighth place.

ثانٍ (الثّاني) second; next; another, one
more.

ثانِيًا secondly, in the second place;
again, anew, once again.

ثاني أُكسيدِ الكَرْبُون carbon dioxide.

ثانويّ secondary, minor, unimportant,interior.

ثانوية secondary school, college, high school.

ثانية second.

ثبات firmness, steadiness, constancy; stability, perseverence, persistence, endurance; sureness; permanence, endurance, continuation, continuance; immobility; stillness; compliance with, observance of; resolution, resistance, boldness; certainty; truth, correctness, validity; staying, remaining, stay; retention, adherence to; durability.

ثبت to be stable, steady, strong, unshakable; to be constant, unchangeable; to be stationary, motionless, immovable; to be established, proven; to maintain, adhere to, comply with; to persist in, persevere in; to remain firm, stand up against.

ثبت to be steadfast, brave, courageous, unyielding.

ثبّت to fix, secure, settle, stabilize; to make firm, stable; to consolidate, strengthen; to reinforce, cement; to valorize (prices); to gaze at; to gain a foothold; to appoint permanently (an employee).

ثبّط to frustrate, hold back, prevent from doing; to hinder, handicap, impede; to slow down; to bring about the failure; to discourage, disappoint, demoralize.

ثبور destruction, density, consistency, compactness.

ثخين thick, dense, consistent, compact.

ثدي breast, bosom (human); udder, dug (animal).

ثديي mammary, mammal.

ثرى earth, ground, soil.

ثراء wealth, affluence, prosperity, fortune.

ثرثار talkative, prattler, chatterbox.

ثرثر to chatter, prattle, blabber.

ثروة wealth, fortune, treasure, affluence, riches.

ثريّ wealthy, rich, well-to-do.

ثريّا chandelier.

ثريّا pleiades (astr.).

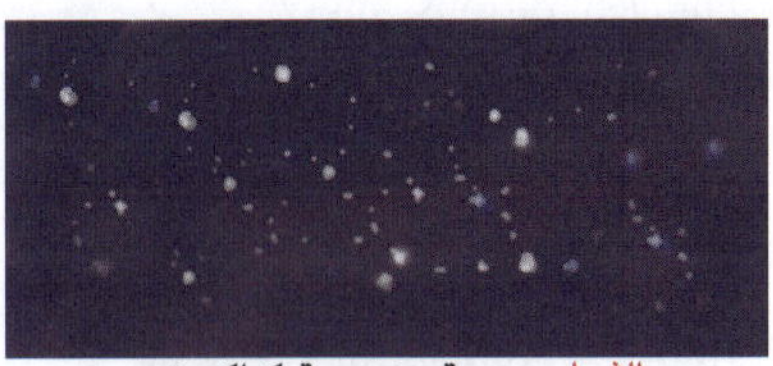

الثريا مجموعة من سبعة كواكب ترى بالعين المجردة خلال الليل

The pleiades is a group of seven stars that could be seen by the naked eye during nights

ثعبان snake, serpent (reptile).

ثعلب fox (animal).

ثغاء bleating, bleat (sheep).

ثغر to perforate, pierce, punch, indent.

ثغر mouth; port, harbor; bay, inlet; coastal city.

الثعلب حيوان ماكر يغدر بفريسته

Foxes are reputed for being cunning in catching their prey

ثُغْرَة breach, crack, rift, crevice, gap, cavity, hole.

ثُفْل sediment, residue, dregs, lees.

ثِقَاب matches.

ثَقَافَة culture, education.

ثَقَافِيّ cultural, educational, intellectual.

ثَقَبَ to perforate, pierce, punch, bore a hole in; to puncture.

ثَقَّبَ to light, kindle.

ثَقْب hole, bore, puncture; piercing, perforation.

ثَقْبُ الإبْرَة eye.

ثِقَة confidence, trust, faith, reliance; expert.

ثِقَةٌ بالنفس self-confidence, self-reliance.

ثَقَّفَ to educate, train, form, teach; to straighten, adjust.

ثَقُلَ to weigh heavily; to become heavy; to slacken one's steps; to lag, tarry; to be burdensome, cumbersome.

ثِقَل heaviness, sluggishness, dullness.

ثِقْل weight, burden, load; heaviness, gravity.

ثَقِيل heavy, weighty; grave, serious; burdensome, troublesome, oppressive; disagreeable, unpleasant.

ثَكِلَ to lose a child by death.

ثَكْلَى bereaved of a child by death.

ثُكْنَة barracks.

ثُلاثَ three at a time.

الثُّلاثَاء، الثَّلاثاء Tuesday.

30

ثَلاثَة three.

ثَلاثَةَ عَشَرَ thirteen.

ثَلاثُون، الثَّلاثُون thirty; the thirtieth.

ثُلاثِيّ tripartite; consisting of three; threefold, triple, triad; threesome; trinity.

ثُلاثِيُّ الأبعاد three-dimensional, tridimensional.

ثُلاثِيُّ الزَّوايا triangular.

ثُلاثِيُّ اللُّغات trilingual.

ثَلاَّجَة ice-box, refrigerator.

ثُلَّة band, group; detachment (military).

ثُلُث one third.

ثَلَّجَ to freeze, refrigerate, congeal.

ثَلْج snow, ice.

ثَلْجِيّ snowy, icy; glacial; white (color).

ثَلَمَ to blunt, indent, groove, furrow, dent.

أ ب ت **ث** ج ح خ د ذ ر ز س ش ص ض ط ظ ع غ ف ق ك ل م ن هـ و ي

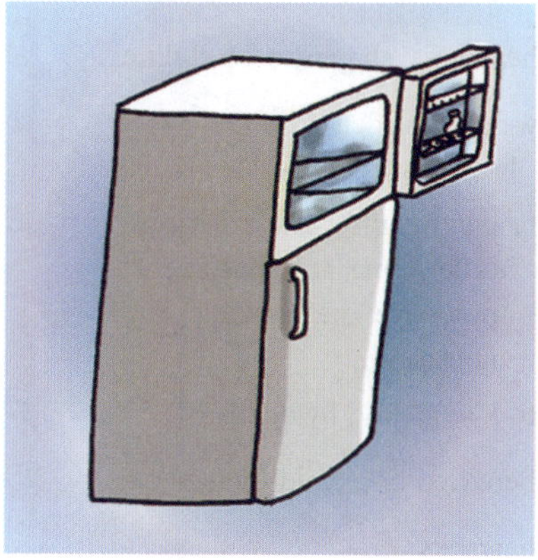

أضع الطعام في الثلاجة لحفظه من التعفن
I put the food in the refrigerator to preserve it from rotting

ثَلَمَ السُّمْعَة to dishonor; to tarnish, besmirch, defame, defile, sully; to slander, calumniate.

ثَلْم notch, breach, opening, gap; crack, fissure.

ثَلْم السُّمْعَة defamation, slander, calumny.

ثَمَّ there; over there, in that place.

مِنْ ثَمَّ hence, therefore, thus, as a result; consequently.

ثُمَّ then, afterwards, later on; besides.

يغطي الثلج سطوح المنازل في فصل الشتاء
Snow covers the roofs of houses during winter

ثُمالَة residues, sediment, dregs, lees; scum, foam.

ثُمانَ eight at a time; by eights.

ثَمانُون، الثَّمانُون eighty; the eightieth.

ثُمانِيُّ الزَّوايا أو الأضلاع octagonal, octagon.

ثَمانِيَة عَشَرَ eighteen.

ثَمَّة there, there is.

ثَمَر fruits, produce.

ثَمَرَة fruit; result, outcome; benefit.

ثَمِلَ to become drunk, intoxicated.

ثَمَل intoxication, inebriety, drunkenness.

ثَمِل drunken, intoxicated, inebriated; drunk.

ثَمَّنَ to estimate, value, assess, appraise; to esteem, prize, appreciate, cherish.

ثَمَن price, cost, value, worth.

ثُمُن، ثُمْن one-eighth, eighth.

ثَمين valuable, costly, precious.

ثَنَى to fold, double up, fold under; to bend, flex.

ثَنَى to dissuade, prevent, divert someone from.

ثَناء praise, laudation, tribute, compliment.

ثُنائِيّ twofold, double, dual, binary; duo; duet (music, song).

ثُنائِيُّ البعد two-dimensional.

ثُنائِيُّ الجنس bisexual.

ثُنائِيُّ الطور diphase, biphase.

ثُنائِيُّ القُطْب	bipolar, dipolar.
ثُنائِيُّ اللُّغَة	bilingual.
ثُنائِيُّ اللَّون	bicolored, dichromatic.
ثَنْي	folding, flexing, bending; discouraging, deterring someone from doing something.

ثَنْيَة	fold, pleat, crease, ply, cuff.
ثَنِيَّة	mountain pass; middle incisor (teeth).
في ثَنَايا	inside, within, amidst; in one's heart.
ثَوَى	to stay, live at a place; to pass away, to be buried.
ثَوَاب	requital, recompence, reward for good deeds; merit, credit.
ثَوْب	dress, cloth, material, garment; outward appearance, guise, mask.
ثَوْبُ السِّبَاحَة	swimsuit, bathing suit.
ثَوْر	bull, ox, bison (animal).
ثَوْرَة	revolution, revolt, upheaval, uprising, insurrection, riot, rebellion; outbreak (of fury); eruption (of a volcano).

حصلت ثورة في البلد أدت إلى قلب نظام الحكم فيها
A rebellion took place in the country and overthrew the ruling regime in it

ثَوْرَةٌ بَيْضاء	bloodless revolution.
ثَوْرَةٌ أَهْلِيَّة	civil war, internal strife.
ثَوْرَةٌ مُضادَّة	counterrevolution.
ثَوْرِيّ (ص)	revolutionary, insurgent, insurrectionary.
ثَوْرِيّ (اسم)	mutineer, rebel, revolutionary.
ثُوْم	garlic; chive (plant).

جَاءَ to come; to get to; to reach, arrive, bring to; to bring forth, produce, set forth; to do, perform; to occur, to be mentioned, said (in a document).

جائِر (ص) unjust, unfair; tyrannical, despotic.

جائِر (اسم) tyrant, oppressor, despot.

جَائِز permitted; conceivable, lawful, allowable; possible, probable.

مِنَ الجائِز perhaps, probably, maybe.

جائِزة prize, reward, award.

جَائِع hungry, starved.

جابَ to travel, traverse, roam, wander; to pierce, penetrate, cut through; to cruise about a place.

جابٍ (الجابِي) tax collector.

جَابَهَ to face, confront, encounter, oppose, defy.

نال الرياضي المتفوّق جائزة من رئيس النادي
The winning athlete received an award from the club's president

جَاثِم squatting; perching; prostrate, prone.

جَاحِد infidel, atheist; defector; denying; ungrateful.

جادَ to become good, improve; to grant generously; to be openhanded; to bestow liberally upon; to grant, give lavishly; to sacrifice oneself; to shed tears from his eyes; to be copious, abundant (rain).

جادّ earnest, serious; adept, efficient.

جادّة street, avenue; middle of the road.

جادَلَ to argue with, dispute with, quarrel with; to contest, contend, dispute in.

جاذَبَ to contend with someone at pulling; to engage someone in conversation, discussion.

جاذِبيّة gravitation, gravity; attraction, charm, sex appeal; magnetism.

جارَ to deviate from, commit an outrage on; to encroach on another's territory; to oppress, tyrannize.

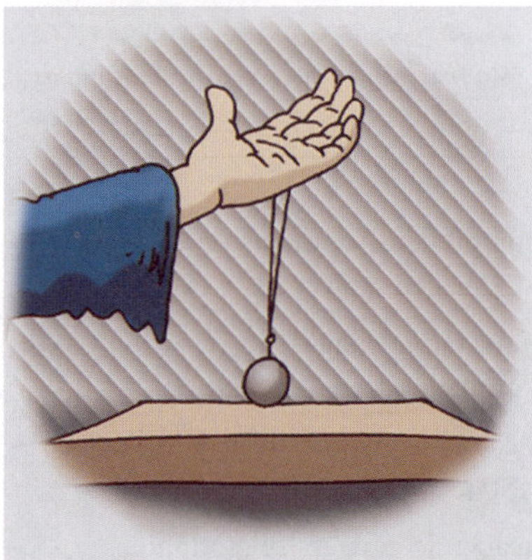

تشدّ جاذبية الأرض جميع الأجسام إلى سطحها

The Earth gravity pulls all bodies to its surface

جار neighbor.

جارّ preposition (grammar); pulling, towing, tugging.

جارٍ (الجاري) flowing, running; current, present; taking place, in progress.

جارى to keep pace with, keep abreast with; to act in agreement with, in conformity with, in line with; to take the same course as; to adapt oneself.

جارِح injurious, stinging, hurting; rapacious, predatory (beast); ferocious.

جارِف torrential (stream), stormy; violent (emotions).

جارور drawer.

جازَ to be permissible, allowable, allowed; to become possible, thinkable, probable; to cross, leave behind; to exceed, surpass, traverse.

جازى to reward, recompense; to punish, chastise.

جازَفَ to risk; to act at random, take a chance; to risk (one's life).

جازِم decisive, final, firmly established; absolutely certain of, positive about.

جاسِئ tough, rough, rugged.

جاسوس spy.

جاسوسيّة espionage, spying.

جاشَ to be agitated, convulsed with pain; to boil, simmer.

جَأْش emotional agitation, anxiety, worry; heart, soul.

يحاول الجاسوس معرفة أسرار العدو متخفياً وبسرية تامة

The spy tries to uncover the enemy's secrets in hiding and in full secrecy

جاعَ to be hungry; to feel hungry; to starve, famish.

جافّ dry, arid, dehydrated; dull, tedious; rough, rude, blunt.

جَافَى to offend; to disagree with; to be in conflict with.

جَالَ to roam, rove, wander about; to engage, absorb, preoccupy (one's mind); to cross someone's mind.

جَالَى to announce publicly.

جَالَسَ to sit down with someone; to keep someone's company.

جالِيَة colony, community.

جَامِح headstrong, unruly, untamable, runaway, unrestrained, inordinate in manners.

جامِد solid, hard, stiff; frozen, congealed; motionless, inanimate; defective (grammar); dry, dull; ossified; inorganic, mineral.

جامَعَ to have sexual intercourse with; to copulate with.

جامِع (اسم) mosque; collector; compiler, typesetter.

الجامع هو المسجد الذي يؤمّه المسلمون للصلاة

Moslems frequent mosques to perform prayers

جامع (ص) comprehensive, inclusive, extensive, universal.

جامِعَة university; league, confederation, association.

جامِعَةُ الدُّوَلِ العَرَبِيَّة League of Arab States, Arab League.

جامِعِيّ academic; university graduate.

جَامَلَ to flatter; to show courtesy to; to be polite, courteous, friendly to; to make a compliment to.

جَامُوس buffalo (animal).

يُستخدم الجاموس في الحراثة وفي جرّ الأثقال

Buffalos are used to till the land and to draw weights

جانٍ (الجاني) criminal, culprit, felon; reaper, harvester.

جَانَبَ to walk by the side of; to run alongside of; to skirt, flank; to avoid, keep away.

جانِب side, flank, wing; part, portion; aspect, phase; quantity, amount of a certain number of, a few, some of.

جانِبًا aside, apart, out of the way.

من جانبٍ واحد unilateral.

من جانِب on his part, on the part of.

من جانِبٍ آخر on the other part.

إلى جانِبِه at his side, next to him.

بجانِبِه next to him, side with.

في كلِّ جانِب everywhere, on all sides.

إلى جانِبِ ذلِك in addition to, furthermore, moreover.

جانِبِيّ lateral; marginal.

جانِبِيَّة profile.

جانِح (ص) delinquent, pervert, depraved; inclined, leaning.

جانح (اسم) wing, side, flank.

جَاه rank, dignity, honor; fame; power; prestige.

جَاهَدَ to strive, endeavor, take pains, fight; to wage holy war (Jihad); to battle against.

جَاهَرَ to declare publicly, announce, proclaim in public; to raise one's voice; to express frankly; to disclose, make known, state, expose openly.

جاهِز ready, prepared, equipped; ready-made, ready-to-wear (clothes); available, handy, obtainable.

جاهِل ignorant, uncultivated, unaware of, illiterate; foolish, uneducated, ignoramus.

جاهِلِيَّة pre-Islam, pre-Islamic epoch; state of ignorance.

جاوَبَ to reply, respond, answer.

جاوَرَ to neighbor; to be the neighbor of; to live next door to; to be adjacent, in the immediate vicinity of; to border, be close to.

جاوَزَ to go beyond something; to overstep, cross; to exceed, surpass; to traverse, leave behind; to disregard, pay no attention to; to give up, relinquish, refrain from.

جُبّ well, pit.

جَبَّار giant; oppressor; omnipotent (God); gigantic, colossal, huge; powerful, mighty; arrogant, haughty.

جَبَّالَة mixer.

جَبَان — coward, cowardly, weakhearted, poltroon.

جَبَّان — cheesemonger, cheesemaker.

جِبَايَة — collection (of taxes); tax, duty, (charge).

جَبَرَ — to splint (bones); to repair, correct, restore; to help, assist, relieve; to be charitable to; to comfort, console, gratify, oblige, treat with kindness.

جَبْر — splinting of bones; reparation; forcibly, by force; splint; haughtiness, arrogance; power, strength, might; fate, destiny; predestination; act of God.

جَبْر — algebra.

جَبْرًا — forcibly, by force, compulsorily.

جَبَرُوت، جَبْروت، جُبْروت — omnipotence, power, might; tyranny.

جَبْرِيّ — compulsory, obligatory; fatalist.

جِبْس — gypsum, plaster.

جَبَلَ — to mold, form, shape, fashion; to knead (flour); to create; to make.

جُبِلَ — to have a natural disposition for; to be born for; to be naturally disposed to; to have a propensity for.

جَبَل — mountain.

جَبَلُ جليد — iceberg.

جَبَلُ طارق — Gibraltar.

جَبَلِيّ (ص) — mountainous, hilly.

جَبَلِيّ (اسم) — highlander, mountaineer.

جَبُنَ — to be a coward, be fearful; to shrink from.

جُبْن — cowardice, cowardliness.

جُبْن — cheese.

جَبْهَة — forehead, brow; frontline, battlefront; bloc, front.

جَبين — forehead, brow, front.

جَثَا، جَثَى — to kneel, rest on the knees; to genuflect, fall on one's knees.

جَثَمَ — to perch, roost (bird); to crouch, lie face down; to prostrate oneself; to sit or lie heavily on.

جُثَّة، جُثْمان — corpse, cadaver, body.

جَحَدَ — to deny, negate, disavow; to refuse, repudiate; to renounce, adjure; to be ungrateful to; to deny someone his right.

جُحْر — hole, den, lair.

جَحْش — ass, young donkey (animal).

جَحْش خَشَبِيّ — trestle.

جُحُود — denial, evasion, shirking, ingratitude, disavowal, disclaimer; unbelief, apostasy, atheism.

جَحيم — hell, inferno, fire.

جَدَّ — to be new; to have happened lately; to crop up; to enter as a new factor; to be serious, weighty, grave, significant; to strive, seek, work earnestly; to make every effort; to be serious; to mean business; to hurry, hasten, rush; to cut, cut off.

جَدّ grandfather, ancestor, forefather.

جِدّ seriousness, earnestness; diligence, perseverence.

بِجَدٍّ seriously, in earnest.

جِدًّا very much, enormously, highly,by far.

جِدَار wall.

يمنع الجدار الغرباء من الدخول إلى حديقة المنزل

Walls surrounding a house prevent trespassers from entering to its garden

---

جِدارُ الصَّوْتِ sound barrier.

جَدارَة worthiness, worth, merit, fitness, suitability; aptitude, qualification, ability, competence, efficiency.

جِدَال argument, quarrel, dispute, discussion, debate; polemics, dialectics, squable, arguing, contention.

جَدَبَ to be dry, arid (soil); to suffer from drought; to be barren, sterile.

جَدْب sterility, barrenness; infertility, aridity.

جَدَّة grandmother.

جِدَّة newness, novelty, modernity.

جَدَّدَ to renew, make anew, remake, modernize, restore, renovate, remodel, recondition, refurbish; to regenerate, rejuvenate, revive, freshen up; to repeat, remake.

جَدُرَ to be worthy of, deserve, merit; to be suitable, fit, proper for, appropriate for; to befit, behoove.

جُدَرِيّ smallpox.

مرض الجدريّ من الأمراض التي أصبحت على وشك الزوال

Smallpox is a disease on the way of extinction

جُدَرِيُّ الماء chicken pox.

جَدَعَ to amputate, mutilate, maim.

جَدَّفَ to blaspheme; to row.

جَدَلَ to twist, braid, plait, entwine, strand.

جَدْل twining, interweaving, braiding, plaiting, twisting.

جَدَلِيَّة dialectics.

جَدْوَى utility; advantage; feasibility; benefit, gain.

بِلا جَدْوَى useless, of no use; futile; unprofitable; worthless, of no effect; in vain, of no avail.

جَدْوَل creek, brook, stream; list, chart, table, schedule, scroll, roll, panel.

جَدْوَلُ الأَعْمال agenda.

جَدْوَلٌ بيانِيّ chart, diagram, graph.

جَدْوَلٌ دِراسِيّ curriculum.

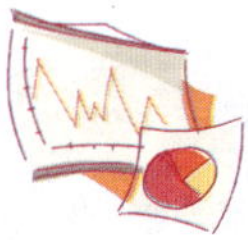

جَدْوَلُ الرَّواتِب payroll.

جَدْوَلٌ زَمَنِيّ timetable.

جَدْوَلُ الضَّرْب multiplication table.

جَدْوَلَة tabulation, classification, indexing; scheduling.

جَدْي young goat, kid (animal).

جِدِّيّ serious, grave, weighty; earnest, momentous.

جِدِّيًا seriously, in earnest, earnestly.

جِدِّيَّة seriousness, earnestness, gravity of a situation.

جَديد new, recent, modern, novel, brand-new, unused.

مِن جَديد again, once more.

جَدير worthy of, deserving, meriting; meritorious, worthwhile; suitable for, fit for, appropriate for, eligible; qualified, competent; capable.

جَديلَة braid, plait.

جَذَّ to cut off, clip; to hurry, hasten, rush.

جَذّاب attractive, charming, enticing, captivating; magnetic, magnetizing, engaging.

جُذاذات (ج) clippings, bits, small pieces, shreds.

جُذام leprosy.

جَذَب to attract, pull, draw, drag; to appeal; to magnetize, captivate, fascinate, charm.

جَذْب attraction, gravitation; appeal, lure, enticement, captivation; ecstasy; sex appeal.

جَذَّر to uproot, pull out; to deracinate, eradicate; to extract the root of a number.

جِذْر root; base, stem, radical (grammar); origin, bottom, base.

جِذْرٌ تَرْبيعيّ square root.

جِذْرٌ تَكْعيبِيّ cubic root.

جِذْع trunk, stem, stump, torso; shaft, arbor (of a machine).

جَذَّف to row.

جَذَل gaiety, hilarity, exuberance, happiness, joy.

جَذِل happy, cheeful, gay, joyful, exuberant, elated.

جَرَّ to draw, tug, haul, pull, tow, trail, drag along; to lead to, cause, entail, give rise to, provoke.

جَرَّ الكَلِمَة to put a word into the genitive.

جَرَّ to draw, tug, haul, pull, tow, trail, drag along; to lead to, cause, entail, give rise to, provoke.

أ ب ت ث ج ح خ د ذ ر ز س ش ص ض ط ظ ع غ ف ق ك ل م ن هـ و ي

جَرَّ الكَلِمَة to put a word into the genitive.

جَرّ drawing, tugging, dragging, hauling, towing; causing, bringing about; genitive.

جَرَى to flow, stream (water); to rush, hurry; to take place, come to pass, happen, occur; to be current; to head for, proceed in accordance with; to entail; to spread, circulate, pass from mouth to mouth.

جَرَى مَجْراه to take the same course as; to pursue the same way as; to imitate, be guided by, analogous to.

جَرُؤَ to dare, venture, risk, hazard; to take the risk of; to have the courage for; to be daring, venturesome; to have the audacity to; to be bold, courageous.

من جَرَّاء because, of , due to, in view of, for, for the sake of.

جِراب bag, sack, knapsack; cover; sheath, scabbard (of a sword); pouch, sac.

جُرْأة courage, boldness, intrepidity, bravery, daring, insolence, audacity.

جَرَّاح surgeon.

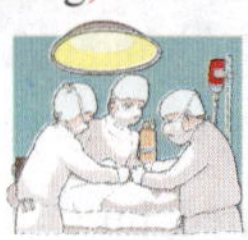

جِراحة surgery.

جِراحةٌ تَجْميلية plastic surgery.

جَراد، جَرادَة locusts, locust; grasshoppers, grasshopper.

جَرَّار (اسم) tractor, bulldozer; potter.

جَرَّار (ص) huge, tremendous, massive.

خضع جدّي لجراحة في معدته

My grandfather had a surgery operation in his stomach

جَرَّافَة rake, dredger, harrow, earth mover.

جَرِبَ to be scabby, mangy; to fade (color).

جَرَّبَ to try, try out, essay; to sample, test, rehearse; to put to a test, rehearse; to experience, to have experienced.

جَرَّة jar; trail, track.

جَرَّةُ قلم stroke of a pen.

جُرْثُوم، جُرثُومة microbe, bacterium; root, origin.

جَرْجَر to gargle; to trail, drag one's feet.

جَرَحَ to wound, injure, hurt; to offend, insult, affront; to challenge, invalidate (testimony); to declare unreliable (a witness); to defame, slander.

جُرْح wound, injury, lesion.

جَرَدَ to take stock; to make an inventory of goods on hand; to peel, pare; to remove the shell, peel, rind, husk of a fruit, vegetable; to denude, divest, strip bare.

جَرَّدَ to denude, divest, strip, dispossess, deprive of; to draw, unsheathe (a sword); to unleash something against someone; to dispatch troops against; to isolate, abstract; to divest someone of his right, rank; to disarm someone; to free oneself from; to give up something; to empty, vacate, evacuate; to disrobe, undress, lay bare.

جُرْد high and barren mountains.

جَرْداء arid, desolate, without vegetation; hairless, bald.

جَرْدَة inventory (of goods on hand).

جِرْذَوْن rat.

الجرْذون حيوان من القواضم ينقل الأوبئة وبالأخص الطاعون

Rats carry the microbes of epidemics particularly plague

جَرَس bell, gong.

جَرَشَ to grind; to crush; to grate, mill.

جَرْش grinding; crushing; grating, milling.

جَرَعَ to swallow, gulp down, drink.

جَرْعَة، جُرْعَة، جِرْعَة dose, potion, mouthful, gulp.

جَرَفَ to sweep away; to wash away; to remove, tear away, carry off, carry along; to dredge, scoop, erode.

جُرْف، جُرُف cliff, precipice, escarpment, slope, shelf.

جَرَّمَ to incriminate, charge with a crime, condemn.

جَرْم boat, barge.

جُرْم crime, offense.

جِرْم criminal, delinquent.

جَرْو، جُرْو puppy, cub, young dog.

جَرْي running, racing.

جَرْيًا على according to, after the manner of, in accordance with, in conformity with.

جَرِيء bold, intrepid, brave courageous; fearless; audacious; insolent; foolhardy, reckless.

جَرَيان flow, course, stream, flux.

جَريح wounded, injured, hurt.

جَريدَة newspaper, daily, journal.

جَريدَة رَسْمِيَّة official gazette.

جَريدَةٌ مُسَنَّنَة rack (mechanics).

جَريرَة guilt, misdeed, crime.

جَريمَة crime, offense, guilt, sin.

جَزَّ to cut off, clip, shear off (wool of sheep); to mow, cut down (grass).

جَزَّأَ to divide, part, separate, break up, split, subdivide, section.

جَزَى to recompense, reward; to punish; to give satisfaction to; to compensate for.

جُزْء part, portion, fraction, piece, component, division; volume, tome.

جُزْءٌ لا يَتَجَزَّأ part and parcel, integral part.

جَزاء reward, retribution; punishment, penalty; fine.

جَزائِيّ penal, criminal, vindictive, retributory.

جَزَّار butcher.

جُزازَة label, tag, index card; clip, clipping, slip (paper).

جُزافًا، جِزافًا at random, haphazardly, aimlessly.

جَزالَة eloquence of language; abundance, amplitude; plenty, ampleness.

جُزْئِيّ partial, part; minor; trivial, insignificant; petty, unimportant.

جُزْئِيًّا partly, in part.

جُزْئِيّات (ج) details, particulars; minor issues.

جَزَرَ to slaughter, kill, butcher (an animal); to sink, fall, drop; to ebb (water); to recede, subside.

جَزَر، جَزَرَة carrots, carrot (plant).

يعشق الأرنب أكل الجزر

Carrots are the favorite food of rabbits

جَزْر ebb, flow back; slaughtering, killing, butchering.

جَزِعَ to be anxious, worried, concerned; to become sad, grieved; to pity, compassion, mourn for.

جَزَع anxiety, worry; concern, apprehension; unrest, anguish, fear; sadness; sorrow, grief.

جَزَلَ to cut, cut off; to coo (birds).

جَزُلَ to abound; to be abundant, plentiful; to be eloquent, pure, lucid (language).

جَزْل abundant, plentiful, ample, much; eloquent, pure, lucid; judicious, prudent; generous, openhanded, liberal; cooing (birds).

جَزَمَ to cut off, sever, clip; to judge, decide, settle something; to be positive about; to be absolutely certain; to make up one's mind; to impose upon, obligate upon; to put a verb into the acopocate or imperative form; to pronounce the final consonant of a word without a vowel.

جَزْم resolve, resolution, judgment; apocopate form; assertion; imposition; obligation.

جَزْمَة boots.

أرتدي الجزمة خلال فصل الأمطار
I wear boots during the rain season

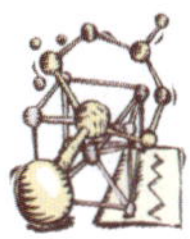

جُزَيْء molecule.

جُزَيْئِيّ molecular.

جِزْيَة tribute, capitation, tax.

جَزيرَة island, isle.

جَزيل abundant, plentiful, ample, much; pure, lucid, eloquent (style); generous, open-handed.

جَسَّ to touch, feel; palpate, examine by touch; to probe, sound, test; to search for; to feel someone's pulse; to spy out, scout, explore, pry, snoop.

جَسَأَ to be callous, tough, hard, rugged.

جَسارَة boldness, intrepidity, audacity; impudence, insolence, impertinence.

جَسامَة largeness; bulkiness; hugeness; fatness, obesity, corpulence; gravity, seriousness; enormity; importance; size, volume, magnitude.

جَسَّدَ to make corporeal, embody, incarnate; to give concrete form to; to represent in corporeal form; to materialize, personify, symbolize.

جَسَد body.

جَسَدِيّ (ص) bodily, corporeal, carnal, physical.

جَسَرَ to venture, risk, have the courage to do something; to span, cross, traverse; to build a bridge; to bridge.

جِسْر bridge, dam, dike, embankment, viaduct; axle, beam, girder, axletree.

يسهّل بناء الجسر
اجتياز الأنهار والشوارع المزدحمة
The bridge facilitates the crossing of rivers and congested roads

جَسَّمَ to enlarge, to make big, bulky; to exaggerate; to embody, materialize; to protrude, bring out; to cause to stand out; to raise in relief; to make a three-dimensional model; to give a concrete form to.

جِسْم body; substance; mass; object; form, shape; institution, corps, board; size of type; hull of a ship or a plane.

جُسْمان body, mass.

جِسْمانيّ corporeal, bodily, carnal, physical, corporal.

جُسُوء callousness, hardness, rigidity, ruggedness.

جَسُور bold, intrepid, audacious, daring; impudent, insolent, impertinent.

جَسيم large, huge, bulky, massive; fat, obese, stout; flagrant; heavy, grievous, enormous; important, grave.

جَشَأَ to belch, burp.

جَشَع greed, covetousness, avarice.

جَشِع greedy, covetous, avaricious.

جَشَّمَ to make someone suffer, bear something; to impose on, burden with, charge with.

جَصّ، جِصّ plaster, gypsum.

جَصَّصَ to plaster, whitewash.

جِعال، جَعالَة، جُعالَة bribe, wages, allowance; prize.

جَعْبَة quiver (for arrows); gun barrel, cartridge pouch.

جِعَة beer.

جَعْجَعَة hubbub, rumpus, clamor, roar, bluster, turmoil; vociferation, bellowing, shouting.

جَعَّدَ to crease, pleat, plait (cloth); to curl, frizz (hair); to wrinkle (skin).

جَعْد curly, frizzly, frizzled, wavy, rippled.

جَعَلَ to make, place; to create, effect, bring about; to make (rule, principle); to appoint to an office; to fix, set (sum, price); to think, deem, believe someone to be; to take someone for; to represent as, in the form of; to settle something in someone's favor; to give, grant, concede something to someone; to attribute to someone something; to maintain that something belongs to someone; to entrust something to; to put, get something into a specific state or condition; to provide, supply, furnish, equip with; to begin, start to.

جُعْل salary, emolument; fee, charge; allowance; royalty; commission, brokerage; prize, reward, bonus.

جُغْرافيّ (ص) geographical.

جُغْرافيّ (اسم) geographer.

جُغْرافيا، جِغْرافيا، جُغْرافِيَة geography.

جَفَّ to dry, dry up; to dry out; to dehydrate.

جَفَا to shun, desert, avoid; to walk out on; to treat someone harshly, rudely; to display rude manners.

جَفاء alienation, roughness; aversion, loathing; harshness, antipathy, disgust; avoidance, shunning.

جَفاف desiccation, dryness, drying up; dullness; aridity, drought; tedium, lifelessness.

جَفَّفَ to dry up, dry out, desiccate, dehydrate; to drain, empty.

جَفَلَ to start, jump (with fright); to shy (a horse); to rouse, scare away.

جَفْن eyelid.

جَلَّ to be great, exalted, sublime; to be beyond something; to be far above something; to envelop, clothe; to border, edge.

جُلّ most of; the major part of; the bulk of; the main part.

جُلّ packsaddle, saddle; roses, jasmine.

جَلا to clean, polish; to make clear, plain; to reveal, disclose; to dislodge, remove; to shine; to pull out, move out, go away, depart (from a place); to leave, quit, evacuate (a place); to show, represent; to be dispelled; to vanish, go clarify, unearth, uncover.

جَلاء evacuation, withdrawal; polishing, glazing, cleaning; clarity, distinctness; clarification, elucidation, unveiling, bringing to light.

بِجَلاء clearly, distinctly, obviously, explicitly, plainly.

جَلّاد executioner, hangman; leather merchant.

جَلال loftiness, sublimity, augustness; splendor, glory; majesty, greatness, dignity.

جَلالَة majesty (for king, queen).

صاحِبُ الجَلالَة Your Majesty, His Majesty.

جَلَبَ to attract, fetch, bring; to import (goods); to bring about; to bring a harm upon; to gain, win, obtain; to procure, summon, call in; to incur upon oneself; to clamor, shout; to be noisy; to coagulate (blood).

جَلْب bringing, acquisition, importation, causation; summoning (to court).

جَلَب ، جَلَبَة clamor, uproar, tumult, noise.

جَلْجَل to rattle, jingle.

جَلْجَلَة rattle, clank; resounding; jingle.

جَلَخ to sharpen, whet, hone (a knife); to stretch, grind (metal).

جَلْخ whetstone, grindstone.

جَلَدَ to whip, flog, thrash, lash.

جَلُدَ to be tough, strong, steadfast, patient.

جَلِدَ to be frozen, frosted, iced.

جَلَّدَ to freeze, frost, congeal; to bind (a book).

جَلَد endurance, patience, tolerance, steadfastness, sturdiness.

جَلْد (اسم) whipping, flogging, scourging.

جَلْد (ص) patient, steadfast, tough, hardy.

جَلْدُ عُمَيْرَة masturbation.

جِلْد skin, hide, leather.

جِلْدَةُ الرأس scalp.

جِلْدَةُ الكتاب cover, jacket (of a book).

جِلْدِيّ cutaneous, dermal; skin.

جَلَسَ to sit down; to sit; to keep someone's company.

شعر الرَّجل بتعبٍ فجلس على مقعدٍ ليستريح
The man felt tired so he sat on a chair to have some rest

جَلَّسَ to straighten; to make someone sit; to seat someone.

جَلْسَة session (committee, court); gathering, meeting; manner of sitting.

جَلْسَةٌ سِرِّيَّة meeting in camera, closed-door session.

جَلْسَةٌ بِكَامِلِ الأَعْضَاء plenary session.

جَلْطَة، جُلْطَة clot, lump; blood clot, thrombus.

جِلْف rude, uncivil, impolite, uncouth, crude.

جَلْفَطَ to calk.

جَلْفَنَ to galvanize.

جَلَّلَ to cover, wrap, drape, clothe; to honor, dignify, revere; to deem too exalted, sublime.

جَلَل important, significant, momentous, grave.

جَلْمَد، جُلْمُود boulder, rock.

جُلُوس sitting down; audience.

جَلِيّ obvious, express, evident, conspicuous.

جَلِيَّة obvious matter, plain fact, sure thing.

جَلِيد ice.

جَلِيس table companion; person with whom someone sits.

جَلِيل exalted, sublime, venerable; important, momentous, great; glorious, splendid; grave; respectable.

جَمّ much, abundant, many, numerous; major part; crowd, group of people.

جَمَاد solid, inorganic body, inanimate body.

جَمَاد soil, earth; neutral (grammar).

جِمَاع sexual intercourse, copulation, coition.

جَمَاعَة group of people, gang, party; squad (military); company, body, community.

جَمَاعَاتٍ وأَفْرَادًا in groups and individually.

جَمَاعِيّ collective, communal.

جَمَال beauty, aesthetics (science); prettiness.

جَمَّال cameleer, camel driver.

جُمْجُمَة skull, cranium.

عُثِر مؤخّراً على **جمجمة** رجل عاش قبل 50 ألف سنة

The skull of a man who lived 50 thousand years ago was discovered recently

---

جَمَح to bolt (horse); to be defiant, capricious, whimsical; to run away from home (wife).

جَمَدَ to freeze, congeal, stiffen; to become hard, solid; to be rigid, inflexible; to stagnate, be indolent, dull, indifferent toward; to be motionless, inactive, inert.

جَمَّدَ to freeze, frost, congeal; to solidify, harden; to make solid, hard; to coagulate, clot (blood); to curdle (milk).

جَمْر، جَمْرَة live coal, firebrand, ember; resentment; carbuncle.

جُمْرُك customs, customhouse.

جَمَعَ to gather, collect, combine; to unite, bring together; to join, set, compose; to sum up, summarize, add; to pile up, amass, accumulate, assemble; to make plural (grammar); to link; to contain, hold; to raise (funds).

جَمَّعَ to assemble, rally; to pile up, accumulate; to clutter; to unite, gather, collect; to sum up, summarize.

جَمْع gathering, combining, collecting, assembling, joining; collection (of funds); accumulation, piling up; banding, rounding up; rallying; addition, aggregation; plural (grammar).

جُمْعُ اليَد fist.

الجُمُعَة، الجُمْعَة Friday; week.

جَمْعِيَّة society, organization, assembly, association.

جَمعِيَّة تأسيسِيَّة constituent assembly.

جَمْعِيَّةٌ تَشْرِيعيَّة legislative assembly; parliament.

جَمْعِيَّةٌ تَعاوُنِيَّة cooperative society.

جَمْعِيَّةٌ خَيْرِيَّة charitable association; philanthropic organization.

جَمْعِيَّةٌ عامَّة general assembly, plenary session.

جَمَلَ to sum up, summarize; to be beautiful, handsome, pretty, graceful; to be proper; to befit, behoove.

جَمَّلَ to make beautiful; to make oneself pretty, handsome.

جَمَل camel; dromedary.

جُمَّل (حساب الجُمَّل) use of the letters of the alphabet according to their numerical value.

جُمْلَة sum, whole, group; sentence, clause (language).

جُمْلَةٌ إسمِيَّة nominal clause.

جُمْلَةٌ فعلِيَّة verbal clause.

جُمْلَةٌ شَرْطِيَّة conditional clause.

جُمْلَة (ص) completely, wholly, altogether, in general; all at once.

جُمْهُور multitude, crowd, public, the people; audience, attendance, spectators, listeners.

جُمْهُوريّ republican.

جُمْهُورِيَّة republic.

جُمُوح recalcitrance, defiance, unruliness, willfulness.

جُمُود frozen state; solidity, rigidity, stiffness; immobility, standstill, inertia, inactivity; lethargy, apathy; stagnation, dullness; inorganic state; hardness, inflexibility; indifference; stalemate; recession, slump.

جُمَّيز sycamore (tree).

جَميع entire, all, total.

جَميعًا all of, one and all, everyone, everything, wholly, entirely, totally.

جَميل (ص) beautiful, pretty, graceful, handsome, charming.

جَميل (اسم) friendly act, favor, service.

جُنَّ to be insane; to go mad; to be wildly excited; to be crazy; to lose one's head or temper.

جِنّ jinn, demons.

جَنَى to pick, gather; to harvest, reap; to pocket, rake in, collect, derive (profit); to realize, secure (advantage); to incur (harm, punishment); to bring about, cause; to commit (crime); to offend, harm, inflict harm against; to bring into trouble; to cause misery to.

جَنائِزيّ funeral.

جَنائنيّ gardener, horticulturist.

جِنائيّ criminal, penal.

جَناب your honor, mr., sir.

جَناح wing (of a bird, an airplane); side, flank; annex (of a building); suite, ward (hospital, prison); stand, stall (exhibition); division, section, compartment.

جُنّاز، جَنّاز requiem, funeral rites.

جَنازَة، جِنازة funeral procession; funeral ceremony.

جَنان heart, soul.

جِناية felony, crime, capital offense.

جَنَّب to keep away from; to guard against; to avert, ward off; keep out of the way; to spare; to side, walk by someone's side, run alongside; to skirt, flank, avoid.

جَنْب side, flank, waist; beside, near at, next to.

جَنْبًا لِجَنْب side by side with.

جَنْبَة shrub; side; region.

جَنَّة paradise; garden; heaven.

جَنَح to be inclined; to lean toward; to be stranded on a coast (ship); to deviate, turn away from; to be delinquent; to commit a misdemeanor.

جُنْح part (of the night); watch; darkness, gloom.

جُنْحة misdemeanor, delinquency.

جَنَّدَ to draft, enlist, recruit someone; to mobilize troops.

جُنْد soldiers, troops, army.

جُنْدُب grasshopper (insect).

جَنْدَلَ to throw to the ground; to bring down, fell.

جُنْدِيّ soldier.

مهمة الجنديّ حماية حدود الوطن من الأعداء

The soldier's duty is to protect the country from enemies

جُنْدِيٌّ نظاميّ regular soldier.

جُنْدِيٌّ أَوَّل private first class.

الجُنْدِيُّ المَجْهُول unknown soldier.

جُنْدِيَّة military service; the military, the armed forces; military life (career).

جِنْزِير chain.

جَنَّسَ to naturalize, confer citizenship upon.

جِنْس kind, variety, species, sex, category, race, sort, type; genus, gender; sexuality.

الجِنْسُ البَشَرِيّ human race, humankind.

جِنْسِيَّة nationality.

جَنَّنَ to drive someone mad, crazy, to enrage, infuriate.

جَنُوب south.

جَنُوبًا southwards.

جَنُوبِيّ (ص) southern, southerly.

جَنُوبِيّ (اسم) Southerner.

جُنُوح inclination, tendency; delinquency; stranding (of a ship); leaning, bent.

جُنُون insanity, madness, craziness; mania, dementia, folly; frenzy, rage, fury; obsession, possession.

جُنُونِيّ frantic, frenzied, hysterical, crazy, insane, mad, wild, raging.

جَنْي picking, harvest, reaping; earning, gaining, acquisition, achievement.

جِنِّيَّة fairy, female demon.

جَنِين fetus, embryo.

جُنَيْنَة garden.

جِهَاد jihad, holy war; struggle, battle, fighting.

جِهاز appliance, instrument, apparatus, device; gear, set, impliment; system; institution, corps, body.

جِهازُ نَقْلِ الحَرَكَة transmission system.

جِهَازُ الإرْسَال	transmitter.
جِهَازُ الاسْتِقْبَال	receiver.
جِهَازٌ لاسِلْكِيّ	wireless set.

جَهالة — ignorance, stupidity, foolishness.

جِهَة — side, direction; region, part; area, district; authority, body.

لِجِهَة — as regards, as to, with respect to.

من جِهَةٍ أُخرى — on the other hand.

إلى جِهَةِ — towards.

جُهْد، جَهْد — effort, strain, exertion; endeavor, attempt; voltage, tension (elec.).

بِجُهْدٍ جَهيد — with great effort, with strenuous effort.

جُهْدَ طَاقَتِهِ — as mush as he can; to the limits of his abilities.

جَهَرَ — to be brought to light; to show, appear; to reveal, disclose; to be made public, proclaim, announce; to express frankly, declare openly; to raise the voice.

جَهُرَ — to be loud, clearly audible (the voice).

جَهْرًا — publicly, in public, openly, overtly.

جَهَّزَ — to prepare, make ready, equip, provide with; to rig (a ship); to prepare the dead for burial; to provide the bride's trousseau.

جَهِلَ — to be ignorant, not to know; to be irratioal, foolish; to be uneducated, unwitting, unaware of; to have no knowledge of; to be unfamiliar with.

جَهْل — ignorance; foolishness; stupidity; unawareness of, unconsciousness of, lack of knowledge.

جَهُمَ — to frown, scowl, glower; to eye gloomily, coolly, grimly; to regard with displeasure.

جُهَنَّم — hell.

جَهورِيّ — loud (voice); sonorous.

جَوّ — atmosphere, air, weather; sphere, environment, milieu; ambience, tone, situation, mood.

جَوًّا — by air.

جَوَى — love, intense emotion, passion.

جَوَاب — answer, reply; octave (music); letter, message.

جَوَّاب — globe-trotter, wanderer, rover; tramp, vagabond.

جَوَاد (ص) — generous, openhanded, magnanimous.

جَوَاد (اسم) — horse, steed (animal).

جِوَار — neighborhood, proximity, vicinity.

بِجِوار — close to; in the vicinity of, near to.

جَوَاز — permissibility, potentiality; licence, authorization, permit; admissibility, lawfulness.

جَوَازُ سَفَر — passport.

جَوازُ مُرور — laissez-passer, pass.

جَوَّال — wanderer, rover, globetrotter; boyscout, scout; traveler, ambulant.

جَواهِرِيّ jeweler.

جُوخ cloth, broadcloth.

جَوَّدَ to improve; to do well; to ameliorate; to recite the Koran.

جُود generosity, munificence, openhandedness.

جَوْدَة، جُودَة excellence, superiority, perfection, goodness.

جَوْر injustice, tyranny, oppression, inequity.

جَوْرَب sock, stocking.

جَوْز walnut, nut.

قشرة الجوز قاسية يصعب كسرها باليد

The nut's shell is hard and is difficult to break open by hand

الجَوْزاء Gemini (astrology); Orion (astronomy).

جَوَّعَ to starve; to famish; to cause to starve.

جُوع hunger, starvation.

جَوَّفَ to hollow out; to make hollow; to bore, excavate.

جَوْف interior, cavity, inside, center; belly, abdomen; hollow, hole, hold (of a ship).

في جَوْف inside, within, in the middle of; in the interior of.

جَوْفِيّ underground, subterranean; inside, interior; abdominal; inner; subsurface.

جَوْقَة troop, group; choir (mus.); orchestra, band (mus.).

جَوْلَة round (in sports, talks); patrol, tour; journey, excursion, ride, voyage; roundtrip.

جَوْهَر essence, substance, matter, content, core; jewel, atom, monad; intrinsic nature.

جَوْهَرَة jewel, gem, precious stone.

جَوْهَرِيّ substantial, essential, material, intrinsic, radical; fundamental, basic; major, cardinal, crucial; chief, main, inherent.

جَوِّيّ meteorological, aerial.

جَيْئَة، جِيئَة arrival, coming.

جَيْئَةً وذَهَابًا، جِيئَةً وذُهُوبًا to and fro, back and forth.

جَيَّاش agitated, ebullient; impassioned, boiling up; surging, rolling; heaving.

جَيْب pocket; heart, breast; sinus (med.).

جَيْبٌ هَوائِيّ air pocket (in aviation).

جَيِّد good, excellent, perfect, outstanding.

جَيِّدًا thoroughly, excellently, perfectly.

أ ب ت ث ج ح خ د ذ ر ز س ش ص ض ط ظ ع غ ف ق ك ل م ن هـ و ي

جِيْد — neck.

جَيَّرَ — to endorse; to plaster with lime; to calcify.

جِيْر — lime.

جِيْرٌ حَيّ — quicklime.

جَيرٌ مُطْفَأ — slaked, hydrated lime.

جِيْرَة — neighborhood, vicinity.

جِيرِيّ — calcareous, limy.

حَجَرٌ جِيرِيّ — limestone.

جَيْش — army, armed forces, troops.

جَيَشَان — agitation, outburst, surge, upheaval, ebullition.

جَيَشَانُ النَّفْس — nausea.

جِيفَة — corpse, carcass, cadaver (of dead animal).

جِيْل — generation; century, age, epoch, era; people, nation, tribe, race.

جِيولُوجيا — geology.

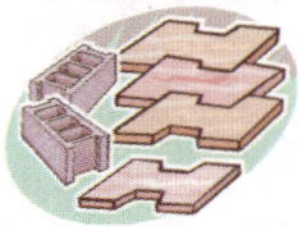

حَائِر perplexed, dismayed, embarrassed, bewildered, confused, baffled; disconcerted, helpless, at a loss; wavering, puzzled, confounded; hesitant, undecided.

حَائِز holder, possessor, tenant.

حَائِط wall.

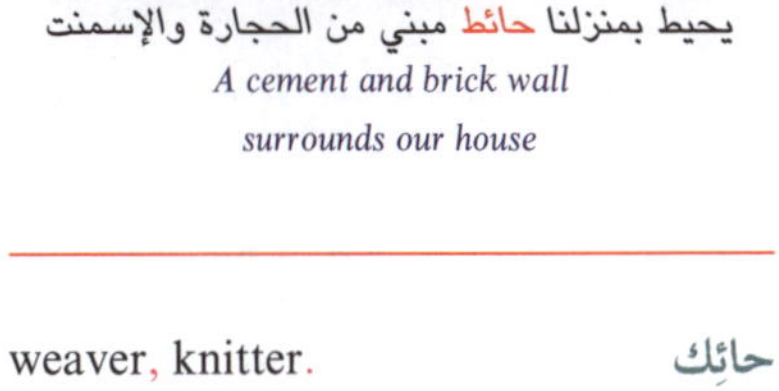

يحيط بمنزلنا حائط مبني من الحجارة والإسمنت
A cement and brick wall surrounds our house

حائِك weaver, knitter.

حائِل obstacle, obstruction, barrier; partition, buffer; changeable, variable; wan, pallid.

حابَى to prefer, favor, take sides with someone or something; to show deference to.

حاجّ pilgrim.

حاجِب doorkeeper, janitor; bailif (of a court); chamberlain (of a king); eyebrow; edge, border; veil, screen, cover.

حاجَة need, want, necessity; demand, deficiency; desire, wish; thing, object.

عِنْدَ الحاجَة in case of need,if need be.

حاجِز obstruction, obstacle; screen, partition; blockade, fence, railing; hurdle, barrier, barricade.

حَاجِزُ الصَّوْت sound barrier.

حاجِزٌ جُمْرُكِيّ customs barrier.

حاجِزُ الأمْواج breakwater.

حادَ to deviate from, turn aside, turn from; to drift from, stay from, alter one's course.

حادّ sharp, keen (mind); vehement, fiery, impetuous (character); fierce, vivid; acute (illness).

حادُّ الطَّبْع hot-blooded, hot tempered, hot-headed; irascible.

حادُّ الطَّعْم acrid, pungent, tart, piquant.

حادُّ الصَّوْت high-pitched, strident.

حادُّ البَصَر sharp-sighted.

حادَثَ to speak to, talk to, discourse with, hold talks with; to call up, converse, chat with.

حادِث happening, occuring, occurrence, event; accident, mishap; new, recent; fresh.

حادِثَة occurrence, event, happening;incident, accident, mishap.

حادِي عَشَرَ eleventh.

حاذَى to be in front of; to face; to neighbor, border, be adjacent to; to be parallel to; to be opposite to.

حاذَرَ to be cautious, wary; to beware of; to watch out, be on one's guard, be careful.

حاذِق skilled, skillful, clever, smart, intelligent; very sour, pungent, acrid (food).

حارَ to be confused, perplexed; to hesitate, waver; to be unable to decide or to choose; to be baffled, dismayed, startled.

حارّ hot, warm; pungent, sharp, piquant; ardent, fervent, zealous; cordial, friendly, hearty.

حارَبَ to fight, engage in a fight, battle; to wage war against.

حارِس guard, sentry, bodyguard; doorkeeper, gatekeeper; guardian, custodian, warden; trustee; ibis (bird).

حارِسُ الصَّيْد gamekeeper.

حارِسٌ قَضائِيّ custodian, receiver, sequestrator.

حارِسُ المَرْمَى goalkeeper.

حارِق arsonist, incendiary; incinerator, burner.

حازَ to obtain, get, possess, seize; to acquire, attain, realize; to win, gain, achieve.

حازِم resolute, firm, strict, drastic, decisive; judicious, prudent, discreet; austere, tough, unwavering.

حاسَبَ to settle an account with, get even with; to hold someone responsible for; to be cautious of; to take care; to take into account; to ask someone for an accounting.

حاسِب calculator, counter, computer.

حاسِبَة calculator, calculating machine.

حاسَّة sense (sense organ), sensation.

الحَوَاسُّ الخَمْس the five senses.

حاسِد envious, grudger.

حاسِر uncovered, unveiled, bareheaded; unarmed.

حاسِم dicisive, definite, crucial, conclusive, absolute.

حاشَا except, save; God forbid.

حاشِد numerous, crowded.

حاشِيَة border, rim, fringe, hem, margin.

حاشِيَة footnote, annotation, commentary, postscript.

حاشِيَة retinue, suite, entourage.

حاصَرَ to besiege, lay siege to; to encircle, ring; to beleaguer, surround, block, blockade.

حاصِل result, sum, product (math); revenues, receipts, gain, income; crop, harvest; essence, substance; briefly, in short; happening, under way; warehouse, depot; remainder, rest.

حاصِلُ الذَّكاء intelligence quotient.

حاضَرَ to deliver a lecture.

حاضِر present; ready; current, actual.

الحاضِر the present time, today; the present.

حاضِرَة capital (of a country), city, metropolis.

حاضِنَة incubator; nurserymaid, baby-sitter.

حاطَ to guard, protect, watch over; to surround, encircle; to build a wall; to comprise, contain; to know thoroughly, comprehend, grasp completely.

حافٍ (الحَافي) barefooted.

حافَّة ، حافَة edge, rim; verge, tip; hem, brink, border.

حافِر hoof (of animal).

حافِز incentive, motive, drive, impulse; catalyst (chemistry).

حافَظَ to guard, observe, comply with; to be mindful, heedful; to keep up, maintain, sustain, retain; to take care of, save, put away, store; to conserve, preserve.

حافِظ keeper, guardian, curator, trustee; conserver, holder; saving, maintaining, preserving; one who knows the Koran by heart; one who learns by heart.

حافِظَة memory; wallet, pocketbook, folder, briefcase, portfolio, satchel.

حافِل full of, filled, replete with; abundant, copious; well-attended by visitors; solemn, festive, ceremonial.

حافِلَة bus, autobus, wagon, railroad car.

حاقَ to surround, enclose, encircle; to happen to, to affect, act upon; to penetrate; to pierce (with a sword).

حاقِد full of hatred, spiteful, malicious; rancorous; resentful; malevolent.

حاكَ to weave, knit; to hatch, contrive, devise; to fabricate, invent, make up.

حاكّ abrasive.

الحاكي phonograph, gramophone; storyteller, narrator.

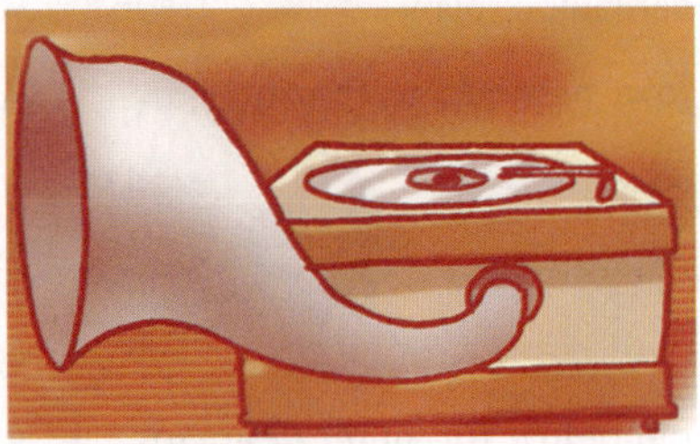

أصبح الحاكي في الوقت الحاضر نادر الاستعمال
Gramophones are rarely used nowadays

حاكى to resemble, imitate, mimic, ape.

حاكَمَ to judge; to pass sentence on; to prosecute, arraign, bring to trial; to litigate, take legal action against.

حاكِم (اسم) ruler, governor; judge; commander, master.

حاكِم (ص) governing, ruling, prevailing.

حالَ to prevent, hinder, block, obstruct, impede, hamper; to intervene, interpose between; to pass, expire, elapse.

حال state of affairs, condition, circumstance, situation, position, case; the present time, this moment.

حال circumstantial expression or phrase (grammar).

حالاً immediately, at once, on the spot, right away.

في حال in case of, in the event of, provided that, whether.

في أيِّ حالٍ by no means, under no circumstances, never.

على كُلِّ حال in any case, anyhow, at any rate.

كَيفَ حالُكَ how are you?.

أحْوالٌ جَوِيَّة weather conditions.

أحْوالٌ شَخْصِيَّة personal status.

حالَة situation, status, condition, state, circumstance; case, mood (grammar).

والحالَة هَذِه under these circumstances, such being the case.

في هذه الحالَة in this case, under this condition.

الحالَةُ الراهِنَة the status quo.

حالَفَ to become an ally with; to enter into an alliance; to keep to, stay constantly with.

حالِك pitch-black, gloomy, murky.

حالِم dreamer, visionary; romantic.

حالَما as soon as, no sooner than, right after, upon, on.

حاليّ present, actual, present-day; instant, immediate.

حَاليًا now, actually, at this time; today, nowadays.

حامَ to circle, hover, glide (in the air); to swarm, buzz around; to loiter about.

حامٍ (الحَامِي) (ص) hot, warm, heated, vehement; intense, fierce, grim (battle, fight).

حامٍ (الحامِي) (اسم) protector, guardian, patron.

حَامَى to defend, guard, protect, shelter.

حامِض sour, acid.

حامِل carrier, transporter, bearer; pregnant, expectant; holder; hanger, stay, prop, girder; brace; easel (for painters).

حامِلَةُ طَائِرات aircraft carrier.

حامِيَة garrison.

حانَ to approach, draw near; to become ripe, mature.

حانَ الوَقْتُ time has come, now is the time, it is high time.

حَانَة bar, pub, tavern.

حَانِق furious, mad, angry, resentful, embittered.

حَانُوت store, shop.

حانُوتِيّ storekeeper, shopkeeper; undertaker.

حاوٍ (الحاوِي) (ص) comprising, including, containing, embracing, enclosing.

حاوٍ (الحَاوِي) (اسم) snake charmer, conjurer.

حاوَرَ to dialogue with; to have talks with; to discourse with; to debate, discuss, argue with.

حاوَلَ to try, attempt, endeavor, seek to.

حُؤُول prevention, hindering, barring, blocking.

حَاوِيَة container, box; bag; tin.

حَبّ grain, seeds, pulse.

حَبّ pimples, boils, blisters; pills, tablets.

حَبُّ الشباب acne.

حَبُّ الهال cardamon (plant).

حُبّ love, passion, attachment.

حُبُّ الذات self-love.

حُبُّ الاسْتِطلاع inquisitiveness.

حُبُّ الوَطَن patriotism.

حُبًّا في out of love for; in the desire to.

حَبَا to crawl, creep; to endow with; to grant to; to bestow upon; to present with.

حَبَّال rope maker, rope dealer.

حَبَّبَ to endear oneself to; to make oneself popular; to court, woo (a woman); to render pleasant, attractive.

حَبَّة grain, seed, pellet; pimple, boil, pustule; pill, tablet; bead (of a rosary).

حَبَّةُ العَيْن eyeball, pupil of the eye.

حَبَّذَ to endorse, support, uphold; to acclaim, praise, recommend; commend, favor.

حَبَّذَا how nice! how lovely it is; how nice it would be if.

حَبِرَ to be happy, glad, delighted.

حَبَّرَ to embellish, decorate; to write (a book).

حَبْر pontiff, bishop; scholar, authority.

الحَبْرُ الأعْظَم the Pope.

حِبْر ink; scholar, authority.

حَبَسَ — to imprison, arrest, jail, apprehend; to obstruct, shut off, confine; to block, bar; to hold back (tears); to hold in custody, detain someone; to tie up (money).

حَبْس — jail, prison, lock-up; imprisonment, confinement, detention, arrest, incarceration; holding back, keeping back, retention; obstruction, prevention, blocking.

يُسجنُ المجرم في الحبس عقاباً لما فعلته يداه

Prisons are constructed to jail criminals in them

حَبَكَ — to weave well and tight; to plait, braid; to twist, knit, tighten, fasten.

حَبَلَ (حَبَلَتِ المَرْأَة) — to be pregnant.

حَبَل — pregnancy, conception.

حَبْل — rope, cord, string; cord, chord (anatomy); vein, tendon.

الحَبْلُ السُّرِّي — umbilical cord.

الحَبْلُ الشَوْكِيّ — spinal cord.

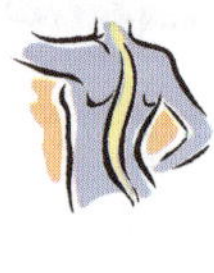

حَبْلٌ صَوْتِيّ — vocal cord.

حَبْلُ الغسيل — clothesline.

حَبْلُ المِشْنَقَة — hangman's rope.

حَبْلُ الوَرِيد — jugular vein.

حُبْلَى — pregnant, expectant.

أتت شقيقتي الحبلى لتقضي نهاراً عندنا

My pregnant sister came to visit me

حُبُور — joy, happiness, gladness.

حُبِّيّ — friendly, cordial, hearty; affectionate; peaceful.

حبيب — lover, beloved, dear.

حَبِيبَة — sweetheart, darling, pet, love; beloved.

حَبِيس — hermit, recluse, ascetic; prisoner, captive, convict.

حَتَّ — to scrape off, abrade, corrode; erode, wear away.

حَتّ — abrasion, erosion, wear, scraping off.

حَتَّى — until, till, up to, as far as; so that, in order to; inclusive, together with, as well as.

حَتّى لا in order not to.

حَتّى لو even if, in spite of the fact that, although.

حِتار rim, edge, margin, lip.

حَتْف death.

حَتَمَ، حَتَّمَ to prescribe; to impose, enjoin upon; to determine definitely; to make necessary; to make incumbent upon.

حَتْمًا definitely, positively, absolutely, by all means, necessarily, inevitably.

حَتْمِيّ definite, positive; unquestionable; obligatory, imperative; decided, final, conclusive; inevitable.

حَثَّ to incite, urge, encourage; to spur on, impel, stimulate, inspire, to exhort, prompt, goad, prod.

حَثّ urging, prompting, prodding; motivation, stimulation; induction (elec.).

حَثا to pour (dust) upon; to leave behind, outstrip; to embarrass; to begrudge, give too little to.

حُثالَة lees, sediment, scum; rubbish; trash; offal.

حَثيث fast, quick, prompt, swift, rapid.

حَجَّ to make a pilgrimage to holy places or lands; to betake upon oneself to; to confute by proof; to vindicate.

حِجا، حَجَى mind, intellect; sagacity; intelligence, wit.

حِجاب veil; screen, mantle; partition, division; amulet, charm; diaphragm; bar, barrier.

أدّى والدي فريضة الحجّ عندما كان شابًا

My father made his pilgrimage to Mecca when he was still young

حَجّار stonecutter, stonemason.

حَجَبَ to veil, screen, hide, conceal; to shroud, clock; to obstruct the view; to separate, keep-part; to ecclipse, outshine; to make invisible.

حُجَّة argument, plea, excuse, pretext, claim; proof, evidence; authority, expert.

حُجَّة deed, document, title deed.

حَجَرَ to deny access, stop, detain; to forbid, prohibit someone from doing something; to place under guardianship; to quarantine.

حَجَر stone.

حَجَرٌ أساسيّ cornerstone, foundation stone.

حَجَرُ الخُفّاف pumice stone.

حَجَرُ الرَّحى millstone.

حَجَرُ الزاوية cornerstone.

حَجَرُ الشَّبّ alum.

حَجَرُ القَدَّاحَة flint.

حَجَرٌ كريم precious stone, gem.

حَجَرُ النار firestone.

حَجْر denying access to; restraint, prohibition, detention; preclusion, confinement; interdiction; limitation of someone's legal competence; quarantine.

حُجْر ، حِجْر room, cell, compartment, chamber; cabin (in a ship).

حُجْرَةُ جُلوس living room, sitting room.

حَجَزَ to hold back, hinder, prevent; to block off, close, isolate, confine, seclude; to set apart; to arrest, detain, seize; to sequester property; to confiscate; to reserve, retain.

حَجْز retention, detention, confinement, seclusion, isolation; arrest, lockup; hindering, prevention; reservation, booking (of a seat); restraint, containment, separation.

حَجْزُ أَمْوَال sequestration, seizure, confiscation.

حَجْم volume, bulk, size, dimension.

حَدَّ to mourn by wearing black clothes.

حَدَّ to sharpen, hone (a knife); to set bounds; to limit, restrict, confine; to hinder, check; to demarcate borders; to punish, castigate (a criminal).

حَدّ boundary, limit, edge, frontier; verge, end, extremity; punishment; restriction, confinement, checking.

حَدٌّ أدنى least; minimum.

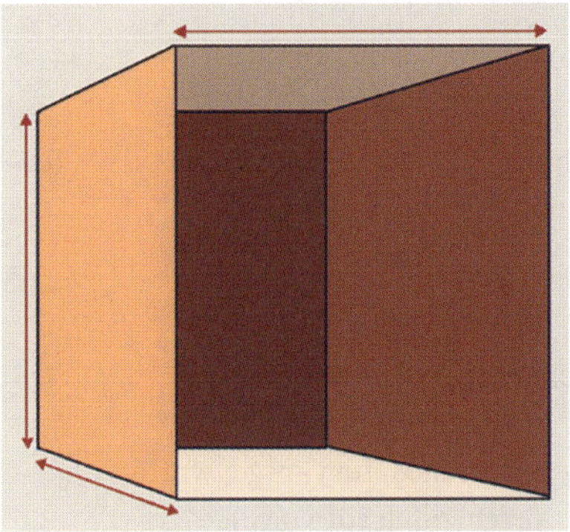

أقيس حجم الشيء قبل أن أوضبه في صندوق
I take beforehand the dimensions of the thing i wish to put in a crate

حَدٌّ أَقْصَى highest; maximum.

إلى حَدّ as far as, till, until; up to.

إلى حَدِّ الآن so far, till now, still, up to now.

إلى حَدٍّ ما to some extent; in a sense, somewhat.

إلى حَدٍّ بعيد to a great degree, considerably, extremely, by far.

على حَدٍّ سَوَاء equally, alike, evenly, all the same, likewise.

في حَدِّ ذاتِه in itself, as such, per se.

إلى غيرِ حَدٍّ unlimited, without limits.

حَدَاثَة newness, modernity, novelty; youthfulness, juvenility; recency.

حَدَّاد blacksmith, ironsmith.

حِداد mourning.

حَدِبَ to become hunchbacked; to be domeshaped, cambered; to be solicitous about someone; to take care of; to be convex, curved, crooked; to sympathize with.

حَدَب — sympathy, care, kindness; upward slope.

حَدَبَة — hump; convexity, curvature, protrusion, boss; cam.

على حِدَة — alone, apart from others; isolated, aside, separately.

حِدَّة — sharpness, acuity; intensity, violence; markedness, vehemence; fury, rage, wrath, anger; pitch (of voice).

حِدَّةُ البَصَر — sharp-sightedness.

حِدَّةُ الذِّهن — perspicacity, astuteness, keenness, discernment.

حِدَّةُ الطَّبع — irascibility, nervousness, hotheadedness.

حَدَث — to happen, occur, take place, come to pass; to befall.

حَدَّث — to tell about; to report to about; to speak, talk, converse with, chat with.

حَدَّث — to modernize, update, renew.

حَدَّثَهُ قَلْبُهُ — to have a presentiment; to presage; to have a premonition of; his heart told him that.

حَدَث — event, phenomenon, incident, happening; a new thing, a novelty; innovation; misdeed, evil symptom, disaster.

حَدَث — young man, youth, youngster, minor.

حَدَج — to stare at, gaze at, look sharply at.

حَدَّد — to define, specify, fix; to designate, determine, stipulate, set, lay down; to demarcate, define, delineate (boundaries); to limit, restrict.

حَدَّد — to forge; to sharpen, hone; to taper, point.

حَدَر — slope, incline, slant, declivity; dip; cliff; steep.

حَدَس — to surmise, guess, conjecture.

حَدْس — surmise, guess, intuition, conjecture, presentiment.

حَدْسِيّ — intuitive.

حَدَّق — to stare at, gaze at, look sharply at.

حَدَقَة — iris (of the eye).

حَدْوَة، حِدْوة — horseshoe.

حَديث (ص) — new, recent, modern, up-to-date.

حَديث (اسم) — speech, conversation, talk; interview; gossip; report, account; tale, narrative.

حَديثًا — recently, of late, newly, lately.

حَديد — iron.

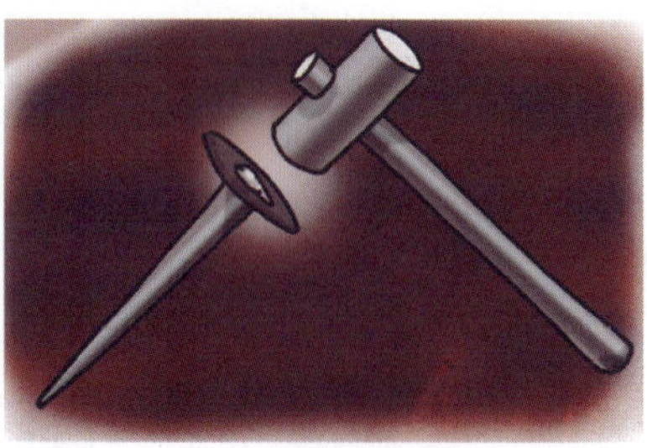

تُصنع من معدن الحديد آلات وأدوات لا تُحصى
Iron is a widely used metal in all industries

حَديدُ الزَّهْر — cast iron.

حَديدٌ مُطاوع — wrought iron.

حَديقة — garden.

حَدِيقَةُ حَيَوانات — zoo.

حَذا — to imitate, copy, emulate, follow suit.

حِذَاء — shoe, footwear, boot.

حِذَاء — opposite to; in front of; parallel; near to, close to; alongside of, beside; next to; facing.

حَذَارِ — beware of! be careful of! watch out for!.

حَذِرَ — to be cautious of; to be careful, alert, on the alert; to take heed, watch out; to be wary of.

حَذَّرَ — to warn, caution; to put someone on his guard; to admonish, exhort, forewarn.

حَذَر — caution, wariness, alertness, prudence, carefulness.

حَذِر — cautious, prudent, alert, watchful, on one's guard.

حَذَفَ — to shorten, clip; to cut off, reduce, cross out; to cancel, delete, omit, suppress; to deduct; to cast away, discard, trim; to write off, cross off; to pelt with, strike with, throw at; to elide (grammar).

حَذْف — deletion, cancellation, crossing out, crossing off, writing off, omitting, omission; trimming, suppression; elision, ellipsis (grammar); deduction, substraction.

حَذَقَ — to be skilled, skillful, proficient; to master, gain mastery at; to be well-versed.

حِذْق — skill, dexterity, cleverness, perspicacity, sagacity, proficiency, expertise, acumen.

حَرّ — heat, warmth.

حُرّ — at liberty, emancipated, freeman, free, liberated; independent; unrestricted; open; noble; genuine; unadulterated.

حَرَاجَة — gravity, seriousness, difficulty.

حَرَارَة — heat, warmth; fever; temperature; ardor, fervor, enthusiasm, zeal; cordiality, friendly feeling, affection.

حرارَةٌ نَوْعِيَّة — specific heat.

حَرارِيّ — thermal, thermic.

حِرَاسَة — protection, safeguarding, custody, trust, tutelage, guarding, keeping watch, patrol, guard duty.

حِرَاسَةٌ قَضَائِيَّة — sequestration, receivership.

حَرَافَة — pungency, acridity, sharpness.

حَرَّاق — burner.

حَرَام — taboo, inviolable, holy; ill-gotten; sin, wrongdoing; forbidden, interdicted, prohibited, unlawful.

بالحَرَام — unlawfully, illegally, illicitly.

حَرَامٌ عليك — you mustn't do or say that.

حِرَام — blanket, woolen blanket or cover.

حَرَامِيّ — thief, burglar.

حَرْب — war, warfare, combat, battle.

حَرْبٌ أهْلِيَّة — civil war.

أ ب ت ث ج ح خ د ذ ر ز س ش ص ض ط ظ ع غ ف ق ك ل م ن هـ و ي

تُستعمل في الحرب كافة أنواع الأسلحة

In wars all kinds of weapons are put to use

حَرْبٌ تَقْلِيدِيَّة conventional war.

حَرْبُ عِصَابات guerilla warfare.

حَرْبٌ نُوَوِيَّة nuclear war.

حَرْبَة bayonet, lance, spear.

حَرْبِيّ military, martial, warlike.

حَرَثَ to plough, till, cultivate.

حَرَّجَ to narrow, tighten, straiten; to forbid, insist, persist; to afforest, plant with trees.

حَرَج embarrassment, disconcertion, perplexity, difficulty, closeness, tightness; oppression; anguish; critical situation; restriction; sin, offense; forest, wood.

حَرِج critical, grave, complicated; narrow, tight.

حَرِدَ to be annoyed, furious, disgruntled with.

حَرِد، حَرْدان angry, cross, disgruntled, furious, annoyed.

حَرَّرَ to free, liberate, release, set at liberty; to emancipate, set free, release from bondage; to save from, rid of, free from; to discharge from an obligation; to absolve from, acquit from, exonerate from a debt, charge, obligation; to unleash, give vent to.

حَرَّرَ to edit, write, compose, formulate, put down in writing.

حَرَّرَ to consecrate to the service of God.

حِرْز inaccessible place; refuge, sanctuary; share, portion.

حِرْز amulet, charm, talisman, fetish.

حَرَسَ to guard, keep watch over; to safeguard, escort, patrol; to oversee, supervise, superintend.

حَرَسَ to guard, keep watch over; to safeguard, escort, patrol; to oversee, supervise, superintend.

حَرَس guard, bodyguard, escort.

حَرَسُ الشَّرَف honor guard.

حِرْش forest, wood, thicket.

حَرَصَ to covet, aspire to; to be greedy, covetous, avid; to stick to, adhere to; to observe, comply with; to be punctual; to be on time; to be devoted; to be attached to.

حِرْص desire, wish, aspiration; covetousness, avidity; stinginess; observance of; care, concern, attention; punctuality.

حَرَّضَ to instigate, goad, prod, incite, provoke; to abet, stir up, agitate, induce.

حَرُفَ to become pungent, piquant, hot, acrid.

حَرَّفَ to slant, incline, make oblique; to deflect, distort, corrupt, twist; to pervert, misconstrue, falsify; to sharpen the pencil; to swerve, tilt, alter, change.

أ ب ت ث ج ح خ د ذ ر ز س ش ص ض ط ظ ع غ ف ق ك ل م ن هـ و ي

حَرْف edge, border, rim, brink, verge; ride, hem; letter, character; particle (grammar, language).

حَرْفُ تَعْرِيف definite article.

حَرْفُ جَرّ preposition.

حَرْفٌ ساكِنٌ consonant.

حَرْفٌ مُصَوَّتٌ vowel.

حَرْفُ عَطْف conjunction.

حَرْفُ عِلَّة weak letter, vowel.

حَرْفٌ صغيرٌ lowercase letter, small letter.

حَرْفٌ كبيرٌ capital letter, uppercase letter.

حِرْفَة craft, occupation, vocation, handicraft.

حَرْفِيًّا literally, word for word, to the letter, exactly.

حِرْفِيّ artisan, craftsman.

حَرَقَ to burn, sting, smart; to vex (someone's heart); to destroy by fire; to scorn, scald; to kindle, ignite, set on fire.

حَرْق scorch, burn, fire; burning, incineration, combustion, kindling, setting afire, arson.

حَرْقَة، حُرْقَة burning, incineration, combustion; torture, torment, agony, pain; intensity; yearning, craving.

حَرَّكَ to move, stir, shake; to stimulate, actuate, drive; to stir up, work up, inspire, excite; to awaken, arouse, foment; to affect the feelings; to vowelize a consonant (grammar); to set in motion; to arouse an emotion.

أحرّك السكر في فنجان الشاي لكي يذوب
I stir sugar in my cup of tea to make it melt

حَرَكَة movement, motion, activity, vivacity; move, gesture; sign; physical exercice; vowel point (grammar).

حَرَمَ to deprive of, bereave, dispossess, divest of; to take away, withhold from; to deny, refuse to someone something; to preclude, exclude from; to excommunicate.

حَرَّمَ to forbid, interdict; to deny, refuse, exclude, preclude; to declare sacred, inviolable, taboo, unlawful, not permissible.

حَرَم sanctuary, sacred place; wife, spouse; campus (of a university); sanctum.

حِرْمَان deprivation, stripping; denial, refusal, preclusion; lack, want; poverty, misery, distress; excommunication (religion); disinheritance; exclusion from inheritance.

حُرْمَة	sanctity, holiness, inviolability, immunity; wife, spouse; lady, woman; that which is holy, sacrosant, taboo.
حَرَنَ	to be obstinate, stubborn, unruly, restive.
حَرُون	restive, obstinate, unruly, ungovernable, reluctant.
حَرِيّ	appropriate for, suitable for, befitting.
حُرِّيَّة	freedom, liberty, independence; license, unrestraint.
حُرِّيَّةُ الاجْتِماع	freedom of assembly.
حُرِّيَّةُ الإرادَة	freedom of will.
حُرِّيَّةُ التَّعْبير	freedom of speech.
حُرِّيَّةُ الصَّحافَة	freedom of the press.
حُرِّيَّةُ العِبادَة	freedom of worship.
حُرِّيَّةُ الفِكْر	freedom of thought.
حَرير	silk.

تنتج دودة القز خيوط الحرير التي
تُصنع منها أقمشة فاخرة

Silkworms produce silk threads from which luxury clothes are made

حَريرٌ صَخْرِيّ	asbestos.
حُرَيْرَة	calorie.

حَرِيز	inaccessible, impenetrable, strong, forbidding, secure.
حَرِيص	greedy, covetous; desiring, eager; stingy, thrifty, frugal; adhering to, observing, abiding by; punctual (time).
حَريق	fire, conflagration.
حَريقٌ مُفْتَعَل	arson.
حَريم	harem, women.
حَزَّ	to notch, indent, dent, groove, furrow; to hurt, pain, torment, sadden, grieve (one's heart).

حَزّ	notch, incision, dent, cut, groove.
حَزازَة	hatred, rancor, spite, hate.
حِزام	belt, girdle, strap.

يشدّ الحزام الخصر لمنع السروال من السقوط

Belts are used to keep trousers attached to the body

حِزامُ الأمان	safety belt, seat belt (car, plane).

حِزْب party, faction; group, band, gang; troop.

حِزْبِيّ factional, party member.

حِزْبِيَّة partisanship, factionalism; bias, partiality.

حَزَّة incision,. notch, dent; the nick of time; critical moment; contingency; pinch; straits; distress, dilemma.

حَزَرَ to guess, surmise; to estimate, assess, make a rough estimate.

حَزَمَ to pack, package, parcel, wrap up; to tie, bind, fasten.

حَزُمَ to make fast; to take matters firmly in hand; to be firm, unwavering.

حَزْم packing, packaging, binding.

حَزْم firmness, resoluteness, resolution, determination; severity; prudence; decision; firm will.

حُزْمَة bundle, bale, bunch, parcel, pack, packet; beam (rays).

حَزِنَ to become sad, grieved, distressed; to be grieved, distressed; to grieve; to feel sorrow; to mourn over (a dead).

حُزْن sadness, grief, sorrow, affliction; mourning over a dead.

حَزيران June.

حَزِين sad, grieved, unhappy, mournful, doleful; mourning.

حِسّ sensation, perception, feeling, sentiment; voice, sound; anticipation, intuition.

حَسَاء soup, broth.

حِسَاب arithmetic, calculation, counting; consideration, accounting, account; statement (of account); appraisal, settlement, caution; bill, invoice.

حِسَابٌ جارٍ current account.

حِسَابُ التَّوْفير savings account.

حِسَابُ المُثَلَّثَات trigonometry.

حِسَابٌ دائِن credit account.

حِسَابٌ مَدين debit account.

حِسَابٌ مَكْشُوف overdrawn account.

حِسَابُ إيْداع deposit account.

حِسَابُ الأَرْبَاح والخَسَائِر profit and loss account.

على الحِسَاب on account, on credit.

حَسَّاس sensitive, sentimental, emotional, delicate, ticklish.

حَسَّاسِيَّة sensitivity, sensibility; allergy (med.); susceptibility.

حُسَام sword, sword edge.

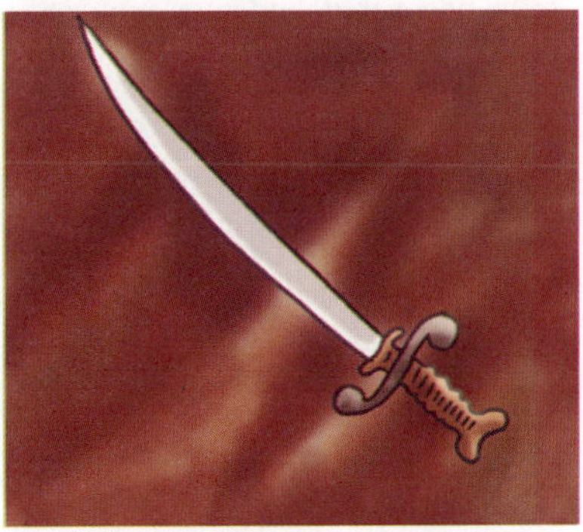

قتلَ الفارس عدوّه بحسامه القاطع
The knight killed his foe by his sword

حَسَبَ to calculate, compute, count; to consider, hold, rate; to think, suppose; to take into account, reckon with, bear in mind; to anticipate.

حَسَب ancestry, noble descent; esteem, respect.

حَسَب extent; measure; number; amount, value.

حَسَبَ according to, in accordance with.

حَسْب counting, thinking; extent; measure; sufficiency.

حَسْب only, merely, solely, and nothing else.

حُسْبَان computation, calculation, counting; supposition, assumption; opinion, view.

حِسْبَة account; salary; price control.

حَسْبَمَا according to, depending on how; as chance will have it.

حَسَدَ to envy, covet; to begrudge; to be envious, covetous.

حَسَد envy, jealousy.

حَسَرَ to uncover, lay bare, lift, raise; to be uncovered, laid bare, removed, raised; to be tired, exhausted, weary.

حَسِرَ to be grieved, sad; to be languid, fatigued, tired.

حَسَر fatigue, tiredness, weariness.

حَسَرُ البَصَر myopia, nearsightedness.

حَسْرَة sorrow, sadness, pain, distress, affliction; sigh.

حَسَك thorns, fishbones, spines.

حَسَمَ to settle, finish, complete, terminate; to decide a matter; to deduct, discount; to cut, sever, cut off.

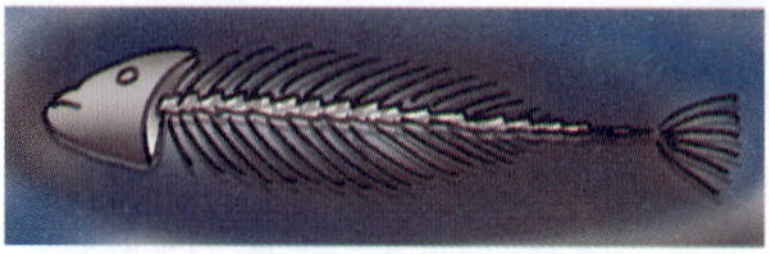

نأكل لحم السّمك ونترك الحسك جانباً
We eat fish meat and leave fishbones aside

حَسْم severence, cutting off; deduction, discount, rebate; substraction; settlement of a matter; termination, resolution.

حَسَّنَ to beautify, embellish, adorn, decorate, improve, ameliorate; to present in a favorable light or state.

حَسَن handsome, nice, beautiful; good; comely, fair, fine; well.

حُسْن beauty, loveliness, gracefulness, prettiness; excellence, superiority, perfection.

حُسْنُ الضِّيافَة hospitality.

بِحُسْنِ نِيَّة in good faith.

لِحُسْنِ الحَظّ luckily, fortunately.

حُسْنُ السُّلوك good conduct.

حُسْنُ التَّعْبير euphemism.

حُسْنَى kindness, kindliness, good outcome.

بالحُسْنَى with kindness, amicably.

حَسْنَاء beautiful (female); beautiful woman.

حَسَنَة charity, handout, alms; good deed, favor, kind act; advantage, merit; good feature, point, quality.

envious, begrudging, jealous.	حَسُود
sensory, perceptible, sensible; tangible, concrete; physical, real; sensual.	حِسِّيّ
highborn, highbred, of noble birth; nobleman.	حَسِيب
enough, sufficient.	حَسِيب
tired, exhausted, weary; sad, grieved.	حَسِير
to stuff, fill up, fill in, pad; to cram, pack, charge; to load (a weapon); to insert, interpolate.	حَشَا
to mass, gather, call up, mobilize (troops); to pile up, store up, accumulate, amass; to side with, support, back up.	حَشَدَ
crowd, gathering, throng, multitude; rallying, assembling; massing, mobilization, calling up (troops).	حَشْد
to gather, rally (people); to cram, crowd, pack, jam (people together); to squeeze, press; to insert, stuff, shove.	حَشَرَ
to poke one's nose into, to meddle, interfere in, intrude upon, obtrude upon.	حَشَرَ أَنْفَهُ في
wedging; cramming, stuffing, jamming, crowding; gathering, assembling	حَشْر
resurrection.	حَشْر
insect.	حَشَرَة
rattling, rattle in the throat.	حَشْرَجَة
glans (of male sexual organ).	حَشَفَة
servants, retinue, entourage.	حَشَم (ج)

تعيش ملايين الأنواع من الحشرات على سطح الأرض

Uncounted multitudes of insect species live on earth

shame; bashfulness, timidity; difference, modesty; descency; decorum.	حِشْمَة
stuffing, filling, dressing, padding; charging, loading (a weapon); insertion, cramming; interpolation; redundancy; wordiness, verbosity.	حَشْو
stuffing, padding, filling; fill, pad, filler; loading, charging (a weapon); panel; cytoplasm (med.).	حَشْوَة
grass, weeds, herbs; hay; hashish, hemp.	حَشِيش
herb, weed.	حَشِيشَة
pearl; saffron.	حُصّ
pebble, small stone; calculus (med.).	حَصَاة
harvesting, harvest, reaping, cropping; harvest time.	حَصَاد
harvester, reaper, cropper, mower; mowing machine, cropping machine, harvesting machine.	حَصَّادَة

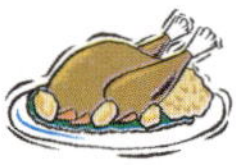

حِصار siege, blockade.

حَصافَة sound judgment, wisdom, sagacity, judiciousness.

حِصان horse, steed, stallion (animal).

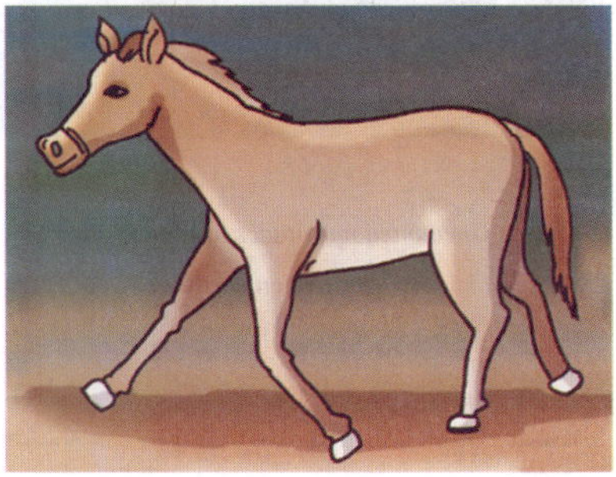

الحصان العربي هو أشهر الأحصنة في العالم
The Arab horse is the most famous among horses in the world

حِصانُ البَحْر hippopotamus (animal).

قُدْرَةٌ حِصانِيَّة horsepower.

حَصانَة immunity; inaccessibility; strength; impregnability.

حِصانَةُ المَرْأة chastity, virtue, decency.

حَصَب، حَصْباء pebbles, gravel, macadam.

حَصْبَة measles; rubella.

حِصَّة share, part, lot; quota, quotient; span of time.

حَصْحَصَ to come to light, manifest itself; to become clear, manifest, plain, patent.

حَصَدَ to harvest, reap, gather, crop, mow; to kill; to claim.

حَصَرَ to limit, surround, encircle, encompass; to enclose; to blockade, lay a siege, besiege; to detain, restrain, contain, restrict; to narrow down, confine; to compile, arrange, bring together; to set up, list, enumerate; to comprise, include, involve; to block, shut off, seclude; to count, calculate, compute; to monopolize, concentrate.

حَصِرَ to be unable to express oneself; to falter, stutter, stumble (in speech).

حَصْر restriction, confinement, constraint, restraint; fixing, limitation, determination; encirclement, blockading, laying siege; narrowing; gathering; enumeration, listing, computing, centralization; monopoly.

عَلامَةُ الحَصْر parenthesis, bracket (grammar).

حِصْرِم sour grapes, unripe grapes.

حَصْرِيّ exclusive, sole, restrictive.

حَصَّصَ to allot, apportion, allocate; to distribute, divide, parcel out, share out, deal out.

حَصَلَ to happen, occur, take place, pass, come to pass; to arise, come about, transpire, befall, overtake.

حَصَلَ to originate from, proceed from, follow from, result from, be caused by.

حَصَلَ to obtain, get, acquire, earn, receive; to accomplish; to possess, own, have.

حَصَّلَ to recover, collect (a debt); to infer, deduce, conclude.

حَصَّنَ to fortify, make inaccessible, strengthen.

أ ب ت ث ج ح خ د ذ ر ز س ش ص ض ط ظ ع غ ف ق ك ل م ن هـ و ي

حَصَّنَ to immunize, make immune, grant immunity to.

حِصْن fortress, port, castle, citadel, stronghold; fortification, entrenchment, protection.

كانت الحصون من أمنع الأمكنة في الأزمنة القديمة

Fortresses were well-fortified constructions built for the protection of cities

حُصُول happening, occurrence, incidence.

حُصُول obtainment, acquisition; earning, realization; possession, owning, having; attainment, achievement.

حَصِير ، حَصِيرَة straw mat.

حَصِيف judicious; having sound judgment; shrewd, discriminating.

حَصِيلَة outcome, result, issue, sequence, sequel; yield, produce, income, revenue; remainder, rest.

حَصِين well-fortified; inaccessible, impenetrable; strong, secure; immune, unsusceptible, impregnable, invulnerable; proof against.

حَضَارَة civilization, culture.

حَضَانَة ، حِضَانَة nursing, rearing, breeding, upbringing; hatching (of eggs); incubation; day nursery.

حَضَرَ to attend; to be present at; to take part, participate, to arrive at; to visit (a place); to appear (before a judge); to show up; to become urbanized; to watch, witness; to come to one's mind.

حَضَّرَ to prepare, make ready, ready; to civilize, urbanize; to fetch, procure, supply; to conjure, evoke (spirits).

حَضَر civilized region with a settled population; town dwellers.

حَضْرَة Mr., your honor, esquire.

حَضَنَ to embrace, clasp, hug in one's arms; to nurse, raise, rear, bring up; to hatch, incubate, brood (eggs of a bird); to concoct, contrive.

حَضْن embrace, cuddle, accolade; nursing, raising, rearing; incubation, hatching, brooding.

حِضْن lap, bosom.

حُضُور presence, attendance, participation, visit; audience, assembly, spectators, viewers, onlookers.

حُضُورُ الذِّهْن presence of mind, shrewdness, perspicacity.

حَضِيرَة squad (army); vanguard, advance guard (army).

حَضِيض bottom, rock bottom, lowest level; perigee (astr.).

حطَّ to descend, come down, fall down; to decline, lower, drop, unload; to decrease, diminish, reduce; to depreciate the value of; to land, touch down (plane); to perch, sit, roost (bird); to halt, stop, dismount, encamp; to demote, degrade, reduce someone in rank; to debase, humiliate, discredit, undervalue someone's value, position, honor.

حطّاب woodcutter, logger, lumberjack.

حُطام debris, remains, wreckage, rubble, broken pieces.

حَطَب firewood, wood.

حطَّمَ to break, shatter, smash, wreck, demolish.

حَظّ luck, chance, fate, destiny; lot, share, part, portion; prosperity, fortune, affluence, wealth.

حَظَرَ to ban, prohibit, forbid; to fence in, hedge in.

حَظْر ban, prohibition, embargo, interdiction.

حَظْرُ التَّجَوُّل curfew.

حِظْوَة، حُظْوَة favor, grace, goodwill; benevolence; prestige, standing, respect; favored position, precedence, rank.

حَظِيَ to acquire, obtain, attain, gain, win; to enjoy the favor of; to obtain the good graces of; to have the privilege from.

حَظيرَة pen, corral, enclosure (of cattle); hangar, shed (of planes, machines, vehicles).

حَفَّ to surround someone of something; to enclose, encompass, border something.

حَفَّ to rub, scrub; to trim, clip, depilate; to create a swish, hiss, murmur.

حَفّار digger, excavator; driller; inscriber; carver; engraver.

حَفّارُ القُبور gravedigger.

حَفّارَة excavator, drill, drag line.

حَفاوَة، حِفاوَة friendly reception, welcoming, welcome, salutation.

حَفَرَ to dig; to excavate, drill, bore; to engrave, incise, inscribe, carve; to engrave, etch.

حَفْر digging, excavation, drilling, boring; engraving, carving, etching; inlaying, marquetry.

حُفْرَة hole, pit, bore, crater, cavity.

أحدثت القنبلة حفرة كبيرة في الأرض

The bomb produced a wide and deep hole in the ground

حَفَّزَ to catalyse; to motivate, incite, urge, prompt.

حَفِظَ to keep, protect, safeguard, maintain, conserve, preserve;to observe, bear in mind, comply with; to retain, uphold, safekeep, store; to retain in one's memory; to know by heart; to memorize, commit to memory; to stay, suspend (a court case); to reserve for oneself, appropriate for oneself; to put away, take care of.

حِفْظ preservation, safeguarding, conservation; upkeep, protection, guarding, safekeeping; storage, custody, retention; compliance with, abidance by; memorization, learning by heart; stay, suspension (legal action); filing (papers, documents).

حَفَلَ to gather, congregate, throng together; to pay attention, attend to; to abound with, overflow with; to feel interest about someone or something; to be replete, teeming with.

حَفْل gathering, meeting, assembly, congregation, crowd; performance, show, celebration; feast, festival; attendance, heed, concern, interest.

حَفْلَة assembly, gathering, congregation; social party, public event; show, performance, concert; festival, festivity, ceremony, celebration.

حَفْلَةُ افْتِتاح opening ceremony; inauguration party.

حَفْلَةٌ تأبينية commemorative ceremony (for a deceased person).

حَفْلَةُ تَخَرُّج أو تَخْريج commencement, graduation ceremony.

حَفْلَةٌ تَنَكُّرِيَّة masked ball.

حَفْلَةٌ خَيْرِيَّة charity performance.

حَفْلَةٌ راقِصَة dance party, ball.

حَفْلَةٌ ساهِرَة soirée, evening party.

حَفْلَةُ زواج أو زِفاف wedding party, marriage ceremony.

حَفْلَةٌ موسيقِيَّة concert, recital, musicale.

حَفْنَة، حُفْنَة handful.

حَفيد grandson, grandchild.

حَفيدَة granddaughter.

حَفيظَة anger, resentment, grudge, rancor, spite.

حَفيف swish, hiss, murmur.

حَقَّ to be true, turn out to be true; to be right, correct; to be necessary, requisite, obligatory; to deserve; to be entitled to; to have the right to.

حَقّ truth; rightful, correct, sound, valid; title, legal claim.

حَقُّ الاقْتِراع suffrage, franchise, right to vote.

حَقُّ تَقْرِيرِ المَصِير right of self-determination.

حَقُّ اللّجوءِ السِّياسِيّ right of asylum.

حَقُّ المرور right to pass, right-of-way.

حُقوقُ الإنْسان human rights.

حُقوقُ التأليفِ أو النَّشر copyright.

بِحَقّ rightly, justly, truly, fairly.

بِحَقِّ by (for swearing).

الحَقُّ عليك you are wrong, you are at fault.

من حَقِّهِ أن he has the right to, he is entitled to.

والحقُّ يُقال one may say, it must be admitted.

حُقّ، حُقَّة hollow, cavity; pot, receptacle, jar.

حَقارَة lowness, vulgarity, baseness, vileness, meanness; insignificance, worthlessness, inferiority.

حِقْبَة stretch of time, period, age, epoch.

حَقَدَ to harbor feelings of hatred against; to bear a grudge against.

حِقْد، حَقْد grudge, hatred, spite, rancor, illwill, bitter feeling.

حَقَرَ to despise, scorn, disdain; to have a low opinion of.

حَقَّرَ to degrade, disparage, depreciate; to debase, humble, humiliate; to scorn, despise, disdain.

حَقَّقَ to realize, carry out, put into effect, fulfill.

حَقَّقَ النَّظَر to look closely, study, examine, explore.

حَقَّقَ مع to interrogate, examine.

حَقْل field, domain, realm, area; column (in a newspaper).

حَقَنَ to inject, shoot; to withhold, detain, retain; to suppress; to spare someone's blood; to give an injection.

حُقْنَة injection, shot.

حَقُود spiteful, hateful, rancorous.

حُقُوقِيّ (ص) legal, juristic.

حُقُوقِيّ (اسم) jurist, jurisconsult, lawyer.

حَقِيبَة suitcase, trunk; briefcase; handbag; satchel.

حَقِير low, base, mean, vulgar, vile; paltry; poor; wretched; miserable; despicable; little, small.

حَقِيقَة truth, reality, fact; essence; true sense.

حَقِيقِيّ real, true, genuine, actual, factual; essential; authentic.

حَكَّ to rub, chafe, scrape, scratch, abrade.

حَكّ rubbing, chafing, scraping, friction, scratching.

حَكَى to tell, report, give an account; to speak, talk; to imitate, resemble, copy.

حِكَايَة story, narrative, tale, narration.

حَكَرَ to hoard and withhold; to monopolize; to hold a monopoly over.

حُكْر monopoly, hoarding of goods.

حَكَمَ to rule over, govern, dominate; to order, command; to pass judgment, express an opinion on; to decide, give a dicision; to pass a verdict; to sentence; to impose, inflict a penalty on; to adjucate, adjudge, award; to ordain, decree, prescribe.

حَكَّمَ to chose someone as arbitrator; to make someone the judge over; to empower, authorize, give a free hand to; to resort; to have recourse; to make use of, employ.

حَكَم arbitrator, arbiter, referee.

حُكْم sentence, judgment, decision; rule, administration, direction, command; government, reign, regime; provision, stipulation.

حُكْمٌ وِجاهِيّ judgment delivered in the presence of the parties in a legal proceeding.

حُكْمٌ ذاتِيّ autonomy, self-rule.

حُكْمٌ عُرْفِيّ martial law.

حُكْمٌ غيابِيّ — judgment by default, judgment in absentia.

حُكْمُ الفَرْد — autocracy.

حُكْمُ الأقَلِّيَة — oligarchy.

حُكْمٌ مُطْلَق — dictatorship, autocracy, totalitarianism.

حُكْمًا — definitely, positively, necessarily, legally.

بِحُكْم — by virtue of, pursuant to, by force of.

حِكْمَة — wisdom, sagacity, maxim, rationale, philosophy.

حِكَمِيّ — aphoristic, gnomic, expressing maxims.

حُكُومَة — government.

حُكُومَةٌ ائْتِلافِيَّة — coalition government.

حُكُومَةٌ اتِّحادِيَّة — federal government.

حُكُومَةٌ انْتِقالِيَّة — caretaker government.

حُكُومِيّ — governmental, public, state controlled; official.

حَكِيم — wise, judicious; wise man, sage, philosopher.

حَلَّ — to untie (a knot); to unfasten, unbind, undo; to solve, resolve, settle (a case, a problem); to decipher, decode (a cipher); to dissolve, liquefy; to analyze, decompose (matter); to disband, break up (an organization); to loosen, unstring, relax; to release, free, liberate, set free someone; to befall, occur; to stop, halt, settle down, stay; to come (for a visit); to take up residence in; to overcome, overwhelm; to fade, dim, pale (color); to be lawful, legal, legitimate.

حَلّ — solution, resolution, settlement; untying, unfastening, undoing, loosening; dissolution, dissolving; release, releasing, freeing; discharge, acquittal, release; abolition, cancellation, annulment.

حَلٌّ وَسَط — compromise.

حَلا — to sweeten, to be sweet; to be beautiful, pretty.

حَلَّى — to sweeten; to adorn, decorate, embelllish.

حَلَّاق — barber, hairdresser.

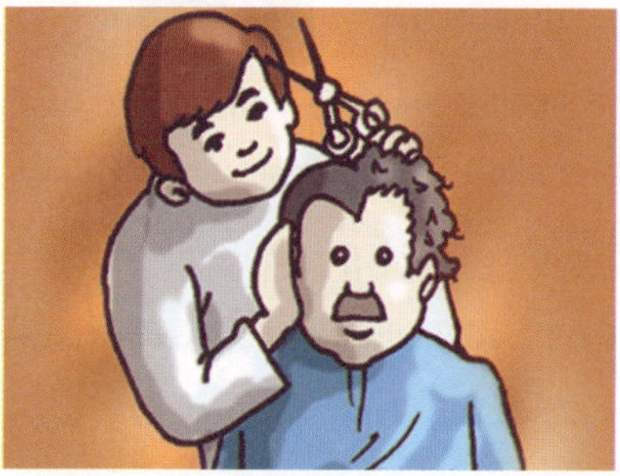

أذهب إلى الحلاق مرة في الشهر لقصّ شعر رأسي

I visit the hairdresser once every month to cut my hair

حِلاقَة — shaving, hairdressing; hairdo; barber's trade.

حَلال — lawful, legitimate; admissible, allowable.

حَلاوَة — sweetness, prettiness; halva.

حَلَبَ — to milk.

حَلْبَة — racetrack, racecourse; arena, field, ring.

حَلَّة — cooking pot.

حُلَّة — garment, dress, suit, uniform.

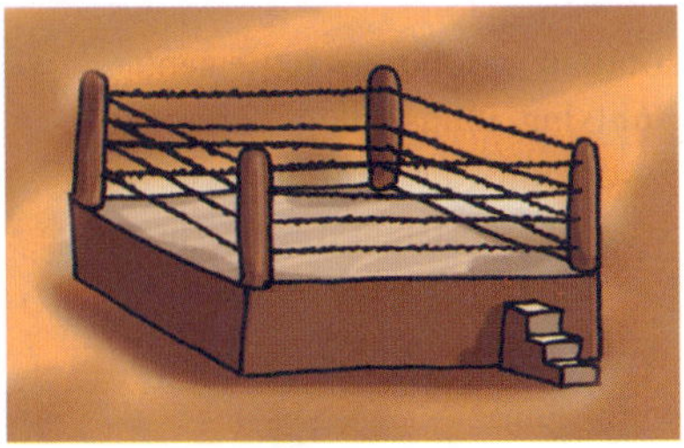

يتصارع الملاكمان داخل حلبة الملاكمة

The boxers fight each other inside a ring

to gin (cotton). حَلَج

snail; spiral, helix. حَلَزُون

spiral, helical. حَلَزونيّ

to swear; to take an oath. حَلَف

to make someone swear; to exact an oath from; to adjure, entreat earnestly someone. حَلَّف

oath, oath taking. حَلْف، حَلِف

alliance; ally; oath, swearing. حِلْف

to shave; to have a haircut. حَلَق

to soar, hover, climb in the air; to rise, tower, climb up; to be high, lofty; to round; to make round, circular. حَلَّق

earring. حَلَق

throat, gullet, pharynx. حَلْق

ring, circle, loop, annulet; earring; group, body of people; episode (of a program, story, sequence). حَلْقَة، حَلَقَة

seminar, colloquium, symposium. حَلْقَةٌ دِراسِيَّة

vicious circle. حَلْقَةٌ مُفْرَغَة

throat, gullet, pharynx. حُلقوم

يحلق الطائر عالياً مستعيناً بجناحيه

Birds soar in the air using their wings

annular, circular, ringshaped. حَلْقيّ

to be deep-black. حَلِك

to dissolve in water; to resolve, analyze; to decompose, disintegrate; to discharge, absolve; to make legitimate, lawful; to justify, declare permissible; to allow, permit; to regard as fair game; to legalize, sanction. حَلَّل

to dream of; to attain puberty. حَلَم

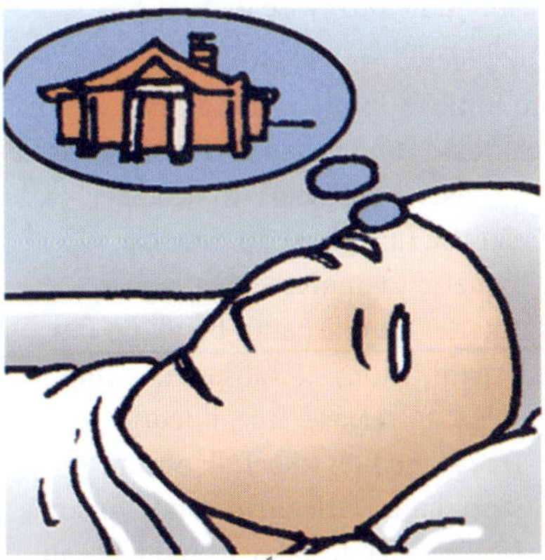

حلمت بأني أصبحت أميراً على إمارة واسعة وغنية

I dreamt of being a ruler over a wide and rich country

أ ب ت ث ج ح خ د ذ ر ز س ش ص ض ط ظ ع غ ف ق ك ل م ن هـ و ي

حَلُمَ	to be patient; to show patience; to be clement, gentle, mild-tempered.
حُلُم	puberty, sexual maturity.
حُلْم	dream.
حِلْم	patience, clemency, mildness, forbearance, insight, understanding, reason, intelligence, indulgence.
حَلَمَة	nipple, teat.
حُلْو	sweet, delicious; nice, beautiful, pretty.
حَلْوَى	candy, confection, dessert, sweet pastry.
حُلُول	stopping, putting up, sojourn, dwelling; beginning, setting in; substitution, replacement; subrogation of.
حَلِيّ	jewelry, trinket.
حَليب	milk.

نحصل على الحليب من ضرع البقرة

We obtain milk from the udder of the cow or goat

حِلْيَة	trinket, decoration, ornament.
حَليف	ally, allied.
حَليق	clean shaven,shaved.
حَليل	husband, spouse, wife.
حَليم	patient, tolerant, clement, indulgent, mildtempered.
حُلَيْمَة	papilla.
حُمَّ	to contract fever; to have a fever.
حَمّ	heat, warmth, hotness.
حَمَى	to defend, protect, shelter, shield; to support, uphold; to follow a diet.
حَمَا، حَمُو	father-in-law.
حُمَّى	fever.
حُمَّى التيفوئيد	typhoid fever.
حِمَى	refuge, shelter, sanctuary.
حَمْأَة	mud, sludge, slime.
حَمَاة	mother-in-law.
حِمَار	donkey, ass (animal).

يشتهر الحمار بصبره ولكنه يرفس من يزعجه

Donkeys are famed for their patience but will kick whoever irritates them

zebra (animal).	حِمَارُ الزَّرْد
she-ass, female donkey.	حِمَارَة
enthusiasm ardor, zeal, fervor, keenness.	حَماس، حَمَاسَة
zealous, ardent, fervent; stimulating, inspiring; fanatic, rousing, electrifying.	حَمَاسِيّ
stupidity, foolishness, imbecility, folly; anger, wrath; dumbness, idiocy, dimwittedness.	حَمَاقَة
porter.	حَمَّال

طلبت من الحمّال أن ينقل حقائب السفر

The porter carried my luggage to my house

beam, girder, support; post, pier; suspenders (of trousers); stretcher, litter (for the sick); hanger (for clothes).	حَمَّالَة
key holder.	حَمَّالَةُ مَفَاتِيح
brassiere.	حَمَّالَةٌ للصَّدْر
pigeon, dove.	حَمام، حَمَامَة
bathroom; bath; lavatory, water closet, washroom.	حَمَّام

الحمام طير داجن يرمز إلى السلام

Pigeons are symbols of peace

blood bath.	حَمَّامُ دَمٍ
death.	حِمَام
heat, warmth.	حَمَاوَة
protection, defense, preservation; supporting, sponsorship.	حِمَايَة
to praise, commend, laud, eulogize.	حَمِدَ
praise, commendation, laudation.	حَمْد
praise be to God; thank God.	الحَمْدُ لله
to roast, grill, broil (food); to redden.	حَمَّرَ
redness; rouge, lipstick, blushing powder.	حُمْرَة
to roast, toast.	حَمَّصَ
to become sour, acid.	حَمُضَ
to make sour; to acidify, acidulate; to develop (a film).	حَمَّضَ
acid.	حَمْض
boric acid.	حَمْضُ البُورِيك
citric acid.	حَمْضُ اللَّيمون
acid, sour.	حَمْضِيّ

حَمْضِيَات (ج) citrus fruits, citrus trees.

حَمُقَ to be stupid, foolish.

حُمْق stupidity, foolishness, imbecility, folly, idiocy.

حَمَلَ to carry, bear, raise, pick up, transport, convey; to bring along; to carry away; to assume the burden.

يحمل مدير المدرسة حقيبة يضع فيها أوراقه الخاصّة

The school's principal carries a satchel in which he puts all his papers

حَمَلَ to induce, cause, prompt, make someone do something.

حَمَلَ to attack, launch an attack, assail.

حَمَلَ (المَرْأة) to become pregnant; to conceive.

حَمَلَ (الشَّجَرَة) to bear fruit, fructify.

حَمَلَ السِّلاحَ to take up arms against.

حَمَّلَ to load with; to make someone carry something; to burden with; bear down on, encumber; to impose on.

حَمَل lamb.

الحمل هو ولدُ النعجة والكَبْش

A lamb is the offspring of an ewe and a ram

حَمْل carrying, carriage; lifting, raising, transportation.

حَمْل pregnancy; embryo, fetus,

حِمْل load, cargo, charge, burden, encumbrance.

حَمْلَة attack, offensive, assault, charge, campaign.

حَمْلَةٌ حَرْبِيَّة military expedition.

حَمْلَةٌ انتِخَابِيَّة election campaign.

حَمْلَقَ to stare at, gaze at, goggle at.

حُمُوضَة acidity, sourness.

حُمُولَة burden, load, cargo, freight.

حَمِيَ to become hot, warm; to become violent; to flare up; to glow; to become angry with; furious at.

حَمِيَّة zeal, enthusiasm, ardor, fanaticism.

حِمْيَة diet, dietary.

حَميد (ص) praiseworthy, laudable, commendable; benign, harmless (disease).

حَميم intimate, close friend; close; hot (water).

حَنَّ to long for, yearn for, crave, desire; to sympathize with; feel sympathy for; to commiserate; to have mercy.

حَنَى to bend, curve, bow, incline; to stoop, hunch; to lean over; to deviate, disgress, turn.

حِنَّاء henna.

حَنَان sympathy, love, affection; tenderness; commiseration, compassion, pity.

حَنِثَ to break one's oath; to perjure; to sin, do wrong.

حَنْجَرَة، حُنْجُور larynx, throat.

حَنَّطَ to embalm, mummify; to stuff (dead animals).

حِنْطَة wheat.

حَنَفِيَّة faucet, tap, cock, hydrant.

حَنِقَ to become enraged by, furious at, mad at; to burst in anger; to lose one's temper; to be annoyed, exasperated, irritated; to be resentful.

حَنَك palate, jaw, jawbone, mandible.

حُنْكَة sophistication; worldly wisdom, experience.

حَنْو twist, curving, flexing, bowing, bending.

حُنُوّ sympathy, compassion, pity, affection, love, kindness.

حَنُون compassionate, merciful, affectionate, kindhearted.

حَنْي bending, curving, twisting, flexing, bowing.

حَنْيَة bend, curve, turn, twist.

حَنيف true, orthodox.

الدِّينُ الحَنيف the true religion (Islam).

حَنين longing, yearning, nostalgia; craving, desire; hankering.

حَوَى to contain, hold, enclose, comprise, include; to gather, collect, unite; to possess, own, have.

حَوَّاء Eve.

حِوار dialogue, conversation, discussion, speech; argument, dispute; script, scenario (of a play, a motion picture).

حَوالَى about, approximately; around; nearly, almost.

حَوالَة draft, order of payment; transfer, remittance of money, money order; cession, transfer, conveyance.

حَوَّامَة helicopter.

حُوت whale, (fish).

بُرْجُ الحُوت Pisces (astr.).

حَوْج need, want, lack, deficiency, destitution.

أ ب ت ث ج ح خ د ذ ر ز س ش ص ض ط ظ ع غ ف ق ك ل م ن هـ و ي

حَوَّلَ to change, alter, convert, mutate; to short, switch, transfer, transform; to shunt (a rail track); to remit, transfer, send, transmit money by mail; to pass on, hand on to; to endorse (a bill of exchange, cheque, promissory note); to direct, turn a glance toward; to divert, distract, avert one's eyes from; to switch off, disconnect (a current); to change the course of; cede (a debt).

حَوَل squint, strabismus, cross-eye.

حَوْل year.

حَوْل power, might, strength.

حَوْل around, about, round; concerning, regarding, with regard to, in respect of, in relation to, re.

حَوَّمَ to circle, hover in circles, rotate, go around; to swarm, buzz around.

حَوْمَة turmoil of battle; main body; quarter (of a city).

حُوَيْصِلَة vesicle, bladder.

حَيّ alive, living, live; lively, animated, energetic, undismayed; living being; organism; tribe; block of apartment houses, quarter of a city.

حَيُّ الضَّمير upright, incorruptible, conscientious.

الحوت هو أكبر الحيوانات البحرية الموجودة

Whales are the largest living sea creatures

حَوَّرَ to modify, alter, change; to distort, corrupt, falsify; to roll out dough; to bleach a wall.

حَوْر poplar (tree).

حُورِيَّة nymph.

حُورِيَّة الماء mermaid, naiad.

حَوْز possession, holding; obtainment, acquisition; occupancy; tenancy; enclosed area, boundary, precinct.

حَوْزَة possession, holding; property; area, territory.

حَوْش enclosure, enclosed area; courtyard, backyard.

حَوْصَلَة craw (of a bird); bladder.

حَوْض basin, trough, cistern, container, reservoir; pool, pond; pelvis (anatomy); dock, shipyard; bed; bathtub; tub.

حَوَّطَ to encircle, surround, enclose, encompass; to build a wall around something; to close in from all sides; to guard, protect, preserve, take care of, look after.

أ ب ت ث ج ح خ د ذ ر ز س ش ص ض ط ظ ع غ ف ق ك ل م ن هـ و ي

حَيَّا	to greet, salute, hail.
حَيَاء	bashfulness, shyness, diffidence, modesty, shame.
حَيَاة	life, living, existence.
حِيَاد	neutrality.
حِيَادٌ إِيْجَابِيّ	positive neutrality.
حِيَادِيّ	neutral.
حِيَازَة	possession, holding; acquisition, obtainment; getting; tenure, occupancy; acquisition of title; attainment.

حِيَاكَة	weaving, knitting.

جدتي تتقن حياكة الصوف

My grandmother likes knitting wool pullovers

حِيَالَ	in view of; in the face of; in front of; before.
حَيَّة	snake, serpent, viper.
حَيْثُ	whereas, wherein, wherever, in which, at which;since, due to the fact that, in as much as; in any case, at any rate; because, considering that.

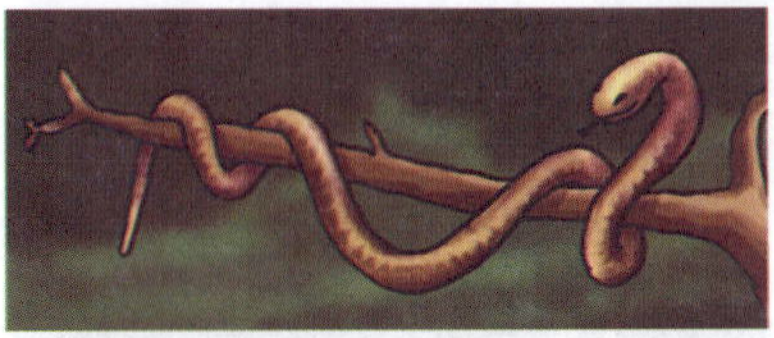

تعرف الحية باسم الأفعى ومنها ما هو سام وقاتل

Vipers are of various kinds: Some are poisonous others are harmless

بِحَيْثُ	so that, so as to, in order to.
مِنْ حَيْثُ	from where, whence, as for, as to, concerning; in respect of; in view of, because of.
حَيْثُمَا	wherever, where, wheresoever, anywhere.
حَيْد	deviation, deviance, swerve, diversion.
حَيْدٌ بَحْرِيّ	reef.
حَيْدٌ مَرْجَانِيّ	coral reef.

حَيَّرَ	to confuse, puzzle, bewilder, confound, dismay, perturb, baffle, embarass, nonplus.
حَيْرَة	confusion, perplexity, bewilderment, embarassment; bafflement, dismay; hesitation, wavering.
حَيِّز ، حَيْز	space, location; extent; expanse, sphere, realm; scope, range, reach, field.
حَيْض	menstruation, period, menses.
حَيْطَة ، حِيْطَة	caution, prudence, circumspection; precaution.
حَيْف	injustice, inequity, prejudice, harm, damage.
حَيْل	strength, vigor, vitality, force, power.

حِيْلَة — trick, ruse, subterfuge, fraud, ploy, stratagem, artifice, maneuver; wile; device; shift.

حَيْلُولَة — separation, interruption, disruption; prevention.

حِيْن — time, period of time; epoch.

حِيْنَ — when, upon, on; at the time when.

حِينًا — for some time, once, at times, sometimes.

حِيْنَئِذٍ — at that time, then, by then.

حِيْنَمَا — when, while, during, as; whilst.

حَيَوان — animal, beast.

حَيَوانٌ ثَدْيِيّ — mammal.

حَيَوانٌ مُجْتَرّ — ruminant.

حَيَوانٌ مَنَوِيّ — spermatozoan.

عِلْمُ الحَيَوان — zoology.

نجم البحر حيوان مائي يعيش في أعماق البحار

The starfish lives in the depth of the sea

حَيَوَانِيّ — animal, zoological; bestial, brute, beastly, ruffian.

حَيَوِيّ — vital, essential, fundamental, crucial; lively.

حَيَوِيَّة — vitality, vigor; life; spirit; vivacity; activity; vim.

حَيِيَ — to live, be alive, exist.

لِيَحْيَ — long live!.

حَيِيّ — shy, bashful, timid, modest.

حُيَيّ — microbe.

حرف الخاء

خائِب unsuccessful, futile, abortive, disappointed.

خائِر weak, languid, strengthless.

خائِف afraid, scared; terrified, frightened; horrified, panicstricken; apprehensive for, worried about.

خائِن، خَؤون (ص) treacherous, unfaithful, disloyal.

خائن (اسم) traitor, betrayer, deceiver.

خابَ to fail, miscarry; to be frustrated, disappointed.

خابَرَ to communicate with; to reach, call by telephone; to exchange letters with; to speak to, talk to, contact.

خابور wedge, peg, pin, cotter.

خاتَلَ to dupe, gull, cheat, double-cross; to deceive.

خاتَم ring, finger ring; last, end.

خاتَمُ الزَّواج wedding ring.

خاتَمُ البَريد postmark.

خاتِمَة end, termination; close, closure; conclusion, final stage; epilogue (of a book); finale (music).

خادَعَ to deceive, mislead, dupe, cheat, double-cross.

خادِع deceptive; swindler, crook; fraudulent.

خادِم servant, manservant, page, waiter.

قدّم الخادم وجبة الطعام إلى الزبون
The waiter served the meal ordered by the customer

أ ب ت ث ج ح خ د ذ ر ز س ش ص ض ط ظ ع غ ف ق ك ل م ن هـ و ي

خادِمَة maid, maid servant, attendant, housemaid.

خَارَ to weaken, languish, flag, decline in vigor; to be weak, feeble, droopy, flabby; to subside, calm down.

خَارَ to moo, bellow (cow, ox).

خَارِج outside, exterior, coming out; leaving, outgoing.

خارِج dissident, insurgent, renegade, apostate.

خَارِجٌ على القانون outlaw, rebel.

خارِجٌ عن المَوْضوع irrelevant, impertinent, outside the topic.

خَارِجيّ external, exterior, outer, outside; foreign.

خارِطَة، خَريطَة map, chart, cartogram.

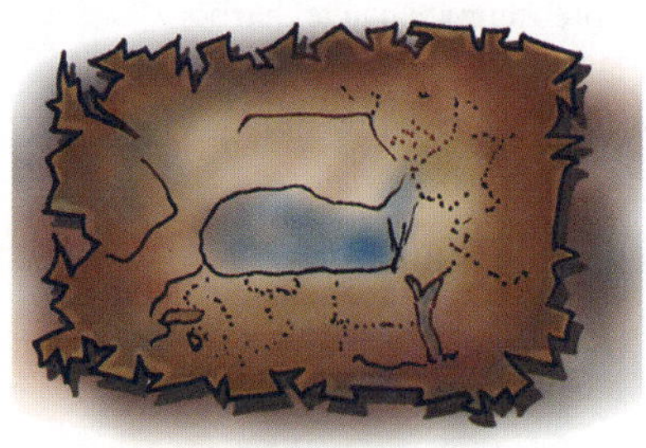

يرسم الخطاط خارطة البلدان وحدودها

Maps show the countries of the world and their boundaries

خارِطَةُ المَسَاحَة cadastral map.

خارِق penetrating, piercing; extraordinary, unusual, supernatural, marvelous; wonderful.

خازِن treasurer, warehouseman, storekeeper.

خَاسِر loser, hopeless; profligate, scoundrel, depraved.

خاشِع humble, submissive, devout, pious.

خاصّ special, particular, specific, personal; related to, pertaining to, connected with.

خاصَّة، خاصِّيَّة characteristic, peculiarity, attribute, feature.

خاصَّتي mine.

خاصَرَ to put one's arm around the waist of; to clasp someone around the waist.

خاصِرَة waist, flank, middle, hip, haunch.

خاصَمَ to quarrel with, fight with; to antagonize; to prosecute, bring suit against; to argue, dispute with, have a fight with someone; to sue, litigate.

خاضَ to wade into; sink into, plunge into, embark upon; to deal with, discuss; to enter the war; to run for election; to face death, peril; to be engrossed in.

خاضِع submissive, humble, obedient; pliant, prone, liable to; subordinate, subject, governed by.

خاطَ to sew, stich.

خاطِئ (ص) wrong, in error; sinful; guilty, at fault; incorrect.

خاطِئ (اسم) sinner; guilty person.

خَاطَبَ to address, speak to, talk to, discourse with.

خاطِب fiancé, suitor, betrothed; matchmaker.

خاطِبَة fiancée, betrothed, engaged; matchmaker.

خاطَرَ to risk, hazard, stake one's life; to incur the danger of; to bet, wager; to make a bet.

خاطِر idea, thought, mind; will, wish, desire, volition.

خاطِف (اسم) kidnapper, abductor, hijacker.

خافَ to fear, apprehend; to be frightened, scared, afraid of; to dread; to be filled with fear; to be apprehensive for, anxious about, concerned about.

خافِت faint, dim, subdued.

خافِق (ص) throbbing, pulsating; palpitating, fluttering; flapping.

خافِق (اسم) flag, banner.

خَالَ to fancy, imagine, think, believe, suppose that; to deem, consider, regard.

خال maternal uncle; mole, beauty spot.

خالٍ، الخَالي empty, vacant, open, free of; past, bygone.

خالَة maternal aunt.

خالِد immortal, eternal, perpetual, everlasting.

خالَصَ to settle an account with; to get even with; to act with integrity, sincerity toward; to treat someone fair; to be devoted, faithful to.

خالِص clear, pure, unadulterated; sincere, frank, candid, true; free, exempt from.

خالِصُ أُجورِ البَريد postpaid.

خالَطَ to blend, merge with; to mingle with, associate with.

خالَفَ to be contradictory, contrary, opposed to; to clash, be at variance with; to contradict; to be different; to break, fail to keep one's word; to disagree, differ in opinion; to breach, violate, infringe, contravene, transgress, disobey.

خام crude, raw, unrefined, unprocessed; calico.

مادَّةٌ خام raw material, ore.

خامّ stinking; rotten; putrid, foul-smelling; spoiled.

خامَة ore (mineral).

خامِد dying, abating, subsiding; calm, still, quiet; extinct, passive.

خامَرَ to preoccupy, engage, harbor, entertain; to suspect, doubt, have doubts, misgivings about.

خامِس، الخامِس fifth, the fifth.

خامِسًا fifth, in the fifth place.

خامِل indolent, inert, inactive; languid; dull.

خامِلُ الذِّكْر unknown, undistinguished, nameless, obscure.

خَانَ to betray, be disloyal to; to act treacherously toward; to be unfaithful to; to deceive, cheat; to mislead, forsake, desert, let down; to fail to keep (a promise, a contract).

خان inn, hostel, khan.

خَانَة digit, column; entry, item.

خانِق (ص) choking, strangling, suffocating, asphyxiating, stifling, smothering, throttling.

خانِق (اسم) throttle, choke; gorge, canyon, ravine.

خاوٍ، الخاوي empty, vacant, unoccupied, desolate.

خَبا to fade, tarnish (color); go out, die, be extinguished (light, fire); to abate, subside (strength, vigor).

خَبَأ to hide, conceal, shelter, cover up, veil.

خَبّاز baker

خَبُثَ to be vicious, wicked, evil, bad, sly, wily, foxy.

خَبُثَ to be noxious, pernicious, repugnant, offensive; to be malignant, virulent (tumor, sickness).

خُبْث malice, molevolence, viciousness, offensiveness, obnoxiousness; malignancy, virulence.

خَبَرَ to try, test, experience; to know by experience; to know well, thoroughly; to be fully acquainted with.

خَبَّرَ to notify, advise, inform, tell; to let know, to report, relate.

خَبَر story, news item, information; predicate (grammar).

خِبْرَة experience, know-how, knowledge, expertise.

خَبَزَ to make bread; to bake.

خُبْز bread.

خَبَطَ to beat, strike; knock, rap (on the door); to bring down, hit, knock down; to bump, collide with; to trample, tread (the ground).

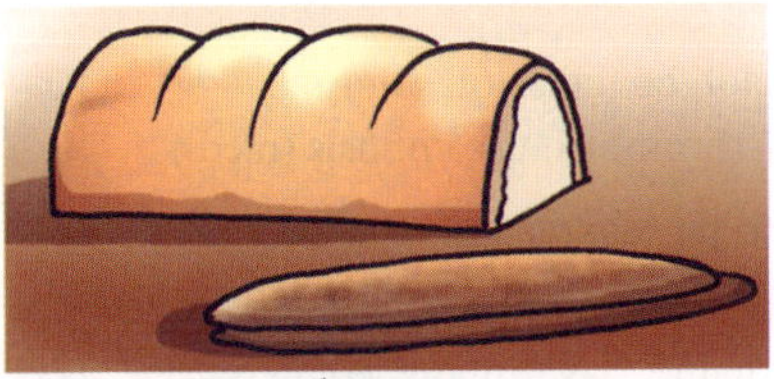

الخبز جزء هامّ من كلّ وجبة طعام

Bread is the staple food for all persons on earth

خَبْطَة blow, stroke, beat, bang, knock, rap; uproar, noise.

خَبَلَ to be mentally deranged, confused; to be crazy, insane.

خَبَل insanity, lunacy, madness, mental derangement or confusion.

خَبيث malicious, bad, evil, wicked; noxious, harmful; malignant (tumor); offensive, repulsive, nauseating (odor, smell).

خَبير expert, specialist, skilled in, conversant with, well versed in, experienced in, proficient in; learned person.

خِتام end, close, conclusion, termination; sealing wax.

خِتامًا in conclusion, finally, lastly, at last.

خِتاميّ final, terminal, closing.

خِتان، خِتانَة circumcision.

خَتَلَ to deceive, dupe, gull, cheat, double-cross.

خَتَمَ to seal, stamp, impress with a stamp; to seal off, close; to conclude, terminate, wind up, finish, complete.

خَتْم sealing, seal, stamping, stamp, impression; conclusion, completion, termination, ending.

خَثْرَة clot, coagulation, lump; thrombus, thrombosis (med.).

خَجِلَ to be ashamed of; to feel embarrassed; to blush, feel shame.

خَجَل shame, bashfulness, coyness, modesty, difference, timidity, shyness.

خَجَّلَ to embarrass, abash, shame; to put to shame.

خَجِل abashed, embarrassed; bashful; diffident, shy, timid, coy; shamefaced.

خدّ cheek; groove, furrow, ridge, trench.

خَدَّاع (ص) deceitful, dishonest, deceptive, illusive, delusive.

خَدَّاع (اسم) imposter, swindler, cheat, crook, double-crosser.

خِداع، خديعَة deception, deceit, fraud, swindling, delusion, dupery, perfidy, trickery, betrayal, treachery, illusion.

خَدَّام manservant, butler, waiter, attendant.

خَدَّدَ to furrow, plow (the ground).

خَدَّرَ to anesthetize, drug, stupefy; to numb, benumb; to deprive of sensation, narcotize.

خَدَشَ to scratch, lacerate, tear to pieces; to violate the rules of decency, the peace; to sully, ruin someone's reputation.

خَدَعَ to deceive, mislead, dupe, beguile, swindle; to double-cross, trick, outwit, fool, bluff, cheat.

خُدْعَة trick, artifice, subterfuge; ruse, deception, fraud; hoax.

خَدَمَ to serve, do service; to work; to wait on someone; to stand up for; to render a service; to till the soil.

خِدْمَة service, duty, work, job.

خِدْمَةٌ مَدَنِيَّة civil service.

خَدين friend, companion, comrade.

خَذَلَ to fail someone when needed; to disappoint, desert, abandon, forsake in time of need.

خَذْل، خَذَلان، خِذلان disappointment, desertion, forsaking.

خَرَّ to bubble (water); to snore (the sleeper); to fall down, tumble down, collapse; to prostrate oneself.

خَرِئَ to defecate, excrete.

خِرَاء excrement, feces, stool.

خَرَاب ruin, destruction, desolation; wreckage.

خُرَاج، خُرَّاج abscess.

خَرَّاط turner, operator of a lathe.

خُرَافَة superstition; fable, fairy tale; legend, myth.

كان الأقدمون يعتقدون بالخرافات الباطلة

Ancient people believed strongly in legends

خُرَافِيّ mythical, fictitious; fabulous; legendary.

خَرَّبَ to destroy, devastate, lay waste, wreck, lay in ruins; to demolish, sabotage, vandalize.

خَرِب ruined, devastated, wrecked, demolished, in ruins.

أ ب ت ث ج ح خ د ذ ر ز س ش ص ض ط ظ ع غ ف ق ك ل م ن هـ و ي

خِرْبَة site of ruins, ruins.

خَرَجَ to go out, walk out, come out of, emerge from; to leave, depart, go away; to protrude, project, stick out; to drive out; to conclude, deduce, infer, figure out; to revolt against, rise against; to attack, assail; to dissent from, disagree with; to violate, transgress, deviate from, go beyond a topic; to oust, dislodge, dissuade from; to be derailed (train).

خَرَّجَ to train,educate, graduate; to explain, expound.

خَرْج duty, land tax; expenditure, cost; output, produce, yield.

خُرْج saddlebag, traveling bag.

خُرْدَوَات (ج) hardware, haberdashery, sundries.

خَرْدَل mustard.

خَرَزَ to pierce, bore.

خَرَزَة bead.

خَرِسَ to keep silent; to hold one's tongue, shut up, stop talking.

خَرَس dumbness, muteness.

خَرْسَاء dumb, mute (female).

خَرْسَانَة concrete, cement.

خَرْسَانَةٌ مُسَلَّحَة reinforced concrete.

خَرَطَ to turn, lathe, shape with a lathe; to cut into small pieces; to mince, chop, dice (meat, vegetables).

خَرْطُوشَة cartridge.

خُرْطُوم trunk (of elephant); hose, hydrant (water).

خَرَعَ to droop; become slack, limp; to sag, weaken.

يستعمل الفيل خرطومه لشرب الماء والتقاط الغذاء

The elephant uses its trunk to drink and to eat its food

خَرِع soft, languid, nerveless, flabby, limp.

خَرِفَ to be senile, feeble-minded; to talk nonsense; to dote.

خَرَف feeble-mindedness, dotage, senility.

خَرِف doting, feeble-minded, senile.

خَرَقَ to tear, rend, make a hole in; to perforate, pierce, bore; to break, pass through, traverse; to violate, impair, encroach upon; to commit a breach of; to be unprecedented, unusual.

خَرُقَ to be clumsy, awkward, stupid, foolish.

خَرْق tearing, laceration, piercing, penetration; crossing, breakthrough; violation, breach; opening, aperture, tear, rip.

خِرْقَة rag, piece of cloth; polishing cloth.

خَرَّمَ to pierce, perforate, bore, tear, rend, rip.

خُرْم hole; eye of a needle; perforation, punch.

going out, emergence, departure, exodus, emigration; attack, assault; getting off; protrusion, projection, bulge. خُرُوج

castor oil. زَيْتُ الخِرْوَع

sheep, lamb. خَرُوف

تُربّى الخراف لصوفها ولحمها اللذيذ
Sheep are raised for their wool and delicious meat

graduate, alumnus. خِرِّيج

murmur, bubble (of water, stream); snoring (of sleeper). خَرير

autumn, fall. خَرِيف

potter, ceramist, dealer in chinaware. خَزَّاف

reservoir, tank; pool, basin; sump; dam. خَزَّان

wardrobe; vault, coffer, safe; locker, closet; cupboard. خِزَانَة

idle talk, joke, hoax; jest; nonsense. خُزَعْبَل ، خُزَعْبَلَة

pottery, china, ceramics, porcelain, earthenware. خَزَف

to pierce, stab, drive, ram; to tear, rip apart. خَزَقَ

rip, rent, tear; hole (in a dress). خَزْق

to store, stock, hoard, amass, accumulate. خَزَنَ ، خَزَّنَ

storing, storage, hoarding, stockpiling; warehousing. خَزْن

to be base, vile, despicable; to be ashamed. خَزِيَ

disgrace, shame; infamy; dishonor, ignominy. خِزْي

treasury; coffer, safe, strong box. خَزِينَة

to be mean, vile; to diminish, depreciate, fall in value. خَسَّ

lettuce (plant). خَسّ

to chase away, kick out. خَسَأَ

loss, damage. خَسَارَة

losses, casualties. خَسَائِر (ج)

meanness, lowness, vileness, baseness. خِسَّة

to lose, incur a loss; to go astray; to perish. خَسِرَ

to sink down, give way, cave in; to be eclipsed (moon). خَسَفَ

lunar eclipse. خُسوفُ القمَر

mean, vile, ignoble; abject; low, base, despicable, contemptible, miserable, lowly. خَسِيس

villainy, infamy, mean trick, vile act. خَسِيسَة

wood merchant, timberman; logger, lumberjack. خَشَّاب

wood, timber, lumber. خَشَب

plywood. خَشَبٌ رقائِقِي

خَشَبَة piece of wood, timber; log, stick, rod, plank.

خَشَبَةُ المَسْرَح stage, boards.

خَشَبَةُ المَيِّت coffin.

خَشَبِيّ wooden, woody, wood.

خَشْخَشَ to clank, clatter, rattle, tinkle, jingle.

خُشْخَيْشَة، خَشْخِيشَة rattle (child's toy).

خَشَعَ to be humble; to be submissive; to humble oneself; to lower one's eyes; to show reverence to.

خَشُنَ to be coarse, rough, harsh, hard; to be rude, tough.

خَشِن coarse, rough; unpolished, uncouth; rude, rowdy, impolite, mannerless; hoarse, husky, gruff (voice).

خُشُوع reverence, awe, submission; godliness, piety, humility.

خُشُونَة roughness, crudeness, coarseness, toughness; grossness, rowdiness (character); hoarseness, huskiness (voice).

خَشِيَ to fear, dread for, be afraid of; to apprehend.

خَشْيَة fear, apprehension, anxiety, dread.

خَشْيَةَ أن for fear that, lest, for fear of.

خَصَّ to single out, distinguish, favor someone; to bestow special honors upon in preference to others; to apportion, allot, assign; to devote, allocate to; to pertain to, belong to; to have to do with; to apply in particular; to become poor, destitute.

خَصَّ نَفْسَهُ بِـ to take exclusive possession of, to appropriate.

خَصَّهُ بِالذِّكْر to make special mention of; to refer specially to.

خُصّ hut, cottage, shack.

خَصَى to castrate, emasculate.

خِصام، خُصُومة quarrel; argument, dispute, feud; controversy, disagreement, contention, antagonism; litigation, prosecution (judicial, legal).

خَصِبَ to be fertile, productive.

خِصْب، خُصُوبَة fertility, productivity, fecundity, abundance.

خَصِب، خَصِيب fertile; fecund; productive; lush, prolific; rich.

خَصْر waist, waistline, hip, haunch.

خَصَّصَ to specify, earmark, allot, set aside; to devote, dedicate, allocate, assign, destine, designate.

خَصْلَة habit, property, attribute, trait, characteristic.

خُصْلَة tuft, lock, wisp (of hair); cluster, bunch.

خَصَمَ to substract, deduct, to discount (a bill).

خَصْم opponent, adversary, antagonist; litigant in a lawsuit; discount, rebate; substraction, deduction.

خُصُوم liabilities (commerce).

خُصُوص respect, regard, concern.

بِخُصُوص in respect of, regarding, as regards; with reference to; about.

بِهٰذَا الخُصُوص in this connection, in this respect, concerning this, in this matter, about this.

خُصُوصًا، خَصِيصًا especially, particularly, in particular, specially.

خُصُوصِيّ particular, specific; personal; connected with, pertaining to; special; private, confidential.

خَصِيّ eunuch, castrated, emasculated.

خُصْيَة، خِصْيَة testicle.

خَضَّ to agitate, stir, shake, jolt; to frighten, scare.

خَضّ، خَضَّة agitation, stirring, shaking, jolting; convulsion, concussion; shock, jolt, jerk.

خِضَاب dye, color, paint; pigment.

خُضَار vegetables, greenery.

خَضَبَ to dye, tint, color, paint.

خَضِرَ to be green, verdant.

خَضْرَاء green, verdant (feminine adj).

خُضْرَة greenness, verdancy, verdure, green color; vegetables.

خُضَرِيّ greengrocer.

خَضَعَ to submit to, surrender to, obey, comply with (orders, laws); to undergo, experience, go through; to humble oneself.

خِضَمّ sea, ocean; crowd, throng, multitude.

خُضُوع submission, surrender; obedience; compliance; humility; subjection; yielding; deference.

خَطَّ to write; to draw, trace a line; to sketch, design, engrave, inscribe; to outline, mark, prescribe; to mark with lines; to map out, trace out, plan, project, devise.

خَطَّ الوَجْهُ to wrinkle, become wrinkled.

خَطَّ شَعْرُهُ الشَّيْبُ his hair turned gray.

خَطّ line, stroke, stripe, streak, curve, bar; handwriting, script, inscription; calligraphy, penmanship.

خَطُّ الإِسْتِوَاء equator.

خَطُّ أنابيب pipeline.

خَطٌّ بَيَانِيّ graph, diagram.

خَطُّ تَمَاس demarcation line.

خَطٌّ جَوِّيّ airline.

خَطُّ السِّكَّة الحَدِيدِيَّة railroad line.

خَطُّ الزَّوَال meridian.

خَطُّ الطول longitude.

خَطُّ العَرْض latitude.

خَطَا to step, pace, walk; to advance, make progress.

خَطَأ error, mistake, incorrectness; offense, fault, blunder.

خَطَأٌ مَطْبَعِيّ misprint, printing error.

خَطَأً by mistake, erroneously.

خِطَاب، خُطْبَة address, speech; letter, message.

خِطَاب اعْتِمَاد credentials (diplomats); letter of credit (banks).

خِطَاب اعْتِمَاد مَصْرَفِي غَيْرُ قَابِلٍ لِلرُّجُوع irrevocable letter of credit (banks).

خَطَابَة elocution, rhetoric, oratory.

خِطَابَة rhetoric, oratory, lecture, discourse.

خَطَّاط calligrapher, sign-writer.

خَطَّاف hook, grapnel; robber, thief; swift, tern (birds).

خَطَبَ to deliver a public speech; to deliver a sermon to the people; to propose to a girl, ask for a girl's hand in marriage; to address, speak, talk.

خَطْب misfortune, trouble; matter, affair, concern.

خِطْبَة، خُطُوبَة engagement, betrothal.

خُطَّة plan, project, scheme, design, policy.

خَطَرَ لَهُ to occur to; to cross someone's mind.

خَطَرَ to swing, sway, wave; to brandish, oscillate; to strut, prance in one's steps; to parade haughtily.

خَطَر danger; consequence, gravity; peril, menace, risk, hazard; stake, bet, wager.

خَطِر dangerous, risky, hazardous; unsafe.

خَطَّطَ to draw, plan, design, scheme, map out; to sketch, trace, line; to demarcate, delineate.

خَطَفَ to snatch, grab, wrest away; to kidnap, abduct (someone); to hijack (a plane, train, car).

خَطْف forcible seizure, abduction, kidnapping, grabbing.

خَطَل nonsense, idle talk, prattle.

خَطْم muzzle, muffle (of animal).

خُطْوَة، خَطْوَة step, stride, pace,

اتَّخَذَ خُطْوَةً حاسِمَةً to take a decisive step.

خُطُورَة gravity, seriousness; significance; importance.

خَطِّي in writting, on paper; handwritten; linear.

خَطِيئَة sin, misdeed, guilt, blunder; offense, crime.

خَطِيب public speaker, orator, lecturer, preacher; suitor, fiancé.

يلقي خطيب الجامع خطبته من فوق منبر

The mosque's preacher delivers his sermon from atop a podium

خطيبة fiancée.

خَطِير grave, serious; important; momentous; critical.

خَفَّ to be lighter, decrease in weight; to diminish, lessen, decline; to be nimble, agile, swift.

خَفَّ إلى to hasten, hurry to, rush to.

خُفّ slipper,mule, sandal, shoe.

خُفُّ الحيوان hoof, sole of the foot.

خَفَى to conceal, hide; to keep secret; to keep out of view.

خَفَاء secrecy, covertness; veil, cover, covering, mantle.

في الخَفَاء secretly, clandestinely, covertly.

خَفَارَة guarding, watching over; sentry duty; vigil.

خَفَّاف، حَجَرُ الخَفَّاف pumice, pumice stone.

خَفَّاقَة egg-beater, whisk.

خَفَتَ to fade; to dim, grow dim; to die down, die away.

خِفَّة levity; frivolity, imprudence, rashness; triviality, pettiness; briskness, quickness, agility; inconstancy.

خِفَّةُ الدم wit, humor, joviality, geniality, charm.

خِفَّةُ العقل feeblemindedness, stupidity, foolishness.

خِفَّةُ اليد deftness, dexterity, legerdemain; jugglery.

خَفَرَ to watch over, guard; to patrol; to do sentry duty.

خَفِرَ to be timid, bashful.

خَفَر shyness, timidity, bashfulness; guard, watch, patrol.

خَفَضَ to lower, decrease, reduce, lessen, diminish, drop.

خَفَّضَ to lower, reduce, lessen, decrease, diminish; to devalue (currency); to demote someone's rank, position.

خَفْض lowering, decreasing, dropping.

خَفَّفَ to make lighter, reduce the weight of; to decrease, lessen, reduce, cut back.

خَفَّفَ to ease, soften, mollify; to alleviate; mitigate; to thin, dilute (a liquid); to slow down, decelerate (speed); to commute a penatly.

خَفَقَ to throb, beat, pulsate, vibrate, tremble, shake (heart); to flutter, wave (flag); to flap (wings); to waver, flicker (light, lightning); to beat (eggs).

خَفَقَان palpitation, throbbing, beating (heart); fluttering, flapping (wing); waving (flag).

خَفْقَة beat, throb, pulse; heart beat (heart); tap, rap, knok; tick, ticking sound.

خَفِيَ to disappear; to conceal, hide oneself; to be hidden, remain unknown, secret.

خَفِيّ hidden, concealed, disguised; dark, covert; clandestine, secret; cryptic.

خِفْيَةً، خُفْيَةً secretly, covertly; clandestinely, in secret; furtively, stealthily; privately.

خَفِير guard, watchman, sentry, escort.

خَفِيض low, soft; subdued; light, mild.

خَفِيض easy, comfortable, smooth (life).

خَفِيف light (of weight); little, trivial; thin, scanty, sparse; nimble, agile; sprightly, lively; diluted (liquid).

خَفيفُ الرُّوح likable, charming, amiable, cheerful, genial.

خَفيفُ العَقْل feebleminded, dim-witted, stupid, foolish.

خَفيفُ اليد deft, nimblefingered, dextrous.

خَلّ vinegar.

خِلّ، خُلّ friend, close friend, pal, comrade.

خَلا to be empty, vacant, unoccupied; to be free from, devoid of, lacking; to be in need of; to pass, elapse, go by.

خَلا إلى نَفْسِهِ to be alone with oneself; to isolate, seclude oneself; to withdraw, retire (for delibration).

خَلاَ للأَمْر to devote oneself to; to apply oneself to; to attend.

خَلاَ، ما خَلا، فيما خَلاَ except, save; but; apart from, aside from.

خَلَّى to abandon, give up; to release, discharge, let go; to give someone a free hand; to empty, vacate, void, drain.

خَلاء emptiness, vacuum, void.

خَلاَّب fascinating, captivating, charming, attractive, winning.

خَلاَّب fraudulent, deceiful; deceptive; fallacious, delusive.

خَلاَص salvation; rescue; escape; deliverance.

خَلاَص placenta, afterbirth.

خُلاَصَة excerpt, extract, substance; abstract, resumé, summary, synopsis; essence.

خَلاَّطَة mixer, blender (machine).

خَلاَعَة wantonness, lewdness, licentiousness, dissipation, profligacy, depravity, debauchery, pornography.

خِلاَف disagreement, dispute; dissimilarity, deviation; contrast, conflict, contradiction, controversy.

خِلاَف beside, apart from, aside from, unlike.

خِلاَفَة succession, caliphate.

خَلاَّق (ص) creative, inventive, fictive, artistic.

خَلاَّق (اسم) maker, creator, inventor, author.

خِلاَلَة toothpick.

خِلال during, in the course of, through, between.

خَلَبَ to charm, fascinate, captivate; cajole, coax; beguile; enchant, bewitch.

خَلَبَ to clutch, seize with the claws; to pounce on.

خَلْخال anklet.

خَلْخَلَ to dislocate, disengage, unloose, unfasten; to shake, rock; to rarefy.

خَلَدَ to remain forever, last forever; to be eternal, everlasting, perpetual, immortal.

خَلَدَ إلى to remain at, abide in, stay at.

خَلَّدَ to perpetuate, immortalize; to make immortal, unforgettable; to commemorate; to abide in, remain at; to grow very old, enjoy a long life.

خَلَد soul; spirit, mind.

خُلْد mole.

يشبه الخلد الفأرة ولكنه يعيش مختبأً تحت الأرض
Moles resemble rats but live underground in hiding

خُلْسَة opportunity, occasion; stealthily, secretly.

خَلَصَ to be unmixed, unadulterated; to get, come, arrive at; to be saved, rescued; to escape from; to be done, over; to clear, purify, refine, clarify; to settle a bill; to restore one's right; to act with integrity, with sincerity.

خَلَّصَ to save, rescue, free from, extricate from; to relieve of, redeem; to clear (goods); to purify, refine.

خَلَطَ to mix, mingle, blend; to confuse, confound between two things; to merge, fuse with, associate with.

خَلْط mixture, blend, ingredient; confusion, mixing up.

خَلَعَ to take off, undress, strip off one's clothes; to cast off, slip off; to pull out, extract, uproot (a nail, a tooth); to depose, remove, dismiss, discharge from an office; to get through, have done with; to confer, bestow upon, arrogate to someone the right of; to divorce one's wife in return for a compensation to be paid by her.

خَلُعَ to be dissolute, morally depraved, lewd, licentious.

خَلْع taking off, slipping off of one's clothes; deposition of a ruler; extraction of a nail, tooth, etc.; dislocation, luxation of a joint; dethronement of a king.

خَلَفَ to succeed, come after, take the place of, substitute, replace; to go back on one's word; to stay behind.

خَلَّفَ to leave behind; to appoint as successsor; to replace someone; to have descendants, offsprings.

خَلَف successor; offspring; issue; substitute, alternate.

خَلْف back, rear, reverse; behind, after; in the rear, at the back of.

خِلْف teat, nipple, mamilla.

خَلْفِي rear, hind, back, posterior, backward.

خَلْفِيَّة background, setting, ground.

خَلَقَ to create, make, originate, shape, form, mold; to invent, contrive, devise, fabricate, concoct, think up; to give rise to, generate; to attribute falsely to.

خَلُقَ to be fit for, suitable for, becomming for, worthy of; to be worn out; to become old and shabby.

خَلَّقَ to perfume.

خَلَق old, worn, shabby, tattered, ragged.

أ ب ت ث ج ح خ د ذ ر ز س ش ص ض ط ظ ع غ ف ق ك ل م ن هـ و ي

خَلْق creation; natural disposition, nature; constitution, generation; origination, production.

خَلْق creatures, people, mankind.

خُلْق، أخْلاق nature, character, natural disposition, temper; morals, ethics, manners.

خِلْقَة nature, natural disposition, character; constitution, makeup, structure, physique, shape, appearance.

خِلْقَةً by birth, congenitally, by nature.

خُلُقِيّ، خُلْقِيّ ethical, ethic, moral.

خِلْقِيّ congenital, inborn, inherent, inbred, native.

خَلَّل to acedify; to acetify; to pickle, marinate; to cure in brine; to run the fingers through; to part, comb (the hair, beard); to pick the teeth.

خَلَل cleft, crack, rupture, fissure; gap, interval; unbalanced state, imperfection; fault, flaw, defect, disturbance, shortcoming, disorder; damage, injury, harm.

خُلُوّ emptiness, vacancy; freedom from, free from; goodwill (of premises, company).

خِلْوٌ free from, devoid of, lacking, without.

خَلْوَة privacy, solitude, seclusion; conclave, closed meeting; retreat, place of seclusion; cell, hermitage; booth, cabin.

خُلُود immortality, eternity, eternal life; endless time; abiding, remaining, staying.

خُلُوص clarity, candor, frankness, sincerity, purity.

خَلُوق noble-minded; well-mannered, well-bred, polite, courteous, good-natured.

خَلَوِيّ cellular; isolated, secluded; rural, rustic.

خَلِيّ devoid of, free from.

خَلِيَّة cell, beehive.

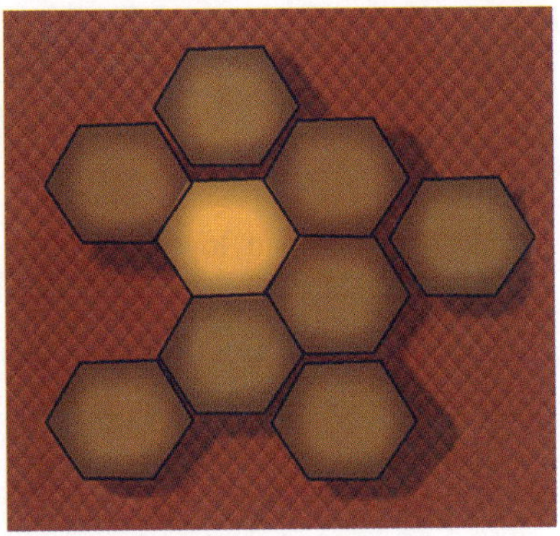

يتكوّن جسم الإنسان من ملايين الخلايا
The human body is formed of millions of cells

خَليج gulf, bay, canal.

خليج مدينة جونيه من أشهر الخلجان في لبنان
The bay of Jounieh is one of the most famous bays in Lebanon

خَلِيط mixture, admixture, blend; alloy (minerals).

خَلِيع dissolute, wanton, profligate, morally depraved; deposed, dismissed, discharged from an office; repudiated, disowned.

خَلِيفَة successor; caliph; deputy.

خَلِيق fit for, suitable for; worthy of, befitting, apt.

خَلِيقَة creation, hummankind; nature, created beings; natural disposition, trait, characteristic.

خَلِيل friend, intimate friend; lover; boyfriend.

خَلِيلَة girlfriend, sweetheart; concubine, mistress.

خَمَّ to stink, emit a foul smell; to be bad-smelling, rotten, decayed, putrefied, spoiled.

خُمّ coop (poultry), pen (cattle).

خَمَّار vintner, wine merchant.

خَمَّارَة wineshop; tavern, bar, saloon.

خُماسِيّ fivefold, quintet (music); pentagon.

خَمِجَ to rot, decay, putrefy.

خَمَج rottenness, rot, decay; infection.

خَمِدَ، خَمَدَ to go out, die; to abate, subside, cease; to die down (fire).

خَمَّرَ to ferment; to leaven (dough); to brew (beer); to veil; cover, hide, conceal with a veil.

خَمْر، خَمْرَة wine, liquor.

خَمْرِيّ wine-colored, reddish brown.

خَمَّسَ to make fivefold, multiply by five; to make pentagonal.

خُمْس one fifth.

خَمْسَة five.

خَمْسَةَ عَشَرَ fifteen.

خَمْسون، الخمسون fifty; the fiftieth.

خَمْسِيّ quinquennial, five-year.

خَمَلَ to be dull, lazy, sluggish, indolent; to be obscure, unknown; to be weak, languid.

خَمَّنَ to guess, estimate, surmise, assess, appraise; to value, rate, evaluate.

خُمُود deterioration, tranquility, immobility, calm, extinction; decline, degeneration; inertia, inactivity.

خُمُول sluggishness, dullness, indolence, languor, weakness; lethargy; apathy, indifference; drowsiness; obscurity.

خَمِيرَة yeast, leaven, ferment; enzyme.

يستعمل الفران الخميرة في صنع الخبز
The baker uses yeast in making bread

brewer's yeast. خَمِيرَةُ البِيرَة

Thursday. الخميس

thicket, wood, scrub. خَمِيلَة

to speak nasally; to twang; to speak through the nose. خَنَّ

to be obscene, vulgar; to use obscence language. خَنَا

the Devil, Satan. الخَنَّاس

suffocation, choking, strangling, throttling. خِناق

hermaphrodite, bisexual, androgyne. خُنْثَى

trench, ditch; moat. خَنْدَق

dagger, stiletto. خَنْجَر، خِنْجر

pig, swine, hog (animal). خِنْزِير

wild boar (animal). خِنْزِيرٌ بَرِّيّ

guinea pig (animal). خِنْزِيرٌ هِنْديّ

warthog. خِنْزِيرٌ وَحْشِيّ

little finger, smallest finger. خِنْصَر، خِنْصِر

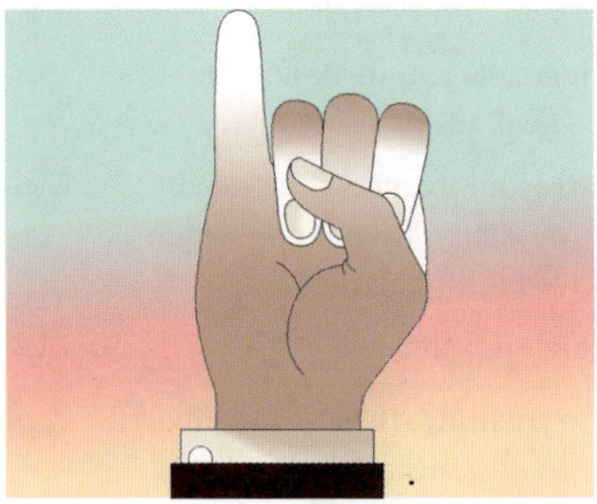

الخنصر صغرى أصابع اليد الخمس
The little finger is the smallest of the hand's fingers

to humble oneself before someone; to yield, surrender, low, stoop to someone; to cringe before. خَنَعَ

to strangle, strangulate; to throttle, suffocate, smother; stifle; to choke to death. خَنَقَ

strangulation, throttling; choking, suffocation. خَنْق

subservience, abjectness, humility, humbleness, meekness, submission. خُنُوع

to be empty, vacant, unoccupied; to be hungry, to feel hungry; to starve. خَوَى

emptiness, void, vacuum, vacancy; hunger, inanition. خَوَاء

moo, bellow, lowing. خُوَار

fearful, timid, fainthearted, coward, poltroon. خَوَّاف

buffet, sideboard, table. خُوَان، خِوَان

kickback. خُوَّة

plum, peach (plant). خَوْخ

الخوخة ثمرة لذيذة الطعم تؤكل طازجة أو مطهية
Plums are delicious and are eaten either fresh or cooked

helmet. خَوْذَة

يرتدي الجندي خوذة لحماية رأسه من الشظايا
The soldier wears a helmet to protect his head from shrapnel

خَوَر weakness, feebleness, languor, impotence, lassitude.

خَوْر wadi, ravine, gorge; inlet, bay, gulf.

خُوري curate, clergyman, vicar, pastor.

خَوْض wading into; plunging into; penetration; search into; examination, discussion, treatment of a subject.

خَوَّفَ to frighten, scare, intimidate, terrorize, horrify.

خَوْف fear, dread, fright; alarm; terror, scare; phobia.

خَوْفًا مِن for fear of.

خَوَّلَ to grant, accord, give, concede to someone the right or the power to do something; to bestow, confer upon someone something; to vest, endow with powers to act.

خَوَّنَ to accuse of betrayal; to regard as faithless, disloyal; to mistrust, distrust.

خِيَار option, choice, alternative; the best, prime, elite.

خِيَار cucumber (plant).

خَيَّاط tailor.

خَيَّاطَة seamstress.

خِيَاطَة sewing, tailoring, dressmaking; suturing (med).

شقيقتي تتعلم فن الخياطة في معهد متخصص
My sister is learning sewing at a tailor's atelier

خَيَال imagination, fancy, fantasy, fiction; ghost, spirit, phantom; shadow; reflection, image.

خَيَّال horseman, rider, cavalier.

خَيَالِيّ imaginary; unreal, fanciful; ideal; utopian; visionary.

خِيَانَة treason, treachery, betrayal; infidelity, deception; breach of faith; violation.

خِيَانَةٌ عُظْمَى high treason.

خَيَّبَ to frustrate, thwart, foil, abort; to disappoint, dash someone's hopes.

خَيْبَة failure, frustation, disappointment, letdown; defeat; fizzle, flop, miscarriage.

خَيَّرَ — to make someone choose; to give someone the choice, option or alternative; to prefer to, favor, choose to.

خَيِّر — charitable, generous, beneficent, benevolent; gracious, kind, liberal, openhanded.

خَيْر — good blessing, wealth, advantage, welfare, affluence.

خَيْرٌ مِن — better than.

خَيْرُ البِرِّ عاجِلُهُ — the sooner the better.

خَيْرَة، خَيْرات — good deed; blessings, resources.

خِيْرَة — choice, prime, cream, elite; the best.

خَيْرِيّ — philanthropic, charitable, benevolent.

خَيْزُران — bamboo, cane, reed.

خَيْش — jute, gunny, burlap, hessian; canvas.

خَيْط — thread, yarn, string, twine, fiber.

خَيَّلَ — to give the impression that; to make as if.

خُيِّلَ إليه — to imagine, fancy, believe, assume, appear to; to suppose, think, deem to be; it appeared to him.

خَيْل — horses.

خُيَلاء — conceit, vanity, vainglory, arrogance, snobbery.

خَيَّمَ — to encamp, camp, tent, pitch a tent; to stay in, remain in, settle down at; to lie down, linger.

خَيَّمَ — to reign in; to prevail in, predominate in; to pervade, spread over.

خَيْمَة — tent, tarpaulin; arbor; bower; pavilion.

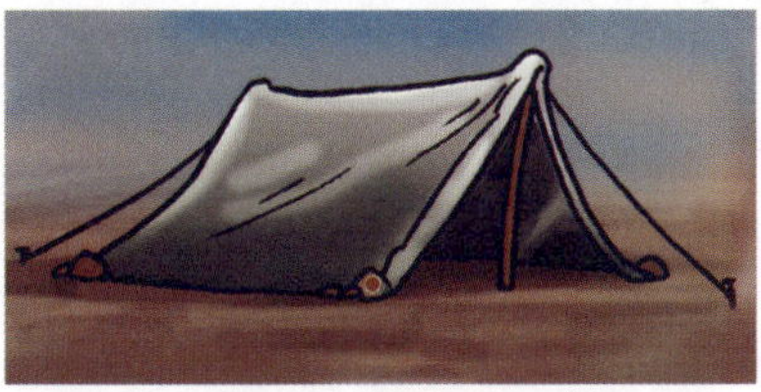

تُصنع الخيمة من وبر الجمل
ويعيش أهل البدو فيها
Bedouins live in tents
made of camel's hairs

داء disease, sickness, ailment.

دائِخ dizzy, vertiginous.

دائِر turning, spinning, circulating; ambulant; in progress, in operation; round; occurring, current.

دائِرَة circle, ring, sphere; domain, realm; field.

الدائرة شكل هندسي مستدير كالكرة
The circle is a geometrical form round as a ball

دائِرة department, section, service, bureau.

دائِرة misfortune, calamity, catastrophe.

دائِرةٌ كَهْرَبائِيَّة electric circuit.

دائِرةٌ انْتِخابِيّة constituency, electoral district.

دائِرةُ المَعارِف encyclopedia.

دائِرةُ البُرُوج Zodiac.

دائِرةُ نُفُوس census department.

دائِرِيّ circular, round.

دائِم lasting, enduring, everlasting; perennial; incessant, constant; permanent; durable.

دائِمُ الخُضْرَة evergreen.

دائِمًا always, all the time, forever; permanently.

دائِن creditor, lender; credit side of an account.

دَأَب to persevere in; to apply oneself eagerly to; to continue to do; to do persistently; to be used to, accustomed to; to have the habit of.

دَأْب — perseverence, persistence, assiduity, eagerness; habit, custom, practice.

دابَّة — pack animal, animal, beast; riding animal (horse, donkey, mule).

دابِر — past, bygone; end, extremity; root, origin.

داجٍ (الدَّاجِي) — dark, gloomy.

داجِن — tamed, domesticated.

دَواجِن (ج) — poultry, domestic animals.

داخَ — to be dizzy; to feel giddy; to submit; to humble oneself; to subdue, conquer, vanquish, subjugate.

داخِل — inside, interior, internal; within.

مِنَ الدَّاخِل — from within, from inside.

داخِلِيّ — internal, inside, inward; domestic, local; indoor.

داخِلِيَّة — interior, inland.

حَرْبٌ داخِلِيَّة — civil war.

مَدْرَسةٌ داخِلِيَّة — boarding school.

مَلابِسُ داخِلِيَّة — underwear.

دارَ — to turn, revolve, rotate, move in a circle around; to circulate; to run; to be in operation, (car, machine); to run around, roam, rove, wander, make the rounds; to take place; to be in progress, underway; to take a different direction.

دارَتِ المَعْرَكَة — to flare up; erupt.

دارَتْ عليهِ الدَّوائِرُ — to be stricken by misfortunes.

دار — house, home, dwelling; seat, center; country, region, territory; business house, commercial firm, establishment, institution.

الدار التي أسكن فيها هي ملك لأبي

The house in which I live belongs to my father

دارُ الآثار — museum.

دارُالأيْتام — orphanage.

دارُ البَقاء — the hereafter, the eternal abode.

دارُ توليد — maternity.

دارُ العَجَزَة — infirmary, old age hospice.

دارُ الكُتُب — library.

دارُ المُعَلِّمين — teachers college, normal school.

دارُ نَشْر — publishing house.

دارَى — to be willing to please; to flatter; to deceive, beguile.

دارَة — circle, loop; villa; halo of the moon.

دارِج — current, prevalent, widespread, popular, in vogue, in circulation, fashionable; colloquial, slang (language).

دارِس (ص) — obliterated, old, dilapidated, crumbling.

دارِس (اسم) learner, scholar, researcher, student.

داسَ to tread on, step on, trample down, stamp; to run over, crush underfoot; to treat with disdain.

داسِر propeller, airscrew, impeller.

داعٍ (الدَّاعِي) cause, motive, exigency; inviter, host; propagandist, herald.

بِداعِي because of, due to, in view of.

لا داعِيَ لِـ it is not necessary; there is no need to.

داعَبَ to play with; to flirt; to play around; to play about; to caress, fondle, stroke gently; to beguile, tempt, delude (hopes); to joke with, make fun with.

داعِر dissolute, wanton; licentious, obscene, immoral; unchaste; lewd, libertine, rake.

داعِيَة cause, reason, necessity; propagandist, herald.

دافِئ warm, hot.

دافَعَ to defend, protect, support; to plead for; to resist, withstand, oppose; to uphold.

دافِع propellant, impellent; propeller, impeller; repellent; incentive, repeller, impulse, impetus; spur, reason, cause, motive, drive, urge.

داكِن dark, dusky, mudcolored, dark-colored.

دالٌّ indicative of; indicator; sign, denotation.

دالَّة familiarity, audacity, boldness, chumminess.

دالَّة function (math).

دالِية vine, grapevine, waterwheel.

تتدلى عناقيد العنب في الدالية

Grapes bunches hang from a vine

دامَ to last, persevere, persist, continue, go on; to spin.

ما دامَ as long as, in as mush as.

دامٍ (الدَّامِي) bloody; bleeding.

دامِس dark, tenebrous, pitch-black, deep-black, dusky.

دانَ to borrow, take up a loan; to be a debtor, indebted; to owe; to bow, yield, obey; to lend money, grant a loan; to subject, subjugate; to condemn, pass judgment on; to find guilty, to convict; to profess, adopt, embrace (a religion).

دانٍ (الداني) near, nearby, close at hand; imminent, impending.

دانَى to come close to; to approximate, be imminent; to get near, get close to; to draw near.

داهَمَ to break in, burst into; to raid, attack suddenly; to surprise, take unawares; to enter suddenly; to invade, fall upon, overtake.

داهَنَ to flatter, cajole, cheat, dupe, outsmart.

داهِيَة smart fellow, old fox, sly dog; calamity, disaster, catastrophe, scourge; resourceful, crafty, clever person.

داوَى to treat, cure, remedy.

دَؤُوب persevering, persistent; untiring, tireless, assiduous.

داوَرَ to dodge; to ensnare, try to deceive, cheat, trick; to get away, escape, duck out; to go around with, turn with.

داوَلَ to rotate, alternate, follow one another; to confer with, hold talks with; to negotiate with, discuss, talk with someone about something.

داوَمَ to persevere in, pursue steadily; to continue, go on.

دَبَّ to creep, crawl (reptile); to advance, move slowly; to spread over, fill, pervade, invade; to flow, stream, run.

دُبّ bear (animal).

دُبٌّ قُطْبِيّ polar bear (animal).

دَبّابَة tank, armored car (military).

دَبّاغ tanner.

دِباغَة tanning.

دَبّاغَة tannery.

يعيش الدب في المناطق القطبية وله فرو سميك
The bear lives in the polar regions and has a thick fur to protect it from cold

دَبَّجَ to embelish, adorn; to write in an elegant style; to write down, compose, pen.

دَبَرَ to elapse, pass, go by (time); to turn one's back; to flee, run away, escape, dodge.

دَبَّرَ to arrange, make arrangements, make plans for; to prepare, organize, design, devise, bring about; to contrive, work up a ruse; to regulate, marshal, steer; to handle with care; to consider, weigh, contemplate; to procure, obtain, accomplish; to economize; to be frugal, thrifty.

دُبْر rear part, hind, hinder part, back; buttocks, rump, behind; end, lower part.

دِبْس molasses.

دَبَش ، دَبْش trash, junk, rubble.

دَبِق sticky, adhesive, gluey; tenacious, viscous.

دبلوماسِيّ diplomat, diplomatic.

دِبْلوماسِيَّة diplomacy.

أ ب ت ث ج ح خ د ذ ر ز س ش ص ض ط ظ ع غ ف ق ك ل م ن هـ و ي

دَبُوس pin, safety pin.

دَبُوسُ شَعْر hairpin.

دَبيب creepage, crawling.

دِثار garment, dress, gown; overcoat; blanket; cushion.

دَثَّر to cover, wrap, envelop.

دَجا to grow dark, murky, tenebrous, gloomy.

دُجى darkness, murkiness, gloominess.

دَجاجة hen, chicken.

طبق الدجاج من الأطباق المفضّلة لديّ

Chicken meal is one of my preferred dishes

دَجّال quack, swindler, cheat; imposter, charlatan.

دَجَّج to arm heavily.

دَجِرَ to be baffled, perplexed, embarrassed.

دَجَلَ ، دَجَّلَ to deceive, fool, delude, lie, cheat, dupe; to cover; to tar; to gild (gold); to fertilize, manure, dung.

دَجَل deceit, trickery, swindle, deception, dupery, imposture.

دَجَنَ to be dusky, gloomy, murky; to darken, blacken; to remain in, settle in, reside in a place; to be tamed, domesticated (animal or bird).

دَحَرَ to defeat, vanquish, rout; to drive away, force out.

دَحْرَجَ to roll, roll along, roll down.

دُحْروجَة roller.

دَحَضَ to disprove, refute, invalidate; to prove invalid, void, untenable; to rebut, falsify.

دُخان ، دُخَّان smoke, fume; tobacco.

دَخَلَ to enter, go, step, walk, move, come, get into; to penetrate, drop in on someone; call on someone; to be newly introduced; to join, participate, take part in.

دَخَلَ ضِمنَ to fall, come under; to belong, pertain, refer to.

دَخَلَ في الموضوع to come to the point; to include, embody.

دَخَلَ على to start, begin, set out on; to visit, call on.

دَخْل income, revenue, receipts, takings; doubt, suspicion; defect, vice, blemish; concern, relationship, pertinence.

دَخْلُ الفَرْد per capita income.

دَخْلٌ قَوْمِيّ national income.

دَخَّنَ to smoke (a cigarette); to smoke, fumigate; to emit smoke, fumes.

دُخْنَة color of smoke.

دُخُول entrance, admittance; penetration, piercing, joining; beginning, commencement, start, rise, advent.

دَخيل foreigner, alien, outsider, extraneous; inner self; stranger; false, spurious, newlyadded; novice, new convert, guest, charge; foreign word or experience.

دَرَّ to flow abundantly; to stream, spurt, gush; to produce, yield; to bestow lavishly upon someone; to overwhelm, shower with.

دُرّ pearls.

دَرَأَ to ward off, avert, repulse, reject something.

دَرَى to know of, be aware of, acquainted with; to come to know, find out about.

دَرابْزين، دَرابْزون railing, handrail, balustrade, parapet.

دَرَّاجةٌ هَوائِيَّة bicycle.

ركوب الدرّاجة رياضة جسديّة مفيدة

Riding bicycles is a rewarding sport for the body

دَرَّاجةٌ نارِيَّة motorcycle.

دَرَّاس eager, zealous student or studier.

دَرَّاس thresher, thrashing machine for grains.

دَرَّاسَة threshing machine; thresher.

دِراسة study, research, treatise, education.

دِراسيّ pertaining to study, scholastic; educational, tuitional, school, academic.

دِرايَة knowledge, awareness, know-how, expertise.

دَرَّبَ to train, exercise, coach; to familiarize with; to habituate, accustom someone.

دَرْب path, trail, track, course, route, way, road.

دِرْباس lion; bolt, latch, lock.

دِرْبَكَّة hand drum.

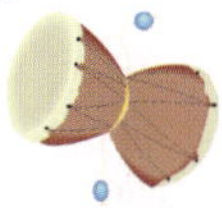

دُرَّة pearl.

دَرَجَ to go, walk, move, proceed, advance slowly; to approach gradually; to move step by step; to proceed along the lines of; to approximate, roll up, fold up; to circulate, to make the general practice of something; to pass away; to get used to; to follow a certain course; to make a habit of doing something.

دَرَّجَ to graduate, gradate, scale; to calibrate, put into circulation; to approximate, approach to; to roll up, fold.

دَرَج stairs, stairway; course, path.

دُرْج drawer, till.

دَرَجة step, stair; degree, rank, level, standing; extent, measure, size, proportion; stage, phase, period; point, class, pitch, tone (music); mark, grade (school).

دَرَجَةُ الحَرَارَة degree of temperature.

دَرَجَةٌ عِلْمِيَّة academic degree.

دَرَجَةٌ أُولَى first-rate, first class.

لِدَرَجَةِ أنْ to the extent that; so much that.

دَرْدار elm (tree).

دُرْدُور whirlpool, eddy current, vortex.

دَرَزَ to sew, stitch; to suture (med.).

دَرْز sewing, stitching; suture (med.).

دَرْزَة stitch, seam; suture (med.).

دُرْزِيّ Druze.

دَرَسَ to study, learn, consider carefully; to deliberate, think about, contemplate; to scrutinize, examine; to discuss, explore.

دَرَسَ to wipe out, obliterate, blot out, efface.

دَرَّسَ to teach, instruct, educate.

دَرْس study, learning, education; perusal, consideration; discussion, scrutiny, deliberation; lesson, class.

دَرْس obliteration, wiping out, extinction, blotting out.

دَرَّعَ to armor; to arm.

دِرْع coat of mail; plate arbor; armor, plate, armature; breastplate, shield, cuirass; carapace, scute (of a tortoise).

دَرْفَة leaf, shutter (of door, window).

كان الجنود في قديم الأزمان يضعون درعاً واقياً يغطي وجههم وصدرهم

Soldiers in old times used to wear shields to protect their face and their breasts from arrows

دَرْك bottom, lowest level; attainment, accomplishment.

دَرَك police force.

دَرَكِيّ policeman.

دَرَن dirt, filth, outgrowth; tuberculosis; tumor.

دَرْوِيش dervish.

دَزِّينَة dozen.

دَسَّ to thrust, insert, shove, slip; to instill, infuse; to foist into; to scheme, plot, intrigue against; to hide, conceal, bury in; to interpolate words in a text; to betray, denounce, conspire.

دَسَّاس intriguer, schemer, plotter, conspirator.

دُسْتُور constitution, law, code.

دُسْتُورِيّ constitutional.

يجب أن يحترم كافة المواطنين **دستور** البلاد

All citizens should respect the country's constitution

دَسَرَ — to push, shove, propel, thrust.

دَسَم — fat, grease (in food).

دَسِم — fatty, oily, greasy (of food).

دَسِيسَة — intrigue, scheme, plot, conspiracy.

دُشّ — shower.

دَشَّنَ — to inaugurate, open, dedicate.

دَعَا — to call, summon, send for, appeal to, invite, urge; to induce, prevail; to name; to wish well; to invoke God in favor of someone; to invoke a blessing upon someone.

دَعَا — to propagate, publicize.

دُعَاء — call; prayer, invocation of God; request, plea.

دُعَابَة — joking, jesting; joke, jest, fun; teasing, banter.

دَعَارَة، دِعَارَة — prostitution, licentiousness, debauchery, lewdness.

دِعَامَة — support, stay, prop, pillar, buttress.

دِعَايَة، دَعَاوَة، دِعَاوَة — propaganda, publicity, advertising.

دَعَسَ — to tread on, step on, trample down, stamp.

دَعَكَ — to rub, scrub, scour.

دَعَمَ — to support, prop up, stay, buttress; to consolidate, reinforce, bolster, further, promote; to advocate, uphold, back up; to subsidize (in funds).

دَعْم — staying, buttressing, underpinning; consolidation, strengthening, promotion, confirmation; support, backing up, upholding; subsidizing; subsidy (in funds).

دَعْوَى — lawsuit, case, legal proceedings; allegation, pretension, litigation.

بِدَعْوَى أَنَّ — on the pretext that, under the pretense that.

دَعْوَة — convocation, summons; call, appeal; invitation; demand, request; missionary activity; imploration, supplication, good wish.

دَعْوَة — imprecation, curse, ill wish.

دَعِيّ — adopted son; bastard; braggart; pretender; swindler, imposter.

دَغِل — covered with dense overgrowth; false, perfidious; secret, mysterious.

دَفّ، دُفّ tambourine (music).

الدف هو شقيق الطبل يصاحبه في كل عزف

The tambourine is a small-sized drum used in playing music

دَفَأَ to warm up, make warm, make hot.

دَفأ، دِفْء، دَفاءَة warmth, heat, hotness.

دِفَاع defense, safekeeping, sheltering, protection; supporting, advocacy, championship, sponsorship, pleading.

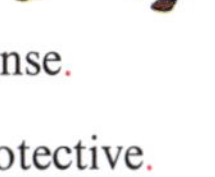

دِفاعٌ عَن النَّفْس self-defense.

دِفاعٌ مَدَنيّ civil defense.

دِفاعٌ وَطَنيّ national defense.

دِفاعِيّ defensive, protective.

دَفَّة rudder, helm, steering wheel (of a boat, ship); side; leaf, shutter (of a door, window); cover (of a book).

دَفْتَر notebook, booklet, copybook; journal, ledger (of accounts); roster, register.

دَفْتَرُ حِساب account book.

دَفْتَرُ حِساب مَصْرِفيّ bankbook, passbook.

دَفْتَرُ شُرُوط book of conditions or stipulations.

دَفْتَرُ شيكات check book.

دَفْتَرُ الصُّنْدُوق cashbook.

دَفْتَرُ الصُّوَر album.

دَفْتَرُ اليومية daybook, journal.

دَفَعَ to push; to shove away, push back, drive back, repel; to remove, dislodge; to get rid of; to reject, repudiate, rebut, refute, disprove; to propel, egg on, goad, incite, induce, compel, oblige someone to do something; to hand over, present; to pay a price; to push, shove one another; to object, challenge; to disburse, pay out.

يدفع الحمّال العربة المملوءة بالحقائب

The porter pushes the cart loaded with baggages

دَفْع pushing away, shoving, repulsion, warding off; getting rid of; removal, elimination; refutation, disproof, confutation; rebuttal, objection, challenge.

دَفْع propulsion, thrusting, rushing; prompting, incitation, stimulation; forcing, coercion; handing over; sending, submitting; payment, settlement, spending, outlay.

دَفْعَة shove, push, thrust; impetus, impact, impulse, drive; payment, disbursement, deposit.

دُفْعَة gush, burst, spurt; time, instance.

دُفْعَة group, batch, lot.

دُفْعَةً واحِدَةً all at once, in one stroke, all at one time.

دَفَقَ to pour out, pour forth, gush, spout forth.

دَفَنَ to bury, inhume, entomb, lay to rest (a dead person); to hide, conceal, keep secret.

دَفْن burial, inhumation, interment; hiding, concealment.

دَفين hidden, concealed; interred, buried.

دَقَّ to be thin, frail; to be little, small, tiny; to be subtle, delicate; to be trifling, unimportant; to be too fine, too subtle.

دَقَّ to pound, crush, bruise, grind, pulverise.

دَقَّ to hammer, strike, knock, hit; to beat, drive (a nail); to type (on a typewriter); to ring (bell); to throb, pulsate (heart).

دَقّ pounding, crushing, pulverization; hammering, striking, hitting, tapping; knocking, beating; ringing; rapping.

دَقَّة beat, throb, pulse (of heart); blow, stroke, bang, thump, knock; ring, sound, peal; hammering sound; ring of a bell, a telephone.

دِقَّة fineness, tininess, smallness.

دِقَّة accuracy, precision, exactness, critical state.

دِقَّة punctuality; delicacy; seriousness, gravity.

بِدِقَّة exactly, accurately, meticulously, sharply.

دَقَّقَ to scrutinize, examine, carefully, investigate, study, verify, check out; to be meticulous, strict, exact.

دَقيق (ص) fine, thin, delicate, frail; little, small, tiny; subtle, paltry, trivial.

دَقيق (ص) precise, accurate, exact.

دَقيق (ص) painstaking; scrupulous, meticulous, strict; critical; serious; precarious.

دقيق (اسم) flour, meal.

دَقيقَة minute, particle; detail, particle; nicety.

دَكَّ to ram, stamp, level (earth, ground); to beat down; to demolish, destroy, ruin, crush; to fill up; to squeeze, press, compress, stuff, load, pack, charge.

دُكّان shop, store; seat; terrace, bench.

دَكَّة bench, seat, terrace; ballast, rubble.

يملك أخي **دكاناً** يقع قرب الملعب الرياضيّ
My brother owns a shop near the stadium

دِكَّة waistband.

دِكْتاتورِيَّة dictatorship.

دُكْتُور doctor of letters.

دُكْتُوراه doctorate, title of a doctor.

دُكْتُوراه فَخْرِيَّة honorary doctorate.

دَلَّ to show, point out, denote, designate, indicate.

دَلَّ على to prove; to furnish evidence, confirm, corroborate; to suggest, be indicative of.

دَلَّ to flirt; to coddle, spoil, pamper.

دَلال coquetry, flirtation, dalliance, coddling, pampering.

دَلَّال auctioneer, broker, go-between.

دَلالَة guidance, indication; sign, token; sense, meaning.

دِلالَة business of a broker; brokerage, commission; public sale, auction.

دِلْتا delta.

دَلَّس to cheat, defraud, deceive; to forge, falsify; to conceal the defects of; to impose on.

دَلَّع to pamper, spoil, caress, fondle, pet.

دَلَف to walk with short steps; to saunter, stroll to, advance toward, approach step by step; to penetrate, reach as far as; to toddle, shuffle.

دَلَف to leak, drip, trickle, ooze, percolate.

دَلَق to spill, pour out (a liquid); to unsheathe, draw (a sword, dagger).

دَلَّك to massage, pass the hand over; to knead (dough); to rub, embrocate, scour.

دَلَّل to pamper, spoil, coddle, fondle, caress, pet (a child).

دَلَّل to show, demonstrate, point out; to prove, establish, verify; to auction, put up at auction, auction off (goods).

دَلْو bucket, pail.

بُرْجُ الدَّلو Aquarius.

دَليل indication, symbol, evidence, proof; clue; guideline.

دَليل guide, conductor, pilot, guide book, manual; index, directory, handbook, timetable.

دَليل exponent (math).

دَم blood.

دَمّ ointment, unguent; paint, pigment, dyestuff.

دَماثة courteousness, politeness, tenderness, mildness, gentleness, friendliness (of character).

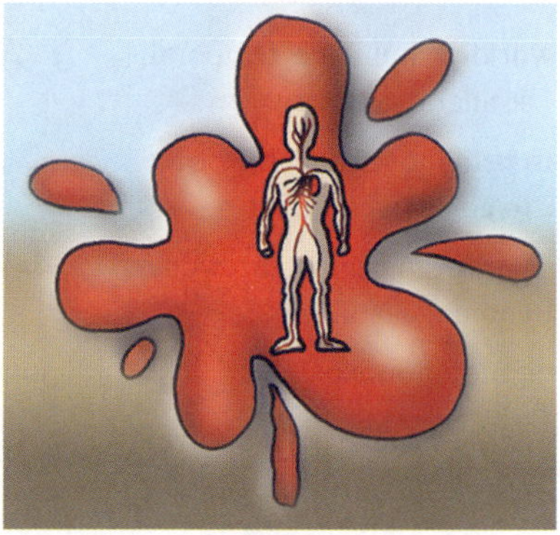

يشكّل الدم خمسة بالمئة من وزن جسم الإنسان
Blood forms five percent of the human body's weight

دَمار destruction, ruin, desolation.

دِماغ brain.

يوجد الدماغ في رأس الإنسان وتحيط به عظام متينة لحمايته
The brain is enclosed in the cranium surrounded by protecting bones

---

دِماغِيّ cerebral.

دَمامَة ugliness, monstrosity, ugly appearance.

دَمِث ، دَمْث gentle, amiable, courteous, polite.

دَمَجَ to insert, include, embody, incorporate; to merge, fuse, amalgamate, blend, mix.

دَمْج merger, fusion, integration; blending; incorporation.

دَمْدَمَ to mumble, murmur, grumble, rumble, snarl, growl.

دَمْدَمَة mutter, rumble, growl, snarl.

دَمَّرَ to destroy, ruin, wreck, devastate, demolish, annihilate.

دَمْع (ج) tears.

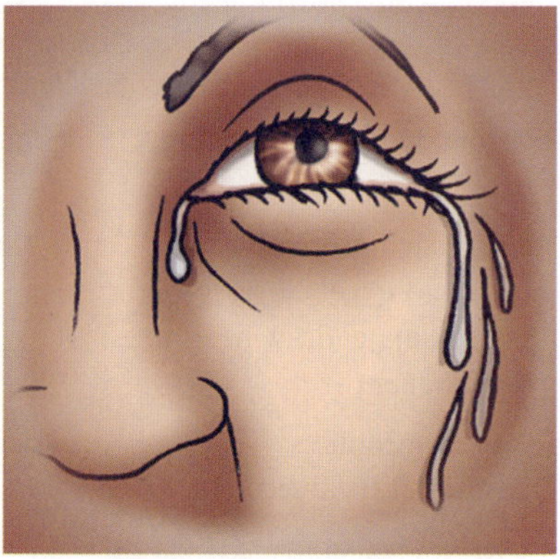

يذرف المصاب الدمع من شدة الألم
The injured shed tears because he felt great pains

دَمْعَة teardrop.

دَمْعِيّ lachrymal, lacrimal.

دَمَغَ to stamp, brand (an animal); to invalidate, refute, disprove; to hallmark (gold or silver articles).

دَمْغَة stamp, imprint, impress; hallmark (of gold articles).

دَمَلَ to manure, dung, fertilize.

دَمِلَ to heal, heal up, cicatrise (wound); to fester, suppurate.

دُمَّل، دُمَّلَة furuncle, abscess, boil, score, tumor, uclcer.

دَمَوِيّ bloody, sanguinary; bloodthirsty; murderer, assassin, murderous, killer.

دَمِيَ to bleed.

دُمْيَة doll, dummy, effigy, statue; puppet; hireling, servant; instrument.

دَميم ugly, hideous, horrid, grisly.

دَنّ vat, cask, jug.

دَنّ، دَنين buzzing, humming, droning; drone, buzz, hum.

دَنَا to approach; to come near, come close, get close; to approximate, draw near; to be imminent.

دَنَاءَة lowness, meanness, despicability, abjectness.

دَنَاوَة، دُنُوّ closeness, proximity, approach, imminence, incoming.

دَنْدَنَة buzzing; humming, droning; intonation.

دَنَّسَ to spoil, pollute, contaminate; to desecrate, dishonor, disgrace, violate, profane.

دَنَس dirt, filth, uncleanness, impurity; squalor, blemish.

دَنِس impure, dirty, polluted, unclean, filthy, stained.

دَنِيء، دِنِيّ low, lowly, mean, base, vile, despicable, infamous, depraved, ignoble, abject.

دُنْيَا world, land, earth; this world; worldly existence.

دُنْيَوِيّ worldly, mundane, temporal; secular, transitory.

دَهَى to befall, overtake, hit, strike; to come over, afflict.

دَهَاء slyness, smartness, shrewdness, cunning, astuteness.

دَهَّان painter, house painter.

دِهَان paint, cosmetic cream, salve, ointment; varnish.

دِهَان hypocrisy, deceit, flattery, cheating.

دَهْر age, epoch, era, period; eternity; lifetime.

دَهِشَ، دُهِشَ to be astonished, amazed, surprised, bewildered; to wonder, marvel; to be perplexed, puzzled, startled.

دَهْشَة astonishment, bewilderment, surprise; perplexity, bafflement, dismay, consternation, amazement.

دِهْلِيز vestibule, gallery, corridor, lobby, hallway.

دَهَمَ to come upon someone suddenly; to take unawares, by surprise; to enter suddenly, unexpectedly; to raid.

دَهَنَ to paint, varnish; to anoint; to rub, smear, oil.

دُهْن fat, grease, oil; sebum (of skin).

دُهْنِيّ fatty, greasy, oily; sebaceous (of skin).

دَهْوَرَ to hurl down, tear down, topple, overthrow.

دَوَّى، دَوَى to sound, ring out; to echo; to reverbate.

دَوَاء medecine, drug, remedy, cure, medicament.

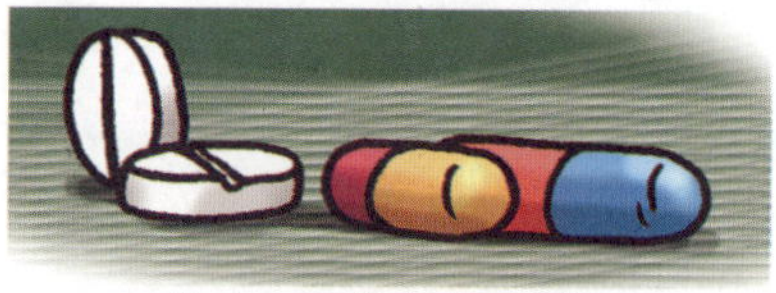

يصف الطبيب الدواء للمرضى لمعالجتهم
The doctor prescribes medicine for patients to cure them

دَوَاة inkwell, inkstand.

دَوَّار revolving, rotary, rotating, turning, spinning, whirling, circulating; ambulant, roving, roaming.

دَوَّار rotary, circle.

دُوَار ، دَوَار vertigo, dizziness, giddiness.

دُوَارُ البَحْر seasickness.

دَوَّارَة compass, pair of dividers; whirlpool, eddy, vortex.

دَوَّاسَة pedal.

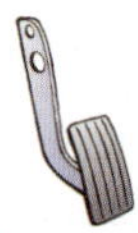

دَوَام duration; endurance; permanence, perpetuity; abiding; working hours.

دُوَّامَة whirlpool, eddy, vortex; spinning top (toy); merry-go-round, whirligig.

دَوْحَة lofty tree; family tree.

دَوَّخ to stun, daze, dizzy; to humiliate, subjugate, subdue; to make someone dizzy; to molest, bother, trouble someone.

دُودَة worm, larva, maggot.

دُودَةُ الحرير أو دُودَةُ القَزّ silkworm.

دُودِيّ wormlike, vermiform, vermicular.

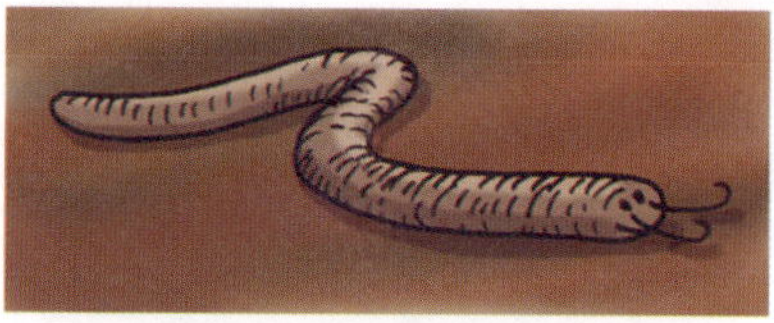

تزحف الدودة على بطنها معتمدة على قوة عضلاتها
Worms crawl on their bellies relying on the power of their muscles

دَوَّر to make round, circular; to start up (an engine); to wind (a watch); to revolve, spin, whirl, turn.

دَوْر role, turn, time, period, era; phase, stage, floor, story; cycle, shift, rotation; circle, round.

دَوْر fit, attack, spell (of sickness, fever).

الدَّوْرُ الأرْضِيّ ground floor.

الدَّوْرُ السُّفْلِيّ basement.

بالدَّوْر alternately, by turns, successively, one by one.

بِدَوْر in the role of, as (actor, film star).

دَوَرَان rotation, turning, revolution, tour; spinning, spin.

دَوْرَة turn, circuit, rotation, revolution, tour; spinning, spin.

دَوْرَة turn, circuit, rotation, revolution; cycle; round trip; detour; session (of parliament); course (of study, training); round (of a competition); tournament, series.

دَوْرَةٌ دَمَوِيَّة blood circulation.

دَوْرَةُ الحَيَاة life cycle.

دَوْرَةُ رَأْسِ المَال turnover.

دَوْرَةٌ زِرَاعِيَّة crop rotation.

دَوْرَةُ المِيَاه lavatory, water closet, toilet.

دَوْرِيّ sparrow

لُقِّبَ هذا الطير بالدوريّ لأنه يعتاد العيش في الدور
Sparrows are accustomed to live atop houses

دَوْرِيًّا periodically.

دَوْرِيَّة patrol, watch, guard; journal, periodical.

دَوْزَنَ to tune a musical instrument; to string, adjust.

دُوش shower.

دُوطَة dowry.

دُوق duke.

دُوقِيَّة duchy, dukedom.

دَوَّلَ to internationalize.

دُولاب wheel, tire.

دَوْلَة state, country, empire, power.

دَوْلَة (فلان) His Excellency.

دَوْلَةٌ عُظْمى superpower, great power.

دُوَلِيّ international.

دَوَّمَ to revolve, turn, whirl, spin, swirl, rotate.

دَوَّنَ to register, record, write down, put in writting; to enter, list, inscribe in a register; to note.

دُون low, lowly, bad; inferior; meager; ignoble.

دُونَ below, under, inferior, beneath; without, exclusion of; before, in front of.

دَوِيّ sound, peal, roar, bang, boom.

دِيَانَة religion, creed, confession, sect, faith, belief.

دِيباجَة preamble, preface, introduction; face; style; renown, standing, prestige.

دِيَة blood money.

دَيْجُور darkness, gloom.

دَيْدُبان guard, sentinel, sentry.

دَيْر monastery, convent, cloister.

دِيك cock, rooster; hammer (of a gun).

يُقال الديك الفصيح من البيضة يصيح
The cock is the male of the hen

أ ب ت ث ج ح خ د ذ ر ز س ش ص ض ط ظ ع غ ف ق ك ل م ن هـ و ي

دِيكُ الحَبَش، دِيكٌ رُومِيّ	turkey.
دَيْماس	dungeon, crypt, vault.
ديمُقْراطِيَّة	democracy.
دَيِّن	religious, devout, pious.
دَيْن	debt, liability, obligation, indebtedness.
بالدَّيْن	on credit.
دَيْنٌ مُمْتَاز	preferred debt.
دَيْنٌ مُوَحَّد	consolidated debt.

دِين	religion, faith, belief, creed.
دِينامِيّ	dynamic.
دِينامِيّة	dynamism, energy.
دِينامِيكا	dynamics.
دَيْنونَة	last judgment, judgment.
دِينِيّ	religious, spiritual.
دِيوَان	divan; collection of poems; book, record; council, office, bureau.

ذا — this, this one, that, that one.

بِذا — by this, thereby.

لِذا — therefore, consequeutly, hence.

كَذا — thus, in this manner, so and so, as such.

هَكَذا — in this manner.

ذَلِكَ أَنَّ — due to, in view of, by reason of.

كَذَلِكَ — thus, like this, as such, too, also, as well, in addition, furthermore, likewise.

مَعْ ذَلِكَ — in spite of this, nonetheless, though, yet, still.

ماذا؟ — what?.

لِماذا؟ — why? what for?; for what reason?.

ذائِب — dissolved, melted, liquefied, soluble.

ذائِع — widespread, common, widely known; prevalent.

ذائِعُ الصِّيت — famous, renowned, noted, illustrious.

ذَاب — to melt, melt away, liquefy.

ذِئْب — wolf (animal).

يهجم الذئب على صغار النعاج ويفترسها

Wolves attack small sheep and devour them

ذابِل — withered, wilted, dry, dried up; languid, dull; weak, feeble; faded (color); languishing (glance).

ذات — self, person, being, nature.

الذّات — ego.

ذاتُ اليَد wealth, affluence.

ذاتَ مَرَّةٍ once, one time.

ذاتَ يومٍ one day.

بالذَّات personally, in person, the same, the very same.

ذاتُ الشيء the same thing.

في حدِّ ذاتِه by itself.

قَائِمٌ بذاتِه self-existent, self-contained, independent.

حُبُّ الذات selfishness, egoism.

ذاتِيّ personal, subjective; spontaneous, automatic.

ذاتِيُّ الحَرَكَة self-driven, self-propelled, automatic.

ذاتِيَّة identity; personality; subjectivity; subjectivism.

ذَادَ to defend, protect; to chase away, scatter.

ذَاعَ to be spread, circulated, disseminated, widespread; to become public, generally known.

ذَاقَ to taste; to test, try; to suffer, undergo, pass through; to get a taste of; to sense, perceive.

ذاكِرَة memory.

ذَاهِب going to, heading for, departing, leaving to.

ذَاهِبُ اللَّون discolored, faded, colorless.

ذَاهِل negligent, distracted, dazed, in a stupor; absent-minded, bewildered, amazed; confused, baffled.

ذاوٍ (الذاوي) withered, faded, dried up, wilted.

ذَبَّ to defend, protect;to expel, drive away (the enemy).

ذُبابَة fly.

يكثر الذباب في الأماكن القذرة
وينقل الأمراض من شخص لآخر
Flies abound in dirty places and carry diseases from one person to the other

---

ذُبابَةُ الخَيْل horsefly, gadfly.

ذَبَحَ to slaughter; to massacre, slay, murder, kill.

ذَبْح massacre, slaying; slaughtering, killing.

ذَبْذَبَ to vibrate, wobble, oscillate, swing, dangle; to waver, hesitate, vacillate.

ذَبْذَبَة oscillation, vibration; pendulous motion.

ذَبَلَ ، ذَبُلَ to wither, wilt, shrivel, dry up, fade; to waste away, become dull; to lose its luster (eye).

ذُبول withering, shrivelling, drying up, fading.

ذَبيحَة sacrifice, offering; carcass; slaughter animal; sacrificial victim.

يعلّق الجزّار الذبيحة ليقتطع منها اللّحم ويبيعه

The butcher hangs the slaughter animal in order to cut its meat

---

ذَخيرَة supplies, provisions, stores.

ذخيرةٌ حَرْبيَّة ammunition, munitions.

ذَرَّ to scatter, spread, sprinkle, strew; to rise, come up (sun); to emerge, sprout, grow, appear (plant).

ذَرّ strewing, scattering, sprinkling; tiny particles, atoms, specks (of dust), motes (of dust).

ذَرَّى to winnow, fan (grain); to scatter, disperse; to atomize; to ablate; to wear away the soil (by the wind).

ذَرَى protection, shelter.

ذِراع arm (human being); cubit (measure); crank (machine).

ذِراعُ التَّوْجيه steering arm.

ذِراعُ التَّوْصيل connecting rod.

ذَرِب sharp, cutting.

ذَرِبُ اللِّسان fluent, eloquent; impudent, obscene, foul, pert.

ذَرَّة atom.

ذُرَة corn, sorghum.

تصنع أطعمة متنوعة من الذرة كما تعصر للحصول على زيتها

Corn is a staple grain used in preparing meals and to produce edible oil

---

ذُرَةٌ بَيْضاء millet. 

ذُرَةٌ صَفْراء maise, corn. 

ذَرَعَ to measure; to take the measurement of; to cover, cross, traverse (a distance).

ذَرْع ability, capability; endurance, toleration.

ضاقَ ذَرْعاً بـ to be unable to bear something or someone; to be fed up with, tired of, oppressed by.

ذَرَفَ to shed (tears).

ذَرَفَ الدَّمْع to flow, drop, shed (tears).

ذَرْق droppings, excrement (of birds).

ذُرْوَة، ذِرْوَة summit, top, peak; climax, apex, acme, pinnacle; highest point; prime.

ذَرور	powder.
ذَرّيّ	atomic.
قُنْبُلَةٌ ذَرِّيَّة	atomic bomb.

مُفاعِلٌ ذَرّيّ	atomic reactor, atomic pile.
ذُرِّيَّة، ذَرِّيَّة، ذِرِّيَّة	progeny, offspring, descendants, children.
ذَريعَة	means; excuse, pretext, claim.
ذُعِرَ	to panic, fear; to be frightened, terrified, scared.
ذُعْر	panic, terror, fear, dread, alarm, fright.

ذَعِنَ	to submit, yield, give in to someone.
ذَقَن، ذِقْن	chin.
ذَكّى	to cause to blaze, fan, kindle (the fire); to immolate, sacrifice, slaughter (an animal).
ذَكاء	intelligence, cleverness; acumen, mental brightness; smartness.
حاصِلُ الذَكَّاء	intelligence quotient (I.Q).
ذَكَرَ	to bear in mind, remember, recall, recollect; to speak, talk of, mention, name, cite, quote; to point to, refer to, state, indicate (facts); to report, relate.

ذَكَرَ إِسْمَ الله	to invoke God; to laud, glorify the name of God.
يُذْكَرُ أو يَسْتَحِقُّ الذِّكر	worth mentioning.
لا يُذْكر أو لا يَسْتَحِقُّ الذِّكر	worthless, negligible, inconsiderable.
ذَكَّرَ	to remind, point out to, call someone's attention to; to make masculine (grammar).
ذَكَر	male; penis.
ذِكْر	mentioning, referring to, stating, citation, pointing out, indicating, naming, quoting; report, narrative.
ذِكْر	invocation of God, mention of God's name.
ذِكْر	remembrance, recollection, reminiscence, memory commemoration.
ذِكْر	reputation, repute, renown.
الذِّكْرُ الحَكيم	the Holy Koran.
على ذِكْر	speaking of.
سَعيدُ الذِّكْر	incidentally.

ذِكْرَيات	memories, memoirs, recollections.
ذُكُورَة	masculinity, virility, manhood.
ذَكِيّ	bright, intelligent, clever, smart, sharp-witted.
ذَكِيّ	fragrant, aromatic; delicious, tasty.
ذَلَّ	to be lowly, humble; to be humiliated, degraded, debased, despised.
ذُلّ	lowliness, disgrace, shame, humiliation, degradation, meekness, submissiveness, humility, humbleness.
ذَلاقَة	eloquence, glibness (of the tongue), fluency (of speech).
ذَلَّل	to overcome, eliminate, surmount (obstacles); to get over, subdue, conquer; to deride, flout, disparage, degrade; to humiliate, humble; to run down.

ذَليل low, humble, servile, submissive, meek; despised, despicable, docile, tractable, abject, cowering, cringing.

ذَمَّ to blame, criticize; to rebuke, censure, slander, defame; to calumniate, dispraise, libel.

ذَمّ slander, blame, libel, defamation, calumny, censure.

ذِمَام security; right, claim; custody.

ذِمَّة protection, care, custody, security; responsibility; financial obligation, liability, debit; safeguard, guarantee, conscience.

بالذِّمَّة؟ really? honestly? seriously?.

أَهْلُ الذِّمَّة the free non-Muslim subjects living in Moslem countries given protection and safety.

ذَنَب tail; follower, servant, henchman.

ذَنْب offense, fault, sin, guilt, crime, misdeed.

ذَهَاب leaving, leave, departure.

ذَهَابًا وإيابًا back and forth, to and fro.

ذَهَبَ to go to, repair to, head for; to go away, leave, depart; to disappear, vanish, dwindle; to perish, die; to be destroyed, annihilated; to take along; to escort; to take away; to be of the opinion that, believe that.

ذَهَبَ بِخَيَالِهِ to let one's imagination wander.

ذَهَبَ مَذْهَبَهُ to embrace, follow someone's teaching; to adopt someone's policy, proceed exactly like.

ذَهَبَ سُدًى to be futile, in vain, of no avail.

ذَهَّبَ to gild.

ذَهَب gold.

تُحفظ سبائك الذهب في البنك المركزي

Gold ingots are kept usually at the central bank

ذَهَبٌ أَبْيَض platinum.

ذَهَبِيّ golden, auric.

ذَهَلَ to forget, omit, overlook.

ذَهِلَ to be distracted, absent-minded, astonished, amazed, startled, bewildered; to be alarmed, dismayed.

ذِهْن mind, intellect.

ذِهْنِيَّة mentality.

ذُهُول absentmindedness; amazement, perplexity, confusion, consternation, stupor, bewilderment, dismay, alarm, fight; distraction, astonishment.

ذُو possessor of, holder of, having, comprising.

ذُو شَأْنٍ important, serious.

ذُو حَدَّين double-edged.

ذُو عَقْلٍ intelligent, reasonable, wise.

ذُو مالٍ wealthy, rich.

ذَوُو القُرْبَى relatives.

ذَوُو influential people, those concerned with the matter, the competent authorities.

ذَوَى to wither, wilt, fade; to be withered, dried up.

ذَوَات notables, dignitaries, upper class.

إِبْنُ ذَوَات descended from a good family, highborn.

ذَوَّاقَة gourmet, gastronome, epicure.

ذَوَّبَ to dissolve, melt, liquefy.

ذَوَبَان dissolution, solution, melting, liquefaction.

سَرِيعُ الذَّوَبان instant.

ذَوْد defense, protection.

ذَوْق taste; liking, relish; tact, suavity, decency; gustation, sampling; inclination; sensitivity; flavor.

ذَيَّلَ to provide with a tail; to append, add, supplement, annex, annotate, comment on; to provide at the end.

ذَيْل tail; end; bottom, lower part; train (of a dress); appendix, annex, postscript, addendum.

يتعلّق السعدان بذيله على غصن شجرة

The monkey swings on the tree branch suspended by its tail

ذُيُوع spread, circulation, publicity, diffusion, dispersion.

حرف الراء

رَأى to see, view, discern; to perceive, notice, observe; to regard as, deem, find, believe; to try, hear, look into a case, a matter, a dispute; to inspect, examine; to contemplate, consider, think that.

رائِب curdled (milk).

رائِج widespread, in vogue; in demand, selling well; brisk (market); circulating.

رائِحَة smell, odor, scent, perfume.

رائِد pioneer, pathfinder; scout; guide; example, pattern.

رائِد major (mil.).

رائِدُ فَضاء astronaut, cosmonaut, space explorer.

رِئاسَة presidency, leadership, chairmanship.

رِئاسِيّ presidential.

رائِع wonderful, admirable, charming; superb, magnificent.

رائِعَة masterpiece, chef d'oeuvre.

رائِق pure; quiet; limpid.

رَأَبَ to patch up, heal, mend; to reconcile, conciliate.

رابِح winner, beneficiary; lucrative, profitable.

رَابَطَ to be positioned; to take up positions; to move into fighting positions (army).

رابِطُ الجأش composed, calm, fearless.

رابِطَة bond, tie, relation; league, confederation, union.

رابع، الرابع fourth, the fourth.

رابعًا fourthly.

رابِيَة hillock, mound, hill.

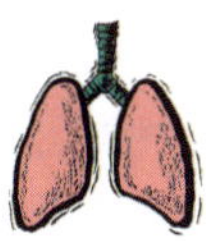

رِئَة lung.

راتِب salary, pay, emolument; monotonous.

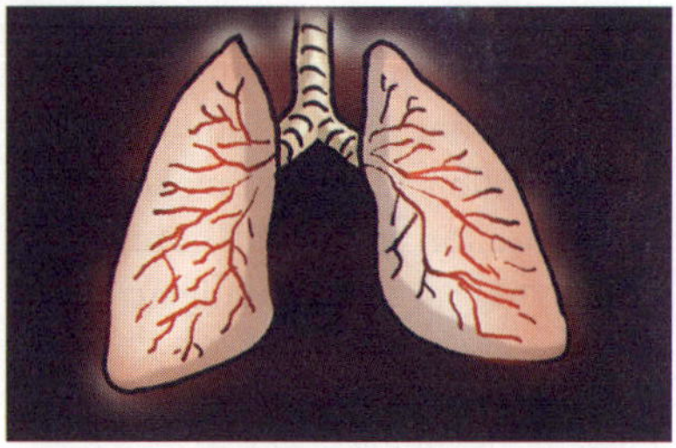

يتنفَّس الإنسان الهواء بواسطة رئتيه

Man breathes air by way of his two lungs

راتِنج — resin.

راجَ — to be current, widespread, popular, in vogue; to be brisk; to sell well, be in demand (goods).

راجِح — preponderant, predominant; preferable; likely; more acceptable; probable.

راجَعَ — to refer to; to revise, go over again, repeat; to go back, apply for information; to consult, check, verify, examine critically; to audit (accounts).

راجِع — returning, going back to; attributable to; subject to.

راجِل — pedestrian, going on foot.

راحَ — to go away, leave; to set out to do.

رَاح — wine.

راحَة — rest, repose, recreation, ease, leisure, vacation, comfort, relaxation, relief.

راحَةُ اليد — palm of the hand.

راحَةُ البال — peace of mind, calmness, security.

بالرّاحَة — leisurely, gently, at one's ease, easily.

راحِل — departing, leaving, going away; traveler, emigrant; deceased, late.

رادِع (ص) — deterring, preventive, inhibitive.

رادِع (اسم) — deterrent, obstacle, impediment, inhibition.

رَأَسَ — to be in charge; to preside over; to head, lead, direct, manage, run; to be the chief, the leader, the head.

رَأْس — head, tip, extremity, summit, top, peak; chief, chieftain; vertex, apex; headland, cape; main part; beginning, top, upper end.

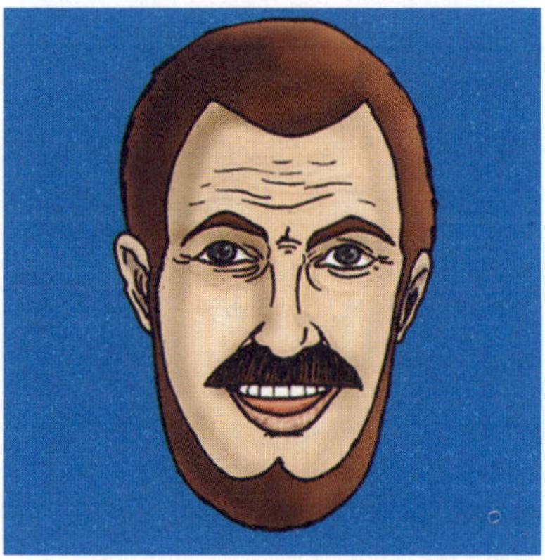

يغطي رأس الإنسان شعر كثيف ما يلبث أن يتساقط مع التقدم في العمر

Hair covers the heads of humans and start to fall with the advance in age

رَأْسًا — directly, straightaway, immediately, forthwith.

رَأْسًا عَلى عَقِب upside down, head over heels.

على رَأْس at the head of, before, prior to.

راسِب precipitate, deposit, sediment; residue; failing, failure (in examination).

راسِخ deep-rooted, well-established, firm, fixed; versed in, skilled in, well acquainted (in a science, art, profession).

راسَلَ to correspond with, write to, exchange letters with.

رَأْسمال capital

رَأْسُمالٌ احْتِياطِيّ reserve capital.

رَأْسُمالٌ عامِل working capital.

رَأْسمال الشَّرِكَة (مقسماً إلى أسْهُم) capital stock.

رَأْسُمالِيّ capitalist.

رَأْسُمالِيَّة capitalism.

رَأْسِيّ vertical, upright, perpendicular; cephalic.

راشِد adult, of legal age; orthodox.

راضَ، رَوَّضَ to tame, domesticate (an animal); to train, coach; to pacify, placate; to regulate; to practice, exercise.

راعَ to frighten, scare, alarm; to startle, surprise, awaken someone's admiration; to please, thrill, delight; to grow, increase, flourish.

راعٍ (الرّاعِي) shepherd, herdsman; cowboy, cowman; guardian, custodian; sponsor, patron, protector.

راعَى to observe, comply with, abide by, respect, honor; to take into consideration, allow for, make allowance for; to stare at, gaze at (stars); to bear in mind, adhere to.

راغِب desirous, wishful, willing.

راغِبٌ عَن reluctant, unwilling, disinclined.

رَأَفَ to have mercy upon; to have compassion for; to show mercy, have pity with; to be kind, gracious, merciful to.

رَأْفَة mercy, clemency, compassion, pity, kindness.

رافِد tributary, branch, affluent (of a river); assistant, aid.

رافِدَة rafter, girder, beam, prop.

رافِض refusing; rejecter, dissenter.

رافَعَ to submit a petition, file a report; to initiate (legal action); to lodge a complaint against someone (in court); to bring legal action against; to plead, summon, defend someone's cause.

رافِعَة lever, crane, winch, hoist, jack.

رافَقَ to keep company with; to be a comrade of; to accompany, attend, be present with.

راقَ to be clear, pure; to please, delight.

راقٍ (الرّاقِي) high, elevated, high-ranking, refined; advanced.

راقٍ (الرّاقِي) charmer, sorcerer, enchanter.

راقَبَ to watch, observe, look closely at; to supervise, control; to await, watch over, guard; to fear (God); to censor (prints).

راقِد sleeping, dormant, resting; quiet, dull.

راقَصَ to dance with.

راقِص dancer, dancing.

راقِصَة dancing girl, ballerina.

رَاكَبَ to overlap, superimpose, lap.

راكِب (ص) riding, mounted, on horseback.

راكِب (اسم) passenger, rider.

راكِبُ دَرَّاجَة cyclist, bicyclist.

راكِد stagnant, static; inactive; sluggish.

تكون المياه في المستنقعات راكدة على الدوام
Water remains stagnant always in swamps

رامَ to desire, wish, want, covet; to crave for, look for; to stay at, remain at (a place).

رامٍ (الرَّامي) thrower, hurler; rifleman (army); sharpshooter.

الرَّامي Sagittarius (astr.).

راهِب monk, friar, hermit.

راهِبَة nun.

راهَنَ to bet, wager, stake.

راهِن (ص) current, present, actual; permanent, established.

راهِن (اسم) mortgagor, pawner.

راوٍ (الرَّاوِي) storyteller, narrator.

راوَحَ to alternate, vary between two things; to fluctuate.

راوَدَ to seek to win, try to entice or tempt someone; to attempt to seduce a woman; to have in mind, be willing to do; to have designs on; to be on the point of doing something.

راوَغَ to dodge, evade, go away; to double-cross, cheat, trick.

رَؤُوف merciful, compassionate, kind.

رَؤُوم affectionate, loving.

رِئَوِيّ pulmonary, pneumonic.

رَأْي opinion, view, concept, suggestion, notion, thought; advice, counsel.

الرَّأْيُ العَامّ public opinion.

فِي رأْيِي in my opinion, in my view.

رُؤْيَا vision, dream; revelation, apocalypse.

رُؤْيَة seeing, view, viewing, sight; visibility; eyesight, sight.

رايَة flag, banner, standard.

رَئيس head, chieftain, leader; boss, chief; director, president; headmaster, principal; chairman.

رَئيسُ الأَرْكان chief of staff.

رَئيسُ البَلَدِيَّة mayor.

رَئيسُ التَّحْرير editor-in-chief.

تزيّن راية بلادي الدوائر الحكومية
The national flag flutters
on top of government buildings

chief of protocol, master of ceremonies. رَئيسُ المَراسِم

foreman. رَئيسُ العُمَّال

speaker, president of parliament. رَئيسُ مَجْلِسِ النُّوَّاب

president of the republic. رَئيسُ الجُمْهُورِيَّة

premier, prime minister. رَئيسُ مَجْلِسِ الوُزَراء

main; chief, primary; cardinal; capital; head, foremost. رَئيسِيّ

God, deity; the lord, God; lord, master. رَبّ، الرَّبّ

owner, possessor, proprietor. رَبّ

father of a family, master. رَبُّ الأُسْرَة

employer, principal. رَبُّ العَمَل

many a (man, time). رُبَّ

to bring up, raise, rear, nurse; to educate, teach; to breed (animals); to promote, develop, make grow. رَبَّى

usury; interest. رِبا

fiddle, rebec, rebab (musical instr). رَبابَة

band, bond, tie, ligature; bandage, dressing, ligament; fetter, shackle; hospice (for the poor). رِباط

shoelace, shoe-string. رِباطُ الحِذاء

necktie. رِباطُ العُنُق

self-control, intrepidity, poise, composure, calmness. رِباطَةُ الجَأْش

weightlifter. رَبَّاع

fourfold, consisting of four, quadruple, foursome, quartet. رُباعِيّ

captain, skipper, shipmaster (of a ship); pilot (of a plane). رُبَّان

to pat, caress, stroke gently. رَبَّتَ

goddess, mistress, lady. رَبَّة

housewife. رَبَّةُ المَنْزِلِ أو الأُسْرَة

muse. رَبَّةُ الشِّعر

to gain, profit, win. رَبِحَ

profit, gain, revenue, yield; interest. رِبْح

gross profit. رِبْحٌ إجماليّ

net profit. رِبْحٌ صافٍ

to lie down, rest (animal); to lurk for someone. رَبَضَ

to bind, tie up, attach; to link, join, unite, tie in, connect; to bandage, dress (a wound); to assess, rate (taxes). رَبَطَ

binding, fastening, connecting, joining, uniting, attaching; assessment, rating (of taxes); bandaging, dressing (a wound). رَبْط

رَبْطَة bundle, ribbon, band, parcel, package; bandage.

رَبْطَةُ العُنُق necktie.

رَبْطَةُ السَّاق garter.

رَبَّعَ to square, multiply a number by itself (math); to quadruple.

رَبْع group of people; quarter; district, region, territory; house, residence, abode.

رُبْع ، رُبُع quarter, one fourth.

رُبْعُ الدائِرة quadrant.

رُبْعٌ نهائِيّ quarter final (of a competition).

رُبْعِيَّة quadrant.

رُبَّما perhaps, may, might, likely, sometimes, possibly, may be.

رَبِيب stepchild, foster child; ally; foster father.

رَبِيبَة stepchild, foster child, foster daughter; foster mother; ally, confederate (female).

رَبِيع spring.

رَتَابَة monotony, dullness.

رِتَاج gate; wicket; lock; latch.

رَتَّبَ to arrange, array; to settle, determine, regulate; to put into proper order; to put together (words); to group; to generate, result in, accrue from; to entail, involve, imply.

رُتْبَة rank, grade, category, standing, order, quality, class.

رَتَجَ to bolt, latch, lock, bar.

رَتَعَ to graze, pasture (cattle); to feast, revel; to indulge freely in.

رَتَقَ to patch, darn, mend.

رَتَّلَ to psalmodize, recite in singing; to sing, chant (hymns); to recite slowly and distinctly the Holy Koran.

رَتَل line, file, row, column, caravan, convoy.

رَثَّ to be ragged, tettered, worn (clothes).

رَثّ ragged, tettered, worn, old, shabby.

رَثَى to bewail, bemoan, lament; to mourn for; to feel sorry for; to elegize (a deceased person); to deplore, pity.

رِثَاء elegizing, bewailing, bemoaning (a deceased person); pity, commiseration, lament, elegy.

رَجَّ to shake, rock, convulse; to quake.

رَجَا to hope, hope for, expect, wish for; to ask, request; to look forward to; to implore, plead with.

رَجَا side, direction, region.

أَرْجَاءُ البلاد all over the country.

رَجَاء hope, expectation, wish, request.

رَجَاحَةُ العَقْل wisdom, equanimity, sagacity; composure; leniency.

رَجَّحَ to give greater weight to; to give preference to; to favor, prefer, consider likely or more probable; to swing back and forth, rock, pendulate, teeter, seesaw.

رَجْرَجَ to shake, convulse, agitate; sway, quiver.

رُجْز dirt, filth; punishment inflicted by God; idolatry.

رَجِس dirty, filthy, squalid.

رِجْس dirt, filth, squalor; atrocity; taboo.

رَجَعَ to return, come back, recur; to withdraw, draw back, retract; to recede, regress; to resort to, have recourse to; to resume, turn again to; to consult (a book); to be dependent on; to be due; to fall under someone's jurisdiction.

رَجَعَ عَن to refrain from, abstain, desist from; to withdraw, retract, revoke, recall, recant.

رَجَعَ عَلى to claim from, demand from.

رَجَعَ بِـ to bring about to, produce, bring in, entail.

رَجَّعَ to return, give back, send back; to turn away from; to sing or chant in a quavering tone; to echo, reverbate.

رَجْعَة coming back, recurrence; retreat, retraction, regress; resumption; recourse to; revocation.

رَجْعِيّ reactionary, old-fashioned, conservative; out of season.

رَجْعِيَّة reaction, retroactivity, narrow-mindedness.

رَجَف to be convulsed, shaken; to tremble, quake, shiver, shudder; to rock; to spread calumnies.

رَجْفَة tremor, quiver, quake, shudder.

رَجُل man.

رَجُلُ أعْمَال businessman.

رَجُلُ دَوْلَة statesman.

رَجُلُ عِصَابَات guerilla.

رِجْل foot, leg.

رَجَمَ to stone, curse, damn, revile.

رَجْم stoning, damning, reviling.

رُجُوع coming back, returning; withdrawal, retreat; regression, recession, fallback.

رُجُوعٌ إلى recourse to; referring to; resumption, taking up again, doing anew.

رُجُوعٌ عَن retraction, revocation, recalling; desistance from, refrainment from.

رُجُوعٌ عَلى claiming.

رُجُولَة manhood, virility.

رَجِيم cursed, damned, evil.

رَحًى hand mill; molar (tooth).

رَحَابَة spaciousness, vastness, amplitude.

رَحَابَةُ الصَّدْر magnanimity, generosity, patience, tolerance.

رَحَّالَة explorer, traveler, nomad, roaming.

رَحُبَ، رَحِبَ to be wide, spacious.

رَحَّبَ to welcome, greet, receive graciously.

رَحْب wide, spacious, roomy.

رَحْبُ الصَّدْر magnanimous, open-minded; carefree; candid.

رَحْبُ الباع generous, open-handed, liberal.

رَحَلَ to depart, set out, leave; to emigrate, go away.

رَحَّلَ to expel, evict, dislodge, send away, deport; to carry forward, post (accounts); to pass away, die.

رَحْل saddle, saddlebag, baggage, luggage.

رَحْلَة، رُحْلَة — trip, journey, voyage, excursion, flight (by air).

رَحِمَ — to have mercy upon; to have compassion for; to spare, let off; to be merciful.

رَحِم، رَحْم — womb, uterus; kinship, relationship.

رَحْمَة — mercy, pity, compassion, sympathy, kindness.

الرَّحْمَن — the Most Merciful (epithet of God).

رَحيق — nectar.

رَحيل — departure, going away, leaving, emigration.

رَحيم — merciful, compassionate, kind.

الرَّحيم — the Most Merciful (epithet of God).

رَخاء — welfare, ease, comfort, happiness, prosperity, abundance.

رُخام — marble.

رَخَاوَة — flaccidity, looseness, softness, laxity, weakness.

رَخُصَ — to be cheap, inexpensive; to be supple, tender.

رَخَّصَ — to make cheap; to authorize, permit, allow, empower; to reduce the price.

رُخْص — cheapness.

رُخْصَة — licence, permit, authorization, permission.

رَخَّمَ — to soften, mellow (the voice); to elide, contract (grammar).

رَخْو، رُخْو، رِخْو — loose, flaccid, languid, lax, limp, soft.

رِخْوِيّ — mollusk.

رَخيص — cheap, inexpensive; mean, low, worthless; supple, tender, soft.

رَخيم — soft, mellow, melodious (voice).

رَدَّ — to give back, send back, return, put back, lay back something in its place; to repel, expel, drive back; to resist, oppose; to refuse, turn down, decline to accept; to ward off, reject; to reply, answer; to reflect (light); to trace back, attribute something to an origin; to yield, produce, bear; to close (the door).

رَدَّ الاعْتِبَار — to rehabilitate; to discharge.

رَدَّ مالاً — to refund, repay, reimburse.

رَدَّ مَعْرُوفاً — to reciprocate, return in kind.

رَدَّ عَلى الشَّيْءِ بِمِثْلِهِ — to retaliate, make reprisal, retort.

رَدّ — return, restitution, reimbursement, repayment, requittal; repulsion, warding off, retort; denial, refusal; reply, answer; reflexion (of light); attribution.

رَدُّ الفِعْل — reaction.

رَدُّ الاعْتِبَار — rehabilitation.

رَدًّا على — in reply to.

رَدٌّ بالمثل — retaliation, reprisal, requittal.

رَدًى — ruin, destruction; death, demise.

رِداء — dress, robe, garment, clothes, suit, wear, gown.

رَداءَة — badness, wickedness, viciousness.

رَدَّة — ugliness, reverbation, echo; apostasy from a religion.

رِدَّة — apostasy, desertion, defection from a creed or a religion.

رَدَّدَ to repeat, echo, reverbate, reiterate.

رَدَعَ to deter from; to prevent from; to curb, check, inhibit.

رَدْع deterrence, prevention, inhibition.

رِدْف rump (of an animal); buttocks, backside, croup (of an animal).

رَدَمَ to fill up with earth; to dam.

رَدْم filling up with earth (swamp, pond); rubble, debris.

رُدْن sleeve.

رَدْهَة hall, lounge, lobby; floor.

رَدِيء bad, evil, inferior; low-grade; base, vile, wicked, vicious; malicious, spoiled; mean.

رَدِيف substitute, standby, reserve; one riding behind another.

رَذَاذ drizzle, spray, sprinkle.

رَذَالَة lowness, baseness, meanness, vileness.

رَذُلَ to be low, base, mean, vile.

رَذِيل low, mean, base, vile, depraved.

رَذِيلَة vice, depravity.

رُزِئَ to be afflicted with; to lose, suffer, incur a loss.

رُزْء disaster, calamity, heavy loss.

رَزَانَة solemnity, sobriety, poise; equanimity; gravity, sedateness; composure, staidness.

رَزَحَ to succumd, collapse, sink to the ground (under a burden); to be burdened with.

رَزَقَ to provide with the means of subsistence; to bestow upon, bless with (a child); to live.

رُزِقَ to be blessed with a child.

رِزْق lievelihood, means of subsistence, nourishment, sustenance, blessing of God; property, wealth, fortune; income, pay, wages.

رَزَمَ to pack, wrap up, bundle, bale.

رِزْمَة parcel, package, pack, packet, bundle, bale.

رَزِين sedate, grave, serious, staid, composed, calm, self-possessed.

رَسَا to anchor, drop anchor, moor, berth (a ship); to land, disembark; to be firm, stable, fixed.

رَسَت عَلَيهِ المُنَاقَصَة to be the successful bidder.

رِسَالَة letter, note, message; missive; mission, vocation, calling; thesis, dissertation, treatise, study.

رَسَّام draftsman; painter; artist.

رَسَبَ to fail, flunk (examination); to settle, subside, deposit.

رَسَخَ to be firmly established, be deeply rooted; to be firm, solid, stable; to be thoroughly conversant with; to be fast.

رَسَّخَ to establish, settle, fix; to make fast, strengthen, consodidate; to stabilize; to make firm, steady; to implant, instill, engrave in someone's mind.

رُسْغ wrist (of hand); ankle (of foot).

رَسَمَ to draw, trace, sketch; to describe, picture, design.

رَسَمَ to decree, ordain (a priest); to plan, scheme, map out; to paint, record in writing; to make, indicate, depict, portray; to work out, conceive (a plan).

أ ب ت ث ج ح خ د ذ ر ز س ش ص ض ط ظ ع غ ف ق ك ل م ن هـ و ي

رَسْم drawing, sketching, designing, painting.

يضع الفنان رسمه على ركيزة ثلاثية الأرجُل

The painter fixes his drawing on a three-legged stand

رَسْم description, portrayal, illustration, pattern.

رَسْم trace, impression, legend, record, imprint.

رَسْم charge, duty, tax, fee.

رَسْمٌ بَيَانِيّ graph, diagram, chart.

رَسْمٌ دِرَاسِيّ tuition fee.

رَسْمٌ مائِيّ watercolor, aquarelle.

رَسْمُ الإِنْتَاج excise tax.

رَسْمُ المشاهِد الطبيعية landscape painting.

رَسْمِيّ official, formal, conventional, ceremonial.

رَسْمِيًا officially.

رَسْو، رُسُوّ anchorage, mooring, landing, berthing; stability, steadiness, firmness.

رُسُوب precipitation, sedimentation; failure, flunking (examination); lees, dregs, settlings.

رُسُوخ firmness, steadfastness, stability; strength; constancy.

رَسُول messenger, envoy, delegate; prophet, apostle, emissary.

النبي محمد وهو رسول الله إلى الناس

Prophet Mohammad is God's Messenger to mankind

الرَّسُول the Prophet, the Messenger of God, Mohammed.

رَسُولِيّ apostolic.

رَشّ to sprinkle, spray, spatter, splash, shower.

رَشَا to bribe, buy off, corrupt.

رَشَاد integrity of conduct, good sense, reason.

رَشَّاش machinegun.

رَشَاقَة gracefulness, elegance; nimbleness, agility.

رَشَحَ to ooze, exude, seep, leak; to sweat, perspire (skin); to percolate, filter.

رَشَّحَ to nominate, put up as a candidate for an office; to filter, percolate, distill.

رَشْح leakage, percolation, filtering; sweat, perspiration (of skin); common cold.

رُشْد integrity of one's actions; sensible conduct, good sense, consciousness, maturity of mind; right guidance.

رَشَفَ to sip, suck, drink up; to drain a vessel.

رَشَقَ to pelt with, strikle with, throw at, hurl at; to shoot at, bombard, attack with bombs.

رَشْوَة، رُشْوَة، رِشْوَة bribe, bribery, corruption, dishonesty.

رَشيد reasonable; wise, judicious, rational; rightly guided, following the right way; mature, major, of full legal age.

رَشيق graceful, lithe; lissome, slender; nimble, agile, brisk, quick; sprightly.

رَصَّ to impact, fit tightly together; to press together, compress; to ram, force into the ground; to pile up, stack up; to align, arrange side by side, line up.

رَصّ compaction, ramming, packing, pressing.

رَصاص lead (mineral); bullets.

قَلَمُ رَصاص lead pencil.

رَصاصَة bullet, pellet.

رَصاصَةُ الرَّحْمَة coup de grace.

رَصاصِيّ leaden, made of lead, lead-colored.

رَصانَة sedateness, composure; calmness.

رَصَدَ to lie in wait; to observe, watch over, control; to conjure a demon; to observe the demon; to observe the stars; to provide, set aside, earmark; to keep account of; to allot, assign.

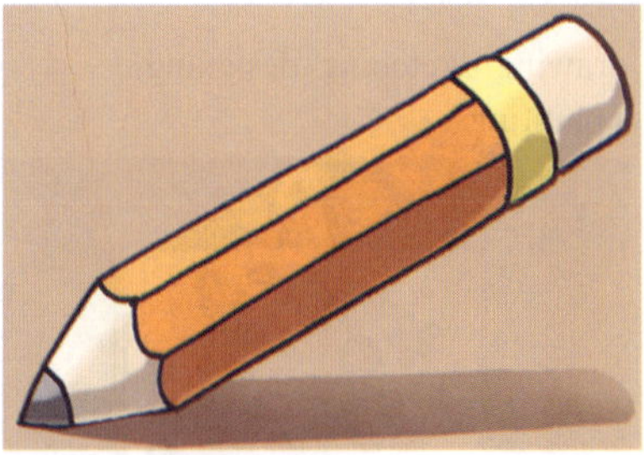

يمكن محو ما يكتب بقلم الرصاص

Words written by a lead pencil could be erased

رَصَّدَ to balance an account.

رَصْد monitoring, observation, watching; earmarking, allotment; meteorology.

رَصَّعَ to inlay, set, stud with gold; to decorate, ornament with.

رَصَفَ to pave, lay with stones; to be firmly joined; to align, line up, arrange, stratify.

رَصْف paving of roads; alignment, arrangement, stratification.

رَصُفَ to be sedate, calm,composed.

رَصيد stock on hand (of merchandise); available funds; balance of an account; capital.

رَصيف sidewalk, pavement; quay, wharf, pier; platform.

رَصيف colleague, associate.

رَصيف compact, solid, firmly joined.

رَصين sedate, calm, composed, firm.

رَضَّ to crush, bruise, contuse.

رَضّ، رَضَّة bruise, contusion.

رِضا، رِضى	contentment, satisfaction; assent, consent; goodwill, favor, approval; delight.
رَضاعة، رِضاعة	suckling, nursing.
رَضّاعة	nursing bottle.
رَضَخ	to yield to, bow, give in, submit to; to break, smash.
رَضَعَ	to suck at its mother's brest; to suckle.
رُضوخ	yielding, sudmission, surrender, obedience, compliance.

رَضِيَ	to be satisfed, content with; to be pleased with.
رَضِيَ	to consent, agree, approve; to accept, sanction; to assent.
رَضِيّ	satisfed, content, pleased; pleasant; affectionate; good-natured, friendly; obedient, compliant.
رَضيع	suckling, sucker, nursling, infant, baby, new-born.
رَطُبَ، رَطِبَ	to dampen; to be moist, humid, damp, wet.
رَطَّبَ	to cool, refresh, humidify, moisten.
رَطْب	humid, moist, damp, wet; fresh, cool; succulent.

رُطَب	ripe dates.
رَطل	pound, measure of weight equalling 450 grams.
رَطَنَ	to speak unintelligibly; to talk gibberish.
رُطوبة	humidity, moisture, dampnesas, wetness.
رَعَى	to take care of; to watch over; to bear in mind; to abide, comply, adhere to, observe; to protect, patronize, sponsor; to govern, rule, control.
رَعَى الماشيةَ	to graze, tend a flock of cattle, sheep, herd.
رَعاع	mob, riffraff, scum, hooligan; ragtag.
رُعاف	nosebleed.
رِعاية	care, custody, charge; patronage, sponsorship; auspices.
رُعْب	fright, fear, terror, panic; dismay; dread.

رَعْد	thunder.
رَعْدِيّ	thunderous.
رِعْديد	cowardly, weakhearted, poltroon, coward.
رَعَشَ	to tremble, shake.
رَعُنَ، رَعِنَ	to be frivolous, lighthearted, thoughtless.
رُعونة	frivolity; folly; carelessness, rashness; imprudence.
رَعْيُ الماشية	grazing, pasturage.
رَعِيّة	citizens, nationals; herd, flock; parish.
رَعيل	squadron of troops; advanced party of men; generation.
رَغا	to foam, froth; to grumble, growl (camel); to rumble, peal (thunder).
رَغادة	ease, comfort, affluence.
رَغام	earth, dust and sand.
رُغام	mucus.

رَغِبَ to desire, wish, want, crave, covet; to request, ask for; to prefer; to like something better than another.

رَغِبَ عن to dislike, detest, shun, avoid, loathe.

رَغَّبَ to make someone desirous of; to interest someone in.

رَغْبَة desire, longing; wish; appetite; lust.

رَغُدَ، رَغِدَ to be pleasant, comfortable, carefree.

رَغَد، رَغْد ease, comfort, opulence, affluence.

رَغْمَ despite, in spite of.

رَغْمَ أنَّ in spite of the fact that; although, though.

رَغْمًا عَن in spite of, despite.

بالرَّغْم مِن، بِالرَّغْم عَن in spite of, despite.

رَغْمَ أَنْفِهِ against his will, forcedly, reluctantly.

رَغْوَة، رُغْوَة foam, froth; spume; scum; lather.

رَغيد pleasant, carefree, agreeable; affluent, easy.

رَغيف loaf of bread.

رَفَّ to quiver, tremble; twitch, flicker; to flap the wings (bird); to flutter; to gleam, shimmer, glitter.

رَفّ shelf, rack; ledge; covey of birds.

رِفاء harmony, accord, love.

بِالرِّفاءِ والبَنِين live in harmony and have many children.

رُفات remains (of a dead); corpse.

رَفَّاص spring (spiral); propeller.

رَفاهة، رَفاهِيَة welfare; opulence; comfort; luxury; comfortable life.

رَفَتَ to break, smash; to reject, decline; to dismiss, discharge from a job or function.

رَفَدَ to support, aid, help; to uphold, carry.

رَفْرَفَ to flap the wings (bird); to flutter (flag); to blow (wind).

رَفَسَ to kick.

رَفْش shovel, spade.

رَفَضَ to refuse, reject, leave, abandon; to dismiss, discard; to decline, refuse to accept, turn down.

رَفْض refusal, dismissal, rejection.

رَفَعَ to raise, lift up, heave up, hoist up, hike up; to boost, elevate, heighten; to enhance, promote.

رَفَعَ to raise, erect, build, construct.

رَفَعَ to remove, take away, eliminate.

رَفَعَ إلى to submit to (petition); to file (report); to present, forward, deliver to, hand over to.

رَفَعَ قَضِيَّة to start, initiate legal action; to bring suit against.

رَفَعَ الكلمة to pronounce the final consonant with damma (grammar) to put a word in the nominative (grammar).

رَفَعَ مِن مكانَتِهِ to speak of someone in glowing terms; to upgrade something; to enhance the importance of someone.

رَفَعَ الجلسةَ to adjourn a meeting, session.

رَفَعَ يدَه عن to leave alone; to desist from.

رَفُعَ to become high; to become thin, delicate.

رَفَّعَ to promote, raise (in rank, position); to make thin.

رَفْع raising, uplifiting, hoisting; stepping up (prices); erection (of building); remission (of duties, penality); submission of a report; pronouncement of the final consonant with a damma (grammar); putting a word in the nominative (grammar).

رَفْعُ الأثقال weightlifting.

رَفْعُ الجَلْسَة adjournment (of a meeting, session).

رَفْعُ الدَّعْوَى على bringing suit against, prosecution, suing.

رِفْعَة high-standing, superiority, eminence, prestige, excellency.

رَفِقَ، رَفَقَ، رَفُقَ to treat with kindness; to be lenient toward; to be kind, friendly, nice, courteous; to show a gentle attitude toward.

رِفْق kindness, gentleness, leniency, clemency, mercy.

رُفْقَة، رِفْقَة company; associates, comrades; group, troop.

بِرِفْقَة accompanied by, in the company of, with.

رَفَّهَ to entertain; to cheer up someone; to soothe the soul of someone.

رَفَّهَ عن نفسه to amuse oneself; to relax; to find recreation.

رَفْو darning, mending, patching, sewing up.

رَفِيع high ranking, exalted, sublime; fine, exquisite.

رَفِيع thin, delicate, slender (body).

رَفِيق (اسم) companion; associate; comrade; consort, mate.

رفيق (ص) kind, gentle, tender, lenient, tolerant; light, soft, mild.

رَقَّ to become thin, delicate, slender; to soften; to pity, commiserate; to have sympathy for, sympathise with.

رَقّ parchment, scroll; turtle; tambourine.

رِقّ slavery, bondage.

رَقَّى to promote to a higher rank or office; to elevate, uplift, upgrade, raise, advance.

رَقَابَة supervision, control, surveillance; observation, watching, monitoring; censorship (of press, opinions).

رُقَاد sleep, slumber; recumbency; lying.

رَقَبَ to observe, watch, regard attentively; to control; to guard; to heed, respect; to take care of.

رَقَبَة neck.

رِقَّة tenderness, gentleness, mercy; softness; thinness, slenderness, slimness; mildness; friendliness.

رِقَّةُ الحاشِية	courteousness, amiability.
رِقَّةُ الشعور	sensitivity, tact.
رِقَّةُ الطبع	kindness, gentleness; mild temper.
رَقَدَ	to sleep, slumber, go to sleep; to lie down, rest; to rest in a grave; to abate, subside, calm down; to stagnate (market); to hatch (hen); to neglect, ignore.
رَقْرَقَ	to mix, dilute (drink with water); to overflow with tears; to glitter, glisten, sparkle; to breathe (wind).

رَقَصَ	to dance; to prance; to tremble (heart).

يرقص الناس في المناسبات السعيدة للتعبير عن فرحهم

People dance on happy events to express their joy

رَقْص	dancing, dance, choreography.
رَقْصَة	dance.
رَقَعَ	to patch (a garment).
رُقْعَة	patch; area; label, tag; coupon; terrain, plot of land.
رَقَّقَ	to make thin; to soften toward; to refine, render delicate; to polish, smooth; to laminate (metal); to dilute.
رَقَّمَ	to number; to page; to punctuate (a text); to imprint, mark; to point, provide with points (a text); to stripe, rule (something); to write.
رَقْم	number, figure, digit, numeral.
رَقْمِيّ	digital, numerical.
رَقِيَ	to ascend, climb, mount; to rise (in rank); to advance; to date back (to a bygone era); to develop upward.
رُقِيّ	progress, advancement, development.
رَقيب	observer, controller, supervisor, watchman, guard, vigilant, keeper, watcher; sergeant (mil.).
رَقيق (ص)	soft, tender, thin, slim, delicate.
رَقيق (اسم)	slave, bondsman, serf.
رَقيقُ الحال	poor, needy.
رَقيقُ الحاشِية	friendly, courteous, amiable.
رَقيقُ الشعور	sensitive, emotional.
رَقيقُ الفؤاد	tender-hearted, affectionate, compassionate.
رَقيقُ الطبع	kind, gentle, friendly.
رَقيقٌ أبيض	white slaves.

رَقيقَة foil, lamina, flake.

رَكاكَة weakness, feebleness, lowliness, poorness.

رُكام pile, heap, lump, cumulus (clouds).

رَكِبَ to ride, mount, go on board, go by; to commit.

رَكِبَ رأسَهُ to be obstinate, stubborn; to act rashly.

رَكَّبَ to assemble, fasten, fit, insert, set (a precious stone); to install, lay, put together, build, construct; to fabricate; to compose, synthesize; to prepare.

رَكْب convoy, riders, caravan; escort; retinue.

رُكْبة knee.

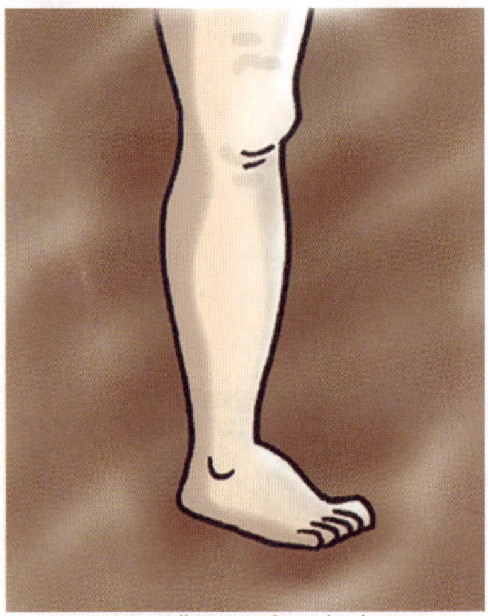

ارتطمت ركبتي عند المفصل بالجدار فآلمتني كثيراً
My knee knocked at the joint with the wall and I felt much pain

رَكَدَ to stagnate; to be dull, slack, stagnant.

رَكَّزَ to fix, stabilize, insert, station, emplace; to focus, localize, center; to concentrate, condense; to emphasize, highlight, underline, stress.

رَكَضَ to run, race, jog, rush.

ركضت بسرعة لأصل إلى الملعب قبل رفاقي
I ran quickly in order to reach the playground before my comrades

رَكْض running, jogging, racing.

رَكَعَ to kneel down; to bow, bend the body (in praying); to drop to one's knees.

رَكَلَ to kick.

رَكَمَ to accumulate, amass, pile up, heap up.

رَكْم pile, heap, accumulation, stacking.

رَكَنَ to lean on, rely on, depend on; to support one's weight on; to quiet down, become calm; to have faith, confidence in.

رُكن corner, prop, pillar; basis, basic element.

رُكوب mounting, embarkation, getting aboard, boarding.

رُكوبُ البَحْر navigation.

رُكوبُ الخَيْل horseback riding.

رُكود stagnancy, stagnation, recession, standstill, slackness, tranquility, stillness.

رُكوع kneeling, bowing.

رَكيزة support, prop, stay, shore, pillar, post, pile.

رَكيك weak, feeble, thin; colorless (style); pitiful, meager.

رَمَى to throw, cast, fling, hurl something; to toss away, throw aside, discard, lay aside.

رَمَى to shoot, fire, pelt, hit; to charge, accuse, blame, reproach someone; to have in view; to intend, plan, drive at.

رَماد ash, ashes, cinders.

رَمادِيّ gray, ash-colored.

رُمّان، رُمّانَة pomegranate; knob, pommel.

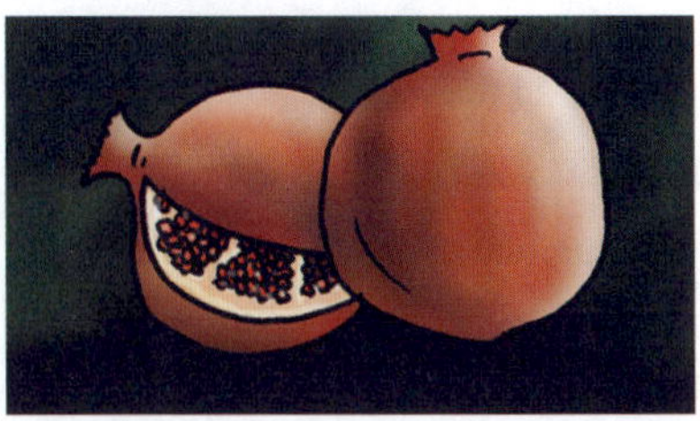

الرمان فاكهة صيفية تكون حلوة أو حامضة المذاق

Pomegranates are summer fruits and are either sweet or sour

رُمّانَةٌ يَدَوِيَّة hand grenade.

رِماية shot, throw, toss.

رُمَّة piece of worn-out rope.

بِرُمَّتِهِ wholly, totally, completely.

رَمَث raft, lighter.

رُمح spear, lance, javelin.

رَمَد ophthalmia, trachoma (eyes).

رَمَزَ to symbolize, represent, indicate; to make a sign, wink, nod, motion; to designate, express symbolically.

رَمْز sign, nod, wink; intimation, allusion; symbol, emblem; character, secret sign; allegory; cipher, code.

رَمْزِيّ allegoric, symbolic, nominal.

رَمْس burial; grave, tomb.

رَمْش، رِمْش eyelashes.

رَمَقَ to regard, glance, look at; to stare, gaze.

رَمَق last spark of life.

رَمَّلَ sprinkle with sand; to cause someone to become a widow.

رَمْل sand.

ضَرْبُ الرَّمْل geomancy.

رَمْلِيّ sandy.

حَجَرٌ رَمْلِيّ sandstone.

رَمَّمَ to repair, rehabilitate, mend, overhaul.

رَمْي throwing, shooting, marksmanship.

رَميم decayed, rotten.

يكون الرمل في الصحراء ناعماً ذهبيّ اللون
Sand in deserts is fine and golden colored

رَنَّ to ring, toll, peal, resound; to echo; to cry, wail, lament.

رَنَا to gaze at, stare at.

رَنَّان ringing, resounding, sonorous, pealing.

رَنَّح to make dizzy, make stagger; to sway.

رَنَّم to intone, chant, sing; to hum a tune.

رَنين peal, ringing, resonance.

رُهَاب phobia.

رُهَابُ الأَجَانِب xenophobia.

رُهَابُ الأَمَاكِنِ المُغْلَقَة claustrophobia.

رَهَافَة slimness, slenderness.

رِهَان bet, wager, stake.

رَهِبَ to fear, dread, apprehend.

رَهَّبَ to frighten, scare, alarm, intimidate.

رَهْبَة dread, fear, fright, terror, awe.

رَهْط، رَهَط group, troop, band; kinsfolk, tribe; persons.

رَهُفَ to be thin, sharp (sword); to be slender, fine.

رَهِلَ، رَهَلَ to be flabby, soft, fat, bloated, flaccid.

رَهَنَ to pawn, mortgage, pledge, hypothecate, wager; to make conditional on.

رَهْن mortgage, lien, pledge, gage, security; hostage.

رَهْن pending, subject to.

رَهْنٌ بِـ subject to, contingent upon.

رَهْنَ إشارته at his beck and call, at his disposal.

رَهْنِيَّة pledge, mortgage.

رَهِيب dreadful, awful, terrible, grave, frightful, ghastly.

رَهينَة hostage (person taken in forced custody).

رَوَى to irrigate, water; to tell, relate, report; to give an account of; to quote from a source; to quench one's thirst.

رِوَائيّ novelist, storywriter, playright, author, writer.

رَوَاج popularity, circulation, marketability.

رُوَاق، رِوَاق portico, gallery, colonnade; tent, curtain; porch, veranda; lobby, vestibule.

رِوَاية story, tale, narrative, report, account, novel, play, drama; recounting, telling, narration.

رِوَايةٌ هَزْلِيَّة comedy.

رِوَايةٌ بُولِيسِيَّة detective story.

رِوَايةٌ مُحْزِنَة tragedy.

رُوتين governmental officialism; routine; bureaucracy.

رَوْث dung, manure.

أحب قراءة الروايات التاريخيّة المشوِّقة

I like reading interesting historical novels

رَوَّجَ to put into circulation, propagate, publicize; to popularize, promote (merchandise).

رَوَّحَ to refresh, soothe, ease, relax; to provide recreation; to go in the evening.

رَوَّحَ عن نَفْسِهِ to amuse oneself; to take rest; to relax.

رُوح soul; spirit; essence, extract.

رُوحٌ رياضية sportsmanship.

الرُّوحُ القُدُس the Holy Ghost.

رُوحانِيّ spiritual, divine, holy, sacred.

رُوحِيّ spiritual, immaterial, incorporeal; alcoholic.

رُوزنامَة calendar, almanac.

رَوَّضَ to tame, domesticate, train, coach; to pacify, placate.

رَوْضَة garden, meadow.

رَوْضَةُ الأَطْفَال kindergarten.

رَوَّعَ to frighten, scare, alarm, intimidate, terrorize.

رَوْع fear, fright, alarm, horror, panic, scare; heart, soul, mind.

أعلق الروزنامة على حائط غرفتي لأعرف التاريخ

I hang the calendar on my room's wall to know the date

رَوْعَة beauty, charm, splendor, magnificence; fright, alarm, fear, awe; surprise, perplexity.

رَوَّقَ to filter, clarify, purify; to pacify, placate someone.

الرُّومُ الأَرْثُوذُكْس the Greek Orthodox (church).

الرُّومُ الكَاثُوليك the Roman Catholic (church).

رُوماتِزْم rheumatism (med.).

رُومانتِيكِيَّة romanticism.

رَوْنَق splendor, glamor, beauty.

رَوِيَ to quench one's thirst; to be irrigated, supplied with water.

رَوِيَّة deliberation, reflection, consideration.

عن رَوِيَّة deliberately, carefully.

رُوَيْدًا slowly, deliberately, without haste.

رُوَيْدَك take it easy; take your time.

رَيّ irrigation, watering.

رِيَاء hypocrisy, duplicity.

رِيَاش furniture; attire, clothes; apparel.

رِيَاضَة sport, athletics, gymnastics, physical training.

الركض رياضة تفيد الجسم وتُبعد التوتّر
Running is a sport that benefits the body and drives away tension

رِياضَةٌ رُوحِيَّة spiritual exercise; devotions.

رِياضِيَّات mathematics.

رِياضِيّ (ص) sportive, sporting, athletic; mathematical.

رِياضِيّ (اسم) athlete, gymnast; mathematician.

رِيَالَة saliva, drool, slobber.

رَيَّان succulent, juicy; plump, chubby, full; sated with liquid; well-irrigated, well-watered.

رَيْب doubt, suspicion, uncertainty.

بلا رَيْب no doubt, doubtless, undoubtedly.

لا رَيْبَ فِيه there is no doubt about it.

رَيْبَة doubt, suspicion, misgiving, distrust.

رَيْثَمَا until, as long as, pending.

رِيح wind, flatulence (gas in stomach); fart; smell, odor.

رِيحٌ مَوْسِمِيَّة monsoon.

رِيش feathers, plumage (of a bird).

رِيشَة feather, plume (of a bird); pen point, nib; brush, paintbrush; blade, vane (of a fan); quill, plectrum (of a musical instrument).

استعمل الأقدمون الريشة لكتابة الرسائل
Ancient peoples used feathers in writing letters

رَيْع income, proceeds, returns; profits, revenue, earnings; yield, produce.

رَيْعان prime, bloom.

رِيف countryside, rural areas.

رِيفِيّ (ص) rural, provincial, rustic.

رِيفِيّ (اسم) countryman, provincial.

رِيق saliva, spittle.

زائِد	additional, extra, plus, excess; superfluous, excessive, immoderate; in addition to, added to.
زائِدَة	outgrowth; appendix.
زائِر	visitor, guest.
زائِغ	abberrant, divergent, digressing.
زائِف	false, falsified, forged, phony; fictitious; feigned, counterfeit; spurious, fake, unreal, mock.
زَائِل	transient, ephemeral, temporal; volatile.
زِئْبَق	mercury, quicksilver.
زاجِر (ص)	deterrent, inhibitory, prohibitory, impediment.
زاجِر (اسم)	conscience; obstacle, handicap.
زاحَ	to go away, depart, leave; to remove, drive away; to pull away; to throw back (a curtain).
زاحِف	creeping, reptant, reptilian, crawling.

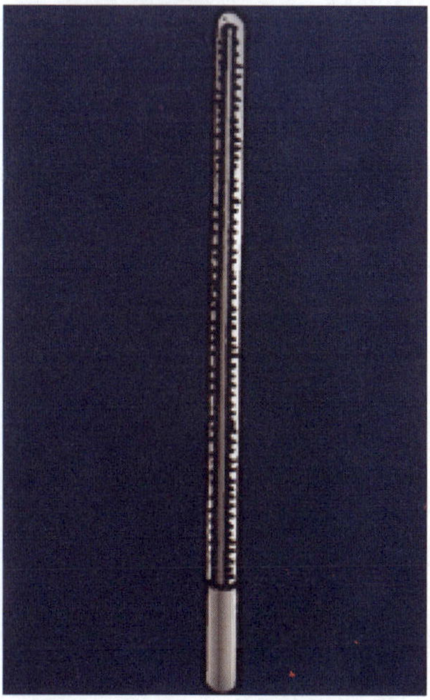

الزئبق أثقل أنواع المعادن وأخطرها للإنسان
Mercury is the heaviest metal and the most lethal to man

زواحِف (ج) reptiles, reptilians.

زاحَمَ to push, shove, jostle, press, hustle; to compete, vie with, contend with; to approach, border on.

زاخِر replete with, loaded with; generous, openhanded; brimful, full, filled to overflowing; abounding.

زادَ to become greater, to increase, multiply; to exceed something; to go beyond an amount or number; to augment, compound, step up, raise; to add, enlarge, expand; to further, promote, intensify.

زاد provisions, supplies, stores; input (computer).

زَأَرَ to roar (lion).

زارَ to visit, call on someone, drop by at some place.

زَاغَ to deviate from, depart from, swerve from, digress from.

زالَ to disappear, vanish, cease to exist; to abate, die down.

ما زالَ، لم يَزَل still, go on doing, yet.

زامَلَ to be a comrade of; to be a colleague of; to be associated with; to accompany someone.

زامَنَ to synchronize.

زانٍ (الزّاني) adulterer, fornicator.

زانية adulteress, whore, harlot.

زاهٍ (الزّاهي) bright, shining, radiant; vivid, gay, lively, gaudy.

زاهِد (ص) indifferent, apathetic, disinterested.

زاهِد (اسم) ascetic; abstinent, self-denying.

زاهِر bright, radiant, brillant, luminous.

زاوَجَ to pair, mate, connect, link, couple.

زاوَلَ to practise, pursue; to engage oneself in.

زاوِيَة angle, corner, nook; small mosque, prayer room.

زَاوِيَةٌ حادَّة acute angle.

زَاوِيَةٌ قائِمَة right angle.

زَاوِيَةٌ مُسْتَقِيمَة straight angle.

زَاوِيَةٌ مُنْعَكِسَة reflex angle.

زَاوِيَةٌ مُنْفَرِجَة obtuse angle.

زَاوِيَةُ النَّجّار square, bevel.

زايَدَ to outbid, overbid, bid more than another.

زئير roar (lion).

زَبّال garbage collector, street cleaner.

زُبالَة garbage, rubbish, refuse, waste.

زَبانِيَة myrmidons; angels who thrust the damned into hell.

زَبَد foam, froth, scum; slag, refuse, cinder.

زُبد، زُبْدَة cream, butter.

زُبْدَة prime, pick, the best part; flower; elite.

زُبْدَة essence, substance, gist, pith, core.

زَبون، زَبائِن client, customer; clientele, patrons.

زَبيب raisins, currants.

زَجَّ to throw, shove, thrust, introduce forcibly; to entangle, involve, implicate.

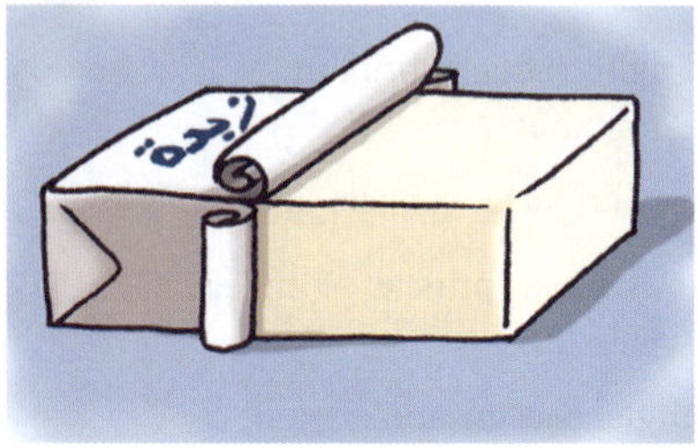

تصنع الزبدة من الحليب وهي سريعة الذوبان
Butter is made of milk and melts quickly when exposed to heat

زَجّاج glassmaker, glassman, glazier.

زُجَاج glass.

زُجاجُ الأمان safety glass.

زُجَاجَة bottle, vial, flask; piece of glass.

زُجاجِيّات glassware, glasswork.

زَجَّجَ to vitrify, glaze, glass.

زَجَرَ to scold, chide, reproach, rebuke; to restrain, prevent, deter; to drive away, oust, drive out.

زِحَام crush, jam; crowd, throng; swarming.

زَحْزَحَ to move, dislodge, displace.

زَحَفَ to crawl, creep on all fours; to advance, march, proceed; to be on the march.

زَحْف advance, march (army); crawl, creepage; army.

زُحَل Saturn (astronomy).

زُحْلُوقَة skid, sledge, sled.

زَحَمَ to crowd, overcrowd, throng; to jam, congest, crush; to push, shove, hustle, jostle; to press, beset.

تُغطى النوافذ بألواح الزجاج لمنع دخول الغبار
Windows are covered with glass panes that prevent dust from entering to the inside

زَحْمَة jam, crowd, throng.

زَخَرَ to be full of, filled with, replete with, abound in; to swell, rise (river); to boast, vaunt.

زَخْرَفَ to adorn, embellish, decorate, ornament.

زُخْرُف، زَخْرَفَة ornament, decor, decoration, embellishment.

زَخْم impetus, momentum, thrust, impulse.

زِرّ button, knob, pommel; bud of a plant.

زِرُّ كُمِّ القَمِيص cufflink.

زِرُّ الطَرْبُوش tassle.

زِراعَة agriculture, cultivation, growing, planting; farming, raising of crops.

زِراعَةُ البَساتِين horticulture, gardening.

زِراعِيّ agricultural, agrarian.

زَرَافاتٍ ووُحْداناً in groups and individually, jointly and separately.

زَرِبَ to leak, seep, flow (water).

زَرَدَ to choke, strangle someone's neck; to gulp, swallow, devour (food, drinks).

زَرَدَة ring, link of a chain.

زَرَدِيَّة pliers.

زَرَّر to button up.

زَرَعَ to sow, plant, grow, cultivate, till; to spread, scatter; to lay (mines).

زَرْع seed, plantation, field; green crop; transplant (of heart, kidney); laying (mines).

زَرَقَ to drop excrement (bird); to hit, pierce; to jab, bore into; to throw, hurl; to inject, give an injection to.

زَرَق glaucoma (eye disease).

زَرْق injection, shooting.

زُرْقَة blueness, blue color; cyanosis (med.).

زَرْكَشَ to brocade, embroider, adorn, decorate.

زِرْنيخ arsenic (chem.).

زَرِيّ despicable, wretched, low, worthless; bad, poor, miserable, contemptible.

زَرِيبَة pen, corral, barn, fold.

زُعاف deadly.

زَعَامَة leadership.

زَعَجَ to disturb, trouble, harass, molest.

زَعْزَعَ to shake, convulse, upset, rock.

زَعْزَعَة convulsion, shock, concussion.

زَعْفران saffron (plant).

زَعَقَ to cry, shout, shriek, yell, scream.

زَعَمَ to claim, allege, pretend; to say, state.

زَعْم allegation, contention, pretension, pretext, claim.

زِعْنِفَة، زَعْنَفَة fin (of fish); flipper (of whale); horde, pack, mob, rifraff.

زَعِيم leader, head, chief; colonel (army rank).

زَغَب pile, fluff, down, fuzz.

زَفَّ to hurry, hasten; to give away the bride; to bring good or glad news to; to inform of.

زِفَاف wedding, marriage ceremony, nuptials.

زَفَّتَ to pitch, cover with pitch; to asphalt (a road).

زِفْت pitch, asphalt.

زَفَرَ to sigh deeply; to pant, groan, moan; to exhaust, puff out (air, breath), expire, breathe out.

زَفْرَة sigh, moan, groan.

زَفير exhalation, expiration; sigh, groan, moan.

زُقَاق lane, alley, corridor.

زَكا to thrive, grow, increase; to be pure in heart, be just, righteous, good; to be suitable for.

زَكَّى to increase, augment, make grow; to purify, chasten; to justify, vindicate someone; to vouch for, bear witness to someone's integrity; to declare someone honest, just, upright; to attest to the truth or credibility of; to commend, praise; to give alms or charity.

زَكَاء moral purity, chastity; integrity, honesty.

زَكَاة justness, integrity, honesty; alms giving, alms tax.

زُكَام common cold.

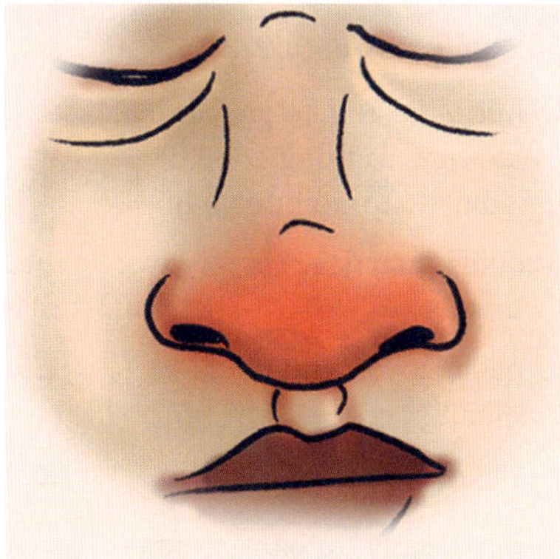

عانيت طويلاً من الزكام خلال الشتاء الماضي
I suffered for a long time from a cold during last winter

زُكِمَ to catch cold.

زَكِيّ pure, chaste, honest, upright; fragrant, sweetsmelling, redolent.

زَلَّ to slip, trip, tumble; to err, commit an error.

زُلال albumin, albumen; fresh and pure (water).

زَلَّة slip, lapse, stumble, error, misstep.

زَلْزَال، زِلْزال، زَلْزَلَة shaking, earthquake, seism.

زَلَقَ، زَلِقَ to slip, stumble, trip, glide, skid.

زَلَّقَ to make slippery; to lubricate, oil, grease; to cause to slip, glide.

تركت الزلزلة شقوقاً عميقة في الأرض
The earthquake left deep clefts in the earth

زَلِق، زَلْق slippery, greasy, soapy.

زَمَّ to tie up, fasten, tighten; to contract, constrict.

زَمَّار piper, flutist.

زَمَّارة wood-wind instrument; siren.

زَمَالَة comradeship, fellowship, scholarship.

زِمَام bridle, reins, halter, leash.

زَمَان time, period, era, epoch; fate, destiny.

زَمْجَرَ to roar, snarl, growl.

زَمَّرَ to blow; to play a wind instrument.

زُمرَة group, set, band, gang, company, clique.

زُمُرُّد emerald.

زَمَن time, period, era, epoch.

زَمَنِيّ temporal, secular, laic; time; transient, temporary.

زَمْهَرِير bitter cold.

زَمِيل colleague, fellow, friend, comrade, companion; classmate, schoolmate (of school).

زَنَى to commit adultery; to fornicate.

زِنًى adultery, fornication.

زِناد hammer, cock, firelock (of gun).

زُنّار belt, girdle, waistband.

زُنْبَرك spring (spiral).

زُنْبور hornet, wasp.

زَنْبيل، زِنْبيل basket (made of palm leaves).

زِنْجار verdigris.

زَنْجِيّ، زِنْجِيّ negro.

زَنِخ to turn rancid.

زَنَخ rancidity.

زَنِخ rancid.

زَنْد forearm, wrist.

زَنْدَقَة atheism, irreligion, unbelief.

زِنْديق atheist, unbeliever, freethinker.

زَنَّرَ to belt, wrap, surround with a belt; to glare at.

زَنْزانَة prison cell, dungeon.

زَنَقَ، زَنَّقَ to tighten, compress, squeeze; to keep on short rations; to scrimp; to be stingy; to be tight-fisted toward.

زِنْك zinc.

زَنيم outsider; ignoble, wicked, miscreant, evil.

زَها to be proud, conceited; to boast, brag of, flaunt, show off; to thrive, prosper; to bloom, flower; to shine, gleam, radiate.

زُهاء roughly, about, some, more or less.

زَهادَة smallness, moderateness, pettiness.

زَهّار florist.

زَهَدَ، زَهُدَ، زَهِدَ to abstain from; to renounce, forsake; to withdraw from; to become an ascetic; to lead a pious life.

زُهْد asceticism, renunciation of, indifference to worldly things; abstinence, disinterest.

زَهَرَ to shine, give light; to glow; to blossom, be in bloom (flower).

زَهْر flowers, blossoms; dice.

حَديدُ الزَّهْر cast iron.

ماءُ الزَّهْر orange-flower water.

زَهْرَة flower, blossom, bloom; splendor, beauty; elite, prime, choice, pick.

الزُّهْرَة Venus (astronomy).

زَهْرِيّ pink, rosy, roseate; floral, flowery.

زُهْرِيّ syphilis (med.).

زَهْرِيَّة flower vase.

زَهَقَ to vanish, disappear; to die, pass away, come to nothing.

زَهِقَتْ روحُهُ to die; to become weary, tired, disgusted with.

زَهْو، زُهُوّ pride, arrogance, conceit; vanity, falsehood; splendor; fun, play, amusement.

زَهُوق perishable, bound to vanish; vain.

زَهيد trivial, trifling, negligible, little, meager, scanty.

زَوَاج marriage, matrimony, wedding, wedlock.

زَوَاجٌ أحادِيّ monogamy.

زَوَاجٌ تَعَدُّدِيّ polygamy.

زَوَاجُ المَصْلَحَة marriage of convenience.

زَوَاجُ المُتْعَة temporary marriage.

زَوَال disappearance, vanishing, cessation, end; setting of the sun; noon, midday.

زَوْبَعَة hurricane, tornado, storm, tempest.

زَوَّج to give in marriage; to marry, wed, join in marriage; to place in pairs or couples; to double.

زَوْج husband, wife, mate; couple, pair.

زَوْجُ الإبْنَة son-in-law.

زَوْجُ الأُخْت brother-in-law.

زَوْجُ الأُمّ stepfather.

زَوْجُ العَمَّة أو الخالة uncle.

زَوْجَة wife, spouse, mate, consort.

زَوْجَةُ الأب stepmother.

زَوْجَةُ الابن daughter-in-law.

زَوْجَةُ الأخ sister-in-law.

زَوْجَةُ العمّ أو الخال aunt.

زَوْجِيّ even, in pairs, double; marital, matrimonial.

زَوْجِيَّة matrimony.

زَوَّدَ to supply with, provide with, equip with, outfit with; to supply provisions; to cater (provisions).

زَوَّرَ to forge, falsify, counterfeit, fake, simulate.

زَوْر inclination, slant; perfidy; squint (eyes); cross-eye.

زَوْر thorax, chest.

زُور falsehood, lie, untruth.

بالزُّور by force, forcibly.

زَوْرَق boat, launch, skiff.

يستعمل الزَّورق لقطع مسافات قصيرة في البحر

Boats are used to traverse small distances in the sea

زِيّ clothing, dress, attire, costume; style of dressing, fashion; guise, form, shape.

زَيَّات oil merchant.

زِيادَة increase, increment, growth; surplus, excess; enchancement, intensification; addition; rise, hike.

زِيادَةً عَن أو عَلى moreover, furthermore, in adition to, besides, over and above, apart from, aside from, beyond.

زِيارَة visit, call.

زَيَّتَ to oil, lubricate, grease.

زَيْت oil.

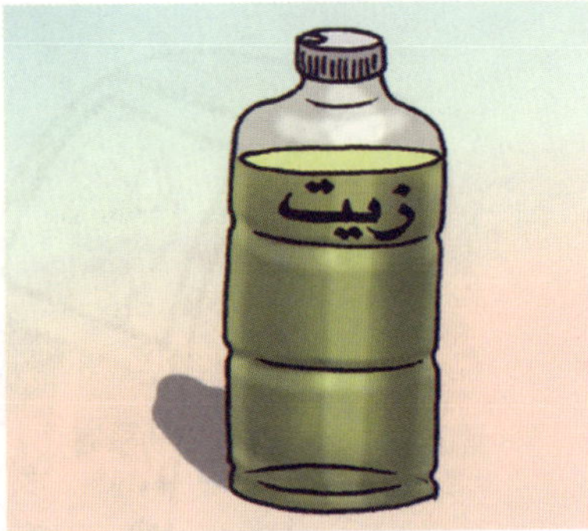

يُستعمل الزيت لطهي معظم الأطعمة

Vegetable oil is used to cook meals

زَيْتُ الخِرْوَع castor oil.

زَيْتُ الزَّيتون olive oil.

زَيْتُ السَّمَك cod-liver oil.

زَيْتٌ مَعْدِنِيّ mineral oil.

زَيْتٌ نباتِيّ vegetable oil.

زَيْتُ الوَقود fuel oil.

زَيْتٌ أَساسِيّ essential oil, volatile oil.

زَيْتون، زَيْتونَة olives, olive tree.

زَيْتِيّ oily, greasy, fatty; olive-green (color).

زيجَة marriage, wedding.

زيجِيّ marital, conjugal, nuptial, matrimonial.

ترمز شجرة الزيتون إلى السلام
وتثمر حبّاً أسود وأخضر اللّون

The olive tree is a symbol of peace
and produces green or black olives

زِير large jar, vat, cask.

زيرُ النِّساء ladies man, philanderer.

زَيْغ، زَيَغان deviation, deflection, digression, turning aside.

زَيَّفَ to forge, counterfeit.

زَيْف falseness, unreality; false, forged, spurious, counterfeit; falsification, forgery, counterfeiting.

زَيَّنَ to decorate, adorn, embellish; to shave, get a shave; to grace, bedeck, dress; to extol, present in a favorable light; to conjure up; to create visions (of something in someone's mind); to suggest to someone to do something.

زَيْن beautiful, handsome, nice, good-looking.

ساءَ to be bad, vile, wicked; to detoriorate, worsen; to grieve, sadden, afflict, hurt, vex, trouble, offend; to displease; to make sorry, pain, torment.

سائِب left, forsaken, derelict; loose, unrestrained.

سائِح tourist, traveler.

سائِد ruling, prevailing, prevalent, common, widespread.

سائِر walking, going on; under way; afoot, in process of; current, common, widespread; remaining, remainder, rest.

سائِس stableman, groom (horse); ruler, leader, governor.

سائِغ savory, palatable, acceptable; permissible, admissible.

سائِق driver, motorist.

سُؤَال question, inquiry, query; request; begging, beggary.

سائِل (ص) flowing, running, streaming.

سائِل (اسم) questioner, inquirer; beggar, mendicant; liquid, fluid; petitioner.

سائِحة grazing livestock.

سَابِح swimmer, bather.

سَابع، السَّابع seventh, the seventh.

سابَقَ to race with; to compete with.

سابِق previous, antecedent, anterior, prior, earlier, former; past, last, preceding.

سابِقًا previously, formerly, at one time.

سابِقٌ لأَوَانِهِ premature, precocious.

كالسَّابِق as before, as usual.

سابِقَة precedent, antecedent.

سابِلَة passers-by; much frequented road.

أ ب ت ث ج ح خ د ذ ر ز س ش ص ض ط ظ ع غ ف ق ك ل م ن هـ و ي

ساتِر (ص) screening, hiding; covering; veiling.

ساتِر (اسم) screen; barricade, mound; obstruction.

سَاجِد prostrate in worship, bowing in adoration, kneeling.

ساجَلَ to compute with; to rival, contend, dispute, debate with; to draw someone into a conversation; to have a talk with.

ساحَ to tour, cruise, rove, roam; to flow, stream.

ساحَة square, plaza, yard, domain, field; arena.

ساحَةُ الحرب battlefield.

ساحَةُ المطار apron.

ساحِر (ص) charming, enchanting, captivating, glamorous.

ساحِر (اسم) magician, sorcerer, wizard, conjurer.

ساحِرة witch, sorceress.

ساحِق crushing, overwhelming, extensive; decisive, conclusive.

ساحِل coast, seashore, seaside.

ساحِلِيّ coastal, littoral, seaboard.

ساخِر sarcastic, sardonic, mocking, cynical, bitter, caustic.

ساخِط discontented, dissatisfied; disgruntled, resentful, angry; annoyed, vexed.

ساخِن hot, warm.

سادَ to be master, sovereign; to rule, govern; to prevail; to be predominant, have the upperhand.

يقوم الساحر بأعمال خفَّة تثير الدهشة
The magician performs magic tricks that surprise the audience

سادّ obstructive.

سُؤْدُد، سُؤْدَد rule, power, dominion, sovereignty; glory, honor, eminence, dignity.

سادِس، السادِس sixth, the sixth.

ساذِج، ساذَج naive, guileless, simple-minded, artless, candid.

سارَ to move on, set out, start, get going; to march, travel, ride, journey; to leave, depart, run; to progress, advance.

سارَ to run, function, operate; to circulate, get about.

سارَ to behave, act; to follow, pursue, adopt.

سارّ delightful, cheering, glad, joyous, gladdening.

سارٍ (السَّارِي) contagious, infectuous (sickness); effective, valid, in force, enforceable, applicable; night traveler.

سارَعَ to hurry to; to be quick, rapid; to speed up, rush, run; to hasten to do something.

سارِق thief, burglar, robber.

سارِيَة column; mast (of ship); pole, post.

ترفع السفينة علماً على ساريتها للتعريف عن جنسيتها

The ship raises a flag on a mast to identify its nationality

سارِيَةُ العَلَم flagpole, flagstaff.

سَاسَ to govern, rule, manage, lead, guide, conduct; to groom (horses).

ساطِع radiant, brillant, shining, luminous; clear, plain, evident, obvious (proof).

ساعٍ (السّاعي) messenger, courier, delivery boy, office boy; slanderer, calumniator.

ساعِيُ البريد postman.

ساعاتِيّ watchmaker, clockmaker.

ساعَة hour; clock, watch; timepiece; counter, meter.

السَّاعَة now, at present, currently; immediately, at once.

ساعَةُ توقيت stopwatch.

ساعَةٌ رَمْلِيَّة sandglass.

ساعَةٌ شَمْسِيَّة sundial.

أعرف الوقت بالنظر إلى عقربَي الساعة

I know time just by looking on the two hands of the watch

ساعَةُ يَدٍ wristwatch.

ساعَدَ to help, assist, aid, support; to contribute; to promote, favor, encourage.

ساعِد forearm.

ساغَ to be allowable, permissible; to be palatable; to be easy to swallow.

سافَرَ to travel, make a trip; to leave, depart, go on a journey.

سافِر unveiled, barefaced; overt, obvious; shameless, flagrant.

سافِل low, base, ignoble, despicable; villain; dirty; vulgar; indecent, mean, lowly.

سافِلة buttocks, behind, rump.

ساقَ to drive, steer; urge on; to transmit, transport, deliver, convey, send, despatch; to carry on a conversation, relate, narrate, recount (a story).

ساق leg; shrank; trunk (of tree); stem (of a plant).

ساق الرجل السيارة ببطء
كي لا يتسبب بحصول حادث
The driver drives his car slowly in order not to cause an accident

---

ساقٍ (السَّاقِي) butler, bartender.

ساقِط falling, fallen; base, vile, mean; disreputable, notorious; omitted, missing; forgotten; null and void, abolished, canceled; failing (in exams).

ساقِيَة barmaid; rivulet, brooklet; irrigation ditch.

ساكِت silent, quiet, still; reticent, tranquil, quiescent.

ساكَنَ to live with; to cohabit with; to share quarters with.

ساكِن (ص) calm, motionless; still; stagnant, standing (water); static (electricity); vowelless (word).

ساكِن (اسم) dweller, inhabitant, resident, occupant.

حرفٌ ساكِنٌ consonant.

سُكَّان (ج) population, inhabitants.

سَأَلَ to ask, inquire, request, demand, implore, adjure; to interrogate; to call to account; to beg for alms.

سالَ to flow, dissolve, seep, melt.

سالِب negative.

سالِف (ص) previous, former, bygone, old; preceding.

سالِف (اسم) sideburn.

سالِفًا previously, formerly, in the past.

سالِك passable, open, clear, unobstructed.

سالَمَ to keep the peace, to make peace with one another; to become reconciled with one another.

سالِم safe, secure; unblemished; flawless, intact; sound; healthy; integral; regular (verb).

سَئِمَ to be bored with; to be tired of; to be weary of.

سامَ to offer for sale; to impose upon someone (a punishment, task); to demand of someone something beyond his power; to humiliate, oppress, treat unjustly; to consecrate, ordain (a priest).

سَأَم boredom, weariness.

سامّ poisonous, toxic, venomous.

سامٍ (السَّامِي) high, elevated, lofty, sublime, august.

سامَحَ to forgive, excuse, pardon.

سامَرَ to chat in the evening with someone.

سانِح auspicious, propitious, favorable.

سَوَانِح (ج) auspices, good omen; ideas, thoughts.

سانِحة opportunity, occasion.

سانَدَ to support, stand by, stand up for, assist, aid, help.

ساهٍ (السَّاهِي) inattentive, inadvertant, absentminded.

ساهِر sleepless, awake; vigilant, watchful.

ساهَمَ to contribute, participate in, take part in; to cast or draw lots with.

ساوَى to equal; to smooth, flatten, level; to equalize, regulate, make up, put in order.

ساوَرَ to beset, assail, attack, overcome, grip.

ساوَقَ to harmonize; to draw out, form a sequence; to be successive, continuous, coherent.

ساوَمَ to bargain with.

سايَرَ to comply with someone's wishes; to appease, pacify, try to satisfy; to keep up with, go along with; to humor; to keep in line with.

سَبَّ to insult, abuse, revile, call names; to rail, curse, blaspheme, swear.

سَبّ، سِبَاب cursing, swearing, abuse, revilement.

سَبَى to capture, take captive; to captivate, fascinate, charm; to beguile, intrigue.

سَبَّابَة forefinger, index finger.

أشار رفيقي بالسبّابة إلى الطائرة
My friend pointed with his index finger toward the aircraft

سُبَات torpor, slumber; coma; lethargy.

سِباحَة swimming, bathing.

سُباعِيّ sevenfold, septet; seven-lettered (word).

سُباعِيُّ الزَّوايا heptagonal, heptagon.

سِباق race, contest, competition.

سِباقُ الخَيْل horse racing, horse race.

سِباقُ السَّيارَات car rally.

سِباقُ الضاحِيَة cross-country race.

سَبَّاك plumber.

سِباكَة plumbing, foundry.

سَبَّبَ to cause, provoke, arouse; to produce, bring about, effect; to occasion, motivate, generate; create, give rise to, bring forth; to trigger, inspire, engender.

سَبَب — reason, cause, motive; rope, tent rope; means for obtaining something.

بِسَبَب — because of, by reason of, in view of, due to, on account of.

السَّبْت — Saturday, Sabbath.

سَبَح — to swim, bathe.

سَبَّح — to praise, glorify, extol, eulogize.

سُبْحَانَ الله — Praise the Lord, Glory to God.

سَبْحَة — rosary, beads.

يمسك جدّي بسبحته طوال النهار

My grandfather holds his rosary during all hours of the day

سَبَخَة، سَبْخَة — marsh, swamp, quagmire.

سَبَرَ — to probe, measure, sound (the depth); to fathom, explore; to get to the bottom of; to study something thoroughly; to examine, test.

سِبْط — grandchild; tribe.

سَبَّع — to multiply by seven.

سَبْع، سَبُع — beast of prey, lion.

سَبْع، سَبْعَة — seven.

سُبْع — one seventh of a whole.

سَبْعَةَ عشَرَ — seventeen.

سَبْعُون، السَّبْعون — seventy, the seventieth.

سَبَقَ — to proceed, happen before; to outstrip, overtake, go past, get ahead of, arrive before; to outdistance; to surpass, beat.

لَم يَسْبِق لَهُ مَثِيل — unprecedented.

سَبَقَ لنا القَوْل — we have previously said that.

سَبَقَ السَّيفُ العَذَل — it is already too late; there is nothing one can do about it; one has to accept the accomplished fact.

سَبْق — antecedence, precedence, priority.

سَبْقٌ صِحَفِيّ — scoop.

سَبْقُ الإصرار — premeditation, willfulness.

سَبَكَ — to found, cast, smelt; to shape, formulate.

سَبُّورَة — blackboard.

سَبِيّ — captive.

سَبْي — capture, captive.

سبيكة — ingot, bullion.

سَبِيل — way, road, path; expedient, means; public fountain.

في سَبيل — for the sake of, in the interest of.

على سبيل — by way of, as, for.

سِتّ — six.

توضع السبورة في غرفة التدريس
ليكتب عليها الأستاذ

The blackboard is put in the classroom in order that the teacher writes on it

سِتار	veil, screen, covering, curtain, drape; pretext, excuse.
تَحتَ سِتار	under the guise of.
وَراءَ السِّتار	behind the scenes.
سِتارة	curtain, drape, blind.
سِتَّة	six.
سِتَّةَ عَشَرَ	sixteen.
سَتَرَ	to cover, veil, conceal, shield, protect, hide; to overlook, condone something done by someone.
سِتْر	curtain, screen, drape, veil; covering; shelter.
سُتْرَة، سِتْرَة	jacket, coat, tunic.
سِتُّون، السِّتُّون	sixty, the sixtieth.
سَجَّاد (ج)	carpets, rugs.
سَجَّادَة	carpet, rug.
سِجَال	contest, rivalry, competition with alternate success.
سَجَّان	warden (of prison).

يستعمل المسلم السجادة للصلاة عليها

The Moslem uses a carpet to pray on it

سَجَدَ	to prostrate oneself in worship; to worship God; to bow in worship; to throw oneself down in worship.
سُجُق	sausage.
سَجَّلَ	to register, record, write down, make a note of; to put on record; to make a statement for the official records; to enter in the accounts books.
سَجَّلَ على شريط	to tape-record.
سَجَّلَ إصابَةً	to score a hit, goal, mark.
سَجَّلَ اخْتِراعًا	to patent an invention.
سَجَّلَ رَقْمًا قِياسِيًّا	to set a record.
سَجَّلَ لِحِساب فُلان	to credit someone's account with.
سَجَّلَ على حِساب فُلان	to debit someone's account with.
سِجِلّ	register, record, logbook; list; scroll; journal.
سِجِلٌّ تِجارِيّ	commercial register.
سِجِلٌّ عَقارِيّ	cadastre, land register.
سِجِلُّ التشريفات	list of visitors.
سَجَنَ	to jail, imprison, lock up, intern.
سَجْن	imprisonment, internment.
سِجْن	prison, jail.

سُجُود prostration (in prayer), bowing down (in worship).

سَجِيَّة nature, natural disposition, trait, characteristic.

سَجين prisoner, inmate; convict; imprisoned, jailed person.

سَحَاب، سَحَابَة clouds, cloud.

سَحَّاب zipper, zip fastener.

سَحَابَةَ throughout, during all.

سَحَبَ to drag along; to pullout; withdraw, take away; to strip, dispossess, divest someone of; to take out, draw (from an account); to unsheathe (a sword); to apply, make applicable (law, statute); to retract, revoke, cancel.

سحبت المرأة وراءها العربة المملوءة بالمشتريات

The woman drew the carriage full of provisions behind her

سَحْبٌ عَلى المَكْشوف overdraft (bank account).

سَحَجَ to scrape off, chafe, abrade; to strip off.

سَحَرَ to bewitch, spell, conjure; to charm, enchant, fascinate.

سَحَر time before daybreak; dawn, early morning.

سِحْر magic, sorcery, witchcraft; bewitchment, fascination, enchantment, charm, spell, infatuation.

سَحَقَ to crush, pound, bruise, pulverize; to annihilate, wipe out (an army, troops); to wear out (clothing); to suppress, quell, stiffle, smash, destroy.

سَحُقَ، سَحِقَ to be distant, remote, faraway.

سَحْق crushing, pounding, pulverization; suppression, smashing, destruction, annihilation, extermination, putting down.

سَحَلَ to file, smooth, peel, shave off; to drag along on the ground; to draw or pull along.

سَحُمَ to become black.

سَحَنَ to pulverise, powder, pound, crush.

سَحْنَة، سَحَنَة، سِحْنَة appearance, looks, visage, facial features.

سَحُور light meal before daybreak (during Ramadhan).

سَحِيق distant, faraway, remote; immemorial; very deep.

سَخَاء generosity,openhandedness.

سَخَافَة folly, childish prank, feeble-mindedness, absurdity.

سَخَّان heater, boiler.

سَخِرَ to mock, scoff, jeer, sneer, ridicule, deride; to make fun of, gibe, taunt.

سَخَّرَ to subject, make subservient to for the purpose of; to employ, utilise, turn to profitable account, make use of; to exploit, subjugate.

سُخْرَة forced labor; joke.

سُخْرِيّ laughing stock, target of ridicule; forced labor.

سُخْرِيَّة، سُخْرِيَة laughing stock, object of ridicule, mockery.

سَخِطَ to be discontented, displeased, angry, annoyed; to resent; to be enraged, irritated.

سُخْط، سُخُط، سَخَط discontent, indignation, anger, wrath.

سُخْف، سَخْف absurdity, foolishness, nonsense, idiocy, folly.

سَخَّمَ to besmut, blacken with soot.

سَخَنَ، سَخُنَ، سَخِنَ to heat, warm up; to be hot, warm.

سُخْن hot, warm.

سُخُونَة heat, hotness, warmth; fever.

سَخِيَ to be generous, openhanded.

سَخِيّ generous, openhanded; bountiful, ample, profuse.

سَخِيف silly, stupid, idiot, absurd, ridiculous, despicable.

سَدَّ to plug up, close up, clog, congest; to obstruct, bar, block up, blockade; to cork, stopper; to pay, defray, settle, cover (debts, expenses); to satisfy, fulfill, meet (a claim); to fill (a gap); to remedy (a shortcoming); to meet someone's needs; to repair, redress, supplement, (deficiencies).

سَدّ clogging, plugging, closing, stopping up; obstruction, blocking, defrayment of costs; payment, settlement of a debt; fulfillment of a claim.

سَدّ obstacle, barrier, dam, dike, barrage; hurdle, barricade, rampart; embankment, weir.

يحجز السدّ مياه الأمطار لاستعمالها عند الحاجة

The dam retains rainwater for use when needed

سُدّ cataract (eyes).

سُدًى in vain, futilely, uselessly.

سَدَاد payment, defrayment, settlement (of a debt); the right thing to do; appropriateness, appositeness.

سِدَاد، سِدَادَة plug, stopper, cork, seal.

سُدَاسِيُّ الأضلاع أو الزوايا hexagonal.

سُدَّة position, post, rank; seat, pulpit; door, gate.

سَدَّدَ to defray, settle, cover, pay (a debt); to fulfill, satisfy, meet (one's obligations); to aim, point at, direct to; to guide someone's steps, show the right way to.

سَدَّسَ to make sixfold; to multiply by six.

سُدْس، سُدُس one sixth.

سَدَلَ to let something hang down; to drop, lower a curtain.

سُدْل	curtain, veil.
سَدُود	tight, impervious, hermetically sealed.
سَديد	apposite, pertinent; appropriate, correct, sound.
سَذاجَة	naiveté, ingenousness, simplemindedness guilelessness, innocence, simplicity.
سَرَّ	to gladden, delight, make happy, cheer; to confide to someone, whisper in one's ear; to confide a secret.
سُرَّ	to be pleased with, delighted at, happy, glad at; to rejoice, cheer up, delight in.
سِرّ	secret, mystery; sacrament (Christianity).
سِرًّا	secretly, in secret,covertly.
في سِرِّهِ	inwardly, in his heart.
سَرَى	to travel by night; to circulate, spread, run, stream.
سَرَى على	to be applicable to.
سَرَى في	to creep into, spread into, pervade, flow into.
سَرَى مَفْعولُهُ	to be valid, in fore, effective, operative.
سَرَّى عن	to comfort, cheer, amuse someone.
سَرَّاء	joy, happiness, welfare.
في السَّرَّاء والضَّرَّاء	for better or for worse, in sorrow and in joy, in good and bad days.
سَرَاب	mirage; phantom.
سَرَاة	top,summit; middle, center; outset, beginning; chief, head, high ranking person.
سِرَاج	lamp, light.
سَرَاح	dismissal, release, discharge.
أَطْلَقَ سَرَاحَهُ	to dismiss, release, discharge, free, set at liberty.
مُطْلَقُ السَّرَاح	free, at liberty, as one chooses and decides.
سُرادِق	pavilion, canopy, large tent.
أَسارير (ج)	features, lines of face.
سِرَاط	path, road, way.
سَرَّبَ	to leak out, spread, circulate (a secret, report).
سِرْب	flock, herd (of animals); flight; flock (of birds); swarm (of locusts); school (of fish); squadron (of airplanes).
سُرَّة	navel, umbilicus.
سَرَّجَ	to braid, plait; tack, baste.
سَرْج	saddle.

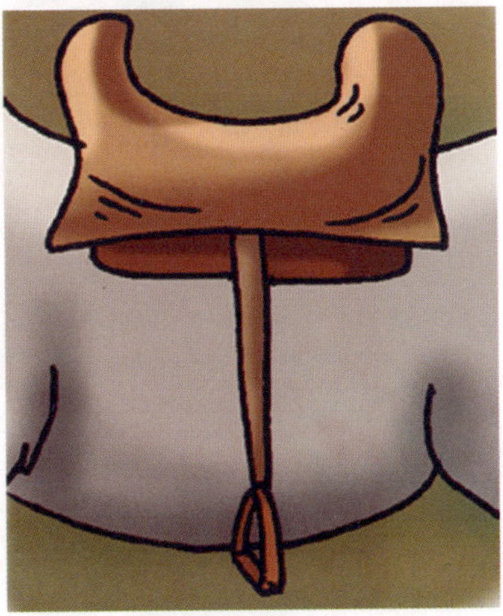

يثبت السرج على ظهر الحصان قبل ركوبه

The saddle is fixed on the horse's back before one rides it

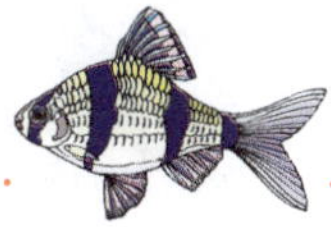

سِرْجين	dung, manure.
سَرَحَ	to go out, depart, go away; to graze freely (cattle).
سَرَّحَ	to send away, dismiss, discharge, release (from employment); to set free, set at liberty (of a detainee); to demobilize, disband (troops); to divorce (one's wife); to comb the hair; to card wool; to relieve, comfort someone; to look around, set ones eyes at.
سَرَدَ	to list, relate, recite, narrate, tell; to set forth, quote,cite, enumerate.
سَرْد	presentation, citing, stating, narrating, telling.
سِرْداب	vault, crypt, cellar, basement.
سَرَطان	crab.

يعيش السرطان بين صخور الشاطئ وله نابان قويان

The lobster lives between the coastal rocks and has two powerful canines

سَرَطانُ البَحْر	lobster.
سَرَطان	cancer (med.).
بُرْجُ السَّرَطان	Cancer (astr.).
سَرَّعَ	to speed up, hasten,accelerate, expedite.
سُرْعانَ ما	in no time, soon, before long, presently.
سُرْعَة	speed, haste, hurry, velocity, pace, rapidity.
سُرْعَةُ الخاطِر	presence of mind, quickwittedness.
بِسُرْعَة	quickly, promptly, rapidly, hastily.
سَرَقَ	to steal, pilfer, filch, rob; to plagiarize (manuscripts).
سَرِقَة	stealing, pilfering, robbing, filching, burglary, theft, plagiarism (manuscripts), larceny.
سَرْمَدِيّ	eternal, everlasting, immortal, perpetual.
سِرْوَال	trousers, panties, underpants.
سُرُور	delight, joy, gladness, pleasure.

سُرِّيّ	umbilical.
سِرِّيّ	secret, private, confidential; covert, clandestine; mysterious; occult.
سَرَيان	spreading, currency, circulation; flowing, streaming.
سَرَيانُ المَفْعول	validity, effectiveness, applicability, coming into force.
سَرِيَّة	company, detachment, brigade (mil.).
سِرِّيَّة	secrecy, privacy, mystery, secretiveness.
سَرير	bed, bedstead.
سَريرَة	inner self, secret thought; mind, heart, soul.
سَريرِيّ	clinical.

سَريع	fast, speedy, quick, swift, prompt, rapid; nimble.
سَريعًا	quickly, rapidly, speedily, promptly.
سَريعُ الخاطِر	quick-witted.
سَريعُ الزَّوال	ephemeral, transient, fleeting.
سريعُ التَّصْديق	credulous.
سريعُ العَطَب	fragile.
سريعُ الغَضَب	quick-tempered, irascible, irritable, bad-tempered, touchy.
سَطا	to burglarize, rob at gunpoint; to usurp, take by force; to attack, assault, raid, pounce, jump upon.
سَطَحَ، سَطَّحَ	to spread out, level off, stretch; to throw down; to unfold, unroll; to make smooth.
سَطْح	surface, plane, face, level; roof, terrace; deck (of ship).
سَطْحٌ مُسْتَوٍ	plane.
سَطْحِيّ	superficial, shallow; external, outside, surface.
سَطَرَ، سَطَّرَ	to rule, draw lines; to write, jot down, record; to draw up, compose something; to line, stripe, bar.
سَطْر	line.
سَطَعَ	to shine; to be radiant, brilliant; to rise; to spread (dust); to be clear, obvious. plain (proof, truth).
سَطْل	bucket, pail.
سَطَمَ	to close, shut.
سَطْو	burglary, attack, assault, house-breaking, robbery; usurpation; storming into, charge, rush, raid.
سَطْوَة	influence, authority, power, upper hand, strength; attack, assault, house-breaking.
سُطوع	brilliance, radiance, glow, brightness, luminosity; diffusion, spreading, emanation.
سَعَى	to seek to, attempt to, endeavor to, pursue, seek after; to go about; to toil, work hard; to proceed to, head for; to move, walk.
سَعَى بِفُلان	to slander, calmuniate, denounce, betray.
سَعادَة	joy, happiness, bliss, felicity, prosperity, welfare.
صاحِبُ السَّعادَة	Your Excellency, His Excellency.
سُعال	cough.
سُعالٌ ديكِيّ	whooping-cough.
سَعَة	capacity, extent, range, volume; faculty, power, ability; plenty, abundance.
سَعَةُ الصَّدْر	patience.
سَعَةُ العَيْش	wealth, ease, comfort.
سَعِدَ، سُعِدَ	to be happy, lucky, fortunate.
سَعْد	good luck, luckiness, good fortune.
سَعَّرَ	to kindle (fire); to price (merchandise).

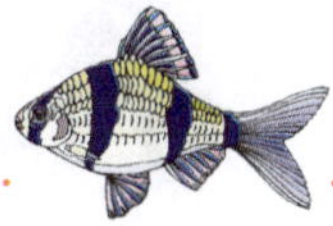

سَعِرَ to be afflicted with rabies; to go mad; to run mad, become mad, furious; to flare up in anger.

سُعْر madness, frenzy; rabies (med.); starvation; heat, hotness; voracity.

سِعْر price, rate, cost; quotation.

سِعْرُ القَطْع discount rate, bank rate.

سِعْرُ الصَّرْف exchange rate.

سِعْرُ الكُلْفَة cost price.

سُعْرَة calorie.

سَعَف (ج) palm leaves.

سَعَلَ to cough.

سَعُوط snuff.

سَعْي effort, endeavor, attempt, pursuit, labor.

سَعيد happy, lucky, fortunate.

سَعيدُ الذِّكر of blessed memory; the late...

سَعير blaze, flame, inferno.

سَفَّاح assassin, murderer, manslayer.

سِفارَة، سَفارَة embassy; mediation, good offices.

سَفَّاك assassin, killer, murderer, manslayer, blood-shedder.

سَفالَة lowness, depravity, vileness; meanness, ignomity; dirtiness; obscenity, indecency.

سَفاهَة foolishness, stupidity, silliness; impudence, insolence; squandering, prodigality.

سَفَحَ to shed, spill, pour out.

سَفْحُ الجَبَل foot, versant.

سَفَرَ to unveil; to shine, glow; to mediate between rivals; to make peace between enemies.

سَفَّرَ to send on a journey; to compel someone to leave; to expedite, despatch, consign (goods).

سَفَر travel, journey, trip, tour, yoyage.

سِفْر book.

سَفْرَة journey, trip, travel, tour, excursion.

سَفَعَ to tan, sunburn, scorch, burn; scald.

سَفْعَة dark spot, black stain; scorch, scald.

سَفَكَ to shed, spill.

سَفْك shedding, spilling.

سَفَلَ، سَفُلَ، سَفِلَ to be vile, despicable, mean, base.

سُفْلِيّ lower, at the bottom.

سَفُهَ، سَفِهَ to be stupid, silly, foolish; to be inpudent, insolent; to be prodigal, wasteful, profligate.

سَفَّهَ to discredit, depreciate, put down as inferior; to disgrace, dishonor; to make a fool of.

سَفَه foolishness, stupidity; impudence, insolence.

سَفير ambassador; mediator.

سَفيرٌ فوقَ العادَة ambassador extraordinary.

سَفيرٌ مُتَجَوِّل ambassador-at-large.

سَفيرٌ مُعَيَّن ambassador designate.

أ ب ت ث ج ح خ د ذ ر ز س ش ص ض ط ظ ع غ ف ق ك ل م ن هـ و ي

سَفيرٌ مُفوَّض	ambassador plenipotentiary.
سَفين	wedge, cotter.
سَفينَة	ship, vessel.
سَفينةٌ تِجاريَّة	merchant ship.
سَفينةٌ حربيَّة	warship, battleship.
سَفينةٌ شِراعيَّة	sailboat, sailer.
سَفينةٌ فَضائيَّة	spaceship, spacecraft.
سَفينةُ نُوح	Noah's Ark.
سَفيه	foolish, stupid; indecent, obscene, vulgar; impudent, indecent, insolent; spendthrift, prodigal, wasteful.
سَقى	to give to drink; to water, irrigate, supply with water.
سَقى المَعْدِنَ	to temper.
سَقّاء	water carrier.
سَقّاطَة	latch, catch, pawl, ratchet.
سِقالَة	scaffold.
سَقام	illness, sickness; thinness; infirmity.
سَقَط	to fall down, drop, tumble, trip, slip, stumble upon, come across; to find, get, come, reach; to decline, sink.
سَقَطَ في الامتحان	to fail, flunk.
سَقَطَ حُكْمُهُ	to cease to be valid, to become null and void.
سَقَطَ رأسُهُ	was born in.
سَقَطَ من عَيْنِهِ	to drop in someone's estimation.
سَقَطَ في يَدِهِ	to stand aghast, be at a loss, be bewildered.

سَقَط	offal, trash, junk, rubbish; mistake, fault.
سَقْطَة	fall, tumble; slip; lapse; fault, error, mistake.
سَقْف	ceiling, roof.
سَقْفُ الحَلْق	palate (of the mouth).
سَقُمَ، سَقِمَ	to be sick, ill, ailing.
سَقَم، سُقْم	illness, sickness, disease; infirmity.
سُقُوط	fall, tumble, lapse; decline, downfall.
سُقُوطُ الحق	extinction, abatement.
سُقُوطُ الشَّعْر	loss of hair.
سَقْي	irigation, watering.
سَقْيُ المَعْدِن	tempering.
سَقيفَة	shed, roofed portico, awning.
سَقيم	sick, ill, ailing, unhealthy; poor, weak.
سَكَّ	to mint (money); to lock (door).
سَكّ	mintage (money); coining, coinage, monetization.
سِكافَة	shoemaking, shoerepairing.
سَكاكِر	candy, confectionery.
سُكّان	rudder, helm (of a ship).
سَكَبَ	to pour out, spill, shed.
سَكَتَ	to be silent, say nothing; to lapse into silence; to calm down, be quiet, subside, pass over in silence, hush up.
سَكَّتَ	to silence, calm down, soothe, pacify; to order to be silent; to hush up.

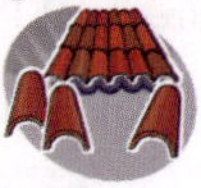

سِكَّة	road, lane; plowshare; die.
سِكَّةُ الحديد	railway.
سَكْتَةٌ قَلْبِيَّة	heart failure (med.).
سَكْتَةٌ دِماغيَّة	apoplexy, stroke (med.).
سَكِرَ	to be or to get drunk, intoxicated.
سَكَّرَ	to sprinkle with sugar; to sweeten with sugar; to make someone intoxicated, drunk, inebriated; to close, shut, lock, bolt.
سُكَّر	sugar.

أضيف القليل من السكر إلى
فنجان الشاي لتحلية مذاقه

I add some sugar to the tea cup in order to sweeten its taste

سُكْر	intoxication, inebriety, drunkenness.
سِكْر	sluice.
سَكْرَان	drunken, intoxicated, inebriated.
سَكْرَة	drunkenness, intoxication, inebriety.
سَكْرَةُ الموت	agony of death.
سِكْرِتير	secretary (male & female).

سِكْرِيتيرية ، سِكْرِيتارية	secretariat.
سُكَّرِيّ	sugary.
داء السُّكَّرِيّ	diabetes.
سُكَّرِيَّة	sugar bowl.
سَكَنَ	to live in, dwell, inhabit.
سَكَّنَ	to make vowelless (letter); to allocate living quarters; to settle, lodge, put up someone in.
سَكَّنَ	to calm, cool, quiet, pacify, tranquilize, soothe, appease.
سَكَن	dwelling, housing, residence, lodging.
سَكَنِيّ	residential.
سُكُوت	silence, quiet.
سُكُون	calmness, tranquility, stillness, silence.
سُكُونِيَّات	statics.
سِكِّير	drunkard, heavy drinker.
سِكِّين ، سِكِّينَة	knife.
سَكِينَة	calmness, peace, quietude.
سَلَّ	to unsheathe, draw, pull out (dagger, sword).
سُلَّ	to be affected with tuberculosis.
سُلّ ، سِلّ	tuberculosis.
سَلاَ	to forget; to console oneself; to think no more of.
سَلَّى	to entertain, distract, amuse; to alleviate, dispel worries.
سَلاَّب	plunderer, looter, robber, thief.

أ ب ت ث ج ح خ د ذ ر ز **س** ش ص ض ط ظ ع غ ف ق ك ل م ن هـ و ي

سِلاح	weapon, arms, armament.

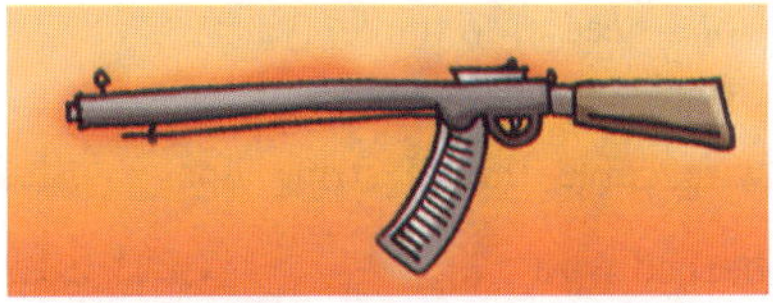

الرّشّاش سلاح يُستعمل في المعارك الحربيّة
The automatic rifle is used in war battles

سِلاحُ الجَوّ	air force.
سِلاحُ البَحْر	navy.
سِلاحُ المَدْفعيّة	artillery.
سَلاسَة	mildness, docility; obedience; smoothness.
سَلاّل	basketmaker.
سُلالَة	progeny, offspring, lineage; breed, race; family, dynasty.
سَلام	peace, safety, security; greeting, salute.
سَلامَة	safety, security, integrity, healthiness.
سلامةُ النِّيّة	good faith, sincerity, good will.
مع السَّلامَة	farewell, so long, goodbye.
سَلَبَ	to steal, plunder, rob, strip; to dispossess, deprive of.
سَلْب	spoilation, spoilage, plunder, loot, robbery, robbing, theft, stealing, rifling; negation.
سَلْبِيّ	negative, passive.
سَلْبِيّة	negativism, passivism, passivity, negative attititude.
سَلّة	basket, scuttle.
سَلّةُ المُهْمَلات	wastebasket, wastepaper basket.
سَلَحَ	to drop excrement, drop dung (birds).
سَلّحَ	to arm, equip with arms.
سَلَخَ	to skin, strip off the skin of; to detach, separate, peel off; to spend, pass (time); to end, terminate, conclude (a period of time).
سَلِسَ، سَلُسَ	to be mild, docile, flexible, obedient.
سَلَسُ البَوْل	incontinence of urine, enuresis (med.).
سَلِس	mild, docile, flexible, obedient, pliable.
سَلْسَلَ	to link together, interlink, interlock, enchain; to trace someone's lineage back to; to form a chain or series.
سِلْسِلَة	chain; series; succession, hierarchy; range (mountain); spinal column (spine); genealogy, ancestral line (family).
سَلَّطَ	to set up as absolute master over; to invest someone with authority over; to empower.
سَلَّطَ الأضْواء	to highlight, shed, throw light upon.
سُلْطان	Sultan, supreme master; power, rule, reign, domination; hegemony, influence, sway.
سُلْطانية	bowl.
سَلَطَة	salad.

سُلْطَة authority, power, rule, command; domination; influence, strength, might, sway; official agency.

السُّلْطَةُ التَّنفيذِيَّة أو الإجرائية the executive power.

السُّلْطَةُ التشريعية the legislative power.

السُّلْطَةُ الرابعة fourth estate.

السُّلْطَةُ الروحية spiritual, religious power or authority.

السُّلْطَةُ الزَّمَنِيَّة temporal power.

السُّلْطَةُ القضائية the judicial power.

سَلْطَنَة sultanate.

سِلْعَة commodity, ware, merchandise, commercial article.

سَلَفَ to be over, be past, be bygone; to precede.

سَلَّفَ to advance, lend, loan, money to.

سَلَف ancestor, forefather, ascendants; predecessor, precursor in rank, position.

سَلَفًا in advance, in anticipation.

سِلْف brother-in-law.

سُلْفَة advance, loan, advance payment.

سِلْفَة sister-in-law.

سَلَقَ to boil, cook in boiling water.

سَلَكَ to behave, act, conduct oneself; to follow, pursue, travel along a road; to take a road, enter upon a course or road; to enter a place; to stick, insert something in; to thread a needle.

سَلَّكَ to insert, stick something in; to pass thread through the eye of a needle; to unreel (yarn); to clean, clear (a pipe).

سِلْك wire, cable, thread, string, line.

سِلْكٌ شائِك barbed wire.

سِلْك cadre, body, vocation, career, profession, corps.

السِّلْكُ السِّياسِيّ أو الدِّبْلوماسِيّ diplomatic corps.

سَلِمَ to escape danger; to be safe, secure; to be sound, intact, unharmed, free from flaws, faults.

سَلَّمَ to hand over, turn over, surrender, deliver; to lay down arms; to give oneself up; to submit, resign oneself to.

سَلَّمَ to greet, salute.

سَلَّمَ to accept to; to approve of, consent to, agree to.

سَلَّمَ جَدَلاً to take for granted, concede, acknowledge as true without proof; to presume, presuppose.

سَلَم، سِلْم، سَلْم peace.

سُلَّم ladder, stairs, flight of steps.

سُلَّمُ السَّفِينة gangway, gangplank.

سُلَّمُ الطائرة ramp.

سُلَّمٌ مُتَحَرِّك أو دَوَّار escalator.

سُلَّمٌ مُوسيقِيّ musical scale.

سِلْمِيّ peaceful, pacific, amicable.

سِلْمِيًا peacefully, amicably.

سَلْوَى consolation, solace, comfort; fun, amusement, distraction, entertainment.

سُلْوَان consolation, solace, comfort; oblivion, forgetting.

سُلُوك behavior, conduct, deportment, attitude, comportment.

سُلِّيّ، سِلِّيّ tubercular.

سَلِيب stolen, taken, wrested away.

سَلِيقَة intuition, instinct, natural disposition.

سَلِيل descendant, offspring, son; unsheathed (sword).

سَلِيلَة polyp; female descendant, daughter.

سَلِيم sound, healthy, intact, unharmed, faultless, secure; whole, complete, perfect, integral.

سَلِيمُ العَقْل sane.

سَلِيمُ النِّيَّة guileless, sincere, good-natured.

سُمّ، سَمّ، سِمّ poison, toxin, venom.

سُم eye, threading hole of a needle; pore.

سَمَا to be elevated, high, raised, lofty, tall, eminent; to be too proud, too high, too difficult for someone; to exceed someone's understanding; to aspire to, aim at, yearn for.

سَمَّى to name, call, nominate, designate.

سَمَاء sky, firmament, heaven.

سَمَاجَة ugliness, odiousness, repulsiveness.

سَمَاح permission; pardon, forgiveness; magnanimity, kindness; indulgence, tolerance; sanction, legitimization.

سَمَاحَة magnanimity, generosity; indulgence, tolerance.

سَمَاحَتُهُ His Eminence.

سَمَاد fertilizer, manure.

سَمَاع hearing, listening, audition; acceptance by usage.

سَمَّاعَةُ التلفون telephone receiver.

سَمَّاعَةُ الراديو earphone, headphone.

سَمَّاعَةُ الطبيب stethoscope.

سماعِيّ acoustic, acoustical, audible; traditional, unwritten law; sanctioned by common usage.

سَمَّاك fishmonger, fisherman.

سَمَاكَة thickness; ichthyology (science of fish).

سِمَاكة pisciculture (culture of fish).

سَمَّان butter merchant, grocer.

سِمانَة grocery.

سَمَاوِيّ heavenly, celestial; sky-blue, azure (color); divine, spiritual.

سَمْت azimuth; way, road, manner, mode.

سِمَة mark, sign, characteristic, feature, trait; stamp, impress; facial expression, mien; bearing; visa; stigma; trademark.

أ ب ت ث ج ح خ د ذ ر ز **س** ش ص ض ط ظ ع غ ف ق ك ل م ن هـ و ي

سَمِج، سَمْج	ugly, uncouth, odious, boring, disgusting.
سَمَح	to allow, permit, let; to admit, sanction, license; to entitle to, authorize to, empower to; to grant generously, give liberally.
لا سَمَحَ اللّٰه	God forbid.
سَمْحُ الصَّدْر	magnanimous, generous, tolerant, lenient.
سِمْحاق	cirrostratus (clouds); periosteum (anat.).
سَمَّدَ	to fertilize, dung, manure the soil.
سَمَّرَ	to nail, fasten with a nail; to tan, brown (the skin).
سَمَر	evening chat, talk, entertainment.
سِمْسار	middleman, go-between, stockbroker, broker.
سَمْسَرَة	brokerage, commission.
سَمِعَ	to hear; to learn; to be told of; to listen; to understand, grasp, comprehend; to obey.
لم يُسْمَعْ بِهِ	unheard of.
سَمَّعَ	to recite, say one's lesson.
سَمْع	hearing, listening; sense of hearing, ear.
سَمْعًا وطاعَةً	at your service; I hear and obey.
سُمْعَة	reputation, repute, renown, fame.
سَمْعِيّ	accoustical, auditive; traditional; auditory.
سَمْعِيٌّ بَصَرِيّ	audiovisual.

سَمُكَ	to become thick.
سَمَّكَ	to thicken, make thick.
سَمَك، سَمَكَة	fish.

تعيش أنواع لا تحصى من السمك
في المياه الحلوة والمياه المالحة
Uncounted numbers of kinds of fish live in sweet and salty waters

سُمْك	thickness.
السَّمَكتان (برج)	Pisces (astronomy).
سَمْكَرَة	plumbing.
سَمْكَرِيّ	plumber, tinsmith.
سَمَلَ، سَمُلَ	to become worn, ragged, shabby (dress).
سَمَل، أَسْمال	tatters, rags.
سَمِل	tattered, worn, shabby.
سَمَّمَ	to poison.
سَمِنَ	to put on weight; to become fat, corpulent, obese, plump, fleshy.
سَمَّنَ	to fatten; to make fat, plump.
سَمْن، سَمْنَة	fat, butter, ghee, shortening.
سُمْنَة	thrush (bird).
سِمْنَة	fatness, corpulence, obesity, overweight, stoutness.
سُمُوّ	exaltedness, eminence, highness; height, altitude.
سَمِيّ	namesake.

سُمّيّ toxic, poisonous.

سُمِّيَّة toxicity.

سَميد semolina.

سَمير companion in night entertainment or chat.

سَميك thick.

سَمين fat, corpulent, obese, stout, overweight.

سَنَّ to whet, sharpen, grind.

سَنَّ القَانون to enact (a law); to make laws, legislate.

سَنّ whetting, sharpening, grinding.

سَنُّ القَوانِين enactment, legislation, law making.

سِنّ tooth; age; point, nib, tip; notch, indentation.

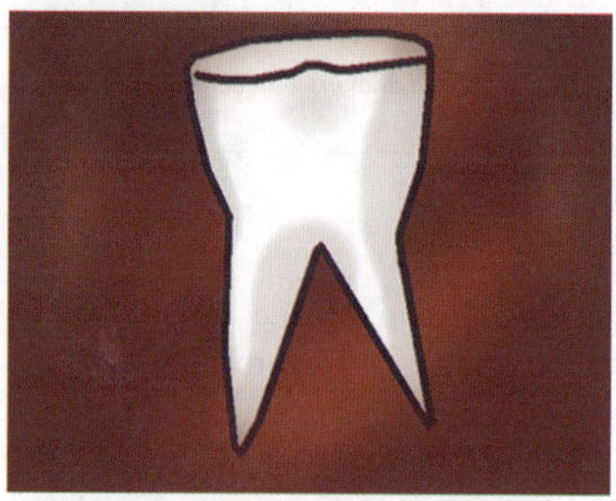

يجب تنظيف الأسنان بالفرشاة كل صباح

One should clean his teeth with the tooth brush every morning

سِنُّ التَّمْييز age of discretion.

سِنُّ العَجَلَة cog, sprocket.

سِنُّ الفيل tusk.

سِنُّ المِحْرَاث plowshare.

سِنُّ اليأس menopause.

سَنَا to flash (lightning); to shine, radiate, glisten.

سَنَاء sublimity, highness, eminence, glory; flash, glare, flare; brilliance, resplendence, splendor.

سِنَاج soot, smut.

سِنَاد support, stay, prop; backing, bracing.

سُنْباذَج emery.

سُنْبُك awl, punch, drill.

سُنْبُلَة ear, spike; Spica (astronomy).

بُرْجُ السُنْبُلَة Virgo (astrology).

سَنَة year.

سَنَةٌ دِراسِيَّة academic year, school year.

سَنَةٌ شَمْسِيَّة calendar year.

سَنَةٌ كَبيسَة leap year.

سُنَّة mode of life, norm, custom, usage, tradition.

سُنَّةُ الرسول Sunna.

سُنَّةُ الطبيعة law of nature.

سَنَح to occur to, come to someone's mind; to present itself (opportunity); to afford; to become easy, possible; to dissuade someone from his opinion; to keep away from.

سَنَدَ to support, prop oneself, rest upon; to lean, recline upon; to back, assisst, aid, help someone.

سَنَد support, prop, stay; bond, bill, debenture; deed, act, voucher, policy.

سَنَد — authority, source.

سَنَدُ خَزينة — treasury bond.

سَنَدُ شَحْن — bill of lading.

سَنَدُ مِلْكِيَّة — deed, title deed.

سَنَدٌ مَالِيّ — security, stock.

سَنْدان، سِنْدان — anvil.

سِنْدِيان، سِنْدِيانَة — oak, oak tree (tree).

سَنَّنَ — to indent, dent, notch, serrate; to whet, sharpen, grind; to clean one's teeth.

سَنَوِيّ — annual, yearly.

سَنَوِيًّا — annually, yearly, per year, per annum.

دَخْلٌ سَنَوِيّ — annuity.

سَنِيّ — sublime, exalted, eminent.

سُنِّيّ — Sunnite, Sunni.

سِنِّيّ — dental.

سَهَا — to forget, overlook, neglect; to be abstracted, inattentive; to be lost in thought.

سُهَاد — insomnia.

سَهْب، سُهُب، سُهْب — steppe.

سَهَّدَ — to make sleepless; to deprive someone of sleep.

سُهْد، سَهَد — insomnia.

سَهِرَ — to stay awake at night; to find no sleep; to stay up at night; to watch, guard, look after, attend to (someone's interests); to attend a gathering at night.

سَهْران — awake; watchful, alert, vigilant.

سَهْرَة — evening party or gathering.

سَهُلَ — to become easy; to become smooth, even.

سَهَّلَ — to facilitate, make easy; to smooth, even, level; to be indulgent, tolerant toward someone.

سَهْل (ص) — easy, simple, uncomplicated; fluent, flowing; smooth, plane, even.

سَهْل (اسم) — plain, level land.

سَهْم — arrow; share; part, lot.

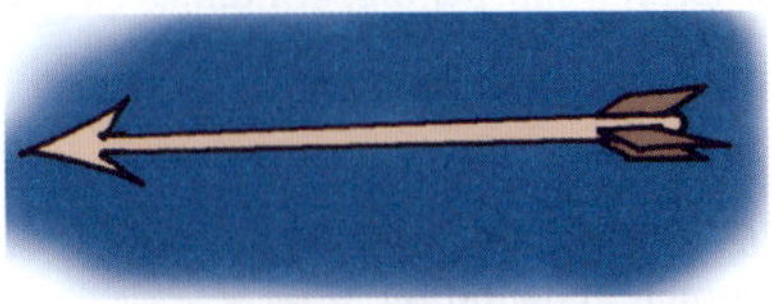

كان الأقدمون يصطادون الحيوانات بالسهام
Ancient peoples used to hunt wild animals with arrows

السَّهْمُ الأَخير — last resort.

سَهْمٌ نارِيّ — firework, rocket.

سَهْو — inadvertance, distraction, absentmindedness, oversight, negligence, forgetfulness.

سَهْوًا — inattentively, inadvertently, by mistake.

سُهُولَة — ease, easiness, facility, convenience.

سُهَيْل — Canopus (astronomy).

سَوَّى — to level off, even, roll, grade; to dress, make, prepare.

سَوَّى — to tear down, raze, pull down, level to the ground.

سَوَّى بَيْنَ to equalize, equate, treat equally; to reconcile, make peace between; bring about an agreement between.

سَوَّى to settle, pay, balance; to fix, adjust, reconcile, make up, regulate, resolve, compose; to compromise.

سُوء evil, ill, iniquity; injury, offense, calamity.

سُوءُ البَخْت، سُوءُ الحظّ misfortune, bad luck.

سُوءُ الخُلُق ill nature, ill-temperedness.

سُوءُ السُّلُوك misbehavior, misconduct.

سُوءُ المُعَامَلَة mistreatment.

سُوءُ الفَهْم misunderstanding.

سُوءُ القَصْد evil intent.

سُوءُ الهَضْم indigestion.

سُوءُ استِعْمال السُّلْطَة abuse of power.

سُوءُ التَّغْذِيَة malnutrition.

سُوءُ السُّمْعَة disrepute, notoriety.

سُوءُ الظَنّ mistrust, distrust.

سِوَى except, save, but, excluding, other than.

سَوَاء equal, equality, sameness; except; normalcy.

سَوَاءٌ بِسَوَاء equally, without distinction.

على السَّوَاء likewise, in like manner, equally.

سَوَاءُ السَّبيل the straight, right path.

سَوَاد blackness; mourning; majority, multitude.

السَّوَادُ الأَعْظَم the great majority.

سَوادُ النَّاس the masses; the common people.

سَوَّدَ to blacken; to make master, lord, chief of.

سَوَّرَ to enclose, wall in, fence in, surround with a wall.

سُوْر wall, fence, rail.

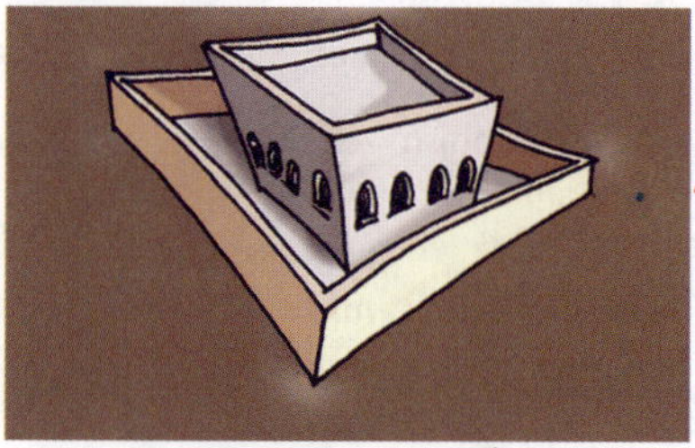

يُبنى السور حول المنزل
لحمايته من اللصوص

The wall is built around the house
to protect it from thieves

سَوْرَة vehemence, severity, intensity.

سُوْرَة Sura, chapter of the Koran.

سُوْس liquorice, licorice.

سَوْط whip, lash, scourge.

سَوَّغَ to allow, permit; to justify, warrant, vindicate.

سَوَّفَ to stall, postpone, delay, put off.

سَوْفَ will, shall.

سَوَّقَ to market, sell (commodities).

سَوْق driving, steering; transportation, conveyance.

سُوْق market, marketplace, trading center.

يضرب الفارس حصانه بالسوط ليحثّه على السرعة

The jockey hits his horse with a whip to urge it to speed up

سُوقٌ خَيرِيَّة — charity fair or bazaar.

سُوقِيّ — vulgar, mobbish.

سَوْقِيَّات — logistics.

سَوَّلَ — to entice, seduce, lure.

سَوَّلَت لَهُ نَفْسُهُ — he let himself be seduced to.

سَوِيّ — straight, intact, sound; straightshaped, even, regular, shapely; harmonious; correct, proper.

سَوِيًّا — jointly, together, in common.

سَوِيَّةً — together, in common, with each other, jointly.

سُوَيق، سُوَيْقَة — stalk, stem (of plants).

سَيِّئ — bad, evil, ill, foul, vile.

سَيِّئُ البَخْت أو الحظ — unlucky, unfortunate.

سَيِّئُ الخُلُق — ill-natured, bad-tempered, morose, surly.

سَيِّئُ السُّمْعَة — disreputable, ill-reputed.

سَيِّئُ النية — evil-minded, ill-intentioned.

سَيِّئَة — sin, offense, misdeed; bad side; evil.

سَيِّئَة — disadvantage, drawback, shortcoming.

سِيَاج — fence, hedge, railing, enclosure.

سِيَاحَة — tourism, journeying, voyaging; tour, travel, journey.

سِيَادَة — sovereignty, dominion, domination, ascendancy.

سِيَادَتُكُم — Your Excellency, Your Eminence, Your Lordship.

سِيَادَةُ القانون — rule of law, supremacy of law.

سَيَّار — mobile, moving, ambulant, itinerant, wandering, roaming.

سَيَّارَة — car, automobile.

السيارة على أنواع منها المدنيّة والعسكرية

Cars are produced in different models, for civilian and military uses

سَيَّارَةُ أُجْرَة — taxi, taxicab.

سَيَّارَةُ إسعاف — ambulance.

سَيَّارَةُ إطفاء — fire engine.

سَيَّارَةُ شحن — truck, lorry.

سَيَّارَةُ مُصَفَّحة — armored car.

سِيَاسَة — policy; administration; management.

سِيَاسَةُ البابِ المَفْتُوح open-door policy.

سِيَاسَةُ حُسْنِ الجِوَار good-neighbor policy.

سِيَاسَةٌ وَاقِعِيَّة أو عَمَلِيَّة realpolitik.

سِيَاسِيّ (ص) political.

سِيَاسِيّ (اسم) politician, statesman.

سِيَاق context, sequence, course.

سِيَّان the same, alike, similar.

سَيَّبَ to relinquish, release, let go, free; to leave, give up, neglect.

سَيَّجَ to fence in, hedge in, surround with a fence, a hedge.

سيجارَة، سيكارة cigarette.

سَيَّحَ to make flow, cause to flow.

سيخ skewer, spit.

سَيِّد master, gentleman, sir, lord; chief, chieftain; title of Prophet Mohammed's direct descendants.

سَيِّدِي sir.

سَيِّدَة lady, madam, mrs, mistress.

سَيَّرَ to make walk; to cause to walk; to drive, set in motion, direct, steer, lead; to start up, operate, run; to manage, handle, conduct; to propel, shove, impel; to send, despatch; to circulate, spread, promote.

سَيْر walking, marching, movement, motion.

سَيْر progress, course; traffic.

سَيْر strap, belt.

سَيْرًا على القَدَمَيْن on foot.

سِيْرَة conduct, deportment; line of conduct; case history; biography, life history.

سِيْرَةٌ ذَاتِيَّة autobiography.

سَيْطَرَ to dominate, command, govern, gain power over; to prevail over; to overcome, subdue, conquer, rule.

سَيْطَرَة rule, dominion, domination, supremacy, power, authority, hegemony, influence, control.

سَيْف sword, saber, foil, rapier.

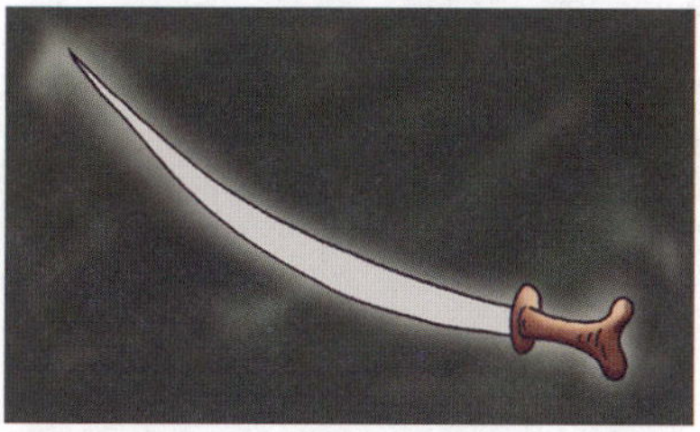

كان السياف في الماضي يقطع رأس المجرم بالسيف

The swordsman in ancient times used to severe the head of the criminal by his sword

سِيف shore, coast; shelf (of continent).

سَيْل flood, inundation, torrent, stream; deluge, hail, volley, shower.

سَيَلان flowing, running, streaming.

سَيَلان gonorrhea (med.).

سِيماء expression, aspect, mien, countenance; sign, mark.

سيناريو scenario.

سينما cinema, motion pictures, movies; movie house.

سِينَمَائِيّ cinematographic; motion picture actor.

سُيُولَة liquidity, fluidity.

شاءَ — to want, wish, desire, intend.

إن شاءَ اللّه — God willing, please God.

إلى ما شاءَ اللّه — forever, perpetually, for good.

شائِب — white-gray hair; old, aged; old man.

شائِبة — stain, spot, flaw, defect, fault; suspicion.

شائِع — widespread, current, prevalent, prevailling, universal.

الشَّائِعُ أن — it is rumored that.

شائِعة — rumor, hearsay.

شائِق — arousing, longing, stimulating desire; brilliant, splendid, beautiful, thrilling, exciting, fascinating, interesting.

شائِك — thorny, spiky, spiny, prickly; delicate, critical (matter); difficult, ticklish (question, issue).

شائِن — discreditable, scandalous, outrageous, indecent.

شابّ — youth, youngster, young man, youthful.

شابَّة — young woman, young girl.

شابَكَ — to interjoin, intertwine, interlace, interweave; to entangle, complicate; to join, unite, combine.

شابَهَ — to resemble, bear a resemblance, be similar to; to look like; to be like.

وما شَابَهَ ذلك — and the like.

شاتَمَ — to vilify one another, abuse one another.

شاجَرَ — to quarrel, fight, dispute with one another.

شاحِب — pale, wan, sallow, emaciated, lean, haggard; dim (light); dull, fade (color); lackluster.

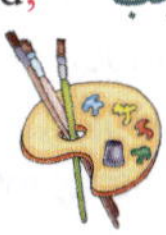

شاحَنَ to quarrel, argue, fight with someone; to hate, detest.

شاحِن shipper, forwarder, carrier; charger (battery).

شاحِنَة truck, lorry.

تنقل الشاحنة البضاعة من مكان لآخر

Trucks transport charges from one place to the other

شاخَ to grow old.

شادَ to erect, set up, construct, build.

شادٍ (الشَّادِي) singer, songster; warbler.

شادِر tent, awning.

شادِيَة songstress, warbler, singer (female).

شاذّ irregular, abnormal, anomalous, unusual; exceptional; curious, queer, odd, peculiar, eccentric; perverted.

شاذُّ الأطْوار أو الطِّبَاع extravagant, eccentric, crazy.

شواذات (ج) peculiarities, idiosyncrasies.

شارٍ (الشارِي) purchaser, buyer.

شارِب drinker; mustache.

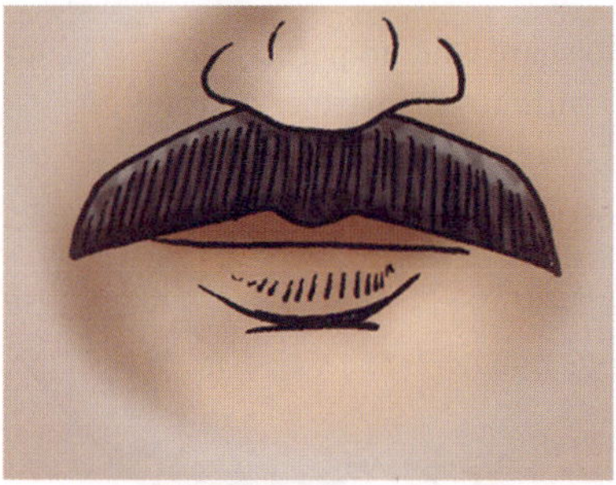

يدل نمو الشارب على بلوغ المراهق

The appearance of a mustache points to an adolescent becoming an adult

شارَة badge, emblem, sign, mark; chevron.

شارِد straying, wandering, roaming, roving; erratic; fugitive, runaway, vagrant.

شارِدُ الذِّهْن absentminded, distracted.

شارَطَ to stipulate; to specify as a condition; to contract to make.

شارع street, thoroughfare.

الشوارع الرئيسيّة في المدينة واسعة ونظيفة

The main thoroughfares in the city are wide and clean

شارَفَ to approach, come within sight; to vie in honor with.

شارَكَ to share with; to participate with; to be a partner of; to associate oneself with.

شاسِع vast, wide, great; remote, distant.

شاش gauze.

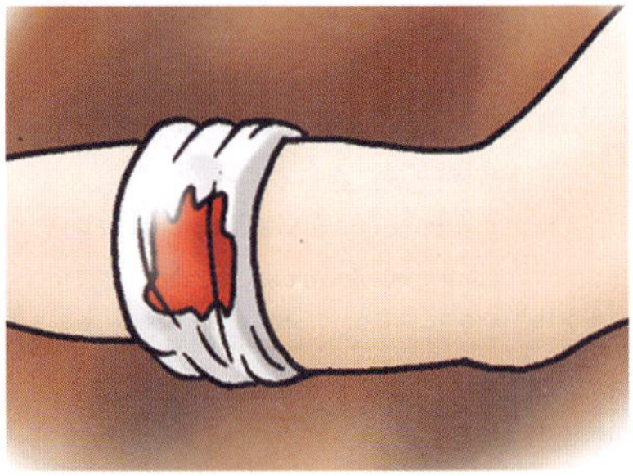

يُلفّ شريط الشاش حول الجرح النازف

A gauze strip is rolled around the bleeding wound

شاشَة screen.

شاطِئ shore, coast, beach, seashore, seaside, seaboard.

شاطَرَ to share equally with; to participate in, partake of.

شاعَ to spread; to be current, widely known, public.

شاعِر (ص) feeling, sensing, noticing, aware of.

شاعِر (اسم) poet.

شاعِريّ romantic, poetic, dreamy.

شاعِريَّة poetic talent, poetship.

شاغَبَ to disturb the peace, to make trouble; to stir up riots, cause an uproar, riot, trouble.

شاغِر (ص) unoccupied, vacant; free, empty; open.

شاغِر (اسم) vacancy.

شاغِل preoccupation; object of concern or worry; occupant, resident, dweller.

شافٍ (الشّافي) healing, remedial; conclusive, decisive; definite; satisfactory; clear.

شاقّ hard, troublesome, wearisome, tedious, arduous, onerous, difficult.

شاقُول plumb line, plummet; spirit level.

شاكِر thankful, grateful.

شاكَسَ to pick a quarrel; to quarrel with.

شاكَلَ to be similar, resemble someone; to be like someone or something; to conform to, correspond to.

شاكِلَة figure, form, shape, appearance.

شالَ to rise, lift, carry; to convey.

شال shawl, muffler.

شُؤْم evil omen, bad luck.

شامَة beauty spot, mole.

توجد على خد الفتاة شامة سوداء جميلة

A black beautiful mole is seen on this girl's face

شامِخ high, lofty, towering.

شامِخُ الأَنْف proud, arrogant, supercilious.

شامِل comprehensive, exhaustive, general, universal, total; all-inclusive, extensive, massive; sweeping.

شَأْن matter, affair, concern, issue; business, connection; condition, state, situation; importance, consequence; standing, prestige, rank.

بِشَأْن concerning, regarding, as regards, with respect of, as to, as for, in reference to, in terms of.

في هذا الشَّأْن in this respect, regarding this.

ذو شَأْن important, significant, grave, serious.

لا شَأْنَ لِي بِهِ I haven't anything to do with; it's none of my business.

شَاه king (in chess); Shah.

شَاه مَات checkmate (in chess).

شاهَدَ to see, view, watch, witness; to observe, attend.

شاهِد witness, eyewitness; evidence, proof; example, illustration; quotation, citation; tombstone.

شَاهِدُ إِثْبات witness for the prosecution.

شاهِدُ نَفْي witness for the defense.

شَاهِدُ زُور false witness.

شاهِدة tombstone; index finger; true copy, duplicate.

شاهَرَ to engage on a monthly basis; to rent by the month.

شاهِق high, towering, lofty, elevated.

شَأْو aim, goal, end.

شاوَرَ to take counsel with; to reflect, bethink oneself; to make a sign, beckon, signal, wink, blink to someone.

شاي tea.

تشتهر بلد سيلان
بإنتاج الشاي من أصناف متنوعة
Ceylon (Sri Lanka) is famous for its production of various kinds of tea

شايَعَ to follow, adopt; to conform, fall in with; to side with; to take sides for in; to make common cause with.

شَبَّ to grow up; to rise, spring, go up suddenly; to break out, flare up (fire); to prance, ramp (horse).

شَبَاب youth, the youths, the young people.

شُبَاط February.

شُبّاك window.

شُبّاكُ التَّذاكِر box office.

شَبَح ghost, specter, phantom.

شِبْر span of the hand.

شَبِعَ to eat one's fill; to be satiated, sated, satisfied.

شَبِعَ مِن to be fed up with; to be tired of, sick of.

شَبَّعَ to sate, satiate, fill someone with; to satisfy, gratify someone's desires, appetite.

شَبْع ، شَبَع satiety, satiation; saturation, repletion.

شِبْع something that fills or satisfies the appetite.

شَبْعان full, satisfied, sated.

شَبَق lewdness, lechery, lust, licentiousness.

شَبِق lewd, lecherous, lustful, licentious.

شَبَكَ to fasten, tighten, attach; to interlace, intertwine, entangle, interweave; to join, combine, unite, connect.

شَبَكَة net, network, mesh, grid, set; system; snare.

شَبَكِيَّة retina (eye).

شِبْل lion cub; cadet (in scouting, army).

شَبَّهَ to liken to, compare to, make similar to.

شُبِّهَ بـ to be doubtful, dubious, uncertain, obscure.

شَبَه resemblance, similarity, likeness; analogue, similar.

شِبْه almost, semi-, para-, quasi-, sub-,.

شِبْهُ جَزيرَة peninsula.

شِبْهُ جُمْلَة phrase.

شِبْهُ رَسْمِيّ semiofficial.

شِبْهُ قارَّة subcontinent.

شِبْهُ مُوَصِل semiconductor.

شُبْهَة suspicion, doubt; obscurity, vagueness, uncertainty.

تَحْتَ الشُّبْهَة suspicious, suspect.

فَوقَ الشُّبْهَة above suspicion.

شَبِيبَة youth, the youth.

شَبِيكَة lattice.

شَبِيه (ص) like, similar to, analogous to, identical with.

شَبِيه (اسم) twin; image, picture; double, duplicate; match, like.

شَتَّ to be scattered, dispersed, dissolved; to disperse, scatter.

شَتَّى various, diverse, sundry, manifold, miscellaneous.

شَتَّى ما بينهما what a difference between the two of them.

شِتاء winter, winter time.

شَتَّتَ to disperse, scatter, break up, disband.

شَتَرَ to cut off, tear off, rip off; to tear up.

شَتَلَ to plant, transplant.

شَتْلَة transplant, sapling.

شَتَمَ to abuse, revile, vilify; to scold, curse.

شَتْم cursing, revilement; vilification, abuse.

شَتيمَة abuse, vilification, vituperation, insult.

شَجَّ to fracture, split, cleave (skull).

شَجًا grief, sorrow.

شَجًا anxiety, worry.

شَجًا affection, emotion.

شِجار quarrel, fight, dispute, argument, squabble, fray.

شُجاع courageous, brave, valiant, bold, fearless, intrepid.

شَجاعَة courage, bravery, boldness, intrepidity, fearlessness.

شَجَبَ to condemn morally; to criticize sharply; to denounce.

شَجَب grief, sorrow, distress.

شَجْب condemnation, censure, criticism, denunciation.

شَجَّرَ to afforest; to plant with trees.

شَجَرَة، شَجَر tree, trees; shrub, shrubs.

تعيش الشجرة في كل مكان تصل إليه الرطوبة

The tree lives in everyplace that moisture reaches

شَجَرَةُ العائِلَة genealogical tree, family tree.

شَجَّعَ to encourage, support, foster, embolden, hearten.

شَجَن anxiety, worry, sorrow, sadness; branch; twig (of tree).

شَجِيَ to be worried, troubled, sad, distressed, anxious.

شَجِيّ sad, grieved, worried, anxious; apprehensive; moving; touching, sentimental; melodious, tender, soft.

شَحَّ to be stingy, avaricious, niggardly, miserly; to become short of supply; to run out, decrease, dwindle.

شُحّ، شِحّ stinginess, miserliness, avarice; scarcity, insufficiency, shortage, lack.

شَحّاذ beggar.

شَحّاذُ العَيْن sty.

شِحاذَة beggary.

شَحَبَ، شَحُبَ، شَحِبَ to be pale, pallid, wan, sallow, emaciated; to look ill, sickly; to be haggard, lean.

شَحَذَ to whet, sharpen, grind; to beg, ask for alms.

شَحَّمَ to grease, lubricate (machinery).

شَحْم grease, fat, tallow, lard (of pig).

شَحْمَة piece of fat.

شَحْمَةُ الأُذُن earlobe.

شَحْمِيّ fatty, greasy, lipoid.

شَحَنَ to ship, transport, consign; to charge with, load with; to fill up with.

شَحْن shipping, shipment, freight, consignment, forwarding; charging, loading, filling up.

شَحْنَة ، شِحْنَة cargo, freight, load, lading; shipment, consignment; charge (elect.).

شُحُوب paleness, palor, wanness; sallowness, emaciation.

شَحِيح stingy, tight-fisted, niggardly, miserly, avaricious; short in supply; scarce, meager, sparse.

شَخَّ to urinate, micturate, piss.

شَخَرَ to snort.

شَخَصَ to rise, tower up; to ascend.

شَخَصَ بِبَصَرِهِ to stare at, gaze at, fix one's eyes on.

شَخَصَ عَن to leave, depart, go.

شَخَّصَ to diagnose; to personify, personate.

شَخْص person, individual, man, party; someone, somebody.

شَخْصٌ طبيعيّ natural person.

شَخْصٌ مَعْنَوِيّ artificial person; juristic person, body corporate.

شَخْصٌ غَيْرُ مَرْغُوبٍ فيه persona non grata.

للشَّخْصِ الواحِد per capita, for each person.

شَخْصِيّ personal, private, of one's own.

شَخْصِيًّا personally, in person.

شَخِير snorting, snort.

شَدَّ to tighten; make firm, hard, strong, brace; to strengthen, pull taut; to tight; to fasten, bind, tie, lash; to drag, tug.

شَدَّ أَزْرَه to support, back up, help, strengthen.

شَدَّ الرِّحَال to pack up, set off, start out; to leave, depart.

شَدّ tightening, drawing tight; tying, binding; dragging, tugging, pulling, hauling.

شَدُّ الحبْل tug-of-war (game).

شَدا to sing, warble, chant.

شَدَّة pull, draw, drag, tug; accent; stress, emphasis.

شِدَّة strength, forcefulness, vehemence, intensity; distress, misfortune, calamity, misery, hardship; affliction.

شَدَّدَ to stress; to put emphasis on a word; to emphasize; to press upon, exert pressure on; to insist on; to highlight, underline; to oppress, harass, restrain, restrict; to accentuate, accent; to intensify, double, geminate a consonant (grammar); to demand emphatically.

شِدْق corner of the mouth; mandible, lower jaw, jawbone.

شَدْو singing, warbling.

شَدِيد strong, powerful, severe; rigorous, hard, intense; violent, acute, grave, serious; extreme, difficult, bad.

شَذَّ to segregate, isolate, separate oneself from; to be isolated, separated from; to elude, be irregular, deviate; to be an exception; to be abnormal, odd, queer, bizarre.

شَذا fragrance, scent, perfume.

شَذَبَ، شَذَّبَ to trim, prune, pare; to refine, polish.

شُذُوذ irregularity, deviation, anomaly, exception; eccentricity, queerness, oddness, strangeness; perversion.

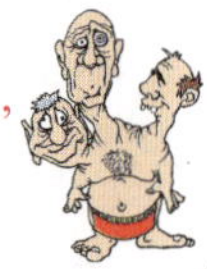

شُذُوذٌ جِنْسِيّ sexual perversion.

شَرّ evil, badness, wickedness, ill, mischief, calamity, disaster, iniquity, injustice; harm, damage, injury; viciousness, malice, vice, sin.

شِراء، شِرَى buying, purchasing.

شَراب drink, beverage, juice, sherbet.

شَرابٌ مُسْكِر alcoholic drink.

شَرابُ التُّفّاح cider, apple juice.

شُرّابَة tassel, tuft.

شَرارَة spark.

شَراسَة wickedness, malice, viciousness, meanness, villainy; ferocity, savagery, fierceness.

شِراع sail.

شَراكَة partnership, participation, collaboration.

شَراهَة gluttony, ravenousness, voracity, greediness, covetousness, avidity.

شَرِبَ to drink, sip.

شَرِبَ السِّيجارة to smoke.

شَرِبَ نَخْبَهُ to toast, drink to someone's health.

تعتمد المراكب الشراعية في مسيرها على أشرعتها

Saiboats rely on their sails for crossing the seas

شَرَّبَ to drench, soak, saturate, impregnate with; to inculcate, imbue with.

شُرْب، شَرْب، شِرْب drinking.

شَرْبَة، شُرْبَة drink; dose, potion.

شَرَج، شَرْج anus; loop, ring, eyelet.

شَرْجِيّ، شَرَجِيّ anal.

شَرَحَ to explain, expound, elucidate, illustrate, describe, comment on, interpret, present, expose, set forth.

شَرَحَ صَدْرَهُ to gladden, delight someone.

شَرَّحَ to cut in slices, cut up, rip open; to dissect, dismember, anatomize.

شَرَّحَ الجُثَّة to autopsy.

شَرْح explanation, exposition, description; commentary, annotation, setting forth.

شَرْخ prime of youth, heyday.

شَرَدَ to bolt, start, run away, flee, escape, break lose; to go astray, wander, roam.

شَرَدَ ذِهْنُهُ to be absentminded.

شَرَدَ به الفِكرُ to be lost in thought.

شَرِس quarrelsome, vicious, aggressive, mischievous, belligerent, wild, fierce, peevish, ferocious.

شَرْشَفُ السَّرير bedsheet, bedspread, bedcover.

شَرْشَفُ المائِدة tablecloth.

شَرَطَ، شَرَّطَ to slash, slit open, cut, scratch, scarify.

شَرَطَ to impose as a condition; to stipulate, make conditional.

شَرْط precondition, condition, clause, stipulation.

شَرْط incision, long cut, slash, slit in the skin.

شَرْطَ أن provided that, as long as.

بدون شَرْط unconditional.

بلا قيدٍ أو شَرْط unconditional, with no strings attached.

شَرْطَة dash, hyphen (grammar).

شُرْطَة police, policemen.

شُرْطَةُ الآداب vice squad.

شُرْطَةُ المرور traffic police.

شُرْطِيّ conditional.

شُرْطِيّ policeman.

شَرَعَ to begin, start, set to; to attempt; to point, aim.

شَرَّعَ to make laws, enact laws, prescrible, give laws.

شَرْع law.

الشَّرْع the canonical law of Islam.

شِرْعَة law, bill, statute, charter.

شَرْعِيّ legitimate, legal, lawful, rightful; fair, just, licit.

الطِبُّ الشَّرْعِيّ forensic medicine.

المَحْكَمَةُ الشَّرْعِيَّة religious court.

غيرُ شَرْعِيّ illegitimate, illegal, illicit, unlawful.

شَرْعِيَّة legitimacy, legality, lawfulness; rightfulness, validity.

شَرَّفَ to honor, confer honor upon; to ennoble, dignify, exalt, raise to distinction, honor.

شَرَف honor, dignity, nobility; honesty, integrity.

على شَرَفِ فُلان in honor of.

شُرْفَة balcony, veranda, terrace.

شَرَقَ to rise (sun); to shine; to choke; to have a fit of choking.

شَرْق east.

الشَّرق the Orient, the East.

الشَّرقُ الأَدْنَى the Near East.

الشَّرقُ الأَوْسَط the Middle East.

الشَّرقُ الأَقْصَى the Far East.

شَرْقًا eastward.

شَرْقِيّ (ص) eastern, oriental, easterly.

شَرْقِيّ (اسم) Oriental, Levantine, Easterner.

شَرَك trap, snare, net.

شَرِكَة، شِرْكَة company, partnership, association, corporation, commercial enterprise, firm, establishment, business.

شَرِكَةٌ تَابِعَة subsidiary company.

شَرِكَةُ تَضامُن joint-liability company, partnership.

شَرِكَةُ تَوْصِيَة limited partnership.

شَرِكَةٌ فَرْعِيَّة affiliate company.

شَرِكَةٌ قابِضَة holding company.

شَرِكَةٌ مَحْدُودَة limited liability company.

شَرِكَةٌ مُساهِمَة، شَرِكَةٌ مُغْفَلَة joint-stock company.

شَرَمَ to spilt, slit, slash, rip.

شَرْم cleavage, ripping, slitting, slashing; cleft, crack, rip, slit; bay, gulf, inlet.

شَرْنَقَة cocoon.

شَرَه gluttony, voracity, greed, avidity, covetousness.

شَرِه gluttonous, greedy, voracious, ravenous, covetous.

شُرُود straying, wandering, roaming; fleeing, escape.

شُرُودُ الفِكر absentmindedness, distraction, distractedness.

شُرُوع beginning, starting; attempt, plan, try.

شُرُوعٌ فِي سَرِقَة attempted theft.

شُرُوق sunrise.

شَرْيَان، شِرْيان artery.

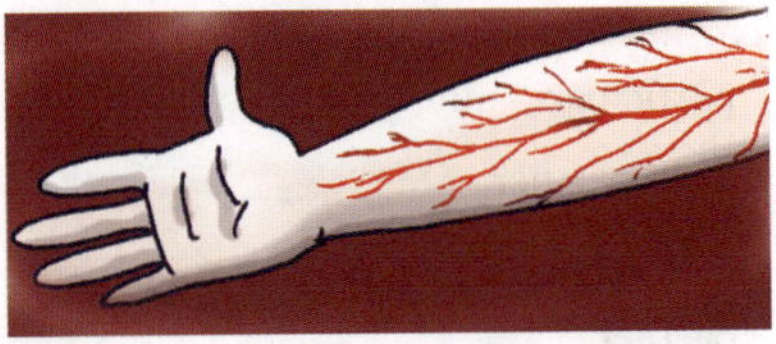

ينقل الشريان الدم من القلب إلى بقية أعضاء الجسم
Arteries carry blood from the heart to all the other members of the body

شَرْيانيّ، شِرْيانيّ arterial.

شَرِيحَة slice, rasher, girth; slide; section.

شِرِّير، شَرِّير vicious, very wicked, scoundrel, very malicious, rascal, villain, evildoer, sinner, wrongdoer.

شَرِيط tape, band, ribbon; string; strap, stripe; line, wire.

شَرِيطُ تَسْجيل magnetic tape.

شَرِيطُ الحِذاء shoelace, shoestring.

شَرِيطُ فيديو videotape.

شَرِيطٌ لاصِق adhesive tape.

شَرِيطٌ وثائقيّ documentary.

على شَرِيطَة on the condition that.

شَرِيعَة law, code.

شَرِيعةُ الغاب law of the jungle.

شَرِيعةٌ إسلامية Islamic law, Sharia.

شَرِيعةٌ كَنَسِيَّة canon law, ecclesiatical law.

شَرِيف noble, highborn, peer, honorable; honest, upright.

شريف — sharif, sherif (title of the descendants of Prophet Mohammed).

شَريك — partner, associate; accomplice, participant; ally.

شريكٌ مُفَوَّض — acting partner.

شريكٌ مُوْصٍ — silent partner, sleeping partner.

شطَّ — to deviate from, disgress, stray from (the topic); to go too far; to exceed the proper limits, bounds.

شَطَارَة — slyness, cunningness, shrewdness, adroitness, cleverness.

شَطَبَ — to scratch, slash, cut; to strike off, cross out, cancel; to erase, efface (a word); to finish off, terminate (work).

شَطْب — slash, cut, slit; striking out, crossing out, writing off; cancellation; effacement; cancelling; termination, completion.

شَطَرَ — to bisect, divide into two halves; to cut through, cut off; to separate from, withdraw from.

شَطْر — dividing in two halves; cutting, severance; bisecting, halving, partitioning.

شَطْر — portion, half, share, lot; hemistich (of a verse of poetry).

شَطْرَ — direction, toward.

شِطْرَنج — chess.

شَطَط — excess, exceeding the bounds, transgression, inroad.

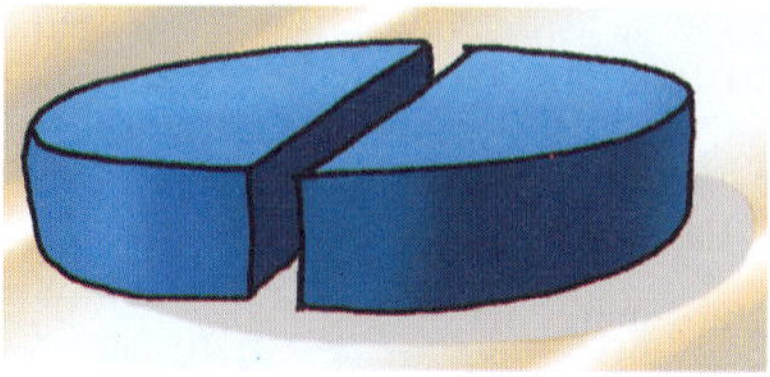

شطرت قطعة الجبن إلى نصفين أعطيت نفصها إلى شقيقتي

I cut the piece of cheese in two halves and I gave one to my sister

شَطَفَ — to rinse, wash with water.

شَظَف — hardship, difficulty, discomfort; ruggedness of life.

شَظِف — hard, difficult, harsh; austere (life).

شَظِيَّة — splinter, chip, fragment, shrapnel; bone, fibula.

شَعَّ — to scatter, diffuse, spread; to radiate, flash up.

شَعائِريّ — ceremonial, ritual.

شِعار — slogan, password, motto, emblem, logo, badge, mark.

شُعَاع — ray, beam.

شُعَاع — radius; spoke (of a wheel).

شَعْب — people, nation.

شُعْبَة — branch, offshoot; section, division, department; bough, ramification; twig; field of study; part, portion.

شَعْبِيّ — popular, public, folk.

شُعَبِيّ — bronchial.

شَعْبِيَّة — popularity.

شَعِثَ — to become disheveled, unkempt, matted (hair).

أ ب ت ث ج ح خ د ذ ر ز س ش ص ض ط ظ ع غ ف ق ك ل م ن هـ و ي

شَعِث	matted, disheveled, unkempt (hair).
شَعَرَ	to feel, sense, realize, notice; to be aware of, conscious of, cognizant of; to percieve; to poetize, compose poetry.
شَعَرَ مَع	to be filled with a feeling toward; to sympathize with.
شَعْر	hair, bristle.
شَعْرٌ مُسْتَعار	wig, toupee.
شِعْر	poetry, verse.
شِعْرٌ حُرّ	free verse.
شِعْرٌ غِنائِيّ	lyric poetry.
بيتُ شِعْر	verse, line of poetry.
شَعْرَة	a hair.
شَعْرِيّ	hairy, capillary.
شِعْرِيّ	poetic.
شَعْرِيَّة	lattice work, wire grill, wire netting; window shade.
شِعْرِيَّة	vermicelli.
شَعْشَعَ	to radiate, shine; to attenuate, water down; to dilute, mix with water.
شُعْلَة	torch, flame.
شَعْوَاء	violent, fierce, large-scale (war, campaign).
شَعْوَذَة	jugglery, sleigh of hand, conjuration, sorcery, quackery, charlatanism.
شُعُور	feeling, sensation, awareness; sentiment, affection, emotion, presentiment, intuition.
شَعير	barley (plant).

يجمع الحصّاد سنابل الشعير في حزمات ويربطها
The harvester collects the spikes of barley in bundles and bind them

شعيرَة	rite, ritual, religious ceremony.
شَغَّال (ص)	very busy, industrious, laborious, active, in operation.
شَغَّال (اسم)	worker, laborer.
شَغَبَ، شَغِبَ	to disturb the peace, stir up trouble; to cause an uproar; to provoke dissension.
شَغْب	riot, trouble, uproar, strife; tumult.
شَغَرَ	to be vacant, unoccupied, empty.
شُغِفَ بِـ	to love, adore, be madly in love with; to be infatuated, passionately fond of.
شَغَف	passionate, love, passion infatuation, craze, love.
شَغِف	madly in love, infatuated, enamored of, fascinated by.
شَغَلَ	to occupy, make busy, take up, engage, fill up; to hold a position, seat.

شُغِلَ بـ to be distracted by; to occupy oneself with; to work at, attend to.

شَغَّلَ to employ, engage, provide employment for; to put to work, make work, put in operation, make run, make start (a machine); to operate, work, run (a machine).

شُغْل work, vocation, profession, career, employment.

شُغْلٌ يَدَوِيّ handwork, handicraft, handcraft, manual work.

شُغُور vacancy.

الشَّغِّيلَة the proletariat.

شَفَى to cure, heal, restore to health.

شَفَى غَلِيلَهُ to quench one's thirst, gratify one's desire; to satisfy one's thirst for revenge.

شَفَا edge, border, rim, verge, brink.

شِفَاء recovery, healing, recuperation, convalescence; cure, remedy, medicine, medicament.

شَفَاعَة intercession, mediation.

شَفَّاف transparent, disphanous, flimsy, thin.

شَفَّافِيَّة transparency, thinness, transluscence.

شَفَة lip; rim, edge; flange; fringe.

شَفْر edge, rim, border; fringe; outer edge of the eyelid; labium (anat.).

شَفْرَة blade; large knife; razor blade; brink, edge.

شِفْرَة، شيفرَة cipher, code.

شَفَعَ to mediate, intercede, plead on behalf of someone; to double; to attach; join; to enclose something; to give someone the right of preemption to.

شَفْعِيّ even (number).

شَفَق twilight, dusk, evening glow; fear, fright; compassion, commiseration, pity, sympathy.

شَفَّقَ to arouse pity, fill with mercy; to move, touch someone's heart.

شَفَقَة pity, commiseration, sympathy, kindness, loving care.

شَفَهِيّ oral, spoken, verbal; labial.

شَفَهِيًّا orally, verbally, by word of mouth.

شَفُوق، شَفِيق compassionate, sympathetic, affectionate, kind.

شَفِير edge of the eyelid; edge, rim; border; fringe.

على شَفِيرِ الهَاوِيَة on the brink of the abyss.

شَفِيع mediator, intercessor; preemptor; patron saint.

شَقَّ to split, cleave, tear, rip; to plow, till the soil; to furrow, traverse, cross something; to pass, travel through a land.

شَقَّ طريقَهُ to force one's way; to hustle, thrust, pass through; to advance, progress.

شَقَّ عَصَا الطَّاعة to rebel, revolt; to renounce allegiance.

شَقَّ عليه الأمْر to become hard for him; to become unbearable for him; to be difficult for him.

شَقّ fissure, crack, cleft, split, slit, slot, rent, gap.

شِقّ half, side, part, section.

بِشِقّ النفس with great difficulty, hardly, scarecely.

شَقَاء unhappiness, misery, distress, suffering, trouble, toil, pain, drudgery.

شِقَاق dissension, disunity, discord, schism.

شَقْلَبَة sommersault, upturning, capsizing (vessel).

شَقِيَ to be unhappy, wretched.

شَقِيّ (ص) unhappy, wretched, unlucky; miserable.

شَقِيّ (اسم) rascal, rogue, villain, scoundrel, criminal, outlaw.

شَقِيق brother.

شَقِيقَة sister.

شَكَّ to pierce with; impale something on; to prick, stab; to doubt, distrust, suspect, question; to entertain doubts, have misgivings about; to stitch, sew; to baste, tack (a dress).

شَكّ doubt, suspicion, distrust, mistrust.

بلا شَكّ، لا شَكَّ undoubtedly, doubtless, no doubt.

شَكا، شَكَى to complain, grumble, express discontent; to suffer from.

شِكَايَة complaint; suffering; grievance.

شَكَرَ to thank, show gratitude; to be thankful, grateful to; to praise, laud, extol someone.

شُكْر، شُكْرَان thanks, gratitude, gratefulness; praise, laudation; acknowledgement, appreciation.

شَكَّكَ to doubt, have doubts; to be skeptical, have misgivings.

شَكَلَ to hobble (an animal with a shackle); to vowel, provide with vowel points (a text); to be dubious, ambiguous.

شَكَّلَ to form, shape, fashion; to create, mold, organize, build up; to diversify, vary, variegate; to vowelize, furnish with vowel points (a text); to braid, plait (hair).

شَكْل form, figure, build; resemblance, similarity, likeness; outward appearance; type, pattern, manner, fashion, style; vowel point, vowel.

شَكلاً in form, formally.

شَكْلِيّ formal, nominal.

شَكْلِيَّات (ج) formalities.

شَكْوَى complaint, protest, claim, grievance, suffering.

شُكوكِيَّة skepticism.

شَكِيمَة bit, snaffle, curb; brake of a wheel.

شَكِيمَة unruliness; contempt; obstinacy; disdain.

قَوِيُّ الشَّكِيمَة vigorous, energetic, active.

شَلَّ to paralize, cripple, immobilize; to overcome, overwhelm.

شُلَّ to become crippled, stunted, paralyzed, lame.

شَلاَّل waterfall, falls, cataract.

منظر الشلال من أجمل مناظر الطبيعة
The view of the waterfall is one of the most beautiful natural landscapes

شَلَل paralysis, palsy (med.).

شَلَلُ الأَطْفَال poliomyelitis, polio (med.).

شَمَّ to smell, sniff, snuff.

شَمَّ to behave haughtily; to be proud, supercilious.

شَمّ smelling, smell.

حاسَّةُ الشَّمّ sense of smell.

شَمَاتَة malicious joy, malice; gloating over someone's grief.

شَمَّاس deacon.

شَمَّاع chandler, maker of candles.

شَمال north; north wind.

شِمال left; left side, left hand.

شَمالِيّ northern, northerner.

شَمِتَ بِـ to rejoice, gloat over someone's grief, misfortune.

شَمَخَ to tower; to be high, tall, lofty; to loom.

شَمَخَ to be arrogant, proud, supercilious, haughty.

شَمَّرَ to gather up, lift, roll up, tuck up (a garment); to prepare oneself; get ready to do something; to apply oneself to, get to work, embark upon, set out to.

شَمَّسَ to expose to the sun's rays.

شَمْس sun.

تنير الشمس الأرض وتبعث الحياة في جميع الأحياء والمخلوقات
The sun lights the earth and instill life in all human beings and creatures

شَمْسِيّ solar.

النِّظامُ الشَّمْسِيّ solar system.

شَمْسِيَّة umbrella, sunshade.

شَمَّعَ to wax, treat with wax.

شَمْع wax.

شَمْعُ الخَتْم sealing wax.

شَمْعُ العَسَل beeswax.

شَمْعَة candle.

شَمْعةُ الإشْعَال spark plug.

شَمْعَدان candelabra, candel holder.

تضيء الشمعة الحجرة بقدر ضئيل لضعف قوتها

The candle lights slightly the room in view of its feeble power

شَمَلَ، شَمِلَ to include, contain, comprise, comprehend, enclose; to prevail in, spread over; to be universal.

شَمْل union, unity; uniting. gathering.

جَمْعُ الشَّمْل reunification.

شَمَم pride, haughtiness, disdain, self-esteem; height, altitude, loftiness.

شُمُوخ pride, haughtiness, arrogance; height, loftiness.

شُمُول inclusion, comprehension; comprehensiveness, universality, fullness, completeness, containment, embracement, encompassment.

شَمِيلة merit, character, trait, good quality.

شَنَّ to make a raid, attack; to launch an attack against; to wage war; to fight.

شَنَار disgrace, dishonor, infamy, ignominy.

شَنَاعَة ugliness; atrocity; outrage; repulsiveness.

شَنَّجَ to contract; shrink.

شَنَّرَ to disgrace, criticize harshly, blame.

شَنَّعَ to vituperate, revile, slander, defame.

شَنِع، شَنيع ugly, unsightly; repugnant; hideous, disgusting; atrocious, outrageous.

شَنَّفَ to delight the ears.

شَنَقَ to hang, execute by hanging.

شَنْق hanging.

شَهَّى to whet, stimulate the appetite (food); to arouse one's desire for.

شِهَاب meteor, shooting star.

الشهاب هو جسم مضيء نراه في بعض الليالي

A meteor is a shining body which we can see in certain nights

شَهَادَة testimony, evidence, attestation, affidavit; certificate, degree, diploma (of studies).

شَهَادَةُ أَسْهُم stock certificate, share certificate, scrip.

شَهَادَةُ حُسْنِ سُلُوك certificate of good conduct.

شَهَادَةُ زور perjury.

شَهَادَةُ منشأ certificate of origin.

شِهادَة martyrdom.

شَهَامَة perspicacity, astuteness; audacity; gallantry; vigor, verve, decency; boldness; chivalry, magnimity.

شَهِدَ to witness; to be witness of; to experience personally; to see with one's own eyes; to be present at; to attend, see.

شَهِدَ to testify, bear witness; confirm, certify; to give evidence, give testimony to or about something.

شَهَّدَ to acknowledge, adjudge, sign as a witness (on a document).

شَهْد، شُهْد honey.

شَهَرَ to make well-known, notorious, famous; to spread, divulge, proclaim, advertize, announce; to unsheathe a weapon; to declare war on; to level a gun at.

شَهَّرَ to defame, slander, revile publicly.

شَهْر month; announcement, proclamation.

شَهْرُ العَسَل honeymoon.

شُهْرَة fame, repute, reputation; good will (of an establishment); surname, family name (of a person).

شَهْرِيّ monthly, every month, per month.

شَهْرِيَّة monthly salary, wages; monthly publication.

شَهَقَ to bray (donkey); to inhale, sign deeply; to sob, gulp, to moan, groan; to burst into tears.

شَهْقَة whoop, moan, groan; gulping.

شَهْم sagacious, gallant, gentleman; astute, clever.

شَهْوَانِيّ lustful, covetous, lecherous, dissolute, debauched; sensual, sensuous, lascivious.

شَهْوَة appetite, craving, yearning, desire; carnal appetite, lust, passion.

شَهِيّ appetizing, appealing to the appetite, delicious; pleasant; inviting; tasty.

شَهِيَّة appetite.

شَهِيد martyr.

شَهِير widely known, famous, renowned; notorious, ill-reputed.

شَهِيق inspiration, inhalation; sob; braying (of donkey).

شَوَى to grill, roast (meat).

شِوَاء، شُوَاء grill, roast, roasted meat.

شَوَّرَ to make a sign, beckon, signal, wink to someone.

شَوْرَى consultation, deliberation, counsel, advice.

مَجْلِسُ الشَّوْرَى state council.

شَوْرَبا، شَوْرَبَة soup.

شَوْرِيّ consultative, advisory.

شَوَّش to muddle, confuse, confound; to disturb, complicate; to perturb, distrupt, mix up; to throw into disorder; to jam.

شَوْط round, game, half, course (in sports); stroke (mechanics).

شَوَّق to fill with longing, craving, desire; to arouse craving, desire, longing in someone; to excite, interest.

شَوْق longing, desire, craving, wish, nostalgia.

شَوْك thorns, spines; fishbones.

شَوْكَة thorn, spine; fork; tuning fork; spur.

شَوْكَة power, might, strength, prowess, valor, dash, verve.

شُوكولاتَة chocolate.

شَوْكِيّ thorny, prickly; spiny, spinal, vertebral.

شَوْلَة comma(,).

شَوْلَةٌ مَنْقُوطَة semicolon(;).

شَوَّه to deform, deface, disfigure, distort; to mar, mutilate, deface; to revile, slander (someone); to sully, tarnish, stain, discredit (someone's reputation).

شَيْء thing, object.

شَيْءٌ ما something.

شَيْءٌ من some, a little of.

شَيْئًا فَشَيْئًا bit by bit, gradually, by steps.

لا شيء nothing.

بعضُ الشَّيْء to a certain extent, somewhat, a little.

شَيَّال porter, carrier.

شَيْخ old man, aged; sheikh, chieftain, head of a tribe; senator; religious man; title of rulers in certain countries.

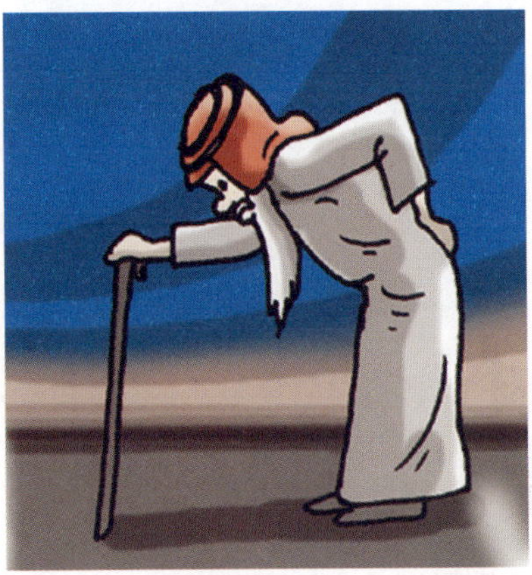

يستند الشيخ على عكاز كي لا يقع أثناء سيره
The old man leans on a walking stick in order not to fall when walking

شَيْخوخَة old age, senility.

شَيْخوخِيّ senile, geriatric.

شَيَّد to build, erect, construct.

شيش saber, epee; skewer, spit.

لُعْبَةُ الشيش fencing.

أ ب ت ث ج ح خ د ذ ر ز س **ش** ص ض ط ظ ع غ ف ق ك ل م ن هـ و ي

شَيْطان، الشَّيْطان devil, demon; the Devil, Lucifer, Satan.

شَيْطانِيّ devilish, satanic, diabolic; hellish, demoniac, infernal; fiendish.

شَيْطَنَة devilry, mischief, villainy; dirty trick.

شَيَّعَ to bid farewell to; to accompany, escort the dead to his final resting place.

شَيعَة sect, faction, denomination; followers, adherents, partisans.

الشِّيعَة the Shiites, the Shiah, Shiism.

شيعِيّ Shiite.

شَيْفَرَة cipher, code.

شِيك check (bank).

شِيك سِياحِيّ traveler's check.

شِيمَة habit, nature, natural disposition, trait, attribute; temper; custom, practice.

شُيُوع spreading, currency; joint ownership, in common.

شُيُوعِيّ communist.

شُيوعِيَّة communism.

صائِب — right, faultless; sound, correct, pertinent.

صائِت — vocal, sonic, acoustic.

صائِغ — goldsmith.

صائِم — faster.

صائِن — preserver, keeper; guardian; protector.

صابِر — patient, enduring; steadfast.

صابورَة — ballast.

صابون، صابونَة — soap, cake of soap.

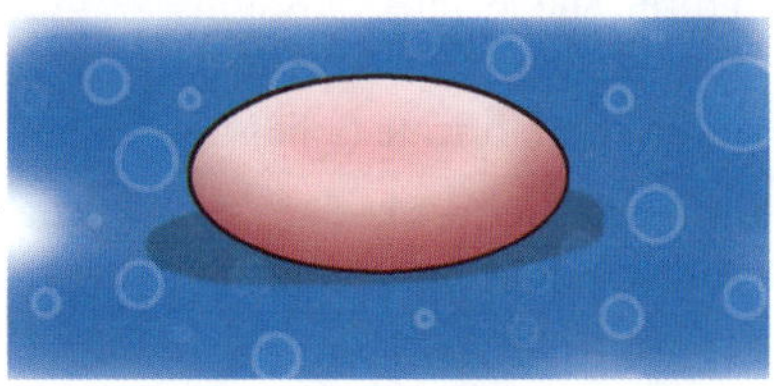

أغسل جسمي وثيابي بقطعة صابون معطرة
I clean my body and clothes with a perfumed cake of soap

صابونِيّ — soapy, soaplike.

صاحَ — to cry, shout, yell, scream, screech; to utter, let out a cry; to bellow, bellow at, call out to.

صاحٍ، (الصَّاحِي) — clear, cloudless, sunny (weather; day); awake, wakeful; watchful, alert; sober.

صاحَبَ — to be a companion, comrade, friend of someone; to accompany, escort, keep company.

صاحِب — companion, comrade, friend, fellow.

صاحِب — owner, possessor, holder, proprietor; author, originator (of an idea); master, overlord, head, chief (of a country, a company).

صاحِبُ الامْتِيَاز — concessionaire, owner.

صاحِبُ الجَلالَة — His Majesty.

صاحِبُ الدَّعْوَة host, inviter.

صاحِبُ السَّعادَة His Excellency, His Honor.

صاحِبُ السُّمُوِّ المَلَكِيّ His Royal Highness.

صاحِبُ الشأن person concerned, involved, interested.

صاحِبُ الغِبْطَة His Beatitude.

صاحِبُ القَداسَة His Holiness.

صاخِب noisy, loud, tumultuous, riotous, raging.

صادَ to hunt, fish, catch; to entrap, ensnare.

صادَ بِصِنّارَة to angle, hook.

صادِح singer, chanter; warbling, singing.

صادَرَ to confiscate, seize, sequester, expropriate.

صادِر issued, published; pronounced, delivered, given (a court verdict); emanating, arising, stemming.

صادِرات (ج) exports.

صادَفَ to happen by chance; to come across, encounter, meet unexpectedly.

صادَفَ to fall on; to correspond to, coincide with (a given date).

صادَقَ to make friends, befriend; to hold true; to give one's consent; to consent, agree, approve, certify, sanction; to substantiate, attest, ratify.

صادِق true, truthful, honest, sincere, loyal; candid; reliable, accurate, genuine, faithful; authentic.

صارَ to become, begin, start to, come to; to occur, happen, come to pass, take place; to end, wind up with, result in.

صارٍ (الصّارِي) mast (of ship).

صارَحَ to make clear, explicate, explain, clarify; to declare, make a statement about; to speak frankly, openly, explicity about.

صارِخ flagrant, clear, blatant; outrageous, shameless; glaring, startling, screaming, sharp.

صارَعَ to wrestle with, struggle with.

صارِم severe, hard, harsh, rigorous, strict; sharp, cutting, acute.

صاروخ rocket, missile.

صاعِد rising, ascending.

مِنَ الآن فَصاعِدًا henceforth, from now on.

صاعِق (ص) astounding, stunning, shocking; sudden, unexpected; abrupt; swift, rapid.

صاعِق (اسم) detonator; flash tube; lightning rod.

صاعِقَة thunderbolt.

صاغَ to form, shape, mold, fashion, formulate; to coin (a word); to invent, fabricate (a lie).

صاغِر low, lowly, despised; contemptible; humiliated; submissive, servile.

صافٍ (الصّافي) clear, fine, pure, unadulterated; limpid, tranquil, calm; cloudless, fair, fine (weather); net.

صافي النِّيَّة well-meaning, bona fide, honest, sincere.

صافَى to be sincere toward someone; to deal honestly with; to be of pure intent toward.

صافَحَ to shake hands with.

تصافح الصديقان بحرارة عندما تقابلا
The two friends shook hands together when they met

صالَ to spring, jump, leap on; to attack, assail, assault.

صالَة hall, room, auditorium.

صالَةُ عرْض showroom.

صالَحَ to make peace with, to be reconciled with.

صالح (ص) good, right, proper, sound; virtuous, pious, devout; usable, useful, suitable, appropriate; competent, duly qualified; deserving, meritorious, eligible.

صالحٌ للأكل edible.

صالحٌ للزِّراعة arable.

صالحٌ للشُّرب potable.

صالحٌ للطيران air worthy.

صالح (اسم) advantage, benefit, interest, welfare.

صالون parlor, reception room.

صالونُ حِلاقَة barbershop.

صامَ to fast; abstain from.

يصوم المسلم طوال شهر رمضان من الصباح إلى المساء
The Moslem fasts during Ramadhan from dawn to sunset

صامِت silent, quiet, noiseless.

حرفٌ صامِت consonant.

صامِد steadfast, unfaltering; resistant; impervious to; eternal; resisting.

صامِدٌ للرَّصَاص bulletproof.

صامِدٌ للنار fireproof.

صامولَة، صَمُولَة nut of a bolt.

صانَ to preserve, conserve, protect, safeguard; to maintain, service, sustain.

صانِع maker, manufacturer, producer; author.

صاهَرَ to be related by marriage to.

صَبَّ — to pour out, pour forth; to shed; to cast in a mould; to shape, cut a key.

صَبّ — pouring out, emptying, shedding; casting, molding, forming, founding.

صَبّ — lover, adorer, infatuated with, ardently in love.

صَبَا — to yearn for, long for, desire, aspire to; to tend, incline to.

صَبًا — east wind, sirocco.

صِبًا — youth, boyhood, youthfulness; longing, craving, aspiration, nostalgia.

صَبابَة — ardent love; craving, desire, longing.

صَباح — morning.

صَباحًا — in the morning.

صَباحُ الخَيْر — good morning.

صَبَّاغ — dyer.

صِباغة — dyeing, coloring; painting.

صَبُحَ — to be pretty, beautiful, graceful, handsome; to light up, radiate, flash up, brighten.

صَبَّحَ — to come in the morning; to wish someone a good morning.

صُبْح — morning.

صَبَرَ — to be patient, take patience; to bear patiently, to endure; to withstand, persevere.

صَبَّرَ — to comfort, solace; to embalm, mummify, stuff; to make durable, preserve, conserve; to ballast (a ship).

صَبْر — patience, forbearance, composure, self-control; perseverance, endurance.

صَبِر — aloe (plant).

صَبَغَ — to dye, color, paint, daub, stain; to transform, change; to give something the air, touch of something.

صَبْغ — dyeing, coloring; painting.

صِبْغ — dye, dyestuff, color; paint; tinge, pigment.

صَبْغَة — tincture.

صَبْغَةُ اليود — tincture of iodine.

صِبْغَة — characteristic, quality, distinctive feature; stamp; color, tint; touch, shade; nature, character.

صَبَّنَ — to rub with soap; to convert into soap.

صَبُوح — radiant, bright, shiny.

صَبُور — patient, enduring, perseverant, steadfast.

صَبِيّ — boy, lad.

صِبْيانِيّ — childish, immature; silly.

صَبِيَّة — girl, maid, young girl.

صَبِيح — radiant; pretty, comely, handsome.

صَحَّ — to be healthy, in order; to recover, recuperate from; to be sound, vigorous, firm, right, correct, unshakable; to be authentic, true, certain; to come into effect; to come true, become a fact.

صَحَا to wake up, get up from slumber; to sober up from, regain consciousness, recover from; to become clear, cloudless (sky, day).

صِحَافَة، صَحَافَة journalism, the press

صِحَافِيّ، صَحَافِيّ journalist, newsman, reporter.

صَحِبَ to associate with, accompany, escort; to be a companion of.

صُحْبَة companionship, comradeship, friendship; companions, comrades, friends.

بِصُحْبَة accompanied by, with.

صِحَّة health; hygiene; truth, verity, validity, soundness; credibility; legality.

صَحَّحَ to correct, amend, rectify; to prepare a critical edition; to legalize, authenticate; to recuperate from; to sanitize; to proofread a text.

صَحْرَاء desert, wilderness.

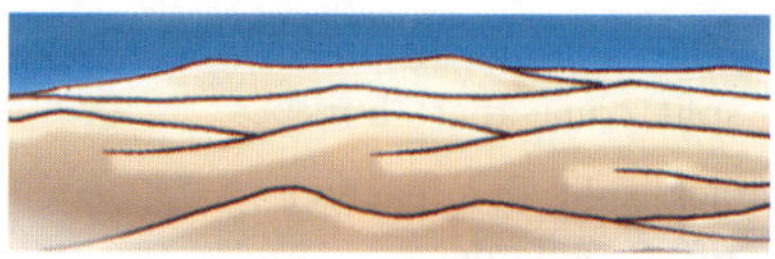

تغطي الصحراء القاحلة أجزاءً واسعة من سطح الأرض

Arid deserts cover wide expanses of the earth surface

صَحَّفَ to misread, misrepresent, corrupt, twist; to misspell, mispronounce, misplace the diacritical marks.

صُحُفِيّ journalistic; newspaperman, journalist.

صَحْن dish, plate, bowl; dish; meal; food.

صَحْنُ الدَّار courtyard, court, patio.

صَحْنُ الفِنْجَان saucer.

صَحْنُ المَسْجِد nave.

صَحْو wakefulness, waking; consiousness; cloudlessness.

صِحِّيّ healthy, healthful, hygienic; wholesome; sanitary.

صَحِيح true, veritable, real; authentic, genuine, credible; valid, legal, lawful; healthy, well, sound; complete, integral, undivided.

جَمْعٌ صَحِيح sound plural (grammar).

عَدَدٌ صَحِيح integer (math); integral number (math).

صَحِيحٌ أنه it is true that....

صَحِيفَة leaf, sheet, page; newspaper, paper, daily, journal.

صَخِبَ to shout, cry, yell, clamor, roar; to be loud.

صَخَب clamor, bellowing, shouting; roaring, raging; cry.

صَخِب vociferous, roaring, raging, noisy.

صَخْر، صَخْرَة rocks, rock, boulder, stone.

يكثر وجود الصخور قرب الشاطئ

Rocks abound near the coast

صَخْرِيّ rocky, petrous.

صَدَّ to repel, repulse, ward off, stave off, avert, rebuff; to hinder, prevent from, inhibit from; to turn away from, avoid, shun; to deter, restrain, dissuade.

صَدّ repulsion, repelling, warding off, parrying, staving off; avoidance, shunning, turning away from.

صَدُؤَ، صَدِئَ to rust, become rusty, oxidized, corroded.

صَدَأ rust, oxidation, corrosion.

صَدَى echo, reverbation; extreme thirst.

صَدَارَة forefront, precedence; preeminence; presidency; priority.

صُدَاع headache, migraine.

صَدَاق dowry.

صَدَاقَة friendship.

صِدَام collision, clash; breakdown, collapse.

صَدَح to sing, warble (a bird).

صَدَد intention, purpose, design; side, direction; respect, regard; relation, concern; matter, subject.

في صَدَد concerning, regarding, with respect to, re.

في هذا الصَّدَد in this respect, with regard to this, in this connection, with relation to this.

صَدَرَ to appear, come out; to be published, issued; to be pronounced, delivered, rendered (a judgment); to happen, occur, take place; to emanate from, arise from, come out of; to reach, arrive at; to go to; to repair.

صَدَّرَ to export (goods); to introduce, preface (a book); to put in the front, give the first place to.

صَدْر chest, breast, thorax, bust, bosom; front, forefront, forepart; beginning, start; dawn; early stage; outset; first hemistich (of a verse); leader, commander.

صَدْرِيّ thoracic, pectoral.

صُدْرِيَّة brassiere; vest, waistcoat.

صَدَعَ، صَدَّعَ to split, cleave, crack, sunder, break; to cause to break; to conquer, overcome (obstacles).

صَدَعَ بالحَقّ to come out openly with the truth.

صُدِعَ to have a headache; to get split, come apart, burst.

صَدْع crack, split, fissure, crevice; rift, flaw; fault.

صُدْغ temple.

صَدَفَ to turn away from, avoid, shun; to dissuade, discourage.

صَدَفَة، صَدَف shell, oyster; helix (of the ear).

صُدْفَة، صِدْفَة chance, coincidence; by chance, by coincidence.

صَدَقَ to say, speak, tell the truth; to be right, hold true; to keep one's promise; to give alms.

الصدف هو غطاء القواقع البحرية ويكثر وجوده في مياه البحر وعلى السواحل

The shell is the cover of oysters and is found plentifully in sea waters and on coasts

---

صَدَقَةُ النَّصِيحَة to advice someone sincerely.

صَدَّقَ to believe, deem credible, accept as true, trust; to certify, authenticate, attest, legalize, ratify; to confirm.

لا يُصَدَّق unbelievable, incredible; unreliable.

صِدْق truth, trueness, veracity, sincerity, honesty; candor.

صَدَقَة alms, almsgiving, charity, handout.

صَدَمَ to shock, bump, strike, knock, bounce; to hit, collide, clash with.

صَدْمَة shock, blow, stroke, hit, jolt; trauma.

صُدُور publication, issue, appearance (of a book); issuance (of an ordinance); emanation.

صَدُوق reliable, trustworthy, sincere, honest, truthful.

صَديد pus, matter.

صَديق friend, comrade.

صَرَّ to bundle, wrap up; to bind, tie up, lace, cord.

صَرَّ to prick one's ears; to shirp, creak, squeak, screech, grate (doors); to chatter (teeth).

صَرَاحَة clarity, distinctness, frankness, sincerity, plainness, candor.

بِصَرَاحَة frankly, expressly, explicitly, unequivocally; honestly, openheartedly, patently.

صُرَاخ crying, yelling, shouting, clamor; screams.

صِرَاط way, path, road.

صِرَاع struggle, fight; wrestling, strife; conflict.

صَرَّاف money-changer, teller, banker.

اذهب إلى الصراف لتبديل النقود الأجنبية بعملة وطنية

I go to the money changer to exchange foreign currency with our national currency

---

صِرَافَة money-changing, exchange, banking.

صَرَامَة sharpness, harshness, severity, rigor, strictness.

صُرَّة bundle, pack, packet, parcel, package.

صَرَّحَ to declare, announce, avow publicly; to speak out, make clear, clarify, explicate, explain; to state, make a statement, be explicit about; to allow, permit, license, grant a license.

صَرْح edifice, palace, high building.

صَرَخَ to cry, yell, shout, scream; to call out, shout to.

صَرْخَة cry, shout, yell, shriek.

آخِرُ صَرْخَة fad, fashion, mode, craze.

صَرَعَ to throw down, fell, bring to the ground.

صَرْع epilepsy (med.).

صَرْعَة fad, craze, style, fashion; rage.

صَرَفَ to dismiss, discharge, fire, sack (from employment).

صَرَفَ to turn away, avert, dissuade, alienate, keep away.

صَرَفَ to spend money; to pay; pay out, disburse money.

صَرَفَ to issue, give out, devote one's time.

صَرَّفَ to discharge, empty, drain; to change money; to sell out, dispose of goods; to market, sell, distribute goods.

صَرَّفَ الأَعْمَال to manage, direct, adminster, take care of.

صَرَّفَ to conjugate (a verb); to decline (a noun); to inflect (a word).

صَرْف dismissal, discharge, turning away from.

صَرْف expenditure, spending, use; application (of time).

صَرْفُ النُّقُود money changing, exchange of currencies.

صَرْفُ المِيَاه drainage.

صَرْف inflection, declension (grammar).

صِرْف pure, unadulterated, plain, straight.

صَرُمَ to be severe, strict, rigorous, harsh, drastic, sharp.

صَرِيح frank, candid, unreserved; forthright, direct; express.

صَرِير creaking, squeaking, screeching; gnashing (of teeth); stridulation (of crickets).

صَرِيع thrown to the ground, felled; mad, crazy, insane; fallen victim to.

صَعُبَ to be difficult, hard.

صَعَّبَ to make difficult, hard; to complicate.

صَعْب difficult, hard, complicated, tough.

صَعْبُ الاحْتِمَال hard to bear, oppressive.

صَعْبُ المِرَاس hard to manage, unruly, recalcitrant, obstinate.

صَعِدَ to ascend, climb, rise, mount up; scale.

صَعَّدَ to escalate, aggravate; to sublimate; to utter wails; to cause to evaporate, vaporize.

صَعَقَ to strike, hit, shock someone; to destroy, slay; to stun, stupefy, make unconscious.

صُعِقَ to be struck, hit (by electricity, lightning); to lose consciousness; to be thunderstruck.

صُعْلُوك pauper, poor, wretched; base, vile, destitute; beggar, tramp, vagabond, loafer.

صُعُوبَة difficulty, toughness.

بِصُعُوبَة with great difficulty; scarcely; just, by a narrow margin.

صُعُود rise, ascension, mounting, ascent, scaling.

صَعِيد highland; upland; level, standard; scene, sphere, field.

صَغُرَ to be small; to shrink, wane; to be lowly, humble.

صَغَّرَ to decrease, reduce, make small; to belittle, disparage; to degrade, debase, humble.

صِغَر smallness.

صِغَرُ السِّنّ youthfulness, youth, boyhood.

صَغِير (ص) small, little; paltry, scanty, tiny; minute.

صَغِير (اسم) minor, juvenile, underage, young.

صَفَّ to set up in a row, line; to align, array, arrange, set; to compose; to class, range, classify.

صَفّ alignment, arraying, arrangement.

صَفّ typesetting, composition.

صَفّ line, row, file, column; class, grade.

صَفَا to be clear, pure, untroubled, limpid, unmixed.

صَفَّى to clarify, purify, refine, filter; to drain.

صَفَّى to dissolve, liquidate (a company); to eliminate; to settle, clear, square, balance (account, debt).

ينتظم الطلاب في صف
قبل أن يدخلوا إلى المدرسة
Students align themselves in rows before entering to the classroom

صَفَاء clearness, purity, limpidity, clarity; happiness, felicity, serenity, gaiety, cheerfulness; honesty, candor.

صَفَارُ البَيْض yolk (egg).

صَفَّارَة whistle, siren.

صِفَة quality, property, character, peculiarity; adjective, attribute (grammar); capacity.

صَفَحَ to forgive, excuse, pardon.

صَفَّحَ to armor, plate, coat with metal plates.

صَفْح pardon, forgiveness, remission; side.

صَفْحَة page, sheet, leaf; surface, face.

صَفَّدَ to fetter, shackle, enchain, tie up, handcuff.

صَفَرَ to whistle, hiss, wheeze on breathing.

صَفَّرَ to make yellow; to whistle; to vacate, empty.

صِفْر (اسم) zero, cipher.

صِفْر (ص) empty, vacant, void.

صَفْراء bile.

صَفَعَ to slap someone's face, smack.

صَفْعَة slap, cuff, blow.

صَفَّفَ to comb (hair).

صَفَقَ to slap; to slam (the door shut); to flap, flutter (wings of a bird); to decant (a liquid); to be thick, heavy.

صَفَّقَ to applaud, clap one's hands; to flap, flutter (wings); to decant.

صفّق الحاضرون تحيةً للزائر الكريم
The audience applauded to welcome the noble visitor

صَفْقَة deal, bargain.

صَفْو clarity, limpidity, serenety, purity, cloudlessness; happiness, felicity, delight; choice, elite, the best pick.

صَفُوح forgiving, ready to forgive, tolerant, merciful.

صَفِيح tin, tin plates.

صَفِيحة plate, sheet, leaf, tinplate; lamina; blade; can, container; table (anatomy).

صَفِير whistling, hissing, wheezing (on breathing).

صِقَالَة scaffold.

صُقْع region, land, territory.

صَقَلَ to polish, smooth, burnish, refine (style); to glaze.

صَقْل polishing, burnishing, smoothing; glazing, finishing; refinement.

صَقِيع frost.

صَكَّ to beat, strike; to shut, lock.

صَكّ cheque, deed, legal instrument, check, bill.

صَكُّ مِلْكِيَّة title deed.

صَلَّى to pray; to warm, heat.

صَلابَة solidity, hardness, rigidity, firmness, stiffness; stubbornness, obstinacy, intolerance.

صَلاة prayer, blessing from God.

يصلّي المسلم خمس مرات في اليوم
The Moslem prays five times a day

صَلاح — validity; fitness, adequacy; utility, usability; righteousness, uprightness, honesty; piety.

صَلاحِيَّة — competence, jurisdiction, power, authority; validity, proper condition, appropriateness, aptness.

صَلادَة — hardness, rigidity.

صَلَبَ — to crucify.

صَلُبَ، صَلِبَ — to be hard, rigid, solid, firm.

صُلْب (ص) — hard, solid, rigid, stiff, inflexible.

صُلْب (اسم) — heart, innermost, core; middle, bottom; essential point; steel.

صِلَة — connection, relation, relevance; link, tie, bond; gift.

صَلَحَ، صَلُحَ — to be fit, suitable, appropriate, adequate; to suit, fit; to be useful, practicable, proper; to be pious, godly.

صُلْح — peace, reconciliation, settlement, peacemaking.

صَلْصَال — clay, argil, earth.

صَلْصَة — sauce, gravy, dressing.

صَلْصَلَة — clatter, rattle, rustle, clank.

صَلِعَ — to be bald, hairless.

صَلَع — baldness.

صَلَف — vainglory, bragging, boasting, conceit, arrogance.

صَلِف — boastful, bragging, vainglorious, swaggering.

صَليب — cross.

صَليبٌ مَعْقوف — swastika.

صَليبيّ — crusader; cruciferous.

صَليل — rattle, clank, clash, clatter.

صَمَّ — to be deaf; to close, plug; to learn by heart, memorize.

صِمَام — valve.

صِمَامُ الأمان — safety valve.

صِمَامٌ خَانق — throttle valve.

صِمَامُ القَلْب — heart valve.

صِمَامٌ مُفَرَّغ — vacuum valve.

صَمَتَ — to be silent; to hush up, stop talking.

صَمْت — silence, quiet.

صَمَدَ — to withstand, resist, oppose, confront, endure, last, defy; to stand up against.

الصَّمَد — the Everlasting (God).

صَمَّغَ — to paste, glue, gum.

صَمْغ — paste, glue, adhesive, gum.

صَمْغٌ عَرَبِيّ — gum arabic.

صَمَّمَ — to make up one's mind; to determine to do someting; to resolve, decide, persist in; to plan, design; to deafen.

صَمَم — deafness.

صُمُود — steadfastness, perseverance, firmness; resistance.

صَمُولَة — nut (of a bolt).

صَميم — real, true, sincere; innermost, heart, core, essence.

في صَمِيمِ المَوْضُوع relevant, in point.

صِنَّارَة hook, fishinghook, needle.

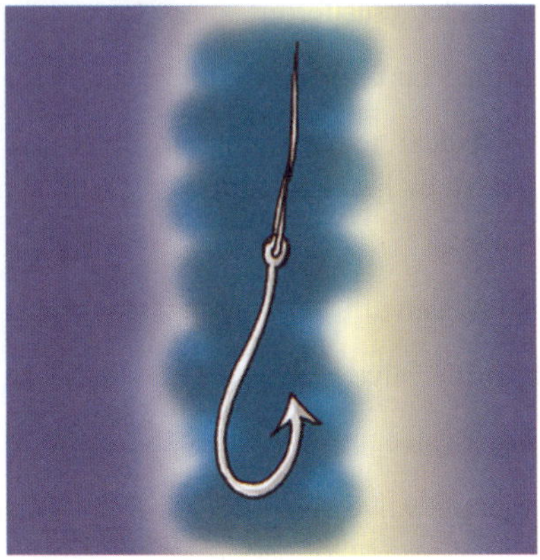

نصطاد الأسماك بواسطة الصنارة

We catch fish by a hook

صِنَاعَة industry, manufacture.

صِنَاعِيّ industrial, industrialist.

صُنْبُور tap, faucet, cock.

نفتح صنبور الماء عندما نريد غسل أيدينا

We open the water tap when we want to wash our hands

صُنْدُوق treasury, coffers, pay office; fund.

صُنْدُوقُ الدُّنيا peep show.

صِنْدِيد valiant, brave; leader, notable.

صَنَعَ to make, do, perform. manufacture; to fabricate, produce.

صُنْع manufacture, production, make.

صَنْعَة craft, trade, vocation, profession, career; workmanship, skill, artistry, finesse.

صُنْعِيّ artificial, synthetic, man-made.

صَنَّفَ to classify, class, arrange, sort out; to compile, compose, write a book; to categorize, tabulate.

صِنْف category, class; grade; group, kind, sort, type, brand.

صَنَم idol, image.

صِنْو، صَنْو counterpart, parallel, twin, duplicate, equal, peer.

صَنَوْبَر pine (tree).

كوزُ صَنَوْبَر pinecone, cone.

صَنِيع deed, act; good deed, kind act; creature; servile, dependent, puppet, willing tool; meal, repast, banquet; favor, benefit.

صَهَرَ to fuse, melt, smelt.

صَهْر fusion, fusing, melting, smelting.

صِهْر son-in-law; brother-in-law.

صِهْرِيج cistern, tank, reservoir; tanker.

صَهَلَ	to neigh, whinny (horse).
صَهيل	neigh, whinnying (of horse).
صَواب	right, accurate, exact, proper; reason, mind, consciousness.
فَقَدَ صَوابَه	to lose one's mind.
غابَ عَن صَوابِهِ	to lose consciousness, faint, swoon.
صَواعِد	stalagmites.
صَوَّان	flint, firestone; granite; silica.
صِوان، صُوان	cupboard, case, buffet; auricle (of the ear).
صَوَّبَ	to aim at, point at, take aim at; to correct, rectify; to approve of, sanction.
صَوْب	direction, quarter; that which is right, proper; in the direction of, toward to.
من كلِّ حدْبٍ وَصَوْب	from all sides, from all quarters, from everywhere, from every place.
صَوَّتَ	to vote, cast a ballot, cast a vote; to poll; to make a noise, shout, sound, ring.
صَوْت	sound, voice,tone; melody, tune; noise; fame, renown; vote.
رَجعَ الصَّوْت	echo, reverbation.
صَوْتٌ مُرَجِّح	casting vote.
بِصَوْتٍ عالٍ	loudly.
بِصَوْتٍ مَسْموع	audibly, aloud.
صَوْتِيّ	sonic, phonic, vocal.
صَوَّرَ	to draw, portray, figure, picture; to describe, depict; to shape, form, fashion; to copy, make an exact copy of, reproduce; to photography, film, snapshoot.

صُور	horn, bugle.
صُورَة	picture, portrait, painting, image, photography; form, shape, figure, copy, reproduction; manner, mode, fashion.
صُورَةٌ جانبيَّة	profile.
صُورَةٌ زَيتيَّة	oil painting.
صُوَرٌ مُتحرِّكَة	cartoon, motion picture.
بِصُورةٍ مَلْحوظَة	noticeably, markedly.
صُورِيّ، صُوَرِيّ	formal, nominal, proforma; fictitious, dummy, simulated, unreal.
صُوص	chick, young chicken.
صُوف	wool.
صُوفِيّ (ص)	woolen, woolly.
صُوفِيّ (اسم)	Sufi, mystic.
صَوْلَة	attack, assault; power, authority, influence.
صَوْلَجان	scepter, wand, crosier.
صَوْم، صِيام	fast, fasting.
صَوْمَعَة	cell, hermitage.
صَوْن	preservation, conservation, protection, safeguarding.
صِياح	crying, shouting, screaming, yelling.
صَيَّاد	hunter, shooter (birds, animals); fisher, fisherman (fish).
صَيَّادُ السَّمك	kingfisher (bird).
صِياغَة	goldsmithing; forming, shaping, forging; drafting, framing, composition; phrasing, wording, coinage (of words).

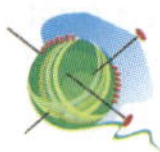

صِيَانَة maintenance, servicing, protection, safeguarding; retention, safeguarding; safekeeping, conservation, preservation.

صِيت reputation, standing, renown, prestige, celebrity.

صَيْحَة cry, yell, shout, scream; fad, craze, rage, fashion.

صَيْد hunting (birds, animals, etc.); fishing (fish).

صَيْد game, quarry, kill.

صَيْدَلَة pharmacology.

صَيْدَلِيّ pharmacist, druggist.

صَيْدَلِيَّة pharmacy, drugstore.

صَيَّرَ to make, cause to be, reduce to, turn into.

صَيْرَفِيّ money-changer.

صَيْرورَة becoming, outcome, result, end, development.

صِيْغَة formula, shape, form, mode; wording, text, version (of a letter etc.); tense (grammar).

صِيغَةُ الأَمْر imperative mood (grammar).

صِيغَةُ التَّفْضيل comparative degree (grammar).

صِيغَةُ التَّفضيل العُليَا superlative degree (grammar).

صِيغَةُ الفَاعل، صِيغَةُ المعلوم active voice (grammar).

صِيغَةُ المفْعول، صِيغَةُ المجهول passive voice (grammar).

صَيْف summer, summertime.

صينيّ porcelain, chinaware.

صينيَّة tray, salver; faceplate (of a drilling machine).

ضَائِع	lost, missing; poor, wretched.
ضَائِقَة	predicament, straits; difficulty, crisis; critical situation.
ضَاءَلَ	to decrease, lessen, reduce.
ضَابِط	officer; regulator, governor (instrument).
ضَابِط	control, check, deterrent; criterion, standard, measure; rule, principle, norm.
ضَابِطُ اتِّصَال أو ارْتِبَاط	liaison officer.
ضَابِطُ أرْكَان	staff officer.
ضَابِطُ صَفّ	noncommisioned officer.
ضَاجَعَ	to sleep with, make love to, have sexual intercourse with.
ضَاحِيَة	suburb, outskirt, precinct.
ضَادَّ	to contradict, oppose; to counteract, antagonize.
ضَارّ	harmful, noxious, evil; maleficent, injurious; adverse.
ضَارٍ (الضَّارِي)	predatory, rapacious, ferocious; savage, wild.
ضَارِبٌ بالرَّمل	geomancer.
قُوَّةٌ ضَارِبَة	striking force.
ضَارَعَ	to match, equal, be like, similar, resemble.
ضَاعَ	to get lost, be lost; to disappear, perish.
ضَاعَفَ	to double, multiply.
ضَاغِط (ص)	compressive, pressing, squeezing.
ضَاغِط (اسم)	compressor.
ضَافٍ (الضَّافِي)	abundant, plentiful; detailed, elaborate.
ضَاقَ	to narrow; to be narrow, tight, confined, cramped; to be anguished, uneasy, depressed because of.
ضَاقَت به الحياة	life depressed him; he had a bad time.

أ ب ت ث ج ح خ د ذ ر ز س ش ص ض ط ظ ع غ ف ق ك ل م ن هـ و ي

ضاقَ صَدْرُهُ to be annoyed, angry.

ضالّ wandering, astray, errant; perverse, false, lost.

ضَآلَة smallness, scantiness, sparsity, paucity, dwindling, waning, diminution, tininess; shrinking; decrease.

ضالَّة goal, aim, objective, wish, desire; object of persistent search, of a long-cheriched wish.

ضامَ to wrong, harm, inflict damage upon; to treat unjustly.

ضامِر atrophied, emaciated; thin, skinny; svelte, slender.

ضامِن guarantor, warrantor, surety, bailsman; insurer; responsible, answerable, liable.

ضَأْن sheep.

لَحْمُ الضَّأْن mutton.

ضاهَى to match, equal, compete with successfully; to imitate, compare with, correspond to, resemble.

لا يُضاهَى incomparable, matchless, peerless, unique, unequalled.

ضايَقَ to annoy, harass, oppress, beset, anger someone; to trouble, inconvenience, disturb, affect gravely someone.

ضَئِيل small, tiny; spare; thin, slight, scanty, meager, little.

ضَباب fog, mist.

يتكون الضباب من الرطوبة وينتشر عادة فوق التلال

Fog is formed from moisture and it spreads usually over hills

ضَبَطَ to catch, seize, arrest, capture, confiscate; to control, contain, subdue, keep under control; to adjust, regulate, fix, set; to verify, determine precisely; to correct, rectify, make right; to vowelize (grammar).

ضَبَطَ أَعْصابَهُ to control oneself; to remain composed, calm.

ضَبْط capture, arrest, restraint, subdual; control, check.

ضَبْط accuracy, correctness, exactitude, precision.

ضَبْط correction, adjustment, amendment, regulation.

ضَبْط vowelization (grammar); bookkeeping (accounts).

ضَبْطُ النَّفْس self-control, temperance, self-restraint.

بِالضَّبْط exactly, precisely.

ضَجَّ to be noisy, boisterous; to shout, roar, cry.

ضَجَّة، ضَجيج noise, din, row, cry, yell, outcry, clamor, tumult.

ضَجِرَ to be bored with, fed up with, weary of, annoyed by; to be angry, irritated, exasperated at; to be dissatisfied, discontent, displeased with.

أ ب ت ث ج ح خ د ذ ر ز س ش ص ض ط ظ ع غ ف ق ك ل م ن هـ و ي

ضَجَر boredom, annoyance, anger; sorrow, worry, grief; displeasure, vexation, dissatisfaction, weariness, tiredness.

ضَجِر annoyed, displeased, angered, irritated, weary of; tired of, troubled, grieved; sullen, vexed, angry.

ضَحَّى to sacrifice, immolate.

ضُحًى، ضَحْو، ضَحْوَة morning.

ضَحَّاك joker, jester, buffoon; constantly laughing.

ضَحِكَ to laugh at; to jeer, scoff, jibe at; to deride, ridicule, mock, scorn; to dupe, fool, bluff, deceive.

ضَحِك، ضِحْك، ضَحْك laughter.

ضَحْكَة، ضِحْكَة laugh.

ضَحِيَّة victim; slaughter animal; immolation; blood sacrifice.

ضَخَّ to pump.

ضَخّ pumping.

ضَخَامَة hugeness, vastness, enormity, largeness, greatness; corpulence, obesity; hypertrophy (med.).

ضَخُمَ to be huge, big, large, bulky, voluminous.

ضَخَّمَ to inflate, swell, blow up, expand, distend; to exaggerate, overstate, magnify; to amplify (elect.).

ضَخْم huge, big, large, great, voluminous, bulky; vast, immense, massive, enormous; formidable; mammoth, colossal; corpulent, obese, fat, plump.

ضِدّ opposite, contrary, contrast, against; versus.

ضِدّ adversary, opponent; antonymn.

ضِدُّ الحريق fireproof.

ضَرَّ to harm, damage, hurt, injure; to cause damage to; to impair, prejudice.

ضَرّ، ضَرَر damage, harm, impairment, prejudice, detriment; injury, loss, disadvantage.

ضَرَّاء distress, misfortune, adversity.

ضَرَاوَة voracity, ferocity, violence, savagery; greed, rapacity.

ضَرَبَ to beat, strike, hit; to shoot, fire, shell, bombard; to play (on a musical instrument); to type (on a typewriter).

ضَرَبَ to knock, rap (on a door); to blow (a trumpet); to beat, whip (eggs); to lay siege to; to pitch, set up (a tent); to set (a record); to beat (a drum); to coin, mint (money); to multiply (a number by another); to give an example; to cite, exemplify (by way of example); to avoid, shun, overlook, bypass, pardon (a bad deed made by someone).

ضَرَبَ في الأرض to roam, wander, travel, migrate.

ضَرَبَ اللَّونُ إلى to incline to (a color).

ضَرَبَ موعِدًا to fix a date, make an appointment.

ضَرَبَ عُنُقَهُ to behead, have someone's head cut off.

ضَرَبَ بِهِ عُرْضَ الحائط to disdain, reject, throw overboard, despise.

ضَرْب beating, striking, hitting, slapping; knocking (the door); ringing (the bell); multiplication (math); giving (an example); minting (coins); typing (on typewriter).

ضَرْب kind, sort, type, variety.

ضَرْبُ الرَّمْل geomancy.

ضَرْبَة blow, stroke, knock, strike, tap, affliction, trial; ordeal.

ضَرْبَةُ القَلْب beat, throb, pulse.

ضَرْبَةُ جَزاء penalty kick (football).

ضَرْبَةُ شَمْس sunstroke.

ضَرْبَةٌ قاضِيَة knockout (boxing); fatal blow.

ضَرْبَةُ مُعَلِّم masterstroke, coup de maitre.

ضَرَّة fellow wife; udder.

ضَرَّجَ to spot, stain, smear.

ضِرْس molar tooth.

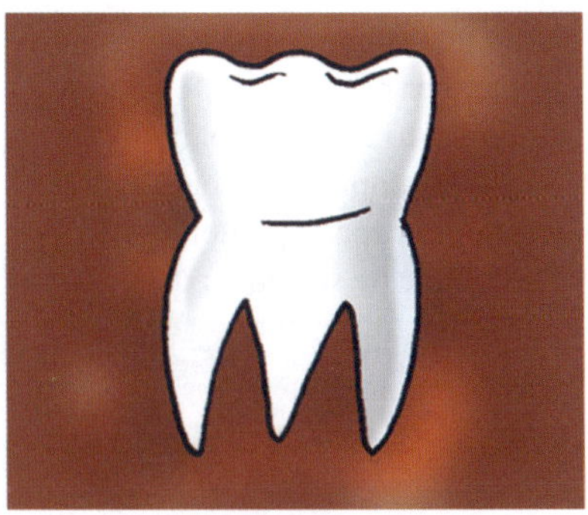

يطحن الضِّرس الطعام ليُسَهِّل ابتلاعه

The molar tooth grinds food to facilitate its swallowing

ضِرْسُ العَقْل wisdom tooth.

ضَرَطَ to break wind.

ضَرْع udder, teat.

ضِرْع like, similar, alike.

ضَرِمَ to catch fire; to burn, flare, blaze, set on fire.

ضَرُورة necessity, need, constraint; distress, plight, want.

بِالضَّرورة if need be,in case of need.

ضَروريّ necessary, prerequisite; essential, imperative, obligatory; inevitable, mandatory.

ضَريبَة tax, duty, levy, imposition, excise.

ضَريبَةٌ إضافِيَّة surtax.

ضَريبَةٌ تَصاعُدِيَّة progressive tax.

ضَريبَةُ الدَّخْل income tax.

ضَريح grave, tomb.

ضَرير blind.

ضَعَة، ضِعَة lowliness, baseness, humbleness.

ضَعْضَعَ to tear down, demolish, raze, ruin, weaken.

ضَعُفَ to weaken; to be weak, feeble, frail, debilitated; to be impotent, flabby, attenuated, enfeebled.

ضَعْف، ضُعْف weakness, feebleness, debility, powerlessness.

ضَعْفٌ جِنْسِيّ impotence.

ضِعْف double, twice as much, multiple.

أضْعافًا مُضاعفَة many times.

ضَعِيف weak, feeble, frail, debilated; powerless, impotent.

ضَعِيفُ العَقْل weak-minded, stupid, idiot, simpleton, fool.

ضَعِيفُ القَلْب weak-hearted, cowardly.

ضَغَطَ to press, squeeze, compress, exert pressure; to oppress, suppress, bear down heavily upon.

ضَغْط pressure, stress, suppression, oppression, tension.

ضَغْطُ الدَّم blood pressure.

ضَغْطُ الهَواء air pressure.

ضَغِنَ to bear a grudge, harbor hatred against, resent.

ضَغِن spiteful, hateful; hater, rancorous.

ضَغِينَة، ضِغْن rancor, spite, malice, illwill, hatred, grudge.

ضِفَّة، ضَفَّة bank, shore, riverside, waterside.

تقع السهول الخصبة على ضفة النهر
Fertile plains stretch alongside the river bank

ضِفْدِع، ضِفْدِعَة frog (animal); toad (animal).

ضَفَرَ، ضَفَّرَ to braid, plait, interweave, intertwist, entertwine.

يعيش الضفدع في المستنقعات
Frogs live in swamps

ضَلَّ to go astray; to lose one's way; to get lost; to be astray; to fail, miss the mark; to be in vain, abortive; to err, wander.

ضَلال، ضَلالَة aberration, error, deception, going astray.

ضِلْع rib; cutlet; vein; stave.

ضِلْع side, role, part, hand.

ضَلَّلَ to mislead, lead astray, misguide; delude, deceive, cheat.

ضَلِيع versed in, knowledgeable, experienced, skilled in; strong.

ضَمَّ to join, unite, bring together; to add up, sum up; to gather, collect, reap, harvest; to embrace, hug; to attach, combine, compress; to grasp, grab, seize; to pronounce with the vowel point for(,) (grammar).

ضِمَاد، ضِمَادَة bandage, compress, dressing.

ضَمَان، ضَمَانَة guaranty, warrant, surety, security; assurance, insurance, guarantee, collateral; liability, responsibility.

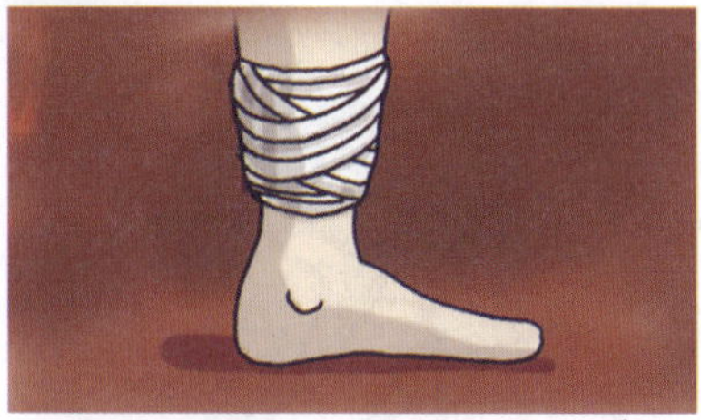

يلفّ الممرض الضماد حول الجرح لوقف النزيف
The nurse rolls a bandage around the wound to stop bleeding

ضَمَّة embrace, hug; the vowel point for (ُ) (grammar).

ضَمَدَ، ضَمَّدَ to bandage, dress a wound.

ضَمَرَ، ضَمُرَ to waste away; to be atrophic; to be lean, skinny, thin, emaciated, slim, slender; to contract, shrink; to make lean, slender; to secrete, conceal, hide, keep secret; harbor a feeling toward.

ضَمِنَ to guarantee, warrant, ensure; to be liable for; to insure, achieve, realize; to vouch, safeguard.

ضَمَّنَ to include, enclose, incorporate, comprise, imply, contain; to modulate (electricity).

ضِمْن inside, inner; within, among, inclusive.

ضِمْنًا inclusively.

ضِمْنَهُ enclosed, herewith attached.

ضِمْنِيّ implied, implicit, underlying.

ضُمُور atrophy, emaciation, leanness, thinness, slimness.

ضَمير conscience, heart, mind, innermost; pronoun (grammar).

فاقِدُ الضَّمير unscrupulous.

حَيُّ الضَّمير scrupulous, conscientious.

ضَنُكَ to weaken; to be weak; to be narrow, hard, difficult (living); to be cramped, confined (circumstances).

ضَنْك poverty, distress, straits, hardship.

ضَنِيَ to be lean, emaciated, gaunt; enervated, worn out.

ضَنين grudging, niggardly; stingy thrifty, sparing.

ضَنين clinging to, adhering to, devoted to, attached to.

ضَوَى to be lean, thin, slight, scrawny; to join, follow, attach oneself to; to flock around; to rally under someone's banner.

ضَوْء، أضْواء light, glow, illumination; limelight.

ضَوْءٌ كَاشِف searchlight.

على ضَوْء in the light of, under the circumstances of.

ضَوْئِيّ luminous, luminary.

ضَوْر starvation, violent hunger.

ضَوْضاء noise, din, uproar, tumult, turmoil.

ضَياع loss, waste, alienation, estrangement; perdition, ruin, destruction.

ضِيافَة entertainment, accomodation, hospitable reception.

أنت في ضِيافَتي your are my guest.

ضَيْر harm, damage, injury, injustice, offense, iniquity.

ضَيْعَة village, hamlet; loss, forfeiture; ruin, destruction.

ضَيْف guest.

ضَيَّقَ to narrow, tighten, straiten; to cramp, confine, restrain, restrict, contract; to pull tight; to opress, besiege.

ضَيِّق tight, limited, confined; narrow.

ضَيِّقُ الخُلُق restless, nervous, impatient; annoyed.

ضَيِّقُ الصَّدْر vexed, angry, upset; depressed, downcast.

ضَيِّقُ النِّطاق limited in extent; restricted, limited.

ضَيِّقُ التَّفكير narrow-minded, intolerant, old-fashioned.

ضَيْق tightness, closeness, narrowness; confinement, restriction, constraint; shortage, scarcity; anguish, depression; lack, want, care, worry, anxiety; anger, annoyance, exasperation.

ضِيقُ ذات اليد poverty, destution.

ضَيْم wrong, injustice, inequity, grievance, oppression.

طَائِر (ص) flying, in flight.

طَائِر (اسم) bird.

يبني الطائر عشّه بين أغصان الأشجار
The bird builds its nest in the fold of tree leaves

طَائِرٌ مُخَوِّض wading bird.

طَائِرٌ مُغَرِّد warbler.

على الطائر المَيْمون have a good trip! happy journey!.

طائِرَة airplane, aircraft, plane.

طائِرَةٌ شِراعِيَّة glider.

طَائِرَةٌ عمودية ، حَوَّامَة helicopter.

طَائِرَةٌ نَفَّاثَة jet plane.

طَائِرَةٌ وَرَقِيَّة kite.

تطير الطائرة بواسطة محركاتها وأجنحتها
The airplane flies by the power of its engines and wings

طائِش reckless, rash, careless; foolhardy, frivolous, imprudent; heedless, thoughtless; lightheaded.

طائِع obedient, compliant, submissive.

طائِف ambulant, itenerant, roving, wanderer.

طائِفة sect, denomination, cult; group, band, party; swarm, community; people; class; part, section, piece; bevy, covey.

طائِفيّ sectarian, confessional.

طائِفيَّة sectarianism, confessionalism.

طائِل enormous, immense, huge, great; use, benefit; might, power, strength.

طائِلَة might, power, force; revenge, retaliation.

تَحْتَ طَائِلَةِ القَانُون subject to punishment by law.

طابَ to be pleasant, agreeable, delicious, delightful; to please, delight, appeal to.

طابَتْ لَيلَتُكُم good night!.

طابَة ball.

طابَع stamp; mark; character, feature, property, trait; tinge; seal, imprint, impress; tablet, pill.

طابَعٌ بَريديّ postage stamp.

طابَقَ to be identical with; to correspond to; to conform harmonize with, match, tally with; to be compatible, consistent with; to bring to coincidence; to correlate, compare, contrast with.

طابِق floor, story.

الطَّابِقُ السُّفْلِيّ basement.

طابور line, file, row, column, queue; battalion.

طاحَ to perish, die; to go astray, wander about; to throw, cast, fling, hurl; toss, carry away.

طاحون، طاحونَة mill, grinder.

حَجَرُ الطَّاحون millstone.

طارَ to fly away; to hurry, hasten to, dash to, fly to.

طارت اليمامة في الجوّ لتلحق برفيقاتها
The pigeon flew in the air to catch up with its companions

طارَ عَقْلُهُ to lose one's mind; to get wildly excited.

طارَ فَرَحًا to exult; to be overjoyed, elated, carried away with joy; to be jubilant, highly pleased.

طارَ صيتُهُ to be famous, renowned, well-known.

طارِئ (ص) accidental, casual, unexpected, unforseen.

طارِئ (اسم) foreigner, stranger, alien; emergency, contingency; accident, mishap, incident.

حالَةُ الطَوارِئ state of emergency.

مَخْرَجُ الطَوارِئ emergency exit.

طارَدَ to chase, pursue, run after; to hunt, track, trail.

طارِد expeller, evictor, banisher.

طارِق night visitor; striker, knocker; banging, beating, rapping.

طازَج fresh, tender, new.

طاس، طاسَة bowl, cup, tumbler, goblet.

طاشَ to be rash, reckless, heedless, frivolous.

طاشَ عن الهَدَف to miss the mark.

طأطأَ to bow one's head; to duck, lower, bend one's head.

طاعَة obedience, compliance, submission, surrender; allegiance, fidelity, loyalty, piety.

طاعِنٌ في السِّنّ old aged.

طاعون plague.

طاغِيَة oppressor.

طافَ to circle around; to walk about, travel about, rove about, run around; to ride, go, walk, circumambulate; to make the rounds; to guide around; to overflow, spill over, flood, inundate; to familiarize oneself with; to become acquainted with.

يطوف المسلمون حول الكعبة المشرفة
Moslems circumambulate the sacred Kaaba during Ramadhan

طافِح replete, full, filled to capacity and overflowing.

طاقَ to be able, in a position to do something; to be capable of doing something; to bear, stand, endure, sustain.

طاقَة energy; ability; faculty, capability, aptitude; power, strength; bunch (of flowers).

طاقَةٌ حَرَكِيَّة kinetic energy.

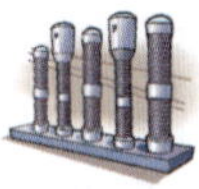

طاقَةٌ كامِنَة potential energy.

قَدْرُ الطاقة as far as possible.

طاقِم crew (of ship, plane, etc).

طالَ to be long; to extend, stretch, grow longer; to be high, tall, elevated; to last long.

طالَبَ to claim, demand, request someone to do something; to want, wish from someone to do something; to reclaim, call for the return of something.

طالِب student; seeker, claimant, demander; appliant, petitioner, suitor.

طالِبٌ داخِلِيّ boarding student.

طالِبٌ عَسْكَرِيّ cadet.

طالِح bad, evil, crooked, wicked.

طالَعَ to read, peruse; to present with, supply with; to look at, inspect, view; to inform, notify, let someone know about.

طالَما often, frequently, repeatedly; as long as; while, the more so as.

طامِح avid, eager, keen, yearning, craving, longing, high-aspiring.

طاهِ (الطاهي) cook

طاهِر pure, immaculate, chaste, virtuous.

طاهِرُ الذَّيْل innocent, blameless, upright, honest.

طاوَعَ to consent to; to comply with someone's wishes; to yield, submit, be obedient to someone; to obey, follow, accede to someone's wishes.

طاوِلَة table.

طاوِلَة الكيّ ironing board.

طاووس peacock (bird).

الطاووس طير له ريش جميل للغاية يتفاخر به لجذب الأنثى

The peacock has very beautiful feathers which it spreads to entice the female

طِبّ medicine.

طِبُّ الأطفال pediatrics.

طِبُّ الأمراض الجلديّة dermatology.

طِبُّ أمراض النِّساء gynecology.

طِبُّ بَيطريّ veterinary medicine.

طِبُّ التَّوليد obstetrics.

طِبٌّ شَرعِيّ forensic medicine.

طِبُّ الشيخوخة geriatrics.

طِبُّ العيون ophtalmology.

الطِبُّ الوِقائي preventive medicine.

طَبّاخ cook; cooking stove, kitchen range.

طباشير (ج) chalk.

تستعمل الطبشورة للكتابة على اللوح الأسود

Chalk is used to write on the blackboard

طَبّاع printer, typographer.

طِباعَة printing, typography.

طِباعَةٌ على الحَجَر lithography.

طَبّال drummer.

طَبَّبَ to treat medically, give medical treatment.

طَبَخَ to cook.

طَبْخ cooking, cookery, cuisine; cooked food.

طَبَعَ to print; to typewrite; to stamp, impress.

طَبَعَ على to shape, create, mold.

طُبِعَ على to have a natural disposition; to be disposed by nature for; to be innate, inborn, inherent.

طَبْع	printing, typewriting, stamping, impression.
طَبْع	natural disposition, inborn character, temper.
طَبْعًا	of course, certainly, for sure, by all means.
طَبْعَة	edition, print, stamp, impression.
طَبَّقَ	to apply, put into effect, implement, enforce; to comply with, put into practice; to follow, stick to, observe; to carry out.
طَبَّقَ	to cover up; to spread through; to be universal.
طَبَق	plate, dish, bowl, tray, cover; layer, tier, stratum.
طِبْقَ	according to; in conformity with; similar to.
طَبَقَة	layer, stratum, bed (of land, sea, air).
طَبَقَة	floor, storey (of a building).
طَبَقَة	class, category; range; degree, rank.
طَبَقَةُ الصَّوت	pitch, tone.
طَبَقَةٌ خَارِجِيَّة	film, screen, coat, layer.
طَبَقِيّ	class.
طَبَّلَ	to beat a drum.
طَبْل، طَبْلَة	drum.
طَبْلَةُ الأُذُن	eardrum.
طِبِّيّ	medical.
طَبِيب	physician, doctor.
طَبِيبُ الأَطْفَال	pediatrician.

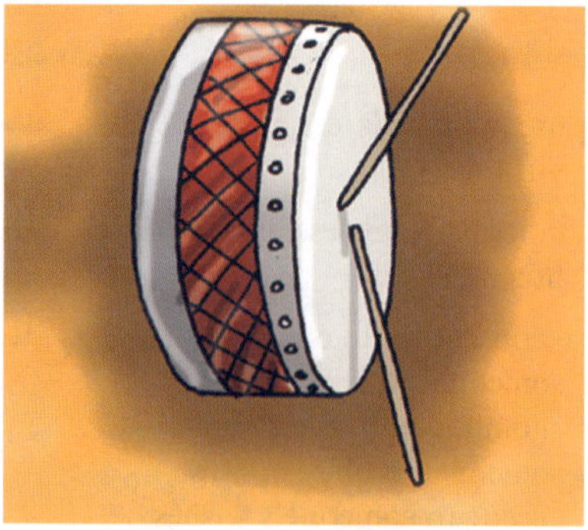

يُصنع الطبل من جلود الحيوانات

Drums are made of animal hide

طَبِيبٌ جَرَّاح	surgeon.
طَبِيبٌ بَيْطَرِيّ	veterinarian.
طَبِيعَة	nature, natural disposition, peculiarity, character.
بِطَبِيعَة الحال	naturally, ipso facto, as a matter of course.
عِلْمُ الطَّبِيعَة	physics, natural science.
فَوقَ الطَّبِيعَة	supernatural, metaphysical.
طَبِيعِيّ	natural, innate, inherent, inborn; normal, usual; simple, plain, ordinary.

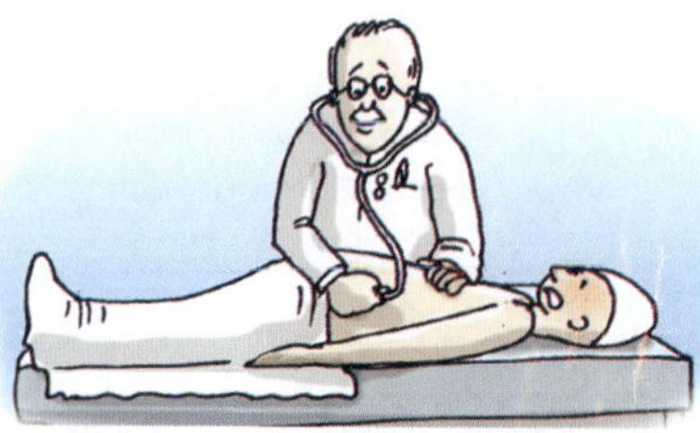

يداوي الطبيب المريض
بعد أن يتفحصه لمعرفة مرضه

The physician treats the patient after he examines him to know the nature of his sickness

شَخْصٌ طَبيعيّ	natural person.
غازٌ طَبيعِيّ	natural gas.
طِحال	spleen.
طحَّان	miller.
طَحَنَ	to mill, grind, crush.
طَحْن	grinding, ,milling, crushing.
طحين	flour.

يصنع الفران الخبز من الطحين

The baker makes bread from flour

طَحينَة	sauce made of sesame oil.
طُخْرُور	cirrus (high clouds).
طُرًّا	altogether, one and all.
طَرَأَ	to happen, occur, take place, develop, come about; to befall.
طَرَّاز	embroiderer.
طِراز	style, fashion; class, type; brand.
طَرافَة	originality, rarity; novelty, curiosity.
طَراوَة	softness, tenderness.
طَرِبَ	to be delighted, enraptured, jubilant, transported with joy.
طَرَب	joy, delight, mirth, rapture, elation; singing, music, chanting.
طَرِب	delighted, joyful, rapt, enraptured, jubilant, touched.
طَرْبوش، طُرْبُوش	fez.

انتشر اعتمار الطربوش خلال القرن التاسع عشر في مصر

Fez became very popular to wear in Egypt during the nineteenth century

طَرَحَ	to substract (math); to deduct; to hurl, throw, toss; to cast off, shed off; to jettison (a ship's load); to miscarry (about a pregnant woman); to put forth, raise, bring up; to introduce.
طَرَّحَ	to cause, induce, effect an abortion to a pregnant woman.
طَرْح	expulsion, rejection, repulsion, repudiation; substraction (math); deduction, discount; miscarriage, abortion (of a pregnant woman); bringing up, posing, presentation.

طَرْحَة scarf, veil.

تضع العروس الطرحة على رأسها في حفلة الزواج
The bride wears a veil on her head during the marriage ceremony

---

طَرَدَ to expel, throw out, oust, evict, eject; to repel, repulse, deport, banish, exile; to dismiss, discharge, fire, expel (from an office).

طَرْد expulsion, repulsion, eviction; dismissal (of an office) banishment, hunt, chase.

طَرْد parcel, package; swarm of bees.

طَرَّزَ to embroider, stitch.

طَرَش deafness.

طَرَفَ to blink, wink (eyes); to twinkle.

طَرَف edge, border, limit; tip, point; side, part; party; limb, extremity; term (math); trace, touch, bit, smack.

طَرَفَا النَّهار morning and evening.

على طَرَفَيْ نَقيض differing in opinion; contradictory; diametrically opposed, contradicting, opposed; disagreeing.

من طَرَف on the part of, from, by.

طَرْف eye; glance, look.

من طَرْفٍ خَفِيّ stealthily, secretly, furtively.

طَرْفَة twinkle, wink, flicker of an eye.

في طَرْفَةِ عين instantly, immediately, in no time.

طُرْفَة anecdote, novelty, rarity, curiosity, rare object; exquisite present, masterpiece; hit, highlight.

طَرَفِيّ extreme, marginal, lateral, terminal.

طَرَقَ to strike, percuss, knock, hit, bang (on a door); to hammer, forge, (metal); to come by night.

طَرَقَ مَوْضُوعًا to broach, raise, treat, deal with.

طَرْق hammering, striking; forging; knocking, tapping, banging.

طَرْقَة knock, rap, blow.

طَرُوب merry, gay, gleeful.

طَرُوق malleable, ductible (metal).

طَرِيّ soft, tender, fresh, mellow.

طريح thrown down, cast down, felled; expelled, rejected.

طريحُ الفِرَاش bedridden, confined to bed.

طَريد expelled, outlawed, banished; fugitive, on the run, outcast, ousted.

طَريدَة game, quarry.

طَريق way, road, path; trail, route; course; street.

عن طريق by means of, by way of, via.

طريقَة way, method, procedure, process, system, manner; means,approach; creed, faith, doctrine, religious community.

طَعام food, foodstuff, victual.

طَعَّمَ to graft, transplant; to inoculate, vaccinate, inject.

طَعْم taste, flavor, savor.

طُعْم bait, lure, decoy; graft (plants); vaccine.

طَعَنَ to stab, thrust, pierce, jab; to defame, slander, vilify; to calumniate; to contest, challenge; to appeal (a judgment).

طَعَنَ في السِّنّ to grow old; to be aged.

طَعْن stabbing, thrusting, piercing, jabbing; defamation, slander, calumny, libel; contestation, challenge; appeal (of a judgment).

طَعْنَة stab, thrust, jab.

طَغا to exceed the proper bounds; to overflow, flood; (river); to surge, heave, swell up (sea):

طَغَى to oppress, rule tyranically; to be despotic, tyrannical, autocratic; to exceed the proper bounds; to be rough, tumultuous (sea); to overflow (river); to prevail, predominate, preponderate, outweigh, outbalance.

طُغْمَة group, band, troop.

طُغْيان tyranny, oppression, despotism; flood, inundation, deluge.

طَفا to float, emerge, surface, spring up,

طَفَحَ to be overflowing; to flow over, spill over.

طَفْح superabundance; skin rash, eruption; overflow.

طَفَرَ to jump, leap, bounce.

طَفْرَة jump, leap, bounce; impulsive motion, rise, upswing; successful step; gust, outburst, surge.

طَفِقَ to set to, begin, set out to do; to do suddenly.

طِفْل infant, baby, child.

طَفْو ، طُفُو floating, flotation, buoyancy; emergency, appearance, rise.

طُفُولَة infancy, childhood.

طُفُوليّ child, pertaining to childhood, infantile, childlike.

طَفيف slight, little, trivial, insignificant, small.

طُفَيْليّ parasite, uninvited guest, intruder, sycophant.

طَقَّ to crack, pop, smack, flap; to burst, explode.

طَقْس weather, climate; rite, ritual; ceremony.

طَقْطَقَة crackle, rattle, clatter, crash, snap.

طَقْم series, set (of tools); suit (of clothes).

طَقْمُ الحِصان harness.

طَقْمُ شاي tea service.

طَقْمُ أسْنان denture, set of false teeth.

طَلَّ to rise, appear, show; to bespray, bedew, bedrizzle.

طَلّ dew, drizzle.

طَلَى to paint, daub, coat; overlay, plate, gild (with gold); galvanize (with electricity); to enamel.

طِلاء coat, paint, overlay, plating; facepaint; galvanization, electroplating; polish.

طَلاق divorce.

طَلاقَة ease, relaxedness, unrestraint.

طَلاقَةُ اللِّسان fluency, eloquence.

طَلاقَةُ الوجه gaiety, cheerfulness of the face.

طَلَبَ to ask for, request, demand, call for, want, wish, desire; to look, search for; to try to obtain, ask, beg, require; to entreat, order, appeal to; to send for, summon.

طَلَبَ يَدَ فَتاةٍ to propose, ask a girl for marriage.

طَلَب demand, request, claim, order, quest; application, petition, appeal; requisition.

تَحْتَ الطَّلَب on order, on demand, by request.

حَسَبَ الطَّلَب made to order, custom-made.

طَلْحِيَّة sheet of paper.

طِلَسْم، طِلَسْم، طِلَّسْم talisman, charm, enigma; mystery.

طَلَعَ to rise, ascend, come up, appear, show, become visible; to erupt, sprout, break forth (plant); to emerge, come suddenly upon; to climb, get on top, get aboard into (car, train, plane).

طَلْعَة looks, appearance, aspect, guise; rise, ascent.

طَلُقَ to be jovial, cheerful, happy (face).

طُلِقَتِ الحاملُ to be in labor.

طَلَّقَ to divorce; to leave, quit, part with, forsake.

طَلَقٌ نارِيّ، طَلَقَةٌ نارِيَّة gunshot.

طَلْق labor, pains (of childbirth).

طَلْق talc.

طَلِق free, unconfined, uninhibited.

طَلِقُ المُحَيّا with a cheerful face, bright-faced.

طَلِقُ اللِّسان eloquent.

طَلِقُ اليَدَيْن openhanded, generous.

طُلُوع rise, ascension, ascent; climbing, mounting; emergency, coming out.

طُلُوعُ الشَّمْس sunrise.

طَلْي painting, daubing, coating, plating; gilding; electroplating, galvanizing, enameling.

طَلِيعَة forefront, foremost, vanguard.

طَلائِع (ج) pioneers, pathfinders, scouts; forerunners, precursors; signs, indications, symptoms; beginnings.

طَلِيعِيّ pioneer, avant-garde.

طَلِيق set free, freed, released; freed man.

طَمَّاع greedy, covetous, avaricious, desirous.

طَمْأَنَ to reassure, give confidence to; to quiet, calm, pacify, appease, soothe, assuage.

طُمَأْنِينَة tranquility, peace of mind, quietude; security, safety; assurance; ease, calmness; trust, confidence.

طَمْث menstruation, period, menses.

طَمَحَ to aspire to, aim to, yearn for; to strive, crave, covet.

طَمَرَ to bury, inter, cover with earth, fill up with earth.

طَمْر burial, interment; filling up with earth.

طَمَسَ to obliterate, erase, efface, wipe out; to destroy, eradicate, blot out; to suppress, hush up.

طَمْس effacement, obliteration, blotting out, suppression, hushing up.

طَمِعَ to covet, desire, wish, crave, strive, aspire; to hope; to be ambitious, covetous, greedy, avaricious; to be filled with greed.

طَمَع greed, cupidity, avarice, covetousness, ambition.

طَمُوح ambitious, aspirant, yearning, eager, covetous, avid.

طُمُوح ambition, aspiration, longing, yearning, avidity; endeavor; craving, loftiness of purpose.

طَمْي alluvium, silt, alluvial mud.

طُنّ ton.

طَنَّان ringing, resonant, buzzing, humming; pompous, famous, renowned, celebrate.

طَنْجَرَة cooking pot, cooking pan, skillet.

تطبخ والدتي الطعام في طنجرة مصنوعة من المعدن
My mother cooks meals in a cooking pot made of metal

طَنْطَنَ to tinkle, peal, ring; to hum, buzz, drone; to clang, boom, roar, rumble, blare out.

طَنْطَنَة ringing, pealing, tinkling, humming, buzzing, droning.

طُنُف، طَنَف، طَنْف ledge, eaves, cornice; top, summit, peak; promontory, bodily prominence.

طَنْفُسَة، طُنْفُسَة، طِنْفِسَة carpet, rug.

طَنِين buzz, hum, drone, whiz; ringing (of the ear).

طَها to cook.

طَهَارَة cleanness, purity; chastity, chasteness, virtue; innocence, honesty, probity righteousness.

طَهُرَ، طَهَرَ to be clean, pure; to clean, purge, expurgate.

طَهَّرَ purify, disinfect, sterilize; to circumcise; to chasten, refine, expurgate.

طَهْو	cooking.
طَهُور	circumcision; cleansing, purging.

طَوَى	to fold, double; to pleat, bend, flex.
طَوَى	to keep secret; to cover up, conceal, hide.
طَوَى	to cross, traverse (a country); to spend, pass.
طَوَى	to end, bring to an end, finish, give up, renounce.
طَوَى صَفْحَةَ المَاضِي	to let bygones be bygones; to turn a new page in one's life.
طَوًى	hunger, starvation.
عن طَوَاعِيَة	voluntarily; to one's own accord.
طَوَاف	circumambulation, circling, walking around; wandering about, roaming, cruising, traveling; round, circuit.
طَوَّاف	ambulant, ambulatory, itenerant, roving, wandering, making the circuit, walking the beat.
طَوَّافَة	helicopter.
طَوَال	during, throughout, all through; along, alongside of.
طُوب (ج)	bricks, adobes, tiles.
طوبوغرافيا	topography.
طَوَّحَ	to hurl, throw; cast, toss; to endanger, expose to danger.
طَوْد	mountain.
طَوَّرَ	to develop, promote, advance, further.
طَوْر	phase, stage, period, degree; state; limit; one time.
طَوْرًا بعد طَوْر	time and again.
خَرَجَ عن طورِهِ	to become upset; to lose one's selfcontrol.
طُور	mountain.
طَوَّعَ	to subdue, render obedient; to enlist, recruit, draft, enroll in the armed forces.

طَوْع	spontaneity; obedient, compliant, submissive.
طَوْعًا	voluntarily.
طَوْعَ يَدِهِ	under someone's beck and call.
طوعيًّا	voluntarily, of one's own accord.
طَوْف	raft, float, pontoon; patrol, nightwatch; enclosure.
طُوفان	flood, deluge.

أغرقت مياه الطوفان البيوت والمزارع

Flood waters inundated houses and farms

طَوَّقَ	to surround, clasp, enwrap, encircle, enclose; to control, contain, check; to embrace, hug, wrap in one's arms.
طَوْق	collar; hoop, circle, ring; strap, girdle, ribbon; ability, power, strength, capability, aptitude.

طَوْل might, power, strength.

طُوْل length, height.

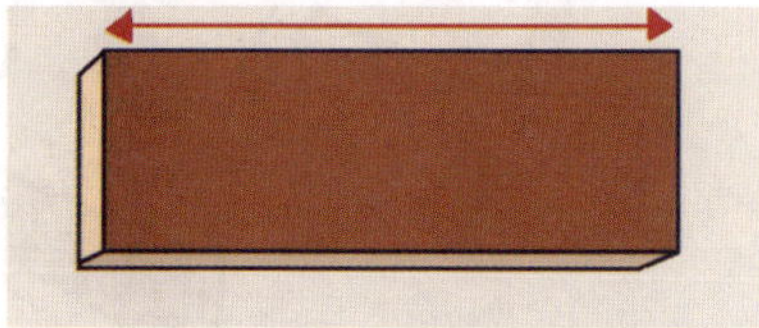

يبلغ طول المكيّف الهوائيّ متراً واحداً

The length of the airconditioning set is one meter

بِالطُّوْل lengthwise.

طولُ الأناة patience, endurance, tolerance.

طولُ الموجة wavelength.

طُوْلِيّ linear, longitudinal.

طَوِيَ to be hungry; to starve.

طَوِيل long, high, tall, big.

طَوِيلُ الأمَد long-term.

طَوِيلُ الأناة patient, tolerant, forbearing.

طَوِيلُ الباع mighty, powerful, capable, able.

طَوِيلُ البصر farsighted, hyperopic.

طَوِيلُ اللِّسان impudent, insolent.

طَيّ folding, doubling, pleating, flexing.

طَيَّهُ enclosed, herewith, attached.

طَيَّار (ص) volatile.

طَيَّار (اسم) pilot, flyer, aviator.

طَيَّبَ to make agreeable, delicious, sweet; to perfume, flavor, spice, season.

طَيَّبَ خاطِرَهُ to soothe, placate, mollify.

طَيِّب good, pleasant, agreeable, delicious; gay; well-disposed; friendly, kindly; well, in good health.

طَيِّبُ الخُلُق good-natured, genial.

طَيِّبُ القلب kind, generous.

طَيِّبُ السَّريرة simplehearted, simpleminded, sincere, naive.

طِيب perfume, scent.

طيبَة goodness; tastiness; deliciousness; geniality.

عن طيبَةِ خَاطِر most willingly, with pleasure.

طَيَّرَ to fly, fly off; to pass on promptly, dispatch quickly; to rush, forward without delay (report, message); to make fly.

طَيْر bird, fowl.

عِلْمُ الطُّيور ornithology.

طَيَران flying, flight, air navigation.

عِلْمُ الطَّيَران aeronautics.

شَرِكَةُ طَيَران airline.

خُطوطُ الطَّيَران airways, airlines.

طَيْش fickleness, recklessness, rashness, frivolity.

طَيْف vision; phantom; fantasy, apparition; specter, ghost.

طَيَّنَ to coat with clay; to whitewash, lute, plaster.

طِين clay, mud, mortar, plaster, mire, argil.

زاد في الطِّين بلَّة to make things worse.

طينة kind, specific character, constitution, nature; clay, plaster; mire, mud; argil, mortar.

حرف الظاء

ظافِر victorious, successful, winner, victor, triumphant.

ظالِم (ص) unjust, unfair, oppressing, iniquitous.

ظالِم (اسم) tyrant, oppressor, transgressor, sinner.

ظاهِر apparent, visible, perceptible, obvious, evident, clear, manifest, conspicuous, external; seeming, presumed, ostensible, alleged; outside, exterior surface.

ظاهِرُ المدينة outskirt.

ظاهِرًا seemingly, ostensibly, outwardly.

ظاهِرُ اللَّفظ literal meaning of an expression.

الظَّاهِرُ أنَّ it seems, it appears.

ظاهِرَة phenomenon.

ظاهِرِيّ outward, exterior; ostensible, apparent; alleged; prima facie.

ظاهِريًا outward, outside, externally, seemingly, allegedly.

ظَرافَة elegance, grace, charm, gracefulness.

ظَرْف envelope, receptacle; circumstance, condition, state; occasion, time, period.

ظَرْف wit, charm, elegance, gracefulness, cleverness.

ظَرْفُ زَمان adverb of time.

ظَرْفُ مَكان adverb of place.

بِظَرْف، في ظَرْف within, during.

حَسَبَ الظَّرْف according to the circumstance.

ظَرْفُ تَخْفيف extenuating circumstance.

ظَرْفُ تَشْديد aggravating circumstance.

ظَرْفيّ adverbial.

ظريف witty, elegant, graceful, charming, nice, fine; humorous, amusing, comical; cute.

ظَفِرَ to win, gain, obtain, get; to conquer, vanquish, beat, overpower, overcome.

ظَفَر trimph, victory, success.

ظُفُر، ظُفْر، ظِفْر fingernail, toenail; claw (of animal).

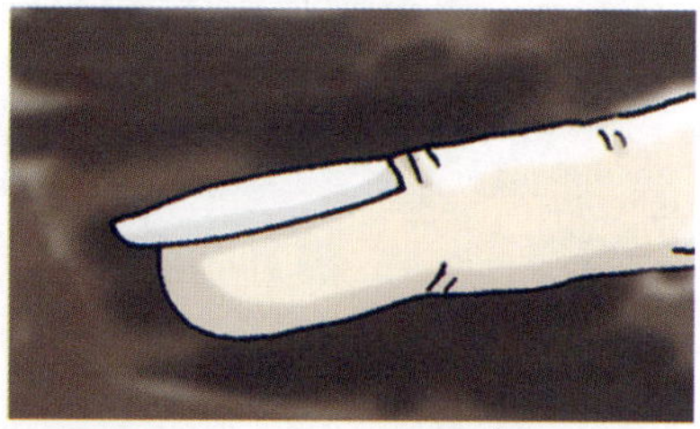

كلّما طال الظفر يجب قصّه

Fingernails should be cut whenever they get longer

ظَلَّ to continue to do, keep doing, persevere in doing; to remain, stay; to last, endure, persist.

ظِلّ shadow, shade.

في ظِلّ، تحتَ ظِلّ under, under the protection of.

ثَقيلُ الظِّلّ insufferable, annoying, vexing, bore, dull.

خفيفُ الظِّلّ likable, nice, funny, charming, amiable, witty.

ظَلام، ظُلْمَة darkness, duskiness, gloom, murkiness.

ظُلامَة grievance, complaint; injustice, misdeed, iniquity.

ظِلْف hoof (of an animal); cloven hoof.

ظَلَّلَ to shade, overshadow, cast a shadow over; to screen, shelter, protect, guard (from the sun).

ظَلَمَ to oppress, tyrannize, maltreat; to be unjust toward; to do injustice to; to harm, commit outrage upon.

ظَلِمَ to be dark, dusky, gloomy, tenebrous.

ظُلْم injustice, wrong, oppression, tyranny, iniquity.

ظليل shady.

ظَمَأ، ظماء thirst.

ظَمِئ، ظَمْآن thirsty.

ظَنَّ to think, assume, suppose, believe, deem, consider; to suspect, doubt; to mistrust, distrust, accuse of, charge.

ظَنّ assumption, belief, view; doubt, mistrust, dubiosity.

في أغْلَب الظَّنّ، أكْثَرُ الظَّنّ most probably, most likely.

ظَنَّان، ظنون، ظنين suspicious, distrusting, unreliable, suspect, untrustworthy.

ظَنّيّ presumptive, supposed, hypothetical, assumed; accusatory, indictment.

ظَهَرَ to be visible, perceptible, distinct, clear, obvious; to give the impression of; to come to light, into sight; to emerge, crop up; to develop, appear; to sound, seem.

ظَهَرَ to occur, happen, take place; to mount, climb, ascend; to gain the upperhand, triumph over, overcome, conquer; to come to know; to gain knowledge of, become acquainted with; to learn; to be cognisant of.

ظَهَّرَ to endorse (a cheque); to develop (a photograph).

ظَهْر surface, upper part, top; deck (of ship); shell.

ظهرًا لِبَطْن upside down, topsy-turvy.

عن ظَهْرِ قَلْب by heart.

ظُهْر noon, midday.

بَعْدَ الظُّهْر afternoon.

قَبْلَ الظُّهْر in the forenoon.

ظُهُور appearance, emergence; occurence, happening.

حُبُّ الظُّهُور exhibitionism, pomposity, ostantatiousness.

ظَهير helper, assistant, aid, supporter, partisan; back (in football); hinterland (geog.).

عَائِد (ص) recurrent; going back to; relating to, connected with, returning, reverting; accruing; (profits); belonging, pertaining to.

عَائِد (اسم) visitor to a sick person; revenue, profit, gain.

عَائِدات (ج) revenues, profits; duties, fees; royalties.

عائِق ، عائِقَة obstacle, hindrance, impediment; barrier; obstruction.

عَائِلة family, household.

عَائِلِيّ domestic, familial.

عَائِم floating, afloat; swimming.

عَابَ to render faulty or defective; to mar, disfigure, spoil; to find fault with; to accuse of a fault; to dishonor, disgrace; to blame, censure, decry, reprimand, chide, reproach.

تتألف العائلة من الأم والأب والأولاد
The family is formed of a father, a mother and their children

عَابِث frivolous, jocular; scornful, wicked, outrageous, wanton.

عَابِر passing, fleeting, transient, ephemeral, temporal.

أ ب ت ث ج ح خ د ذ ر ز س ش ص ض ط ظ ع غ ف ق ك ل م ن هـ و ي

عابِر past, bygone, elapsed (time); casual, incidental; crossing.

عابِرُ سَبيل passer-by.

عابِس frowning, scowling, sullen, sulky; gloomy, morose, grim, stern, austere, severe.

عاتٍ (العاتي) arrogant, haughty, presumptuous, impudent, impertinent; violent, fierce, wild, furious, raging (storm); tyrannical, powerful, highhanded.

عاتَبَ to admonish, blame, reprove, censure, scold (in a friendly manner).

عاثَ to ravage, sow havoc, make trouble, cause mischief.

عاجِز feeble, helpless, unable, incompetent, unqualified; impotent, disabled, decrepit; invalid, incapable of.

عاجِل immediate, prompt, hurried, abrupt, urgent, pressing.

عاجِلاً soon, immediately, instantly, quickly, rapidly.

عادَ to return, come back, go back; to revert, refer, relate; to be due; to belong, appertain; to visit a patient; to resume, recommence.

عادَ عَن to withdraw, give up, abandon, relinquish, abstain from.

عادَى to engage in hostile action; to act unjustly toward; to assail, attack; to treat as an enemy; to be at war with.

عادَة habit, custom, usage.

عادَةً usually, as a rule, normally.

كالعادَة as usual.

فَوْقَ العادَة extraordinary, unusual, special.

على عادتِه according to his habit.

العادَةُ السِّرِّيَّة masturbation.

عادَلَ to equal, match, outweigh, equalize, treat as equal; to straighten up, make straight; to neutralize (chemistry).

عادِل just, fair, equitable, impartial, rightful; honest.

عادِيّ ordinary, usual, customary, conventional, regular; plain, simple, normal; old, ancient, antique.

عادِيَة wrong, outrage; misfortune.

عاذَ to seek the protection of someone from; to take refuge with someone from.

عاذِل، عَذُول censurer, critic, reprover.

عار shame, disgrace; infamy, disrepute, dishonor, discredit; ignominy.

عارٍ (العاري) naked, nude, undressed, bare; devoid, destitute; free, stripped, deprived of; blank, stark.

عاري القَدَمَيْن barefoot.

عارٍ عن الصِّحَّة unfounded, false, untrue.

عارَضَ to oppose, resist, work against; to contradict, protest, object, raise objections; to remonstrate against; to stand up against.

عارِض demonstrator, exposer, exhibitor.

عارِض fit, attack, spell; accident, incident.

عارِضَة beam, girder, prop, transom; jamb (of door); cheek, side of the face.

عارِضَةُ أَزْيَاء mannequin, model.

عارِف familiar, acquainted, cognizant of; expert, authority.

عارِم vicious, violent; tremendous; huge, overwhelming.

عَازَ to need, require; to be in need of.

عازِف player, musician (music).

عازِل insulator, nonconductor of electricity; insulation.

عازِم resolved to; determined to; dead set to.

عاشَ to live, exist, be alive.

عاشَ الملك! long live the king!.

عاشَرَ to associate with; to be associated with; to live with another.

عاشِر ، العَاشِر tenth, the tenth.

عاشِق lover, enamored of, infatuated with.

عاصٍ (العاصي) hard; disobedient, insubordinate, insurgent, rebellious; mutineer, riotous, rebel; sinning, sinful.

عاصَرَ to be a contemporaneous.

عاصِفَة storm, tempest, gale, hurricane, violent wind.

اقتلعت العاصفة الأشجار وهدمت المنازل
The hurricane uprooted trees and destroyed houses

عاصِفَةٌ بَرَدِيَّة hailstorm.

عاصِفَةٌ رَعْدِيَّة thunderstorm.

عاصِمَة capital, metropolis.

بيروت هي عاصمة الجمهورية اللبنانية
Beirut is the capital of Lebanon

عاضَدَ to help, assist, aid; support, advocate, stand up for; give mutual help; to cooperate, work hand in hand.

عاطِر sweet-smelling, fragrant, aromatic.

عاطِفة amorous affection, affection, benevolence; sympathy, compassion, attachment, sentiment, feeling, emotion.

عاطِفِيّ sentimental, emotional, passionate, romantic; touching, emotive, tender, affectionate.

عاطِلٌ عن العَمَل — unemployed, jobless, idle; destitute, inactive, useless; out of work; shut-off.

عافَ — to loathe, have an aversion to; to feel disgust at.

عافَى — to restore to health, heal, cure; to protect from evil; to guard against harm.

عافِيَة — good health.

عاقٌّ، عَقُوق — disobedient; untrue; ungrateful, disloyal.

عاقَبَ — to punish, chastise, discipline, penalize.

عاقَبَ — to alternate, rotate, cause to follow one another.

عاقِبَة — issue, consequence, result, outcome; effect; end.

عاقِر — barren, sterile.

عاقِل — rational, reasonable, wise, sage, discerning, intelligent; sane in mind; prudent.

عاكَسَ — to contradict, oppose, counteract, thwart; to molest, vex, tease, harass.

عاكِس — reflector; commutator; lampshade, screen.

عاكِف — addicted, obsessed by, bent on, busily engaged in.

عالَ — to have a numerous family; to be poor, reduced to poverty, become impoverished; to be unjust, unfair in his judgement.

عالٍ (العالي) — high, elevated, tall; high-ranking, eminent; loud, strident (voice).

عالي الهِمَّة — ambitious, aspiring.

عالَة — dependent, parasite; burden, charge; poverty; canopy, marquee, awning.

عالَجَ — to treat (a patient); to deal with (a subject); to attend to; to take upon oneself; to work on, manipulate, try hard.

عالِق — suspended, undecided (subject); pending, conditioned.

عالَم — world, universe.

عالَمُ الحَيَوان — animal kingdom.

عَالِم (ص) — acquainted with, cognizant of, familiar with.

عَالِم (اسم) — scientist, savant, scholar, erudite, learned, expert.

عَالَمِيّ — worldwide, universal, international.

عامَ — to float, swim.

عام — year.

عامّ — public, universal, common, general.

بِصورة عامَّة، بوجه عامّ — in general, generally, altogether.

أَمْلاكٌ عامَّة — public domain, public property.

العامَّة — the common people, the masses, populace.

عامِر — inhabited, peopled, populated; full, filled, crowded; civilized; cultivated land; flourishing, thriving.

عامِرٌ بالأَمَل — full of hope.

عامَلَ — to treat with, deal with; to handle; to transact business with; to trade with.

عامَلَ بِالمِثْل to repay for like; to treat in like manner.

عامِل (ص) active, effective, functioning, operating.

عامِل (اسم) worker, workman, laborer, wage earner; factor, element, agent, motive power; maker, producer, doer, author.

عامِل تَنْظيفات sweeper, garbage collector.

عامّيّ slang, colloquial, vernacular; common, vulgar.

العامّيّة slang, vernacular, colloquial (language).

عانى to endure, bear, suffer, meet with; to be preoccupied with; to take pains in doing something; to undergo, sustain, labor.

عانَدَ to oppose, resist; to be obstinate, offer resistance.

عانِس spinster.

عانَقَ to embrace, hug; to press someone to the bosom.

عاهَة handicap, disability, deformity, infirmity.

عاهَدَ to promise, pledge, undertake, bind oneself; to make a contract with someone; to obligate oneself to.

عاهِرَة whore, harlot, prostitute, adulteress.

عاهِل king, monarch.

عاوَدَ to return to, revert to, recommence, do again; to recur, affect again (sickness).

عاوَنَ to help, aid, assist, support, relieve, succor.

عايَدَ to wish someone a happy feast.

عايَرَ to gauge, test the accuracy of; to regulate, adjust, fix, standardize, calibrate; to titrate (chem.).

عايَشَ to live with; to cohabit with; to live together.

عايَنَ to check, examine, inspect; to see with one's eyes; to view, look at, scrutinize.

عَبَأَ to care about, pay attention to.

لا يُعْبأُ بِهِ unimportant, insignificant.

غَيْرُ عابِئ indifferent, unconcerned.

عَبَّأَ to fill up, pack, encase, can, package.

عَبَّأَ to call up, mobilize, recruit (army).

عَبَّأَ to charge, load, fill; to wind up (a clock).

عِبء burden, charge, load, onus.

عَباءَة، عَباء cloak, gown, aba.

عِبادَة worship, adoration, cult, devotion.

عِبادَةُ الأوْثان adolatry.

عِبادَةُ الشَّخْصِيَّة personality cult.

عِبارَة phrase, expression, word, idiom, term.

عِبارَةٌ عَن consisting in, equivalent to, meaning.

بِعِبارَةٍ أُخْرى in other words, put another way, that is to say.

عَبِثَ to play with, dally with, tamper with, mess around; to abuse, misuse (something).

يرتدي البدوي عباءة للوقاية من الطقس البارد
The bedouin wears a aba to protect himself in cold weather

عَبَث play, frivolity, toying with, tampering with, messing around; abuse, misuse, absurdity.

عَبَث futility, uselessness, vainness, fruitlessness.

عَبَثًا in vain, vainly, to no avail.

عَبَدَ to worship, adore.

عَبَّدَ to pave (roads).

عَبْد slave, serf, servant, man, human being.

عَبَرَ to cross, traverse, pass across; to go by, elapse (time).

عَبَّرَ to express, voice, declare, state, speak out, make clear (one's opinions, ideas, feelings etc).

عَبْر، عِبْر across, through, via, by way of, by means of; on the other side of.

عَبْرَة teardrop.

عِبْرَة example, lesson, warning, something decisive or crucial; advice, rule, precept to be followed, that which is of consequence, of importance.

عَبَسَ to frown, glower, scowl, look sternly.

عَبِقَ to be fragrant, full of, filled with a scent.

عَبْقَرِيّ، عَبْقَرِيَّة genius.

عُبُوَّة refill.

عُبُوَّةٌ ناسِفَة bomb, explosive.

عُبُودِيَّة slavery, bondage, servitude; homage, adoration, worship.

عُبُور crossing, traversing, transit; passage; fording.

عُبُوس frowning, scowling, glowering, sulkiness, gloominess; austerity, sternness.

عَبِير fragrance, scent, perfume, redolence.

عِتَاب admonition, reproof, friendly reproach, blame.

عَتَاد equipments, materiel, war materiel, ordnance, military supplies, ammunition.

عَتَّال porter.

عِتَالَة porterage.

عَتَبَ to blame, censure, reprove, scold.

ينقل العتّال الأمتعة على ظهره المُقوَّس

The porter carries the luggage on his curved back

عَتَبَة — threshold, doorsill, lintel; step, stair.

عَتَقَ، عَتُقَ — to be old, ancient, antique; to mature, ripen.

عَتَلَة — lever, crowbar.

عَتَّم — to hesitate, waver.

ما عَتَّمَ أن — it did not take long until.

عَتَّمَ — to darken, obscure, cloud, black out.

عَتَمَة — darkness, gloom, dark.

عَتَه، عُتْه — idiocy, imbecility, insanity, lunacy.

عَتِيد — future, forthcoming; intended, prepared, ready.

عَتِيق — old, ancient, antique.

البيتُ العَتِيق — the Kaaba.

عُثَّة — moth, mite.

عَثَرَ — to trip, tumble, stumble.

عَثَرَ على — to find, come across, chance upon, happen upon; to discover, detect.

عَثْرَة — tumble, false step, trip, misstep.

عُثُور — finding, detection, discovery of.

عَجَّ — to vociferate, clamor, cry, yell; to abound, swarm, teem.

عَجَاج — dust, smoke.

عُجَالَة — hurried work, hastily prepared work, rush job.

عَجِبَ — to wonder, marvel; to be astonished, amazed, surprised.

عَجَب — astonishment, amazement, surprise; marvel, wonder.

لا عَجَب — no wonder.

يا للعَجَب — how wonderful, how strange.

عُجَّة — omelet.

عَجْرَفَة — arrogance, haughtiness, insolence, presumption.

عَجَزَ — to fail to, fall short of, be unable to do.

عَجَّزَ — to weaken, debilitate, paralyze, cripple; to grow old; to disable, frustrate, thwart, foil; to defeat.

عِجْز، عَجْز، عَجُز — buttocks, rump, posterior, backside; sacrum (anatomy).

عَجْز — weakness, impotence (sexual); inability, incompetence; failure, incapacity; disability, infirmity; decrepitude, defect, deficiency, shortage, lack, want.

عَجَّل to harry, hasten, speed, rush; to be in a hurry; to expedite, accelerate, speed up, dash, quicken.

عَجَّل to rush, impel, urge, press.

عَجَلَة wheel.

عَجَل، عَجَلَة hurry, haste, precipitation, in a hurry, speedily, expedition, speediness, hastiness.

عَجَمَ to try, test, put to the test; to provide a letter with diacritical points (grammar).

عَجَنَ to knead (dough); to blunge (clay).

عَجُوز old woman, old man

يجب علينا احترام
كلّ عجوز ومساعدته
We must respect and help
every old person we meet

عَجِيب wonderful, marvelous, amazing; strange, odd; remarkable.

عَجِيبَة miracle, wonder, prodigy.

عَجِيج clamor, roar; crying, yelling.

عَجِين، عَجِينَة dough, pasta, paste.

عَدَّ to count, number, reckon; to compute, calculate; to consider, deem, regard, find; to judge, hold.

عَدّ counting, calculation, computation, reckoning.

عَدّ considering, counting; deeming; judging, thinking.

عَدٌّ عَكْسِيّ countdown.

عَدَا to run, dash, race, gallop; to treat unjustly.

لا يَعْدُو كَوْنَهُ merely, solely, just, nothing more than.

عَدَّى to turn away from, abandon, leave; to omit, leave out; to overlook, disregard, bypass; to make a verb transitive (grammar).

عَدا، ما عدا، فيما عدا except, but, excluding, without, save.

فيما عدا ذلك besides, apart from, other, in addition to.

ما عَدا السَّهْو والخَطَأ errors and omission excepted.

عَدَّاء runner.

عِدَاء enmity, hostility, feud.

عِدَائِيّ hostile, antagonistic, offensive, aggressive.

عَدَّاد counter, meter (for electricity, water, etc.).

في عِدَاد among, one of.

عَدَالَة، عَدْل justice, impartiality, fairness; honesty, probity, equitableness, just, compromise; straightness, integrity, equity.

عدليّ	judicial, juridical.
عدِمَ	to be deprived, be devoid, be deficient of; to lack, lose, miss.
عدَم	non existence, nothing, nothingness; lack, want, loss; privation; nullity, banality, trifle.
عدَمُ الأهْلِيَّة	incapacity, incompetence.
عدَمُ الانْحِياز	nonalignment.
عدَمُ التَّدَخُّل	noninterference.
عدَمُ اعْتِداء	nonaggression.
عدَمُ الوجُود	nonexistence.
عدُوّ	enemy, foe.
عدْو	running, race, jogging.
عدْوَى	infection, contagion.
عُدْوان	aggression, assault, attack; wrongdoing.
عُدْوانيّ	aggressive, offensive, hostile, unfriendly.
عديد	numerous, many, several.
عديل	brother-in-law; equal, like, parallel, match.
عديم	lacking, in need of, bereft of, deprived of, devoid of; poor, destitute, impoverished.
عديمُ الأهْلِيَّة	incompetent.
عديمُ الحَياة	lifeless, inanimate.
عديمُ اللَّوْن	colorless.
عديمُ النَّظير	unequaled, incomparable, unique.
عذَاب	torture, torment, agony, pain, affliction, suffering.

عَذُبَ	to be sweet, pleasant, agreeable.
عَذَّبَ	to torture, agonize, afflict, punish, torment.
عَذْب	sweet, pleasant, agreeable.
عَذَرَ	to excuse, forgive.
عُذْر	excuse, pretense, plea.
عَذْراء	virgin, maiden; chrysalis (insect).
بُرْجُ العَذْراء	Virgo (astr.).
العَذْراءُ مَرْيَم	the Virgin Mary, the Madonna.
عُذْرِيّ	platonic, spiritual, pure, chaste.
عَذَلَ	to blame, censure, rebuke, reproach.
عَذْل	blame, censure, reproach, reproof.
عُذُوبَة	sweetness, charm.
عَرَّ	to be a disgrace, a shame; to bring shame upon; to dishonor someone.
عَرَا، عَرَى	to befall, grip, seize, strike, afflict.
عَرَّى	to disrobe, bare, denude, uncover, strip someone of his clothes; to deprive, divest, undress.
عُرْي	nakedness, nudity.
عَراء	outdoors, open air, open space.
في العَراء	outdoors, outside, in the open air, under the open sky.
عَرَّاب	godfather, sponsor.
عَرَّاف	diviner, soothsayer, fortune-teller.

عَرَاقَة ancestry, pedigree, noble descent.

عِرَاك fight, battle, quarrel, brawl.

عَرَّبَ to translate into Arabic; to Arabicize, make Arabic; to give an Arabic form; to express, voice, state clearly; to declare; to make a down payment; to proclaim, utter.

عَرَب، عُرْب، عُرْبَان Arabs.

عَرَبَة carriage, vehicle, wagon; van, cart, car, coach; cab, hack, hackney, hansom.

عَرَبَةُ أَطْفَال pram, go-cart, baby carriage.

عَرَبَةُ شَحْن truck, lorry, van.

عَرَبَةٌ مَقْطُورة trailer.

عَرَبَةُ يد pushcart, barow, wheelbarrow.

عَرْبَدَ to romp, make an orgy; to be quarrelsome, riotous, noisy, boisterous.

عَرْبَدَة revelry, boisterous festivity, orgy, romp, uproar.

عُرْبُون earnest money, down payment; pledge, tribute, token.

عَرَبِيّ (ص) Arab, Arabian, Arabic.

عَرَبِيّ (اسم) an Arab.

العَرَبِيَّة the Arabic language.

عِرْبِيد quarrelsome, noisy, riotous, reveler, romper.

عَرَجَ to limp, hobble; to be lame, walk lamely; to ascend, mount, rise.

عَرَّجَ to stop, halt, stay at; to call on someone; to visit a place; to turn off, swerve from, leave from; to zigzag, follow a zigzag course.

عُرْس wedding, marriage ceremony, nuptials.

عَرْش throne.

عَرَضَ to demonstrate, present, expose, exhibit, show; to offer, tender, extend; to become wide, broad; to widen, broaden; to propose, suggest.

عَرَضَ to review, examine, treat, discuss, study, parade (army); to show off; to follow, ensue.

عَرَضَ له عارِض an obstacle arose in his path.

عَرَضَ له خَاطِر a thought occured to him.

عَرَّضَ to broaden, widen, extend; to expose; to subject to; to make susceptible to.

عَرَّضَ للخطر to endanger, imperil, expose to danger.

عَرَّضَ بِالشَّخص to insinuate, allude, to, suggest indirectly.

عَرَض accident; symptom.

عَرَضًا by chance, incidentally, by coincidence.

عَرْض breadth, width; presentation, exhibition, show, exposure; offer, tender, bid; suggestion, proposal.

عَرْض putting forth, presenting; submission, reference, handing over to; examination, consideration, survey, studying.

عَرْض supply.

بِالعَرْض crosswise, across, widthwise, breadthwise.

عَرْضُ أزْيَاء fashion show.

عَرْضٌ أوّل premiere (film, show).

عَرْضُ حَال petition.

عُرْض side, middle.

عُرْضُ البحر high seas.

عِرْض honor, dignity, repute.

عُرْضَة design, target, intention.

عُرْضَةٌ لـِ subjected, liable to; exposed to, prone to, susceptible to.

عَرَضِيّ accidental, incidental, random, irrelevant, nonessential; fortuitous, casual, random, occasional.

عَرْضِيّ cross, transverse, horizontal.

عَرَفَ to know, recognize, perceive; to be aware of, cognizant of, acquainted with; to discover, find out; to acknowledge something as being right; to be positive about.

عَرَّفَ to introduce someone to another; to define, specify; to inform of, advise of, tell about, explain; to confess.

عَرَّفَ to make a noun definite (grammar).

عُرْف custom, practice, usage, tradition, habit, convention.

عُرْفُ الدِّيك comb, crest.

عُرْفُ الفَرَس mane.

عِرْفَان cognition, knowledge, perception ; acknowledgment.

عِرْفَانُ الجَمِيل gratitude, thankfulness.

عُرْفِيّ conventional, traditional, usual, customary, habitual.

حُكْمٌ عُرْفِيّ martial law.

عَرَّقَ to cause to sweat; to mix with water, add water to;to take root; to vein, strike roots.

عَرَق sweat, perspiration; arack; bond, course.

عِرْق vein, race, descent; root, rib, stem (of plant).

عِرقُ السُّوس licorice.

عَرْقَلَ to hinder, hamper, complicate, encumber, impede, obstruct.

عَرْقَلَة hindrance; impeding, obstruction, blocking.

عِرْقِيّ racial, ethnic.

عَرَكَ to turn, adjust; to play havoc with, damage severely; to rub, scour; to harden by experience.

عَرْكَة fight, battle, combat.

عَرَمْرَم violent, vehement; huge, numerous (army).

عُرُوبَة Arabism, pan-Arabism.

عُرْوَة buttonhole, loop, noose; handle, ear; tie, bond.

عَرُوس bride.

عَرُوسُ الشِّعْر muse.

عَرُوض prosody.

عِلْمُ العَرُوض prosody, metrics (poetry).

عَرِيَ to be naked, bare, undressed; to be divested of, devoid of, deprived.

عُرْي، عُرْيَة nakedness, nudity.

عَرِيس bridegroom.

عَرِيض broad, wide; vast, extensive.

عَرِيضَة petition, pleading, brief (of a court case).

عَرِيف corporal (army rank); monitor; introducer of speakers at a meeting; teaching assistant.

عَرِيق deep-rooted, ancient, of noble descent, highborn.

عَرِين lair, den.

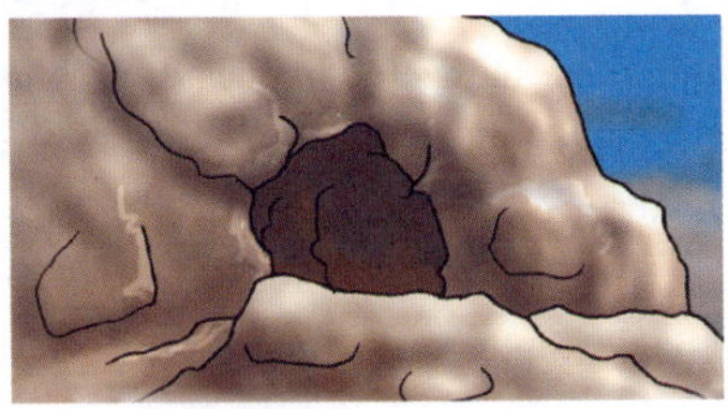

يعيش الأسد في عرينه مع أنثاه وأشباله

The lion lives in a den with its female and cubs

عَزَّ to be strong, powerful, respected; to be rare, scarce, dear, cherished, precious.

عَزَّ عليه أن he was sorry that...

عِزّ glory, prestige, power, might, fame, renown.

عَزَا، عَزَى to attribute to, ascribe, impute to; to incriminate, charge with; to blame, lay the blame on someone.

عَزَّى to console, comfort, give comfort to, express one's sympathy to, offer one's condolences to.

عَزَاء consolation, comfort, solace, condolence.

عُزْبَة، عُزُوبِيَّة، عُزُوبَة celibacy, bachelorhood.

عَزَّزَ to consolidate, make strong, strengthen, reinforce, fortify, confirm, solidify; to raise in esteem, exalt, elevate someone; to make dear, endear; to esteem, value; to enhance, improve, boost, support, bolster.

عَزَفَ to play on a musical instrument, play a tune.

عَزَفَ عن to abstain from, give up, refrain from.

عَزَقَ to hoe, dig up, loosen, break up the soil.

عَزَلَ to separate, isolate, segregate, set apart; to seal off, close tightly.

عَزَلَ to depose, oust, remove from an office; to dismiss, expel; to insulate (from electricity, sound, light etc.).

عَزْل separation, isolation, seclusion, segregation; insulation, displacement; removal from an office.

عُزْلَة isolation, seclusion, solitude, privacy.

عَزَمَ to resolve to; to decide to, embark upon; to be bent on, be determined to; to enchant, spellbind.

عَزْم resolution, resolve, determination, intention.

عَزْم moment (mech.).

عَزْو ascription, imputation, attribution.

عُزوف abstention, abandonment, turning away.

عَزِيز	precious, costly, valuable; dear, beloved, darling.
عَزِيز	rare; noble, revered; august,venerable.
عَزِيزُ الجَانِب	powerful, mighty, strong.
عَزِيمَة	determination, firm will, firm intention, decision.
عَزِيمَة	spell, charm, incantation.
عَسَى	maybe, perhaps, possibly; it may be that.
عَسُرَ، عَسِرَ	to be difficult, hard.
عَسَّرَ	to make difficult, hard; to oppress, bear down hard on.
عَسِر	hard, difficult, trying, distressing, adverse; harsh.
عُسْر، عُسُر، عُسْرَة	difficulty, distressful situation, predicament; plight, straits; poverty, distress; destitution.
عَسَفَ	to oppress, tyrannize, treat unjustly; to act recklessly; to act rashly; to deviate, stray from.
عَسْف	tyranny, despotism,oppression, injustice.
عَسْكَرَ	to camp, encamp.

ينتظم العسكر في صفوف لتحية العلم

Soldiers line up to salute the flag

عَسْكَرِيّ	military; soldier, private.
عَسَل	honey.
عَسَلِيّ	honey-colored.
عُشّ	nest.
عَشَاء	dinner, supper.
عِشَاء	evening, eve.
عَشَائِرِيَّة	tribalism.
عَشَاوَة	night blindness.
عَشُبَ، عَشِبَ، عَشَّبَ	to be grassy, grass-covered.
عُشْب	grass, plants, herbage, pasture.
عُشْبَة	plant, herb.
عُشْبَةٌ ضَارَّة	weed.
عُشْر، عِشْر	one tenth; tithe.
عَشَرَة	ten.
عِشْرَة	fellowship, company; companionship, intimacy, social intercourse, relations; association.
عِشْرُون	twenty.
العِشْرُون	the twentieth.
عَشْرِيّ، عُشْرِيّ	decimal.
كَسْرٌ عَشْرِيّ	decimal fraction.
عَشَّشَ	to build a nest; to nest.
عَشِقَ	to love passionately, adore, be enamored of.
عِشْق	passion, passionate love.
عِشْقُ الذَّات	narcissism.
عَشْوَائِيّ	random, haphazard, aimless.
عَشْوَائِيًّا	at random, randomly, aimlessly.

عَشِيَّة evening, eve, on the eve of.

بين عَشِيَّةٍ وضُحَاهَا overnight; all of a sudden, suddenly.

عَشِيرَة clan, tribe, kinsfolk, kindred.

عَشِيق lover, sweetheart.

عَشِيقَة sweetheart, paramour, beloved; mistress.

عَصَى to disobey, resist, revolt against; to refuse one's obedience; to be difficult, intricate, hard, inaccessible; to be recalcitrant, insubordinate, rebellious.

عَصَا stick, rod, staff, wand; walking stick; cane; scepter.

عَصَا المَارشالِيَّة field marshal's baton.

شَقَّ عَصَا الطَّاعَة to rebel, revolt, renounce allegiance.

عَصَا لُعبَة البليارد cue.

عِصَاب، عِصَابَة gang, band, group, company; band, bandage, dressing.

عِصَابَةُ الرَّأْس headcloth.

عَصَّارَة juicer, press, squeezer, wringer (cloth).

عُصَارَة juice, extract, sap.

عِصَامِيّ self-made.

عَصَبَ، عَصَّبَ to fold, tie, bind, wrap, bandage.

عَصَب nerve; sinews; mainstay.

عُصْبَة league, union, association, coalition; circle, band, gang, faction.

عَصَبِيّ nervous, irritable, irascible.

عَصَبِيَّة team spirit, partisanship, tribalism; nervousness, bigotry, fanaticism, nationalism.

عَصَرَ to press out, squeeze out, compress, wring (clothes).

عَصْر pressing, squeezing, compression, wringing (clothes).

عَصْر afternoon; age, era, epoch, period.

عَصْرٌ ذَهَبِيّ golden age.

عَصْرُ النَّفَقَات economizing, providence, frugality.

عَصْرِيّ modern, recent, present, actual, contemporary.

عَصَفَ to storm, rage, blow violently (wind); to shake thoroughly.

عُصْفُور sparrow, bird.

عَصَمَ to hold back, restrain, curb, check, prevent, hinder; to guard, safeguard, protect, defend; to immunize (med.).

عِصْمَة hindering, prevention; preservation, safeguarding; defense, protection.

عِصْمَة chastity, purity, modesty, infaillibility.

عِصْمَةُ الزَّوَاج bond of marriage.

عِصْيَان disobedience, insubordination, mutiny, rebellion, insurrection, sedition.

عَصِيب crucial, critical, hot, serious, grave, difficult.

عَصِير juice, syrup.

عَضَّ to bite; to torture, torment, afflict; to hold on.

عَضّ biting.

عُضال inveterate, chronic, incurable (disease).

عَضَدَ to support, help, back up, stand up for, cooperate.

عَضْد help, assistance, aid, support, backing; helper, assistant,supporter, backer.

عَضُد upper arm; strength, power, vigor, force.

شَدَّ عَضُدَه to stand by someone; to aid, assist.

عَضِلَ to be muscular.

عَضَلَة muscle.

العَضَلَة ذاتُ الرَّأْسَيْن biceps.

عَضَلَةٌ عاصِرَة sphincter.

عَضَلَةُ القَلْب myocardium.

عَضَلِيّ muscular.

عُضْو organ, member, limb.

عُضْوٌ في مجلس الشُّيوخ senator.

عُضْوِيّ organic.

عُضْوِيَّة membership (in a club, society etc.).

عَطاء gift, present, donation, bonus; tender, bid, offer.

عَطَّار druggist, spice dealer.

عُطارِد Mercury (astronomy).

عَطالَة unemployment; inertia.

عَطِبَ to damage, injure, harm, destroy, spoil, mar.

عَطَب wreck, destruction, ruin, damage, injury, perdition.

سَريعُ العَطَب fragile, delicate.

عَطَّرَ to perfume, aromatize.

عَطِر sweet-smelling, fragant, aromatic, perfumed.

عِطْر perfume, scent, essence, essential oil.

عَطَسَ to sneeze.

عَطْس sneezing, sneeze.

عَطِشَ to be thirsty, feel thirsty; to long, languish, yearn.

عَطِش ، عَطْشان thirsty; covetous, languishing, yearning.

عَطَفَ to bend, incline, bow, lean toward to; to be favorably disposed toward; to harbor affection for; to sympathize with; to feel compassion.

عَطْف sympathy, compassion, pity, affection, love, care, tenderness, kindness.

عَطْف bending, inclination, curving, curvature, inflection, bowing, twisting, turning.

حَرْفُ عَطْف conjunction (grammar).

عَطَّلَ to disable, incapaciate, stop, disrupt, interrupt, neutralize, put out of action; to defuse (a mine, bomb etc.); to hinder, hamper, impede, obstruct.

عُطْل failure, trouble, disorder, defectiveness; devoid of, lacking; damage, loss.

عُطْلَة holidays, vacation.

عُطْلَةُ نهاية الأسبوع weekend.

عُطْلَةٌ قَضائِيَّة court recess.

عَطوف sympathetic, compassionate, loving, warmhearted, kindhearted, kind, tender.

عُطوفة His Excellency.

عَطِيَّة gift, present, grant, donation.

عِظَة sermon; example, lesson.

عَظُمَ to be great, big, large; to be huge, immense, stupendous.

عَظَّمَ to glorify, exalt, extol, honor, prize, esteem; to magnify, enlarge, make greater, bigger, larger.

عَظْم bone.

عِظَم greatness, largeness; magnitude, importance, significance, grandeur.

عَظَمَة greatness, splendor, sublimity, loftiness; might, power; arrogance, pride.

عَظْمَة piece of bone, bone.

عَظِيم great, big, large, huge, tremendous, considerable; mighty, strong, powerful; grandiose, imposing, glorious, magnificent, majestic; significant, important, weighty, momentous.

عَفَّ to refrain from, abstain from; to be abstinent, virtuous, chaste, decent, pure.

عَفا to forgive, excuse, pardon; to exempt, free, relieve.

عَفَا to be effaced, obliterated, eliminated, wiped out.

عِفَّة، عَفَاف abstinence, continence, chastity, modesty; virtue, decency, purity; integrity, honesty, probity.

عَفَرَ، عَفَّرَ to cover with dust.

عِفْرِيت demon, devil, fiend; crafty, cunning; malicious, wicked; jack (of a car).

عَفِنَ to rot, decay, decompose, putrefy; to mildew.

عَفَّنَ to rot, decompose, decay.

عَفَن mold, mildew, rot; decay; putridity, putrefaction.

عَفِن putrid, rotten, decayed; foul; putrescent, moldy, musty; septic.

عَفُوّ forgiving, indulgent, tolerant.

عَفْو pardon, forgiveness; effacement, obliteration; favor, courtesy.

عَفْوًا I beg your pardon! pardon me! excuse me!.

عَفْوًا incidentally, spontaneously.

عَفْوٌ عامّ amnesty.

عُفُونَة putridity, putrefaction, decay; moldiness, mold, must; mildew, rot, rottenness.

عَفْوِيّ spontaneous, impulsive.

عَفْوِيَّة spontaneity.

عَفِيف chaste, modest, virtuous, pure.

عَقّ، عَقُوق disobedient, disrespectful, undutiful; refractory.

عُقُوق disobedience, unruliness; recalcitrance of a child.

عَقائِدِيّ ideological, dogmatic, doctrinal.

عِقاب punishment, punition, penalty, sanction.

عِقابِيّ punitive, penal, retributive.

عَقار real estate, real property, immovable property.

عَقَبَ to follow, come after, ensue.

عَقَّبَ to follow up with; to comment on, review, criticize; to come after; to be the father of a son; to have an offspring; to cause to succeed, follow.

عَقِب heel.

عَقِب offspring, progeny, descendants.

عَقِب end, remainder, rest; stub, stump, butt.

عَقِبَ subsequent to, in the wake of; immediately after.

رَأْسًا على عَقِب head over heels, topsy-turvy.

عَقَبَة obstacle, difficulty, obstraction; steep road or track, steep incline, mountain pass.

عَقَدَ to tie, fasten, lock; to conclude, agree, reach to an agreement; to hold, convene, convoke (a meeting).

عَقَدَ أَمَلَهُ على to set one's hopes on.

عَقَدَ العَزْمَ على to be firmly determined to do something.

عَقَدَ النِّيَّة على to resolve, make up one's mind to do something.

عَقَدَ على امْرَأَةٍ to marry a woman.

عَقَّدَ to complicate; to make complicated, complex, difficult; to knot tightly; to congeal, clot, thicken, set, solidify.

عَقْد contract, agreement, deed, bill, legal instrument.

عَقْد vault, arch.

عَقْد decade, group of ten, tens.

عَقْد tying, knotting, fastening.

عَقْد conclusion of an agreement.

العَقْدُ الاجتِماعِيّ social contract.

عَقْدُ إيجار lease, contract of tenancy.

عَقْدُ بَيْع bill of sale.

عَقْدُ تأسيس شركة articles of association.

عَقْدُ تأمين insurance policy.

عِقْد necklace.

عُقْدَة knot, loop; knob, nodule; growth; joint.

عُقْدَةٌ نَفْسِيَّة complex.

عُقْدَةُ النَّقْص inferiority complex.

عَقَرَ to wound; to slaughter, slay; to bite.

عُقْر barrenness, sterility.

في عُقْرِ دارِهِ on his own ground; in his own place.

عَقْرَب scorpion; pointer, hand (of a clock); Scorpio (astronomy); sting, prick;lock, curl.

عَقَلَ to intern, confine, detain, arrest, put under arrest; to be reasonable, have intelligence, be conscious; to realize, comprehend; understand; to shackle, hobble (a horse).

لا تقترب من العقرب خشية أن يلسعك فتموت

Do not come near a scorpion for fear of biting you and you will die thereafter

عَقَّلَ	to bring to reason.
عَقْل	mind, reason, comprehension; insight, intellect; intelligence; blood money; sense.
مُخْتَلُّ العَقْل	mentally deranged, insane, mad.
العَقْلُ الباطن	the unconscious.
العَقْلُ المُمَيِّز	the conscious.
عَقْلِيّ	mental, rational, reasonable, intellectual.
عَقْلِيَّة	mentality, mind.
عَقَمَ، عَقُمَ، عَقِمَ	to be sterile, barren (womb, woman).
عَقَّمَ	to sterilize, pasteurize, disinfect.
عُقْم، عَقَم، عَقْم	sterility, barrenness.
عُقُوبَة	punishment, penalty, sanction.
عُقُوبَةُ الإِعْدَام	capital punishment, death penalty.
عُقُوق	undutifulness, disobedience, ungratefulness (of a child).
عَقِيد	colonel (army rank).
عَقِيدَة	belief, doctrine, dogma, creed, faith, ideology.
عَقِيق	agate (precious stone); onyx; canyon, ravine.
عَقِيلَة	wife, spouse.
عَقِيم	sterile, barren; futile, useless, fruitless, ineffective, vain; of no avail, of no use.
عُكَّاز	crutch, walking stick, cane.

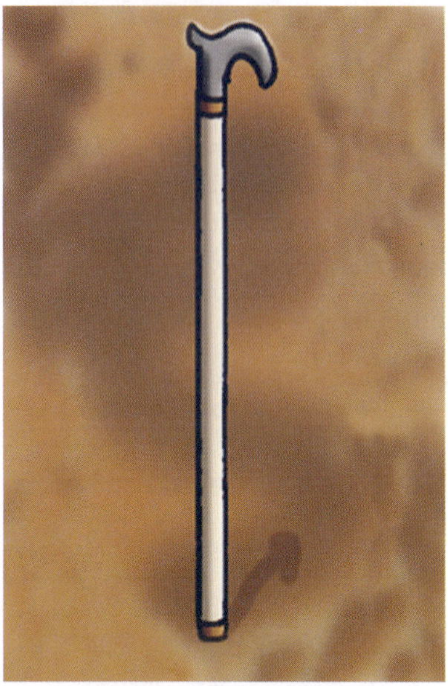

يتوكأ العجوز على عكاز أثناء سيره

The old man leans on his walking stick when walking

عَكَّرَ	to disturb, trouble; to make turbid, muddy, roily
عَكِر	turbid, muddy, roily; troubled, disturbed, deranged, muddled, confused.
عَكَسَ	to reverse, invert, reflect (light); to mirror, show, demonstrate, state, express.

عكس reversal, reversion, reflexion; opposite, contrary, reverse, counter.

بالعكس on the contrary.

والعكسُ بالعكسِ vice versa, conversely.

عكسيًا contrary, opposite, adverse, counter, inverse, reverse.

عكسيًا backwards, backwardly, conversely, inversely.

عكفَ to devote oneslf to; to dedicate oneself with; to be engaged in, busy with; to adhere to, stick to, cling to.

عكفَ to seclude oneself, isolate oneself in, retire to; to restrain, hold back, keep away from.

علّ perhaps, maybe.

علُ ، من علُ، من علِ from above.

علا، علِيَ to rise high, ascend; to be elevated, sublime, lofty, high.

علا، على to overtop, tower over, rise above, surmount.

عَلَى on, upon, on top of, above, over; at, on, by; for, toward; according to, in accordance with, pursuant to, on the basis of, by virtue of; against, in spite of; in addition to, on top of, over and above; by, through.

عَلى أنْ provided that, as long as.

عَلى أنَّ however, but, on the other hand, yet, still, though.

عَلى أنَّهُ in view that.

عَلَى الرَّأس والعَيْن with pleasure, very gladly.

عَلَى كُلِّ حَال in any case, at any rate.

عَلَى الخُصوص particularly, especially.

عَلَى الإطْلاق absolutely, without exception, under any circumstances.

عَلَى التَّوالِي incessantly, continuously.

عَلَيْهِ، وعَلَيْهِ accordingly, consequently, therefore, hence.

عُلّى، عَلاء highness, high rank, high standing; prestige; superiority, glory; loftiness.

عِلاج remedy, medical treatment, cure, therapy.

عَلاقَة relationship, connection, contact, relevance, bond, tie, link; attachment, devotion, affection.

عَلاقاتٌ عامَّة public relations.

عَلاقَاتٌ مُتَبادَلَة mutual relations.

عَلاّقَةُ ثِياب coat hanger.

عَلاّقَةُ مفاتيح key holder.

عَلامَة mark, sign, token; badge, emblem; characteristic, indication, symptom.

عَلامَةٌ تِجارِيَّة trade-mark.

عَلامَةُ التَّعَجُّب exclamation mark.

عَلامَةُ الاسْتِفْهام question mark.

عَلامَةٌ مدرَسيَّة grade mark.

عَلامَةٌ فارِقَة identifiying mark, peculiarity, attribute.

عَلاَّمَة most erudite, very learned person.

عَلانِية openness, openly, publicly; in public, overtly.

عِلاوَة increase, raise, allowance, subsidy, bonus.

عِلاوَةً على ذلك in addition to, over and above, on top of, along with, as well as, aside from, besides, moreover.

عُلْبَة box, case, pack, package; can, tin.

تحتوي علبة الثقاب حوالى أربعين عود ثقاب

The matchbox contains about forty matchsticks

عِلَّة disease, illness, sickness, malady; deficiency, defect; weakness; cause, reason, occasion; excuse, pretense, pretext, plea; imperfection, shortcoming, blemish, flaw.

عِلَّةُ الوُجُود raison d'etre.

حَرْفُ عِلَّة weak letter, vowel (grammar).

على عِلاَّتِه in spite of its defects, such as he is.

عَلَف fodder, forage, feed.

عَلِق to get caught in; to catch in, get stuck in; to stick, cling, cleave, adhere to; to be attached, devoted to.

عَلَّق to suspend, dangle, attach to, fasten to, affix to; to stick, post (a poster); to hold back, defer action on; to ban temporarily; to adjourn (a meeting); to make conditional on, contingent on (an agreement); to comment on, remark with regard to; to criticize, annotate.

عَلَّق الآمَالَ على to pin one's hopes on, depend on.

عَلَك to chew, masticate.

عِلْك، عِلْكَة chewing gum.

عَلَّل to justify, warrant, explain, give reasons for; to make an excuse, offer a pretext; to busy oneself with.

عَلَّل النَّفْسَ بِالآمَال to entertain hopes; to indulge in hopes.

عَلَّل بِالوعود to put off someone with promises.

عَلِمَ to know of, have knowledge of; to be aware of, cognizant of, familiar with; to learn about; to find out about; to perceive, discern.

عَلَّمَ to teach, instruct, educate; to mark, distinguish, designate, label something; to let know, tell about; to inform, apprise, notify, advise.

عَلَم flag, banner, standard.

عَلَم distinguished personality, authority; chief, head.

إِسْمُ عَلَم proper noun, proper name.

عِلْم science, knowledge, education, cognition, perception.

عِلْمُ الآثَار archaelogy.

عِلْمُ الاجْتِمَاع sociology.

عِلْمُ الأجناس البَشَرِيَّة ethnology.

عِلْمُ الإحْصاء statistics.

عِلْمُ الأحْياء biology.

عِلْمُ الأخْلاق ethics, morals.

عِلْمُ الأرصاد الجَوِيَّة meteorology.

عِلْمُ الأساطير mythology.

عِلْمُ الأعْصاب neurology.

عِلْمُ الاقْتِصاد economics.

عِلْمُ الأمْراض pathology.

عِلْمُ أمْراض النِّساء gynecology.

عِلْمُ الأنساب genealogy.

عِلْمُ البَشَرِيَّات anthropology.

عُلومٌ إنسانيَّة humanities.

عِلْمُ البَديع، عِلْمُ البلاغة rhetoric.

عِلْمُ البصريَّات optics.

عِلْمُ البيئة ecology.

عِلْمُ التَّربية pedagogy, pedagogics, education.

عِلْمُ التَّشْريح anatomy.

العِلْمُ التَّطْبيقيّ applied science.

عِلْمُ التَّغْذِية dietetics.

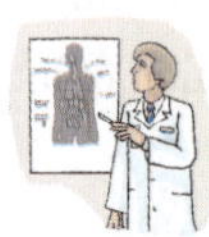

عِلْمُ التَّنْجيم astrology.

عِلْمُ الجَراثيم bacteriology.

عِلْمُ الجَمال aesthetics.

عِلْمُ الحَشرات entemology.

عِلْمُ الحَيوان zoology.

عِلْمُ دَلالات الألفاظ semantics.

عِلْمُ الزَّلازِل seismology.

عِلْمُ السُّكان demography.

عِلْمُ الأسماك ichthyology.

عِلْمُ السُّموم toxicology.

عِلْمُ طبقات الأرض geology.

عِلْمُ الطَّيران aeronautics.

عِلْمُ الطُّيور ornithology.

عِلْمُ الأدوية pharmacology.

عِلْمُ الفَلَك astronomy.

عِلْمُ التَّوليد obstetrics.

عِلْمُ اللاَّهوت theology.

عِلْمُ اللُّغة linguistics.

عِلْمُ المُداواة therapeutics.

عِلْمُ المُناخ climatology.

عِلْمُ المَناعة immunology.

عِلْمُ المَنْطق logic.

عِلْمُ المِياه hydrology.

عِلْمُ النَّبات botany.

عِلْمُ الوراثة genetics.

عِلْمُ وظَائِف الأعْضاء physiology.

عِلْمانيّ (ص) secular, laic.

عِلْمانيّ (اسم) layman, secularist.

عِلْمِيّ scientific, academic.

عَلَنًا openly, overtly, publicly, in public.

عَلَنِيّ open, overt, public.

عُلُوّ height, altitude, elevation; loftiness, superiority; loudness (of voice); exaltedness, highness, grandeur.

عُلْوِيّ upper, higher; upstairs, overhead; supreme; celestial, heavenly, divine.

العَلِيّ the Most High, the Supreme (epithet of God).

عُلِّيَّة attic, upper room.

عُلِّيَّةُ القَوْم elite, people of distinction, upper class, prominent people, dignitaries, leading personalities.

عَليل (ص) sick, ill, ailing; soft, gentle, mild.

عَليل (اسم) sick person, patient.

العَليم the Omniscient (epithet of God).

عَمَّ to be universal, prevalent, all-embracing; to spread, prevail, include, embrace, extend; to be spread, diffused.

عَمّ uncle;father-in-law (father of the bride or the bridegroom).

عَمَّ، عَمَّا where of, what, about what.

عَمَّى to make blind, obscure, make vague, cryptic; to disguise, hide, blind, conceal.

عَمًى blindness.

عَمَى الألوان color blindness.

عِماد support, stay, buttress; pillar, prop, post.

عِماد major general (army rank).

عِماد baptism (Christianity).

عِمادة deanship.

عِمارة building, edifice, structure.

عَمالَة، عُمالَة، عِمالة employment; brokerage, commission.

عَمالَة treason.

عَمَّة aunt, paternal aunt.

عَمَدَ to resort to, undertake, go, set about, proceed, apply oneself, embark upon; to do on purpose, aim intentionally; to support,shore up, buttress.

عَمَّدَ to baptize, christen; to confirm.

عَمْد intent, purpose; premeditation, willfulness.

عَمْدًا، عَمْدِيّ purposely, deliberately, intentionally, willfuly.

عُمْدَة mayor, governor, chief of a village, faculty; support, prop, shore; basic issue of a controversy.

عَمَرَ to inhabit, live, dwell in; to be inhabited, populated; to live long; to thrive, prosper, flourish, bloom.

عَمَّرَ to live long.

عَمَّرَ to build, erect, construct, set up; to populate, make inhabited; to restore, rebuild, reconstruct; to repair, overhaul; to load a gun; to fill the lamp with oil; to perform the (Umra).

عُمْر age, life, duration of life, lifespan.

عُمْران building, development, construction; culture, civilization, structure, edifice; bustling life, prosperity of a country.

عَمَّقَ to deepen, make deeper.

عُمق، عُمُق، عَمق depth, profoundness, bottom.

في العُمْق in depth.

عَمِلَ to do, act, operate, work; to make, produce, manufacture, carry out; to perform, execute, put into operation; to plan, contrive, seek to accomplish, pursue, strive for; to endeavor, exert oneself to do; to toil, labor, run.

عَمِلَ بموجب أو حَسَبَ to act according to, pursuant to, on the basis of; to enforce, execute, practise.

عَمِلَ في to act upon, affect; to govern; to process, treat.

عَمَل act, action, doing, deed, activity, work, performance; making, production, manufacture; execution; practical work, operation; job, labor; feat, achievement, exploit; occupation, business, trade, craft.

أعْمالٌ مَنْزِليَّة household chores.

أعْمالٌ يَدَويَّة handworks, manual work.

عَمَلٌ فَنّي work of art.

صاحِبُ العَمَل employer.

رَجُلُ أعْمال businessman.

عِيدُ العَمَل Labor Day.

يومُ عَمَل workday.

عَمَلٌ حَربِيّ belligerent act, military operation.

عَمَلٌ ميدانِيّ field work.

عَمَلٌ جَماعِيّ teamwork.

عَمَلاً بِـ pursuant to, in execution of, according to, on the basis of, as stipulated by, by virtue of; under, in conformity with.

عِمْلاق (ص) giant, colossal, mammoth, enormous, huge.

عِمْلاق (اسم) giant.

عُمْلَة، عِمْلَة currency, money.

عُمْلَةٌ صَعْبَة hard currency.

عُمْلَةٌ مُزَيَّفَة counterfeit money.

عُمْلَةٌ وَرَقِيَّة paper currency.

عَمَلِيّ practical, applied, serving practical purposes.

عَمَلِيًّا practically, in practice.

عَمَلِيَّة work, job, action, activity; transaction (commerce); operation; making, manufacture, production; procedure, process; surgery.

عَمَّمَ to generalize, spread universally, popularize; to introduce universally; to circulate; to make accessible to all; to open to the public at large; to put a turban on someone's head.

عَمود column, pillar, post, pole, shaft; flagpole (of a standard, flag); shore, buttress, prop.

عَمودٌ في صَحيفة column.

العَمُودُ الفِقَرِيّ spine, vertebral column.

عَمودِيًّا vertically, perpendicularly.

عُمولَة commission, brokerage.

عُموم universality; whole, totality, all.

العُمُوم the public, the masses, the people, all everybody; the public at large, the general public.

عُمُومًا، على العُمُوم in general, generally, on the whole, altogether; as a whole, en masse, en bloc; in the main; generally speaking.

عُمُومِيّ public, common, general, universal.

عَمِيَ to become blind; to be blind to; to lose one's eyesight.

عَمِيد chief, leader; president, dean (of a faculty); headmaster; brigadier general (military rank); doyen (of a diplomatic corps).

عَمِيق deep, profound.

عَمِيل agent; representative; customer, client, patron.

عَمِيلٌ سِياسِيّ hireling, traitor, mercenary, agent.

عَنْ from, off, away from; out of, by reason of, due to; about, on, over; regarding, in respect of, in connection with; on behalf of, for; after; to, towards, at, on.

عَنْ طَرِيق through, by way of, by means of.

عَنْ حُسْنِ نِيَّة in good faith, bona fide.

عَنْ عِلْم on the basis of sound knowledge.

عَنَى to mean, intend, have in mind; to worry, preoccupy oneself with; to be worried, concerned about; to take care of, look after, attend to a sick person.

عَنَاء trouble, effort, toil, labor, hardship, distress.

عِنَاد opposition, stubbornness, obduracy, obstinacy; resistance.

عِنَاق embrace, cuddle, accolade, hug.

عَنَان clouds; firmament, sky.

عِنَان rein

أَطْلَقَ لَهُ العِنَان to give free rein to someone.

عِنَايَة care, protection, attention, concern; caution, prudence.

العِنَايَةُ الإلهِيَّة divine providence.

عِنَايَةٌ فَائِقَة intensive care.

عِنَايَةٌ طِبِّيَّة medical care.

عِنَب grapes (plant).

يصنع من العنب الخل والنبيذ

Vinegar and wine are produced from grapes

عَنْبَر warehouse, storehouse, depot, storeroom; hangar, shed.

عَنِتَ to fall on hard days; to come to grief, be in distress; to commit a sin, commit adultery.

عَنَّتَ to force someone; to perform a difficult task; to afflict, distress, harass someone, bring hardship upon.

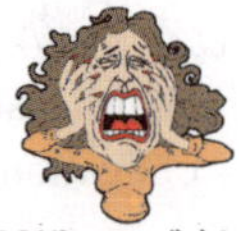

عنت distress, affliction, agony, pain, adversity; constraint, coercion, harassment.

عَنْجَهِيَّة haughtiness, pride, self-importance.

عِنْد at, by, near; off, on, upon, in the opinion of.

عِنْدَ الحَاجَة if need be, if necessary.

مِنْ عِنْد from , of.

مِنْ عِنْده for his part, in his turn.

عِنْدِي I have.

عَنْدَ ذَلك thereupon, then, at that moment.

عِنْدَئِذٍ then, at that time, thereupon.

عِنْدَمَا when, at the time when, as, while.

عُنْصُر race, stock; origin, root; element, component, factor.

عُنْصُرِيّ racial, ethnic, racist; elemental.

عَنُفَ to intensify, heighten; to be more violent, more vehement; to be harsher, fiercer, more intense.

عَنَّفَ to treat severely, harshly, with rigor; to deal with someone roughly; to reprimand, rebuke, scold, chide.

عُنْف، عَنْف، عِنْف violence, severity, bluntness, ruggedness, vehemence, bitterness, toughness, use of force.

عُنْفُوان bloom, vigor, prime; power, force, pride.

عُنُق، عُنْق neck.

عُنْقُود cluster, bunch.

عَنْكَبُوت spider (insect).

بَيْتُ العَنْكَبُوت cobweb, spiderweb.

عُنْوَان title, heading; address; epitome, embodiment, symbol; incarnation.

لكل كتاب عنوان على غلافه

Each book has a title printed on its outside cover

عَنْوَة by force, forcibly.

عَنْوَنَ to entitle, address, label.

عُنِيَ to take pains in doing something; to spend effort on; to see to it, bear in mind, make sure that; to concern oneself with.

عَنِيد stubborn, obstinate, obdurate, pigheaded, headstrong, inflexible, adamant, intransigent.

عَنيف violent, severe, rigorous, harsh, hard, rude; blunt, vehement, tough, fierce; strenuous, exacting, stern.

عَهِدَ to know, be acquainted with, observe closely, heed; to delegate, entrust, assign to; to vest in; to commission, charge, authorize, empower; to impose, enjoin, obligate, commit someone to do something; to fulfill, keep one's promise.

فيما أعْهَدُ as far as I know, to my knowledge.

عَهْد knowledge; contact with well-known, familiar nature of; close observance, strict adherence to.

عَهْد delegation, assignment; committing, vesting in, commissioning, charging, entrusting with.

عَهْد commitment, liability, obligation, reponsibility; vow, pledge, promise, oath.

عَهْد contract, covenant, pact, treaty, agreement.

عَهْد time, epoch, era; reign, rule, term of office.

عَهْد affection, friendship, love.

حَديثُ العَهْد recent, new, young.

مِن عَهْدٍ قَريب of late, recently, the other day.

العَهْدُ الجَديد the New Testament.

العَهْدُ القَديم the Old Testament.

على عَهْدِه at his time, in his time.

ما زَالَ على عَهْدِهِ to be unchanged; to be as always.

قَطَعَ عَهْدًا على نَفْسِهِ to assume an obligation; to commit oneself.

عُهْدَة care, custody, guaranty; guardianship; contractual obligation, responsibility, charge.

عَهْر، عِهْر adultery, fornication, prostitution.

عَوَى to howl, yelp (dog).

عَوَّاد lutist.

عَوَّامَة buoy, raft, pontoon, float.

عَوَّامَةُ النَّجاة life buoy.

عَوَّجَ to bend, twist, curve, crook.

عَوَّدَ to accustom, habituate, condition, insure, season to; to make someone used to.

عَوْد، عَوْدَة return, reversion, recidivism; repetition, resumption, doing again, taking up again.

عُود stick, rod, pole, branch of tree; stem, stalk of plant; lute (musical instrument); body, build, physionomy; strength, force, intensity.

عَوْدَةٌ عَن withdrawal, retraction, revocation, repeal; refrainement from, abstention from, relinquishment.

عُودُ أَسْنَان toothpick.

عُودُ الثِّقاب matchstick.

عَوْرَة private parts (of man, woman); genitals, sexual organs.

عَوْرَة defect, fault, deficiency, imperfection, weak spot.

أ ب ت ث ج ح خ د ذ ر ز س ش ص ض ط ظ ع غ ف ق ك ل م ن هـ و ي

عَوِزَ	to become poor, needy, destitute; to need, require; to be in want or in need of; to lack, to be absent, non-existent, wanting, missing (a thing).
عَوَز	poverty, neediness, destitution, penury.
عَوَّضَ	to compensate, indemnify, remedy, redress; to replace, substitute for, recompense for.
عِوَض	substitute, compensation, indemnity, reparation.
عِوَضًا عَن	as a substitute for, in return for, instead of.
عَوَّلَ	to rely on, depend on, trust in; to resolve to; to intend to, decide to; to make up one's mind to .

عَوَّلَ	to lament, wail, howl, cry, yelp.
عَوْم	floating, buoyancy, swimming.
عَوْن	helper, assistant, bodyguard, servant.
عَوِيل	wailing, lamentation; lament, crying; howling.
عَيَاء	incapacity, weakness, fatigue, feebleness.
عِيَادة	visit, call; clinic.
عِيَاذ	act of taking refuge; refuge, shelter, asylum.
العِيَاذُ بِالله	God forbid; God save me from that.
عِيَار	standard, gauge, measurement, caliber; fineness.
عِيَارٌ نَارِيّ	gunshot.

عِيَارِيّ	standard.
عِيَان	seeing, viewing.
شَاهِدُ عِيَان	eyewitness.
عَيَّبَ	to find fault with; to take exception to; to dishonor, disgrace, blame, denounce, censure, reprove, reproach.
عَيْب	defect, fault, flaw, deficiency, failing, shortcoming; shame, disgrace.
عَيَّدَ	to celebrate a feast.
عِيْد	feast, festival, holiday.
عِيْدُ الأَضْحَى	Greater Bairam.
عِيْدُ الأُمّ	Mother's Day.
عِيْدُ جميع القدّيسين	All Saints Day.
عِيْدُ رأسِ السَّنة	New Year's Day.
عِيْدُ البِشَارَة	Annunciation Feast.
عِيْدٌ سَنَوِيّ	anniversary.
عِيْدُ الغِطاس	Epiphany.
عِيْدُ العَمَل	Labor Day.
عِيْدُ العَنْصَرَة	Whitsunday.
عِيْدُ الفِصْح	Easter.
عِيْدُ الفِطْر	Lesser Bairam.
عِيْدٌ مِئَوِيّ	centenary, centennial.
عِيْدُ المَرْفَع	Carnival.
عِيْدُ ميلاد [شخص]	birthday.
عِيْدُ ميلاد المسيح	Christmas.
عِيْدُ المَوْلِدِ النَّبَوِيّ الشَّرِيف	the Prophet's Birthday.

أ ب ت ث ج ح خ د ذ ر ز س ش ص ض ط ظ ع غ ف ق ك ل م ن هـ و ي

عَيَّرَ to taunt, rebuke, upraid, to humiliate, degrade, discredit; dishonor, shame, condemn; abuse, insult, revile.

عَيْش life, living, existence; subsistence; bread.

عَيَّنَ to individualize, particularize, specify, itemize, designate; to fix, determine, set down, define, stipulate; to appoint, nominate; to set aside, single out, earmark; to allot, assign, allocate, appropriate funds to.

عَيَّنَ سَبَبًا to give a reason.

عَيْن eye; spring, source, fountain.

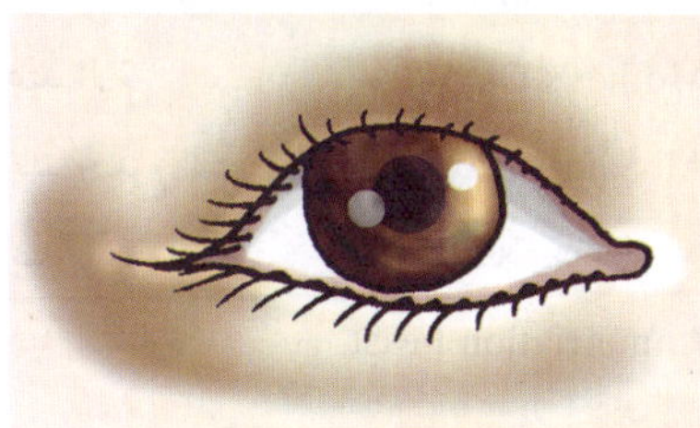

نرى الأشياء من حولنا بواسطة العين

We see things around us with our eyes

عَيْن spy, scout, overseer; lookout, watchman.

عَيْن eminent man, man of distinction, leader, notable.

عَيْن chattel, property, capital asset, ready money, cash.

عَيْن substance, essence.

بِعَيْنِه ، عَيْنُهُ the same, the very same, in person.

عَيْنًا in kind.

العَيْنُ بِالعَيْنِ an eye for an eye.

عَيِّنَة sample, specimen.

عَيْنِيّ real estate; in rem (law); corporeal, material; in kind; ocular, ophthalmic, optic.

عَيِيَ to fail to, break down, malfunction; to falter, stammer, stutter; to be incapable of; to lack the strength for; to fail sick, ill.

غَائِب absent, absentee, truant; hidden, concealed.

صِيغَةُ الغَائِب third person (grammar).

غائِر hollow, cavernous, sunken.

غَائِط feces, stool, excrement.

غَائِم cloudy, overcast.

غَابَ to be absent; to stay away, to vanish from sight; to disappear; to be hidden, concealed from; to go down (sun).

غَابَ عن وَعْيِهِ to lose consciousness, faint, swoon.

غَاب ، غَابَة forest, wood, thicket, jungle.

تعيش في الغابة الطيور والحيوانات المفترسة

Rapacious birds and animals live in the jungle

غَابِر bygone, past.

غَادَة young girl, delicate woman.

غَادَرَ to leave, depart from a place to another.

غادِر ، غَدَّار perfidious, disloyal, treacherous; false, deceitful.

غَارَ to sink, penetrate deeply into; to become hollow (eyes); to seep away (water); to dry up (spring).

غارَ مِن to be jealous of.

غارَ على to guard, protect jealously; to show care or concern for; to display zeal, vie for, be solicitous about.

غَارَة incursion, raid, invasion, inroad, foray, attack.

غارِق drowned; sunken, submerged, flooded; completely taken aback, deeply shocked, engrossed in, absorbed.

أ ب ت ث ج ح خ د ذ ر ز س ش ص ض ط ظ ع غ ف ق ك ل م ن هـ و ي

غاز	gas; flatulence, wind (in body).
غازٌ مُسَيلٌ للدُّموع	tear gas.
مِياهٌ غازِيَّة	mineral water, carbonated water, soda water.
غازٍ (الغازي)	invader, raider, attacker, marauder, warlord.
غازَلَ	to court, woo, speak words of love (to a woman); to flirt, dally, philander (with a woman).
غاشِم	oppressive, outrageous, brutal, tyrannical.
غاصَ	to dive into, plunge into.
غاصِب	usurper; brutal, violent; outrageous; ravisher, violator (of a woman).
غاضِب، غضْبان، غَضِب	angry, exasperated, irate, furious, enraged; vexed, annoyed, irritated, angered, infuriated.
غاطِس	diver; draft (of a ship).
غاظَ	to anger, enrage, infuriate, irritate, vex.
غافٍ (الغافي)	asleep, slumbering, dozing.
غافَلَ	To take advantage of someone's inadvertance.
غافِل	inattentive, unaware, heedless, negligent, unwary.
غالٍ (الغالي)	expensive, costly, dear; valuable, precious; well-beloved; cherished person; to be high-priced.
غالٍ	boiling, ebullient.
غالَى	to exaggerate, magnify; to raise the price of; to overcharge for; to ascribe great value to, rate highly.
غالَبَ	to fight, combat; to contend with, wrestle with; to try to defeat someone.
غالِب	winner, victor, triumphant; predominant, prevailing, prevalent; the majority of.
غالِبِيَّة	majority, greater portion.
غالَطَ	to seek to involve someone in mistakes; to deceive, beguile, cheat, swindle.
غامَرَ	to venture, risk; to plunge blindly, throw oneself headlong into.
غامِر	overwhelming risk, hazard, stake; copious.
غامِض	obscure, vague, ambiguous, hazy, incomprehensible, mysterious, enigmatic, unclear; dark, dim.
غامِق	dark, deep.
غانِيَة	belle, beautiful woman, beauty.
غاوٍ (ص)	aberrant, deviating, misled, misguided.
غاوٍ (الغاوي) (اسم)	tempter, seducer, enticer, allurer; amateur; lover.
غايَة	extreme limit, extremity, aim, goal, end, objective; intent, intention, purpose.
لِغايَة	as far as, up to, to the extent of, until, till.
غايَرَ	to alter, modify, make different; to be at variance with, to be different from, unlike to, in contrast with.
غِبَّ	after, following.
غباء، غباوة	stupidity, foolishness, idiocy, imbecility.

غُبار، غَبَرَة dust.

لا غُبارَ عليه irreproachable, faultless, unmatched, peerless.

غَبَرَ to pass, elapse, go by; to be bygone, past, elapsed.

غِبْطَة envy; happiness; beatitude, blessedness.

غِبْطَة، صاحِبُ الغِبْطَة His Beatitude, His Eminence.

غَبَنَ to cheat, dupe, gull, defraud, deceive, prejudice.

غَبْن، غُبْن، غَبَن injustice, prejudice, fraud, deceit, cheating; imposture, swindle, duping.

غَبِيّ stupid, silly, dumb, unwise, imbecile, idiot; ignorant, unjudicious, foolish.

غَثْي، غَثَيان nausea; disgust, qualmishness, indisposition.

غَجَرِيّ gypsy.

غَد (الغَد) tomorrow, the following day.

بَعْدَ غَد the day after tomorrow.

غدا to go in the early morning; to become, grow, turn into.

غَداء lunch.

غَداة، غُدْوَة early morning.

غَدَّار perfidious, disloyal, treacherous, traiterous, deceitful.

غُدَّة gland.

غَدَرَ to betray; to act treacherously toward; to deceive, delude; to act perfidiously toward.

غَدْر perfidy, breach of faith, breach of trust, betrayal, treason, treachery, deception.

غَدير brook, creek, river, pond, stream.

غَديرَة braid, plait, pigtail, lock of hair.

غَذَّى to feed, nourish; to supply with.

غِذاء nourishment, food, foodstuff, victual.

غِذائِيّ alimentary, nutritive, nourishing.

مَوادّ غِذائِيَّة foodstuffs, victuals.

غَرَّ to deceive, mislead, beguile; to delude, gull, dazzle, blind; to entice, allure, tempt, seduce.

غِرّ inexperienced, gullible, new, green, inadvertent; naive, untrained, tenderfoot; recruit (army).

غَرا، غَرَّى to glue, fix with glue.

غِراء glue.

يُستعمل الغراء لإلصاق قطعتين من الخشب أو البلاستيك

Glue is used to fix together two pieces of wood or plastic

غَرابَة strangeness, curiousness, oddness, peculiarity, oddity.

غِرار lead, example, model, pattern.

على غِرار like, similar to, in the manner of, after.

أ ب ت ث ج ح خ د ذ ر ز س ش ص ض ط ظ ع غ ف ق ك ل م ن هـ و ي

inexperience, naivety, gullibility, heedlessness. غرارة

arboriculture, cultivation, planting, growing. غِراسة

love, passion, infatuation. غَرام

fine, penalty, damages, amends, compensation. غَرامة

amorous. غَرامِيّ

romances, love affairs, love adventures. غَرامِيّات

to set, go down; to go away, depart, emigrate. غَرَبَ

to be a stranger; to be strange, queer, obscure, difficult to comprehend. غَرُبَ

to banish, exile, estrange, alienate; to go away, depart; to go westward; to emigrate. غَرَّبَ

west; the West, the Occident; vehemence, violence. غَرْب، الغَرْب

westward, toward the west. غَرْبًا

sieve. غِرْبال

نستعمل الغربال لتنقية الطحين والمواد الأخرى

We use the sieve to sift flour and other material

---

life away from, home, emigration; banishment, exile. غُرْبَة

to sift, sieve, riddle. غَرْبَلَ

western, westerly. غَرْبِيّ (ص)

Occidental, Westerner. غَرْبِيّ (اسم)

beginning, start of the month. غُرَّةُ الشَّهْر

to sing, warble. غَرِدَ، غَرَّدَ

to expose to danger, deceive, beguile, mislead; to entice, allure, tempt; to endanger, imperil; to dazzle, blind. غَرَّرَ

risk, hazard, jeopardy, danger, peril. غَرَر

to stick into, drive into, insert into; to stab, ram, push, bore, plant, implant. غَرَزَ، غَرَّزَ

to plant; to implant, embed, insert, inculcate. غَرَسَ

purpose, design, aim, end, objective, goal, intent. غَرَض

effects, possessions, materials, objects, things. أغْراض (ج)

to gargle; to simmer, bubble, gurgle. غَرْغَرَ

to scoop, ladle, spoon. غَرَفَ

room, cell, compartment, cabin, chamber. غُرْفَة

chamber of commerce. غُرْفَةُ تِجارَة

living room, sitting room. غُرْفَةُ جُلوس

dining room. غُرْفَةُ طعام

clearing house. غُرْفَةُ مُقاصَّة

bedroom. غُرْفَةُ نَوْم

chamber of industry. غُرْفَةُ صِناعَة

to sink; to drown (person); to plunge, dive, be immersed; to be engrossed, absorbed in; to be wholly engaged, lost in (thought, work). غَرِقَ

أخذ الرَّجل يلوِّح بيديه وهو يغرق
The man began to wave his hands while he was drowning

غَرَق sinking, drowning.

غَرَّمَ to fine, impose a fine.

غَرْو، غَرْوَى < 22w.[لاغَرْوَ، لاغَرْوَ] no wonder

غُرُوب setting of the sun, sunset; nightfall.

غُرُور conceit, vanity, vainglory, pride, arrogance.

غُرُور deception, delusion, illusion.

غريب strange, foreign, alien, extraneous; odd, queer, quaint; peculiar; amazing, astonishing, startling; wondrous, marvelous; obscure; remote; rare, uncommon, outlandish.

غريبة oddity, curiosity, wonder, marvel.

غِرِّيد singing, warbling.

غريزة instinct, impulse, urge, nature.

غريزِيّ instinctive.

غريق drowned, sunken.

غريم opponent, adversary, rival; creditor, debtor.

غَزَا to invade, attack, raid; to flood, inundate; to overrun, overspread, overwhelm, overccome; to aspire; to mean, intend.

غَزَارَة abundance, profusion, plenty, large quantity.

غَزُرَ to abound; to be plentiful, copious, abundant.

غَزَلَ to spin.

غَزَل flirt, flirtation, courtship, wooing, love, words of love; love poetry.

غَزْو، غَزْوَة invasion, incursion, raid, military campaign; foray, assault, inroad, attack, aggression; military expedition.

غزير abundant, copious, plentiful, profuse, ample, rich in.

غَسَّالَة washerwoman, washing machine.

غَسَق dusk, twilight before nightfall.

غَسَلَ، غَسَّلَ to wash, launder, clean, cleanse; to purge, rinse.

غَسْل washing, cleaning, laundering, cleansing, purging, rinsing.

غَسُول wash water; lotion; lye; marshmallow (plant).

غسيل washing; dirty or washed clothes.

غَشّ to cheat, swindle, double-cross, delude, trick; to act dishonestly toward; to deceive, fool, mislead, dupe; to vitiate, adulterate, debase.

أمي تغسل الثياب المتسخة ثم تنشرها على الحبل لتجف

My mother washes the dirty clothes and then hangs them on a clothes-line to dry

غِشّ adulteration, corruption, debasement; fraud, deceit; double-cross, perfidy, treachery, bluffing, trickery.

غَشَّى to cover, envelop, conceal, veil; to overlay, coat, plate.

غِشَاء membrane, thin layer, diaphragm, screen, film, coating.

غِشَاءُ البَكَارَة hymen.

غِشَاءُ القَلْب pericardium.

غِشَاءٌ مُخَاطِيّ mucuous membrane.

غَشَّاش (ص) deceitful, dishonest; deceptive; fallacious, false.

غَشَّاش (اسم) fraud, swindler, impostor, double-crosser, crook, deceiver.

غَشِيَ to come to a place; to cover, wrap up, conceal, veil; to come, descend upon, overcome, overwhelm; to be dark (night); to sleep with, have sexual intercourse with, copulate with.

غَشْيَة swoon, faint, unconsciousness, trance.

غَصَّ to choke on some food; to be overcrowded, congested, packed, crammed with.

غَصَّ بهم المكان the place was overcrowded.

غَصَبَ to force, compel, coerce; to take away by force or illegally; to extort from, usurp.

غَصْب forcing, force; compulsion, coercion, constraint.

غَصْبًا عَنْهُ in spite of him, unwillingly, forcedly.

غُصْن branch, bough, twig (of a tree).

غَضَّ to lower, cast down one's eyes.

غَضَّ الطَّرْفَ أو النَّظَر to overlook, disregard, ignore, pay no attention to.

غَضَّ من قَدْرِهِ to derogate from, disparage, detract from.

غَضَّ النَّبات to become fresh, tender, succulent.

غَضّ tender,fresh, succulent; lowering one's eyes.

غَضَاضَة shortcoming, deficiency, fault, defect.

لم يَجِد غَضَاضَةً في he found nothing wrong with; he took no offense at; he had no objection to.

غَضِبَ to be angry, cross, mad, vexed, irritated, furious, exasperated, annoyed, enraged, infuriated.

غَضَب	fury, rage, anger, vexation, exasperation, irritation.
غَضَّنَ	to wrinkle, pucker, crease, fold, crumple.
في غُضُون	during, within, in.
في غُضُون ذلِكَ	meanwhile, in the meantime.
غَطَّ	to immerse, dip, plunge something in.
غَطَّ	to snore.

غَطَّى	to cover, cover up, wrap, envelope, veil, conceal; to cover (expenses); to outshine, overshadow, outweigh.
غِطاء	cover, wrapping, veil, envelope, covering; lid, cap; housing; bonnet, jacket; hull,case.
غِطاءُ السَّرير	bedsheet, bedcover.
غِطاءُ المائِدَة	tablecloth.
غِطاءُ مُحرِّك السَّيَّارَة	hood.

غَطْرَسَة	haughtiness, vainglory, insolence, presumption, arrogance, impudence, conceitedness.
غَطَسَ	to dive, dip, plunge, immerse, submerse into water.
غَطْس	diving, plunging, immersion, sinking, submersion.
غَفَا	to slumber, doze, take a nap, fall asleep.
غَفَرَ	to forgive, grant pardon, remit, absolve.
غُفْران ، غَفْر	pardon, forgiveness, remission, absolution.

يغطس السباح في الماء من علو كبير
The swimmer plunges in water from a high board

عِيدُ الغُفْران	Day of Atonement.
غَفَلَ	to neglect, disregard, ignore; to pay no attention to.
غَفَل ، غَفْلَة	inadvertence, inattention, negligence, carelessness.
غَفْوَة	slumber, sleep, doze, nap.
غَفُور	forgiving, indulgent, merciful tolerant.
غَفير	great, large, numerous.
جَمْعٌ غَفير	crowd, swarm, throng.

غلَّ ، غَلَّل	to handcuff, fetter, shackle, chain.
غَلَّ	to produce, yield.
غَلَّ	to insert, penetrate, put in, enter, introduce.
غُلّ	handcuff, fetter, shackle, chain.
غِلّ	rancor, spite, grudge.
غَلا	to increase in price; to become expensive, high-priced; to exceed the proper bounds; to exaggerate.
غَلَى	to boil, simmer.

غلاء high cost, high price, high level of prices.

غلاءُ المَعيشَة high cost of living.

غِلاف envelope, cover; coating, case; tegument.

غِلالَة diaphanous dress; night shirt, night dress, veil, gown; mantilla.

غُلام boy, youth, lad; servant, waiter; slave; valet.

غَلاَّيَة kettle, caldron; boiler.

غَلَبَ to defeat, beat, vanquish, subdue, overpower.

غَلَبَ على to prevail, predominate, preponderate.

غَلَبَ عليه النُّعاس he was overcome by drowsiness.

غَلَبَة victory, triumph, predominance, superiority, upperhand, mastery.

غَلَّة yield, produce, harvest, crop; revenue, yield, proceeds, returns.

غَلِطَ to commit a mistake; to be mistaken, in error, at fault.

غَلَط (ص) wrong, incorrect.

غَلَط (اسم) mistake, error, fault, blunder.

غَلْطَة mistake, error, fault, blunder.

غَلْطَة مَطْبَعِيَّة erratum, misprint.

غَلُظَ to thicken; to be thick, coarse, rough, crude, gross; to become viscous, sirupy.

غَلَّظَ to make thick, gross, big, crude, rough, rugged.

غَلْغَلَ to penetrate into, enter into.

غَلَفَ، غَلَّفَ to envelop, wrap in a cover; to cover, encase; to bind (a book).

غَلَقَ، غَلَّقَ to close, shut, lock, bolt (a door).

غَلِق obscure, dark, ambiguous, dubious, difficult to comprehend, recondite.

غَلْق closing, shutting, locking, bolting; foreclosure of a mortgage.

غُلُوّ، غُلْواء extravagance, immoderation; exaggeration.

غَلْي، غَلَيان boiling, ebullition.

غَليظ thick, heavy, dense, viscous, sirupy (liquid); rough, coarse, harsh, crude; inconsiderate, boorish; antipathetic, repulsive, disgusting, dull, tedious; fat and uncouth, burly, gross (person); solid, stringy (food).

غَليظُ الرَّقَبة obdurate, obstinate, stubborn, stiff-necked.

غَليل burning thirst; rancor, illwill; ardent desire.

غَمَّ to fill with sadness, pain, grief; to pain, grieve, distress; to cover, veil, conceal.

غَمَّازَة dimple.

غَمام (ج) clouds.

غَمامَة cloud.

غَمَدَ to sheathe, put into the scabbard (a sword); to plunge, thrust the sword in someone's breast; to shelter, protect, cover.

غَمَّدَ	to conceal, cover up someone's faults, offences.
غِمْد	scabbard, sheath; case, outer covering, housing.
غَمَرَ	to flood, inundate with; to immerse, submerge, soak in a liquid; to cover, spread over, fill, pervade.
غَمُرَ	to be plentiful, copious, abundant, abound.
غَمْر	flooding, inundation, submersion, plunging.

غَمْر	flood, deluge.
غَمْر	generous, openhanded; inexperienced, simple, unskilled.
غَمْرَة	deluge, flood, inundation, emotional exuberance; distress, adversity, hardship; jam, crowd, throng.
غَمْرَةُ المَوْت	pang of death, mortal throe.
غَمَزَ	to beckon, make a sign with one's eyes; to wink, twinkle, blink with one's eyes; to feel, touch, palpate.
غَمَزَ	to slander, caluminate, defame, speak evil of.
غَمْزَة	sign, signal, hint, wink with the eye.
غَمَسَ	to tip, plunge, submerse, sink, immerse.
غَمَضَ، غَمُضَ	to be obscure, vague, ambiguous, mysterious; to be difficult to comprehend.
غَمَّضَ	to obscure, make obscure; to close one's eyes; to pretend not to see; to feign blindness, overlook.

غَمْضَة	blink, twinkle, wink.
في غَمْضَةِ عَيْن	in a moment, in no time, in a jiffy.
غَمَطَ، غَمِطَ	to despise, scorn, hold in contempt, belittle.
غَمَطَهُ حَقَّهُ	to refuse to recognize his rights.
غَمَطَ النِّعْمَة	to be ungrateful.
غَمْغَمَة	mumble, muttering; battle cry.
غُمُوض	obscurity, ambiguity, mystery; vagueness, uncertainty, incertitude; equivocation, confusion.
غَنَّى	to sing, chant, vocalize; to enrich, make rich.
غِنًى، غَنَاء	wealth, affluence, riches; sufficiency, satisfaction.
لا غِنى عنه	indispensable, essential, inevitable, imperative.
غِناء	singing, chanting, song.
غِنائِيّ	lyric, lyrical.

شِعْرٌ غِنائِيّ	lyric poetry, lyric poem.
غَنَّام	shepherd.
غَنَّجَ	to pamper, spoil, coddle, pet, fondle.
غَنِمَ	to take as booty, capture, gain, obtain, loot, plunder.
غَنَمَ الفُرصَة	to seize the opportunity.
غَنَم	sheep, small, cattle.
غَنِيّ	wealthy, prosperous, rich, well-to do; abounding in.
غَنِيٌّ عن البيان	self-evident, self-explanatory.
غَنِيمَة	booty, loot, pillage, prize; gain, profit, benefit.

غَنيمَةٌ بارِدَة easy prey.

غَوَى to stray from the right path; to go astray, err in one's actions; to misguide, mislead, lead astray; to seduce, tempt, entice, lure, induce, ensnare, beguile.

غَوَّاص diver, plunger.

يغوص الغواص لاكتشاف الحيوانات البحرية

The diver dives into deep water to discover sea animals

غَوَّاصَة submarine.

غَوايَة error, sin; seduction, temptation, allurement, enticement.

غَوْث relief, aid, help, succor.

غَوْر depression, declivity, depth.

بَعِيدُ الغَوْر deep, unfathomable, profound.

غَوْص diving, plunging; dive, plunge.

غَوْغَاء mob; rabble, noise, clamor, tumult.

غَيّ error, sin; temptation, enticement, offense, transgression.

غِياب، غَيْبَة absence, failure to attend; truancy, absenteeism.

غِيابُ الشَّمْس setting of the sun.

غِيابِيًا in abstentia, judgement by default.

غِيار exchange, replacement; dressing, bandage.

قِطَعُ الغِيار spare parts.

غَيَّبَ to take away, remove; to cause to disappear; to hide, conceal.

الغَيْب the invisible; the supernatural; the divine secret.

عن ظهر الغَيْب، غَيْبًا by heart, from memory.

عَالَمُ الغَيْب the invisible world.

غَيْبُوبَة trance, unconsciousness, swoon, daze, faint; coma, syncope, stupor.

غَيْث rain.

غَيَّرَ to change, alter, modify, vary; to make different; to exchange, switch, transform, mutate.

غَيْر other than, different from, unlike; save, except, but.

الغَيْر third party or parties, the others, neighbors.

غَيْرَ أنَّ yet, however, still, on the other hand, except that, but.

وغَيْرَ ذلك etcetera, and so on, and the like, et al.

لا غير، لَيْسَ غير only, just, merely, soley, and nothing else, nothing but, no more than.

مِنْ غَيْر without, excluding, with the exclusion of.

غَيْرَة، غِيرَة jealousy; zeal, fervor, earnest concern, solicitude; sense of honor, self-respect; enthusiasm.

غَيْظ rage, anger, fury, wrath, ire, irritation.

غَيْم clouds; mist, fog.

غَيْمَة cloud.

غَيُور jealous, zealous, enthusiastic, eager, keen; zealot, solicitious, ardent, fervid, earnestly concerned.

أ ب ت ث ج ح خ د ذ ر ز س ش ص ض ط ظ ع غ ف ق ك ل م ن هـ و ي

فَائِت past, elapsed; transient; lost, missing, absent.

فُؤَاد heart.

فَائِدَة benefit, profit, use, interest; welfare; usefulness.

عَديمُ الفَائِدَة useless, futile, fruitless, of no avail.

فَائِر ebullient, boiling up, gushing, jetting forth; seething, inflamed; hot; wild; frantic.

فَائِز winner, victor, successful.

فَائِض superabundant, superfluous; surplus, excess, spare; copious, effluent, pouring forth; superfluity, overflow.

فَائِق superior, outstanding, extraordinary; exquisite, excellent, remarkable; exceeding, extensive, stepped up, extreme, severe.

فَائِق awake, wakeful.

فاتَ to pass away, vanish; to be over, past; to escape, elude, slip away; to abandon, leave behind, relinquish; to exceed, surpass, transcend to.

فاتَ الأوان it escaped him that; he omitted, neglected, failed, forgot to, failed to see, note.

فاتَهُ القِطار he missed the train.

فِئَة group, category, party, faction, class, kind, sort, type; rate (of taxation); value, denomination (of money, stamp).

فِئَةُ الدم blood group.

فاتَحَ to speak first, address first someone; to begin, start, commence a conversation.

فاتِح light, bright; first, beginner; originator; launcher.

الفَاتِح the conqueror, the victor.

فاتِحَة introduction, foreword, preamble, preface; beginning, start, onset, dawn, opening, prelude (mus.).

الفاتِحَة [من القرآن الكريم] the opening chapter of the Holy Koran.

فاتِر lukewarm, tepid; cool; frigid, unenthusiastic, unfriendly, indifferent (character); dull, stagnant (business).

فاتِرُ الهِمَّة listless, slack, weak, languid, feeble.

فاتِك، فتّاك deadly, lethal, murderous.

فاتِن، فتّان fascinating, captivating, thrilling, spellbinding, glamorous; tempting, alluring, seductive, enchanting.

فاتُورَة invoice, bill.

فاتُورَةٌ أوَّلِيَّة proforma invoice.

فاجَأَ to surprise, take by surprise, take aback, overtake; to attack, assail suddenly.

فاجِر dissolute, libertine, debauched, rake; liar, insolent, impudent; indecent, bawdy, immoral; adulterer.

فاجِعَة disaster, calamity, catastrophe, tragedy, misfortune.

فاحَ to diffuse a pleasant odor; to be fragrant.

فاحِش obscene, shameless, lewd, ribald, filthy, indecent; exorbitant, excessive (price); unreasonable; grievous, oppressive (act); flagrant, monstrous, outrageous, vile, shameless, impudent.

فاحِص examiner, tester, investigator, inspector; auditor, comptroller (of accounts).

فاحِم black, coal-back, jet black.

فاخَرَ to vie in glory with; to be proud of, pride oneself upon; to vaunt, boast, brag.

فاخِر excellent, choice, first-class, splendid, deluxe, luxurious; perfect, sumptuous, glorious, outstanding; vainglorious.

فادِح gross, burdensome, oppressive, grave, serious (mistake).

فارَ to boil, simmer, bubble; to boil over; to burst into passion; to gush forth, shoot up, spout forth, spurt, jet.

فارَ to irritate, rankle.

فأر mouse, rat (animal).

يُستعمل الفأر الأبيض في المختبرات لإجراء التجارب العلمية عليه

White rats are used in laboratories to make scientific tests on them

فارّ (الفارّ) fugitive, runaway, fleeing, escapee; deserter (army).

فأْرَةُ النَّجّار plane, jointer.

أ ب ت ث ج ح خ د ذ ر ز س ش ص ض ط ظ ع غ ف ق ك ل م ن هـ و ي

فارِس horseman, rider, cavalier, cavalryman.

فارِع tall, lofty, towering; slender, slim; beautiful, pretty.

فارِعُ القامَة tall and slender.

فارِغ empty, void, vacant, unoccupied; idle, useless, pointless, vain.

بِفارِغِ الصَّبْر impatiently.

فارَقَ to part with; to make a distinction between; to differentiate; to dissociate oneself from, abandon, detach oneslf from.

فارِه active, agile, brisk; beautiful, pretty, handsome,sturdy, big.

فازَ to win, gain, succeed, triumph over; to defeat, overcome.

فأس ax, hatchet, hoe.

يستعمل الحطّاب الفأس لقطع أغصان الأشجار

The lumberjack uses the ax to cut the tree branches

فاسِد bad, foul, rotten, putrid; depraved, immoral, wicked; empty, vain; false, wrong, vicious; incorrect.

فاسِق dissolute, wanton, lecherous, debauchee, lewd, lascivious; nefarious; offender, sinner; adulterer, trespasser.

فاشِل unsuccessful, futile, failing, worthless.

فاصِل (اسم) separator; insulator (elect.); interval, intermission, pause; screen, partition, barrier.

فاصِلَة comma (,).

فاصِلَةٌ مَنْقُوطَة semicolon (;).

فاضَ to flow over, spill over, inundate, flood, flow, pour forth, issue, outflow; to abound; to be superabundant, plentiful, copious.

فاضِح shameful, infamous, scandalous, outrageous, dishonorable, ignominious, disgraceful, glaring, gross.

فاضَلَ to compare two things in order to determine which deserves preference.

فاضِل (ص) virtuous, excellent, distinguished, deserving, eminent; remaining, exceeding.

فاضِل (اسم) remainder, remnant, residue, surplus, excess.

فاعِل (ص) active, effective, efficient.

فاعِل (اسم) worker, laborer, doer, perpetrator; active subject of a verb or verbal clause (grammar).

إسْمُ الفاعِل active participle (grammar).

فاعِلُ خَيْر philanthropist, almsgiver.

صيغَةُ الفاعِل active voice (grammar).

فاقَ to surpass, excell, tower, above; to outweigh, outbalance, exceed; to show outstanding skill.

أ ب ت ث ج ح خ د ذ ر ز س ش ص ض ط ظ ع غ ف ق ك ل م ن هـ و ي

فاقة poverty, need, penury, want, destitution, indigence.

فاقِد bereaved of, deprived of, devoid of, lacking, wanting.

فاكَه to amuse someone with jokes; to joke with, banter with.

فاكِهَة fruit.

فَأْل good omen, auspice.

فالِت loose, unchained, free, at large; wanton, dissolute, debauched, libertine; good-for-nothing.

فالِج hemiplagia (med.).

فالِح successful, lucky, fortunate.

فانٍ (الفاني) transient, ephemeral, perishing; mortal, transitory; far advanced in years, very old; must eventually perish, die.

فانُوس lantern.

فاهَ to utter, pronounce, say.

فاه mouth.

فاوَضَ to negotiate with, confer with.

فَتِئَ عَن to refrain from, desist from.

ما فَتِئَ still, yet; to continue to do, go on doing.

فَتًى youth, young boy, lad, youngster.

فُتات (ج) crumbs, fragments; fractions; scraps, detritus.

فَتاة young woman, girl, lass.

فَتَّاحَة can opener.

فَتَّاك deadly, lethal, murderous, of disastrous effect.

فَتَّتَ to crumble, fritter, divide into small fragments, pieces.

فَتَحَ to open, turn on (a faucet); to switch on (an instrument); to dig (a canal); to build (a road); to introduce, begin; to conquer, capture; to reveal, disclose.

يفتح الصبيّ الباب ليدخل الضيوف
The boy opened the door to let guests enter

فَتَحَ الشَّهِيَّة to stimulate the appetite.

فَتَحَ حِسَاباً في مصرف to open an account with a bank.

فَتَحَ النَّار to open fire; to shoot.

فَتْح opening; conquest; occupation; victory.

فُتْحَة opening, aperture, gap, hole, slot, orifice.

فَتَرَ to become tepid, lukewarm; to abate, subside, calm down, cool down (temper); to languish, lag, slacken, relax.

فَتَّرَ to cause to abate, mitigate, soothe; to make languid; to weaken, sap; to make tepid (liquid).

فَتْرَة period, time, interval, epoch; stage, phase.

فَتْرَةُ انْتِقال transitional period, interim period.

بين فَتْرَةٍ وأُخرى now and then, from time to time, at times.

فَتَّشَ to search, inspect, investigate; to look for, search for.

فَتَكَ to kill, assassinate, murder, slay; to ravage, stamp out, annihilate, attack with violence, destroy.

فَتْك assassination, murder; destruction, annihilation.

فَتَلَ to twist, twine, entwine, curl, spin.

فَتَنَ to fascinate, infatuate, enchant, captivate, enthrall, charm; to subject to temptations, seduce, entice, beguile.

فُتِنَ to be infatuated, fascinated, enchanted, charmed by; to be in love, enamored of, crazy over.

فِتْنَة charm, temptation, enchantment, captivation, fascination; temptation; intrigue; sedition, riot, civil strife; distress, trial.

فَتْوى advisory opinion, legal opinion.

فُتُوَّة youth, adolescence; generosity, chivalry.

فُتُور tepidity; coolness, frigidity; apathy, lack of emotion.

فُتُور الهِمَّة languor, laxity, weakness.

فَتِيل (اسم) wick, fuse, slow match.

فَجّ mountain pass; gate; defile.

من كلِّ فَجٍّ عَميق from all sides, from everywhere.

فِجّ unripe, green (fruit); blunt, rude (speech); coarse, blunt, crude (character).

فَجْأَةً suddenly, unexpectedly, inadvertently, unawares.

فَجَرَ to lead a dissolute life, to act immorally; to sin; to indulge in debauchery; to commit adultery.

فَجَّرَ to cause to overflow; to let waterpour forth; to explode, detonate; to blow up, to dynamite.

فَجْر dawn, outbreak, outset, beginning, start.

فَجَعَ ، فَجَّعَ to distress, torment, afflict; to make miserable by bereaving.

فُجِعَ to be painfully affected; to suffer the loss of.

فَجْوَة gap, opening, aperture, crevice, fissure, crack; crater.

فُجُور immorality, depravation, debauchery, licentiousness; fornication, dissolution, wantonness, lewdness, prostitution.

فَجيعَة disaster, calamity, catastrophe, tragedy.

فَحُشَ to become obscene, foul, indecent; to become excessive, immoderate, grave, serious, outrageous, unreasonable.

فُحْش، فَحْشاء obscenity, indecency, bawdiness; monstrosity, atrocity, vile deed; crime; adultery, fornication.

فَحَصَ to examine, test, check up; to investigate, inspect, explore.

فَحَصَ الحِسَابَات to audit accounts.

فَحْص test, examination, checkup (med.); investigation, inquiry.

يجري الطبيب فحصاً للمريض

The doctor executes a checkup on his patient

فَحُمَ to become black; to blacken; to be dumbfounded, nonplused, unable to answer.

فَحَّمَ to carbonize, char; to blacken with coal.

فَحْم coal; charcoal; carbon, coke.

فَحْوَى meaning, sense, signification, import, purport; tenor; contents; substance.

فَخّ trap, snare.

فَخَار glory, pride, honor.

فَخَّار pottery, earthenware.

فَخَامَة splendor, magnificense, eminence, stateliness.

صاحِبُ الفَخَامَة His Excellency.

فَخْذ، فَخِذ thigh; leg; moiety of a tribe.

فَخْر، فَخَر glory, pride, honor.

فَخْرِيّ honorary.

فَخُمَ to be splendid, magnificent, grandiose, majestic.

فَخَّمَ to exalt, dignify, ennoble, magnify, glorify; to make a consonant emphatic (grammar).

فَخَّمَ الكلام to make a speech grandiloquent, pompous.

فَخْم stately, splendid, magnificent, majestic, superb, sumptuous, luxurious.

فَخُور proud of, boastful, bragging, vainglorious.

فَدَى to redeem, ransom with, sacrifice for; to risk life for.

فِدىً ، فِدَاء redemption, ransoming, sacrifice.

فِدَائِيّ commando; one who sacrifices himself for his cause.

فَداحَة enormity, oppressiveness, gravity, seriousness.

فِدْيَة ransom; redemption.

فَذّ unique, individual, matchless, peerless, unrivaled; single, sole, unusual.

فَذْلَكَة summary, abstract, epitome, brief outline.

فَرَّ to escape, flee, run away, run off from; to desert (army).

فِراء، فَرْو fur.

فُرَادَى individually, separately, one, by one, one after the other.

فِرار	escape, flight, running away.
فِراسَة	physiognomy; insight, perspicacity, clairvoyance.
فَرَاش	wheel (of a mill); propeller (of a ship).
فِراش	bed, mattress.
فِراشُ المَوْت	deathbed.
فَرَاشَة	butterfly, moth.

للفراشة أجنحة ذات ألوان جذّابة للغاية

The butterfly has most attractive colored wings

فَرَاغ	vaccum, void, empty space, gap.
فِراق	separation, departure, parting; disunion, disunity.
فَرَّان	baker.
فَرَّجَ	to open up, spread out, unfold, open wide; to separate, split, make an opening in; to dispel, drive away (grief); to relieve, comfort, solace someone.
فَرَج	relief, ease, repose, comfort; freedom from grief or sorrow; joy, relaxation, happy ending.
فَرْج	opening, gap; pudendum, vulva of the female.
فِرْجَار	compass, dividers.
فُرْجَة	opening, gap, aperture, hole, crack, crevice; state of happiness, pleasure, delight; sight, spectacle.
فَرِحَ	to be glad, happy, delighted; to rejoice; to be gay, merry, cheerful over.
فَرَح	joy, gaiety, mirth, happiness, merriment, gladness.
فَرَح	wedding ceremony, feast, celebration, festival.
فَرِح، فَرْحان	glad, happy, merry, jubilant, cheerful.
فَرَّخَ	to hatch (eggs); to germinate, sprout (tree, shrub); to spread, gain ground.
فَرْخ	yound bird, nestling, fledgling (bird).
فَرْخ	shoot, sprout (plant).
فَرْخ	sheet (paper).
فَرْد	sole, single, only; solitary, lone, lonely.
فَرْد	unique, unrivaled, peerless.
فَرْد	person, individual.

فَرْد	odd, uneven (number).
فَرْدًا فَرْدًا	one at a time, one after the other, one by one, singly.
فِرْدَوْس	paradise, heaven.
فَرْدِيّ	solitary, single, solo; pertaining to a single person; individual, personal; odd, uneven (number).

فَرَزَ to sort out, categorize, assort, group, to set apart, isolate, classify; to partition (land).

فَرْز separation, sorting out, setting apart; classification, sorting, grouping, grading; partition (land).

فَرَسٌ horse, mare; knight (in chess).

فَرَشَ to spread out; to pave, flag, slab; to furnish, provide with furniture (office, house).

فَرْش furniture, household effects; spreading out; paning, flagging, slabbing, flooring; mat, rug.

فُرْشَاة brush.

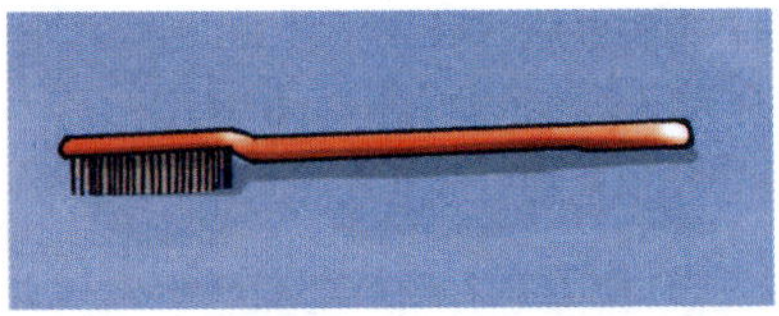

يجب تنظيف أسناننا كل صباح بالفرشاة

we should clean our teeth every morning with a brush

فُرْشَاةُ الحِلاقَة shaving brush.

فُرْشَاةُ الرَّسْم paint brush.

فُرْصَة opportunity, chance, occasion; vacation, recess, holiday.

انْتَهَزَ الفُرْصَة to seize the opportunity.

فَرَضَ to decide, determine, decree, order, ordain; to impose upon, enjoin upon; make incumbent upon; to dictate, prescribe; to appoint, assign, allot; to notch, make incisions in; to suppose, presume, presuppose, postulate.

فَرَّضَ to notch, incise, indent, make incisions in.

فَرْض assumption, supposition, postulate, hypothesis, given (math).

فَرْض imposition, injunction, prescription, dictation.

فَرْضُ الضَّرائِب taxation.

فَرْض obligation, duty, task, assignment; order, command, decree.

فَرْضٌ مَدْرَسِيّ homework.

على فَرْض أن supposing that, on the assumption that.

فُرْضَة notch, incision, indentation, groove, furrow, gap.

فَرَطَ to precede; to slip, escape inadvertently; to get lost on; to neglect; to be lax, remiss with regard to; to strip off (fruits).

فَرَّطَ to waste, squander, forsake, give up, neglect; to lose, forfeit; to abuse, misuse.

فَرْط excess, immoderation, exaggeration, surplus, hyper.

فَرْطُ ضَغْطِ الدَّم hypertension.

فَرْطُ الحَسَاسِيَّة hypersensitivity.

فَرْع branch, ramification; section; division, department; bough, twig, offishoot, branch (of tree, plant).

فَرْع descendant, offspring.

فَرْعِيّ branch, subsidiary, tributary; marginal.

فَرَغَ — to be empty, void, vacant, unoccupied.

فَرَغَ مِن العَمَل — to finish, terminate, end, bring to an end.

فَرَغَ إلى نَفْسِهِ — to collect one's thoughts.

فَرَّغَ — to empty, void, vacate, discharge; to drain; draw water from; to unload, unlade; to disembark, land (goods from ship); to remove the contents of, unpack; to pour, pour forth, empty.

فَرَقَ، فَرَّقَ — to separate, part, divide; to scatter, disperse, spread; to distribute, allot, apportion, parcel out; to part one's hairs.

فَرَّقَ — to distinguish between, differentiate between; to discriminate between; to frighten, scare, terrify.

فَرَّقَ بين — to sow dissension between; to stir up discord among.

فَرْق — difference, dissimilarity, disparity, variation.

لا فَرْق — all the same, likewise, in manner; it does not make any difference.

الفُرْقان — the Holy Koran.

فِرْقَة — group, part, portion, division, section, unit; band, company, party, detachment, troop; class, grade; troupe, ensemble (music); team, crew, sect.

فِرْقَةُ المَطافِئ — fire brigade.

فِرْقَةٌ موسيقيَّة — band, orchestra.

فَرْقَعة — cracking, snapping, crackle, explosion, blast.

فَرَكَ — to rub, scrub.

فَرَمَ — to mince, hash, chop up.

فُرْن — oven, stove, cooking stove, cooker; furnace, kiln; bakery.

فَرْو، فَرْوَة — furs, fur.

فَرْوَةُ الرَّأس — scalp.

فَرُّوج — chicken, chick, pullet.

فُروسِيَّة — horsemanship, equitation; chivalry, knighthood.

فُروغ — emptiness, voidness, vacancy.

فُروغُ الصَّبْر — impatience.

فِرْيَة — lie, falsehood, falsity; slander, calumny.

فَريد — unique, matchless, peerless, unrivaled; alone, lone, lonely; singular, solitary.

فَريسَة — prey, victim.

يلتهم الحيوان المفترس فريسته بنهم شديد

The predatory animal devours its prey greedily

فَريصَة — muscle below the shoulder blade.

ارْتَعَدَتْ فَرائِصُهُ — to tremble, shake all over.

فَريضَة — duty, obligation; religious duty, divine precept; obligatory prayer (in Islam); lawful share; legal portion (in Islam).

فَريق party, side; team,group; troop; company.

فَريق lieutenant general (army rank).

فَزّاعَة scarecrow; one who inspires fear.

فَزِعَ to be afraid, scared of, frightened by; to panic, fear, dread; to take refuge, flee to; to seek asylum with.

فَزَّعَ to frighten, scare, alarm, terrify, startle, dismay.

فَزَع fear, fright, dismay, panic, terror, anxiety.

فَزِع frightened, terrified, scared, alarmed, dismayed.

فَسا to break wind, fart.

فَساد decay, rottenness, corruption, decomposition, putridity, putrefaction; depravity, wickedness; weakness, immorality.

فَساد invalidity, nullity, voidness.

فُسْتان woman's dress.

فَسُحَ to become wide, spacious, roomy (place).

فَسَّحَ، فَسَحَ to widen, make wide or broad; to extend, expand; to make room for; to open or pave the way for.

فُسْحَة space, interval; open space; enough time, time margin.

فُسْحَة wideness, roominess, vastness, spaciousness.

فَسَخَ to dislocate, disjoint; to sever, tear; to cancel, abolish, rescind, revoke, abrogate, annul, invalidate; to dissolve, void, vacate (jurisdiction).

فَسْخَة splinter, chip, sliver, fragment, slice.

فَسَدَ to decay, rot, decompose; to be rotten, decayed, decomposed, putrid, spoiled; to be corrupted, depraved, perverted.

فَسَّدَ to spoil, deprave, ruin, corrupt, degrade, demoralize.

فَسَّرَ to explain, expound, explicate, elucidate, interpret, construe.

فَسَقَ، فَسُقَ to stray, deviate from the right path; to act sinfully, immorally; to lead a dissolute life.

فِسْق، فُسُوق debauchery, moral depravity, dissolute life, lewdness, immorality, profligacy, wantonness.

فَسِيح wide, spacious, roomy; broad; vast, ample.

فُسَيْفُساء mosaic.

فَشَا to spread, circulate, disclose, divulge (a secret, etc.).

فَشَخَ to stride over, straddle, take wide steps over.

فَشِلَ to fail, miss the mark, miss, be unsuccessful, miscarry; to lose courage, despair; to be disappointed.

فَشَّلَ to thwart, foil, frustrate something or someone.

فَشَل failure, fizzle, frustration, disappointment; fiasco.

فَشِل weakhearted, cowardly, craven, fearful.

فَصّ stone (of a ring, etc.); clove (of garlic, etc.); lobe (anatomy).

فَصاحَة eloquence, purity of language.

فِصْح، عيدُ الفِصْح Easter.

الفُصْحى، العَرَبيَّة الفُصْحَى classical Arabic.

فَصَدَ to bleed, draw blood from.

فَصَلَ to cut off, detach, disjoin, divide, separate, set apart.

فَصَلَ to discharge, dismiss, fire, sack from an office.

فَصَلَ to decide a controversy; to make a decision; to render judgment about, with respect to a dispute.

فَصَّلَ to divide into particular sections; to arrange in sections; to group, classify, categorize; to detail, particularize; to make clear, plain, distinct; to make to measure (a garment).

فَصْل parting, severance, separation; division, partition.

فَصْل discharge, dismissal, sacking, firing from an office.

فَصْل rendering judgment, decision, determination, resolution.

فَصْل chapter (of book); act (of a play); season, quarter; semester, term, trimester, quarter (study year); class, grade (of school).

فَصْلِيّ، فَصْلِيًّا quarterly.

فَصَمَ to cause to crack; to crack, split, cleave.

فَصِيح eloquent, well-spoken; pure, literary.

فَصِيل، فَصِيلَة family; platoon (army); squad (police); faction, group.

فَضَّ to open, unlock, unwrap, break open; to unseal, remove the seal of; to pierce, bore; to scatter, break up; to adjourn, conclude (a meeting).

فَضَّ بَكَارَةَ فَتاة to deflower a girl.

فَضَّ النِّزاع to solve, resolve, settle a dispute.

فَضّ opening, breaking, unlocking; scattering, disbanding; adjournment, conclusion (of a meeting); disengagement; defloration; settlement.

فَضَاء space, open space, outer space.

فَضَائِيّ spatial.

فُضَالَة remnant, residue, leftover; refuse, offal, surplus.

فِضَّة silver.

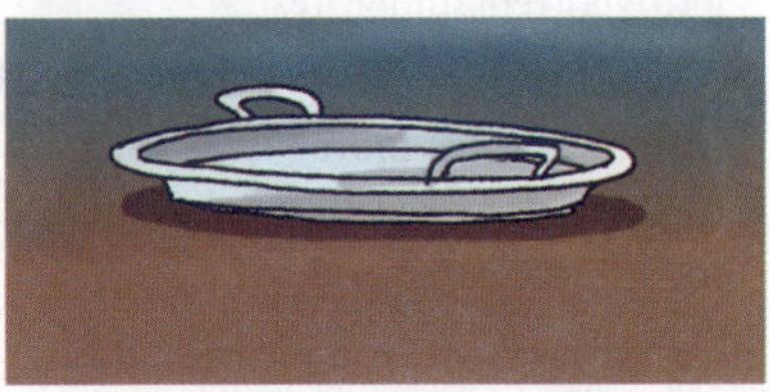

تُصنع بعض آنية الطعام والأقداح من الفضة

Some kitchen utensils and drinking cups are made of silver

فَضَحَ to disclose, uncover someone's offenses; to expose, show up, compromise; to shame, disgrace someone; to ravish, violate, rape a woman.

فَضْح exposure; degradation, disgracing, dishonoring; disclosure to the public; unmasking, unveiling someone's secrets or offenses.

فَضْفَاض loose, flowing (garment); bombastic, flowery, aureate, pompous (speech); plump, corpulent (girl).

فَضَلَ to remain, be left over, be in excess, in surplus; to excel, surpass, outshine; to be better than.

فَضُلَ to be virtuous, honest, good; to be generous, pious.

فَضَّلَ to prefer to, favor, choose to; to deem wise to; to give precedence to over.

فَضْل favor, kindness, service; gift, present; merit, credit; preference, priority, precedence; benefit, favor.

فَضْل surplus, excess, superfluity; leftover, remainder, rest.

فَضْلاً عَن ذلك besides, beside, aside from, let alone; moreover, furthermore, as well as, in addition to.

مِن فَضْلِك if you please! will you please!.

فَضْلَة leftover, rest, surplus, residue, remnant; waste, offal, rubbish, trash, refuse.

فُضُول curiosity, inquisitiveness, meddling, obstrusion.

فُضُولِيّ curious, inquisitive, meddlesome, obstrusive.

فِضِّيّ silvery, argentine, silver.

فَضِيحَة scandal.

فَضِيل eminent, outstanding, distinguished; learned, erudite.

فَضِيلَة virtue, moral excellence, morality; merit, advantage.

صَاحِبُ الفَضِيلَة His Eminence (title of a sheikh).

فِطَام weaning.

فَطَرَ to create, make; to split, cleave; to have breakfast; to break the fast.

فُطِرَ to have a natural disposition for; to be innate in someone; to be split, cleft, broken.

فَطْر crack, fissure, rift, rupture, split.

فِطْر fast breaking.

عِيدُ الفِطْر Lesser Bairam.

فُطْر mushroom, fungus.

فِطْرَة nature, natural disposition, innate character; instinct; creation.

بِالفِطْرَة by nature, by birth, innately.

فُطْرِيّ fungal, fungous.

فِطْرِيّ natural, primitive, innate, inborn, inherent.

فَطَمَ to wean.

فَطَنَ، فَطُنَ، فَطِنَ to realize, discern, comprehend, grasp; to be aware of, find out about; to be shrewd, astute, intelligent, sagacious.

فَطِن، فَطُن، فَطْن discerning, sagacious, astute, intelligent, clever, smart, bright.

فِطْنَة discernment, sagacity, intelligence, astuteness, wit, insight, acumen, perspicacity, cleverness.

فُطُور breakfast.

فَطِيرَة pastry, pancake.

فَظّ rude, rough, crude, coarse, impolite, uncouth, ill-mannered.

فَظَاظَة rudeness, crudeness, coarseness, bluntness, impoliteness, uncouthness, gruffness, bad manners.

فَظَاعَة ugliness, repulsiveness, atrocity, horror, hideousness.

فَظِيع ، فَظِع abominable, atrocious, detestable, disgusting, heinous, horrid, horrible, ugly, shocking, hideous.

فَعَّال effective, efficient, active, operative, efficacious.

فَعَالِيَّة efficiency, efficacy, effectiveness; activity.

فَعَل to do, act, perform; to act upon, affect, influence.

فِعْل deed, act, action, performance; effect, influence, impact; verb (grammar).

فِعْلاً، بِالفِعْل، فِعْلِيًا actually, as a matter of fact, indeed.

بِفِعْل out of, because, due to, on account of.

فِعْلٌ تامّ perfect verb (grammar).

فِعْلٌ غير قِياسِيّ irregular verb (grammar).

فِعْلٌ قِياسِيّ regular verb (grammar).

فِعْلٌ لازِم، غير مُتَعَدٍّ intransitive verb (grammar).

فِعْلٌ مُتَعَدٍّ transitive verb (grammar).

فِعْلٌ مَجْهُول passive verb (grammar).

فِعْلٌ مُساعِد auxiliary verb (grammar).

فِعْلٌ مَعْلُوم active verb (grammar).

فِعْلٌ ناقِص defective verb (grammar).

فِعْلِيّ actual, factual, real; active, effectual; verbal (grammar).

فَغَر to gape, open the mouth wide.

فَقَأ to rip open, slit open (a tumor).

فُقَاعَة bubble.

فَقَدَ to lose, forfeit; to be deprived of, bereft of; to lack, want, miss.

فَقَدَ الأمَل to lose hope, despair.

فَقْد ، فُقْدان، فِقْدان loss, bereavement; lack, want, absence; forfeiture, privation, deprivation.

فَقْدُ الأهْلِيَّة incapacity, incompetence; disability.

فَقْدُ الذّاكِرَة amnesia, loss of memory.

فَقْدُ الوَعْي unconsciousness, faint, swoon.

فَقْدُ الصَّواب folly, madness.

فَقَرَ ، فَقَّر to pierce, bore, perforate; to make poor, impoverish, reduce to poverty.

فَقْر ، فُقْر poverty, need, destitution, penury, lack, want.

فِقْرَة paragraph, clause, section, part.

فَقَس to hatch, incubate (eggs).

فَقَّط to write the word (only) after the total; to spell out the figures; to write figures in words.

فَقَط only, just, solely, nothing but, no more; total.

فَقِهَ، فَقُهَ to understand, grasp. comprehend, realize; to know of; to have jurisprudential knowledge; to be a jurist, jurisprudent, legal scholar.

فِقْه jurisprudence, doctrinal writings; understanding; philology (of the language); comprehension.

فِقْهِيّ jurisprudent, doctrinal.

فَقِيد lost, missing; dead, deceased.

فَقِير poor, pauper, mendicant; destitute; meager, scanty.

فَقِيه jurist, legist, jurisprudent.

فَكَّ to disassemble, dismantle, break up; to separate, disjoin, detach, disunite; to untie, unfasten, undo, unwind, disengage; to lift, raise, put an end to; to unbotton, unscrew; to solve a problem; to change money; to set free, liberate, ransom, redeem a person; to unseal, break open (a seal); to decipher, decode (a code); to pay off, redeem (a mortgage); to dislocate, luxuate (a bone).

فَكّ untying, unbinding, loosening, disengagement, disassembly, dismounting; separation, disconnection; dissociation; dislocation; setting free, releasing, emancipation; redemption of a lien.

فَكّ jaw, jawbone; mandible (upper jaw), maxilla (lower jaw).

فُكَاهَة humor, jesting, funmaking, joking, wisecrack.

فُكَاهِيّ humorous, comical, funny; wit.

فَكَرَ، فَكَّرَ to think of; to reflect on, medidate on, ponder on; to revolve in one's mind; to contemplate, consider, cogitate.

فِكْر thinking, reflection, speculation, consideration; thought, idea, notion, concept, opinion, view; intellect, mind.

فِكْرَة idea, thought, notion, concept, view, opinion.

عَلى فِكْرَة incidentally, speaking of, by the way.

فِكْرِيّ intellectual, mental, ideational, speculative.

فَكَّكَ to disassemble, dismantle, take apart, dismember, disjoin, disconnect, disunite; to dislocate, disjoint; to dissociate (chem.).

فَلَّ to dent, notch, blunt (sword, knife); to flee, run away; to weaken, subdue.

فَلّ group, company, band.

فَلاح success, prosperity; salvation, deliverance; welfare.

فَلاَّح tiller of the soil, peasant, farmer.

يحرث الفلاح الأرض ثم يزرعها ويعتني بها

The peasant tills the soil then plant seeds in it and look after it

فِلاحَة cultivation, tillage (of land); farming, agriculture.

فُلان so-and-so, unnamed person or thing.

فَلَتَ to escape from, slip away from, get away from; to extricate oneself from; to free oneself from.

فَلْتَة unexpected event; extravagance; oversight, error, lapse.

فَلْج cleft, crack, crevice, fissure.

فَلَحَ to till, plow, cultivate (land); to split, cleave; to thrive, prosper; to be lucky, successful.

فِلْذَة piece, portion, slice.

فَلَّسَ to declare bankrupt; to cause bankruptcy or insolvency to someone; to bankrupt.

فُلُوس money; scales of fish.

فَلْسَفَة philosophy.

فَلْسَفِيّ philosophical.

فُلْفُل، فِلْفِل pepper.

فَلَقَ، فَلَّقَ to split, cleave, rend, break open, tear apart.

فَلَق dawn, daybreak.

فَلْق crack, split, crevice, fissure, cleft, rift; fault.

فِلْقَة lobe, one half of a split thing.

فَلَك orbit of celestial bodies; star, celestial body.

فَلَكِيّ (ص) astronomical.

فَلَكِيّ (اسم) astronomer.

فَلِّين، فِلِّين، فَلِّينَة، فِلِّينَة cork.

فَم mouth; orifice, opening, aperture; muzzle (of animal).

فَمُ النَّهْر embouchure, mouth of river.

فَمُ آلَةِ النَّفْخ المُوسيقيَّة mouthpiece,

فَمَوِيّ، فَمِيّ، فَمِّيّ oral, buccal.

فَنّ art, technique; kind, sort, type, variety.

فَنٌّ تَجْريدِيّ abstract art.

فَنٌّ تشكيليّ plastic art.

الفُنون الجميلَة fine arts.

فَنَى، فَنِيَ to pass away, perish, cease to exist; to wane, perish, vanish, become extinct, consumed, spent.

لا يُفْنَى، لا يَفْنَى imperishable, inexhaustible.

فَنَاء passing away; ruin, annihilation, vanishing, perdition; extinction, exhaustion.

فِنَاء courtyard, open hall.

فَنَار lighthouse.

فَنَّان، فَنَّانَة artist.

فِنْجان cup, teacup, coffee cup.

فَنَّدَ to refuse, rebut, confute, disprove, challenge as false; to classify, specify, detail, itemize.

فُنْدُق hotel, inn, hostel.

فَنَن twig, branch (of a shrub).

فَنِّيّ (ص) technical, artistic.

فَنّي (اسم) technician.

فِهْرِس، فِهْرِسْت table of contents, index, catalogue.

فَهِمَ to understand, comprehend, realize, perceive, know of, learn about, grasp.

فَهَّمَ to instruct, give someone to understand; to make someone understand, grasp the meaning of.

فَهِم quick-witted, astute, keen.

فَهْم understanding, comprehension, conception, perception; brains, intellect; acumen, insight; intelligence.

سُوءُ الفَهْم misunderstanding, miscomprehension.

فَهِيم discerning, perspicacious, judicious, shrewd, intelligent.

فُو mouth.

فَوَات passage, elapsing, expiry, expiration, lapse.

قَبْلَ فَوَاتِ الأَوَان before it is too late.

فَوَّاح redolent, fragrant, aromatic, diffusing fragance.

فَوَّار effervescent, bubbling, ebullient, jetting forth.

فَوْج battalion, regiment; group, band, company; crowd.

فَوْر، فَوَران boiling, bubbling, ebullition; agitation, upheaval.

فَوْر، فَوْراً at once, right away, instantly, immediately.

على الفَوْر forthwith, without delay, promptly, immediately.

فَوْرَة outburst, flare-up, gust, surge; boom, prosperity; intensity, violence, severity.

فَوْرِيّ instant, instantaneous, immediate, on the spot, direct.

فَوْز victory, triumph, success; winning, gaining, achievement.

فَوَّضَ to authorize, commission, empower, entrust; to delegate, give full power to; to deputize, depute.

فَوْضَى anarchy, chaos, disorder, confusion, muddle, jumble.

فَوْضَوِيّ anarchist; chaotic, disarrayed, disordered, messy.

فَوْضَوِيَّة anarchism, anarchy.

فُوطَة apron, towel, napkin; diaper; dishcloth.

فَوْق up, upstairs, on top, above, over, on; beyond, more than.

فَوْقَ ذَلِك on top of, in addition to, plus, over and above, moreover, furthermore.

فَوْقَ البَنَفْسَجِيّ ultraviolet (radiation).

فَوْقَ صَوْتِيّ supersonic.

فَوْقَ الطَّبِيعَة supernatural, transcendental, metaphysical.

فَوْقَ العَادَة extraordinary, unusual, exceptional, supernatural.

وما فَوْق and upward, and more, upwards.

فَوْقِيّ higher, upper, located higher or above.

أ ب ت ث ج ح خ د ذ ر ز س ش ص ض ط ظ ع غ ف ق ك ل م ن هـ و ي

فُولاذ steel.

فُولاذٌ لا يَصْدأ stainless steel.

فُولاذُ الزَّهْر cast steel.

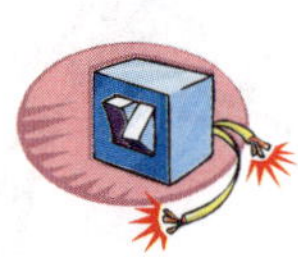

فُولت volt.

فُولْتِيَّة voltage.

فُوَّهَة ، فُوْهَة mouth, opening, vent, orifice; nozzle, spout.

فُوَّهَةُ البُرْكَان crater.

فُوَّهَةُ البُنْدُقِيَّة muzzle.

في in, at, on; during, within, among, with, about, over; because of, according to; multiplied by; whilst, during, as.

فِيما مَضَى in the past, formerly, previously, once.

فِيما يَلي hereinafter, hereinbelow, below, in the following.

فَيء shade; shadow; booty, loot, pillage; prize.

فَيَّاض effluent, outflowing, torrential; exuberant, elaborate, exhaustive (speech); bountiful, generous, munificent (person).

فَيروز turquoise.

فِيزياء physics (science).

فِيزياءٌ حَيَوِيَّة biophysics.

فِيزياءُ الأرض geophysics.

فِيزياءٌ فَلَكِيَّة astrophysics.

فِيزيائِيّ (ص) physical.

فِيزيائِيّ (اسم) physicist.

فَيْض flood, deluge, inundation; effluence, excess.

فَيْض superabundance, surplus, plenty, profuseness; exuberance; emanation, outpouring.

فَيَضان deluge, flood, inundation.

فِيل elephant; bishop (in chess).

فَيْلَسُوف philosopher.

فَيْلَق army corps, legion.

فِيلْمٌ سينمائِيّ motion picture, cinema film.

فِيلْمُ رُسومٍ مُتَحَرِّكَة animated cartoon.

فِيلْمٌ وَثائِقِيّ documentary.

فَيْنَة time, period; instant, moment.

بين فَيْنَةٍ وأُخرى from time to time, now and then, occasionally.

حرف القاف

قَائِد — leader, chief; commander, commandant.

قَائِدُ الجَيْش — army commander.

قَائِدُ الطَّائِرَة — captain, pilot.

قَائِدُ فِرقَةٍ مُوسِيقِيَّة — conductor, maestro.

قَائِم — rising, getting up; standing, erect, upright; vertical, perpendicular.

قَائِم — situated, located; existing, existent; present; standing; actual, current.

قَائِم — gross, total, entire, (weight).

قَائِمٌ على — based on, founded on.

قَائِمٌ بِالأَعْمَال — chargé d'affaires.

قَائِمٌ بِذاته — self-existent, independent, separate.

قَائِمُ الزَّوايا — right-angled, rectangular.

قَائِمة — post, pillar, pole; list, roster, roll; table, schedule.

قَائِمةٌ أَمَامِيَّة — foreleg, forelimb.

قَائِمةٌ خَلْفِيَّة — hindleg, hindlimb.

قَائِمةُ أَسْعَار — price list.

قَائِمةُ الجَرْد — inventory.

قَائِمةُ الحِساب — invoice, bill.

قَائِمةُ الطَّعَام — menu.

قَائِمةُ المُحْتَويات — table of contents, index.

قَائِمُ مَقام — district commissioner, deputy governor.

قَائِمَّقامِيَّة — district (administrative district).

قَابِس — plug (elect.).

قَابِض (ص) — grievous, distressing, embarrassing; astringent, constrictive, constringent.

قَابِض (ص) — holding, grasping, catching, clutching, clasping; controlling, dominant, dominating.

قابِض (اسم) receiver; arrester; clutch (mech.).

قابع staying at, remaining at, withdrawn into, retired at.

قابَلَ to meet with, encounter; to come upon, come across; to get together with, have a meeting with; to face, confront.

قابَلَ to compare with; to correspond to, be similar to; to place opposite to, in front of; to oppose, set against.

قابَلَ بِالمِثْل to reciprocate, return in kind, repay, payback.

قابِل accepting, consenting, approving, willing; capable of, susceptible of, liable to, apt to, allowing, predisposed to.

قابِلٌ للاحْتِراق combustible.

قابِلٌ للتَّجْدِيد renewable.

قابِلٌ للتَّجْزِئَة divisible.

قابِلَة midwife.

قابِلِيَّة disposition, tendency, inclination; predisposition; faculty, power, capacity, ability, aptitude, competence; appetite.

قاتَلَ to fight, combat, battle with.

قاتِل (ص) deadly, mortal, fatal, killing.

قاتِل (اسم) killer, murderer, assassin.

قاتِل الحَشَرات insecticide.

قاتِم dark, gloomy; cloudy, overcast; black, pitch-black.

قاحِل arid, barren, dry.

قادَ to lead, guide, conduct, direct; to drive, pilot, steer.

قادِر possessing power, powerful, potent; capable, able, efficient, talented.

قادِم coming next, following, forthcoming; incoming.

قادوس hopper, waterwheel bucket.

قاذِف ejector, expeller, thrower.

قاذِفَةُ القَنابِل bomber.

انهمرت القنابل من قاذفة إسرائيلية كانت تحلق فوق الجنوب اللبناني

Bombs fell heavily from an Israeli bomber on the southern region of Lebanon

---

قار tar, bitumen.

قارِئ reader, reciter.

قارِئُ البَخْت fortune-teller, soothsayer.

قارِئُ الكَفّ chiromancer, palmist.

قارَبَ to get near to; to border on; to be about to do something, reach something.

قارِب boat, dinghy, canoe.

قارِبُ النَّجاة lifeboat.

قارَّة continent.

تتكوّن الكرة الأرضية من خمس قارات وبحار

The Planet Earth is formed of five continents and several oceans

قارِس — chilly, severe, biting; sharp, chilling, cutting.

قارِص — biting, stinging; bitter, acrid; cutting.

قارَعَ — to come to blows with; to fight with; to draw lots with.

قارِعُ الطَّبْل — drumbeater.

قارِعَةُ الطَّريق — middle of the road, pavement.

قارَنَ — to compare with, contrast with; to be associated with, linked with, coupled with.

قارِنَة — coupling (mech.).

قارُورَة — flask, vial, bottle.

قارِّيّ — continental.

قاسَ — to measure, gauge, take the measurements of; to try on a garment; to weigh, judge, draw conclusions from; to compare, correlate with or between two things.

قاسٍ (القاسي) — hard; grim, austere, inexorable; difficult; cruel, severe, merciless, inflexible; tough, drastic.

قاسَى — to suffer, undergo, sustain, bear.

قاسَمَ — to share with; to divide with.

قاسِمٌ مُشْتَرَك — common denominator, common divisor.

قاصِد — going to, heading for; direct, straight way.

قاصِر — minor, underage, legally minor.

قاصِر — incapable, unable; confined to, reserved for.

قاصِرُ اليد — powerless, impotent, helpless, weak.

قاضٍ (ص) — deadly, lethal, fatal, mortal.

قاضٍ (القاضِي) (اسم) — judge, magistrate, justice.

قاضِي القُضاة — chief justice.

قاضَى — to prosecute, summon before a judge, arraign; to sue, take legal action, bring suit against.

قاطِبَةً — all together, one and all, all and sundry.

قاطِرَة — locomotive; towing machine; trailer.

قاطَعَ — to interrupt, cut off, boycott; to part company with; to break off from; to withdraw from.

قاطِع — cutting, sharp, incisive; convincing; dogmatic, decisive, conclusive, definitive, positive, absolute; migratory (bird).

قَاطِع — cutter; secant (engineering); partition, screen, division; section, sector, strip.

قَاطِعُ التَّيَّار — cutout, switch.

قَاطِعُ الدَّائِرَة الكَهْرَبائِيَّة — circuit breaker.

قَاطِعُ طَرِيق — highwayman, bandit, brigand.

قَاطِن (ص) — residing, living, dwelling.

قَاطِن (اسم) — inhabitant, resident, dweller.

قاع — bottom, bed; depth; floor.

قَاعَة — hall, room, auditorium.

قَاعِدة — foundation, groundwork; basis, fundament, base; support base, socle, pedestal, foot; chassis, undercarriage.

قَاعِدَة — precept, rule, principle, maxim; formula, method, manner; mode, model.

قَوَاعِدُ اللُّغَة — grammar.

قَوَاعِدُ السُّلوك — rules of conduct.

قَافِلَة — caravan, convoy.

كانت القوافل تجوب الصحاري
ناقلة السلع من بلد إلى آخر

Caravans used to traverse deserts carrying merchandise from one country to the other

قَافِيَة — rhyme.

قَالَ — to speak, say, tell, utter, voice; to state, maintain, assert, propound, profess, advocate; to allege; to speak ill of someone.

قَالَ — to nap; take a nap, a siesta.

قَالَب، قَالِب — mold, die, block, matrix.

قَالِبُ الأَحْذِيَة — last, shoe tree.

قَالِبُ جُبْن — chunk or loaf of cheese.

قَالِبُ صَابُون — cake of soap.

قَلْبًا وقَالِبًا — with heart and soul.

قَامَ — to get up, rise, stand up; to set out, start out, get going, start off; to be located in, lie in, situated in.

قَامَ الدَّلِيلُ — it has been proven, established, demonstrated that.

قَامَتِ الحَرب — to break out.

قَامَ المَيِّت — to be resurrected; to rise from the dead.

قَامَ بِالعَمَل — to perform, carry out, execute; to assume, take over, take upon oneself to carry, shoulder.

قَامَ بِأَوَدِهِ — to support, sustain, provide for someone's needs.

قَامَ بِدور — to stage, carry out (a role); perform a role or part in.

قَامَ بِزِيارَة — to pay visit; to visit, call on someone.

قَامَ على — to be based on; to look after, attend to; to manage, handle, operate.

قَامَ في وَجْهِهِ — to resist, oppose, challenge, stand in his ways.

قَامَ مَقَامَهُ — to replace; to be substituted for; to take the place of.

قَامَ (بانقلاب، مُظاهَرَة) — to stage, carry out; to make a coup d'etat, demonstration, etc.

قامَة — figure, stature, build, body.

قامَرَ — to gamble, bet on.

قامُوس — dictionary, lexicon.

قانِط — despairing, desperate, disheartened.

قانِع — contented, satisfied.

قانُون — law, statute, act, legislation, code; canon, established principle, basic rule; axiom; norm, regulation, ordinance; precept.

يجب أن نعيش تحت ظل القانون

We must live under the law of the country

قانُونٌ أَساسِيّ لِشرِكَة — articles of association, statutes.

قانُونٌ أَساسِيّ — fundamental law.

قانُونُ البِحار — law of the sea, maritime law.

قانُونٌ جِنائِيّ — criminal law, penal law or code.

قانُونُ حِمايَةِ المِلْكِيَّةِ الأَدَبِيَّة — copyright law.

قانُون حِمايَةِ المِلْكِيَّةِ الصِّناعِيَّةِ والاخْتِراعات — patent law.

قانُونٌ داخِلِيّ لِشَرِكَة — rules of procedures.

قانُونٌ دُسْتورِيّ — constitutional law.

قانُونٌ طَبِيعِيّ — natural law.

قانُونٌ عُرْفِيّ — martial law.

قانُونٌ مَدَنِيّ — civil code.

قانُونُ المُوجِبات والعُقُود — law of obligations and contracts.

قَانُونٌ دُوَلِيّ — international law.

قَانُونُ أَحْوال شَخْصِيَّة — personal status law.

قَانُونُ الضَّمان الاجْتِماعِيّ — social security law.

قانونِيّ (ص) — legal, juristic, statutory; lawful, legitimate, valid, de jure.

قَانُونِيّ (اسم) — jurist, jurisprudent, legist.

غَيْرُ قَانُونِيّ — illegal, unlawful, illegitimate.

قَاهِر (ص) — forcible, irresistible, cogent; overpowering.

قَاهِر (اسم) — vanquisher, conqueror, victor; despot, tyrant.

قُوَّةٌ قَاهِرَة — force majeure.

قَاوَلَ — to confer, parley, negotiate with; to make a contract; to conclude a bargain, make a deal with.

قَاوَمَ — to resist, oppose, counter; to withstand, hold out.

قَايَضَ — to barter, exchange, swap, bargain, give on exchange.

قَباحة — ugliness, ignominy, infamy, shamefulness.

قُبالة	opposite to, facing, face to face with.
قَبّان	platform scale, steelyard.
قَبَّة	collar.
قُبَّة	dome, cupola.

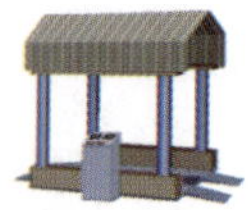

قَبُح	to be ugly, repulsive; to be ignominious, infamous, disgraceful, shameful.
قَبَّح	to make ugly; to reprove, rebuke, censure, condemn; to distort, disfigure, find fault with.
قُبْح، قَبْح	ugliness, repulsiveness.
قَبَرَ	to bury, inhume, lay to rest.
قَبْر	grave, tomb, sepulcher; burial, interment, inhumation, burying.
قَبَضَ	to grasp, grip, hold, take hold of, grab, clasp, seize.
قَبَضَ على	to arrest, apprehend, capture, detain.
قَبَضَ مالاً	to receive, get, collect money.
قَبَضَ	to contract, constipate (bowels); to oppress, deject, dispirit, depress someone.
قَبَضَ يَدَهُ عَنْ	to keep oneself from seizing something; to be stingy toward; to be ungenerous toward.
قَبْض	grasping, grip, hold, catching, seizure; arresting, apprehension, capture; receipt of money; contraction; constipation (of bowels).
قَبْضَة	grip, hold, clasp; handful; control, domination.
قَبْضَةُ اليد	fist.
في قَبْضَةِ يَدِهِ	in one's possession, under one's control.
قُبْطان	captain, shipmaster; pilot, skipper.
قَبَعَ	to stay at, remain at, seclude oneself at; to grunt (pig); to trumpet (elephant).
قُبَّعة	hat.
قَبِلَ	to accept, agree, consent, assent, accede to; to approve, subscribe to; to sanction, content oneself with; to yield, give in to, submit to someone's command; to guarantee, be surety for.
قَبَّلَ	to kiss.
قَبْلُ، قَبْلاً، من قَبْلُ	before, formerly, once, in the past.
قَبْلَ	prior to, previous to.
قَبْلَ أنْ	before.
قَبْلَ أوانِه	premature, too early.
قَبْلَ فَواتِ الأَوان	before it is too late.
قَبْلَ كُلِّ شَيء	above all, first of all, to begin with.
قَبْلَ الميلاد	BC; Before Christ.
من قَبْل	prior to, before.
ما قَبْلَ التّاريخ	prehistory.

من قِبَلِ	from, on the part of.
قُبْلَة	kiss.
قِبْلَة	Kiblah (direction to which Moslems turn in prayer).
قِبْلَة	Mecca.
قَبَلِيّ	tribal.
قَبْلِيّ	anterior, antecedent.

قَبْو vault, cellar; tunnel, drift, gallery (in mine).

قَبُول، قُبُول acceptance, assent, approval, admittance, admission.

قُبُول reception, receipt, taking in, admission.

قَبِيح ugly, hideous, repugnant, abominable, monstrous; infamous, disgraceful, shameful; obscene, indecent, foul, vile, base, mean; impudent, insolent, impertinent, shameless.

قَبِيل guarantor, surety.

مِن قَبِيلِ كَذا by way of, as a matter of.

مِن هَذا القَبِيل of this kind, of this type, like this.

قُبَيْل shortly before, just prior to.

قَبِيلَة tribe.

قِتَال combat, fight, warfare, battle.

قَتَرَ، قَتَّرَ to be stingy toward; to be tightfisted, niggardly.

قَتَلَ to kill, slay, murder; to alleviate, soothe; to mix with water.

قَتَلَ المَوضوعَ بَحْثاً to study the subject thoroughly; to master completely.

قَتَلَ الوَقْت to kill, waste, squander time.

قَتْل killing, murder, manslaughter, assassination.

قَتْلٌ جَماعِيّ genocide.

قَتْلٌ رَحِيم mercy killing.

قَتْلٌ عَمْد premeditated murder.

قَتِيل killed, slain, murdered, assassinated.

قُحّ pure, unmixed, genuine.

قَحَّ to cough.

قَحَطَ، قَحِطَ، قُحِطَ to be rainless (year); to be withheld (rain); to scrape off, scratch off.

قَحْط rainlessness, lack of rain, aridity, dryness, drought; famine; lack, want; scarcity.

قَحِلَ to become dry, arid; to wither, dry up.

قَدَّ to cut lengthwise, cut into stripes; to cut off, chop off.

قُدَّ قَلْبُهُ من حَجَرٍ to have a heart of stone.

قَدّ figure, frame, physique, height, build; size, bulk, volume, quantity.

عَلى قَدِّهِ of the same size, of equal size or measure.

قَدْ already; may, might, perhaps, possibly, at times.

قَدَّاحَة lighter.

قُدَّاس mass.

قَدَاسَة holiness, sanctity, sainthood.

صَاحِبُ القَدَاسَة His Holiness.

قُدَّام forepart, front, face.

قُدَّامَ in front of, before.

قَدَحَ to bore, pierce; to slander, defame, malign; to vilify, censure, blame, reprove, chide.

قَدَح cup, glass, goblet, tumbler.

قَدْح slander, libel, calumny, censure, rebuke, reproach.

قَدَّدَ to slit, cut lengthwise, cut into long narrow strips; to chop off; to cure, dry in the sun (slices of meat).

قَدَرَ، قَدِرَ to possess strength, power, ability to do something; to be master of, up to, equal to; to be in a position to do something; to be capable.

قَدَّرَ to estimate, assess, appraise, evaluate, value, rate.

قَدَّرَ to anticipate, foresee, surmise, guess, presume, suppose, believe, be of the opinion that; to enable someone to do something.

قَدَّرَ حَقَّ قدره to esteem highly; to appreciate, treasure, cherish.

قَدَّرَ الله to predetermine, foreordain, predestine (of God).

لا قَدَّرَ الله God forbid.

لا يُقَدَّر invaluable, immense, huge, enormous.

قَدَر fate, destiny, divine foreordainment, lot.

قَدْر extent, scope, scale; number, amount, value, degree; worth, rank, prestige.

قَدْرَ، على قَدْر in proportion to, in accordance with, corresponding to, equal to, equivalent to.

بِقَدْرِ ما in the same measure as; to the same extent as; as much as, as large as.

على قَدْرِ ما to a certain extent.

قَدْرَ المُسْتَطاع، بِقَدْرِ المُسْتَطاع as far as feasible, as much as possible; to the best of one's abilities.

قِدْر cooking pot.

قُدْرَة ability, capability, capacity, power, strength, might; output; power (physics).

قُدْرَةُ حِصان horsepower.

قُدْرَةُ شَمْعَة candlepower.

قُدْرَةٌ كُلِّيَّة omnipotence.

قَدَّسَ to sanctify, consecrate, dedicate, glorify, hallow; to canonize; to celebrate mass; to officiate a mass.

قُدْسِيّ holy, sacred, divine, sacrosanct.

قُدْسِيَّة sanctity, holiness, saintliness.

قَدُمَ to be old, ancient, antique; to become antiquated, grow obsolete, old.

قَدِمَ to come, arrive, get to a place.

قَدَّمَ to bring forward to let precede; to place at the head; to do earlier or beforehand; to give preference to over; to prefer to; to offer, tender, present; to exhibit, display, show, demonstrate; to give, donate, grant, award, accord.

قَدَّمَ إلى to submit to, file to, present to, lay before, put before; to provide with, supply with, furnish with.

قَدَّمَ استِدْعاءً to make a formal request, petition, application.

قَدَّمَ اسْتِقالَتَهُ to resign, tender one's resignation.

قَدَّمَ امْتِحاناً to sit for an examination.

قَدَّمَ خِدْمَةً to render a service to, do someone a favor.

قَدَّمَ دَعْوَى ضِد to bring suit against; to take legal action against; to institute legal proceedings against, sue, prosecute.

قَدَّمَ السَّاعَة to set the clock forward.

قَدَّمَ عَطاءً to tender, bid, offer a bid.

قَدَّمَ شَخْصًا إلى آخر to introduce someone to another.

قَدَّمَ الشُّكر to thank.

قَدَّمَ شَكْوَى to lodge a complaint.

قَدَّمَ طَلَبًا to apply, submit an application, a request.

قَدَّمَ لِكِتابٍ to preface, introduce.

قَدَم foot; foot (measure of length).

على قَدَم وسَاق in progress, under way, in full swing.

عَلى قَدَمِ المُساواة on an equal footing, on a par, evenly.

قُدُمًا ahead, forward, onward.

قِدَم antiquity, oldness; ancient times.

مُنْذُ القِدَم from ancient times, from time immemorial.

قُدْوَة، قَدْوَة، قِدْوَة example, model, pattern, ideal.

قَدُّوم adze.

قُدُوم arrival, coming, advent.

قَدير powerful, potent, capable, possessing power or strength.

قِدِّيس saint.

قَدِيم old, ancient, antique; existing from time immemorial.

قَدِيماً in old times, in ancient times, in the past, of old.

قَديمُ العَهْد بِـ long-aquainted with, long-familiar with; long-experienced.

قَذارَة dirtiness, filthiness, impurity, uncleanliness.

قَذُرَ، قَذِرَ، قَذَرَ to be dirty, unclean, filthy.

قَذَّرَ to dirty, soil, stain, pollute.

قَذَر dirt, filth, dirtiness, uncleanness, filthiness.

قَذِر، قَذْر، قَذُر dirty, filthy, unclean, impure, polluted.

قَذَفَ to throw, cast, discard, throw away; to fling, hurt, toss; to push, shove; to emit, expel, oust, evict.

قَذَفَ to defame, slander, accuse, charge with.

قَذَفَ بِالقَنابِل to bomb, shell, attack with bombs, fire guns at.

قَذْف throwing, casting, hurling, flinging, tossing, pelting; ejection, emitting, discharge.

قَذْف defamation, slander, libel, calumny.

قَذْف ejaculation (of sperm); vomiting; bombing, bombardment, bombarding, shelling, gunfire, artillery fire.

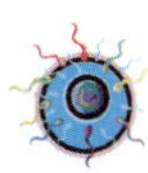

قَذِيفَة missile, projectile, shell, bomb.

قَرَّ عَيْناً to be delighted, glad, happy.

قَرَّ الرَّأْيُ على it was decided to.

لا يَقِرُّ له قَرار to be restless, restive, uneasy, undecided.

قَرَأَ to read, recite.

قرأت الكتاب بكامله فوجدته مفيداً جداً
I read the whole book and found it very useful

قَرَأَ بين السُّطور to read between the lines.

قَرَأَ عليه السَّلام to greet, salute someone.

قِرَاءَة reading, recital, recitation.

قَرَابة relationship, kinship, blood relation.

قُرَابَة approximately, about, some.

قَرَار decision, resolution; sentence, judgment; decree; verdict; sedentariness, sedentation; firmness, solidity; steadiness, constancy, stability, repose, stillness; abode, dwelling, residence, place; bottom, depth (of sea).

قَرَار refrain, keynote (music).

قَرَار depression, low ground.

قَرَّاضَة pincers, nippers.

قُرَاضَة cuttings, shavings.

القُرْآنُ الكَرِيم the Holy Koran.

القرآن أنزله جبريل على النبي محمد من الله عز وجل
The Holy Koran was descended from God by Angel Gabriel on Prophet Mohammad

قِران marriage, wedding; close connection, close union.

قَرُبَ to approach; to be near, close to; to get near, close to; to be imminent; to draw near.

ما يَقْرُبُ من، تَقْرِيبًا approximately, about, some, circa.

قَرَّبَ to approximate to, bring near to; to advance toward.

قَرَّبَ بَيْنَهُم to bring them close together; to make peace between them; to reconcile them.

قَرَّبَهُ إليه to take him as close companion; to show favor to him.

قُرْب nearness, closeness, proximity; vicinity, neighborhood.

بِقُرْب، بِالقُرْبِ مِن near, close to, in the vicinity of, next door to.

عَن قُرْب closely, from a short distance.

قِرْبة skin, bottle, canteen; bagpipe.

قُرَّة deposit, sediment.

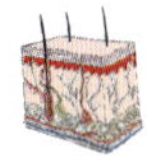

قُرَّةُ العَين delight of the eye, joy, pleasure, darling, dear one.

قَرَّحَ to injure, ulcerate, wound.

قَرْح ulceration, cankering.

قَرْحَة، قُرْحَة، قَرْح ulcer, sore, fester, abscess.

قَرَّرَ to decide, determine, resolve, make up one's mind; to establish, settle, fix; to make someone confess.

قَرَصَ to pinch, nip, bite, sting.

قُرْص disk, disc, plate; discus; tablet, pill (med.); dial (of watch, radio).

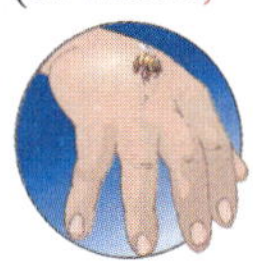

قُرْصَان pirate, corsair.

قَرْصَنَة piracy.

قَرَضَ، قَرَّضَ to gnaw, nibble at; to corrode, clip, cut off.

قَرَضَ الشِّعْر to compose poetry.

قَرْض، قِرْض loan, advance.

قُرْط earring.

قِرْطَاسِيَّة stationery.

قَرَعَ to knock, rap (at a door); to hit, bump against; to strike, beat, thump against; to thrash, spank; to clink, touch, (glasses); to ring, sound.

قَرَعَ الجَرَس to ring the bell.

قَرَعَ سَمْعَهُ to reach someone's ear.

قَرَعَ الكَأْسَ to drink to someone's health.

قَرِعَ to become bald.

قَرْع knocking, rapping, beating, striking, ringing.

قَرَع baldness, bareness, starkness.

قَرَّعَ to scold, upraid, berate, reprove, rebuke, blame, censure.

قَرْعَة knock, rap, tap, blow, beat, bang, toll, ring.

قُرْعَة lot.

قَرِفَ to be disgusted of, nauseated by, sick of; to loathe, detest, abhor.

قَرَّفَ to cause to be disgusted; to arouse disgust; to disgust, nauseate, sicken.

قَرَف disgust, revulsion, loathing, nausea.

قِرْمِيدَة tile, brick.

قَرَنَ to pair, join, couple, connect, link, unite.

قَرْن coupling, joining, juncture, connection, connecting, linking, linkage.

قَرْن horn, antenna, feeler.

قَرْن peak of mountain; pod of bean.

قَرْن century, age, generation.

قَرْنُ الحِذاء shoehorn.

قَرَوِيّ (ص) rural, provincial.

قَرَوِيّ (اسم) villager, countryman, provincial, peasant.

قَرِيب (ص) near, close, nearby, next-door; neighboring, adjacent.

قَرِيبُ الحُدُوث imminent, impending, forthcoming.

قَرِيبُ الفَهْم easily understood, simple.

قَرِيب (اسم) relative, kinsman, kindred, related by blood.

قَرِيبًا، عمَّا قَرِيب shortly, in the near future.

قَرْيَة village, hamlet.

قَرِيحَة natural disposition, genius, talent, gift, faculty.

قَرِين husband, spouse; companion, associate, fellow, mate.

قَرِينَة wife, spouse.

قَرِينَة presumption, evidence, indication; context (speech).

قَرِينَة connection, relation, link, tie, bond.

قُزَح، قَوسُ قُزَح rainbow.

قُزَحِيَّة iris (of eye).

قَزَم dwarf, midget, pygmy.

قَسّ priest, clergyman, pastor, vicar, curate, parson.

قَسَا to be hard, solid, stiff; to harden, toughen, solidify; to treat harshly, cruelly, roughly.

قَسَّى to harden, solidify, stiffen.

قَسَاوَة hardness; cruelty, severity; rigor.

قَسَرَ to compel, constrain someone to do something.

قَسْر coercion, compulsion, constraint.

قِسْرًا forcibly, by force; necessarily, compulsorily.

قَسَطَ to act justly, establish justice; to act equitably.

قَسَّطَ to pay in installments; distribute.

قِسْط share, portion, part, lot; quantity, amount, measure, extent; installment; justice, equitable; premium (insurance policy); tuition fee (school).

على أقْسَاط in installments.

قَسَمَ، قَسَّمَ to divide, part, split; to distribute, deal out, parcel out; to partition; to assign, apportion, destine, foreordain (by God); to divide a number by another (arith.).

قَسَم oath.

قَسَمًا بِـ I swear by.

قِسْم part, division, portion, section, lot, share; department, service, administration, office; district, province, area.

قَسَمَات (ج) features.

قِسْمَة division, partition, separation, splitting, allotment; division by (math); share, part, lot; destiny, fate, (foreordained by God).

قَسْوَة severity, rigor, hardness, harshness, cruelty, inhumanity.

قِسِّيس priest, clergyman, minister, parson, vicar, pastor.

قَسِيمَة coupon, receipt.

قِشْدَة cream of milk.

قَشَرَ، قَشَّرَ to peel, pare, shell, bark, skin, scale, shave off.

قِشْر، قِشْرَة peel, rind, skin, shell, husk; crust (of earth); epicarp (of fruit); cortex (of an organ); scab (of a wound); layer (of wood); scales (of fish); bark, rind (of trees).

قِشْرَةُ الرَّأْس dandruff.

قَشَطَ to take off, strip off, scrape off, plane, raze, rasp.

قُشَعْرِيرَة shudder, shivering, trembling, gooseflesh, quiver.

قَشُفَ، قَشِفَ to live in misery; to pay no attention to cleanliness; to lead an ascetic life.

قَصَّ to cut, cut off, clip, shear; to trim, crop, lop; to follow someone's tracks; to tell, relate exactly, recount.

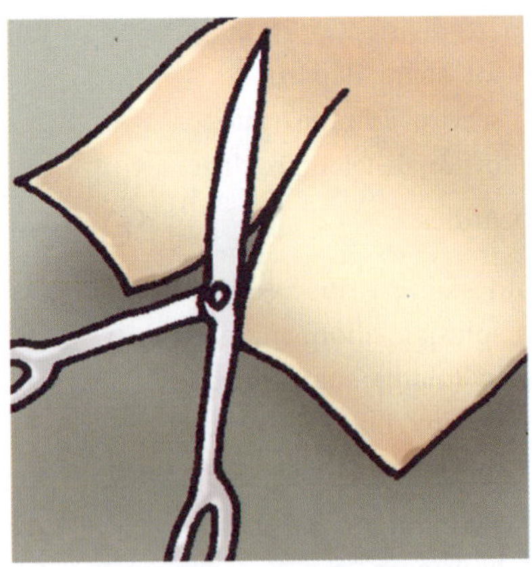

استعمل المقص لأقص الورق أو القماش

I use the scissors to cut paper or cloth

قَصّ cutting, clipping, shearing, mowing; trimming, paring; narration, recounting, telling.

قَصُّ الشَّعْر haircutting.

قَصَّاب butcher.

قَصار، قُصَارَى the utmost, the limit; the most you can accomplish, is to do this; you must limit yourself to doing this.

بَذَلَ قَصَارَ جُهده to exert every conceivable effort in order to; to go to great lengths, do one's best.

قُصَارَى القَوْل in short, in brief.

قَصَّاص novelist, storywriter, storyteller, narrator; shearer; tracer of tracks.

قِصَاص punishment, reprisal, chastisement, castigation; retaliation, revenge, requital; penalty, sanction, punition.

قَصَب cane, reed; gold or silver threads.

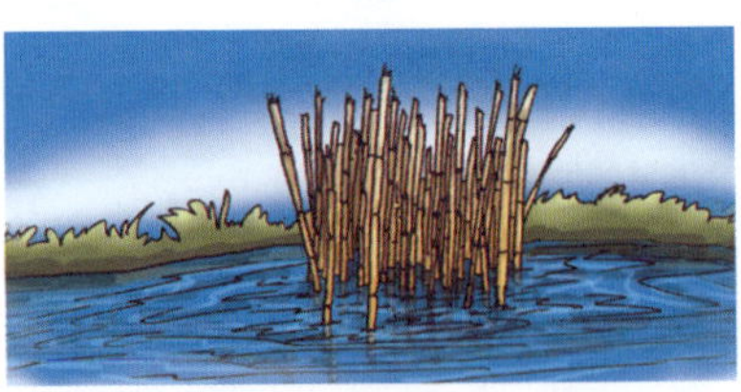

ينمو القصب في المستنقعات وعلى ضفاف الأنهر

Cane grows in swamps and along the banks of rivers

قَصَبُ السُّكَّر sugar cane.

قَصَبَة cane, reed; perch, rod; reed pipe, flute, clarinet; writing pen; trachea (anat.); citadel, capital city, metropolis.

قَصَّةُ شَعْر haircut.

قِصَّة story, tale, narrative.

قِصَّةٌ غَرَامِيَّة love story.

قِصَّةٌ رَمْزِيَّة allegory.

قِصَّةٌ هَزْلِيَّة comedy.

قِصَّةٌ مُحْزِنَة tragedy.

قَصَدَ إلى to go to, repair to, head for; to be headed for.

قَصَدَ to intend, design, plan, aim at, drive at, strive for; to seek; to have in mind; to have in view, contemplate, consider.

قَصَدَ to be frugal, economical, thrifty, provident; to save, economize.

قَصَدَ to follow, imitate.

قَصْد intent, purpose, aim, object, design, goal, objective.

قَصْد temperance, moderation.

قَصْد frugality, thrift, economy.

عن قَصْد purposely, intentionally, on purpose, deliberately.

قَصْدِير tin.

قَصَرَ to limit to, restrict to; to confine; to fall short of, fail to, be unable to do; to fail to operate in the usual manner.

قَصُرَ to become short.

قَصَّرَ to shorten, make short or shorter; to neglect, omit; to fail; flunk (an exam); to bleach; to be insufficient, inadequate; to fall short of, fail to attain, achieve, realize; to curtail, abridge, reduce, restrain, check, control, restrict.

قَصْر palace, mansion, castle.

قِصَر shortness, smallness.

قِصَرُ النَّظَر myopia, nearsightedness.

قَصَصِيّ، قِصَصِيّ narrative, fictional; fiction.

قَصَفَ to shell, bombard, bomb, fire guns at.

قَصَفَ to snap, break, smash.

قَصَفَ to roll, peal, rumble (thunder).

قَصْف roar of canons; revelry, carousal, romp; shelling, bombing, gunfire; snapping, breaking, smashing; roll, peal, rumble of thunder.

قَصَمَ to break, shatter.

قَصَمَ ظَهْرَهُ to deal a fatal blow to; to destroy, kill.

قُصُور failure to do something; inability, inadequacy, deficiency, shortcoming, lack; decrease; slackness, laxity, negligence, indolence, inertness; impotence, helplessness.

قُصُورٌ ذَاتِيّ inertia (mech.).

قُصُورُ القلب heart failure.

قَصِيّ far, distant, remote, far off.

قَصِيد، قَصِيدَة poetry, poem.

قَصِير short; stubby, dumpy.

قَصِيرُ الأَجَل short-term.

قَصِيرُ البَاع impotent, helpless, weak, incapable, unable.

قَصِيرُ النَّظَر myopic, nearsighted; myope.

قَضّ to pierce, bore, perforate; to crush, bruise, pulverize, tear down, demolish, pullout, tear off, tear out (a peg).

قَضَّ عليهِ المَضْجَع to be rough, hard, make sleepless.

جَاءَ القَوْمِ قَضُّهُم all the people came, everybody came.

قَضَى to carry out, finish, terminate, conclude, end, wind up; to complete, achieve, accomplish, perform, effectuate.

قَضَى to fulfill a request, comply with, gratify a wish, satisfy, meet, answer a demand; to pay, settle a debt, to spend, pass time; to order, command, require.

قَضَى أَجَلَهُ، قَضَى نَحْبَهُ to pass away, die.

قَضَى أَمْرًا to impose, ordain, decree, prescribe.

قَضَى حُكْمًا to judge, rule, decide, pass sentence in favor of or against; to inflict a penalty on.

قَضَى على to annihilate, extirpate, terminate, root out, kill; to do away with, put an end to; to thwart, foil, frustrate.

قُضِيَ الأَمْرُ the die is cast.

قَضَاء the judiciary, courts, judicial authorities; administration of justice; judgment, ruling, decision, sentence, verdict; award.

قَضَاء constituency, district, province.

قَضَاء carrying out, execution, effectuation, conclusion; compliance, meeting, satisfaction.

قَضَاء imposition, injunction, ordainment, prescription.

قَضَاءٌ عَلى annihilation, extermination, eradication, killing, destruction, wiping out, suppression, stamping out; doing away with, getting rid of, elimination.

قَضَاءُ الله death.

القَضَاءُ والقَدَر fate and divine decree.

قَضَائِي judicial, judicatory, forensic, legal, judiciary.

حَارِسٌ قَضَائِي receiver in bankruptcy, liquidator; legally appointed trustee or administrator.

قَضِيب stick, rod, staff, wand, bar; cut-off branch of a tree; twig; switch; penis, phallus (male organ of generation); rail, guide rail.

قَضِيبُ الصَّاعِقَة lightning rod.

قَضِيَّة suit, lawsuit, case, legal proceeding; cause, matter, case, issue, question, problem; theorem, proposition (math).

قَطُّ never, not at all, ever.

قَطْ enough, sufficient; only, just, merely.

قِطّ cat, male cat (animal).

قِطَار train; caravan, convoy.

قَطَّارَة eyedropper, pipette, dropper.

قِطَاع sector, section.

قِطَاعٌ عَرْضِي cross section.

للقط شاربان وأذنان صغيرتان ومخالب قوية
The male cat has two mustaches,
two small ears and strong claws

قِطاف، مَوْسِمُ القِطَاف — picking, harvest; picking season, harvest time.

قَطَّبَ — to frown, contract the brows, scowl, lower, glower; to sew, stitch.

قَطْب — pole, axis, pivot.

قُطْب — leading personality, leader, magnate.

قُطْبٌ سَالِب — negative pole; cathode (elect.).

قُطْبٌ مُوجِب — positive pole; anode (elect.).

قُطْبٌ كَهْرَبائِيّ — electrode.

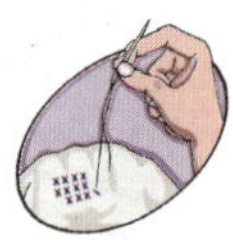

قُطْبَة — stitch, seam.

قُطْبِيَّة — polarity.

قَطَرَ — to fall in drops, drip, dribble, trickle; to percolate, ooze, seep.

قَطَرَ — to tow, tug, haul, trail; to smear with tar; to tar.

قَطَّرَ — to filter, percolate, distill, extract; to let fall or flow in drops; to infuse in drops; to refine; to drip, drop, dribble something; to extract by distillation.

قَطْر — towing, tugging, hauling, trailing; dripping, dribbling, trickling; trickle, drip, dribble.

قَطْر — drops, rain.

قَطْر — syrup.

قُطْر — region, district, section; tract of land, zone, country, land.

قُطْر — bore (of a tube), caliber

قُطْرُ الدَّائِرَة — diameter.

نِصْفُ قُطْر — radius.

قَطْرَان، قِطْرَان — tar.

قَطْرَة — drop (eyedrop, raindrop, dewdrop, eardrop).

قُطْرِيّ — regional, territorial; diametral, diametrical, diagonal.

قَطَعَ — to cut off, chop off, lop off, amputate, cut through; to tear apart, sunder, disjoin, separate, sever, break; to interrupt, cut short, silence; to turn off, switch off, disconnect, (an electric current); to prevent, hinder someone from; to forbid, prohibit someone from doing something; to intersect, cross; to stop, suspend, cease, put an end to; to assert, affirm authoritatively; to be absolutely certain about.

قَطَعَ الأَمَل — to give up hope, lose hope.

قَطَعَ دَابِرَ كَذَا — to eradicate, exterminate, uproot, deracinate.

قَطَعَ رَأْسَ فُلان — to decapitate, behead, cut off someone's head.

قَطَعَ الطَّرِيق — to engage in high robbery.

قَطَعَ العَهْد — to pledge, vow, promise, make a pledge to.

قَطَعَ الوَقْت — to spend time, kill time.

قَطَّعَ — to cut up, cut into pieces, divide, separate, dismember; to tear apart, lacerate, rip apart.

قَطْع — cutting, cutting off, chopping off, cutting down (tree).

قَطْع — amputation, sectioning, segmentation, sundering.

قَطْع — stoppage, blockage; ban; suspension, interruption.

قَطْعُ التَّيَّار الكَهْرَبَائِيّ — disconnection, turning off, switching off.

قَطْعُ شَجَرَةٍ — felling.

قَطْعُ العَلاقَة — rupture, breakoff.

قَطْع — crossing (river, road, bridge).

قَطْعُ الوَقْت — passing, spending time.

قَطْعُ الطَّرِيق — highway robbery.

قَطْعُ الأَمَل — despair.

قَطْعًا — definitely, decidedly, certainly, of course, absolutely.

قَطْعٌ نادِر — hard currency.

مُعَدَّلُ القَطْع — discount rate.

بِقَطْعِ النَّظَر عن — irrespective of, aside from, apart from, without regard to, regardless of.

قُطْعَة — plot (of land), tract, area, piece (of land); stump.

قِطْعَة — piece, lump, chunk; part, portion, section, division; segment (geometry); unit (military formation).

قِطْعَة — passage, excerpt.

قِطَعُ الغِيَار — spare parts.

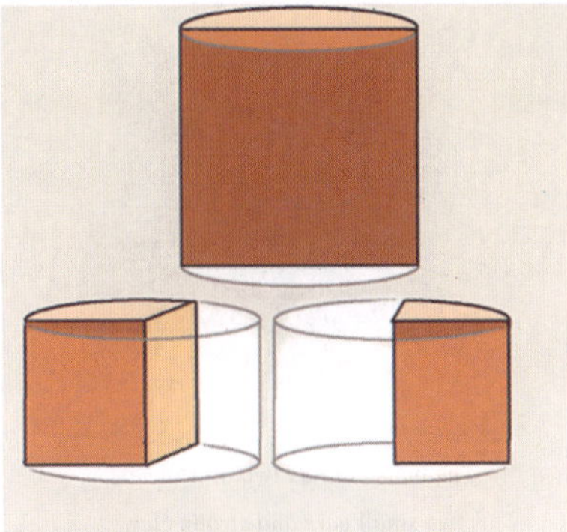

أجمع القطع إلى بعضها لأصنع شكلاً متكاملاً

I join the pieces to make an integral form

قِطَعٌ إضَافِيَّة — accessories.

قِطْعَةٌ نَقْدِيَّة — specie, coin; paper money.

قِطْعَةٌ فَنِّيَّة، أَدَبِيَّة، مُوسِيقِيَّة — piece, work, composition.

قَطْعِيًّا — decidedly, definitely.

قَطَفَ، قَطَّفَ — to pick, gather, reap, harvest, pluck out.

قطفتُ وردة من الحديقة وقدّمتها إلى والدتي

I picked a rose from the garden and offered it to my mother

أ ب ت ث ج ح خ د ذ ر ز س ش ص ض ط ظ ع غ ف ق ك ل م ن هـ و ي

قَطْف picking, gathering, reaping, harvesting, plucking out.

قَطَنَ to live, dwell, reside (in a place); to inhabit (a place).

قَطَن dwelling, living, inhabiting, residence; lumbar region (anat.).

قُطْن، قُطُن cotton.

تصنع الثياب الداخلية من القطن عادة

Underwears are usually made of cotton

قَطِيع flock, herd, drove, group.

قَطِيعَة rupture, breakoff (of relations); alienation, separation.

قَعَدَ to sit down, take a seat; to sit, stay, abide, lie in wait; to desist, abstain from; to renounce, waive.

قَعَّرَ to make concave; to hollow out, make hollow.

قَعْر bottom, foot, floor, bed, depth, cavity, depression.

قُعُود sitting, taking a seat; omission, neglect, abstention from, desistance from, renunciation of.

قَفَا to follow someone's tracks.

قَفَّى to rhyme, put into rhyme.

قَفًا back, reverse; nape, occiput, back of the head.

قَفَّاز jumper, leaper; jumping, leaping.

قُفَّاز glove.

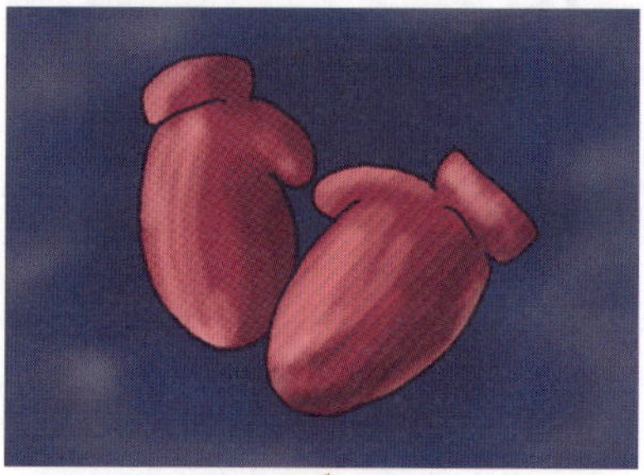

يرتدي الملاكم قفّازين أثناء المباراة

The boxer wears gloves during the competition

قُفَّة basket.

قَفْر (ص) empty, bleak, forsaken, deserted, lifeless, desolate.

قَفْر (اسم) desert, wasteland, desolate region.

قَفَزَ to jump,leap, spring, hop.

قَفْزٌ بِالعَصَا pole vaulting.

قَفَص cage; coop; pen; crate; basket; thorax, chest.

قَفَلَ to come back; to shut up, bolt.

قُفْل lock, latch, padlock.

قَفِير beehive, hive.

قَلَّ to become small, few, little; to lessen, decrease; to become less, smaller than, fewer than.

يقفز الرياضي فوق الحاجز العالي للفوز في مباراة القفز

The athlete jumps over the high hurdles to win in the high-jump competition

قَلَّما seldom, rarely, barely, hardly.

قَلَى ، قَلا to fry (food); to hate, detest, loathe, abhor.

قَلَّاب reversible, tiltable.

شَاحِنَةٌ قَلَّابة tipper, dump truck.

قِلادَة necklace, collar, pendant.

قَلَبَ to turn, turn about, turn around, turn over; to tip over, overturn, upset, capsize, turn upside down.

قَلَبَ to reverse, overthrow, topple, bring down; to convert, transform, change, alter, transmute.

قَلَبَهُ رَأساً على عَقِب to turn something upside down.

قَلَبَ لَهُ ظَهرَ المِجَنّ to show someone the back of the shield; to give someone the cold shoulder; to become hostile to.

قَلَّبَ فِيهِ النَّظَر to scrutinize, regard something.

قَلَّبَ الصَّفَحات to turn over, flip, leaf the pages of a book.

قَلَّبَ الرَّأْي to think over, reflect on, consider carefully.

قَلْب reversal, transformation, transmutation, inversion; perversion, alteration; overthrow (of a rule, government).

قَلْب heart, center, core, essence; mind, soul, spirit.

إذا توقف قلب الإنسان عن الخفقان يموت فوراً

If man's heart stops beating he dies instantly

قَلْبُ الأَسَد Regulus (astrology).

قَلْبًا وقَالِبًا heart and soul, wholly, entirely, fully.

قَلْبِيّ hearty; cardiac; sincere, most cordial.

قِلَّة dearth, rarity, shortage, deficiency; littleness, fewness; triviality; paltriness, scantiness; minority, scarcity, insufficiency; lack, want..

قِلَّةُ الحَياء impudence, insolence, impertinence.

قِلَّةُ الصَّبْر impatience.

قَلَّدَ to copy, ape, imitate; to forge, counterfeit; to award someone a decoration; to confer, grant someone a favor; to entrust someone with the rule or government; to give authority over something to someone.

قَلَّصَ to shrink, deflate, decrease, contract, constrict, draw together something; to tuck up, roll on something.

قَلَعَ to pluck out, pull out, uproot, extirpate; take off one's clothes.

قَلْع extraction, pulling out, extirpation, plucking out.

قَلْعَة fortress, fort, castle, stronghold; rook, castle (in chess).

قَلِقَ to worry; to be worried, anxious, uneasy; to be upset, ill at ease; to be troubled, disturbed, restless, sleepless.

قَلَق unrest, anxiety, apprehension, fear, worry, alarm.

قَلِق disquieted, worried, anxious, excited, upset, troubled, restless; sleepless, perturbed; uneasy, apprehensive.

قَلْقَلَ to shake, move, convulse, disturb, trouble, harass; to agitate, disquiet, stir up, alarm, excite.

قَلْقَلَة unrest, commotion, convulsion, disturbance, stir.

قَلَّلَ to lessen, decrease, reduce, make less (smaller, fewer).

قَلَّلَ من شَأْنِهِ to belittle, underestimate, underrate, disdain.

قَلَّمَ to clip, trim, pare, prune; to stripe, striate.

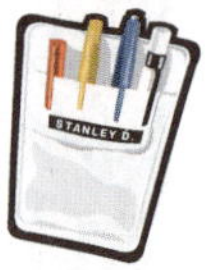

قَلَم pen.

قَلَمُ حِبْر fountain pen.

قَلَمُ حِبْرٍ جافّ ball-point pen.

قَلَمُ رَصاص lead pencil.

قَلَم stripe, streak, line.

قَلَم office, bureau, department.

بِقَلَم by, written by.

قَليل little, small (in number or quantity); scarce, rare, few, insignificant, trifling, scant, spare, meager.

قَليلاً ما sedlom, rarely.

بَعْدَ قَليل a little later, shortly afterward.

عَمَّا قَليل before long, shortly, soon.

قَليلُ الأَدَب impolite, uncouth.

قَليلُ الحَياء brazen, insolent, impertinent.

قَليلُ الصَّبْر impatient.

قَليلُ الوُجود scanty, scarce, rare.

قِمار gambling, speculation, staking, betting.

قُماش، أَقْمِشَة fabric, cloth; textiles, dry goods.

قِماط swaddle (of baby); diaper (of baby).

قُمامَة garbage, refuse, waste.

قِمَّة summit, peak; vertex, zenith; crest; pinnacle, top.

قَمْح wheat.

يُزرع القمح في مختلف أنحاء العالم
وبه يقتات الإنسان
Wheat is grown in all parts of the world and man gets nourished by it

قَمْحَة grain of wheat; grain (measure of weight).

قَمَر moon.

قَمَرٌ صِنَاعِيّ artificial satellite, man-made moon.

قَمَطَ ، قَمَّطَ to swaddle a baby; to fetter, shackle.

قَمَعَ to tame, bridle, curb; to restrain, check, suppress, repress, subdue; to hinder, prevent.

قَمْع repression, suppression, restraint, crushing, putting down, prevention, subdual, taming, quelling.

قِمْع funnel; cupule; pericarp; stem (of fruit).

قَمْعِيّ repressive, suppressive, restraining.

قَمِلَ to be lice-infected

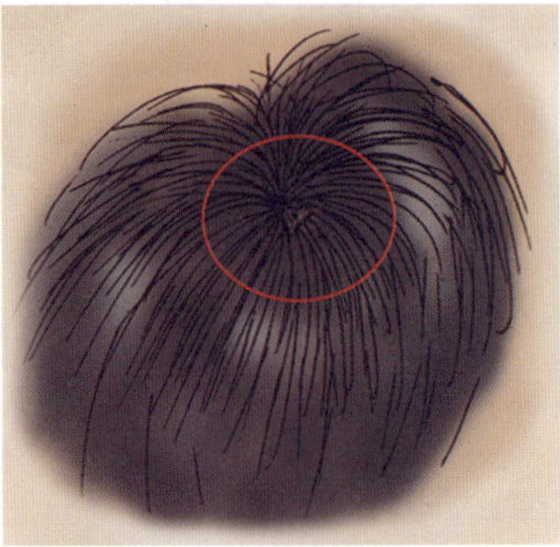

قَمِلَ شعر رأس الفتاة فأخذت تحكّه باستمرار
The girl's hair got lice-infected and she began to scratch her head

قَمْل lice.

قَمْلَة louse.

قَمِيص shirt; jacket (of book).

قَمِيصٌ تَحْتَانِيّ undershirt.

قَمِيصُ النَّوْم nightgown, nightshirt, nightdress.

قِنّ chicken coop; slave.

قَنَاة ، قَنَال canal, stream, waterway, channel, conduit, tube, duct, path, passage; shaft; spear, lance.

قَنَاة ditch (for irrigation); gutter (for rain water).

قَنَاةُ الصَّفْرَاء bile duct.

قَنَاةُ الرَّحْم ، قَنَاةُ فَالوب fallopian tube.

قَنَّاص hunter; sniper (of persons).

قِنَاع mask, veil, disguise.

قَناعَة satisfaction, contentment; frugality, temperance; conviction, persuasion; moderation.

خَيْطُ قِنَّب twine, rope, cord.

قَنْبَلَة bombardment, bombing, shelling.

قُنْبُلَة bomb, shell, grenade.

تحتوي القنبلة اليدوية على مواد متفجرة خطرة

The hand grenade contains dangerous explosive materials

قُنْبُلَةٌ ثاقِبَةٌ لِلدُّروع armor-piercing bomb.

قُنْبُلَةٌ ذَرِّيَّة atom bomb.

قُنْبُلَةٌ ضِدَّ الأَشْخاص anti-personnel bomb.

قُنْبُلَةٌ عُنْقُودِيَّة cluster bomb.

قُنْبُلَةٌ مُحْرِقَة incendiary bomb.

قُنْبُلَةُ مِدْفَع cannonball.

قُنْبُلَةٌ مَوْقُوتَة time bomb.

قُنْبُلَةٌ يَدَوِيَّة hand grenade.

قَنَصَ to hunt; to snipe (persons).

قَنْص hunting, shooting, sniping (persons).

قُنْصُل consul.

قُنْصُلِيَّة consulate.

قَنِطَ ، قَنَطَ ، قَنُطَ to despair, lose hope, lose all courage.

قَنَّطَ to drive someone to despair; to dishearten, discourage someone.

قَنَط ، قُنُوط despair, despondency, desperateness, hopelessness.

قَنِط ، قَنُوط despairing, desperate, despondent, discouraged.

قَنُوع satisfied, contented.

قِنِّينَة bottle, flask, vial.

قَهَّار ، القَهَّار conquering, vanquishing; the Subduer (God).

قَهَرَ to subdue, subjugate, vanquish, overcome; to surmount, master; to compel, coerce, force, oblige.

قَهْر vanquishing, subdual, subjection; compulsion, coercion, force; sorrow, trouble, annoyance.

قَهْرًا by force, forcibly.

قَهْقَرى ، قَهْقَرَة backward movement, recession, retrogression; retreat; fallback; decline, retrogradation.

قَهْقَهَة guffaw, loud burst of laughter.

قَهْوَة coffee; coffeehouse, cafe.

قَوَّى to make strong, strengthen, consolidate, fortify, brace; to encourage, hearten, embolden; to intensify, boost, enrich.

تصنع القهوة من طحن بذور البن بعد تحميصها

Coffee is made by grinding coffee beans after their roasting

قَوام upright posture; erect bearing, stature, physique, build, body; strength, vigor; firmness, consistency; support, stay; living, livelihood.

قَوّام caretaker, custodian, keeper; superintendent, guardian.

قِوَام support, prop, stay; basis, foundation; staple, main ingredient; sustenance, subsistence; provider, supporter.

قُوَّة strength, force, might, power, potency, vigor; violence, vehemence, severity; authority, leverage; ability, capability; energy, capacity; courage, pluck, faculty, potential.

قُوَّةُ الإرادَة will power.

قُوَّةُ الشِّراء purchasing power.

قُوَّةُ القانُون legal force.

قُوَّةٌ قاهِرَة force majeure.

قُوَّةٌ مَرْكَزِيَّة طارِدَة centrifugal force.

قُوَّةٌ مَعْنَوِيَّة moral strength, morale.

قُوّاتٌ مُسَلَّحَة armed forces.

قُوّاتُ احْتِياط reserves.

قُوَّةٌ مَرْكَزِيَّة جاذِبَة centripetal force.

قُوّاتُ حِفْظِ السَّلام peace-keeping forces.

قُوَّةٌ ضاغِطَة pressure group, lobby.

بالقُوَّة by force, compulsorily.

قُوَّةٌ دافِعَة كَهرِبائِيَّة electromotive force.

قُوَّةٌ مَركَزِيَّة central power.

قُوت food, foodstuff, aliment, victual, nourishment.

قَوَّس to bend, curve, crook.

قَوْس bow, arc,arch, vault; parenthesis, bracket.

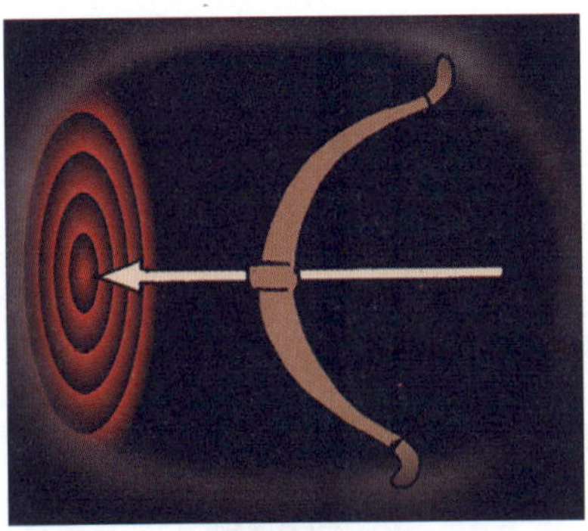

كان القوس أداة حربية منتشرة الاستعمال في القرون الخالية

The bow was a military weapon widely used during the past centuries

قَوْسُ قُزَح rainbow.

أ ب ت ث ج ح خ د ذ ر ز س ش ص ض ط ظ ع غ ف ق ك ل م ن هـ و ي

قَوْسُ النَّصر — triumphal arch.

قَوَّضَ — to demolish, tear down, wreck, ruin, destroy.

قَوْل — speech, word, utterance, saying; opinion, view; statement, testimony; doctrine, teaching.

قَوْلٌ مَأْثُور — saying, adage, maxim.

بِالقَوْلِ والفِعْل — by word and deed.

قَوْلَبَ — to mold, cast, block, shape, fashion.

قَوْلَبَة — casting, molding, forming, shaping, fashioning.

قَوَّمَ — to straighten, rectify, correct, adjust, set right; to evaluate, estimate, appraise.

قَوْم — people, nation, kindred, kinsfolk, race, tribe.

قَوْمِيّ — national, nationalist.

قَوْمِيَّة — nationalism, nationality.

قَوِيَ — to become strong, more powerful, mighty; to strengthen, grow; to surmount, overcome; to be able to cope with.

قَوِيّ — strong, powerful, mighty, potent, sturdy; intense, violent, vehement; firm; solid, robust, hardy.

قَوِيُّ الإِرادَة — strong-willed.

قَوِيم — straight, erect, authentic, upright, right, sound; firm. solid, true (religion).

قِيادَة — leadership, guidance; driving, steering; command.

عَجَلَةُ القِيادَة — steering wheel.

قِيادِيّ — leading, main, master, major; leader, chief, head.

قِياس — measurement, gauging, measuring; dimension, scale; record (athletics); comparison, analogy, syllogism (logic).

قِياساً على ذلك — by analogy with, correspondingly.

عَلى القِياس — by analogy, regular, after the model.

بِغَيْرِ قِياس — illogical.

أَخَذَ قِياسَه — to take someone's measure (tailor).

قِياسٌ عالَمِيّ — world record (athletics).

شَرِيطُ القِياس — tape measure.

قِياسٌ فاسِد — paralogism, fallacy, sophism.

قِياسِيّ — standard, normal, analogical; syllogistic (logic); record; analogous, comparable, logical.

قِيام — standing up, getting up, rise, rising; takeoff, departure; outbreak, flare-up, breaking out; performance, execution, accomplishment; discharge, carrying out.

قِيامَة — resurrection; turmoil, tumult, upheaval, commotion.

يَوْمُ القِيامَة — Day of Final Judgment.

قامَتْ قِيامَتُهُ — to get angry; to become furious; to be upset.

قيثار ، قيثارَة — guitar, harp, lyre.

قَيْح — pus.

قَيَّدَ — to bind, tie up, fetter, shackle, manacle; to limit, restrict, confine; to check, curb, bridle.

أ ب ت ث ج ح خ د ذ ر ز س ش ص ض ط ظ ع غ ف ق ك ل م ن هـ و ي

قَيَّدَ to register, record, note down, set down, enter, list; to enroll, list.

قَيَّدَ عَلَيهِ أو على حِسَابِهِ to debit with; to charge to someone's account.

قَيَّدَ لَهُ أو لِحِسَابِهِ to credit with.

قَيْد tie, bond, fetter, shackle, chain, thong, strap; recording, entry, registration, registering; determination, fixation, stipulation, specification; confinement, restriction; condition, proviso; measure, degree; distance.

بِلا قَيْدٍ أو شَرْط without any reservation, unconditional.

عَلى قَيْدِ الحَياة alive, living.

قَيْدَ شَعْرَةٍ within a hair's breadth.

عَلى قَيْدِ سَاعَةٍ واحِدة within one hour.

قَيْدَ under, on, in, at, subject to, pending.

قَيْدَ البَحْث under discussion or consideration.

قَيْدَ التَّحْضِير in preparation.

قَيْدَ التَّداوُل in circulation, common.

قَيْدَ الطَّبْع in press.

قِير tar, pitch, bitumen, asphalt.

قَيْصَر Caesar, czar, kaiser.

قَيْصَرِيّ Caesarian, czarist, tsarist.

قَيَّضَ اللَّهُ له to destine to; to foreordain to.

قَيْظ oppressive heat, heat of summer, draught.

قِيلٌ وقَال gossip, idle talk, chitchat.

قَيْلُولَة siesta, midday nap.

قَيَّمَ to evaluate, estimate, appraise.

قَيِّم (ص) valuable, precious, priceless, costly, worthy.

قَيِّم (اسم) guardian, curator, custodian, keeper, trustee, superintendent, caretaker.

قِيمَة value, worth, amount; price, cost; quantity.

قِيمَةٌ اسْمِيَّة par value, nominal value, face value.

حَسَبَ القِيمَة ad valorem.

لا قِيمَةَ لَهُ worthless, valueless.

القَيُّوم the Everlasting, the Eternal (God).

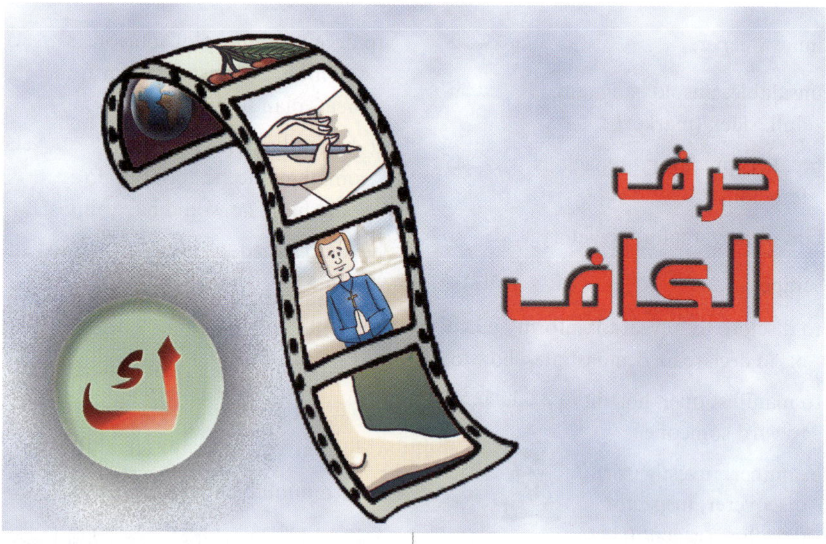

كَ — just as, like, similar to.

كَهٰذَا — such, like this.

أنا كَمُسْلِم — I, as a Moslem.

كائِد — cunning, crafty, foxy; plotter, conspirator, schemer.

كائِن — being, existing, existent; entity, creature, organism.

كائِن — situated, located.

كائِناً مَن كان — whoever, whosoever, whoever it may be.

كائِناً ما كان — whatever it may be.

كَئِبَ — to be dejected, dispirited, downcast, sad.

كَئِب ، كَئِيب — sad, dispirited, dejected, downcast, depressed.

كَآبَة ، كَأْبَة ، كَأْب — grief, sorrow, depression, dejection.

كَابَدَ — to suffer, bear, endure, stand,sustain, undergo.

كَابَرَ — to contend stubbornly on; to vie with.

كَابْل ، كَبل — cable.

كَاتَبَ — to write to, exchange letters with.

كَاتِب — writer, author, clerk, copyist.

الكَاتِبُ العَدْل — notary public.

كَاتِم — one who keeps a secret.

كَاتِمُ السِّرّ — secretary.

كَاتِمُ الصَّوت — muffler, silencer.

كَاحِل — ankle.

يقال صَلُبَ كاحله بمعنى أنه أصبح قوياً

It is said that someone has a solid ankle meaning that he became strong

كَادَ to deceive, dupe; plot someone's downfall; to conspire against; to cheat, plan to do harm to.

كَادَ to be on the point of doing something; to be about to do something; he would have almost.

كَادَ يَمُوت he almost died.

مَا كَادَ no sooner than; as soon as he; hardly, barely.

بِالكَاد almost, nearly, with great difficulty.

كَادّ، كَدُود industrious, hard working, diligent.

عَقَبَةٌ كَأْدَاء insurmountable obstacle.

كَادِح (ص) toiling, hardworking, industrious.

كَادِح (اسم) worker, laborer.

كَاذِب dishonest, untruthful; false, untrue, deceptive, fake, phony, unreal, mimic, simulated.

كَارِثَة catastrophe, disaster, calamity.

كَارِه averse, loath, reluctant, grudging.

كَاز kerosene.

كَاسَ to be courteous, polite, refined, elegant, nice.

كَأْس glass, drinking glass, cup, goblet; chalice.

كَأْسُ الزَّهْرَة calyx.

كَأْسُ المُبَارَاة trophy cup.

كَاسِب winner.

كَاسِح sweeping, crushing, overwhelming; decisive; total.

كَاسِحَة dredge; harrow; scavenging machine.

كَاسِحَةُ أَلْغَام minesweeper.

كَاسِد unsalable, unsold; stagnant, dull, slack (market).

كَاسِر breaker; predatory, repacious, ferocious.

طَيْرٌ كَاسِر bird of prey, raptor, predatory.

كَاشِطَة scraper.

كَاشَفَ to disclose to, reveal to, inform of; to declare to, demonstrate, show to.

كَاشَفَهُ بِالعَدَاوَة to manifest open hostility toward someone.

كَاشِف examiner, investigator, discoverer, inspector; detector; reagent (chem.).

ضَوْءٌ كَاشِف searchlight.

كَاعِب buxom, busty (girl); well-developed bosom.

كَافٍ (الكَافِي) enough, sufficient, adequate, appropriate, proper; capable, able, qualified, skilled, efficient, competent.

كَافَأَ to reward, recompense, remunerate, compensate.

كَافَأَ to match, be similar to, equal to, compare favorably with.

كَافَى to reward, recompense; to be enough, sufficient; to meet all requirements.

كَافَّة all, all of, the whole of, entirely, wholly.

كَافَّةُ النَّاس all the masses, all the people.

كَافَحَ to struggle against, fight, contend against.

كَافِر unbeliever, infidel, atheist; ungrateful, thankless.

كَافِل، كَفيل	reponsible, answerable; vouching, guaranteeing; protector, guardian, bailsman, surety, sponsor, guarantor.
كَالَ	to measure, gauge, weigh.
كَالَ لَهُ الشَّتائِم	to heap abuses upon.
كَالَّ، كَليل	to become tired, weary, exhausted, weak.
كَالِح	gloomy, grim, sullen, stern, grave, livid; colorless, faded; dull grey (color).
كَالَمَ	to speak, talk to.
كَامِد، كَمِد	sad, grieved, worried; gloomy, dark-colored.
كَامِل	perfect, consummate, complete, full, genuine; whole, entire, integral.
بِكَامِلِه	wholly, entirely, totally, in its entirety.
كَامِن	hidden, latent, secret, concealed, underlying.
كَانَ	to be, exist; to take place, happen.
فَلْيَكُن	let it be, all right.
أَصْبَحَ في خَبَرِ كانَ	to disapper, belong to the past.
كَأَنَّ	as if, as though, like.
كَانِسَةُ أَلْغام	minesweeper (navy ship).
كَانُون	brazier, stove.
كَانُون الأَوَّل	December.
كَانُون الثَّاني	January.
كَاهِل	upper part of the back.
أَثْقَلَ كَاهِلَهُ	to burden, load, encumber someone.

كَاهِن	priest, minister, parson.

يضع الكاهن المسيحي صليباً
حول عنقه للتعريف عن نفسه

The Christian priest puts a Cross around his neck to identify himself

كَؤُود	insurmountable obstacle.
كَئِيب	gloomy, depressing, cheerless; desolate, dreary (place); distressing, saddening, melancholic; dismal; sad, grieved.
كَايَدَ	to deceive, dupe, outwit someone.
كَبَّ	to overturn, turn upside down, overthrow, topple, upset; to pour out, pour away (a liquid).
كَبا	to stumble, trip, fall, miss.
كَبا	to grow dim, gloomy; to fade, pale, lose luster.
كَبَّاس، كَبَّاسَة	stappler.
كَبَّاس	piston, press (mech.).
كَبَتَ	to suppress, repress, subdue, stifle, restrain, inhibit.
كَبَتَ أَنْفاسَهُ	to get someone out of breath.

كَبتَ غَيْظَهُ to suppress one's anger.

كَبْت suppression, repression, restraint, inhibition.

كُبَّة ball of thread.

كَبَح to bridle, curb, contain, withhold; to restrain, repress, subdue, inhibit; to hamper, prevent, control; to brake, to stop a car with a brake.

كَبَح جِمَاحَهُ to repress someone; to curb someone's defiance.

كَبْح checking, controlling, containment, restraint, repression, suppression, inhibition; braking (a car).

كَبَّد to inflict damage upon; to cause losses to someone.

كَبِد middle, center; interior, heart; zenith of the sky.

كَبِد، كَبْد، كِبْد liver (anat.).

كَبُر فُلاناً to be older than.

كَبُرَ to become great, big, large; to grow, increase, augment; to become famous, important; to become too big, great, large for something.

كَبِرَ في السِّنّ to grow old, get old, grow up.

كَبَّرَ to make great (er), big (ger); large (r); to magnify, enlarge, enhance; to extend, expand, widen, amplify; to intensify; to exaggerate, aggravate.

كَبَّرَ to praise, laud, extol, glorify; to exclaim, (Allahu Akbar) (God is Great).

كُبْر greatness, bigness, eminence, grandeur; expanse, extent; glory, fame, prestige; might, power; main part.

كِبْر bigness, greatness, eminence, importance, nobility, prestige, standing; pride, haughtiness, arrogance.

كِبَر bigness, largeness, greatness, eminence; old age.

كِبْرياء pride, haughtiness, arrogance.

كِبْريت sulfur.

عودُ الكِبريت matchstick.

كَبَسَ to press, compress, squeeze; to attack suddenly, raid; to preserve in vinegar; to marinate.

كَبْس pressure, squeeze, pressing; attack, raid; preservation in vinegar; surprise attack.

كَبْسُولَة capsule.

كَبَشَ to take a handful of; to grasp with the hand.

كَبْش chief, head, leader.

كَبْش battering ram, pile driver.

كَبْشُ الفداء scapegoat.

كَبَلَ، كَبَّلَ to shackle, fetter, enchain, bind, tie up; to handcuff.

كَبْل shackle, fetter, handcuff; cable.

كَبْو، كُبُوّ failure.

كَبْوَة stumble, trip, slip.

كَبير great, big, huge; immense, enormous; considerable, grand, massive; senior, powerful, eminent (person).

كَبيرٌ في السِّنّ old-aged; old.

كَبيرُ القُضَاة Chief Justice.

senior officers.	كِبَارُ الضبَّاط
great sin, grave offense, atrocious crime.	كَبيرة
leap year.	كَبيسَة (سنة)
book; letter, message; document, deed.	كِتَاب
credentials; letter of credit.	كِتَابُ اعْتِمَاد
pocket book.	كِتَابُ الجيب
yearbook.	كِتَابٌ سَنَوِيّ
textbook, school book.	كِتَابٌ مَدْرَسِيّ
the Bible; the Scriptures.	الكِتَابُ المُقَدَّس
bill of divorce.	كِتَابُ الطَّلاق
writing, script, inscription.	كِتَابة
in writing, written.	كِتَابِيّ
clerical work, desk work.	عَمَل كِتَابِيّ
linen, flax.	كَتَّان
to write, put down in writing, inscribe, record, register; to compose, draw up, draft.	كَتَبَ
to predestine to, foreordain to.	كَتَبَ الله
to be foreordained to, predestined to.	كُتِبَ عَلَيه
bookseller, librarian.	كُتُبِيّ
to bind, tie up the hands behind the back; to fetter, shackle; to cross, fold one's hands or arms.	كَتَفَ، كَتَّفَ
shoulder; mountain slope; buttress, pier.	كَتِف، كَتْف، كِتْف
to lump, mass, cluster; to agglomerate, press into a lump, pile up, gather in a mass.	كَتَّلَ

كتبت رسالة إلى شقيقي في الخارج أسأل عن أحواله

I wrote a letter to my brother abroad inquiring about his health

lump, mass, cluster, clod, clot, bulk, block; beam, joist, linter, girder; bloc (political).	كُتْلَة
crowd, throng, mass.	كُتْلَةٌ بَشَرِيَّة
to hide, conceal, keep secret; to suppress, repress, restrain, hold back, keep back; to muffle (sound); to stifle, smother (fire); to keep silent; to confide to.	كَتَمَ، كَتَّمَ
secrecy, silence, restraint, control; suppression.	كِتْمَان، كَتْم
reserved, secretive, discreet, reticent, taciturn.	كَتُوم
booklet, pamphlet, manual.	كُتَيِّب
battalion, detachment (army).	كَتِيبَة
buttress, bracket, pier.	كَتِيفَة
shut tight; hermetically sealed; impermeable, impervious, hermetic.	كَتِيم

أ ب ت ث ج ح خ د ذ ر ز س ش ص ض ط ظ ع غ ف ق ك ل م ن هـ و ي

كَثّ bushy, thick, dense; densely crowded.

كَثافَة density, thickness, intensity, consistency, compactness, fullness; degree of viscosity; capacity, intensity (electric current).

كَثَب nearness, proximity, vicinity.

عَن كَثَب، من كَثَب near; from nearby, at a short distance.

كَثُرَ to be much, many, numerous, more than; to increase, augment, multiply; to abound, exist in large numbers.

كُثْر large quantity, plenty, abundance.

كَثْرَة large quantity, great number, multitude; abundance; plurality; majority, major portion.

بِكَثْرَة plentifully, abundantly, a lot.

كَثَّفَ to condense, concentrate, intensify, thicken; to make thick, dense; to increase the capacity of.

كَثير much, many, abundant, copious, plenty; a lot, a great deal.

كَثيراً ما often, frequently.

بِكَثير by far, far.

كَثيراً very, much, to a large extent; often, frequently.

كَثيف dense, thick, concentrated, intensive, intense.

كَحَلَ، كَحَّلَ to paint or smear the eyes with kohl.

كُحْل antimony, kohl.

كُحْلِيّ navy blue, dark blue.

كُحُول alcohol.

كَدَّ to work hard, exert oneself, toil, labor; to overwork, exhaust, weary, tire someone.

كَدّ pain, labor, hard work; assiduity, diligence.

كَدَرَ، كَدُرَ، كَدِرَ to be turbid, muddy, soiled (color); to be dreary, unhappy (life).

كَدَّرَ to trouble, render turbid, soil, muddy, disturb, spoil; to ruffle someoene's peace of mind; to annoy, molest someone.

كَدَر turbidity, muddiness, griminess; trouble, disturbance, vexation; grief, distress, worry, sorrow; irritation.

كَدِر turbid, muddy, grimy; troubled, disturbed; spoiled; embittered, unsettled.

كَدَسَ، كَدَّسَ to accumulate, amass, heap up, stack up, pile up.

كَدْم، كَدْمَة bruise, contusion.

كَدُود industrious, hard-working; painstaking, diligent.

كَذَّاب، كَذوب (ص) liar, dishonest, deceitful, false.

كَذَّاب، كَذوب (اسم) liar, swindler.

كَذَبَ to lie, tell a lie.

كَذَبَ على to deceive, delude, mislead; to lie, tell a lie.

كَذَّبَ to disclaim, disavow, disprove, belie, deny, disown.

كَذِب، كِذْب lying, lie, deceit, falsehood, untruth.

كِذْبَة lie.

كِذْبَةُ نيسان April's fool.

كَرَّ to attack, bear down upon; to turn around and attack; to recur; to withdraw, retreat, fall back; to alternate, roll on, pass, elapse; to succeed one another.

كَرّ attack, assault, charge.

كَرٌّ وفَرٌّ attack and retreat (in a battle).

بَيْنَ كَرٍّ وفَرّ intermittently, alternately.

على كَرِّ الزَّمَن in the course of time.

كَرَى slumber, sleep.

كُرَّاس booklet, pamphlet, brochure, handbook; notebook, copybook.

كَرَامَة dignity, honor, respect, repute; nobility; generosity, munificence; mark of honor, token of esteem; miracle.

صَاحِبُ كَرَامَة worker of miracles.

كَرَاهَة، كَرَاهِيَّة hatred, hate, aversion, antipathy; distaste, repugnance, loathing, dislike, disgust.

كَرَبَ to oppress, distress, grieve, trouble.

كَرْب worry, grief, fear; distress, trouble, agony, torment.

كَرْبُون carbon, coal.

أوَّلُ أوكسيد الكَرْبون carbon monoxide.

ثاني أوكسيد الكَرْبون carbon dioxide.

وَرَق الكَرْبون carbon paper.

كَرَّة time, turn; attack, assault.

كَرَّةً بعد كَرَّةٍ time and again, again and again, repeatedly.

كُرَة ball, globe, sphere.

الكُرَة الأرضِيَّة earth, terrestial globe, world.

كُرَةُ ثَلْج snowball.

كُرَةُ السَّلَّة basketball.

الكُرَةُ الطَّائِرَة volleyball.

كُرَةُ الطَّاوِلَة ping-pong, table tennis.

كُرَةُ القَدَم football, soccer.

كُرَةُ المَاء water polo.

كُرَةُ المَضْرِب tennis.

نصف الكُرَة الأرْضِيَّة hemisphere.

كَرْتُون cardboard, paperboard, carton.

كَرَّر to repeat, reiterate, do repeatedly, do again.

كَرَّر to clarify, filter; to rectify; to purify, refine.

كَرَزَ to preach.

كَرْز sermon, preaching.

كَرَّسَ to dedicate, consecrate, devote; to sancitify; to lay the foundation of; to set up, found, settle, fix; to confirm, corroborate.

كُرْسِيّ chair, seat; throne; see; professorial chair; base, pedestal, socle

كُرْسِيّ تَحْمِيل bearing.

كُرْسِيٌّ بِلا ظَهْر stool.

كُرْسِيٌّ ذُو ذِرَاعَيْن armchair.

كُرْسِيٌّ دَوَّار swivel chair.

كُرْسِيٌّ هَزَّاز rocking chair.

كُرْسِيٌّ كَهربائِيّ electric chair.

كُرْسِيٌّ طَوِيل chaiselongue.

كَرِش، كِرْش stomach, paunch, potbelly; tripe, intestines.

كَرَعَ، كَرِعَ to sip, suck; to belch, burp.

كَرُمَ to be generous, openhanded, munificent; to be precious; to be noble, high-minded.

كَرَّمَ to honor, revere, venerate, treat with deference; to exalt someone above another; to bestow honor upon someone before others; to entertain, welcome, receive hospitably, treat with respect.

كَرَم generosity, liberality, munificence.

كَرَمُ الأَخْلاق noble character.

كَرَمُ المَحْتِد noble descent.

كَرْم vine, vineyard; garden, orchard; grapes.

كَرْمَى لك، كُرْمَاناً لَكَ for your sake; just to please you.

كَرِهَ to hate, detest, abhor.

كَرَّهَ to make someone hate someone or something; to alienate from; to make someone averse to.

كُرْه، كَرْه hatred, hate, aversion, dislike, antipathy.

كُرْهاً، كَرْهاً، على كُرْهٍ منه unwillingly, reluctantly, under duress.

كُرَوِيّ globular, global, spherical, ball-shaped.

كُرَيَّة corpuscule, globule; pellet.

كَرِيم generous, munificent, openhanded; noble, high-ranking, eminent; noble-hearted; beneficent, benefactor, kind; amicable, gracious; honorable; valuable, costly.

كَرِيمُ الأَخْلاق noble, noblehearted.

كَرِيمُ الأَصْل أو المَحْتِد of noble descent, highbred.

كَرِيه unpleasant, repulsive, detestable, odious, foul, ugly.

كَرِيهُ الرَّائِحَة stinging, bad smelling, smelly, fetid.

كُزَاز tetanus (med.).

كَسَا to clothe, dress, garb, attire someone with; to hang, drape, face, line with; to cover, coat with.

كِسَاء garment, dress, robe; clothing, uniform.

كُسَاح rickets (of babies).

كَسَاد depression, slump, recession, stagnation; unmarketability, unsalability (of goods).

كَسَّارة nutcracker; crusher; crushing plant.

كَسَبَ to gain, win, acquire; to earn; to profit; to gather, obtain, get; to attain.

كَسْب acquisition, earnings, gain, profit, winnings.

كَسَحَ to sweep, scavenge.

كَسَح paralysis, lameness, rickets (med.).

كَسْح sweeping, cleaning, emptying; lameness; paralysis; palsy.

كَسَدَ to be unsalable, unmarketable, remain unsold (goods); to stagnate, slump, become stagnant (market).

كَسَرَ to break, break open, force open; to violate, infringe (a legal duty); to destroy, defeat, rout (an army); to provide with the vowel (kasra) (grammar); to fragmentise, shatter, smash.

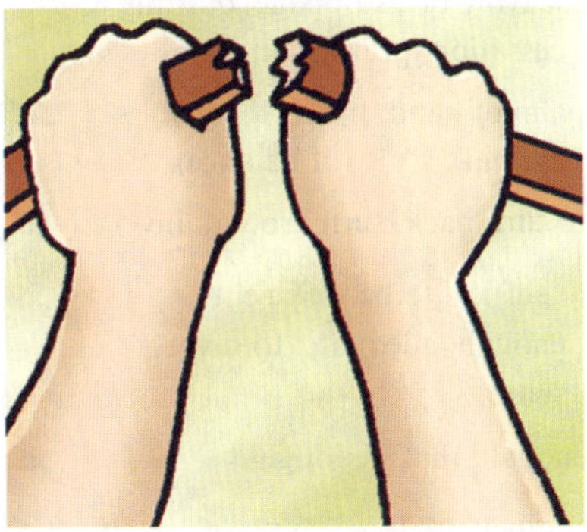

كسر الرَّجل بيديه قضيباً خشبيّاً رقيقاً

The man broke a thin wooden bar with his hands

كَسَرَ خاطِرَهُ to disappoint, offend someone.

كَسَرَ من حِدَّتِهِ to tone down, curb, temper; to extenuate, allay; to dilute, thin down (liquid); to blunt the edge of.

كَسَرَ شَوْكَتَهُ to subjugate, subdue, overcome, overpower; to degrade, humiliate.

كَسْر breaking, shattering, fragmentation; break; breach, fracture, crack, rupture; fraction (math).

كَسْرٌ عُشْرِيّ decimal fraction (math).

كِسْرَة fragment, piece, bit, morsel.

كَسَفَ to eclipse; to be eclipsed; to reprimand, reprove; to abash, shame, put to shame.

كَسِلَ to be lazy, idle, sluggish, indolent, negligent.

كَسَلٌ sluggishness, laziness, idleness, loafing, indolence.

كَسِلٌ، كَسْلان، كَسول lazy, idle; sluggish, indolent, inactive.

كُسْوَة، كِسْوَة clothing, attire, clothes; uniform; draping, lining, facing, wainscoting; garment, dress.

كُسُوف eclipse; solar eclipse.

يقال الكسوف للشمس والخسوف للقمر

For the sun it is said solar eclipse and for the moon it is said lunar eclipse

كَسِيح crippled, lame, paralyzed, palsied.

كَشَّاف boyscout, scout.

كَشَرَ، كَشَّرَ to grin, grimace, bare one's teeth; to scowl, glower.

كَشَطَ to scrape off, scratch off, rub off; to abrade, graze, remove.

كَشْط scraping, abrasion.

كَشَفَ to pull away, remove, take off, throw open; to lift, raise a covering, a curtain; to reveal, uncover, expose, bare; to shed light on; to show, demonstrate, lay open, bring to light; to investigate, examine medically.

أ ب ت ث ج ح خ د ذ ر ز س ش ص ض ط ظ ع غ ف ق ك ل م ن هـ و ي

كَشَفَ القِنَاعَ عن — to unveil, unmask, disclose.

كَشْف — uncovering, exposure, baring, laying bare; disclosure, unveiling; detection; examination, survey, inquiry; search, inspection; revelation, vision.

كَشْف — list, roster, statement, table; checkup (med.).

كُشْك، كِشْك — kiosk, booth, stand, stall.

كَشْكُول — beggar's bag; patchwork.

كَظَمَ — to suppress, repress, stiffle, contain.

كَظِيم — filled with anger, angry; anguished.

كَعَبَ — to be full and round (breast).

كَعَّبَ — to cube; to dice; to make cubic; to form a cube.

كَعْب — heel, anklebone, talus; knot, knob; foot, tail, bottom; glory, dignity, honor; dice.

الكَعْبَة — the Kaaba.

يطوف المسلمون حول الكعبة المشرفة خلال الحج
Moslems circumambulate al-Kaaba during the pilgrimage season

كُعْبُرَة — knotty excrescence, knob, node; radius (anat.).

كَعْك — cake, pastry.

كَفَّ — to refrain from, desist, abstain from, cease, stop; to give up, leave off, renounce; to waive, forego; to prevent.

كُفَّ بَصَرُهُ — to become blind.

كَفّ — abstention, desistance, discontinuation, giving up; leaving off, stoppage, quitting, cessation, prevention.

كَفّ — palm of hand, hand, paw (of animal); scale (of balance).

كَفَأَ — to turn back, turn around, invert.

كَفَى — to suffice; to be sufficient, enough, adequate; to save, spare.

كَفَى! — enough! that's enough!.

كُفْؤ، كَفْء، كُفْء، كِفْء — competent, adequate, suitable, qualified, capable; fit, fitted, efficient.

كَفَاءَة — qualification, capability, efficiency, competence, aptitude, merit, adequacy, ability.

كِفَاح — struggle, contention, fighting; opposition; battle, strife.

كَفَاف — subsistence.

كِفَاف — border, edge; outline.

كَفَالَة — guaranty, guarantee, warranty, security, bail, surety, collateral; bail, bond.

كِفَايَة — sufficiency, adequacy; full supply; capacity, ability, adequacy, competence, efficiency.

كَفَّة، كِفَّة scale or pan of a balance.

كَفَرَ to be an atheist; to be ungrateful; to cover, hide; to curse, swear; to renege one's faith.

كَفَّرَ to atone for, make amends for; to expiate; to grant remission to of; to forgive, pardon.

كَفر hamlet, small village.

كُفر unbelief, disbelief, atheism; ingratitude, ungratefulness.

كَفكَفَ to hold back tears; to wipe off one's tears.

كَفَلَ to guarantee, warrant, secure, vouch for; to bail out; to support, provide for, feed.

كَفَنَ، كَفَّنَ to shroud, wrap in a shroud (a dead person).

كَفَن shroud, winding sheet (of a dead).

كَفِيف blind.

كَفِيل guarantor, sponsor, surety, bondsman, security, bailsman; protector; legal guardian.

كَلَّ to be tired, weary, exhausted; to become dim (eyesight); to become blunt (knife).

كَلّ exhausted, tired, weary, faint, fatigued, weak, feeble; dull, blunt; dim, languid.

كُلّ all, all of, each, every, entire, total, totality.

الكُلّ the whole of, everyone, altogether, all of.

بِالكُلّ، كَكُلّ on the whole of, in bulk, taken altogether.

على كُلٍّ in any case, at any rate.

كُلُّهُ all of it or him, entirely.

كُلُّ شَيءٍ everything, all.

كُلُّ مَن whoever, whosoever.

بِكُلّ for each, per, for every.

كَلأَ to guard, protect, watch.

كَلأ grass, pasture.

كَلَّا no! never! not at all! by no means.

كِلا both of, the two.

كَلَّاب hook, clamp, grapnel, cramp.

كَلام talk, speech, conversation, words, statement, discussion, debate; dispute, utterance; language; sentence, clause.

كَلَامٌ فَارِغ nonsense, idle talk, prattle.

كَلَامِيّ verbal, spoken, oral; scholastic, theological.

كَلِبَ to covet, crave for; to become rabid, to run mad.

كَلَب rabies, madness, hydrophobia (med.); thirst.

كَلِب rabid, mad; greedy, hydrophobic.

كَلْب dog, hound (animal).

كَلَحَ to frown, scowl, look gloomy, morose.

كَلَّسَ to plaster with lime, whitewash; to calcify.

كِلْس lime; quicklime, limestone.

مَاءُ الكِلْس limewater, white-wash.

كِلْسٌ مُطْفَأ slaked lime, hydrated lime.

الكلب حيوان أليف ومخلص لصاحبه
The dog is a domestic animal faithful to its master

كِلْسِيّ calcareous, limy.

حَجَرٌ كِلْسِيّ limestone.

كَلِفَ to become freckled, covered with freckles.

كَلِفَ to like, be intent, bent, set, keen on; to be very attached to, very fond of, in love with.

كَلَّفَ to commission, charge, entrust someone with; to assign to; to cost someone a certain amount; to impose (a tax).

كَلَّفَ خاطِرَه to take the trouble; to bother someone.

مَهْما كَلَّفَ الأمْر whatever it may cost, at any cost.

كَلَف freckles.

كَلَف love, passion.

كَلِف very fond of, deeply in love with, very attached to.

كُلْفَة trouble, discomfort, hardship.

كُلْفَة cost, charge, expenditure.

كُلْفَةُ المَعِيشَة cost of living.

سِعْرُ الكُلْفَة cost price.

كَلَّلَ to crown; to perform the marriage ceremony; to become blunt; to become dull, obstuse, expressionless (of face).

كَلَمَ to wound, injure.

كَلَّمَ to speak to, talk to, converse with, address.

كُلَّمَا whenever.

كَلِمَة word, term, expression; speech, address, statement, remark; opinion, view.

كَلِمَةُ السِّرّ password.

كَلِمَاتٌ مُتَقاطِعَة crosswords.

كَلِمَةً كَلِمَة word for word, word by word, literally, verbatim.

بِكَلِمَة in a word, in short, to sum up, in brief.

بِكَلِمَةٍ أخْرى in other words, namely, to wit.

قالَ كَلِمَتَهُ he said what he had to say.

اجْتَمَعَتْ كَلِمَتُهُم they joined forces, came to an agreement.

كُلْوَة، كُلْيَة kidney (anat.).

كُلِّيّ total, entire, complete, whole; universal; general; aggregate, to be all-round; sweeping, comprehensive; absolute.

كُلِّيُّ القُدْرَة Omnipotent (God).

كُلِّيُّ الوُجُود Omnipresent (God).

كُلِّيَّة faculty, college, academy.

كُلِّيَّة totality, entirety, wholeness, universality.

بِكُلِّيَّتِهِ wholly, totally, in full, entirely, absolutely.

كُلِّيَّةُ الحُقوق faculty of law.

كُلِّيَّةُ الآداب faculty of arts.

كَمَّ to muzzle someone's mouth; to cover, hide, mask, conceal.

كَمّ muzzling.

كَمّ quantity, amount.

كَمّاً ونَوْعاً quantitatively and qualitatively.

كَمْ how many? how much?.

كَمْ بالأحرى how much more, with greater reason, the more so.

بِكَمْ how much does it cost? how much is it?

كُمّ sleeve.

كَمَا just as, as.

كَمَا لَوْ as if, as though.

كَمَا يلي as follows.

كِماد، كِمادَة compress, pack.

كَمَّاشَة pincers.

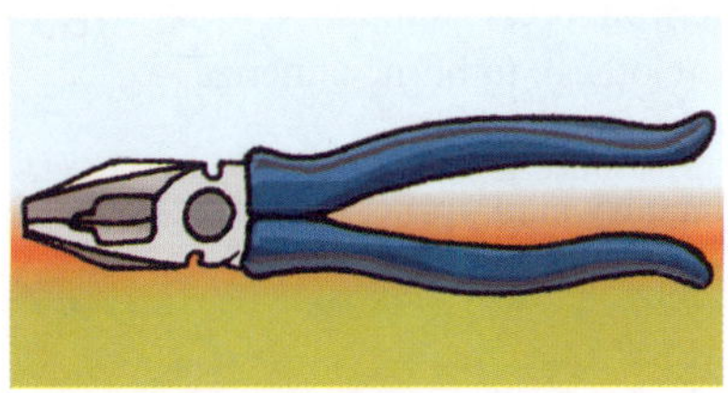

يستعمل النجار الكماشة لإخراج المسامير المغروزة في الخشب

The carpenter uses pliers to extract nails inserted in the piece of wood

---

كَمال perfection, completeness, ripeness, maturity.

كَمالِيّ luxury, luxurious.

كَمالِيّات luxuries.

كِمامَة muzzle (of animal); mask, respirator.

كَمان violin.

العزف على الكمان يثير العاطفة والحنان

Playing on the violin arouses feelings of sympathy and affection

---

كِمْبِيالَة bill of exchange, draft, promissory note.

كَمِدَ to become sad, grieved, depressed; to become opaque, dull, dusky; to fade, lose luster.

كَمَد، كُمْد sadness, depression; grief, worry; dull, swarthy color; dullness, duskiness.

كَمِد sad, grieved; gloomy, dark, dull, dusky.

كَمَلَ، كَمُلَ، كَمِلَ to be complete, full, whole, entire, perfect; to be concluded, finished, consummated.

كَمَّمَ to muzzle; to provide with sleeves.

كَمَنَ، كَمِنَ to hide; to be hidden, concealed, latent; to ambush, waylay someone; to lie in wait for someone.

كَمِّيَّة quantity, amount, magnitude; size, measure; number.

كَمِّيَّةٌ غير مُتَّجِهَة scalar.

كَمِّيَّةٌ مُتَّجِهَة vector.

كَمِين ambush, trap, snare.

كَنَّ to hide, conceal, cover, shelter, contain; to calm.

كَنَى، كَنَّى to surname, nickname, call, denominate.

كَنَّاس sweeper, scavenger, street cleaner, garbage collector.

كُنَاسَة sweepings, refuse, garbage, waste.

كِنَايَة عَن consisting in, equivalent to, meaning.

كَنَّة daughter-in-law.

كَنَزَ to bury a treasure in the ground; to pile up, heap up, accumulate, amass, collect, gather; to save, hoard.

كَنْز treasure; hoarding; heaping up, collection, amassment.

كَنَسَ to sweep, scavenge.

كَنْس sweeping scavenging vacuum-cleaning

كَنَسِيّ ecclesiastic

كَنَفَ to guard, protect, shelter; to help, aid, assist; to fence in, hedge, surround, enclose.

كَنَف side, wing; shadow, shade; bosom.

كَنَف protection, care, keeping, support.

في كَنَفِهِ under the auspices of; under the protection of; under the sponsorship of; sponsored by.

كُنْه essence, substance, true nature, core; extreme, gist, pith.

كُنْيَة، كِنْيَة surname, nickname, agnomen.

كَنِيس synagogue (of Jews).

كَنِيسَة church (of Christians).

كَنِيف toilet, water closet; enclosure, fold, pen, yard.

كَهْرَبَ to electrify.

كَهْرَباء electricity; amber.

كَهْرَبائِيّ (ص) electric, electrical.

كَهْرَبائِيّ (اسم) electrician.

كَهْرَبَة electrification.

كَهْرَطِيس electromagnet.

كَهْف cave, cavern, grotto.

كَهَلَ، كَهُلَ to be middle-aged.

كَهْل middle-aged, man of mature age.

كُهُولَة middle age.

كَوَى to iron, press, launder (clothes); to burn, cauterize (a wound).

كَوَّاء laundry man, ironer (of clothes).

كَوالِيس lobby, hallway; coulisse, backstage area.

كُوب cup, tumbler, drinking glass.

كُوَّة opening, skylight, louver, scuttle.

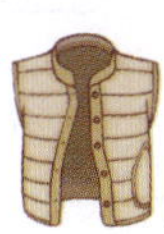

كُوخ hut, cottage.

كَوَّرَ to roll, make into balls; to conglomerate; roll up, coil, wind; to clench one's fist.

استعمل المكواة لكيّ الثياب وهي رطبة

I use the iron to press the clothes while damp

كُور forge; saddle; bellows, furnace.

كَوْرَس chorus, choir.

كُوز mug, jug.

كُوزُ الذُّرَة corncob, ear.

كُوع elbow; curve, bend, turn; wristbone (anat.).

كَوْكَب star, planet.

كَوْكَبَة constellation, group, troop; squad, squadron (army).

كَوْكَبِيّ astral, stellar, star-shaped.

كُوليرا cholera (med.).

كَوَّمَ to heap up, pile up, amass, accumulate.

كَوْمَة، كُومَة heap, pile, stack, pack.

كَوَّنَ to form, shape, fashion, create, produce, originate, bring forth; to bring into being.

كَوْن being, existence; event, occurence, incident.

الكَوْن the existent; the world; the cosmos; the universe.

عِلْمُ الكَوْن cosmology.

لِكَوْنِهِ because of, for, on account of, due to the fact that; in view of the fact that, since, owing to, as.

مَع كَوْنِهِ although, in spite of the fact that.

كُونفِدِرَالِيّ confederative.

كَوْنِيّ cosmic, universal.

كَيّ ironing, pressing, laundering (clothes); burning; cauterization (wound); branding (animals).

كَيْ، لِكَيْ so that, in order that, that, in order to, so as, with the aim of, for the purpose of.

كَيْ لا، كَيْلا، لِكَيْ لا lest, in order not to, so as not to.

كِيَاسَة courtesy, civility, politeness, refinement; complaisance, decency, propriety; dexterity, skill, smartness, sagacity; fineness, gracefulness, elegance.

كِيَان entity, being, structure; nature, existence, essence.

كَيْتَ وكَيْتَ such and such, so and so.

كَيْد cunning, ruse, craftiness, subtlety, deceit, deception, trick, artful plot, stratagem.

كِيس sack, bag, purse, pouch; cyst (anat.).

كِيسُ المِخَدَّة	pillowcase.
كَيَّفَ	to put in high spirits, amuse, delight someone.
كَيَّفَ	to adapt, accomodate, condition, fashion, make fit.
كَيَّفَ الهَواء	to air-condition.
كَيْفَ	how? in what way?.
كَيْفَ حَالُكَ	how are you?.
كَيْفَما	however, howsoever.
كَيْفَما كان الحَالُ	whatever the case may be, in any case, no matter how, any way, whatever may come.
كَيْفِيّ	arbitrary, despotic, dictatorial; qualitative.
كَيْفِيَّة	manner, modem, quality; nature, state, condition; mode; particulars.

كَيْفِيَّةُ الاسْتِعْمَال	directions for use.
كَيْل	measure.
كيلوغرام	kilogram.
كيلومِتْر	kilometer.
كيلوسيكل	kilocycle.
كيلوواط	kilowatt.
كيلوواط ـ ساعة	kilowatt-hour.
كِيمياء	chemistry.
كِيميائِيّ (ص)	chemical.
كِيميائِيّ (اسم)	chemist.
تَحْليلٌ كِيميائِيّ	chemical analysis.
مُرَكَّبٌ كِيميائِيّ	chemical compound.
تَفاعُلٌ كِيميائِيّ	chemical reaction.
كَيْنُونَة	existence, being, entity.

لَ	truly, verily, certainly, surely.
لَعَمْرُكَ	by your life.
لِـ	for, on behalf of, in favor of, to, because of, for the sake of, due to, owing; for, for the purpose of; when, as, by, as to.
ما لَهُ وما عَلَيه	his assets and his liabilities; his rights and his duties.
لَهُ أن	he has a right to; he may, he can.
أَلَكَ في	would you like? do you want?.
أَخُوهُ لأَبِيه	his brother on the paternal side.
لِيَسْقُطْ	down with!.
لا	no, not; don't.
لا أَحَد	nobody, no one, none.
لا إِلَهَ إِلاَّ اللهُ	There is no god but God.
لا سِيَّمَا	especially, particularly; specially, in particular.

لا شَيْء	nothing, none, nonentity.
لا شَكَّ	no doubt, doubtless.
لا هذا، ولا ذاك	neither this nor that.
لا خَيْر فيه	there is no good in it; it's no good.
لا أنانِيَّة	selflessness.
لا اجْتِماعِيّ	antisocial, unsocial.
لا أَخْلاقِيّ	immoral, unethical.
لا تَمْييز	indiscrimination.
لا حِزْبِيّ	non-partisan.
لا دِينِيّ	anti-religious, irreligious.
لا سَامِيَّة	anti-semitism.
لاسِلْكِيّ	wireless, radio.
لا شَرْعِيّ	illegal, illegitimate.
لا شُعُور	unconsciousness.
لا طائِفِيّ	non-sectarian.
لا عَقْلانِيّ	irrational.

لا مُبالاة indifference, nonchalance, carelessness, apathy.

لا مَرْكَزِيَّة decentralization.

لا مَسْئولِيَّة irresponsibility.

لا مَعْقول absurd.

لا مَنْطِقِيّ illogical, irrational.

لا نِهائِيّ، لا مُتَناهٍ infinite, eternal, perpetual.

لائِحَة list, table, schedule, panel; draft (of law); bylaw (of a company); bill (of indictment); aspect, outward looks.

لائِق suitable, appropriate, befitting, deserving, proper, fit.

لأَمَ to suit, harmonize with; to be adequate to, convenient for; to reconcile, unite, combine, stick or join together.

لائِمَة censure, rebuke, reproach, reproof, blame.

لابِس wearing, clad, clothed, dressed.

لاجِئ refugee.

لاحَ to loom, appear, come into sight; to become visible, apparent; to flash, shine, glimmer; to tan (skin).

يَلُوحُ لي أن it seems to me that.

لاحَظَ to observe, notice, view, see, perceive, remark; to take into consideration; to supervise, superintend.

لاحَقَ to follow up, pursue, go after, trail, chase.

لاحِق subsequent, following, succeeding, future, ulterior; appended, attached, joined.

لاحِقاً later on, subsequently.

لاحِقَة appendage, appurtenance, suffix, addendum, postscript, supplement; tag, label.

لاذَ to resort to, have recourse to, seek refuge with.

لاذَ to observe, comply with, abide by, adhere to.

لاذَ بِالصَّمْت to maintain silence.

لاذَ بِالفِرار to run away, escape, get away.

لاذِع burning; biting; sharp; pungent, acrid, bitter; sarcastic, caustic, snappish, waspish.

لازَمَ to accompany, attend; to adhere to, stick to; to haunt, persevere in, hang on to.

لازِم necessary, requisite, obligatory, mandatory; proper, fitting; intransitive (grammar).

لَوازِم necessaries, necessities, requisites; fixtures, fittings, supplies; outfit.

لاسِع stinging, burning, biting; acrid, pungent

لاشَى eliminate, annihilate, destroy; to suppress, ruin, crush.

لاصَقَ to adjoin, be adjacent to, be in contact with.

لاصِق adhesive, cohesive, sticking, adhering.

شَريطٌ لاصِق adhesive tape.

لاطَفَ to treat with kindness; to be civil and polite to; to be complaisant, obliging, indulgent toward; to flatter, humor, caress, fondle, pet.

لاعَبَ to play with, joke with, toy with; to jest, dally, trifle with.

لاعِب player, sportsman, athlete.

لاغٍ (اللاغي) null, void, invalid, inoperative, ineffective; canceled, invalidated, nullified, obsolete.

لافِتٌ للنَّظَر eye-catching, noticeable, remarkable.

لافِتَة signboard, billboard, sign.

لافِح burning, scorching, searing.

لاقَ to befit, become, be proper, suitable, befitting to.

لاقَى to encounter, meet, come across; to find, experience, undergo; to light upon; to get, obtain, achieve; to receive; to go to meet, come to meet.

لاقِط pickup, receiving set, receiver; catcher, finder.

لاكَ to chew, masticate.

لاكَ سُمْعَتَهُ to slander, defame, calumniate, speak evil of.

لاكَمَ to fight with; to box with.

لِئَلاَّ lest, so as not to.

لُؤلُؤ، لُؤلُؤَة pearls, a pearl.

لُؤلُؤِيّ، لُؤلُئِيّ pearly.

لأَمَ to dress, bandage; to repair, mend.

لَؤُمَ to be mean, base, vile, miscreant, evil, wicked.

لامَ to reproach, blame, admonish.

لُؤْم ignoble mind, baseness, meanness, vileness, wickedness, sordidness, miserliness.

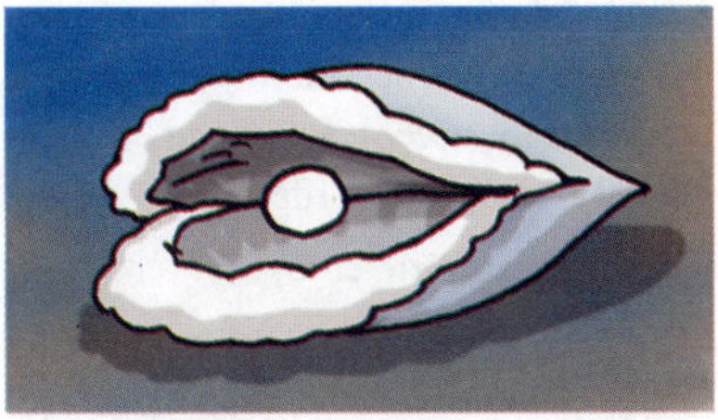

نجد اللآلئ في بعض الرخويات
Pearls are found in certain mollusks

لامَسَ to be in touch with; to touch, feel, palpate, finger.

لامِع bright, brilliant, lustrous, shining, polished, glazed.

لانَ to become flexible, pliable, tender, supple; to yield, soften, calm down, relax.

لَئِن indeed if.

لأَنَّ because, for, on the grounds that; in view of the fact that; due to, owing to, on account of.

لأن so that, in order that, in order to.

لاهٍ (اللاهي) heedless of, inattentive of, forgetful of.

لاهِث panting, gasping, out of breath.

لاهُوت theology, divinity.

لأْي tardiness; distress, hardship.

بَعْدَ لأْيٍ eventually, in the end, finally.

لَئِيم lowly, ignoble, base; mean, evil, vile, wicked; miserly; sordid, depraved.

لايَنَ to treat with leniency; to be kind to, gentle to.

لُبّ core, heart, essence; marrow, pith, gist; mind, intellect, reason; kernel, pulp; crumb (of bread).

لَبّى to comply with, accede to consent to, accept; to answer, satisfy, carry out (orders).

لُباب marrow, gist, pith, core; cellulose (of wood).

لَبّاد، لِبّاد felt.

لِباس dress, garment, clothing, clothes, wear.

لَباقَة tactfulness, skill, adroitness, subtlety, cleverness; propriety, decency; elegance, gracefulness.

لُبان frankincense, benzoin.

لَبِثَ to stay in, remain in, keep to.

ما لَبِثَ أنْ in no time he; before long he, soon he.

لَبَدَ، لَبِدَ to remain in, stay in; to stick to, cling to.

لَبَّدَ to compress, press, flocculate; to form a dense mass; to cause to adhere and mat together; to line with felt.

لَبِد compact, coherent.

لُبْدَة matted, compacted or compressed hair, wool.

لُبْدَة الأسَد mane.

لَبِسَ to wear, put on; to be clad in, get dressed, clothe oneself; to be clothed in.

لَبَّسَ to dress, clothe, attire; to drape, line; to coat, overlay, plate, encrust.

لُبْس wearing, dressing, putting on one's clothes.

لُبْس confusion, tangle, obscurity, ambiguity, doubt.

لَبَطَ to kick with one's foot; to throw down, fell (a person).

لَبُقَ، لَبِقَ to be tactful, skilled; to fit, suit; to be clever, suave, elegant, refined.

لَبَق cleverness, subtlety, adroitness; decency, propriety, skill, slyness, smartness.

لَبِق clever, subtle, skilled; elegant; becoming; proper.

لَبَكَ، لَبَّكَ to mix, mingle, confuse, muddle.

لَبَن yoghurt

لَبَنِيّ milky, milklike, lacteous.

لَبُون giving milk.

لَبيب intelligent, sensible, understanding, wise, rational.

لِثام veil, cover, wrapping.

لِثَة gum; gingiva.

لَثِغَ to lisp (in his talk).

لَثَمَ to kiss.

لَثَّمَ to veil the face.

لَثْم kissing.

لَثْمَة kiss.

لَجَّ to insist on; to persist, persevere in; to continue, keep doing something; to importune, pester, trouble, bother.

لَجَأَ to resort to, take refuge in, seek pretection in; to refer to, have recourse to.

لَجاجَة importunity, insistence, obstinacy, persistence.

لِجام — bridle, rein.

لَجَب — clamor, uproar, noise, tumult.

لُجَّة — depth of the sea.

لَجْلَجَ — to stammer, stutter, repeat words in speaking.

لَجَمَ — to bridle, rein in; to retain, curb, check, control.

لَجْنَة — committee, commission, panel, board.

لَجْنَةٌ فَرْعِيَّة — subcommittee.

لُجُوء — resorting to, taking refuge or shelter in; seeking protection in; reference to, consulting.

اللُّجوءُ السِّياسِيّ — political asylum.

لَجُوج — insisting, insistent; obstinate, unyielding, stubborn; obtrusive; importunate.

لِحاء — bark; cortex.

لِحاف — quilt, cover.

لَحاق — accession to, joining of, enrollment in, entry; following, sequence; catching up with, reaching, overtaking.

لَحَّام — butcher; welder.

لِحام — welding, soldering; solder.

لَحَدَ — to dig a grave; to bury, inter; to deviate from the right path; to abandon one's faith; to become a heretic.

لَحْد — grave, tomb.

لَحِسَ — to lick, lick up; to eat away, devour, lap.

لَحَظَ — to regard, view, eye; to look at, notice, see, perceive, observe; to catch sight of, remark, heed, take into consideration; to supervise, superintend.

لَحْظ — glance, eye, look.

لَحْظَة — moment, instant, second; look, glance, glimpse.

لَحِقَ — to catch up with; to overtake, catch, reach; to follow, succeed; to stick to, cling to, keep close to, hang on to; to befall, afflict, affect, come upon; to join, enter; to trail, pursue, chase.

لَحَمَ، لَحَّم — to weld, solder.

لَحْم — flesh, meat.

لَحْمُ البَقَر — beef.

لَحْمُ الخِنْزِير — pork, ham, bacon.

لَحْمُ الضَّأْن أو لَحْمُ الغَنَم — mutton.

لَحْمُ العِجْل — veal.

لَحْمٌ هَبْر — lean meat.

لُحْمَة — relationship, kinship; decisive factor, motif.

لَحَنَ — to speak ungrammatical Arabic.

لَحَّنَ — to compose, set to music; to intone, chant.

لَحْن — tune, air, melody; grammatical mistake.

لِحْيَة — beard, goatee.

لَخَّصَ — to summarize, sum up, recapitulate, condense, outline; to make an excerpt or extract of; to sketch (a passage).

لَدَى at, near, by (place and time); in front of, before, in the presence of.

لَدائِن plastics.

لَدَانَة plasticity, softness, pliability, flexibility, suppleness; resilience, elasticity, ductility, malleability.

لَدَغَ to sting, bite; to taunt, hurt, offend.

لَدْغَة sting, bite (of snake).

لَدَّنَ to soften, mollify, anneal, plasticize.

لَدُن، لَدْن، لُدُن، لُدْن at, by, near, close to, in front of.

مِن لَدُن from, on the part of, since.

لَدُود mortal enemy, bitter enemy; vehement, violent disputer.

لَذَّ to be delicious, pleasant, sweet; to please, gratify, delight; to give pleasure.

لَذَّة pleasure, delight, joy, rapture, bliss, delectation; sensual delight, lust, voluptuousness.

لَذَعَ to burn, bite, sting; to hurt, offend, insult.

لَذْع burning, fire; sharpness; acridity, pungency.

لَذِيذ delicious, delighful, pleasing, delectable, dainty, pleasant, nice, sweet; beautiful, splendid, magnificent.

لِزَام، لُزُوم necessity, requirement, duty.

كان لِزَاماً عليه to be incumbent upon; to be someone's duty.

لَزِجَ to become sticky, gluey; to stick to.

لَزِج sticky, gluey; glutinous, viscid, viscous; adhesive.

لَزَّزَ to compress, press, cram together; join firmly.

لَزِقَ to stick to, adhere to, cling to.

لَزَّقَ to affix, attach, stick, glue, plaster, cement, fix.

لَزِق glutinous; gluey, sticky; adhesive.

لَزِمَ to keep to, stay at, remain at (a place); to stick to, adhere to, cling to, abide by; to maintain, keep close to; to keep doing.

لَزِمَ to be necessary, imperative, indispensable.

لَزِمَ دارَه (فِرَاشَه) to stay at home (in bed).

لَزِمَ الصَّمْت to keep silent, maintain silence.

إذا لَزِمَ الأَمْر if need be, in case of need, if necessary.

لُزُوجَة viscosity, stickiness.

لُزُوم need, necessity, exigency; implication.

عِنْدَ اللُّزُوم in case of need, when necessary.

لِسان tongue; language; headland, cape; tab; tenon.

لِسَانُ القَوْمِ أو الحُكُومَة mouthpiece, spokesman.

لَسَعَ to sting, bite; to hurt, injure, offend (with words).

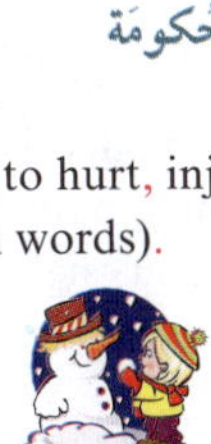

لَسْعَة sting, bite.

لَسْعَةُ الصَّقِيع frost bite.

لَسَغَ to criticize; to slander, defame; to sting, bite.

لَسِنَ — to be eloquent.

لَسِن — eloquent.

لِصّ — thief, robber, burglar.

لَصِقَ — to adhere, cleave, cling, stick to; to hang on, get stuck to; to fit closely; to cling to.

لَصِق — sticky, gluey, adhesive, viscous.

لِصْق — adjoining, adjacent, near, close to.

لُصُوصِيَّة — robbery, theft, larceny, burglary.

لَصُوق — plaster; paste; adhesive, glue; cement.

لَطَافَة — gracefulness, loveliness, kindness, politeness; thinness, fineness; suavity, sophistication.

لَطَّخَ — to stain, blot, sully, soil; to spatter, splash, tarnish.

لَطْخَة — stain, blot, spot; blotch, smear; smudge, patch.

لُطْخَة — stupid, idiot, fool, dolt.

لَطَفَ — to be kind to; to treat someone kindly.

لَطُفَ — to be thin, fine, delicate, dainty; to be graceful, elegant, nice; to be amiable, friendly.

لَطَّفَ — to soften; to make mild, soft, gentle; to mitigate, alleviate, ease, soothe, palliate, extenuate; to temper, moderate, reduce, diminish, tone down.

لُطْف — kindness, friendliness; mildness, daintiness; gracefulness, gentleness; courtesy, civility, politeness; thinness; delicacy; tenuity.

لَطَمَ — to slap, buffet; to strike, hit.

لَطْمَة — slap; buffet; flap, blow, hit, strike.

لَطِيف — kind, nice, friendly; gentle, soft, mild, light; pleasant, agreable, civil, polite, courteous; affable, witty, elegant; little, small; thin, fine, delicate.

لَطِيفَة — witticism, joke, jest.

لُعَاب — saliva, spittle, drool, slobber, drivel.

لَعَبَ — to drool, drivel, slobber (saliva).

لَعِبَ — to play, play with, toy with, dally with.

ألعب في الحديقة مع أصدقائي
بعد أن أنهي فروضي المدرسية
I play in the garden with my friends
after finishing my homework

لَعِب، لَعْب، لِعْب — play, game, fun, amusement; joke, jest.

لَعِبُ القِمار — gambling.

الألْعَابُ الأولِمْبِيَّة olympic games, olympiad.

ألْعابٌ سِحْرِيَّة jugglery, magic, prestidigitation.

ألْعَابٌ نارِيَّة fireworks.

لُعْبَة puppet, tool, instrument; hireling, agent (in the service of another).

لَعِقَ to lick, lick up, lap up.

لَعلَّ perhaps, maybe.

لَعْلَعَ to reverberate, boom, roar, rumble, peal.

لَعَنَ to curse, damn, imprecate, execrate.

لَعْنَة curse, imprecation, malediction.

لَعُوب playful, sportive, frolicsome; coquettish, flirtatious.

لَعِين، مَلْعُون cursed, damned, wicked, execrable, detestable.

اللَّعِين the Evil One (the Devil).

لَغَا to speak, talk; to be null, void, invalid; to be canceled, outdated, obsolete; to talk nonsense; to make mistakes in speaking.

لُغَة language, tongue, parlance, idiom.

لُغَةٌ اصْطِلاحِيَّة، عَامِّيَّة jargon.

لُغَةٌ مَحَلِّيَّة dialect.

لُغْز riddle, puzzle, enigma, mystery.

لَغَطَ، لَغَّطَ to clamor, shout; to raise a din; to be clamorous and noisy.

لَغْط clamor, shouting, uproar, tumult, turmoil.

لَغَمَ to mine, lay a mine; to booby-trap.

لَغْم mining, minelaying.

لُغْم mine.

تزرع الألغام الأرضية لمنع تقدم جيوش العدوّ
Land mines are planted in order to prevent the advance of the enemy armies

---

لَغْو nonsense, drivel; chatter, chat; foolish talk.

لَغْو mistake, error, blunder.

لَغْو null, void, ineffective.

لُغَوِيّ (ص) linguistic, lingual.

لُغَوِيّ (اسم) linguist, lexicologist, philologist.

لَفَّ to roll up, wind, coil, twist, wrap up, fold up; to envelop, cover, swathe; to join, connect, attach; to grow densely from a tangled mass; to make a round of calls; to go about something; to beat about the bush.

لَفَّ لَفَّهُ to do just like someone; to belong to the same sort as.

لَفّ wrapping up, coiling, winding, curling, twisting; enwrapping; detour, circumvention.

لِفافَة bandage, dressing; wrapper, covering, jacket.

لِفافَةُ تَبْغ cigarette.

لَفَتَ، لَفَّتَ to turn, bend, turn away from; to draw someone's attention; to point out to.

لَفَتَ الانْتِباه أو النَّظَر to attract attention; to catch the eye.

لَفَّة coil, twist, curl, roll; turn, revolution, turning.

لَفْتَة turn, sideglance, gesture, furtive look; turnabout.

لَفَحَ to scorch, sear, burn.

لَفَظَ to eject, discharge, expel, reject extrude.

لَفَظَ to pronounce, speak, articulate, utter, express, say.

لَفَظَ النَّفَسَ الأَخِير to die, expire, be in the throes of death.

لَفْظ ejection, discharge, expulsion, rejection.

لَفْظ pronunciation, utterance, articulation; delivery of a sentence (by the judge); expression, term.

لَفْظاً ومَعْنًى in letter and spirit.

لَفْظَة word, term, expression, saying.

لَفْظِيّ phonetic, verbal, oral, literal.

لَفَّقَ to invent, make up, create, fabricate, feign, fake, concoct, contrive, devise; to falsify, trump up.

لَفْلَفَ to cover up, conceal; to wrap up, envelop.

لَفِيف multitude, crowd, swarm, cluster, group of people.

لَفِيفَة roll, coil, scroll, winding; reel, spool, bobbin; bundle, package, pack, packet.

لِقَاء encounter, meeting, get-together, reunion, interview.

لِقَاء in exchange for, in return for.

إلى اللِّقاء! goodbye!, so long!.

لَقَاح vaccine; pollen, seed, semen, sperm; virus.

لَقَّبَ to surname, nickname; to denominate, designate.

لَقَب surname, agnomen, nickname; title, designation; family name.

لَقَّحَ to impregnate, fecundate, pollinate; to vaccinate; to graft (a tree).

لَقْح impregnation, fecundation, pollination.

لَقَطَ to pick up, take up, catch, gather.

لُقْطَة that which is picked up; bargain; pickup.

لَقْطَة shot, photogtraph, snap; catch.

لَقَّمَ to feed; to provide with; to load (a gun).

لُقْمَة morsel, mouthful, bite; bit (of a punch).

لُقْمَةٌ سائِغَة choice morsel.

لَقَّنَ to teach, dictate to; to prompt, cue (an actor on stage); to instruct; to instill, infuse, inspire; to insinuate, suggest to someone something.

لَقِيَ to encounter, meet with someone or something; to come across someone or something; to find, experience, undergo, suffer, endure.

لُقْيا encounter, meeting.

لَقِيط foundling.

لكّ lac, lacquer, varnish, resin.

لَكَزَ to strike with the fist; to poke; to thrust someone, nudge.

لَكَمَ to punch, box, strike with the fist.

لَكْمَة punch, blow with the fist.

لَكِنَّ، لَكِن but, however, yet, still, nevertheless.

لُكْنَة accent; stutter, stammer; ungrammatical language, incorrect pronunciation, usage.

لَمَّ to collect, gather, assemble.

لَمَّ شَمْلَهُم to rally, gather together, reunite.

لُمَّ to suffer from a slight mental derangement.

لَمّ gathering, collection, assembly; crowd, throng.

لَمْ not.

إنْ لَمْ، ما لَمْ unless, if not, except if.

لَمَّا when, at the time when, as; whereas, since, because, in view of the fact that; not, not yet.

لِماذا why? what for? wherefore?.

لَمّاع bright, brilliant, flashing, lustrous, sparkling; glossy, polished, glazed.

لَمَّة collection, gathering, assembly; hardship, misfortune.

لَمَحَ to glance at, glimpse at, catch sight of; to behold, notice, see; to become aware that.

لَمَّحَ to insinuate, intimate, hint, allude, refer to.

لَمْحَة glance, glimpse, quick look; general view, comprehensive look; summary, synopsis, outline.

لَمَزَ to find fault with, criticize, censure, blame; to defame, wink at, give someone a wink.

لَمَسَ to touch, feel, sense, notice, realize, become conscious of, become aware of.

لَمْس touching, touch, feeling.

حاسَّةُ اللَّمْس touch.

لَمْسَة touch.

لَمَساتٌ أَخِيرَة finishing touches, final touches.

لَمَعَ to gleam, glitter, twinkle, sparkle, shimmer, shine.

لَمَعَ بيده to wave one's hand.

لَمَعَ في رَأْسِهِ خاطِرٌ a thought flashed through his mind.

لَمَّعَ to polish, burnish, shine, gloss.

لَمَعان، لُمْعَة، لَمْع luster, gloss, shine, shimmer, gleam, glow; brightness, light.

لَمْلَمَ to gather, collect.

لِمَن to whom, whose.

لَنْ not, never.

لَها to play, toy, dally, amuse oneself, have fun; to love, be fond of.

لَها عَن to try to forget; to pay no attention to.

لُهاث pant, gasp.

لَهِبَ to flame, burn, blaze.

لَهَب flame, blaze, flare.

لَهَثَ، لَهِثَ to pant, gasp, be out of breath, breathe heavily.

لَهِجَ to be devoted, dedicated to; to be attached to, very fond of, in love with.

لَهِجَ بِالثَّناء عليه to extol someone fervently.

لَهِجَ بِشُكْرِهِ to launch forth into profuse praise.

لَهِجَ بِذِكْرِهِ to speak constantly of someone; to mention someone's name continually with praise.

لَهْجَة dialect, accent, tone, tongue; vernacular, language.

لَهِفَ to regret, deplore, lament, sigh, grieve for; to fret, worry about; to yearn for.

لَهْف، لَهْفَة regret, grief, lament, sigh; desire, eagerness, yearning, longing, hankering; impatience.

لَهْو amusement, diversion, entertainment, distraction; sport, fun, play.

لَهِيب flame, blaze, flare.

لَوْ أَنَّ if.

لَوْلا except for, if not.

فِيما لَوْ in case that, in the event that.

وَلَوْ although, even if, albeit, though.

لَوَى to twist, kink, wrench, bend, turn, curve, flex; to contort, warp, distort, pervert.

لا يَلوي على شيء not to care about anything.

لِوَاء banner, flag; brigade (army); major general (army rank); district, county, province.

لِوَاط sodomy, pederasty, homosexuality, buggery.

لَوَّثَ to pollute, contaminate, defile, soil, sully, tarnish.

لَوَّثَ سُمْعَتَهُ to tarnish someone's reputation; to slander, debase, dishonor, defame, calumniate someone's repute.

لَوْثَة foolishness, idiocy, imbecility, stupidity; stain, blot, spot.

لَوْثَة mental derangement, slight madness; languor, lassitude, fatigue; passion; weakness for.

لَوَّحَ to wave, beckon, make a sign, signal; to allude, hint, insinuate; to intimate, give to understand.

لوّحت له بيدي كي يتوقف ويكلمني
I waved to him with my hand to stop and speak to me

أ ب ت ث ج ح خ د ذ ر ز س ش ص ض ط ظ ع غ ف ق ك **ل** م ن هـ و ي

لَوَّحَ — to brandish; turn grey; to burn, tan (with sun).

لَوَّحَ بِيده — to wave with his hand.

لَوْح — board, table, slab, plate, sheet; panel, slate.

لَوْحٌ أَسْوَد — blackboard.

لَوْحٌ خَشَب، لَوْحٌ خَشَبِيّ — board, plank.

لَوْحُ صَابُون — bar, cake.

لَوْحُ الكَتِف — shoulder blade.

لَوْحَة — painting, tableau, drawing; plaque.

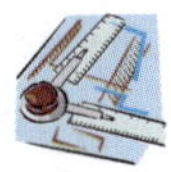

لَوْحَةُ الإسْم — nameplate.

لَوْحَةُ إعْلانات — bulletin board, notice board.

لَوْحَةٌ إعْلانِيَّة — signboard, billboard.

لَوْحَةُ القِيادَة — dashboard.

لَوْحَةُ المَفَاتيح — keyboard, switchboard.

اللَّوْزَتان — tonsils (anat.).

التِهابُ اللَّوْزَتَيْن — tonsilitis (med.).

لُوطِيّ — homosexual, pederast, bugger.

لَوَّعَ — to torment, torture.

لَوْعَة — agony, torment, pain, grief, sorrow; ardor of love, amorous rapture.

لَوْلَب — screw; spiral, helix; loop; spring.

لَوْلَبِيّ — spiral, helical, winding, volute.

لَوَّمَ — to reprove, blame, reprimand.

لَوْم، لَوْمَة — censure, blame, rebuke, reproach, reproof.

وَضَعَ اللَّوْمَ على — to blame, lay the blame on.

لَوَّنَ — to color, paint, tint, daub; to variegate, dapple, hue.

لَوْن — color, coloring, tint, shade.

لَوْن — kind, sort, specimen, category, class.

لَوْنُ طَعَام — dish, course.

لَوِيَ — to be crooked, bent, twisted, curved; to writhe, wriggle, squirm (serpent).

لَيّ، لَوْي — twisting, wrenching, bending, flexion; kinking; contorsion; curling; turning.

لِياقَة — decency, propriety, etiquette, civility, courtesy, good manners; competence, aptitude, fitness; merit, capability, qualification; worthiness.

لَيَّة — twist, fold, ply, bend, curve, turn.

لَيْتَ، يا لَيْتَ — if only, would that.

ليث — lion

اللَّيث اسم آخر من أسماء الأسد العديدة

«Leith» is another word in Arabic meaning a lion

لَيس إلاّ	nothing but, just, simply, merely, no more than.
أَلَيسَ كَذلك	isn't it so?.
لَيَّفَ	to clean, wash, rub with a sponge.
لِيف	coir, fiber.
لِيفَةُ الاسْتِحْمَام	sponge.
لَيل	night.
لَيلاً	at night, by night.
لَيلَة	night, evening.
اللَّيلَة ، هَذِه اللَّيلَة	tonight.
لَيلَةَ أمْس	last night.
بَيْنَ لَيلَةٍ وضُحَاها	overnight, all of a sudden.
لَيلِيّ	nocturnal, nightly.
لَيمُون	lemon, citrus.
حَامِضُ اللَّيمُون	citric acid.
شَرابُ اللَّيمُون	lemonade.
لَيَّنَ	to soften, soothe, allay, mitigate, temper, moderate.

أعصر ليمونة حامضة فوق الطعام
الذي يتطلب ذلك كصحن الفول مثلاً

I press a lemon over the meal that requires a sour taste like baked beans

لَيِّن	soft, tender; flaccid, limp, lax; flexible, pliable, elastic, supple; ductile, malleable; flabby, feeble.
لَيِّنُ الجَانِب	docile, flexible, compliant, obedient.
لِين، لُيونَة	tenderness, flaccidity, laxity; leniency, gentleness; clemency; flexibility, elasticity, resilience, plasticity, ductility, malleability; suppleness.

مَ، ما، ماذا؟	what?.
بِمَ؟	with what?.
عَمَّ؟	about what?.
مِمَّ؟	of what?.
ما لكَ؟	what's the matter with you?.
ما أَجْمَلَه!	how beautiful it is!.
شَيءٌ ما	something.
بِما فيهِ	including, inclusive.
لأَمْرٍ ما	because of something, for some reason or other.
يَوْماً ما	someday, sometime in the future.
ما دُمْتُ حَيًّا	as long as I live.
ما لَم	not, unless, so long as.
ما قَبلَ التَّاريخ	prehistory.
ما وَراءَ البِحار	overseas.
ما وَراءَ الطَّبيعة	metaphysics.

لِما، لِماذا؟	why? what for? for what?.
ماء، مِيَاه	water.

الماء أساس كل حياة على وجه الأرض
Water is the basis for every life on earth

مِياهٌ إقْليمِيَّة	territorial waters.
مِياهٌ جَوْفِيَّة	ground water.
ماءٌ عَذْب	fresh water.
ماءٌ عَسِر	hard water.

ماءٌ عكِر — troubled water.

مِياهٌ غازِيَّة — soda water, carbonated water.

مِياهٌ مَعْدِنيَّة — mineral water.

ماءٌ مُقطَّر — distilled water.

ماءُ الوَجْه — honor, dignity, prestige, self-respect.

حَفْظُ ماءِ الوَجْه — to save face.

مائِت — dying, moribund, in the throes of death; mortal.

مُؤاتٍ (المُؤاتي) — favorable, propitious, opportune.

مَائِج — heaving, swelling, stormy, high (sea).

مُؤاخَذَة — blame, censure; objection.

مائِدَة — table, dining table.

أوَاني المائِدَة — tableware, table utensils.

مُؤازَرَة — support, backing up, assistance.

مُؤاساة — consolation, condolence, solace.

مائِع — liquid, fluid.

مائِل — inclined, slanting, bent, tilted; diagonal, sloping.

حَرْفٌ مائِل — italic.

مُؤامَرَة — plot, conspiracy, intrigue.

مُؤانِس — amusing; friendly, genial; intimate or close friend.

مُؤانَسَة — intimacy, familiarity, friendliness, cordiality.

مائِيّ — aquatic, aqueous, hydraulic.

مَآب — retreat, recourse, resort.

مُؤبَّد — eternal, everlasting, for life.

سِجْنٌ مُؤبَّد — life imprisonment.

مَأبِض — hollow of the knee; popliteal space.

ماتَ — to die, pass away, meet death, expire, part with life.

مَاتَ — to perish, die down; to subside; to abate.

مِئَة — one hundred.

مِئَة وواحد — one hundred and one.

بالمِئَة — percent, %.

مُؤْتَلَف — harmonious, in harmony with; friendly; combined, united, joint, in agreement.

مَأتَم — funeral ceremony.

مُؤْتَمَر — conference, convention, congress.

مُؤْتَمَرُ قِمَّة — summit meeting, summit conference.

مُؤْتَمَن — entrusted with; trustworthy, reliable; confidant.

مُؤَثَّث — furnished, provided with furniture (house, office).

مُؤَثِّر — effective, operative; influential; affecting, influencing; moving, touching, impressive.

مُؤَثِّرات خاصَّة — special effects.

مَأْثُرَة — exploit, achievement. remarkable deed.

مَاثَلَ — to look alike, bear a likeness to; to compare, imitate; to make similar, analogous; to assimilate.

ماثِل — standing, appearing, present; manifest, visible, obvious.

مَأثُور — related, quoted, transmitted, handed down.

ماجَ — to heave, swell up, roll, welter, surge; to be agitated, excited.

مُؤَجَّر — let out, leased, hired out; chartered (ship).

مُؤَجَّرٌ من الباطِن — subleased, sublet.

مُؤَجِّر — lessor, landlord.

مُؤَجَّل — postponed, adjourned, deferred; fixed in time.

ماجِن — impudent, shameless, brazen, impertinent; dissolute, profligate; joker, jester.

مَأْجُور — mercenary, hireling; employed, hired; bribed; salaried.

ماحِق — destructive, devastating.

ماحَكَ — to wrangle with, bicker with, quarrel with.

ماحِل — barren, bare, bleak, sterile.

مَأْخَذ — source, spring; defect, flaw; objection, criticism, complaint; way, method.

مَأْخَذٌ كهرَبائِيّ — outlet, plug, socket.

قَريبُ المَأْخَذ — easy to handle, at hand, near at hand.

مُؤَخَّر (ص) — delayed out, postponed, adjourned.

مُؤَخَّر (اسم) — end, rear part; stern (of ship); remainder of a sum to be paid later.

مُؤَخَّراً — recently, lately; at last, finally, eventually.

مُؤَخَّرة — rear, end, hind, posterior, tail; stern (of ship).

مادَ — to be shaken, upset, shocked, moved.

مادَ — to swing; to feel giddy, dizzy.

مُؤَدٍّ (المُؤَدِّي) — leading to; contributing to; bringing about; giving rise to, causing, resulting in.

مُؤَدَّب — polite, well-mannered, courteous, cultivated, civil.

مَأْدُبَة — banquet.

مادَّة — matter, substance, material; ingredient, constituent, component; article, item, section; provision, stipulation, term.

مادَّةٌ دِراسِيَّة — course, subject.

مادَّةٌ خام — raw material.

مادِّيّ — material, concrete, tangible, corporeal, physical.

مُؤْذٍ (المُؤْذِي) — harmful, injurious, detrimental, noxious, damaging, evil, unhealthy; bothersome, offensive; prejudicial, annoying, irksome, troublesome, insulting.

مُؤَذِّن — muezzin, (person who calls for prayer).

مِئْذَنَة — minaret of a mosque.

يُبنى في كل مسجد مئذنة لدعوة المؤمنين إلى الصلاة منها

A minaret is built in every mosque to call the faithful to prayers therefrom

مَأْذون (ص) authorized, licensed, permitted, allowed.

مَأْذون (اسم) marriage official (in Islam).

مارّ passer-by, pedestrian, walker; passing through, crossing, traversing, going through.

مارَى to dispute with, argue with.

مَأْرَب wish, desire, need; purpose, aim, goal.

مُؤَرِّخ dated.

مُؤَرِّخ historian.

مارِد giant, demon, devil; refractory, recalcitrant, rebel.

مارَسَ to exercise, practise, pursue; to carry out, execute; to be in practical contact, have actually to do with.

مارَسَ ضَغطاً على to exert a pressure.

مارِق apostate, renegade, defector, deserter; heretic.

ماركَة mark, trademark, brand.

ماركسِيَّة Marxism.

مارونِيّ Maronite.

مازَجَ to intermix, intermingle with; mix with; blend with.

مِئْزَر apron, loin cloth.

مَأْزِق deadlock, dilemma, plight, predicament; bottleneck, critical situation, narrow path.

مازوت gas oil, fuel oil.

ماسَّ to touch; to be in contact with.

ماس، ماسَة diamond.

حاجَةٌ ماسَّة urgent need, pressing need, exigency.

مَأْساة drama, tragedy.

مَأْساوِيّ tragic, disastrous, catastrophic.

ماسَحَ to cajole, coax, sweet-talk.

ماسِحُ الأحْذِيَة shoeblack, bootblack.

ماسِحَة wiper.

مُؤَسَّس established, founded, instituted.

مُؤَسِّس founder.

مُؤَسَّسَة foundation, establishment, institution, organization, firm, institute.

مُؤَسَّسَةٌ تابِعَة subsidiary.

مُؤَسَّسَةٌ فَرْعِيَّة affiliate.

مُؤَسَّسَةٌ خَيْرِيَّة philanthropic organization, charitable foundation.

مؤْسِف regrettable, deplorable; unfortunate, pitiful; distressing; sad.

ماسِكُ حِسابات bookkeeper.

مَأْسور (ص) captured, arrested, jailed; captivated, fascinated.

مَأْسور (اسم) captive, prisoner.

ماسُورَة pipe, tube, gun barrel.

مَأْسُوفٌ عَليه mourned, the late, the deceased.

ماسُونِيّ Freemason, Mason.

ماسُونِيَّة Freemasonry.

ماشٍ (الماشِي) walker, pedestrian.

ماشِياً on foot.

ماشَى to keep abreast; to go along, agree with, harmonize with; to be consistent, compatible with.

مِنْشار saw.

مُؤَشَّرٌ عليه marked, stamped, signed, endorsed.

مُؤَشِّر indicator, pointer, sign, index.

ماشِيَة livestock, cattle.

ماصّ absorbent, soaking up.

ماصَّة suction (pump); suction (pipe); siphon; sucker.

ماضٍ (المَاضِي) past, previous; prior, preceding; bygone days.

المَاضِي the past tense, perfect tense (grammar).

في المَاضِي in the past.

ماضٍ sharp, cutting, acute, penetrating, incisive; energetic, effective.

ماضِي العَزِيمَة resolute, determined.

ماطِر rainy.

ماطَلَ to temporize, put off, delay, procrastinate.

ماعَ to melt, dissolve; to be liquefied, melted.

ماعُون ream of paper; vessel, utensil; lighter, barge.

مَأْفُون imbecile, idiot, stupid, moron.

مُؤَقَّت temporary, transitory, provisional, interim; transient, ephemeral, momentary, temporal.

مُؤَقَّتاً temporarily, ad interim, for the time being.

مُؤَكَّد certain, definite, proved; emphasized, emphatic.

مِنَ المُؤَكَّد most certainly, of course.

ماكَرَ to try to deceive.

ماكِر sly, cunning, wily, crafty.

مَأْكَل food, meal, repast; fodder, feed.

مَأْكَل . مَأْكُولات edible; foods, victuals.

ماكِينَة machine.

ماكِينَات machinery; hardware (of computers).

مالَ to incline, slope, tilt, tip, slant; to tend to; to be inclined to, have an inclination (propensity, liking) for; to favor; to take sides with; to be partial to.

مالَ عَن to deviate from, depart from, diverge from; to turn away from; to avoid, shun, abandon, relinquish, renounce; to be averse to; to have an antipathy for; dislike, hate.

مَآل end, consequence, issue; return, resort.

مال money, chattel, property, wealth, goods; fortune, estate; affluence; income, revenue.

مال assets, capital, stock, fund.

بيتُ المال treasury.

رأسُ المال capital.

أمْوالٌ ثابِتَة landed property, real estate, immovable property.

ذُو مال wealthy, rich, prosperous.

مالأَ to help, assist, side with, be partial to.

مالَج، مالَق trowel.

مالح salty, saline, briny.

مُؤَلَّف (ص) set up, established, made, formed by, composed.

مُؤَلَّف (اسم) book, work, compilation, publication.

مُؤَلِّف author, composer, writer.

مالِك owner, proprietor, possessor, holder.

مالِكُ الأرْض، العِقَار landlord, landowner.

مُؤْلِم painful, tormenting, grievous; sad; aching.

مَأْلوف familiar, customary, usual, accustomed.

ماليّ financial, monetary, fiscal.

مالِيَّة finance, public finance.

مَأمَل hope, expectation.

مُؤَمِّل hopeful.

مُؤَمَّم nationalized.

مَأمَن place of safety, safe place, shelter, refuge.

مُؤَمَّن ensured, safe, secure; available, provided.

مُؤَمَّنٌ عليه insured.

مُؤَمِّن insurer, insurance company.

مُؤْمِن faithful, believer, believing.

مَأْمور (ص) commanded, commissioned, charged.

مَأْمور (اسم) commissioner, civil officer, official; servant.

مَأْمورُ تَسْجيل registrar.

مَأْمورُ تَفْليسَة receiver in bankruptcy.

مَأْمورُ صَرْف paymaster.

مَأْمُورِيَّة mission, assignment, task, job, commission.

مَأْمُول hoped for, expected, anticipated.

مَأْمُون trustworthy, reliable, faithful, honest; safe, secure.

مُؤَنَّث feminine, feminine gender (grammar).

مانِح donor, giver, donator.

مُؤْنِس entertaining, amusing; sociable, amiable; domestic; close comrade.

مانَعَ to oppose, resist; to object to; to forbid, prohibit; to defend, protect; to obstruct, bar.

مانِع (ص) hindering, forbidding, preventive, prohibitive.

مانِع (اسم) obstacle, obstruction, hindrance, impediment, deterrent, restraint; objection.

مانِعٌ لِلحَمَل contraceptive.

لا مانِعَ عِنْدي I have no objection.

مأْنوس familiar, customary, habitual.

ماهِر skilled, clever, adept, skillful, proficient.

مُؤَهَّل qualified for, competent, able, deserving; fit for, suited for, worthy of; meritorious.

مُؤَهِّلات (ج) qualifications, abilities, aptitudes, merits.

مَأْهُول inhabited.

ماهِيَّة essence, nature, substance.

مَأْوَى shelter, refuge, haven, asylum.

مَأْوَى dwelling, habitation, lodgings, house.

مَؤُونَة provisions, supplies, victuals; materiel (army).

مِئَوِيّ centesimal; centenary, centennial (anniversary).

قِياسٌ مِئَوِيّ centigrade measure.

نِسْبَةٌ مِئَوِيَّة percentage.

دَرَجَةٌ مِئَوِيَّة degree centigrade.

مُؤَيَّد supported, upheld, confirmed, corroborated, endorsed, approved, sustained.

مُؤَيِّد supporter, upholder, partisan, proponent, endorser, countenancer, backer, advocator.

مُباح permissible, allowed, lawful, legal, authorized.

مُباح public, common, open to everyone.

مُباحَثَة discussion, dialogue, debate, talk, conversation; negotiation, parley.

مُبادَرَة initiative, enterprise; undertaking; starting, initiation.

مُبادَلَة interchange, exchange; barter, swap, trade-off, reciprocity; requital, returning in kind.

مُباراة match, competition, contest, test, game.

مُباراةٌ نِهائِيَّة finals, play-off game.

مُبارَزَة competition, contest; duel; fencing.

مُبارَك blessed, fortunate, lucky; congratulations.

مُبارِك blesser, well-wisher.

مُبارَكَة blessing, benediction, well-wishing, congratulation; sanction, endorsement, consent, approval.

مُباشِر (ص) direct, immediate, firsthand.

مُباشِر (اسم) court usher, bailiff.

مُباشَرَة pursuit, practice, start, commencement, carrying out.

مُباشَرَةً directly, immediately, firsthand.

مُباع sold.

مُباعَدة separation, alienation, estrangement; isolation, elimination; sowing of dissension.

مُباغِت surprising, sudden, unexpected, unforseen.

مُباغَتَة surprise; sudden event; sudden attack.

مُبالٍ (المُبالي) mindful of, attentive to, concerned about.

مُبالاة attention, heed, concern, interest.

مُبالَغٌ فيه exaggerated, overstated, magnified; unreasonable.

مُبالَغَة exaggeration, overstatment; hyberbole (language).

مُباهٍ (المُباهي) vainglorious, boastful, proud, braggart, boaster, show-off.

مُباهاة pride, vainglory, boastfulness.

مُبايَعَة homage, pledge of allegiance; induction, inauguration; appointment, assignment.

مُبْتَدَأ beginning, start; subject of a nominal clause (grammar).

مُبْتَدِئ	beginner, untrained, novice; unskilled, inexperienced; freshman.
مُبْتَدَع	contrived, invented, created, conceived.
مُبْتَدَع	innovation, invention, novelty, creation.
مُبْتَدِع	inventor, innovator, author, creator.
مُبْتَذَل	trite, banal, common, vulgar, commonplace.
مُبْتَزّ	extortioner, extortionist, blackmailer, usurer.
مُبْتَسَر	premature.
مُبْتَسِم	smiling.

مُبْتَغَى	sought after, desired, coveted.
مُبْتَغَى	desire, goal, endeavor, effort, wish, aim.
مُبْتَكَر	novel, innovated, original, new, created, designed; invented, unique, contrived,introduced.
مُبْتَكِر	creator, inventor, designer, innovator, deviser, maker, originator, author.
مُبْتَلّ	moist, damp, wet.
مُبْتَلًى بِـ	afflicted with, stricken by, suffering from.
مُبْتَهِج	rejoicing, jubilant, happy, glad, joyful, merry.
مَبْتُور	broken, unconnected; cut, severed.
مُبَجَّل	revered, respected, honored, venerable, exalted, esteemed; glorified; venerated, honorable.
مَبْحُوح	hoarse (voice).
مَبْحَث	theme, subject, field of investigation, discussion; object of research, study, examination.
مِبْخَرة	censer; fumigator; steamer.

يُحرق البخور في المبخرة فتتصاعد رائحته الذكيّة
Incense is burned in the censer and its sweet smell spreads everywhere

مَبْدَأ	principle, conviction of a person, ideology, concept; beginning, start , starting point; origin, basis.
مِنْ حَيْثُ المَبْدَأ	in principle.
مَبَادِئ (ج)	principles, rules, rudiments elements, concepts.
مَبْدَئِيّ	initial, fundamental, main, primary.
مَبْدَئِيًا	in principle, initially, tentatively.

مُبَدَّد scattered, dispersed, eliminated, driven away; wasted, squandered, dissipated.

مُبَدِّد scatterer, squanderer; wastrel, spendthrift, dissipator; extravagant, prodigal, lavish, profligate.

مُبْدِع producing, creating, creative; unique, exceptional, outstanding (in achievement); innovator, marvelous.

مُبَدَّل altered, changed, converted, transformed.

مُبَدِّل alterant, changer; commutator (elect.).

مُبَدِّلُ السُّرعَة gearshift (in car, machine).

مُبَذِّر squanderer, spendthrift, prodigal, lavish, extravagant, wastrel, careless spender.

مَبْذُول exerted, made, sacrificed, offered, spent, expended.

مِبْراة penknife; pencil sharpener.

مَبَرَّة act of charity; philanthropic foundation, charitable institution; benefaction; good deed.

مُبَرَّد frozen, cooled.

مُبَرِّد cooler, chiller, refrigerant, air cooler.

مِبْرَد file, rasp.

مُبَرَّر (ص) justified, justifiable, warranted.

مُبَرِّر (اسم) justification, excuse, warrant, reasonable grounds.

مُبَرِّرُ الوُجُود raison d'etre.

مُبَرِّز excelling, outstanding, distinguished, excellent; surpassing, superior; winner, victor (in a contest).

مُبْرَز (ص) brought out, exhibited, displayed, emphasized, exposed, presented, shown; accentuated.

مُبْرَز (اسم) exhibit.

مُبْرَم firm, strong; irrevocable, confirmed, ratified.

مِبْرَم spindle.

مُبَرْمَج programmed, scheduled.

مُبَرْمِج programmer.

مُبَرْهَن proved, established, substantiated, verified.

مَبْرُور accepted into the grace of God; blessed; valid, sound.

مَبْرُوم twisted, twined, rolled, curled; circular.

مُبَسَّط simplified, plain, uncomplicated.

مَبْسِم mouth; mouthpiece.

مَبْسِمُ السِّيجارَة cigarette holder.

مَبْسُوط extended, outstretched; extensive, great.

مَبْسُوط happy, glad, cheerful, feeling well, in good health.

مُبَشِّر preacher, missionary; harbinger, forerunner, precursor, bringer of good tidings.

مِبْشَرَة scraper, grater, rasp.

مَبْشُور grated, peeled, pared, scraped off.

مُبْصِر endowed with eyesight; acutely aware of; possessing knowledge of; discerning, discriminating.

مِبْضَع scalpel, dissecting knife.

مُبَطَّن lined, filled, padded (dress).

مُبَطَّن hidden, disguised; secret; implied, concealed.

مُبَعْثَر disarrayed, scattered, dispersed, strewn about; overturned, upturned, turned upside down, disordered; wasted, squandered, dissipated.

مُبْعَد removed, kept away, isolated, secluded; disqualified; excluded, repulsed; dropped.

مُبْعَد deported, banished, exiled, expatriated.

مَبْعُوث (ص) sent, dispatched, forwarded.

مَبْعُوث (اسم) envoy, delegate, emissary.

مَبْعُوج dented, notched.

مَبْغًى brothel, bordello, whorehouse; desire, goal, aspiration, endeavor, effort.

مُبْغِض hater, malicious, resentful, spiteful.

مَبْغُوت taken aback, surprised, stunned, dumbfounded, shocked, taken by surprise, flabbergasted.

مُبْكٍ (المُبْكِي) causing the flow of tears; lamentable, mournful, sad, deplorable.

مُبَكِّر، مُبْكِر premature, early in the morning; precocious.

مُبَلْبَل confused, disturbed, perturbed, upset, mixed up, deranged, disconcerted.

مُبَلَّط paved, tiled, slabbed.

مَبْلَغ amount, sum; extent, scope; range, limit.

مَبْلَغٌ مَقْطُوع lump sum.

مُبَلَّل، مَبْلُول wet, moist, damp, bedewed, drenched.

مُبَلْوَر crystallized.

مَبْنًى building, structure, edifice; form, structure, shape; style, phraseology, wording; foundation, basis.

مُبَنَّج anesthetized.

مُبَنِّج anesthetist.

مَبْنِيّ built, constructed, set up, developed, made, formed.

مَبْنِيٌّ على based on, founded on.

مَبْنِيّ indeclinable, with an undeclinable ending (language).

مُبْهِج pleasant, charming, delightful; beautiful, resplendent.

مُبَهْرَج ornate, flamboyant, pompous, adorned, embellished, bedecked, garnished, showy, tawdry, gaudy; cheap, trashy, rubbishy, inartistic.

مُبْهَم obscure, dark, cryptic, vague, ambiguous, dim, unintelligible, incomprehensible, enigmatic, mysterious.

مَبْهُوت astonished, astounded, amazed, shocked, dumbfounded, flabbergasted, bewildered, startled.

مَبْهُور dazzled, dazed, breathless, overwhelmed; startled.

مُبَوَّب — classified, categorized, assorted, grouped; arranged in groups.

مِبْوَلَة — chamber pot, urinal; latrine, water closet.

مُبَيَّت — hatched, premeditated, prearranged; hidden, concealed; contrived, plotted, schemed.

مُبيد — destructive, annihilative, lethal, eradicative.

مُبيدُ الأعْشاب — herbicide.

مُبيدُ الجَراثيم — germicide.

مُبيدُ الحَشَرات — insecticide.

مُبَيِّضُ الآنِيَة النُّحاسِيَّة — tinner, tinsmith.

مَبيع — sold, sale, selling.

مُبَيَّن — shown, demonstrated, manifested, displayed, revealed, exposed, indicated, stated, explained.

مَتَّ — to stretch, spread.

مَتَّ إلَيهِ بِصِلَة — to be related to, connected to, belong to.

مَتى؟ حَتّى مَتى؟ — when? whenever; till when?.

مُتابَعَة — following, pursuing, pursuit, prosecution, continuation; watching, study, inquiry; agreement, consent.

مُتَأثِّر — affected, influenced; impressed, touched, excited.

مُتاجَرَة — trade, business, commerce, dealing; exploitation.

مُتاح — available, at one's disposal, handy, accessible; granted, given; predestined, preordained.

مُتَأخِّر — late, delayed, tardy; backward, underdeveloped; overdue, outstanding, unpaid.

مُتَأخِّرٌ عن الدَّفع — defaulter, in arrears.

مُتاخِم — adjacent, contiguous, adjoining, touching, proximate.

مُتاخَمَة — adjacency, contiguity, proximity.

مُتَأرْجِح — fluctuating, vacillating, vibrating.

مُتآزِر — cooperating, collaborating, synergic.

مُتَأزِّم — aggravated, critical, strained.

مُتَأسِّف — sad, sorry, regretful.

مُتَأصِّل — deep-rooted, deep-seated; chronic, ingrained.

مَتاع، أمْتِعَة — effects, goods, chattels, belongings.

أمْتِعَةُ السَّفَر — luggage, baggage, suitcases.

مُتَأقْلِم — acclimatized, adapted, adjusted.

مُتَأكِّد — sure, convinced, assured, confident.

مُتآكِل — corroded, eroded.

مُتآلِف — harmonious, in harmony, in agreement, symphonic; friendly, familiar; united.

مُتَألِّق — brilliant, radiant, dazzling, bright, shining.

مُتَألِّم — aching, painful, in pain; suffering, deeply affected; tormented, anguished, excruciated.

مُتآمِر — conspirator, intriguer.

مُتأمِّل meditating, reflecting, contemplating, speculating; pensive, wistful.

مَتانَة solidity, firmness, sturdiness, strength.

مُتأنِّق spruced up, elegant, fashionable, smartly dressed; flowery, bombastic, pompous (speech).

مُتأهِّب ready, prepared, on call, on the alert.

مُتبادَل mutual, reciprocal.

مُتبارٍ (المُتَبارِي) participant in a contest; contestant, contender, competitor.

مُتَباعِد separate, far, faraway, remote; discordant, alienated, estranged.

مُتَباهٍ (المُتَباهِي) boastful, braggart, vainglorious.

مُتَبايِن different, differing; dissimilar, unlike, varying; opposed, contrary; disparate.

مُتَبحِّر well-versed in, proficient in, erudite, expert, authority.

مُتَبَخْتِر strutting, prancing, mincing

مُتَبَدِّل changeable, variable, inconstant, unstable.

مُتَبرِّع donator, grantor, donor; volunteer.

مُتَبَرِّم cross, peevish, vexed, annoyed.

مُتَبَصِّر discerning, understanding, discriminating, versed, proficient, knowledgeable, astute, shrewd.

مُتبَقٍّ (المُتَبقّي) residue, remnant, remainder, rest.

مُتَبَلْوِر crystallized.

مُتَبَنَّى (ص) adopted; embraced.

مُتَبَنَّى (اسم) adopted child.

مُتَتابِع successive, consecutive, sequential.

مُتَتالٍ (المُتَتالي) successive, consecutive, sequential, alternating; constant, uninterrupted.

مُتَثاقِل sluggish, dull, sullen, indolent, lazy.

مُتَجاذِب mutually attractive, inseparable.

مُتَجاسِر bold, daring, insolent, impudent.

مُتَجانِس akin, related, of the same kind or nature; homogeneous, identical, similar, alike, comparable.

مُتَجاوِب responsive, harmonious.

مُتَجاوِر having a common border, adjoining, adjacent.

مُتَجاوِز passing, overtaking, exceeding; trespassing, transgressing, overlooking; disregarding, letting pass.

مُتَجَبِّر haughty, arrogant, despotic, overbearing.

مُتَجَدِّد renewed; regenerated; new, novel, up-to-date, evolving, progressing.

مَتْجَر store, shop.

مَتْجَرٌ كَبير supermarket, departmental store.

مُتَجَرِّد just, unbiased, evenhanded, impartial.

مُتَجَعِّد curled, frizzed, wavy; furrowed, creased, wrinkled.

مُتَجَمِّد frozen, congealed, frosted; hard, solid; rigid; coagulated, clotted, curdled.

مُتَجَنِّس naturalized.

مُتَّجِهٌ إلى going to , heading for, aiming at.

مُتَجَهِّم sullen, grim, sulky, morose (face).

مُتَجَوِّل (ص) wandering, roving, ambulatory, strolling.

مُتَجَوِّل (اسم) traveler, rover, wanderer.

مُتَحَارِب belligerant, warring, in a state of war.

مُتَحَامِل discriminating, prejudiced, biased, partial.

مُتَحَجِّر petrified; antiquated, obsolete; narrow-minded, fanatic, bigoted; fossil; ossified.

مُتَحَجِّرُ الفُؤَاد stony-hearted, ruthless, cruel, merciless.

مُتَّحِد united, combined, integrated, merged, joined.

مُتَحَدِّث spokesman, speaker, narrator, teller.

مُتَحَدِّر descending from, born from, originating from; slanting, sloping, descending, declining.

مُتَحَرِّر freed, released, liberated; liberal, broad-minded, open-minded, emancipated.

مُتَحَرِّك moving, mobile; vowelized consonant (grammar).

مُتَحَزِّب biased, partial; party follower, partisan, adherent to a party, supporter.

مُتَحَسِّر sorrowful, sad, grieved, regretful.

مُتَحَضِّر civilized, cultured, urbanized; urbanite.

مُتْحَف، مَتْحَف museum.

يحتوي متحف بيروت على تحف وآثار تاريخية ثمينة

The museum of Beirut contains valuable historical antiquities and works of art

مُتَحَفِّز ready, on the alert, prepared, all set, ready to jump.

مُتَحَفِّظ reserved, vigilant, wary, cautious, reticent, sedate, staid.

مُتَحَكِّم despotic, absolute, high handed, domineering, arbitrary.

مُتَحَمِّس (ص) enthusiastic, zealous, passionate, eager, keen.

مُتَحَمِّس (اسم) zealot, fanatic, advocate, ardent supporter.

مُتَحَيِّر disconcerted, dismayed, embarrassed, perplexed, startled, at a loss, baffled, bewildered, confused.

مُتَحَيِّز partial, prejudiced, biased.

مُتَخَاذِل weak, languid; exhausted, spent, effete.

مُتَخَرِّج graduate, alumnus.

مُتَخَصِّص specialized, competent, duly qualified.

مُتَخَطٍّ (المُتَخَطِّي) overstepping, surpassing, going past, overtaking, transgressing, trespassing; transgressor, trespasser.

مُتَخَفٍّ (المُتَخَفِّي) disguised, masked, concealing oneself.

مُتَخَلًّى عنه abandoned, surrendered, relinquished; ceded, dropped, forsaken, yielded, disclaimed.

مُتَخَلِّف lagging, left behind, left over, retarded, backward, underdeveloped (mentally, in growth).

مُتَخَلِّف absent, absentee, truant; defaulter; residue, remainder, overplus, remains; waste, scrap.

مُتْخَم satiated, stuffed, sated, glutted, full.

مُتَدَاخِل overlapping, superimposed, intertwined, meshed.

مُتَدَاعٍ (المُتَدَاعِي) faltering, threatening to fall, ramshackle, shaky, unsteady, insecure, precarious.

مُتَدَاوَل current, circulating, in circulation, common.

مُتَدَخِّل meddlesome, interfering, obtrusive, nosy, prying.

مُتَدَخِّل meddler, intruder, prier, obtruder.

مُتَدَرِّب trained, drilled, schooled; apprentice.

مُتَدَرِّج progressive, graduated, gradated.

مُتَدَفِّق flowing out, gushing forth, streaming, jetting, pouring out, bursting forth; incessant, continuous.

مُتَدَلٍّ (المُتَدَلِّي) suspended, hanging, dangling, drooping.

مُتَدَنٍّ (المُتَدَنِّي) descending, falling; sinking, declining; inferior, poor, low, low-grade.

مُتَدَهْوِر deteriorating, declining, slumping, retrogressive.

مُتَدَيِّن pious, devout, religious.

مُتَذَبْذِب oscillating, vibrating; wavering, hesitating, vacillating; undecided, uncertain.

مُتَذَلِّل servile, submissive, abject.

مُتَذَمِّر complaining, nagging, grumbly, grumbling.

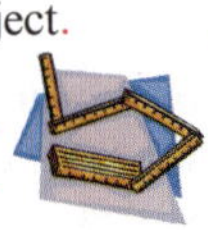

مِتْر meter (measure of length).

مُتَرَابِط correlated, interrelated, associated, attached, coupled, joined; inherent, cohesive.

مُتَرَادِف synonymous; synonym.

مِتْرَاس barricade, rampart.

مِتْرَاس الباب bolt, latch, lock.

مُتَرَاصِف aligned, well set, compact; stratified.

مُتَرَافِق associated, joined, accompanying one another.

مُتَرَاكِب overlapping, superimposed.

مُتَرَاكِم accumulated, heaped up, piled up.

مُتَرَامٍ (المُتَرَامِي) wide, vast, extensive.

مُتَرَتِّب على resulting from, consequent, following from, ensuing from, arising from, caused by; occasioned by.

مُتَرْجِم translator, interpreter.

مُتَرَدٍّ (المُتَرَدِّي) declining, deteriorating; low, inferior.

مُتَرَدِّد hesitant, undecided, uncertain, wavering.

تَيَّارٌ مُتَرَدِّد alternating current.

مُتْرَف luxurious, sumptuous, splendid; self-indulgent.

مُتَرَفِّع lofty, haughty, disdainful.

مُتَرَقِّب expecting, anticipating, awaiting, looking forward to.

مُتَرَهِّل flabby, flaccid.

مَتْرُوك abandoned, renounced, foresaken; left out, neglected, disregarded.

مَتْرُوك left over, remainder, residue, remains.

مِتْرِيّ metric.

مُتَزَامِن synchronous, synchronized, concurrent; contemporary.

مُتَزَايِد increasing, growing, heightening, augmenting.

مُتَزَعْزِع shaky, unsteady, unstable, precarious.

مُتَزَلِّف adulator, flatterer, sycophant, bootlicker.

مُتَزَمِّت rigorous, rigid, austere, strict, stern.

مُتَّزِن sober-minded, grave, solemn, composed; judicious, prudent, reasonable; having sound judgment.

مُتَزَوِّج married.

مُتَسَابِق contestant, competitor, contender; racer, runner.

مُتَسَارِع accelerated, accelerating, hurrying, running.

مُتَسَامِح indulgent, merciful, lenient, tolerant.

مُتَسَاهِل indulgent, tolerant, lenient, forbearing.

مُتَسَاوٍ (المُتَسَاوِي) equal, even, similar, equipoised, like.

مُتَسَاوِي الأَضْلاع equilateral (geometry).

مُتَسَاوِي الزَّوايا equiangular (geometry).

مُتَسَاوِي الأَبْعَاد equidistant.

مُتَسَتِّر disguised, in disguise, incognito; hidden, concealed.

مُتَسَرِّع hasty, quick, fast, prompt, rapid, precipitate.

مُتَّسَع vast expanse, room, space.

مُتَّسَعٌ من الوقت enough time, plenty of time.

مُتَّسِع vast, wide, extensive; spacious, roomy; large, ample.

مُتَّسِق in good order, balanced, harmonious.

مُتَسَكِّع loiterer, loafer, wanderer, idler.

مُتَسَلْسِل serial, successive, consecutive, interlinked.

مُتَسَلِّط domineering, dominating; ruling, governing.

مُتَسَلِّق climbing, ascending, mounting.

مُتَسَلِّق climber, mounter, scaler.

مُتَسَلِّل sneaking, slipping, penetrating.

مُتَسَلِّل infiltrator, sneaker.

مُتَّسِم marked by, characterized by, distinguished by.

مُتَسَوِّل beggar, mendicant.

مُتَشَائِم pessimistic, pessimist.

مُتَشَابِك intertwisted, intertwined, interwoven; tangled, twined; complicated, intricate.

مُتَشَابِه similar, alike, akin, identical.

مُتَّشِح clad in, attired in, dressed in, garbed in.

مُتَشَدِّد strict, severe, rigorous, tough, austere; inflexible, intransigent, unyielding.

مُتَشَرِّد vagabond, vagrant; rogue, tramp, homeless.

مُتَشَعِّب ramified, branching; subdivided, divergent, manifold, diverse; forked.

مُتَشَوِّش muddled, jumbled, confused, disturbed, deranged.

مُتَشَوِّش الفِكْر bewildered, baffled.

مُتَشَوِّق longing, yearning, craving, desirous, covetous.

مُتَصَارِع wrestling, struggling, fighting.

مُتَصَاعِد rising, mounting, soaring, growing, increasing; emanating; emitted, discharged; ascending.

مُتَصَدِّع cracked, split, cleft.

مُتَصَرِّف governor, administrative officer.

مُتَّصِف characterized by, distinguished by.

مُتَّصِل persistent, continued, unceasing, uninterrupted; contiguous, closely connected; related to, relevant to.

ضَمِيرٌ مُتَّصِل pronominal suffix (grammar).

مُتَّصِلُ الحَلَقَات interlinked.

مُتَصَلِّب inflexible, adamant, relentless, hard, unyieding.

مُتَصَوَّر imagined, concieved, visualized, envisioned, assumed.

مُتَصَوِّف mystic, Sufi.

مُتَضَائِل dwindling, decreasing, diminishing, declining.

مُتَضَارِب conflicting, discordant, contradictory, opposite, inconsistent, incompatible, opposed.

مُتَضَافِر collaborative, cooperative, synergic.

مُتَضَامِن consolidated, joined; jointly liable, responsible.

مُتَضَايِق irritated, disturbed, annoyed, vexed.

مُتَضَخِّم inflated, exaggerated, magnified.

مُتَضَرِّر injured, harmed, damaged, aggrieved.

مُتَضَمَّن included, contained, comprised in, incorporated.

مُتَضَمِّن including, containing, comprising, implying, involving.

مُتَطَاوِل impudent, insolent, impertinent; lengthened, elongated, extended, protracted.

مُتطرِّف، المُتطرِّف extreme; immoderate, unrestrained; radical, extremist.

مُتطفِّل، المُتطفِّل parasitic, intrusive, prying; intruder, prier, meddler, obtruder.

مُتطلِّب demanding, exacting, requiring, needing.

مُتطلَّبات (ج) requirements, requisites, prerequisites, demands, exigencies, necessities.

مُتطوِّر developed, sophisticated, advanced.

مُتطوِّع volunteer, unsalaried trainee.

مُتظاهِر demonstrator; pretender, faker, simulator.

متَّع to make enjoy; to enjoy oneself, have a good time.

متَّع النَّظر to feast one's eyes on.

مُتعادِل equal, even; balanced, on a par, in equilibrium.

مُتعارِض conflicting, inconsistent, contradictory, opposed.

مُتعارَفٌ عليه conventional, prevailing, practised, accepted, recognized, customary, common.

مُتعاطِفٌ مع sympathetic with, favorably disposed to.

مُتعاظِم increasing, growing, rising; proud, arrogant, haughty, presumptuous, supercilious.

مُتعاقِب successive, sequential, consecutive.

مُتعاقِد، مُتعاهِد contracting party, contractor.

مُتعالٍ (المُتعالي) transcendental; the Most High (God).

مُتعامِد perpendicular, rectangular, orthogonal.

مُتعاوِن، المُتعاوِن cooperating, collaborating, synergic; collaborator, cooperator.

مُتعِب wearing, tiring, exhausting, strenuous, uncomfortable, vexing, onerous, wearisome, troublesome.

مُتعبِّد devout, pious, worshiper.

مُتْعة enjoyment, pleasure, delight, gratification.

مُتعجِّب astonished, amazed, surprised, befuddled.

مُتعجرِف arrogant, supercilious, presumptious, concerted.

مُتعدٍّ (المُتعدّي) aggressor, assailant; transitive (grammar).

مُتعدِّد manifold, multiple, plural, numerous, diverse.

مُتعذِّر impossible, unfeasible, too difficult to achieve or to reach, impracticable.

مُتعرِّج zigzag, winding, twisting, tortuous, sinuous.

مُتعسِّر difficult, adverse, hard.

مُتعصِّب (ص) fanatic, prejudiced, bigoted, enthusiastic.

مُتعصِّب (اسم) fanatic, bigot, zealot, enthusiast.

مُتعطِّش yearning, longing, desirous, anxious, eager, aspiring; thirsty; languishing; craving, covetous.

مُتعلِّق related to, concerning, regarding, pertaining to, associated with, relevant to; clinging to, adhering to, sticking to, hanging on to; in love with, fond of; conditional on, dependent on.

مُتعلّم educated, literate.

مُتعمّد deliberate, premeditated, intentional, willful.

مُتعنّت obstinate, stubborn, inflexible, unyielding, adamant.

مُتعهّد contractor; bound by. committed by.

مُتعوّد used to, habituated to, accustomed to.

مُتغضّن wrinkled, puckered, corrugated, crumpled, creased.

مُتغطرِس haughty, arrogant, supercilious, conceited, presumptuous, insolent, overproud.

مُتغيّر variable, changeful, inconstant, unstable.

مُتغيّرات (ج) variables.

مُتفائِل optimist, optimistic.

مُتفاعِل interacting, interactive; reacting, reactive.

مُتفاقِم aggravated, grave, critical, intense; growing in gravity, spreading dangerously.

مُتفاوِت differing, divergent, disparate, uneven.

مُتفجّر explosive, blasting.

مُتفجّرات (ج) explosives, bombs.

مُتفرّج spectator, onlooker, viewer; bystander.

مُتفرّجون، نظّارة (ج) audience, spectators, onlookers, viewers.

مُتفرّع ramified, branching; bifurcating, subdivided

مُتفرّغ devoted to, dedicated to, exclusively occupied with.

مُتفرّق separated, divided, dispersed, irregular.

مُتفرّقات sundries, miscellaneous items, odds and ends.

مُتّفق عليه agreed upon, customary, conventional, acceptable.

مُتّفِق congruous, concordant, analogous; suitable, fit, appropriate; acceptable, convenient.

مُتفهّم understanding, sympathetic, broad-minded.

مُتفوّق surpassing, outstanding, excellent, preponderant.

مُتقابِل opposite, to each other, facing each other.

مُتقارِن coupled, connected, associated, paired, joined.

مُتقاطِع crisscross, intersecting.

مُتقاعِد retired, pensioner.

مُتّقِد burning, flaming, blazing, aflame; ardent, fervent, passionate, zealous, vehement; hot, ebullient.

مُتقدّم advanced, developed, moving forward, going ahead.

مُتقدّم in progress, under way.

مُتقدّم front, frontal, foremost; first, ahead.

مُتقدّم preceding, antecedent, previous, prior, earlier, old, ancient; advanced in years, aged.

مُتقطّع intermittent, sporadic, occasional, interrupted.

مُتقلّب inconstant, unsteady, unstable, whimsical, wavering.

مُتقلّص contracted, shrunken, dwindling, decreasing, declining.

مُتْقَن accurate, masterly, skillful, excellent, well-done, dextrous, perfect, superior, brought to perfection.

مُتَقَهْقِر retreating, retracting, receding, declining, moving backward, regressive.

مُتَقَيِّد بِـ complying with, abiding by, respecting, honoring, conforming to; bound, tied, committed, obligated.

مُتَّكَأ support, prop; pillow, rest; couch, sofa.

مُتَكَاثِر increasing, growing, proliferating.

مُتَكَافِئ equivalent, equal, even; corresponding, commensurate.

مُتَكَافِل guaranteeing each other, jointly liable; joined, combined, consolidated.

مُتَكَامِل integral, complementary, total, thorough.

مُتَكَبِّر proud, haughty, supercilious, insolent, arrogant.

مُتَكَرِّر recurring, recurrent, repeated, frequent.

مُتَّكِلٌ على relying on, depending on, trusting in.

مُتَكَلِّف affected; artificial; constrained, feigned, assumed.

مُتَكَلِّم speaker, talker, spokesman; theologian.

مُتَكَيِّف adaptive, pliable, adjustable.

مُتَلائِم suitable, agreeable, convenient, appropriate, adequate, timely, in harmony with, concordant, conforming, congruent, apt; feasible, proper, adapted.

مُتَلاحِق successive, consecutive, continuous, unceasing.

مُتَلازِم correlative, inseparable, inherent, associated, concurrent, attached, connected.

مُتَلاشٍ (المُتَلاشِي) vanishing, dwindling, declining, fading; transient, fleeting, transitory, volatile.

مُتَلألِئ shining, glimmering, sparkling, radiant.

مُتَلامِس touching, in contact with, adjoining to, tangent.

مُتَلَعْثِم stuttering, stammering; stumbling, hesitating.

مُتَلَكِّئ laggard, tardy, hesitant, late, slow.

مُتَلَهِّف yearning, anxious, eager, longing; regretful, sorry, sad, grieved.

مُتَلَوِّن fickle, unsteady, whimsical, changeable.

مُتَماثِل similar, analogous, corresponding, homologous, even, homogenous, identical, alike, akin.

مُتَمارِض feigning illness; malingering.

مُتَماسِك cohesive, coherent, sticking, together, consistent, solid, concrete, firm, firmly connected; tenacious.

مُتَمايِل reeling, staggering, wavering, swaying, tottering.

مُتَمَدِّد lying down, prostrate, reclining; expansible, expandable; distended, expanded, stretched, spread out.

مُتَمَدِّن civilized, cultured, civil, urban, refined, educated, sophisticated.

مُتَمَرِّد refractory, recalcitrant, disobedient, insubordinate, mutinous, rebellious.

مُتَمَرِّس experienced, sophisticated.

مُتَمَرِّن experienced, trained, skilled, seasoned, used to.

المُتَمَرِّن probationer, apprentice, trainee.

مُتَمَسِّكٌ بـ holding fast, hanging on, clinging, adhering to; tenacious of, devoted to, attached to, holding on to.

مُتَمَكِّن versed in, skilled with, learned, proficient, conversant with, well-acquainted with; adept, master.

مُتَمَكِّن strengthened, cemented, firmly established, consolidated, deep-rooted, deeply ingrained; lasting, enduring, declinable (grammar).

مُتَمَلِّص، المُتَمَلِّص evasive, elusive; dodger, evader.

مُتَمَلِّق adulator, flatterer, sycophant, cajoler.

مُتَمَلِّك possessor, proprietor, holder.

مُتَمَلْمِل fidgety, restless, nervous.

مُتَمِّم complementary, integral, completing, perfecting.

مُتَمَهِّل slow, deliberate, easygoing.

مُتَمَوِّج wavy, curly, curled, frizzled; undulating, undulatory; undulated, waved.

مُتَمَوِّل wealthy, rich, financier, capitalist, well-to-do.

مُتَمَيِّز distinguished, marked, notable, outstanding, prominent, characterized by distinctive traits.

مَتَّنَ to strengthen, consolidate, fortify.

مَتْن back; text, body (of book); middle of the road.

على مَتْن aboard, on board of.

مُتَناثِر scattered, dispersed.

مُتَنازَعٌ عليه disputed, contested, controversial, at issue, litigated matter.

مُتَنازِع disputing party, contending party, litigant.

مُتَنازَلٌ عنه relinquished, abandoned, surrendered, waived, renounced, ceded, disclaimed; assigned, alienated.

مُتَنازِل assignor, transferor, alienator (of property).

مُتَناسِب proportionate, proportional, mutually corresponding, analogous, even, regular, symmetrical.

مُتَناسِق well-ordered, well-arranged, regular, symmetrical.

مُتَناظِر (ص) corresponding, analogous, homologous, similar, alike, symmetrical.

مُتَناظِر (اسم) debater, disputant, analog, interlocutor.

مُتَناغِم in harmony, in agreement, consonant, concordant.

مُتَنافِر discordant, conflicting, incompatible, inconsistent, not in accord, disagreeing, incoherent; dissonant (voice).

مُتَنافِس competitor, contestant, rival, contender.

مُتَناقِص decreasting, diminishing, growing less, shrinking, waning, dwindling, declining.

مُتَناقِض contradictory, incompatible, inconsistent, conflicting.

مُتَناقِضات (ج) contrasts, contrarieties, contradictions, paradoxes.

مُتَناوِب alternating, rotating.

تَيّارٌ مُتَناوِب alternating current.

مُتَناوَل taken, obtained.

مُتَناوَلٌ (للبَحْث) dealt with, handled, treated, tackled, discussed, studied, considered, covered, comprised.

في المُتَناوَل within reach, at hand, available, on hand.

مُتَنَزِّه walker, stroller, excursionist, picnicker.

مُتَنَصِّت eavesdropper.

مُتَنَفِّذ influential, powerful.

مُتَنَفَّس vent, outlet.

مُتَنَقِّل mobile, movable, moving; portable; itinerant, ambulant, roaming, migratory; nomadic, nomad.

مُتَنَوِّع various, varied, variegated, diverse, diversified, manifold.

مُتَهاوِد moderate, low, reduced (price).

مُتَهاوِن negligent, careless, indifferent, remiss, lax.

مُتَهَتِّك dissolute, insolent, impudent, shameless, immoral.

مُتَهَدِّج trembling, wavering, quavering (voice).

مُتَهَدِّل hanging loosely, flowing, dangling.

مُتَهَدِّم torn down, destroyed, devastated, ruined, in ruins.

مُتَهَرِّب، المُتَهَرِّب evasive, elusive; evader, dodger, eluder.

مُتَهَكِّم sarcastic, satirical, mocking, derisive, sneering.

مُتَّهَم accused, charged, indicted, impeached, suspect.

مُتَهَوِّر rash, hasty, precipitate, frivolous, thoughtless, light-headed, imprudent, careless, reckless, foolhardy.

مُتَهَيِّب respectful, reverential; timid, timorous, shy, diffident, dreadful.

مُتَهَيِّج agitated, upset, excited; impassioned.

مُتَوائِم harmonious, in harmony with, concordant.

مُتَواجِد found, available, on hand, existing, present, in existence.

مُتَواجِه opposite to each other, facing each other.

مُتَوارَث hereditary, inherited, bequeathed.

مُتَوازٍ، (المُتَوازِي) parallel; corresponding, equivalent, equal.

مُتَوازِي الأضْلاع parallelogram.

مُتَوازِن equally balanced, in equilibrium, even, equal, stable.

مُتَواصِل continuous, continued, presistent, unceasing; interconnected, unbroken.

مُتَواضِع humble, modest, unpretentious; small, trivial, negligible, slight.

مُتَوافِر available, obtainable; abundant, plentiful, profuse, ample, numerous.

مُتَوافِق harmonious, agreeing, concordant, compatible, conforming, analogous; suitable, fit, appropriate, convenient, congruous, consistent.

مُتَوالٍ (المُتَوالي) successive, consecutive, continuous, unbroken, alternating, alternate, rotating.

مُتَوَتِّر strained, tense, uptight.

مُتَوَّج crowned, enthroned; topped, capped.

مُتَوَحِّش wild (animal); savage, barbarous, brutal, cruel (person).

مُتَوَرِّط involved, implicated, embroiled.

مُتَوَرِّم swollen, tumid, tumescent, turgescent.

مُتَوَسِّط middle, central, median, intermediate, medium; mean, midway; moderate; average, mediator; intermediary.

مُتَوَسِّل ، المُتَوَسِّل entreating, imploring, begging; supplicant, suppliant, solicitor, petitioner.

مُتَوَعِّد threatening, menacing.

مُتَوَعِّك indisposed, unwell, ill, not feeling well.

مُتَوَفًّى dead, deceased, defunct.

مُتَوَفِّر available, obtainable; ample, abundant, plentiful.

مُتَوَقِّد الذِّهن impulsive; having a lively mind, sharp, witty.

مُتَوَقَّع expected, anticipated, foreseen.

مُتَوَقِّف dependent on, conditional on, subject to; motionless, coming to a stop, stopped, halted.

مُتَوَلٍّ (المُتَوَلّي) in charge of, entrusted with, taking care of, assuming, undertaking, carrying, occupying.

مُتَوَهِّم imagining, suspecting, fancying, mistaken, misled.

مُتَيَسِّر available, obtainable, feasible, simplified.

مُتَيَّم enthralled by, infatuated by, crazy about, madly in love with, captivated by, enchanted by.

مَتين solid, strong, firm, tough, sturdy.

مُثابِر persevering, diligent, industrious.

مُثابَرَة perseverance, diligence, industry, assiduity.

مَثّال sculptor.

مِثال type, model, pattern, paradigm; ideal, example; epitome, embodiment, symbol; illustration, ease; quantity.

على سبيل المِثال for example, for instance, e.g..

مِثاليّ ideal, typical, exemplary, perfect, utopian.

مُثَبَّت fixed, fastened, stabilized, braced, consolidated; established, confirmed, sure, certain, proven.

مُثَبِّت fixer, stabilizer, fastener; mordant (of color).

مُثْبَت proven, established, substantiated; confirmed, corroborated, upheld, positive; registered, recorded, put down in writing, listed.

مُثَبِّط frustrating, disappointing, discouraging, depressing, demoralizing.

مِثْقَب drill, auger, perforator, punch.

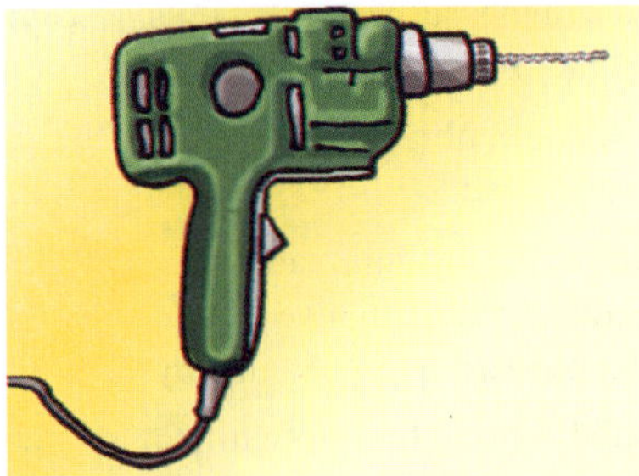

المثقب آلة كهربائية تستعمل
لقدح الثقوب في الجدران

The drill is an electrical instrument used to perforate holes in walls

مُثَقَّف cultured, educated, literate, refined, erudite.

مُثْقَل ، مُثَقَّل overburdened, overloaded, surcharged.

مَثْقُوب pierced, punctured, perforated, bored.

مَثَلَ to appear before, present oneself to; to appear, come into view; to resemble, look alike; to compare, to represent, mean, signify; to stand for; to come forward.

مَثَّلَ to represent, stand for, symbolize, exemplify, serve as an example; to portray, depict, describe; to compare to, liken to; to assimilate food (after digestion).

مَثَّلَ دَوْراً to act, perform a role or part (in a play); to star in.

مَثَّلَ to make an example of; to punish someone most cruelly; to mutilate, maim a victim's body.

مَثَل example, instance; proverb, saying, maxim, aphorism; lesson, warning; ideal, pattern, model.

مَثَلاً for example, for instance, e.g., such as.

مِثْل similar to, analogous, just as, one like, the same as; likewise, equally, also, too.

مُثْلَى ideal, exemplary, perfect (feminine case).

مُثَلَّث triangle.

يقال للجسم الهندسي ذي
ثلاثة جوانب بأنه شكل مثلث

A geometrical body having three sides is called a triangle

مُثَلَّثٌ حادُّ الزَّوايا acute triangle.

مُثَلَّثٌ قائِمُ الزَّوايا right triangle.

مُثَلَّثٌ مُتساوي الأَضْلاع equilateral triangle.

مُثَلَّثٌ مُنْفَرِجُ الزَّاوِية obtuse triangle.

مُثَلَّثُ الشَّكل	triangular.
مُثَلَّج	iced, frozen, ice-cold.
مُثْلِج	snowy.
مُثَلَّم، مَثْلوم	blunt, notched, indented, grooved, corrugated.
مِثْلَما	as, just as, like.
مُثْمِر	fruitful, profitable, productive.
مُثَمَّن	estimated, assessed, evaluated, appraised.
مُثَمَّنُ الزَّوايا	octagon, octagonal.
مُثَمِّن	estimator, evaluator, valuer, appraiser.
مُثَنَّى	double, twofold, dual; doubled, duplicated; repeated, reiterated.
مَثْنِيّ	folded, bent, twisted, curved, flexed.
مَثْوَى	abode, dwelling; inn, boardinghouse, motel.
مُثُول	appearance, presence.
مُثير (ص)	exciting, rousing, arousing, stimulating, provocative, instigating, breathtaking, spectacular, sensational.
مُثير (اسم)	inciter, instigator, rouser, stimulator; incentive, stimulus, impulse, motive.
مَثيل	like, identical, analogous, similar; equal, match; parallel, twin; image, picture.
لا مَثيلَ لَهُ	incomparable, matchless, peerless, unrivaled, unique.
مُجابَهَة	confrontation, facing, meeting, defiance, coping with.

مُجادَلَة	dispute, quarrel, argument, debate, discussion.
مُجاراة	keeping pace with, going along with; in conformity with, in accordance with.
مَجاز	passage, corridor, way, path; metaphor, allegory (grammar).
مَجازاً	figuratively, metaphorically.
مُجاز	permitted, allowed, authorized, licensed.
مُجازاة	repayment, remuneration; punishment, penalization.
مُجازِف (ص)	reckless, foolhardy.
مُجازِف (اسم)	adventurer.
مُجازَفَة	risk, venture, hazard; rashness, temerity.
مَجاعَة	famine, starvation.
مَجال	field, domain, sphere, province, area, range, extent, room, space; opportunity, chance.
مَجالٌ مَغْنَطِيسِيّ	magnetic field.
في هذا المَجال	in this connection, in this field, in this respect.
لا مَجالَ للشَّك فيه	to be incontestable, undoubted, irrefutable.
مُجالَسَة	company, social intercourse.
مُجامِل	courteous, polite flatterer, civil.
مُجامَلَة	courtesy, civility, compliment, flattery.
مُجامَلَةٌ دَوْلِيَّة	comity of nations.
مَجّان	impudent, shameless, brazen, insolent.

مَجّاناً، بِالمَجّان free, free of charge, gratis, at no cost; complimentary.

مُجانِب near, nearby, close, next to, neighboring, adjacent.

مَجّانِيّ free, free of charge, gratis, complimentary, at no cost.

مُجاهِد fighter, combatant, struggler, warrior.

مُجاهَرَة candor, frankness, avowal, announcement, disclosure.

مَجاهِل unexplored territory, unknown land or region.

مُجاوِر neighboring, proximate, adjacent, bordering, close to, nearby.

مُجاوَرَة neighborhood, vicinity, adjacency, closeness.

مُجَبِّر bonesetter, orthopedist, osteopath.

مَجْبُول formed, shaped, made; kneaded.

مَجْبُولٌ على naturally disposed for, having a natural property of.

مُجْتَزَأ shortened, cut short discounted, taken off, divided.

مُجْتَمَع society, human society, community; meeting place, gathering place.

مُجْتَمِع meeting, assembled, convened in session; combined, united, joined.

مُجْتَهِد (ص) diligent, industrious.

مَجْثَم roost, perch (of bird).

مُجْحِف unjust, unfair, prejudicial, harmful, inequitable.

مَجَّدَ to glorify, exalt, praise highly, eulogize.

مَجْد glory, honor; splendor, magnificence; nobility, distinction, grandeur.

مُجِدّ diligent, industrious, laborious, hard worker, assiduous, painstaking.

مُجْدٍ (المُجْدِي) useful, profitable, effective, workable, advantageous, beneficial, helpful.

مِجْداف oar.

مُجَدَّد renewed, renovated, updated, modernized; revived, regenerated, revitalized; repeated, remade.

مُجَدَّداً again, anew, once again, another time.

مُجَدِّد renewer, innovator, modernizer, reformer.

مُجَدِّف blasphemer; oarsman, rower.

مَجْدول twisted, woven, interwoven; braided, plaited.

مِجْذاف oar.

مُجَذِّف oarsman, rower.

مَجْذوب attracted, tugged, hauled; captivated, enchanted.

مَجْرَى watercourse, stream, canal, channel; conduit, duct.

مَجْرَى الأَحْداث course of events, direction of progress.

مَجْرَى النَّهْر riverbed.

مَجْرَى هَواء air stream, draft.

مُجَرَّب tried, tested, proven by experience, time-tested; experienced, seasoned, skilled.

مُجَرِّب tester, examiner, sampler.

مُجَرَّد mere, sheer, simply, just, no more than; abstract; first stem of a verb (grammar).

مُجَرَّدٌ من ثِيابِهِ bare, naked, undressed.

مُجَرَّدٌ مِن divested of, deprived of, stripped of; freed, disentangled from; devoid of; unsheathed (sword); emptied.

بِمُجَرَّد as soon as, immediately after.

مِجْرَشَة grinder, hand mill.

مِجْرَفَة shovel, scoop, spade, hoe.

يجرف الفلاح الرمل بواسطة المجرفة

The farmer moves earth with a spade

مُجْرِم criminal, culprit, delinquent.

مُجْرِمٌ عائِد recidivist, habitual criminal.

مَجْرُوح wounded, injured.

مَجْرُود (اسم) shovel, scoop, dustpan.

مَجْرُور (اسم) genitive case (grammar); sewer, drain, sink.

مَجْرُوش ground, crushed, grated.

مُجَزَّأ divided, partitioned, separated, fragmented.

مَجْزَرَة massacre, slaughter, blood path.

مَجْزُوم cut off, severed; decided, determined; in the apocopate form (grammar).

مَجَسّ tentacle, feeler, antenna (of insect).

مِجَسّ probe, sound; tentacle, feeler, antenna (of insect).

مُجَسَّد embodied, incarnate, corporeal, typified, symbolized.

مُجَسَّم embodied, incarnate, corporeal, shaped, formed; three-dimensional form, in relief, embossed; enlarged, exaggerated.

مُجَسَّم solid (engineering).

مُجَعَّد curly, frizzled, crimped, waved, wavy, kinky (hair); wrinkled, furrowed, creased, crinkled, crumpled, corrugated.

مُجَلٍّ (المُجَلِّي) excelling, distinguished, brilliant; winner; superior.

مَجَلَّة magazine, review, periodical.

مُجَلْجِل ringing, reverberating, rattling, clanking.

مُجَلِّخ sharpener, whetter, honer.

مُجَلَّد frozen, congealed; bound (book); volume, tome.

مُجَلِّد bookbinder.

مَجْلِس council, assembly, board; court, tribunal; seat; meeting, session; conference room, assembly hall.

مَجْلِسُ الإدارَة board of directors.

مَجْلِسُ الأعْيان senate, upperhouse.

مَجْلِسٌ إقْتِصادِيّ	economic council.
مَجْلِسُ الأمن	Security Council.
مَجْلِسُ أُمَناء	board of trustees.
مَجْلِسٌ بَلَدِيّ	municipal council, city council.
مَجْلِسٌ تَأدِيبِيّ	disciplinary board.
مَجْلِسٌ تَأْسِيسِيّ	constituent assembly or council.
مَجْلِسٌ تَشْرِيعِيّ	legislative assembly.
مَجْلِسُ ثورة	junta, revolutionary council.
مَجْلِسُ الخِدمَة المَدَنِيَّة	civil service board.
مَجْلِسُ الشَّعب	people's assembly.
مَجْلِسُ الشُّورى	state council.
مَجْلِسُ شُيوخ	senate.
مَجْلِسٌ عِرْفِيّ	court-martial.
مَجْلِسُ العُموم	House of Commons, Lower House.
مَجْلِسُ قِيادَةُ الثَّوْرَة	Revolutionary Command Council.
مَجْلِسُ اللُّوردات	House of Lords, Upper House.
مَجْلِسُ الملك الخاص	Privy Council.
مَجْلِسُ النُّوَّاب	parliament, chamber of deputies.
مَجْلِسُ الوزراء	council of ministers, cabinet.
مَجْلِسُ الوصاية على العرش	regency council.
مُجَمَّد	frozen, congealed, frosted, iced.
مُجَمَّد	coagulated, clotted, curdled.

مَجْمَع	assembly, congregation.
مَجْمَعٌ عِلْمِيّ	scientific academy.
مَجْمَع	junction, place of assembly, confluence of two rivers; box, case, can.
مَجْمَعٌ كَنَسِيّ	synod.
مُجَمَّع	accumulated, piled up, stacked; grouped, congregated.
مُجَمَّع	assembled, fitted together.
مُجَمَّع	complex (building); compound, collection, group.
مُجَمِّع	collector, storage battery, accumulator.
مُجْمِع	unanimous, agreed, of one accord.
مُجْمَل	concise, brief, summed up, abridged, synopsized.
مُجْمَل	summary, abstract, synopsis, resumé.
مُجْمَل	sum, total, whole.
مَجْمُوع	collected, grouped, united, assembled, accumulated, aggregated, stacked, crowded; added, added up.
مَجْمُوع، جُمِعَت الكلمة	put in the plural (grammar).
مجموع	sum, total, aggregate, score.
المَجْمُوع	everyone, the public, the masses.
مَجْمُوعٌ إجْمالِيّ	grand total.
مَجْمُوعَة	group, collection (of books, works of art, etc), list, series; alliance, league, bloc; aggregate, complex, block (of buildings); periodical, bulletin; team, body, bloc.

مَجَنَ — to joke, jest, scoff, mock, jeer; to be impudent, dissolute, uninhibited, dissipated.

مُجَنَّح — winged.

مُجَنَّد — enlisted, recruited, drafted; mobilized.

مُجَنَّد — recruit, conscript, draftee.

مُجَنَّس — naturalized.

مَجْنُون — insane, mad, lunatic, demented, crazy.

مَجْنُون — madman, maniac, lunatic, fool.

مَجْنِيٌّ عَليه — victim, aggrieved, injured, harmed party.

مُجْهَد — strained, overworked, exhausted, weary, fatigued.

مُجْتَهِد — strenuous, onerous, exhausting, tiring, fatiguing.

مِجْهَر — microscope.

يستعمل المجهر في المختبرات الطبية لمشاهدة الجراثيم

The microscope is used in laboratories to detect germs

مِجْهَرِيّ — microscopic.

مُجَهَّز — prepared, made ready; equipped with, furnished with, supplied with, provided with.

مُجَهِّز — supplier, furnisher, provider.

مَجْهُود — endeavor, effort, exertion, pains, trouble, work.

بَذَلَ مَجْهُودَهُ — to make every effort.

مَجْهُول — unknown, anonymous.

صِيغَةُ المَجْهُول — passive voice (grammar).

فِعْلٌ مَجْهُول — passive verb (grammar).

مُجَوَّف — hollow, concave, sunken, hollowed.

مُجُون — impudence, shamlessness; clowning, buffoonery.

مُجَوْهَرات — jewelry

مَجِيء — arrival, coming, incoming, advent.

مُجِيب — answering, answerer; respondent (to a case); responsive, susceptible, impressible, resonant.

مَجِيد — glorious, praiseworthy, admirable, splendid, illustrious, celebrated.

مُجِيد — proficient, skilled, excellent, brilliant.

مُخّ — yolk (of egg); essence, gist, pith.

مَحَا — to erase, wipe off, rub out, scratch out, strike out; to efface, blot out, obliterate; to wipe out, eradicate, exterminate, eliminate, abolish, extinguish.

مُحَاباة — favoritism, partiality, bias, prejudice; nepotism.

مُحَادَثَة — conversation, dialogue, discourse, talk, discussion.

مُحَاذٍ (المُحَاذِي) — opposite to, in front of, alongside of; parallel to, adjoining, neighboring, near.

مُحاذاة adjacency, neighborhood, vicinity, proximity.

مَحار oysters, mussels, shellfish.

مُحارِب warrior, combatant, fighter.

مُحارِبٌ قَدِيم veteran.

مُحارَبَة combat, battle, fighting, waging war against.

مُحازِب partisan.

مُحاسِب accountant, comptroller.

مُحاسِبٌ قانُونِيّ chartered accountant.

مُحاسَبَة accounting, settlement, clearing; accountancy.

مُحاصَر besieged, surrounded, blockaded, confined.

مُحاصَرَة besieging, beleaguering; blockade, siege.

مُحاضِر lecturer, speaker, reader.

مُحاضَرَة lecture.

مُحاطٌ بِـ surrounded by, encircled by, enclosed by.

مُحافِظ governor; conservative, old-fashioned; protector, defender, preserver; keeper, guardian, custodian, caretaker.

مُحافِظٌ عَلى المَوْعِد punctual.

مُحافَظَة preservation, guarding, protection, safekeeping; conservation, sustaining, upholding, retention, maintenance; compliance with, adherence to; governorate, province, administrative district.

مُحافَظَة على المَوْعِد punctuality, being on time.

مُحاكاة imitation, mimicry; resemblance, similarity.

مُحاكَمَة trial, prosecution, lawsuit, case, litigation.

مُحال impossible, unfeasible, hopeless, inconceivable, out of the question, absurd, preposterous.

لا مَحالَة certainly, definitely, absolutely, inevitably, by all means, unavoidably.

مُحالَفَة alliance.

مُحامٍ (المُحامِي) lawyer, attorney, barrister, advocate.

مُحاماة the bar, legal profession.

مُحاوِر interlocutor, talker.

مُحاوَلَة attempt, trial, effort, bid, endeavor.

مُحايِد neutral.

مُحايَدَة neutrality, neutralization.

مُحِبّ loving, affectionate; fond of, in love with; lover, fan, adorer.

مُحِبٌّ لِذاتِهِ egoistic, selfish, egocentric; egoist.

مُحِبٌّ لِلغَيْر altruistic; altruist.

مُحِبٌّ لِوَطَنِهِ patriotic; patriot.

مُحَبَّب lovable, attractive, agreeable, pleasing, charming.

مُحَبَّب granular, granulated, grainy.

مَحَبَّة love, affection, attachment.

مَحْبَرَة، مِحْبَرَة inkwell, inkstand.

مَحْبَس jail, prison, cell.

مِحْبَس trap, clasp, spigot.

مَحْبُوب beloved, dear, derisable; favorite, beloved one.

تُغمس ريشة الكتابة في المحبرة المملوءة بالحبر
The writing pen is dipped in the inkstand full of ink

مَحْبُوس imprisoned, jailed, detained; prisoner, convict.

مَحْبُوس isolated, secluded, separated, confined.

مَحْبُوك woven, knitted, meshed, tightened, fastened tight; well-knit, firm, solid, compact.

مُحْتَاج in need, in want; needing, wanting, calling for; requiring.

مُحْتَاج needy, poor, destitute, indigent.

مُحْتَار disconcerted, startled, perplexed, confused, dismayed, embarrassed, baffled, bewildered, uncertain.

مُحْتَال swindler, artful, treacherous, perfidious, cunning; cheat, imposter, fraud, crook, scoundrel; deceitful.

مُحْتَجّ، المُحْتَجّ protesting, remonstrating, objecting; protestant, remonstrant, protester, objector.

مُحْتَجَز restrained, confined, hindered; detained, arrested; attached, sequestered, impounded; confiscated.

مُحَدَّب convex, arched; crooked, curved, bent.

مُحَدِّث speaker, talker, narrator; moderniser, renewer.

مُحْدِث causer, author, maker, producer, causative.

مُحَدَّد specific, particular, concrete, determined, defined, fixed, decided upon, indicated, explicit, set, specified; limited, restricted, confined.

مُحَدَّد sharpened; hammered; pointed, tapering.

مُحَدِّد determining, distinctive, peculiar, specific; restrictive, limitative, limiting; determinant (math).

مُحْدِق surrounding, encircling, enclosing; imminent, impending.

مِحْدَلَة road roller, steamroller.

مَحْدُود bounded, bordered, circumscribed, confined, limited, delimited, determinate, fixed, definite, definitive.

مُحْدَوْدِب convex, hunched, arched, crooked, bent, curved, cambered.

مَحْذُور danger; misfortune, trouble, adversity.

مَحْذُوف deleted, canceled, removed, omitted, dropped; deducted, substracted; thrown away, discarded.

مِحْرَاب mihrab, prayer recess in a mosque.

مِحْرَاث plow.

مُحْرَج embarrassed, disconcerted, ill at ease.

مُحْرِج embarrassing, disconcerting, uneasy, perplexing.

مُحَرَّر liberated, freed, emancipated; consecrated to God.

مُحَرَّر edited, written, composed, compiled; document, deed, instrument in writing.

مُحَرِّر liberator; editor, writer, clerk.

مُحْرَز acquired, obtained, gained, attained, accomplished.

مُحَرَّض instigated, aroused, motivated, incited, provoked.

مُحَرِّض inciter, provoker, motivator, agitator, troublemaker.

مُحَرَّف distorted, perverted, corrupted, falsified, altered, changed.

مَحْرَقَة crematorium, holocaust.

مُحَرَّك vocalized (grammar).

مُحَرِّك driver, mover, engine, motor; motive, incentive, drive, impulse; stimulator, actuator, stirrer, inciter, instigator, agitator; stimulating, rousing, stirring.

مُحَرِّكُ المَشَاعِر touching, pathetic, emotional, exciting.

مُحَرِّكٌ دَاخِلِيّ الإِحْتِرَاق internal combustion engine.

مُحَرِّكٌ نَفَّاث jet engine.

مُحَرَّم prohibited, forbidden, interdicted, banned, outlawed, illegal, taboo, unlawful, illicit, unauthorized.

مَحْرَمَة handkerchief, tissue, napkin.

مَحْرَمَة holy, sacrosanct, sacred; forbidden, prohibited, unlawful; offense, sin; cursed action.

مَحْرُوس guarded, protected, shielded, kept safe from harm.

مَحْرُوق burned, charred, destroyed by fire.

مَحْرُوقَات fuel.

مَحْرُوم deprived of, bereaved of, bereft of; excluded, precluded, debarred from; underprivileged; disadvantaged; destitute, poor.

مُحَزَّز notched, indented; jagged, grooved, furrowed.

مُحْزِن saddening, doleful, depressing, melancholic, distressing, sorrowful, mournful; pathetic, tragic, heartrending, heartbreaking, dismal.

مَحْزُون grieved, pained, sad, mourning (for a deceased person).

مُحَسَّن improved, embellished, ameliorated.

مُحَسِّن ameliorative, improving, embellishing.

مُحْسِن beneficent, charitable, philanthropic, benefactor.

مَحْسَنَة ، مَحَاسِن advantage, merit; amenity; charms; advantages; good qualities, charming qualities.

مَحْسُوب calculated, reckoned, counted.

مَحْسُوبِيَّة patronage, favoritism nepotism.

مَحْسُود envied.

مَحْسُور bared, uncovered, tired, weary, exhausted; dim, dull; nearsighted (eyes); afflicted with near sightedness or myopia.

مَحْسُوس felt, palpable, tangible, perceptible, sensed; appreciable, considerable; real, physical, material.

مَحْسُوم severed; decided, determined, resolved, concluded; discounted, deducted, substracted.

مَحْشُوّ stuffed, padded, packed; loaded, charged (firearm).

مَحْشُور crammed, wedged, squeezed, jammed together, compressed, pressed; close, compact, tight.

مُحْصًى counted, computed, calculated.

مُحَصِّل collector.

مُحَصِّلُ ضَرائِب tax collector, revenue officer.

مُحَصَّن fortified, strengthened, reinforced; immunized (against an infection).

مَحْصُود harvested, reaped, cropped, mown.

مَحْصُور limited, confined, encircled, constrained; fixed, specified, determined; condensed, concentrated, squeezed, pressed; listed, compiled; exclusive, sole.

مَحْصُول yield, crop, produce, harvest; proceeds, receipts, output; content, import, meaning (of a speech).

مَحْض pure, unmixed, unadulterated; plain, straight, absolute.

بِمَحْضِ اخْتِيَارِهِ entirely of his own accord or choice.

لِمَحْضِ صَالِحِهِ solely in his own interest or good.

مَحْضَر minutes, procès verbal, report, record.

مُحَضَّر prepared, ready, made, produced.

مِحْضَن، مِحْضَنَة incubator.

مَحَطّ station; roost, perch (of birds); pause, finale (music).

مَحَطُّ الأَنْظَار focus of attention (attraction, interest).

مَحَطَّة station, terminal, stopping place, stopping point.

مَحَطَّةُ الإِذاعَة broadcasting station.

مَحَطَّةُ البَنزِين gas station.

مَحَطَّةُ سِكَّةِ الحَدِيد railway station.

مَحَطَّةٌ طَرَفِيَّة terminal.

مَحَطَّةٌ كَهْرَبَائِيَّة power plant.

مُحَطَّم smashed, crashed, broken crushed, wrecked, demolished.

مَحْظُور banned, prohibited, interdicted, outlawed, taboo.

مَحْظُوظ lucky, fortunate; happy, glad, contented.

مَحْفَظَة wallet, purse, billfold.

مَحْفَظَة handbag, purse, satchel.

مَحْفَظَةُ أوْراق folder, file, portfolio, briefcase.

مَحْفِل board; gathering, meeting; meeting place; lodge (Masonry).

مَحْفُور excavated, bored, drilled, dug; engraved, inscribed; carved, chased.

مَحْفُوظ kept, preserved, guarded; committed to memory; conserved, ensured, reserved, secured.

مَحْفُوظات archives; memorized material.

مَحْفُوفٌ بِـ fraught with, full of, involving, surrounded by.

مُحِقّ right, truthful, equitable, just, correct.

مُحَقَّق certain, beyound doubt, unquestionable; affirmed; realized, carried out, fulfilled, performed; ensured, secured; examined, investigated, verified, checked out.

مُحَقِّق investigator, examining magistrate, inquiry officer.

مِحْقَن، مِحْقَنَة syringe.

مِحَكّ standard, yardstick, gauge, criterion; touchstone (gold).

مُحَكِّم arbitrator, arbiter, umpire, referee.

مُحْكَم strengthened, reinforced, firm, solid, sturdy; tight, taut; perfect, masterly, masterful; well-aimed (shot); accurate, precise, exact; airtight, hermetic, impervious, tightly shut.

مَحْكَمَة court, tribunal.

مَحْكَمَةُ بِدايَة court of first instance.

مَحْكَمَةُ أحْداث juvenile court.

مَحْكَمَةُ اسْتِئْناف court of appeals.

مَحْكَمَةُ تحكيم court of arbitration.

مَحْكَمَةُ تمييز court of cassation.

مَحْكَمَةُ جنايات criminal court.

مَحْكَمَةُ أحْوالٍ شَخْصِيَّة personal status court.

مَحْكَمَةُ صُلْح court of peace, district court.

مَحْكَمَةُ العَدْل الدَّوْلِيَّة International Court of Justice.

مَحْكَمَةٌ عِرْفِيَّة court-martial.

المَحْكَمَةُ العُليا Supreme Court.

مَحْكُومٌ عَلَيْه convicted, condemned, sentenced; guilty.

مَحْكُومٌ عَلَيْه بِالفَشَل doomed to fail.

مَحْكِيّ told, related, narrated, reported.

مَحَلَ، مَحُلَ to be barren, arid.

مَحَلّ place, spot, site, location; scene, position, venue.

تباع مختلف الخضار والفاكهة في محل خضار
All kinds of vegetables and fruits are sold in the greengrocery

مَحَلٌّ تِجارِيّ	store, shop, firm, business firm.
مَحَلُّ إقامَة	domicile, address, residence.
مَحَلُّ نِزاع	object of dispute, controversial matter.
في مَحَلِّهِ	in place of, as a substitue for.
كانَ في مَحَلِّهِ	to be appropriate, advisable, justified.
في غَيرِ مَحَلِّهِ	misplaced, unsuitable, ill-suited, inappropriate.
لا مَحَلَّ لَهُ	there is no room for, it is out of place.
مَحَلُّ العَمَل	place of employment.
مَحَلُّ رُهونات	pawnshop.
مَحَلُّ اللَّهْو	amusement center.
مَحَلُّ نَظَر	deserving attention, remarkable.

مَحْل	barrenness, aridity; famine, dearth; deceit.
مُحَلًّى	sweetened; adorned, decorated, embellished.
مَحَلَّة	district, quarter, part of town.
مُحَلَّف	bound by oath; jury, member of a jury.
مُحَلِّق	in flight, flying.
مُحَلَّل	authorized, permitted, allowed, lawful, legal, legitimate; analyzed, resolved; disintegrated.
مُحَلِّل	analyser, analyst.
مُحَلِّلٌ نَفْسِيّ	psychoanalyst.
مَحْلول	solved, resolved, worked out; free, freed, liberated.
مَحْلول	solution.
مَحْلولٌ كَهْرَبائِيّ	electrolyte.
مَحَلِّيّ	local, indigenous, domestic, internal.
مُحَمَّص	roasted, toasted, grilled.
مَحْمَصَة	roastery.
مِحْمَصَة	roaster; toaster (of bread).
مُحَمَّل	loaded with, laden with, burdened with, encumbered with.
مَحْمود	commended, lauded; praiseworthy, laudable.
مَحْمول	carried, borne, transported, loaded; bearable, tolerable; predicate, attribute (logic).
مَحْمولٌ جَوًّا	airborne.
مَحْموم	feverish; frantic, frenetic, hectic, hysterical, raging, nervous, wild, stormy.
مَحْمِيّ	protected, safeguarded, sheltered, shielded.
مَحْمِيَّة	protectorate.

مِحْنَة	trial, affliction, calamity, disaster, ordeal, distress.
مُحَنِّط	embalmer (of dead persons); stuffer (of animals, birds).
مُحَنَّك	experienced, sophisticated.
مَحْو	erasure, wiping off; obliteration; eradication, elimination, abolition; effacement.
مِحْوَر	axis, pivot; center, heart, core, hub.
مِحْوَرُ العَجَلَة	axle, arbor.
مِحْوَرُ العَرَبَة	axletree.

مِحْوَرُ التَّمَاثُل axis of symmetry.

مُحَوِّل converter, transformer (elect.); switch.

مُحَيًّا countenance, face, mien, looks.

مُحَيِّر confusing, perplexing, enigmatic, confounding.

مُحِيط (ص) surrounding, encircling, enclosing, enveloping; acqainted with, familiar with; comprehensive, inclusive, complete, total.

مُحِيط (اسم) circumference, perimeter, periphery; environment, surroundings; ocean.

مُخّ cerebrum, brain.

مُخُّ العِظَام bone marrow, medulla.

مُخَابَرَة telephone call, communication.

مُخَاتِل deceitful, tricky, insincere, fraudulent, deceiver.

مُخَادِع deceitful, tricky, double-dealer, deceiver, fraud, cheat, crook, swindler, impostor.

مَخَاض labor pains (of childbirth).

مُخَاط nasal mucus.

مُخَاطَب addressee.

صِيغَةُ المُخَاطَب second person (grammar).

مُخَاطِب addresser, speaker.

مُخَاطَبَة، المُخَاطَبَة addressing, speaking to; speech, address, talk.

مُخَاطَرَة risk, hazard, venture.

مُخَاطِيّ mucous.

مُخَالَصَة acquittal, quittance, discharge; receipt.

مُخَالِف contrary to; divergent, varying, different; inconsistent, contradictory, contrasting, conflicting; in violation of, disagreeing with.

مُخَالِف dissident, dissenter.

مُخَالَفَة breach, violation, contravention, infringement; contrast, contrariety; mindemeanor; contradiction, inconsistency, disagreement, conflict.

مَخَاوِف apprehensions, anxieties, fears.

مَخْبَأ shelter, refuge, retreat, hideout, hideaway.

مَخْبَر laboratory.

مُخْبِر informer, informant; denouncer; detective, sleuth.

مَخْبَز bakery.

مَخْبُول insane, mentally deranged, crazy, imbecile.

مُخْتَار، المُخْتَار chosen, selected; choice, select; chief.

مُخْتَارَات (ج) selections, collected excerpts, selected writings.

مُخْتَال swaggering, prancing, vainglorious, arrogant, snob.

مُخْتَبَر، المُخْتَبَر tested, tried out, experimented upon; laboratory.

مُخْتَرِع inventor, maker, author, creator.

مُخْتَزِل stenographer, shorthand typist.

مُخْتَصّ competent, responsible, relevant, concerning, pertaining to, relative to.

مُخْتَصَر (ص) abbreviated, abridged, summarized, condensed; brief, short, concise.

مُخْتَصَر (اسم) summary, abridgment, synopsis, abstract, digest, resumé, précis, outline.

مُخْتَلّ disturbed, deranged, confused, upset.

مُخْتَلُّ التوَازُن out of balance.

مُخْتَلُّ العَقْل mentally deranged, demented, insane.

مُخْتَلِس embezzler, pilferer, stealer.

مُخْتَلِس السَّمْع eavesdropper.

مُخْتَلِس النَّظَر peeper, voyeur.

مُخْتَلَط mixed.

مُخْتَلِط mixed, mingled, combined; confused, muddled, mixed up, disarranged, disorganized.

مُخْتَلِف different, dissimilar, divergent, varying; various, diverse, sundry.

مُخْتَلِف disagreeing, discordant, at odds, at variance, dissenting.

مُخْتَلَق fabricated, trumped up, fictitious, concocted, pretended, false, contrived, invented, faked.

مُخْتَلِق inventor, faker, concocter, contriver.

مُخْتَمِر fermented, fermenting, leavened; ripe, mature.

مُخْتَنَق bottleneck, straits.

مَخْتُوم sealed, stamped, impressed; shut off, closed up.

مُخَثِّر thickener, curdling, congealing, coagulating, clotting.

مُخْجِل shameful, disgraceful, infamous, dishonorable.

مِخَدَّة pillow, cushion.

مُخَدَّد furrowed, grooved, corrugated, wrinkled.

مُخَدِّر anesthetic, narcotic, drug.

مَخْدَع، مُخْدَع، مِخْدَع room, bedroom.

مَخْدُوع deceived, fooled, bluffed, swindled, duped, tricked.

مُخَرِّب ravager, saboteur, subverter, destroyer, subversive.

مَخْرَج exit, way out, outlet, escape; articulation, vocalization.

مَخْرَجٌ مُشْتَرَك common denominator (math).

مُخْرِج director (screen or stage).

مِخْرَز drill, gimlet, auger, punch, perforator, awl.

مِخْرَطَة lathe.

مُخَرَّم perforated, punched; laced, done in filigree.

مَخْرُوط cone.

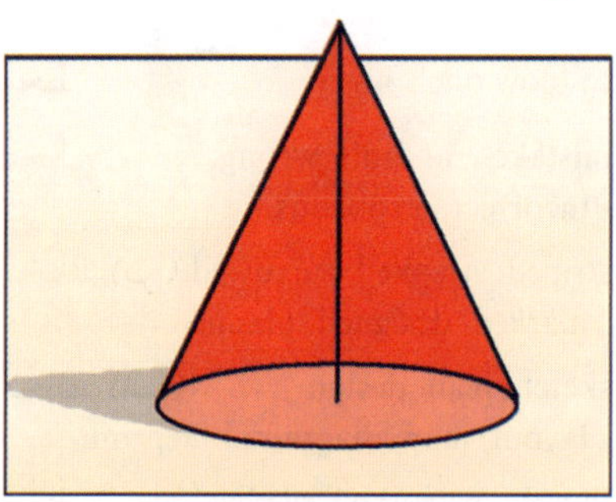

رسم الأستاذ شكل مخروط
يشبه القمع على السبورة
The teacher drew a cone on the blackboard resembling a funnel

أ ب ت ث ج ح خ د ذ ر ز س ش ص ض ط ظ ع غ ف ق ك ل **م** ن هـ و ي

مَخْرُوطِيّ — conic, conical.

مُخْزٍ (المُخْزِي) — disgraceful, dishonorable, shameful, scandalous, infamous.

مَخْزَن — warehouse, store, depot; shop.

مَخْزُون (ص) — stocked, stored, kept in stock, stockpiled.

مَخْزُون (اسم) — stock, supplies, hoard, stockpile.

مُخْزِيّ — ashamed, shamefaced, embarrassed, confused.

مُخَصَّص — specified, specialized, earmarked, assigned, designed for; dedicated, devoted, consecrated for; allotted, allocated.

مُخَصَّصَات (ج) — allowances, emoluments; appropriations, allocations.

مَخْصُوم — discounted, deducted, subtracted.

مُخَضْرَم — one who lived through paganism and Islam; one who lives through two epochs or generations.

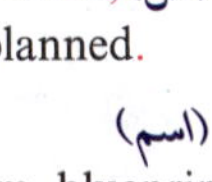

مَخَط — to blow one's nose.

مُخْطِئ — mistaken, at fault, wrong, incorrect, erroneous.

مُخَطَّط (ص) — striped, streaked, furrowed; marked, designed, planned.

مُخَطَّط (اسم) — sketch, plan, design, layout, map, diagram, blueprint.

مَخْطُوبَة — fiancée, betrothed, pledged in marriage.

مَخْطُوطَة — manuscript.

مَخْطُوف — kidnapped, abducted; hijacked, skyjacked (plane).

مُخَفَّض — reduced, lowered, low; moderate, lessened, decreased.

مُخَفَّف — diluted, thinned, watered; eased, softened, mitigated, relieved, appeased, relaxed, moderated, tempered.

مُخَفِّف — mitigative, alleviating, sedative (of pain); analgesic (of pain), palliative, allaying.

مُخْفِق — unsuccessful, failing, unfruitful.

مَخْفِيّ — hidden, concealed, veiled, covered.

مُخِلّ بِـ — infractor, contravener, defaulter; inconsistent with; in violation of; immoral, indecent, obscene (ethics).

مُخْل — crowbar, lever.

مِخْلَب — claw, paw.

مُخَلْخَل — disjointed, dislocated; rocked, convulsed; worn, shabby, tattered; rarefied, rare.

مُخَلِّص — rescuer, saver; savior, liberator.

مُخْلِص — sincere, honest, true; faithful, devoted, earnest, frank, loyal, candid, purehearted, righteous.

مَخْلُوط — mixed, blended, combined, admixed.

مَخْلُوع — taken off, extracted, uprooted; deposed, discharged, ousted, removed from an office; uninhibited, wanton, crazy, mad.

مَخْلُوق — created, fashioned, shaped; creature, created being.

مُخَمَّسُ الأضْلاع	pentagonal, pentagon.
مُخْمَل	velvet, plush.
مُخَمِّن	assessor, appraiser, estimator, valuer.
مَخْنُوق	strangled, throttled, suffocated, asphyxiated; smothered, suppressed, constricted (voice).
مُخَوَّل	entitled to, empowered to, authorized to; granted, accorded, conferred.
مُخَيَّر	free to choose, having the choice.
مُخِيف	fear-inspiring, frightful, dreadful, terrible, horrible, terrifying, appalling, horrifying, awesome, ghastly.
مُخَيِّلَة	imagination, fantasy, vision.
مُخَيَّم	camp, encampment.
مَدَّ	to extend, distend, expand, dilate; to stretch, stretch out; to draw out, protract, spread out, lay out; to lengthen, elongate, prolong; to rise (river); to help, aid, assist, support someone; to supply, provide, reinforce (an army).

مَدَّ البَصَر إلى	to turn one's eyes to.
مَدَّ رِجْلَيْهِ بِقَدْرِ لحافِهِ	to adjust oneself to the circumstances.
مَدَّ إلَيْهِ يَدَهُ	to extend one's hand to someone.
مَدَّ يَدَ المُسَاعَدَة	to lend a helping hand to.
مَدّ	extension, distention, expansion; stretching, spreading, lengthening, elongation, prolongation, protraction; rising, rise (of water); supply with.
مَدُّ البَصَر	range of vision; as far as the eye can see.
مَدُّ النَّظَر	farsightedness, foresight; hyperopia.
مَدَى	extent, range, stretch, expanse, scope, space; distance, interval; degree, scale, proportion, extreme, limit; duration, period.
على مَدَى	throughout, all through, all during, during.
مَدَى البَصَر	range of vision.
مَدَى الحياة	for life.
مَدَى العُمْر	lifetime.

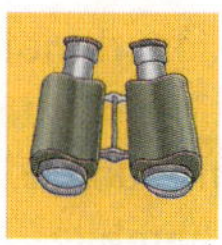

إلى مَدًى بعيد	at a great distance.
بَعِيدُ المَدَى	far-reaching; long-range.
مُداخَلَة	interposition, interference, intervention, participation.
مِداد	ink; manure, fertilizer; pattern, model, type.
مَدار	orbit, cycle, axis, pivot.
مَدارُ البَحْث	topic, subject, theme.
مَدارُ الجَدْي	Tropic of Capricorn.
مَدارُ السَّرطان	Tropic of Cancer.
على مَدارِ السَّنَة	all year round, throughout the year.
مُداراة	favoring, indulgence; flattery, cajolery; sociability.
مَدارِك	mental faculties, perception; the five senses.
مَداس	shoes, sandals.
مُداعَبَة	dalliance, joke, flirtation, making fun, jest.

مُدَافِع defender, protector, supporter; patron, sponsor.

مُدَافَعَة defense of, protection of.

مُدَان convicted, condemned, incriminated, denounced.

مُدَاهَمَة police raid, house search; raid, attack.

مُدَاوَاة treatment (of a sickness); medication, curing, therapy.

مُدَاوَاةٌ طَبِيعِيَّة physiotherapy.

مُدَاوَرَة evasion, elusion, deviousness, circumvention; cheating, trickery, shift, dodge, ensnaring, humbug.

مُدَاوَلَة parley, negotiation, deliberation, consultation, discussion, talk.

مُدَاوَلَةً alternately, one at a time.

مُدَاوَمَة persistence, perseverance, endurance, duration, continuation.

مُدَبَّج adorned, embellished; written in an elegant style.

مُدَبَّر arranged, planned, prepared; plotted, schemed; devised, contrived; concocted, hatched; deliberate, premeditated; procured, obtained, acquired; achieved, accomplished.

مَدْبَغَة tannery.

مَدْبُوغ tanned (skin).

مُدَّة period of time, duration, interval, term, while.

في مُدَّة in the course of, during.

مُدَّة من الزمن for some time.

مُدَجَّجٌ بالسِّلاح heavily armed, armed to the teeth.

مَدَحَ to praise, laud, extol.

مَدْح praise, laudation, extolment, eulogy, compliment, tribute.

مَدْخَل entrance, entry, inlet, access.

مَدْخَلٌ إلى موضوع دِراسِيّ introduction to a subject of study.

مُدَخِّن smoker.

مِدْخَنَة chimney, stack, funnel; brazier.

مَدْخُول revenue, income, receipts, returns; sickly, diseased, mentally abnormal, disordered, of weak character.

مَدَد aid, help, support, assistance; supplies, resources.

مِدْرَار torrential, flowing copiously, pouring forth; abundant, copious.

مُدَرِّب trainer, instructor, coach, drillmaster (army).

مَدْرَج runway, route, course.

مُدَرَّج (ص) gradated, scaled, progressive.

مُدَرَّج (اسم) amphitheater, stadium.

مُدْرَجٌ في included in, registered in, recorded in.

مُدَرِّس teacher, instructor, tutor, lecturer.

مَدْرَسَة school; doctrine.

مَدْرَسَةٌ ابْتِدَائِيَّة primary school, elementary school.

مَدْرَسَةٌ إعْدَادِيَّة preparatory school.

مَدْرَسَةٌ ثَانَوِيَّة secondary school, high school.

يذهب الأولاد إلى المدرسة لتلقي الدروس
Children go to school to attend classes

مَدْرَسَةٌ داخِلِيَّة boarding school.

مَدْرَسَةٌ رَسْمِيَّة public school.

مَدْرَسَةٌ مِهَنِيَّة technical training school.

مَدْرَسِيّ scholastic, academic.

كِتَابٌ مَدْرَسِيّ textbook.

قِسْطٌ مَدْرَسِيّ tuition fee.

مُدَرَّع armored.

مُدَرَّعَة cruiser, warship; armored vehicle, armored car.

مُدْرِك rational, reasonable, endowed with reason, intelligent; sexually mature; of legal age.

مَدْرُوس studied, deliberate, measured, carefully thought out, well planned, elaborate; obliterate, extinct; threshed.

مُدَّعٍ (المُدَّعِي) claimer, pretender, simulator, faker; assuming, pretending, simulating, faking; pretentious, presumptious, self-conceited, arrogant, vainglorious.

مُدَّعٍ (المُدَّعِي) impostor, cheat, swindler; claimant, plaintiff; prosecutor.

المُدَّعِي العام attorney general, prosecutor.

مُدَّعَى alleged, claimed, pretended, simulated, feigned.

مُدَّعَى عَلَيه defendant, respondent.

مَدْعُوّ invited, guest; called upon, requested; called, named, designated.

مَدْعُوم propped up, stayed, supported; consolidated, strengthened; corroborated, subsidized (from the state).

مِدْفَأَة heating stove, heater, fireplace.

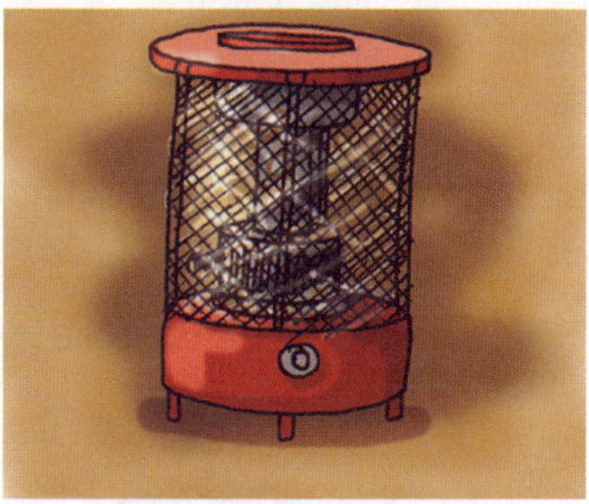

نستعمل المدفأة في فصل الشتاء البارد لتدفئة الغرف
The heating stove is used in cold weather to heat rooms

مِدْفَع gun, cannon.

مِدْفَعٌ مُضَادٌّ للطَّائِرات antiaircraft gun.

مِدْفَعُ هاون mortar.

مِدْفَعِيّ gunner, artilleryman.

مِدْفَعِيَّة artillery, battery.

مَدْفَن cemetery, graveyard.

مَدْفُوع paid, settled; disbursed, expended, spent.

مَدْفُوع driven back, repulsed, repelled, shoved away.

مَدْفُوع propelled, impelled, thrusted, pushed forward.

مَدْفُوع compelled, forced, obliged, coerced.

مَدْفُون buried; entombed.

مِدَقَّة pestle, mallet, gravel, hammer.

مُدَقِّق examiner, investigator, researcher.

مُدَقِّق حِسَابات auditor, comptroller.

مَدْقُوق pounded, ground, crushed, pulverized.

مِدَكّ ramrod (of gun); tamper, rammer.

مُدَلًّى dangled, hanging, suspended.

مُدَلِّك masseur, massagist.

مُدَلَّل pampered, spoiled, caressed, fondled, petted; pet.

مُدَلَّلٌ عليه proved, proven, verified, substantiated.

مُدَلَّه madly in love, bewildered.

مَدْلُول meaning, sense, significance, purport, content.

مُدْمَج ، مُدَمَّج compact, built-in.

مُدَمَّر destroyed, wrecked, demolished, in ruins.

مُدَمِّر destroyer, devastator, saboteur, destructive.

مُدْمِن addicted, addict, inveterate, habitual.

مَدَنِيّ urban, urbanized; townsman, citizen, city dweller.

مَدَنِيّ civilized, cultured; civilian, secular, civil.

مَدَنِيَّة civilization.

مُدْهِش amazing, astonishing, surprising, wonderful.

مُدْهِن fatty, greasy, oily.

مُدَوَّر round, circular, rotund.

مُدَوَّن recorded, set down in writing, entered, listed.

مَدْيَة ، مُدْيَة ، مِدْيَة knife, pocketknife.

مَدِيد long.

مُدِير director, manager, administrator.

مُدِيرُ مَدْرَسَة principal, headmaster.

مُدِيرُ المَرَاسِم chief of protocol.

مُدِيرِيَّة directorate, department, division; province, county, territory.

مَدِين debtor, indebted.

مَدينَة city, town, township.

بيروت هي المدينة الرئيسية في لبنان وعاصمة الجمهورية

Beirut is the metropolis of Lebanon and its capital

مَدِينيّ civic, city.

مَدِينِيَّة urbanism, urbanization, civilization.

مُذَاب dissolved, liquefied, molten, solute.

مُذَاع disseminated, announced, published; broadcast.

مَذَاق taste, flavor, savor.

مُذَاكَرَة deliberation, consultation, discussion, parley, debate.

مَذْبَحَة massacre, butchery, carnage, blood bath.

مِذْراة winnow, pitchfork, winnowing fork.

مَذْعُور terrified, horrified, frightened, scared.

مُذَكَّر masculine gender.

مُذَكَّرَة memorandum, note, reminder, warrant.

مُذَكَّرَة تَفْتِيش search warrant.

مُذَكَّرَات memoirs, autobiography.

مَذْكُور mentioned, referred to, specified, stated, cited.

مُذِلّ degrading, debasing, humiliating.

مُذَنَّب comet.

مُذْنِب guilty, wrongdoer, evildoer, criminal.

مَذْهَب faith, belief, creed, doctrine, ideology, rite.

مَذْهَبِيّ denominational, sectarian, confessional.

مُذْهِل astounding, astonishing, amazing, stupendous, stunning.

مِذْيَاع microphone, radio, receiving set; tell-tale, gossip, blabber.

يوجد في كل بيت تقريباً مذياع
يعمل بواسطة الكهرباء

There is in almost every house a radio operating by electricity

مُذِيب solvent.

مُذِيع announcer, broadcaster, newscaster; spreader, proclaimer, promulgator.

مَرَّ to pass, go, walk, saunter, stroll by; to march past; to elapse, run out (time); to skirt; to travel, move, cross, traverse; to flow through, run through; to head; run out (through an area).

مَرَّ ذِكْرُهُ it has been mentioned above.

مَرَّ بِسَلام to go off without mishap.

مَرَّ مَرَّ الكِرَام to pass as if nothing had happened.

مَرَّ to become bitter.

مَرّ passing, going by; transition; crossing, lapse, course of time.

على مَرِّ الزَّمان in the course of time.

مُرّ bitter, painful; myrrh.

المَرْء man, person.

مَرْأى view, sight.

أ ب ت ث ج ح خ د ذ ر ز س ش ص ض ط ظ ع غ ف ق ك ل م ن هـ و ي

مَرْأَب، مِرْأَب garage; hanger (for plane).

مُرابٍ (المُرابِي) usurer.

مِرْآة mirror, looking glass.

مُراجَعَة review, revision, verification; study, consultation, having recourse to; repetition; application, petition.

مُرَاد purpose, intent, aim, goal; desire, wish.

مُرادِف synonym, analogous, corresponding in meaning.

مَرَارَة bitterness; gallbladder (anat.).

مِرَاس strength, power.

سَهْلُ المِراس tractable, docile, compliant.

صَعْبُ المِراس intractable, unruly, refractory.

مُرَاسِل correspondent, reporter.

مُرَاسَلَة correspondence, exchange of letters.

مَرَاسِم ceremonies, protocol.

مُرَاعَاة observance of, adherence to, honoring, living up to; consideration, deference, respect, regard.

مع مُرَاعَاة taking into consideration; subject to.

مُرَافَعَة pleading, defense.

مُرَافِق escort, bodyguard, companion; attendant, collateral; accompanying, concomitant, aide.

مُرَافَقَة association; escort, accompaniment, company.

مُرَاقَب observed, inspected; censored, controlled.

مُرَاقِب observer, supervisor, inspector, controller; censor.

مُرَاقَبَة observation, supervision, surveillance, inspection, control; censorship (of the press).

مُرَاهِق adolescent, teenager.

مُرَاهَقَة adolescence.

مُراهِن bettor, wagerer.

مُرَاهَنَة betting, wagering, staking; bet, wager.

مَرْؤُوس subordinate, subaltern; subject.

مُرَاوِغ dodgy, elusive, devious, sly, deceitful.

مُرَاوَغَة evasion, elusion, deviousness, slyness, trickery.

مَرْئِيّ visual, viewed.

مُرَبٍّ (المُرَبِّي) educator, pedagogue, teacher; breeder (animals).

مُرَبًّى (ص) brought up, raised, reared, educated, cultured.

مُرَبًّى (اسم) jam.

مُرْبِح profitable, lucrative.

مَرْبِض pen; fold; launching pad.

مَرْبَع night club.

مُرَبَّع square, checkered.

مُرْبِك confusing, disturbing; upsetting, embarrassing; bewildering, disconcerting; confounding, perplexing.

مَرْبُوط tied up, bound, attached; connected, linked, coupled.

رسم الصغير مربعات مختلفة
ولوّنها بالأصفر والأحمر والأزرق

The young boy drew various squares and colored them in yellow, red and blue

مُرَبِّيَة governess, nursemaid, baby sitter.

مَرَّة once, one time.

مَرَّتين twice.

مَرَّةً أُخرى once more, anew, a second time.

مِرَارًا وتَكْرارًا time and again, repeatedly.

مَرَّةً وإلى الأَبَد once and for all.

مُرْتاب doubtful, suspicious; uncertain; distrustful, skeptic.

مُرْتاح comfortable; feeling at ease, at rest; satisfied.

مُرْتاحُ البَال at ease, relaxed, tranquil.

مُرَتَّب (ص) arranged, organized, regulated, set up, tidy.

مُرَتَّب (اسم) salary, pay, emolument.

مُرْتَبِك confused, confounded, perplexed, upset, embarrassed.

مُرْتَجّ shaking, trembling, vibrating.

مُرْتَجَى hope, expectation.

مُرْتَجَع returned, sent back.

مُرْتَجَل improvised, extemporised; extemporaneous, impromptu.

مُرْتَزِق mercenary, hireling.

مَرْتَع pastureland; hotbed, breeding ground.

مُرْتَعِد trembling, quivering, shaking, shivering.

مُرْتَفَع height, hill, mound, upland.

مُرْتَفِع high, elevated, rising, ascending; resounding; loud (sound); climbing, towering.

مُرْتَكِب perpetrator.

مُرْتَكَز pivot, center, fulcrum, abutment.

مَرْج pasture, pastureland; meadow, lawn, turf.

مَرْجَان coral.

مُرَجَّح likely, probable, preponderant, preferred.

مَرْجِع return; resort, recourse; refuge, retreat; reference, source; authority, authoritative source.

مِرْجَل boiler.

مَرْجُوّ hoped for, expected; requested, desired.

مَرِحَ to frolic; to rejoice, exult; to be gay, happy, merry, cheerful, exuberant; to be in high spirits.

مَرَح joy, cheerfulness, gaiety, mirth, merriment.

مَرِح — joyful, gay, happy, merry, cheerful, hilarious.

مَرْحَى — well done! bravo!.

مِرْحَاض — toilet, lavatory, water closet.

مُرَحَّل — deported, evicted, ousted, banished.

مُرَحِّل — relay (elect.).

مَرْحَلَة — stage, phase; a day's journey, leg of a journey.

مَرْحَلِيّ — temporary, temporal, transitory, provisional.

مَرْحُوم، المَرْحُوم — deceased, dead, late; the late.

مُرَخَّص — reduced, lowered, cheap, inexpensive; authorized, licensed, permitted; legal, legitimate.

مَرْدُود (ص) — rejected, refused, repelled, parried.

مَرْدُود (اسم) — yield, return, produce, output.

مَرْذُول — rejected, discarded; low, mean, inferior, depraved, despicable, wicked, evil.

مَرْسًى — anchorage, moorage, berth.

مِرْسَاة — anchor, hawser, grapnel.

مَرَسَة — rope, cord, line, cable.

مُرْسَل — sent, dispatched,forwarded; transmitted; long and flowing hair); free, unrhymed (poetry); missionary.

مُرْسِل — sender, consignor, forwarder; transmitter.

مَرْسَم — studio (of painter, artist).

مِرْسَمَةُ الرِّيح — anemograph.

مِرْسَمَةُ الزَّلازِل — seismograph.

مِرْسَمَةُ الطَّيف — spectograph.

مِرْسَمَةُ القَلْب — cardiograph.

مَرْسُوم (ص) — drawn, sketched, illustrated; painted, planned; designed, devised, contrived; deliberate, calculated, premeditated, decreed.

مَرْسُوم (اسم) — decree, ordinance, act.

مِرَشَّة — sprinkler, watering can; shower, sprayer, atomizer.

مُرَشَّح — candidate, nominee.

مُرَشِّح — filter.

مُرْشِد — guide, pilot, usher, counselor, adviser; beacon; instructor, leader to the right way.

مِرْصَاد — lookout, observatory, observation post.

مَرْصَد فَلَكِيّ — observatory.

مَرْصُود — observed, watched; appropriated, earmarked, allocated, allotted, assigned (funds, money).

مَرْصُوف — paved, slabbed, parqueted; stratified, aligned.

مَرِضَ — to become sick; to fall ill.

مَرَض — disease, malady, ailment, illness, sickness.

مَرَضٌ تَنَاسُلِيّ — venereal disease.

مَرَضٌ عُضْوِيّ — organic disease.

مَرَضٌ عَقْلِيّ — mental disease.

مَرَضٌ مُزْمِن — chronic disease.

مَرَضٌ مُسْتَوْطِن — endemic disease.

مَرَضٌ مُعْدٍ contagious disease.

مَرَضٌ وَبائِيّ epidemic disease.

مَرْضاة satisfaction, gratification, pleasing.

لِمَرْضاةِ الله to please God.

مُرْضٍ (المُرْضِي) satisfactory, pleasing, gratifying.

مُرْضِع breast-feeding mother.

مُرْضِعَة wet nurse; foster mother.

مُرَطِّب moisturizer; refreshment; soft drink.

مَرْعًى pasture, pasture land, grazing ground.

مُرْعِب frightful, frightening, terrifying; horrible, awful.

مَرْعِيُّ الإجْراء observed, effective, in force, valid, operative.

مَرَّغ to roll in, rub over; to rub; to sully, make dirty.

مُرْغَم compelled, obliged, forced.

مَرْغُوبٌ فيه desirable, coveted, sought after, in demand.

غيرُ مَرْغُوبٍ فيه undesirable; persona non grata.

مَرْفَأ port, harbor, haven.

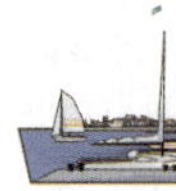

مُرْفَقٌ بِهِ enclosed, attached.

مُرْفَقات (ج) enclosures.

مِرْفَق، مَرْفِق، مِرْفَق elbow (anat.).

مِرْفَقٌ عام، مَرافِق عامَّة public utility, appurtenance, facilities.

مَرْفُوض refused, rejected, turned down.

مَرْفُوع raised, lifted up, hoisted; submitted to.

مَرْفُوع noun in the nominative, verb in the indicative (grammar).

مَرَق to pierce, penetrate, pass through; to dart, rush, shoot, fly past, pass swiftly; to digress, deviate; to renege, renounce (the true faith).

مَرَق broth, gravy, stock.

مِرْقاة ladder; stairs, step, stair.

مِرْقَب telescope.

مَرْقَد bed, couch, resting place; mausoleum.

مَرْقَص ballroom, dance hall.

مُرَقَّم numbered, paged, paginated.

مَرْكَب ship, boat, vessel.

مَرْكَبٌ بُخارِيّ steamship, steamer.

مَرْكَبُ الصَّيد fishing smack, trawler.

مَرْكَبٌ شِراعِيّ sail boat.

مُرَكَّب (ص) mounted, fastened, fixed, fitted, inserted, assembled; made up, composed, consisting of.

مُرَكَّب (اسم) compound, complex, composite.

مُرَكَّبُ نَقْص inferiority complex.

مَرْكَبَة vehicule, carriage, cab.

مَرْكَبَةٌ فَضائِيَّة spacecraft, spaceship.

مَرْكَز center; focus, position, post; location, station, locality; job; situation; status, standing.

مَرْكَزُ الإدارة headquarters, central office.

مَرْكَزُ الثِّقل — center of gravity.

مَرْكَزٌ شَاغِر — vacant post.

مُرَكَّز — fixed, fastened; concentrated, centralized; condensed.

مَرْكَزِيّ — central, centralized.

مَرْكَزِيَّة — centralism.

مَرْكَم — storage battery, accumulator.

مَرْكُوب، المَرْكُوب — ridden, mounted; mount, riding animal.

مَرْمًى — goal,aim, end, purpose; range (of a gun); reach, extent.

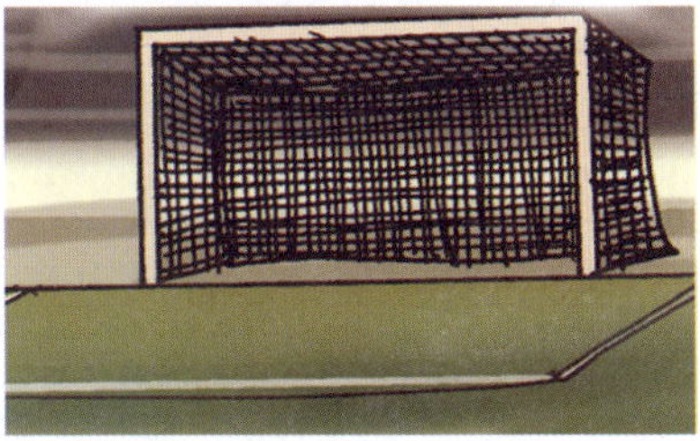

يحاول لاعب كرة القدم تسجيل هدف في المرمى
The football player tries to enter the ball into the goal

مَرْمَر — marble.

مَرْمُوق — remarkable, notable, significant, important; lofty, proud, distinguished, eminent.

مَرَّنَ — to train, drill, accustom, condition, season someone to; to make someone get used to; to practise, exercise, coach.

مَرِن — pliant, pliable, flexible; elastic, supple, lithe, ductile, extensible; yielding, compliant.

مُرْهَف — thin, fine, sharpened, sharp.

مُرْهَفُ الحِسّ — sensitive, delicate.

مُرْهَق — exhausted, weary, tired out, overburdened, oppressed.

مُرْهِق — oppressive (burden); exhausting, tiring, wearisome, burdensome, strenuous, laborious, exacting, onerous.

مَرْهَم — ointment, salve, cream, pomade.

مَرْهُون — mortgaged, pawned, pledged; subject to.

مُرُوءَة — chivalry, generosity, manhood.

مِرْوَحَة — fan, ventilator, propeller.

يتم تشغيل المروحة في فصل الصيف لجلب الهواء البارد
Fans are used during summer to introduce cold air in the room

مِرْوَحِيّ — fan-shaped.

مُرُور — passing, parade, march past; journey, trip through; transit, flow, crossing; flying over.

مُرُور — traffic; progression; process, course, lapse (of time).

مُرُورُ الزَّمان — expiration of the deadline; prescription.

حَرَكَةُ المُرُور — traffic.

شُرْطَةُ المُرُور — traffic police.

مُرَوَّض — domesticated, tamed, subjugated, trained, drilled; accustomed to, habituated to.

مُرَوِّض — trainer.

مُرَوِّع — frightening, dreadful, terrible.

مُرُونَة — flexibility, pliancy, pliability, elasticity; ductility, agility, nimbleness, resilience, plasticity.

مَرْوِيّ — irrigated, watered; narrated, related, told, recounted; cited, quoted, reported.

مُرِيب — arousing, suspicious, doubtful.

مُرِيح — comfortable, calmful, soothing; cozy; flatulent.

المِرِّيخ — Mars (planet).

مَرِير — bitter, strong.

مَرِيض (ص) — sick, ill, ailing, diseased, unwell, indisposed.

مَرِيض (اسم) — sick person, patient.

مِزَاج — temperament, temper, mood, nature, state of mind.

مِزَاجِيّ — temperamental, moody, whimsical.

مُزَاح — joking, jesting, funmaking; joke, jest, banter.

مُزَاحِم — competitor, rival.

مُزَاحَمَة — competition, rivalry.

مَزَادٌ عَلَنِيّ — public auction.

مَزَار — shrine, sanctuary.

مُزَارِع — farmer, peasant, cultivator.

مَزَاعِم — allegations claims, pretexts, contentions.

مُزَامَنَة — synchronization.

مُزَاوَجَة — coupling, pairing, mating; duplication, doubling.

مُزَاوَلَة — practice, pursuit, engagement in.

مُزَايَدَة — outbidding.

مَزْبَلَة — dunghill.

مَزَجَ — to mix, mingle, blend; to intermix, interblend, admix.

مَزَحَ — to joke, jest, banter, make fun.

مُزَخْرَف — ornamented, adorned, embellished, decorated.

مُزْدَحِم — crowded, swarming, packed, crammed with people.

مُزْدَهِر — flourishing, thriving, prospering.

مُزْدَوِج — double, twofold, binary, in pairs, dual.

مِزْرَاب، مِيزَاب — drain, gutter, spout.

مَزْرَعَة — farm, plantation, ranch, country estate.

مُزَرْكَش — embellished, ornamented, brocaded, embroidered.

مَزْرُوع — planted, sown, cultivated.

مُزْعِج — disturbing, annoying, troublesome, irksome, inconvenient, unpleasant, disquieting, harrying.

مَزْعُوم — alleged, pretended, claimed, so-called.

مَزَّقَ — to tear, rend, rip apart, shred, cut to pieces.

مِزْلاج — bolt, bar; latch, lock.

مَزْلَج، مِزْلَج، مِزْلَجَة — ski, sled, skate.

مَزْلَق، مِزْلَقَة — slide, chute, slip, skids, pitfall; abyss, pit; slippery ground, slippery place.

مُزَلَّق — lubricated, oiled, greased.

مُزَلِّق — lubricant, lubricator.

مِزْمَار — reed pipe, flute, clarinet.

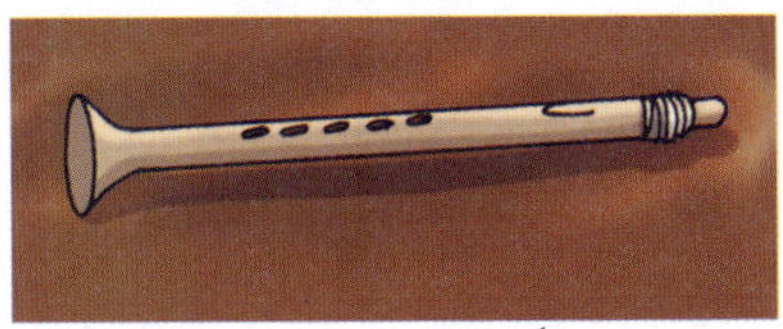

أطرب كثيراً عند سماع صوت المزمار الذي يعزف عليه صديقي

I feel enraptured on hearing the sound of the clarinet that my friend plays on

مِزْمَارُ القِرْبَة — bagpipe.

مُزْمَع — determined, decided, intended, scheduled to be held.

مُزْمِن — chronic; old, lasting.

مُزْهِر — blooming, in bloom, flowering.

مَزْهَرِيَّة — flower vase.

مَزْهُوّ — vainglorious, self-conceited, haughty, arrogant.

مُزَوَّدٌ بِـ — supplied with, provided with, furnished with, equipped with.

مُزَوِّد — supplier, furnisher, caterer.

مِزْوَد — knapsack, haversack.

مُزَوَّر — forged, counterfeit, false, falsified.

مُزَوِّر — forger, falsifier.

مَزِيَّة — merit, characteristic, advantage, feature, virtue.

مُزَيَّت — lubricated, oiled.

مُزَيِّت — lubricant; oiler; lubricative.

مِزْيَتَة — oilcan, oiler.

مَزِيج — mixture, medley, blend; combination, compound, alloy.

مَزِيد — increased, additional, extra; greater, larger; exceeding, maximum; many, much.

مَزِيد — derivative stem of a verb (grammar).

مُزَيَّف — counterfeit, forger, falsified.

مُزَيِّف — forger, falsifier.

مُزِيل — remover, eliminator.

مُزِيلُ الأوساخ — detergent, cleaning compound.

مُزِيلُ الرَّوائح — deodorant, deodoriser.

مُزِيلُ الشَّعْر — depilatory.

مُزَيَّن — adorned, ornamented, decorated, ornate.

مُزَيِّن — haidresser, barber; ornamenting, decorative.

مَسَّ — to feel, finger, handle, palpate, touch.

مَسَّ — to violate, infringe upon; to hit, befall.

مَسَّهُ بِأَذَى — to harm, wrong, hurt someone; to impair.

مَسَّت الحَاجَةُ إلى	it is urgently needed, circumstances require; to necessitate, require, to become necessary to.
مَسّ	touching, contact; misfortune, calamity; attack, fit (of a disease); insanity, madness, frenzy.
مَساء	evening.
مَساءً	in the evening.
مَساءُ الخير، عِمْ مَساءً	good evening.
مُسابَقة	contest, race, competition, test.
مُساجَلَة	contest, competition; debate, discussion.
مَسَّاح	land surveyor.
مِساحَة	area, plane, surface; floor space, surface extent; terrain, sector.
مِساحَة	surveying, survey, geodesy, cadastre.
مُساحَقة	lesbianism.
مُساحِقة	lesbian.
مِساحِيّ	cadastral.
مَسار	path, track, course, trajectory; trend, tendency, progress; route, current, channel.
مِساس	touching, feeling, handling, fingering, palpation.
مَساس	infringement, violation, encroachement upon a right.
مِساس	connection, relation, contact.
مع عَدَم المِساس بـ	without prejudice to.
لَهُ مِساسٌ بِـ	it touches upon.
مُساعِد (ص)	additional, auxiliary, supplementary, secondary, accessory.

مُساعِد (اسم)	assistant, help, supporter, aide.
مُساعِد (ص)	helpful, useful, serviceable, advantageous.
مُساعِدٌ لـ	conductive to, contributory to, leading to.
فِعْلٌ مُساعِد	auxiliary verb (grammar).
مُساعَدَة	help, aid, assistance, support, relief; contribution, subsidy, allowance, subvention.
مَسافَة	distance, space, interval, stretch.
مُسافِر	traveler, passenger.
مَسْأَلَة	question, issue, matter, affair, case; theorem; proposition.
مُسالِم	peaceful, pacific, peace-loving; lenient, gentle, mild-tempered.
مُسالَمَة	reconciliation, making peace with, pacification.
مُسامِح (ص)	forgiving, excusing, indulgent, tolerant.
مُسامِح (اسم)	pardoner, forgiver.
مُسامَحَة	pardon, forgiveness.
مَسامِيّ	porous.
مَسامِيَّة	porosity.
مُسانَدَة	support, backing, aid, help.
مُساهِم	contributor, participant; shareholder, stockholder.
مُساهَمَة	contribution, participation, sharing.
مُساوٍ (المُساوِي)	equal to, equivalent to, amounting to.
مُساواة	equality, parity, sameness; settlement.

على قَدَمِ المُساواة equally, on the same footing, on a par.

مَسْؤُول responsible, liable, accountable.

مَسْؤُول (اسم) in charge of, supervisor, executive, head; official, civil servant, functionary.

مَسْؤُولِيَّة responsibility, liability, charge.

مُساوَمَة bargaining.

مُسايَرَة humoring, indulgence, willingness to please; adaptation, keeping in line with.

مِسْبار probe.

مُسَبِّب، المُسَبِّب causative, resulting, bringing about; originator, author, maker, creator; cause, reason.

مَسْبَح bath, beach, swimming pool.

مِسْبَحَة rosary, beads.

مِسْبَر probe, sound.

مُسَبَّق advance.

مُسْبَقاً beforehand, prematurely, in advance.

مَسْبَك foundry.

مَسْبُوك cast, molded.

مُسْتاء displeased, dissatisfied, annoyed, indignant.

مُسْتَأْجَر rented, leased, hired, chartered (ship).

مُسْتَأْجِر tenant, leaseholder.

مُسْتَأْجِرٌ من الباطِن subtenant.

مُسْتَأْصَل uprooted, eradicated, rooted out, extracted.

مُسْتَأْنَف resumed, recommenced, renewed.

مُسْتَأْنَفٌ عليه appellee, respondent.

مُسْتَأْنِف appellant (of a verdict).

مُسْتَأْهَل deserved, merited, earned.

مُسْتَأْهِل deserving, meriting, worthy of.

مُسْتَبِدّ، المُسْتَبِدّ despotic, autocratic, absolute, totalitarian, tyrannical, arbitrary; despot, autocrat, tyrant, dictator.

مُسْتَبِدٌّ بِرَأْيِهِ stubborn, obstinate, unyielding, inflexible, headstrong, obdurate, uncompromising.

مُسْتَبْشِر optimistic about, regarding as auspicious.

مُسْتَبْعَد unlikely, improbable; put aside, dropped, excluded; ruled out.

مُسْتَتِبّ stabilized, constant, orderly; quiet, steady.

مُسْتَتِر hiding, hidden, concealed, veiled.

ضَميرٌ مُسْتَتِر implied pronoun (grammar).

مُسْتَثْمِر investor, exploiter, beneficiary.

مُسْتَثْنًى مِن excluded from, exempted from; the thing excepted.

مُسْتَجِدّ new, recent, late.

مُسْتَجِدّات latest developments.

مُسْتَجْدٍ (المُسْتَجْدي) beggar, mendicant; supplicant.

مُسْتَجْمَع catchment basin (for rain water).

مُسْتَجْوِب interrogator, questioner, inquirer, investigator.

مُسْتَجِيب reponsive to complying with, consenting to.

مُسْتَحٍ (المُسْتَحِي) abashed, ashamed, embarrassed; bashful, shy, timid, diffident.

مُسْتَحَبّ desirable, nice, pleasant; preferred, chosen.

مُسْتَحْدَث new, novel, original, unprecedented; novelty, invention, creation, innovation.

مُسْتَحْسَن advisable, recommendable, agreeable, appropriate; recommended, proper.

مُسْتَحْضَر preparation, compound, confection.

مُسْتَحَقّ deserved, merited, appropriate.

مُسْتَحِقّ deserving, meriting, worthy of, fit for.

مُسْتَحِقُّ الدَّفع due, payable, matured.

مُسْتَحِقّ beneficiary (of a right).

مُسْتَحْكَم intense, strong, forceful, drastic, serious; deep-rooted, firmly established, ingrained.

مُسْتَحْوِذ obsessing, absorbing, gripping, engrossing.

مُسْتَحِيل impossible, unthinkable of, absurd.

مُسْتَخْدَم employee, servant; employed, hired; used, utilized, applied; secondhand.

مُسْتَخْدِم employer, principal; user, utilizer.

مُسْتَخْرَج extracted from, derived, taken, deduced.

مُسْتَخْلَص abstract, extract; excerpt.

مُسْتَدْعٍ (المُسْتَدْعِي) applicant, petitioner.

مُسْتَدِقّ slender, delicate, thin; tapering, pointed, cuspidated, cusped, sharp.

مُسْتَدِير round, circular, rotund.

مُسْتَرْخٍ (المُسْتَرْخِي) relaxing, slack, languid.

مُسْتَرْسِل long flowing (hair); free, uninhibited, loose, at ease.

مُسْتَرِقُّ السَّمْع eavesdropper.

مُسْتَرِقُّ النَّظَر voyeur, peeping tom, snooper.

مُسْتَرِيح relaxing, at rest, at ease, resting.

مُسْتَشَار adviser, counselor, counsel, consultant.

مُسْتَشْرِق orientalist.

مُسْتَشْفَى hospital, infirmary.

مُسْتَشْفَى الأَمْرَاض العَقْلِيَّة lunatic asylum.

مُسْتَضْعَف weak, oppressed, wretched, poor.

مُسْتَطَاع possible, feasible.

مُسْتَطِيل rectangle; oblong; rectangular.

مُسْتَعَار borrowed.

مُسْتَعَار false, fake, artificial, fictitious.

مُسْتَعْجِل hurried, in a hurry, hasty, speedy, fast, rapid.

مُسْتَعِدّ prepared, ready, all-set.

مُسْتَعْصٍ (المُسْتَعْصِي) incurable, irremediable; obstinate, refractory, difficult, hard; intricate, intractable.

مُسْتَعْطٍ (المُسْتَعْطِي) beggar, mendicant.

مُسْتَعْمَر colonized.

مُسْتَعْمِر colonist, settler, colonialist, imperialist.

مُسْتَعْمَرَة colony, settlement.

مُسْتَعْمَل used, in use,utilised; second hand.

مُسْتَعْمِل user, utilizer.

مُسْتَغْرَب unfamiliar, upsetting; unusual; surprising.

مُسْتَغْرِب surprised, astonished, amazed.

مُسْتَغَلّ exploited.

مُسْتَغِلّ exploiter, utilizer.

مُسْتَفْحِل serious, grave; widespread, rampant, growing; aggravated; spreading dangerously.

مُسْتَفِيد beneficiary, payee.

مُسْتَفِيض elaborate, detailed, exhaustive, lengthy.

مُسْتَقًى مِن derived from, taken from, drawn from.

مُسْتَقْبَل، مُسْتَقبِل future.

مُسْتَقْبِل receiver, receiving set.

مُسْتَقَرّ seat, center, site; abode, residence.

مُسْتَقِرّ stable, settled, constant; quiet, peaceful, steady; firmly established, fixed, unvarying, enduring, lasting; stationary, immobile, firm.

مُسْتَقِلّ independent, autonomous, self-governing, free.

مُسْتَقِلّ unattached, separate, distinct, individual.

مُسْتَقِيل resigned.

مُسْتَقِيم straight, upright, erect; correct, proper, straight forward; honest, sincere, just, righteous.

المُسْتَقِيم rectum (anat.).

مُسْتَكْشِف explorer, pathfinder, scout.

مُسْتَكِين submissive, yielding, resigned, humble.

مُسْتَلِف borrower, debtor.

مُسْتَلْقٍ (المُسْتَلْقِي) lying down, reclining, prone, prostrate.

مُسْتَلِم recipient, receiver.

مُسْتَمِرّ continuous, continuing; permanent, lasting; persistent, enduring, unceasing, incessant; regular.

تَيَّارٌ مُسْتَمِرّ direct current (elect.).

مُسْتَمِع listener.

مُسْتَمِعون audience.

مُسْتَمِيت desperate, death-defying.

مُسْتَنْبَت culture (med.); nursery, greenhouse (plants).

مُسْتَنْبَط invented, devised, contrived; derived, extracted.

مُسْتَنَد document, instrument (legal); record, bill, voucher; exhibit (legal).

مُسْتَنِد leaning on, reclining on, relying on, depending on.

مُسْتَنَدِيّ documentary.

مُسْتَنْزَف exhausted, consumed, depleted.

مُسْتَنْطِق examining magistrate, investigator, inquisitor.

أ ب ت ث ج ح خ د ذ ر ز س ش ص ض ط ظ ع غ ف ق ك ل م ن هـ و ي

مُسْتَنفَر put on alert, mobilized, combat-ready.

مُسْتَنْقَع swamp, marsh, moor.

يكثر وجود المستنقعات في جنوب العراق

Swamps are numerous in south Iraq

مُسْتَنْكَر condemned, censured, denounced.

مُسْتَنْكِر condemner, disapprover, decrier, deprecator.

مُسْتَهْتِر reckless, careless, irresponsible, unrestrained, thoughtless, heedless, wanton.

مُسْتَهْدَف exposed to, subject to, susceptible to.

مُسْتَهَلّ (ص) begun, started, commenced.

مُسْتَهَلّ (اسم) beginning, start, outset; opening verse of a poem.

مُسْتَهِلّ beginner, starter, initiator.

مُسْتَهْلَك consumed, exhausted, wasted; amortized, paid off, written off (debt); redeemed (bonds).

مُسْتَهْلِك consumer.

مُسْتَوَى level, standard, plane.

مُسْتَوَى سَطْح البَحْر sea level.

مُسْتَوَى التَّمَاثُل plane of symmetry.

مُسْتَوَى مائِل inclined plane.

مُسْتَوَى المَعِيشَة standard of living.

على مُسْتَوًى عالٍ on a high level.

مُسْتَوْحًى مِنْ inspired by, drawn from.

مُسْتَوْدَع warehouse, depot, store, depository.

مُسْتَوْدَع أَسْلِحَة arsenal.

مَسْتُور hidden, veiled, covered, concealed, masked.

مُسْتَوْرَد imported.

مُسْتَوْرِد importer.

مُسْتَوْصَف clinic, dispensary, infirmary.

يشرف طبيب وممرضة عادة على المستوصف

A doctor and a nurse usually supervize a clinic

مُسْتَوْطَنَة settlement, colony.

مُسْتَوْعَب، مُسْتَوْعِب container.

مُسْتَوْفِي الشُّرُوط fulfilling conditions, meeting requirements.

مُسْتَوْلَى عَلَيه seized, captured, taken over, appropriated, confiscated, expropriated, usurped.

مُسْتَيْقِظ awake, wakeful; vigilant, watchful, cautious, attentive, on the alert, wide,-awake.

مَسْجِد mosque.

يؤمّ المسلمون المسجد للصلاة نهار الجمعة

Moslems pray in the mosque every Friday

مُسَجَّل registered, listed, recorded; enrolled (as a member).

مُسَجِّل recorder, registrar.

مُسَجِّلَة tape recorder.

مَسَحَ ، مَسَّحَ to stroke with the hand; to wipe off, wipe away; to rub off; to wash, wash off; to wipe out, blot out; to erase, clean, polish; to smooth with a plane; to anoint (with sacred oil); to survey (land); to scan (television).

مَسْح wiping, rubbing, cleaning, polishing; anointment; scanning.

مَسْحُ الأَرَاضِي land survey.

مِسْحَاة spade, shovel.

مَسْحُوب withdrawn, recalled, revoked, repealed; retracted, pulled, drawn, dragged, hauled; tugged, towed, trailed.

مَسْحُوبٌ عَلَيه drawee, drawn on.

مَسْحُور bewitched, fascinated, infatuated, spellbound.

مَسْحُوق (ص) crushed, pounded, pulverized; broken-hearted.

مَسْحُوق (اسم) powder.

مَسَخَ to transform, disfigure, deform; distort (the truth); to metamorphose.

مَسْخ metamorphosis, transformation; deformation, distortion (of the truth); metempsychosis (of human spirit).

مِسْخ monster, freak, monstrosity.

مَسْخَرَة butt, joke, laughing-stock.

مُسَخَّن heated, warmed up.

مُسَخِّن heater, boiler.

مُسَدَّد paid, settled, discharged; directed, pointed, aimed at.

مُسَدَّس pistol, revolver, handgun.

يحمل الشرطي مسدساً على وسطه حفاظاً على الأمن والنِّظام

The policeman carries a revolver on his waist to keep security and order

مُسَدَّسُ الزَّوايا hexagon, hexagonal.

مَسْدُود closed up, stopped up, sealed, shut off; obstructed, clogged, choked up, congested; stuffed up (nose).

طَرِيقٌ مَسْدُود blind alley, dead-end street, impasse.

مَسْرَب intake, sewer, duct, drain, conduit.

مَسْرَح theater, stage.

مَسْرَحُ الدُّمَى puppet theater.

مَسْرَحُ اللامَعْقُول theater of the absurd.

مَسْرَحِيّ dramatic, theatrical.

مَسْرَحِيَّة play, performance, drama, theatrical show.

مَسْرَد index, glossary.

مُسَرِّع accelerator, precipitator.

مُسْرِع hurried, in a hurry, hasty, rushing, speeding; quick, fast, rapid, speedy.

مُسْرِف wastrel, spendthrift, squanderer; excessive, extravagant, intemperate, unrestrained.

مَسْرُور happy, glad, pleased, delighted, merry, joyful.

مَسْرُوق stolen, pilfered, robbed.

مَسْرُوقات (ج) stolen objects or goods.

مُسَطَّح (ص) level, flat, even; spread out; supine, prostrate, prone.

مُسَطَّح (اسم) surface, area, flat area.

مُسَطَّر lined; drafted, written down; striped, ruled, barred.

مَسْطَرَة، مِسْطَرَة ruler; sample, specimen; procedure.

مَسْعًى effort, endeavor.

مُسْعِف succorer, helper, rescuer; first-aid man.

مَسْفُوح shed, spilled.

مَسْقَط projection (eng.).

مَسْقَطُ الرَّأْس birthplace, hometown.

مَسْقَطُ الماء waterfall, falls.

مَسْقُوف roofed, provided with a roof.

مَسَكَ to grab, grasp, clasp, seize, take hold of; to hold fast, stick, cling, cleave, adhere, hang on to.

مَسَكَ دَفَّةَ الأُمُور to be at the helm.

مَسَكَ لِسَانَه to keep one's tongue in check.

مَسْك seizure, grip, hold, detention.

مَسْكُ الدَّفاتِر bookkeeping.

مَسْكُ الحِسَابات accountancy.

مِسْك musk.

مَسْكَة handle, grip, knob, hilt, clasp.

مُسَكِّر sweetening.

مُسْكِر (ص) intoxicating, inebriant.

مُسْكِر (اسم) alcoholic beverage, alcohol.

مَسْكَن، مَسْكِن residence, domicile, house, dwelling.

مُسَكِّن analgesic, painkiller, sedative, tranquilizer.

مَسْكُوك minted, coined.

مَسْكُوكَة coin.

مَسْكُون inhabited, occupied; haunted; possessed (person).

المَسْكُونَة the world.

مِسْكِين poor, miserable, beggar, humble; servile.

مُسَلٍّ (المُسَلِّي) amusing, entertaining, diverting, pleasant; comforting, solacing; consoler, comforter, condoler.

مِسَلَّة large needle; obelisk.

مُسَلَّح، المُسَلَّح armed; gunman.

مَسْلَخ slaughter house.

مُسَلْسَل serial, successive, consecutive; series, chain, succession; serial story.

مُسَلْسَلَة serial story.

مَسْلَك way, road, path; passage, canal, conduit; behavior, comportment, manners, conduct, attitude.

مَسْلَكِيّ behavioral, professional.

مُسَلَّمٌ بِهِ conceded, admissible, accepted, unquestionable, undeniable, undisputed, admitted.

مُسْلِم Moslem.

مُسَلَّمَة postulate, axiom.

مَسْلُوب unsuccessful; stolen, plundered, looted.

مَسْلُوخ skinned, flayed; detached, separated, stripped off.

مَسْلُوق boiled.

مَسْلُول tuberculous, tuberculator; unsheathed, drawn (sword).

مُسَمًّى named, called, by name of; known, designated, given.

إلى أجَلٍ مُسَمًّى for a limited period.

إلى أجَلٍ غير مُسَمًّى for an indefinite time, until further notice.

غَيْرُ مُسَمًّى anonymous, nameless, unnamed.

مِسْمَار nail, pin; corn (of the foot); rivet, bolt.

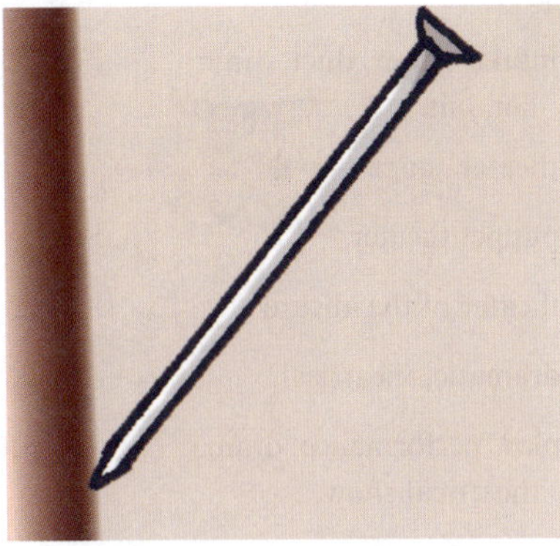

يستعمل النجّار المسامير لتثبيت القطع الخشبيّة في صنع الكراسي والطاولات

The carpenter uses nails to fasten wood pieces in making chairs and tables

مُسَمَّر nailed, fastened with a nail; tanned, browned.

مَسْمَع earshot, hearing.

على مَسْمَعٍ مِن within earshot of; for him to hear.

مَسْمَكَة fish store.

مُسَمَّم poisoned.

مُسَمَّن fattened.

مَسْمُوح permissible, allowed, admissible, licensed, authorized.

مَسْمُوع heard, audible, easily heard.

مَسْمُوم poisoned.

مُسِنّ old, aged.

مِسَنّ whetstone, grindstone, sharpener.

مُسْنَد predicate, attribute (grammar).

مُسْنَدٌ إليه subject (grammar).

مَسْنَد، مِسْنَد	rest, cushion, pillow, bolster; prop, rest.
مُسَنَّن	toothed, indented, notched; pointed, sharp, serrated.
مَسْنُود	supported, consolidated, strengthened, sustained.
مُسْهَب	detailed, elaborate, redundant, lengthy.
مُسْهِل، مُسَهِّل	laxative, purge.
مُسَوَّدَة	draft, rough copy, outline; proof sheet.
مُسَوَّدَةُ قانون	draft law.
مُسَوَّغ	allowed, permitted, justified, warranted.
مُسَوِّغ	justification, warrant.
مُسِيء	injurious, harmful, evil, offensive, offending.
مُسَيَّج	fenced in, hedged in, surrounded with a fence.
المَسِيح	Christ, Messiah.
مَسِيحِيّ	Christian.
المَسِيحِيَّة	Christianity.

مُسَيَّر	directed, controlled by; guided; having no free will; propelled, driven forward; striped, streaked.
مُسَيِّر	propeller, impeller; propulsive.
مَسِيرَة	distance, travel, journey; tour, trip; demonstration, march, procession.
مُسَيْطَرٌ عَلَيه	dominated, controlled, governed, subjected to; influenced, ruled.
مُسَيْطِر (ص)	dominating, controlling, ruling.
مُسَيْطِر (اسم)	ruler, governor, master, overlord.
مُسَيَّل	liquefied, melted; dissolved.
مُسِيل	solvent.
مُسِيلٌ للدُّمُوع	causing tears to flow.
غازٌ مُسِيلٌ للدُّمُوع	tear gas.
مَشَى	to walk, go on foot; to pace, stride, move along; to proceed, march.

مشى الرجل بسرعة ليصل إلى عمله باكراً

The man walked speedily to reach his office early

مُشَابِه	similar, resembling.
مُشَابَهَة	similarity, resemblance, likeness.
مُشَاجَرَة	fight, quarrel, dispute, argument.
مُشَاحَنَة	wrangle, squabble, brawl; quarrel, fight; enmity, rancor; grudge, hatred, controversy.
مَشَادَّة	heated debate, squabble; wrangle, quarrel.

مُشارٌ إلَيه	referred to, stated, cited, aforementioned; indicated above, pointed at.
مُشَارِك	participant, contributor, sharer.
مُشَارَكَة	participation, contribution, collaboration, cooperation, sharing.
مُشَاطَرَة	sharing, participation.
مُشاع	common, public; diffused, spread, well-known.
مِلْكٌ مُشَاع	public domain, no man's land, common estate; joint tenancy, joint property.
مُشَاغِب	troublemaker, agitator, rioter, subverter.
مُشَاغَبَة	unrest, trouble, disturbance, dissension, riot, commotion, uproar, strife; quarrel, controversy.

مُشَاكِس	quarrelsome, conspirator, morose, surly, grumpy.
مُشَاكَسَة	controversy, quarrel, dispute, wrangle; surliness, petulance, moroseness, pugnacity, grumpiness.
مُشَاهَد	seen, viewed, watched, observed.
مُشَاهِد	spectator, viewer, watcher.
مُشَاهَدَة	seeing, viewing, witnessing; sight, spectacle; apparition, vision, view.
مُشَاوَرَة	consultation, deliberation, discussion.
مَشْؤُوم	inauspicious, ill-boding, unfortunate, fateful.
مُشْبَع	saturated, sated, replete; appeased, gratified.
مُشْبِع	satisfying, gratifying, satiating.
مِشْبَك	hook, pin, clasp, clip.
مِشْبَكُ الوَرَق	paper clip.
مِشْبَكُ الشَّعْر	hair pin.

مَشْبُوبُ العاطِفَة	ardent, passionate, zealous, impassioned.
مَشْبُوه	suspect, suspected; doubtful, dubious, equivocal.
مُشْتَاق	longing, desirous, covetous, craving, yearning.
مُشْتَبِك	entangled, complicated, intricate, involved; fighting, battling; engaged in a fight, quarrel.
مُشَتَّت	dispersed, dispelled, scattered.
مُشَتَّتُ الفِكْر	distracted, distraught.
مُشْتَدّ	intense, serious, severe, aggravated.
مُشْتَرٍ (المُشْتَرِي)	buyer, purchaser.
المُشْتَرِي	Jupiter (planet).
مُشْتَرَيات (ج)	purchases.

مُشْتَرَط	stipulated, provided for, under condition.
مُشْتَرِع	legislator, lawgiver, jurist, legist.
مُشْتَرَك	common, combined, concurrent, collective, joint.
عامِلٌ مُشْتَرَك	common factor.
قاسِمٌ مُشْتَرَك	common denominator, common divisor.
مُشْتَرِك	participant, subscriber; taking part, contributing, sharing; contributory, participating.

مُشْتَعِل	burning, afire, on fire, ablaze, in flames.
مُشْتَغِل	working, functioning, operating, in operation; worker, laborer; busy, occupied with.

مُشْتَقّ	derived, derivative.
مَشْتَل	nursery.
مُشْتَمِلٌ على	containing, comprising, covering; including, embodying, involving.
مُشْتَهٍ (المُشْتَهِي)	covetous, craving, desirous, longing for; greedy, avid, lustful.
مُشْتَهِر	well-known, widely-known, famous, renowned, notorious, wide-spread.
مِشْجَب	rack, stand, clothes peg.
مُشَجِّع	encouraging, heartening; encourager, promoter, sponsor; proponent, advocate.
مَشْجُوب	condemned morally, criticized; sharply.
مِشْحَذ، مِشْحَذَة	whetstone, grindstone, sharpener, grinder.
مِشْحَمَة	grease box, grease can.
مَشْحُون	loaden, laden, freighted (in a ship); charged with, filled with; replete.
مِشَدّ	corset, girdle.

مُشَدَّد	intense, severe, stern; emphatic.
مَشْدُود	taut, tight, strained; tied, bound, fastened; pulled, drawn, dragged, hauled.
مَشْدُوه	perplexed, appalled, baffled, confused, astonished, stunned, puzzled, shocked, flabbergasted.
مُشَذَّب	trimmed, clipped, pruned, pared.
مَشْرَب	drinking place; bar, pub; taste, inclination, trend.
مَشْرَحَة	morgue, autopsy room.
مُشَرَّد	homeless, fugitive, refugee, displaced person.
مُشَرَّدُ البَال	confused, disconcerted.
مِشْرَط	scalpel.
مُشَرَّع	legislated, enacted.
مُشَرِّع	legislator, lawmaker, lawgiver, lawmaking.
مُشْرِف	controller, supervisor; overlooking, commanding; near to, close to, on the verge of, about to.
مَشْرِق، المَشْرِق	the Orient, the East; place of sunrise.
مُشْرِق	shining, radiant, resplendent, brilliant, bright.

مَشْرُوب	drink, beverage.
مَشْرُوط	conditional, qualified, stipulated.
مَشْرُوط	slashed, ripped open, cut open.
مَشْرُوع (ص)	legal, lawful, legitimate, rightful, licit; permissible, allowed; legislated, enacted.
مَشْرُوع (اسم)	project, plan, scheme.
مَشْرُوعُ قانُون	draft law.
مَشْرُوعُ مُعاهَدَة	draft treaty.

مَشَطَ، مَشَّطَ to comb (hair); to card (wool); to rake, comb (earth).

أمشط شعري بعد أن أغسل وجهي صباح كل يوم
I comb my hair every morning after washing my face

مُشْط comb; rake; bridge (of a stringed musical instrument); cartridge.

مُشْطُ الرِّجل metatarsus (anat.).

مُشْطُ اليَد metacarpus (anat.).

مَشْطُوب scratched, incised, slit; struck off, canceled, deleted; bevelled, chamfered.

مَشْطُور split, bisected, cut through, severed, halved.

مُشِعّ radiant, radiating, emitting rays, radioactive.

مِشْعَاع radiator.

مُشَعْشَع diluted, mixed with water, thinned out, weakened; shining, radiating; tipsy, half-drunk.

مَشْعَل torch.

مُشَعْوِذ juggler, conjurer; magician, sorcerer; charlatan, quack, swindler, trickster.

مَشْغَل workshop, atelier, factory.

مَشْغُوف passionately fond of; madly in love with, infatuated with, enamored of, fascinated by.

مَشْغُول busy, occupied with; distracted, diverted from; worked on, processed; occupied.

مَشْغُولُ البَال anxious, apprehensive, concerned, worried.

مَشْفَى infirmary, hospital.

مَشْفُوعٌ بِـ accompanied by, attached to; enclosed with.

مَشَقَّة hardship, difficulty, discomfort.

مَشْقُوق split, cleft, cracked, fissured; ripped, slit, halved.

مِشْكَاة lantern; lamp; niche.

مُشَكِّك skeptic, doubting, uncertain, unbelieving, distrustful, suspicious, incredulous, in doubt.

مُشَكَّل different, diverse, manifold, miscellaneous, variegated; formed, shaped, worked, wrought, made, built.

مُشَكَّلٌ مِن consisting of, made up of.

مُشْكِل، مُشْكِلَة (اسم) problem, unsolved issue, difficulty.

مَشْكُوٌّ مِنه complained of, accused, charged.

مَشْكور worthy of thanks, meritorious, praiseworthy.

مَشْكوكٌ فِيه doubtful, dubious, suspected, suspicious.

مَشْلُول paralyzed, crippled, paralytic, lame.

مُشْمَئِزّ disgusted, nauseated, revolted.

مُشْمِس sunny.

مُشَمَّع waterproof, impermeable (cloth); waterproof material; oilcloth, linoleum; waxed; raincoat.

مَشْمُول included, contained, comprised, implied.

مَشْمُولٌ بِرِعَايَتِه enjoying the patronage or protection of.

مِشْنَقَة، مَشْنَقَة gallows, scaffold, hangman's rope.

مَشْنُوق hanged.

مُشَهٍّ (المُشَهِّي) appetizer, hors d'oeuvre; stimulating to the appetite, savory, tasty, delicious.

مَشْهَد place of assembly, meeting; place where a hero died; religious shrine; funeral procession.

مَشْهَد view, aspect, spectacle, sight; scene; act, scene (in a theater).

مَشْهُود taking place in the presence of witnesses; happening before a large audience; memorable event.

بِالجُرْمِ المَشْهُود redhanded, flagrante delicto.

مَشْهُور famous, well-known, celebrated, famed; current, common, widespread, notorious; renowned; ill-reputed.

مِشْوَاة grill, roaster, broiler.

مَشُوب mixed, adulterated, vitiated; spoiled, corrupted.

مَشُوبٌ بِالهُموم troubled with worries.

مَشُورَة، مَشْوَرَة consultation, counsel, advice, deliberation.

مُشَوَّش muddled, befuddled, confused, disturbed, deranged.

مُشَوَّشُ الفِكْر bewildered, confused, baffled.

مُشَوِّق arousing desire; stimulating, exciting, breathtaking; thrilling, absorbing, fascinating, attractive.

مُشَوَّه disfigured, defaced, deformed, mutilated; distorted, falsified, twisted; warped (truth).

مَشْوِيّ grilled, broiled, roasted.

مَشْي walking, walk.

مَشْيٌ خِلالَ النَّوم noctambulism, somnambulism, sleepwalking.

مَشِيئَة will, wish, desire.

مُشَيَّد built, constructed, set up.

مُشِير advisor, counselor, consultant; field marshal (army rank).

مَشِين dishonorable, scandalous, disgraceful.

مَصَّ to suck, suck up, soak up, suck in, absorb; to sip, lap, lap up, lick up; to drink in small sips; swallow up.

مَصّ sucking, suction, suck, soaking up, suck, absorption.

مُصابٌ بِـ stricken by, hit by, afflicted with, suffering from.

مُصَاب	casualty, victim, wounded person; sick, ill, injured.
مُصَاحِب	accompanying, escort; escorting.
مُصَاحَبَة	accompanying; company, escort; accompaniment (music).
مُصَادَر	confiscated, sequestered, expropriated.
مُصَادَرَة	seizure, confiscation, expropriation, sequestration.
مُصَادِف	falling on a given date, concurrent with.
مُصَادَفَة	chance, haphazard; coincidence, concurrence.
مُصَادَفَةً	by chance; by coincidence, accidentally.
مُصَادَقَة	consent, assent; ratification, legalization; concurrence in; authentication (of a document).
مُصَادَمَة	collision, clash, impact.
مُصَارِع	wrestler, gladiator; bullfighter, matador (bulls).
مُصَارَعَة	wrestling, fighting.
مُصَارَعَةُ الثِّيرَان	bullfighting.
مَصَّاص	absorbent, absorber.
مَصَّاصُ الدِّمَاء	blood sucker, vampire; extortioner, usurer.
مَصَّاصَة	feeding bottle; nipple of a feeding bottle (babies).
مَصَاعِب (ج)	difficulties, hardships.
مُصَافَحَة	handshake.
مُصَالَحَة	conciliation, compromise, settlement; peace.

مُصَاهَرَة	relationship by marriage.
مَصَبّ	mouth (of river); estuary; outlet, escape, drain.
مِصْبَاح	lamp; burner.
مِصْبَاحٌ كَهْرَبَائِيّ	light bulb.
مَصْبَغَة	laundry; dyeworks.
مَصْبَنَة	soap factory.
مَصْبُوب	poured, spilled; cast, molded.
مَصْبُوغ	dyed, tinted, painted, colored.
مَصَحّ، مَصَحَّة	sanatorium.
مُصَحَّح	corrected, rectified; mended, repaired.
مُصَحِّح	corrector, adjuster, rectifier; proofreader.
مَصْحُوب	accompanied by, attended with, associated with.
مِصَدّ	buffer, fender, bumper.
مِصْدَاقِيَّة	credibility.
مَصْدَر	origin, source, starting point, point of origin.
مَصْدَر	infinitive, verbal noun (grammar).
مُصَدَّر	exported.
مُصَدِّر	exporter.
مُصَدَّق	credible, reliable, trustworthy; certified, authenticated, ratified, sanctioned, approved.
مِصْدَم	buffer, bumper, fender, shock absorber.
مَصْدُوع	split, cracked, broken; having a headache.

مُصِرّ insistent, insisting, persistent, persisting; determined, resolved, resolute.

مِصْر country, land, territory; Egypt.

مِصْرَاع shutter, leaf; hemistich.

مُصْرَان intestines, bowels, guts, viscera.

مُصَرَّح بِهِ declared, announced, proclaimed; licensed, authorized, allowed; permissible, permitted.

مَصْرَع death.

مَصْرَف drainage canal, drain; outlet, escape.

مَصْرِف bank.

مَصْرُوف، المَصْرُوف spent, outlaid, disbursed; dismissed, discharged (from service, duty); expenditure, outlay, expenses, costs.

مَصْطَبَة، مِصْطَبَة seat, terrace; stone bench.

مُصْطَفَى chosen, selected, preferred.

مَصْطَكَى، مُصْطَكَى، مُصْطَكَاء mastic, mastic tree.

مُصْطَلَى fireplace.

مُصْطَلَح generally accepted, followed, established; conventional, customary; technical term, expression, idiom.

مُصْطَنَع artificial, synthetic; affected, bogus, imitated, simulated, phony, sham.

مِصْعَد elevator, lift; anode.

مَصْعُوق struck, hit, shocked; stunned, startled, aghast, amazed, astounded, flabbergasted, stupefied; thunderstruck.

مُصَغَّر diminished, decreased, minimized; miniature; tiny.

مُصَفٍّ (المُصَفِّي) liquidator, receiver in equity.

مُصَفًّى clarified, purified, clear, limpid, filtered; dissolved (company); eliminated (athletic team); discharged, liquidated, paid, settled (account).

مِصْفَاة sieve, screen, filter; refinery; strainer.

مُصَفَّح plated, coated, laminated; armored, reinforced.

مُصَفَّحَة armored car.

مَصْفُوف lined up, aligned, ranged, arranged; set, composed.

مَصْقُول burnished, polished, cut; refined, acute (wit); glossed, glazed, lapped; glossy, shiny; smooth, refined; cultivated.

مَصْل serum, plasma (med.); whey (of milk).

مُصَلًّى place of prayer, oratory (in a mosque).

مُصَلَّب، المُصَلَّب hardened, solidified; crossing, interjunction (of roads).

مُصْلِح peacemaker, conciliator, reformer, reformist.

مَصْلَحَة interest, advantage, welfare; service, administration, department, division, office.

مَصْلَحَة commonwealth, public interest, general welfare.

لِمَصْلَحَة	in the interest of, in favor of.
مَصْلُوب	crucified.
مُصَمَّم	designed, planned, sketched, drawn, modeled.
مُصَمِّم (ص)	determined to, intent on, resolute, unwavering.
مُصَمِّم (اسم)	designer, styler, planner; couturier (dresses).
مَصْنَع	factory, plant.

يعمل في المصنع عادة عدد كبير من العمال

A great number of workers usually work in a factory

مُصَنَّع	industrialized; produced, manufactured.
مُصَنَّف (ص)	classified, categorized, assorted, grouped, composed.
مَصْنُوع	made, produced, fabricated, fashioned, wrought, worked.
مَصْهَر	smelter.
مِصْهَر	fuse.
مَصْهُور	melted, fused.

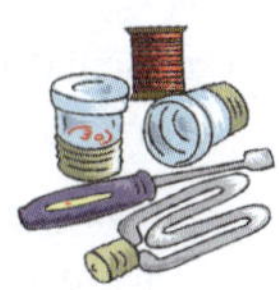

مُصَوَّب	aimed at, pointed at; corrected, rectified.
مُصَوِّت (اسم)	voter, elector.
مُصَوَّر	painted, depicted, illustrated, pictured; shaped, formed; filmed, photographed.
مُصَوِّر	photographer, painter; maker.

يلتقط المصور صور الأشخاص بواسطة آلة تصوير صغيرة يحملها

The photographer snapshoots the pictures of people with a small camera that he carries

مُصَوِّرٌ صُحُفِيّ	press photographer.
مُصَوِّرٌ تَلفزيونيّ أو سينمائيّ	cameraman.
مَصُون	preserved, conserved; well-kept, sheltered, maintained.
مُصِيب	correct, pertinent, faultless, right.
مُصِيبَة	misfortune, calamity, disaster, affliction, ordeal, catasrophe.
مِصْيَدَة	trap, snare.
مَصِير	development, progress (of work); outcome, end, issue, result; destiny, fate, lot.
مَصِيف	summer resort, summer residence.
مَضَّ	to hurt, pain; to burn, sting; to torment, harass, molest.

مَضَى — to go, go away, leave, depart; to pass, elapse, slip by; to continue to do, proceed in.

مَضَى — to conclude, accomplish, execute; to go ahead, progress.

مَضَى — to be sharp, cutting.

مَضَى لِسَبِيلِه — to die, pass away.

مَضَى قائِلاً — he went on to say, he added.

فِيما مَضَى — formerly, previously, in the past.

مُضَاء — lighted, illuminated.

مُضَاجَعَة — sexual intercourse, copulation, lovemaking.

مُضَادّ — contrary, opposite, counter, against.

مُضَادٌّ للالْتِهاب — anti-inflammatory.

مُضَادٌّ للحُمَّى — antipyretic.

مُضَادٌّ للحُمُوضَة — antacid.

مُضَادٌّ للجَراثِيم — antibiotic.

مُضَادٌّ للدَّبّابات — antitank.

مُضَادٌّ للطّائِرات — antiaircraft.

مُضَادٌّ للغَوّاصات — antisubmarine.

مُضَادٌّ للعُفُونَة — antiseptic.

ثَوْرَةٌ مُضَادَّة — counterrevolution.

جِسْمٌ مُضَادّ — antibody.

هُجُومٌ مُضَادّ — counterattack, counteroffensive.

مُضَارَبَة — speculation (in stocks).

مُضَارِع — present, present tense, imperfect (grammar).

مُضَارِع — like, similar, equal to; parallel.

مُضَارَعَة — similarity, equality paralleling.

مُضَاعَف — double, twofold, multiple; multiplied, redoubled.

مُضَاعَفٌ مُشْتَرَك — common multiple (math).

مُضَاعَفٌ مُشْتَرَكٌ أَصْغَر — least common multiple (math).

مُضَاعَفَة — doubling, compounding, multiplying.

مُضَاعَفَات (ج) — complications (of illness).

مُضَاف — added, annexed, attached, adjunct; governing word (grammar).

مُضَافٌ إليه — governed, governed noun (grammar).

مُضَاهٍ (المُضَاهِي) — like, similar to, analogous to, parallel, match; corresponding to, equal to.

مُضَاهَاة — similarity, resemblance, likeness, analogy; correspondence; comparison.

مُضَايِق — annoying, vexing, irksome, irritating.

مُضَايَقَة — annoyance, annoying, vexation, harassment, nuisance.

مَضْبُوط — accurate, exact, precise, correct, true, sound; verified; adjusted, fixed; corrected, rectified.

مَضْبُوط — seized, caught, arrested; seized, confiscated; controlled, under control; restrained, subdued, held back.

مُضْجِر — boring, annoying, irritating, exasperating, irksome.

مَضْجَع bed, couch.

مُضْحِك comic, funny, ridiculous, droll.

مِضَخَّة pump.

مُضَخَّم inflated, expanded, exaggerated, overstated, overdone; amplified, enlarged, swollen.

مُضَخِّمُ الصَّوْت loud speaker.

مَضْرِبُ المَثَل exemplary, cited as an example.

مِضْرَب mallet, racket, bat; large tent.

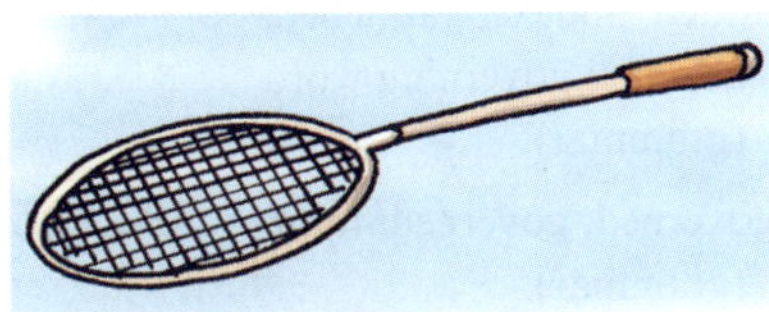

يستعمل اللاعب المضرب
لقذف الكرة باتجاه خصمه
The tennis player uses his racket
to throw the ball toward his opponent

مَضَرَّة harm, damage, detriment, loss, disadvantage.

مُضَرَّجُ اليَدين caught in the act, caught red-handed.

مَضْرُوب beaten, stricken, punched; coined, minted; fixed, appointed, specified; multiplication (math).

مَضْرُوبٌ في multiplied by, times.

مَضْرُوبٌ فيه multiplier (math).

مَضَض pain, suffering, torture, agony, affliction.

على مَضَضٍ unwillingly, reluctantly.

مُضْطَجِع lying down, reclining, prone, prostrate.

مُضْطَرّ obliged, coerced, compelled.

مُضْطَرِب disturbed, confused, disarranged, uneasy, disquited, ill at ease, troubled, upset, anxious, excited.

مُضْطَرِب rough, surging, heaving (sea waves).

مُضْطَرِب ailing, sick, ill, unhealthy, unwell.

مُضْطَرِم burning, flaming, blazing, afire.

مُضْطَهَد persecuted, oppressed, tyrannized.

مُضْطَهِد persecutor, oppressive, tyrant.

مَضَغَ to chew.

مَضَغَ الكَلام to speak indistinctly.

مَضْغُوط pressed, compressed, squeezed; tight, compact.

مُضِلّ misleading, misguiding, deceptive, delusive, fallacious.

مُضَلَّع ribbed; polygon (eng.).

مُضَلَّل misled, misguided, perverted, deceived, fooled.

مُضَلِّل misleading, misguiding, false, fallacious, deceptive.

مِضْمَار recetrack, course, turf; arena, field, domain, area.

مُضَمَّن included, implied.

مَضْمُوم closed, tight, compressed; assembled, fitted together, joined, combined; collected; annexed, appended, attached.

أ ب ت ث ج ح خ د ذ ر ز س ش ص ض ط ظ ع غ ف ق ك ل م ن هـ و ي

مَضْمُون guaranteed, secured, ensured; secure, sure; registered (mail).

مَضْمُون content, import, tenor, significance, meaning.

مُضْنٍ (المُضْني) exhausting, grueling, wearisome.

مُضِيء luminous, shining, radiant, brilliant.

مُضِيّ going, departure, leaving; passing, elapsing.

مُضِيّ المُدَّة superannuation, lapse of time.

مِضْياف hospitable.

مَضْيَعَة loss, waste, ruin.

مُضِيف host, steward (on a plane).

مُضِيفَة hostess, air hostess, stewardess.

مَضيق strait; bottleneck.

مَطَّ to expand by pulling; to stretch, draw out, draw tight, tighten; to tauten, distend; to lengthen.

مُطَابِق identical, corresponding, confirming, concordant, in harmony, in agreement, congruous.

مَطَار airport, airfield.

مُطَارَدَة pursuit, chase, hunt; tracking, trailing.

مَطَّاط (ص) elastic, extensible, stretchable.

مَطَّاط (اسم) rubber.

مُطَاع obeyed, complied with.

مَطَاف travel, touring.

انْتَهى بِهِ المَطَاف wind up with, arrive eventually at; to reach.

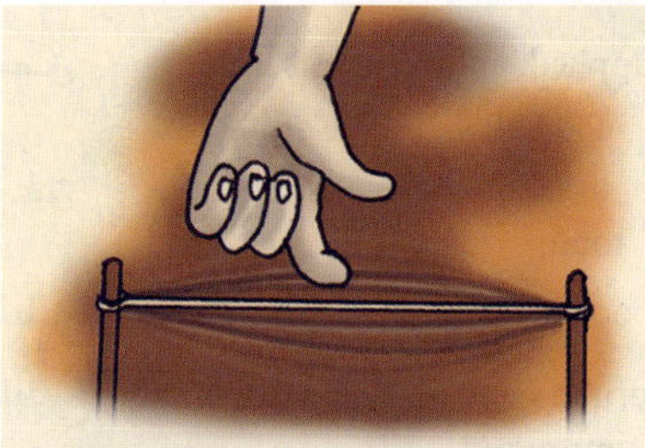

يمغط المطّاط عندما نشدّه بالإصبع

The elastic expands when you draw it by the finger

خَاتِمَةُ المطَاف end of the matter, the final issue, conclusion, windup, upshot, outcome, result.

مُطَالَب accountable, responsible; called upon, requested; claimed, demanded; one of whom something is demanded.

مُطَالِب claimant, requesting someone to do something.

مُطَالَبَة claim, demand, request, calling upon, asking someone to do something, appeal.

مُطَالِع reader.

مُطَالَعَة reading, examination; research; study; findings.

مُطَاوِع obedient, compliant, submissive, yielding; pliable, pliant, malleable.

مَطْبَخ kitchen.

مِطْبَخ cooking stove, cooker.

مَطْبَعَة printing press.

مَطْبَعِيّ typographical.

خَطأٌ مَطْبَعِيّ misprint, erratum, typographical error.

مُطَبَّق applied, enforced, effective, applicable, implemented.

مُطْبِق entire, complete, absolute, total.

مَطْبُوخ cooked.

مَطْبُوع printed, typed, typewritten; impressed.

مَطْبُوعٌ على naturally disposed for, having the innate property of being characterized by.

مَطْبُوعَة printed material, periodical, print.

مَطْبُوعَات printed matter.

مِطْحَنَة mill, grinder, grinding machine.

مِطْحَنَةٌ يَدَوِيَّة quern, hand mill.

مَطْحُون ground, crushed.

مَطَر rain.

تساقط المطر بغزارة فبقيت العائلة في المنزل

Rain poured densely obliging the family to stay home

مَطَرٌ خَفِيف drizzle, shower, dribble.

مَطَرٌ غَزِير downpour.

مِقْيَاس المَطَر pluviometer.

مِطْران، مَطْران archbishop.

مِطْرانِيَّة، مَطْرَانِيَّة archbishopric, diocese.

مُطْرِب (ص) melodius, mellow; delightful, ravishing.

مُطْرِب (اسم) singer, chanter.

مُطْرِبَة songstress, chanteuse.

مُطَّرِد incessant, uninterrupted, continuous, constant.

مُطَرَّز embroidered, brocaded.

مِطْرَقَة hammer, mallet, gavel.

مَطْرُوح subtracted; cast away, pitched, dumped, discarded; prostrate; subtrahend (math); put for discussion, raised, set forth, introduced, presented.

المَطْرُوح منه minuend (math).

مَطْرُود expelled, evicted, ousted, outcast; banished, exiled, expatriated, outlaw; dismissed, discharged (from an office).

مَطْرُوق hammered, forged; knocked, beaten, tapped; much frequented (place); well-trodden (place); previously treated, frequently discussed or debated.

مَطْعَم restaurant.

مُطَعَّم inoculated, injected; grafted; inlaid.

مُطْفَأ extinguished, extinct; mat, dull (color); slaked (lime).

مِطْفَأة fire extinguisher

مَطْلَب demand, claim, quest, pursuit; question, issue, problem, case, subject; postulate (logic).

أمرت الحكومة بتزويد كل سيارة مطفأة حريق

The government ordered that each car should be provided with a fire extinguisher

مَطْلَع start, beginning, outset, early stage; starting point; introduction, preface (of a book); prelude (a piece of music); ladder, stairs, steps; place of sunrise; dawn (of an era).

مُطَّلِع acquainted with, aware of, conversant with, knowing.

مُطَلَّق، مُطَلَّقَة divorced, divorcee.

مُطْلَق absolute, unbounded, sheer, outright, unconditional, ultimate, unrestricted.

مُطْلَقاً absolutely, without exception, under any circumstances, general.

مَطْلُوب desired, wished for, wanted, required; due, owed (money); unknown (of a quantity) (math).

مَطْلُوبات (ج) liabilities.

مَطْلِيّ painted, coated, plated, overlaid.

مُطْمَئِنّ peaceful, at ease, free from fear, confident, reassured, sure, certain.

مَطْمَح aspiration, hope, ambition, desire, goal, aim.

مَطْمُور buried, interred; underground.

مُطْنِب lengthy, elaborate, detailed, verbose, exaggerated.

مُطَهَّر disinfected, sterilized, purged, purified, decontaminated; circumcized.

مُطَهِّر antiseptic, disinfectant, detergent, purifier.

مَطْهُوّ cooked.

مَطْوَى pocketknife, penknife.

مِطْوَاع obedient, compliant; pliant, pliable; ductile, malleable; flexible, resilient, yielding.

مُطَوَّر developed, advanced, sophisticated.

مُطَوِّف ambulant, ambulatory; wanderer, traveler; pilgrims' guide in Mecca.

مُطَوَّق surrounded, encircled, ringed, enclosed.

مُطَوَّل lengthened, elongated, prolongated, protracted, elaborate.

مَطْوِيّ folded, pleated, rolled up; bent, flexed.

مَطِيَّة mount, riding animal.

مُطِيع obedient, compliant, submissive, tractable, docile, dutiful, loyal, faithful, pious.

مُظَاهَرَة demonstration; help, assistance, support; patronage.

مُظَفَّر victorious, triumphant.

مِظَلَّة umbrella, sunshade; parachute.

بات الآن سعر المظلة في السوق رخيصاً جداً

The cost of an umbrella is very low in the market at present

مِظَلَّةٌ جَوِّيَّة air cover.

مُظَلَّل shady, shaded.

مُظْلِم dark, dim, tenebrous.

مَظْلوم wronged, oppressed, maltreated, aggrieved.

مِظَلِّي parachutist, paratrooper.

مَظْنون assumed, imagined; suspected, suspect.

مَظْهَر outward appearance, aspect, semblance, form, shape; expression, indication, manifestation; comportment, conduct; sight, looks, view; phenomenon, symptom, expression.

مُظَهَّر endorsed; developed (film).

مُظَهِّر endorser (of a cheque).

مَعَ، مَعْ with, together with, accompanied by; plus, added to; supporting, for; despite, in spite of.

مَعَ أَنَّ، مَعْ أَنَّ although, though.

مَعَ ذَلِك، مَعْ ذَلِك in spite of this, still, and yet.

مَعاً together, jointly, at the same time.

مِعًى، مَعِيّ intestine (anat.).

أَمْعاء (ج) intestines, bowels.

مُعاتَبَة censure, blame, reproof, reprimand, rebuke.

مُعاد returned, repeated.

مُعادٍ (المُعادِي) hostile, antagonist, adversary, enemy, foe.

مُعاداة hostility, antagonism, enmity.

مُعادِل equal to, equivalent to; amounting to.

مُعادَلَة equality, equivalence, equilibrium; assimilation, approximation, balancing; evenness, levelling.

مُعادَلَة equation (math); neutralization (chem.).

مَعاذ shelter, sanctuary, refuge.

مَعاذَ الله God forbid; God protect us from that.

مُعارِض، المُعارِض opposed to, objecting to, reluctant, resisting; adversary, antagonist, dissenter, contrary to, inconsistent with, in disagreement with.

مُعارَضَة opposition, resistance, objection, dissent, disagreement; comparison.

مَعاش salary, wages, subsistence, living.

مُعاشِر companion, fellow, associate, friend, comrade.

مُعَاشَرَة intimacy, company, companionship, social intercourse.

مُعَاصِر contemporary, contemporaneous.

مُعَاضَدَة support, backing, assistance.

مُعَافَى healthy, sound.

مُعَافَاة recuperation, convalescence, recovery (from illness).

مُعَاق handicapped, disabled, invalid; retarded (mentally); delayed, hindered, impeded, obstructed.

مُعَاقَب punished, penalized; following, alternated.

مُعَاقِب punisher, chastiser; alternate.

مُعَاقَبَة punishment, sanctions, infliction of punishment; alternation, rotation.

مُعَاكِس counter-, contra-, anti-, adverse, opposite, unfavorable, inconvenient.

مُعَاكَسَة contradiction, opposition; molestation.

مُعَالَج treated, dealt with; processed, worked.

مُعَالِج curer, physician.

مُعَالَجَة treatment, therapy, curing; dealing with, handling, tackling, discussion; processing, working, manipulation.

مُعَالَجَة طَبِيعِيَّة physiotherapy.

مُعَامِل coefficient (math).

مُعَامَلَة treatment, handling, processing, treating.

مُعَامَلَة dealing, transaction; application, request; petition.

مُعَامَلَةٌ بِالمِثْل reciprocity.

مُعَامَلَةٌ تَفْضِيلِيَّة preferential treatment.

مُعَانَاة effort; suffering, endurance.

مُعَانَدَة opposition, resistance; stubbornness, obduracy; pigheadedness, willfulness, pertinacity, obstinacy.

مُعَانَقَة embrace, hug, accolade.

مُعَاهَدَة treaty, pact, convention , agreement.

مُعَاهَدَةُ عَدَمِ اعْتِدَاء nonaggression pact.

مُعَاوِن assistant, aide, supporter.

مُعَاوَنَة help, aid, assistance, relief, support, backing.

مُعَايَدَة wishing someone a merry feast; exchange of felicitations.

مُعَايَرَة standardization, calibration, gauging; titration (chem.).

مُعَايَنَة viewing, examination, surveying; inspection; surveillance, supervision, control, observation.

مُعَبَّأ mobilized; filled, packed, canned, tinned; bottled (in bottles); charged, filled up.

مَعْبَد temple.

مُعَبَّد paved.

مَعْبَر crossing, way across, passage, path, corridor.

مُعَبِّر expressive of, indicative of.

مَعْبُود، المَعْبُود worshiped, adored; idol; diety; God.

مُعْتَاد used ,accustomed, habituated; conditioned, seasoned to; being in the habit; customary, normal.

كَالمُعْتَاد as usual.

مُعْتَدٌّ بِنَفْسِهِ self-conceited, proud.

مُعْتَدٍ (المُعْتَدِي) aggressor, assaulter, attacker, assailant; transgressor; wrongdoer; assailing, invading, attacking.

مُعْتَدًى عليه victim, aggrieved person; wronged; encroached upon, impinged upon.

مُعْتَدِل straight, even, proportionate, symmetrical, harmonious; moderate, temperate; mild; clement (weather).

مُعْتَرِض lying across, transversal; adversary ,opponent, opposer, contradicter.

مُعْتَرَفٌ بِهِ recognized, accepted, conceded, acknowledged; approved, granted, admitted, licensed, authorized.

مُعْتَزِل retired, isolated, secluded, recluse.

مُعْتَقَد (ص) believed, thought, considered, deemed.

مُعْتَقَد (اسم) belief, faith, creed, doctrine, dogma, ideology.

مُعْتَقَل concentration camp, prison camp, detention camp; arrested, confined, apprehended; detainee, internee.

مُعْتَكِف secluded, isolated, solitary, recluse, withdrawn.

مُعْتَلّ sick, ill, ailing, sickly; unhealthy, unwell; weak, defective (grammar).

مُعْتِم dark, dim, gloomy, cloudy.

مُعْتَمَد، المُعْتَمَد reliable, dependable, object of reliance; sanctioned, approved, authorized, accredited; commissioner; authorized agent, proxy; envoy, representative.

مُعْتَمَدٌ تِجَارِيّ agent, representative.

مُعْتَمَدُ قَبْضٍ أو صَرْف paymaster.

مُعْتَمَدٌ على relying on, depending on, trusting in, based on, having confidence in, counting on.

مَعْتُوه idiotic, insane, mad, crazy; idiot, lunatic, imbecile, demented person.

مُعْجَب admirer, fan, devotee, pleased with.

مُعْجَبٌ بِنَفْسِهِ conceited, vainglorious, arrogant, vain.

مُعْجِب wonderful, admirable, charming, appealing.

مُعْجِزَة wonder, miracle.

مُعَجَّل urgent, pressing; accelerated; summary (jurisdiction).

مُعْجَم (ص) obscure, ambiguous

مُعْجَم (اسم) dictionary.

مَعْجُون، المَعْجُون kneaded; paste, putty, cream.

مُعَدٌّ لِـ designed for, intended for.

مُعْدٍ (المُعْدِي) infectious, contagious.

مُعَدَّات equipments, materials, furnishings, fittings, appliances, implements, instruments.

مَعِدَة، مِعْدَة stomach.

مُعَدَّل (ص) modified, altered, adjusted, revised, amended.

مُعَدَّل (اسم)	average, rate.
مُعَدَّلُ الخصْم	discount rate, bank rate.
مُعَدَّلُ الفائِدَة	interest rate.
مُعَدَّلُ المَواليد	birth rate.
بِمُعَدَّل	as an average, at the rate of.
مَعْدِن	mineral, metal.
مَعْدِنِيّ	mineral, metallic.
مَعْدُود	countable, calculable; little, few in number.
مَعْدُوم	nonexistent, vanished, gone; wanting, lacking, absent, missing, lost.
مُعَذَّب	anguished, afflicted, tormented, suffering, in pain.
مَعْذِرَة	excuse, pardon; excuse me! forgive me!.
مَعْذُور	excused, justified, warranted, excusable.
مُعَرَّب	translated into Arabic, Arabicized.
مُعَرْبِد	quarrelsome, contentious, boisterous, riotous.
مَعْرِض	exhibition, exposition, show, fair.
في مَعْرِض الحدِيث	on the occasion of conversation, while.
مُعَرَّضٌ لِـ	exposed; determined, identified.
مَعْرِفَة	knowledge, learning, information, skill, know-how; experience, acquaintance, perception; an acqaintance, a friend.
اسم معْرِفَة	definite noun (grammar).

مَعْرَكَة	battle, fight, combat.
مَعْرُوض	demonstrated, exhibited, displayed, exposed; offered, tendered, presented; submitted to, put before; petition, application, proposal, offer, tender.
مَعْرُوف	known, widely-known, renowned.
مَعْرُوفٌ بِـ	commonly known or called as; alias.
مَعْرُوف	favor, fairness, equity; kindness, beneficence.
بِالمَعْرُوف	in all fairness, with appropriate courtesy, amicably.
المَعْرُوفُ أنّ	it is known that; it is commonly understood that.
مُعَزٍّ (المُعَزِّي)	consoler, condoler, comforter.
مُعَزَّز	made strong, stengthened, reinforced, fortified, corroborated, confirmed; hardened, supported,consolidated; raised in esteem, elevated, exalted; endeared.
مَعْزِل	retreat, seclusion, isolation.
بِمَعْزِلٍ عن	separated, detached, apart, secluded, isolated from.
مَعْزُوفَة	recital, piece of music.
مَعْزُول	far, distant, remote from; isolated, insulated (elect.); deposed, discharged, expelled, dismissed.
مُعَسْكَر	camp, encampment.
مُعَسْكَرُ الاعْتِقال	concentration camp.
مَعْسُول، مَعْسُولُ اللِّسان	honeyed; smooth tongued.

مَعْشَر	company, society, group, people, kinsfolk.
مَعْشُوق، مَعْشُوقَة	lover; beloved, sweetheart.
مَعْصَرَة، مِعْصَرَة	mill, press.
مِعْصَم	wrist.
مَعْصُوب	tied, folded; bandaged.
مَعْصُوبُ العَيْنَيْن	blindfold.
مَعْصُوم	infallible, inviolable, sacrosanct; sinless, protected; impeccable.
مَعْصِيَة	sin; insubordination, insurrection, revolt, sedition, rebellion; guilt, wrongdoing.
مُعْضِلَة	problem, enigma, puzzle, dilemma.
مُعْطَى	given, granted, accorded, conferred.
مِعْطَف	overcoat, smock, frock, coat.
مُعَطَّل	inactive, idle; jobless, unemployed; inoperative, out of service, stopped, shut-down, shut-off.
مَعْطُوب	damaged, ruined; impaired; spoiled, wrecked.
مُعْطَيَات (ج)	data, informations, facts.
مُعَظَّم	glorified, exalted, extolled; glorious, splendid.
مُعْظَم	most of, the majority of, bulk, maximum.
في مُعْظَمِهِ	largely, mostly, for the most part of.
مُعْفَى	exempt from, free from.
مُعَقِّب	commentator, investigator, reviewer; pursuer, chaser.

أرتدي المعطف في الطقس الممطر لأتقي المطر
I wear an overcoat in rainy weather to protect myself from rainwater

مُعَقَّد	complicated, intricate, snarled, entangled, difficult; knotted, gnarled, knotty.
مَعْقِل	stronghold, castle, fort, fortress.
مُعَقَّم	sterilized, disinfected, pasteurized.
مُعَقِّم	sterilizer, disinfectant.
مَعْقُود	knotted, knit, tied, joined; concluded; arched; coagulated, curdled; held, convened.
مَعْقُوف	crooked, bent, hooked, bent at the ends.
الصَّلِيبُ المَعْقُوف	swastika.
مَعْقُول	reasonable, sensible, comprehensible, understandable, plausible, rational.

اتخذ الألمان تحت حكم هتلر
الصليب المعقوف رمزاً لوطنهم
Germans under Hitler's regime
took the Swastika
as their national emblem

مَعْكُوس reversed, opposite; reflected (light).

مِعْلاق pluck (of a slaughtered animal).

مُعَلَّب canned, tinned, boxed, packed.

مُعَلَّبَات canned foodstuff.

مُعَلَّق suspended, hanging; in suspense, in abeyance, pending, depending, dependent, conditional on.

مُعَلِّق commentator, reviewer (press etc).

مُعَلَّل justified, motivated, explained.

مَعْلَم road sign, landmark, signpost; peculiarity; track, abode, place, spot, trace.

مَعَالِم (ج) characteristic traits; outlines, features (of face).

مُعَلَّم marked, labeled; taught, instructed.

مُعَلِّم teacher, tutor, professor, instructor; master (in a profession).

مُعْلَن announced, declared, advertised.

مُعْلِن advertiser, announcer.

مَعْلُول، المَعْلُول ill, sick, ailing; effect.

مَعْلُوم known, given, determined.

صِيغَةُ المَعْلُوم active sense (grammar).

فِعْلٌ مَعْلُوم active verb (grammar).

مَعْلُومات (ج) information, data.

مَعْلُوماتِيَّة informatics, data processing.

مِعْمَار architect; mason, builder.

مُعَمِّر long-lived, perennial.

مَعْمَعَة tumult, turmoil; war, battle.

مَعْمَل factory, plant, mill, works, workshop, atelier.

المَعْمُورَة the world.

مَعْمُول done, made, fabricated, produced, manufactured.

مَعْمُولٌ بِهِ in force, in effect, effective, valid, in use.

مَعْنًى meaning, sense; notion, idea, concept; connotation.

اسم مَعْنًى abstract noun (grammar).

بِكل مَعْنَى الكَلِمَة in the full sense of the word, absolutely, downright, outright, utterly, in full, fully.

لا مَعْنًى له meaningless, pointless, senseless.

مُعَنْوَن entitled, addressed, labeled.

مَعْنَوِيّ moral, abstract, incorporeal.

مَعْنَوِيَّات morale, spirit.

مَعْنِيّ meant, intended; concerned, involved, interested in.

مَعْهَد institute, institution.

مَعْهَدٌ مُوسِيقِيّ conservatory.

مَعْهُود known, familiar, usual, ordinary, customary.

مَعْهُودٌ إليه entrusted to, assigned to; commissioned with.

مُعْوَجّ crooked, curved, bent, twisted; tortuous, sinuous; wry, odd, queer.

مِعْوَزٌ، مُعْوَز needy, pauper, destitute, indigent.

مُعَوِّض compensator, indemnifier.

مُعَوَّل reliance, dependence.

مُعَوَّلٌ عليه depending on, relying upon.

مِعْوَل pickaxe, hoe, pick.

مَعُونَة help, aid, assistance, succor, relief, support.

مِعَوِيّ intestinal, enteric.

مِعْيَار criterion, standard, yardstick, norm.

مِعْيَارِيّ standard, normative.

مُعِيب disgraceful, shameful, discreditable.

مَعِيَّة accompaniment, accompanying, company.

بِمَعِيَّة in the company of, with.

مُعِيد repetitor, tutor, coach, assistant; reader.

مَعِيشَة living, life, way of living, form of life; livelihood, subsistence.

مُعِيل breadwinner, family provider.

مَعِين spring, source of water.

مُعَيَّن fixed, designated; scheduled, prescribed, stipulated; nominated, appointed; earmarked, assigned, set aside.

مُعَيَّن rhombus, lozenge (eng.).

مُعِين helper, help, aide, assistant, supporter, backer.

مُغَادِر leaving, departing from, going away from.

مُغَادَرَة departure, leaving, going away.

مَغَارَة cave, cavern, grotto.

تعتبر مغارة قاديشا في لبنان
من أشهر المغاور في البلاد
Kadisha Grotto in Lebanon is one of the most famous caverns in the country

مُغَازَلَة flirt, flirtation, dalliance, dallying.

مُغَالًى فيه exaggerated, overdone, magnified, overstated.

مُغالَطة swindle, deceit, fraud, falsification, distortion, fallacy; cheating; sophism.

مُغامِر adventurer.

مُغامَرَة adventure, risk, venture.

مَغَبَّة consequence, result, issue, effect, outcome.

مَغْبون wronged, aggrieved, prejudiced, cheated, defrauded.

مُغْتاظ angry, furious, irate, enraged, incensed, angered, furious, wrathful, vexed, out of temper.

مُغْتَبِط happy, glad, delighted, jubilant, pleased, satisfied with, gratified by.

مُغْتَرِب emigrant, immigrant, expatriate.

مُغْتَصَب extorted, usurped, raped (woman).

مُغْتَصِب usurper; rapist.

مُغْتَمّ grieved, sad, dejected, distressed; upset, worried.

مِغْدَف paddle.

مُغَذٍّ (المُغَذِّي) nutrient, nutritive, nourishing; feeder.

مُغْرٍ (المُغْرِي) seductive, tempting, inviting, enticing; seducer, tempter.

مِغْراة glue pot.

مَغْرِب sunset, sundown.

مَغْرِب، المَغْرِب the West; the Occident.

المَغْرِب Morocco, Maghreb.

مُغَرِّد singing, warbling (bird).

مِغْرَفَة laddle, scoop.

مُغْرَمٌ بـ in love with, infatuated with, deeply fond of.

مَغْرُور conceited, vain, proud, haughty; fooled, misled, tempted, deluded, blind; snobbish.

مَغْرُوس planted, implanted; embedded; engraved.

مَغْزَى sense, meaning, import, tenor; moral of a story.

مِغْزَل spindle.

مَغْسَل washhouse.

مِغْسَل washtub, washbowl.

مِغْسَلَة washing machine.

مَغْسُول washed, rinsed.

مَغْشُوش tricked, duped; adulterated.

مَغْص colic.

مَغْصُوب forced, compelled, coerced; acquired by unlawful means, extorted.

مُغْضِب angering, infuriating, irritating, enraging.

مَغْضُوبٌ عليه hated, object of anger.

مُغَطًّى covered, wrapped, veiled.

مِغْطَس bathtub, tub.

مَغْفِرَة pardon, forgiveness.

مُغَفَّل stupid, simple-minded, artless, gullible, easily duped; apathetic, indifferent, inattentive.

مُغْفَل anonymous.

شركة مُغْفَلَة joint-stock company.

مِغْلاق lock, padlock; breech (of a gun).

مُغَلَّف (ص) enveloped, wrapped, enfolded; coated; bound.

مُغَلَّف (اسم) envelope.

مُغْلَق closed, shut, locked; ambiguous, obscure, dark, dubious; difficult to comprehend.

مَغْلُوب defeated, vanquished, beaten, overpowered.

مَغْلُوبٌ على أمْرِهِ helpless, powerless.

مَغْلُول fettered, shackled; exhausted; burning with thirst, very thirsty.

مَغْلِيّ boiled.

مُغِمّ grievous, depressing, gloomy; desolate, distressing.

مَغْمُور obscure, unrenowned; flooded, inundated, drowned.

مَغْمُوس dipped, immersed, submerged.

مُغَنٍّ (المُغَنِّي) singer, melodist, vocalist.

مِغْنَاج coquettish, flirtatious.

مَغْنَطَة magnetization.

مَغْنَطِيس magnet.

مَغْنَطِيسِيّ magnetic.

مَغْنَم booty, spoils, loot, prey; gain, profit, benefit.

مُغَنِّيَة songstress, chanteuse.

مِغْوَار invader, fighter; bold; courageous, daring; swift, fast; commando.

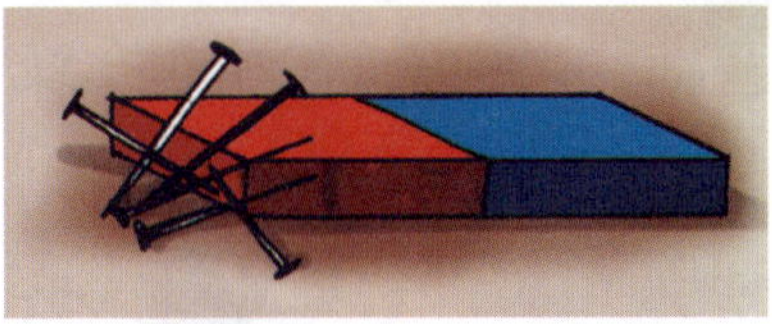

يجذب المغنطيس إليه جميع المسامير المتفرّقة على الطاولة
The magnet attracts all nails dispersed on the table

مَغِيب sunset, sundown; concealed, invisible, absence.

مُغَيَّر changed, modified, altered.

مُغِير raider, invader, marauder.

مُغِيظ vexing, irritating, exasperating, infuriating.

مَفَاتِن charms, attractions, charming qualities.

مُفَاجِئ sudden, unexpected, surprising.

مُفَاجَأَة surprise.

مُفَاخَرَة boasting, vainglory, bragging.

مُفَارَقَة leaving, departure; paradox, anachronism; difference, dissimilarity, distinction.

مُفَاضَلَة comparison; differentiation (math).

مُفَاعِل reactor, reactive.

مُفَاعِلٌ ذَرِّيّ atomic reactor, atomic pile.

مُفَاوِض negotiator.

مُفَاوَضَة negotiation.

مُفتٍ، المُفْتِي deliverer of legal opinions; official expounder of Islamic law; (Mufti).

مِفْتاح key (to door); switch (elect.); lever, pedal (of a car); knob; stop (of a wind instrument); valve, peg, pin.

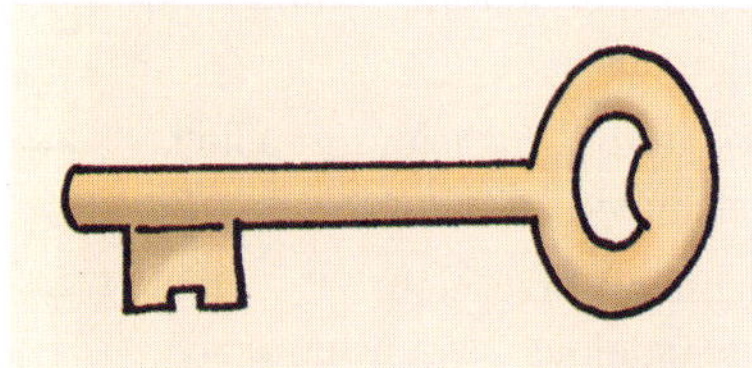

أفتح باب منزلي مستعملاً المفتاح
I open the door of my house using a key

مِفْتاح clue, key, guide (to a riddle).

مِفْتاحٌ إنْكليزيّ monkey wrench.

مِفْتاحُ رَبْط spanner.

مِفْتاحٌ عُمُوميّ master key.

مُفَتَّت crumbled, fragmented.

مُفْتَخِر proud, vianglorious, boastful; outstanding, excellent, first-rate; perfect, splendid; glorious, superb.

مُفْتَرٍ (المُفْتَري) slanderer, calumniator, liar, false accuser.

مُفْتَرِس rapacious, predatory, voracious, ferocious.

مُفْتَرَض supposed, assumed, premised, hypothetic.

مُفْتَرَق crossroads, intersection, crossing, junction.

على مُفْتَرَقِ الطُّرُق at the crossroads.

مُفَتِّش inspector, investigator, examiner.

مُفْتَعَل artificial, fabricated, forged, falsified, false, spurious; intentional, deliberate, intended.

مُفْتَقِر in need of, wanting, needing; lacking, deficient in.

مَفْتُوح open, opened.

مَفْتُول twisted, twined.

مَفْتُولُ السّاعِد muscular, robust, strong, fascinated by, infatuated by, captivated by; enamored of, in love with.

مُفَجِّر detonator.

مُفْجِع painful, grievous, distressing.

مَفْجُوع distressed, afflicted, suffering the loss of, bereaved.

مُفْحِم confusing, convincing, irrefutable.

مَفْخَرَة object of pride; something to boast of, glorious deed; exploit, feat; glorious trait or quality.

مَفَرّ escape, flight.

لا مَفَرَّ منه unavoidable, inevitable; obligatory, mandatory, imperative; inescapable.

مُفْرِح، مُفَرِّح gladdening, cheering, exhilarating; joyous, delightful, pleasant, happy, glad.

مُفْرَد single, one, only, sole; singular (grammar); odd, uneven (number); singled out, destined, allocated for.

بِمُفْرَدِهِ alone, singlehanded, singly; apart, aside, in seclusion.

مُفْرَدَات words, expressions; terminology, technical terms.

مُفْرَز secreted, excreted, discharged.

مَفْرَزَة، مُفْرَزَة group, detachment, squad, platoon.

مِفْرَش tablecloth, tablecover; bedspread, counterpane.

مُفْرِط excessive, extreme, extravagant, exorbitant, superfluous, too much, superabundant, immoderate; hyper-.

مُفْرِطُ الحَسَاسِيَّة hypersensitive.

مُفَرَّغ emptied, vacuumed, discharged; hollow.

مُفْرَغ cast, formed.

مَفْرَق، مَفْرِق crossing, intersection, bifurcation, junction.

مَفْرَقُ الشَّعْر parting of the hair.

مُفَرِّق distributor, retailer.

مُفَرَّق retail.

مَفْرُوز separated, isolated; sorted out, classified; partitioned, divided; secreted, excreted, discharged.

مَفْرُوش spread, spread out; furnished.

مَفْرُوشات (ج) furniture.

مَفْرُوض imposed, ordained, decreed; obligatory, compulsory, mandatory; supposed, assumed, hypothetic.

مَفْرُوغٌ مِنْه incontestable; settled, finished (problem, question); exhausted, carried out, achieved, completed, performed (subject).

مَفْرُوم minced, chopped.

مَفْزَع place of refuge, retreat, sanctuary, shelter.

مُفْزِع terrible, dreadful, alarming, horrible.

مُفْسِد corrupting, malicious, spoiling, depraving, fouling.

مَفْسَدَة cause of corruption; scandalous deed; heinous act.

مَفَاسِد (ج) dirty acts, malicious practices.

مُفَسَّر explained, expounded, interpreted, construed.

مُفَسِّر explainer, expounder, interpreter.

مَفْسُوخ revoked, cancelled, abolished, abrogated, nullified; dislocated, luxated (joint); severed, sundered, torn.

مِفْصَد scalpel, lancet.

مُفَصَّل set forth minutely; described in great detail; elaborate, circumstantial; custom-made (suit); made to measure.

مُفَصَّلَة hinge.

مَفْصِلِيّ articular, articulated; anthropod (specie of animals).

مَفْصُول separated, detached, severed; partitioned; dismissed (from an office); rendered (a decision); determined, resolved.

مُفَضَّل favorite, most preferred chosen.

مَفْضُوح unmasked, compromised, disgraced, notorious; covered with shame; shameful, infamous.

مَفْطُورٌ عَلى naturally disposed for.

مَفْطُوم weaned (baby).

مُفْعَم brimful, filled to capacity, replete, crammed.

مَفْعُول done; effect, impact; validity; object (grammar).

مَفْعُولٌ بِه direct object (grammar).

مَفْعُولٌ فِيه adverbial object (grammar).

مَفْعُولٌ مُطْلَق cognate accusative (grammar).

اسمُ المَفْعُول passive participle (grammar).

صِيغَةُ المَفْعُول passive voice (grammar).

سارِي المَفْعُول، نافِذُ المَفْعُول valid, effective, in force.

مَفْقُود lost, missing, nonexistent.

مِفَكُّ بَراغٍ screwdriver.

مُفَكِّر thinker, intellectual; meditator.

مُفَكِّرَة notebook, calendar, diary; journal.

مُفَكَّك، مَفْكُوك dissassembled, loose, disjoined, disjointed; incoherent (speech); separated, detached, disengaged, dislocated.

مُفْلِح successful, lucky, fortunate.

مُفْلِس bankrupt, broke.

مُفَلْطَح oblate, flat, flattened.

مُفَهْرَس indexed, catalogued.

مَفْهُوم، المَفْهُوم understood, comprehensible; notion, concept, meaning; connotation (logic).

مَفْهُومٌ ضِمْناً implied, implicit, tacit.

مُفَوَّض (ص) authorized, empowered, deputized, entrusted with.

مُفَوَّض (اسم) proxy, deputy, agent, commissioner.

مُفَوَّضِيَّة legation, commissariat.

مُفِيد useful, beneficial, advantageous, favorable, profitable.

مُقابِل opposite; counter, contrary; corresponding to; equivalent, substitute; compensation; price, rate.

مُقابِل in front of, facing, alongside of; in return for, against,for, upon, on.

بِلا مُقابِل gratis, free of charge.

مُقابَلَة interview; meeting; encounter; comparison; opposition, setting against.

مُقابَلَةَ ذلك in exchange for that, for, that, therefor.

المُقابَلَةُ بالمِثْل retaliation, reprisal, requital.

مُقاتِل fighter, combatant, belligerant.

مُقاتَلَة fight, combat, battle.

مُقارِب mediocre, approximate, medium; asymptotic (math).

مُقارَبَة approach

مُقارَعَة fight, struggle.

مُقارَن comparative.

مُقارَنَة comparison.

بالمُقارَنَةِ مَع in comparison with; compared to.

مُقاسِم sharer, partner, participant.

مُقاسَمَة sharing, participation, partnership.

مُقاضاة suing, bringing suit against, taking legal action against; trial, hearing (in court).

مُقاطَعَة boycott; severance of relations, breaking up with, breaking away from; interruption (during a speech).

مُقاطَعَة province, district, county.

مَقال، مَقالَة article, essay.

مَقالَةٌ افْتِتاحِيَّة editorial, leader.

مَقام rank, dignity, position; site, seat, location, shrine; context, occasion; key (music).

في هذا المَقام on this occasion.

مَقامُ الكَسْر denominator of a fraction (math).

مُقام، المُقام raised, set up, erected; stay, sojourn, abode, habitat, whereabouts; place of residence.

مُقامِر gambler.

مُقاوِل contractor.

مُقاوَلَة contract, deal.

مُقاوِم، المُقاوِم resisting, resistant; reluctant, unwilling; opponent, adversary, antagonist, fighter, adversary; resistor (elect.).

مُقاوَمَة resistance, opposition; fight, battle.

مُقايَضَة barter, trade-off.

مَقْبَرَة cemetery, graveyard.

مِقْبَض، مَقْبِض handle, grip, knob; hilt (of sword).

مُقْبِل next, coming, to come, forthcoming, upcoming.

مَقْبُوضٌ عليه seized, arrested, detained; caught, gripped, clutched; detainee, prisoner, in legal custody.

مَقْبُول accepted, approved, reasonable, satisfactory; pleasing, obliging, amiable; well-liked, likable, welcome, admissible, allowed, permitted, tolerable, fair.

مَقَتَ to detest, abhor, hate, loathe.

مَقْت detestation, hate, repugnance, disgust, loathing.

مُقْتَبَس، المُقْتَبَس adapted, cited, borrowed; excerpt, extract.

مُقْتَبَلُ العُمْر prime of youth.

مُقْتَدِر possessing power, ability, strength; powerful, potent, able, capable, efficient, talented.

مُقَتِّر، مُقْتِر (ص) stingy, miserly, parsimonious, niggardly.

مُقْتَرِب approaching, forthcoming, imminent.

مُقْتَرَح proposal, suggestion, motion, proposition.

مُقْتَرِض borrower.

مُقْتَرِع voter, elector.

مُقْتَرِف perpetrator (of a crime).

مُقْتَرِن coupled, joined, linked, associated; married.

مُقْتَصِد economical, economizing, frugal, saving, thrifty.

مُقْتَصِر short, brief, concise; succinct, summary.

مُقْتَضَى — required, necessary.

مُقْتَضَيَات (ج) — requisites, prerequisites, exigencies, demands.

بِمُقْتَضَى — according to, in conformity with, pursuant to; by virtue of, on the basis of, commensurate with.

مُقْتَضَب — short, abridged, condensed, improvised, unprepared.

مُقْتَطَف، المُقْتَطَف — selected, excerpted, quoted; selection; extract.

مُقْتَطَفَات (ج) — selected writings, anthology.

مَقْتَل — death, murder; mortal spot, vulnerable point.

مُقْتَنَيَات (ج) — acquisitions, possessions, property.

مُقْتَنِع — convinced, persuaded.

مُقْحَم — inserted, thrusted, put in, implicated in; crammed, wedged, pushed, forced in.

مِقْدَار — quantity, amount; size, volume; number, extent, range, degree; rate, scope.

بِمِقْدَار ما — in as much as, in so far as, as far as, as much as.

بِمِقْدَار — to a ceratin extent, somewhat, a little.

مِقْدَام — fearless, intrepid, courageous, brave, audacious.

مُقَدَّر — predestined, preordained, fated; estimated, evaluated, valued, assessed; implied, underlying; supposed, assumed, presumed, judged, figured up, thought; anticipated, expected.

مُقَدَّرات — destiny, fate.

مَقْدَرَة، مَقْدُرَة، مَقْدِرَة — power, ability, capability, potency.

مُقَدَّس — sacred, holy, hallowed, divine, sanctified.

مَقْدَم — arrival, coming, advent.

مُقَدَّم — offered, presented, awarded; tendered (bid); displayed, demonstrated; submitted to, put before, handed over.

مُقَدَّم، المُقَدَّم — given, priority over, preferred to; front, face, forefront, lead; prow (of ship); major (mil. rank); antecedent (grammar).

مُقَدَّماً — in advance, beforehand.

مُقَدِّم — donator, presenter; applicant (of petition).

مُقَدِّمَة — lead, front, forefront; prow (of ship); vanguard, advance guard (mil.); introduction, preface, foreword, preamble, prelude (of a book); premise (logic); prelude (mus.).

في المُقَدِّمَة — in the forefront, at the top of, foremost.

مَقْدُور، المَقْدُور — decreed by fate; destiny, fate; faculty, ability; potential resources.

في مَقْدُورِهِ أن — to be able to, capable of; to be in a position to.

مَقْذُوف (اسم) — missile, projectile.

مَقَرّ — seat, site, abode, habitation, domicile, headquarters, center.

مُقَرَّب — close, intimate, favorite.

مَقْرَبَة، مَقْرُبَة closeness, proximity, vicinity.

على مَقْرُبَةٍ مِنْ in the vicinity of, near, close.

مُقَرَّر (ص) established, settled, fixed, determined, confirmed.

مُقَرَّر (اسم) course, curriculum; manual; textbook.

مُقْرِض lender, creditor.

مِقْرَعَة whip, scourge, lash; knocker (of door).

مُقْرِف disgusting, nauseating, repulsive.

مُقْرَن coupled, paired, joined, united.

مِقْرَن yoke.

مَقْرُوء read, legible, readable.

مَقْرُونٌ بِـ coupled with, connected with.

مُقَسًّى hardened, solidified, set, stiffened.

مُقَسَّط installment, by installments.

مُقَسَّم (ص) divided, parted, divisioned, partitioned; distributed, apportioned, allotted, shared out.

مُقَسِّم (اسم) switchboard.

مَقْسُوم dividend (math); divided, partitioned, distributed, shared out.

مَقْسُومٌ عَلَيْه divisor (math).

مِقْشَدَة skimmer, creamer.

مُقَشَّر peeled, skinned, shaved off, pared, husked.

مِقْشَطَة scraper, rasp, plane, jointer.

مِقَصّ scissors, shears.

مَقْصِد، مَقْصَد destination; intention; design, purpose; object, goal, aim, end; sense, meaning, import, significance.

مُقَصَّر shortened, curtailed, abridged; bleached.

مُقَصِّر neglectful, delinquent; failing, failure (in an exam).

مَقْصَف، مَقْصِف buffet, refreshment room, canteen, cafeteria.

مِقْصَلَة guillotine.

مَقْصُود intended, aimed at; intentional, designed, meant, done on purpose.

مَقْصُورٌ على limited to, restricted to, confined to.

مَقْصُورَة compartment, cabin, cabinet, loge, stall, booth; cockpit.

مَقْصُوص cut off, clipped, sheared; narrated, recounted.

مُقَطَّر distilled; dribbled, percolated.

مَقْطَع section, division, portion, piece (of a speech); excerpt; syllable (grammar); stanza, verse (poetry).

مَقْطَعٌ عَرَضِيّ cross section.

مُقَطَّع cut up, cut into pieces, sectioned; separated; lacerated.

مِقْطَع cutter, cutting machine or instrument.

مَقْطُور towed, tugged, trailed, hauled.

مَقْطُورَة trailer.

مَقْطُوع cut off, severed; amputated (limb); broken, sundered; lump (sum), fixed (sum).

مَقْطُوعَة — piece of music, strophe or stanza of a poem.

مَقْعَد — seat, chair.

مُقْعَد — crippled, lame, infirm, invalid.

مَقْعَدَة — buttocks, posterior, backside, rump.

مُقعَّر — concave, hollow.

مُقْفَل — closed, shut, locked.

المِقْلاة — frying pan.

تقلي والدتي البيض في المقلاة

My mother fries eggs in the sauce pan

مِقْلاع — sling, catapult.

مَقْلَب — dump (of waste); prank, practical joke, trick.

مُقْلَةُ العَيْن — eyeball.

مُقَلَّد — imitated, forged, counterfeited, falsified; fake, spurious, false; tradition-bound.

مُقَلِّد — imitator; mimic; counterfeiter, forger.

مَقْلَعُ الحِجارَة — stone quarry.

مُقْلِق — worrisome, troubling, upsetting, disturbing, perturbing.

مِقْلَمَة — pen case.

مَقْلُوب — turned upside down, inverted, reversed, overturned.

بِالمَقْلُوب — upside down, inside out, in reverse, conversely.

مَقْلِيّ — fried.

مُقْمِر — moonlit.

مُقَنْطَر — vaulted, arched, arcaded.

مُقْنِع — convincing, persuasive.

مُقَنَّن — codified; rationed.

مَقْهَى — café, coffeehouse.

مَقْهُور — coerced, constrained; subdued, subjugated, vanquished.

مُقَوَّى — strengthened, fortified, reinforced, consolidated.

مِقْوَد — halter (of animal); steering wheel (of car); handlebars (of bicycle).

مُقَوْلَب — cast, molded, shaped, formed.

مُقَوَّم — valued, rated, evaluated; rectified, adjusted, fixed; straightened, made straight.

مُقَوِّم — appraiser, valuer, estimator; rectifier, corrector; constituent, component, element.

مُقَوِّمُ الأَسْنان — orthodontist.

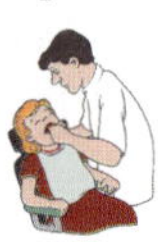

مُقَوِّمُ العِظام — orthopedist.

مُقَوِّمات (ج) — constituents, components, elements, basics, fundamentals, essentials.

مِقْياس — measure, measurement; amount; quantity; gauge, scale; standard, criterion, unit of measure; meter, counter.

مِقْياسُ الارْتِفاع — altimeter.

مِقْياسُ التَّيار الكَهْرَبائِيّ — ammeter.

مِقياسُ الحرارة	thermometer.
مِقياسُ الرُّطوبَة	hygrometer.
مِقياسُ الزَّلازل	seismometer.
مِقياسُ الزَّوايا	protractor.
مِقياسُ الضَّغطِ الجَوّيّ	barometer.
مِقياسُ ضَغطِ الغَازات	manometer.
مِقياسُ الطَّيف	spectrometer.
مِقياسُ الجُهدِ الكَهْربائيّ	voltmeter.
مِقياسٌ مِئَوِيّ	centigrade.
مِقياسُ المَطَر	pluviometer.
مِقياسُ المَغنطيسيَّة	magnetometer.

مَقيت — loathsome, detestable, disgusting, repulsive.

مُقيت — nourishing, nutrient.

مُقيَّد — bound, tied, shackled, chained; obligated; limited, confined, restrained; registered, recorded, listed.

مُقيم — resident, inhabitant, habitant, dweller, settler; residing, remaining, domiciled; lasting, permanent.

مُكابَدَة — suffering, enduring, endurance.

مُكابِر — stubborn, obstinate, arrogant, supercilious, haughty, contentious, stickler.

مُكابَرَة — haughtiness, superciliousness, pomposity, stubbornness, obstinacy, self-will.

مُكاتَبَة — correspondence, communication, exchange of letters.

مُكافَأَة — reward, recompense, retribution, compensation, bonus.

مُكافِح — struggler, fighter, combatant.

مُكافَحَة — opposition ;fight, battle, struggle; contention, strife.

مُكالَمَة — conversation, addressing, telephone call.

مَكان — place, spot, location, site, locality, seat; standing.

مَكان — in the place of, in lieu of, instead of.

في كلّ مَكان — everywhere.

ظَرْفُ المَكان — adverb of place (grammar).

من الأهَمِّيَّة بِمَكان — of considerable importance.

مَكانَة — standing, rank, position, status.

مِكَبّ — spool, reel, bobbin; ball of thread.

مِكْبَح — brake.

مُكَبَّر — enlarged, magnified, expanded, amplified.

مُكَبِّر — amplifier (elect.); loudspeaker.

مِكْبَس — press, compressor; piston, ramrod (of rifle).

مُكَبَّل — shackled, fettered, enchained.

مَكْبُوت ، مَكْبُوح — suppressed, subdued, restrained, in check.

مَكْبُوس — compressed, squeezed, pressed.

مُكْتَئِب — sad, dispirited, dejected, downcast, depressed; gloomy, morose, grave.

مَكْتَب — office, bureau, desk.

أعمل في المكتب من الصباح إلى المساء بدون انقطاع

I work in the office from morning till evening nonstop

مَكْتَبٌ سِياسِيّ politbureau. 

مَكْتَبَة library, bookshop.

مُكْتَتِب subscriber, underwriter (in shares or bonds).

مُكْتَرِب sad, worried, grieved, sorrowful, distressed; anxious, alarmed; troubled, scared, confused.

مُكْتَرِث attentive to, mindful of, concerned about.

غَيْرُ مُكْتَرِث indifferent, uninterested, disinterested, careless.

مُكْتَسَب acquired, gained, won, earned.

مُكْتَشِف discoverer, explorer.

مُكْتَظّ overcrowded, packed, jammed, densely populated.

مُكْتَمِل complete, full, whole, entire; concluded, perfected.

مُكْتَنِز compact, sturdy (body); compressed; massive, strong.

مُكْتَنَز accumulated, amassed, hidden, buried.

مُكْتَنَف surrounded, enclosed.

مَكْتُوب written, put down in writing, composed, compiled, drafted.

مَكْتُوبٌ بِاليَد handwritten.

مَكْتُوب fated, destined, foreordained.

مَكْتُوب letter, note, message, missive.

مَكْتُوفُ اليَدين having the arms folded.

مَكْتُوم hidden, concealed, kept secret.

مَكَثَ to remain, abide, stay, live, dwell, reside in a place.

مُكَثَّف condensed, concentrated, thickened; massive, intense.

مُكَثِّف capacitor (elect.); condenser.

مُكَدَّس amassed, accumulated, piled up.

مَكْدُود worn out, exhausted, overworked.

مَكَرَ to deceive, delude, cheat, dupe, double-cross someone.

مَكْر craftiness, delusion; cheating, deception, cunning, slyness, double-crossing.

مُكَرَّر repeated, bis; refined, filtered.

مُكَرَّس dedicated, consecrated; sanctified; firmly established, stabilized, confirmed, corroborated.

مُكَرَّم honored, revered, venerated.

مُكْرَه coerced, obligated to, compelled.

مَكْرُوب sad,worried; sorrowful, grieved; anxious, apprehensive, alarmed, fearful, scared; confused, troubled.

مَكْرُوه (ص) detested, hated, odious; loathsome, distasteful, disagreable, unpleasant.

مَكْرُوه (اسم) discomfort, adversity, mishap, misadventure, nuisance, inconvenience, harm, injury, accident.

مَكْسَب، مَكْسِب gain, profit.

مُكْسِب profitable, gainful, lucrative.

مُكَسَّر fragmented, broken, shattered, smashed.

مُكَسَّرات almonds and nuts.

مَكْسُوّ clothed, attired in, dressed; plated, covered.

مَكْسُور broken; defeated; frustrated; fractured, shattered.

مَكْسُور having a kasra (grammar).

مِكْشَاف detector.

مَكْشُوف bared, exposed, open, coverless, unveiled, naked.

مَكْشوفُ الرَّأس bareheaded.

على المَكْشُوف openly, publicly, overtly, for anyone to see.

مُكَعَّب cube-shaped, cubiform, cubic, cube.

مُكْفَهِرّ dim, dusky; clouded, overcast (sky); grave, sullen.

مَكْفوفُ البَصَرِ blind

مَكْفُول guaranteed, ensured, secured.

مُكَلَّس calcified.

مُكَلَّف commissioned, charged with; obligated, liable to do; responsible for; bound, obliged to do.

مُكَلَّف subject to taxation, taxable, tax-payer.

مُكَلَّل crowned.

مَكْلُوم wounded, injured, sore.

مُكَمَّل completed, finished, concluded, terminated, finalized; complete; whole, full, total.

مُكَمِّل complementary; supplementary; integrant, integral.

مَكْمَن ambush, hiding place.

مَكُنَ to be strong, to become influential; to have power.

مَكَّنَ to make strong, establish firmly, deepen; to lend weight to; to give a firm place; to put someone in a position to do something; to enable, make possible; to furnish, provide someone with.

مُكَنًّى surnamed, nicknamed.

مِكْنَسَة broom.

مِكْنَسَةٌ كَهْرَبائِيَّة vacuum cleaner.

مَكْنَنَة mechanization.

مَكْنُون hidden, concealed, sheltered; cherished, well-kept.

مُكَهْرَب electrified; electrically charged, electrically conductive, ionized.

مِكْوَاة iron.

مُكُوث staying, lingering, abiding; stay, sojourn.

تنظف والدتي أرض الحجرة بواسطة مكنسة
My mother cleans the room's floor with a broom

مَكُّوك shuttle.

مَكُّوكٌ فَضائِيّ space shuttle.

مُكَوَّم heaped up, piled up, stacked, amassed.

مُكَوَّن formed, shaped, made; constituted of, composed of.

مُكَوِّن maker, originator; ingredient, constituent, component, element.

مِكْيال measure.

مَكِيدَة plot, scheme, intrigue, conspiracy; stratagem, ruse, subterfuge, trick.

مُكَيَّف adapted, accomodated, conditioned, regulated.

مُكَيَّفُ الهَواء air-conditioned.

مُكَيِّف adaptor, conditioner.

مُكَيِّفُ الهَواء air conditioner.

مَكِين firm, solid, strong; deep-rooted, ingrained; influential; powerful, potent, of rank, distinguished.

مَلَّ to become weary, tired, bored, impatient, fed-up with.

مَلأَ to fill up, fill out a form; to wind (a clock).

مَلأ crowd, gathering, congregation, general public.

على المَلأ in public.

مِلْء filling, quantity which fills something; fill, quantity contained in something.

مِلْءُ قَدَح cupful.

مِلْءُ اليد handful.

بِمِلْءِ الفَم in a loud voice.

مَلاءة solvency.

مُلاءَةُ السَّرير bedsheet.

مُلائِم adapted, suited, appropriate, suitable, fit, proper, convenient, favorable, propitious for; agreeing, consistent with; compatible, in comformity, conforming with.

مُلاءَمَة suitability, convenience, expedience, appropriateness, adequacy, aptness, concord, agreement, harmony; accomodation; suiting, reconciliation, matching; peacemaking.

مُلابَسَة intimacy, association, close relations.

مُلابَسات (ج) surrounding conditions.

مَلاّح sailor, seaman, mariner; pilot, aviator; astronaut.

مَلاحَة beauty, grace, prettiness, comeliness; saltiness, saltness, salinity.

مِلاحَة navigation, shipping.

مِلاحَةٌ جَوِّيَّة aviation.

مِلاحَةٌ نَهرِيَّة inland navigation.

مُلاحَظ noticeable, obvious, distinct, remarkable.

مُلاحِظ supervisor, superintendent.

مُلاحَظَة observation, remark, comment, note; heed, notice, attention, supervision, superintendence, surveillance, control; N.B; P.S., statement, postscript.

مُلاحَق، المُلاحَق pursued, chased; fugitive, runaway.

مُلاحَقَة pursuit, chasing, chase; hunting; trailing, tracking.

مَلاذ refuge, retreat, shelter, asylum, harbor, haven.

مُلازِم accompanying, collateral; inherent, innate; adhering to, sticking to, inseparable from.

مُلازَمَة adhesion, clinging, sticking; remaining, staying, dwelling; dependence, inherence; following, assiduity, perseverance in; keeping close to.

مُلاصِق adjacent, contiguous, adjoining, bordering, in close contact with, close to, next to.

مُلاصَقَة adjacency, contiguity, touching, proximity.

مِلاط mortar.

مُلاطَفَة kind treatment, friendliness, courteousness; humoring, flattery; fondling, petting.

مُلاعَبَة joking, dalliance, pleasantry, frolic.

مُلاقاة encounter, meeting, get together, reunion, preception.

مَلاك angel.

مَلّاك landowner, landlord, real estate owner.

مِلاك cadre.

مِلاكُ المُوَظَّفين personnel, staff.

مُلاكِم boxer, pugilist, fighter.

مُلاكَمَة boxing.

شاهدت على التلفزيون مباراة الملاكمة التي انتصر فيها محمد علي كلاي

I watched on television the boxing match in which Mohammad Ali Clay won

مَلّالَة troop carrier.

مَلامَة censure, rebuke, blame, reproof.

مَلامِح features.

مُلامَسَة touching, touch, contact; feeling, palpation.

مَلآن full, filled, replete.

مُلايَنَة gentle treatment, kindness, friendliness.

مُلَبَّد matted, felted, compressed, flocculated.

مُلَبَّدٌ بالغُيوم overcast, cloudy.

مَلْبَس garment, dress, apparel, suit.

مَلابِس (ج) clothes, clothing, garments.

مَلابِسٌ داخِلِيَّة underwear.

مِلَّة sect, denomination, confession, creed.

مُلْتَئِم convened, assembled, in session.

مُلْتَبِس ambiguous, vague, dubious, doubtful, unclear.

مُلْتَحِم cohesive, coherent, united, merged, fused.

مُلْتَحِمٌ في قِتَال engaged in battle, fighting.

مُلْتَزّ compact, close; crowded together, dense; solid, firm.

مُلْتَزِمٌ بِـ bound by, obligated by, committed by; complying with, abiding by, adhering to.

مُلْتَزِم contractor, concessionaire, concessionary.

مُلْتَصِق attached, affixed, sticking; adjacent, bordering; connected, touching each other, close to, neighboring.

مُلْتَفّ winding, twisting, coiled; spirally wound; entwined, grouped around; enclosing, encircling.

مُلْتَفِت turning around, looking at; attentive, heedful.

مُلْتَقَى meeting place, gathering point; intersection, junction, crossroads, confluence.

مُلْتَمِس solicitor, petitioner, applicant.

مُلْتَهِب flaming, blazing, on fire; inflamed (med.).

مُلْتَوٍ (المُلْتَوِي) devious; meandering, twisting, tortuous.

مَلْجَأ refuge, shelter, asylum, resort; recourse.

مِلْح salt.

مُلْحِد atheist, apostate, unbeliever.

مُلْحَق (ص) attached, annexed, added, joined, appended, subjoined, enclosed; adjoining,adjacent, contiguous.

مُلْحَق (اسم) appendant, accessory, auxiliary, supplementary; supplement, appendix, addendum, annex, postscript; appurtenance; annex, wing (of a building); codicit (of a will); attaché (in an embassy).

مُلَحَّم، مَلْحُوم welded, fused.

مَلْحَمَة butchery, slaughterhouse; bloody fight, massacre.

مَلْحَمَةٌ شِعْرِيَّة epic, epopee.

مُلَحِّن music composer.

مَلْحُوظ noted, noteworthy, remarkable.

مَلْحُوظَة observation, remark, note, P.S; N.B.

مُلَخَّص، المُلَخَّص summarized, summed up, recapitulated, abridged summary; recapitulation, resumé, abstract, synopsis, compendium.

مُلْزَم obligated, committed, under obligation.

مُلْزِم binding, obligatory.

مَلْزَمَة section, fascicle (of a manuscript).

مِلْزَمَة vise, clamp.

مَلَّسَ to make smooth; to caress, pass the hand over, stroke lightly with the hand.

مُلْصَق، المُلْصَق attached, affixed, pasted, glued; poster, bill, sticker, label.

مُلَطَّخ stained, blotted, splashed, soiled, tarnished.

مُلَطَّخٌ بِالدَم bloodstained, bloody.

مُلَطَّف softened, mitigated, mollified, alleviated, soothed, allayed, appeased, moderated, tempered.

مُلَطِّف softening, mitigating, alleviating, palliative.

مَلْعَب playground, playfield, stadium, athletic field.

مِلْعَقَة spoon, teaspoon, tablespoon.

مَلْعُون cursed, damned, detested, abominable.

مُلْغَى canceled, invalidated, nullified, annulled, voided, abrogated, repealed; expired, suppressed.

مُلْغِز enigmatic, puzzling, mysterious, ambiguous.

مَلَفّ، مِلَفّ file, folder; coil; reel, spool; wrapping,covering.

مُلْفِتٌ لِلنَّظَر attracting attention, striking, conspicuous.

مُلَفَّق fabricated, invented, trumped up; fake, fictitious, contrived, devised; patched up, embellished with lies.

مَلْفُوظ ejected, emitted; pronounced, uttered, spoken.

مَلْفُوف (ص) wound, coiled, rolled up, voluted, spiraled; intertwined; surrounded, encircled, enclosed; enveloped, covered, wrapped.

ملفوف (اسم) cabbage

سمّي الملفوف بهذا الاسم لأن أوراقه تلتف حول بعضها البعض

The cabbage is called in Arabic «malfouf» which means wound because its leaves are wound up

مُلَقَّب surnamed, nicknamed.

مُلَقَّح inoculated, vaccined; pollinated, fertilized, impregnated.

مِلْقَط tongs, tweezers; clip; forceps; clothespin.

مَلَكَ to possess, own, have, take possession of, acquire; to control, master, overcome; to rule, reign, exercice power; to be capable of, be able to.

مَلَكَهُ الغَيْظ anger overwhelmed him.

مَلَكَ عليه حِسَّهُ to take possession of someone's feelings.

مَلَكَ نَفْسَهُ	to restrain, control oneself.
لَمْ يَمْلُكْ ان	he could not refrain from; he had to.
مَلِك	king, monarch, sovereign.
مُلْك	reign, rule, sway, domination; ownership, property.
مِلْك	property, wealth, estate, landed property.
مَلَكَة	faculty, talent, aptitude, ability.
مَلِكَة	queen.

مَلَكُوتُ الله	the Kingdom of Heaven.
مَلَكِيّ	royal, regal, monarchist.
مِلْكِي، مِلْكُهُم	mine; theirs.
مَلَكِيَّة	monarchy, kingship.
مِلْكِيَّة	ownership, property.
مَلَل	weariness, boredom, tedium.
مُلِمٌّ بِـ	versed in, acquainted with, familiar with.
مُلِمَّة	calamity, misfortune, disaster.
مَلْمَس، مِلْمَس	touch, feel; tentacle, feeler (of insect).
مَلْمُوس	touched, felt; palpable, tangible.
مَلْهَى	cabaret, nightclub, amusement center.
مَلْهَاة	comedy.
مُلْهَم	inspired.

مَلْهُوف	troubled, apprehensive, concerned; anxious, eager for, desirous of, longing, yearning.
مُلَوَّث	polluted, contaminated, soiled.
مُلَوِّث	pollutant, polluter, contaminant, contaminating.
مُلَوَّع	anguished, tormented, languishing with love.
مُلُوكِيّ	royal, majestic, kingly.
مَلُوم، مَلِيم، مُلام	censured, blamed, reprehensible, at fault, in the wrong, blameful, blamable.
مُلَوَّن	colored, tinted.
مُلَوِّن	colorant, coloring.
مَلْوِيّ	twisted, kinked, bent, crooked; tortuous, meandering.
مَلِيء	full, filled, replete; rich, well-to-do, wealthy; solvent; stout, fat, corpulent (person).
مَلِيًّا	for a long time; carefully, thoroughly.
مَلِيح	beautiful, pretty, handsome, comely; nice, pleasant, agreeable; salty, briny, salted.
مُلَيِّن	laxative, purgative; softening, soothing.
مَلْيُون	million.
مِمَّ، مِمَّا	of what, of which, whereof.
مُمَاثِل	similar, analogous, corresponding, identical.
مُمَاحَكَة	wrangle, quarrel, bickering.
مُمَارِس	practitioner; exercising, practicing.
مُمَارَسَة	exercise, practice, pursuit; action, act.
مُمَاطَلَة	procrastination, stalling, postponement, putting off.

مُمالأة partiality, favoritism, bias.

مُمانَعَة opposition, revolt, objection, resistance.

مُمْتَاز first-rate, first-class, excellent; distinguished, exquisite, select, outstanding; special, superb.

دَيْنٌ مُمْتَاز preferred debt.

مُمْتَدّ extended, stretched out, spreaded, prolonged, wide, extensive, outspread, outstretched, laid out.

مُمْتَصّ absorbent, absorptive, soaking up.

مُمْتِع delicious, pleasant, enjoyable, delightful, gratifying, interesting, pleasurable.

مُمْتَعِض resentful, displeased, indignant.

مُمْتَقِع pale, wan.

مُمْتَلِئ full, filled up, replete.

مُمْتَلِئُ الجسم plumb, fleshy, rotund, obese, fat, stout.

مُمْتَلَكَات (ج) possessions, belongings.

مُمْتَنّ obliged, grateful, very thankful.

مُمْتَنِع abstaining from, refraining from, forbearing; refusing, rejecting; impossible; forbidden, interdicted, prohibited, banned, inaccessible; forbidding, elusive, impenetrable.

مُمَثِّل representing, representative; agent; actor, player, film star; deputy; exponent.

مُمَثِّلَة actress.

مِمْحَاة eraser, rubber.

مَمْحُوّ erased, wiped off, effaced, wiped out, eradicated; extinct, abolished, eliminated.

مَمَرّ passage, passageway, path, track, aisle, corridor, lane.

مَمَرٌّ جَبَلِيّ mountain pass, col.

مُمَرِّض، مُمَرِّضَة nurse, hospital attendant.

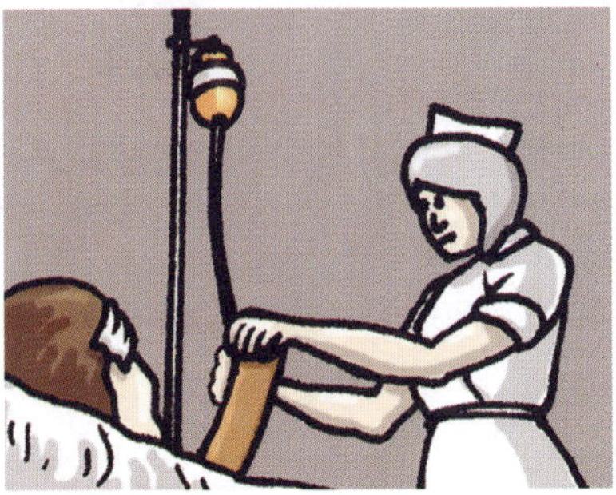

تهتم المرضة براحة المريض وتعطيه الأدوية التي يصفها الطبيب له في الأوقات المحددة

The nurse takes care of the patient's comfort and administer to him the medicine prescribed by the doctor in the specified times

مُمَرَّن trained, drilled, tutored, disciplined, skilled; trainee.

مُمَرِّن trainer, instructor, coach; drillmaster.

مُمَزَّق torn, lacerated, shredded, tattered.

مَمْزُوج mixed, mingled, blended, combined.

مِمْسَحَة mop, wiper, rag, dustcloth, duster.

مُمْسِكٌ بِـ holding, grasping, seizing, catching, clasping.

مَمْسُوح wiped, mopped, cleaned; anointed (with sacred oil); surveyed (land).

مَمْسُوخ metamorphosed, transformed, disfigured, deformed.

مَمْشُوق slender, slim, svelte.

مِمَصّ pipette; sucker, suction tube.

مُمْطِر rainy, wet.

مُمَغْنَط magnetized.

مُمْكِن possible, potential, contingent, conceivable, thinkable, probable, feasible, practicable.

مِنَ المُمْكِن perhaps, maybe, possibly, probably, may, might.

مُمِلّ boring, wearisome, weary, tiresome, tedious, irksome.

مُمَلَّح salted, salty, cured.

مِمْلَحَة saltcellar.

مَمْلَكَة kingdom.

مِمَّن of whom, whereof.

مَمْنُوح granted, awarded, donated, given.

مَمْنُوع forbidden, prohibited, banned, interdicted, barred.

مَمْنُوعٌ من الصَّرف indeclinable (grammar).

مَمْنُون indebted, obligated; grateful, thankful; weak, languid.

مُمَهَّد paved, leveled, facilitated, flattened.

مَمْهُور sealed, stamped, impressed.

مُمَوَّل financed.

مُمَوِّل financier.

مُمَوَّه camouflaged, disguised, concealed; falsified, distorted; coated, plated.

مُمِيت deadly, lethal, fatal.

مُمَيَّز distinguished, distinct, privileged; separate.

مُمَيِّز distinguishing, distinctive, peculiar, rational, discerning.

مَنَّ to be kind, benign, gracious, benevolent to; to do, grant bestow blessings, benefits, favor upon; to award, present, give someone something; to confer graciously upon someone something.

مَنّ honeydew, manna; gift, present, favor.

مَنْ who, whom, he who.

مِنْ from, of, one of a group, some of; consisting of; away from; since; through, by.

يَوْمٌ مِنَ الأَيَّام some day or other.

ما مِن شَخْص there is absolutely none who...

ثَوْبٌ مِنَ الحَرير a dress made of silk.

دَخَلَ مِنَ الباب he entered through the door.

مَنًى ، مَنِيَّة death, fate, destiny.

مَنْأًى distant place.

في مَنْأًى عن away from, apart from, isolated from.

نابَ مَنابَة to act in someone's behalf or name.

مُناجاة confidential talk; soliloquy.

مَناحَة lamentation, wailing.

مُناخ، مَناخ — climate.

مُناخِيّ، مَناخِيّ — climatic.

مُنادٍ (المُنادِي) — caller, herald; auctioneer (in an auction).

مُنادَى — noun in the vocative, vocative sense (grammar).

مُناداة — calling, shouting.

مَنارَة — lighthouse, beacon; lightstand; minaret.

مُنازِع — disputing with, fighting with; opponent, antagonist; litigant; dying, in extremis, at the point of death.

مُنازَعَة — fight, struggle, strife, contention, quarrel, dissension; matter in controversy; case at issue before a court.

مُناسِب — suitable, fitting, proper; correspondent, analogous.

مُناسَبَة — suitability, appropriateness; aptness, adequacy; relation, reference, relevancy, pertinence; opportunity, occasion.

بِمُناسَبَة — on the occasion of.

بِهذِهِ المُناسَبَة — in this connection.

في كلِّ مُناسَبَة — at every suitable occasion.

وبالمُناسَبَة — by the way, speaking of.

مُناشَدَة — urgent request, earnest appeal, adjuration.

مَناص — escape, flight, way out; avoidance; evasion.

لا مَناصَ منه — inevitable, unavoidable.

مُناصَفَة — in half, in two equal parts, fifty-fifty.

مُناضِل — struggler, combatant, fighter, militant.

مُناطٌ بِهِ — entrusted, commissioned with, in charge of.

مُناظِر — corresponding, analogous, similar, like, equal; debator, disputant; rival, adversary, opponent; supervisor.

مُناظَرَة — debate, dispute, discussion; supervision, inspection.

مَناعَة — inaccessibility, strength, impregnability; sturdiness, immunity (to a decease); imperviousness, impenetrability.

مُناغَمَة — harmonization, tuning, matching.

مُنافٍ (المُنافِي) — contradicting with, inconsistent with.

مُنافِس — competitor, rival.

مُنافَسَة — competition, rivalry.

مُنافِق — hypocrite, insincere, two-faced, double-dealer.

مُنافَقَة، نِفاق — hypocrisy, dissimulation, dissemblance.

مَناقِب — virtues, outstanding traits, feats, exploits, morals, ethics.

مُناقَشَة، نِقاش — debate, dispute, disputation, argumentation.

مُناقَصَة — bid, invitation for tenders.

مُناقِض — contradictory to, contrary to, inconsistent with, incompatible with.

مُناقَضَة — contradiction, conflict, clash, inconsistency, contrast.

مَنَال	obtainment, attainment, achievement, acquisition.
بَعِيدُ المَنَال	intangible, unattainable, far away from reach.
مَنَامَة	dormitory; nightgown.
مُنَاهِض	resistant, opposing, opponent, unfavorable to.
مُنَاهَضَة	resistance, opposition.
مُنَاوِئ	hostile to, opposed to, opponent, antagonist, foe.
مُنَاوَأة	resistance, opposition, antagonism, enmity.
مُنَاوَبَة	in rotation, by turns, successively, one by one.
مُنَاوَرَة	maneuver, gambit.
مُنَاوَشَة	skirmish, engagement, armed clash.
مُنَاوَشَات (ج)	hostilities.
مُنَاوَلَة	handling, presenting, delivery.
مَنْبِت	source, springhead, birthplace; hotbed, nursery.
مُنْبَثِق	emanating, springing, emerging, arising, originating.
مِنْبَر	platfrom, tribune, stand, pulpit.
مُنْبَسِط	extending, spreading; gay, happy; level surface.
مُنْبَطِح	prostrate; flat, level, plain land.
مَنْبَع	source, fountainhead, springhead, origin, spring.
مَنْبَعُ النَّهْر	riverhead.
مُنْبَعِث	emitted, sent out, discharged, released, emanated; revived, reanimated, revitalized.

مُنَبِّه	stimulant, exciter; awakening, rousing (from sleep); warning, cautioning.
مَنْبُوذ	cast-off, discarded, ostracized, banished, expelled, repudiated; abandoned, foundling; neglected, disregarded.
المَنْبُوذ	untouchable, pariah.
مُنْتَبِه	attentive, heedful, observant; watchful, vigilant, cautious.
مُنْتِج (ص)	productive, fertile, bearing, generating.
مُنْتِج (اسم)	producer, manufacturer, maker.
مُنْتَجَع	health resort, retreat.
مُنْتَحِل	impersonator, plagiarist.
مُنْتَخَب	elected, selected; elected candidate; selection, excerpt.
مُنْتَخَبَات (ج)	selections, selected writings; anthology.
مُنْتَخِب	elector, voter, constituent.
مُنْتَدَى	forum, place of assembly.
مُنْتَدَب	delegated, deputized, accredited, commissioned with; entrusted with.
مُنْتَزَه	recreation ground.
مُنْتَسِب	affiliate, associated, belonging.
مُنْتَشِر	widespread, current, prevalent, in circulation; diffused, scattered, unfolded, extended; deployed.
مُنْتَصِب	erect, upright, vertical.
مُنْتَصِر	victorious, triumphant, conqueror, victor.
مُنْتَصَف	middle, mid-.

في مُنْتَصَفِ الطَّريق midway.

مُنْتَظَر expected, likely, anticipated.

مُنْتَظِر awaiting, expecting, anticipating.

مُنْتَظِم regular, systematic, steady, methodical; even.

مُنْتَعِش refreshed, stimulated, invigorated.

مُنْتَفِخ blown up, puffed up, inflated, swollen.

مُنْتَقِم avenger, revengeful, vindictive.

مُنْتَمٍ (المُنْتَمِي) belonging, pertaining; affiliate, associate.

مُنْتِن stinking, evil-smelling, putrid, rotten.

مُنْتَهٍ (المُنْتَهِي) finished, complete, done, ceasing, expired.

مُنْتَهًى finished, done; extreme, utmost limit.

بِمُنْتَهَى الشِّدَّة wiht extreme force.

بَلَغَ مُنْتَهَاه to reach its highest degree.

مُنْتَهِك violator, desecrator.

مَنْثُور scattered, strewn about, spread, dispersed; prosaic, in prose (writing); wallflower (plant).

مَنْجًى safety, security from; refuge, shelter.

مَنْجَاة safe place, haven, refuge; protection, rescue, salvation.

بِمَنْجَاةٍ مِن safe from, safeguarded from.

مُنْجَذِب attracted to; fascinated with.

مُنْجَرِف carried away, swept away, washed away.

مُنْجَز carried out, completed, executed, realized, achieved, finalized, fulfilled, concluded, performed; full, total, entire, whole, absolute; outright, unqualified.

مِنْجَل scythe, sickle.

مَنْجَم mine, source, origin.

مَنَحَ to grant, give, accord, award, bestow, confer upon.

مَنْحًى aim, goal, object; mode of action, behavior, direction; field, domain, realm, sphere, walk of life.

مُنْحَاز secluded, retired; removed; partial, biased, prejudiced.

مُنْحَبِس secluded, shut-off.

مِنْحَة gift, present, donation, favor, remuneration, allowance, indemnity; scholarship (study).

مُنْحَدَر depression, slope, incline, talus, descent, declivity.

مُنْحَدِر descending, dipped, lowered; slanting, sloping, declining; in a state of decadence, run-down, waning; being on the downgrade.

مُنْحَرِف oblique, slanted, slanting, sloping, inclined; deviating, corrupted, perverted; twisted, divergent; trapezium; (geometry), delinquent; indisposed, unwell, ill, sicky.

مُنْحَرِفُ المِزَاج out of humor, not in good humor, out of sorts.

مُنْحطّ degraded, fallen (woman); mean, vile; inferior, low, base, low-grade, low-level; decadent, degenerate.

مُنْحَلّ dissolved, broken up; disbanded; languid, prostrate, weak; solved; permitted, allowed; unwound, disengaged, untied, undone.

مُنْحَلُّ الأَخْلاق degraded, corrupt, perverted, immoral, perverse.

مُنْحَنًى bend, flexure, curvature, twist, break, angle, curve (of road), slope.

مُنْحَنٍ (المُنْحَنِي) bent, curved, bowed, inclined, twisted.

مَنْحُوت sculptured, carved.

مَنْحُوتَة sculpture, statue.

مَنْحُوس unlucky, luckless, ill-fated, ill-starred; ill-omened, ill-boding, ominous.

مَنْخَر، مَنْخِر، مِنْخُر، مُنْخُر nostril.

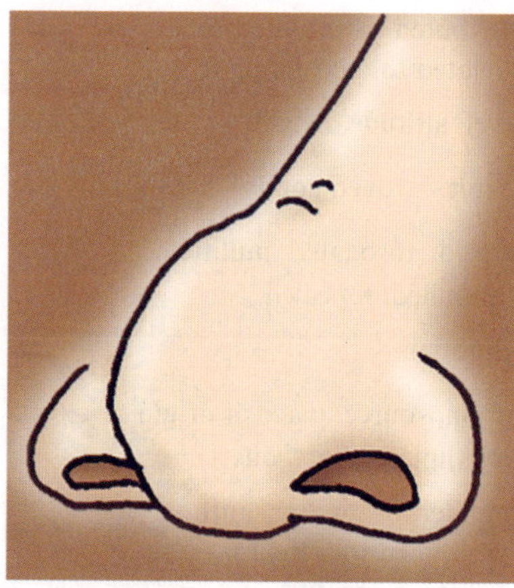

يجب التنفس من المنخر قدر الإمكان وليس من الفم

Breathing should be performed from the nostril as much as possible and not from the mouth

مُنْخَفَض depression.

مُنْخَفِض depressed, low; fading; soft, inaudible (voice).

مُنْخُل sieve, screen.

مُنْدَثِر blotted out, effaced, obliterated; old, obsolete, bygone.

مُنْدَحِر defeated, vanquished, routed.

مُنْدَرِج inserted, interpolated, incorporated; entered, contained in, comprised by; falling under, belonging to; registered in.

مُنْدَرِجات (ج) terms, clauses, stipulations, provisions.

مُنْدَرِس obliterated, old, dilapidated, crumbling, crumbled, extinct, wiped out, expunged, blotted out.

مُنْدَفِع erupting, dashing, bursting out; zealous, enthusiastic; impetuous, hasty, foolhardy.

مُنْدَمِج merged; firm, compact, tight; included, embodied, inserted, incorporated; affiliated; combined, blended, fused.

مَنْدُوب (اسم) deputy, delegate, functionary, commissioner, agent; representative, emissary, envoy, correspondent (of a newspaper).

مَنْدُوبٌ سامٍ high commissioner.

مَنْدُوبٌ مُفَوَّض authorized agent, minister plenipotentiary.

مَنْدُوبٌ فَوْقَ العادَة ambassador extraordinary.

مَنْدُوبٌ خاصّ special envoy.

مَنْدُوحَة alternative, choice, freedom of action.

لا مَنْدُوحَةَ لي عَنْ — it is absolutely necessary for me.

لم يَرَ مَنْدُوحاً مِنْ — he felt compelled to.

مَنْدِيل، مِنْدِيل — handkerchief, scarf.

مِنْدِيلُ المَائِدَة — napkin.

مِنْدِيلٌ وَرَقِيّ — tissue paper.

مِنْدِيلٌ صِحِّيّ — sanitary napkin (for women).

مُنْذُ — since, for, in, ago.

مُنْذُ عَهْدٍ قَرِيب — of late, lately, recently, not long ago.

مُنْذُ الآن — from now on, henceforth; since, ever since.

مُنْذُ أن كُنْتُ تلميذاً — since I was a student.

مُنْذِر — cautioner, harbinger, precursor; warner.

مُنْذِرٌ بِشَرٍّ — foreboding, ominous, ill-boding.

مُنْذَهِل — alarmed, dismayed, perplexed, startled, baffled; distracted, absent-minded.

مُنْزَعِج — disturbed, annoyed, irritated, ill at ease.

مَنْزِل — home, house, residence, domicile; dwelling.

مُنْزَل، مُنَزَّل — revealed; inlaid; sent down from heaven.

مَنْزِلَة — rank, position, status, standing; dignity; degree, grade.

مُنْزَلِق — sliding, gliding.

مَنْزِلِيّ — domestic, homemade, house.

مُنَزَّهٌ عَن — infaillible, unerring, impeccable; free from.

مُنْزَوٍ (المُنْزَوِي) — secluded, solitary, isolated; remote, distant.

مَنْزُوع — removed, extracted, pulled out, torn out.

مُنْسَجِم — harmonious, in accord, concordant

مُنْسَحِق — ground, grated.

مُنْسَحِقُ القَلْب — contrite, penitent, repentant; brokenhearted.

مُنَسَّق — coordinated, in harmony, well-arranged, in good order; classified, assorted, grouped together.

مُنَسِّق — coordinator.

مَنْسَك، مَنْسِك — place of sacrifice; cell, hermitage.

مُنْسَكِب — poured, spilled, shed.

مُنْسَلِخ — peeled off, discarded, skinned; detached, alienated.

مَنْسُوبٌ إلى — attributed to, imputed to; related to, pertaining to.

مَنْسُوب — level, altitude, height.

مَنْسُوجات (ج) — textiles, woven goods.

مَنْسُوخ — copied; abrogated, nullified, annulled, repealed.

مَنْسِيّ — forgotten.

مَنْشَأ — origin, source, place of origin, birthplace; start, onset.

مُنْشِئ — founder, originator, author; writer, editor; creator, creating, creative.

مُنْشَأَة — establishment, foundation, institution; firm, plant, factory.

مِنْشَار — saw.

مِنْشَارٌ شَرِيطِيّ — bandsaw.

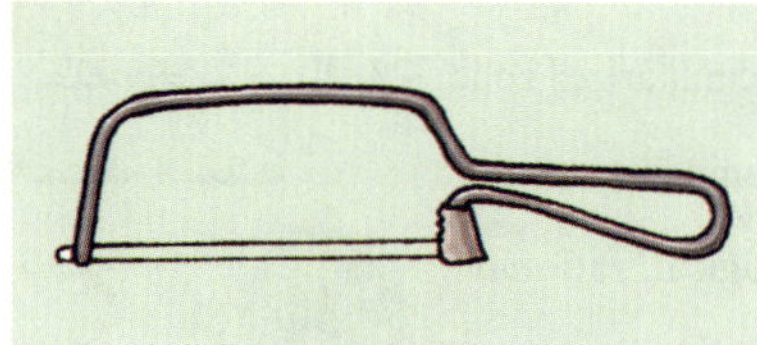

يُستعمل المنشار لنشر الخشب
أو الحديد ويُصنع من الفولاذ
The saw is used to cut wood
or iron and is made of steel

مِنْشَارُ المَعَادِن hacksaw.

مِنْشَارٌ يَدَوِيّ handsaw.

مُنْشِد، مُنْشِدَة singer, songstress.

مُنْشَرَة sawing machine, sawmill.

مُنْشَرِح cheerful, happy, delighted.

مُنَشِّط (ص) stimulating, inspiring, invigorating.

مُنْشَغِل distracted, diverted from, occupied; busy; concerned, worried.

مِنْشَفَة towel.

مُنْشَقّ، المُنْشَقّ dissenting, separatistic, breakaway; seceder, separatist, secessionist, dissident, dissenter.

مَنْشُود sought, aspired, desired, pursued.

مَنْشُور (ص) spread widely, propagated, made public, published; sawn; outstretched, expanded; unfolded, diffused, disseminated.

مَنْشُور (اسم) leaflet, pamphlet, circular, prospectus; decree, ordinance, edict; prism (math).

مُنْصَاع yielding, submitting, obeying, compliant, submissive.

مَنْصِب office, position, standing, rank.

مُنْصَبّ poured out, shed forth, flowing; intent on, bent on; directed to, tending to, turning toward.

مِنْصَب stand, rack, tripod.

مَنَصَّة، مِنَصَّة platform, tribune, rostrum, stand.

مِنَصَّةُ الوَثْب springboard.

مُنْصَرِف leaving, departing; devoted to, dedicated to, engaged in.

مُنْصَرِف inflected, triptote (grammar).

مُنْصَرِم elapsed, past, bygone.

مُنَصِّف halving, bisecting, divider; bisector (geometry).

مُنْصِف just, fair, equitable, impartial.

مَنْصُوب erected, raised, set up, installed; planted; aimed, noun in the accusative (grammar), verb in the subjunctive (grammar).

مَنْصُور، المَنْصُور supported, aided; victorious, triumphant; victor.

مَنْصُوصٌ عليه provided for; stipulated.

مُنْضَبِط disciplined.

مُنَضَّد compact, regularly set, arranged, one above the other, arrayed, put in order; composed, typeset (text).

مِنْضَدَة table, stand, desk.

مُنْضَمّ affiliated, associated; affiliate, associate.

أ ب ت ث ج ح خ د ذ ر ز س ش ص ض ط ظ ع غ ف ق ك ل م ن هـ و ي

مُنْطاد balloon, airship, zeppelin.

يطير المنطاد عالياً بواسطة الهواء الساخن

The airship rises high in the sky by the power of hot air

مُنْطَرِح thrown down, cast down, dumped; thrown off, discarded, expelled, banished, rejected, repudiated.

مُنْطَفِئ extinguished, gone out; mat, dull (color).

مَنْطِق speech, logic.

مِنْطَقَة area, region, territory, land; district, zone, section; belt, girdle.

مِنْطَقَةُ البُروج Zodiac.

المِنطَقَةُ الحارَّة، الاسْتِوائِيَّة، المَدارِيَّة the Tropics.

مِنْطَقَةٌ حَرامٌ no-man's-land, forbidden area.

مِنطَقَةٌ حُرَّة free zone.

المِنطَقَةُ القُطْبِيَّة الجَنُوبِيَّة Antarctic Circle or Zone.

المِنطَقَةُ القُطْبِيَّة الشَّمالِيَّة Arctic Circle or Zone.

مِنْطَقَةٌ مُجَرَّدَةٌ من السِّلاح demilitarized zone.

المِنطَقَةُ المُعْتَدِلَة temperate zone.

مَنْطِقِيّ logical, rational.

مِنْطَقِيّ zonal.

مُنْطَلِق dashing, darting, rushing; going off, exploding; launched, released; setting out, proceeding, moving, in progress; unrestrained, open, liberated, unchained.

مُنْطَوٍ (المُنْطَوِي) على نفْسه self-absorbed, depressed, introverted.

مُنْطَوٍ (المُنْطَوِي) على involving, including, embracing, covering.

مَنْطُوق (اسم) wording, text, statement, formulation.

مَنْطُوقُ القانُون text of the law, legal text.

مَنْطُوقُ الكَلِمَة literal meaning of the word.

مَنْطُوقُ العَقْد the exact terms of the contract.

مِنْظار telescope, speculum (med.).

مِنْظارُ المِيدان binoculars.

مِنْظارُ الوِقايَة goggles.

مَنْظَر view, sight, spectacle, scenery, landscape; outlook; scene, setting.

مُنَظِّر theorist, theoretician.

مُنَظِّف detergent, cleansing compound.

مُنَظَّم well-organized, in good order, orderly, neat, tidy, organized, arranged, kept in order, regular.

مُنَظِّم organizer, control, governor, adjuster, controller.

مُنَظَّمَة organization.

مُنَظَّمَةٌ غير حُكُومِيَّة non-governmental organization.

مَنْظُور (ص) seen, viewed, visible; promising; envied.

مَنْظُور (اسم) perspective.

مَنْظُوم، المَنْظُوم rhythmical; poetrical; poetry.

مَنَعَ to detain, stop, hinder, prevent from; to restrain, hold, back from; to bar, block, obstruct someone's way or access to; to deprive of; to forbid, interdict, prohibit; to protect, guard, defend someone against; to avert, obviate, prevent, ward off, stand by someone against.

مَنْع prevention, prohibition, interdiction, banning, obstructing, hindering, proscription, averting, warding off.

مَنْعُ التَّجَوُّل curfew.

مَنْعُ الحَمْل contraceptive.

مَنَعَة، مِنْعَة resistance, power, force, vigor, strength, invincibility.

مُنْعَتِق freed, liberated, released; uninhibited.

مُنْعَزِل isolated, solitary, recluse.

مُنْعِش (ص) refreshing, reviving, reanimating, fresh, cool.

مُنْعِش (اسم) refreshment; reviver; reanimator

مُنْعَطَف turn, bend, curve; turning point.

مُنْعَطِف bent, curved, twisted, turned.

مُنْعَقِد convened, assembled, in session, sitting, thickened, solidified, set, coagulated.

مُنْعَكِس reflected; reversed; reflex.

مُنْعِم benefactor, donor.

مَنْعُوت substantive (grammar); described, characterized, qualified.

مُنْغَمِس immersed in, absorbed in, wholly engaged in, engrossed in.

مَنْفَى place of exile.

مِنْفَاخ bellows; air pump; blowpipe (for forming glass).

مُنْفَجِر explosive, exploding, detonating, bursting; eruptive, spurting, pouring out, streaming, flowing out; ruptured.

مَنْفَذ، مَنفِذ passage, window, exit, outlet, escape, way out; entrance, access, gateway; loophole, air hole, opening.

مَنْفَذُ المِياه flood gate, sluice gate.

مُنَفَّذ executed, carried out, implemented, realized, fulfilled, accomplished, performed.

مُنَفِّذ executor.

مُنْفِر، مُنَفِّر repulsive, repellent.

مُنْفَرِج wide-open, diverging, separated; relaxed, at ease.

مُنْفَرِد isolated, detached, separated; lone, alone, solitary.

حاكِمٌ مُنْفَرِد district judge, justice of the peace.

مَنْفَس vent, breather, air hole, escape, way out.

مُنْفَصِل separate, detached.

مِنْفَضَة ashtray; feather duster.

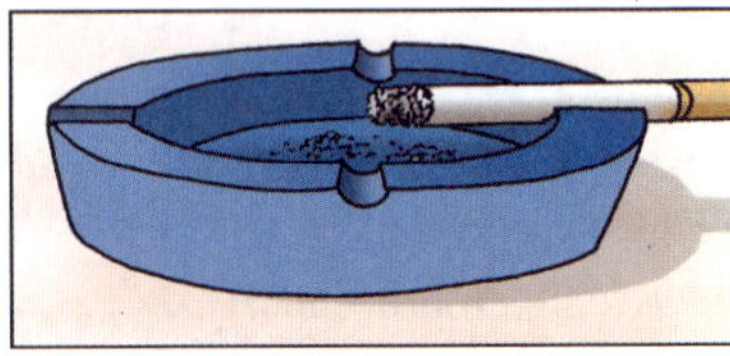

يضع أبي سيكارته في المنفضة القريبة من سريره

My father puts his cigarette in the ashtray near his bed

مَنْفَعَة usefulness, utility, benefit, profit.

مُنْفَعِل excited, upset, irritated, nervous, deeply stirred; influenced, affected.

مُنْفَق spent, paid out, disbursed; passed (time).

مَنْفُوخ blown up, puffed up, inflated; swollen, pumped up.

مَنْفُوخ paunchy, obese, fat; conceited, snobbish.

مَنْفِيّ banished, exiled, deported; denied, disowned, disavowed, disallowed; negated (grammar).

مُنْقَاد led, guided, driven, directed; obedient, compliant.

مِنْقَار beak, bill (of bird); pickax, pick.

مُنَقِّب explorer; examiner, researcher, scholar.

مَنْقَبَة virtue, exploit, feat; laudable act, good traits; mountain pass, gap, col, defile (of mountain).

مُنْقَبِض contracted, shrunken; stiff, rigid.

مُنْقَبِضُ الصَّدْر depressed, dispirited, downcast, gloomy, melancholic.

مُنْقَبِضُ الأَمْعَاء constipated.

مُنَقَّح corrected, redacted; refined, retouched, revised.

مُنْقِذ rescuer, saver, savior.

مُنْقَرِض extinct.

مُنْقَسِم divided, partitioned, sectioned; parted, split; separated; divisible (math).

مُنَقَّط spotted, speckled, dotty; punctuated (grammar).

مُنْقَطِع cut off, severed, torn apart, switched off, stopped, halted, interrupted, sundered.

مُنْقَطِعٌ إلى devoted to, exclusively occupied with.

مُنْقَطِعُ النَّظِير unmatched, peerless, matchless, unrivaled; unequaled, incomparable, singular, unique.

مُنْقَلِب turned over, turned upside down, inverted, reversed.

مُنْقَلَب the way of all flesh; final destiny; the hereafter; tropic.

مُنْقَلَبٌ شَتَوِيّ Tropic of Capricorn.

مُنْقَلَبٌ صَيْفِيّ Tropic of Cancer.

مِنْقَلَة protractor (for measuring angles).

أ ب ت ث ج ح خ د ذ ر ز س ش ص ض ط ظ ع غ ف ق ك ل م ن هـ و ي

مَنْقُوش puffed up, ruffled, disheveled (hair); fluffy (wool).

مَنْقُوش engraved, sculptured, inscribed; painted, colored, dappled, variegated.

مَنْقُوص deficient, incomplete, inadequate, insufficient.

مَنْقُوض broken, violated, repealed, abrogated, annulled.

مَنْقُوع soaked, macerated, drenched; infusion.

مَنْقُول transferred, transported, removed, moved, shifted, conveyed, delivered, hailed; movable, mobile, portable; copied, translated; reported, recounted, cited; traditional.

مَنْكِب shoulder, side; highland, hill.

مُنْكَبّ devoted to; fully occupied with; busy with.

مُنَكَّر indeterminate, indefinite (grammar).

مُنْكَر (ص) denied, unacknowledged, disowned, disavowed; shocking, detestable, abominable.

مُنْكَر (اسم) abomination, atrocity, enormity.

مُنَكَّس inverted, reversed; hung at half mast (flag).

مُنْكَسِر broken, fractured, shattered, fragmented; defeated.

مُنْكَمِش shrunk, cramped, convulsed; self-absorbed, introverted.

مَنْكُوب afflicted with disaster, unhappy, unfortunate, ill-fated, miserable, fate-stricken; victim of a catastrophe.

مَنْكُود unhappy, unforfunate, ill-fated, ill-starred.

مَنْكُودُ الحَظّ unlucky.

مُنَمَّق adorned, embellished, in good style, ornate; flowery (language).

مُنْهَار collapsed, collapsing, fallen, falling.

مَنْهَج، مِنْهَج method, manner, procedure; program, course.

مَنْهَجُ التَّعْلِيم curriculum.

مَنْهَجُ البَحْث methodology of research.

مَنْهَجِيّ methodical, systematic, formal.

مُنْهَك exhausted, weary, tired out; run-down.

مُنْهِك exhausting, grueling, wearying, burdensome.

مَنْهَل watering place, spring, well, fountain.

مُنْهَمِر pouring out, torrential (rain).

مُنْهَمِك engrossed in, absorbed in, preoccupied with.

مَنْهُوك worn out, exhausted, consumed, tired out, weary.

مِنْوَال loom (of spinner).

مِنْوَال manner, way, method, pattern, mode.

على هذا المِنْوَال in this manner, like this.

على مِنْوالٍ واحد alike, lighted, illuminated; enlightened, shining, brilliant.

مَنُوط بِـ entrusted with, charged with, commissioned to do something; dependent on, depending on; contingent on.

مُنَوَّع different, diverse, various, sundry, miscellaneous.

مُنَوَّعات selection, collection, assortment, variety.

مُنَوِّم (ص) soporific, sleep inducing, hypnotic.

مُنَوِّم (اسم) hypnotist; narcotic, sleeping pill.

مَنُون، مَنِيَّة death.

مَنْوِيّ intended, determined, planned.

مُنِيَ بِـ to be afflicted with, tested with; be sorely tried by; to suffer, undergo, sustain; to be stricken by a calamity.

مَنِيّ semen, sperm.

مَنِيع inaccessible, impenetrable, forbidding; well-fortified, mighty, powerful; impregnable, insurmountable, invincible; immune; impervious; unapproachable.

مُنِيف high, lofty, subblime, towering, eminent.

مَهَابَة dignity, solemnity, sublimity; awe, reverence; fear, fright, terror, dread.

مُهاتَرَة vituperation, abuse; wrangle, dispute, quarrel.

مُهاجِر emigrant, immigrant, expatriate; migratory.

مُهاجِم attacker, assailant, aggressor; forward (in football).

مُهاجَمَة attack, charge, assault, onslaught, raid.

مُهادِن tame, peaceful, mild, gentle, submissive.

مُهادَنَة conclusion of a truce, reconciliation, making peace.

مَهَارَة skill, skillfulness, dexterity, expertness, proficiency, expertise, craftsmanship, adroitness, workmanship.

مُهَان insulted, offended, scorned, degraded.

مَهَانَة contempt, degradation, abasement, humiliation, disgrace, shame.

مُهايِئ adapter, conditioner, adjuster.

مُهايَأة adaptation, conditioning, adjustment.

مَهَبُّ الرِّيح windward, direction of the wind.

مِهْبَاج pestle, mallet, pounder.

مَهْبِط place of descent, landing place, air strip (planes); runway (airport); birthplace, place of origin; cathode (elect.).

مَهْبِل vagina (anat.).

مُهْتَرِئ torn, lacerated, mangled, worn out, shabby; overdone.

مُهْتَزّ shaking, quivering, trembling, tremulous, vibrating.

مُهْتَمّ interested, concerned.

مُهْجَة heart, blood, soul.

مَهْجَر place of emigration.

مُهَجَّر displaced, homeless.

مَهْجَع dormitory, quarters, bedroom.

مَهْجُور abandoned, deserted, forsaken; obsolete, antiquated, archaic; lonesome, in disuse, out of use.

مَهَّدَ to spread out evenly; to smooth; to pave (a road); to flatten, make even; to arrange, settle, put in order; to free from obstacles, clear the way for; to make easy, facilitate, make (a bed); to prepare, make (a bed); to pass (a ball); to bring about, set in motion by.

مَهْد cradle, bed.

من المَهْدِ إلى اللَّحْدِ from cradle to grave.

قَتَلَهُ في مَهْدِهِ to nip something in the bud.

كان في مَهْدِهِ to be still in its infancy or beginnings.

مُهَدِّئ tranquilizer, sedative, alleviating, calming.

مِهَدَّة rock crusher (instrument).

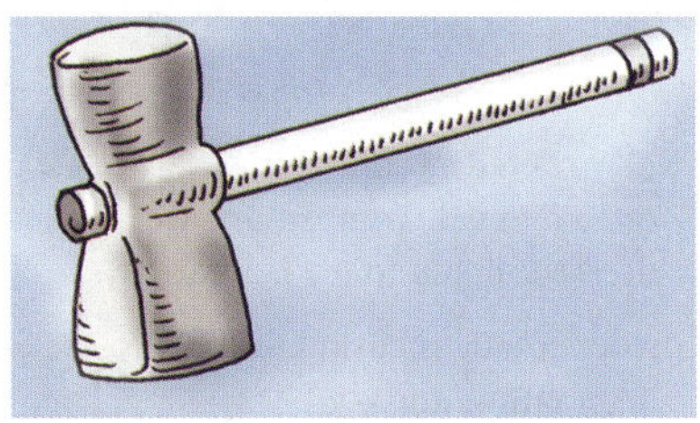

يحطم العامل الحجارة بواسطة مهدة ثقيلة

The worker crushes stone with a heavy rock crusher

مُهَدَّد threatened, menaced.

مُهَدِّد threatening, menacing.

مُهَدَّم torn down, demolished, wrecked, destroyed, in ruins.

مَهْدُود destroyed, demolished, wrecked; exhausted, worn out.

مَهْدُور squandered, futile, vain, useless; shed, spilled.

مَهْدِي rightly guided; the Mahdi; donated, presented, offered.

مُهَذَّب well-mannered, refined, polite, courteous, cultured; purified, rectified.

مَهَرَ to be skillful, dextrous, skilled, proficient, expert, experienced; to seal, stamp, impress; to give a dowry to a woman.

مَهْر dowry, stake, ransom; sealing, stamping.

مُهْر foal, colt (animal); seal, signet, stamp, rubber stamp.

مَهْرَب escape, retreat, refuge, flight, getaway.

لا مَهْرَبَ مِنْه inescapale, unavoidable.

مُهَرِّب smuggler, contrabandist, illicit dealer, trafficker.

مُهَرِّج clown, jester, bufoon.

يؤدي المهرج حركات يضحك لها الأطفال

The clown performs acts that make children laugh

مِهْرَجَان festival, carnival, fair, celebration.

مَهْرُوس crushed, mashed, squashed; bruised.

مَهْزَأة derision, scorn, disdain, contempt, sneer.

مَهْزَلَة comedy, farce.

مَهْزُول emaciated, wasted, haggard; feeble, weak.

مَهْزُوم defeated, vanquished, conquered.

مُهَشَّم destroyed, crushed.

مَهْضُوم digested, digestible; oppressed, outraged.

مَهْل ، مَهَل slowness, ease, leisure.

مَهْلاً، على مَهْل slowly, leisurely, in no hurry.

مُهْلَة respite, time limit, delay.

مُهْلِك devastating, scathing, ruinous; perilous, deadly, destructive; dangerous, lethal, pernicious.

مَهْلَكَة، مَهْلُكَة، مَهْلِكَة dangerous place, danger spot, peril, danger.

مُهَلْهَل thin, diaphanous, finely woven (fabric, poem); worn, shabby, tattered, ragged (clothing).

مُهِمّ important, interesting, grave, significant, momentous.

مَهْمَا whatever, whatsoever, however much.

مَهْمَا يَكُن من الأمْر whatever the case may be.

مِهْمَاز، مِهْمَز spur, prod.

مُهِمَّة، مَهَمَّة function, task, duty, mission, commission, assignment, errand, job; important matter.

مُهْمَل neglected, disregarded, omitted; obsolete, antiquated; lacking, devoid of; unpointed, undotted.

مُهْمِل negligent, neglectful, remiss, slack, careless, reckless, slovenly, heedless, inattentive.

مَهْمُوم concened, worried, anxious, distressed, grieved, sorrowful, preoccupied.

مُهَنِّئ congratulator, well-wisher.

مِهْنَة work, job, occupation, calling, vocation, trade, profession, business, career, pursuit.

سِرُّ المِهْنَة trade secret.

مُهَنْدِس engineer, architect.

مُهَنْدِسُ ديكور interior designer.

مُهَنْدِسٌ زِراعِيّ agronomist.

مُهَنْدِسٌ مَدَنِيّ civil engineer.

مُهَنْدَم well-ordered, well-arrayed, orderly; neat, trim, smart; well-dressed, made to measure (suit).

مِهَنِيّ professional, vocational, occupational.

مَهْوًى shaft, abyss, chasm,gulf; place of one's longing; object of desire; atmosphere.

مِهْوَاة ventilator, fan.

مَهْوُوس maniac, infatuated, crazy, mad, obsessed.

مُهَيَّأ prepared, ready, all set, designed; destined for.

مَهيب awesome, awful, awe-inspiring; dreadful; venerable; solemn, dignified, imposing, majestic.

أ ب ت ث ج ح خ د ذ ر ز س ش ص ض ط ظ ع غ ف ق ك ل م ن هـ و ي

مُهَيِّج (ص) exciting, stirring, rousing, stimulating, provocative, inciting, inflammatory; angry, furious.

مُهَيِّج (اسم) agitator, troublemaker, incendiary, rabble-rouser; stimulant, excitant; demagogue.

مَهِيض broken, shattered.

مَهِيضُ الجَناح helpless, feeble.

مُهَيْمِن، المُهَيْمِن dominant, prevailing, governing, ruling, commanding, controlling; master, overlord, protector.

مُهِين insulting, abusive, offending, humiliating, disgraceful; outrageous, degrading, debasing.

مُوائِم suitable, convenient, appropriate, concordant, harmonious, fit, suiting.

مُوَاءَمَة suitability, convenience, fitness; harmony; adaptation, conformity, fitting, concord.

مُواجِه facing, opposite to.

مُواجَهَة opposite direction; opposition; meeting, facing; countering, confrontation; interview.

مُواجَهَةً face to face, from person to person.

مُوارِب deceitful, devious, tricky; indirect, round about.

مُوارَبَة equivocation, ambiguity, circumlocution.

بدون مُوارَبَة unequivocally.

مُوازٍ (المُوازِي) parallel to, equivalent to.

مُوازَاة parallelism, correspondence, equivalence.

مُوازِن counter-balancing, equal, equivalent, outweighting.

مُوازَنَة balance, equilibrium, counter-balance, counter-weight; budget, balance sheet; timetable; stabilization, equalization.

مُواصَلَة continuation, following up, pursuit; conductance (elect.); line of communication.

مُواصَلاتٌ سِلْكِيَّة wire communications.

طُرُقُ المُواصَلات traffic routes.

مُواصَلاتٌ سِلْكِيَّة ولاسِلْكِيَّة telecommunications.

مُواطِن fellow citizen, countryman, compatriot, native.

مُواظِب diligent, assiduous, persevering, persistent.

مُواظَبَة perseverence, assiduity, persistence.

مُوافاة arrival, communication of a message; delivery, conveyance, presenting, transmission.

مُوافِق (ص) consistent, concordant, corresponding; suitable, fit, appropriate; propitious, wholesome, agreeable; assenting, consenting, approving; concurrent with; falling on a given date.

مُوافِق (اسم) consenter, approver, endorser.

مُوافَقَة approval, consent, assent; endorsement; suitability, fitness, expedience; agreement, consistency, harmony, accordance, conformity; compatibility.

مُواكَبة escort, convoy.

مَوْئِل refuge, asylum, sanctuary.

مُوالٍ (المُوالي) supporter, helper, client, vassal; partisan, follower, adherent, loyalist, upholder.

مُوالاة supporting friendship; constancy, continuance of an action.

مُوبِقة grave offense, crime, mortal sin, atrocity; danger.

مَوْبُوء infested.

مَوْت death, decease.

مَوْتٌ زُؤام sudden or violent death.

مُوَثَّق consolidated, cemented, documented, authenticated, certified, notarized, registered; strengthened.

مُوثَق tied, shackled, enchained; trustworthy, credible, trusty, reliable.

مَوْج، مَوْجَة waves, wave.

مُوجَب positive, affirmative (grammar); necessary, requisite, effect, consequence.

مُوجِب obligating, necessitating, requiring, motivating.

مُوجِب cause, reason, motive, exigency, necessity, obligation.

بِمُوجِب according to, on the basis of, by virtue of; in conformity with, pursuant to.

مُوجِد originator, author, creator.

مُوجَز، المُوجَز abridged, summarized, synopsized, digested, outlined; abstract, epitome, outline, summary, digest, synopsis.

مُوجِع painful; grievous, causing pain, suffering.

مُوَجَّه sent, forwarded, aimed, directed; guided, planned, steered, oriented.

مُوَجَّهٌ من بُعْد remote-controlled.

مُوَجِّه guide, controller, pilot.

مَوْجُود found, available; present, existent, existing; at hand.

المَوْجُود، المَوْجُودات living being; creatures, creation.

المَوْجُودات assets, stock in trade.

مَوْجُوع feeling pain, in pain, ailing, suffering.

مُوحٍ (المُوحي) inspiring, revealing.

مُوحًى به revealed, inspired.

مُوَحَّد (ص) united, unified, combined, integrated, amalgamated, consolidated (debt).

مُوَحِّد (اسم) monotheist; Druze; upholder of the unity of God.

مُوحِش desolate, waste, deserted; oppressed, anxious; weird, eerie; cheerless, gloomy.

مُوحِل muddy.

مُودَع lodged, deposited.

مُودِع lodger, depositor.

مُوَرَّث inherited, transmitted, hereditary; gene.

مَوْرِد watering place, spring, well; resource, source; supply, income, revenue.

مَوارِد (ج) resources, means, finance.

مُوَرِّد	supplier, furnisher, provider; importer.
مُوَرَّق	leafy, foliated; papered.
مُوَرَّم	swollen.
مَوْزَة، مَوْز	banana, bananas.

يطيب للسعدان أكل الموز بعد أن يقشره بأصابعه
A monkey likes to eat bananas after peeling them

مُوَزَّع	scattered, dispersed; distributed, allotted, shred out; apportioned, parceled out.
مُوَزِّع	distributor, retailer.
مُوَزِّعُ البَريد	postman.
مَوْزُون	weighed; balanced, in equilibrium, evenly poised; deliberate, well-balanced, well-measured; rhythmically balanced; of sound judgment, judicious.
مُوسَى	razor; Moses (prophet); sole (fish).
مُوسِر	rich, wealthy, well-to-do, prosperous; solvent.
مُوَسَّع	expanded, widened, broadened, enlarged; detailed.
مَوْسِم	season, feast day.
مَوْسِمِيّ	seasonal.
مُوَسْوَس	obsessed, overconcerned, scrupulous.
مَوْسُوعَة	encyclopedia.
مَوْسُوم	branded, stigmatized, marked, characterized with.
مُوسيقى	music.
مُوسيقِيّ	musician, musical.

مُوَشَّى	embroidered, ornamented, variegated, dappled.
مُوصٍ (المُوصِي)	testor, legator, mandator.
مُوصًى به	bequeathed, willed; decreed, ordered, recommended; entrusted to someone's charge or care.
مُوصًى عليه	made to order, custom-made, tailor-made; (suit); registered (letter).
مُوصَد	closed, shut.
مُوصِل، مُوَصِّل	conductor (elect.); connecting, linking, uniting; conductive to, leading to.
مُوصِلِيَّة	conductance, conductivity (elect.).
مَوْصُوف	described, depicted, characterized; prescribed (medicine); substantive (grammar).
مَوْصُول	connected, linked, joined, united, attached.
اسمٌ مَوْصُول	relative pronoun (grammar).
مَوْصُوم	disgraced, dishonored, blemished, branded.

مُوَضَّب arranged, processed, packaged, encased.

مَوْضِع place, spot, site, location, position, station.

في مَوْضِعِهِ in its right place.

في غير مَوْضِعِه in the wrong place, out of place.

مَوْضِعُ الإعْجاب object of admiration.

مَوْضِعِيّ local, topical.

مَوْضُوع (ص) placed, laid down, set, deposited; compiled, composed, produced, drawn up, drafted; invented, fabricated, spurious.

مَوْضُوع (اسم) subject, topic, theme, matter, question, issue; motif, merits (of a case); article, essay, thesis.

مَوْضُوعِيّ objective, substantive.

قانُونٌ مَوْضُوعِي substantive law.

مَوْضُوعِيَّة objectivity, objectivism.

مَوْطِئُ قَدَم foothold.

مُوَطَّد stabilized, consolidated, reinforced; firm, strong, solid.

مَوْطِن domicile, residence, home, habitat; homeland, fatherland, native country; place, locality; point, spot.

مَوْطِنُ الضُّعْف soft spot, weak spot.

مُوَظَّف (ص) employed, hired, recruited, appointed; invested.

مُوَظَّف (اسم) employee, official, officer, civil servant.

مُوَظَّفٌ إداريّ كَبير executive, administrator, manager.

مُوَظِّف employer, principal.

مَوْعِد appointment, date, time, appointed time or date.

المَوْعِدُ الأخير deadline.

مُوْعَزٌ بِه suggested, insinuated, advised, instructed.

مَوْعِظَة sermon, exhortation, lecture, severe reprimand.

مَوْعُود promised, fixed, appointed, stipulated (time).

مُوفَد، المُوْفَد delegated; envoy, legate, emissary.

مُوَفَّق successful, prosperous, lucky; fortunate, proper, apt, fit.

مَوْفُور ample, abundant, plentiful; complete, rich, moneyed.

مُوَقَّت، مُؤَقَّت scheduled for a given time, appointed, fixed, set; temporal, temporary, passing, transient, transitory; provisional, interim.

مَوْقِد fireplace, hearth, stove, burner, blowtorch.

مُوْقَد ignited, kindled, lit.

مُوَقَّر venerable, venerated, honored, honorable, respected, held in respect.

مَوْقِع place, spot, location, site.

مَوْقِعٌ عَسْكَرِيّ garrison.

مُوَقِّع signatory, signer.

المُوَقِّعون أدناه the undersigned.

مَوْقِعَة، مَوْقَعَة battle, combat; roost, perch.

مَوْقِف stop, station, stand, parking; position, stance; situation, position; scene, scenery; attitude, opinion.

مَوْقُوف arrested, apprehended, detained; delayed, postponed, deferred; suspended from duty; removed from office; established as a wakf; donated, granted; dedicated, devoted, reserved for, dependent, conditional on; based, resting on; suspended.

مَوْقُوفٌ قيد المُحاكَمَة detained pending investigation or trial.

مَوْكِب procession, caravan, convoy, parade, escort.

مُؤَكَّد sure, certain, definite, confirmed, asserted, stressed.

مُوَكَّل commissioned, charged with, in charge of, authorized to act on behalf someone; responsible, answerable; deputized, delegated, empowered.

مُوَكِّل constituent; principal, client (of an advocate); mandator.

مَوْكُولٌ إليه entrusted to; assigned, entrusted with.

مَوَّلَ to finance.

مَوْلًى، المَوْلَى master, lord; God the Lord.

مَوْلِد birth, origin; birthday; birthplace.

عِيدُ المَوْلِدِ النَّبَوِيّ the Prophet's Birthday.

مُوَلَّد (ص) generated, produced, originated; begotten, bred; caused, occasioned.

مُوَلِّد generator, producer, maker; obstetrician (med.); dynamo.

مُوَلِّدُ التَّيَّار المُتَرَدِّد alternator (elect.).

مُوَلِّدَة midwife.

مُوْلَعٌ بِـ fond passionately of, attached deeply to; madly in love with.

مَوْلُود born, newborn.

مُومِس . مُومِسَة prostitute, whore, harlot.

مُومِيَاء mummy.

مَوَّنَ to supply with provisions; to cater.

مَوَّهَ to falsify, adulterate, misrepresent; to feign, camouflage; to coat, plate (a base metal with gold or silver); to add water to; to admix water to; to abound in water; to dilute, thin down, water down.

مَوْهِبَة talent.

مَوْهُوب donated, granted, awarded, bestowed; talented, gifted, endowed.

مَوْهُوم imaginary, apparent, presumed, supposed, delusive, hypothetical; thought, believed, imagined.

مَيَّاس swinging, walking with a proud gait.

مَيَّال inclined to, disposed to; interested in.

مَيْئوس hopeless, desperate.

مُيَاوِم day laborer, daily-paid worker.

مَيِّت، مَيْت mortal, subject to death; lifeless, dead, deceased.

مَيْتَة dead animal, dead meat; corpse, carcass.

مَيْتَم orphanage.

مِيثاق covenant, convention, pact, treaty, charter.

ميدان field, domain, province, area; square, plaza, park, racecourse, motordrome; battleground.

ميدانيّ field.

ميراث heritage, inheritance, legacy, estate.

مَيَّزَ to distinguish, honor, favor someone above someone else; to set aside; to prefer, segregate, single out, select, choose; to grant a special right or privilege to someone; to differentiate, discriminate between.

مَيَّزَ الحُكْم to bring appeal for cassation.

مِيزاب gutter, spout, drain.

ميزان balance, scales, weight, measure.

ميزانُ البناء spirit level.

ميزانُ الضَّغط الجَوِّي barometer.

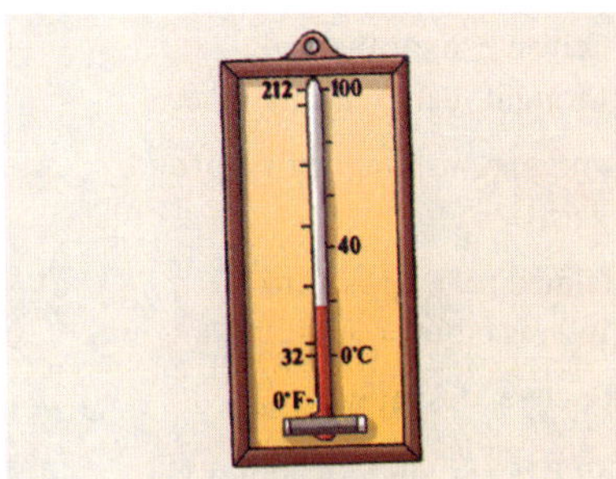

علّق والدي ميزان الضغط الجويّ على الحائط لنعرف درجة الضغط الجوي

My father hanged the barometer on the wall in order that we could know the atmospheric pressure

---

برجُ الميزان Libra, Balance (astrology).

مِيزَانيّة budget, balance sheet.

مِيزَة particularity, peculiarity, distinguishing feature, characteristic, property, trait; advantage, merit.

مَيْسَر gambling.

مُيَسَّر simplified, facilitated, made easy; possible, available.

مَيْسَرَة left, left side, left hand, left wing (of an army).

مَيْسَرَة، مَيْسُرَة، مَيْسِرَة ease, prosperity, affluence, wealth.

مَيْسُور easily done, easily accomplished, within easy reach; feasible without difficulty; easy, successful; lucky, fortunate, prosperous, rich, well-to-do.

ميعاد promise, appointment, date, due date.

في ميعَادِهِ on time, punctually.

مِنْ غَيْرِ مِيعاد all of a sudden, unexpectedly, suddenly.

ميكانيكيّ، الميكانيكي mechanical, automatic; mechanic.

مَيَّلَ to tip, tilt, bend, bow, incline; to catheterize (med.).

مَيْل tendency, trend, inclination, preference, liking; tilt, bend, turn, deflection, slant, slope, incline; affection for, attachment to ; declination (astrology).

ميلاد birth, birthday, time of birth, nativity.

عيدُ الميلاد Christmas (Christian faith).

قبل الميلاد B.C., Before Christ.

بعد الميلاد A.D., After Christ.

مَيْمَنَة — right, right hand, right side, right wing (of an army).

على الطَّائِرِ المَيْمُون — happy journey! godspeed!.

مَيْمُون — mandrill, baboon (animal).

ميناء — port, harbor, seaport, haven.

ميناءٌ جَوِّيّ — airport.

ميناءُ السَّاعَة — dial.

ميناء — enamel.

مُيُوعَة — liquidity, fluidity.

ناءَ to sink under, fall down under; to collapse under.

ناءَ بِهِ الحِمْلُ to weigh heavily upon him, overburden.

نَأَى to be far, distant, remote from; to stay away, keep at a distance from; to remain aloof, move away from; to be at a distance, separated, apart from.

ناءٍ (النَّائِي) remote, distant, outlying, far, far away.

نائِب deputy, representative; agent, proxy, vice.

نائِبُ رئيس vice-president, vice-chairman.

النَّائِبُ العام attorney general, prosecutor, district attorney.

نائِبُ فاعِل subject of the passive (grammar).

نائِبُ الملك viceroy.

نائِبَة calamity, disaster, misfortune.

نائِل acquirer, earner, gainer, winner; boon, benefit, gain.

نائِم asleep, sleeping.

نابَ عَن to represent, act as a representative for; to act on behalf someone; to take the place of.

ناب canine tooth.

نابُ الفيل tusk.

نابُ الحَيَّة fang.

نابِت growing, germinating.

نابِض (ص) pulsating, pulsatory, throbbing, palpitating.

نابِض (اسم) spring, coil.

نابِغَة genius, eminent scholar.

ناتِئ protruding, swollen, projecting, jutting out, salient, protuberant, bulging; hump, protuberance.

ناتِج resulting from, resultant from, consequential on, ensuing from, proceeding from, engendered by.

ناثِر prose writer; scatterer, sprinkler.

ناجَى to whisper to, confide in; to talk to oneself, to soliloquize; to say to oneself.

ناجِح successful, having passed examination.

ناجِز completed, full, total; whole, entire, consummate.

ناجِع useful, healthful, salutary.

ناجِم resulting from; following, ensuing, arising, deriving, originating from.

ناحَ to wail, lament, bemoan, mourn, bewail.

ناحِل thin, slim, slender, lean, skinny; enervated, gaunt.

ناحِيَة side, direction; standpoint; aspect; region, area, section; sphere, domain, field; district, county; secluded part, corner (of a room).

من ناحِيَة with regard to, in respect to; as to, as for, concerning, regarding.

من نَاحِيَةٍ أُخرى on the other hand.

من نَاحِيَةٍ قانونية de jure.

من نَاحِيَةٍ واقِعيَّة de facto.

مُتَعَدِّدُ النَّواحِي many-sided.

من جميع النَّواحِي in every respect.

ناخِب elector, voter, constituent.

نادٍ (النَّادِي) club, society, association.

نادٍ لَيْليّ nightclub.

نادَى to call out, cry out; to call, summon, invite someone; to proclaim, announce, emphasize; to cry one's wares, hawk.

نادِب mourner, wailer.

نادِر، (النادِر) rare, scarce, uncommon, unusual, extraordinary, exceptional, priceless; a crank, an odd fellow, an eccentric.

نادِراً، في النادِر rarely, seldom.

نادِرُ المثال unparalleled, unique, singular.

نادِرَة rarity; anecdote; uncommon word; phenomenon, prodigy; funny story; joke; accident, incident.

نادَمَ to drink together, carouse together with someone.

نادِم، نَدْمان repentant, repenting, rueful, remorseful, regretting, regretful.

نار fire; conflagration; hell.

جَبَلُ النَّار volcano.

أشْهَرُ من نارٍ على عَلَم very famous.

خَطُّ النَّار firing range.

وقْفُ إطْلاقِ النَّار ceasefire.

نارجِيلَة، نارَكِيلَة hubble-bubble, hookah.

نارِيّ fiery, burning, blazing, red-hot.

سِلاحٌ نارِيّ firearm.

دَرَّاجَةٌ نارِيَّة motorcycle.

طَلَقٌ نارِيّ gunshot, shot.

ألْعابٌ نارِيَّة fireworks.

أ ب ت ث ج ح خ د ذ ر ز س ش ص ض ط ظ ع غ ف ق ك ل م ن هـ و ي

مَقْذُوفٌ نارِيّ projectile, bullet, shell (of a firearm).

نازِح emigrant, moving to other lands, going away from home; faraway, distant.

نازَعَ to dispute, fight, struggle, contend with; to contest, challenge, attempt to wrest from someone something.

نازَعَ to be on the throes of death.

نازَعَ to wish, long, yearn; to tend, have an inclination to.

نازَلَ to attack, assail, assault, get into a fight, clash with; to challenge, compete with.

نازِل descending, sloping, falling, going down; living, resident, dweller; residing, dwelling.

نازِلَة mishap, accident, calamity, disaster.

ناس people, humans, mankind, humankind.

ناسَبَ to suit, correspond to, tally with, fit, become, befit, behoove; to harmonize, agree, be compatible, consistant with; to bc in conformity, in agreement with.

ناسَبَ to be related by marriage to; to belong to a clan, faction, party.

ناسِخ، النَاسِخ abrogative, abolishing; copyist, transcriber.

ناسِف، ناسِفَة exploding device or matter.

ناسِك hermit, recluse, ascetic.

ناشِئ growing, growing up, arising from, originating from; emanating, resulting from; inexperienced, beginner.

ناشِئ junior, youngster, youth.

ناشِئَة young generation.

ناشَدَ to adjure, implore; to beseech, entreat, appeal to.

ناشِر publisher.

ناشِزَة recalcitrant woman, insubordinate wife.

ناشِط، نَشِيط brisk, spirited, animated; cheerful; stirring, busy, active, energetic.

ناشِف desiccated, dried up, dry; stiff, tough, hard.

ناصَبَ to be hostile to; to display enmity to.

ناصَبَهُ الحرب to declare war on someone.

ناصَبَهُ العَدَاء to declare oneself the enemy of someone.

ناصِب tiring, exhausting; word governing the subjunctive (grammar).

ناصِح sincere, good counselor, sincere adviser; sincere, true, faithful, loyal.

ناصَرَ to help, aid, assist someone against; to let triumph; to defend, protect, support; to come to someone's aid; to be on someone's side; to side with someone.

ناصِر، نصير helper, protector; ally, adherent, follower, partisan, patron; promoter.

ناصِع — pure, clear, evident, obvious, manifest; white.

ناصَفَ — to share with someone half of something; to share equally with someone.

ناصِيَةُ الشَّارِع — street corner.

أَخَذَ بِنَاصِيَتِهِ — to seize, take by the forelock; to tackle properly.

مَلَكَ ناصِيَتَه — to become master of; to control, master.

ناضِب — dried up, dry, arid, barren.

ناضِج — mature, ripe; well-cooked (food).

ناضِر — flourishing, blooming; verdant, fresh, tender; glowing.

ناضَلَ — to struggle, strive, vie with; to compete, stand up for.

ناطَحَ — to ram, bump on; to thrust with the head.

ناطِح — butting, ramming.

ناطِحَةُ السَّحاب — skyscraper.

ناطِق — talking, speaking, eloquent; endowed with the faculty of speech; plain, distinct; reasonable, rational being.

النَّاطِق — speaker, spokesman.

النَّاطِقُون بالضَّاد — Arabic speaking people.

ناظِر — observer, viewer, onlooker, spectator, inspector, superintendent, administrator.

ناظِرُ مَدْرَسَةٍ — principal, inspector, headmaster.

ناظِرَةُ مَدْرَسَةٍ — headmistress, matron.

ناظِر — look, glance; eye.

بينَ ناظِرَيْه — before his eyes.

ناظِم — regulator, arranger, adjuster.

ناظِمُ الشِّعْر — poet; versifier.

ناعِس — sleepy, dozing, slumbering.

ناعِم — smooth, soft, tender; fine, powdery.

ناغَى — to talk tenderly to a baby, to flatter, babble.

ناغَمَ — to match, harmonize, attune.

نافَى — to contradict, negate, chase, pursue.

نافِخ — blower, blowing.

نافِذ — valid, in force, in operation; penetrating, permeating, infiltrating.

نافِذُ الكَلِمَة — influential, powerful.

نافِذَة — window.

أفتح النافذة في الصباح
لأستنشق الهواء النقي
I open the window in the morning
to breathe fresh air

نافِر fleeing, fugitive; shy, timid; having an aversion to; swelling, bulging, protruding, jutting out, in relief.

نافَسَ to compete with, vie with; to fight, struggle for.

نافِع salutary, usable, useful, advantageous, profitable, beneficial, serviceable.

نافَقَ to play the hypocrite, dissimulate one's true feelings toward someone.

نافِق selling well, in demand, easily marketable (goods).

نافِلَة supererogatory performance; spoils, booty; gift, present.

من نافِلَةِ القول أن it goes without saying that.

نافُورَة ماء fountain, jet.

ناقِد critic (literary works).

ناقَشَ to argue, dispute with; to discuss, debate, criticize; to object, raise an objection to; to hear, examine, study.

ناقَشَ شَاهِداً to cross-examine, interrogate, hear a witness (in court).

ناقِص decreasing, diminished, decreased, reduced; faulty, defective; deficient, lacking, imperfect; less than, minus.

ناقِص defective (grammar).

ناقَضَ to contradict, disagree with; to be in disagreement with, to be opposite to, incompatible, inconsistent with.

ناقِل carrier, forwarder, shipper, transporter; bearer; copyist; translator.

ناقِلُ السُّرعَة gearshift.

ناقِلُ الضَّوء conductor of light; light emitting.

ناقِلٌ للعَدْوَى contagious.

ناقِلَة carrier.

ناقِلَةُ بترول tanker.

ناقِم avenger; hostile to; angry, indignant at; spiteful, resentful, disgruntled.

ناقوس bell, tocsin.

ناكَبَ to butt, abut on.

ناكَدَ to harass, torment, pester, molest.

ناكِر denying, disavowing; unfriendly, hostile.

ناكِرُ الجميل ungrateful.

نالَ to obtain, attain, achieve, get hold of, get possession of; to win, gain, acquire, earn; to procure, accomplish, succeed in; to affect, influence, bear upon; to cause damage, do harm; to prejudice, impair.

نالَ من عِرْضِهِ to discredit, defame, slander someone.

نالَهُ بِسُوءٍ to harm someone.

نالَ من قَدْرِهِ to disparage, belittle, degrade, humiliate, debase.

نامَ to sleep, be asleep, fall asleep, slumber; to go to bed; to abate, subside, calm down; to neglect, omit, ignore; to trust in, have confidence in.

أ ب ت ث ج ح خ د ذ ر ز س ش ص ض ط ظ ع غ ف ق ك ل م ن هـ و ي

ينام الشخص خلال الليل بعد عناء النهار ليستريح

Man sleeps during night following a hard day in order to have a rest

---

نامٍ (النّامي) growing, augmenting, mounting; developing.

ناموس (اسم) mosquitoes; law, code.

ناموسيَّة mosquito net.

ناهٍ (النّاهي) interdictory, prohibiting.

ناهيكَ مِن how excellent is; suffice it to; to say nothing of, let alone, not to mention, take for instance.

ناهِج open, plain road; clear.

ناهَدَ to resist, oppose, contend with; to dispute with.

ناهِد buxom, bosomy, full-bosomed; full, round, swelling (breasts).

ناهَزَ to be near, approach, attain, reach something.

ناهَزَ الخَمْسين he was close to fifty.

ناهَضَ to resist, oppose, defy, challenge; to argue, dispute.

ناهِض rising, getting up; active, energetic; high, lofty; established, proven (evidence).

ناوَأَ to resist, oppose, challenge; to act in a hostile manner toward; to antagonize; to vie, compete with.

ناوأه العَداء to be hostile to; to treat someone with hostility.

ناوَبَ to take turns, alternate with.

ناوَلَ to give, hand, pass, present, offer, serve, handover, deliver, administer (communion to).

نأي remoteness; trench, ditch.

ناي flute.

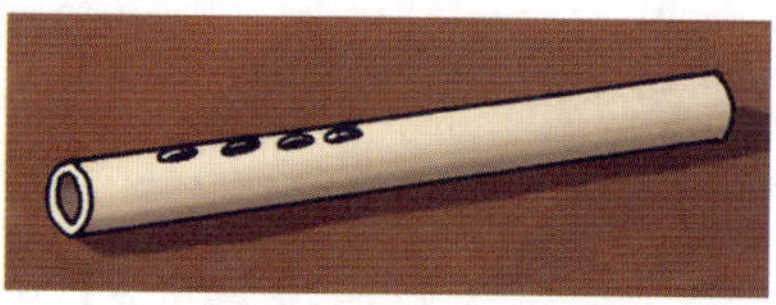

يعزف الراعي على النّاي وهو يراقب قطيعه

The shepherd plays on the flute while watching his herd

نَبَأَ to be raised, elevated, protruding, projecting; to overcome, overwhelm; to turn away, withdraw, shrink from.

نَبا to miss the goal; to fail to hit the goal; to be contradictory to, in conflict with, inconsistent with; to be offensive, repugnant; to dislike, find repugnant; to turn away from; to disagree with.

نَبأ، أنْباء news, information, story, news report.

نَشْرَةُ أنْباء news bulletin.

وِكالَةُ أنْباء news agency.

نَبات plants, vegetables.

نَباتٌ حَوْلِيّ annual plant.

نَباتٌ طِبِّيّ medicinal plant.

نَباتٌ مُعَمِّر perennial plant.

نَباتِيّ ، النَباتِيّ botanical; botanist.

نَباتِيّ vegetarian (man.); herbivore (animal).

نُباح barking, bark (of dog).

نَبالَة nobillity, nobleness, eminence; generosity, magnanimity.

نَباهَة fame, renown, celebrity; vigilance, alertness; nobility intelligence, insight, perception, brilliance.

نَبَتَ to grow, sprout, germinate.

نَبَتَ المكان to produce plants, bring forth vegetation.

نَبَّتَ to sow, plant, grow plants.

نَبْتَة plant, shoot, sprout.

نَبَحَ to bark (dog).

نَبَذَ to throw away, discard, hurl, fling, toss away; to cast out, ostracize, expel, banish; disown, repudiate; to eliminate, dismiss, abandon, forsake, give up, renounce; to relinquish, violate, infringe (an agreement, a contract).

نَبْذ discarding, rejection, repudiation, renunciation, dismissal, disavowal; ostracision; a trifle, a little.

نُبْذَة ، نَبْذَة brief extract, section, part; summary ,abstract, digest, synopsis, outline.

نُبْذَة عن حياة شخص biography, curriculum vitae (c.v).

نِبْراس lamp, light.

نَبْرَة accent, stress, emphasis; tone of voice; swelling, protruberance, tumor.

نَبَسَ to speak, utter, talk, say.

ما نَبَسَ بِكَلِمَة he did not say a word.

نَبَشَ to exhume, excavate, unearth, dig up; to unveil, disclose, reveal, bring to light.

نَبَّشَ to search, burrow in, ransack, ruffle something.

نَبَضَ to beat, throb, pulsate, palpitate (heart); to flow off, run off (water).

نَبْض ، نَبْضَة pulse, pulsation, palpitation, throb, throbbing.

نَبَط depth; inner self; profundity; core, heart.

نَبَعَ to well up, well out, gush out, gush forth; to flow, flow out, spring, originate.

نَبْعُ النَّهر head of river.

نَبَغَ to be a genius; to excel in; to spread about, prevail; to arise, emerge, appear; to be outstanding in.

نَبُلَ to become noble, high-minded, generous, highborn.

نَبُلَ عَن to be above, too high-minded for.

نُبْل nobility, nobleness, magnanimity; generosity.

نَبْلَة arrow, dart.

نَبَهَ، نَبِهَ، نَبُهَ to be well-known, renowned, famous; to heed, mind, note, observe, pay attention to, take notice of; to wake, awaken, rouse (someone from sleep).

نَبَّهَ to call someone's attention to; to point out, show, indicate to; to tell, inform, notify, remind, instruct; to warn, caution; to rouse someone from sleep; to alert, excite, stimulate someone.

نُبُوَّة prophecy, prophethood.

نَبِيّ prophet.

النَّبيذ wine.

نَبيل noble, highborn, high-minded, generous, gallant.

نَبيل honorable, peer, nobleman.

نَبيه discerning, judicious, perspicacious; famous, renowned, eminent, distinguished; highborn, noble.

نَتَأَ to swell, bulge, bulge out, protrude, project; to be in relief, prominent, protuberant.

نِتَاج product, output (of a machine); act of bearing of animals, brood, litter, young ones, young animals; yield, harvest, crop; offspring; result, returns.

نَتَانَة evil smell, decay, stink, stench; putrefaction, decomposition.

نَتَجَ to result from, issue from, arise from; to be the result of; to bear, bring forth (a young one).

نَتَرَ to grab, wrest away, wrench, snatch, snap, take away by force.

نَتَفَ، نَتَّفَ to pluck out, pull out, tear out (hairs, feathers).

نُتْفَة tuft of hair; a small amount, a little of something.

نَتِن stinking, evil-smelling, rotten, putrid, decayed.

نُتُوء protrusion, projection, bulge; swelling; hill, elevation, protuberance.

نَتيجَة result, outcome, issue, consequence, product, effect; yield, produce; gain, profit, output; conclusion, inference, deduction; because of, due to, owing to.

بالنَّتيجَة consequently, hence, therefore.

نَثَرَ to scatter, sprinkle, disperse; to write in prose.

نَثْر scattering, dispersal, sprinkling; prose.

نَثْريّ in prose.

نَجا to save oneself, to be saved, rescued; to escape from; to be delivered from.

نَجَّى to deliver, save, rescue, bring to safety from.

نَجابَة nobility, noble descent; excellence, superiority.

نَجاة salvation, escape, flight, rescue, safety; redemption.

نَجاح successful outcome, favorable result, happy ending; success, good progress; passing an examination.

نَجَّاد	boyscout; upholsterer.
نِجَادَة	upholstery.
نَجَّار	carpenter, cabinetmaker.

يقطع النجار الخشب بواسطة المنشار
The carpenter cuts wood with a saw

نِجَارَة	carpentry.
نَجَاسَة	impurity, pollution, dirtiness.
نَجُبَ	to be highborn, highbred, generous; to be superior, to excel, be excellent, magnanimous.
نَجَحَ	to succeed, progress well, develop satisfactorily; to be successful, have success; to pass an examination.
نَجَّدَ	to upholster; to comb, card (cotton, wool).
نَجْد	highland, plateau, upland.
نَجْدَة	relief, help, aid, succor, assistance, support, salvage.
نَجْدَة	courage, bravery, intrepidity.
نَجَزَ	to be completed, carried out, executed, implemented, achieved, fulfilled.

نَجَّدَ العامل المقعد القديم فأعاده جديداً
The worker upholstered the old chair and made it a new one

نَجُسَ	to be impure, unclean, soiled, dirty, sullied, stained, contaminated, polluted, squalid.
نَجَّسَ	to soil, dirty, pollute, defile, stain, sully.
نَجِس	impure, unclean, dirty, foul, filthy, soiled, sullied, polluted, squalid, contaminated.

نَجَعَ	to be useful, beneficial, salutary.
نَجَف، نَجَفَة	hill, mound, elevation.
نَجَلَ	to beget, sire, father a son.
نَجْل	son, offspring; progeny.
نَجَمَ	to result from, follow from, arise from, derive from, originate from; to be caused by; to appear, come out.

نَجم — star, planet, heavenly body.

يمكن رؤية النجوم في السماء خلال الليل
Stars could be seen in the firmament during night

نَجْمٌ ذو ذَنَب — comet.

نَجْمٌ من دين — installment.

نَجْمٌ سينمائيّ — film star.

نَجْمِيّ — astral, stellar, starlike, stelliform.

نَجْوَى — confidential talk; intimate discourse.

نَجيب — highborn, highbred, of noble descent; excellent, superior, distinguished, outstanding.

نَجيع (اسم) — blood.

نَحا — to wend one's way; to go, walk, move, turn toward; to take the road to; to go in the direction of.

نَحا نَحْوَهُ — to follow someone's example; to imitate someone; to be like, of the same kind as someone.

نَحَّى — to put aside, push away, remove, take away from.

نَحّات — sculptor, stonecutter.

نُحاتَة — shavings, chips, splinters, parings.

يصنع النحات تماثيلَ بنحت الصخر بأزميله
The sculptor makes statues through carving stones with his chisel

نَحّاس — coppersmith.

نُحاس — copper.

نُحاسٌ أصْفَر — brass.

نُحاسِيّ — coppery, brazen, brassy, cupreous.

نَحافَة — thinness, slimness, slenderness.

نَحْب — death; time, period, span; wailing, lamenting.

قَضَى نَحْبَهُ — to die, pass away, expire.

نَحَتَ — to hew out, carve, sculpture.

نَحَتَ كَلِمَةً — to coin a word.

نَحْت — wood or stone carving; sculpture, sculpturing.

نَحَرَ — to cut the throat of an animal; to slaughter, kill, butcher (an animal).

نَحْر — slaughtering, butchering.

نَحْر — upper part of the chest.

يوم النَّحْر — Day of Immolation (Moslem rite).

أ ب ت ث ج ح خ د ذ ر ز س ش ص ض ط ظ ع غ ف ق ك ل م ن هـ و ي

نِحرير skilled, adept, proficient, versed in.

نَحُسَ، نَحِسَ to be unlucky, luckless, unfortunate.

نَحَسَ to make unhappy, bring someone bad luck.

نَحَّسَ to cover, coat with copper.

نَحْس bad luck, disaster, misfortune.

نَحُفَ to become lean, slim, slender; to lose weight.

نَحَّفَ to make thin; to weaken, debilitate.

نَحُلَ، نَحِلَ to become emaciated; to waste away; to lose weight, grow thin.

نَحل، نَحْلَة bees, bee.

تعيش النحلة داخل قفير تحكمه ملكة

Bees live in a beehive ruled by a queen

نَحْنُ we.

نَحْو manner, way, course, method, mode, fashion; analogous to, similar to, like; grammar, syntax.

نَحْوَ towards, in the direction of.

نَحْواً مِن about, around, circa, nearly, more or less.

على هَذا النَّحْو in this manner, in this respect.

نُحُول emaciation, wasting away, slenderness, slimness.

نَحْوِيّ، النَّحْوِيّ grammatical; grammarian.

نَحِيب wail, wailing, lamentation, lament, crying.

نَحِيف thin, slim, slender, emaciated, skinny; delicate, lean; gaunt, enervated.

نَحِيل thin, slim, slender, lean, skinny; enervated, gaunt; emaciated.

نُخَاع spinal cord; bone marrow; medulla (anat.).

نُخَالَة bran.

نَخْب selection, choice; a drink to someone's health, toast.

نُخْبَة choice, selected item, selected passage (of a book); the elite; the pick; the cream of the society.

نَخَرَ to snort; to gnaw, wear away, eat into, bore, pierce, corrode; to burrow (worm); to enervate, ruin, decay.

نَخِر worm-eaten, decaying, decayed, rot.

نَخْر snorting, snoring; decay, rot; tooth decay, caries (of teeth).

نَخَزَ to prick, sting, bore through (worm).

نَخَسَ to goad, prod, urge on, spur, prick (an animal).

نَخَلَ to sift, sieve, strain.

نَخْل palm trees, date palms; sifting, sieving out.

نَخْلَة palm tree, date tree, palm.

نَخْوَة chivalry, gallantry, sense of honor; zeal, enthusiasm; arrogance, haughtiness, pride, self-respect.

نَخِيل palm, date palm, date tree.

نَدَّ to run away, slip away, flee, escape.

نَدّ high hill; incense.

نِدّ peer, equal, match, equivalent; opponent, antagonist.

نَدَا to meet, get together; to invite, summon, convoke a meeting, assemble, gather.

نَدَّى to moisten, wet, bedew.

نَدًى dew, moistness, dampness, wetness; generosity, magnanimity, liberality.

نِداء call, appeal, announcement, address.

نِداء vocative (grammar).

حرفُ النِّداء interjection (grammar).

نَدَبَ to mourn, lament, bewail (a deceased); to appoint, assign someone to an office; to send someone as a representative or agent for oneself; to delegate, depute, deputize someone; to commission, charge, entrust someone.

نَدْب lamentation, bewailing over.

نَدِبَ to scar over, cicatrize, heal up.

نَدْبَة، نَدَبَة scar, cicatrix.

نُدْبَة lamentation for the dead, elegy (for a dead person).

نَدَّدَ to criticize, condemn, denounce; to revile, defame, slander, vilify.

نَدَرَ to be rare, uncommon, unusual.

نَدُرَ to be strange, odd, queer, extraordinary, unusual.

نُدْرَة، نَدْرَة rarity, rareness; shortage, lack, scarcity.

نَدَفَ، نَدَّفَ to card, comb (cotton, wool).

نُدْفَة صُوف flock of wool.

نُدْفَة ثَلْج snowflake.

نَدِمَ to repent of, regret.

نَدَم repentance, remorse, penitence, contrition.

نَدْوَة symposium, seminar, study group, debating group; club.

نَدِيَ to be moist, damp, wet, dewy.

شَيءٌ يُنْدَى له الجَبين an embarassing thing, a disgraceful action.

نَدِيّ wet, dewy, moist, damp.

نَدِيُّ الكَفّ generous, openhanded.

نَدِيم drinking companion, friend, confidant.

نَذالَة depravity, meanness.

نَذَرَ to vow, make a vow; to consecrate, dedicate.

نَذَرَ لله to vow to God; to consecrate to God.

نَذْر vow, votive, offering.

نَذْل mean, low, depraved, base, vile, rescal, villain.

نَذير herald, harbinger, forerunner, precursor, omen, augury, warner, cautioner; warning, alarm.

نَرْد dice; backgammon, trictrac.

نَزَّ to seep, ooze, leak through; to trickle (water).

نَزّاع tending, having an inclination to, leaning toward.

نِزاع dispute, fight, controversy, struggle, strife, conflict, quarrel, squabble, clash, litigation (in courts).

نِزاع agony of death.

بِلا نِزاع indisputably, incontestibly, indubitably, undeniably.

لا نِزاعَ فيه undisputed, uncontested.

نِزال encounter, combat, battle, fight.

نَزاهَة impartiality, fairness; honesty, integrity; chastity, purity, virtue, righteousness.

نَزَحَ to be far off, distant; to leave, depart, emigrate from; to immigrate to.

نَزَحَ to drain, empty, dry out.

نَزْح drainage, draining, emptying, scooping out.

نَزْر little, trivial, trifle, small amount, negligible number.

نَزَعَ to pull out, extract, pluck out; to remove, take away, take off; to shed a garment; to strip, divest, deprive, rob someone of something; to depose, dismiss, demote, reduce in rank; to tend to; to be inclined to; to long for.

نَزَعَ السِّلاح to disarm.

نَزَعَ الفتيل to defuse (bomb).

نَزَعَ المِلْكِيَّة to expropriate, dispossess (an estate).

نَزَعَ عَن to desist from, abstain from.

نَزْع removal, withdrawal, elimination; deposition, removal from office; agony of death.

نَزْعَة tendency, inclination, trend, disposition.

نَزَفَ to drain, empty, dry up (a well); to draw off (blood).

نَزْف، نَزيف hemorrhage, bleeding; loss of blood.

نَزِقَ، نَزَقَ to rush forward; to be hasty; to be rash, impetuous, frivolous, reckless, ruthless, lightheaded.

نَزِق hasty, rash, impetuous, thoughtless, heedless, careless, imprudent, reckless.

نَزَلَ to dismount, alight; to descend, come down, get down, step down, get off (a train, a car); to get out, step out (of a car); to debark, disembark (from a ship); to fall, drop, sink.

نَزَلَ الوَحْيُ to be revealed, descended from heaven.

نَزَلَ عِنْدَ to stop at, stay at, take up quarters at; to reside in, dwell in, inhabit.

نَزَلَ بِهِ الأمْرُ to befall, afflict, occur to.

نَزَلَ عِنْدَ إرادَتِهِ to yield to, submit to, give in to; to comply with someone's demand or will.

أ ب ت ث ج ح خ د ذ ر ز س ش ص ض ط ظ ع غ ف ق ك ل م ن هـ و ي

نَزَلَت الطَّائِرَة to land, touch down.

نَزَلَ عن to cede, waive, relinquish, abandon; to resign from, refrain from.

نَزَلَ مَنْزِلَةَ فُلان to hold the position of; to serve as.

نَزَّلَ to cause to come down; to make someone descend, dismount, step down; to lower (a bucket); to send down, decrease, diminish, lessen, curtail, reduce; to depose, dethrone; to unload; to deduct, substract something from; to demote (in rank); to inlay, set.

نُزُل hotel, inn, boardinghouse.

يسكن المسافرون في النزل القريب من المطار
Travelers reside in the hotel adjacent to the airport

نَزُهَ، نَزِهَ to be impartial, fair, upright; to be virtuous, chaste; to keep away from, refrain from.

نَزِه، نَزِيه impartial, fair, just, unbiased; honest, upright, chaste, pure, virtuous; scrupulous, decent.

نُزْهَة stroll, promenade, excursion, pleasure trip, recreation, amusement, diversion, fun; picnic, picnic ground, excursion spot.

نُزُوح emigration, exodus, immigration to, moving away.

نُزُوع inclination, leaning, trend; desire, wish; impulse.

نُزُول descending, descent; falling, decline; affliction, striking.

نُزُول من وسيلة الانْتِقال disembarkation, debarkation (ship); dismounting (animal); alighting, getting off (car); landing, touchdown (plane).

نُزُولٌ في stopping, residence, residing, staying in.

نُزُولٌ عِنْد complying with, deference to.

نَزِيل lodger, boarder, inmate, occupant, guest.

نِسَاء women.

نِسَائِيّ female, womanly, for women.

نَسَّاخ copyist, transcriber, scribe.

نَسَّافَة torpedo boat.

نُسَالَة lint, tow, ravelings, fibrous waste.

نَسَبَ to relate, refer something to; to link, correlate; to trace someone's ancestry to; to ascribe, attribute, impute, lay something to; to charge, accuse of.

نَسَب lineage, ancestry, genealogy, stock, parentage; family relationship, relationship by marriage, affinity.

عِلْمُ الأَنْسَاب genealogy.

نِسْبَة ratio, rate, measure, proportion; ascription, imputation; kinship, relationship, affinity, relationship by marriage; connection, link; agreement, conformity; relation, reference.

نِسْبَةٌ مِئَوِيَّة percentage.

نِسْبَةُ الوَفَيات death rate, mortality rate.

بِالنِّسْبَةِ إلى with regard to, concerning, as to, compared with; in comparison with, as for.

نِسْبَةُ المَوَاليد birthrate, natality.

نَسَبِيّ genealogical.

نِسْبِيّ relative, comparative, proportional.

نِسْبِيًّا relatively, comparatively.

نِسْبِيَّة relativity.

نَسَجَ to weave; to knit; to spin.

نَسَجَ على مِنْوَالِهِ to imitate, copy, take after, tread in the steps of.

نَسَخَ to abrogate, invalidate, abolish, cancel, repeal, revoke; to supersede; to replace, take the place of.

نَسَخَ الكِتاب to copy, transcribe, make an exact copy of.

نَسْخ abrogation, abolition, cancellation, invalidation; copying, transcription, duplication.

نُسْخَة copy, transcript (of a book, a text).

نُسْغ sap, juice.

نَسَفَ to blow up, blast; to pulverise, spray; to carry away and scatter the dust (by the wind); to screen, sift (grain).

نَسْف blowing up, blow up, blasting, torpedoing; winnowing.

نَسَّقَ to coordinate, harmonize, arrange, put in order, classify; group together, range; to set up, line up, align.

ينسق الطالب كتبه على الرف بطريقة جميلة
The student aligns his books in a beautiful manner on the shelf

نَسْق lining up, alignment, arrangement.

نَسَق order, array, layout; arrangement, disposition, sequence, manner, mode, system, method, symmetry.

على نَسَق in the manner of.

على نَسَقٍ واحد in the same manner, equally, uniformly.

نَسَك، نَسُكَ to lead a life of an ascetic; to be devout.

نَسْك، نُسْك، نُسُك piety, ascetism, reclusion.

نَسَلَ to beget, procreate a child; to pluck out, ravel out, unravel, untwist.

نَسْل progeny, offspring, children, descendants.

نَسَمَ to blow gently (wind).

نَسَّمَ to commence, start, begin something.

نَسْمَة breath of air, whiff, puff, breath of life; person, human being; aura; asthma (med.).

نِسْوَة، نُسْوَة women.

نَسَوِيّ feminine, women's affairs.

نَسِيَ to forget, neglect, omit to do something.

نَسْي، نِسْيَان oblivion, forgetfulness.

نَسِيب relative, kinsman; related by blood or marriage to.

نَسِيب son-in-law; brother-in-law.

نَسِيب highborn, noble, of noble descent.

نَسِيج texture, web, tissue; woven fabric, textile.

نَسِيجُ العَنْكَبُوت spider's web, cobweb.

نَسِيجُ وَحْدِهِ unique in his kind, unparalleled.

نَسِيم breeze, fresh air, breath of air.

نَشَأَ to rise, emerge, appear, come into being, come into existence, originate, arise, crop up, spring, proceed from.

نَشَأَ مِنْ أو عَنْ to grow out, to follow, ensue, result, drive from, develop, evolve of, thrive, flourish.

نَشَّأَ to cause to grow, bring up, raise (a child).

نَشْء the youth, young people, youngsters, young generation.

نَشَا starch; smell, odor, scent.

نَشَاء starch.

نشأة origin, birth, rise, start, emergence; early youth; formation, culture, refinement, genesis.

نُشَارَة sawdust.

نَشَاز dissonance, discord, discordance; elevation, elevated place.

نَشَاط activity, energy, vitality, liveliness, vivacity, verve; briskness, animation, agility, alacrity; ardor, zeal, vim, action, operation; strength, power, vigor.

نَشَاطٌ إشْعَاعِيّ radioactivity.

نَشَّال pickpocket.

نَشِبَ to be fixed, attached, cling, stick, adhere to; to attend; to get involved in, meddle with.

نَشِبَت الحربُ to break out, flare up, erupt (war).

نَشِبَ بَعْضُهُ بِبَعْض to snarl, interweave; to be intertwined, interwoven, knitted, tangled.

نَشَجَ to sob.

نَشَدَ to seek, look, search for; to adjure, implore someone by.

نَشَرَ to spread, spreadout, outspread, stretch out; to extend, unfold, unroll, unwind; to diffuse, release; to propagate, disseminate, circulate, promulgate, publish; to deploy (troops); to hang on a clothes line (laundry).

نَشَرَ to resurrect, raise from the dead.

نَشَرَ to saw (wood, metal).

نَشْر spreading out, stretching out, extention, unfolding; diffusion, propagation, dissemination, publishing, issue.

نَشْرُ الكُتُب publishing, publication, issue.

نَشْرُ القوّات deployment of forces.

نَشْرُ المَوْتَى resurrection of the dead.

نَشْرُ الخَشَب أو المَعْدن sawing.

يومُ النَّشْر Day of Resurrection.

نَشْرَة bulletin, brochure, leaflet, pamphlet, circular.

نَشْرَةُ أخبار newscast, news bulletin.

نَشْرَةٌ جَوِّيَّة weather report.

نَشْرَةٌ دَوْرِيَّة periodical.

نَشْرَةٌ رَسْمِيَّة official bulletin.

نَشَزَ to be elevated; to rise, protrude.

نَشِطَ to be lively, animated, brisk, sprightly, vivacious, spirited, active, eager, keen, zealous, brave; to be cheerful, gay; to be energetic, work actively for; to be in the mood for; to be enthusiastic about; to apply oneself eagerly; to attend attentively to some activity; to embark briskly upon.

نَشِطَ من عِقَالِهِ to be unfettered.

نَشَّطَ to incite, spur on, goad, enliven, stimulate, activate, excite; to strengthen, invigorate, animate, energize; to embolden, encourage someone; to knot, tie up.

نَشِط ، نَشِيط lively, animated, brisk, sprightly, vivacious, energetic, active, agile, full of activity, busy, in full swing; cheerful, gay, glad, enthusiastic about.

نَصَّ to provide for, lay down, stipulate; to dictate to; to compose, write; to attribute to, ascribe to (a declaration); to stack; to set up, line up, pile up in layers.

نَصّ text, wording, version; sentence, expression, language, phraseology, style; stipulation, term, condition, manifestation.

نَصًّا وروحًا in letter and spirit.

نَصَّاب swindler, imposter, cheat, fraud, crook, deceitful.

نِصَاب origin, beginning, original condition.

نِصَابٌ قانُونيّ quorum.

في نِصَابِهِ in its proper place.

عادت الأمور إلى نِصَابِها the situation returned to normal.

وَضَعَ الحَقَّ في نِصَابِهِ — to restore justice.

نَصَبَ — to raise, rear, erect, set up, put up; to prepare, get ready, fit up something.

نَصَبَ خَيْمَةً — to pitch a tent.

نَصَبَ شَجَرَةً — to plant a tree.

نَصَبَ عَلَمًا — to hoist a flag.

نَصَبَ مِدْفَعاً — to mount a canon.

نَصَبَ على — to dupe, cheat, defraud, deceive; to embezzle.

نَصَبَ لَهُ الشَّرَّ — to show open hostility to.

نَصَبَ لَهُ فَخًّا — to set a trap for.

نَصَبَهُ المَرَض — to be exhausted by a disease.

نَصَّبَ — to set up, set upright, rear, raise, lift up; to install, appoint someone to an office.

نَصْب — erection, setting up, placing; planting, raising (a flag); appointment; installation; illness; swindle, embezzlement.

نَصْبُ الكَلِمَة — putting a noun in the accusative, a verb in the accusative case, subjunctive mood (grammar).

نُصْبَ — in front of, opposite, facing.

نُصْبَ عَيْنَيَّ — before my eyes.

جَعَلَ الأَمْرُ نُصْبَ عَيْنَيْه — to direct one's attention to; to have the matter in view.

نَصْب، نُصُب — statue, monument

نَصَحَ — to advise, counsel; to admonish, exhort; to be sincere.

يوجد نصب الشهداء في ساحة الشهداء في بيروت

The martyrs statue is placed at the Martyrs Square in Beirut

نُصْح — advice, recommendation, counsel, guidance; admonition, exhortation.

نَصَرَ — to help, assist, aid against; to render victorious; to let triumph someone over (by God); to deliver, keep, protect, save.

نَصْر — victory, triumph.

نَصْرانِيّ — Christian.

النَّصْرانِيَّة — Christianity.

نُصْرَة — help, aid, assistance, backing, support.

نَصَعَ — to become clear, plain, evident, obvious.

نَصَفَ — to reach its middle or half.

نَصَّفَ — to half, bisect, divide into two equal parts.

نِصْف half, moiety; middle; medium, average, regular; middle-aged; semi-.

نِصْفُ أُسْبُوعِيّ semiweekly.

نِصْفُ خُطْوَة half step.

نِصْفُ قُطْر radius.

نِصْفُ الكُرَة الأرضِيَّة hemisphere.

نِصْفُ النَّهار، مُنْتَصَفُ النَّهار midday.

نِصْفُ اللَّيل، مُنْتَصَفُ اللَّيْل midnight.

نِصْفُ نِهائِيّ semifinal (exam).

نِصْفِيّ half, semi-, hemi-, demi-,.

نَصْل blade, arrowhead, spearhead; lamina (of plant leaf).

نَصوح sincere, honest, loyal, faithful.

نَصِيب share, dividend (of profits); luck, chance, fate, lot; quota, allocation, portion.

كانَ مِنْ نَصِيبِه to fall to someone's lot.

نَصِيحَة advice, counsel, friendly reminder, exhortation.

بَذَلَ النَّصِيحَة to give advice.

نَصِير helper, supporter, ally, backer, partisan, follower; promoter, patron, adherent, devotee, sponsor, proponent.

نَضارَة bloom, freshness, vigor, beauty, health, gracefulness.

نِضال struggle, fight, battle, contest, dispute, defense.

نَضَبَ to run out; to be depleted; to dwindle, drain away, decrease, diminish; to dry up (spring, well); to drain; seep away in the ground (water).

نَضِجَ to become ripe; to ripen; to be well-cooked (food); to become well done (meat); to maturate (tumor).

نُضْج، نُضُوج maturity, ripeness.

نَضَحَ to sprinkle, spray, shower; to wet, moisten; to water; to seep, leak, filter, percolate; to sweat, perspire.

نَضَحَ عَطَشَهُ to quench one's thirst.

نَضْح sprinkling, spraying; leakage, seepage.

نَضَدَ to pile up, stack, arrange in layers; to put in order, array, arrange.

نَضَدَ to compose, set, typeset (printing press).

نَضَد bedstead, pile, stack; rows; tiers (of sacks, bags); bench.

نَضَرَ، نَضُرَ، نَضِرَ to be flourishing, blooming; to be fresh, tender; to be bright, brilliant, radiant.

نَضِر flourishing, blooming; fresh, glowing, radiant, verdant.

نُضُوب depletion, exhaustion.

نَطَّ jump, leap, hop.

نَطاسِيّ، نِطاسِيّ learned, erudite, scholar, expert, authority; skilled physician, specialist.

نِطاق range, extent, scope, sphere, field, domain, limit, boundary, bound, zone.

نِطاق girth, girdle, belt, strap, strip.

نِطاق circle, garrison; belt; enclosure; compass, cordon.

أ ب ت ث ج ح خ د ذ ر ز س ش ص ض ط ظ ع غ ف ق ك ل م ن هـ و ي

واسعُ النِّطاق comprehensive, extensive, large-scale.

نَطَحَ to butt.

نُطْفَة sperm, semen.

نَطَقَ to pronounce, utter, say, speak, talk; to deliver (a verdict).

نَطَّقَ to girdle, encircle with a strap.

نُطْق pronunciation, utterance, articulation, speech; pronouncement of a court sentence; vocalization.

نَظارة jail, prison, lock up.

نَظَّارة spectators, audience, watchers.

نَظَّارة، نَظَّارات eye glasses, spectacles.

نَظَّارةٌ أُحادِيَّةُ الزُّجاجة monocle.

نَظَّارةٌ أَنْفِيَّة pince-nez.

نَظَّاراتٌ شَمْسِيَّة sunglasses.

نضع النظارات الشمسية اتقاءً لوهج الشمس

We wear sunglasses to protect our eyes from the sun glare

نَظَّارةٌ مُكَبِّرة magnifying glass.

نِظارة supervision, control, superintendence.

نَظافة cleanness, cleanliness, tidiness, purity.

نِظام system, order, method; arrangement, regularity, organization; discipline, orderly conduct.

نِظامُ الحُكْم regime, system of government.

نِظام rule, regulation, law.

نِظامٌ أساسِيّ constitution, statute, charter.

نِظامٌ إقْطاعِيّ feudalism, feudal system.

نِظامُ التَّقْنين rationing system.

نِظامٌ داخِلِيّ bylaw, rules of procedure.

نِظامُ الشَّرِكة الأساسِيّ articles of association.

النِّظامُ العِشْرِيّ decimal system.

النِّظامُ المِتْرِيّ metric system.

نِظامِيّ regular, orderly, methodical, systematic, normal; organizational, disciplinarian, disciplinary.

نَظَرَ to look at, regard, see, eye, view, watch, observe, consider.

نَظَرَ في to consider carefully; to think over deeply, contemplate, reflect on, mediate on.

نَظَرَ في دَعْوَى to try, hear, examine, study; to judge, rule, decide.

نَظَرَ لِـ to take care of, look after, help, aid, assist.

نظرت من النافذة إلى لاعب الكرة النشيط

I looked through the window to watch the active football player

نَظَرَ بِعَيْنِ العَطْفِ إلى — to sympathize with; to feel sympathy for; to be favorably disposed to.

نَظَرَ إليه شَذْراً — to give someone a sidelong glance; to look askance at someone.

نَظَرَ بين — to make comparisons, draw parallels between.

نَظَر — seeing, eyesight, vision, look, glance, gaze, sight; prospect; view, aspect, appearance.

نَظَر — insight, discernment, perception, contemplation.

نَظَر — inspection, study, perusal, consideration, reflection.

نَظَرٌ في دَعْوى — trial, hearing.

بِالنَّظَرِ إلى — in view of, due to, owing to, because of; concerning, in respect of, since, as, because.

بِصَرْفِ النَّظَرِ عن — regardless of, irrespective of, let alone, aside from, apart from, not to mention.

في نَظَري — in my opinion, in my view.

مَسْأَلَةٌ فيها نَظَر — an unsettled matter, a debatable case.

تحت النَّظَر — under consideration.

إعَادَةُ النَّظَر — reconsideration; retrial; revision, re-examination.

اسْتَرَقَّ النَّظَرَ إلى — to glance furtively at, give someone a surreptitious look.

تحت نَظَر فُلان — under the protection of.

نَظْرَة — look, glance, sight, view; reflection, perspective.

نَظْرَةٌ شامِلَة — general view, overall look, review.

من النَّظْرَةِ الأولى — at first sight.

نَظَرِيّ — theoretical, academic, abstract; optical, visual; speculative.

نَظَرِيًا — theoretically, in theory.

نَظَرِيَّة — theory, notion, theorem.

نَظَّفَ — to clean, cleanse, polish; to purify, purge.

نَظَّمَ — to organize, array, dispose, put in order; to adjust, regulate, fix, set; to lay out, make, prepare; to plan, draw up, draft; to write, formulate.

نَظْم — order, arrangement, system; string of pearls; poetry.

نَظير ، النَّظير — counterpart, parallel; analogue, peer, equal, like, similar; comparable; isotope.

نَظِيرَ — as a compensation for, in consideration of, for, on.

نَظيف — clean, pure, neat, tidy.

نَعَى — to annouce the death of; to find fault with; to criticize, censure, blame someone's actions.

نُعَاس — drowsiness, sleepiness, lethargy.

نَعَتَ — to describe, qualify.

نَعْت — description, qualification, property, attribute; adjective (grammar), epithet; surname.

نَعَرَ — to grunt (pig); to cry, scream, roar; to spurt, gush forth (blood).

نَعْرَةٌ طائِفِيَّة — confessional feud, sectarianism; religious fanatism.

نَعَسَ — to be sleepy, drowsy; to take a nap, doze; to slumber.

نَعَسَ السُّوق — to be dull, listless, slack, stagnant.

نَعْش — coffin, casket (of a deceased person).

نَعَقَ — to croak, caw (raven); to hoot, whoop (owl).

نَعَّلَ — to furnish with shoes; to shoe a horse.

نَعْل — shoe, boot, sandal; sole of a shoe.

نَعِمَ — to live in comfort; to lead a life of ease; to be delighted by, be happy, glad about, be pleased with; to enjoy, savor, experience.

نَعِمَ — to be fine, powdery; to be green, tender (twig); to be soft, smooth.

نَعَّمَ — to smooth, soften, pulverise, powder; to accustom someone to luxury; to pamper, coddle.

نَعَمْ — yes, indeed, certainly, surely.

نِعْمَة — benefit, blessing, boon; favor, grace, kindness.

بِنِعْمَةِ الله — by the grace of God.

وَلِيُّ نِعْمَتِهِ — his benefactor.

نُعُومَة — softness, smoothness, fineness, delicacy.

مُنْذُ نُعُومَةِ أظْفارِهِ — from his tender age.

نَعْي، نَعِيّ — obituary, death announcement.

نَعيب، نَعيق — caw, croak (raven); hoot, whoop (owl).

نَعيم، النَّعيم — peaceful, gentle; ease, comfort, happiness, felicity.

نَغَزَ — to tickle; prick someone with a needle, sharp rod.

نَغَّصَ — to disturb, ruffle; to spoil someone's pleasure (joy, life); to make loathsome something to someone.

نَغِل — bastard, illegitimate child.

نَغْل — hybrid, crossbred.

نَغَّمَ، نَغَمَ، نَغِمَ — to hum a tune; to sing.

نَغَم، نَغْم — tune, sound, tone, air, melody.

نَغْمَة — tone, tune, sound; melody, song, chant.

نَفَى — to deny, refute, disprove, repudiate; to disclaim, disallow; to exclude, preclude; to negate (grammar); to remove, expel; to banish, exile, deport, expatriate someone.

نَفّاث، نَفّاثَة — jet (engine, plane, etc.).

نَفاد — exhaustion, depletion, consumption (of stores); wastage, waste.

نَفادُ الصَّبْر — impatience.

نَفاذ penetration, permeation; realization, effectuation; effectiveness, execution; infiltration, percolation; validity.

نِفَاس delivery, childbirth, confinement, puerperium.

نَفاسَة preciousness, costliness.

نِفَاق hypocrisy, duplicity, dissemblance.

نُفَايَة garbage, rubbish, trash, junk, waste, scrap, offal.

نَفْتَالين naphtalene.

نَفَثَ to expectorate, cough out, spit out; to discharge, let out, let off, release; to emit, send out; to exhale, puff (smoke).

نَفْثَة expectoration, spittle, emission, effusion.

نَفَثاتُ الأقلام literary works.

نَفَحَ to make someone a present of; to present someone with; to spread; to be diffused, exhale a pleasant smell; to be fragrant; to blow (wind).

نَفْحَة gift, present, donation; fragrance, scent, perfume; gust, whiff (of wind).

نَفَخَ to blow, puff; to breathe, inflate, fill with air; to pump up (a tire); to fill with gas (a balloon); to blow tunes (on a wind musical instrument); to swell, distend.

نَفَخَ في شَخص to inspire, elate, flush with success, fill with pride.

نَفَخَ في البُوق to blow the trumpet.

ينفخ الولد الهواء في البالون لتعبئته بالهواء
The boy blew in his balloon to fill it with air

نَفَخَ في رُوحِهِ to animate, give birth to.

نَفْخ blowing, inflation, filling with, pumping up, swelling, distension; conceit, pride.

نَفْخَة blow, puff; gust, whiff (of wind).

نَفِدَ to be exhausted, depleted, used up.

نَفِدَ الكِتَاب to be out of print, sold out.

نَفِدَ صَبْرُهُ to be at the end of his patience.

نَفَذَ to pierce, bore, penetrate, pass through something; to break through; to get, arrive, reach at; to lead to; to give, open on (a window); to be connected with; to be carried out, executed, effective, operative, valid.

نَفَّذَ to cause to pierce or penetrate; to carry out, execute, perform, accomplish, fulfill; to discharge a duty; to implement a plan or idea; to enforce a resolution; to transmit, convey, send, forward something to someone; to honor, observe, comply with; to levy execution on.

أ ب ت ث ج ح خ د ذ ر ز س ش ص ض ط ظ ع غ ف ق ك ل م ن هـ و ي

نَفَذ، مَنْفَذ opening, orifice, hole, vent, outlet, escape, access, gateway, loophole.

نَفَرَ to shy, bolt, stampede (animal); to flee, run away; to feel a distate for; to avoid, shun, keep away from; to swell, protrude, jut out, bulge out.

نَفَر band, group; person, individual, soldier.

نَفُسَ to be valuable, precious.

نَفَّسَ to give vent to; to release, discharge (air); to relieve one's chest (of anger); to dispel, banish someone's worries; to uncover, reveal; to desist from, cease doing.

نَفَّسَ عن فُلان to cheer up, entertain, amuse.

نَفَس breath, whiff, puff; style; freedom, liberty.

حتّى النَّفَس الأخير to the last breath.

فاضَت أنْفاسُهُ to give up the ghost; to die, pass away.

نَفْس soul, spirit, life, living creature, human being, person, individual; essence, nature; inclination, liking, appetite, desire.

بِنَفْسِهِ personally, in person.

جاءَ مِنْ نَفْسِهِ he came of his own accord.

نَفْسُ الأمر، نَفْسُ الشَّيْء the thing itself, the same thing.

بِشَقِّ النَّفْس with the greatest difficulty.

عفيفُ النَّفْس selfless, unselfish, altruistic.

مَحَبَّةُ النَّفْس selfishness.

نَفْسِيّ، نَفْسانِيّ psychic, psycho-; mental, spiritual; psychological, psychologic.

عالِمٌ نَفْسِيّ psychologist.

علاجٌ نَفْسِيّ psychotherapy.

مُحَلِّلٌ نَفْسِيّ psychoanalyst.

طبيبٌ نَفْسِيّ psychiatrist.

نَفْسِيَّة mentality, disposition, character, mood, state of mind.

نَفَشَ، نَفَّشَ to tease (wool); to swell out; to comb, card cotton; to ruffle its feathers (bird).

نَفَضَ to shake off dust from; to knock the ashes from a burning cigarette; to recover, recuperate from.

نَفَضَ عَنهُ الكَسَل to shake off, get rid off one's laziness.

نَفَضَ يَدَهُ من الأمر to refuse to have something to do with.

نَفَضَ يَدَه من يَدِ فُلان to dissociate oneself from someone.

نَفْط petroleum, oil.

نَفْط خام crude, crude oil.

نَفَعَ to be useful, profitable, of use, of service.

نَفْع usefulness, profit, benefit, utility, welfare.

نَفْعِيّ opportunist, utilitarian.

نَفَقَ to run out of stock; to be exhausted, depleted, fully sold, used up.

نَفَقَ to perish (animal); to be brisk, active (market).

نَفَق tunnel.

تمّ مؤخراً توسيع نفق نهر الكلب لتسهيل حركة السير
Nahr al-Kalb tunnel was recently widened to facilitate traffic

---

نَفَقَة expense, cost, expenditure, disbursement, maintenance costs; support of the divorced wife; charitable gift, handout to the needy; alimony; fee, charge.

على نَفَقَتِهِ at someone's expense.

نَفَقَات ثابِتَة overheads.

نُفُوذ influence, authority, power, weight, prestige.

نَفُور shy, timid; fearful; disinclined, reluctant.

نُفُور reluctance, unwillingness.

نُفُور alienation, disinclination, aversion, distate; fight.

نَفْي denial, disavowal, refutation; banishment, exile, deportation, expulsion; negation (grammar).

نَفير trumpet, bugle; horn; band, group.

نَفِيس precious, valuable, costly, priceless.

نَفِيسَة gem, rarity, masterpiece, chef d'œuvre.

نَقَّى to purify, refine, clarify; to clean; to select, pick out, sift, sort; to hand-pick.

نَقاء purity, fineness, clarity, clearness.

نِقَاب veil.

نِقَابَة union, syndicate, association.

نِقَابَةُ عُمَّال trade union, labor union.

نِقَابِيّ unionist, syndicalist.

نَقَّاش house painter, sculptor, engraver, painter.

نِقَاش argument, dispute, debate, discussion.

نَقَّال portable, mobile, movable.

نَقَّالَة stretcher, litter.

نَقَاهَة convalescence, recovery (from sickness).

نَقَاوَة purity, fineness; selection, elite, pick, best.

نَقَبَ to bore, pierce, perforate, breach; to punch, drill a hole; to dig up, excavate, hollow out; to inquire, ask, look, search for; to examine thoroughly, investigate, delve into.

نَقَّبَ to drill a hole in search of a mineral; to study, investigate thoroughly; to penetrate, delve into, look for.

نَقَّحَ to amend, revise, redact, improve, refine (a style of writing).

نَقَدَ to pay in cash; to peck at; to examine critically; to criticize.

نَقْد criticism, review; cash, ready money, currency.

نَقْداً in cash.

وَرَقُ النَّقْد banknotes, paper money.

نَقْدِيّ cash; monetary; critical.

نَقَرَ to dig, excavate, drill, bore, pierce; to carve, cut, engrave, inscribe; to peck (bird).

نَقَرَ to knock, rap, beat, percuss, drum; to toss.

نَقَرَ إصبَعَهُ to snap one's finger.

نَقْر digging, piercing, boring; carving, engraving.

نَقْر knocking, rap, beating, banging, percussion, drumming; snapping (fingers); tapping.

نُقْرَة pit, cavity, hole; depression.

نُقْرَةُ العَين eye socket, eye hole, orbit.

نُقْرَةُ الذقن أو الخد dimple.

نِقْرِس gout (med.).

نَقَزَ to bound, leap, skip, hop.

نَقَشَ to engrave, inscribe, carve out, sculpture.

نَقَّشَ بالألوان to variegate, dapple, paint.

نَقْش engraving, inscription, sculpture, carving; variegation, dappling; figure, picture, pattern, design.

نَقَصَ to decrease, diminish, lessen; to become less, to be reduced; to be prejudicial; to detract from; to lower, peg down; to be deficient, lacking, insufficient, faulty, imperfect.

نَقَّصَ to decrease, diminish, lessen, reduce, lower, peg down; to curtail, cut.

نَقْص decrease, diminution, loss; shortage, deficiency, lack, want; defect, shortcoming, fault, inferiority.

نَقَضَ to revoke, repeal, rescind, annul, nullify, abrogate; to break, breach, veto, violate, contravene; to invalidate, refute, disprove; to recant, abjure, retract, undo.

نَقَّضَ to tear down, destroy, demolish.

نَقْض destruction, demolition; breach, violation; refutation, veto, invalidation; contradiction; undoing.

نَقْضُ الحُكْم reversal of a court sentence.

نَقَطَ، نَقَّطَ to provide with diacritical points (a letter); to dot, dab, stain, speckle; to cause to drip; to let fall in drops; to give a wedding present (to the bride).

نُقْطَة point, dot, diacritical point; period, fullstop (in writing); speckle, spot, drop.

نُقْطَة matter, issue, subject; item, particular; locality, site, place, position; outpost, base (army).

نُقْطَةُ ارْتِكَاز fulcrum, support.

نُقْطَةُ الانْصِهار melting point.

نُقْطَةُ التَّحَوُّل، نُقْطَة تَحَوُّل turning point.

نُقْطَةُ التَّشَبُّع saturation point.

نُقْطَةٌ حَرِجَة critical point.

نُقْطَتان (:) colon (:).

نَقَعَ to soak, infuse.

نَقَلَ to transport, carry, move, transfer, shift; to convey, transmit, impart; to transcribe, copy; to translate, report, relate, recount, quote from.

نَقَلَ الحِسابات to carry over, carry forward; to post.

نَقَلَ الدم to transfuse blood.

نَقَلَ المَرَض to communicate, transmit, spread disease.

نَقَلَ المِلْكِيَّة to assign, convey, cede (right).

نَقْل carrying, carriage, conveyance, transportation, transport; removal, transfer, relocation (of an official); move, change of residence; transmission; translation, transcription, copy; report, account; entry, posting (in an account book); assignment, cession, transfer (of right).

نَقْلاً عَن according to, based on.

نَقْلُ الدم blood transfusion.

نَقْلَة move, step.

نَقْلِيّات transport services, transports, means of transportation, conveyances.

نَقَمَ على، نَقِمَ على to revenge, avenge oneself; to be hostile, full of rancor against; to be mad, angry at because of; to hate, loathe, detest; to hold a grudge against.

نَقْمَة، نِقْمَة indignation, resentment, wrath; grudge, spite, rancor, bitter feeling; revenge, vengeance; misfortune, punishment, adversity, trial.

نَقِيَ to become pure, clear, clean.

نَقِيّ pure, clean, fresh, fine, immaculate.

نِقْي bone marrow, medulla.

نَقِيب president, chief; captain (army rank).

نَقِيبُ الأشْراف head of the descendants of the Prophet.

نَقِيبَة soul, spirit, mind, intellect; temper, natural disposition.

نَقِير tiny spot on a date pit; an utterly worthless thing.

لا يَمْلِكُ شَرْوى نَقِير he has absolutely nothing.

نَقِيصَة defect, fault, shortcoming, failing; deficiency, flaw.

نَقِيض antithesis, opposite, contrary; reverse, converse.

على النَّقِيض on the contrary.

على نَقِيضٍ مِن، على النَّقِيض مِنْ contrary to, in contrast with, unlike.

نَقِيق croaking (of frog).

نَكَى to cause damage; to harm, hurt, injure someone; to vex, annoy, offend someone; to subdue, conquer, defeat.

نَكّات joker, jester, wit, scoffer, mocker; avocet (bird).

نِكَاح marriage, wedlock.

نِكَايَة spite, vexation , grievance, prejudice, offense, outrage, wrong, harm; subdual, defeating.

نِكَايَةً فيه in spite of him, in defiance of him.

نَكَبَ to afflict, distress; to make unhappy, miserable; to put someone out of favor; to veer, shift (wind).

نَكْب، نكوب، نَكْبَة misfortune, disaster, catastrophe, calamity.

نُكْتَة joke, wisecrack, anecdote, pun, witticism, witty remark; speck, spot.

روحُ النُّكْتَة sense of humor.

نَكَثَ to infringe, renege, break one's promise.

نَكْث breach, violation, infringement of promise.

نَكَحَ to marry, wed, take as a spouse.

نَكِدَ to be unhappy, miserable; to pester, molest.

نَكَّدَ to trouble, vex, annoy; to make life hard, miserable for; to embitter someone's life.

نَكِد troublesome, unhappy, cross, bad-tempered, sulky.

نَكَد hardship, misfortune, adversity, molestation, trouble, nuisance; worry, concern, ill-humor, morosity.

نَكِرَ to be ignorant, have no knowledge of.

نَكَّرَ to disguise; to use a noun in its indefinite form (grammar).

نُكْرَان denial, contestation, disavowal; rejection, refusal.

نُكْرَانُ الجميل ingratitude.

نُكْرَانُ الذَّات self-denial.

نَكِرَة unknown person; indefinite noun (grammar).

نَكَسَ to turn around, turn over, invert, reverse; to lower, retract; to bow, bend one's head; to cause a relapse (illness).

نَكَّسَ to hang at half mast (flag).

نَكْسَة relapse, decadence, setback.

نَكَشَ to clear out, dredge, clean (a well); to stir up, hoe up, rake up, dig up (the soil); to rummage, search, ruffle, tousle, dishevel.

نَكَصَ to draw back, fall back, retreat, recoil, regress.

نَكَصَ على عَقِبَيْه to retreat, fall back, recoil.

نَكَفَ to stop, arrest; to disdain, scorn; to reject, refrain from doing something.

نَكَلَ to recoil from, draw back from, shirk; to abstain from; to refuse, desist, refrain from.

نَكَّلَ to punish severely; to teach someone a lesson; to maltreat, torture.

نَكْهَة flavor.

نُكُوص regress, withdrawal, fall back, shrinking; involution.

نُكُول refusal to testify in court; abstention, desistance.

نَكير denial, disavowal, disapproval, rejection; vile, revolting, atrocious, abominable; difficult, tough.

نَمَّ to indicate, show; to give evidence; to report in a libelous manner; to betray, reveal, disclose; to sow dissension between or among.

نَمّ، نَميمَة slander, calumniation, calumny; slanderer.

نما، نَمَى to develop, increase, grow, prosper, flourish.

نَمَا إلى to ascribe to, attribute to.

نَمَى الخَبَرُ إليه to come to someone's knowledge; to hear of, get wind of, learn about.

نَماء، نُمُوّ growth, increase, accretion, development, progress.

نَمَّام slanderer, informer, calumniator, telltale.

نَمَط manner, mode, pattern, type, fashion, sort, kind.

على هذا النَّمَط in this manner, in this way.

نَمَّقَ to embellish, decorate, adorn; to write in an elegant style.

نَمِلَ to tingle, prickle; to be numb, be benumbed (limb).

نَمِل creepy, creeping, crawling; teaming with ants.

نَمْلَة، نَمْل ant, ants.

نَمْنَمَ to adorn, decorate, embellish; to miniaturize.

نَمُوذَج sample, pattern, specimen; type, model, example.

نَمُوذَجُ طَلَبٍ form, application form.

يعيش مجتمع النمل في مستعمرات تحت الأرض

Ants live in underground colonies

نَمُوذَجٌ أَصْلِيّ prototype, archetype.

نَمُوذَجِيّ typical, exemplary, standard.

نمير healthy, salubrious, delicious, pure, clean.

نَهَى to forbid, prohibit, ban, prevent.

نُهِيَ إليه to reach someone (news); to come to someone's knowledge; to be told about, to learn about.

نُهَى intelligence, reason, intellect.

نِهائِيّ final, ultimate, last.

نِهائِيّ conclusive, final, definitive, absolute.

نِهائِيًا ultimately.

عِلاجٌ نِهائِيّ last resource.

فَوْزٌ نِهائِيّ ultimate triumph, eventual success.

نَهار day, daytime.

نَهاراً ولَيْلاً by day and by night.

نَهارِيّ relating to daytime, diurnal.

نِهايَة end, termination, windup, conclusion, ending; outcome, result; extremity, terminus, terminal point; utmost, extreme.

أ ب ت ث ج ح خ د ذ ر ز س ش ص ض ط ظ ع غ ف ق ك ل م ن هـ و ي

نِهايَة — fate, destiny.

نِهايَةُ الأُسْبوع — weekend.

في النِّهايَة — in the end, at last, finally, eventually.

إلى ما لا نِهايَة — to infinity, endlessly, forevermore.

نَهَبَ، نَهِبَ — to plunder, loot, spoil, rob, take by force.

نَهَبَ الأَرْض — to cover the distance at tremendous speed.

نَهْب — plundering, looting, pillaging, spoilation, spoilage, robbery; plunder, loot, booty.

نَهَجَ — to pursue, enter upon, proceed, act; to clarify; to be clear, distinct; to pant, gasp, be out of breath.

نَهَجَ على مِنْوالِهِ — to follow someone's example.

نَهْج — road, method, manner, precedure, open way.

نَهَدَ الثَّدْيُ — to become round, full; to swell.

نَهَدَتِ الفَتاة — to become buxom, have developped breasts.

نَهْد — breast, bust, bosom.

نَهَرَ — to flow copiously, gush forth; to chide, scorn, reproach; to brush off, rebuff, reject, repulse, drive away.

نَهْر — river, stream.

نَهْرٌ جَليديّ — glacier.

نَهْر — rebuke, reprimand, reproof, rebuff, repulse.

نَهَزَ — to push, shove, prick, prod, urge on.

يروي النهر في جريانه الأراضي الزراعيّة المحيطة به
The river irrigates the agricultural lands surrounding its banks

نَهَشَ — to grasp with the teeth; to tear to pieces; to mangle, bite, snap.

نَهَضَ — to rise, get up; to raise, lift, carry; to upgrade; to pounce on; to practise, pursue, tackle, handle, encourage, promote, further; to give a boost, bring new life into; support, endorse something; to get ready; to begin, start, undertake a mission; to enter, embark upon; to be pertinent, opposite (argument).

نَهَضَ إلى — to rush toward.

نَهَضَ بِالأَمْر — to assume, take the command.

نَهْضَة — upswing, advancement, progress, revival, rebirth, renaissance; getting up, rising, awakening, rise, growth.

نَهَقَ، نَهِقَ — to bray (donkey).

نَهِلَ — to drink.

نَهِمَ — to be gluttonous, greedy (eating food); to have a ravenous appetite; to be insatiable.

نَهَم — gluttony, greed, greediness, avidity, voracity.

نَهِم — gluttonous, greedy, insatiable, glutton, voracious.

أ ب ت ث ج ح خ د ذ ر ز س ش ص ض ط ظ ع غ ف ق ك ل م ن هـ و ي

نُهوض rising, rise; raising, lifting, upgrading, promotion, advancement.

نَهي prohibition, ban, interdiction; inhibition (soul).

نُهَيْز rivulet, creek, brook, stream.

نَهيق bray, braying (donkey).

نَوّ tempest, storm, hurricane, gale; surging, upheaval.

نَوى to intend, have in mind, make up one's mind, plan, design; to go far away; to absent oneself.

نَوى remoteness, destination.

نَوى date pits, fruit kernels, stones, pips.

نَواة kernel, pit, pip, stone; nucleus; core.

نُواح lamentation, lament, wailing, wail.

نَوّار (اسم) month of May; blossoms, flowers.

نَوال gift, favor, benefit; right; incumbent; a duty.

نَوْبَة minfortune, calamity, mishap; heavy blow; reverse.

نَوْبَة turn (in duty); shift, rotation (in duty).

نَوْبَةُ مَرَضٍ fit, attack, spell, spasm.

نَوْبَةٌ قلبية heart attack.

نُوتِيّ sailor, mariner, seaman.

نَوَّرَ to flower, blossom; to light, illuminate, fill with light; to enlighten; to shed light on.

نَوَر gypsies, vagabonds.

نُور light, glow, illumination; lamp, lantern.

نُورٌ كَشّاف searchlight.

رأى النُّور to be born.

نَوْط something suspended; medal, decoration, order.

نَوَّعَ to diversify; to vary, variegate; to charge, alter, modify; to change the appearance of.

نَوْع kind, sort, type; variety; species; way, manner, form, character, quality, grade.

نَوْعاً ما somewhat, in a way, more or less.

نَوْعاً وَكُمّاً qualitatively and quantitatively.

بِنَوْعٍ خاصّ in particular, especially.

نَوْعِيّ qualitative, characteristic, typical, peculiar.

نَوْعِيَّة quality, kind, nature.

نَوْل loom; fare, freight charge.

نَوَّمَ to put to sleep; to put to bed; to hypnotize, anesthetise.

نَوْم sleep, slumber, nap, doze.

نَوَّنَ to provide a noun with the nunnation (grammar).

نَوَّهَ to praise, commend, laud, extol, speak highly of; to mention, refer to, specify, indicate, point out; to hint at, allude to; to stress, emphasize; to imply, intimate.

نَوَوِيّ nuclear.

نَوَوِيٌّ حَرارِيّ thermonuclear.

نيء raw, uncooked (food); unripe.

نِيابَةٌ عَامَّة office of the district attorney; office of the attorney general.

نِيابَةُ الرِّئاسة vice-presidency.

بِالنِّيابَة عن acting, on behalf of, in the name of.

وكيلُ النِّيابَة prosecutor, prosecuting attorney.

نِيابِيّ representative, parliamentary.

مَجْلِسٌ نِيابِيّ parliament.

نِيَّة intent, intention, purpose, design; resolution, resolve.

في النِّيَّةِ أن it is intended to.

سَلامَةُ النِّيَّة good intention, sincerity, innocence, bona fides.

سُوءُ النِّيَّة evil intent, malice, cunning, deceit.

بِسُوءِ نِيَّة in bad faith, mal fides.

عَقَدَ النِّيَّة على to determine on something; to resolve to do something; to direct one's attention to do something.

نَيِّر luminous, shining, brilliant, radiant.

نَيْزَك meteor, shooting star.

نيسان April.

كذبَةُ نيسان April's fool.

نَيِّف ، نَيْف more than, above, over.

نَيْل obtainment, getting, acquirement, gaining, earning.

هــا here! look! ha! there!.

هاكَ herein after, in the following.

ها أنْتُم you there!.

هذا، هذي، هَذِهِ this one.

ها هو ذا، ها هُوَ there he is!.

هاء name of the letter.

هائِج excited, agitated, inflamed, irritated, enraged; rough, rolling (sea); rage, fury, anger.

هائِل huge, big, large, immense, massive; colossal, gigantic, enormous; frightful, terrifying, horrible, awful.

هائِم perplexed, baffled, puzzled, confused; in love, mad with love; roaming, wandering, roamer, wanderer.

هابَ to fear, dread; to be afraid of; to be awed.

هابَ to honor, respect, revere, venerate.

هابِط descending, falling, dropping; sinking.

هاتَرَ to revile, insult, abuse.

هاتِف telephone; invisible caller; shouter, crier.

عندما يرنّ جرس الهاتف أرفع السماعة لأتحدث مع المنادي

When the telephone rings I raise the receiver to speak with the caller

هاجَ to become excited, stirred up, agitated; to rise, spring up; to be very upset, furious, indignant; to be rough stormy.

هاجَى to ridicule each other in satiric verse; to defame, satirize, ridicule, mock someone.

هاجَرَ to emigrate, immigrate.

هاجِرَة midday, noon; midday heat; obscene language.

هاجِس thought, notion, concept, idea; fear, apprehension, anxiety, concern, misgiving, scruple, presentiment.

هاجِع dormant, sleeping.

هاجَم to attack, assault, assail, raid, pounce upon.

هادٍ (الهادِي) guide, pilot, conductor.

هادِئ calm, quiet, serene, peaceful, pacific; composed, self-possessed.

المُحِيطُ الهادِئ the Pacific Ocean.

هادِر thunderous, roaring, raging, surging (sea).

هادِف purposeful, constructive.

هادَنَ to conclude a truce with; to make peace with; to be reconciled with.

هاذٍ (الهاذِي) delirious, raving.

هارِب fugitive, runaway; deserter (from a mission, army).

هازِئ mocker, scoffer, contemptuous, derisive, ironic.

هازَلَ to joke with; make fun with.

هازِل joker, jester; jocular, funny, humorous, amusing.

هاشَ، هَوِشَ to be excited; to be in a state of commotion.

هاضَ to be broken; to break; to crumble.

هاطِل pouring out, raining heavily, torrential.

هالَ to terrify, frighten, strike with terror.

هالَ التُّراب to pour sand, pile up.

هالَة halo, corona, nimbus, aureole (around a saint's head); ring, circle (around the eye).

هالِك perishable, irredeemable, destructible; doomed to perdition, damned.

هامَ to wander, roam, rove; to be thirsty.

هامَ بِـ to fall in love with, love, adore, be very fond of.

هامَ على وَجْهِهِ to wander aimlessly about; to ramble.

هامّ important, serious, crucial, substantial.

هامَة head, summit; crown, vertex (of head).

هامِد still, motionless; inactive; dormant, lifeless; calm, quiet; dead.

هامِش margin, footnote.

على الهامِش، هامِشِيّ marginal, fringe.

على هامِش in connection with, on the occasion of, apropos of, on the periphery of.

هانَ	to be easy; to be of little importance.
هانَ عليهِ أن	to attach no importance to the fact that.
هانَ	to be despicable, contemptible.
هانِئ	happy, glad, delighted.
هاوٍ (الهاوِي)	fan, amateur, hobbyist; lover; falling down, tumbling, sinking.
هاوَدَ	to be indulgent, forbearing, complaisant, obliging.
هاوَدَ في الثمن	to charge a moderate price for.
هاوِيَة	abyss, chasm, pit; hell; ditch, trench.
هَايأَ	to adapt; to make ready, fix up, set up; to array, arrange; to agree with someone about; to concur with someone in; to adjust oneself.
هَبَّ	to start moving, attack, tackle; to embark upon; to begin with, start doing; to get up (from sleep); to rebel, revolt against.

هَبَّ	to blow (wind); to rage (storm); to break out (fire).
هَبَّ للحرب	to take up arms.
هَبَّ واقِفاً	to stand abruptly.

هَبَّت الرَّائِحة	to drift, waft.
هَباء	dust, fine dust, dust particles in the air.
ذَهَبَ هَباءً	to vanish, end up in smoke, come to nought; to dissolve into nothing.
هَبَّة	gust, squall (of wind); whiff, waft; rise, rising.
هِبَة	grant, donation, gift.
هَبَطَ	to descend, go down, fall down, drop; to sink, dip, slope down, collapse; to land (air plane); to lose weight, become lean, (body); to abate, subside, let up, stop, die down (wind, fire); to slump (prices).
هَبْطَة	descent, decline, fall, drop; depression.
هُبُوب	blowing (of wind).
هُبُوط	sinking,fall, decline, descent; lowering, reduction (of price); decrease, weakness, slum (of a market); landing (air craft, passengers); collapse, fall, cave-in (a roof, building); depression.
هُبُوطٌ اضْطِرَارِيّ	forced landing.
هُبُوطٌ بالمَظَلَّة	parachuting.
هُتاف	shout, cry, call, exclamation of joy; hurrah, acclaim, applause, cheer.
هَتَرَ عِرْضَهُ	to disgrace, discredit, dishonor, degrade, debase, defame, slander.
هِتْر	delirium, nonsense; lie, untruth, falsehood.
هَتَفَ	to shout, rejoice, acclaim, hail, cheer, extol.
هَتَفَ	to jeer, boo.
هَتَفَ بِـ	to call out someone.

هَتَكَ	to tear apart, rip apart (a curtain); to unveil, uncover, disclose, reveal something; to rape (a woman).

هَتَكَ عِرْضَهُ to disgrace someone.

هَتْك tearing, ripping apart; disclosure, exposure.

هَتْك rape, ravishment, dishonoring, debasement.

هَجَّ to burn, be on fire, be aflame; to flame, blaze (fire).

هَجَا to mock, disparage, satirize, ridicule; to lampoon.

هَجَّى to spell.

هِجاء satire, lampoonery, defamatory poem.

هِجاء spelling.

هِجَائِيّ alphabetic; defamatory, satirical.

هَجَرَ to part company with; to give up, abandon, leave behind; to relinquish, leave, emigrate; to vacate, give up.

هَجْر desertion, relinquishment, breakaway, renunciation, separation from the beloved one.

هَجْر midday, noon; midday heat.

هِجْرَة emigration, exodus, departure, immigration.

الهِجْرَة the Hegira (the emigration of Prophet Mohammed from Mecca to Medina in 622 A.D.).

هِجْرِيّ (تَقْوِيم) Moslem calendar; of the Hegira.

هَجَسَ to occur all a sudden to someone; to come to someone's mind; to mumble, mutter, talk to oneself.

هَجَعَ to sleep, slumber; to calm down, rest, abate.

هَجَمَ to rush, pounce upon; to attack, assail, charge; to force one's way into; to intrude, trespass, invade.

هَجَّنَ to hybridize, interbreed, crossbreed.

هُجْنَة fault, defect, meanness, baseness.

هُجُوع slumber, sleep; abatement, lull, remission.

هُجُوم attack, assault, charge, raid, onslaught, offensive.

هُجُومٌ جانِبِيّ flank attack (army).

هُجُومٌ مُضادّ counterattack.

هُجُومِيّ offensive, aggressive.

هَجِين low, lowly, ignoble; hybrid, crossbred, half-bred.

هَدَّ to demolish, crush, pull down, tear down, wreck, undermine, destroy; to sap, weaken, ruin.

هَدّ pulling down, wrecking, ruining, demolition; undermining, sapping, weakening.

هَدَأَ to calm down, cool down; to become calm, quiet, still; to abate, die down, cease; to settle down at, rest, remain, stay at a place.

هَدَّأَ أعْصابَهُ to soothe the nerves of someone.

هَدَى to guide, direct, conduct, pilot, show the way to.

calm down! take it easy!. هَدِّئ من رَوْعِك

guidance; right path, true religion; manner, mode, fashion. هُدَى

to be on the right way; to embrace the true religion. كانَ على الهُدَى

to wander aimlessly. سَارَ على غير هُدَى

sharpshooter, marksman. هَدَّاف

destructive, subversive. هَدَّام

guidance. هِدَايَة

border, hem. هُدْب

eyelashes, lash. هُدْب

to shamble, shuffle along; walk with unsteady steps; to totter, hobble, limp. هَدَجَ

to threaten, menace, scare, frighten, terrify, intimidate, daunt, blackmail. هَدَّدَ

to snarl, growl, peal, rumble, roll (thunder); to bray (camel); to clamor, be noisy, storm, rage, shout; to bubble, boil, simmer; to be in vain, be made to no avail; to be spent uselessly (money); to shed uselessly, squander (money or effort); to ruin (health); to coo (pigeon). هَدَرَ

waste, squandering. هَدْر

uselessly, vainly, futilely. هَدْراً

to aim; to aproach someone. هَدَفَ

target, goal, aim, purpose, intent. هَدَف

with the aim of, in order to, so as, for, with a view to, in order that. بِهَدَف

to be exposed, open to. كان هَدَفاً لـِ

to tear down, raze, wreck, destroy. هَدَمَ

armistice, truce; peace, tranquility. هُدْنَة

calm, quiet, tranquility, serenity, silence; composure, calmness, poise; part of the night. هُدُوء

guidance, showing the way to; line of conduct, course, way; offering, immolation, sacrifice. هَدْي

gift, present, offering, donation. هَدِيَّة

قدّمت هدية لأخي عند نجاحه في الثانوية

I offered to my brother a present on his passing successfully the secondary school exam

roar, snarl, growl. هَدير

cooing (of pigeon). هَديل

to talk irrationally, rave; to be delirious. هَذَى

this, this one. هَذا، هَذِه

therefore. لِهذا

أ ب ت ث ج ح خ د ذ ر ز س ش ص ض ط ظ ع غ ف ق ك ل م ن **هـ** و ي

مَع هذا nevertheless, in spite of.

هذا وَ besides, moreover, on the other hand.

هَذَبَ to prune, trim; to clean, purify, smooth, polish.

هَذَّبَ to refine, polish, trim, prune; to discipline, set right; to purify, clean.

هَذَرَ to prattle, babble, talk nonsense, blab.

هَذَيَان delirium, rave, hallucination.

هِرّ cat (male cat) (animal).

هَرَأَ to tear, wear out, wear off; to harm, hurt, irritate, (the skin); to be very cold (wind).

هُراء nonsense, prattle, idle talk.

هِراوَة cudgel, club, bat, bludgeon.

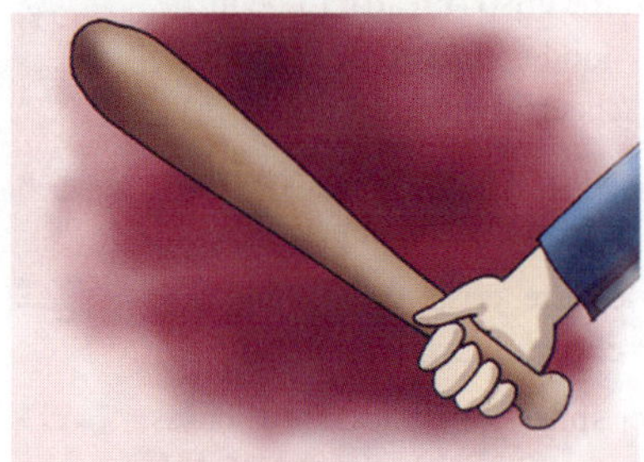

يحمل الشرطي هراوة لتفريق المتظاهرين
The policeman carries a cudgel to disperse demonstrators

هَرَبَ to flee to; to escape (a danger); to run away, desert, elope.

هَرَّبَ to smuggle (goods); to help someone to escape; to put someone to flight; to liberate, free a prisoner; to rescue a distrained thing (by a court); to engage in illicit trade.

هَرَب escape, flight, fleeing, runaway, getaway.

هَرَجَ to be in great commotion; to be agitated; to speak excitedly.

هَرَج excitement, disorder, muddle, confusion.

هَرَجٌ وَمَرج turmoil, confusion, chaos, commotion, agitation.

هَرَسَ to crush, mash, bruize; to pound until tender (meat).

هَرَّشَ to sow dissension among.

هَرَعَ to hurry to, hasten to, rush to.

هَرَع hurry, haste; hysteria.

هَرَقَ to shed, spill.

هَرِمَ to become senile.

هَرَّمَ to mince, chop.

هَرَم pyramid.

اشتهر المصريون القدامى ببناء الأهرام
Ancient Egyptians were famed for building the pyramids

هَرَمٌ ناقِص truncated pyramid (math).

هَرِم senile, aged, old; old man.

هَرَمِيّ — pyramidical, pyramidlike.

هُرُوب — flight, escape, fleeing.

هَرْوَلَ — to trot, jog, hasten, hurry, rush to.

هَرْوَلَة — quick pace, hustle, jogging.

هَزَّ — to shake, swing; to jolt to and fro, jog, rock; to make tremble; to convulse, upset, sway.

هَزَّ كَتِفَيْهِ — to shrug one's shoulders.

هَزَّ ذَنَبَهُ — to wag its tail.

هَزّ — shaking, jolting, swaying, jogging, rocking.

هَزَأَ، هَزِئَ — to scoff, jeer, sneer, make fun of; to deride, ridicule, mock someone.

هُزْء، هَزْء، هُزُؤ — ridicule, mockery, scoff, sneer, contempt.

هَزَّاز — rocking, swinging, shaking.

هُزَال — emaciation, leanness.

هَزَّة — motion, movement, commotion; jolt, push, shock; vibration, oscillation, tremor.

هَزَّةٌ أَرْضِيَّة — earthquake.

هَزَّةُ الطَّرَبِ أو الفَرَح — joyous excitement, delight, rupture.

هَزَّةُ الجِمَاع — orgasm.

هَزِجَ، هَزَّجَ — to sing, chant.

هَزَرَ — to laugh, joke.

هَزَعَ — to hurry, be quick.

هُزِلَ، هَزَلَ — to be emaciated, lean; to lose weight, become lean, skinny, emaciated.

هَزَلَ — to joke, jest, make fun.

هَزْل — joking, jesting,fun.

هَزْلِيّ — comical, jocular, funny, amusing, humorous.

هَزَمَ — to defeat, neutralize, put out of action (an opponent); to rout, vanquish (the enemy); to beat, overcome, crush.

هَزْم — routing, defeat, vanquishing.

هَزِيع — part of the night.

هَزِيل — skinny, emaciated, lean, wasted; meager, slight, thin, slender; trivial, insignificant.

هَزِيمُ الرَّعْد — thunder, thunderpeal.

هَزِيمَة — defeat, rout.

هَشَّ — to be crisp (bread); to be in good spirits; to display a cheerful mien; to smile.

هَشَّ — to meet courteously, receive cheerfully someone.

هَشّ — delicate, crisp, fragile; gay, cheerful; brisk, frail, brittle.

هَشَاشَة — crispness, briskness, brittleness; gaiety, joyfulness, cheerfulness.

هَشَّمَ — to destroy, crush, break into pieces, smash.

هَشِيم — straw, chaff; frail, fragile.

هَصَرَ — to bend down; to produce a crack; to crack, break.

هَضْبَة — hill, plateau, tableland.

هَضَمَ — to digest (food); to oppress; terrorize, outrage, wrong; to stand, bear, endure, stomach, put up with.

تتكاثر الهضاب وتتنوّع على سطح القمر
Plateaus abound in different forms on the moon surface

هَضْم digestion (of food); patience, long-suffering.

هَضْمِيّ digestive, alimentary.

هَطَلَ to pour down, fall heavily (rain).

هَفَّ to pass swiftly, flash, brush, touch lightly; to spread, waft (fragrance); to blow (wind).

هَفَا to slip, commit a lapse, make a mistake; to be famished, starved; to hurry, rush to; to yearn to snatch; to induce, tempt someone to do something.

هَفَا الطيرُ to flutter, fly, float in the air.

هَفَا القَلْبُ to throb violently, beat feverishly; to be passionately excited with love.

هَفَتَ to fly, float in the air; to fall down, collapse; to talk nonsense.

هَفْهَاف slender, slim, svelte, slight, frail, delicate, thin, sparse; diaphanous, transparent; light.

هَفْهَاف waving, fluttering, flowing.

هَفْوَة sin, error, lapse, fault, slip, mistake.

هَلْ interrogative particle introducing a question (are you happy? will you go? did you write?).

هَلَّ to appear, show (new moon); to begin, set in (month).

هَلَاك loss, ruin, total destruction or loss; perdition; eternal damnation.

هِلال new moon, half-moon, cresent.

يظهر الهلال في أول وآخر الشهر الهجري
The crescent appears on the first and the last days of the Hegira month

هِلالان parentheses (in writing).

هِلالٌ معقوف bracket (in writing).

هِلالِيّ lunar, crescent-shaped, semi-lunar.

هُلام jelly, gel.

هُلامِيّ jellylike, gelatinous.

هَلِعَ to be anxious, in despair; to be impatient.

هَلِعَ to be horrified, panic-stricken, appalled.

هَلَع impatience, uneasiness, fear, anxiety, dismay.

هَلَكَ to perish, die; to be annihilated, destroyed.

هُلْك، هَلْكَة، هَلَكَة death, destruction, ruin.

هَلَّلَ to shout with joy, exult, rejoice; to applaud, cheer, acclaim; to say the words (La Ilaha Illa Llah).

هَلُمَّ come! bring me! let's go! get up.

هَلُمَّ جَرًّا and so an, and so forth, etc..

هَلْوَسَ to hallucinate; to talk nonsense.

هَلْوَسَة hallucination, vision, talking nonsense.

هَمَّ to disquiet, make uneasy, distress, fill with anxiety; to preoccupy, interest, concern, regard; to worry; to be important; to have in mind, intend, plan to do something; to be about, on the point of doing something; to begin, start doing something; to rise, get up.

إلى من يَهُمُّهُ الأَمْرُ to whom it may concern.

هَمّ concern, anxiety; care; sorrow, grief, affliction; interest; design, plan; important matter; moment, importance, consequence.

هُمْ they (grammar).

هَمَا، هَمَى to flow, pour forth.

هُمَام generous, heroic, gallant, magnanimous, brave.

هِمَّة resolution; intention; endeavor; ardor, zeal, fervor; energy, vitality, liveliness, vivacity, verve.

عالي الهِمَّة high-aspiring, high-minded, ambitious.

هَمَجِيّ savage, barbarian, barbaric, wild, uncivilized.

هَمَجِيَّة barbarism, savagery, inhumanity, wildness.

هَمَدَ to abate, calm down, cool off, die away.

هَمَّدَ to quiet, still, calm, appease; to soothe, mitigate.

هَمَرَ to pour out, shed.

هَمَزَ to spur, goad, prod, urge on; to slander, calumniate.

هَمَسَ to whisper, murmur, mutter, mumble.

هَمْس، هَمْسَة whisper, whispering, mutter, muttering.

هَمْهَمَة hum, murmur, mutter, snarl, buzz, growl.

هُمُود extinction, cooling off, lull, fatigue, tiredness; torpor, rigor, stiffness; death.

هُنَّ they (grammar) (for the females).

هَنِئَ to enjoy, take pleasure in.

هَنَّأَ to congratulate, felicitate; to make happy.

هُنا، هَهُنَا here, over here, in this place; now, by now, at this point.

إلى هُنا over here, up to here, so far, up to this point.

من هُنا from here, of this, hereof, hence, therefore, for this reason, thereby.

هُنا وهُناك here and there.

هَنَاء bliss, felicity, happiness.

هُنَاك، هُنالِك there, over there, in that place.

إلى هُناك — to that place, over there.

ماذا هُناك — what's up? what's the matter?.

هِنْدام — trimness, smartness, spruceness; symmetry, neatness, tidiness; attire, dress, garb.

هَنْدَسَة — engineering, architecture, geometry, geodesy, surveying.

علم الهَنْدَسَة — geometry.

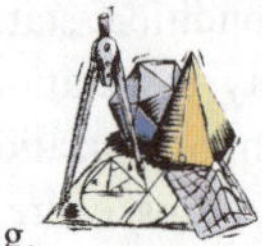

هَنْدَسَةٌ زِراعِيَّة — agronomy.

هَنْدَسَةُ المُدُن — town planning.

الهَنْدَسَةُ المَدَنِيَّة — civil engineering.

هَنْدَسَةٌ داخِلِيَّة — interior design.

هَنْدَسَةٌ مِعْمارِيَّة — architecture.

هَنْدَسِيّ — geometrical, engineering.

وَسَطٌ هَنْدَسِيّ — geometric mean.

هَنْدَمَ — to order, array, adjust; to make smart; to dress up.

هَنيء — comfortable, smooth; pleasant, salutary.

هَنيئًا مَريئًا — good appetite! enjoy your meal!.

هُنَيْهَة — little while, instant, moment, short while.

هُوَ — he.

هَوَى — to fall down, drop, sink; to swoop down; to die, pass away; to blow (wind); to love; to become fond of.

هَوَّى — to air, ventilate, expose to wind, fan the air.

هَوًى — love,passion, affection, liking; inclination, fancy, whim, caprice; fantasy; prejudice, bias.

على هَواه — as he likes, as he pleases.

بِنْتُ الهَوى — prostitute, whore, harlot.

هَواء — air, atmosphere, weather, climate, wind, breeze.

على الهَواء — on the air, live.

هَواءٌ طَلِق — open air, fresh air.

في الهَواء الطَلِق — outdoors, in the open air.

هَوائِيّ — aerial, pneumatic; antenna; capricious, whimsical.

يلتقط الهوائي الموجات اللاسلكية فيشتغل جهاز التلفزيون

The aerial captures wireless waves and the television set will operate

---

هَوادَة — leniency, clemency, indulgence, forbearance.

هَوان — disgrace, shame, humiliation, insignificance.

هِوايَة — hobby ,amateurism.

هَوّايَة — ventilator.

هُوَّة — abyss, chasm, gap, pit.

هَوْجاء — cyclone, tornado, hurricane.

هَوْر — lagoon, lake.

هَوِسَ to become a maniac, infatuated, crazy, perplexed.

هَوَّسَ to baffle, startle, confuse, bewilder, confound; to beguile, delude, dazzle, infatuate, craze, blind.

هَوَس folly, craze, madness; fancy, fantasy, frenzy, delusion, ecstasy, rapture, infatuation.

هَوَسُ السَّرِقَة kleptomania.

هَوَّشَ to excite, agitate, unsettle, rouse, incite, stir up, inflame; to sow dissension among.

هَوَّلَ to alarm, dismay, frighten, terrify, horrify; to menace, scare, threaten; to exaggerate, over-emphasize; to make a great fuss about; to make something appear terrible.

هَوْل terror, fright, alarm, shock, horror, dismay, enormity.

هَوَّنَ to make easy, ease, facilitate; to belittle; to minimize, deride, disparage.

هَوْن ease, tranquility, calmness; disgrace, shame.

هُوْن disgrace, shame, abasement.

هَوِيَ to love, fall in love, be fond of, like, take fancy to.

هُوِيَّة identity, personality.

هَوِيس thought, idea, concept; look.

هُوَيْنَى، هُوَيْنا slowness, leisure, ease.

مَشَى الهُوَيْنا to stroll, walk leisurely or slowly.

هِيَ she, it.

هَيَّأَ to prepare, make ready, arrange, set up; to pave the way for, facilitate.

هَيَّا come on! make haste!.

هَيَّاب timid, timorous, fearful, fearsome.

هَيْئَة form, shape, aspect, mien; attitude, position, condition, state; group, class, society, association; body, corporation, organization, board, committee, corps, cadre.

هَيْئَةٌ تَدْرِيسِيَّة faculty, teaching staff.

هَيْئَةٌ دِبْلُومَاسِيَّة diplomatic corps.

هَيْئَةٌ عَامَّة plenary session, general assembly.

هِيَاج excitement, agitation, commotion, turmoil, fury, irritation, indignation, bitterness, raging, uproar.

هُيَام، هِيَام passionate love, ardent love, passion.

هَيْبَة fear, dread; awe, veneration; dignity, prestige, standing.

هَيَّجَ to excite, agitate, stir, arouse, inflame, stimulate, provoke; to disturb, trouble; to incense, urge on, spur on; to scare up (a bird).

هَيْجَاء battle, war, combat.

هَيَجَان excitement, agitation, commotion, tumult; turmoil, eruption, outburst, fury, uproar (of the elements).

هيدروجين hydrogen.

هيدرولي hydraulic.

هِيرُوغليفي hieroglyphic.

هَيْفَاء svelte, slender, slim.

هَيْكَل temple; altar; skeleton; frame; structure, setup.

هَيْكَلُ السَّرير bedstead.

هَيْكَلُ السيَّارة body, hull.

هَيَّلَ to pile up (sand); to pour, sprinkle.

هَيْمَان madly in love, passionately in love; very thirsty.

هَيْمَنَ to dominate, control, overrule, hold sway over; to prevail over, guard, watch over.

هَيْمَنَة supervision, control, surveillance, ascendancy, hegemony; suzerainty, domination; supremacy.

هَيِّن ، هَيْن easy; negligible, inconsiderable; simple, plain, modest; of little value.

هَيْهَات how preposterous! wrong! far from the mark! how impossilble! how far!.

حرف الواو

و

وَ and, and also, as well as; with.

وَاللّه by God.

واءَمَ to agree, tally, harmonize; to suit; to be in harmony with; to adapt, adjust, conform, accomodate.

وِئام harmony, concord, accord, unity.

وابِل heavy downpour, hail, shower.

واثِق confident, certain, trusting, sure.

واثِقٌ من نَفْسِهِ self-confident, self-assured.

واجِب duty, obligation, job; necessary, required, obligatory; inevitable, unavoidable; due; adequate.

واجِبٌ عليه it is his duty.

واجِد finder; in love, lover; angry, furious; sad, grieved.

واجِس disquieting thought, foreboding, evil premonition.

واجِف throbbing, beating (heart).

واجِم silent, speechless; despondent; dejected.

واجَهَ to face, front, meet face to face, confront, withstand.

واجِهَة face, front, facade; show window.

واحَة oasis.

تنتشر الواحات في الصحارى
وتنبت فيها نباتات معينة
Oases abound in the deserts and certain plants grow in them

أ ب ت ث ج ح خ د ذ ر ز س ش ص ض ط ظ ع غ ف ق ك ل م ن هـ و ي

واحِد one, someone, a certain person; sole, only; single, solitary, separate, individual, isolated.

واحِدًا واحِدًا، واحِدًا بعد واحِد one by one, separately, one at a time.

كُلُّ واحِد everyone, everbody.

ولا واحِد not a single one, not one.

وادٍ (الوادي) valley, ravine, canyon, wadi.

وادِع gentle, mold, meek, calm, composed, moderate; depositor; lodger; consignor.

وارَى to hide, conceal, disguise.

واراهُ الثَّرَى to bury, inhume, inter.

وارِث، وارِثة heir, inheritor; heiress.

وارِد incoming, arriving, newcomer; mentioned, stated; possible, conceivable.

وارِدات (ج) receipts, returns, proceeds, earnings, revenues; imports.

وارِف verdant, flourishing, luxuriant, shady.

وارِم swollen.

وازَى to correspond, be equal; to equal, match.

وازِع obstruction, obstacle, impediment.

وازَنَ to equal in weight; to equilibrate, balance, offset; to equate, equalize, make equal; to compare with; to stabilize (a plane); to even up; to draw a parallel (between two things).

يوازن البائع السلعة عند بيعها إلى الزبون
The vendor balances the goods when he sells them to the client

واسَى to console, comfort someone; to nurse (a patient).

واسِطَة means, medium, expedient; mediator, intermediary.

بِوَاسِطَة by means of, through, by way of, via.

واسِع wide, broad, large, roomy, spacious, vast, extensive.

واسِعُ الانْتِشار widespread.

واسِعُ الصَّدر patient, forbearing, indulgent, generous.

واسِعُ النِّطاق far-reaching, extensive, large-scale, comprehensive.

واسِعُ الحيلة resourceful, ingenious.

واسِعُ النِّعْمَة rich, wealthy.

واشٍ (الواشي) informer, slanderer, calumniator, denunciator, traitor.

واصَلَ to bring into relation; to continue, proceed, persist, persevere in; to have sexual intercourse; to communicate with; to see.

واصَلَ اللَّيل بالنَّهار to work day and night.

واصَل جَهْدَهُ to make untiring efforts for.

واضِح clear, evident, plain, lucid, manifest, visible, apparent.

من الواضِح أن it is obvious that.

واطِئ low, muffled, subdued.

واظَبَ to persevere, persist in, take pains with; to apply oneself steadily to; to keep doing, continue to do, pursue steadily, devote oneself assiduously to.

واعٍ (الواعي) conscious, aware, mindful, rational, heedful, vigilant, alert, cautious.

واعَدَ to make an arrangement; to arrange for a meeting; to make an appointment with.

واعِظ preacher, exhorter.

وافٍ (الوافي) complete, entire, sufficient, ample, adequate.

وافَى to come to; to surprise; to show up; to bring, take, deliver to; to supply, provide, furnish with; to comply with; to fulfill someone's wish.

وافاه أَجَلُهُ his fate overtook him; to die, expire.

وافِد coming, arriving, incoming; immigrant.

وافِر abundant, copious, ample, profuse, plentiful; abounding in; superabundant, numerous.

وافَقَ to befit, become, suit; to be suitable, agreeable, convenient to, consistent with someone's wishes; to agree with; to be unanimous; to concur with; to correspond to; to be in conformity with; to harmonize with; to coincide with; to be wholesome, beneficial; to consent, assent, subscribe to, confirm, approve, licence, authorize, ratify; to bring to agreement, reconcile; to balance, equilibrate between.

واقَعَ to fight with, attack; to have sexual intercourse (with a woman).

واقِع (ص) falling, dropping, tumbling; occurring, happening; actual, real, factual; material, tangible; located.

واقِع (اسم) event, fact, matter of fact; reality, truth.

في الواقِع in fact, indeed, as a matter of fact, actually, really.

الأمرُ الواقِع the accomplished fact.

الواقِعُ أنَّ it is a fact that, actually.

بِواقِع in the amount of, as much as, as far as.

أمرٌ واقِع fait accompli, accomplished fact.

واقِعة incidence, event, happening; fact, accident; battle.

واقِعِيّ actual, factual, real, defacto, positive; practical, authentic; true; pragmatic, realist.

واقِعِيَّة reality, realism.

واقِف stopping; standing; still; upright, erect; familiar with; bystander, spectator (during a street scene); donor (for a wakf); suspensive, suspensory.

واكَبَ to accompany, escort, convoy.

والٍ (الوالي) ruler, governor, administrator, wali.

وَالَى to be a friend, supporter, patron, protector of; to help, assist; to do incessantly, continue without interruption; to pursue, practice; to follow immediately.

والِد father.

الوالِدان father and mother, parents.

والِدة mother.

والِدِيّ paternal, fatherly.

واهٍ (الواهي) weak, frail, fragile, flimsy; thin, brittle; insignificant, trivial; unfounded, groundless (excuse).

واهِم mistaken, deceived, wrong, deluded.

واهِن weak, feeble, weakened, debilitated; sapless, effete, despondent, languid, impotent, frail.

وئيد deliberate, slow, unhurried.

وَئيداً slowly, unhurriedly.

وَبِئَ، وَبُؤَ، وُبِئَ to be infected, infested.

وَباء، وَبأ epidemic, pestilence.

وَبَّخ to reprimand, rebuke, censure, scold, chide.

وَبَر hair (of animals); down, fluff, fuzz.

وَبيل unhealthy, (climate, food); noxious, calamitous, pernicious, harmful, evil.

وَتَّدَ to drive in a peg or stake.

وَتَد peg, stake, wedge.

وَتَّرَ to strain, tighten, draw tight, pull taut.

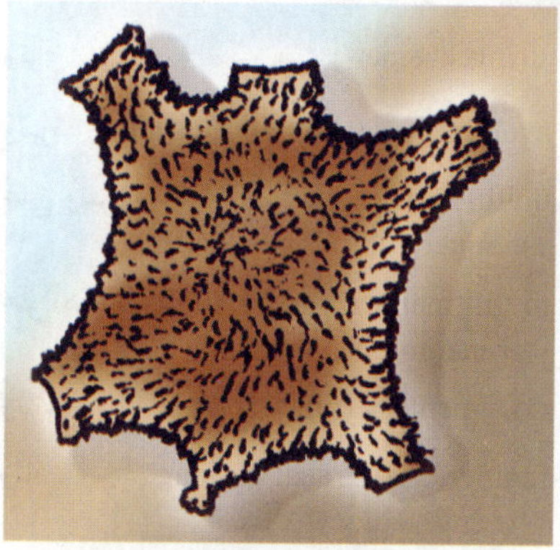

يكسو الوبر جلود الحيوانات

Hair covers the skin of animals

وَتَر string, bowstring (of a bow); string, chord, gut (of a musical instrument); tendon, cord (anat.).

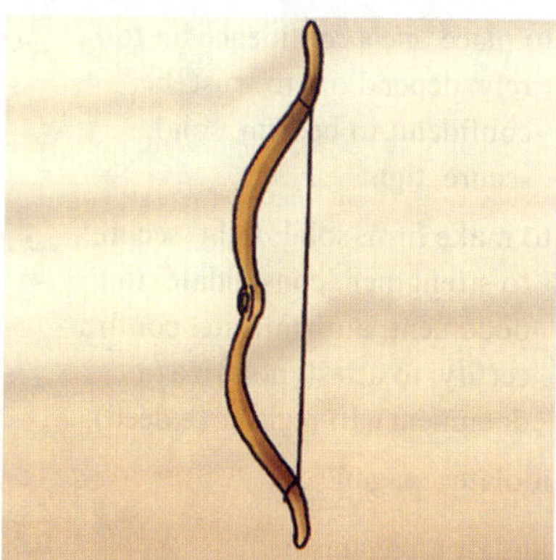

يُستعمل الوتر في الكمان كما في القوس

String is used in the violin as well as in a bow

وَتَرٌ صَوْتِيّ vocal chord.

وَتَرُ العُرْقُوب Achilles Heel.

أ ب ت ث ج ح خ د ذ ر ز س ش ص ض ط ظ ع غ ف ق ك ل م ن هـ و ي

وَتَرِيّ stringed, sinewy.

وَتيرَة manner, mode, way, style, method.

على وَتيرَةٍ واحِدَة uniformity, in the same manner.

عَلى هَذِهِ الوَتيرَة in this manner or way or method.

وثائِقِيّ documentary (film).

وَثَّاب jumper, hotheaded, dashing, daring, bouncy.

وِثاق tie, fetter, bond, shackle.

وَثَبَ to jump, leap, bounce, dash, hop; to pounce, fall upon; to rush, skip, spring.

وَثْب jump, jumping; leap, leaping; hop, hopping.

وَثْبَة jump, leap, bound, attack; daring enterprise; awakening, rise.

وَثِقَ to place one's confidence in; to rely, depend on; to trust, be confident; to be firm, solid, secure, tight.

وَثَّقَ to make firm, solid, tight, secure; to strengthen, consolidate; to document, authenticate, confirm, certify; to attest, notarize (a document); to register (a deed).

وَثَني idolater, pagan.

وَثَنِيَّة idolatry, paganism.

وَثير soft, comfortable, cozy.

وَثيق firm, strong, solid; secure; dependable; close, intimate.

وثيقُ الصِلَة بِالمَوْضُوع relevant, pertinent.

وَثيقَة document, deed, paper, instrument, record.

يركع الوثني أمام تمثال من حجر

The pagan kneels in front of a stone statue

وَجاهَة distinction, eminence, honor, prestige, glory.

وَجاهَة validity, reasonability, plausibility; worth, value.

وَجاهِيّ، وَجاهِيًا in presence of.

وَجَبَ to be necessary, requisite, indispensable; to be incumbent; to collapse, sink down.

وَجَبَ عليه he has to; he should, must, ought to; to owe; to be indebted.

كما يَجِب as it should be, as required, properly, suitably, satisfactorily.

وَجَبَ القَلْب to palpitate, throb, beat.

وَجْبَة meal, repast, ration.

وَجَدَ to find, come across something; to meet with something; to get, obtain; to invent; to discover, detect, spot.

وَجَدَ بِـ to love passionately.

وَجَدَ على to be angry with.

وَجَدَ لِـ to be sad for; to feel sorry for.

وُجِدَ to be found; to exist, be present, show up; to be available; to be impassioned, long ardently for.

وُجْد passion, love; ecstasy.

وِجْدان sentiment, emotion, conscience.

وِجْدانيّ sentimental, emotional, conscientious.

وَجُزَ to be concise, terse, brief (speech, text).

وَجَسَ to be apprehensive, be afraid; to apprehend, fear.

وَجَع pain, ache, anguish, agony.

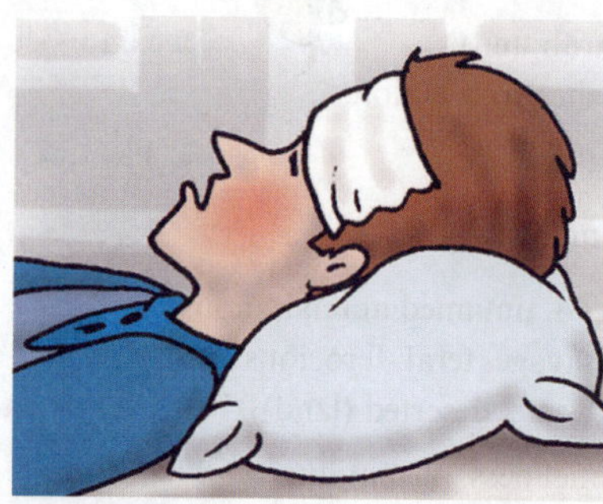

شعرت بوجع شديد في الرأس فاستدعت والدتي الطبيب

I felt a severe pain in the head,
so my mother called upon the doctor to treat me

وَجَفَ to be agitated, excited, troubled; to throb (heart).

وجِلَ to be afraid, scared; to be a coward.

وَجَل fear, dread, apprehension.

وجَمَ to become silent, speechless (with fear, rage); to be shy, despondent, dejected, depressed.

وَجْنَة cheek.

وَجَّهَ to send, despatch; to aim, level at; to direct, steer, guide, channel to; to turn one's attention, one's face to; to address a question, a letter etc. to; to raise an accusation, bring a charge against; to lead, point to, to orientate; to control, govern.

وَجَّهَ to honor, distinguish.

وَجَّهَ إليه دَعْوَةً to invite someone; to send an invitation to.

وَجْه visage, face, front, facade; surface, exterior, outside; dial (of a clock); face (of a coin); phase of the moon); look, appearance, indication; aspect, facet, guise; respect, regard; side, direction; meaning, significance, intent, content, design, purpose; way, manner; reason; beginning, start.

وَجْهُ الشَّبَه point of resemblance, similarity.

وَجْهٌ مُسْتَعار mask, falseface.

وَجْهًا لِوَجْه face to face, opposite, vis-a-vis.

لِوَجْهِ الله for God's sake; for nothing, gratis.

بِوَجْهِ العُمُوم on the whole, by and large, in general.

بِوَجْهِ التَّقْريب، على وَجْهِ التَّقْريب approximately, roughly, nearly.

بِوَجْهٍ خاص، على وَجْهٍ خاص in particular.

بِوَجْهٍ ما some way or other, somehow.

بِدون وَجْهِ حق without any legitimate claim, in an entirely, unlawful manner.

على غَيْرِ وَجْهِهِ incorrectly, improperly.

مَضَى على وَجْهِهِ to go one's way.

على وَجْهِ الإِجْمَال on the whole, in general.

على وَجْهِ التَّفْصيل at great length, in detail.

من وُجوهٍ كثيرة in many respects.

من كُلِّ الوُجُوه in every respect, all the way through.

وَجْهُ النَّهَار during the daytime.

لا وَجْهَ له من الصِّحَّة it has no validity at all; it has no truth in it; it is completely untrue, false.

وُجْهَة، وِجْهَة direction, trend, drift, course; intention, design, aim, goal, objective; respect, regard.

وُجْهَةُ النَّظَر viewpoint, point of view, outlook, perspective.

من وُجْهَةٍ أُخْرَى from another standpoint; from a different point of view.

وُجُود funding, discovery; being, existence; presence, stay, visit; occurrence; availability.

وُجُوم silence, gloom, sulkiness, apprehensive silence; shyness, anxiety, concern, sorrow, grief.

وَجيز brief, succint, short, concise, terse, summary.

بِوَجِيز العِبَارَة briefly stated, in a few words.

وَجيه notable, distinguished, eminent man; person of distinction; outstanding, acceptable, sound (reason).

وَحَّدَ to make into one, unite, unify; to standardize, regularize; to connect, join, bring together, combine, consolidate, amalgamate, merge.

وَحَّدَ الله to declare God to be one.

وَحْدَهُ alone, solely, singlehanded; in seclusion.

وَحْدَانِيّ single ,alone, solitary, lonely, only; unique.

وَحْدَانِيَّة soleness, isolation, seclusion, privacy; oneness (of God); singularity, uniqueness.

وَحْدَة unity, integrity (of a country); solidarity (of interests); identity, sameness; oneness (of God); loneliness, solitude.

وَحْدَة unit, group.

وَحْدَةُ الزَّمَن time unit.

الوِحْدَةُ العَرَبِيَّة Arab unity; the Arab Union.

وَحْدَةٌ حَرارِيَّة calorie.

وَحْدَوِيّ unionist.

وَحْش wild, untamed animal; monster; savage, feral, ferocious animal; waste, deserted (land).

وَحْشَة loneliness, alienation, melancholy.

وَحْشِيّ wild, savage, untamed, feral (animal); barbarous, barbarian, uncivilized (human); brutal, cruel, merciless; repulsive, ugly; bestial, brutish.

وَحْشِيَّة savagery, brutality, barbarism, ferocity, bestiality, wildness, savageness.

وَحِل muddy, dirty.

وَحْل mud, mire, slough, dirt.

وَحْي inspiration, revelation.

وَحيد alone, solitary, lonely, single; individual; separate; unique, unequaled.

وَخَزَ to prick, sting, jab, pierce; to vex, pester, harass.

وَخْز stinging, pricking, twinge.

وَخْزُ الضمير pangs of remorse, qualms, remorse.

الوَخْزُ بالإبَر acupuncture.

وَخُمَ to be unhealthy, unwholesome; to suffer from indigestion.

وَدَّ to love, like, be fond of; to want, wish.

وَدّ، وُدّ، وِدّ cordiality, love, affection, friendship; wish, desire, intimacy.

كانَ بِوُدّي لَوْ I should be pleased if.

وَداع farewell, leave-taking.

وَداعًا God be with you! farewell! good-by!.

وَداعَة gentleness, meekness.

وَدَعَ to leave; to lodge, deposit; to let, stop, cease; to give up, skip, omit.

وَدَّعَ to see off someone; to bid farewell; to take leave of; to say farewell.

وَدود affectionate, warmhearted; friendly, sociable.

وُدّي friendly, amicable, cordial, sincere; sympathetic.

وُدِّيًا amicably.

وَديع meek, mild, gentle, docile, mild-tempered.

وَديعَة deposit, something entrusted to someone's custody, charge, or trust.

الوَرَى mankind, human beings, people.

وَراء behind, in the rear of, at the back of; after; beyond, past, overhand, above, in addition to.

إلى الوَراء to the rear, backward.

وَراءَ الأكَمَةِ ما وَراءَها there is more in it than meets the eye.

ما وَراءَ البِحار overseas.

ما وَراءَ الطبيعة the supernatural; the transcendental.

وَراءَ الكَواليس behind the scenes, backstage.

وَراثَة heredity, succession, inheritance.

وِراثِيّ hereditary.

وَرِثَ to be heir to someone, be someone's heir; to inherit.

وَرَّثَ to bequeath; to give by will.

وَرَدَ to come, arrive; to appear, show up; to be said (in a book, lecture); to be mentioned in; to come to, get to, travel to; to accrue (revenues).

وَرَّدَ to blossom, be in bloom (plant); to dye red; to supply, provide, furnish; to import from; to get, procure from.

وَرْد blossoms, flowers.

وَرْدَة rose, rosebush,

وَرْدِيّ roseate, rosy, pink.

وَرْشَة workshop.

وَرَّطَ to entangle, embroil, involve in (difficulties); to put in an unpleasant situation.

أ ب ت ث ج ح خ د ذ ر ز س ش ص ض ط ظ ع غ ف ق ك ل م ن هـ و ي

يتميَّز الورد بجمال ألوانه وتنوعها

Roses are characterized by the beauty of their colors and their varieties

وَرْطَة predicament, flight, dilemma, critical situation.

وَرِع pious, devout, godly; reserved, cautious.

وَرَع piety, godliness, devoutness; caution, carefulness.

وَرَّقَ to leaf, put forth leaves (tree, plant); to thumb, leaf (a book); to paper (a wall).

وَرَق paper; leaves, foliage (of trees, plants).

وَرَقُ الجُدْران wall-paper.

وَرَقُ الحَمّام toilet paper.

وَرَقٌ شَفّاف tracing paper.

وَرَقُ الكَرْبُون carbon paper.

وَرَقُ اللَّعِب playing cards.

وَرَقُ اللَّفّ wrapping paper.

أَوْراقٌ مالِيَّة securities, bonds.

أَوراقٌ نَقْدِيَّة paper money.

وَرَقٌ مُقَوًّى cardboard, board, paperboard.

وَرَقٌ نَشّاف blotting paper.

وَرَقَة piece of paper, paper; leaf (plant or tree); folio, sheet; card; document, deed.

وَرَقَةُ اتِّهام bill of indictment.

وَرَقَةٌ تِجارِيَّة commercial paper, bill of exchange.

وَرَقَةُ جَلْبٍ إلى المَحْكَمَة summons, subpoena, writ.

وَرَقَةُ عَمَل working paper.

وَرَقَةُ يانَصِيب lottery ticket.

وَرَقِيّ paper, leafy.

وِرْك، وَرِك، وَرْك hip, haunch.

وَرِمَ to swell, bulge ,become swollen.

وَرَم tumor, swelling.

وَرَمٌ حَميد benign tumor.

وَرَمٌ خَبيث malignant tumor.

وَرْنيش varnish, lacquer, polish.

وُرُود arrival, advent, coming.

وَرِيد vein.

وِزارَة ministry, cabinet, council of ministers, government.

وِزارَةُ الإسْكان ministry of housing.

وِزارَةُ الأوْقاف ministry of religious endowments.

وِزارَةُ التَّرْبِيَة ministry of education.

وِزارَةُ الشُّؤونِ البَلَدِيَّة والقَرَوِيَّة ministry of municipal and rural affairs.

وِزارَةُ المَوارِد المائيّة والكهربائيّة ministry of hydroelectric resources.

وِزارِيّ ministerial.

وَزَرَ to sin, commit a sin.

وِزْر burden, heavy load; sin, offense.

وِزرة loincloth, gown.

وَزَّعَ to distribute, allot, apportion, parcel out, dispense.

وَزَنَ to weigh, balance, equilibrate, even up.

وَزْن weight; meter (poetry); importance, significance, gravity.

وَزْنٌ بالطّنّ tonnage.

وَزْنٌ قائم gross weight.

وَزْنٌ ذَرِّيّ atomic weight.

وَزْنٌ صافٍ net weight.

وَزْنُ الذُّبابَة flyweight (athletics).

وَزْنُ الرِّيشَة feather weight (athletics).

وزير minister.

وزيرُ دَوْلَة minister of state.

وزيرٌ بِلا وزارة minister without portfolio.

وزيرٌ مُطْلَقُ الصَّلاحِيَّة minister plenipotentiary.

مَجْلِسُ الوُزَراء council of ministers, cabinet.

وَساخَة dirtiness, filthiness, dirty filth, squalor.

وِسادة pillow, cushion, pad.

أتمدّد على الفراش وأضع الوسادة تحت رأسي
I lay on the bed and put a pillow under my head

وَساطَة mediation, intervention, good offices.

وِسام decoration, badge, medal, order.

وَسامَة beauty, gracefulness, comeliness, charm, grace.

وَسِخ dirty, unclean, filthy, soiled.

وَسَّدَ to put a pillow under someone's head; to rest, lay someone's head on.

وَسَّطَ to set in the middle; to appoint someone as mediator between.

وَسَط middle, center, heart; waist; milieu, environment, surroundings, sphere; means, agent, instrument, medium; medium quality, average.

أَوْساط (ج) circles, classes.

وَسَط median, central, in the middle, moderate; in the midst of, in the center of, among, amid.

وَسَطٌ حِسابِيّ arithmetic mean.

وَسْطَ amid, among, in between, surrounded by.

الوُسْطى middle finger (of hand).

وَسَطِيّ average ,mean, medial.

وَسِعَ ، وَسُعَ to be wide, roomy, spacious, vast, extensive; to hold, accomodate, house, seat; to contain, comprise, include; to be large enough, be sufficient; to suffice; to be adequate, enough for.

وَسَّعَ to make wider, roomier, more spacious; to extend, expand, widen, enlarge ,broaden.

وَسَّعَ عَليه to be generous, liberal, openhanded toward someone; to make rich, enrich someone.

وُسْع capacity, ability, capability.

في وُسْعِهِ أن it is in his power to.

في وُسْعِي أن أقول I can say.

بَذَلَ وُسْعَهُ to go to great pains; to do one's best to.

وَسَمَ to brand (cattle); to stamp, mark, impress.

وَسَمَهُ بالعار to brand someone as infamous; to stigmatize someone.

وَسِنَ to doze off, slumber, sleep lightly.

وَسَن sleepiness, somnolence, slumber, doze.

وَسِن ، وَسْنَان sleepy, drowsy, somnolent.

وَسْوَاس develish insinuation, temptation, wicked thoughts; misgiving, doubt, suspicions, scruple, anxiety, concern.

وَسْوَسَ to whisper to; to instil evil thoughts; to tempt someone with wicked suggestions; to awaken doubts, arouse scruples in someone's mind.

وَسْوَسَة temptation, devilish insinuation, disturbance, scruple, suspicion, rustle, whisper.

وَسيط mediator, intermediary, go-between; agent, middleman; broker; medium, median, middle.

وَسيلَة means, medium, device, measure, step.

وسائلُ الإعْلام mass media, news media.

وسائلُ سَمَعِيَّة وَبَصَرِيَّة audiovisual aids.

وسائلُ النَّقْل means of transport.

وَسيم graceful, comely, pretty, goodlooking.

وَشَى to slander, defame someone with; to inform against; to denounce, betray.

وَشَّى to embellish, ornament with many colors; to embroider.

وِشاح sash, scarf.

وِشَايَة calumny, slander, defamation.

وَشَّجَ to entwine, intertwist, interlock, mesh, snarl.

وَشْك ، وُشْك speed, hurry; imminence.

على وَشْكِ أن about to, on the point of, on the verge of.

وَشم tattooing, tattoo.

وَشْوَشَ to whisper in someone's ear.

أ ب ت ث ج ح خ د ذ ر ز س ش ص ض ط ظ ع غ ف ق ك ل م ن هـ و ي

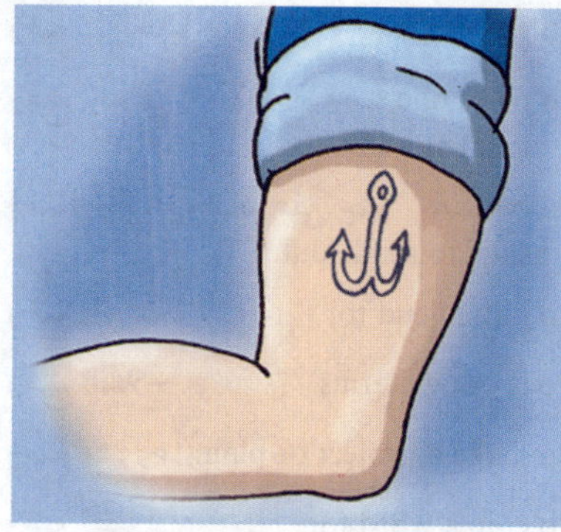

وشم الذراع منتشر بين بحارة السفن
Tattooing arms is a widespread habit among sailors

وَشيعَة reel, spool, bobbin; shuttle, spindle.

وَشيك imminent, impending, about to happen.

وِصال reunion of lovers; sexual intercourse.

وِصايَة guardianship, custodianship; custody, care.

وِصايَةٌ على العَرْش regency.

وِصْر bond, covenant.

وَصَفَ to describe, depict, portray; to qualify; to prescribe.

وَصْف description, portrayal, qualification.

وَصْف adjective, attribute (grammar).

وَصْفَةٌ طِبِّيَّة prescription.

وَصْفَةُ طَعام recipe.

وَصْفِيّ descriptive, depictive.

وَصَلَ to reach, arrive, (to a place); to come to someone's hands; to amount to; to enter a phase.

وَصَلَ to connect, join, unite, combine link, interlink; to attach, establish a connection; to bring into relation; to bestow, confer upon, award something to someone.

وَصْل connection, linkage; junction, coupling.

وَصْل receipt.

وُصْلَة joint, link; elbow, union, connecting piece; hinge.

وَصَمَ to disgrace, tarnish, blemish (honor); to put the blame for something on someone; to brand, stigmatize.

وَصْمَة disgrace, mark of disgrace, blot, blemish; defect, stain, taint, smirch, stigma, brand.

وُصول arrival, access, achievement.

وُصوليّ opportunist.

وُصولِيَّة opportunism.

وَصِيّ guardian, curator, custodian, trustee; executor (of will); administrator (of an estate); regent (of a throne).

وَصِيَّة testament, will, legacy, bequest; directive, order, injunction, commandment; recommendation, advice; admonition.

وَصيف، وَصيفَة page, butler, servant; maid of honor, maid-in-waiting, lady-in- waiting.

وَصيفَةُ شَرَف maid of honor.

وَصيفَةٌ في انْتِخابات جَمال runner-up.

وَضّاح bright, clear, brilliant, shining, luminous; beautiful, pretty, comely, good-looking.

وَضَّبَ to arrange, put on order; to pack, box, encase.

وَضَحَ to be clear, plain, patent, evident; to appear, show, come out, become visible.

وَضَّحَ to make clear, make plain, explain, explicate; to clear up, elucidate, set forth; to show, indicate, designate, express, denote.

وَضَح light, brilliance, brightness.

في وَضَحِ النَّهار in broad dayight.

وَضَعَ to put, place, laydown, deposit, station, emplace; to affix, attach; to write, compose (a book); to make, work out, establish, set up; fabricate, invent, devise.

تعبَ الرّجل من حمل العلبة فوضعها على الطاولة
The man got tired from carrying the box so he laid it down on the table

وَضَعَتِ الحامِلُ to give birth to.

وَضَعَ ثِقَتَهُ في to place one's confidence in.

وَضَعَهُ جانِباً، وَضَعَهُ على حِدَة to put aside; to single out.

وَضَعَ حَدًّا لَهُ to put an end to.

وَضَعَ السِّلاح to lay down arms.

وَضَعَ مَشْروعاً to make a project or plan.

وَضَعَ لَفْظاً لِـ to coin a word for.

وَضَعَ نُصْبَ عينيهِ to demonstrate, point out.

وَضَعَ مَوْضِعَ التَّنْفيذ to put into force; to implement, enforce.

وَضَعَ نَفْسَهُ في مَوْضِعِ فُلان to put oneself in someone's position.

وَضَعَ يَدَهُ على to take possession of, lay hold of; to seize.

وَضَعَهُ تَحْتَ يَدِهِ to put someone or something in someone's power.

وَضَعَ البَيْض to lay eggs.

وَضَعَ على الرَّفّ to shelve, put aside.

وَضَعَ اللَّوْمَ على to blame, put the blame on.

وَضُعَ to be lowly, humble, base, menial.

وَضْع putting, placing, setting down, depositing; writing, composing; drawing up (document); creation, invention, coining (of a treaty); delivery (of child); rule, sketch, draft; attitude, bearing.

أ ب ت ث ج ح خ د ذ ر ز س ش ص ض ط ظ ع غ ف ق ك ل م ن هـ و ي

وَضع carriage, posture, pose (of body); location; statement (math); foundation; humiliation; circumstance.

أوْضاع (ج) circumstances, conditions; rules, principles, manners, practices, customs.

الوَضْعُ الحالِيّ the present situation; the status quo.

وَضْعُ اليَد occupancy, seizure, taking possession of.

وُضوح clearness, clarity, plainness, obviousness.

بِوُضوح clearly, distinctly, expressly, evidently.

وَضِيع lowly, humble, menial, vile, mean, base.

وَطؤَ to be low, flat, level.

وَطِئَ to tread on, step on, walk on.

وَطِئَ المرأة to have sexual intercourse with a woman.

وَطَّأَ to pave, level, make smooth; to prepare, fix up; to make comfortable (seat, bed); to reduce, force down, press down, lower.

وَطْأة pressure, stress, oppression, weight, burden, gravity; violence.

وَطَّد to establish, settle, strengthen, consolidate; to stamp down, ram (earth); to pave the way for.

وَطَّد العَزْمَ على to resolve firmly to.

وَطَّد عُرى المحَبَّة to strengthen the bonds of friendship.

وَطَر wish, desire, purpose, aim.

وَطَّنَ to settle down, get settled in.

وَطَّنَ نفسه على to get used to, adjust oneself to; to make up one's mind to do something; to resolve to; to cope with.

وَطَن homeland, fatherland, country, native country.

وَطَنِيّ (ص) national, native, domestic; homemade.

وَطَنِيّ (اسم) nationalist, patriot, native, citizen.

وَطَنِيَّة patriotism, nationalism.

وَطِيد firm, stable, strong, steady, solid, sturdy.

وَطيدُ الأمَل بِـ having strong hopes of.

وَطيس battle, fight, combat.

وَظَّفَ to employ, engage, hire, appoint to an office; to invest (money).

وَظِيفَة office, position, post, job; duty, task, assignment; employ, service, work, function.

وَظِيفِيّ functional.

وَعَى to contain, include, comprise; to be conscious, aware of; to know by heart, remember.

وَعَّى to warn, caution; to englighten, educate.

وِعاء vessel, container, receptacle.

وِعاءٌ دَمَوِيّ blood vessel.

وِعاءُ الضَّريبَة basis of assessment, taxable income.

وَعَدَ to promise, pledge; to threaten.

وَعْد promise, word, pledge.

وَعْر، وَعِر rugged, wild, rough, hard, difficult.

الطريق الجبلي وعر يصعب السير فيه

The mountain pass is rugged and is difficult to drive on it

وَعَظَ to preach, appeal to someone's conscience; to exhort; to warn, admonish, caution against.

وَعْظ admonition, warning, sermon.

وَعْكَة indisposition, illness.

وُعُورَة ruggedness, hardness, difficulty.

وَعْي consciousness, perception, alertness, awareness.

فاقِدُ الوَعْي unconscious, in a swoon.

دُونَ الوَعْي unconsciously.

وَعِيد threat, menace.

وغى war, battle; din, tumult, turmoil.

وَغْد scoundrel, rogue, rascal, wretched, miserable.

وغَرَ to be furious, angry.

وَغْر، وغَر anger, wrath, rancor, hatred.

وَفَى to live up to a promise; to redeem, fulfill, carry out; to satisfy, gratify, (a wish); to supply (a need); to serve (a purpose); to discharge, meet (an obligation); to pay, settle a debt; to cover costs; to be sufficient, suffice, compensate, make up, counterbalance; to fulfill the function of, substitute for; to carry out completely.

وَفَّى فُلاناً حَقَّهُ to give someone his due in full.

وَفَّى المَوْضُوعَ حَقَّهُ to treat exhaustively the subject; to develop in detail (a subject); to set forth exhaustively (a topic).

وَفَاء keeping, fulfillment, redemption; discharge, settlement; payment (of a debt); compensation, set off; satisfaction.

وَفَاء faithfulness, fidelity, allegiance, devotion.

وَفَاة death, decease, demise.

وِفادة coming, arrival.

أَحْسَنَ وِفادَتَهُ to receive someone hospitably, with deference.

وِفاض travelling bag.

وِفاق concord, harmony, assent, consent; agreement, accordance, conformance; unity; reconciliation, conciliation.

وَفَدَ to come, travel, arrive to; to visit, come to see, call on someone.

وَفْد delegation, deputation; arrival, coming.

وَفَّرَ to increase, augment, make available, abundant; to provide, furnish; to save (money); to economize, lay by, put by (money).

وَفْر saving, savings, surplus, excess; abundance, wealth.

وَفْرَة plenty, abundance, profusion, superabundance.

وَفَّقَ to make fit, adapt, adjust, accomodate.

وَفَّقَ بين to bring to agreement between; to reconcile ,make peace between (two parties).

وُفِّقَ to be helped, assisted (by God); to prosper, win, be lucky, be fortunate; to be succesful.

وَفْقًا لِـ، وَفْقَ in accordance with, according to, pursant to; on the basis of, on the strength of.

وَفِيّ faithful, loyal, devoted, true, to one's words; trustworthy; whole, total, complete, integral, perfect.

وَقَى، وَقَّى to preserve, protect, guard, shelter; to offer protection against; to prevent, obviate (a danger).

وِقَاء، وَقَاء protection, shelter, cover, housing.

وَقَائِع (ج) happenings, developments; factual findings, evidence (of a legal case); proceedings, facts (of an assembly); record, report, procès-verbal (of a meeting).

وِقَائِيّ preventive, precautionary; preemptive (attack).

وَقَاحَة impudence, insolence, impertinence, effrontery.

وَقَار gravity, sobriety, dignity, sedateness; precaution; prevention, warding off; fending off, defense.

وَقَّتَ to time, schedule a time for; to set a time limit for.

وَقْت period of time, point of time, moment, instant.

أحدِّد الوقت بالنظر إلى ساعتي

I know the time by looking at my watch

وَقْتُ الطَّعام mealtime.

وَقْتُ الفَرَاغ sparetime.

في الوَقْتِ الحَاضِر temporarily, for, the time being.

في هَذا الوَقْت now, at present, at this time, actually, nowadays; meanwhile, meantime.

في هَذا الوَقْتِ الذي whilst, as during, while.

في الوَقْتِ نَفْسِهِ at the same time, simultaneously.

في وَقْتِهِ at the time, duly, on time, at the right time.

مع الوَقْت in due time, eventuallly, gradually in time.

من وَقْتٍ لآخَر from time to time, now and then, once in a while.

وَقْتَئِذٍ then, by then, at that time.

وَقْتِيّ temporal, of time; temporary, transient, passing, provisional, momentary, interim.

وَقِح shameless, impudent, impertinent, insolent.

وَقُر to be grave, sedate, solemn.

وَقَّر to revere, respect, honor.

وَقَعَ to fall down, drop, tumble, sink, fall; to happen, occur, befall; to arrive at, run across, meet with.

وَقَعَ في to get caught in;to lie, be located; to impress; to consist of, made of, comprise, contain; to slander, defame, calumniate.

وَقَعَ على to come across, hit upon, find, discover; to alight on (bird).

وَقَعَ بِـ to attack, assault, set upon, pounce upon; to fight, combat.

وَقَعَ القِتَال to break out, erupt.

وَقَعَ على عَاتِقِهِ to fall upon; to bear the duty of.

وَقَّعَ to sign, subscribe; to let fall; to cause to fall.

وَقَّعَ بِالأَحْرُفِ الأُولى to initial.

وَقَّعَ حَجْزًا على to seize, confiscate, impound.

وَقْع falling, dropping; fall, drop; thud, blow; effect, impression, impact.

وَقْعَة fall, drop; shock, blow, impact; encounter, battle, fight; incident, occurrence; meal, repast (food).

وَقَفَ to stand, stand up, rise, get up, stand erect; to cease to move onwards; to pause, stop, cease, abstain from; to end, terminate, come to a halt; to be interrupted, stopped.

يقف العامل منتظراً وصول الباص للعودة إلى منزله

The worker stands erect waiting for the bus to take him to his house

وَقَفَ على to be aware of, familiar with, informed about; to discover, find out about; to understand, comprehend, perceive; to inquire about; to inspect, examine, see.

وَقَفَ مَكْتُوفَ اليَدَيْن to fail to take action; to do nothing; to simply watch; to remain indifferent.

وَقْف stop, stopping, halt, pause; cessation, stoppage, desistance, abstention; dedication, consecration, endowment, mortmain; religious endowment.

وَقْفُ إطلاقِ النّار cease-fire.

وَقْفُ التَّنْفيذ stay of execution.

وَقْفَة posture, stand, stance, position; halt, stop, pause.

وَقُود fuel.

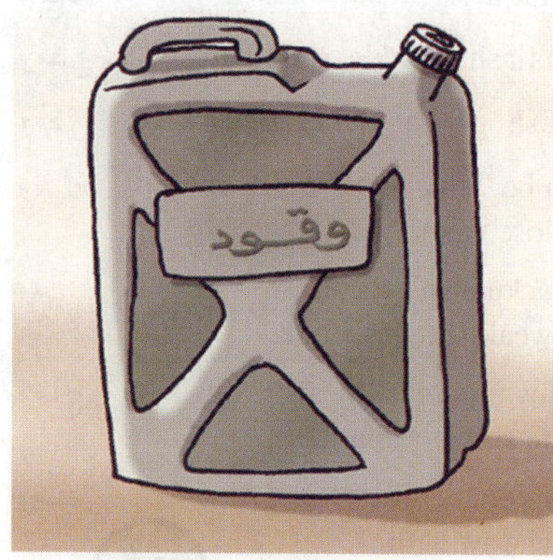

تسير السيارة بواسطة الوقود ويعرف بالبنزين

Cars operate on a fuel known as petrol

وَقُور grave, solemn, dignified, venerable.

وُقُوع fall, drop, tumble; occurrence, happening, incidence.

وُقُوف standing, getting up.

وُقُوفٌ على cognizance, familiarity with; understanding, perception, comprehension; inquiry; inspection, seeing.

وَقيعَة backbiting, slander; roost (of a bird); battle, fight, engagement; incident, event.

وَكالَة power of attorney, proxy; agency, representation, mandate, procuration.

وكالَةُ اسْتِخْبارات intelligence agency.

وَكالَةٌ حَصْرِيَّة sole agency.

وكالَة عامَّة general power of attorney.

بِالوَكالَة acting; deputy, by proxy.

وَكْر nest, den, retreat, haunt, abode.

وَكَّل to authorize, empower, deputize, delegate (someone to act on one's behalf); to commission, charge with, entrust with.

وَكيل authorized representative, agent, deputy, proxy; trustee, attorney; defense counsel.

وَكيلٌ تجارِيّ commission agent.

وَكيلٌ حَصْرِيّ sole agent, exclusive dealer.

وَكيلُ شَحْن forwarder, freighter, carrier.

وَكيلُ نِيابَة prosecutor, district attorney.

وَكيلُ وِزارَة undersecretary (of state).

وَلّى to appoint as a ruler, governor, administrator; to install in an office, appoint to an office; to put someone in charge of; to entrust with, charge with, commission with.

وَلّى الزَّمَن to pass, go by; to be past, bygone; to expire.

وَلّى الأَدْبار to run away, flee, escape.

وَلاء	allegiance, fidelity, devotion; friendship.
وِلادَة	birth, delivery; beginning, start, outset; origin, dawn, rise.
وَلاّعَة	lighter.
وِلايَة	rule, reign, regime, tenure, term of office; custody, care, guardianship; jurisdiction, competence.
وِلايَة	state, province, territory, district.
وَلَجَ	to penetrate into, enter into.
وَلَدَت المَرأة	to give birth to; to beget.
وَلَّدَ	to generate, produce from; to engender, breed, cause, occasion; to raise (a child); to assist a woman in childbirth; to propagate, reproduce.
وُلِدَ	to be born; to arise, originate; to be bred, brought forth, caused, occasioned by.
وَلَد	descendant, offspring; child, son, boy; young one.
وَلَّفَ	to blend, mix, mingle, combine.
وَلَهَ، وَلِهَ	to be infatuated, spellbound, bewildered; to be sad, grieved.
وَلَه	passionate love, distraction; infatuation; fascination; sadness, grief.
وَلْهان	distracted, deeply in love, infatuated, spellbound; sad, grieved, depressed.
وُلوج	entry, penetration.
وُلوع	love, passion, fondness, liking.
وَلْوَلَ	to lament, howl, wail.
وَلِيَ	to be near to; to follow.
ما يَلي	the following, what follows.
كما يَلي	as follows, like this.
وَلِيّ	guardian, custodian, patron, protector; friend; holy man (in Islam); master, lord; owner, possessor.
وَلِيّ الأمر	master, leader, someone in charge, head, chief.
وَلِيّ العَهْد	heir apparent, crown prince.
وَليد	newborn, infant, baby.
وَلِيمَة	banquet.
وَمَضَ	to flash, sparkle, scintillate.
وَمْض، وَمْضَة	flash, gleam, flicker, blink.
وَنَى	to be faint, weak, tired, effete, lose vigor.
وَنًى	slackening, relaxation, weakness, lassitude.
وَهّاج	glowing, blazing, sparkling, flashing, radiant.
وَهَبَ	to donate, grant, accord, endow with.
وَهْد	lowland.
وَهِلَ	to be frightened, scared.
وَهَّلَ	to frighten, scare.
وَهْم	illusion, delusion, fantasy, fiction, phantasm, doubt; misgiving, surmise, conjecture, imagination.
وَهْمِيّ	illusory, illusive, delusory, delusive, fanciful, imaginary, fictitious; false, bogus, phony, make-belief; hypothetical, presumed.

وَهُنَ، وَهِنَ، وَهَنَ to be weak, feeble, incapable of; to lose vigor, courage, strength.

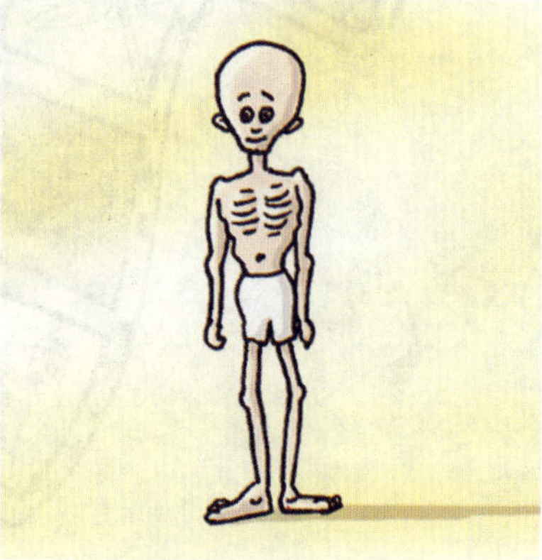

وهن الرجل حتى بات هزيلاً للغاية
The man became so weak to the extent of appearing very skinny

لا يَهِن untiring, unflagging.

وَهْن weakness, feebleness, debilitation, impotence.

وَيْحٌ لَهُ، وَيْحاً لَهُ، وَيْحَهُ woe unto him!.

وَيْل woe, grief, distress; destruction, down, perdition.

حرف الياء

يا	o! oh!.
يائِس	desperate, hopeless, discouraged.
يابِس	dry, dried up; arid, rigid, hard.
اليابِسَة	land, earth, ground.
يَأْس	despair, hopelessness.
يافِع	adolescent, pubescent, juvenile, youngster.
ياقَة	collar.
ياقُوت	corrundum, ruby, sapphire, topaz.
يانَصِيب	lottery.
يانِع	ripe, mellow.
يَبِسَ	to become dry, dry up, shrivel, harden.
يَبَّسَ	to dry up, dry out, desiccate, harden, solidify.
يُبُوسَة	dryness, rigidity, stiffness, aridity (of land).
يُتْم، يَتَم، يَتْم	orphanhood, orphanage.
يَتِيم	orphan, fatherless, motherless, parentless.
يَتِيم	unique, singular, matchless, incomparable.
يَحْمُور	wild ass (animal); hemoglobin.
يَد	hand, arm; handle, tiller (of boat); part, role.

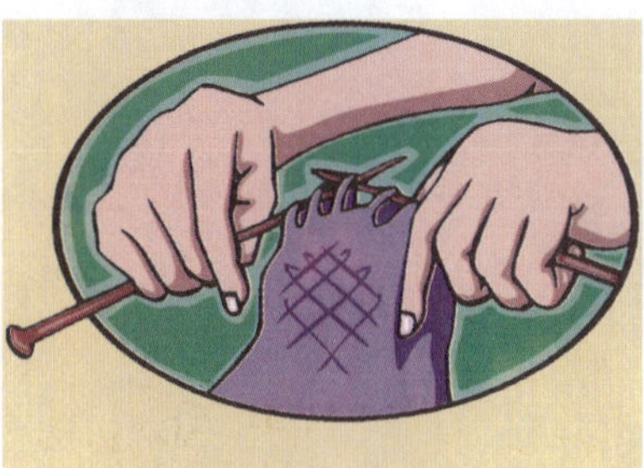

لكل شخص يدان، يد يمنى ويد يسرى

Every human being has two hands: the right hand and the left hand

يَدٌ power, authority; assistance help, aid.

يَداً بِيَد from hand to hand.

في اليد in hand, on hand, available.

عَرَبَةُ اليد hand cart.

يَدَوِيّ manual, handmade.

يَرَاع، يَرَاعَة pen; cane; coward; firefly (insect).

يَسَار solvency; Left, left side, left hand.

يَسَارِيّ Leftist (politics); left, left-handed.

يَسَّرَ to facilitate, ease, make easy; to simplify; to make available, accessible.

يُسْر ease, easiness, facility; wealth, affluence, abundance.

يَسير easy, facile, simple; small, little, slight.

يَقِظ، يَقْظَان watchful, vigilant, alert, careful, cautious; awake, wakeful.

يَقَظَة wakefulness, awakening; vigilance, alertness, caution, advertence.

يَقين certainty, assurance, conviction.

يَقيناً surely, certainly.

حَقُّ اليَقين absolute certainty.

يَمّ sea.

يَمام، يَمامَة dove, pigeon.

يَمَّمَ to head for; to be bound for; to go toward.

يَمَنَ، يَمُنَ، يَمِنَ، يُمِنَ to be lucky, fortunate, prosperous.

يَمَّنَ to go to the right.

يُمْن fortune, good luck, prosperity, happiness.

يَمين oath; right, right side, right hand.

يَمينٌ كاذِبَة perjury.

يَميناً ويَساراً right and left.

يَمِينِيّ Rightist (politics); right-hand, right-handed.

يَنْبُوع spring, source, fountain, spring head; stream, brook.

يُوبيل jubilee.

يُود iodine.

صَبْغَةُ اليُود tincture of iodine.

يَوْم day, time.

اليوم today.

يَوْماً ما someday, sometime.

يومُ القِيامَة، يَومُ النَّشر، يَومُ الدِّين Day of Resurrection; Judgment Day, Doomsday.

يَوْمُ رأسِ السَّنَة New Year's Day.

ذاتَ يَوْم one day, once.

في يومنا هذا nowadays, today, at present, currently.

يَوْمَئِذٍ at that time, on that day.

يَوْمِيّ daily, diurnal, per diem, everyday, quotidian.

يَوْمِيًّا daily, everyday, per day, per diem.

يَوْمِيّات diary, journal, chronicle.

يَوْمِيَّة daily (newspaper); daily wages; diary, journal; daybook; daily allowance.

The Mosque
المسجد

1 - The mosque
2 - The minaret
3 - Reciter of the Qur'an
4 - Prayer
5 - Preacher
6 - Imam
7 - The adorators
8 - The praying congregation

1 ـ المسجد
2 ـ المئذنة
3 ـ قارئ القرآن
4 ـ المصلي
5 ـ الخطيب
6 ـ الإمام
7 ـ الساجدون (السجود)
8 ـ المصلّون

Fruits فاكهة

1 - Apple
2 - Strawberry
3 - Orange
4 - Water melon
5 - Grapes
6 - Banana
7 - Cherry
8 - Avocado
9 - Pomegranate
10 - Kiwi
11 - Mango
12 - Melon
13 - Pineapple
14 - Mulberry
15 - Pear
16 - Peach
17 - Plum
18 - Apricot

1 ـ تفاح
2 ـ فريز (فراولة)
3 ـ ليمون (برتقال)
4 ـ بطيخ (رقي) (حبحب) (جبس)
5 ـ عنب
6 ـ موز (طلح)
7 ـ كرز
8 ـ أفوكا
9 ـ رمان
10 ـ كيوي
11 ـ مانجا
12 ـ شمام (دلاع
13 ـ أناناس
14 ـ توت
15 ـ إجاص (انجاص)
16 ـ خوخ
17 ـ دراق
18 ـ مشمش (لقّيس)

Herbs & Plants

أعشاب ونباتات

الفُطر : جنس نبات يُطلق على طائفة من اللاّزهريات، تنتمي إلى فصائل عديدة، منها ما يُؤْكَل، وما هو سامٌ، وما هو طُفَيْليٌّ على النبات.
جمعها : أفطارٌ، فُطورٌ

1 - Pin mould
2 - Vine mildew
3 - Wheat rust
4 - Ergot of rye
5 - Tremella mesenterica
6 - Death cap
7 - Panther cap
8 - Peziza aurantia
9 - Piptoporus betuilinus
10 - Scleroderma citrinum
11 - Russula atropurpurea
12 - Fly agaric
13 - Destroying angel
14 - Devil's boletus

15 - Yellow stainer
16 - Inocybe patouillardi
17 - Sickener russula emetica
18 - Field mushroom
19 - Parasol mushroom
20 - Shaggy ink cap
21 - Blusher
22 - Fairy ring mushroom
23 - Cep
24 - Giant puffball
25 - Chanterelle
26 - Oyster mushroom
27 - Truffle
28 - Morel

1 - عفن الدَّبُّوس
2 - عفن الكرمة
3 - صـدأ الحـنـطـة - صدأ القمح
4 - قمح
5 - قطن
6 - قبَّعة الموت
7 - قبَّعة الفهد
8 - فطر مفتوح
9 - رأس الفطر
10 - قبعة الفطر
11 - الفطر
12 - عيش الغراب
13 - الملاك المدمِّر
14 - فطر عريض

15 - فطر مثلَّث
16 - الملاك
17 - فطر بري
18 - حقل عشّ الغراب
19 - شمسيَّة عش الغراب
20 - قبَّعة الحبر الشَّعناء
21 - أحمر الخدود
22 - حلقات الفطر الجني
23 - زهر الفطر
24 - الفطر النَّفَّاث العملاق - عملاق الفطر النَّفَّاث
25 - الإنائية (فطر يُؤكل)
26 - محارة عيش الغراب
27 - الكمأ - الكمأة
28 - الغوشنة

Herbs & Plants أعشاب ونباتات

1 - Primrose
2 - Ragged robin
3 - Holly
4 - Scots pine
5 - Spruce
6 - Rhododendron
7 - Handkerchief tree
8 - Bluebell
9 - Larch
10 - Cedar
11 - Cypress
12 - Oak
13 - Beech
14 - Hart's tongue fern
15 - Maidenhair fern
16 - Ash
17 - Field maple
18 - Bracken
19 - Buckler fern

1. زهر الرَّبيع
2. اللُّخنيس (نبات ذو زهر قرنفلي أو أبيض)
3. البهشيَّة - الايكلس (نبات ذو ورق صقيل شائك الأطراف)
4. صنوبر اسكتلندي
5. البيسيه - الرَّاتينجية (شجر من الفصيلة الصَّنوبرية)
6. الورديَّة (جنس جنبات من الفصيلة الخلنجيَّة)
7. شجرة المنديل
8. الجُريس (عشبة ذات أزهار زرقاء)
9. اللاركس - الأرزية (شجر من الفصيلة الصَّنوبريَّة)
10. الأرز
11. السَّرو (شجر من الفصيلة الصَّنوبريَّة)
12. البلُّوط
13. الزَّان
14. سرخس - الخنشار لسان الأيل
15. سرخس كزبرة البئر (نوع من السَّرخسيَّات)
16. شجرة الدَّردار
17. قيقب الحقل
18. السَّرخس
19. سرخس التِّرس

Medicinal Herbs and Plants أعشاب ونباتات طبية

1 - Licorice roots
2 - Fishbone
3 - Cardamom
4 - Sabbah
5 - Lupine
6 - Almond
7 - Walnut
8 - Chamomile
9 - Laurel leaf
10 - Pitcher plant
11 - Fenugreek
12 - Red lentils
1 - Fennel
14 - Ginger
15 - Mustard
16 - Aniseed
17 - Terebinth
18 - Linseed
19 - Wheat
20 - Zinc powder
21 - Black cumin

1 - الحرقوس
2 - عظم سمك
3 - حب هال
4 - سَبه
5 - ترمس
6 - لوز
7 - جوز
8 - زهرة البابونيج
9 - ورق غار
10 - سلمكي
11 - حلبة
12 - عدس أحمر
13 - شمّر
14 - زنجبيل
15 - خردل
16 - يانسون
17 - كركاديه
18 - بزر خله
19 - القمح
20 - بودرة الزنك
21 - حبة البركة (حبة السوداء)

على الشاطئ

1 ـ جرف
2 ـ بنغل
3 ـ منزل على الساحل
4 ـ حاجز صخري
5 ـ عامل الإنقاذ
6 ـ مظلة

7 ـ حمام شمسي
8 ـ منشفة بحر
9 ـ مقعد ينطوي
10 ـ طابة بحر
11 ـ سلة مأكولات

12 معول
13 ـ قصر من الرمال
14 ـ حصى
15 ـ زورق
16 ـ سابحون

17 ـ زورق بخاري
18 ـ مركب صيد
19 ـ مركب شراعي
20 ـ طائرة ورقية
21 ـ صياد سمك

On the Beach

1 - Cliff
2 - Bungalow
3 - Seaside house
4 - Seaside wall
5 - Life guard
6 - Sunshade
7 - Sunbathing
8 - Beach towel
9 - Deck chair
10 - Beach ball
11 - Food basket
12 - Spade
13 - Sand castle
14 - Pebbles
15 - Canoe
16 - Swimmers
17 - Motor boat
18 - Fishing boat
19 - Sail
20 - Kite
21 - Fisherman

Orchids

الأوركيديا

Orchids grow in spring and summer.

They are subject to variances in climatic conditions.

They need a wet soil and need time for reproduction. Their seeds bear well the cold climate in winter.

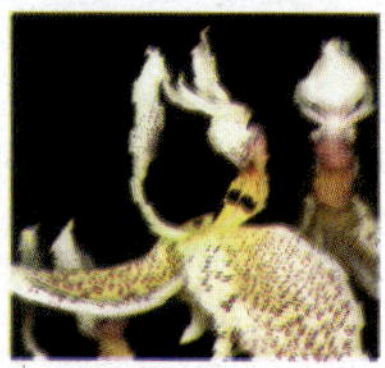

أزهار الأوركيديا

نباتات الربيع والصيف.

وهي دائمة التعرض الى التغييرات الموسمية في الأحوال المناخية خارج المناطق الاستوائية والتي يمكن ملاحظتها بوضوح في المناطق المعتدلة.

تحتاج الى تربة رطبة وبذورها تمتص الماء وتحتاج إلى وقت للتفريخ، وهي أقل مقاومة للبرودة مما لو كانت في حالتها الجافة، رغم أنها قادرة على تحمُّل الشتاء على هيئة بزور.

Aircraft طائرة الركاب

1 - Di-electric nose cone
2 - Curved windshield to cockpit
3 - Airconditioning pipes
4 - Overhead sliding passenger door
5 - Six abreast passenger seating
6 - Passenger floor level
7 - Forward freight hold
8 - Galley
9 - Fuselage skin
10 - Galley service door
11 - Overhead coast stowage
12 - Galley elevator
13 - Floor support members
14 - Inboard leading edge salt
15 - Fuel tank
16 - Engine inlet
17 - Rolls Royce RB-211 turbofan engine
18 - Variable nozzle exhaust outlet
19 - Outboard leading edge salt
20 - Wing skin
21 - Forward position light
22 - Outboard aileron
23 - Outboard flaps
24 - Spoilers
25 - Inboard aileron
26 - Inboard double slotted flaps
27 - Centre seat stowage
28 - Eight abreast passenger seating
29 - Rear passenger door
30 - Hold access door
31 - Emergency exit
32 - Rear freight hold
33 - Rear engine inlet
34 - Toilets
35 - Tailplane
36 - Elevator
37 - Rear engine exhaust
38 - Rail fin
39 - Rudder

1 - مخروط الأنف المزدوج.
2 - حاجب الريح المقوس لركن الطيار.
3 - أنابيب تكييف الهواء.
4 - باب ركاب ينزلق من الأعلى.
5 - مقاعد للركاب.
6 - مستوى أرضية حجرة الركاب.
7 - مخزن الشحن الأمامي.
8 - المطبخ.
9 - غلاف جسم الطائرة.
10 - باب الخدمة المؤدي إلى المطبخ.
11 - أماكن علوية لتعليق الملابس.
12 - مصعد يؤدي إلى المطبخ.
13 - قضبان دعم الأرضية.
14 - أضلاع طرفية تؤدي إلى الداخل.
15 - خزان الوقود.
16 - منفذ دخول الهواء إلى المحرك.
17 - الآت رولز رويس بمراوح توربينية.
18 - مخرج هواء العادم بفوهة متغيرة القياس.
19 - أضلاع طرفية تؤدي إلى الخارج.
20 - غلاف الجناح.
21 - ضوء أمامي لتحديد الوضعية.
22 - جناح صغير خارجي.
23 - جنيحات إضافية خارجية.
24 - أدوات مساعدة للهبوط.
25 - جناح صغير داخلي.
26 - جنيحات إضافية محززة مزدوجة داخلية.
27 - مخزن مقاعد الوسط.
28 - مقاعد الركاب.
29 - باب الركاب الخلفي.
30 - باب احتياطي للدخول.
31 - مخرج طوارئ.
32 - مخزن الشحن الخلفي.
33 - المدخل الخلفي للهواء إلى الآلة.
34 - مراحيض.
35 - سطح الذيل الأفقي.
36 - مصعد.
37 - مخرج هواء العادم الخلفي.
38 - الزعنفة.
39 - سكان الطائرة.

Helicopter طائرة الهليكوبتر

1 - Pilot's seat
2 - Cyclic pitch stick
3 - Tail rotor control pedals
4 - Co-pilot's seat collective-pitch lever
5 - Co-pilot's seat
6 - Main door
7 - Wheel attachments
8 - Forged frame
9 - Rolls-Royce BS.360 gas turbine engines
10 - Rotor blade
11 - Exhaust outlet
12 - Tail rotor power unit
13 - Tail rotor
14 - Tailplane
15 - Intermediate gearbox
16 - Tail rotor drive
17 - Rotor hub
18 - Drag hinge damper
19 - Pitch control rod
20 - Main gearbox
21 - Collective pitch linkages

1 ـ مقعد السائق.
2 ـ قضيب الحط الدائري.
3 ـ دواسات التحكم بدوار الذيل.
4 ـ عتلة الخط المشتركة لمساعد الطيار.
5 ـ مقعد مساعد الطيار.
6 ـ الباب الرئيسي.
7 ـ وصلات تثبيت العجلات.
8 ـ إطار مصنوع بالتشكيل.
9 ـ آلة توربينية غازية رولز رويس.
10 ـ شفرة الدوار.
11 ـ مخرج هواء العادم.
12 ـ وحدة طاقة دوار الذيل.
13 ـ دوار الذيل.
14 ـ سطح الذيل الأفقي.
15 ـ علبة التروس المتوسطة.
16 ـ جهاز تشغيل دوار الذيل.
17 ـ محور الدوار.
18 ـ مخمد مفصلة السحب.
19 ـ قضيب تحكم بالحط.
20 ـ علبة التروس الرئيسية.
21 ـ روابط جماعية للحط.

Hovercraft الهوفركرافت

What are the component parts of a hovercraft?

The hovercraft sails at a height of 3 meters above water level relying on an air cushion. Its main components are:

1 - Air intakes
2 - Main bevel drive gearbox
3 - 12 blade lift fan
4 - Skirt fingers
5 - Flexible skirt
6 - Extention shaft from turbine
7 - Main passenger cabin
8 - Baggage racks
9 - Door to car deck
10 - Passenger entrance door
11 - Retractable stairs
12 - Dinghy pack
13 - Pylon
14 - Engine air intakes
15 - Accoustic baffles
16 - Marine proteus gas turbine
17 - Fin
18 - Rear car ramp
19 - Car deck
20 - Hatch to auxiliary power unit
21 - HS dynamics propeller
22 - Propeller gearbox
23 - Radio aerials
24 - Radar scanner
25 - Control deck
26 - Crew entry ladder
27 - Forward car ramp
28 - Cabin ventilation pack
29 - Forward passenger cabin
30 - Forward fuel tank

ما هي الأجزاء المكونة للهوفركرافت؟

تسير الهوفركرافت على ارتفاع 3 أمتار فوق سطح الماء اعتماداً على وسادة هوائية. أما أجزاؤها المكونة فهي:

1 ـ مداخل الهواء.
2 ـ علبة التروس المشطوبة الرئيسية.
3 ـ مروحة من 12 شفرة للرفع.
4 ـ أصابع الغلاف.
5 ـ غلاف مرن.
6 ـ عمود إدارة متمدد من التوربين.
7 ـ حجرة الركاب الرئيسية.
8 ـ رفوف الأمتعة.
9 ـ الباب المؤدي إلى السطح.
10 ـ باب دخول الركاب.
11 ـ سلالم قابلة للسحب إلى الداخل.
12 ـ مجموعة الأطواف.
13 ـ برج الأسلاك.
14 ـ مداخل الهواء للمحركات.
15 ـ موانع سمعية.
16 ـ توربين غازي.
17 ـ الزعنفة.
18 ـ منحدر السيارات الخلفي.
19 ـ السطح المخصص للسيارات.
20 ـ فتحة تؤدي إلى وحدة الطاقة الاحتياطية.
21 ـ دفاعة مروحية.
22 ـ علبة تروس الدفاعة المروحية.
23 ـ هوائيات اللاسلكي.
24 ـ جهاز مسح الرادار.
25 ـ سطح التحكم.
26 ـ سلم دخول طاقم الباخرة.
27 ـ منحدر السيارات الأمامي.
28 ـ مجموعة تهوية حجرة الركاب.
29 ـ حجرة الركاب الأمامية.
30 ـ خزان الوقود الأمامي.

الغواصة بولاريس

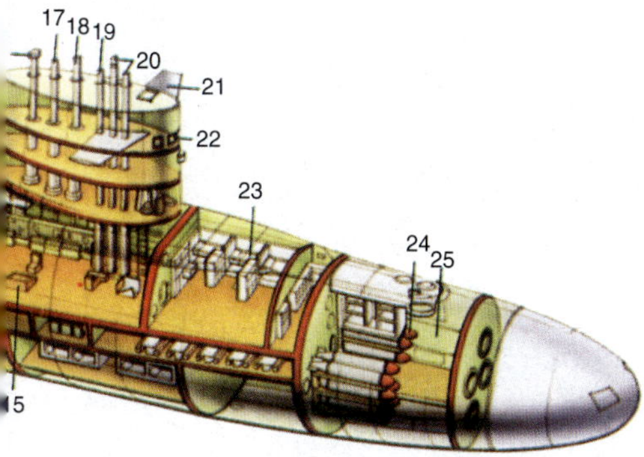

1 ـ الداس
2 ـ سطح الغطس على الجانب الأيمن
3 ـ السكان الاسفل
4 ـ السكان الأعلى
5 ـ حجرة الآلات
6 ـ التوربين
7 ـ حجرة آلة السير إلى الأمام
8 ـ باب أرضي للهبوط
9 ـ سطح المفاعل
10 ـ المفاعل
11 ـ المرجل
12 ـ كوات الصواريخ
13 ـ صواريخ بولاريس
14 ـ أنابيب الصواريخ
15 ـ سطح التحكم
16 ـ مخرج آداة التزود بالهواء النقي
17 ـ هوائي اللاسلكي
18 ـ مدخل آداة التزود بالهواء النقي
19 ـ هوائي اللاسلكي
20 ـ منظار الأفق
21 ـ سطح الإبحار
22 ـ منصة ربان الغواصة
23 ـ أسِرّة النوم
24 ـ الطوربيدات
25 ـ غرفة الطوربيدات

Polaris Submarine

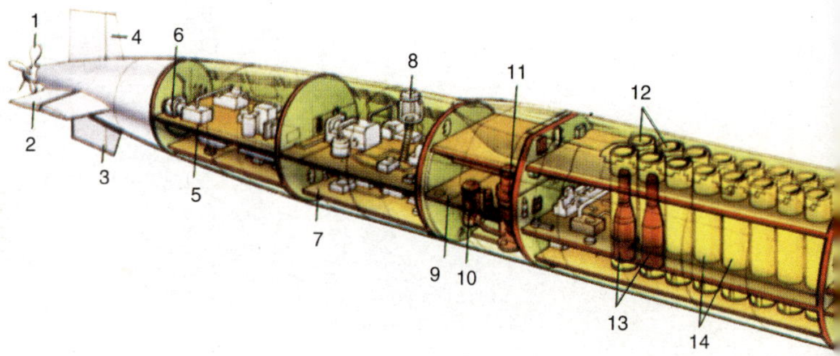

1 - Propeller
2 - Starboard diving plane
3 - Lower rudder
4 - Upper rudder
5 - Engine room
6 - Turbine
7 - Forward engine room
8 - Hatch
9 - Reactor deck
10 - Reactor
11 - Boiler
12 - Missile hatches
13 - Polaris missiles
14 - Missile tubes
15 - Control deck
16 - Snorkel exhaust
17 - Radio antenna
18 - Snorkel intake
19 - Radar antenna
20 - Periscopes
21 - Port sail plane
22 - Bridge
23 - Bunks
24 - Torpedoes
25 - Torpedo room

Warships
السفن الحربية

Development of modern warships began in the middle of the nineteenth century when the French Battleship "La Gloire", the first steel-armored warship was put to water in 1859, followed by the British destroyer "Bristol". Its main components were:

1 - Laundry
2 - Anti-submarine mortar
3 - Helicopter flight deck
4 - Sea dart missiles
5 - Mess decks
6 - Missile control radar
7 - Funnels for gas turbines
8 - Surface search radar
9 - Engine rooms
10 - Funnel for steam turbines
11 - Air search radar
12 - Ikara control radar
13 - Ikara missiles
14 - 4.5 in gun

بدأ تطوير السفن الحربية الحديثة في منتصف القرن التاسع عشر عندما تم إنزال أول سفينة حربية بخارية مدرعة بالفولاذ وكانت المدمرة الفرنسية لاغلوار في عام 1859.

ثم المدمرة البريطانية بريستول مع أجزائها وهي:

1 ـ حجرة غسل الملابس.
2 ـ مدفع هاون مضاد للغواصات.
3 ـ سطح هبوط وإنطلاق طائرات الهليكوبتر.
4 ـ صواريخ نوع سي دارت.
5 ـ اسطح المطعم.
6 ـ رادار مراقبة الصواريخ.
7 ـ مداخن للتوربينات الغازية.
8 ـ رادار الكشف عن سطح البحر.
9 ـ غرف الآلات.
10 ـ مدخنة للتوربينات الغازية.
11 ـ رادار البحث الجوي.
12 ـ رادار التحكم بالصواريخ ايكارا.
13 ـ صواريخ ايكارا.
14 ـ مدفع بقطر 4,5 بوصة.

Camera آلة التصوير

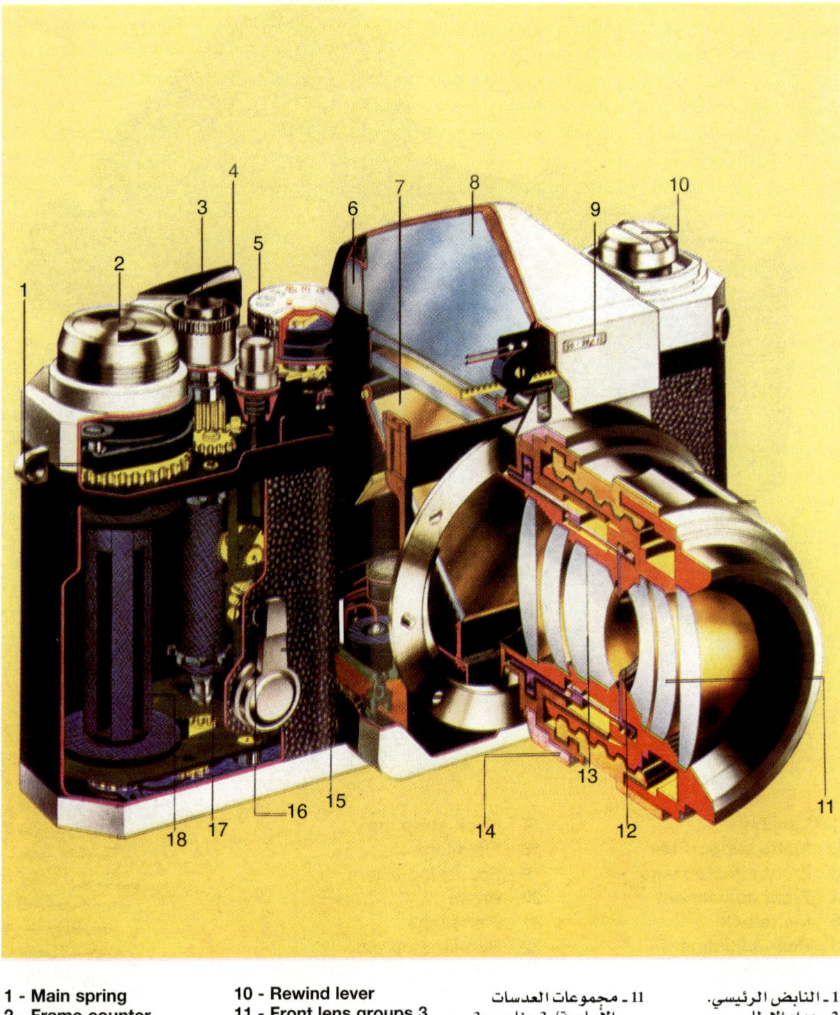

1 - Main spring
2 - Frame counter
3 - Shutter release
4 - Cocking lever
5 - Shutter speed control
6 - Eyepiece
7 - Mirror
8 - Pentaprism
9 - Maximum aperture setting indicator
10 - Rewind lever
11 - Front lens groups 3 elements/3 groups
12 - Iris diaphragm
13 - Rear lens groups (4 elements / 3 groups)
14 - Lens mounting
15 - Self timer lever
16 - Self timer mechanism
17 - Film transport sprocket
18 - Film take-up spool

1 ـ النابض الرئيسي.
2 ـ عداد الإطار.
3 ـ أداة إطلاق المصراع.
4 ـ عتلة التصويب.
5 ـ أداة التحكم بسرعة إغلاق المصراع.
6 ـ عينية لتأطير المنظر.
7 ـ مرآة.
8 ـ موشور خماسي.
9 ـ مؤشر الضبط الأقصى للفتحة.
10 ـ عتلة إعادة اللف.
11 ـ مجموعات العدسات الأمامية/ 3 عناصر، 3 مجموعات.
12 ـ الحجاب القزحي.
13 ـ مجموعات العدسات الخلفية / 4 عناصر، 3 مجموعات.
14 ـ تركيب العدسة.
15 ـ عتلة التوقيت الذاتي.
16 ـ آلية التوقيت الذاتي.
17 ـ العجلة المسننة لنقل الفيلم.
18 ـ بكرة التقاط الفيلم.

Motion picture camera
آلة التصوير السينمائية

1 ـ صمولة الإقفال.
2 ـ قضيب إسناد من خليط معدني.
3 ـ مرحلة تصوير التأثيرات الخاصة.
4 ـ تعديل أمامي.
5 ـ صندوق قضبان الإسناد المصنوعة من خليط معدني.
6 ـ تعديل خلفي.
7 ـ عدسة أولى.
8 ـ صف ترشيح أمامي للصور.
9 ـ صف ترشيح خلفي للصور (يمكن تدويره).
10 ـ شبكة من الزجاج المسحوق.
11 ـ خلف العدسة الأولى.
12 ـ محور البرج المركزي.
13 ـ مصراع مرآة مثبتة عند زاوية 180 درجة.
14 ـ مخلب متقطع للفيلم.
15 ـ حامل العدسة 3.
16 ـ عدسة بديلة (الثانية).
17 ـ عروة شريط العنق.
18 ـ عدسة ميدانية.
19 ـ عتلات تركيز البؤرة.
20 ـ الموشور.
21 ـ مسطح الفيلم.
22 ـ دبوس التسجيل.
23 ـ بوابة الفيلم.
24 ـ مخزن الفيلم.
25 ـ إقفال برميل العدسة.
26 ـ مسامير إزاحة البرج.
27 ـ دلانين الضغط.
28 ـ أجهزة تحديد المنظر.
29 ـ برج بثلاث عدسات منفرجة.
30 ـ بكرة القام الفيلم.
31 ـ أسنان التروس.
32 ـ بكرة التقاط الفيلم.
33 ـ تركيز بؤرة تحديد المنظر.
34 ـ كأس العينية.

1 - Locknut
2 - Matte support bar
3 - Front effects stage
4 - Front adjustment
5 - Matte box
6 - Rear adjustment
7 - Prime lens
8 - Front filter rack
9 - Rear filter rack (revolving)
10 - Ground glass screen
11 - Rear of prime lens
12 - Centre turret pivot
13 - 180° mirror shutter at 45° to the film plane
14 - Intermittent film claw
15 - Mount for lens 3
16 - Alternative lens (2nd)
17 - Neck strap lug
18 - Field lens
19 - Focussing levers
20 - Prism
21 - Film plane
22 - Registration pin
23 - Filmage
24 - Film stock
25 - Lens barrel locks
26 - Turret shift tabs
27 - Pressure rollers
28 - Viewfinder optics (10x)
29 - 3 lens divergent turret
30 - Feed film spool
31 - Geared sprockets
32 - Take-up film spool
33 - Viewfinder focus
34 - Eyepiece cup

The Car of the Future — سيارة المستقبل

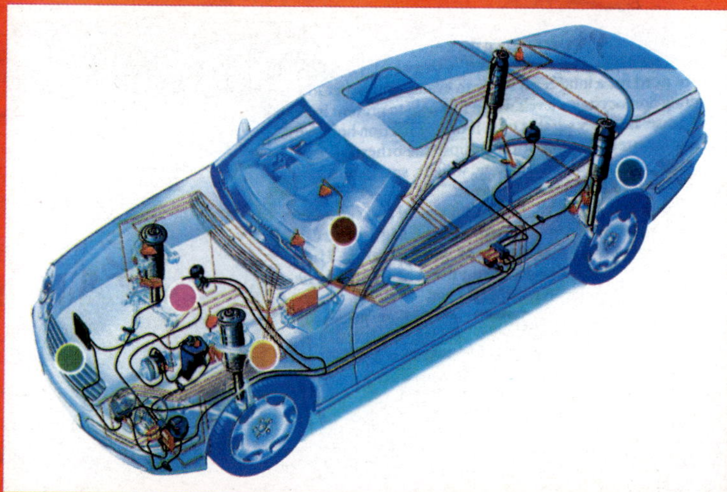

How will look the car of the future?

1- The car of the future shall be provided with an intelligent speed regulator operating by way of a small radar.

2- It will be equipped with a movement-control devise that sends its orders to the car's hydraulic brakes.

3- It will be equipped also with a stabilator devise operated by a computer to help the driver when crossing a bend.

4- It will be equipped with a video camera to control the direction and return the steering wheel to the correct direction.

5- It will be provided with a computer that controls the degree of pollution that the car produces.

كيف ستكون عليه سيارة المستقبل؟

1 ـ سوف يتم تجهيز سيارة المستقبل بجهاز تحكم ذكي بسرعة السيارة يعمل بواسطة رادار صغير يستطيع أيضاً وقف السيارة عند الاقتضاء.

2 ـ وسوف تجهز أيضاً بجهاز مراقبة يتحكم بحركة السيارة ويرسل معلوماته إلى المكابح الهيدروليكية لتثبيت حركة السيارة واهتزازها على الطرق غير المعبدة.

3 ـ سوف تجهز أيضاً بجهاز تحكم يضمن استقرار السيارة يعمل بواسطة كومبيوتر لمنع السائق من ارتكاب خطأ في قيادة السيارة عند اجتيازه أحد المنعطفات.

4 ـ سوف تجهز أيضاً بآلة تصوير ڤيديو لمراقبة خطوط الفصل بين مسارات الاتجاه وإعادة عجلة القيادة إلى الاتجاه الصحيح في حال لاحظت آلة التصوير بأن السائق بدأ يخرج عن الخط الفاصل الذي يحدد الاتجاه.

5 ـ سوف تجهز السيارة بكومبيوتر يراقب مدى التلوث الذي تصدره السيارة ويعدل سلوك السائق قبل أن يتلقى صدمة محتملة.

السيارة

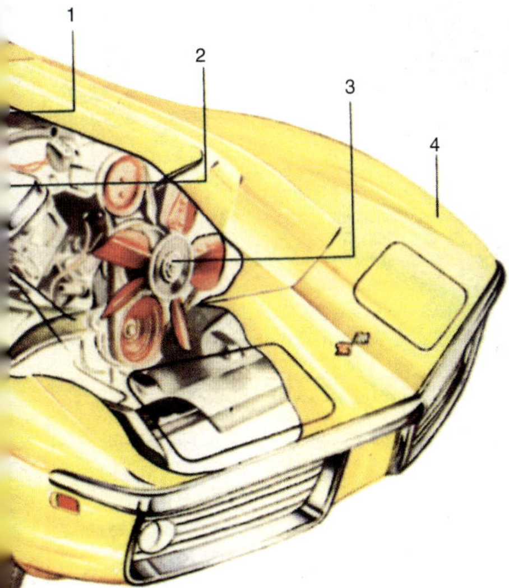

متى تم صنع أول سيارة ذات احتراق داخلي وما هي أهم أجزاؤها؟

ابتكر كارل بينز وغوتلب دايملر أول سيارة تعمل بالبنزين وفق نظام الاحتراق الداخلي في عام 1885م. ولكن النمساوي سيغفريد ماركوس صنع أول سيارة تسير بغاز الهيدروجين.

أما أهم أجزاء السيارة فهي:

1 ـ علبة تروس تغيير السرعة.

2 ـ المحرك.

3 ـ مروحة التبريد.

4 ـ الهيكل الخارجي الخفيف الوزن.

5 ـ علبة التروس.

6 ـ الهيكل المعدني.

7 ـ عمود الإدارة.

8 ـ الترس التفاضلي.

The Automobile

1875 Marcus
1875 ماركوس

1886 Benz
1886 بنز

1902 Wosley
1902 واسلي

1908 Ford
1908 فورد

When was the first internal combustion automobile invented and what are its main component parts?

Karl Benz and Gottlieb Daimler invented the first internal combustion automobile operated by petrol in 1885, but the Austrian, Siegfried Markus, invented the first automobile operated by hydrogen.

The main component parts of the automobile are:

1 - Gearshift
2 - Engine
3 - Cooling fan
4 - Lightweight body
5 - Gearbox
6 - Chassis
7 - Drive shaft
8 - Differential

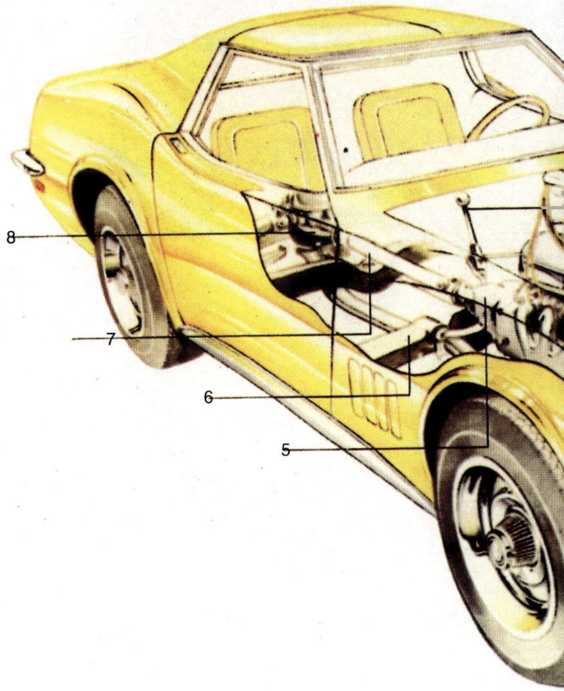

1948 Vauxhall
1948 فوكسهول

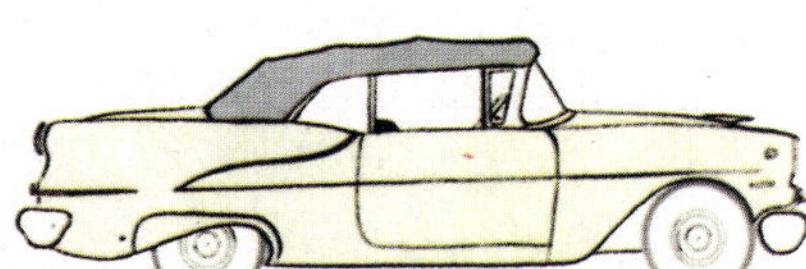

1954 Oldsmobile
1954 أولدز موبيل

1955 Citroe
1955 يتروان

آلة الحصاد

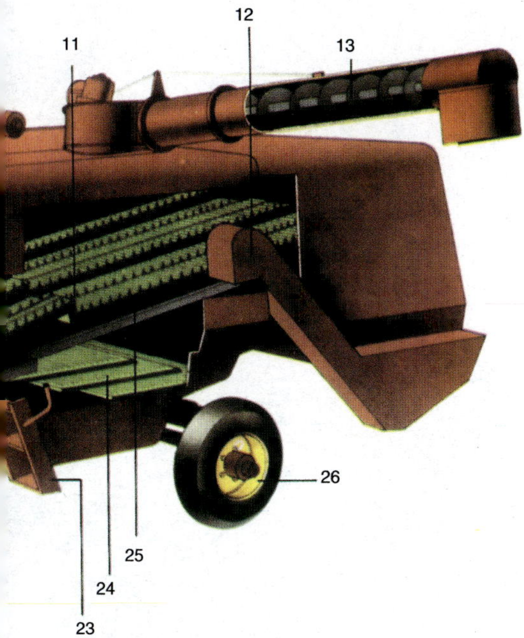

ما هي الأجزاء المكونة للآلة الموحدة لحصاد ودرس وتكديس الحبوب؟

1 ـ بكرة الحصاد.
2 ـ رافعة المحصول.
3 ـ سلاسل مزودة بقوابض.
4 ـ أضواء.
5 ـ حجرة الآلة.
6 ـ عجلة القيادة.
7 ـ أنبوب العادم.
8 ـ أجهزة التحكم الهيدرولية.
9 ـ مقعد السائق.
10 ـ الخافقة الخلفية.
11 ـ دواسة القش.
12 ـ وحدة متعددة الانسياب.
13 ـ برمجة تفريغ الحبوب.
14 ـ عجلة قيادة البكرة.
15 ـ سكين.
16 ـ سير بكرة الالتقاط.
17 ـ برمجة إدارة (تنقل المحصول إلى الداخل)
18 ـ اسطوانة إدارة دافعة المحصول.
19 ـ اسطوانة الدرس.
20 ـ مقعر الحبوب.
21 ـ العجلات الرئيسية.

The Harvester

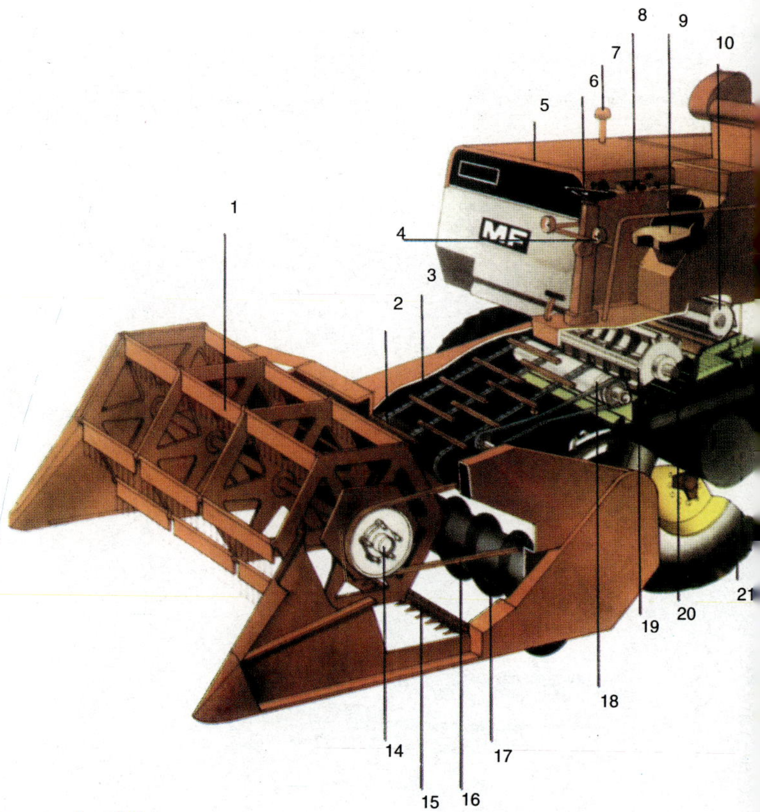

What are the components of the combined harvester-thrasher stacker of grains?

1 - Pick up reel
2 - Crop elevator
3 - Spring loaded chains
4 - Lights
5 - Engine compartment
6 - Steering wheel
7 - Exhaust pipe
8 - Hydraulic controls
9 - Driver's seat
10 - Rear heater
11 - Straw thresher
12 - Multi-flow unit
13 - Grain unloading auger
14 - Reel drive wheel
15 - Knife
16 - Pick up reel belt drive
17 - Rotating auger (moves crop inwards)
18 - Crop elevator drive cylinder
19 - Threshing cylinder
20 - Grain concave
21 - Main wheels

القطار

Midland 4-4-0 compound 1902

القطار ميدلاند 1902

متى تمّ صنع القطار البخاري وما هي أجزاؤه المكونة؟

كان البريطاني ريتشارد تريفيثيك أول من فكر في بناء محرك يعمل بضغط عالي يسير على عجلات. وفي 21 شباط 1804م بدأ القطار الذي ابتكره تريفيثيك أول رحلة له لنقل البضائع. أما القطار البخاري فقد ابتكره جورج ستيفنسون عام 1825م واصبح أول قطار بخاري ينقل بضائع على خط سكة حديد في العالم.

أما الأجزاء المكونة للقطار البخاري فهي التالية:

1 ـ الاسطوانة.
2 ـ عاكسات البخار.
3 ـ صندوق البخار.
4 ـ الكباس.
5 ـ المدخنة.
6 ـ ترس الصمام.
7 ـ قضيب الوصل.
8 ـ قضبان الربط.
9 ـ أنابيب الرمل.
10 ـ أداة حقن المياه.
11 ـ صمام الأمان.
12 ـ أنابيب المرجل.
13 ـ صندوق النار.
14 ـ المنظم.
15 ـ عتلة المكبح البخاري.
16 ـ الصفارة.
17 ـ عتلة المكبح الهوائي.
18 ـ ترس عكس السير.
19 ـ عتلة الرمل.

The Locomotive

Trevithick's engine 1803
محرك تريفيثيك 1903

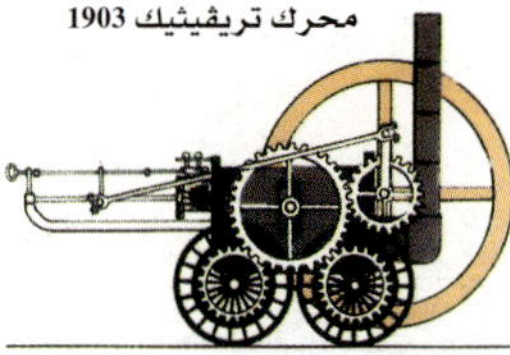

The Firefly 1840
القطار فايرفلاي 1840

The Stirling1840
القطار سترلينغ 1840

How was the steam locomotive invented and what are its component parts?

The British Engineer Richard Trivetic was the first who thought of constructing an engine operated by high pressure and running on wheefls. On 21 February 1804 the first locomotive invented by Trivetic made its maiden Journey transporting goods but the steam locomotive invented by George Stevenson in 1825 became the first steam locomotive running on rails in the world.

Its main component parts are:

1 - Cylinder
2 - Smoke deflectors
3 - Steam chest
4 - Piston
5 - Chimmey
6 - Valve gear
7 - Connecting rod
8 - Coupling rods
9 - Sanding pipes
10 - Water injector
11 - Safety valve
12 - Boiler tubes
13 - Fire box
14 - Regulator
15 - Steam brake lever
16 - Whistle
17 - Vacuum brake lever
18 - Reversing gear
19 - Sand lever

Truck الكميون

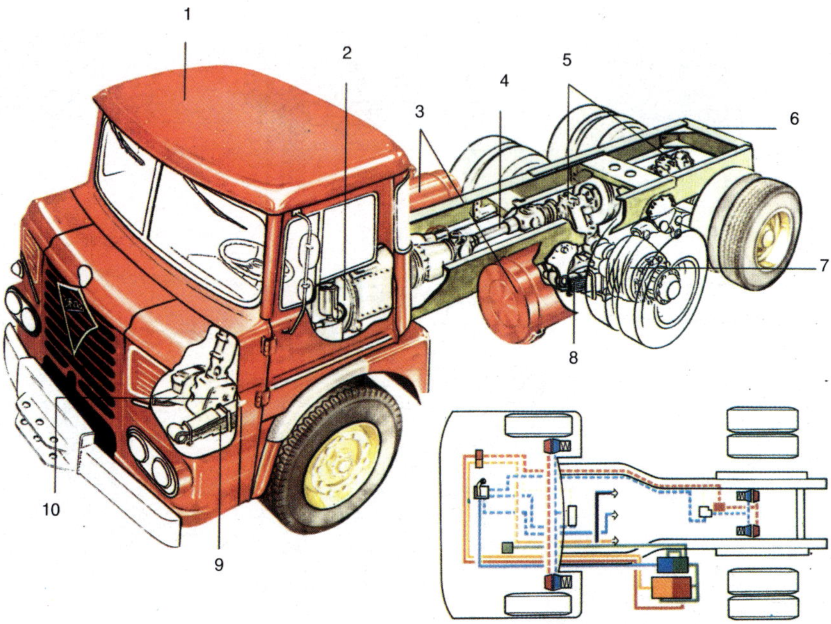

- Air from compressor
- Tractor pressure line
- Tractor brake line
- Trailer pressure line
- Trailer brake line
- Park brake pressure line
- Park brake line
- Emergency line
- Anti-compounding line

- الهواء من الضاغط
- خط حفظ الجرار
- خط كبح الجرار
- خط ضغط المقطورة
- خط كبح المقطورة
- خط ضغط مكبح الإيقاف
- خط مكبح الإيقاف
- خط مكبح حالة الطوارئ
- خط مضاد للتركيب

1 - Driver's cab	1 ـ حجرة السائق
2 - Engine and gearbox	2 ـ المحرك وعلبة التروس
3 - Fuel tanks	3 ـ خزانات الوقود
4 - Drive shaft	4 ـ عمود الإدارة
5 - Final drive gearboxes	5 ـ علب تروس القيادة النهائية
6 - Frame chassis	6 ـ الهيكل الخار جي
7 - Brake drum	7 ـ طبلة المكبح
8 - Rear suspension	8 ـ نوابض التعليق الخارجية
9 - Front suspension	9 ـ نوابض التعليق الأمامية
10 - Steering box	10 ـ جهاز التوجيه

Clothes and near the River ملابس/ بجوار النهر

1 - Trees	8 - Hat	15 - River	15 ـ النهر	8 ـ قبعة	1 ـ أشجار
2 - Handbag	9 - Jacket	16 - Blouse	16 ـ بلوزة	9 ـ سترة	2 ـ حقيبة يدوية
3 - Scarf	10 - Ball	17 - Backpack	17 ـ حقيبة ظهر	10 ـ كرة	3 ـ لفاح
4 - Sweater	11 - Sock	18 - Skirt	18 ـ تنورة	11 ـ جورب	4 ـ قميص
5 - Trousers	12 - Sneakers	19 - Chick	19 ـ صوص	12 ـ حذاء خفيف	5 ـ سروال
6 - Shoe	13 - Bird	20 - Hen	20 ـ دجاجة	13 ـ عصفور	6 ـ حذاء
7 - Cat	14 - Sail Boat			14 ـ مركب شراعي	7 ـ قطة

On the Farm

في المزرعة

1 - Field	7 - Harvester	13 - Lama	13 ـ نعجة	7 ـ حاصدة	1 ـ حقول زراعية
2 - Farmhouse	8 - Cow	14 - Cock	14 ـ ديك	8 ـ بقرة	2 ـ منزل في المزرعة
3 - Barn	9 - Tractor	15 - Horse	15 ـ حصان	9 ـ جرار، تراكتور	3 ـ حظيرة الحيوانات
4 - Fence	10 - Shepherd	16 - Hen	16 ـ دجاجة	10 ـ راعٍ	4 ـ سياج
5 - Trees	11 - Dog	17 - Rabbit	17 ـ أرنب	11 ـ كلبٌ	5 ـ أشجار متنوعة
6 - Pond	12 - Sheep			12 ـ خروف	6 ـ بركة

At the Park

في المتنزه

1 - Painting
2 - Picture Frame
3 - Belt
4 - Peanuts
5 - Boy
6 - Wooden Bench
7 - Man
8 - Trousers
9 - Shoes
10 - Cat
11 - Umbrella
12 - Tree
13 - Sunglasses
14 - Cap
15 - Golf Player
16 - Overall
17 - Tree Leaves
18 - Hen

1 - رسم زيتي
2 - إطار الرسم
3 - حزام
4 - فول سوداني
5 - ولد
6 - مقعد خشبي
7 - رجل
8 - سروال
9 - حذاء
10 - قطة
11 - مظلة
12 - شجرة
13 - نظارة شمسية
14 - قبعة
15 - لاعب غولف
16 - رداء سروالي
17 - أوراق الشجر
18 - دجاجة

البادية

1 ـ قافلة
2 ـ بدو
3 ـ راعٍ
4 ـ قطيع
5 ـ واحة
6 ـ خيمة
7 ـ جمل
8 ـ حصان
9 ـ موقد
10 ـ قرية
11 ـ بساط
12 ـ قنديل
13 ـ ربابة
14 ـ تنور
15 ـ صقر
16 ـ يمامة
17 ـ صبَّار
18 ـ دلَّة القهوة

The Desert

1 - Caravan
2 - Bedouins
3 - Shepherd
4 - Herds
5 - Oasis
6 - Tent
7 - Camel
8 - Horse
9 - Fire
10 - Water jar
11 - Mat
12 - Kerosene lamp
13 - Rebec
14 - Oven
15 - Hawk
16 - Pigeon
17 - Cactus
18 - Coffee-pot

المدينة

1 ـ طرق (طريق)
2 ـ أرصفة (رصيف)
3 ـ أبنية سكنيّة وتجاريّة
4 ـ إشارات سير
5 ـ محلات تجارية
6 ـ مؤسسات صحيّة وخدماتيّة
7 ـ جسر
8 ـ كشك هاتف
9 ـ إشارة ضوئية
10 ـ حافلة (باص)
11 ـ بائع الصحف والمجلات
12 ـ بائع الخضار
13 ـ مستوصف
14 ـ جبل (مرتفعات) تلال
15 ـ شرفة (بلكون)

The City

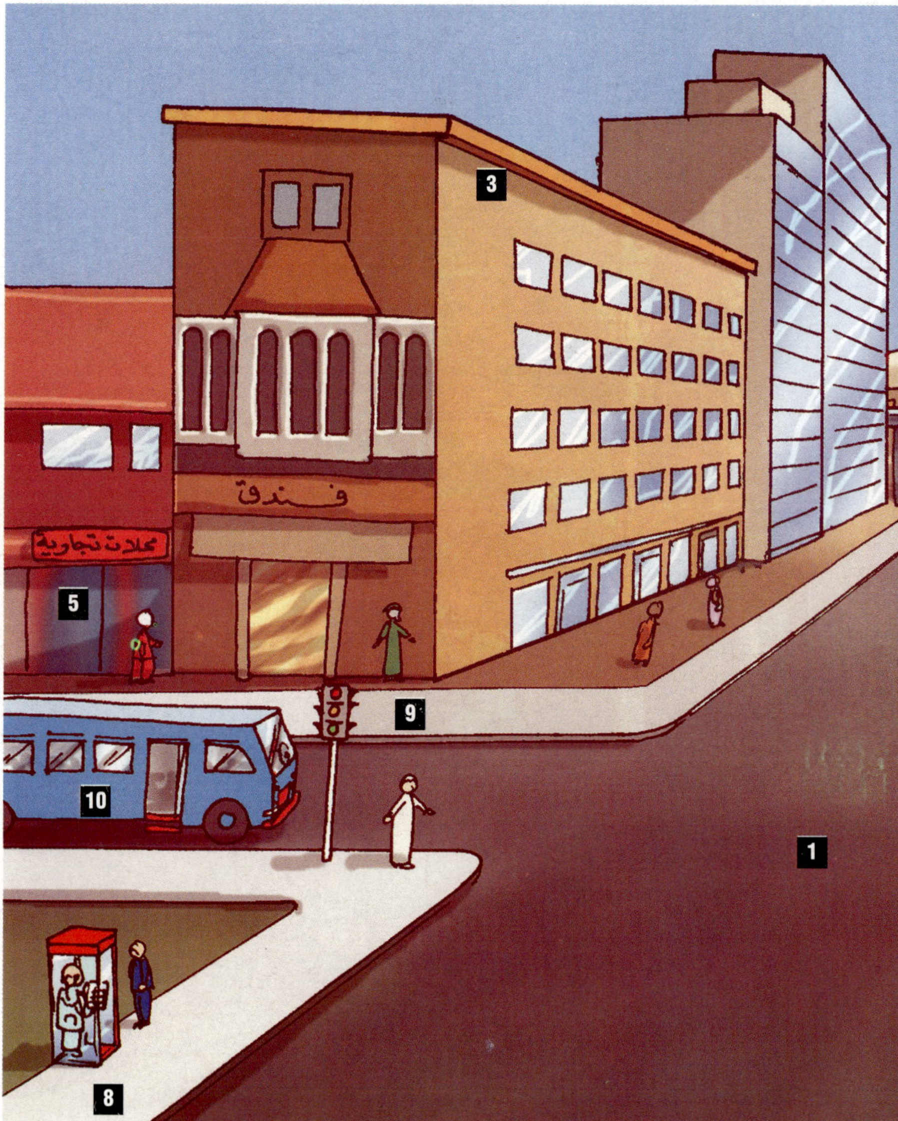

1 - Street
2 - Pavement
3 - Housing and commercial buildings
4 - Direction sign
5 - Commercial shops
6 - Services and health establishments
7 - Bridge
8 - Telephone booth
9 - Traffic lights signals
10 - Bus
11 - Newspaper seller
12 - Vegetable seller
13 - Health clinic
14 - Hill
15 - Balcony

In the Country
في الريف

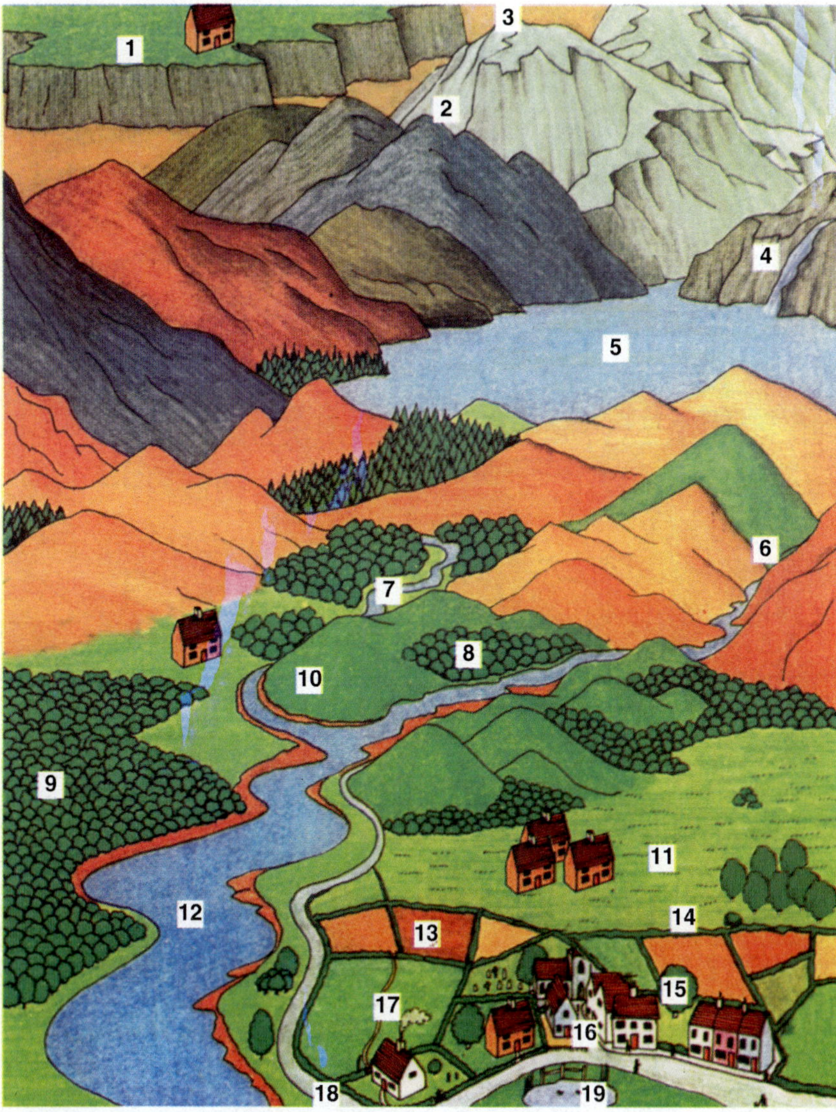

1 - Plateau
2 - Mountain
3 - (Mountain) peak
4 - Waterfall
5 - Lake
6 - Valley
7 - Stream
8 - Wood
9 - Forest
10 - Hill
11 - Mat
12 - River
13 - Meadow
14 - Field
15 - Hedge
16 - Village
17 - (Foot) path
18 - Road
19 - Pound

1 - نجد
2 - جبل
3 - قمة (جبل)
4 - شلال ماء
5 - بحيرة
6 - واد
7 - جدول
8 - حرج
9 - غابة
10 - تلّ
11 - مرج
12 - نهر
13 - حقل
14 - سياج
15 - شجرة
16 - قرية
17 - ممرمشاة
18 - طريق
19 - بركة

The Law & The Court — القانون والمحكمة

1 - Policeman's cap
2 - Prisoner
3 - Truncheon
4 - Handcuffs
5 - Torch
6 - Badge
7 - Police car
8 - Gavel
9 - Magnifying glass
10 - Pistol
11 - Policeman
12 - Police dog
13 - Justice balance
14 - Court Membres
15 - Judge
16 - Defendant lawyer
17 - Court's clerk
18 - Jury
19 - Defendant
20 - Plaintiff
21 - Prosecutor
22 - Audience

1 - قبعة رجل الشرطة
2 - سجين
3 - هراوة
4 - أصفاد
5 - مصباح يدوي
6 - شارة رجل الشرطة
7 - سيارة الشرطة
8 - مطرقة القاضي
9 - زجاجة مكبرة
10 - مسدس
11 - رجل الشرطة
12 - كلب رجل الشرطة
13 - ميزان العدل
14 - أعضاء المحكمة
15 - القاضي
16 - محامي الدفاع
17 - كاتب المحكمة
18 - هيئة المحلفين
19 - المدعى عليه
20 - المدعي
21 المدعي العام
22 الحضور

At the Restaurant في المطعم

1 - Beer mug
2 - Icecream cup
3 - Glass
4 - Ashtray
5 - Bottle
6 - Can opener
7 - Matches box
8 - Corkscrew
9 - Bottle opener
10 - Tankard
11 - Cup of drink
12 - Petrol lamp
13 - Bar customer
14 - Mineral Water bottle
15 - Barman
16 - Waitress
17 - Orders book
18 - Menu
19 - Water cup
20 - Plate
21 - Salt cellar, mustard and pepper pots
22 - Knife
23 - Restaurant customer
24 - Chair
25 - Stool
26 - Juke - box

1 ـ قدح للجعة
2 ـ قدح بوظة
3 ـ كأس
4 ـ منفضة سجائر
5 ـ زجاجة
6 ـ فتاحة علب
7 ـ علبة كبريت
8 ـ فتاحة زجاجات مرطبات
9 ـ فتاحة زجاجات
10 ـ دورق
11 ـ كأس ماء
12 ـ مصباح كاز
13 ـ زبون
14 ـ قنينة ماء معدني
15 ـ خادم الحانة
16 ـ الخادمة
17 ـ سجل الطلبات
18 ـ قائمة الطعام
19 ـ كأس للماء
20 ـ صحن
21 ـ مملحة وإناء للخردل والزيت والبهار
22 ـ سكينة طعام
23 ـ زبونة المطعم
24 ـ مقعد
25 ـ مقعد بلا ظهر
26 ـ صندوق موسيقى

At the Theater, Cinema & the Public Library
في المسرح، السينما والمكتبة العامة

1 - Screen	10 - Music group	10 - الفرقة الموسيقية	1 - شاشة العرض
2 - Stage	11 - Spotlights	11 - أضواء كاشفة	2 - خشبة المسرح
3 - Audience	12 - Actress	12 - الممثلة	3 - الحضور
4 - Upper curtain	13 - Actor	13 - الممثل	4 - الستارة العلوية
5 - Projector	14 - Singer	14 - المطربة	5 - آلة العرض
6 - Projectionist	15 - Book shelves	15 - رفوف كتب	6 - مشغل آلة العرض
7 - Side curtain	16 - Reception desk	16 - طاولة الاستقبال	7 - ستارة جانبية
8 - Aisle	17 - Librarian	17 - أمين المكتبة	8 - ممر بين صفوف المشاهدين
9 - Singer	18 - Book shelves	18 - رفوف كتب	9 - المطرب

الإبحار

1 ـ سفينة حوامة
2 ـ كبل
3 ـ طافية
4 ـ رافعة مشعبة
5 ـ سفينة قطر
6 ـ ألينك
7 ـ سفينة شحن السيارات
8 ـ مركب للركمجة
9 ـ سفينة ترولة
10 ـ سفينة شحن
11 ـ البضاعة
12 ـ مكتب الميناء
13 ـ رافعة
14 ـ سفينة شحن
15 ـ عنبر
16 ـ ناقلة نفط

Navigation

1 - Hovercraft	5 - Tug	9 - Trawler	13 - Crane
2 - Cable	6 - Junk	10 - Cargo ship	14 - Cargo ship
3 - Buoy	7 - Ferry boat	11 - Cargo	15 - Hold
4 - Fork-lift truck	8 - Surfing vessel	12 - Port office	16 - Oil taker

Containers
الحاويات

1 - Dust bin
2 - Crate
3 - Cage
4 - Suitcase
5 - Barrel
6 - Briefcase
7 - Carrier bag
8 - Hold all

9 - Cat basket
10 - Handbag
11 - Trunk
12 - Shopping basket
13 - Mother
14 - Child
15 - Package box

1 ـ صندوق القمامة
2 ـ صندوق للشحن
3 ـ قفص
4 ـ حقيبة سفر
5 ـ برميل
6 ـ محفظة جلدية
7 ـ حاملة أوراق
8 ـ حاوية شاملة

9 ـ سلة القطة
10 ـ حقيبة يد
11 ـ صندوق ثياب
12 ـ سلة التسوق
13 ـ الوالدة
14 ـ فتاة
15 ـ صندوق أمتعة

Verbs Conjugation

سَرْد الأفعال

انْحنى ـ يَنْحني

To bow

نامَ ـ ينامُ

To sleep

نَفخَ ـ يَنْفُخُ

To blow

وَضعَ ـ يَضعُ

To put

ضَبَطَ ـ يَضْبِطُ

To adjust

نَظّفَ ـ يُنَظِّفُ

To clean

رَمَى ـ يَرْمي

To throw

كَتَبَ ـ يَكْتُبُ

To write

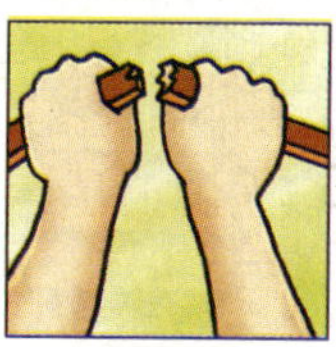

كَسَرَ ـ يَكْسِرُ

To break

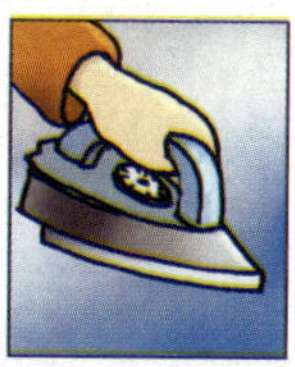

كَوَى ـ يَكْوي

To press

رَكَضَ ـ يَرْكُضُ

To run

أكَلَ ـ يأكُلُ

To eat

قَفَزَ ـ يَقْفِزُ

To jump

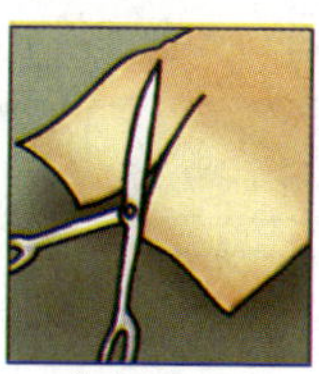

قَصَّ ـ يَقُصُّ

To cut

تَجمّدَ ـ يَتَجَمَّدُ

To freeze

عانَقَ ـ يُعانِقُ

To cuddle

At the Post Office

في مكتب البريد

1 - Globe
2 - Parliament building
3 - Mail box
4 - Pigeon hole
5 - Weighing machine
6 - Letters
7 - Post employee
8 - Notice board

1 ـ كرة أرضية
2 ـ مبنى البرلمان
3 ـ صندوق بريد
4 ـ خانات الرسائل
5 ـ ميزان
6 ـ رسائل
7 ـ موظفة بريد
8 ـ لوحة إعلانات

At Home

في المنزل

1 - Painting
2 - Picture frame
3 - Computer screen
4 - Father
5 - Plant
6 - Grandfather
7 - Cushion
8 - Grandmother
9 - Granddaughter
10 - Flower vase
11 - Table-cloth
12 - Sitting cushion
13 - Mother
14 - Baby
15 - Book
16 - Teddy bear
17 - Photo album

1 - رسم زيتي
2 - إطار
3 - شاشة الكومبيوتر
4 - الأب
5 - نبتة
6 - الجد
7 - وسادة
8 - الجدة
9 - الحفيدة
10 إناء أزهار
11 - غطاء
12 - وسادة للجلوس
13 - الأم
14 - الرضيع
15 - كتاب
16 - دب محشو
17 - ألبوم صور

غرفة الجلوس، غرفة الطعام، وغرفة النوم

1 ـ مصباح كهربائي
2 ـ صورة زيتية
3 ـ أريكة
4 ـ طاولة صغيرة
5 ـ وسادة
6 ـ مكتبة
7 ـ الكرة الأرضية
8 ـ ستارة
9 ـ ثريا
10 ـ نافذة
11 ـ مدفأة
12 ـ جهاز تلفزيون
13 ـ كرسي ذو ذراعين
14 ـ طاولة شاي
15 ـ مقعد، كرسي
16 ـ راديو
17 ـ كأس
18 ـ إبريق قهوة
19 ـ ملعقة
20 ـ سكينة
21 ـ شوكة
22 ـ إبريق شاي
23 ـ مائدة طعام
24 ـ تماثيل للزخرفة
25 ـ مصباح سقفي
26 ـ رف كتب
27 ـ سرير نوم
28 ـ خزانة ثياب
29 ـ سرير الطفل
30 ـ مِبْوَلة للطفل
31 ـ سجادة
32 ـ سروال
33 ـ مشط
34 ـ شال
35 ـ زجاجة الإرضاع
36 ـ فرشاة أسنان
37 ـ لعبة محشوة بالقطن
38 ـ سترة

Living Room, Dining Room, Bedroom

1 - Lamp
2 - Painting
3 - Sofa
4 - Small table
5 - Cushion
6 - Chest of drawers
7 - Globe
8 - Curtain
9 - Chandelier
10 - Window
11 - Fireplace
12 - Television set
13 - Armchair
14 - Tea table
15 - Chair
16 - Radio
17 - Cup
18 - Coffee pot
19 - Spoon
20 - Knife
21 - Fork
22 - Teapot
23 - Dining table
24 - Decoration
25 - Ceiling lamp
26 - Book shelf
27 - Bedspread
28 - Wardrobe
29 - Baby pot
30 - Chamber pot
31 - Rug
32 - Trousers
33 - Comb
34 - Scarf
35 - Feeding bottle
36 - Tooth brush
37 - Teddy bear
38 - Jacket

Household Objects أدوات منزلية

1 - Hanger	11 - Laundry basket	11 ـ سلة الغسيل	1 ـ مشجَب
2 - Heater	12 - Towel	12 ـ منشفة	2 ـ مَدفأة
3 - Brush	13 - Vacuum cleaner	13 ـ مكنسة كهربائية	3 ـ فرشاة ثياب
4 - Hair dryer	14 - Broom	14 ـ مكنسة يدوية	4 ـ مجففة الشعر
5 - Clock	15 - Ironing board	15 ـ طاولة لكي الملابس	5 ـ ساعة حائط
6 - Locker	16 - Washing machine	16 ـ غسالة كهربائية	6 ـ خزانة صغيرة
7 - Brush	17 - Bucket	17 ـ دلو	7 ـ فرشاة
8 - Table lamp	18 - Dust pan	18 ـ مجرود	8 ـ مصباح طاولة
9 - Laundry bag	19 - Mop	19 ـ ممسحة	9 ـ كيس للثياب القذرة
10 - Shelf	20 - Cat	20 ـ قطة	10 ـ رف

The Bedroom غرفة النوم

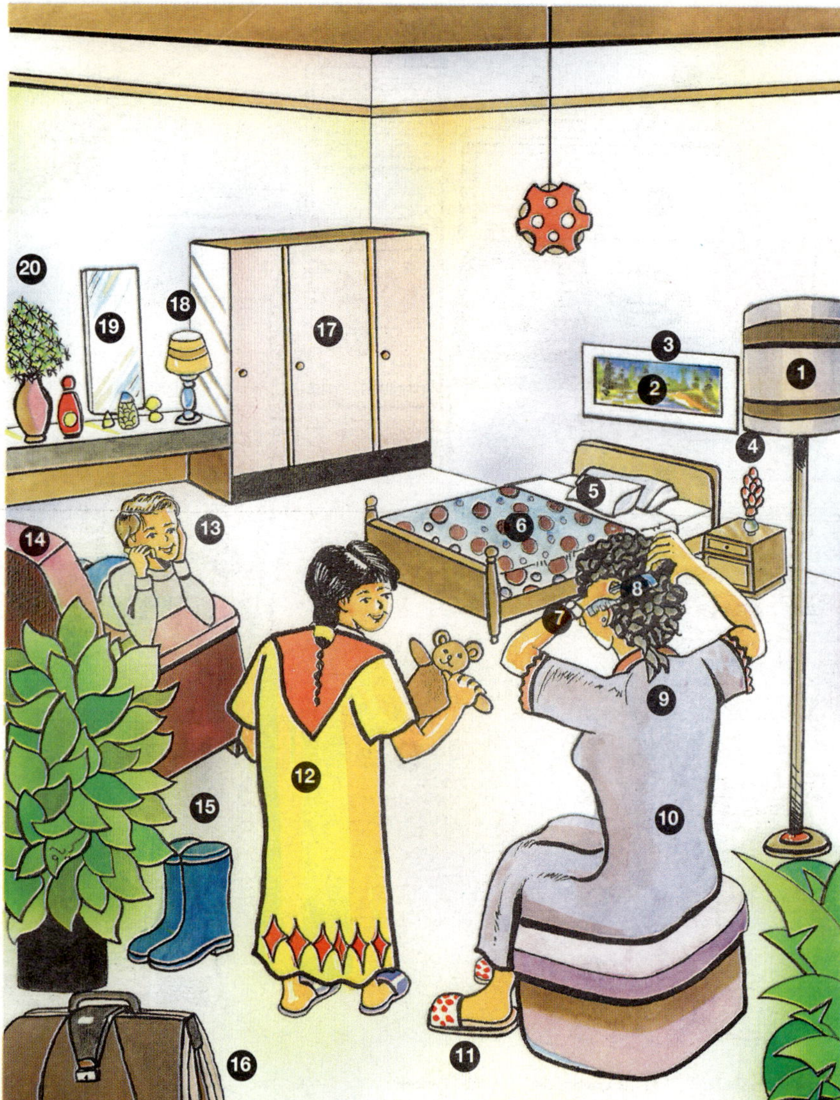

1 - Lampshade
2 - Painting
3 - Picture frame
4 - Plant
5 - Pillow
6 - Bed
7 - Bracelet
8 - Comb
9 - Night dress
10 - Mother
11 - Slippers
12 - Daughter
13 - Son
14 - Sofa
15 - Boots
16 - Schoolbag

1 ـ كُمَّة مصباح
2 ـ صورة زيتية
3 ـ إطار
4 ـ نبتة
5 ـ مخدة
6 ـ سرير نوم
7 ـ إسوارة
8 ـ مشط
9 ـ قميص النوم
10 ـ الأم
11 ـ خف
12 ـ الإبنة
13 ـ الإبن
14 ـ مقعد وثير
15 ـ جزمة
16 ـ حقيبة مدرسية

The Kitchen

المطبخ

1 - Kitchen scale	12 - Bread basket	23 - Faucet	21 ـ ملح	12 ـ سلة الخبز	1 ـ ميزان المطبخ
2 - Toaster	13 - Rolling pin	24 - Dish cloth	22 ـ منفضة	13 ـ شوبك	2 ـ محمصة خبز
3 - Cupboard	14 - Tea towel	25 - Sink	23 ـ صنبور	14 ـ منشفة	3 ـ خزانة آنية
4 - Computer	15 - Refrigerator	26 - Vegetable rack	24 ـ منشفة أوانٍ	15 ـ ثلاجة	4 ـ كمبيوتر
5 - Pot	16 - Cat	27 - Kitchen floor	25 ـ المجلى	16 ـ قطة	5 ـ قدر
6 - Jar	17 - Clothes bin		26 ـ رف الخضار	17 ـ وعاء الغسيل	6 ـ مرطبان
7 - Jug	18 - Set of pots		27 ـ أرضية غرفة المطبخ	18 ـ مجموعة من القدور	7 ـ إبريق
8 - Grill	19 - Microwave			19 ـ طباخ بالموجات الدقيقة	8 ـ شواية لحم
9 - Cooker	20 - Strainer			20 ـ مصفاة	9 ـ طباخ
10 - Ketchup botlle	21 - Salt				10 ـ زجاجة الكتشاب
11 - Salt & pepper	22 - Ashtray				11 ـ الملح والبهار

In the Classroom
غرفة الصف

1 - Wall clock
2 - Painting
3 - Agenda
4 - Teacher
5 - Map of Lebanon
6 - Photocopier
7 - Waste basket
8 - Platform
9 - Television set
10 - Student
11 - Chair
12 - Glue bottle
13 - Protractor
14 - Paint brushes
15 - Set square
16 - School book
17 - Pencil
18 - Exercise copybook
19 - Eraser
20 - School bag
21 - Ruler
22 - School books
23 - Blackboard
24 - Electric plug

1 - ساعة حائط
2 - رسم زيتي
3 - جدول العمل
4 - المعلمة
5 - خارطة لبنان
6 - آلة ناسخة (فوتوكوبي)
7 - سلة المهملات
8 - مصطبة
9 - جهاز تلفزيون
10 - تلميذ
11 - مقعد
12 - صمغ
13 - المنقلة
14 - فراشي الرسم
15 - الكوس
16 - كتاب مدرسي
17 - قلم رصاص
18 - دفتر تمارين
19 - ممحاة
20 - حقيبة كتب مدرسية
21 - مسطرة
22 - كتب مدرسية
23 - السبورة
24 - مقبس كهرباء

The Science Laboratory
المختبر العلمي

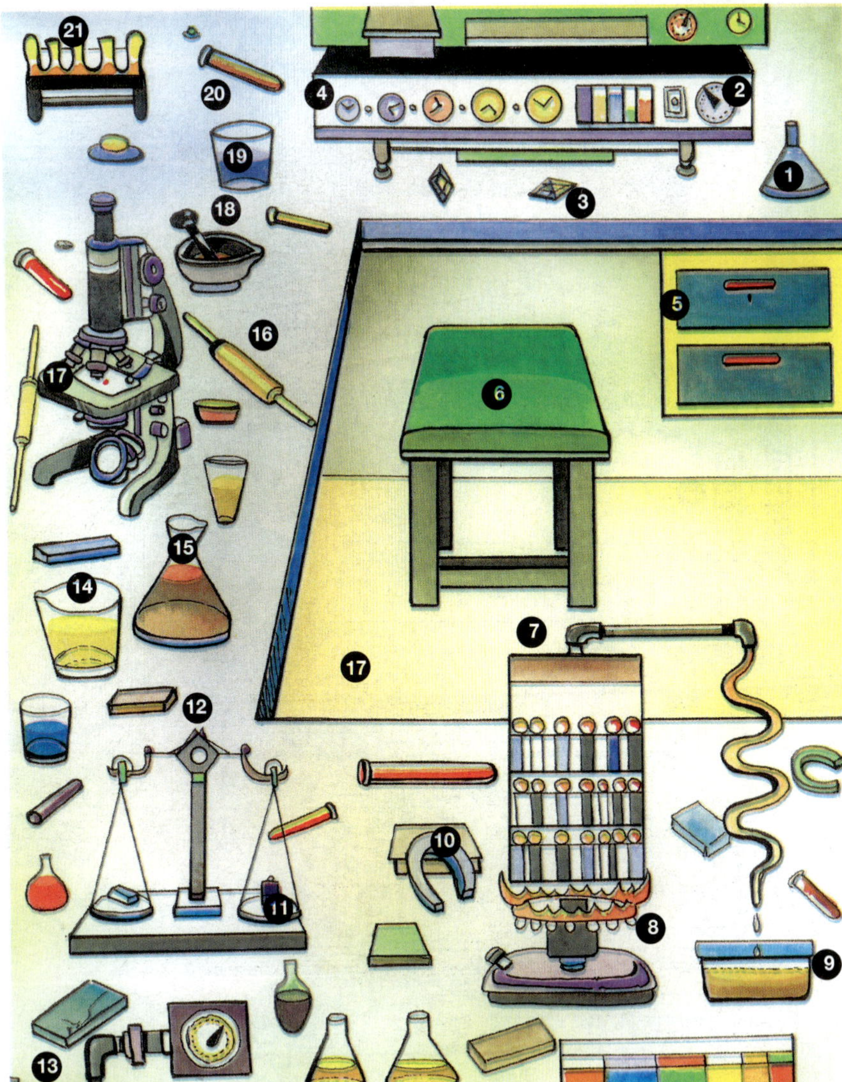

1 - Funnel
2 - Metering needle
3 - Crystal
4 - Metering gauge
5 - Drawer
6 - Stool
7 - Condenser
8 - Burner
9 - Collecting flask
10 - Magnet
11 - Balance scales
12 - Balance
13 - Pipes
14 - Beaker
15 - Liquid container
16 - Pipette
17 - Microscope
18 - Mortar
19 - Container
20 - Test tube
21- Test tube rack

1 - قمع
2 - إبرة مقياس
3 - بلورة
4 - جهاز القياس
5 - جارور
6 - مقعد بدون ذراعين
7 - مكثف
8 - الحراق
9 - إناء التجميع
10 - مغنطيس
11 - كفة الميزان
12 - الميزان
13 - أنابيب
14 - كأس كبيرة
15 - دورق
16 - سحاحة
17 - مجهر
18 - هاون
19 - وعاء
20 - أنبوب إختبار
21 - حامل أنابيب الإختبار

The Skeleton الهيكل العظمي

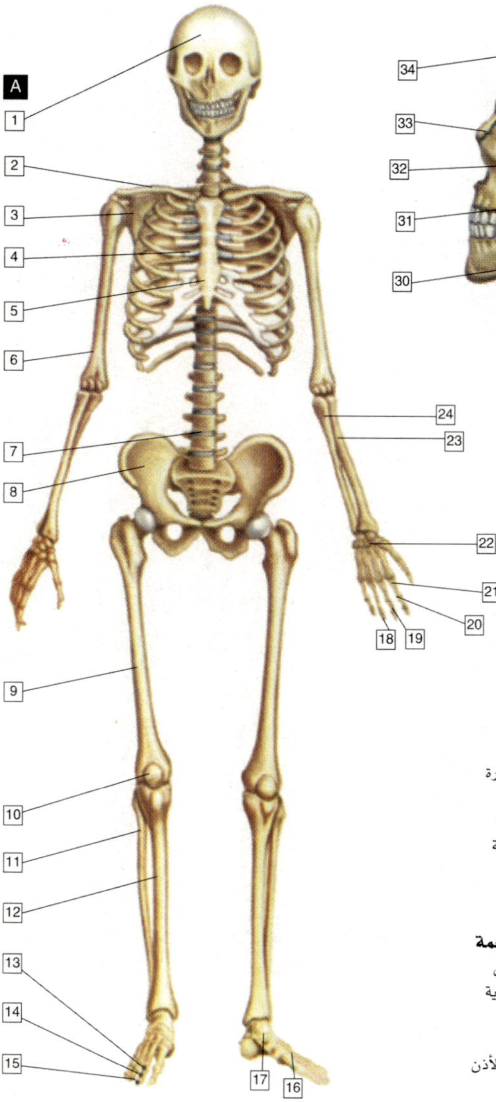

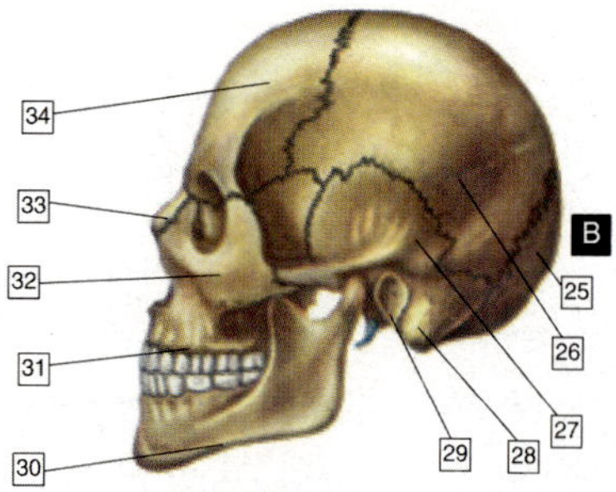

A - SKELETON
1 - SKULL
2 - CLAVICLE
3 - SCAPULA
4 - RIB
5 - STERNUM
6 - HUMERUS
7 - SPINAL COLUMN
8 - ILIAC FOSSA
9 - FEMUR
10 - PATELLA
11 - FIBULA
12 - TIBIA
13 - PHALANGES
14 - PROXIMAL PHALANGES
15 - DISTAL PHALANGES
16 - TARSAL BONES
17 - METATARSAL BONES
18 - DISTAL PHALANGES
19 - PROXIMAL PHALANGES
20 - PHALANGES
21 - METACARPAL BONES
22 - CARPAL BONES
23 - ULNA
24 - RADIUS

B - CRANIAL BONES
25 - OCCIPITAL BONE
26 - PARIETAL BONE
27 - TEMPORAL BONE
28 - MASTOID AREA
29 - EXTERNAL AUDITORY MEATUS
30 - JAW
31 - MAXILLA BONE
32 - ZYGOMATIC BONE
33 - NASAL BONES
34 - FRONTAL BONE

A - الهيكل العظمي
1 ـ الجمجمة
2 ـ الترقوة
3 ـ الكتف
4 ـ الضلع
5 ـ عظم الصدر
6 ـ العضد
7 ـ العمود الفقري
8 ـ تجويف المرقفي
9 ـ عظمةالفخذ
10 ـ العظم
11 ـ القصبة الصغرى
12 ـ قصبة الساق
13 ـ السلامى
14 ـ السلامى المجاورة
15 ـ السلامى البعيدة
16 ـ عظام الرسغ
17 ـ العظام الخاصة بمشط القدم
18 ـ السلامى البعيدة
19 ـ السلامى المجاورة
20 ـ السلامى
21 ـ العظام المشطية
22 ـ العظام الرسغية
23 ـ العظم
24 ـ عظم الساعد

B - عظام الجمجمة
25 ـ العظمة القذالي
26 ـ العظمة الجدارية
27 ـ عظم الصدغ
28 ـ منطقة عظمة صغيرة خلف الأذن
29 ـ صماخ الأذن
30 ـ الفك
31 ـ عظمة الفك
32 ـ العظم الوجني
33 ـ العظام الأنفية
34 ـ العظم الجبهي

The Muscles
العضلات

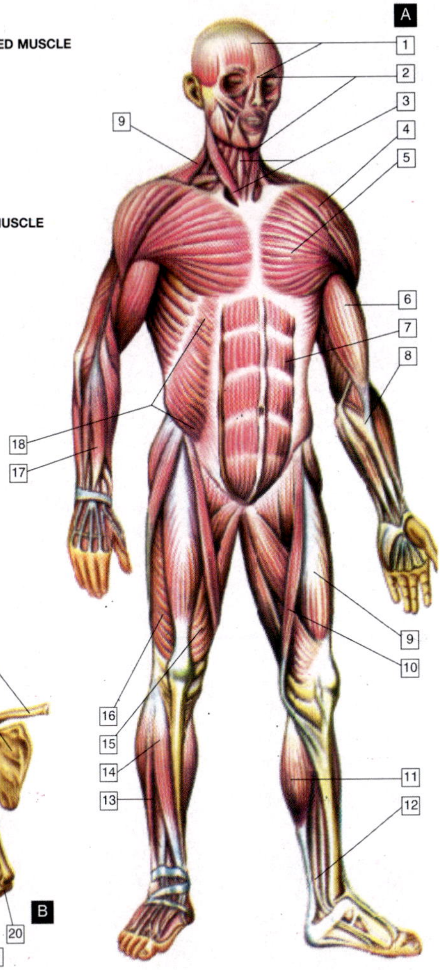

A - MUSCLES
1- SCALP MUSCLES
2 - FACIAL MUSCLES
3 - NECK MUSCLES
4 - DELTOID
5 - PECTORALIS MAJOR
6 - BICEPS
7 - RECTUS ABDOMINIS
8 - FLEXOR MUSCLE
9 - RECTUS FEMORIS
10 - SARTORIUS
11 - GASTRONEMIUS
12 - FLEXOR MUSCLE
13 - EXTENSOR DIGITORUM LONGUS
14 - TIBIALIS ANTERIOR
15 - VASTUS MEDIALIS
16 - VASTUS LATERALIS
17 - EXTENSOR DIGITORUM
18 - ABDOMINAL MUSCLES
19 - TRAPEZUS

B - CONTRACTED MUSCLE
20 - ELBOW
21 - OLNA
22 - RADIUS
23 - MUSCLE
24 - TENDON
25 - SCAPULA
26 - CLAVICLE

C - RELAXED MUSCLE
27 - TENDON
28 - HUMERUS
29 - MUSCLE

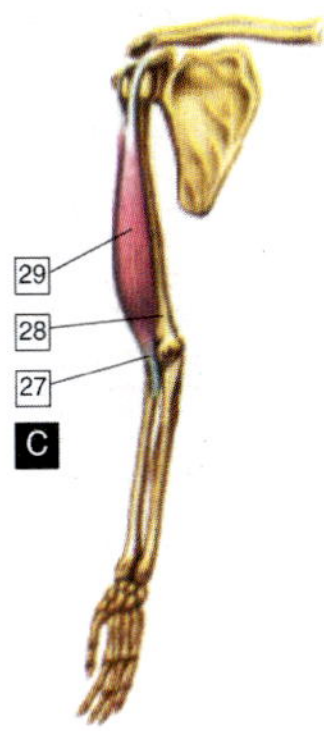

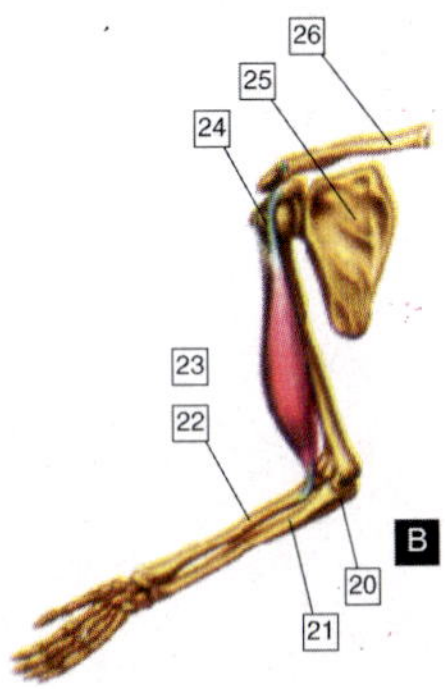

A - الهيكل العظمي
1 ـ عضلات فروة الرأس
2 ـ العضلة المتعلقة بالوجه
3 ـ عضلات الرقبة
4 ـ عضلة داليه
5 ـ عضلة الصدر
6 ـ العضلة
7 ـ أبدومينيس العضلة المستفيحة
8 ـ عضلة الثني
9 ـ فيموريس العضلة المستقيمة
10 ـ عضلة خياطية
11 ـ جاستروكنيميس
12 ـ عضلة الثني
13 ـ العضلة الباسطة
14 ـ عضلة الساق
15 ـ عضلة الفخذ الداخلية
16 ـ عضلة الفخذ السفلي
17 ـ العضلة الباسطة
18 ـ العضلات البطنية
19 ـ العضلة الشبه المنحرفة (في كل من جانبي الظهر

B - تقلص العضلة
20 ـ المرفق
21 ـ عظم
22 ـ عظم الساعد
23 ـ عضلية
24 ـ وتر
25 ـ كتف
26 ـ الترقوة

C - العضلة المسترخية
27 ـ الوتر
28 ـ عضد
29 ـ عضلة

The Respiratory System/Mouth/Teeth جهاز التَّنفُس / الفم / الأسنان

A - RESPIRATORY SYSTEM
1 - NASAL CAVITY
2 - PHARYNX
3 - THYROID CARTILAGE
4 - THYROID GLAND
5 - TRACHEA
6 - BRONCHUS
7 - RIGHT LUNG

B - MOUTH
8 - PALATE
9 - UVULA
10 - PALATINE ARCHES
11 - TONSIL
12 - TONGUE

C - TEETH
12 - MOLAR TOOTH
14 - PREMOLAR TOOTH
15 - CANINE TOOTH
16 - INCISOR TOOTH

A - جهاز التنفس
1 ـ تجويف الأنف
2 ـ البلعوم
3 ـ غضروف الدرقية
4 ـ الغدة الدرقية
5 ـ القصبة الهوائية
6 ـ الشعبة
7 ـ الرئة اليمنى

B - الفم
8 ـ الحنك
9 ـ اللهاة
10 ـ الأقواس المتمتعة بامتيازات ملكية
11 ـ اللوزة
12 ـ اللسان

C - الأسنان
13 ـ الطاحن
14 ـ سن قبل الطاحن
15 ـ الناب
16 ـ السن القاطعة

A

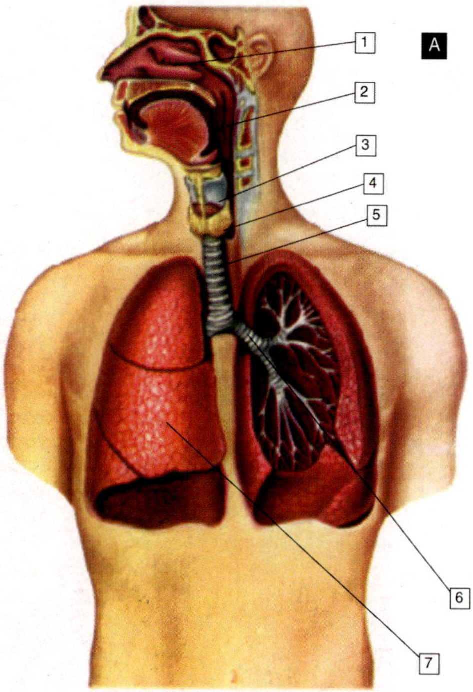

B

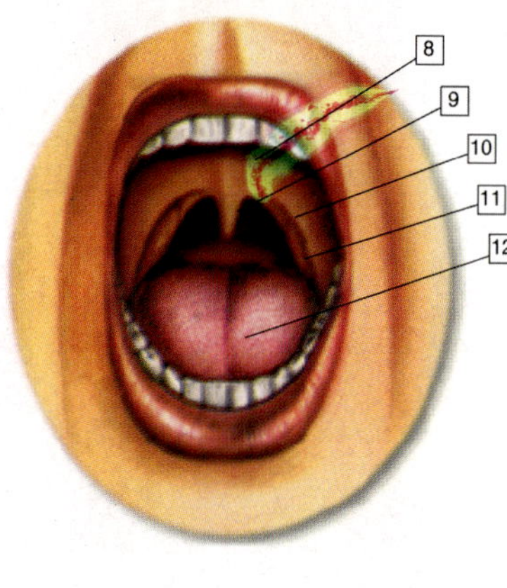

C

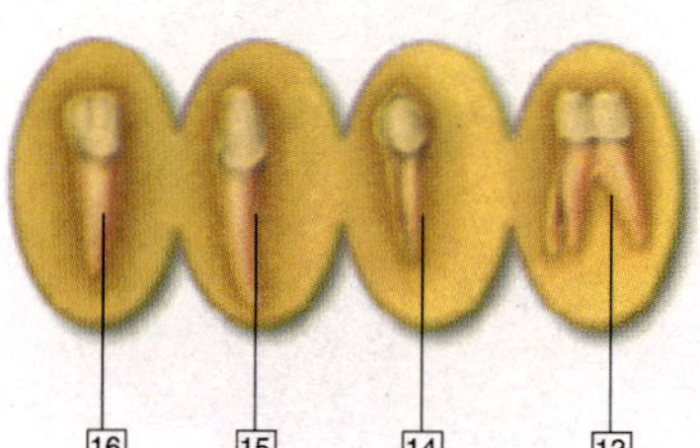

The Nervous System
الجهاز العصبي

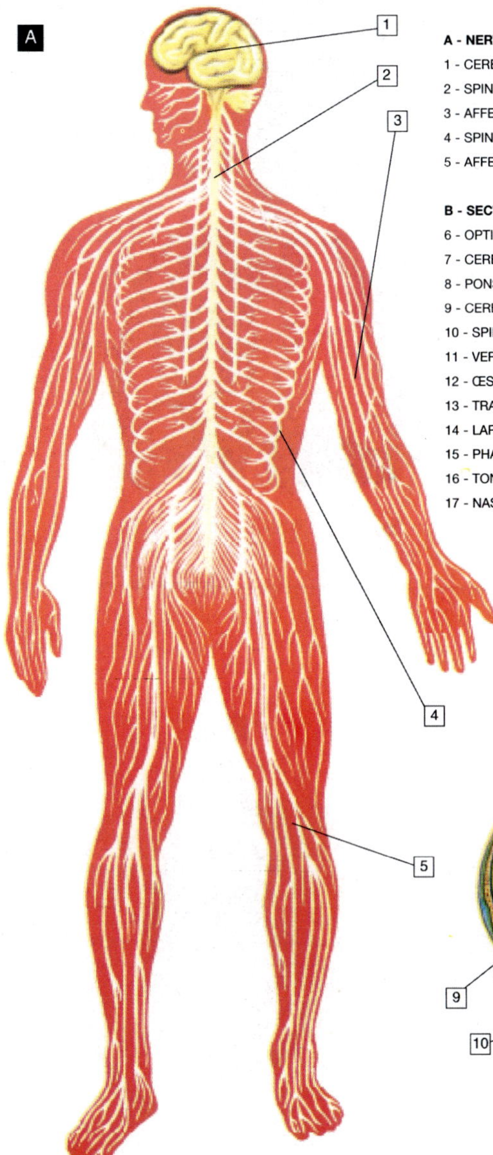

A - NERVOUS SYSTEM	**A - الجهاز العصبي**
1 - CEREBRUM	1 ـ المخ
2 - SPINAL CORD	2 ـ العصب الشوكي
3 - AFFERENT NEURON	3 ـ العصب الناقل
4 - SPINAL NERVE	4 ـ الغدة الفقرية
5 - AFFERENT NEURON	5 ـ العصب الناقل
B - SECTION OF THE BRAIN	**B - قسم المخ**
6 - OPTIC CHIASMA	6 ـ التصالب البصري
7 - CEREBRUM	7 ـ المخ
8 - PONS	8 ـ الجسر ڤارول
9 - CEREBELLUM	9 ـ المخيخ
10 - SPINAL CORD	10 ـ النخاع الشوكي
11 - VERTEBRAL COLUMN	11 ـ العمود الفقري
12 - ŒSOPHAGUS	12 ـ المريء
13 - TRACHEA	13 ـ القصبة الهوائية
14 - LARYNX	14 ـ الحنجرة
15 - PHARYNX	15 ـ البلغوم
16 - TONGUE	16 ـ اللسان
17 - NASAL FOSSAE	17 ـ الحفر الأنفية

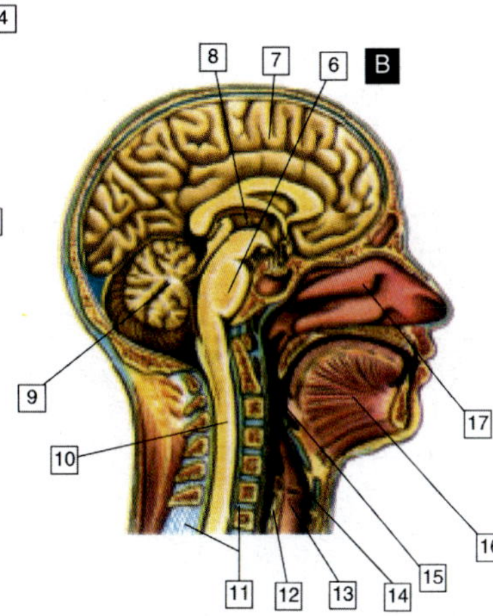

The Digestive System — الجهاز الهضمي

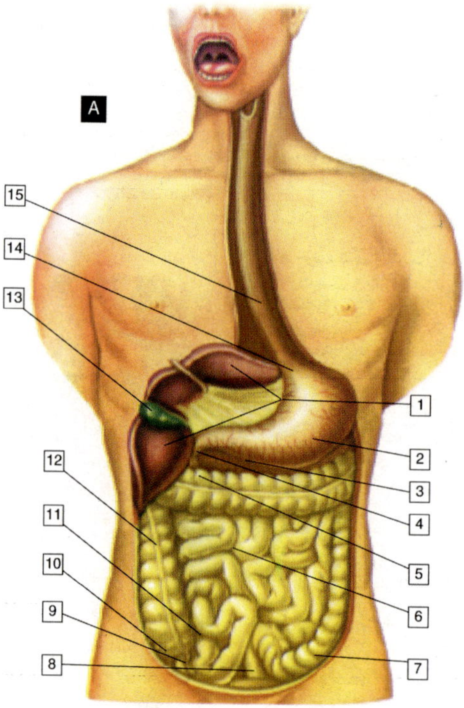

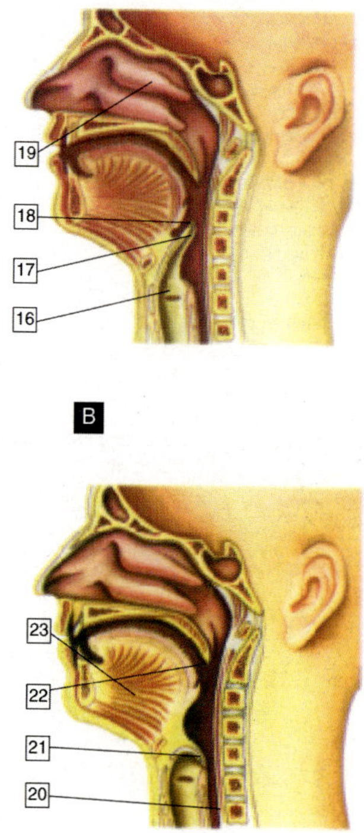

A - DIGESTIVE ORGANS
1 - LIVER
2 - STOMACH
3 - PANCREAS
4 - PYLORUS
5 - TRANSVERSE COLON
6 - SMALL INTESTINE
7 - DESCENDING COLON
8 - RECTUM
9 - APPENDIX
10 - CAECUM
11 - ILEOCAECAL VALVE
12 - ASCENDING COLON
13 - GALL- BLADDER
14 - CARDIAC STOMACH
15 - OESOPHAGUS

B - MECHANISM OF SWALLOWING
16 - LARYNX
17 - PHARYNX
18 - RAISED EPIGLOTTIS
19 - NASAL CAVITY
20 - OESOPHAGUS
21 - EPIGLOTTIS CURVED TO CLOSE THE TRACHEA
22 - PHARYNX
23 - TONGUE

A - الأعضاء الهضمية
1 ـ الكبد
2 ـ المعدة
3 ـ البنكرياس
4 ـ البواب (فتحة بين المعدة المعي)
5 ـ القولون المستعرض
6 ـ الأمعاء الدقيقة
7 ـ القولون الهابط
8 ـ المستقيم
9 ـ الزائدة الدودية
10 ـ المصران الأعور
11 ـ الأمعاء الغليظة
12 ـ القولون الصاعد
13 ـ المرارة
14 ـ المعدة القلبية
15 ـ المريء

B - ميكانيكية البلع
16 ـ الحنجرة
17 ـ البلعوم
18 ـ لسان المزمار المرفوع
19 ـ تجويف الأنف
20 ـ المريء
21 ـ انحنى لسان المزمار لإغلاق القصبة الهوائية
22 ـ البلعوم
23 ـ اللسان

The Digestive System & Heart
الجهاز الهضمي والقلب

A - DIAGRAM OF THE DIGESTIVE SYSTEM
A - OF A RUMINANT
1 - RETICULUM
2 - OMASUM
3 - RENNET
4 - INTESTINES
5 - PAUNCH
6 - OESOPHAGEAL GROOVE

B - OF A CARNIVORE
7 - OESOPHAGUS
8 - OESOPHAGUS
9 - STOMACH
10 - PANCREAS
11 - DESCENDING COLON
12 - INTESTINES
13 - RECTUM
14 - APPENDIX
15 - CAECUM
16 - ASCENDING COLON
17 - DUODENUM
18 - GALL- BLADDER
19 - LIVER

b - Diagram of the Respiratory System
20 - BRONCHIAL TUBE
21 - LUNG
22 - TRACHEA
23 - LARYNX
24 - CHOANES

C - HEART
25 - AORTA
26 - PULMONARY ARTERY
27 - PULMONARY VEIN
28 - MITRAL VALVE
29 - LEFT VENTRICLE
30 - INFERIOR VENA CAVA
31 - TRICUSPID VALVE
32 - RIGHT AURICLE
33 - SUPERIOR VENA CAVA

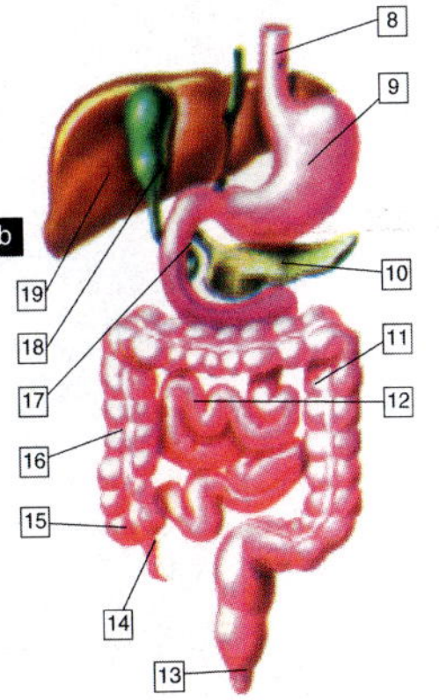

A - رسم للجهاز الهضمي
a - المجتر
1 - طاقية
2 - وريقة
3 - جلطة ثانوية
4 - معي
5 - كرش - بطن - جوف
6 - ميزاب البلعوم
7 - الحريء

B - للاحم
8 - الحريء
9 - معدة
10 - غدة البنكرياس
11 - الجزء الأعلى من المعي الغليظ
12 - معي
13 - مستقيم
14 - زائدة
15 - مصران أعور
16 - الجزء الأعلى من المعي الغليظ
17 - عفج (المعي الاثنا عشري)
18 - حويصله صفراوي (خاص بالصفراء)
19 - كبد

b - رسم للجهاز التنفسي
20 - قصبة الرئة (شعبة الهواء الداخل إلى الرئة والخارج منها)
21 - رئة
22 - أنبوب
23 - حنجرة
24 - المنخر الداخلي

C - القلب
25 - الوتين
26 - الشريان الرئوي
27 - الأوردة الرئوية
28 - الصمام التاجي
29 - البطين الشمالي
30 - الوريد الأجوف الأسفل
31 - الصمام الثلاثي الأطراف
32 - أذين القلب الأيمن
33 - الوريد الأجوف الأعلى

B

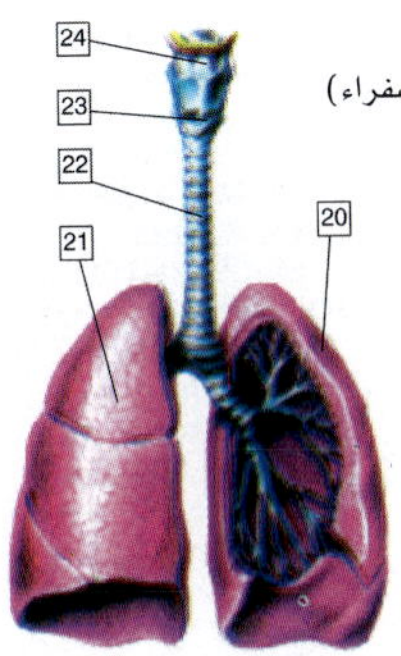

C

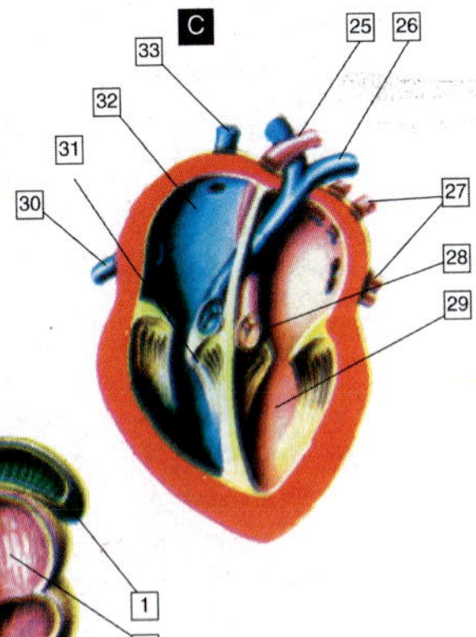

A
a

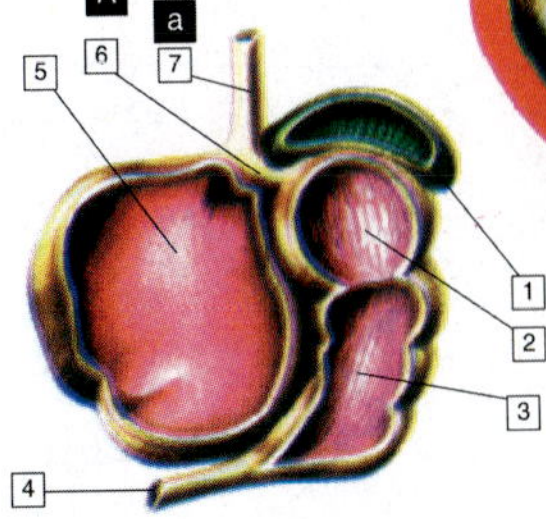

The Senses الحواس

A - OLFACTORY ORGAN

1 - OLFACTORY NERVE

2 - OLFACTORY CELLS

B - ORGAN OF TASTE

3 - EPIGLOTTIS

4 - TONSILS

5 - VALLATE PAPILLAE

6 - FUNGIFORM PAPILLAE

7 - FILIFORM PAPILLAE

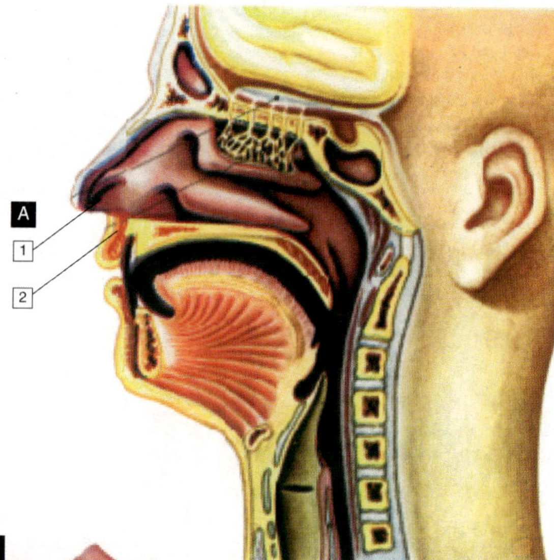

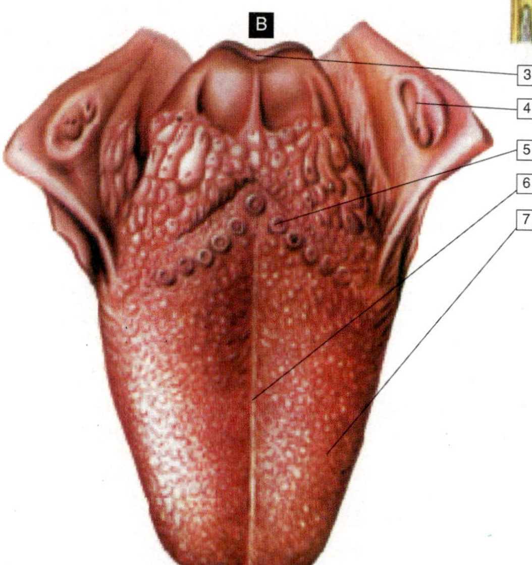

A - عضو الشم

1 - عصب الشم

2 - خلايا الشم

B - عضو المذاق

3 - لسان المزمار

4 - اللوزات

5 - حلمة كأسية الشكل

6 - حلمة فطرية الشكل

7 - الحلمات الخيطية

The Senses الحواس

A - THE EYE | **A - العين**

1- EYEBALL — 1ـ المقلة
2 - LEVATOR OF UPPER LID — 2ـ عضلة دافعة الجفن العلوي
3 - RECTUS SUPERIOR MUSCLE — 3ـ العضلة المستقيمة الرئيسية
4 - RECTUS LATERALIS MUSCLE — 4ـ العضلة المستقيمة الجانبية
5 - RECTUS INFERIOR MUSCLE — 5ـ العضلة المستقيمة السفلى
6 - OBLIQUE INFERIOR MUSCLE — 6ـ العضلة المنحرفة السفلى

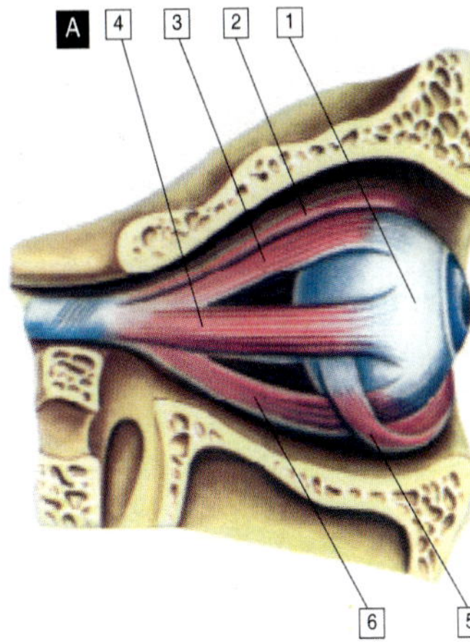

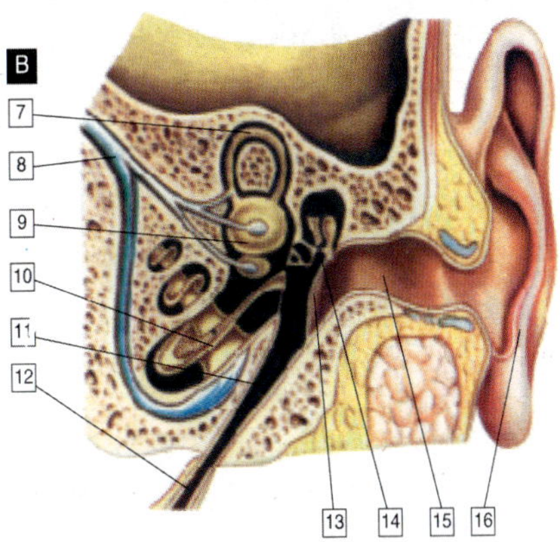

B - THE EAR | **B - العين**

7 - SEMICIRCULAR CANALS — 7ـ قنوات شبه دائرية
8 - AUDITORY NERVE — 8ـ العصب السمعي
9 - UTRICULUS — 9ـ أذن الباطنة
10 - COCHLEA — 10ـ القوقعة
11 - TYMPANIC — 11ـ التجويف المتعلق بطبلة الأذن
12 - EUSTACHIAN TUBE — 12ـ القناة السمعية
13 - EAR- DRUM — 13ـ طبلة الأذن
14 - CHAIN OF AUDITORY OSSICLES — 14ـ سلسلة العظيمات السمعية
15 - AUDITORY DUCT — 15ـ الماسورة السمعية
16 - EXTERNAL EAR — 16ـ الأذن الخارجية

C - SKIN RECEPTORS | **C - أعضاء حس الجلد**

a - Section of skin under the microscop | **a - قسم الجلد تحت الميكروسكوب**

17 - HAIR — 17ـ الشعر
18 - SENSORY CORPUSCLES — 18ـ كرات الدم الحسية
19 - DERMIS — 19ـ الأادمة
20 - SWEAT GLAND — 20ـ الغدة العرقية
21 - HAIR BULB — 21ـ بصلة الشعرة
22 - NERVES — 22ـ الأعصاب
23 - EPIDERMIS — 23ـ البشرة

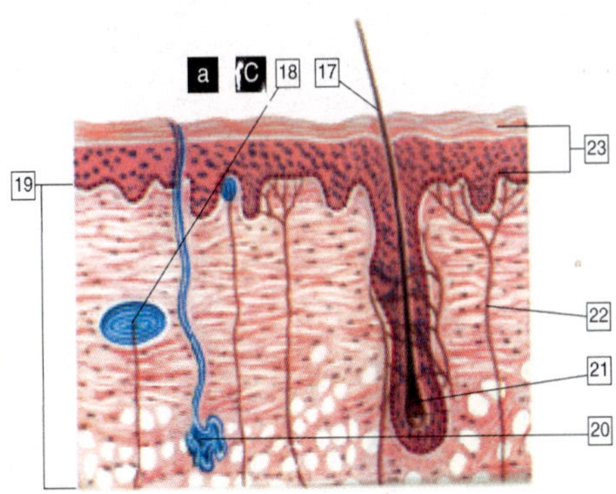

Electric Drill — المثقب الكهربائي

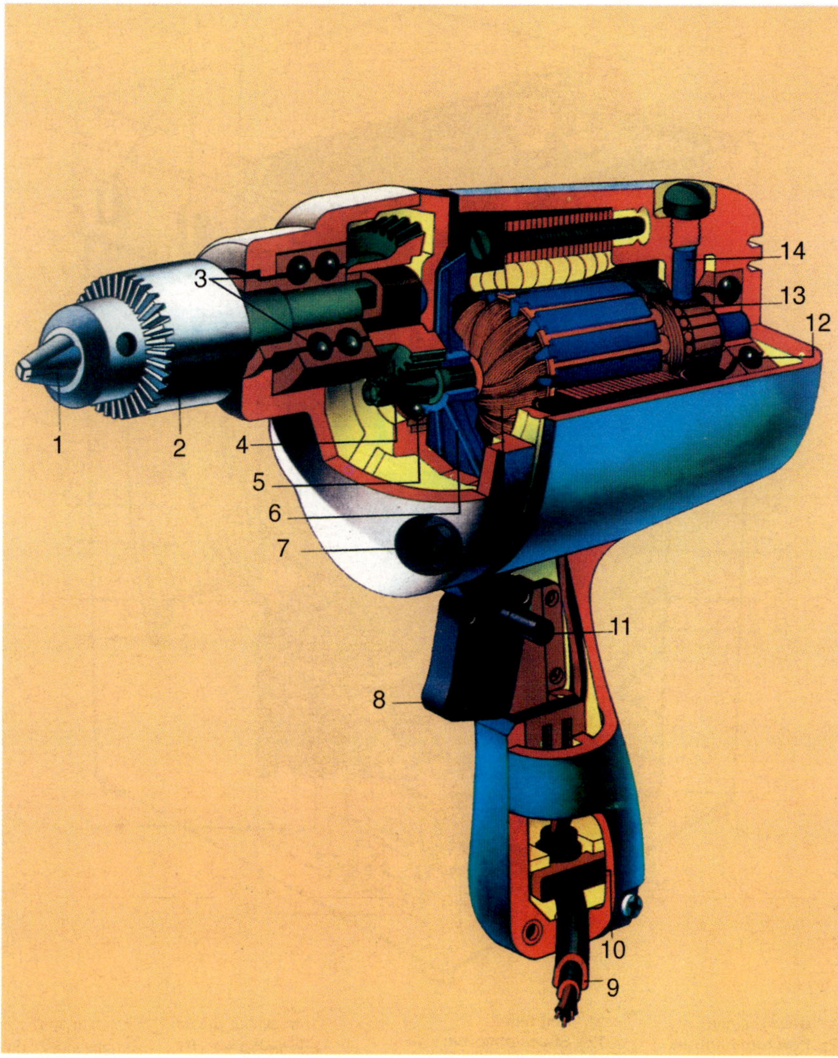

1 - Chuck jaws
2 - Chuck
3 - Chuck bearings
4 - Gears
5 - Front motor bearings
6 - Cooling fan
7 - Rotor windings
8 - On-off switch
9 - 3-Core cable
10 - Cable grip
11 - Switch lock
12 - Rear motor bearings
13 - Commutator
14 - Brush

1 ـ فك الظرف.
2 ـ الظرف.
3 ـ دلانين الظرف.
4 ـ التروس.
5 ـ دلافين المحرك الأمامية.
6 ـ مروحة التبريد.
7 ـ لفائف الدوار.
8 ـ مفتاح وصل/ قطع.
9 ـ كبل بثلاثة قلوب.
10 ـ مسكة الكبل.
11 ـ قفل مفتاح التشغيل.
12 ـ دلافين المحرك الخلفية.
13 ـ عاكس التيار.
14 ـ الفرجون (الفرشاة).

Washing Machine الغسالة

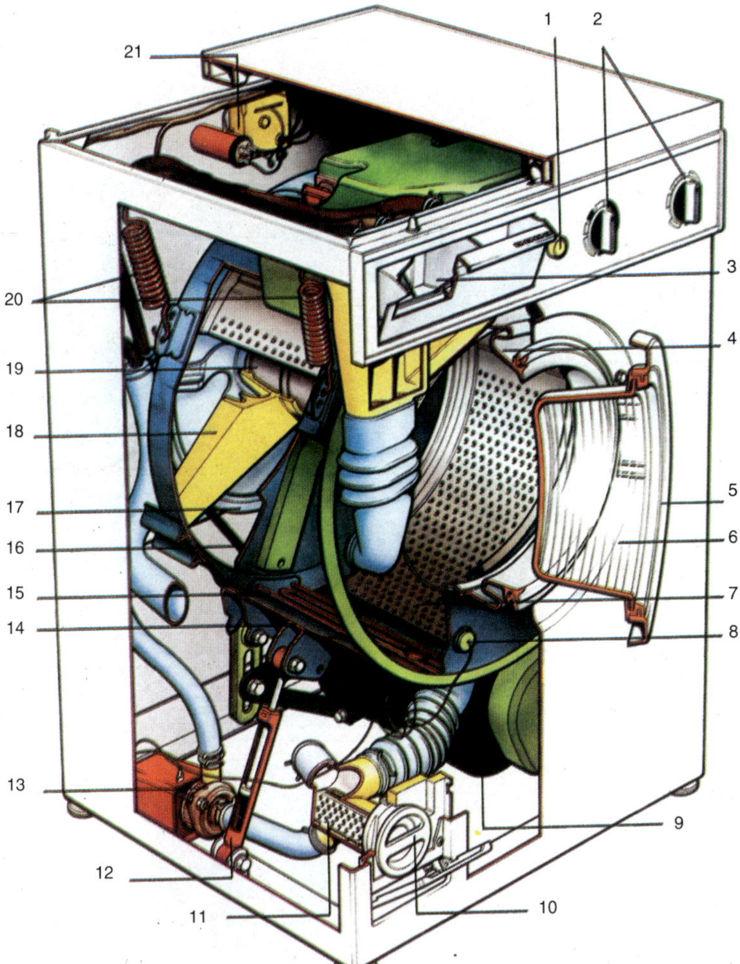

1 - Door release
2 - Program controls
3 - Dispensers for detergent and fabric conditioner
4 - Door seal
5 - Door glass
6 - Cooling fan
7 - Revolving inner drum
8 - Thermostat sensor
9 - Motor
10 - Filter access panel
11 - Lint filter
12 - Shock absorber
13 - Drain pump
14 - Fixed outer drum
15 - 3 K W heater
16 - Drive belt
17 - Drum pulley
18 - Drum support
19 - Drum bearings
20 - Outer drum suspension springs
21 - Control circuits

1 ـ زر اعتاق الباب
2 ـ زر التحكم بالبرامج
3 ـ أوعية مادة التنظيف وتكييف كميتها
4 ـ مسكة الباب
5 ـ زجاج الباب
6 ـ مروحة التبريد
7 ـ الطبلة الداخلية الدوارة
8 ـ مجَس الترموستات
9 ـ المحرك
10 ـ لوحة الوصول إلى المرشح
11 ـ مرشح الغسالات
12 ـ ممَص الصدمات
13 ـ مَضخة تصريف المياه
14 ـ الطبلة الخارجية الثابتة
15 ـ سخان بقوة 3 كيلواط
16 ـ سير التشغيل
17 ـ رافعة الطبلة
18 ـ دعامة الطبلة
19 ـ دلافين الطبلة
20 ـ زنبركات تعليق الطبلة الخارجية
21 ـ دوائر التحكم بالتشغيل

The Lathe المخرطة

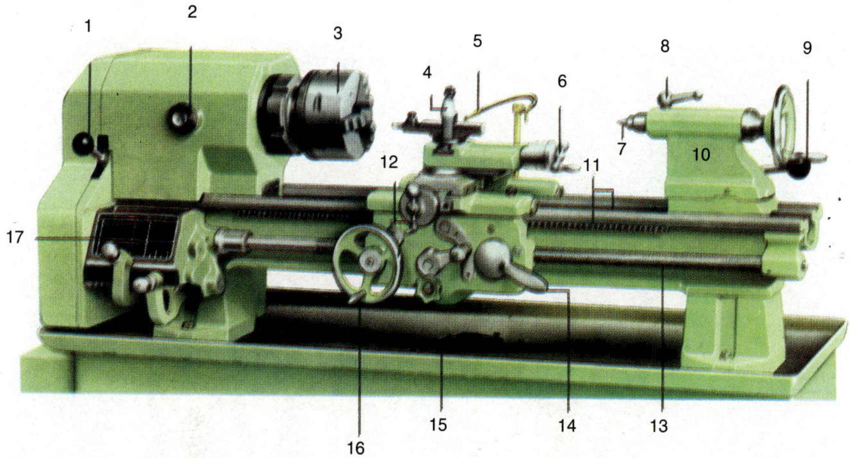

How does the Lathe operate and what are its components?

The Late is used to cut cylindrical parts or to groove screws. The toolpost is pixed inside a chuck installed on the headstock. The headstock contains the feedscrews that transmit movement from an electric motor to the chuck. On the other side of the lathe is the tailstock that can be used to fix the right end in a longitudinal clamp during operation. The cutting tool is clamped in a feed-shaft along the base of the lathe between the headstock and the tail stock.

The main components of the lathe are:

1 - Lever for reversing spindle direction
2 - Spindle lock
3 - Three jawed chuck
4 - Toolpost
5 - Cutting oil delivery
6 - Toolpost traverse
7 - Centre
8 - Longitudinal clamp
9 - Tailstock clamp
10 - Tailstock
11 - Slideways
12 - Crossfeed
13 - Feedscrew (feed shaft is between sideways)
14 - Feedscrew clamp
15 - Drain for cutting oil
16 - Carriage traverse
17 - Feed gaar box

كيف تعمل المخرطة وما هي أجزاؤها المكونة؟

تستعمل المخرطة لقطع وتدوير أجزاء اسطوانية أو لتحزيز اللوالب على هذه الأجزاء. تثبت لوحة العمل داخل ظرف مركب على غراب الرأس (أي لمحمل الجزء الدوار) الموجود على الطرف الأيسر للآلة. يحتوي غراب الرأس على التروس التي تنقل الحركة من محرك كهربائي إلى الظرف. يوجد في الطرف الآخر من الآلة غراب الذيل الذي يمكن استعماله لتثبيت الطرف الأيمن في قطعة محمل طويلة خلال عملية الخرط. تقمط أداة القطع في قضيب عدة مركب على تجحيفة الحامل التي تتحرك على مسارات انزلاقية على امتداد قاعدة المخرطة بين غراب الرأس وغراب الذيل وتوجيه أداة القطع بواسطة لولب رئيسي.

أما الأجزاء المكونة للمخرطة فهي:

1 ـ عتلة لعكس اتجاه المبرم.
2 ـ قفل المبرم.
3 ـ ظرف بثلاثة فكوك.
4 ـ قضيب العدة.
5 ـ أنبوب تزويد الزيت لأداة القطع.
6 ـ أداة لإحداث الحركة الجانبية لقضيب القطع.
7 ـ المركز.
8 ـ القامطة الطولية.
9 ـ قامطة ذيل الغراب.
10 ـ ذيل الغراب.
11 ـ التغذية المستعرضة.
12 ـ التغذية الجانبية.
13 ـ علبة تروس جهاز التغذية.
14 ـ أداة لإحداث الحركة الجانبية للحامل.
15 ـ مصرف زيت القطع.
16 ـ قامطة لولب التغذية.
17 ـ لولب التغذية.

The Sewing Machine آلة الخياطة

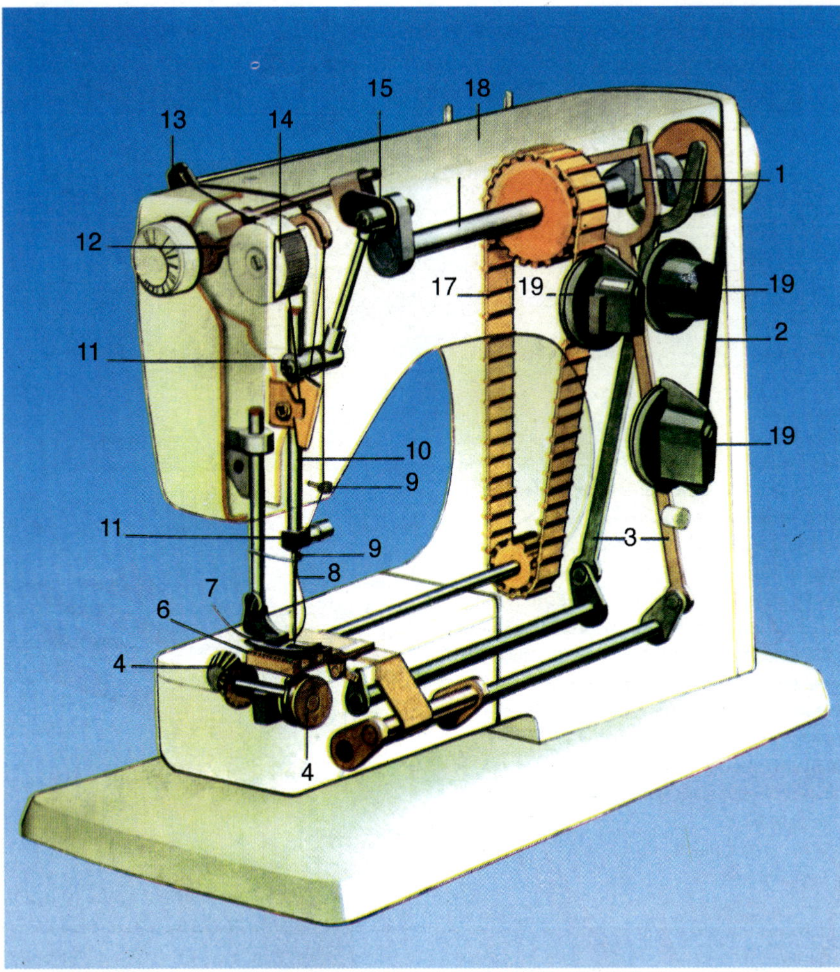

1 - Feed dog cams
2 - Drive belt from motor via gearbox
3 - Feed dog linkages
4 - Bobin and rotary hook
5 - Rotary hook drive
6 - Feed dog
7 - Upper thread
8 - Needle
9 - Thread guides
10 - Needle bar
11 - Needle bar guides
12 - Thread take-up
13 - Thread guide
14 - Thread tensioner
15 - Drive linkage for needle bar and thread take-up
16 - Upper shaft
17 - Thoothed belt drives lower shaft at double speed
18 - Outer casing
19 - Control switches

1 ـ كامات كلاب التغذية.
2 ـ سير الإدارة من المحرك عبر علبة التروس.
3 ـ وصلات ربط كلاب التغذية.
4 ـ المكوك والكلاب الدوار.
5 ـ آلية إدارة الكلاب الدوار.
6 ـ كلاب التغذية.
7 ـ الخيط الأعلى.
8 ـ الإبرة.
9 ـ موجهات الخيط.
10 ـ قضيب الإبرة.
11 ـ موجهات قضيب الإبرة.
12 ـ أداة التقاط الخيط.
13 ـ موجه الخيط.
14 ـ أداة توتير الخيط.
15 ـ وصلة ربط آلية الإدارة لقضيب الإبرة وأداة التقاط الخيط.
16 ـ عمود الإدارة الأعلى.
17 ـ عمود الإدارة الأسفل لتشغيل السير المسنن عند سرعة مزدوجة.
18 ـ الغلاف الخارجي.
19 ـ مفاتيح التحكم بالتشغيل.

The Bicycle الدراجة الهوائية

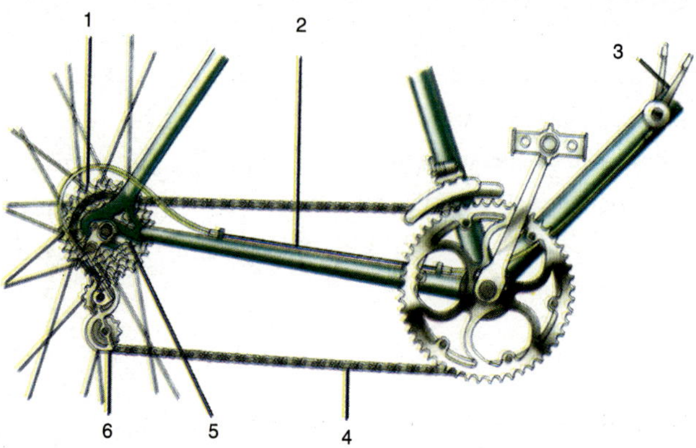

When was the bicycle invented?

In 1839, Kirkpatrick Memillan made the first bicycle operated by way of a foot pedal. Bicycles are manufactured in many countries across the world.

1 - Low gear
2 - Gear control cable
3 - Hand lever
4 - Chain
5 - High gear
6 - Tension pinion

متى تمّ ابتكار الدراجة الهوائية؟

في عام 1839م صنع كيركباتريك ماكميلان أول دراجة هوائية تسير بدواسة قدم. تصنع الدراجات الهوائية في العديد من الدول عبر العالم.

1 ـ الترس الأسفل
2 ـ كبل التحكم بالترس
3 ـ عتلة يدوية
4 ـ السلسلة
5 ـ الترس الأعلى
6 ـ الترس الصغير للتوتير

The Motorcycle · الدراجة النارية

When was the first motorcycle produced? And what are its component parts?

The German Goetleb Daimler made the first single-cylinder motorcycle operating on petrol.

Its main component parts are:

1 - Fuel tanks
2 - Cockpit airing
3 - Turn indicator
4 - Telescopic front fork
5 - Twin disc brakes
6 - Horizontaly-opposed twin cylinder engine
7 - Carburettor
8 - Footbrake
9 - Gearbox and final drive shaft
10 - Rear suspension
11 - Drum brake
12 - Rear lights
13 - Saddle

متى تمَّ صنع الدراجة النارية وما هي أجزاؤها المكونة؟

صنع غوتليب ديملر الالماني أول دراجة نارية ذات أسطوانة واحدة تسير بالبنزين.

أما أجزاؤها المكونة فهي:

1 ـ خزانات الوقود.
2 ـ تهوية ركن السائق.
3 ـ مؤشر الاستدارة.
4 ـ مشعب أمامي متراكب.
5 ـ مكابح قرصية مزدوجة.
6 ـ محرك بأسطوانتين متقابلتين أفقياً.
7 ـ المكربن (كاربوريتور).
8 ـ مكبح قدمي.
9 ـ علبة التروس وعمود الإدارة النهائي.
10 ـ زنبرك التعليق الخلفي.
11 ـ طبلة الكبح.
12 ـ أضواء خلفية.
13 ـ سرج السائق.

The Missile
الصاروخ

كيف يعمل الصاروخ وما هي أجزاؤه المكونة؟

الصاروخ هو ببساطة جهاز أو مركبة يدفعها طرد دفق من الغاز. تولد المادة (الغاز) المنطلق قوة معادلة ومعاكسة للمركبة بالذات. لا يطير الصاروخ ولكنه يستمر في رحلته تحت تأثير الزخم أو كمية التحرك. وهكذا يستمر الصاروخ في الارتفاع إلى أن تتوقف قوة الزخم أو كمية التحرك فيبدأ بالهبوط نحو الأرض تحت تأثير جاذبيتها على شكل قوس يماثل القوس الذي اتخذه لدى إطلاقه. استعمل للمرة الأولى الصاروخ من قبل الفرنسيين ضد القوات البريطانية في نيو اورليانز، الولايات المتحدة.

إن الأجزاء المكونة للصاروخ هي بالنسبة للصاروخ ساتورن 5.

1 ـ المحرك جاى 2.
2 ـ مرحلة صعود المركبة القمرية.
3 ـ مرحلة نزول المركبة القمرية.
4 ـ خزان الهيدروجين السائل.
5 ـ خزان الأوكسجين السائل.
6 ـ كرات الهليوم.
7 ـ المحرك جاى 2.
8 ـ خزان الهيدروجين السائل.
9 ـ خزان الأوكسجين السائل.
10 ـ 5 محركات جاى 2.
11 ـ خزان الأوكسجين السائل.
12 ـ حواجز خزان الأوكسجين السائل.
13 ـ أنابيب نقل الأوكسجين السائل.
14 ـ خزان الكيروسين.
15 ـ أنابيب تحويل الوقود.
16 ـ 5 محركات نوع اف 1.

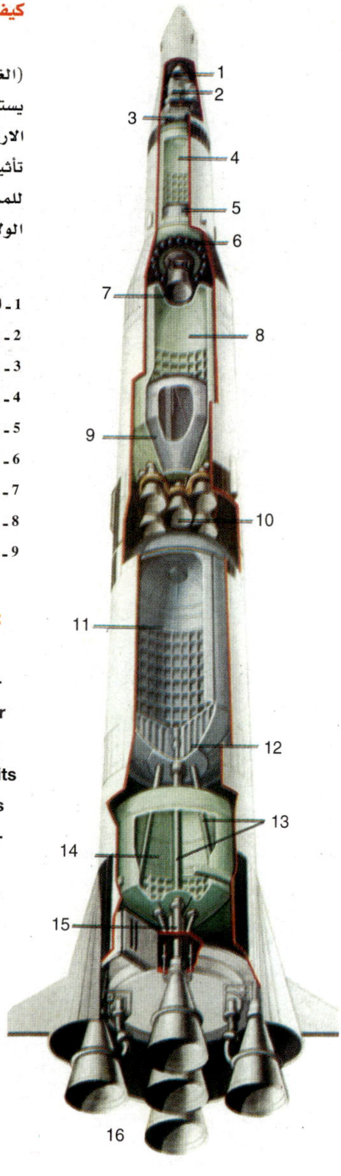

How does a missile operate? And what are its component parts?

The missile is an engine or a vehicle propelled by the expulsion of gas that creates the equalizing and counteracting power of the vehicle itself. The missile does not fly but continues its journey under the influence of momentum. Thus it proceeds in its ascent until the force of momentum ceases its influence. At this moment, it starts its descent toward the ground under the influence of the farth's gravitational force. The French army used in New Orleans, U.S. for the first time a missile against the British forces there.

The main components of a Saturn-5 Missile are:

1 - J-2 engine
2 - Lunar module ascent stage
3 - Lunar module ascent stage
4 - Fuel tank (L/hydrogen)
5 - Lox tank
6 - Helium spheres twin
7 - J-2 engine
8 - Fuel tank (L/hydrogen)
9 - Lox tank
10 - 5 J-2 engines
11 - Lox tank
12 - Lox tank baffles
13 - Liquid oxygen (lox) transfer pipes
14 - Fuel tank (kerosene)
15 - Fuel transfer pipes
16 - Five F-1 engines

Power الطاقـة

1 - Reservoir
2 - Dam
3 - River
4 - Cables
5 - Power plant
6 - Cooling tower
7 - Fuel Reservoir
8 - Fuel waste
9 - Crane
10 - Oil rig
11 - Storage tank

1 ـ خزان مياه
2 ـ سد مائي
3 ـ نهر
4 ـ كابلات كهربائية
5 ـ محطة توليد الطاقة
6 ـ برج تبريد
7 ـ خزان وقود
8 ـ نفايات الوقود
9 ـ رافعة
10 ـ منصة حفر لاستخراج النفط
11 ـ صهريج تخزين

World Writers and Poets — أدباء وشعراء عالميون

Burns, Robert
بيرنز، روبرت

Scottish poet 1759 -1796

شاعر اسكتلندي 1759 ـ 1796

Browning, Elizabeth Barrett
براوننغ، اليزابيت باريت

A cripple British poetess of world repute 1806 -1861

أديبة بريطانية مقعدة ذات شهرة عالمية

1806 ـ 1861

Austen, Jane
أوستن، جين

A British novelist that described in her novels the life of the Middle Classes in England 1775 -1817

روائية بريطانية تحدثت في مؤلفاتها عن حياة الطبقة المتوسطة في بريطانيا.

1775 ـ 1817

Browning, Robert
براوننغ، روبرت

British poet who sympathized with the poor in his poems 1812 -1889

شاعر بريطاني. تميزت اعماله بالعطف الشامل على الطبقة الفقيرة 1812 ـ 1889

Byron, George Gordon
بايرون، جورج غوردون

British poet, fighter and supporter of the Greek independence 1788 -1824

شاعر بريطاني حارب من اجل استقلال اليونان 1788 ـ 1824

Alcoforado, Marianna
الكوفورادو، ماريانا

Portuguese novelist, known as the Portuguese Saint 1683 -1733

روائية برتغالية اشتهرت باسم القديسة البرتغالية 1683 ـ 1733

Cervantes, Saavedra De
سرفانتس، سافيدرا دي

Spanish writer author of "Don Quixote" 1547 - 1616

روائي اسباني كتب قصة «دون كيشوت» التي ترجمت الى 80 لغة عالمية

1547 ـ 1616

Baudelaire, Charles
بودلير، شارل

French poet, author of the book "Fleurs du Mal" 1821 -1867

شاعر فرنسي مؤلف ديوان الشعر «ازهار الشر» 1821 ـ 1867

Balzac, Honoré De
بلزاك، هونوريه دي

French writer. One of the pillars of the Existensialist School 1799 -1850

روائي فرنسي من اشهر مؤلفاته «المهزلة البشرية» وهو أحد رواد المدرسة الوجودية 1799 ـ 1850

World Writers and Poets أدباء وشعراء عالميون

Dostoevski, Feodor Mikhailovich
دستويفسكي، فيودور ميخايلوفيتش

Russian novelist author of "The Brothers Karamazov" 1821-1881

قصصي روسي مؤلف قصة «الاخوة كارامازوف» 1821 ـ 1881

D'Annunzio, Gabriele
دانونزيو، غبريال

Italian poet, novelist and playright 1863 -1938

شاعر وكاتب مسرحيات ايطالي شهير 1863 ـ 1938

Caroll, Lewis
كارول، لويس

British novelist author of "Alice in Wonderland" 1832 - 1898

مؤلف قصصي بريطاني ألّف كتاب «أليس في بلاد العجائب» 1832 ـ 1898

Dickens, Charles
ديكنز، شارلس

British popular novelist 1812 -1870

قصصي بريطاني كتب قصصاً شعبية ناجحة 1812 ـ 1870

Dumas, Alexandre, (Père)
دوماس، الكسندر (الاب)

French novelist wrote several historical novels 1802 -1870

روائي فرنسي، وضع عدداً كبيراً من الروايات التاريخية 1802 ـ 1870

Chaucer, Geoffrey
شوسر، جيوفري

One of the greatest British poets author of "Canterbury Tales" 1340 -1400

احد كبار الشعراء البريطانيين مؤلف ديوان الشعر «حكايات كانتربوري» 1340 ـ 1400

Emerson, Ralph Waldo
اميرسون، رالف والدو

American philosopher and poet 1803 -1882

كاتب وفيلسوف وشاعر اميركي 1803 ـ 1882

Dreiser, Theodore
درايسر، ثيودور

American novelist. One of the pillars of the Naturalist School 1871 -1945

أديب ومؤلف وقصصي أميركي، أحد رواد المدرسة الطبيعية 1871 ـ 1945

Dante, Alighieri
دانتي، اليجيري

The greatest and world-known Italian poet author of "The Divine Comedy" 1265 -1321

اشهر شاعر ايطالي مؤلف ديوان «المهزلة الالهية» 1265 ـ 1321

World Writers and Poets أدباء وشعراء عالميون

Henry, O
هنري، أو

American novelist who described in his books the popular life in New York 1862 - 1910

أديب اميركي، وصف في مؤلفاته الحياة الشعبية في نيويورك 1862 ـ 1910

Hardy, Thomas
هاردي، توماس

British novelist and poet. One of the greatest writers in the Victorian Era 1840 -1928

أديب وروائي بريطاني. احد اشهر الأدباء في العصر الفكتوري 1840 ـ 1928

Hugo, Victor Marie
هوغو، فكتور

French poet, playright and novelist. Author of "Les Misérables" 1802 - 1885

شاعر وروائي وكاتب مسرحي فرنسي. مؤلف قصة «البؤساء» 1802 ـ 1885

Grimm, Jakob & Wilhelm
جريم، جاكوب وويلهلم

Two German writers who wrote popular legends under the form of novels

كاتبان المانيان ألّفا اساطير شعبية على شكل قصص

Gorki, Maxim
غوركي، ماكسيم

Russian novelist and playright 1868-1936

روائي وكاتب مسرحي روسي 1868 ـ 1936

Goethe, Johann Wolfgang
غوته، جوهان وولفغانغ

The greatest German poet of all times. Author of "The Misfortunes of Fritz" 1749 -1832

شاعر الماني شهير. ألّف ديوان آلام فرتز 1749 ـ 1832

Eliot, George
ايليوت، جورج

The pen name of the British novelist Anne Evans author of "Silas Marner" 1819 - 1880

الاسم المستعار للكاتبة البريطانية آن ايفانز مؤلفة كتاب «سيلاس مارنر» 1819 ـ 1880

France, Anatole
فرانس، اناتول

French novelist and writer. Obtained the Noble Prize for Litterature 1844 - 1924

اديب فرنسي حاصل على جائزة نوبل للادب. 1844 ـ 1924

Fenelon, François
فينيلون، فرانسوا

French novelist author of "The Adventures of Télémaque" 1651 -1715

كاتب فرنسي من اشهر مؤلفاته «مغامرات تيليماك» 1651 ـ 1715

World Writers and Poets أدباء وشعراء عالميون

Longfellow, Henry Wadsworth
لونغفيللو، هنري وودزوورث

American poet famous for his historical poems 1807 - 1882

شاعر اميركي اشتهر باشعاره التاريخية 1807 ـ 1882

Johnson, Samuel
جونسون، صموئيل

British writer, critic and author of encyclopedias 1709 -1784

كاتب وناقد ادبي ومؤلف موسوعات بريطاني 1709 ـ 1784

Heine, Heinrich
هاينه، هاينريخ

German poet considered as the greatest lyrical poets of Germany 1797 - 1856

شاعر الماني اعتبر اعظم شاعر غنائي الماني 1797 ـ 1856

Lagerlof, Selma
لاغرلوف، سلما

Swedish novelist. Holder of the Noble Prize for Litterature 1858 - 1940

روائية واديبة سويدية. حصلت على جائزة نوبل للآداب. 1858 ـ 1940

Kipling, Rudyard
كيبلنغ، روديارد

British poet and novelist. Author of the famous novel "Kim" 1865-1936

شاعر وقصصي بريطاني ألّف رواية كيم 1865 ـ 1936

Homer
هوميروس

Greek poet. Author of "The Iliad" and "The Odyssey". The dates of his birth and death are unknown (probably around the end of the eighth century B.C)

شاعر اغريقي مؤلف ملحمتيّ الإلياذة والاوديسة لا يعرف بالضبط تاريخ ولادته ولا تاريخ وفاته (ربما في اواخر القرن الثامن قبل الميلاد)

Mickiewicz, Adam
ميكييفيش، آدام

The greatest polish poet 1798 -1855

اشهر شعراء بولونيا على الاطلاق 1798 ـ 1855

Keats, John
كيتس، جون

One of the pillars of the romantic school in Britain 1795 -1821

شاعر بريطاني احد قادة المدرسة الرومنطيقية في الادب 1795 ـ 1821

Ibsen, Henrik
ابسن، هنريك

One of the greatest Norwegian poets and playrights of all times 1828 -1906

شاعر نرويجي. من أشهر روائيّي المسرح العالمي 1828 ـ 1906

World Writers and Poets

أدباء وشعراء عالميون

Raleigh, Walter
رالي، والتر

British explorer and politican. King James I ordered his execution 1554 -1618

مستكشف وكاتب وسياسي بريطاني حكم عليه الملك جيمس الأول بالاعدام

1618 ـ 1554

Paine, Thomas
بين، توماس

American writer of British origin. Author of the book "The Rights of Man" 1737 - 1809

مؤلف اميركي من اصل بريطاني ألّف كتاب حقوق الانسان 1737 ـ 1809

Maupassant, Guy De
موباسان، غي دي

French writer of short stories 1850 -1893

مؤلف فرنسي للقصة القصيرة

1893 ـ 1850

Rabelais, François
رابليه، فرانسوا

French writer. Author of the book "Pentagruel" 1493 -1553

كاتب فرنسي مشهور. له كتاب «بنتاغرويل» 1493 ـ 1553

Pope, Alexander
بوب، الكسندر

British poet, translated in English Homer's Odyssey 1688 -1744

شاعر بريطاني ترجم ملحمة «الأوديسة» لهوميروس 1688 ـ 1744

Milton, John
ملتون، جون

British poet considered the greatest affer Shakespeare. Author of "The Lost Paradise". 1608 -1674

شاعر واديب بريطاني احتل المقام الثاني بين شعراء ما بعد شكسبير. له «الفردوس المفقود» 1608 ـ 1674

Rousseau, Jean -Jacques
روسو، جان ـ جاك

French writer. The pillar of the Romantic School in litterature 1712 -1778

مؤلف وفيلسوف فرنسي، رائد المدرسة الرومنطيقية في الادب 1712 ـ 1778

Pushkin, Alexander
بوشكين، الكسندر

Russian poet, novelist and playright 1799 - 1837

شاعر وروائي وكاتب مسرحيات روسي

1837 ـ 1799

Poe, Edgar Allan
بو، ادغار آلان

American poet and writer. Author of several short stories 1809 -1849

شاعر وروائي رومنطيقي اميركي اشتهر بقصصه 1809 ـ 1849

World Writers and Poets أدباء وشعراء عالميون

Shelley, Percy Bysshe
شيلي، بيرسي بيش

British poet. One of the greatest lyrical poets 1792 -1822

شاعر بريطاني احد اشهر الشعراء الرومنطيقيين 1792 ـ 1822

Scott, Walter
سكوت، والتر

Scottish novelist, author of "Ivanhoe" 1771 -1832

روائي وشاعر اسكتلندي مؤلف قصة ايفانهو 1771 ـ 1832

Sand, George
ساند، جورج

Pen name of Armentine Aurore. French novelist and writer 1804-1876

الاسم المستعار للكاتبة الفرنسية ارمنتين اورور. الفت روايات عديدة 1804 ـ 1876

Stael, Madame De
ستايل، مدام دي

Fren :h novelist of world fame 1766 -1817

قاصّة فرنسية ذات شهرة عالمية 1766 ـ 1817

Shakespeare, William
شكسبير، ويليام

The greatest British poet of world repute 1564 -1616

روائي مسرحي وشاعر بريطاني يملك شهرة عالمية لا مثيل لها 1564 ـ 1616

Sappho
سافو

Greek poetess. The dates of her birth and death are unknown (Probably at the beginning of the seventh century B.C.)

شاعرة اغريقية، تاريخ ولادتها كما تاريخ وفاتها غير مؤكدين (ربما في أوائل القرن السابع واواخر القرن السادس قبل الميلاد)

Stowe, Harriet Beecher
ستو، هارييت بيشر

American novelist, author of the book "The Cabin of Uncle Tom" 1811-1896

قصصية اميركية الفت قصة «كوخ العم طوم» 1811 ـ 1896

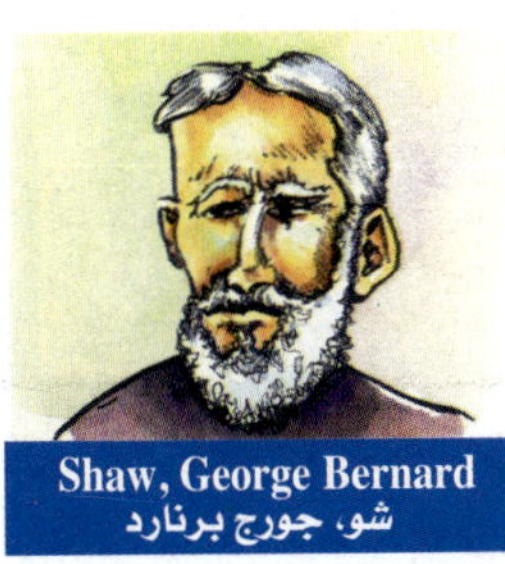

Shaw, George Bernard
شو، جورج برنارد

British playright of Irish origin. A genius of sarcasm 1856-1950

اديب بريطاني من اصل ايرلندي عبقري في السخرية والانتقاد 1856 ـ 1950

Schiller, Von Friedrich
شيلر، فون فريدريك

German poet and novelist. Author of the book "William Tell" 1759-1805

شاعر وروائي الماني مؤلف كتاب «ويليام تيل» 1759 ـ 1805

World Writers and Poets
أدباء وشعراء عالميون

Twain, Mark
توين، مارك

American satirical writer. Author of "The Adventures of Tom Sawyer" 1835 -1910

كاتب اميركي ساخر مؤلف كتاب «مغامرات توم سوير» 1835 ـ 1910

Tennyson, Alfred
تنيسون، الفرد

British poet considered the greatest poet of the Victorian Era 1809 -1892

شاعر بريطاني اعتبر اعظم شاعر في العصر الفكتوري 1809 ـ 1892

Strindberg, August
ستريندبرغ، اوغست

Swedish playright and writer 1849 -1912

كاتب ومؤلف مسرحيات سويدي 1849 ـ 1912

Vigny, Alfred De
فينيي، الفريد دي

French poet. One of the most illustrious romantic poets 1797 -1863

شاعر فرنسي. احد اشهر الشعراء الرومنطيقيين 1797 ـ 1863

Tolstoy, Leo
تولستوي، ليو

Russian novelist, author of "War and Peace" 1828 -1910

روائي روسي من اشهر مؤلفاته «الحرب والسلام» 1828 ـ 1910

Swovatski, Julius
سفو واتسكي، جوليوس

One of the greatest Polish poets. He wrote his poem "Anhily" on one of his visits to Lebanon 1809 -1849

احد اشهر الامراء البولونيين. زار لبنان وكتب ديوان شعره «انهيلي» 1809 ـ 1849

Verne, Jules
فيرن، جول

French writer. Wrote several imaginary scientific stories 1828 -1905

روائي فرنسي، مؤلف قصص علمية خيالية 1828 ـ 1905

Turgenev, Ivan Sergevitch
تورجنيف، ايفان سرجيفيتش

Russian novelist and playright 1818 -1883

روائي وكاتب مسرحيات روسي 1818 ـ 1883

Tagore, Rabindranath
تاغور، رابيندرانات

Indian poet and playright. Holder of the Nobel Prize for Litterature 1913. (1861-1941)

شاعر ومؤلف مسرحي هندي حاز على جائزة نوبل للآداب عام 1913. (1861 ـ 1941)

World Writers and Poets
أدباء وشعراء عالميون

Virgil
فيرجيل

The greatest Roman poet. Author of the epic "Aeneid" 70-19 B.C.

اشهر شاعر روماني ألّف الملحمة الشعرية «اينيد» 70 ـ 19 قبل الميلاد

Voltaire
فولتير

French philosopher and playright 1694 -1778

فيلسوف وكاتب مسرحي فرنسي 1694 ـ 1778

Whitman, walt
ويتمان، والت

American poet. He was known by his advocacy of the rights of man 1819 -1892

شاعر اميركي اشتهر بدفاعه عن حقوق الانسان 1819 ـ 1892

Whittaker, John Greenleaf
ويتيكر، جون غرينليف

American poet. Writer of popular legends of America 1807-1871

شاعر اميركي كتب اساطير شعبية عن الحياة في اميركا 1807 ـ 1871

Wilde, Oscar
وايلد، اوسكار

American poet and playright of Irish origin 1854 -1900

اديب وروائي وكاتب مسرحي اميركي من اصل ارلندي 1854 ـ 1900

Wells, H.G.
ويلز، ايتش.جي

British novelist and writer. Author of several scientific novels 1866 -1946

مؤلف قصصي بريطاني شهير كتب عدة مؤلفات علمية 1866 ـ 1946

Zola, Emile
زولا، اميل

French novelist. Founder of the Naturalist School in litterature 1840 -1902

روائي فرنسي شهير ومؤسس المدرسة الطبيعية في الأدب 1840 ـ 1902

Music

موسيقى

1 - Maestro
2 - Double Bass
3 - Drums
4 - Saxophone
5 - Trumpet
6 - Trombone
7 - Guitar
8 - Violin
9 - Lute
10 - Clarinet
11 - Flute
12 - Drum
13 - Loud Speaker
14 - Piano
15 - Piano Keys
16 - Guitar Player
17 - Amplifier
18 - Zither
19 - Cymbals
20 - Musical Note

1 ـ قائد الأوركسترا
2 ـ الدبلبس
3 ـ آلات الإيقاع
4 ـ الساكسوفون
5 ـ البوق
6 ـ المترددة
7 ـ الغيتار
8 ـ الكمان
9 ـ البزق
10 ـ الكلارينت
11 ـ الناي
12 ـ الطبل
13 ـ مكبر الصوت
14 ـ البيانو
15 ـ منصة المفاتيح
16 ـ عازف الغيتار
17 ـ مكبر الصوت
18 ـ قانون
19 ـ الصناجة
20 ـ نوتة موسيقية

At the Carpenter عند النجار

1 - Bolt	9 - Trowel	17 - Paint	17 ـ دهان	9 ـ مالج	1 ـ برغي
2 - Screw	10 - Screwdriver	18 - Barrel	18 ـ برميل	10 ـ مفك براغي	2 ـ لولب
3 - Nail	11 - Hacksaw	19 - Broom	19 ـ مكنسة	11 ـ منشار معادن	3 ـ مسمار
4 - Washer	12 - Hammer	20 - Carpenter	20 ـ النجار	12 ـ مطرقة	4 ـ فلكه
5 - Nut	13 - Lathe	21 - Bits	21 ـ مجموعة لقم المثقب	13 ـ مخرطة	5 ـ صمولة
6 - Wrench	14 - Angles	22 - Pincers	22 ـ كماشة	14 ـ زوايا	6 ـ مفتاح إنكليزي
7 - Spade	15 - Planks	23 - Boring Pistol	23 ـ مثقب	15 ـ ألواح خشب	7 ـ رفش
8 - Plane	16 - Saw	24 - Broom	24 ـ مكنسة	16 ـ منشار خشب	8 ـ مسحاج

Building Site
موقع الإنشاءات

1 - Mattock
2 - Cement mixer
3 - Water truck
4 - Tipper
5 - Hook
6 - Ladder
7 - Trowel
8 - Structure
9 - Laborer
10 - Construction worker
11 - Pebbles container
12 - Crane
13 - Excavator
14 - Sand
15 - Shovel
16 - Tractor
17 - Pebbles

1 ـ معول
2 ـ جبالة باطون
3 ـ شاحنة خزان
4 ـ شاحنة قلابة
5 ـ كلاّب
6 ـ سلم
7 ـ مالج
8 ـ هيكل البناء
9 ـ عامل
10 ـ عامل بناء
11 ـ وعاء للأحجار
12 ـ رافعة
13 ـ حفارة
14 ـ رمل
15 ـ رفش
16 ـ جرار (تراكتور)
17 ـ كومة حصى

فرقة المطافي، عند طبيب الأسنان، وغرفة المستشفى

1 ـ سيارة إطفاء
2 ـ بلطة وخوذة
3 ـ صنبور ماء
4 ـ جهاز إتصال لاسلكي
5 ـ مصباح يدوي
6 ـ طائرة
7 ـ منزل يحترق
8 ـ رجال الإطفاء
9 ـ ميزان حرارة
10 ـ أطباء يتشاورون
11 ـ محقنة
12 ـ سرير مستشفى
13 ـ طبيب أسنان
14 ـ ضوء كاشف
15 ـ ضمادة
16 ـ محفة لنقل المرضى
17 ـ كرسي بعجلات لنقل المرضى
18 ـ مساند فولاذية للإتكاء عليها
19 ـ حبوب أدوية وبرشامات

Fire Brigade, at the Dentist and a Hospital Ward

1 - Fire Engine
2 - Axe and Helmet
3 - Hydrant
4 - Radio
5 - Torch
6 - Aircraft
7 - Fire
8 - Firemen
9 - Thermometer
10 - Doctors in consultation
11 - Syringe
12 - Hospital bed
13 - Dentist
14 - Spotlight
15 - Bandage
16 - Stretcher
17 - Wheel chair
18 - Crutches
19 - Pills of medicine

Careers and Professions
مهن ووظائف

سائق شاحنة
Truck driver

ميكانيكي
Car mechanic

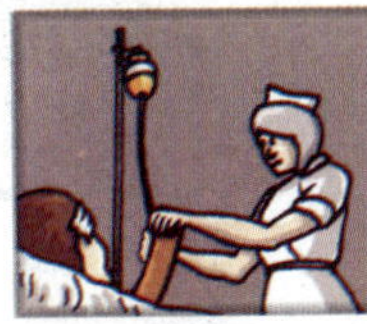
ممرضة
Nurse

ربة منزل
Housewife

حلاق
Barber

رسام
Painter

طبيب
Doctor

مصوّر
Photographer

نادل (جرسون)
Waiter

مذيع
Broadcaster

فرّان
Baker

حمّال، (شيّال، عتّال)
Porter

خيّاطة
Seamstress

سكرتيرة
Secretary

صرّاف
Money-Changer

مدرّس (أستاذ)
Teacher

مزارع
Farmer

مهرّج
Clown

لص وشرطي
Thief and a policeman

طبيب عيون
Ophtalmologist

The Office المكتب

1 - Portable computer
2 - Waste basket
3 - Drawer
4 - Envelope
5 - Computer
6 - File cabinet

7 - Punching machine
8 - Fixed telephone
9 - Stapler
10 - Stamp pad
11 - Cellular telephone
12 - Fax machine

1 ـ الحاسب الآلي
2 ـ خزانة الملفات
3 ـ أدراج المكتب
4 ـ ظرف
5 ـ حاسب نقَّال
6 ـ سلة المهملات

7 ـ مثقاب
8 ـ الهاتف الثابت
9 ـ كباس
10 ـ ختم
11 ـ هاتف خليوي
12 ـ فاكس

The Market Place السُّوق

1 - Merchandise
2 - Shelves
3 - Cart
4 - Umbrella
5 - Salesman
6 - Cash box
7 - Waiting
8 - Waiting queue
9 - Bill

1 ـ حاملات البضائع
2 ـ رفٌ (رفوف)
3 ـ عربة
4 ـ شمسية
5 ـ بائع
6 ـ الصندوق المالي
7 ـ الانتظار
8 ـ حاجز (المانع)
9 ـ الفاتورة

Means of Communication المواصلات

1 - Ship
2 - Airplane
3 - Bicycle
4 - Car
5 - Truck

6 - Bus
7 - Ambulance car
8 - Train
9 - Motorcycle
10 - Caravan

1 ـ باخرة
2 ـ طائرة
3 ـ دراجة
4 ـ سيارة
5 ـ شاحنة

6 ـ حافلة
7 ـ إسعاف
8 ـ قطار
9 ـ موتور سيكل (دراجة نارية)
10 ـ قافلة

حركة المرور

1 ـ إشارة اتجاه
2 ـ دراجة نارية
3 ـ شاحنة
4 ـ طريق عام
5 ـ طريق فوق الجسر
6 ـ جسر للسير
7 ـ نفق
8 ـ ماشٍ، مارّ
9 ـ شاحنة
10 ـ شجر السرو

Circulation

- 1 - Direction Signal
- 2 - Motorcycle
- 3 - Truck
- 4 - Main Road
- 5 - Street above the bridge
- 6 - Bridge
- 7 - Tunnel
- 8 - Pedestrian
- 9 - Rocks Truck
- 10 - Cypress Tree

Traffic Signs

1 - Circulation direction
2 - Circulation direction
3 - Circle
4 - Circulation direction
5 - Circulation direction
6 - Circulation direction
7 - Circulation direction
8 - Stop
9 - No traffic
10 - No parking
11 - Speed limit
12 - Height limit
13 - Breadth limit
14 - Tonnage limit
15 - Left turn
16 - Right turn
17 - Traffic sign
18 - Two-lanes traffic
19 - Crossing
20 - Crossroads
21 - Tunnel
22 - Zigzag road ahead
23 - Narrow road ahead
24 - Slipping road ahead
25 - Slope
26 - Dangerous slope ahead
27 - Fall of rocks
28 - Dangerous road ahead
29 - No detour
30 - No turn
31 - No turn
32 - No horns
33 - No traffic for trucks
34 - No traffic for all vehicles
35 - Priority road
36 - Bicycle lane
37 - Airport
38 - Beware! School
39 - Beware! Straying animals
40 - Railway crossing
41 - Pedestrians crossing
42 - Animals crossing
43 - Motorcycle lane
44 - Works ahead
45 - Holes ahead
46 - Bumps ahead
47 - Moving bridge
48 - No overtaking
49 - No overtaking by trucks
50 - Highway
51 - End of highway
52 - Parking
53 - Hospital
54 - Impasse
55 - Handicapped crossing
56 - Give way

إشارات السير (حفظ النِّظام أمانةٌ)

1 ـ اتجاه السَّير
2 ـ اتجاه السَّير
3 ـ مستديرة
4 ـ اتجاه السَّير
5 ـ اتجاه السَّير
6 ـ اتجاه السَّير
7 ـ اتجاه السَّير
8 ـ قف
9 ـ ممنوع المرور
10 ـ ممنوع الوقوف
11 ـ تحديد السُّرعة
12 ـ تحديد الارتفاع
13 ـ تحديد العرض
14 ـ تحديد الوزن
15 ـ منعطف إلى اليسار
16 ـ منعطف إلى اليمين
17 ـ إشارة مرور
18 ـ السَّير على خطين
19 ـ تقاطع
20 ـ تقاطع طرق
21 ـ نفق
22 ـ طريق متعرِّج
23 ـ طريق ضيِّق
24 ـ طريق منزلق
25 ـ منحدر
26 ـ منحدر خطر
27 ـ تساقط صخور
28 ـ طريق حذر
29 ـ ممنوع الالتفاف
30 ـ ممنوع الالتفاف إلى اليسار
31 ـ ممنوع الالتفاف إلى اليمين
32 ـ ممنوع استعمال الزَّمور
33 ـ ممنوع مرور الشَّاحنات
34 ـ ممنوع المرور لكافة الآليات
35 ـ طريق أفضلية
36 ـ ممرُّ درَّاجات هوائيَّة
37 ـ مطار
38 ـ انتبه مدرسة
39 ـ انتبه حيوانات شاردة
40 ـ ممرُّ سكة حديد
41 ـ ممرُّ مشاة
42 ـ ممرُّ خيل
43 ـ ممرُّ درَّاجات ناريَّة
44 ـ انتبه أشغال
45 ـ انتبه حفر
46 ـ انتبه مطبَّات
47 ـ جسر متحرِّك
48 ـ ممنوع التَّجاوز
49 ـ ممنوع تجاوز الشَّاحنات
50 ـ أوتوستراد
51 ـ نهاية الأوتوستراد
52 ـ موقف
53 ـ مستشفى
54 ـ طريق غير نافذ
55 ـ ممرّ للمعاقين
56 ـ افسح الطريق

السفر جوّاً

1 ـ منطاد مسيَّر
2 ـ مضيفة طائرة
3 ـ مسافر
4 ـ ذيل الطائرة
5 ـ جسم الطائرة
6 ـ جناح الطائرة
7 ـ محرك نفاث
8 ـ الطائرة
9 ـ مدرج الطائرات
10 ـ طائرة صغيرة
11 ـ مرآب الطائرات
12 ـ برج المراقبة
13 ـ مروحة الهليكوبتر
14 ـ الهليكوبتر
15 مأمور الجمرك
16 المسافر
17 حقيبة السفر
18 قائد الطائرة
19 ـ منطاد

Travel by Air

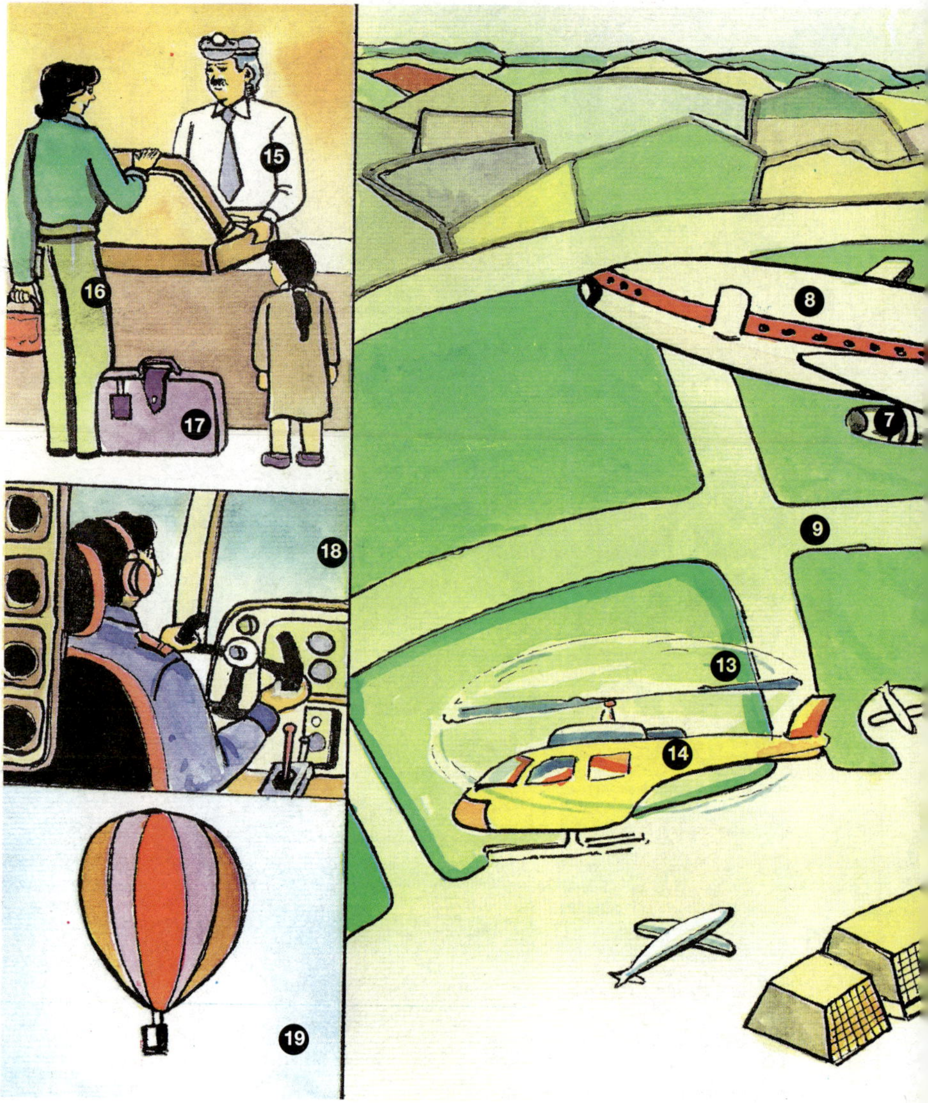

1 - Airship
2 - Air hostess
3 - Traveller
4 - Tail
5 - Fuselage
6 - Wing
7 - Jet engine
8 - Aeroplane
9 - Runway
10 - Light aircraft
11 - Hangar
12 - Control towel
13 - Popeller
14 - Helicopter
15 - Customs officer
16 - Traveller
17 - Luggage
18 - Captain
19 - Balloon

Lines and Measures
خطوط ومقاييس

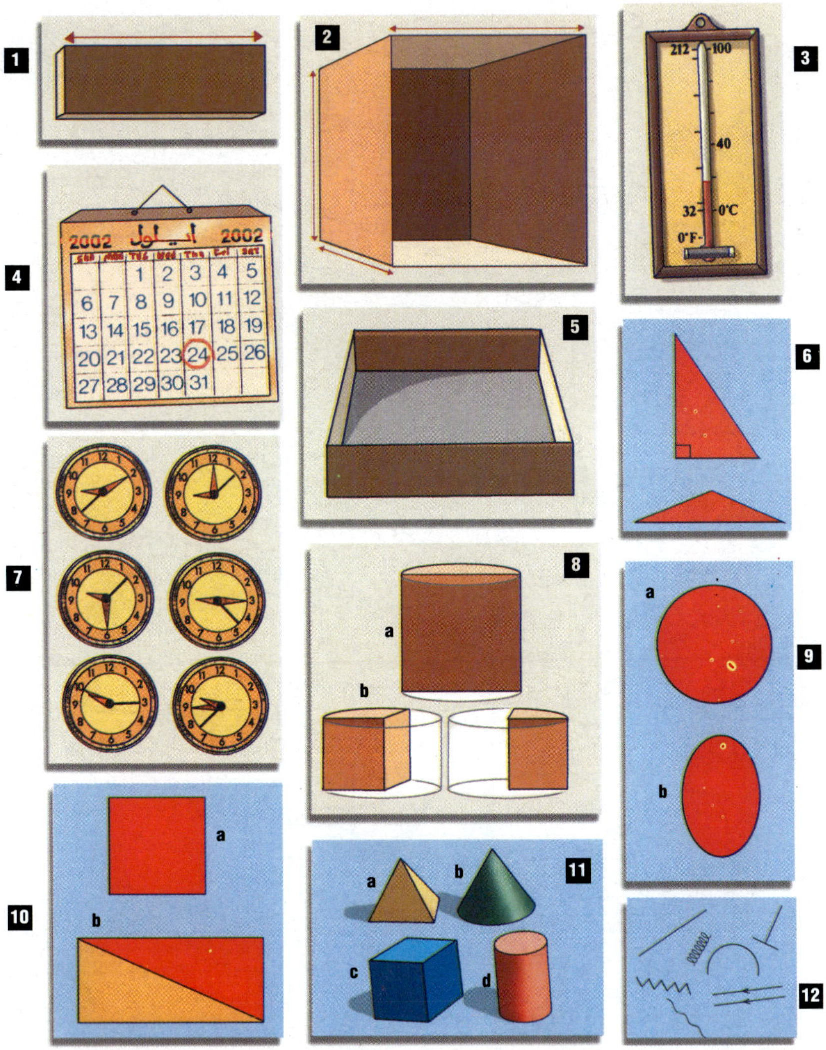

1 - Rectangle
2 - Cube
3 - Thermometer
4 - Calendar
5 - Square void
6 - Triangle
7 - Timing instruments
8-a - Cylindrical
8-b - Sections of cylinder
9-a - Circle
9-b - Ovoid, oval
10-a - Square
10-b - Rectangular
11-a - Pyramidical
11-b - Conic
11-c - Cube, Cubic
11-d - Cylindrical

1 ـ متوازي الأضلاع
2 ـ مكعَّب
3 ـ ميزان الحرارة
4 ـ تقويم شهر (روزنامة)
5 ـ فراغ مربع
6 ـ مثلث
7 ـ الوقت
8 ـ أ ـ أُسطواني
8 ـ ب ـ أجزاء من الأُسطوانة
9 ـ أ ـ دائرة
9 ـ أ ـ بيضاوي
10 ـ أ ـ مربَّع
10 ـ ب ـ مستطيل
11 ـ أ ـ هرمي
11 ـ ب ـ مخروط الشَّكل
11 ـ ج ـ مكعَّب
11 ـ د ـ أُسطواني
12 ـ تخطيط / أشكال

Military Life — عسكريّات

﴿وأَعِدُّوا لَهُمْ مَا اسْتَطَعْتُمْ مِنْ قُوَّةٍ﴾ ـ سورة الأنفال، الآية (٦٠) ـ

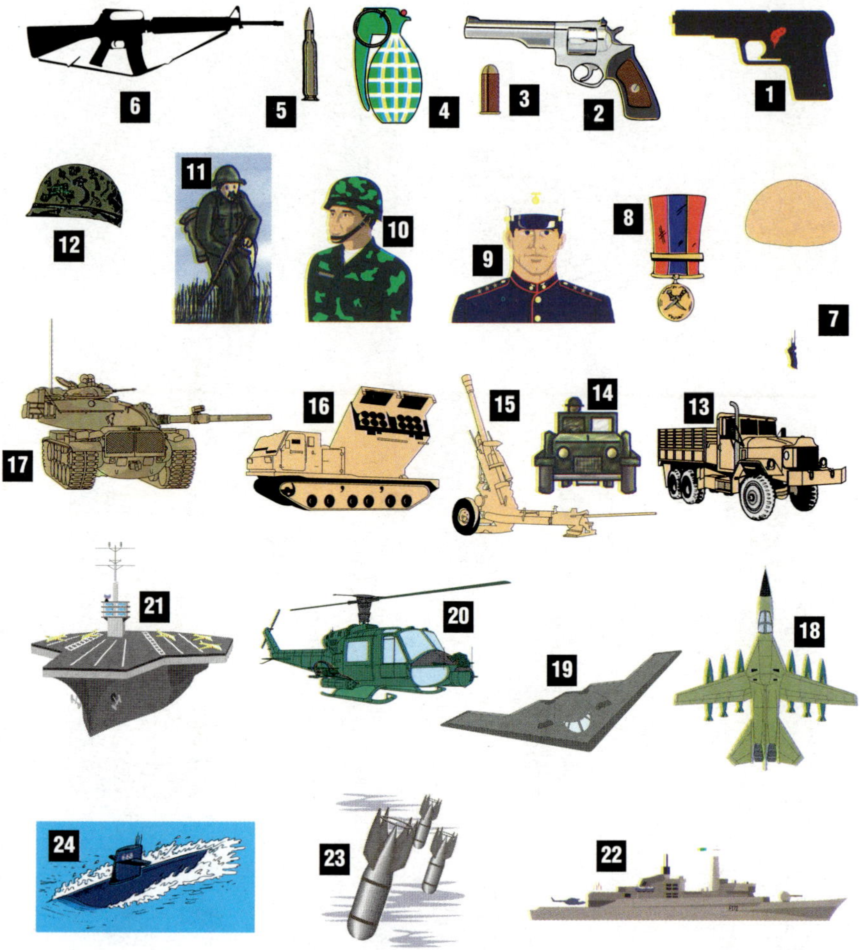

1 - Automatic pistol
2 - Magnum
3 - Bullet
4 - Hand grenade
5 - Machine gun bullet
6 - Machine gun
7 - Parachutist
8 - Medal
9 - Admiral
10 - Soldier
11 - Infantry soldier
12 - Helmet

13 - Troop carrier
14 - Jeep
15 - Field gun
16 - Rocket launcher
17 - Tank
18 - Military aircraft
19 - Phantom
20 - Helicopter
21 - Aircraft carrier
22 - Cruiser
23 - Missiles, rockets
24 - Submarine

1 ـ مسدس أُوتوماتيكي
2 ـ مسدس ماغنوم
3 ـ طلقة مسدس
4 ـ قنبلة يدويّة
5 ـ طلقة رشّاش
6 ـ مدفع رشّاش
7 ـ مظلّي
8 ـ وسام
9 ـ أميرال (ضابط سرية)
10 ـ جندي
11 ـ جندي مشاة
12 ـ خوذة

13 ـ ناقلة جنود (مدرّعة)
14 ـ سيارة جيب
15 ـ مدفع ميدان
16 ـ راجمة صواريخ
17 ـ دبّابة
18 ـ طائرة حربيّة
19 ـ طائرة حربيّة تسمّى (الشّبح)
20 ـ طائرة هليوكبتر
12 ـ حاملة طائرات
22 ـ طراد
23 ـ قذائف صاروخيّة
24 ـ غوّاصة

Sports رياضة

1 - Tennis court
2 - Olympic stadium
3 - Football field
4 - Basketball field
5 - Tennis player
6 - Referee
7 - Goaler
8 - Football player
9 - Basketball player
10 - Racing
11 - Golf player
12 - Baseball player
13 - Athlete
14 - Karate
15 - Boxing
16 - Volley-ball

1 ـ ملعب كرة مضرب
2 ـ استاد أولمبي
3 ـ ملعب كرة قدم
4 ـ ملعب كرة سلة
5 ـ لاعب كرة مضرب
6 ـ حكم
7 ـ حارس مرمى
8 ـ لاعب كرة قدم
9 ـ لاعب كرة سلة
10 ـ سباق
11 ـ لاعب غولف
12 ـ لاعب بايسبول
13 ـ جمباز
14 ـ كراتيه
15 ـ الملاكمة
16 ـ كرة يد

Sports رياضة

1

2

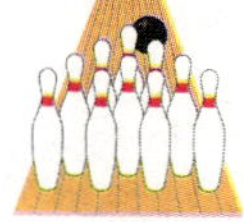
3

4

5

6

7

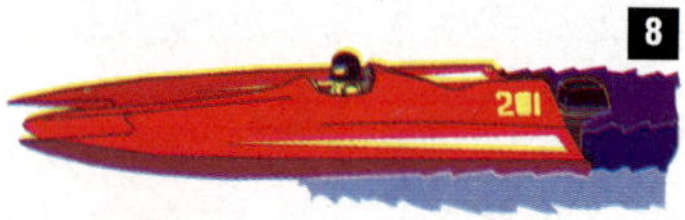
8

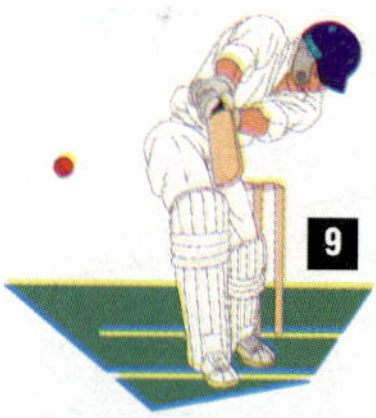
9

10

11

1 - Horse racing
2 - Table tennis
3 - Bowling
4 - Medals gold, silver & bronze
5 - Swimming
6 - Skiing
7 - Baseball
8 - Speed boat racing
9 - Cricket
10 - Car rally
11 - Hockey

1 ـ سباق الخيل
2 ـ كرة الطّاولة
3 ـ بولينغ
4 ـ مداليّة ذهبيّة، فضيّة، برونزيّة
5 ـ سباحة
6 ـ التزلّج على الثّلج
7 ـ كرة قدم (أمريكية)
8 ـ سباق الزوارق السّريعة
9 ـ كريكت
10 ـ سباق سيّارات
11 ـ هوكي

Nouns of Quantity أسماء الكميات

1 - Ball (of string, wool)
2 - Bar (of chocolate)
3 - Tablet / bar (of soap)
4 - Joint (of meat)
5 - Line (of washing)
6 - Loaf (of bread)
7 - Lump (of sugar)
8 - Slice / piece (of cake)
9 - Reel (of cotton)
10 - Box (of matches) Carton (of cigarettes)
11 - Packet (of tea)
12 - Roll (of paper)
13 - Tube (of toothpaste)
14 - Bowl (of soup)

1 ـ كرة من الخيط/الصُّوف
2 ـ قطعة من الشُّوكولاته
3 ـ قرص/قطعة من الصَّابون
4 ـ قطعة من اللَّحم
5 ـ حبل من الغسيل
6 ـ رغيف من الخبز
7 ـ قطعة من السُّكَّر
8 ـ شريحة/ قطعة من الكعكة
9 ـ بكرة من القطن
10 ـ علبة كبريت/ علبة سَجائر
11 ـ علبةُ من الشَّاي
12 ـ لفافةٌ من الورق
13 ـ انبوب من معجون الأسنان
14 ـ وعاءٌ من الحساء

Nouns of Quantity

أسماء الكميات

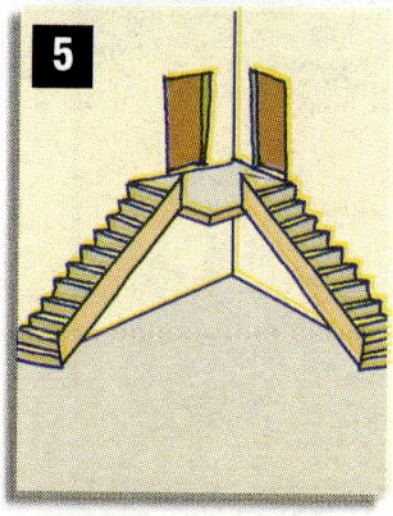

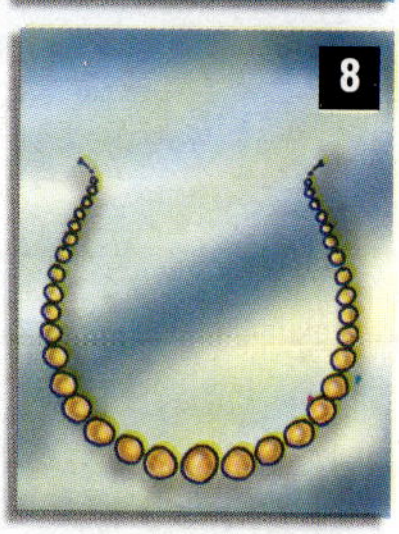

1 - Bunch (of flowers)
2 - Bundle (of sticks)
3 - Crowd (of people)
4 - Fleet (of ships)
5 - Flight (of stairs)
6 - Flock (of sheep or birds)
7 - Gang (of workmen)
8 - String (of beads)
9 - Heap (of stones)
10 - Herd (of cows)
11 - Party (of tourists)
12 - Pile (of blankets)
13 - Plate (of sandwiches)
14 - Row (of houses)
15 - Team (of players)
16 - Swarm (of bees)

1 - باقةٌ من الأزهار
2 - مجموعة من العصيّ
3 - حشدٌ من النّاس
4 - اسطول من السُّفن
5 - مجموعةٌ درجات السُّلَّم
6 - قطيعٌ من الغنم / من الطُّيور
7 - مجموعةٌ من العمال
8 - عقدٌ من حبات اللُّؤلؤ
9 - كومةٌ من الأحجار
10 - قطيعٌ من البقر
11 - حفلٌ/فوج من السُّيَّاح
12 - كومةٌ من البطاط
13 - طبقٌ من السَّاندويشات
14 - صفٌ من البيوت
15 - فريقٌ من اللاَّعبين
16 - قفيرٌ من النَّحل

Adjectives الصِّفات

1. a) Narrow أ) ضيق
   b) Wide ب) واسع / عريض
2. a) Young أ) صغير / شاب
   b) Old ب) عجوز
3. a) New أ) جديد
   b) Old ب) قديم
4. a) Calm أ) هادئ
   b) Rough ب) عنيف
5. a) Rough أ) خشن
   b) Smooth ب) ناعم
6. a) Strong أ) قوي
   b) Weak ب) ضعيف
7. a) Tidy أ) منظم
   b) Untidy ب) مهمل / غير مرتب
8. a) Good أ) جيد
   b) Bad ب) سيئ
9. a) Pretty/ Beautiful أ) جميل / لطيف / ب) بشع /
   b) Ugly كريه
10. a) First أ) الأول
    b) Last ب) الأخير
11. a) Light أ) مضيء
    b) Dark ب) مظلم
12. a) Light أ) خفيف
    b) Heavy ب) ثقيل
13. a) Loud أ) مرتفع / عال
    b) Soft ب) ناعم/لطيف
14. a) Solid أ) صلب
    b) Hollow ب) رخو/لين
15. a) Thick أ) سميك/ثمين
    b) Thin ب) رقيق/رفيع
16. a) Lose أ) طليق/رخو
    b) Tight ب) مشدود / محكم

Adjectives الصِّفات

1. a) Big / Large أ) كبير / ضخم
   b) Little / Small ب) صغير
2. a) Blunt أ) غير حاد
   b) Sharp ب) عاص / حاد
3. a) Clean أ) نظيف
   b) Dirty ب) قذر
4. a) Closed / Shut أ) مغلق / مقفل
   b) Open ب) مفتوح
5. a) Crooked أ) متعرج
   b) Straight ب) مستقيم
6. a) Shallow أ) ضحل
   b) Deep ب) عميق
7. a) Wet أ) مبلل
   b) Dry ب) جاف
8. a) Empty أ) فارغ
   b) Full ب) مليء
9. a) Fast أ) سريع
   b) Slow ب) بطيء
10. a) Fat أ) سمين
    b) Thin ب) رفيع
11. a) Happy أ) سعيد
    b) Sad ب) حزين
16. a) Easy أ) سهل
    b) Difficult / Hard ب) صعب / قاسٍ
13. a) Soft أ) لين
    b) Hard ب) صلب
14. a) High / أ) عالٍ / مرتفع
    b) Low / ب) منخفض / واطئ
15. a) Hot أ) ساخن
    b) Cold ب) بارد
16. a) Long أ) طويل
    b) Short ب) قصير

The Family

العائلة

1

2

الجَدُّ : أبو الأب، وأبو الأم، الجمع: أجدادٌ، وجدودٌ، وجُدودةٌ.

الجَدَّة : أمّ الأمّ، وأمّ الأب.

3

الأب : الوالد، مثنّاه: أبوان، الجمع: آباء، وأُبَوَّة.

يقال: آدم أبو البشر.

4

الأم : الوالدة، الجمع: أُمّهات (لمن يعقل)، وأُمّات (لمن لا يعقل)، ومُصَغّر الأم: أُميمةٌ.

يقال: حوّاء أمُّ البشر.

7

8

العمُّ : أخو الأب، الجمع: أعمامٌ، وعُمومةٌ

«العَمُّ بِمَنْزِلَةِ الوَالِدِ» (حديث شريف)

العمة: أُخت الأب، الجمع: عمّات.

5

الأخ : من ضمّتهُ وإيّاك ولادةُ أبويك أو أحدهما. مثنّاه : أخوان، الجمع: إخوةٌ وإخوان.

9

10

6

الأخت : مؤنّث الأخ، الجمع: أخوات، وتصغير الأخت: أُخَيَّة.

الخال : أخو الأمّ، الجمع: أخوال، وخُؤول، وخؤولة.

«الخَالُ أبٌ» (حديث نبويّ)

الخالة : أخت الأمّ، الجمع : خالات.

«الخَالَةُ أُمٌّ» (حديث نبويّ)

1 - Grandfather	6 - Sister	6 ـ أخت	1 ـ جدّ
2 - Grandmother	7 - Uncle	7 ـ عم	2 ـ جدّة
3 - Father	8 - Aunt	8 ـ عمة	3 ـ أب
4 - Mother	9 - Uncle	9 ـ خال	4 ـ أم
5 - Brother	10 - Aunt	10 ـ خالة	5 ـ أخ